Online Research and Reference Aids

Whether you want to investigate the ideas behind ... conduct in-depth research for a paper, our Online R... help you refine your research skills, find the informat... se that information effectively. You can access these resources through the companion Web site for *America: A Concise History*, Third Edition, at **bedfordstmartins.com/ henrettaconcise** or by using the URLs given below.

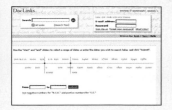

DocLinks

bedfordstmartins.com/doclinks

Annotated links to primary documents online. Search by topic, date, or textbook chapter.

HistoryLinks

bedfordstmartins.com/historylinks

Annotated links to selected U.S. history Web sites, including those containing image galleries, maps, and audio and video clips for supplementing research. Search by date, subject, medium, keyword, or textbook chapter.

A Student's Online Guide to History Reference Sources

bedfordstmartins.com/benjamin

A collection of links to history-related electronic reference sources such as databases, indexes, and journals, plus contact information for state, provincial, local, and professional history organizations. Based on the appendix to Jules Benjamin's *A Student's Guide to History*, Ninth Edition.

Research and Documentation Online

bedfordstmartins.com/resdoc

Clear advice on how to conduct research, integrate primary and secondary sources into research papers, and cite sources correctly.

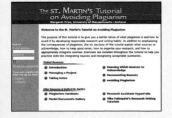

The St. Martin's Tutorial on Avoiding Plagiarism

bedfordstmartins.com/plagiarismtutorial

An online tutorial that explains what plagiarism is and how to avoid it by keeping good notes, staying organized, knowing what to ask, and integrating sources appropriately. Includes exercises on integrating sources and recognizing acceptable summaries.

Third Edition

America

A CONCISE HISTORY

CANADA

MINNESOTA
Duluth
Fargo

Lake Superior

MICHIGAN

Lake Huron

WISCONSIN

St. Paul
Minneapolis
Sioux Falls
Madison
Milwaukee
Lansing
Detroit

Lake Michigan

IOWA
Des Moines
Omaha
Lincoln

ILLINOIS
Springfield

Chicago
Gary

Wabash R.

INDIANA
Indianapolis

Toledo

Lake Erie

Cleveland

Columbus

OHIO
Wheeling

Cincinnati

Louisville

Frankfort

KENTUCKY

Ohio R.

WEST VIRGINIA
Charleston

Pittsburgh

Harrisburg

PENNSYLVANIA

Allegheny R.

Lake Ontario

Buffalo

NEW YORK

Albany

Hudson R.

St. Lawrence R.

MAINE
Augusta

Burlington
Montpelier
VT.
Manchester

N.H.
Concord

Portland

Boston

MASS.
Hartford
Providence
RHODE ISLAND
CONNECTICUT

Newark
New York
Trenton
NEW JERSEY
Philadelphia

Baltimore
MD.
Washington, D.C.
Annapolis

Dover
DELAWARE

Potomac R.

VIRGINIA
Richmond

Roanoke R.

Norfolk

Topeka
Kansas City
Jefferson City
St. Louis

Missouri R.

Wichita

MISSOURI

Illinois R.

TENNESSEE

Nashville

Cumberland R.

Knoxville

NORTH CAROLINA

Raleigh
Charlotte

Cape Fear R.

Tulsa
Oklahoma City

ARKANSAS

Arkansas R.

Little Rock

Memphis

Mississippi R.

Birmingham

SOUTH CAROLINA
Columbia

Santee R.

Charleston

ATLANTIC OCEAN

Fort Worth
Dallas

Austin

Houston

LOUISIANA

MISSISSIPPI
Jackson

ALABAMA
Montgomery

Mobile

Tennessee R.

APPALACHIAN MOUNTAINS

Chattahoochee R.

Alabama R.

Altamaha R.

GEORGIA

Savannah

Jacksonville

Sabine R.
Red R.
Trinity R.

Baton Rouge
New Orleans

Tallahassee

FLORIDA

Tampa

Miami

Gulf of Mexico

BAHAMAS

ATLANTIC OCEAN
67°W   66°W
San Juan
PUERTO RICO
18°N   Ponce
Caribbean Sea
0   25   50 miles
0   25   50 kilometers

CUBA

0   200   400 miles
0   200   400 kilometers

95°W   90°W   85°W   80°W

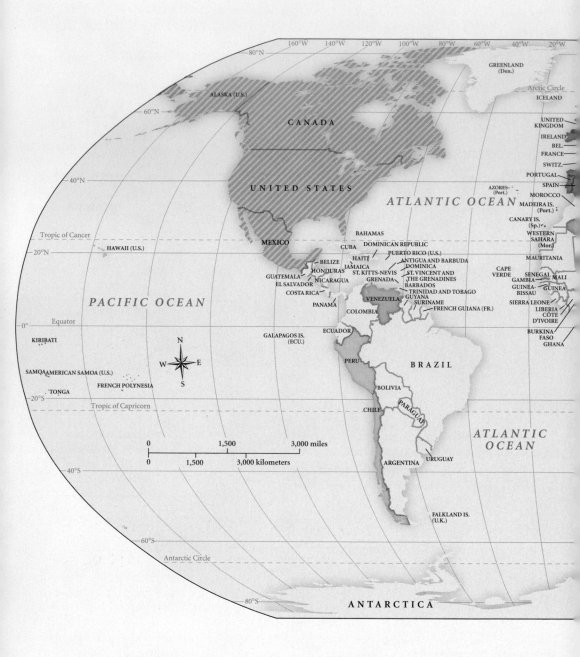

Political divisions as of May 2004

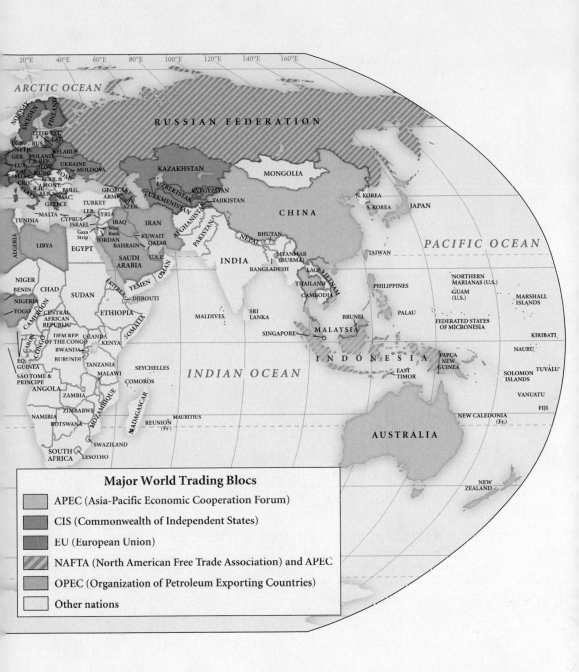

20°E 40°E 60°E 80°E 100°E 120°E 140°E 160°E

ARCTIC OCEAN

NORWAY
SWEDEN
FINLAND

RUSSIAN FEDERATION

LITH. EST.
LAT.
DEN. RUS.
NETH. BELARUS
GER. POLAND
LUX. CZ. REP.
AUS. HUNG. SLOV. UKRAINE
SWITZ. SERB. & MOLDOVA
CRO. MONT. ROM.
ITALY B.H. MAC. BULG.
ALB. GREECE TURKEY

KAZAKHSTAN

MONGOLIA

N. KOREA
S. KOREA   JAPAN

MALTA CYPRUS
TUNISIA   LEB. SYRIA
ISRAEL IRAQ   IRAN
Gaza West
Strip Bank JORDAN KUWAIT
BAHRAIN QATAR

GEORGIA
ARM.
AZER.

UZBEKISTAN KYRGYZSTAN
TURKMENISTAN TAJIKISTAN

CHINA

TAIWAN

PACIFIC OCEAN

ALGERIA

LIBYA   EGYPT

SAUDI
ARABIA   U.A.E.
OMAN

AFGHANISTAN
PAKISTAN

NEPAL   BHUTAN

INDIA   BANGLADESH
MYANMAR
(BURMA)

NORTHERN
MARIANAS (U.S.)

GUAM
(U.S.)

MARSHALL
ISLANDS

NIGER
BENIN   CHAD
NIGERIA
TOGO
CAMEROON

SUDAN

CENTRAL
AFRICAN
REPUBLIC

ERITREA
YEMEN
DJIBOUTI

ETHIOPIA

LAOS
THAILAND VIETNAM
CAMBODIA

PHILIPPINES

PALAU

FEDERATED STATES
OF MICRONESIA

KIRIBATI

MALDIVES
SRI
LANKA

SINGAPORE   MALAYSIA

BRUNEI

NAURU

GABON
CONGO
EQ.
GUINEA

DEM. REP. UGANDA
OF THE CONGO
RWANDA
BURUNDI   KENYA

SOMALIA

INDIAN OCEAN

I N D O N E S I A

EAST
TIMOR

PAPUA
NEW
GUINEA

SOLOMON
ISLANDS

TUVALU

SÃO TOMÉ &
PRÍNCIPE
ANGOLA

TANZANIA
MALAWI

SEYCHELLES
COMOROS

ZAMBIA

VANUATU

FIJI

NAMIBIA
BOTSWANA

ZIMBABWE
MOZAMBIQUE
MADAGASCAR

REUNION
(Fr.)

MAURITIUS

NEW CALEDONIA
(Fr.)

AUSTRALIA

SOUTH
AFRICA

SWAZILAND
LESOTHO

NEW
ZEALAND

Major World Trading Blocs

- APEC (Asia-Pacific Economic Cooperation Forum)
- CIS (Commonwealth of Independent States)
- EU (European Union)
- NAFTA (North American Free Trade Association) and APEC
- OPEC (Organization of Petroleum Exporting Countries)
- Other nations

Third Edition

America
A CONCISE HISTORY

James A. Henretta
University of Maryland

David Brody
University of California, Davis

Lynn Dumenil
Occidental College

BEDFORD / ST. MARTIN'S
Boston • New York

For Bedford / St. Martin's

Executive Editor for History: Mary Dougherty
Director of Development for History: Jane Knetzger
Development Editor: William J. Lombardo
Senior Production Editor: Lori Chong Roncka
Production Supervisor: Jennifer L. Wetzel
Senior Marketing Manager: Jenna Bookin Barry
Editorial Assistant: Elizabeth Wallace
Production Assistants: Kristen Merrill and Amy Derjue
Art Director: Donna Lee Dennison
Text Design: Wanda Kossak
Copy Editor: Mary Lou Wilshaw-Watts
Indexer: EdIndex
Photo Research: Pembroke Herbert and Sandi Rygiel/Picture Research Consultants & Archives
Cartography: Mapping Specialists, Ltd.
Cover Design: Billy Boardman
Cover Art: Boomtown, by Thomas Hart Benton. Cover art © T. H. Benton and R. P. Benton
    Testamentary Trusts/UMB Bank. Trustee/Licensed by VAGA, New York, NY.
Composition: TechBooks
Printing and Binding: R.R. Donnelley & Sons Company

President: Joan E. Feinberg
Editorial Director: Denise B. Wydra
Director of Marketing: Karen Melton Soeltz
Director of Editing, Design, and Production: Marcia Cohen
Managing Editor: Elizabeth M. Schaaf

Library of Congress Catalog Card Number: 2004110495

Manufactured in the United States of America.

0 9 8
f   e

For information, write: Bedford / St. Martin's, 75 Arlington Street, Boston,
MA 02116 (617-399-4000)

ISBN-10: 0–312–41364–5 (Combined Volume)   ISBN-13: 978–0–312–41364–4
ISBN-10: 0–312–41563–X (Volume 1: To 1877)   ISBN-13: 978–0–312–41563–1
ISBN-10: 0–312–41641–5 (Volume 2: Since 1865)   ISBN-13: 978–0–312–41641–6
ISBN-10: 0–312–44587–3 (hardcover high-school edition) ISBN-13: 978–0–312–44587–4

Credits

For Emily and Rebecca;
Siena, Cameron, Alex, Lea, and Eleanor;
and Norman

PREFACE

Now, as never before, Americans realize the importance of History. When the administration of George W. Bush invaded Iraq in the spring of 2003, it hoped in a single dramatic act to transform the Middle East and, indeed, to change the course of history. But History—the cumulative weight of the past—is not so easily overthrown. As the sobering events that followed the toppling of Saddam Hussein's dictatorial regime have shown, the hope of swiftly creating an American-style democracy in Iraq has come up against the historical identity and institutions of its people, as well as their ethnic and religious diversity. In the pages that follow, we will tell that story and many similar stories of the collision in American history between the grand hopes of ambitious individuals and governments and the stubborn persistence of past customs and institutions.

The interaction between past and present is one of the motifs of this third edition of the concise version of our comprehensive text, *America's History*. As we develop this perspective, we remain committed to the historical vision that has informed this textbook project from its very inception. We are bent on writing a democratic history, one that captures the experiences of ordinary people even as it records the achievements of the great and powerful. Throughout the book, we focus not only on the marvelous diversity of peoples who became American but also on the institutions—political, economic, social and cultural—that forged a common national identity. We want to show how people of all classes and groups make their own history while simultaneously being influenced and constrained by circumstances, by the customs and institutions inherited from the past, and by the hierarchy of power in the present. And we believe that the best way to convey the agency of historical actors is through a narrative, but a narrative that is harnessed to historical argument and explanation—not simply a retelling of "this happened, then that happened." The story, we hope, tells not only what happened, but *how* and *why*.

Organization and Structure

Good narrative history is, of course, primarily a product of good sentences and good paragraphs. So our labors have been mostly in the trenches, so to speak, in a line-by-line striving toward the vividness and human presence that are the hallmarks of narrative history. But there are also larger strategies that can be called into play. Within chapters we have been especially attentive to chronology, which sometimes involved a significant reordering of the material. For example, we now begin Chapter 13 with a section on "The Mature Cotton Economy," whose existence encouraged westward expansion, the annexation of Texas, and the fateful war with Mexico. For reasons of continuity we have also reordered Chapters 18 and 19 so that "Politics in the Age of Enterprise" now follows "The Rise of the City." This new organization provides students with a seamless transition to our discussion of the political reforms of the Progressive Era (Chapter 20). Chapter 31 likewise received considerable revision and now provides a compact and coherent overview of the period from the early 1980s to the present. By being forced to think hard about how to organize materials, we have come up with a stronger periodization and clearer thematic development.

To assist students in grasping the meaning and complexity of the past, we have grounded *America: A Concise History* in a clear chronology and strong conceptual framework. Each of the two volumes is divided into three parts, with each part corresponding to a distinct phase of development. Every part begins at a crucial turning point, such as the American Revolution or the Cold War, and emphasizes the dynamic forces at work. Part openers contain **thematic timelines** that highlight key developments and **part essays** that set out clearly and concisely the main themes of our story and, through a combination of quotations from historical actors and careful analysis, explore the crucial engines of historical change that create new conditions of life. This structure will help students understand the major themes in each period of American history, to discover how the bits and pieces of historical data acquire significance as part of a larger pattern of development.

Moreover, to capture the reader's attention, each chapter opens with an anecdote or scene that establishes the chapter's main ideas and topics. Our chapter endings eschew the usual textbook summary in favor of apt statements bringing the discussion to a satisfying close and opening the way for what follows.

New Perspectives

The revising process is also an opportunity to incorporate new scholarship. Our treatment of Native Americans in the colonial era incorporates recent anthropologically influenced work showing how Indian peoples maintained elements of their traditional culture in the face of European domination. We draw on new work dealing with the role of women and gender in eighteenth-century religion and antebellum politics and recent scholarship on the crisis over slavery after Independence. We offer an expanded treatment of the role of state policy during the antebellum Market Revolution, and we make full use of recent Reconstruction scholarship that sees the transition from slavery to freedom as largely a battle over labor systems. We continue to incorporate more about the Far West into the nation's historical narrative, relying on the new western history for insight into the interactions among environment, peoples, and economic development.

Advances in gender history enable us to offer a new discussion of bachelorhood and masculinity in the late nineteenth century and to temper our treatment of progressive welfare policy as we become aware of its patriarchal underpinnings. New scholarship on ethnic minorities similarly enables us to amplify our discussion of Native Americans during World War I and the New Deal, Asian Americans during the Great Depression, and black women during the 1920s and the later civil rights struggles. Recent scholarship based on hitherto closed Soviet and U.S. archives continues to inform our treatment of the Cold War, and an analysis of the turbulent years following the attack by Muslim extremists on September 11, 2001, brings the book to a thoughtful close. In these ways, and others, we strive to maintain the reputation of *America: A Concise History* as a fresh and timely text.

Features in This Edition

In the first edition of *America: A Concise History*, our main goal was to shorten the original text by 40 percent—in effect, to make six words do the work of ten—without compromising its balanced coverage and explanatory power. In the second edition, we undertook the equally ambitious objective of writing a more compelling *narrative* text. Our goal was to produce a book that students would actually enjoy reading, not merely a set of assignments to be gotten through. The number of instructors who now use our text on a regular basis suggests the success of that endeavor.

In this third edition we have turned our attention to some nuts-and-bolts issues of teaching history. Keenly aware that today's students lack geographic literacy, we have beefed up the **map program**. We have added over thirty new maps, redrawn every existing map to reflect recent advances in cartography, and, to assist students to become better map readers, have added "call-outs" to particular maps. As a further aid to readers, we have included a **glossary** that provides a historically appropriate definition of challenging or unfamiliar terms and concepts. Recognizing also that students increasingly live in a mental world shaped by the World Wide Web, we have combed through hundreds of **Web sites** to find those that best supplement the material in the text and integrated them with the "**For Further Exploration**" bibliographical essays found at the end of each chapter. To assist instructors and advanced students, a **full bibliography** is available on the Web at bedfordstmartins.com/henrettaconcise. Our goal is ultimately to write a history that moves seamlessly between the written text and the bountiful images and sources available at the click of a mouse.

To strengthen our commitment to putting a human face on historical experience, each chapter contains two boxed **voices**, first-person excerpts from letters, diaries, autobiographies, and public testimony that paint a vivid picture of the social or political life of the time. Some are **American Voices**; others, new to this edition, are **Voices from Abroad**. These voices deepen the international dimension to our analysis of American life. To enliven students' understanding of history, we have peppered the text with more than 150 paintings, illustrations, and photographs, most of them in full color and many new to this edition. We have also provided detailed captions that set the illustrations in context and extend the discussion in the text.

Taken together, these documents and illustrations provide instructors with a trove of teaching materials, and students with a chance to enter the life of the past and see it from within.

Supplements

Readers of *America: A Concise History* often cite its ancillary package as a key to the book's success in the classroom. Most of the ancillaries are customized for the concise edition, providing a flexible yet targeted collection of resources for instructors and a helpful set of study tools for students.

For Students

Online Study Guide at bedfordstmartins.com/henrettaconcise. The popular Online Study Guide for *America: A Concise History* is a free and uniquely personalized learning tool to help students master themes and information in the textbook and improve their historical skills. Assessment quizzes help students evaluate their textbook comprehension and provide customized plans for further study through a variety of activities. Instructors can monitor student progress through the online Quiz Gradebook or receive e-mail updates.

Documents to Accompany AMERICA'S HISTORY, Fifth Edition. Edited by Melvin Yazawa (University of New Mexico) and Kevin J. Fernlund (University of Missouri, St. Louis), this collection of over 350 primary source documents with editorial apparatus is constructed to facilitate students' comprehension and analysis of the readings, and is easily assigned with the concise edition.

NEW **Maps in Context: A Workbook for American History.** Written by historical cartography expert Gerald A. Danzer (University of Illinois at Chicago), this skill-building workbook helps students comprehend the essential connections between geographic literacy and historical understanding. Organized to correspond to the typical U.S. survey course, *Maps in Context* presents a wealth of map-centered projects and convenient pop-quizzes that give students hands-on experience working with maps.

NEW **History Matters: A Student Guide to U.S. History Online.** This new resource, edited by Alan Gevinson, Kelly Schrum, and Roy Rosenzweig (all of George Mason University), provides an illustrated and annotated guide to 250 of the most useful Web sites for student research in U.S. history, as well as advice on evaluating and using Internet sources. This essential guide is based on the acclaimed "History Matters" Web site developed by the American History Social Project and the Center for History and New Media.

Bedford Series in History and Culture.   Over 70 titles in this highly praised series combine first-rate scholarship, historical narrative, and important primary documents for undergraduate courses. Each book is brief, inexpensive, and focused on a specific topic or period. Package discounts are available.

Historians at Work **Series.**   Brief enough for a single assignment yet meaty enough to provoke thoughtful discussion, each volume in this series examines a single historical question by combining unabridged selections by distinguished historians, each with a differing perspective on the issue, with helpful learning aids. Package discounts are available.

NEW **PlaceLinks at bedfordstmartins.com/henrettaconcise.**   PlaceLinks provides access to resources on the Web for over 100 historical sites in all fifty states, such as specific monuments, parks, and museums that connect students to the places where history happened. This new online feature makes history tangible and local.

DocLinks at bedfordstmartins.com/doclinks.   This Web site provides over 750 annotated Web links to online primary documents, including links to speeches, legislation, treaties, social commentary, Supreme Court decisions, essays, travelers' accounts, personal narratives and testimony, newspaper articles, visual artifacts, songs, and poems. Students and teachers alike can search documents by topic, date, or specific chapter of *America: A Concise History.* Links can be selected and stored for later use or published to a unique Web address.

HistoryLinks at bedfordstmartins.com/historylinks.   Recently updated, HistoryLinks directs instructors and students to over 500 carefully selected and annotated links to history-related Web sites, including those containing image galleries, maps, and audio and video clips for supplementing lectures or assignments. Users can browse these Internet starting points by date, subject, medium, keyword, or specific chapter in *America: A Concise History.* Instructors can assign these links as the basis for homework assignments or research projects, or students can use them in their own history research. Links can be selected and stored for later use or published to a unique Web address.

A Student's Online Guide to History Reference Sources at bedfordstmartins .com/benjamin.   This Web site provides links to history-related electronic reference sources such as databases, indexes, and journals, plus contact information for state, provincial, local, and professional history organizations.

Research and Documentation Online at bedfordstmartins.com/resdoc.   This Web site provides clear advice on how to integrate primary and secondary sources into research papers, how to cite sources correctly, and how to format in MLA, APA, Chicago, or CBE style.

The St. Martin's Tutorial on Avoiding Plagiarism at bedfordstmartins.com/plagiarismtutorial.   This online tutorial reviews the consequences of plagiarism and explains what sources to acknowledge, how to keep good notes, how to organize research, and how to appropriately integrate sources. The tutorial includes exercises to help students practice integrating sources and recognizing acceptable summaries.

Critical Thinking Modules at bedfordstmartins.com/historymodules.   This Web site offers over two dozen online modules for interpreting maps, audio, visual, and textual sources, centered on events covered in the U.S. history survey. An online guide correlates modules to textbook chapters and books in the Bedford Series in History and Culture.

For Instructors

Instructor's Resource Manual.   This popular manual by Bradley T. Gericke (U.S. Army Command and General Staff College) offers both experienced and first-time instructors a wealth of tools—annotated chapter outlines and summaries, lecture strategies, discussion starters, and suggested research assignments—for presenting textbook material in exciting and engaging ways.

Computerized Test Bank.   This test bank by Thomas L. Altherr (Metropolitan State College of Denver) and Adolph Grundman (Metropolitan State College of Denver) provides easy-to-use software to create tests. Over 80 exercises are provided per chapter, including multiple-choice, fill-in-the-blank, map analysis, short essay, and full-length essay questions. Instructors can customize quizzes, add or edit both questions and answers, as well as export them to a variety of formats, including WebCT and Blackboard. The disc includes correct answers and essay outlines.

Transparencies.   This set of over 250 full-color acetate transparencies includes all maps and many images from *America: A Concise History* and the parent text, *America's History*, Fifth Edition. A guide correlating all the maps and art to the concise edition is available on the Book Companion Site.

Instructor's Resource CD-ROM.   This disc provides instructors with ready-made and customizable PowerPoint multimedia presentations built around chapter outlines, maps, figures, and selected images from the textbook. The disc also includes images in JPEG format, an electronic version of the *Instructor's Resource Manual*, outline maps in PDF format for quizzing or handouts, and quick-start guides to the Online Study Guide.

Book Companion Site at bedfordstmartins.com/henrettaconcise.   The companion Web site gathers all the electronic resources for the text, including the Online Study Guide and related Quiz Gradebook, at a single Web address, providing convenient links to such helpful lecture, assignment, and research materials as PowerPoint chapter outlines, a transparency correlation guide, DocLinks, HistoryLinks, and Map Central.

Map Central at bedfordstmartins.com/mapcentral.   Map Central is a searchable database of over 750 maps from Bedford/St. Martin's history texts for classroom presentation and over 50 basic political and physical outline maps for quizzing or handouts.

Using the Bedford Series in History and Culture in the U.S. History Survey at bedfordstmartins.com/usingseries.   This online guide helps instructors integrate volumes from the highly regarded Bedford Series in History and Culture into their U.S. history survey course. The guide not only correlates themes from each series book with the survey course but also provides ideas for classroom discussions.

Blackboard Course Cartridge and WebCT e-Pack.   Blackboard and WebCT content are available for this book.

Videos and Multimedia.   A wide assortment of videos and multimedia CD-ROMs on various topics in American history is available to qualified adopters.

Acknowledgments

The scholars and teachers who reviewed *America: A Concise History* made suggestions that we gratefully incorporated into the new edition. Most of our reviewers have used concise texts in their courses, and their classroom experience has helped us to craft a book that meets the needs of today's diverse students. Thanks are due to: Ginette Aley, Virginia Tech; Rosemary Brogan, Cabrillo Community College; Nichole Etcheson, University of Texas at El Paso; Paul Faler, University of Massachusetts–Boston; David Farber, University of New Mexico; Linda Gies, Eastern New Mexico University; Craig Hendricks, Long Beach City College; Johanna Hume, Alvin Community College; Susan Johnson, Ohio State University; Kathleen Kennedy, Western Washington University; Andrew Kersten, University of Wisconsin, Green Bay; Michael Mangus, Ohio State University, Newark; Jimmie McGee, South Plains College; Carol O'Connor, Arkansas State University; Eric Rauchway, University of California, Davis; Paul Rosier, Villanova University; Bradford Sample, Indiana University; Rhonda Smith, Eastern Kentucky University; Sean Taylor, Minnesota State University, Moorehead; Michael Topp, University of Texas at El Paso; Robert Zeidel, University of Wisconsin, Stout.

As the authors of *America: A Concise History*, we know better than anyone else how much this book is the work of other hands and minds. We are grateful to Mary Dougherty, Jane Knetzger, and Patricia Rossi who oversaw the project, and William

Lombardo, who used his extensive knowledge and critical skills as a well-trained historian to edit our text and suggest a multitude of improvements. Elizabeth M. Welch offered invaluable insight and guidance along the way. As usual, Joan E. Feinberg has been generous in providing the resources we needed to produce the third edition. Lori Chong Roncka did more than we had a right to expect in producing an outstanding volume. Karen Melton Soeltz and Jenna Bookin Barry in the marketing department have been instrumental in helping this book reach the classroom. We also thank the rest of our editorial and production team for their dedicated efforts: Elizabeth Wallace, Kristen Merrill, Amy Derjue, and Anne True; Pembroke Herbert and Sandi Rygiel at Picture Research Consultants and Archives; Jennifer Wetzel and Sandy Schechter. Finally, we want to express our appreciation for the invaluable assistance of Patricia Deveneau, Jonathan White, David Axeen, James Halstead, and Norman S. Cohen, whose work contributed in many ways to the intellectual vitality of this new edition of *America: A Concise History*.

James A. Henretta
David Brody
Lynn Dumenil

BRIEF CONTENTS

Part One

THE CREATION OF AMERICAN SOCIETY, 1450–1775 **2**

1 WORLDS COLLIDE: EUROPE, AFRICA, AND AMERICA, 1450–1620 6

2 THE INVASION AND SETTLEMENT OF NORTH AMERICA, 1550–1700 37

3 THE BRITISH EMPIRE IN AMERICA, 1660–1750 68

4 GROWTH AND CRISIS IN COLONIAL SOCIETY, 1720–1765 99

5 TOWARD INDEPENDENCE: YEARS OF DECISION, 1763–1775 131

Part Two

THE NEW REPUBLIC, 1775–1820 **162**

6 WAR AND REVOLUTION, 1775–1783 166

7 THE NEW POLITICAL ORDER, 1776–1800 196

8 THE DYNAMICS OF WESTERN SETTLEMENT AND EASTERN CAPITALISM, 1790–1820 227

9 THE QUEST FOR A REPUBLICAN SOCIETY, 1790–1820 257

Part Three

ECONOMIC REVOLUTION AND SECTIONAL STRIFE, 1820–1877 **288**

10 THE ECONOMIC REVOLUTION, 1820–1860 292

11 A DEMOCRATIC REVOLUTION, 1820–1844 322

12   RELIGION AND REFORM, 1820–1860   352

13   THE CRISIS OF THE UNION, 1844–1860   382

14   TWO SOCIETIES AT WAR, 1861–1865   412

15   RECONSTRUCTION, 1865–1877   442

Part Four

A MATURING INDUSTRIAL SOCIETY, 1877–1914   **472**

16   THE AMERICAN WEST   476

17   CAPITAL AND LABOR IN THE AGE OF ENTERPRISE, 1877–1900   505

18   THE RISE OF THE CITY   535

19   POLITICS IN THE AGE OF ENTERPRISE, 1877–1896   566

20   THE PROGRESSIVE ERA   597

21   AN EMERGING WORLD POWER, 1877–1914   628

Part Five

THE MODERN STATE AND SOCIETY, 1914–1945   **658**

22   WAR AND THE AMERICAN STATE, 1914–1920   662

23   MODERN TIMES: THE 1920s   692

24   THE GREAT DEPRESSION   723

25   THE NEW DEAL, 1933–1939   752

26   THE WORLD AT WAR, 1939–1945   780

Part Six

AMERICA AND THE WORLD, 1945 TO THE PRESENT   **812**

27   COLD WAR AMERICA, 1945–1960   816

28   THE AFFLUENT SOCIETY AND THE LIBERAL CONSENSUS, 1945–1965   848

29   WAR ABROAD AND AT HOME: THE VIETNAM ERA, 1961–1975   880

30   THE LEAN YEARS, 1969–1980   915

31   A NEW DOMESTIC AND WORLD ORDER, 1981–2004   946

CONTENTS

Preface   xi

List of Maps   xxxviii

About the Authors   xlii

Part One

THE CREATION OF AMERICAN SOCIETY, 1450–1775   **2**

Chapter 1
WORLDS COLLIDE: EUROPE, AFRICA, AND AMERICA, 1450–1620   6

Native American Worlds   7

The First Americans   7   •   The Mayas and the Aztecs   9   •   The Indians of the North   10

Traditional European Society in 1450   14

The Peasantry   14   •   Hierarchy and Authority   16   •   The Power of Religion   17

Europe Encounters Africa and the Americas, 1450–1550   18

The Renaissance   18   •   West African Society and Slavery   **20**   •   Europe Reaches the Americas   23   •   The Spanish Conquest   25

The Protestant Reformation and the Rise of England   29

The Protestant Movement   29   •   The Dutch and the English Challenge Spain   31
•   The Social Causes of English Colonization   33

> VOICES FROM ABROAD
> FATHER LE PETITE: The Customs of the Natchez, 1730   13

> AMERICAN VOICES
> FRIAR BERNARDINO DE SAHAGÚN: Aztec Elders Describe the Spanish Conquest   26

Chapter 2
THE INVASION AND SETTLEMENT OF NORTH AMERICA, 1550–1700   37

Imperial Conflicts and Rival Colonial Models   38

New Spain: Colonization and Conversion   38   •   New France: Furs and Souls   41
•   New Netherland: Commerce   43   •   English Virginia: Settlers and
a Staple Crop   44

The Chesapeake Experience   47

Settling the Tobacco Colonies   47   •   Masters, Servants, and Slaves   50   •   The
Seeds of Social Revolt   51   •   Bacon's Rebellion   52

Puritan New England   53

The Puritan Migration   53   •   Puritanism and Witchcraft   57   •   A Yeoman
Society, 1630–1700   58

The Eastern Indians' New World   59

Puritans and Pequots   59   •   Metacom's (King Philip's) Rebellion   61   •   The Fur
Trade and the Inland Peoples   63

> VOICES FROM ABROAD
> SAMUEL DE CHAMPLAIN: Going to War with the Hurons   42

> AMERICAN VOICES
> MARY ROWLANDSON: A Captivity Narrative   64

Chapter 3
THE BRITISH EMPIRE IN AMERICA, 1660–1750   68

The Politics of Empire, 1660–1713   69

The Great Aristocratic Land Grab   69   •   From Mercantilism to Imperial Dominion
70   •   The Glorious Revolution in England and America   72   •   Imperial Wars
and Native Peoples   74

The Imperial Slave Economy   76

The South Atlantic System   77   •   Slavery in the Chesapeake and
South Carolina   80   •   The Emergence of an African American Community   84
•   Resistance and Accommodation   85   •   The Southern Gentry   87   •
The Northern Maritime Economy   88

The New Politics of Empire, 1713–1750   91

The Rise of Colonial Assemblies   91   •   Salutary Neglect   92   •   Protecting the
Mercantile System   94   •   The American Economic Challenge   95

VOICES FROM ABROAD
OLAUDAH EQUIANO: The Brutal "Middle Passage"   81

AMERICAN VOICES
GOVERNOR JOSEPH DUDLEY AND JOHN WINCHESTER: A "Leveling" Spirit in the Colonies   93

Chapter 4
GROWTH AND CRISIS IN COLONIAL SOCIETY, 1720–1765   99

Freehold Society in New England   100

Farm Families: Women's Place   100   •   Farm Property: Inheritance   102   •
The Crisis of Freehold Society   103

The Middle Atlantic: Toward a New Society, 1720–1765   104

Economic Growth and Social Inequality   104   •   Cultural Diversity   106
•   Religious Identity and Political Conflict   111

The Enlightenment and the Great Awakening, 1740–1765   112

The Enlightenment in America   112   •   American Pietism and the Great
Awakening   114   •   Religious Upheaval in the North   116   •   Social and
Religious Conflict in the South   117

The Midcentury Challenge: War, Trade, and Social Conflict, 1750–1765   119

The French and Indian War Becomes a War for Empire   119   •   British Economic
Growth and the Consumer Revolution   122   •   The Struggle for Land in
the East   124   •   Western Uprisings and Regulator Movements   125

AMERICAN VOICES
Runaway Servants and Slaves   107

AMERICAN VOICES
CHARLES WOODMASON: Social Chaos on the Carolina Frontier   127

Chapter 5
TOWARD INDEPENDENCE: YEARS OF DECISION, 1763–1775   131

The Imperial Reformers, 1763–1765   132

The Legacy of War   132   •   The Sugar Act and Colonial Rights   134   •   An Open
Challenge: The Stamp Act   137

The Dynamics of Rebellion, 1765–1766   138

Politicians Protest and the Crowd Rebels   138   •   Ideological Roots
of Resistance   142   •   Parliament Compromises, 1766   143

The Growing Confrontation, 1767–1770   145

The Townshend Initiatives   145   •   America Again Debates and Resists   147
•   Lord North Compromises, 1770   149

The Road to War, 1771–1775   151

The Compromise Ignored   151   •   The Continental Congress Responds   153
•   The Rising of the Countryside   155   •   The Failure of Compromise   158

> AMERICAN VOICES
> SAMUEL ADAMS: An American View of the Stamp Act   144
>
> VOICES FROM ABROAD
> LIEUTENANT COLONEL FRANCIS SMITH: A British View of Lexington and
> Concord   159

Part Two

THE NEW REPUBLIC, 1775–1820   **162**

Chapter 6
WAR AND REVOLUTION, 1775–1783   166

Toward Independence, 1775–1776   167

The Second Continental Congress and Civil War   167   •   Common Sense   168
•   Independence Declared   171

The Trials of War, 1776–1778   172

War in the North   172   •   Armies and Strategies   174   •   Victory at Saratoga   175
•   Social and Financial Perils   176

The Path to Victory, 1778–1783   178

The French Alliance   179   •   War in the South   180   •   The Patriot
Advantage   183   •   Diplomatic Triumph   183

Republicanism Defined and Challenged   184

Republican Ideals under Wartime Pressures   184   •   The Loyalist Exodus   187
•   The Problem of Slavery   188   •   A Republican Religious Order   190

> AMERICAN VOICES
> MARY HOOKS SLOCUMB: The Meaning of War   169
>
> VOICES FROM ABROAD
> ALEXANDER COVENTRY: The Character of Northern Slavery   191

Chapter 7
THE NEW POLITICAL ORDER, 1776–1800   196

Creating Republican Institutions, 1776–1787   197

The State Constitutions: How Much Democracy?   197   •   The Articles
of Confederation   202   •   Shays's Rebellion   206

The Constitution of 1787   207

The Rise of a Nationalist Faction   **207**   •   The Philadelphia Convention   **208**   •
The People Debate Ratification   **211**   •   The Federalists Implement the
Constitution   **214**

The Political Crisis of the 1790s   215

Hamilton's Financial Program   **216**   •   Jefferson's Agrarian Vision   **218**   •
The French Revolution Divides Americans   **219**   •   The Rise of Political
Parties   **221**   •   Constitutional Crisis, 1798–1800   **222**

> AMERICAN VOICES
> ABIGAIL AND JOHN ADAMS: The Status of Women   **200**

> VOICES FROM ABROAD
> WILLIAM COBBETT: Peter Porcupine Attacks Pro-French Americans   **223**

Chapter 8
THE DYNAMICS OF WESTERN SETTLEMENT AND EASTERN CAPITALISM, 1790–1820   227

Westward Expansion   228

Native American Resistance   **228**   •   Migration and the Changing Farm Economy
232   •   The Transportation Bottleneck   **235**

The Republicans' Political Revolution   237

The Jeffersonian Presidency   **237**   •   Jefferson and the West   **239**   •   Conflict with
Britain and France   **240**   •   The War of 1812   **242**

The Capitalist Commonwealth   246

Banks, Manufacturing, and Markets   **246**   •   Public Policy: The Commonwealth
System   **249**   •   Federalist Law: John Marshall and the Supreme Court   **250**

> AMERICAN VOICES
> RED JACKET: A Seneca Chief's Understanding of Religion   **232**

> VOICES FROM ABROAD
> ALEXIS DE TOCQUEVILLE: Law and Lawyers in the United States   **254**

Chapter 9
THE QUEST FOR A REPUBLICAN SOCIETY, 1790–1820   257

Democratic Republicanism   258

Social and Political Equality for White Men   **258**   •   Toward a Republican Marriage
System   **260**   •   Republican Motherhood   **261**   •   Raising and Educating
Republican Children   **263**

Aristocratic Republicanism and Slavery   266

The North and South Grow Apart   **266**   •   Toward a New Southern Social Order   **268**   •   Slave Society and Culture   **271**   •   The Free Black Population   272   •   The Missouri Crisis   **275**

Protestant Christianity as a Social Force   277

The Second Great Awakening   **277**   •   Women's New Religious Roles   **284**

> AMERICAN VOICES
> JACOB STROYER: A Child Learns the Meaning of Slavery   273

> VOICES FROM ABROAD
> FRANCES TROLLOPE: A Camp Meeting in Indiana   279

Part Three
ECONOMIC REVOLUTION AND SECTIONAL STRIFE, 1820–1877   **288**

Chapter 10
THE ECONOMIC REVOLUTION, 1820–1860   292

The Coming of Industry: Northeastern Manufacturing   293

Division of Labor and the Factory   **293**   •   The Textile Industry and British Competition   **294**   •   American Mechanics and Technological Innovation   **297**   •   Wage Workers and the Labor Movement   **299**

The Market Revolution   301

Migration to the Southwest and the Midwest   **301**   •   The Transportation Revolution Forges Regional Ties   **302**   •   The Growth of Cities and Towns   **308**

Changes in the Social Structure   309

The Business Elite   **310**   •   The Middle Class   **311**   •   Urban Workers and the Poor   **313**   •   The Benevolent Empire   **314**   •   Revivalism and Reform   **315**   •   Immigration and Cultural Conflict   **317**

> AMERICAN VOICES
> LUCY LARCOM: Early Days at Lowell   **298**

> AMERICAN VOICES
> JOHN GOUGH: The Vice of Intemperance   **318**

Chapter 11
A DEMOCRATIC REVOLUTION, 1820–1844   322

The Rise of Popular Politics, 1820–1829   323

The Decline of the Notables and the Rise of Parties   **323**   •   The Election of 1824   **325**   •   The Last Notable President: John Quincy Adams   **327**   •   "The Democracy" and the Election of 1828   **328**

The Jacksonian Presidency, 1829–1837   330

Jackson's Agenda: Patronage and Policy   **332**   •   The Tariff and Nullification   **333**   •   The Bank War   **334**   •   Indian Removal   **336**   •   The Jacksonian Impact   **340**

Class, Culture, and the Second Party System   342

The Whig Worldview   **342**   •   Labor Politics and the Depression of 1837–1843   **345**   •   "Tippecanoe and Tyler Too!"   **347**

> AMERICAN VOICES
> MARGARET BAYARD SMITH: Republican Majesty and Mobs   331

> AMERICAN VOICES
> BLACK HAWK: A Sacred Reverence for Our Lands   338

Chapter 12
RELIGION AND REFORM, 1820–1860   352

Individualism   353

Emerson and Transcendentalism   **353**   •   Emerson's Literary Influence   **355**   •   Brook Farm   **357**

Communalism   358

The Shakers   **358**   •   The Fourierist Phalanxes   **361**   •   John Humphrey Noyes and the Oneida Community   **361**   •   The Mormon Experience   **362**

Abolitionism   367

Uplift, Race-Equality, and Rebellion   **367**   •   Garrison and Evangelical Abolitionism   **368**   •   Opposition and Internal Conflict   **371**

The Women's Rights Movement   374

Origins of the Women's Movement   **374**   •   Abolitionism and Women   **376**   •   The Program of Seneca Falls and Beyond   **378**

> AMERICAN VOICES
> An Illinois "Jeffersonian" Attacks the Mormons   365

> AMERICAN VOICES
> KEZIAH KENDALL: A Farm Woman Defends the Grimké Sisters   377

Chapter 13
THE CRISIS OF THE UNION, 1844–1860   382

Manifest Destiny   383

The Mature Cotton Economy, 1820–1860   **383**   •   The Independence of Texas   **386**   •   The Push to the Pacific: Oregon and California   **387**   •   The Fateful Election of 1844   **390**

War, Expansion, and Slavery, 1846–1850   392

The War with Mexico, 1846–1848   392   •   A Divisive Victory   393   •   1850: Crisis and Compromise   396

The End of the Second Party System, 1850–1858   398

Resistance to the Fugitive Slave Act   399   •   The Political System in Decline   400 • The Kansas-Nebraska Act and the Rise of New Parties   401   •   The Election of 1856 and Dred Scott   403

Abraham Lincoln and the Republican Triumph, 1858–1860   406

Lincoln's Political Career   407   •   The Party System Fragments   409

        AMERICAN VOICES
        MARY BOYKIN CHESNUT: A Slaveholding Woman's Diary   385

        AMERICAN VOICES
        AXALLA JOHN HOOLE: "Bleeding Kansas": A Southern View   404

Chapter 14
TWO SOCIETIES AT WAR, 1861–1865   412

Secession and Military Stalemate, 1861–1862   413

Choosing Sides   413   •   Setting War Aims and Devising Strategies   418

Toward Total War   423

Mobilizing Armies and Civilians   423   •   Mobilizing Resources   426

The Turning Point: 1863   428

Emancipation   428   •   Vicksburg and Gettysburg   430

The Union Victorious, 1864–1865   432

Soldiers and Strategy   432   •   The Election of 1864 and Sherman's March to the Sea   436

        VOICES FROM ABROAD
        ERNEST DUVEYIER DE HAURANNE: German Immigrants and the Civil War within Missouri   417

        AMERICAN VOICES
        DOLLY SUMNER LUNT: Sherman's March through Georgia   439

Chapter 15
RECONSTRUCTION, 1865–1877   442

Presidential Reconstruction   443

Lincoln's Approach   443   •   Johnson Seizes the Initiative   444   •   Acting on Freedom   446   •   Congress versus President   450

Radical Reconstruction   452

Congress Takes Command   **453**   •   Woman Suffrage Denied   **456**   •   Republican Rule in the South   **457**   •   The Quest for Land   **460**

The Undoing of Reconstruction   464

Counterrevolution   **465**   •   The Acquiescent North   **468**   •   The Political Crisis of 1877   **469**

> AMERICAN VOICES
> JOURDON ANDERSON: Relishing Freedom   447

> AMERICAN VOICES
> HARRIET HERNANDES: The Intimidation of Black Voters   466

Part Four

A MATURING INDUSTRIAL SOCIETY, 1877–1914   **472**

Chapter 16
THE AMERICAN WEST   476

The Great Plains   476

Indians of the Great Plains   **478**   •   Wagon Trains, Railroads, and Ranchers   **479**   •   Homesteaders   **482**   •   The Fate of the Indians   **486**

The Far West   491

The Mining Frontier   **491**   •   Hispanics, Chinese, Anglos   **495**   •   Golden California   **500**

> AMERICAN VOICES
> IDA LINDGREN: Swedish Emigrant in Frontier Kansas   483

> VOICES FROM ABROAD
> BARON JOSEPH ALEXANDER VON HÜBNER: A Western Boom Town   493

Chapter 17
CAPITAL AND LABOR IN THE AGE OF ENTERPRISE, 1877–1900   505

Industrial Capitalism Triumphant   506

The Age of Steel   **506**   •   The Railroad Boom   **507**   •   Large-Scale Enterprise   **511**

The World of Work   514

Labor Recruits   **515**   •   Working Women and the Family Economy   **519**   •   Autonomous Labor   **521**   •   Systems of Control   **523**

The Labor Movement   525

Reformers and Unionists   525   •   The Triumph of "Pure and Simple" Unionism   527
•   Industrial War   530   •   American Radicalism in the Making   531

> VOICES FROM ABROAD
> COUNT VAY DE VAYA UND LUSKOD: Pittsburgh Inferno   518

> AMERICAN VOICES
> ROSE SCHNEIDERMAN: Trade Unionist   529

Chapter 18
THE RISE OF THE CITY   535

Urbanization   536

City Innovation   537   •   Private City, Public City   539   •   A Balance Sheet:
Chicago and Berlin   541

Upper Class/Middle Class   542

The Urban Elite   542   •   The Suburban World   544   •   Middle-Class
Families   545

City Life   549

Newcomers   551   •   Ward Politics   555   •   Religion in the City   557   •   City
Amusements   560   •   The Higher Culture   561

> AMERICAN VOICES
> M. CAREY THOMAS: "We Did Not Know . . . Whether Women's Health
> Could Stand the Strain of College Education"   547

> AMERICAN VOICES
> ANONYMOUS: Bintel Brief   554

Chapter 19
POLITICS IN THE AGE OF ENTERPRISE, 1877–1896   566

The Politics of the Status Quo, 1877–1893   567

The National Scene   567   •   The Ideology of Individualism   571
•   The Supremacy of the Courts   572

Politics and the People   574

Cultural Politics: Party, Religion, and Ethnicity   574   •   Organizational
Politics   576   •   Women's Political Culture   578

Race and Politics in the New South   581

Biracial Politics   581   •   One-Party Rule Triumphant   584   •   The Case of
Grimes County   586

The Crisis of American Politics: The 1890s   587

The Populist Revolt   588   •   Money and Politics   591   •   Climax: The Election of 1896   592

> AMERICAN VOICES
> HELEN POTTER: The Case for Women's Political Rights   580

> AMERICAN VOICES
> TOM WATSON: The Case for Interracial Unity   583

Chapter 20
THE PROGRESSIVE ERA   597

The Course of Reform   598

Progressive Ideas   598   •   Women Progressives   600   •   Reforming Politics   604   •   Racism and Reform   605   •   Urban Liberalism   608

Progressivism and National Politics   611

The Making of a Progressive President   611   •   Regulating the Marketplace   615   •   The Fracturing of Republican Progressivism   620   •   Woodrow Wilson and the New Freedom   622

> AMERICAN VOICES
> DR. ALICE HAMILTON: Tracking Down Lead Poisoning   612

> VOICES FROM ABROAD
> JAMES BRYCE: America in 1905: "Business Is King"   616

Chapter 21
AN EMERGING WORLD POWER, 1877–1914   628

The Roots of Expansion   629

Diplomacy in the Gilded Age   629   •   The Economy of Expansionism   632   •   The Making of a "Large" Foreign Policy   634   •   The Ideology of Expansionism   635

An American Empire   636

The Cuban Crisis   637   •   The Spoils of War   639   •   The Imperial Experiment   642

Onto the World Stage   646

A Power among Powers   646   •   The Open Door in Asia   650   •   Wilson and Mexico   652   •   The Gathering Storm in Europe   654

> AMERICAN VOICES
> GEORGE W. PRIOLEAU: Black Soldiers in a White Man's War   643

> VOICES FROM ABROAD
> JEAN HESS, ÉMILE ZOLA, AND RUBEN DARIO: American Goliath   648

Part Five

THE MODERN STATE AND SOCIETY, 1914–1945   **658**

Chapter 22
WAR AND THE AMERICAN STATE, 1914–1920   662

The Great War, 1914–1918   663
War in Europe   **663**   •   The Perils of Neutrality   **665**   •   "Over There"   **669**

War on the Home Front   674
Mobilizing Industry and the Economy   **674**   •   Mobilizing American Workers   **676**
•   Wartime Reform: Woman Suffrage and Prohibition   **679**   •   Promoting National
Unity   **681**

An Unsettled Peace, 1919–1920   683
The Treaty of Versailles   **683**   •   Racial Strife, Labor Unrest, and the Red
Scare   **687**

> AMERICAN VOICES
> HARRY CURTIN: Trench Warfare   **666**

> AMERICAN VOICES
> Southern Migrants   **678**

Chapter 23
MODERN TIMES: THE 1920s   692

Business-Government Partnership of the 1920s   692
Politics in the Republican "New Era"   **693**   •   The Economy   **696**   •   Economic
Expansion Abroad   **699**

A New National Culture   702
A Consumer Culture   **702**   •   Mass Media and New Patterns of Leisure   **704**

Dissenting Values and Cultural Conflict   707
The Rise of Nativism   **708**   •   Legislating Values: The *Scopes* Trial and
Prohibition   **713**   •   Intellectual Crosscurrents   **716**   •   Cultural Clash in the
Election of 1928   **718**

> VOICES FROM ABROAD
> The Ford Miracle: "Slaves" to the Assembly Line   **698**

> AMERICAN VOICES
> KAZUO KAWAI: A Foreigner in America   **710**

Chapter 24
THE GREAT DEPRESSION 723

The Coming of the Great Depression 723

Causes of the Depression 724 • The Worldwide Depression 725

Hard Times 726

Families Face the Depression 728 • Popular Culture Views the Depression 733

Harder Times for the Down and Out 735

African Americans in the Depression 735 • Dust Bowl Migrations 737 • Mexican American Communities 740 • Asian Americans Face the Depression 742

Herbert Hoover and the Great Depression 744

Hoover Responds 744 • Rising Discontent 745 • The 1932 Election: A New Order 748

> AMERICAN VOICES
> LARRY VAN DUSEN: A Working-Class Family Encounters the Great Depression 729

> AMERICAN VOICES
> Public Assistance Fails a Southern Farm Family 746

Chapter 25
THE NEW DEAL, 1933–1939 752

The New Deal Takes Over, 1933–1935 752

The Roosevelt Style of Leadership 753 • The Hundred Days 754 • The New Deal under Attack 758

The Second New Deal, 1935–1938 761

Legislative Accomplishments 761 • Stalemate 763

The New Deal's Impact on Society 765

New Deal Constituencies and the Broker State 765 • The New Deal and the Land 772 • The New Deal and the Arts 773 • The Legacies of the New Deal 776

> AMERICAN VOICES
> Americans Respond to the Fireside Chats 755

> AMERICAN VOICES
> SUSANA ARCHULETA: A Chicana Youth Gets New Deal Work 770

Chapter 26
THE WORLD AT WAR, 1939–1945   780

The Road to War   781

The Rise of Fascism   781   •   Depression-Era Isolationism   782   •   Retreat from Isolationism   783   •   The Attack on Pearl Harbor   785

Organizing for Victory   787

Defense Mobilization   787   •   Workers and the War Effort   789   •   Politics in Wartime   793

Life on the Home Front   794

"For the Duration"   794   •   Japanese Internment   796

Fighting and Winning the War   799

Wartime Aims and Strategies   799   •   The War in Europe   799   •   The War in the Pacific   802   •   Planning the Postwar World   806

> VOICES FROM ABROAD
> GERMAN POWs: American Race Relations   792

> AMERICAN VOICES
> JUANITA REDMOND: An Army Nurse in Bataan   803

Part Six

AMERICA AND THE WORLD, 1945 TO THE PRESENT   **812**

Chapter 27
COLD WAR AMERICA, 1945–1960   816

The Cold War Abroad   817

Descent into Cold War, 1945–1946   817   •   The Truman Doctrine and Containment   819   •   Containment in Asia and the Korean War   823   •   Eisenhower and the "New Look" of Foreign Policy   827   •   The Cold War in the Middle East   829

The Cold War at Home   831

Postwar Domestic Challenges   831   •   Fair Deal Liberalism   833   •   The Great Fear   835   •   "Modern Republicanism"   837

The Emergence of Civil Rights as a National and International Issue   839

Civil Rights under Truman   839   •   Challenging Segregation   840

The Impact of the Cold War   842

Nuclear Proliferation   843   •   The Military-Industrial Complex   844

VOICES FROM ABROAD
JEAN MONNET: Truman's Generous Proposal   822

AMERICAN VOICES
RON KOVIC: Memories of a Cold War Childhood   845

Chapter 28
THE AFFLUENT SOCIETY AND THE LIBERAL CONSENSUS, 1945–1965   848

The Affluent Society   849

Economic Expansion and the Affluent Society   849   •   The Suburban Explosion   851

American Life during the Baby Boom   853

Consumer Culture   854   •   The Search for Security: Religion and the Family   855   •   Contradictions in Women's Lives   856   •   Youth Culture and Challenges to Conformity   857

The Other America   860

International and Domestic Migration to Cities   860   •   The Urban Crisis   862

John F. Kennedy and the Politics of Expectation   863

The New Politics   863   •   Activism Abroad   864   •   The New Frontier at Home   868   •   New Tactics for the Civil Rights Movement   868   •   The Kennedy Assassination   872

Lyndon B. Johnson and the Great Society   873

The Momentum for Civil Rights   873   •   Enacting the Liberal Agenda   874

AMERICAN VOICES
A Woman Encounters the Feminine Mystique   858

AMERICAN VOICES
ANNE MOODY: We Would Like to Be Served   870

Chapter 29
WAR ABROAD AND AT HOME: THE VIETNAM ERA, 1961–1975   880

Into the Quagmire, 1945–1968   881

America in Vietnam: From Truman to Kennedy   881   •   Escalation: The Johnson Years   884   •   American Soldiers' Perspectives on the War   887

The Cold War Consensus Unravels   889

Public Opinion on Vietnam   889   •   Student Activism   891   •   The Counterculture   892   •   The Widening Struggle for Civil Rights   893   •   The Rights Revolution   897   •   The Revival of Feminism   901

The Long Road Home, 1968–1975   903

1968: A Year of Shocks   **904**   •   Nixon's War   **908**   •   Withdrawal from Vietnam and Détente   **909**   •   The Legacy of Vietnam   **911**

> AMERICAN VOICES
> DAVE CLINE: A Vietnam Vet Remembers   **888**

> AMERICAN VOICES
> MARY CROW DOG: The Trail of Broken Treaties   **899**

Chapter 30
THE LEAN YEARS, 1969–1980   515

The Nixon Years   916

The Republican Domestic Agenda   **917**   •   The 1972 Election   **918**   •   Watergate   **919**

Lean Economic Times   921

Energy Crisis   **921**   •   Economic Woes   **924**

Reform and Reaction in the 1970s   928

The New Activism: Environmental and Consumer Movements   **928**   •   Challenges to Tradition: The Women's Movement and Gay Rights   **930**   •   Racial Minorities **933**   •   The Growth of Conservatism   **937**

Politics in the Wake of Watergate   939

Ford's Caretaker Presidency   **939**   •   Jimmy Carter: The Outsider as President   **939** •   Carter and the World   **940**   •   The Reagan Revolution   **942**

> AMERICAN VOICES
> ELIZABETH DREW: Watergate Diary   **922**

> AMERICAN VOICES
> DAVID KOPAY: The Real Score: A Gay Athlete Comes Out   **934**

Chapter 31
A NEW DOMESTIC AND WORLD ORDER, 1981–2004   946

Reagan-Bush Domestic Policy, 1981–1993   947

Reaganomics   **948**   •   Reagan's Second Term   **949**   •   The First Bush Presidency   **950**

Foreign Relations under Reagan and Bush   952

Interventions in Developing Countries and the End of the Cold War   **952**   •   War in the Persian Gulf, 1990–1991   **954**

Uncertain Times: Economic and Social Trends at the Turn of the Millennium 954

The Economic Roller Coaster 956 • Globalization 958 • Popular Technology 961 • An Increasingly Pluralistic Society 962 • Backlash against Women's and Gay Rights 965

Restructuring the Domestic and International Order: Public Life, 1992–2004 967

Clinton's First Term 967 • Limiting the Federal Government 968 • Clinton's Impeachment 970 • Clinton's Foreign Policy 971 • An Unprecedented Election 973 • George W. Bush's Early Presidency and September 11 975 • Politics and the Economy after 9/11 978

VOICES FROM ABROAD
SADDAM HUSSEIN: Calling for a Holy War against the United States 955

AMERICAN VOICES
JOHN LEWIS: We Marched to Be Counted 974

DOCUMENTS D-1
The Declaration of Independence D-1
The Articles of Confederation and Perpetual Union D-4
The Constitution of the United States D-9
Amendments to the Constitution D-18

APPENDIX A-1
Territorial Expansion A-1
The Labor Force A-2
Changing Labor Patterns A-3
American Population A-4
Presidential Elections A-5

GLOSSARY G-1

CREDITS C-1

INDEX I-1

LIST OF MAPS

1.1 The Ice Age and the Settling of the Americas 8
1.2 West Africa and the Mediterranean in the Fifteenth Century 21
1.3 The Spanish Conquest of the Great Indian Civilizations 28

2.1 New Spain Looks North, 1513–1610 39
2.2 River Plantations in Virginia, c. 1640 49
2.3 Settlement Patterns within New England Towns, 1630–1700 60

3.1 Britain's American Empire, 1713 76
3.2 Africa and the Atlantic Slave Trade, 1700–1810 78
3.3 The Rise of the American Merchant, 1750 89

4.1 The Hudson River Manors 105
4.2 Religious Diversity in 1750 108
4.3 European Spheres of Influence, 1754 120
4.4 Westward Expansion and Land Conflicts, 1750–1775 126

5.1 Britain's American Empire in 1763 133
5.2 British Troop Deployments, 1763 and 1775 149
5.3 British Western Policy, 1763–1774 154

6.1 The War in the North, 1776–1777 174
6.2 The War in the South, 1778–1781 181
6.3 The Status of Slavery, 1800 192

7.1 The Confederation and Western Land Claims 203
7.2 Land Division in the Northwest Territory 205
7.3 Ratifying the Constitution of 1787 214

8.1 Indian Cessions and State Formation, to 1840 231
8.2 The War of 1812 243
8.3 Defining the National Boundaries, 1800–1820 245

9.1 The Expansion of Voting Rights for White Men, 1800–1830   259
9.2 Distribution of the Slave Population in 1790 and 1830   269
9.3 The Missouri Compromise, 1820–1821   276
9.4 The Second Great Awakening, 1790–1860   283

10.1 Western Land Sales, 1830–1839 and 1850–1862   303
10.2 The Transportation Revolution: Roads and Canals, 1820–1850   306
10.3 Railroads of the North and South, 1850–1860   307

11.1 Presidential Election of 1824   326
11.2 The Removal of Native Americans, 1820–1843   340

12.1 Major Communal Experiments before 1860   359
12.2 The Mormon Trek, 1830–1848   364
12.3 Women and Antislavery, 1837–1838   373

13.1 American Settlements in Texas, 1821–1836   387
13.2 Routes to the West, 1835–1860   389
13.3 The Mexican War, 1846–1848   394
13.4 The Compromise of 1850 and the Kansas-Nebraska Act of 1854   399
13.5 Political Realignment, 1848–1860   405

14.1 The Process of Secession, 1860–1861   414
14.2 The Eastern Campaigns of 1862   419
14.3 The Western Campaigns, 1861–1862   422
14.4 Lee Invades the North, 1863   431
14.5 The Closing Virginia Campaign, 1864–1865   435
14.6 Sherman's March through the Confederacy, 1864–1865   438

15.1 Reconstruction   453
15.2 The Barrow Plantation, 1860 and 1881   463

16.1 The Natural Environment of the West, 1860s   477
16.2 The Sioux Reservations in South Dakota, 1868–1889   488
16.3 The Mining Frontier, 1848–1890   492
16.4 The Settlement of the Pacific Slope, 1860–1890   495

17.1 Iron and Steel Production, 1900   508
17.2 The Expansion of the Railroad System, 1870–1890   511
17.3 The New South, 1900   516

18.1 The Expansion of Chicago, 1865–1902   538
18.2 The Lower East Side, New York City, 1900   553

19.1 Presidential Elections of 1880, 1884, and 1888   570
19.2 Disfranchisement in the New South   585
19.3 Presidential Elections of 1892 and 1896   594

20.1 Woman Suffrage, 1890–1919   603
20.2 National Parks and Forests, 1872–1980   614
20.3 Presidential Election of 1912   623

21.1 The Spanish-American War of 1898   641
21.2 Policeman of the Caribbean   650
21.3 The Great Powers in East Asia, 1898–1910   651

22.1 European Alliances in 1914   664
22.2 U.S. Participation on the Western Front, 1918   671
22.3 The Great Migration and Beyond   677
22.4 Europe after World War I   685

23.1 Ku Klux Klan Politics and Violence in the 1920s   695
23.2 The Shift from Rural to Urban Population, 1920–1930   708
23.3 Presidential Election of 1928   720

24.1 The Spread of Radio, to 1939   734
24.2 The Dust Bowl, 1930–1941   738
24.3 Presidential Election of 1932   749

25.1 Public Works in the New Deal: The PWA in Action, 1933–1939   762
25.2 The Tennessee Valley Authority, 1933–1952   773

26.1 World War II in the North Atlantic, 1939–1943   786
26.2 Japanese Relocation Camps   798
26.3 World War II in Europe, 1941–1943   800
26.4 World War II in Europe, 1944–1945   801
26.5 World War II in the Pacific, 1941–1942   804
26.6 World War II in the Pacific, 1943–1945   805

27.1 Cold War in Europe, 1955   819
27.2 The Korean War, 1950–1953   825
27.3 American Global Defense Treaties in the Cold War Era   829
27.4 The Military-Industrial Complex   844

28.1 Connecting the Nation: The Interstate Highway System, 1930 and 1970   853
28.2 Decolonization and the Third World, 1943–1990   866
28.3 Black Voter Registration in the South, 1964 and 1975   875

29.1 The Vietnam War, 1954–1975   **883**
29.2 Racial Unrest in America's Cities, 1965–1968   **896**
29.3 Presidential Election of 1968   **907**

30.1 From Rust Belt to Sun Belt, 1940–2000   **927**
30.2 States Ratifying the Equal Rights Amendment, 1972–1977   **932**
30.3 American Indian Reservations   **935**

31.1 U.S. Involvement in Latin America and the Caribbean, 1954–2004   **953**
31.2 U.S. Involvement in the Middle East, 1979–2004   **956**
31.3 Latino Population and Asian Population, 2000   **963**

The United States (physical)   **at the front of the book**
Major World Trading Blocs   **at the front of the book**

ABOUT THE AUTHORS

James A. Henretta is Priscilla Alden Burke Professor of American History at the University of Maryland, College Park. He received his undergraduate education at Swarthmore College and his Ph.D. from Harvard University. He has taught at the University of Sussex, England; Princeton University; UCLA; Boston University; as a Fulbright lecturer in Australia at the University of New England; and at Oxford University as the Harmsworth Professor of American History. His publications include *The Evolution of American Society, 1700–1815: An Interdisciplinary Analysis;* *"Salutary Neglect": Colonial Administration under the Duke of Newcastle; Evolution and Revolution: American Society, 1600–1820;* and *The Origins of American Capitalism.* Recently he coedited and contributed to a collection of original essays, *Republicanism and Liberalism in America and the German States, 1750–1850,* as part of his larger research project on "The Liberal State in America: New York, 1820–1975." In 2002–2003, he held the John Hope Franklin Fellowship at the National Humanities Center in North Carolina.

David Brody is Professor Emeritus of History at the University of California, Davis. He received his B.A., M.A., and Ph.D. from Harvard University. He has taught at the University of Warwick in England, at Moscow State University in the former Soviet Union, and at Sydney University in Australia. He is the author of *Steelworkers in America; Workers in Industrial America: Essays on the Twentieth-Century Struggle;* and *In Labor's Cause: Main Themes on the History of the American Worker.* He has been awarded fellowships from the Social Science Research Council, the Guggenheim Foundation, and the National Endowment for the Humanities. He is past president (1991–1992) of the Pacific Coast branch of the American Historical Association. His current research is on labor law and workplace regimes during the Great Depression.

Lynn Dumenil is Robert Glass Cleland Professor of American History at Occidental College in Los Angeles. She is a graduate of the University of Southern California and received her Ph.D. from the University of California, Berkeley. She has written *The Modern Temper: American Culture and Society in the 1920s* and *Freemasonry and American Culture: 1880–1930.* Her articles and reviews have appeared in the *Journal of American History;* the *Journal of American Ethnic History; Reviews in American History;* and the *American Historical Review.* She has been a historical consultant to several documentary film projects and is on the Pelzer Prize Committee of the Organization of American Historians. Her current work, for which she received a National Endowment for the Humanities Fellowship, is on World War I, citizenship, and the state. In 2001–2002 she was the Bicentennial Fulbright Chair in American Studies at the University of Helsinki.

Third Edition

America

A CONCISE HISTORY

Part One

THE CREATION OF AMERICAN SOCIETY

1450–1775

ECONOMY	SOCIETY	GOVERNMENT
From Staple Crops to Internal Growth	**Ethnic, Racial, and Class Divisions**	**From Monarchy to Republic**
1450 ▸ Native American subsistence economy Europeans fish off North American coast	▸ Sporadic warfare among Indian peoples Spanish conquest of Mexico (1519–1521)	▸ Rise of monarchical nation-states in Europe
1600 ▸ First staple export crops: furs and tobacco	▸ English-Indian warfare African servitude begins in Virginia (1619)	▸ James I claims divine right to rule England Virginia House of Burgesses (1619)
1640 ▸ New England trade with sugar islands Mercantilist regulations: first Navigation Act (1651)	▸ White indentured servitude in Chesapeake Indians retreat inland	▸ Puritan Revolution Stuart restoration (1660) Bacon's Rebellion in Virginia (1675)
1680 ▸ Tobacco trade stagnates Rice cultivation expands	▸ Indian slavery in the Carolinas Ethnic rebellion in New York (1689)	▸ Dominion of New England (1686–1689) Glorious Revolution ousts James II (1688–1689)
1720 ▸ Mature yeoman farm economy in North Imports from Britain increase	▸ Scots-Irish and German migration Growing rural inequality	▸ Rise of the colonial representative assemblies Challenge to "deferential" politics
1760 ▸ Trade boycotts encourage domestic manufacturing	▸ Uprisings by tenants and backcountry farmers Artisan protests	▸ Ideas of popular sovereignty Battles of Lexington and Concord (1775)

RELIGION	CULTURE
From Hierarchy to Pluralism	**The Creation of American Identity**
▶ Protestant Reformation begins (1517)	▶ Diverse Native American cultures in eastern woodlands
▶ Persecuted English Puritans and Catholics migrate to America	▶ Puritans implant Calvinism, education, and freehold ideal
▶ Religious liberty in Rhode Island	▶ Aristocratic aspirations in the Chesapeake
▶ Rise of toleration	▶ Emergence of African American language and culture
▶ German and Scots-Irish Pietists in Middle Atlantic region Great Awakening	▶ Expansion of colleges, newspapers, and magazines Franklin and the American Enlightenment
▶ Evangelical Baptists in Virginia Quebec Act allows Catholicism (1774)	▶ First signs of an American identity Republican innovations in political theory

Societies are made, not born. They are the creation of decades, even centuries, of human endeavor and experience. The first American societies were formed by hunting and gathering peoples who migrated to the Western Hemisphere from Asia many centuries ago. Over numerous generations these migrants—the Native Americans—came to live in a wide variety of environments and cultures. In much of North America they developed kinship-based societies that relied on farming and hunting. But in the lower Mississippi Valley, Native Americans developed a hierarchical social order similar to that of the great civilizations of the Aztecs, Mayas, and Incas of Mesoamerica. The coming of Europeans and their diseases tore the fabric of most Native American cultures into shreds. Nearly everywhere, men and women of European origins—the Spanish in Mesoamerica, the French in Canada, the English along the Atlantic coast—gradually achieved domination over the native Indian peoples.

The Europeans who settled in the English mainland colonies initially sought to transplant their traditional society to the New World—their farming practices, their social hierarchies, their culture and heritage, and their religious ideas. But in learning to live in the new land, the English, Germans, and Scots-Irish who came to England's North American colonies eventually created societies that were distinctly different from those of their homelands in their economies, social character, political systems, religion, and culture.

ECONOMY Many European settlements were very successful in economic terms. Traditional Europe was made up of poor, overcrowded, and unequal societies that periodically suffered devastating famines. But with few people and a bountiful natural environment, the settlers in North America created a bustling economy and, in the northern mainland colonies, prosperous communities of independent farm families. Indeed, this region became known to migrants from the British Isles and Germany as "the best poor man's country."

SOCIETY Some of the European settlements, however, became places of oppressive captivity for Africans. Aided by African traders and political leaders, Europeans bought hundreds of thousands of enslaved workers, from many African regions. They transported these slaves to the West Indies and the southern mainland colonies and forced them to labor on sugar, tobacco, and rice plantations. Slowly and with great effort, the slaves and their descendants created an African American culture within a social order dominated by Europeans.

GOVERNMENT In the meantime, whites in the emerging American societies created an increasingly free and competitive political system. The first English settlers transplanted authoritarian institutions to America, and the English government continued to manage their lives. However, after 1689 traditional controls gradually gave way to governments based in part on representative assemblies. Eventually, the growth of self-rule would lead to demands for political independence from England.

RELIGION The American experience profoundly changed religious institutions and values. Many migrants left Europe because of the conflicts among rival Christian churches in the wake of the Protestant Reformation and came to America seeking to practice their religion without interference. The societies they created became increasingly religious, especially after the evangelical revivals of the 1740s. By this time, many Americans had rejected the harshest tenets of Calvinism (a strict Protestant faith), and others had embraced the rationalist view of the European Enlightenment. As a result, American Protestant Christianity became increasingly tolerant, democratic, and optimistic.

CULTURE The new American society witnessed the appearance of new forms of family and community life. The first English settlers lived in patriarchal families ruled by dominant fathers and in communities controlled by men of high status. By 1750, however, many American fathers no longer strictly managed their children's lives. As these communities became more diverse and open, many men and some women began to enjoy greater personal independence. This new American society was increasingly pluralistic, composed of migrants from many European ethnic groups — English, Scots, Scots-Irish, Dutch, and Germans — as well as enslaved West Africans and many different Native American peoples. Distinct regional cultures developed in New England, the Middle Atlantic colonies, and the Chesapeake and Carolina areas. Consequently, an overarching American identity based on the English language, English legal and political institutions, and shared experiences emerged very slowly.

The story of the English colonial experience is thus both tragic and exciting. The European settlers warred with Native Americans and condemned most African Americans to bondage while themselves enjoying rich opportunities for economic security, political freedom, and spiritual fulfillment.

Chapter 1

WORLDS COLLIDE: EUROPE, AFRICA, AND AMERICA
1450–1620

Soon there will come from the rising sun a different kind of man from
any you have yet seen . . . [after that,] the world will fall to pieces.

A SPOKANE INDIAN PROPHET

"**B**efore the French came among us," an elder of the Natchez people
of Mississippi exclaimed, "we were men . . . and we walked with boldness every
road, but now we walk like slaves, which we shall soon be, since the French already
treat us . . . as they do their black slaves." Before the 1490s the native peoples of the
Western Hemisphere knew absolutely nothing about the light-skinned inhabitants
of Europe and the dark-complexioned peoples of Africa. However, Portuguese
merchants hungry for the riches of Asia were already sailing along the west coast
of Africa and were trading for African slaves. When Christopher Columbus, another European searching for a sea route to Asia, encountered the peoples of the
Western Hemisphere, the destinies of four continents quickly became intertwined.
On his second voyage, Columbus carried a cargo of enslaved Africans, beginning
the centuries-long trade that created a multitude of triracial societies in the
Americas.

As the Natchez elder knew well, the resulting mixture of peoples was based not
on equality but on exploitation. By the time he urged his people to resist, the
European invaders were too numerous and strong to be dislodged. Aided by Indian
allies, the French killed hundreds of the Natchez rebels and sold the survivors into
slavery on the sugar plantations of the West Indies. The fate of the Natchez was
hardly unique. In the three centuries following Columbus's voyage, many Native
American peoples came under the domination of the Spanish, Portuguese, French,
English, and Dutch who colonized the Western Hemisphere and used enslaved
Africans to work agricultural plantations.

How did this happen? How did Europeans become leaders in world trade and
extend their influence across the Atlantic? What made Native American peoples

vulnerable to conquest by European adventurers? And what led to the transatlantic trade in African slaves? In the answers to these questions lie the origins of the United States and the dominant position of people of European descent in the modern world.

Native American Worlds

When the Europeans arrived, most Native Americans—about 45 million—lived in Mesoamerica (present-day Mexico and Guatemala) and along the western coast of South America (present-day Peru); another 15 million resided in lands to the north (present-day United States and Canada). Some lived in simple hunter-gatherer or agricultural communities governed by kin ties, but the majority resided in societies ruled by warrior-kings and priests. In Mesoamerica and Peru, Indian peoples created civilizations whose art, religion, society, and economy were as complex as those of Europe and the Mediterranean.

The First Americans

According to the elders of the Navajo people, history began when their ancestors emerged from under the earth; for the Iroquois, the story of their Five Nations began when people fell from the sky. However, most twenty-first-century anthropologists and historians believe that the first inhabitants of the Western Hemisphere were migrants from Asia. Some migrants came by water, but most probably came by land. Strong archaeological and genetic evidence suggests that late in the last Ice Age, which took place from 20,000 B.C. until 9000 B.C., small bands of Asian tribal hunters followed herds of game across a hundred-mile-wide land bridge between Siberia and Alaska. An oral history of the Tuscarora Indians, who lived in present-day North Carolina, tells of a famine in the old world and a journey over ice toward where "the sun rises," a trek that brought their ancestors to a lush forest with abundant food and game.

Most anthropologists believe that the main migratory stream from Asia lasted from about 13,000 B.C. to 9000 B.C., when the glaciers melted and the rising ocean waters submerged the land bridge and created the Bering Strait. A second movement of peoples around 6000 B.C., now traveling by water across the narrow strait, brought the ancestors of the Navajos and the Apaches to North America, while a third migration around 3000 B.C. introduced the forebears of the Aleut and Inuit peoples—the "Eskimos." Subsequently, the people of the Western Hemisphere, who were now settled as far south as the tip of South America and as far east as the Atlantic coast of North America, were largely cut off from the rest of the world for three hundred generations (Map 1.1).

For many centuries the first Americans lived as hunter-gatherers, subsisting on the abundant vegetation and wildlife. Gradually, the larger species of animals— mammoths, giant beaver, and horses—died out because of overhunting and

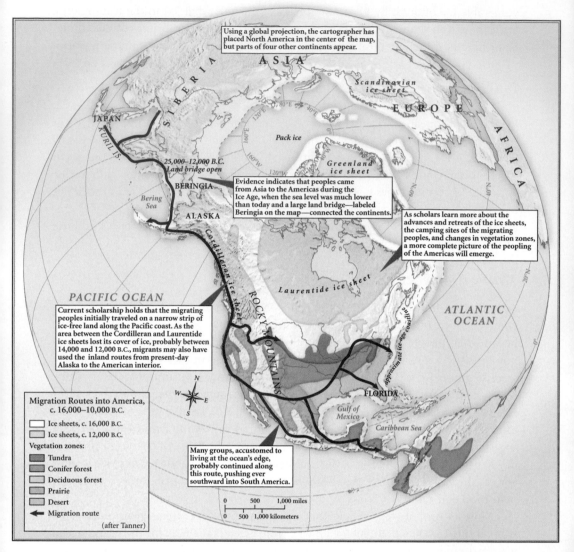

Using a global projection, the cartographer has placed North America in the center of the map, but parts of four other continents appear.

Evidence indicates that peoples came from Asia to the Americas during the Ice Age, when the sea level was much lower than today and a large land bridge—labeled Beringia on the map—connected the continents.

As scholars learn more about the advances and retreats of the ice sheets, the camping sites of the migrating peoples, and changes in vegetation zones, a more complete picture of the peopling of the Americas will emerge.

Current scholarship holds that the migrating peoples initially traveled on a narrow strip of ice-free land along the Pacific coast. As the area between the Cordilleran and Laurentide ice sheets lost its cover of ice, probably between 14,000 and 12,000 B.C., migrants may also have used the inland routes from present-day Alaska to the American interior.

Many groups, accustomed to living at the ocean's edge, probably continued along this route, pushing ever southward into South America.

Migration Routes into America, c. 16,000–10,000 B.C.

- ☐ Ice sheets, c. 16,000 B.C.
- ☐ Ice sheets, c. 12,000 B.C.

Vegetation zones:
- ■ Tundra
- ■ Conifer forest
- ☐ Deciduous forest
- ☐ Prairie
- ☐ Desert
- ← Migration route

(after Tanner)

25,000–12,000 B.C. Land bridge open

0   500   1,000 miles
0   500   1,000 kilometers

MAP 1.1 The Ice Age and the Settling of the Americas

Some sixteen thousand years ago, a sheet of ice covered much of Europe and North America. Taking advantage of a broad bridge of land connecting Siberia and Alaska, hunting peoples from Asia migrated into North America, searching for large game animals, such as woolly mammoths, and ice-free habitats. By 10,000 B.C. the descendants of the migrant peoples had moved as far south as present-day Florida and central Mexico.

climatic change, and hunters became adept at killing more elusive and faster rabbits, deer, and elk. About 3000 B.C. some Native American peoples began to develop farming, most notably in the region near present-day Mexico. These inventive horticulturists planted beans, squash, and maize (corn), as well as tomatoes, potatoes, and manioc—crops that would eventually enrich the food supply of the entire world. Indeed, the Indian peoples gradually bred maize into an extremely nutritious plant that had a higher yield per acre than wheat, barley, and rye, the staple cereals of Europe. They also learned to plant beans and squash together with corn, creating a mix of crops that provided a nutritious diet and preserved soil fertility. The resulting agricultural surplus laid the economic foundation for populous and wealthy societies in Mexico, Peru, and the Mississippi River Valley.

The Mayas and the Aztecs

The flowering of civilization in Mesoamerica began among the Olmec people, who lived along the Gulf of Mexico around 700 B.C. Subsequently, the Mayan peoples of the Yucatán Peninsula of Mexico and the neighboring rain forests of Guatemala built large urban religious centers with elaborate systems of water storage and irrigation. By A.D. 300 the Mayan city of Tikal [*t-CALL*] contained at least 20,000 inhabitants, mostly farmers whose labor built huge stone temples. An elite class claiming descent from the gods ruled Mayan society and lived in splendor on goods and taxes extracted from peasant families. Drawing on religious and artistic traditions that stretched back to the Olmecs, skilled Mayan artisans decorated temples and palaces with art depicting warrior-gods and complex religious rituals. Mayan astronomers created a calendar that recorded historical events and accurately predicted eclipses of the sun and the moon. Mayas drawn from the elite class also developed hieroglyphic writing to record royal lineages, wars, and other noteworthy events. These skills in calculation and writing enhanced the authority of the priestly class and provided the Mayan peoples with a sense of their history and identity. By facilitating the movement of goods and ideas, they also increased the prosperity of Mayan society and the complexity of its culture.

Beginning around A.D. 800, Mayan civilization went into decline. Evidence suggests that a two-century-long dry period caused an economic crisis and prompted overtaxed peasants to desert the temple cities and retreat to the countryside. By A.D. 900 many religious centers had been abandoned, but some Mayan city-states lasted until the Spanish invasion in the 1520s.

A second major Mesoamerican civilization developed in the central highlands of Mexico around the city of Teotihuacán [*tea-o-ti-hue-CON*], with its magnificent Pyramid of the Sun. At its zenith about A.D. 500, Teotihuacán had more than one hundred temples, about four thousand apartment buildings, and a population of at least 100,000. By A.D. 800 Teotihuacán had also declined, probably because of a long-term drought and recurrent invasions by seminomadic warrior peoples. Eventually one of these peoples, the Aztecs, established an even more extensive empire.

The Aztecs entered the highlands of Mexico from the north and settled on an island in Lake Texcoco. There, in A.D. 1325, they began to build a new city, Tenochtitlán [*ten-och-tit-LAWN*] (present-day Mexico City). The Aztecs learned the settled ways of the resident peoples, mastered their complex irrigation systems and written language, and established an elaborate culture with a hierarchical social order. Priests and warrior-nobles ruled over twenty clans of free Aztec commoners who farmed communally owned land. The nobles also used huge numbers of non-Aztec slaves and serfs to labor on their private estates. Skilled artisans worked in stone, pottery, cloth, leather, and especially obsidian (hard volcanic glass that made sharp-edged weapons and tools).

The Aztecs remained an aggressive tribe and soon subjugated most of central Mexico. Their rulers demanded both economic and human tribute from scores of subject tribes, gruesomely sacrificing untold thousands of men and women to ensure agricultural fertility and the daily return of the sun. Aztec merchants created trading routes that crisscrossed the empire and imported furs, gold, textiles, food, and obsidian from as far north as the Rio Grande and as far south as present-day Panama. By A.D. 1500, Tenochtitlán had grown into a great metropolis with magnificent palaces and temples and over 200,000 inhabitants. Its splendor dazzled subject peoples as well as Spanish soldiers. "These great towns and pyramids and buildings arising from the water, all made of stone, seemed like an enchanted vision," marveled one Spaniard. The Aztecs' wealth, strong institutions, and military power posed a formidable challenge to any adversary, at home or from afar.

The Indians of the North

The Indians who resided north of the Rio Grande lived in societies that were less complex and less coercive because, unlike those to the south, they lacked a diversity of occupations and a social hierarchy. Most of the northern peoples lived in self-governing tribes composed of **clans**—groups of related families with a common identity and a real or legendary common ancestor. Clan elders and local chiefs conducted ceremonies, resolved personal feuds, and disciplined individuals who violated customs. They also decided war policy and banned marriage between members of the same clan, a rule that helped prevent inbreeding. However, the elders and chiefs did not form a distinct ruling class—like that of the Mayan and Aztec nobles—and, because their kinship system of government was locally based and worked by consensus, they had only limited powers. Moreover, the culture of these lineage-based societies did not encourage the accumulation of material goods. Indeed, the individual ownership of land was virtually unknown; as a French missionary among the Iroquois noted, they "possess hardly anything except in common." The elders urged individuals to share food and other scarce goods, encouraging an ethic of reciprocity rather than one of accumulation. "You are covetous, and neither generous nor kind," the Micmac Indians of Nova Scotia told acquisitive-minded French fur traders around 1600. "As for us, if we have a morsel of bread, we share it with our neighbor."

Over the centuries some Indian peoples did develop a materialistic outlook and engaged in trade or conquest. The earliest expansive Indian cultures appeared in the areas of present-day Ohio. By A.D. 100 the vigorous Hopewell people had increased the food supply by domesticating plants, organized themselves in large villages, and set up a trading network that stretched from Louisiana to Wisconsin and beyond. They imported obsidian from the Yellowstone region of the Rocky Mountains, copper from the Great Lakes, and pottery and marine shells from the Gulf of Mexico. The Hopewell built large burial mounds and surrounded them with extensive circular, rectangular, or octagonal earthworks that in some cases still survive. Skilled craftsmen fashioned striking ornaments that they buried with the dead: copper beaten into intricate artistic designs, mica cut into the shapes of serpents and human hands, and stone pipes carved to represent frogs, hawks, bears, and other animals—figurines evidently representing spiritually powerful beings. For unknown reasons, the elaborate trading network of the Hopewell gradually collapsed around A.D. 400.

A second complex culture developed among the Pueblo peoples of the Southwest—the Hohokams, Mogollons, and Anasazis. By A.D. 600 Hohokam [ho-HO-kam] peoples in the high country along the border of present-day Arizona and New Mexico were using irrigation to grow two crops a year, fashioning fine pottery with red-on-buff designs, and worshiping their gods on Mesoamerican-like platform mounds; by A.D. 1000, they were living in elaborate multiroom stone structures (or pueblos). To the east, in the Mimbres Valley of New Mexico, the Mogollon [mo-gee-YON] peoples developed a distinctive black-on-white pottery. In the north of present-day New Mexico, the Anasazi (now known as the people of the Ancestral Pueblo) culture emerged around A.D. 900. The Anasazis were master architects, building residential-ceremonial villages in steep cliffs, a pueblo in Chaco Canyon that housed 1,000 people, and four hundred miles of straight roads. However, the culture of the Anasazis, Mogollons, and Hohokams gradually collapsed after A.D. 1150 as long periods of drought and soil exhaustion disrupted maize production and prompted the abandonment of Chaco Canyon and other long-established communities. The descendants of these Pueblo peoples—including the Zunis and the Hopis—later built strong but smaller and more dispersed village societies.

The last large-scale culture to emerge north of the Rio Grande was the Mississippian civilization. Beginning about A.D. 800, the advanced farming technology of Mesoamerica spread into the Mississippi River Valley, perhaps carried by Mayan emigrants from the Yucatán Peninsula. By planting new strains of maize and beans, the Mississippian peoples produced an agricultural surplus and a robust culture based on small, fortified temple cities. By A.D. 1150 the largest city, Cahokia [ca-HO-key-ah] (near present-day St. Louis), boasted a population of 15,000 to 20,000 and more than one hundred temple mounds, one of them as large as the great Egyptian pyramids. As in Mesoamerica, the tribute paid by peasant cultivators supported a privileged class of nobles and priests who waged war against neighboring chiefdoms, patronized skilled artisans, and may have been worshiped as quasi-sacred beings related to the sun god.

By A.D. 1350, this six-hundred-year-old Mississippian civilization was in rapid decline, undermined by overpopulation, warfare, and urban diseases such as

Chaco Canyon

Chaco Canyon was a major center of ancestral Pueblo culture between A.D. 850 and 1250. In this high desert landscape, with its long winters, short growing seasons, and marginal rainfall, the Chacoan peoples constructed massive stone buildings. Well-built roads connected these "great houses," which were used for ceremonial and administrative purposes, to more than 150 other great houses scattered throughout the region. NPS Photo / D. Six.

tuberculosis. Nonetheless, its values and institutions endured for centuries. When the Spanish adventurer Hernán de Soto invaded the region in the 1540s, he found the Apalachee [*ap-a-LA-chee*] and Timucua [*tee-MOO-cwa*] Indians living in permanent settlements and fiercely resistant to his commands. "If you desire to see me, come where I am," a chief told de Soto, "neither for you, nor for any man, will I set back one foot." A century and a half later, French traders and priests who encountered the Natchez people (and who would soon help to conquer them) found a society rigidly divided among hereditary chiefs, two groups of nobles and honored people, and a bottom class of peasants. "Their chiefs possess all authority," a Frenchman noted. "They distribute their favors and presents at will." Undoubtedly influenced by Mayan or Aztec rituals, the Natchez marked the death of a chief by sacrificing his wives and burying their remains in a ceremonial mound (see Voices from Abroad, "The Customs of the Natchez, 1730," p. 13).

Other peoples in the region, such as the Creeks, Chickasaws, Cherokees, and Seminoles, resided in small and dispersed agricultural communities. In these societies—and among the Algonquian peoples who lived farther to the east—farming was the work of women. While men hunted and fished, Indian women

VOICES FROM ABROAD

The Customs of the Natchez, 1730

FATHER LE PETITE

*B*eliefs and institutions from the earlier Mississippian culture (A.D. 1000–1450) lasted for centuries among the Natchez, who lived in present-day Mississippi. Father le Petite was one of the hundreds of Jesuits who lived among—and wrote detailed accounts of—the Indians in the French colonies of Louisiana and Canada. Here, he accurately describes many Natchez customs but fails to understand that the rules governing the succession of the chief simply follow the normal practice of descent in a matrilineal society.

My Reverend Father, This Nation of Savages inhabits one of the most beautiful and fertile countries in the World, and is the only one on this continent which appears to have any regular worship. Their Religion in certain points is very similar to that of the ancient Romans. They have a Temple filled with Idols, which are different figures of men and of animals, and for which they have the most profound veneration. Their Temple in shape resembles an earthen oven, a hundred feet in circumference. They enter it by a little door about four feet high, and not more than three in breadth. Above on the outside are three figures of eagles made of wood, and painted red, yellow, and white. Before the door is a kind of shed with folding-doors, where the Guardian of the Temple is lodged; all around it runs a circle of palisades, on which are seen exposed the skulls of all the heads which their Warriors had brought back from the battles in which they had been engaged with the enemies of their Nation. . . .

The Sun is the principal object of veneration to these people; as they cannot conceive of anything which can be above this heavenly body, nothing else appears to them more worthy of their homage. It is for the same reason that the great Chief of this Nation, who knows nothing on the earth more dignified than himself, takes the title of brother of the Sun, and the credulity of the people maintains him in the despotic authority which he claims.

The old men prescribe the Laws for the rest of the people, and one of their principles is . . . the immortality of the soul, and when they leave this world they go, they say, to live in another, there to be recompensed or punished.

In former times the Nation of the Natchez was very large. It counted sixty Villages and eight hundred Suns or Princes; now it is reduced to six little Villages and eleven Suns. [Its] Government is hereditary; it is not, however, the son of the reigning Chief who succeeds his father, but the son of his sister, or the first Princess of the blood. This policy is founded on the knowledge they have of the licentiousness of their women. They are not sure, they say, that the children of the chief's wife may be of the blood Royal, whereas the son of the sister of the great Chief must be, at least on the side of the mother.

SOURCE: *The Jesuit Relations and Allied Documents*, ed. Reuben Gold Thwaites (Cleveland: Murrow Brothers, 1900), 68:121–35.

became adept horticulturists, using flint hoes to plant corn, squash, and beans. Because of the importance of farming, a **matrilineal** inheritance system developed among many eastern Indian peoples, including the Five Nations of the Iroquois (the Mohawks, Oneidas, Onondagas, Cayugas and Senecas who lived in present-day New York State). Women cultivated the fields around semi-permanent settlements and passed the right to use them to their daughters. In these matrilineal societies, fathers stood outside the main lines of kinship; the principal responsibility for childraising fell upon the mother and her brothers, who often lived with her (rather than with their wives). The ritual and religious lives of these farming peoples focused on the agricultural cycle, such as the Iroquois green corn and strawberry festivals. Because of women's labor, the eastern Indian peoples of A.D. 1500 ate better than their ancestors had, but they enjoyed few material comforts and their populations grew slowly.

When Europeans intruded into their lives after 1500, most Indians north of the Rio Grande had resided on the same lands for generations. However, the strong city-states that had once flourished in the Southwest and in the Mississippi valley had vanished. Consequently, there were no great Indian empires or religious centers that could lead a sustained campaign of military and spiritual resistance. "When you command, all the French obey and go to war," the Chippewa chief Chigabe [*chig-AH-be*] remarked to a general, but "I shall not be heeded and obeyed by my nation." Because household and lineage were the basis of his society, Chigabe explained, "I cannot answer except for myself and for those immediately allied to me."

Traditional European Society in 1450

In A.D. 1450 few observers would have predicted that the European peoples would become the overlords of the Western Hemisphere. A thousand years after the fall of the great Roman empire, Europe was divided into many small kingdoms. Indeed, around 1350 a vicious epidemic from the subcontinent of India—the Black Death—had killed one-third of Europe's peoples. Other areas of the world, such as China, were much more economically advanced and were dispatching commercial fleets to far-flung lands, including the eastern coast of Africa.

The Peasantry

There were only a few large cities in Western Europe—in A.D. 1450 only Paris, London, and Naples had 100,000 residents and thus equaled the size of Teotihuacán at its zenith. More than 90 percent of the European population consisted of **peasants** living in small rural communities. Peasant families usually owned or leased a small dwelling in the village center and had the right to farm the surrounding fields. The fields were "open"—not divided by fences or hedges—making cooperative farming a necessity. The village community decided which crops would be grown,

Artisan Family

Work was slow and output was limited in the preindustrial world, and survival required the efforts of all family members. Here a fifteenth-century French woodworker planes a panel of wood while his wife twists flax fibers into linen yarn for the family's clothes and their son fashions a basket out of reeds.

Giraudon / Art Resource, NY.

and every family followed its dictates. Because there were few merchants or good roads, most families exchanged surplus grain and meat with their neighbors or bartered their farm products for the services of local millers, weavers, and blacksmiths. Most peasants yearned to be **yeomen**—members of a household that owned enough land to support its members in comfort—but relatively few achieved that goal.

As among the Native Americans, the rhythms of European peasant life followed the seasons. The agricultural year began in March or April, when the ground thawed and dried and the villagers began the exhausting work of spring plowing and the planting of wheat, rye, and oats. During these busy months men sheared the thick winter wool of their sheep, which the women washed and spun into yarn. Peasants cut the first crop of hay in June and stored it as winter fodder for their livestock. In the summer, life became more relaxed, and families repaired their houses and barns. Fall brought the strenuous harvest time, followed by solemn feasts of thanksgiving and riotous bouts of merrymaking. As winter approached, peasants slaughtered excess livestock and salted or smoked the meat. During the cold months peasants completed the tasks of threshing grain and weaving textiles, visited friends and relatives, and held celebrations to mark the pagan winter solstice or birth of Christ. Just before the farming cycle began again in March, rural residents held carnivals to celebrate with drink and dance the end of the long winter night.

Even births and deaths followed the seasons. Many rural people died in January and February, victims of viral diseases, and again in August and September, casualties of epidemics of fly-borne dysentery. More mysteriously, in European villages (and later in rural British America), the greatest numbers of babies were born in February and March, with a smaller peak in September and October. The precise causes of this pattern are unknown; most likely, seasonal fluctuations in female work patterns or the food supply altered a woman's ability to carry a child to full term. One thing is certain. This pattern of births does not exist in modern urban societies, so it must have reflected the rigors of the traditional agriculture cycle.

For most peasants survival required unremitting labor. Horses and oxen strained to break the soil with primitive wooden plows, while workers harvested hay and grain with small hand sickles. Because of the lack of high-quality seeds, chemical fertilizers, and pesticides, output was pitifully small—less than one-tenth of present-day yields. The margin of existence was thin and corroded family relations. Malnourished mothers fed their babies sparingly, calling them "greedy and gluttonous," and many newborn girls were "helped to die" so that their older brothers would have enough to eat. Disease killed about half of all peasant children before the age of twenty-one. Violence—assault, murder, rape—was part of the fabric of daily life, and hunger was a constant companion. "I have seen the latest epoch of misery," a French doctor reported as famine and plague struck. "The inhabitants . . . lie down in a meadow to eat grass, and share the food of wild beasts."

Often destitute, usually exploited and dominated by landlords and aristocrats, many peasants simply accepted their condition. Others hoped for a better life for themselves and their children. In Spain, Germany, and Britain, the deprived rural classes would supply the majority of white migrants to the Western Hemisphere.

Hierarchy and Authority

In the traditional European social order, as among the Aztec and Mayan peoples, authority came from above. Kings and princes owned vast tracts of land, conscripted men for military service, and lived in splendor off the labor of the peasantry. Yet monarchs were far from supreme because of the power of local nobles, each of whom also owned large estates and controlled hundreds of peasant families. Collectively, these noblemen challenged royal authority. They had their own legislative institutions, such as the French *parlements* and the English House of Lords, and enjoyed special privileges. However, after 1450 kings expanded their powers by fashioning new royal courts of law and forming alliances with wealthy merchants. These initiatives gradually undermined the power of the nobility and created more centralized and better financed states, thereby laying the administrative basis for overseas expansion.

Just as kings and nobles ruled society, so men governed families. Among rich and poor, the man was the head of the house, his power justified by the teachings of the Christian Church. As one English clergyman put it, "The woman is a weak creature not embued with like strength and constancy of mind"; law and custom consequently "subjected her to the power of man." Upon marriage, an English woman assumed her husband's surname and had to submit (under threat of legally sanctioned physical "correction") to his orders. Moreover, she surrendered to her husband the legal right to all her property; upon his death she received a **dower**, usually the use during her lifetime of one-third of the family's land and goods.

A father controlled the lives of his children with equal authority, demanding that they work for him until their middle or late twenties. Then landowning peasants would provide land to sons and dowries to daughters and choose marriage partners of appropriate wealth and status. In many regions fathers bestowed most of the land on the eldest son, an inheritance practice known as **primogeniture**, which forced many younger children to join the ranks of the roaming poor. In such a society few men—and even fewer women—had much personal freedom or individual identity.

Hierarchy and authority prevailed in traditional European society both because of the power of established institutions, such as the family, church, and village community, and because, in a violent and unpredictable world, they offered ordinary people a measure of security. These values of order and security, which migrants carried with them to America, would shape the character of family life and the social order there well into the eighteenth century.

The Power of Religion

For centuries, the Roman Catholic Church was the only Christian Church in Western Europe and served as one of the great unifying social institutions. By A.D. 1000, Catholic priests had converted most of pagan Europe. The pope, as head of the Catholic Church, directed a vast religious hierarchy of cardinals, bishops, and priests. Catholic books and theologians preserved Latin, the great language of classical scholarship, and Christian dogma provided a common understanding of God, the world, and human history. Equally important, the Church provided a bulwark of authority and discipline. Every village had a church, and the holy shrines that dotted the byways of Europe were constant reminders of the Church's power and teachings.

Christian doctrine penetrated deeply into the everyday lives of peasants. Originally, most Europeans were pagans; like many of the Indians of North America, they were animists who believed that the entire natural world contained unpredictable spiritual forces that had to be paid ritual honor. Then, Christian priests taught them that spiritual power came from outside of nature, from a great God who had sent his divine son, Jesus Christ, into the world to save humanity from its sins. The Church also devised a religious calendar that transformed pagan agricultural festivals into Christian holy days. Thus, the winter solstice, which for pagans marked the return of the sun, became the feast of Christmas, to mark the coming of the Savior. To avert famine and plague, Christianized peasants did not make ritual offerings to nature but offered prayers to Christ and the saints.

The Church also taught that Satan, a lesser and evil supernatural being, constantly challenged God by tempting people to sin. If a devout Christian fell mysteriously ill, the sickness might be the result of an evil spell cast by a witch in league with Satan. If prophets spread unusual doctrines, or **heresies**, they were surely the tools of Satan. Suppressing false doctrines among Christians became an obligation of rulers, while combating Islam was a principal task of new orders of Christian knights. Following the death in A.D. 632 of the prophet Muhammad, the founder of Islam, the newly converted Arab peoples of the Mediterranean used force and persuasion to spread the Islamic faith and Arab civilization into sub-Saharan Africa, India, and Indonesia and deep into Spain and the Balkan region of eastern Europe. Between A.D. 1096 and 1291 Christian armies undertook a series of Crusades to halt this advance.

The Crusaders had some military successes against their Muslim Arab foes, but their most profound impact was on European society. Religious warfare intensified Europe's Christian identity and prompted the persecution of Jews and their expulsion from many European countries. The Crusades also broadened the intellectual and economic horizons of the privileged classes of Western Europe, who absorbed the advanced scholarship of the Arab world and set out to capture the Arab-dominated trade routes that stretched from Mongolia to Constantinople and from the East Indies to the Mediterranean.

Europe Encounters Africa and the Americas, 1450–1550

Around A.D. 1400 Europeans experienced a major revival of learning—the **Renaissance** (from the French word for "rebirth"). Drawing inspiration from classical Greek and Roman (rather than Christian) sources and from Europe's rapid recovery from the devastating Black Death of the 1340s, Renaissance intellectuals were optimists. They saw themselves not as victims of the forces of nature but as many-sided individuals with the capacity to change the world. Inspired by new knowledge, the rulers of Portugal and Spain commissioned Italian mariners to find trade routes to India and China. These maritime adventurers soon brought Europeans into direct contact with the peoples of Africa, Asia, and the Americas, beginning a new era in world history.

The Renaissance

Stimulated by exposure to the Arab world, first Italy and then the countries of northern Europe experienced a rebirth of learning and cultural life. Arab traders had access to the silks and spices of the East, and Arab societies had acquired

Astronomers at Istanbul, 1581

Arab and Turkish scholars transmitted ancient texts and learning to Europeans during the Middle Ages and provided much of the geographical and astronomical knowledge used by European explorers during the sixteenth century, the great Age of Discovery.

Ergun Cagutay, Istanbul.

magnetic compasses, water-powered mills, and mechanical clocks. Moreover, Arab scholars carried on the legacy of Byzantine civilization, which, in the centuries following the collapse of the Roman empire in Western Europe, had preserved the great achievements of the Greeks and Romans in medicine, philosophy, mathematics, astronomy, and geography. As the Crusades of the twelfth and thirteenth centuries exposed Europeans to Byzantine and Arab learning, they reacquainted themselves with their own classical heritage.

The Renaissance had the most profound impact on the upper classes. Merchants from the Italian city-states of Venice, Genoa, and Pisa dispatched ships to Alexandria, Beirut, and other eastern Mediterranean ports, where they purchased goods from China, India, Persia, and Arabia and sold them throughout Europe. The enormous profits from this commerce created powerful merchants, bankers, and textile manufacturers who conducted trade, lent vast sums of money, and spurred technological innovation in silk and wool production. This moneyed elite ruled the republican city-states of Italy and created the concept of **civic humanism**, an **ideology** that celebrated public virtue and service to the state and would profoundly influence European and American conceptions of government.

Perhaps no other age in European history has produced such a flowering of artistic genius. Michelangelo, Andrea Palladio, and Filippo Brunelleschi [*bru-nel-LESS-key*] designed and built great architectural masterpieces, while Leonardo da Vinci, Jacopo Bellini, and Raphael produced magnificent religious paintings, creating styles and setting standards that have endured into the modern era.

This creative energy inspired Renaissance rulers. In *The Prince* (1513), Niccolò Machiavelli provided unsentimental advice on how monarchs could increase their political power. The kings of Western Europe followed his advice, creating royal law courts and bureaucracies to reduce the power of the landed classes and forging alliances with merchants and urban artisans. Monarchs allowed merchants to trade throughout their realms and granted privileges to artisan guilds, thereby encouraging domestic manufacturing and foreign trade. In return, kings and princes extracted taxes from towns and loans from merchants to support their armies and officials. This alliance of monarchs, merchants, and royal bureaucrats (which eventually became known as **mercantilism**) propelled Europe into its first age of overseas expansion.

Under the direction of Prince Henry (1394–1460), Portugal led a great surge of maritime commercial expansion. Henry was at once a Christian warrior and a Renaissance humanist. As a general of the Crusading Order of Christ, he had fought the Muslims in North Africa. As a humanist, Henry patronized Renaissance thinkers. And, as an explorer, he retained the services of Arab and Italian geographers. Imbued with the spirit of the Renaissance, he tried to fulfill the mission assigned to him by an astrologer: "to engage in great and noble conquests and to attempt the discovery of things hidden from other men."

Because Arab and Italian merchants dominated trade in the Mediterranean, Henry sought an alternative route to Asia. In the 1420s he established a center for exploration near Lisbon and sent newly designed and strongly constructed three-masted ships (caravels, with a lateen—or triangular—sail) to navigate the African coast. His seamen soon discovered and settled three sets of islands—the Madeiras, the Canaries, and the Azores. By 1435 Portuguese sea captains were roaming the coast of West Africa, seeking ivory and gold in exchange for salt, wine, and fish. By the 1440s they were trading in humans as well, the first Europeans to engage in the long-established trade in African slaves.

West African Society and Slavery

Vast and diverse, West Africa stretches along the coast from present-day Senegal to Angola. In the 1400s tropical rain forest covered much of the coast, but a series of great rivers—the Senegal, Gambia, Volta, Niger, and Congo—provided relatively easy access to the woodlands, plains, and savanna of the interior (Map 1.2).

Most West Africans farmed modest plots and lived in extended families in small villages. Normally, men cleared the land and women planted and harvested the

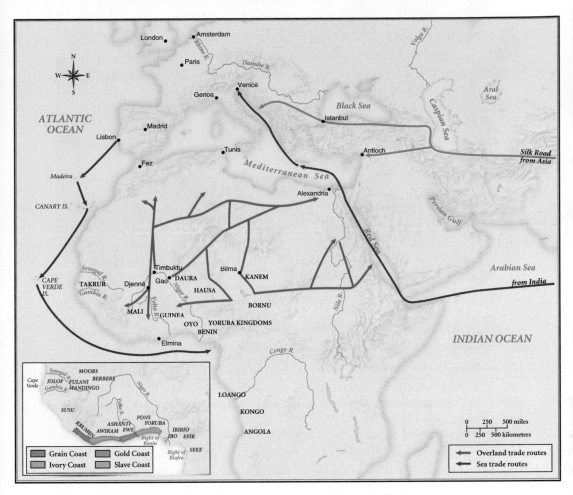

MAP 1.2 West Africa and the Mediterranean in the Fifteenth Century

Trade routes across the Sahara Desert had long connected West Africa with the Mediterranean region. Gold, ivory, and slaves moved northward; fine textiles, spices, and the Muslim faith traveled to the south. Beginning in the 1430s, the Portuguese opened up a maritime trade with the coastal regions of West Africa, which were home to many peoples and dozens of large and small states.

crops. On the plains of the savanna, millet, cotton, and livestock were the primary products, while the forest peoples grew yams and harvested oil-rich palm nuts. Forest dwellers exchanged palm oil and kola nuts, a mild stimulant, for the textiles and leather goods produced by savanna dwellers. Similarly, salt produced along the seacoast was traded for iron or gold mined in the hills of the interior.

West Africans spoke many different languages and lived in hundreds of distinct cultural and political groups. A majority of the people resided in hierarchical, socially stratified societies ruled by princes. Other West Africans dwelled in stateless societies organized by household and lineage (much like those of the woodland

Fulani Village in West Africa

Around 1550 the Fulani people conquered the lands to the south of the Senegal River. To protect themselves from subject peoples and neighboring tribes, the Fulani constructed fortified villages, such as the one depicted here. Previously the Fulani had been nomadic herders and, as the enclosed pasture shows, continued to keep livestock. Note the cylindrical houses of mud brick, surmounted by thatched roofs. Frederic Shoberl, ed., *The World in Miniature*, 1821.

FOR MORE HELP ANALYZING THIS IMAGE, see the Online Study Guide at **bedfordstmartins.com/henrettaconcise**.

Indians of eastern North America). Most peoples had secret societies, such as the Poro for men and the Sande for women, that united people from different lineages and clans. These societies provided education in sexual practices, conducted adult initiation ceremonies, and, by shaming individuals and officials, enforced codes of public conduct and private morality.

Spiritual beliefs varied greatly. Although some West Africans had been converted to Islam by Arab missionaries and believed in a single god, most recognized a variety of deities—ranging from a remote creator-god who seldom interfered in human affairs to numerous animistic spirits that lived in the earth, animals, and plants. Africans viewed their ancestors with great respect, believing that they inhabited a nearby spiritual world from which they could intercede on behalf of their descendants.

At first European traders had a positive impact on life in West Africa by introducing new plants and animals. Portuguese merchants carried coconuts from East Africa, oranges and lemons from the Mediterranean, pigs from Western Europe, and (after 1500) maize, manioc, and tomatoes from the Americas. Portuguese merchants also expanded existing African trade networks. From small, fortified trading posts on the coast, they shipped metal products and manufactures to inland areas and took gold, ivory, and pepper in return. Africans handled this trade; yellow fever, malaria, and dysentery quickly struck down Europeans who ventured inland, and their death rate often reached 50 percent a year.

Europeans soon joined Arab merchants and Africans in the slave trade. Unfree labor was the norm in most premodern societies, and in West Africa it took the form of slavery. Some people were held in bondage as security for debts; others were sold into servitude by their kin, often in exchange for food in times of famine; still others were war captives. Although treated as property and exploited as agricultural laborers, slaves were usually considered members of the society that had enslaved them. Most retained the right to marry, and their children were often free. A small proportion of unfree West Africans were **trade slaves**, mostly war captives and criminals sold from one kingdom to another or carried overland in caravans by Arab traders to the Mediterranean region. Thus, the first Portuguese in Senegambia found that a Wolof [WOE-*lof*] king

> supports himself by raids which result in many slaves. . . . He employs these slaves in cultivating the land allotted to him; but he also sells many to the Azanaghi [Arab] merchants in return for horses and other goods.

Subsequently, Portuguese traders established "forts" at small port cities—Gorée, Elmina, Mpinda, and Loango—where they bought slaves from African princes and warlords. Initially they carried a few thousand African slaves each year to sugar plantations in Madeira and the Canary Islands and to Lisbon, which soon had a black population of 9,000. After 1550 the maritime slave trade expanded enormously as Europeans set up sugar plantations in Brazil and the West Indies. By 1700, slave traders were carrying hundreds of thousands of enslaved Africans to toil and die on American plantations.

Europe Reaches the Americas

As they traded with Africans, Portuguese adventurers continued their quest for an ocean route to Asia. In 1488, Bartolomeu Dias rounded the Cape of Good Hope, the southern tip of Africa, and ten years later Vasco da Gama reached India. Although the Arab, Indian, and Jewish merchants who controlled the trade along India's Malabar Coast tried to exclude him, da Gama acquired a highly profitable cargo of cinnamon and pepper—spices used to flavor and preserve meat. To capture the trade in spices and Indian textiles, da Gama returned to India in 1502 with twenty-one fighting vessels, which outmaneuvered and outgunned the Arab fleets. Soon the Portuguese government set up fortified trading posts for its merchants at key points around the Indian Ocean, in Indonesia, and along the coast of Asia to China and

Japan. In a transition that helped to lay the foundations for the momentous growth of European wealth and power, the Portuguese replaced Arabs as the leaders in world commerce.

Spain quickly followed Portugal's example. As Renaissance rulers, King Ferdinand of Aragon and Queen Isabel of Castile saw national unity and commerce as the keys to power and prosperity. Married in their teens in an arranged match, the young rulers (r. 1474–1516) combined their kingdoms and completed the centuries-long *reconquista* by ousting the Muslims from their realm. In 1492 their armies captured Granada, the last outpost of Islam in Western Europe. Using Catholicism to build a sense of "Spanishness," Ferdinand and Isabel launched a brutal Inquisition against suspected Christian heretics and expelled or forcibly converted thousands of Jews and Arabs. Simultaneously they sought trade and empire and enlisted the services of Christopher Columbus, a mariner from Genoa. Misinterpreting the findings of Italian geographers, Columbus believed that the Atlantic Ocean, long feared by Arab sailors as a ten-thousand-mile-wide "green sea of darkness," was little more than a narrow channel of water separating Europe from Asia. Although dubious about Columbus's theory, Ferdinand and Isabel arranged financial backing from Spanish merchants and charged Columbus to find a new trade route to Asia and carry Christianity to its peoples.

Columbus set sail in three small ships in August 1492. Six weeks later, after a perilous voyage of three thousand miles, he found land, disembarking on October 12 on an island in the present-day Bahamas. Believing he had reached Asia— "the Indies," in fifteenth-century parlance—Columbus called the native inhabitants Indians and the islands the West Indies. Surprised by the rude living conditions of the native people, Columbus expected them to "easily be made Christians, for it appeared to me that they had no religion." With ceremony and solemnity, he bestowed the names of the Spanish royal family and Catholic holy days on the islands, thereby intending to claim them for Spain and for Christendom. Columbus then explored the neighboring Caribbean islands and demanded tribute from the local Taino [*TIE-no*], Arawak [*AR-a-wak*], and Carib peoples. Buoyed by the natives' stories of rivers of gold lying "to the west," Columbus left forty men on the island of Hispaniola (present-day Haiti and the Dominican Republic) and returned triumphantly to Spain.

Although Columbus brought back no gold, the Spanish monarchs supported three more voyages over the next twelve years. During those expeditions Columbus began the colonization of the West Indies, transporting more than a thousand Spanish settlers—all men—and hundreds of domestic animals. He also began the transatlantic trade in slaves by carrying hundreds of Indians to bondage in Europe and importing black slaves from Africa to work as artisans and farmers in the new Spanish settlements. Because Columbus failed to find either golden treasures or great kingdoms, his death in 1506 went virtually unnoticed.

Other explorers continued the quest, and a German geographer named the continents after a Genoese mariner, Amerigo Vespucci, who had traveled to South

America around 1500 and called it a *nuevo mundo*, a new world. For its part, the Spanish crown continued to call the new lands *Las Indias* (the Indies) and determined to make them part of a new Spanish world.

The Spanish Conquest

Columbus and other Spanish adventurers ruled the peoples of the Caribbean islands with an iron hand. After subduing the Arawaks and Tainos on Hispaniola, the Spanish probed coastal settlements on the mainland in search of gold and slaves. In 1513 Juan Ponce de León explored the coast of Florida and gave the peninsula its name. That same year Vasco Núñez de Balboa crossed the Isthmus of Darien (Panama), becoming the first European to see the Pacific Ocean. Rumors of rich Indian kingdoms in the interior encouraged other Spaniards, including many hardened veterans of the wars against the Muslims, to launch an invasion. To encourage these adventurers to expand its American empire, the Spanish crown offered successful conquistadors (conquerors) titles of nobility, the ownership of vast estates, and Indian laborers to farm them.

The first great success of the conquistadors came in present-day Mexico. In 1519 the ambitious and charismatic adventurer Hernán Cortés landed on the Mexican coast with 600 men and marched toward the Aztec capital of Tenochtitlán. Fortunately for the Spaniards, Cortés arrived in the very year that Aztec mythology had predicted for the return of the god Quetzalcoatl. Fearful that Cortés might be the returning god, Moctezuma [*mock-ta-zoo-ma*], the Aztec ruler, acted indecisively. After an Aztec ambush failed, Moctezuma allowed Cortés to proceed without challenge to Tenochtitlán and received him with great ceremony, only to become Cortés's captive.

When Moctezuma's forces finally attempted to expel the invaders, they faced superior European military technology. The sight of the Spaniards in full armor, with guns that shook the heavens and inflicted devastating wounds, made a deep impression on the Aztecs, who knew how to purify gold but not how to produce iron tools or weapons. Moreover, the Aztecs had no wheeled carts or cavalry, and their warriors, fighting on foot with flint- or obsidian-tipped spears and arrows, were no match for mounted Spanish conquistadors wielding steel swords and aided by vicious attack dogs. Although heavily outnumbered and suffering great losses, Cortés and his men were able to fight their way out of the Aztec capital (see American Voices, "Aztec Elders Describe the Spanish Conquest," p. 26).

Still, the Indian peoples of Mexico could easily have crushed the European invaders if they had remained united. But Cortés deftly exploited the widespread resentment against the Aztecs. With the assistance of Malinche, his Indian interpreter and mistress, he formed military alliances and raised thousands of troops from subject peoples who had seen their wealth expropriated by Aztec nobles and their people sacrificed to the Aztec sun god. The Aztec empire collapsed, the victim not of superior Spanish military technology but of a vast internal rebellion of Indian peoples.

AMERICAN VOICES

Aztec Elders Describe the Spanish Conquest

FRIAR BERNARDINO DE SAHAGÚN

During the 1550s Friar Bernardino de Sahagún published the Florentine Codex: General History of New Spain. *According to Sahagún, the authors of the codex were Aztec elders who lived through the conquest. Here the elders describe their reaction to the invading Europeans and the devastating impact of smallpox.*

Moctezuma enjoyed no sleep, no food, no one spoke to him. Whatsoever he did, it was as if he were in torment. Ofttimes it was as if he sighed, became weak, felt weak. . . . Wherefore he said, "What will now befall us? Who indeed stands [in charge]? Alas, until now, I. In great torment is my heart; as if it were washed in chili water it indeed burns." . . .

And when he had so heard what the messengers reported, he was terrified, he was astounded. . . . Especially did it cause him to faint away when he heard how the gun, at [the Spaniards'] command, discharged: how it resounded as if it thundered when it went off. It indeed bereft one of strength; it shut off one's ears. And when it discharged, something like a round pebble came forth from within. Fire went showering forth; sparks went blazing forth. And its smoke smelled very foul; it had a fetid odor which verily wounded the head. And when [the shot] struck a mountain, it was as if it were destroyed, dissolved . . . as if someone blew it away.

All iron was their war array. In iron they clothed themselves. With iron they covered their heads. Iron were their swords. Iron were their crossbows. Iron were their shields. Iron were their lances. And those which bore them upon their backs, their deer [horses], were as tall as roof terraces.

And their bodies were everywhere covered; only their faces appeared. They were very white; they had chalky faces; they had yellow hair, though the hair of some was black. . . . And when Moctezuma so heard, he was much terrified. It was as if he fainted away. His heart saddened; his heart failed him. . . .

[Soon] there came to be prevalent a great sickness, a plague. It was in Tepeilhuitl that it originated, that there spread over the people a great destruction of men. Some it indeed covered [with pustules]; they were spread everywhere, on one's face, on one's head, on one's breast. There was indeed perishing; many indeed died of it. No longer could they walk; they only lay in their abodes, in their beds. No longer could they move. . . . And when they bestirred themselves, much did they cry out. There was much perishing. Like a covering, covering-like, were the pustules. Indeed, many people died of them, and many just died of hunger. There was death from hunger; there was no one to take care of another; there was no one to attend to another.

SOURCE: *The Florentine Codex: General History of New Spain*, translated by Arthur J. O. Anderson and Charles E. Dibble. Copyright © 1975 by the University of Utah Press and the School of American Research. Reprinted Courtesy of the University of Utah Press.

The Spanish also had a silent ally—disease. Separated from Eurasia for thousands of years, the inhabitants of the Western Hemisphere had no immunities to common European diseases. A massive smallpox epidemic lasting seventy days ravaged Tenochtitlán following the Spanish exodus, "striking everywhere in the city," according to an Aztec source, killing Moctezuma's brother and many others. "They could not move, they could not stir. . . . Covered, mantled with pustules, very many people died of them." Subsequent outbreaks of smallpox, influenza, and measles killed hundreds of thousands of Aztecs and their subject peoples and sapped the morale of the survivors. Exploiting this demographic weakness, Cortés quickly extended Spanish rule over the entire Aztec empire. His lieutenants then moved against the Mayan city-states in the Yucatán Peninsula, eventually conquering them as well.

In 1532 the Spanish conquest entered a new phase. Francisco Pizarro led a military expedition to Peru, home of the rich and powerful Inca empire that stretched 2,000 miles along the Pacific coast of South America. To govern this far-flung empire, the Inca rulers had built 24,000 miles of roads and dozens of carefully placed administrative centers, which were constructed of finely crafted stone. A semidivine Inca king ruled the empire, assisted by a hierarchical bureaucracy staffed by noblemen, many of whom were his relatives. By the time Pizarro and his small force of 168 men and 67 horses reached Peru, half of the Inca population had died from European diseases, which had been spread by Indian traders. Weakened militarily and fighting over succession to the throne, the Inca nobility was easy prey for Pizarro's army. In little more than a decade Spain had become the master of the wealthiest and most populous regions of the Western Hemisphere (Map 1.3).

The Spanish invasion and European diseases changed life forever throughout the Americas. Disease and warfare wiped out virtually all the Indians of Hispaniola—at least 300,000 people. In Peru the population plummeted from nine million in 1530 to fewer than half a million a century later. Likewise, diseases carried by Spanish adventurers into the area of the present-day United States inflicted catastrophic losses on the Pueblo peoples of the Southwest and the Mississippian chiefdoms of the Southeast. Mesoamerica suffered the greatest decline. In 1500, it boasted a population of 40 million; by 1650, its Native American population had fallen to a mere 3 million people—one of the greatest demographic disasters in world history.

Once the conquistadors had triumphed, the Spanish government quickly created an elaborate bureaucratic empire. From its headquarters in Madrid, the Council of the Indies issued laws and decrees to viceroys and other Spanish officials in America. Nonetheless, the conquistadors remained powerful because they held royal grants (*encomiendas*) giving them legal control of the native population. They ruthlessly exploited the surviving Native Americans, forcing them to raise crops and cattle for local consumption and export to Europe. The Spaniards also permanently altered the natural environment by introducing grains and grasses that supplanted the native flora. Horses, once native to the Western Hemisphere but now extinct, were

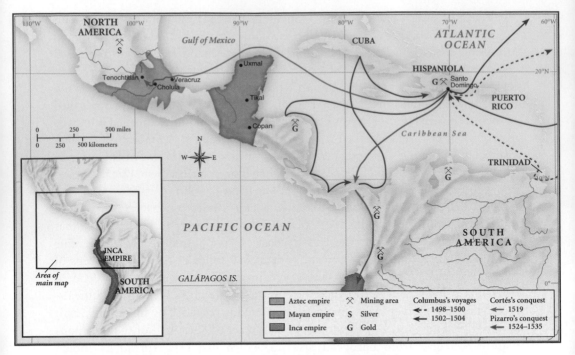

MAP 1.3 The Spanish Conquest of the Great Indian Civilizations

The Spanish first invaded the islands of the Caribbean. Rumors of a magnificent golden civilization led to Cortés's invasion of the Aztec empire in 1519. By 1535 other Spanish conquistadors had conquered the Mayan temple cities and the Inca empire in Peru, completing one of the great conquests in world history.

FOR MORE HELP ANALYZING THIS MAP, see the Online Study Guide at **bedfordstmartins.com/henrettaconcise**.

reintroduced by Cortés and dramatically changed the way of life of many Indian peoples, especially on the Great Plains.

The Spanish invasion of the Americas had a significant ecological impact on Europe and Africa as well. In a process of transfer known to historians as the **Columbian Exchange**, the food products of the Western Hemisphere—especially maize, potatoes, and cassava (manioc)—became available to the peoples of other continents, significantly increasing agricultural yields and stimulating the growth of population. Similarly, the livestock and crops—and weeds and human diseases—of African and Eurasian lands became part of the lives of residents of the Americas. Nor was that all. The gold and silver that had formerly honored Aztec gods now gilded the Catholic churches of Europe and flowed into the countinghouses of Spain, making that nation the richest and most powerful in Europe.

By 1550 the once magnificent civilizations of Mexico and Peru lay in ruins. "Of all these wonders"—the great city of Tenochtitlán, the rich orchards, the overflowing markets—"all is overthrown and lost, nothing left standing," recalled the Spanish chronicler Bernal Díaz, who had been a young soldier in Cortés's army. Moreover, the surviving Indian peoples had lost vital parts of their cultural identity, as Spanish priests suppressed their worship of traditional gods and converted them to Catholicism. As early as 1531 an Indian convert reported a vision of a dark-skinned Virgin Mary, later known as the Virgin of Guadalupe, a Christian version of the "corn mother" who traditionally protected the maize crop.

A new society took shape on the recently emptied land. Between 1500 and 1650, no fewer than 350,000 Spanish migrants settled in areas previously occupied by the native peoples of Mesoamerica and South America. Because over 75 percent of the Spanish settlers were men who took Indian women as wives or mistresses, the result was a substantial **mestizo** (mixed-race) population and an elaborate race-based **caste system**. Around 1800, at the end of the colonial era, Spanish America was a vast empire that stretched from the tip of South America to present-day Oregon and contained about 17 million people: a dominant caste of 3.2 million Europeans; 5.5 million people of mixed race and cultural heritage; 7.5 million Indians, most of whom were poor; and 1 million enslaved Africans. For the original Native American peoples, the consequences of the European invasion in 1492 were tragic and irreversible.

The Protestant Reformation and the Rise of England

Religion formed a central aspect of European life and played a crucial role in the settlement of America. Even as Catholic fervor in Spain prompted the forced conversion of Muslims, Jews, and Native Americans, Christianity ceased to be a unifying force in European society. New religious doctrines preached by Martin Luther and other reformers divided Europe between Catholic and Protestant states and plunged the continent into religious wars. These struggles resulted in the emergence of Holland and England as Protestant nations determined to challenge Spain's dominant position in the Western Hemisphere.

The Protestant Movement

Over the centuries, the Catholic Church had become a large and wealthy institution. Renaissance popes and cardinals used the Church's wealth to patronize the arts and some clerics used their power for personal gain. Pope Leo X (r. 1513–1521) received half a million ducats a year from the sale of religious offices. Corruption at the top encouraged ordinary priests and monks to use status to obtain economic or sexual favors. One English reformer denounced the clergy as a "gang of scoundrels" who should be "rid of their vices or stripped of their authority," but he was ignored. Other reformers, such as Jan Hus of Bohemia, were tried and executed as heretics.

In 1517 Martin Luther, a German monk and professor at the university in Wittenberg, took up the cause of reform. His Ninety-five Theses condemned many Catholic practices, including the use of **indulgences**—church certificates that allegedly pardoned a sinner from punishments in the afterlife. Outraged by Luther's charges, the pope dismissed him from the Church and the Holy Roman Emperor, King Charles I of Spain (r. 1516–1556), threatened Luther with punishment. However, the princes of northern Germany, who were resisting the emperor's authority for political reasons, protected Luther from arrest, thus allowing the Protestant movement to survive.

Luther broadened his attack and took issue with Roman Catholic doctrine in three major respects. First, he rejected the doctrine that Christians could secure salvation through good deeds or the purchase of indulgences; instead, Luther argued that people could be saved only by grace, which came as a free gift from God. Second, the German reformer downplayed the role of the clergy and the pope as mediators between God and the people, proclaiming, "Our baptism consecrates us all without exception and makes us all priests." Third, Luther said that believers must look to the Bible (not Church officials or doctrine) as the ultimate authority in matters of faith. So that every literate German-speaking believer could read the Bible, he translated it from Latin into German.

Peasants as well as princes heeded Luther's attack on authority and, to his dismay, mounted social protests of their own. In 1524 some German peasants rebelled against their manorial lords. Fearing social revolution, Luther urged obedience to established political institutions and condemned the teachings of new groups of religious dissidents, such as the Anabaptists (so called because they rejected infant baptism). Reassured of Luther's social conservatism, most princes in northern Germany embraced his teachings and broke from Rome, thereby gaining the power to appoint bishops and control the Church's property within their domains. To restore Catholic doctrine and his political authority, the emperor dispatched armies to Germany, unleashing a generation of warfare. Eventually, the Peace of Augsburg (1555) restored order by dividing Germany into Lutheran states in the north and Catholic principalities in the south.

John Calvin, a French theologian, established the most rigorous Protestant regime in Geneva, Switzerland. Even more than Luther, Calvin stressed the weakness of men and women and the omnipotence of God. His *Institutes of the Christian Religion* (1536) depicted God as an awesome and absolute sovereign who governed the "wills of men so as to move precisely to that end directed by him." Calvin preached the doctrine of **predestination**—the idea that God had chosen certain people for salvation even before they were born and condemned the rest to eternal damnation. In Geneva he set up a model Christian community, eliminating bishops and placing spiritual power in the hands of ministers chosen by the members of each congregation. Ministers and pious laymen ruled the city, prohibiting frivolity and luxury and imposing religious discipline on the entire society. "We know," wrote Calvin, "that man is of so perverse and crooked a nature, that everyone would scratch out his neighbor's eyes if there were no bridle to hold them in." Calvin's doctrines won converts all over Europe, becoming the theology of the Huguenots in France, the Reformed churches in Belgium and Holland, and the Presbyterians and Puritans in Scotland and England.

In England, King Henry VIII (r. 1509–1547) initially opposed Protestantism. However, in 1534, when the pope refused to annul his marriage to Catherine of Aragon, Henry broke with Rome and placed himself at the head of a national Church of England (which promptly approved the annulment). Although Henry made few changes in Church doctrine, organization, and ritual, he allowed the spread of Protestant beliefs and teachings. Faced with popular pressure for religious reform, Henry's daughter and successor, Queen Elizabeth I (r. 1558–1603) approved a Protestant confession of faith that incorporated both the Lutheran doctrine of salvation by grace and the Calvinist belief in predestination. To mollify traditionalists, Elizabeth retained the Catholic ritual of Holy Communion—now conducted in English rather than in Latin—as well as the hierarchy of bishops and archbishops.

Elizabeth's compromises angered radical Protestants, who condemned the power of bishops as "anti-Christian and devilish and contrary to the Scriptures." Many of these reformers took inspiration from the Presbyterian system pioneered in Calvin's Geneva and developed by John Knox for the Church of Scotland; in Scotland local congregations elected lay elders (presbyters), who assisted ministers in running the Church, and sent delegates to synods (councils) that decided Church doctrine. By 1600, at least five hundred ministers in the Church of England wanted to eliminate bishops and install a Presbyterian form of church government.

Other radical English Protestants called themselves "unspotted lambs of the Lord" or "Puritans." These extraordinarily intense and devout Calvinist Protestants wanted to "purify" the Church of Catholic teachings and magical or idolatrous practices. Thus, Puritan services avoided appeals to dead saints or the burning of incense; instead, they focused on a carefully argued sermon on ethics or dogma. Puritans also placed special emphasis on the "conversion experience," the felt infusion of God's grace, and the "calling," the duty to serve God in one's ordinary life and work. To ensure that all men and women had access to God's commands, they encouraged everyone to read the Bible, thus promoting widespread literacy. Finally, most Puritans wanted authority over spiritual and financial matters to rest primarily with local congregations or Presbyterian synods (elected church councils). Eventually, thousands of Puritan migrants would establish churches in North America based on these radical Protestant doctrines.

The Dutch and the English Challenge Spain

Luther's challenge to Catholicism in 1517 came just two years before Cortés conquered the Aztec empire, and the two events remained linked. Gold and silver from Mexico and Peru made Spain the wealthiest nation in Europe and King Philip II

Elizabeth I (r. 1558–1603)

Attired in richly decorated clothes that symbolize her power, Queen Elizabeth I relishes the destruction of the Spanish Armada (pictured in background) and proclaims her nation's imperial ambitions. The queen's hand rests on a globe, asserting England's claims in the Western Hemisphere. By kind permission of His Grace the Duke of Bedford and the Trustees of the Bedford Estates.

(r. 1556–1598), the successor to Charles I, its most powerful ruler. In addition to Spain, Philip presided over wealthy city-states in Italy, the commercial and manufacturing provinces of the Spanish Netherlands (present-day Holland and Belgium), and, after 1580, Portugal and all its possessions in America, Africa, and the East Indies. "If the Romans were able to rule the world simply by ruling the Mediterranean," a Spanish priest boasted, "what of the man who rules the Atlantic and Pacific oceans, since they surround the world?"

Philip, an ardent Catholic, tried to root out Protestantism in the Netherlands, which had become wealthy from trade with the vast Portuguese empire and from the weaving of wool and linen. To protect their Calvinist faith and political liberties, the Dutch and Flemish provinces revolted in 1566, and in 1581, the seven northern provinces declared their independence, becoming the Dutch Republic (or Holland). When Elizabeth I of England dispatched 6,000 troops to assist the Dutch cause,

Philip found a new enemy. In 1588, he sent the Spanish Armada—130 ships and 30,000 men—against England. Philip planned to reimpose Catholicism in England and then wipe out Calvinism in Holland. However, the Armada failed utterly, as English ships and a fierce storm destroyed the Spanish fleet. Philip continued to spend his American gold on religious wars, undermining the Spanish economy and prompting the migration of hundreds of thousands of Spaniards to America. By the time of his death in 1598, Spain was in serious decline.

As Spain faltered, Holland prospered—the economic miracle of the seventeenth century. Amsterdam emerged as the financial capital of northern Europe, and the Dutch Republic became the leading commercial power by replacing Portugal as the dominant trader in Indonesia and West Africa. The Dutch merchants also looked across the Atlantic and created the West India Company, which invested in sugar plantations in Brazil and established the fur-trading colony of New Netherland in North America.

England also emerged as an important European state, its economy stimulated by a rise in population from 3 million in 1500 to 5 million in 1630. Equally important, the royal government supported the expansion of commerce and manufacturing. English merchants had long supplied European weavers with high-quality wool, and around 1500, they created their own textile industry. In this **outwork** (or putting-out) system merchants bought wool from the owners of great estates and provided it to landless peasants, who spun and wove the wool into cloth. The government helped these textile manufacturers by setting low rates for wages and by opening up foreign markets. To encourage merchant enterprise, Queen Elizabeth granted special monopoly privileges to the Levant Company (Turkey) in 1581, the Guinea Company (Africa) in 1588, and the East India Company (India) in 1600.

This system of state-assisted manufacturing and trade became known as mercantilism. Elizabeth encouraged domestic manufacturing in order to reduce imports and increase exports—and give England a favorable balance of trade. The queen and her advisors wanted gold and silver to flow into the country in payment for English goods, stimulating further economic expansion and enriching the merchant community. Increased trade also meant higher revenues from import duties, which swelled the royal treasury and enhanced the power of the national government. By 1600 these merchant-oriented policies had laid the foundations for overseas colonization. The English (as well as the Dutch) now had the merchant fleets and economic wealth needed to challenge Spain's monopoly in the Western Hemisphere.

The Social Causes of English Colonization

The growth of the English population combined with unsettling economic changes to provide a large body of settlers willing to go to America. The massive expenditure of American gold and silver by Philip II had doubled the money supply of Europe and sparked a major inflation between 1530 and 1600—known today as the **Price Revolution**.

In England the nobility was the first casualty of the Price Revolution. Aristocrats had customarily rented out their estates on long leases for fixed rents, giving them a secure income and plenty of leisure. As one English nobleman put it, "We eat and drink and rise up to play and this is to live like a gentleman." Then inflation struck. In less than two generations the price of goods more than tripled while the nobility's rent income barely increased. As the wealth of the aristocracy declined, that of the **gentry** and the yeomen rose. The gentry (nonnoble landholders with substantial estates) kept pace with inflation by renting land on short leases at higher rates. Yeomen, described by a European traveler as "middle people of a condition between gentlemen and peasants," owned small farms that they worked with family help. As wheat prices tripled, yeomen used the profits to build larger houses and provide their children with land.

Economics influenced politics. As aristocrats lost wealth, their branch of Parliament, the House of Lords, declined in influence. At the same time, members of the rising gentry entered the House of Commons, the political voice of the propertied classes. Supported by the yeomen, the gentry demanded new rights and powers for the Commons, such as control of taxation. Thus the Price Revolution encouraged the rise of representative institutions in which rich commoners and small property owners had a voice, a development with profound consequences for English—and American—political history.

The Price Revolution likewise transformed the lives of peasants and landless farm laborers, who made up three-fourths of the population. The rise of the textile industry increased the demand for wool and led profit-minded landlords and wool merchants to persuade Parliament to pass **enclosure acts**. These acts allowed owners to fence in the open fields that surrounded many peasant villages and put sheep to graze on them. Now dispossessed of land, peasant families lived on the brink of poverty, spinning and weaving wool or working as wage laborers on large estates. Wealthy men had "taken farms into their hands," an observer noted in 1600, "whereby the peasantry of England is decayed and become servants to gentlemen."

A series of crop failures caused by cold weather precipitated the migration across the Atlantic. Between 1590 and 1640, land prices rose and the danger of starvation increased, prompting thousands of yeomen families to look to America for land for their children. Dispossessed peasants and weavers, their livelihoods threatened by a recession in the cloth trade, were likewise on the move. "Thieves and rogues do swarm the highways," warned one justice of the peace, "and bastards be multiplied in parishes." Seeking food and security, tens of thousands of young propertyless laborers contracted to go to America in the lowly condition of indentured servants. This massive migration of English yeomen families and impoverished laborers would bring about a new collision between the European and Native American worlds.

TIMELINE			
13,000–3000 B.C.	Main settlement of North America	1492	Christopher Columbus's first voyage to America
		1513	Juan Ponce de León explores Florida
3000–2000 B.C.	Cultivation of crops begins in Mesoamerica	1517	Martin Luther sparks Protestant Reformation
100 B.C.–A.D. 400	Flourishing of Hopewell culture	1519–1521	Hernán Cortés conquers Aztec empire
300	Rise of Mayan civilization	1531–1538	Francisco Pizarro vanquishes Incas in Peru
500	Zenith of Teotihuacán civilization	1534	Henry VIII establishes Church of England
600	Emergence of Pueblo cultures	1536	John Calvin, *Institutes of the Christian Religion*
700–1100	Spread of Arab Muslim civilization		
800–1350	Development of Mississippian culture	1550–1630	Price Revolution English mercantilism Enclosure acts
1096–1291	Crusades link Europe with Arab learning	1556–1598	Philip I, king of Spain
1325	Aztecs establish capital at Tenochtitlán	1558–1603	Elizabeth I, queen of England
1400–1550	Italian Renaissance		
		1560s	English Puritan movement begins
1440s	Portugal enters trade in African slaves		

For Further Exploration

Kenneth Pomeranz, *The Great Divergence: Europe, China, and the Making of the Modern World Economy* (2000), sets the settlement of America in the perspective of world history. Alvin M. Josephy Jr., ed., *America in 1492: The World of the Indian Peoples before the Arrival of Columbus* (1991), offers a panorama of early Indian societies. Recent scholarship on the prehistoric Indians of the United States is brought to life by Brian M. Fagan, *The Great Journey: The People of Ancient America* (1987). For the European background of colonization, begin with George Huppert, *After the Black Death* (2nd ed., 1998), a highly readable introduction to Western Europe's recovery from the devastating epidemic of the mid-fourteenth century. William D. Phillips with Carla Rahn Phillips continue the story of European expansion in *The Worlds of Christopher Columbus* (1992), an engaging biography that describes the enormous consequences of Columbus's voyages.

Peter Laslett, *The World We Have Lost* (3rd ed., 1984), offers a vivid portrait of society in seventeenth-century England, while Susan Doran and Christopher Durston, *Princes, Pastors, and People: The Church and Religion in England, 1529–1689* (1991), discuss the impact of the Protestant Reformation on theology, the role of the clergy, and church services.

Two interesting Public Broadcasting Service (PBS) videos examine the ancient civilizations of Mesoamerica: *Odyssey: Maya Lords of the Jungle* (1 hour) and *Odyssey: The Incas* (1 hour). For additional information log on to "1492: An Ongoing Voyage" at <http://lcweb.loc.gov/exhibits/1492/intro.html>, which provides a survey of the native cultures of the Western Hemisphere, the impact of discovery, and full-color images of artifacts and art. Material on an early Indian civilization in the southwestern United States is available at "Sipapu: The Anasazi Emergence into the Cyber World," <http://sipapu.gsu.edu/>.

For definitions of key terms boldfaced in this chapter, see the glossary at the end of the book.

To assess your mastery of the material covered in this chapter, see the Online Study Guide at **bedfordstmartins.com/henrettaconcise**.

For map resources and primary documents, see **bedfordstmartins.com/henrettaconcise**.

Chapter 2

THE INVASION
AND SETTLEMENT
OF NORTH AMERICA
1550–1700

Human life is reduced to real suffering, to hell, only when . . .
cultures and religions overlap.

ALBRECHT VON HALLER

Establishing colonies in the distant land of North America was not for the faint of heart. First came a long voyage in small ships over stormy, dangerous waters. Then the migrants, weakened by weeks of travel, spoiled food, and shipboard diseases, faced potentially hostile Indian peoples. "We neither fear them or trust them," declared Puritan settler Francis Higginson, but rely on "our musketeers." Although the risks were great and the rewards uncertain, Europeans by the tens of thousands crossed the Atlantic during the seventeenth century. They were either driven by poverty and religious persecution at home or drawn by the lures of the New World: land, gold, and—as another Puritan migrant put it—the hope of "propagating the Gospel to these poor barbarous people."

For Native Americans, the European invasion was nothing short of catastrophic. Whether they came as settlers or missionaries or fur traders, the white-skinned people spread havoc, bringing new diseases and religions and threatening Indians with the loss of their cultures, lands, and lives. "Our fathers had plenty of deer and skins, . . . and our coves were full of fish and fowl," the Narragansett chief Miantonomi reminded the neighboring Montauk people in 1642, "but these English having gotten our land . . . their cows and horses eat the grass, and their hogs spoil our clam banks, and we shall all be starved." The Narragansetts called for united resistance. "We [are] all Indians," Miantonomi continued, and must "say brother to one another, . . . otherwise we shall all be gone shortly." But Indian unity was fragmentary and brittle, and foretold the course of North American history: the advance of the European invaders and the dispossession of the Indian peoples.

Imperial Conflicts and Rival Colonial Models

In Mesoamerica the Spanish converted the Indians to Catholicism and made them dig gold and farm large estates. In the more sparsely populated region of eastern North America, the French and the Dutch created fur-trading empires and the native peoples retained their lands and political autonomy. However, in the English colonies, settlers sought to expel Indians from their lands. Whatever the goals of the invaders, nearly everywhere Indian peoples eventually rose in revolt.

New Spain: Colonization and Conversion

In their ceaseless quest for gold, Spanish adventurers penetrated deeply into the southern and western United States. In the 1540s Francisco Vásquez de Coronado searched in vain for the fabled seven golden cities of Cíbola, but his men discovered the Grand Canyon in Arizona, the Pueblo peoples of New Mexico, and the grasslands of central Kansas. Simultaneously, Hernán de Soto and a force of 600 adventurers cut a bloody swath across the Southeast, doing battle with the Apalachees of northern Florida and the Coosas of northern Alabama but finding no gold and few other riches (Map 2.1).

By the 1560s Spanish officials gave up the search for rich Indian peoples and focused on the defense of the existing empire. Roving English "sea dogs" were plundering Spanish treasure ships and Caribbean seaports, and French Protestants began to settle in Florida, long claimed by Spain. Following King Philip II's order to cast out the trespassing Frenchmen "by the best means," Spanish troops massacred 300 members of the "evil Lutheran sect." To safeguard Florida, in 1565 Spain established a fort at St. Augustine, which became the first permanent European settlement in the future United States. However, Indian raids wiped out a dozen other Spanish military outposts and religious missions, one as far north as Chesapeake Bay.

These military setbacks prompted the Spanish crown to adopt a new policy toward the Indian peoples. The Comprehensive Orders for New Discoveries, issued in 1573, placed the "pacification" of new lands primarily in the hands of missionaries, not conquistadors. Franciscan friars promptly set up missions among the settled agricultural Pueblo peoples visited by Coronado two generations before and named the area *Nuevo México*. Although the friars often learned Indian languages, they systematically attacked the natives' culture. Protected by Spanish soldiers, missionaries whipped sexual sinners and smashed the Indians' religious idols. To win the allegiance of Native Americans to the Christian God, they tried to impress them with rich vestments, gold crosses, and silver chalices.

For the Franciscans, religious conversion and cultural assimilation went hand in hand. They introduced the European practice of having men instead of women grow most of the crops and encouraged the Indians to talk, cook, dress, and walk like Spaniards. Moreover, they generally ignored Spanish laws intended to protect

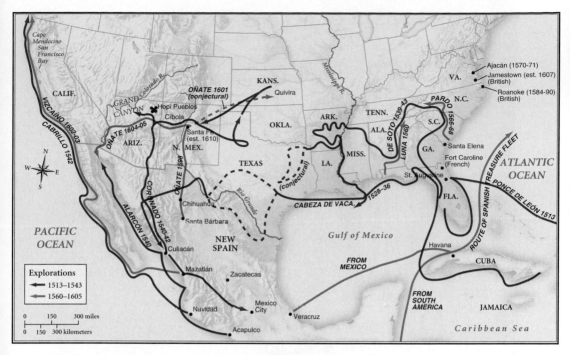

MAP 2.1 New Spain Looks North, 1513–1610

The quest for gold drew Spanish adventurers first to Florida and then deep into the present-day United States. When the wide-ranging expeditions of Hernán de Soto and Francisco Vásquez de Coronado failed to find gold or flourishing Indian civilizations, authorities in New Spain confined northern settlements to St. Augustine in Florida (to protect the treasure fleet) and Santa Fe in the upper Rio Grande Valley.

FOR MORE HELP ANALYZING THIS MAP, see the Online Study Guide at **bedfordstmartins.com/henrettaconcise**.

the native peoples from coerced labor. This neglect allowed privileged Spanish landowners (**encomenderos**) to collect tribute from the native population, both in goods and in forced labor. The missions also depended on Indian workers, who grew the crops and carried them to market, often on their backs.

Native Americans initially tolerated the Franciscan rule out of fear of military reprisals or in hopes of learning their spiritual secrets. But when Christian prayers failed to protect their communities from European diseases, droughts, and raids by the nomadic Apaches, many Pueblo people returned to their ancestral religions and blamed Spanish rule for their ills. Thus, the people of Hawikuh refused to become "wet-heads" (as the Indians called baptized Christians) "because with the water of baptism they would have to die."

In 1598 the tense relations between Indians and Spaniards in New Mexico exploded into open warfare. An expedition of 500 Spanish soldiers and settlers led

Conversion in New Mexico

Franciscan friars, assisted by nuns of various religious orders, introduced Catholicism to the Indian peoples north of the Rio Grande. This 1631 engraving shows one of those nuns, María de Jesús de Agreda, preaching to a nomadic people (*los chichimecos*) in New Mexico.

Nettie Lee Benson Latin American Collection, University of Texas at Austin.

by Juan de Oñate seized corn and clothing from the Pueblo peoples and murdered or raped those who resisted. When Indians of the Acoma pueblo killed 11 soldiers, the Spanish troops destroyed the pueblo, killing 500 men and 300 women and children. Now faced by bitterly hostile Indian peoples, most of the settlers withdrew from New Mexico.

However, in 1610 the Spanish returned, founded the town of Santa Fe, and reestablished the system of missions and forced labor. Over the next two generations, European diseases, forced tribute, and raids by nomadic Navajos and Apaches threatened many Pueblo peoples with extinction. By 1680 their population, which had once numbered 60,000, had declined to a mere 17,000. In desperation the Indian shaman (priest) Popé led the peoples of two dozen pueblos in a carefully coordinated rebellion that killed over 400 Spaniards. As the uprising continued, the Indians forced the remaining 2,000 Spanish colonists to flee three hundred miles to El Paso. Repudiating Christianity, the Pueblo peoples desecrated churches and tortured and killed 21 missionaries.

Reconquered a decade later, the Indians rebelled again in 1696, only to be subdued. Exhausted by a generation of warfare, the Pueblo peoples agreed to a compromise that allowed them to practice their own religion and avoid forced labor. In return, they accepted a dependent position in New Mexico and joined with the Spanish to defend their settlements and farms against attacks by nomadic Indians.

Spain had maintained its northern empire but had largely failed to achieve its goals of religious conversion and cultural assimilation. Taken aback by the military costs of expansion, Spanish officials delayed settlement of the distant region of California until the 1760s. For the time being, Florida and New Mexico stood as the defensive outposts of Spain's North American empire.

New France: Furs and Souls

Far to the northeast the French likewise tried to convert the native peoples to Catholicism. In the 1530s Jacques Cartier had claimed the lands bordered by the Gulf of St. Lawrence for France, but the first permanent French settlement came only in 1608, when Samuel de Champlain founded Quebec. Despite a series of brutal famines in northwestern France and the offer of leaseholds in the fertile St. Lawrence Valley, few peasants migrated to America. France's Catholic monarchs discouraged migration to preserve an ample supply of military recruits at home. They also barred Huguenots (French Protestants) from Quebec, fearing they would not be loyal to the crown. Moreover, French peasants held strong legal rights to their village lands and feared the long, bitter winters in Quebec. Many regarded Canada "as a country at the end of the world" and living there a virtual sentence of "civil death." Of the 27,000 men and women who migrated to Quebec, nearly two-thirds eventually returned to France. In 1698 the European population of New France was only 15,200, compared with 100,000 settlers in the English colonies.

Rather than developing as a settler colony, New France instead became a vast enterprise for acquiring furs, which were in great demand in Europe. To secure plush beaver pelts from the Huron Indians (who lived to the north of the Great Lakes), Champlain provided them with guns to fight the expansionist-minded Five Nations of the Iroquois (see Voices from Abroad, "Going to War with the Hurons," p. 42). Searching for furs and a water route to Asia, the French explorer Jacques Marquette reached the Mississippi River in present-day Wisconsin in 1673 and traveled as far south as Arkansas. In 1681 Robert de La Salle traveled down the Mississippi to the Gulf of Mexico, completing exploration of the majestic river and claiming new lands for France, while also enriching himself. As a French priest noted with disgust, La Salle's expedition hoped "to buy all the Furs and Skins of the remotest Savages, who, as they thought, did not know their Value; and so enrich themselves in one single voyage." To honor King Louis XIV (r. 1643–1714), La Salle named the region he explored Louisiana; soon it included the thriving port of New Orleans on the Gulf of Mexico.

Despite their small numbers, French traders had a disastrous impact on Native Americans of the Great Lakes region. By unwittingly introducing European diseases, they triggered epidemics that killed 25 to 90 percent of the residents of many Indian villages, including those of their Huron allies. Moreover, by buying furs for export to Europe, the French sparked a devastating series of wars among Indian peoples. In the 1640s, the New York Iroquois defeated the Hurons, forced them to migrate to the north and west, and took control of their rich fur-bearing territory.

VOICES FROM ABROAD

Going to War with the Hurons

SAMUEL DE CHAMPLAIN

B est known as the founder of Quebec, Samuel de Champlain was primarily a soldier and an adventurer. Champlain joined the Company of New France and in 1603 traveled to North America, determined to create a French empire there. To ensure French access to western fur trade, in 1609 Champlain joined the Hurons in a raid against the Iroquois, which he described in a book of his American adventures.

Pursuing our route, I met some two or three hundred savages. . . . We made a reconnaissance, and found that they were tribes of savages called Ochasteguins [Hurons] and Algonquins, on their way to Quebec to assist us in exploring the territory of the Iroquois, with whom they are in deadly hostility. . . .

In all their encampments, they have their Pilotois, or Ostemoy, a class of persons who play the part of soothsayers, in whom these people have faith. One of these builds a cabin, surrounds it with small pieces of wood and covers it with his robe: after it is built, he places himself inside, so as not to be seen at all, when he seizes and shakes one of the posts of his cabin, muttering some words between his teeth, by which he says he invokes the devil, who appears to him in the form of a stone, and tells them whether they will meet their enemies and kill many of them. . . .

Now, as we began to approach within two or three days' journey of the abode of our enemies, we advanced only at night. . . . By day, they withdraw into the interior of the woods, where they rest, without straying off, neither making any noise, even for the sake of cooking, so as not to be noticed in case their enemies should by accident pass by.

In order to ascertain what was to be the result of their undertaking, they often asked me if I had had a dream, and seen their enemies, to which I replied in the negative. . . . [Then one night] while sleeping, I dreamed that I saw our enemies, the Iroquois, drowning near a mountain, within sight. When I expressed a wish to help them, our allies, the savages, told me we must let them all die. . . . This, upon being related [to our allies], gave them so much confidence that they did not doubt any longer that good was to happen to them. . . .

[After our victory over the Iroquois] they took one of the prisoners, to whom they made a harangue, enumerating the cruelties which he and his men had already practiced toward them without any mercy, and that, in like manner, he ought to make up his mind to receive as much.

Meanwhile, our men kindled a fire; and, when it was well burning, they brand, and burned this poor creature gradually, so as to make him suffer greater torment. Sometimes they stopped, and threw water on his back. Then they tore out his nails, and applied fire to the extremities of his fingers and private member. Afterwards, they flayed the top of his head, and had a kind of gum poured all hot upon it. . . .

SOURCE: Samuel de Champlain, *Voyages of Samuel de Champlain, 1604–1618*, ed. W. L. Grant (New York: Charles Scribner's Sons, 1907), 79–86.

French priests sought converts among both the defeated Hurons and the belligerent Iroquois. Most were Jesuits, members of the Society of Jesus—a religious order originally founded to combat the Reformation. Between 1625 and 1763, hundreds of Jesuits lived among the Indian peoples and, to a greater extent than the Spanish Franciscans, came to understand their values. Thus, one Jesuit noted the Huron belief that "our souls have desires which are inborn and concealed, yet are made known by means of dreams." As among the Pueblo peoples, many eastern Indians initially welcomed the French "Black Robes" as powerful spiritual beings with magical secrets, such as the ability to forge iron. But when prayers to the Christian God did not protect them from disease and attack, they grew skeptical. A Peoria chief charged that the priest's "fables are good only in his own country; we have our own [religious beliefs], which do not make us die as his do." When epidemics came, some Indians vented their anger by killing French missionaries and fur traders.

Whatever their shortcomings, the French Jesuits did not exploit the labor of the Indian peoples. Moreover, they tried to keep alcoholic beverages, which wreaked havoc among the natives, from becoming a bargaining item in the French fur trade. Finally, the French Jesuits won converts by adapting Christian beliefs to address Indian needs. Thus, in the 1690s they introduced the cult of the Virgin Mary to the young women of the Illinois people, who used its emphasis on chastity to assert the Algonquian belief that unmarried women were "masters of their own body."

Still, the French fur-trading system brought war and cultural devastation to the Indian peoples. According to an oral history of the Iroquois, "Everywhere there was peril and everywhere mourning. Feuds with outer nations, feuds with brother nations, feuds of . . . sister towns and feuds of families and of clans made every warrior a stealthy man who liked to kill."

New Netherland: Commerce

By 1600 the Dutch Republic was the trading hub of northern Europe, and its agents in North America had little interest in religious conversion. Their eyes were fastened on commerce. In 1609 Henry Hudson, an Englishman employed by the Dutch East India Company, encountered and named the Hudson River in present-day New York. Soon Dutch merchants established fur-trading posts on Manhattan Island and at Fort Orange (present-day Albany). In 1621 the Dutch government chartered the West India Company, giving it a monopoly of trade in West Africa and in the Americas. Three years later the company founded the town of New Amsterdam on Manhattan Island and made it the capital of New Netherland.

Few Dutch settlers moved to these fur-trading posts, making them vulnerable to a takeover by rival European nations. To encourage migration, the West India Company granted huge estates along the Hudson River to wealthy Dutchmen and stipulated that each proprietor settle fifty tenants within four years or lose his grant; by 1646 only one proprietor, Kiliaen van Rensselaer, had succeeded. The population in Dutch North America remained small, reaching only 1,500 in 1664.

Although New Netherland failed to attract settlers, it flourished briefly as a fur-trading enterprise. In 1633 Dutch traders at Fort Orange exported thirty thousand beaver and otter pelts. Subsequently, the Dutch seized prime farming land from the Algonquian-speaking peoples and took over their trading network, in which corn and wampum from Long Island were exchanged for furs from Maine. The Algonquians responded with force. A bloody two-year war killed more than 200 Dutch residents and 1,000 Indians, many in brutal massacres of women, children, and elderly men. After the war the Dutch provided guns and entered into an alliance with the Mohawks, one of the Iroquois Nations of New York and a long-time foe of the Algonquians. However, the West India Company now largely ignored its crippled North American settlement and concentrated on the profitable importation of African slaves to its sugar plantations in Brazil.

In New Amsterdam, Dutch officials ruled shortsightedly. Governor Peter Stuyvesant rejected the demands of English Puritan settlers on Long Island for a representative system of government and alienated the colony's increasingly diverse population of Dutch, English, and Swedish migrants. Consequently, in 1664, during an Anglo-Dutch war, the residents of New Amsterdam offered little resistance to an English invasion and subsequently accepted English rule. For the rest of the century, the renamed towns of New York and Albany remained small fur-trading centers, Dutch-English outposts in a region still dominated by Native Americans. In Albany, Mohawk remained the language of business until the 1720s.

English Virginia: Settlers and a Staple Crop

The first English ventures in North America, undertaken by minor nobility in the 1580s, were abject failures. Sir Humphrey Gilbert's settlement in Newfoundland collapsed for lack of financing, and Sir Ferdinando Gorges's colony along the coast of Maine floundered because of the harsh climate. Sir Walter Raleigh's three expeditions to North Carolina likewise ended in disaster when the colony at Roanoke vanished without a trace (and today is known as the "lost" colony). Following these failures, merchants replaced landed gentry as the leaders of English expansion; initially, their goal was trade rather than settlement. To provide adequate funding, the merchants formed **joint-stock companies** that sold shares to many investors and sought royal support. In 1606, King James I (r. 1603–1625) granted a group of ambitious London merchants a trading monopoly in the lands stretching from present-day North Carolina to southern New York. To honor the memory of Elizabeth I, the "Virgin Queen," the company's directors named the region Virginia. To prevent the spread of Spanish Catholicism among the natives, they promised to "propagate the [true] Christian religion" among the "infidels and Savages."

However, trade remained the main goal of the Virginia Company. The first expedition in 1607 included only adventurers—no farmers, ministers, or women. The company retained ownership of the land and appointed a governor and a small

Carolina Indians Fishing, 1585

The artist John White was one of the English settlers in Sir Walter Raleigh's ill-fated colony on Roanoke Island, and his watercolors provide a rich visual record of Native American life. Here the Indians who resided near present-day Albemarle Sound in North Carolina are harvesting a protein-rich diet of fish from its shallow waters. Trustees of the British Museum.

council to direct the adventurers, who were its employees or "servants." The directors expected them to procure their own food and ship gold, exotic crops, and Indian merchandise to England. Some adventurers were young gentlemen with personal ties to the shareholders of the company: a bunch of "unruly Sparks, packed off by their Friends to escape worse Destinies at home." The rest were cynical men bent on turning a quick profit by trading for gold or finding it. All they wanted, as one of them said, was to "dig gold, refine gold, load gold."

Unfortunately, such traders were unprepared for the challenges of the new environment. Arriving in Virginia after a hazardous four-month voyage, the newcomers settled on a swampy and unhealthful peninsula. They named both their new home (Jamestown) and the waterway (James River) after the king. Because the adventurers lacked access to fresh water and refused to plant crops, their fate was sealed. Of the 120 Englishmen who embarked on the expedition, only 38 were alive nine months later, and death continued to take a high toll. By 1611 the Virginia Company had sent 1,200 settlers to Jamestown, but fewer than half had survived. "Our men were destroyed with cruell diseases, as Swellings, Fluxes, Burning Fevers, and by warres," reported one of the leaders, "but for the most part they died of meere famine."

Native American hostility gradually developed into a major threat. The Pamunkey [pa-MUN-key] chief Powhatan, leader of the Algonquian-speaking tribes of the region, initially treated the traders as a source of valuable goods. A "grave majestical man," according to the adventurer John Smith, Powhatan allowed his followers—some 14,000 people in all—to exchange their corn for English cloth and iron hatchets. As conflicts over food and land increased, Powhatan accused the English of coming "not to trade but to invade my people and possess my country" and threatened war. In 1614 the Indian leader tried to integrate the newcomers into his chiefdom through a family alliance, by marrying his daughter Pocahontas to the adventurer John Rolfe. This tactic also failed, partly because Rolfe imported tobacco seed from the West Indies and cultivated the crop, which fetched a high price in England. Eager to become rich by planting tobacco, English settlers embarked for Virginia by the thousands, threatening to overrun Powhatan's kingdom.

To attract migrants to its increasingly valuable colony, the Virginia Company instituted a new set of policies. In 1617 it allowed individual settlers to own land, granting one hundred acres to every freeman and allowing masters to claim an additional fifty acres for every servant. Next, the company issued a "greate Charter" that swept away the military-style regime of Governor Sir Thomas Dale and created a system of representative government. The House of Burgesses, which first convened in Jamestown in 1619, could make laws and levy taxes, although the governor and the company council in England could veto its legislative acts. By 1622 these incentives of land ownership, self-government, and a judicial system based on "the lawes of the realme of England" had attracted about 4,500 new recruits. Virginia was on the verge of becoming a settler-colony.

However, the influx of English migrants sparked all-out war with the Indians. Land-hungry tobacco planters demanded access to Native American farming lands, alarming Opechancanough, Powhatan's brother and successor. Mobilizing the peoples of many Chesapeake tribes, in 1622 Opechancanough launched a surprise attack that killed nearly a third of the white population. The English fought back by seizing the Indians' cornfields and harvesting the food for themselves. By depriving the native peoples of sustenance, they gradually secured the safety of the colony.

The cost of the war was high for both sides. The Indian revolt killed many settlers and destroyed much property but failed to halt English expansion. The victorious invaders sold captured warriors into slavery, "destroy[ing] them who sought to destroy us," and took control of "their cultivated places . . . possessing the fruits of others' labour." By 1630 the colonists in Virginia had created a flourishing tobacco economy and a stable English-style local polity, controlled by landed gentlemen sitting as justices of the peace.

The Chesapeake Experience

The English colonies in the Chesapeake brought wealth to some people but poverty and moral degradation to many more. Settlers forcefully dispossessed Indians of their lands, and prominent families ruthlessly pursued their dreams of wealth by exploiting the labor of English indentured servants and enslaved African laborers.

Settling the Tobacco Colonies

Shocked by the Indian uprising, James I accused the Virginia Company of misman-agement and, in 1624, made Virginia a royal colony. Under the terms of the colony's charter, the king and his ministers appointed the governor and a small advisory council. The king allowed the House of Burgesses to continue but stipulated that his Privy Council ratify all legislation. James also decreed the legal establishment of the Church of England, which meant that all property owners had to pay taxes to support its clergy. These institutions—a royal governor, an elected assembly, and an established Anglican Church—became the model for royal colonies throughout English America.

A second tobacco-growing settler-colony, which developed in neighboring Maryland, had a different set of institutions. In 1632 King Charles I (r. 1625–1649), the successor to James I, conveyed the territory bordering the vast Chesapeake Bay to Cecilius Calvert, an aristocrat who carried the title Lord Baltimore. As the pro-prietor of Maryland (named in honor of Queen Henrietta Maria, Charles's wife), Baltimore could sell, lease, or give this land away as he pleased. He also had the authority to appoint public officials and to found churches and appoint ministers.

Baltimore wanted Maryland to become a refuge from persecution for his fellow English Catholics. He therefore devised a policy of religious restraint to minimize confrontations between Catholics and Protestants, instructing the governor (his brother, Leonard Calvert) to allow "no scandall nor offence to be given to any of the Protestants" and to "cause All Acts of Romane Catholicque Religion to be done as privately as may be." In 1634, twenty gentlemen (mostly Catholics) and two hundred artisans and laborers (mostly Protestants) established St. Mary's City, which over-looked the mouth of the Potomac River. Maryland's population grew quickly, for the Calverts carefully supervised its development by hiring skilled artisans and offering ample grants of land to wealthy migrants. However, political conflict constantly

The Tobacco Economy

Most farmers—poor or rich—raised tobacco because it grew just as well in small fields as on vast plantations. Large-scale operations, such as the one pictured here, used indentured servants and slaves to grow and process the crop. The workers cured the tobacco stalks by hanging them for several months in a well-ventilated shed; then they stripped the leaves and packed them tightly into large plantation-made barrels, or "hogsheads," for shipment to Europe. Library of Congress.

FOR MORE HELP ANALYZING THIS IMAGE, see the Online Study Guide at **bedfordstmartins.com/henrettaconcise**.

threatened Maryland's stability. When Governor Leonard Calvert violated the terms of the charter by governing without the "Advice, Assent, and Approbation" of the freemen, they elected a representative assembly and insisted on the right to initiate legislation, which Lord Baltimore grudgingly granted. Uprisings by Protestant settlers also endangered Maryland's religious mission. To protect his Catholic coreligionists, who remained a minority, Lord Baltimore persuaded the assembly to enact a Toleration Act (1649) granting religious freedom to all Christians.

In Maryland, as in Virginia, tobacco was the basis of the economy. Indians had long used tobacco as a medicine and a stimulant. By the 1620s English men and women had come to crave tobacco and the nicotine it contained, smoking, chewing, and snorting it with abandon. Initially James I condemned tobacco as a "vile Weed" whose "black stinking fumes" were "baleful to the nose, harmful to the brain, and dangerous to the lungs." But the king's attitude changed as revenues from an import tax on tobacco filled the royal treasury.

European demand for tobacco set off a forty-year economic boom in the Chesapeake. "All our riches for the present do consist in tobacco," a planter

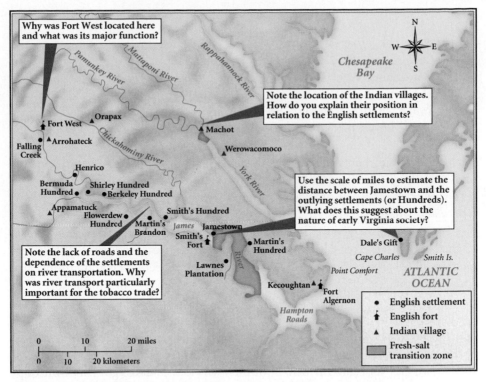

Why was Fort West located here and what was its major function?

Note the location of the Indian villages. How do you explain their position in relation to the English settlements?

Use the scale of miles to estimate the distance between Jamestown and the outlying settlements (or Hundreds). What does this suggest about the nature of early Virginia society?

Note the lack of roads and the dependence of the settlements on river transportation. Why was river transport particularly important for the tobacco trade?

English settlement
English fort
Indian village
Fresh-salt transition zone

MAP 2.2 River Plantations in Virginia, c. 1640

The first migrants settled in widely dispersed plantations—and different disease environments—along the James River. The growth of the tobacco economy continued this pattern as wealthy planter-merchants traded with English ship captains from their riverfront plantations. Consequently, few substantial towns or trading centers developed in the Chesapeake region.

remarked in 1630. Exports rose from about 3 million pounds in 1640 to 10 million pounds in 1660. Newly arrived planters moved up the river valleys, establishing large farms (plantations) that were distant from one another but easily reached by water (Map 2.2).

Despite the economic boom, life in the Chesapeake colonies remained harsh, brutish, and short. The scarcity of towns deprived settlers of mutual assistance and the benefits of community life. Families were equally scarce because there were few women settlers, and marriages were often disrupted by early death. Pregnant women were especially vulnerable to malaria, which was spread by the mosquitoes that flourished in the mild Chesapeake climate. Many mothers died after bearing a first or second child, so that orphaned children (along with unmarried young men) formed a large fraction of the society. In Middlesex County, Virginia, more than 60 percent of children had lost one or both of their parents by the time they were thirteen. Although 15,000 settlers arrived in Virginia between 1622 and 1640, the number of English colonists rose only from 2,000 to 8,000.

Masters, Servants, and Slaves

Nonetheless, the prospect of owning land continued to lure migrants to the Chesapeake region. By 1700 more than 80,000 English settlers had moved to Virginia, and another 20,000 had arrived in Maryland, the great majority not as free men and women but as indentured servants. English shipping registers provide insight into their backgrounds. Three-quarters of the 5,000 indentured servants who embarked from the port of Bristol were young men; many had traveled hundreds of miles searching for work. Once in Bristol, these penniless wanderers were persuaded by merchants and sea captains to sign labor contracts called **indentures** and embark for the Chesapeake. The indentures bound servants to work for a master for four or five years, after which they would be free men and women, able to marry and work for themselves.

For merchants, servants represented valuable cargo because their contracts fetched high prices from Chesapeake planters. For the plantation owners, they were an incredible bargain. During the tobacco boom a male servant could produce five times his purchase price in a single year. To ensure maximum production, most masters ruled their servants strictly, beating them for bad behavior and withholding permission to marry. If servants ran away or became pregnant, masters went to court to increase the term of service. Female servants were especially vulnerable to abuse. As a Virginia law of 1692 stated, "dissolute masters have gotten their maids with child; and yet claim the benefit of their service." Planters got rid of uncooperative servants by selling their contracts to new masters. As an Englishman remarked in disgust, in Virginia "servants were sold up and down like horses."

Despite this ordeal, most indentured servants did not escape from poverty. Half the men died before receiving their freedom, and another quarter remained poor. Only a quarter acquired the property and respectability they had sought. If they survived, female servants generally fared better because men in the Chesapeake had grown "very sensible of the Misfortune of Wanting Wives." Many female servants married their masters or other well-established men. By migrating to the Chesapeake, these few— and very fortunate—men and women escaped a life of landless poverty in England.

The first African workers fared worse. In 1619 John Rolfe noted that "a Dutch man of warre . . . sold us twenty Negars," but for a generation the numbers of Africans remained small. About 400 Africans lived in the Chesapeake colonies in 1649, making up 2 percent of the population, and by 1670 the proportion of blacks had reached only 5 percent. Although many Africans served their English masters for life, they were not legally enslaved. English common law acknowledged indentured servitude but not **chattel slavery**—the ownership as property of one human being by another. Moreover, some of these Africans had labored as slaves in African seaports and had some knowledge of European traders and Atlantic commerce. By cunning calculation, hard work, or conversion to Christianity many of them escaped bondage. Some ambitious African Christian freemen even purchased slaves, bought the labor contracts of white servants, or married English women, suggesting that at that time religion and personal initiative were as important as race in determining social status. By becoming a Christian and a planter, an enterprising African could aspire to near equality.

This mobility for Africans came to end in the 1660s because legislatures in the Chesapeake colonies enacted laws that lowered their status. One cause was the growing consciousness of race among the English-born elite. Even more important, the end of the tobacco boom prompted planters to turn to slave labor. The "low price of Tobacco requires it should bee made as cheap as possible," declared Colonel Nicholas Spencer, and "blacks can make it cheaper than whites." By 1671 the Virginia House of Burgesses had forbidden Africans to own guns or join the militia. It had also barred them—"tho baptized and enjoying their own Freedom"—from buying the labor contracts of white servants and from winning their freedom by converting to Christianity. Being black was a mark of inferior legal status, and slavery was becoming a permanent and hereditary condition. As an English clergyman observed around 1680, "These two words, Negro and Slave, had by custom grown Homogeneous and convertible."

The Seeds of Social Revolt

By the 1660s the growing size of the tobacco crop triggered a collapse of the market. Tobacco had once sold for 24 pence a pound; now it fetched one-tenth as much. As the economic boom turned into a "bust," long-standing social conflicts flared up in political turmoil.

Political decisions in England were one reason for the decline of tobacco prices. In 1651, Parliament passed an Act of Trade and Navigation designed to exclude Dutch ships from England's colonies. As revised in 1660 and 1663, the Navigation Acts permitted only English or colonial-owned ships to enter American ports, thereby excluding Dutch merchants, who paid the highest prices for tobacco. The acts also required the colonists to ship tobacco and other "enumerated articles" only to England, where monarchs continually raised the import duty on tobacco, thereby stifling growth of the market. By the 1670s planters were getting only one penny a pound for their crop.

Nonetheless, the number of Chesapeake planters continued to grow and tobacco exports doubled between the 1670s and the 1690s. Profit margins grew thin, and yeomen families earned just enough to scrape by. Even worse off were newly freed indentured servants, who could not pay the fees to claim the 50 acres of land to which they were entitled or to buy the necessary tools and seed. Many former servants had to sell their labor again, by signing new indentures or becoming wageworkers or tenant farmers.

Gradually the Chesapeake colonies came to be dominated by an elite of planter-merchants whose power rivaled that of the English gentry. Owners of large estates prospered by leasing small plots to the growing army of former servants. They also lent money at high interest rates to hard-pressed yeomen families. Some well-to-do planters became commercial middlemen, setting up retail stores or charging a commission for selling the tobacco of their poorer neighbors to English merchants.

In Virginia this elite accumulated nearly half the land by securing grants from royal governors. In Maryland well-connected Catholic planters were equally powerful; by 1720 Charles Carroll owned 47,000 acres of land, which was farmed by scores of tenants, indentured servants, and slaves.

As these aggressive planter-entrepreneurs confronted a multitude of young, landless laborers, social conflicts intensified. In Virginia, they reached a breaking point during the corrupt regime of Governor William Berkeley. Berkeley first served as governor between 1642 and 1652; appointed governor again in 1660, he made large land grants to members of his council, who promptly exempted their lands from taxation and appointed friends as local justices of the peace and county judges. To suppress dissent in the House of Burgesses, Berkeley bought off legislators with land grants and appointments to lucrative positions as sheriffs, tax collectors, and estate appraisers. Unrest increased when the corrupt Burgesses changed the voting system to exclude landless freemen, who constituted half of all adult white men. Property-holding yeomen retained the vote but—distressed by tobacco prices, rising taxes, and political corruption—they were no longer willing to support the rule of Berkeley and the power-hungry landed gentry.

Bacon's Rebellion

An Indian conflict lit the flame of social rebellion. By 1675 the number of Native Americans in Virginia had dwindled from 30,000 in 1607 to a mere 3,500, as compared to 38,000 Europeans and about 2,500 Africans. Although most Indians lived on treaty-guaranteed lands along the frontier, their presence remained controversial. Hundreds of impoverished English **freeholders** and aspiring tenants wanted cheap land and insisted that the natives be expelled or exterminated. Wealthy seacoast planters, who wanted a ready supply of white labor, opposed expansion into Indian territory, as did Berkeley and the planter-merchants who traded with the Native Americans for furs.

Fighting broke out late in 1675 when a band of Virginia militia murdered 30 Indians. Defying orders from Governor Berkeley, a larger force of 1,000 militiamen then surrounded a fortified Susquehannock village and killed five chiefs who came out to negotiate. The militarily strong Susquehannocks, recent migrants from present-day northern Pennsylvania, retaliated by raiding outlying plantations and killing 300 whites. To avoid war, Berkeley proposed a defensive military policy. However, settlers dismissed his strategy of building frontier forts as useless militarily and simply a plot by planters and merchants to impose high taxes and take "all our tobacco into their own hands."

Nathaniel Bacon emerged as the leader of the protesters. An English migrant, Bacon had settled on a frontier estate and commanded the respect of his neighbors because of his youthful vigor and his English connections, which had secured him an appointment to the governor's council. When Berkeley refused to grant Bacon a military commission, the headstrong planter marched his frontiersmen against the Indians anyway and slaughtered some of the peaceful Doeg [DO-g] people. Condemning the frontiersmen as "rebels and mutineers," Berkeley expelled Bacon from the council and arrested him. But Bacon's men quickly won his release and forced the governor to hold legislative elections. The newly elected House of Burgesses enacted far-reaching political reforms that curbed the powers of the governor and the council and restored voting rights to landless freemen.

These much-needed reforms came too late. Bacon was bitter about Berkeley's arbitrary actions, and the poor farmers and indentured servants in his army resented years of exploitation by wealthy men and arrogant justices of the peace. As one yeoman rebel put it, "A poor man who has only his labour to maintain himself and his family pays as much [in taxes] as a man who has 20,000 acres." Backed by 400 armed men, Bacon seized control of the colony and issued a "Manifesto and Declaration of the People," that demanded the death or removal of all Indians and an end to the rule of wealthy "parasites." "All the power and sway is got into the hands of the rich," Bacon proclaimed, as his army burned Jamestown to the ground and plundered the plantations of Berkeley's allies. When Bacon died suddenly from dysentery in October 1676, the governor took his revenge, dispersing the rebel army, seizing the estates of well-to-do rebels, and hanging 23 men.

Bacon's Rebellion was a pivotal event in Virginia's history and, indeed, in American history. Thereafter, landed planters remained dominant in Virginia by curbing corruption and finding public positions for politically ambitious yeomen. They also appeased the lower social orders by cutting their taxes and supporting the expansion onto Indian lands. Finally, the uprising confirmed the planters' growing commitment to African slavery. To forestall another rebellion by poor whites, Chesapeake planters turned away from indentured servitude, explicitly legalized slavery in 1705, and imported thousands of African laborers. Those decisions committed subsequent generations of Americans to a social system based on racial exploitation.

Puritan New England

The Puritan exodus from England between 1620 and 1640 was both a worldly quest for land and a spiritual effort to preserve the "pure" Christian faith. By creating a "holy commonwealth" in America, pious migrants hoped to reform the established Church of England. By distributing land broadly, they tried to build a society of independent property-owning farm families. And by defining their mission in spiritual terms, the Puritans gave a moral dimension to American history.

The Puritan Migration

From the beginning New England differed from other European colonies. Unruly male adventurers began New Spain and Jamestown, and commercial-minded fur traders dominated life in New France and New Netherland. By contrast, women and children as well as men settled Plymouth, the first permanent community in New England, and its leaders were pious Protestants—the Pilgrims.

The Pilgrims were Puritans who had left the Church of England, thus earning the name "Separatists." When King James I threatened to harry Puritans "out of the land, or else do worse," the Pilgrims left England and settled among Dutch Calvinists in Holland. Subsequently, 35 of these exiles resolved to migrate to America to maintain their English identity. Led by William Bradford and joined by 67 other migrants from England, they sailed to America aboard the *Mayflower* in 1620. Arriving in America without a royal charter, they created their own covenant of government, the Mayflower Compact, to "combine ourselves together into a civill body politick." This document was the first "constitution" adopted in North America and used the Puritan model of a self-governing religious congregation as the blueprint for political society.

The first winter in America tested the Pilgrims. As in Virginia, hunger and disease took a heavy toll; of the 102 migrants who arrived in November, only half survived until the spring. Thereafter the Plymouth colony—unlike Virginia—became a healthy and thriving community. The cold climate inhibited the spread of mosquito-borne diseases, and the Pilgrims' religious discipline established a strong work ethic. Moreover, because a severe smallpox epidemic in 1618 had killed most of the local Wampanoag people, the migrants faced few external threats. The Pilgrims built solid houses, planted ample crops, and their numbers grew rapidly to 3,000 by 1640. To ensure political stability, they issued a written legal code that provided for a colony-wide system of representative self-government, broad political rights, and a prohibition of government interference in spiritual matters.

Meanwhile, England was plunging deeper into religious turmoil. King Charles I repudiated some Protestant doctrines, such as the role of grace in salvation. English Puritans, who had gained many seats in Parliament, accused the king of "popery"—holding Catholic beliefs. In 1629 Charles dissolved Parliament, claimed the power to rule by "divine right," and raised money through royal edicts and the sale of monopolies. When Archbishop William Laud, whom Charles chose to head the Church of England, dismissed hundreds of Puritan ministers, thousands of Puritans fled to America.

The exodus began in 1630, when 900 Puritans sailed across the Atlantic under the leadership of John Winthrop, a well-educated country squire. Calling England morally corrupt and "overburdened with people," Winthrop sought land and opportunity for his children and a place in Christian history for his people. "We must consider that we shall be as a City upon a Hill," Winthrop told his fellow passengers. "The eyes of all people are upon us." Like the Pilgrims, the Puritans envisioned a reformed Christian society, a genuinely "New" England that would preserve the true faith and inspire religious change in England.

Winthrop and his associates established the Massachusetts Bay colony in the area around present-day Boston and transformed their joint-stock business corporation, the General Court of shareholders, into a colonial legislature. Over the next decade about 10,000 Puritans migrated to the colony, along with 10,000 others fleeing hard times in England. The Puritans created representative political institutions, with an elected governor, council, and assembly. However, to ensure rule by the godly, the Puritans limited the right to vote and hold office to men who were church members. Eschewing the policy of religious toleration in Plymouth colony, they established Puritan congregationalism as the state-supported religion, barred other faiths from conducting services, and used the Bible as a legal was well as a spiritual guide. "Where there is no Law," the colony's government advised local magistrates, they should rule "as near the law of God as they can."

In establishing churches, New England Puritans tried to re-create the simplicity of the first Christians. They eliminated bishops and placed power in the hands of the laity, or the ordinary members of the congregation—hence their name, Congregationalists. Influenced by John Calvin, Puritans embraced **predestination**, the doctrine that God had decided, or "predestined," the fates of all people before they were born and had chosen only a few "elect" men and women (the Saints) for salvation. Many church members lived in great anxiety, for they could never be sure whether God had selected them for salvation or damnation.

Puritans dealt with the uncertainties of divine election in three ways. Some congregations stressed the conversion experience—the intense spiritual sensation of being "born again" upon receiving God's grace. Other Puritans stressed ministerial "preparation," the confidence in salvation that came from years of spiritual guidance. Still others believed that God considered the Puritans as his "chosen people," who would be saved as long as they obeyed his laws.

To maintain God's favor, the Puritan magistrates of Massachusetts Bay purged their society of religious dissidents. One target was Roger Williams, who in 1634 had become the minister of the Puritan church in Salem, a new coastal town just north of Boston. Williams endorsed the Pilgrims' separation of church and state in Plymouth colony and condemned the legal establishment of Congregationalism in Massachusetts Bay. He taught that political magistrates should have authority over only the "bodies, goods, and outward estates of men," not their spiritual lives. Moreover, he questioned the Puritans' seizure (rather than purchase) of Indian lands. In response, the Puritan magistrates banished him from Massachusetts Bay.

In 1636 Williams and his followers resettled in Rhode Island, founding the town of Providence on land purchased from the Narragansett Indians. Other religious dissidents founded Portsmouth and Newport. In 1644 these towns obtained a corporate charter from the English Parliament that granted them full authority "to rule themselves." In Rhode Island as in Plymouth, there was no legally established church; every congregation was autonomous, and individual men and women could worship God as they pleased.

Puritan magistrates in Massachusetts Bay also felt threatened by Anne Hutchinson, the wife of a merchant and a mother of seven who worked as a midwife. Hutchinson held weekly prayer meetings for women in her house and accused certain Boston clergymen of placing undue emphasis on good behavior. In words that recalled Martin Luther's rejection of indulgences, Hutchinson argued that salvation could not be earned through good deeds; there was no "covenant of works." Rather, God bestowed salvation through the "covenant of grace" and "revealed" divine truth directly to the individual believer. The doctrine of revelation diminished the role of ministers, and Puritan magistrates denounced it as heretical.

The magistrates also resented Hutchinson because of her sex. Like other Christians, Puritans believed that both men and women could be saved. When it came to the governance of church and state, however, women were seen as distinctly inferior to men. As the Pilgrim minister John Robinson put it, women "are debarred by their sex from ordinary prophesying, and from any other dealing in the church wherein they take authority over the man." Puritan women could never be ministers, lay preachers, or even voting members of the congregation.

In 1637 the magistrates put Hutchinson on trial for the heresy of teaching that inward grace freed an individual from the rules of the church. Hutchinson defended her views with great skill, and even Winthrop admitted that she was "a woman of fierce and haughty courage." But the judges scolded her for not attending to "her household affairs, and such things as belong to women" and found her guilty. Banished, she followed Roger Williams into exile in Rhode Island.

These coercive policies, along with the desire for better land, prompted other Puritans to leave Massachusetts Bay. In 1636 pastor Thomas Hooker led his congregation to the Connecticut River Valley, where they established the town of Hartford; other migrants settled along the river at Wethersfield and Windsor. In 1639 the Connecticut Puritans adopted the Fundamental Orders, a plan of government that included an established church, a popularly elected governor and assembly, and voting rights for most property-owning men—not just church members.

As Puritans established themselves in America, England fell into a religious war. When Archbishop Laud imposed a Church of England prayer book on Presbyterian Scotland in 1642, a Scottish army invaded England. Thousands of English Puritans (and hundreds of American Puritans) joined the invaders, demanding greater authority for Parliament and reform of the established church. After four years of civil war, the Parliamentary forces led by Oliver Cromwell were victorious. In 1649 Parliament executed Charles I, proclaimed a republican Commonwealth, and banished bishops and elaborate rituals from the Church of England.

The Puritan triumph was short-lived. Popular support for the Commonwealth ebbed, especially after 1653 when Cromwell took dictatorial control. Following Cromwell's death, moderate Protestants and a resurgent aristocracy summoned the son of Charles I from Europe and restored the monarchy and the power of bishops in the Church of England. For many Puritans, Charles II's accession in 1660 represented the victory of the Antichrist—the false prophet described in the final book of the New Testament.

For the Puritans in America, the restoration of the monarchy began a new phase of their "errand into the wilderness." They had come to New England to preserve the "pure" Christian Church, expecting to return to Europe in triumph. When that sacred mission was dashed by the failure of the English Revolution, Puritan ministers exhorted their congregations to create a new society in America based on their faith and ideals.

The PROTESTANT

ALMANACK,

For the Year 1700.

The Creation of the World ———————— 5706
The Incarnation of Jesus Christ ——— ———— 1700
England received the Christian Faith ———— 1510
Martin Luther wrote against the Pope ——— ——— 184
Our first Deliverance from Popery by K. *Edward* VI.— 152
Our second deliverance from Popery by Q. *Elizabeth*— 141
The horrid design of the Gun-Powder Plot———— 95
The Burning of the City of *London* ———— 34
Our Third Deliverance from Popery, by K.*Will*, & Q. *Mary* 12

Being the

BISSEXTILE or LEAP-YEAR.

WHEREIN

The Bloody Aspects, Fatal Oppositions, Diabolical Conjunctions, and Pernicious Revolutions of the Papacy against the Lord and his Anointed, are described.

With the Change of the Moon, some probable Conjectures of the Weather, the Eclipses, the Moons place in the Zodiack, and an account of some principal Martyrs in each Month.

Calculated according to Art, for the Meridian of *Babylon*, where the Pope is elevated a hundred and fifty degrees above all Right and Religion; above Kings, Canons, Councils, Conscience, and every thing therein called God. *2 Thess. 2.* And may without sensible Errour, indifferently serve the whole Papacy.

By *Philoprotest*, a well-willer to the Mathematicks.

London, Printed by *John Richardson* for the Company of STATIONERS, 1700.

The Protestant Almanack, 1700

The conflict between Protestants and Catholics took many forms. To reinforce the religious identity of English Protestants, the Company of Stationers (or printers) published a yearly almanac that charted not only the passage of the seasons but also the "Pernicious Revolutions of the Papacy against the Lord and his Anointed."

By permission of the Syndics of Cambridge University Library.

Puritanism and Witchcraft

Like the Native Americans they encountered in New England, Puritans thought that the physical world was full of supernatural forces. This belief in "spirits" stemmed in part from Christian teachings, such as the Catholic belief in miracles and the Protestant faith in the powers of "grace." Devout Christians saw signs of God's (or Satan's) power in blazing stars, birth defects, and other unusual events. Noting that many ministers' houses "had been smitten with Lightning," Cotton Mather, a prominent theologian, wondered "what the meaning of God should be in it."

The Puritans' respect for spiritual forces also reflected widespread pagan assumptions. When Samuel Sewall, a well-educated Puritan merchant and judge, moved into a new house, he fended off evil spirits by driving a metal pin into the floor. Thousands of ordinary Puritan farmers followed the pagan astrological charts printed in almanacs to determine the best times to plant crops, marry, and make other important decisions.

Zealous ministers attacked many of these beliefs and practices as "superstition" and condemned "cunning" individuals who claimed to have special powers as healers or prophets. Indeed, many Christians looked on such conjurers as "wizards" or "witches" who acted at Satan's command. The people of Andover, Massachusetts, "were much addicted to sorcery," claimed one observer, and "there were forty men in it that could raise the Devil as well as any astrologer." Between 1647 and 1662 civil authorities in New England hanged 14 people for witchcraft, mostly older women who, their accusers claimed, were "double-tongued" or "had an unruly spirit."

The most dramatic episode of witch-hunting took place in Salem, Massachusetts, in 1692. Initially, a few young girls experienced strange seizures and accused various neighbors of bewitching them. When judges allowed the introduction of "spectral" evidence—visions seen only by the young accusers—the number of accusations spun out of control. Eventually, Massachusetts authorities arrested 175 people and executed 20 of them. The causes of this mass hysteria were complex and are still hard to fathom. Some historians point to group rivalries: many of the accusers were the daughters and young servants of poor farmers in a rural area of Salem, whereas many of the accused witches were wealthier church members or their friends. Because 14 women were executed, other historians view the witchcraft trials as part of a broader attempt to keep women in a subordinate position. Still other scholars focus on the fears raised by recent Indian attacks in nearby Maine, which killed the parents of some of the young accusers who sparked the Salem prosecutions.

Whatever the cause, the Salem episode marked a turning point. Popular revulsion against the executions brought an end in New England to legal prosecutions for witchcraft and heresy. The European Enlightenment, a major intellectual movement that began around 1675, also discouraged witchcraft accusations by promoting a more rational view of the world. Increasingly, educated people explained accidents and sudden deaths through theories that drew upon the "laws of nature," not through religion, astrology, and witchcraft. In contrast to Cotton Mather (d. 1728), who believed that lightning might be a supernatural sign, well-read men of the next generation—such as Benjamin Franklin—would conceive of lightning as a natural phenomenon.

A Yeoman Society, 1630–1700

In building communities in New England, Puritans consciously shunned the worst features of traditional Europe. They did not wish to live in towns dominated by a few wealthy landowners or controlled by a distant government that levied oppressive taxes. Consequently, the migrants created self-governing towns and encouraged broad property ownership. Instead of granting thousands of acres to wealthy planters (as occurred in the Chesapeake colonies), the General Courts of Massachusetts Bay and Connecticut bestowed the title to a township on a group of settlers, or **proprietors**, who distributed the land among themselves.

Widespread ownership of land did not mean equality of wealth or status. "God had Ordained different degrees and orders of men," proclaimed the Boston merchant

John Saffin, "some to be Masters and Commanders, others to be Subjects, and to be commanded." Town proprietors normally gave the largest plots to men of high social status, who often became selectmen and justices of the peace. However, all male heads of families received some land, creating a freehold society of independent households. Even as the sons of smallholders were forced, at least temporarily, into the ranks of tenants and laborers, the vast majority of men remained landowners with a vote in the **town meeting**, the main institution of local government (Map 2.3).

Consequently, ordinary farmers in New England communities had much more political power than did most European peasants and most yeomen in the planter-dominated Chesapeake colonies. Each year the town meeting chose selectmen to manage its affairs. The meeting also levied taxes; enacted ordinances regarding fencing and road building; and regulated the use of common fields for grazing livestock. Finally, towns elected representatives to the General Court, which gradually displaced the governor as the center of political authority.

Because of these Puritan-inspired policies, nearly all New England households had an opportunity to acquire freehold property, participate in the political life of the community, and enjoy some economic security. When he died in the 1690s, Nathaniel Fish was one of the poorest men in Barnstable, Massachusetts, yet he owned a two-room cottage, eight acres of land, an ox, and a cow. For him and thousands of other settlers, New England had proved to be the promised land, a new world of opportunity.

The Eastern Indians' New World

Native Americans throughout the eastern woodland region were also living in a new world, but for them it was a bleak, dangerous, and conflict-ridden place. Some Indian peoples, like the Pequots in New England, the Susquehannocks in Virginia, and the Iroquois in the trans-Appalachian region, resisted the invaders by force. Others retreated into the mountains or moved farther west to preserve their traditional culture or to band together in new tribes.

Puritans and Pequots

Even before the Puritans came to New England, they pondered the morality of intruding on Native American lands. "By what right or warrant can we enter into the land of the Savages?" they asked themselves. John Winthrop answered this query by detecting God's hand in a disastrous smallpox epidemic that reduced the Indian population from 13,000 to 3,000. "If God were not pleased with our inheriting these parts," he asked, "why doth he still make roome for us by diminishing them as we increase?" Citing the book of Genesis, the magistrates of Massachusetts Bay declared that the Indians had not "subdued" their land and therefore had no "just right" to it.

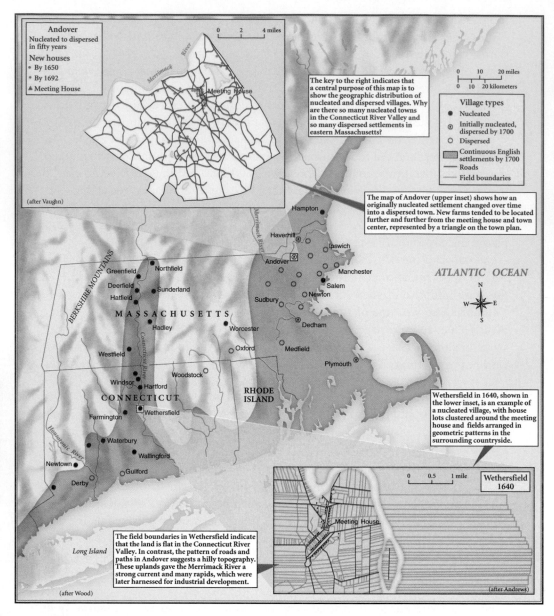

Andover
Nucleated to dispersed
in fifty years
New houses
• By 1650
• By 1692
▲ Meeting House

The key to the right indicates that a central purpose of this map is to show the geographic distribution of nucleated and dispersed villages. Why are there so many nucleated towns in the Connecticut River Valley and so many dispersed settlements in eastern Massachusetts?

Village types
● Nucleated
⊙ Initially nucleated, dispersed by 1700
○ Dispersed
▨ Continuous English settlements by 1700
— Roads
— Field boundaries

The map of Andover (upper inset) shows how an originally nucleated settlement changed over time into a dispersed town. New farms tended to be located further and further from the meeting house and town center, represented by a triangle on the town plan.

ATLANTIC OCEAN

Wethersfield in 1640, shown in the lower inset, is an example of a nucleated village, with house lots clustered around the meeting house and fields arranged in geometric patterns in the surrounding countryside.

The field boundaries in Wethersfield indicate that the land is flat in the Connecticut River Valley. In contrast, the pattern of roads and paths in Andover suggests a hilly topography. These uplands gave the Merrimack River a strong current and many rapids, which were later harnessed for industrial development.

Wethersfield
1640

(after Vaughn)   (after Wood)   (after Andrews)

MAP 2.3 Settlement Patterns within New England Towns, 1630–1700

Initially, most Puritan towns were compact. Regardless of the local topography (hills or plains), families lived close to one another in the nucleated village center and traveled daily to work in the surrounding fields. This pattern is clearly apparent in the 1640 map of Wethersfield, Connecticut, which is situated on the broad plains of the Connecticut River Valley. The first settlers of Andover, Massachusetts, also chose to live in the village center. However, the rugged topography of eastern Massachusetts encouraged a dispersed form of settlement, and by 1692 many residents of Andover lived on their own farms.

Because of their moral righteousness, the Puritans often treated Native Americans with a brutality equal to that of the Spanish conquistadors and Nathaniel Bacon's frontiersmen in Virginia. When Pequot warriors attacked English farmers who had intruded into the Connecticut River Valley in 1636, Puritan militia and their Indian allies led a surprise attack on a Pequot village and massacred about 500 men, women, and children. "God laughed at the Enemies of his People," one soldier boasted, "filling the Place with Dead Bodies."

Like most Europeans, English Puritans viewed the Indians as "savages," culturally inferior people who did not deserve civilized treatment. But the Puritans were not racist as the term is understood today. To them, Native Americans were not genetically inferior—they were white people with sun-darkened skins—and "sin" or Satan, rather than race, accounted for their degenerate condition. "Probably the devil" delivered these "miserable savages" to America, the Puritan minister Cotton Mather suggested, "in hopes that the gospel of the Lord Jesus Christ would never come here to destroy or disturb his absolute empire over them."

This interpretation of the Indians' history inspired the Puritan minister John Eliot to convert them to Christianity. Eliot translated the Bible into Algonquian and undertook numerous missions to Indian villages in eastern Massachusetts. Because Puritans demanded that Indians understand the complexities of Protestant theology, only a few Native Americans became full members of Puritan congregations. However, the Puritans created "**praying towns**" that, like the Spanish Franciscans' missions in New Mexico, supervised the Indian population; by 1670, more than 1,000 Indians lived in fourteen special mission towns. At the close of the seventeenth century, the combination of Christianization, European diseases, and military force had destroyed the autonomy and culture of many of the Algonquian-speaking peoples in coastal New England.

Metacom's (King Philip's) Rebellion

By the 1670s there were three times as many whites as Indians in New England. The English population now totaled some 55,000, while the number of Indians had plummeted: from an estimated 120,000 in 1570, to 70,000 in 1620, to barely 16,000. To Metacom, leader of the Wampanoags, the future looked grim. When his people copied English ways by raising hogs and selling pork in Boston, Puritan officials accused them of selling at "an under rate" and placed restrictions on their trade. When they killed wandering livestock that damaged their cornfields, authorities denounced them for violating English property rights. Like Opechancanough [*op-e-CHAN-canoe*] and the Susquehannocks [*sus-kwa-HAN-oks*] in Virginia and Popé in New Mexico, Metacom finally concluded that only military resistance could save Indian lands and culture. So in 1675 Metacom (whom the English called King Philip) forged a military alliance with the Narragansetts and Nipmucks and attacked white settlements throughout New England. Bitter fighting continued into 1676, ending only

Metacom (King Philip), Chief of the Wampanoag

The Indian uprising of 1675 left an indelible mark on the historical memory of New England. This painting from the 1850s, done on semitransparent cloth and lit from behind for dramatic effect, was used by traveling performers to tell the story of King Philip's War. Note that Metacom is not depicted as a savage but as a dignified man; freed from fear of Indian attack, nineteenth-century New England whites could adopt a romanticized version of their region's often brutal history. Shelburne Museum.

when Indian warriors ran short of guns and powder, and Mohegans and Mohawks in alliance with the Massachusetts Bay government ambushed and killed Metacom.

The rebellion was a deadly affair. The Indians had fought long and hard, a party of Narragansetts told Roger Williams, because the English "had forced them to it." Indeed, the Indians destroyed 20 percent of the English towns in Massachusetts and Rhode Island and killed 1,000 whites, about 5 percent of the adult population. Almost every day, recalled settler William Harris, he had heard new reports of the Indians' "burneing houses, takeing cattell, killing men & women & Children: & carrying others captive." But the Indians' own losses—from famine and disease as well as battle—were much larger: as many as 4,500, or 25 percent of an already diminished population. Many of the surviving Algonquian peoples migrated farther into the New England backcountry, where they intermarried with other Algonquian tribes tied to the French. Over the next century, these displaced Indian peoples would take their revenge, allying with the French to attack their Puritan enemies (see American Voices, "A Captivity Narrative," p. 64).

The Fur Trade and the Inland Peoples

As English settlers slowly advanced up the river valleys from the Atlantic coast, the Indians who lived near the Appalachian Mountains and in the great forested areas beyond remained independent. Yet these distant Indian peoples felt the European presence because they entered the fur trade to obtain woolen blankets, iron cookware, knives, and guns, which they used to kill deer and their enemies. Thanks in part to their strategic geographic location in present-day central New York, which enabled them to bargain for goods from different European officials and merchants, the militarily aggressive and diplomatically astute Iroquois peoples were the most successful. Iroquois warriors moved quickly to the east and south along the Mohawk, Hudson, Delaware, and Susquehanna Rivers to exchange goods with (or threaten) the English and Dutch colonies. They traveled north via Lake Champlain and the Richelieu River to deal with French traders in Quebec. And they journeyed west by means of the Great Lakes and the Allegheny-Ohio river system to exploit the rich fur-bearing lands of the Mississippi Valley.

The rise of the Iroquois was breathtakingly rapid, just as their subsequent decline was tragically sobering. In 1600 the Iroquois in New York numbered about 30,000 and lived in large towns of 500 to 2,000 inhabitants. Two decades later they had organized themselves in a great "longhouse" confederation of the Five Nations: the Senecas, Cayugas, Onondagas, Oneidas, and Mohawks. Although a virulent smallpox epidemic in 1633 cut their numbers by a third, the Iroquois waged a successful series of wars against the Iroquoian-speaking Hurons (1649), Neutrals (1651), Eries (1657), and Susquehannocks (1669). The victorious warriors carried hundreds of captives to New York, where Iroquois kin tortured and killed many of the captives to atone for those lost in battle.

These triumphs gave the Iroquois control of the fur trade with the French in Quebec and the Dutch in New York. Equally important, it replenished the populations of villages hard hit by epidemics and wartime losses. To assimilate war captives that were spared, Iroquois families conducted "requickening" ceremonies that transferred to the captives the names of their dead relatives, along with their social roles and duties. By 1667 half of the population of many Mohawk towns consisted of adopted prisoners. Cultural diversity within Iroquoia increased because the Five Nations now

A Captivity Narrative

MARY ROWLANDSON

*M*ary Rowlandson, a minister's wife in Lancaster, Massachusetts, was one of many settlers taken captive by the Indians during Metacom's war. Mrs. Rowlandson spent
twelve weeks in captivity, traveling constantly, until her family ransomed her for the consider-
able sum of £20. Her account of this ordeal, The Sovereignty and Goodness of God, *published*
in 1682, became one of the most popular prose works of its time.

On the tenth of February 1675, came the Indians with great numbers upon Lancaster: their
first coming was about sunrising; hearing the noise of some guns, we looked out; several
houses were burning, and the smoke ascending to heaven. . . . [T]he Indians laid hold of us,
pulling me one way, and the children another, and said, "Come go along with us"; I told
them they would kill me: they answered, if I were willing to go along with them, they would
not hurt me. . . .

The first week of my being among them I hardly ate any thing; the second week I found
my stomach grow very faint for want of something; and yet it was very hard to get down
their filthy trash; but the third week . . . they were sweet and savory to my taste. I was at this
time knitting a pair of white cotton stockings for my [Indian] mistress; and had not yet
wrought upon a sabbath day. When the sabbath came they bade me go to work. I told them
it was the sabbath-day, and desired them to let me rest, and told them I would do as much
more tomorrow; to which they answered me they would break my face. . . .

During my abode in this place, Philip [Metacom] spake to me to make a shirt for his
boy, which I did, for which he gave me a shilling. I offered the money to my master, but he
bade me keep it; and with it I bought a piece of horse flesh. Afterwards he asked me to make
a cap for his boy, for which he invited me to dinner. I went, and he gave me a pancake,
about as big as two fingers. It was made of parched wheat, beaten, and fried in bear's grease,
but I thought I never tasted pleasanter meat in my life. . . .

My master had three squaws, living sometimes with one, and sometimes with another
one. . . . [It] was Weetamoo with whom I had lived and served all this while. A severe and
proud dame she was, bestowing every day in dressing herself near as much time as any of
the gentry of the land: powdering her hair, and painting her face, going with necklaces, with
jewels in her ears, and bracelets upon her hands. When she had dressed herself, her work
was to make girdles of wampom and beads. . . .

On Tuesday morning they called their general court (as they call it) to consult and
determine, whether I should go home or no. And they all as one man did seemingly consent to it, that I should go home. . . .

SOURCE: C. H. Lincoln, ed., *Original Narratives of Early American History: Narratives of Indian Wars,*
1675–1699 (New York: Barnes and Noble, 1952), 14: 139–41.

made peace with their traditional French foes and allowed Jesuit missionaries to live among them. Soon about 20 percent of the Iroquois were Catholics, some living under French protection in separate mission-towns.

In 1680 the Iroquois repudiated their ties to the French and traded with the English and Dutch merchants in New York. Seeking furs, they embarked on a new series of western wars. Warriors of the Five Nations pushed a dozen Algonquian-speaking peoples allied with the French—the Ottawas, Foxes, Sauks, Kickapoos, Miamis, and Illinois—out of their traditional lands north of the Ohio River and into a newly formed multitribal region (present-day Wisconsin) west of Lake Michigan. The cost of these victories was high. After losing about 2,200 warriors, in 1701 the Iroquois again made treaties with the French, bringing peace to the inland region for two generations.

However, the character of Indian society throughout the eastern woodland region had been permanently altered. Most tribes had diminished in size as warfare, European diseases, and the rum and corn liquor sold by fur traders took their toll. "Strong spirits . . . Causes our men to get very sick," a Catawba leader in Carolina protested, "and many of our people has Lately Died by the Effects of that Strong Drink." Many Indian peoples also lost their economic independence. As they exchanged furs for European-made iron utensils and woolen blankets, Indians neglected traditional artisan skills—making fewer flint hoes, clay pots, and skin garments. As a Cherokee chief complained in the 1750s, "Every necessity of life we must have from the white people." Religious autonomy vanished as well. When French missionaries won converts among the Hurons and Iroquois, they divided Indian communities into hostile religious factions.

Equally striking, constant warfare altered the dynamics of tribal politics by shifting power from cautious elders, the sachems, to headstrong young warriors. The sachems, one group of Seneca warriors said with scorn, "were a parcell of Old People who say much but who Mean or Act very little." The position and status of women changed in complex and contradictory ways. Traditionally, eastern woodland women had asserted authority as the chief providers of food and handcrafted goods. As a French Jesuit noted of the Iroquois, "The women are always the first to deliberate . . . on private or community matters. They hold their councils apart and . . . advise the chiefs . . . , so that the latter may deliberate on them in their turn." The influx of European goods and the disruption of farming by warfare threatened the economic basis of women's power. At the same time, the influence of women in victorious tribes increased because they assumed responsibility for the cultural assimilation of hundreds of captives.

Finally, the sheer extent of the fur industry—the trapping and killing of hundreds of thousands of beaver, deer, otter, and other animals—profoundly altered the natural environment. Streams ran faster and forest underbrush grew denser because there were fewer beavers to build dams and fewer deer to trim the vegetation. Native animals as well as the native peoples now lived in a new American world.

TIMELINE

1539–1543	Coronado and de Soto seek gold and explore parts of present-day United States	1625–1649	Charles I, king of England
1565	Spain establishes St. Augustine, Florida	1630	Puritans found Massachusetts Bay colony
1598	Acoma rebellion in New Mexico	1634	Maryland settled
1603–1625	James I, king of England	1636–1637	Pequot war
1607	English adventurers settle Jamestown, Virginia		Roger Williams and Anne Hutchinson banished
1608	Samuel de Champlain founds Quebec	1640s	Puritan revolution in England
			Iroquois go to war over fur trade
1613	Dutch set up fur-trading post on Manhattan Island	1651	First Navigation Act
		1660	Restoration of English monarchy
1619	First Africans arrive in the Chesapeake region		Tobacco prices fall and remain low
	Virginia House of Burgesses convened	1664	English conquer New Netherland
1620	Pilgrims found Plymouth colony	1675–1676	Bacon's Rebellion
			Metacom's uprising
1620–1660	Tobacco boom in Chesapeake colonies		Expansion of African slavery in the Chesapeake region
1621	Dutch West India Company chartered	1680	Popé's Rebellion in New Mexico
1622	Opechancanough's uprising	1692	Salem witchcraft trials
1624	Virginia becomes a royal colony		

For Further Exploration

For a comprehensive and insightful narrative of the Spanish exploration and settlement of the lands to the north of the Rio Grande, consult David Weber, *The Spanish Frontier in North America* (1992). Bernard Bailyn, *The Peopling of British North America: An Introduction* (1986), presents a brief, vivid history of English migration and settlement. In *American Slavery, American Freedom* (1975) Edmund Morgan offers a compelling portrayal of white servitude and black slavery in early Virginia, while John Demos, *The Unredeemed Captive: A Family Story from Early America* (1994), relates the gripping tale of Eunice Williams, a captured Puritan girl who lived her life among the Mohawks. Two other fine studies of Native American life are James Merrell, *The Indians' New World: Catawbas and Their Neighbors from European Contact through the Era of Removal* (1989), and Colin Calloway, *New Worlds for All: Indians, Europeans, and the Remaking of Early America* (1997). William Cronon, *Changes in the Land: Indians, Colonists, and the Ecology of New England* (1983), is a succinct analysis of the impact of the Indians and the English on the ecology of New England. Arthur Quinn, *A New World: An Epic of Colonial America from the Founding of Jamestown to the Fall of Quebec* (1994), is a lively narrative filled with portraits of important political figures, macabre events, and high hopes that end disastrously.

A PBS video, *Surviving Columbus* (2 hours), traces the experiences of the Pueblo Indians over 450 years. "First Nations Histories," at <http://www.tolatsga.org/Compacts.html>, presents short histories of many North American Indian peoples and information on their politics, language, culture, and demography. Two fine Web sites explore the history of the Pilgrims at Plymouth: "Caleb Johnson's Mayflower History," at <http://www.mayflowerhistory.com/>, and "The Plymouth Colony Archive Project," at <http://etext.lib.virginia.edu/users/deetz/>. "Colonial Williamsburg," at <http://www.colonialwilliamsburg.org/history/>, offers an extensive collection of documents, illustrations, and secondary texts about colonial life, as well as information about the archeological excavations at Williamsburg. Extensive materials on the Salem witchcraft episode can be viewed at <http://etext.lib.virginia.edu/salem/witchcraft/>.

For definitions of key terms boldfaced in this chapter, see the glossary at the end of the book.

To assess your mastery of the material covered in this chapter, see the Online Study Guide at **bedfordstmartins.com/henrettaconcise**.

For map resources and primary documents, see **bedfordstmartins.com/henrettaconcise**.

Chapter 3

THE BRITISH EMPIRE
IN AMERICA
1660–1750

> These two words, Negro and Slave, [have become] Homogeneous and
> convertible; even as Negro and Christian, Englishman and Heathen,
> are [now] ... made opposites.
>
> Reverend Morgan Godwyn, 1680

When Charles II came to the throne in 1660 England was a second-class trading country, picking up the crumbs left by Dutch merchants. "What we want is more of the trade the Dutch now have," declared the duke of Albemarle. To secure this trade, the English government passed the Acts of Trade and Navigation, which excluded Dutch merchants from its growing colonies, and then went to war to enforce the new legislation. By the 1720s the newly unified kingdom of Great Britain (comprising England and Scotland) controlled the North Atlantic trade. "Our trade is our chief support," Lord Carteret told the House of Lords in 1739. As the ardent imperialist Malachy Postlethwayt put it a few years later, the British empire "was a magnificent superstructure of American commerce and naval power on an African foundation."

As Postlethwayt noted, the wealth of the British empire rested on the predatory trade in African slaves and the sugar those slaves produced on the plantations of the West Indies. To protect these valuable sugar colonies from European rivals—the Dutch in New Netherland, the Spanish in Florida, and especially the Catholic French in Quebec and the West Indies—British officials repeatedly went to war. Boasted one English pamphleteer, "We are, of any nation, the best situated for trade, . . . capable of giving maritime laws to the world."

As the Navigation Acts regulated colonial commerce, British officials tried to subject colonial political institutions to imperial direction. Although this initiative met with less success, by 1713 Britain had become a significant power in Europe and the Western Hemisphere. The cost was high. While most white colonists on the North American mainland enjoyed modest prosperity, thousands of enslaved Africans endured brutal work and early death.

The Politics of Empire, 1660–1713

In the first decades of settlement England governed its Chesapeake and New England colonies in a haphazard fashion. Taking advantage of this laxity and the English civil war, local oligarchies of Puritan magistrates and tobacco-growing planters ran their societies as they wished. Following the restoration of the monarchy in 1660, royal bureaucrats imposed order on the unruly settlements and, with the aid of Indian allies, went to war against rival European powers.

The Great Aristocratic Land Grab

In 1660 Charles II ascended the English throne and quickly created a string of new settlements: the Restoration Colonies, as historians call them. A generous but extravagant man who was always in debt, Charles rewarded eight aristocratic supporters with a gift of the Carolinas, an area long claimed by Spain and populated by thousands of Indians. Then in 1664 he granted all the territory between the Delaware and Connecticut Rivers to his brother James, the duke of York. That same year James took possession of the conquered Dutch province of New Netherland, renaming it New York, and conveyed the ownership of the adjacent province of New Jersey to two of the Carolina proprietors.

In one of the great land grabs in history, a few English aristocrats took title to vast provinces. Like Lord Baltimore's Maryland, their new colonies were proprietorships; the aristocrats owned all the land and could rule as they wished, if their laws conformed broadly to those of England. Most proprietors envisioned a traditional social order presided over by a gentry class and a legally established Church of England. Thus, the Fundamental Constitutions of Carolina (1669) prescribed a **manorial system** with a powerful nobility and a mass of serfs.

This aristocratic scheme proved to be a pure fantasy. The first settlers in North Carolina, poor families from Virginia, refused to work on large manors and grew grain and tobacco on modest family farms. Indeed, farmers in Albemarle County, inspired by Bacon's Rebellion in Virginia and angered by taxes on tobacco exports, rebelled in 1677. They deposed the governor and forced the proprietors to abandon most of their feudal powers.

In South Carolina, the colonists refused to accept the Fundamental Constitutions. Instead, white settlers who had migrated from the overcrowded sugar-producing island of Barbados created their own version of the hierarchical European social order. They used slaves — both Africans and Native Americans — to raise cattle and food crops for export to the West Indies. Carolina merchants also opened a lucrative trade with Indian peoples by exchanging English manufactured goods for deerskins. Because of the Carolinians' reliance on slave labor, they encouraged their Indian allies to take captives from Native American settlements in Florida. These slave raids raised the threat of war with Spain and, in 1715, prompted a brutal war with the Yamasee people, which took the lives of four hundred settlers.

Until the 1720s South Carolina remained an ill-governed, violence-ridden frontier settlement.

In dramatic contrast to the Carolinas, the new proprietary colony of Pennsylvania (which included present-day Delaware) pursued a pacifistic policy toward Native Americans and quickly became prosperous. In 1681 Charles II bestowed the colony on William Penn in payment of a large debt owed to Penn's father. Born to wealth and seemingly destined for courtly pursuits, the younger Penn had converted to the Society of Friends (Quakers), a radical Protestant sect, and used his money and prestige to spread its influence. He designed Pennsylvania as a refuge for Quakers, who were persecuted in England because they refused to serve in the army and would not pay taxes to support the Church of England.

Like the Puritans, the Quakers wanted to restore the simplicity and spirituality of early Christianity. However, the Quakers rejected the pessimistic religious doctrines of Puritans and other Calvinists, who restricted salvation to a small elect. Rather, Quakers followed the teachings of the English visionaries George Fox and Margaret Fell, who argued that God had imbued all men and women with an inner "light" of grace or understanding.

Penn's Frame of Government (1681) applied Quaker radicalism to politics. Rejecting a legally established church, Penn's constitution allowed all Christians to join the church of their choice and all property-owning men to vote and hold office. Thousands of Quakers, mostly middling farm families from northwestern England, flocked to Pennsylvania. Initially, they settled along the Delaware River near the city of Philadelphia, which Penn himself laid out in an orderly grid pattern of main streets and back alleys. To attract European Protestants, the proprietor published pamphlets in Dutch and German that promised cheap prices for land and freedom from religious warfare and persecution. In 1683 migrants from the German province of Saxony founded Germantown (just outside Philadelphia) and thousands of other Germans soon followed. Ethnic diversity, pacifism, and freedom of conscience made Pennsylvania the most open and democratic of the Restoration Colonies.

From Mercantilism to Imperial Dominion

Since the 1560s Elizabeth I and her successors had used government subsidies and charters to stimulate English manufacturing and foreign trade. Beginning in the 1650s, the English government extended these policies—known as **mercantilism**—to its American colonies. According to mercantilist theory, the colonies were to produce agricultural goods and raw materials, which English merchants would carry to the home country, where they would be reexported or manufactured into finished products. Consequently, the Navigation Act of 1651 excluded Dutch merchants from the English colonies and required that goods imported into England or its American settlements be carried on ships owned by English (or colonial) merchants. New parliamentary acts in 1660 and 1663 strengthened the ban on foreign traders and

Power and Race in the Chesapeake

Lord Baltimore holds a map of his proprietary colony, Maryland, in this 1670 painting by Gerard Soest. The colony will soon belong to his grandson Cecil Calvert, who points to his magnificent inheritance. The presence of a young African servant foreshadows the importance of slave labor in the post-1700 Chesapeake economy.

Enoch Pratt Free Library of Baltimore.

FOR MORE HELP ANALYZING THIS IMAGE, see the Online Study Guide at **bedfordstmartins. com/henrettaconcise**.

stipulated that colonial sugar, tobacco, and indigo could be shipped only to England. To provide even more business for English merchants, the acts required that European exports to America pass through England. To pay the customs officials that enforced these mercantilist laws, the Revenue Act of 1673 imposed a "plantation duty" on sugar and tobacco exports.

The English government backed its mercantilist policy with the force of arms. In three commercial wars between 1652 and 1674, the English navy drove the Dutch from New Netherland and ended Dutch supremacy in the West African slave trade. Meanwhile, English merchants expanded their fleets and seized control of North Atlantic commerce.

Many Americans resisted these mercantilist laws as burdensome and intrusive. Edward Randolph, an English customs official in Massachusetts, reported that the Puritan-dominated government took "no notice of the laws of trade," welcomed Dutch merchants, imported goods from the French sugar islands, and claimed that its royal charter exempted it from the new regulations. Outraged, Randolph called for English troops to "reduce Massachusetts to obedience." Instead, the Lords of

Trade—the administrative body charged with colonial affairs—pursued a punitive legal strategy. In 1679 the lords denied the claim of Massachusetts Bay to the
adjoining province of New Hampshire and created a separate colony there with a
royal governor. Then, in 1684, the lords persuaded the English Court of Chancery
to annul the charter of Massachusetts Bay on the grounds that the Puritan government had violated the Navigation Acts and virtually outlawed the Church of
England.

That was just the beginning. The accession to the throne of James II
(r. 1685–1688) prompted new imperial initiatives. James had grown up in France
during the reign of Oliver Cromwell and was an admirer of France's authoritarian
king, Louis XIV. Believing that monarchs had a "divine-right" to rule, James instructed the Lords of Trade to subject the American colonies to royal control. In
1686 the Lords revoked the corporate charters of Connecticut and Rhode Island
and merged them with the Massachusetts Bay and Plymouth colonies to form a new
royal province, the Dominion of New England. Two years later the home government added New York and New Jersey to the Dominion, creating a vast colony that
stretched from the Delaware River to Maine.

This administrative innovation went far beyond mercantilism, which regulated
trade while respecting the political autonomy of the American colonies. Rather, it
extended to America the authoritarian model of colonial rule imposed on Catholic
Ireland. When James II took control of New York in 1674, he refused to allow an
elective assembly and ruled by decree. Now he imposed absolutist rule on the entire
Dominion by appointing Sir Edmund Andros, a former military officer, as governor
and empowering him to abolish the existing legislative assemblies. In Massachusetts,
Andros immediately banned town meetings, angering villagers who prized local self-
rule. He also advocated public worship in the Church of England, offending Puritan
Congregationalists. Even worse from the colonists' perspective, the governor challenged all land titles granted under the original Massachusetts charter. Andros offered to provide new deeds but only if the colonists would agree to pay an annual
fee (or quit-rent).

The Glorious Revolution in England and America

Fortunately for the colonists, James II angered English political leaders as much
as Andros alienated the Americans. The king revoked the charters of many
English towns, rejected the advice of Parliament, and aroused popular opposition by openly practicing Roman Catholicism. When James's Spanish Catholic
wife gave birth to a son in 1688, it raised the prospect of a Catholic heir to the
throne. To forestall such an event, English parliamentary leaders led a quick and
bloodless coup known as the Glorious Revolution. Backed by popular sentiment
and military leaders, they forced James into exile and enthroned Mary, his
Protestant daughter by his first wife, and her Dutch Protestant husband, William

of Orange. Queen Mary II and King William III agreed to rule as constitutional monarchs loyal to "the Protestant reformed religion." They accepted a bill of rights limiting royal prerogatives and increasing personal liberties and parliamentary powers.

To justify their coup, parliamentary leaders relied on the political philosopher John Locke. In his *Two Treatises on Government* (1690), Locke rejected divine-right theories of monarchical rule; he argued that the legitimacy of government rests on the consent of the governed and that individuals have inalienable natural rights to life, liberty, and property. Locke's celebration of individual rights and representative government had a lasting influence in America, where many political leaders wanted to expand the powers of the colonial assemblies.

More immediately, the Glorious Revolution sparked rebellions by colonists in Massachusetts, Maryland, and New York. When the news of the coup reached Boston in April 1689, Puritan leaders seized Governor Andros and shipped him back to England. Responding to American protests, the new monarchs broke up the Dominion of New England. However, they refused to restore the old Puritan-dominated government; instead, in 1692 they created a new royal colony of Massachusetts (which included Plymouth and Maine). The colony's charter empowered the king to appoint the governor (and customs officials) and stipulated that the Massachusetts assembly be elected by all male property owners (not just Puritan church members). It further undermined Puritan rule by prohibiting restrictions on members of the Church of England.

In Maryland the uprising of 1689 had economic as well as religious causes. Since 1660 falling tobacco prices had threatened the livelihoods of smallholders, tenant farmers, and former indentured servants. These economically vulnerable people were mostly Protestant, and they resented the rising taxes and the high fees imposed by wealthy proprietary officials, who were primarily Catholic. When Parliament ousted James II, a Protestant association in Maryland quickly removed the Catholic officials. The Lords of Trade supported this Protestant initiative; they suspended Baltimore's proprietorship, imposed royal government, and legally established the Church of England. This arrangement lasted until 1715, when Benedict Calvert, the fourth Lord Baltimore, converted to the Anglican faith, and the king restored the proprietorship to the Calvert family.

In New York the rebellion against the Dominion of New England began a decade of violent political conflict. New England settlers on Long Island, angered by James's prohibition of representative institutions, began the uprising and quickly won the support of Dutch Protestant artisans in New York City, who welcomed the succession of Queen Mary and her Dutch husband. The Dutch militia ousted Lieutenant Governor Nicholson, an Andros appointee and an alleged Catholic sympathizer. They rallied behind a new government led by Jacob Leisler, a militant German Protestant merchant who had married into a prominent New York Dutch family. Leisler hoped to win the support of all classes and ethnic groups, but his denunciations of political rivals as "popish dogs" and "Roages, Rascalls, and Devills" alienated many New Yorkers. When Leisler imprisoned his opponents, imposed new taxes, and championed the artisans' cause, the wealthy merchants who had traditionally controlled the city's government condemned his rule. In 1691 the merchants won the support of the new English governor, who had Leisler indicted for treason. Convicted by an English jury, Leisler was hanged and then decapitated, an act of vengeance that corrupted New York politics for a generation.

In both America and England the Glorious Revolution of 1688 and 1689 began a new historical era. The uprisings in Boston and New York toppled the authoritarian Dominion of New England and, because King William wanted colonial support for a war against Catholic France, won the restoration of internal self-government. In England, William and Mary ruled as constitutional monarchs and promoted an empire based on commerce. Although Parliament created a new Board of Trade (1696) to supervise the American settlements, it had little success. Settlers and proprietors resisted the board's attempt to install royal governments in every colony, as did many English political leaders, who feared an increase in monarchical power. The result was a period of lax administration. The home government imposed only a few laws and taxes on the colonies and allowed enterprising merchants and financiers to develop them as a source of trade.

Imperial Wars and Native Peoples

In a world of competing mercantilist nations, the expansion of British trade depended on the growth of its military power. Between 1689 and 1815 Britain fought a series of increasingly intense wars with France for dominance in western Europe. To win this struggle, British political leaders created a powerful central state that spent three-quarters of its revenue on military expenses. As these wars spread to the Western Hemisphere, they involved growing numbers of colonists and Native American warriors, who were now armed with European guns. Indeed, many Indian peoples were now familiar enough with European goals and diplomacy to turn the fighting to their own advantage.

The first significant battles in North America occurred during the War of the Spanish Succession (1702–1713), which pitted Britain against France and Spain and prompted English settlers in the Carolinas to attack Spanish Florida. The Carolinians armed the Creeks, whose 15,000 members lived in matrilineal clans and farmed the fertile lands along the present-day Georgia-Alabama border. A joint English-Creek expedition burned the Spanish town of St. Augustine but failed to capture the nearby fort. Fearing that future Carolinian-backed Indian raids would endanger its colony of Florida and pose a threat to Havana in nearby Cuba, the Spanish reinforced St. Augustine and unsuccessfully attacked Charleston, South Carolina.

The Creeks had their own quarrels to settle with the pro-French Choctaws to the west and the Spanish-allied Apalachees to the south and used this opportunity to become the dominant tribe in the region. Beginning in 1704 a force of Creek and Yamasee warriors destroyed the remaining Franciscan missions in northern Florida, attacked the Spanish settlement at Pensacola, and captured 1,000 Apalachees, whom they sold to South Carolinian slave traders for sale in the West Indies. Simultaneously, a Carolina-supplied Creek expedition attacked the Iroquois-speaking Tuscarora people of North Carolina, killing hundreds, executing 160 male captives, and sending 400 women and children into slavery. The surviving Tuscaroras migrated to the north and joined the New York Iroquois (who then became the Six Nations). Having ruled by the guns of their Indian allies, the Carolinians now died by them. When traders demanded the payment of debts in 1715, the Yamasee and Creek revolted and killed 400 colonists before being overwhelmed by the Carolinians and their new Cherokee allies.

Native Americans also played a central role in the fighting in the Northeast, where French Catholics from Canada confronted English Protestants from New England. Aided by the French, Abenaki and Mohawk warriors took revenge on their Puritan enemies. They destroyed English settlements in Maine and in 1704 attacked the western Massachusetts town of Deerfield, where they killed 48 residents and carried 112 into captivity. In response, New England militia attacked French settlements and, in 1710, joined British naval forces and troops to seize Port Royal in French Acadia (Nova Scotia). However, a major British-American expedition against the French stronghold at Quebec failed miserably.

The New York frontier remained quiet because France and England did not want to disrupt the lucrative fur trade and because most of the Iroquois Nations had tired of war and adopted a policy of "aggressive neutrality." In 1701 the Iroquois concluded a peace treaty with France and its Indian allies. Simultaneously, they renewed their "covenant chain" of military alliances with the English governors of New York and the Algonquian tribes of New England. For the next half-century the Iroquois exploited their geographic location by trading with both the English and the French but refusing to fight for either one. The Delaware leader Teedyuscung urged an alliance with the Iroquois by showing his people a pictorial message: "You see a Square in the Middle, meaning the Lands of the Indians; and at one End, the Figure of a Man, indicating the English; and at the other End, another, meaning the French. Let us join together to defend our land against both."

Despite the military stalemate in the colonies, Britain won major territorial and commercial concessions through its victories in Europe. In the Treaty of Utrecht (1713), Britain obtained Newfoundland, Acadia, and the Hudson Bay region of northern Canada from France, as well as access to the western Indian trade (Map 3.1). From Spain, Britain acquired the strategic fortress of Gibraltar at the entrance to the Mediterranean and a thirty-year contract to supply slaves to Spanish America. These

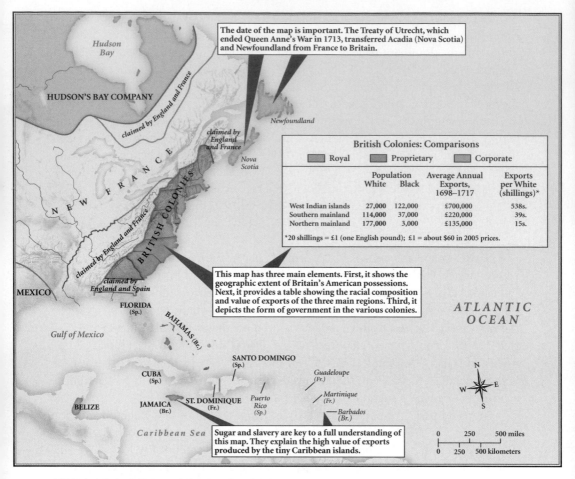

The date of the map is important. The Treaty of Utrecht, which ended Queen Anne's War in 1713, transferred Acadia (Nova Scotia) and Newfoundland from France to Britain.

British Colonies: Comparisons

■ Royal   ■ Proprietary   ■ Corporate

	Population White	Black	Average Annual Exports, 1698–1717	Exports per White (shillings)*
West Indian islands	27,000	122,000	£700,000	538s.
Southern mainland	114,000	37,000	£220,000	39s.
Northern mainland	177,000	3,000	£135,000	15s.

*20 shillings = £1 (one English pound); £1 = about $60 in 2005 prices.

This map has three main elements. First, it shows the geographic extent of Britain's American possessions. Next, it provides a table showing the racial composition and value of exports of the three main regions. Third, it depicts the form of government in the various colonies.

Sugar and slavery are key to a full understanding of this map. They explain the high value of exports produced by the tiny Caribbean islands.

MAP 3.1 Britain's American Empire, 1713

Britain's possessions in the West Indies consisted of tiny islands—mere dots on the Caribbean Sea. However, in 1713 they were by far the most valuable parts of the empire. Their sugar crops brought wealth to English merchants, trade to the northern colonies, and a brutal life (and early death) to African workers.

gains solidified Britain's commercial supremacy, preserved the Protestant monarchy instituted in 1689, and brought peace to eastern North America for a generation.

The Imperial Slave Economy

Britain's increasing interest in American affairs reflected the growth of a new agricultural and commercial order—the South Atlantic system—which produced sugar, tobacco, rice, and other subtropical products. At the center of this economic regime stood plantations worked by enslaved labor from Africa.

The South Atlantic System

The South Atlantic system had its center in Brazil and the West Indies and had sugar as its main product. Before 1500 people in most lands had few sweeteners—mostly honey and the juices of fruits, such as apples and oranges. Then Portuguese planters developed sugar plantations in the Madeira Islands and, after 1550, in Brazil. As the production of sugarcane spread, first Europeans and then other peoples developed a craving for the potent new sweetener.

European merchants, investors, and planters ran the system. They provided the organizational skill, ships, and money needed to grow and process sugarcane, carry the refined sugar to market, and supply the plantations with European tools and equipment. To provide labor for the sugar plantations, the merchants imported slaves from Africa. Between 1550 and 1700, Portuguese and Dutch traders annually transported about 10,000 Africans across the Atlantic. Subsequently, British and French merchants took over this commerce. They developed African-run slave-catching systems that extended far into the interior of Africa and funneled captives to the slave ports of Elmina, Whydah, Loango, and Cabinda. Between 1700 and 1810 European ships carried about 7 million Africans—800,000 in the 1780s alone—to toil in the Americas (Map 3.2).

Beginning in the 1620s, Dutch merchants introduced sugar cultivation to English and French settlements in the West Indies, and a "sugar revolution" quickly transformed their economies. In the 1650s most residents of the island of Barbados were English planters and their white indentured servants, who exported tobacco and livestock hides. Fifty years later, the majority of Barbadians were enslaved Africans, and hundreds of English settlers were departing for the Carolinas. By 1700 English sugar planters were investing heavily in the Leeward Islands and Jamaica, which soon had populations that were 85 to 90 percent African. In 1750 Jamaica—the largest island in the British West Indies—had seven hundred large sugar plantations worked by more than 105,000 slaves.

Sugar was a rich man's crop because it required many laborers to plant and cut the cane and expensive equipment to process it into raw sugar and molasses. Consequently, an affluent planter-merchant elite financed the sugar industry and grew even wealthier from its produce, drawing annual profits of more than 10 percent on their investment. As the Scottish economist Adam Smith noted in his famous treatise *The Wealth of Nations* (1776), sugar was the most profitable crop in Europe and America.

In fact, the South Atlantic system brought wealth to the entire European economy. To take England as an example, the owners of most British West Indian plantations lived as absentees in England and spent their profits there. Moreover, the Navigation Acts required that sugar produced in the British West Indies be sold to British consumers or exported by British merchants to continental markets. By 1750 British reshipments of sugar and tobacco from America accounted for half of all British exports. Substantial profits also flowed into Britain from the

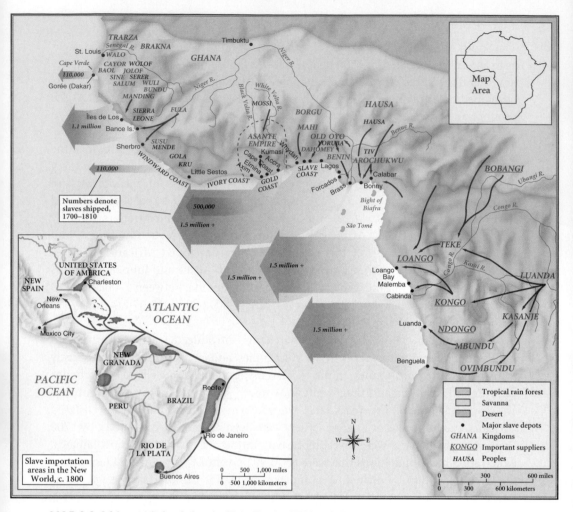

MAP 3.2 Africa and the Atlantic Slave Trade, 1700–1810

The tropical rain forest region of West Africa was home to scores of peoples and dozens of kingdoms. Some kingdoms, such as Dahomey, became aggressive slavers, taking tens of thousands of war captives and funneling them to the seacoast, where they were sold to European traders. About 15 percent of the Africans died during the grueling Middle Passage, the transatlantic voyage between Africa and the Americas. Most of the survivors labored on sugar plantations in Brazil and the British and French West Indies.

FOR MORE HELP ANALYZING THIS MAP, see the Online Study Guide at **bedfordstmartins.com/henrettaconcise**.

slave trade because the Royal African Company and other English traders sold male slaves in the West Indies for three to five times what they paid for them in Africa. In addition, the trade in American sugar and tobacco stimulated British manufacturing. To transport slaves (and machinery and settlers) to America, English shipyards built hundreds of vessels. Thousands of English and Scottish

Shipping Sugar from Antigua

Sugar was a valuable commodity and also a heavy one. Few sugar plantations had wharves that could accommodate large vessels. Consequently, slaves had to maneuver the heavy barrels of sugar onto small boats and row them to the oceangoing ships, which used winches and pulleys to lift them on board. National Maritime Museum, London.

men and women worked in trade-related industries: building port facilities and warehouses, refining sugar and tobacco, distilling rum from molasses (a by-product of sugar), and manufacturing textiles and iron products for the growing markets in Africa and America. Finally, commercial expansion provided Britain with a supply of experienced sailors and thus helped the Royal Navy become the most powerful fleet in Europe.

As the South Atlantic system enhanced prosperity in Europe, it brought economic decline, political change, and human tragedy to West Africa. Between 1550 and 1870 the Atlantic slave trade uprooted about 15 million Africans, diminishing the population and wealth of much of the continent. Moreover, the value of the guns, iron, rum, cloth, and other European products that entered the African economy in exchange for slaves amounted only to about one-tenth (in the 1680s) to one-third (by the 1780s) the value of the goods those slaves subsequently produced in America.

Equally important, the slave trade changed the nature of West African society by promoting centralized states and military conquest. In 1739 an observer noted that "whenever the King of Barsally wants Goods or Brandy . . . the King goes and ransacks some of his enemies' towns, seizing the people and selling them." War and slaving became a way of life in Dahomey, where the royal house made the sale of slaves a state monopoly and used the resulting access to European guns to create a military despotism. Dahomey's army, which included a contingent of 5,000 women, systematically raided the interior for captives and exported thousands of slaves each year. The Asante kings also used the firearms and wealth acquired through the Atlantic trade to create a bureaucratic empire of 3 million to 5 million people. Yet slaving remained a choice for Africans, not a necessity. The old and still powerful kingdom of Benin, famous for its cast bronzes and carved ivory, prohibited the export of slaves for over a century.

The trade in humans produced untold misery—bringing early death to hundreds of thousands of Africans and lifelong slavery to millions more. In many African societies class divisions hardened as people of noble birth enslaved and sold those of lesser status. Gender relations shifted as well. Men constituted two-thirds of the slaves sent across the Atlantic both because European planters paid more for "men and stout men boys," "none to exceed the years of 25 or under 10," and because African traders directed women captives into local slave markets for sale as agricultural workers and house servants. The resulting imbalance between the sexes in Africa allowed some men to take several wives, changing the nature of marriage. Moreover, the Atlantic trade prompted harsher forms of slavery in Africa and eroded the dignity of human life there as well as in the Western Hemisphere.

Those Africans sold into the heart of the South Atlantic system had the bleakest fate. Torn from their village homes, captives were marched in chains to coastal ports such as Elmina on the Gold Coast. From there they made the perilous **Middle Passage** to the New World in hideously overcrowded ships. The captives had little to eat and drink, and the stench of excrement was nearly unbearable. Some slaves jumped overboard, choosing to drown rather than endure more suffering (see Voices from Abroad, "The Brutal 'Middle Passage,'" p. 81). Nearly a million Africans (15 percent of the 8 million who crossed the Atlantic between 1700 and 1810) died on the journey, mostly from dysentery, smallpox, or scurvy.

For the survivors of the Middle Passage, things only got worse. Life on the sugar plantations of northwest Brazil and the West Indies was a lesson in relentless exploitation and systematic violence. Enslaved Africans labored for ten hours a day under a hot semitropical sun, slept in flimsy huts, lived on a starchy diet of corn, yams, and dried fish, and were subject to brutal discipline. With sugar prices high and the cost of slaves low, many planters worked slaves to death and then imported more. Between 1708 and 1735, British planters imported about 85,000 Africans into Barbados, but the island's black population increased by only 4,000 (from 42,000 to 46,000) during those three decades.

Slavery in the Chesapeake and South Carolina

In the aftermath of Bacon's Rebellion, planters in Virginia and Maryland took advantage of the increased British trade in slaves to import thousands of Africans (see Chapter 2). In a "tobacco revolution," they created a new plantation regime based

The Brutal "Middle Passage"

OLAUDAH EQUIANO

Olaudah Equiano, known also as Gustavus Vassa, claimed to have been born in the ancient kingdom of Benin (in present-day southern Nigeria). However, two scholars, writing independently, have recently argued that Equiano was actually born into slavery in America and drew upon conversations with African-born slaves to create a fictitious history of an idyllic childhood, kidnapping and enslavement at the age of eleven, and a traumatic Middle Passage across the Atlantic. Whatever the validity of their arguments, Equiano apparently endured plantation slavery in Barbados and Virginia, where he was purchased by an English sea captain. Buying his freedom in 1766, Equiano settled in London, became an antislavery activist, and, in 1789, published the memoir containing this selection.

My father, besides many slaves, had a numerous family of which seven lived to grow up, including myself and a sister who was the only daughter. . . . I was trained up from my earliest years in the art of war, my daily exercise was shooting and throwing javelins, and my mother adorned me with emblems after the manner of our greatest warriors. One day, when all our people were gone out to their works as usual and only I and my dear sister were left to mind the house, two men and a woman got over our walls, and in a moment seized us both, and without giving us time to cry out or make resistance they stopped our mouths and ran off with us into the nearest wood. . . .

At length, after many days' travelling, during which I had often changed masters, I got into the hands of a chieftain in a very pleasant country. This man had two wives and some children, and they all used me extremely well and did all they could to comfort me, particularly the first wife, who was something like my mother. . . . I was again sold and carried through a number of places till . . . at the end of six or seven months after I had been kidnapped I arrived at the sea coast.

The first object which saluted my eyes when I arrived on the coast was the sea, and a slave ship which was then riding at anchor and waiting for its cargo. I now saw myself deprived of all chance of returning to my native country . . . ; and I even wished for my former slavery in preference to my present situation, which was filled with horrors of every kind. . . . I was soon put down under the decks, and there I received such a salutation in my nostrils as I had never experienced in my life; so that with the loathsomeness of the stench and crying together, I became so sick and low that I was not able to eat, nor had I the least desire to taste any thing. I now wished for the last friend, death, to relieve me; but soon, to my grief, two of the white men offered me eatables, and on my refusing to eat, one of them held me fast by the hands and laid me across I think the windlass, and tied my feet while the other flogged me severely. . . . One day, when we had a smooth sea and moderate wind, two of my wearied countrymen who were chained together (I was near them at the time), preferring death to such a life of misery, somehow made it through the nettings and jumped into the sea.

At last we came in sight of the island of Barbados; the white people got some old slaves from the land to pacify us. They told us we were not to be eaten but to work, and were soon to go on land where we should see many of our country people. This report eased us much; and sure enough soon after we were landed there came to us Africans of all languages.

SOURCE: *The Interesting Narrative of the Life of Olaudah Equiano, or Gustavus Vassa, the African, Written by Himself* (London, 1789), 15, 22–23, 28–29.

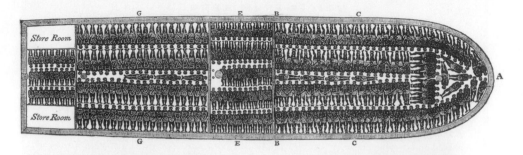

Two Views of the Middle Passage

As the slave trade boomed during the eighteenth century, ship designers packed in more and more human cargo, treating enslaved Africans with no more respect than hogsheads of sugar or tobacco. By contrast, a watercolor of 1846, painted by a ship's officer on a voyage to Brazil, captures the humanity and dignity of the enslaved Africans.

Peabody & Essex Museum / National Maritime Museum, London.

on African slavery rather than English indentured servitude. By 1720 Africans numbered 20 percent of the Chesapeake population, and slavery had become a defining principle of the social order, not just one of several forms of bound labor. Equally important, slavery was now defined in racial terms. A Virginia law of 1692 prohibited sexual intercourse between the English and Africans, and in 1705 another statute defined virtually all resident Africans as slaves: "All servants imported or brought into this country by sea or land who were not Christians in their native country shall be accounted and be slaves."

Living conditions for enslaved Africans in Maryland and Virginia were much less severe than in the West Indies, and they lived relatively long lives. In terms of labor, tobacco was not as physically demanding a crop as sugar. Slaves planted the young tobacco seedlings in the spring, hoed and weeded the crop throughout the summer, and in the fall picked and hung up the leaves to cure over the winter. Moreover, epidemic diseases did not spread easily in the Chesapeake because the plantation quarters were small and dispersed. Also, because tobacco profits were low, planters could not afford to buy new slaves and therefore treated those they had less harshly than West Indian planters did.

Indeed, some tobacco planters increased their workforce through reproduction by purchasing female slaves and encouraging large families. In 1720 women made up about a third of the African population of Maryland, and the black population had begun to increase naturally. One absentee owner instructed his plantation agent "to be kind and indulgent to the breeding wenches, and not to force them when with child upon any service or hardship that will be injurious to them." And, he added, "the children are to be well looked after." By midcentury slaves constituted over 30 percent of the Chesapeake population, and over three-quarters of them were American born.

Slaves in South Carolina labored under much more oppressive conditions. The colony grew slowly until 1700, when Africans from rice-growing societies, who knew how to plant and process that nutritious grain, turned it into a profitable export. To expand production, white planters imported tens of thousands of slaves—and a "rice revolution" changed the face of the colony. By 1720 a majority of South Carolinians were of African birth or descent, and slaves constituted 80 percent of the population in rice-growing areas. Growing rice in inland swamp areas was dirty and dangerous work. Slaves planted, weeded, and harvested the crop in ankle-deep mud, amidst pools of putrid water. Mosquitoes were legion and transmitted epidemic diseases to densely populated plantations, where they took hundreds of African lives. Other slaves died from exhaustion as they moved tons of dirt to build irrigation works. "The labour required for [growing rice] is only fit for slaves," a Scottish traveler remarked, "and I think the hardest work I have seen them engaged in." As in the West Indies, there were many deaths and few births, and the importation of new slaves constantly "re-Africanized" South Carolina's black population.

"Virginian Luxuries"

This painting by an unknown artist (c. 1810) depicts the exploitation inherent in a slave society. On the right, an owner chastises a male slave by beating him with a cane; on the left, ignoring the cultural and legal rules prohibiting such affairs, a white master prepares to engage in sex with his black mistress. Abby Aldrich Rockefeller Folk Art Collection, Colonial Williamsburg Foundation.

The Emergence of an African American Community

Slaves came from many regions of West Africa. South Carolina slave owners preferred laborers from the Gold Coast and Gambia, who had a reputation as hardworking farmers. However, as African sources of slaves shifted southward after 1730, more than 30 percent of the colony's workforce came from the Congo and Angola. Some white planters welcomed such ethnic diversity as a deterrent to slave revolts. "The safety of the Plantations," declared a widely read English pamphlet, "depends upon having Negroes from all parts of Guiny, who do not understand each other's languages and Customs and cannot agree to Rebel."

In fact, slaves initially did not think of themselves as "Africans" or "blacks" but as members of a specific family, clan, or people—Mende, Hausa, Ibo, Yoruba—and they associated mostly with those who shared their language. Gradually, however, enslaved peoples transcended these cultural barriers. In the West Indies and the Carolina lowlands, the largely African-born population created new languages, such as the Gullah dialect, that combined English and African words in an African grammatical structure. "They have a language peculiar to themselves," a missionary reported, "a wild confused medley of Negro and corrupt English, which makes them very unintelligible except to those who have conversed with them for many years." In the Chesapeake, where there were more American-born slaves, most people of African descent gradually gave up their native tongues. In the 1760s a European visitor to Virginia reported with surprise that "all the blacks spoke very good English."

A common language, whether Gullah or English, was a prerequisite for the creation of an African American community. A more equal sex ratio, which encouraged marriage and stable families, was another. In South Carolina a high death rate undermined ties of family and kinship, but after 1725 Chesapeake-area blacks created strong nuclear families and extended kin relationships. For example, all but 30 of the 128 slaves on one of Charles Carroll's estates in Maryland were members of two extended families. These "African Americans" had gradually developed a culture of their own, passing on family names, traditions, and knowledge to the next generation. As one observer suggested, blacks had created a separate society, "a Nation within a Nation."

As enslaved blacks forged a new identity, they integrated some African practices into their new American existence. Many Africans arrived in the colonies with ritual scars that white planters called "country markings" but these signs of tribal identity fell into disuse because slaves no longer lived in ethnic-based communities. However, their African heritage took tangible form in wood carvings inspired by traditional motifs, the large wooden mortars and pestles that slaves used to hull rice, and the design of dwellings, which often had rooms arranged from front to back in a distinctive "I" pattern (not side by side, as was common in English houses). African values also persisted, as some slaves retained Muslim religious beliefs and many more relied on the spiritual powers of conjurers, who knew the ways of African gods. As an English missionary reported from Georgia in the 1750s, many slaves clung to "the old Superstition of a false Religion." Other slaves adopted Protestant Christianity but reshaped its doctrines, ethics, and rituals to fit their needs.

Resistance and Accommodation

There were drastic limits on African American creativity because slaves were denied education, accumulated few material goods, and had little leisure time. A well-traveled European who visited a slave hut in Virginia in the late eighteenth century found it "more miserable than the most miserable of the cottages of our peasants. The husband and wife sleep on a mean pallet, the children on the ground; a very bad fireplace, some utensils for cooking. . . . They work all week, not having a single day for themselves except for holidays."

Slaves resisted this rigorous work routine at their peril. To punish slaves who refused to work or ran away, planters resorted to the lash and the amputation of fingers, toes, and ears. Declaring the chronic runaway Ballazore an "incorrigeble rogue," a Virginia planter ordered all his toes cut off: "nothing less than dismembering will reclaim him." Thomas Jefferson, who witnessed such cruelty on his father's Virginia plantation, noted that each generation of whites was "nursed, educated, and daily exercised in tyranny," for the relationship "between master and slave is a perpetual exercise of the most unremitting despotism on the one part, and degrading submission on the other."

The extent of white violence depended on the size and density of the slave population. Because their numbers were small, blacks in rural areas of the northern colonies endured low status but little violence. Conversely, assertive slaves on the predominantly African sugar plantations in the West Indies routinely suffered branding with hot irons. In the South Carolina rice districts, where Africans outnumbered Europeans eight to one, planters prohibited slaves from leaving the plantation without special passes and forced their poor white neighbors to patrol the countryside.

Slaves dealt with their plight in a variety of ways. Some newly arrived Africans fled to the frontier, where they tried to reestablish traditional villages or married into Indian tribes. Blacks who were fluent in English fled to towns, where they tried to pass as free. But most African Americans worked out their destinies as enslaved agricultural laborers and bargained continually with their masters over the terms of their bondage. Some blacks undertook extra work to obtain better food and clothes; others seized a small privilege and dared the master to revoke it. Thus, Sundays gradually became a day free of labor—a right rather than a privilege. When bargaining failed, slaves protested silently by working slowly or stealing. Other blacks, provoked beyond endurance, attacked their owners or overseers, although such assaults were punishable by mutilation or death. A few blacks even plotted rebellion, despite white superiority in guns and, usually, in numbers as well.

Predictably, South Carolina witnessed the largest slave uprising—the Stono Rebellion of 1739. The governor of the neighboring Spanish (and Catholic) colony of Florida instigated the revolt by promising freedom to slaves who ran away from their English owners. By February 1739 at least sixty-nine slaves had escaped to St. Augustine, and rumors circulated "that a Conspiracy was formed by Negroes in Carolina to rise and make their way out of the province." When war between England and Spain broke out in September, seventy-five Africans—some of them Portuguese-speaking Catholics from the African kingdom of Kongo—rose in revolt and killed a number of whites near the Stono River. Displaying their skills as former soldiers in the war-torn Kongo, the rebels took up arms and marched south toward Catholic Florida "with Colours displayed and two Drums beating." Unrest swept the countryside, but the white militia killed many of the Stono rebels and prevented a general uprising. Frightened whites imported fewer new slaves and tightened plantation discipline.

The Southern Gentry

As the southern colonies became full-fledged slave societies, the character of life changed for whites as well as for blacks. After 1675 most colonists in the Chesapeake region no longer lived in the disease-ridden swampy lowlands and consequently lived longer and formed stable families. Similarly, white rice planters in South Carolina maintained their health by moving to Charleston during the hot, mosquito-ridden summer months. As longevity increased, men reassumed their customary control of family property. When death rates had been high and took the lives of kin, husbands gave their widows large inheritances and named them as the executors of their estates and the legal guardians of their children. After 1700 most wealthy planters had living male kin and named them as executors and guardians. They also favored their male children by limiting the widow's portion of the estate to the traditional one-third share during her lifetime.

The reappearance of **patriarchy** within the family mirrored broader social developments. A planter and merchant elite used its financial power to control yeomen families and white tenant farmers and resorted to brute power to exploit the labor of enslaved blacks, the American equivalent of the oppressed peasants and serfs of Europe. Wealthy planters used Africans to grow food as well as tobacco; build houses, wagons, and tobacco casks; and make shoes and clothes. By making their plantations self-sufficient, the Chesapeake elite survived the depressed tobacco market between 1660 and 1720. Small-scale planters who used family labor to grow tobacco fared less well and fell into debt.

To prevent another rebellion like Bacon's uprising, the Chesapeake gentry addressed the concerns of middling and poor whites. With some success, they urged smallholders to seek wealth by investing in slaves; by 1770, 60 percent of the English families in the Chesapeake owned at least one slave. In addition, the gentry gradually reduced the taxes paid by poorer whites; in Virginia the annual poll tax fell from 45 pounds of tobacco in 1675 to 5 pounds in 1750. The political elite also allowed poor yeomen and some tenants to vote. The strategy of the leading families—the Carters, Lees, Randolphs, Robinsons—was to curry favor with these voters by bribing them with rum, money, and the promise of minor offices in county governments. In return, they expected yeomen and tenants to elect them to office and defer to their authority. This "horse trading" solidified the social position of the planter elite, which used its control of the House of Burgesses to undermine the power of the royal governor to dispense patronage and land grants. Hundreds of yeomen farmers benefited as well, tasting political power and garnering substantial fees and salaries as deputy sheriffs, road surveyors, estate appraisers, and grand jurymen.

Even as wealthy Chesapeake gentlemen created alliances with yeomen farmers, they consciously set themselves apart from their less affluent neighbors. Until the 1720s the ranks of the gentry were filled with boisterous, aggressive men who enjoyed the amusements of common folk—from hunting, hard drinking, and gambling on horse races to sharing tales of their manly prowess in seducing female servants and slaves. As time passed, however, affluent Chesapeake landholders took on the trappings of wealth and modeled themselves on the English aristocracy. Beginning in the 1720s they replaced their modest wooden houses with mansions of brick and mortar. The plantation house of Robert "King" Carter was over seventy-five feet long, forty-four feet wide, and forty feet high. Genteel planters entertained their neighbors in lavish style and sent their sons to London to be educated as lawyers and gentlemen. Most of the young men returned to America, married well-to-do heiresses, and followed in their fathers' footsteps, managing plantations, socializing with fellow gentry, and running the political system.

Wealthy Chesapeake and South Carolina women likewise emulated the refined ways of the English elite. They read English newspapers and fashionable magazines, wore English clothes, and dined in the English fashion, with an elaborate afternoon tea. To improve their daughters' marriage prospects, they hired English tutors to teach them etiquette. Once married, affluent gentry women deferred to their husbands' authority, reared pious children, and maintained elaborate social networks—gradually creating the new ideal of the southern genteel woman. Using the profits of the South Atlantic system, the planter elite formed an increasingly well-educated, refined, and stable ruling class.

The Northern Maritime Economy

The South Atlantic system had a broad geographic reach. As early as the 1640s, New England farmers provided the sugar islands with bread, lumber, fish, and meat. As a West Indian explained, planters in the islands "had rather buy food at very dear rates than produce it by labour, so infinite is the profit of sugar works." By 1700 the economies of the West Indies and New England were tightly interwoven. Soon farmers and merchants in New York, New Jersey, and Pennsylvania were also shipping wheat, corn, and bread to the sugar islands.

The South Atlantic system tied together the entire British empire. In return for the sugar they sent to England, West Indian planters received bills of exchange (credit slips) from London merchants. The planters used those bills to buy slaves from Africa and to reimburse North American farmers and merchants for their provisions and shipping services. The American farmers and merchants then exchanged the bills for British manufactures, primarily textiles and iron goods (Map 3.3).

The West Indian trade created the first American merchant fortunes and the first urban industries. Merchants in Boston, Newport, Providence, Philadelphia, and New York invested their profits in new ships and in factories that refined raw sugar into finished loaves (which previously had been imported from England). They also distilled West Indian molasses into rum; by the 1740s Boston distillers were exporting half a million gallons of rum annually. In addition, merchants in smaller ports, such as Salem and Marblehead, built a major fishing industry by selling salted mackerel and cod to the sugar islands and to southern Europe.

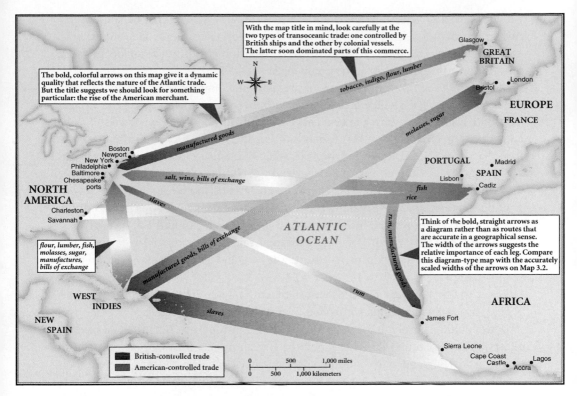

With the map title in mind, look carefully at the two types of transoceanic trade: one controlled by British ships and the other by colonial vessels. The latter soon dominated parts of this commerce.

The bold, colorful arrows on this map give it a dynamic quality that reflects the nature of the Atlantic trade. But the title suggests we should look for something particular: the rise of the American merchant.

Think of the bold, straight arrows as a diagram rather than as routes that are accurate in a geographical sense. The width of the arrows suggests the relative importance of each leg. Compare this diagram-type map with the accurately scaled widths of the arrows on Map 3.2.

tobacco, indigo, flour, lumber

molasses, sugar

manufactured goods

salt, wine, bills of exchange

slaves

manufactured goods, bills of exchange

rum, manufactured goods

fish

rice

rum

slaves

flour, lumber, fish, molasses, sugar, manufactures, bills of exchange

GREAT BRITAIN — Glasgow, Bristol, London

EUROPE — FRANCE

PORTUGAL — Lisbon

SPAIN — Madrid, Cadiz

NORTH AMERICA — Boston, Newport, New York, Philadelphia, Baltimore, Chesapeake ports, Charleston, Savannah

ATLANTIC OCEAN

WEST INDIES

NEW SPAIN

AFRICA — James Fort, Sierra Leone, Cape Coast Castle, Accra, Lagos

■ British-controlled trade
■ American-controlled trade

0   500   1,000 miles
0   500   1,000 kilometers

MAP 3.3 The Rise of the American Merchant, 1750

In accordance with mercantilist doctrine, British merchant houses controlled most of the transatlantic trade in manufactures, sugar, tobacco, and slaves. However, merchants in Boston, New York, and Philadelphia dominated trade between the mainland and the West Indies. In addition, Newport traders played a small role in the slave trade from Africa, while Boston and Charleston merchants grew rich by carrying fish and rice to southern Europe.

FOR MORE HELP ANALYZING THE MAP, see the Online Study Guide at **bedfordstmartins.com/henrettaconcise**.

Southern merchants transformed Baltimore into a major port by developing a bustling trade in wheat, while Charleston traders exported deerskins, indigo, and rice to European markets.

The expansion of Atlantic commerce fueled the rapid growth of American port cities and coastal towns. Seeking jobs and excitement, British and German migrants and young people from the countryside —servant girls, male laborers and apprentice artisans—flocked to urban areas. By 1750 Newport, Rhode Island, and Charleston had nearly 10,000 residents apiece, Boston had 15,000, and New York had almost 18,000. The largest port was Philadelphia, whose population by 1776 reached 30,000, the size of a large European provincial city. Smaller coastal towns emerged as centers of the shipbuilding and lumber industries. Seventy sawmills dotted the Piscataqua River in New Hampshire, providing low-cost wood for homes, warehouses, and especially shipbuilding. Taking advantage of the Navigation Acts, which allowed colonists to build and own trading vessels, scores of shipwrights turned out oceangoing vessels, while hundreds of other artisans made ropes, sails, and metal fittings for the new fleet. By the 1770s colonial-built ships made up about one-third of the entire British merchant fleet.

The impact of the South Atlantic system extended far into the interior. A small fleet of trading vessels sailed back and forth between Philadelphia and the villages along the Delaware Bay, exchanging cargoes of European goods for barrels of flour and wheat for export to the West Indies and Europe. By the 1750s hundreds of professional teamsters in Maryland moved 370,000 bushels of wheat and corn and 16,000 barrels of flour to market each year—over 10,000 wagon trips. To service this traffic, entrepreneurs and artisans set up taverns, horse stables, and barrel-making shops in small towns along the wagon roads. The prosperous interior town of Lancaster, Pennsylvania, boasted more than 200 German and English artisans. The South Atlantic system not only provided markets for northern farmers but also opportunities for artisans in country towns and merchants and laborers in seaport cities.

Wealthy landowners and prosperous merchants dominated seaport society. In 1750 about forty merchants controlled over 50 percent of Philadelphia's trade and had taxable assets averaging £10,000, a huge sum at the time. Like the Chesapeake gentry, these urban merchants imitated the British upper classes, importing design books from England and building Georgian-style mansions to showcase their wealth. Their wives created a genteel culture by decorating their houses with fine furniture and entertaining guests at elegant dinners.

Artisan and shopkeeper families formed the middle ranks of seaport society and numbered nearly half the population. Innkeepers, butchers, seamstresses, shoe-makers, weavers, bakers, carpenters, masons, and dozens of other specialists formed mutual self-help societies and worked to gain a competency—an income sufficient to maintain their families in modest comfort and dignity. Wives and husbands often worked as a team, teaching the "mysteries of the craft" to their children. Some artisans aspired to wealth and status, an entrepreneurial ethic that prompted them to hire apprentices and expand production. However, most craft workers were not well-to-do, and many of them were quite poor. In his entire lifetime a tailor was lucky to accumulate £30 worth of property—far less than the £2,000 owned at death by an ordinary merchant or the £300 listed in the **probate inventory** of a successful blacksmith.

Laboring men and women formed the lowest ranks of urban society. Merchants needed hundreds of dockworkers to unload manufactured goods and molasses from inbound ships and reload them with barrels of wheat, fish, and rice. Sometimes they filled these demanding jobs with black slaves, who numbered 10 percent of the workforce in Philadelphia and New York City; otherwise, they hired unskilled men who worked for wages. Poor women—whether single, married, or widowed—eked out a living by washing clothes, spinning wool, or working as servants or prostitutes. To make ends meet, most laboring families sent their children out to work at an early age. Indispensable to the economy yet without property, urban laborers rented rooms in crowded tenements in back alleys. In good times, their jobs bought security for their families or as much cheap New England rum as they could drink.

Periods of stagnant commerce threatened merchants with bankruptcy and artisans with irregular work. For laborers and seamen, whose household budgets left no margin for sickness or unemployment, depressed trade meant hunger, dependence on charity from the overseers of the poor, and—for the most desperate—a life of petty thievery. Involvement in the sugar- and slave-based South Atlantic system between 1660 and 1750 brought economic uncertainty as well as jobs and opportunities to farmers and workers in the northern colonies.

The New Politics of Empire, 1713–1750

The success of the South Atlantic system of production and trade changed the politics of empire. British ministers, pleased with the prosperous commerce in staple crops, ruled the colonies with a gentle hand. The colonists took this opportunity to strengthen their political institutions and, eventually, to challenge the rules of the mercantilist system.

The Rise of Colonial Assemblies

Before 1689 the authority of the representative assemblies in most colonies was weak. Political power rested in the hands of proprietors, royal governors, and authoritarian elites and reflected the traditional view that "Authority should Descend from Kings and Fathers to Sons and Servants," as a royal-minded political philosopher put it. In the Glorious Revolution of 1688 the political faction known as the Whigs challenged that hierarchical outlook in England and secured a constitutional monarchy that limited the authority of the crown. English Whigs did not advocate democracy but wanted substantial property owners in the House of Commons to have political power, especially over the levying of taxes. When Whig politicians forced King William and Queen Mary to accept a Declaration of Rights in 1689, they strengthened the powers of the Commons at the expense of the crown.

American representative assemblies also wished to limit the powers of crown officials. In Massachusetts during the 1720s the assembly repeatedly rebuffed the king's instructions to provide the royal governor with a permanent salary. Legislatures in North Carolina, New Jersey, and Pennsylvania likewise declined for several years to pay a salary to their governors. Through such tactics, the colonial legislatures gradually won control over taxation and local appointments, which angered imperial bureaucrats and absentee proprietors. "The people in power in America," complained the proprietor William Penn during a struggle with the Pennsylvania assembly, "think nothing taller than themselves but the Trees."

The rising power of the colonial assemblies created an elitist rather than a democratic political system. Although most property-owning white men had the right to vote after 1700, only men of considerable wealth and status stood for election. In Virginia in the 1750s seven members of the influential slave-owning Lee family sat in the House of Burgesses and, along with other powerful families, dominated its major committees. In New England descendants of the original Puritans intermarried and formed a core of political leaders. "Go into every village in New England," John Adams noted in 1765, "and you will find that the office of justice of the peace, and even the place of representative, have generally descended from generation to generation, in three or four families at most."

However, neither elitist assemblies nor wealthy property owners could impose unpopular edicts on the people. The crowd actions that overthrew the Dominion of New England in 1689 were a regular part of political and social life in America. In New York mobs closed houses of prostitution, while in Salem, Massachusetts, they ran people with infectious diseases out of town. In Boston in 1710 angry crowds prevented merchants from exporting scarce grain, and in New Jersey in the 1730s and 1740s they battled with proprietors who were forcing tenants from disputed lands. When Boston officials restricted the sale of farm produce to a single public market, a crowd destroyed the building and defied the authorities to arrest them. "If you touch One you shall touch All," an anonymous letter warned the sheriff, "and we will show you a Hundred Men where you can show one" (see American Voices, "A 'Leveling' Spirit in the Colonies," p. 93). Such expressions of popular power, combined with the growing authority of the assemblies, undermined the old hierarchical system. By the 1750s colonial political institutions were broadly responsive to popular pressure and increasingly immune from British control.

Salutary Neglect

British colonial policy during the reigns of George I (r. 1714–1727) and George II (r. 1727–1760) contributed significantly to the rise of American self-government. Royal bureaucrats relaxed their supervision of internal colonial affairs, focusing instead on defense and trade. Two generations later the British political philosopher Edmund Burke would praise this strategy as "**salutary** [healthy] **neglect**."

Salutary neglect was a by-product of the political system developed by Sir Robert Walpole, the leader of the British Whigs in the House of Commons between 1720 and 1742. By strategically dispensing appointments and pensions in the name of the king, Walpole won parliamentary support for his policies. However, Walpole's use of patronage weakened the imperial system because it filled the Board of Trade and the royal governorships with men of little talent. When Governor Gabriel Johnson arrived in North Carolina in the 1730s, he vowed to curb the powers of the assembly and "make a mighty change in the face of affairs." Quickly discouraged by the lack of support from the Board of Trade, Johnson renounced

AMERICAN VOICES

A *"Leveling" Spirit in the Colonies*

GOVERNOR JOSEPH DUDLEY AND JOHN WINCHESTER

*I*n 1705 legal authorities in Massachusetts prosecuted two woodcutters, John Winchester and Thomas Trowbridge, for insubordination because they defied orders from the royal governor, Joseph Dudley. The following extracts from the testimony during their trial illustrates both the disdain of the upper classes for ordinary folk and popular resistance to the arbitrary exercise of authority.

Account of Governor Joseph Dudley:

The Charet [coach] wherein the Governour was had three sitters and their Servants . . . drawn by four horses, one very unruly, & was attended only at that instant by Mr. William Dudley, the Governour's son.

When the Governour saw the two carts approaching he directed his son to bid them to give him the way . . . Who accordingly did Ride up & told them the Govr was there, & they must give way. Immediately upon it the second Carter came up to ye first . . . & one of them says aloud he would not go out the way for the Governour whereupon the Govr came out of the Charet and told Winchester he must give way to the Charet. Winchester answered boldly . . . I am as good flesh & blood as you. I will not give way. You may go out the way, & came towards the Governour. Whereupon the Governour drew his sword to secure himself & command the Road & went forward . . . and again commanded them to give way. Winchester answered that he was a Christian & would not give way & as the Governour came toward him he advanced & at length laid hold of the Govr & broke the sword in his hands. . . . And this is averred upon the honour of the Governour. . . .

Then came up John Winchester . . . who gives the following account.

. . . I left my cart and . . . asked Mr. William Dudley why he was so rash. He replied this dog [Trowbridge] won't turn out the way for the Governour. . . . I then told his excellency, if he would have patience a minute or two I would clear that way for him. . . . The Governour followed me with his drawn sword and said run the dogs through and with his naked sword stabbed me in the back. I facing about, he struck me on the head . . . giving me there a bloody wound. . . . I caught hold of his sword and broke it.

SOURCE: David Brion Davis and Steven Mintz, *The Boisterous Sea of Liberty: A Documentary History of America from Discovery through the Civil War* (New York: Oxford University Press, 1998), 105–6.

reform and decided "to do nothing which can be reasonably blamed, and leave the rest to time, and a new set of inhabitants."

Walpole's tactics also weakened the empire by undermining the integrity of the political system. **Radical Whigs** protested that Walpole had betrayed the Glorious Revolution by using patronage and bribery to create a strong Court Party. A Country

Sir Robert Walpole, the King's Minister

All eyes are on Walpole (left) as he offers advice to the Speaker of the House of Commons. A brilliant politician, Walpole used patronage to command a majority in the Commons and to win the support of George I and George II — the German-speaking monarchs from the duchy of Hanover. Walpole's personal motto, "Let sleeping dogs lie," helps to explain his colonial policy of salutary neglect. © National Trust Photographic Library / John Hammond.

Party of landed gentlemen likewise warned that Walpole's policies of high taxes and a bloated royal bureaucracy threatened British liberties. Politically minded colonists adopted these arguments and complained that royal governors likewise abused their patronage powers. To preserve American liberty, they set about enhancing the powers of the representative assemblies, unintentionally laying the foundation for the American independence movement.

Protecting the Mercantile System

Apart from patronage, Walpole's American policy had as its prime goal the protection of British commercial interests from military threats from the Spanish and French colonies. Initially, Walpole pursued a cautious foreign policy to allow Britain to recover from the generation of war (1689–1713) against Louis XIV of France. However, in 1732 he provided a parliamentary subsidy for the new colony of Georgia, which had been founded by its reform-minded trustees as a refuge for Britain's poor. Envisioning a society of independent family farmers, the trustees limited most land grants to 500 acres and initially outlawed slavery.

Walpole had little interest in social reform and subsidized Georgia to protect the valuable rice colony of South Carolina. Britain's expansion into Georgia, where

Spanish Franciscans had Indian missions, outraged Spanish officials. They were also angry because British merchants were taking over the trade in slaves and manufactured goods to Spain's American colonies. To resist Britain's commercial and geographic expansion, in 1739 Spanish naval forces stepped up their seizure of illegal traders—and mutilated the English sea captain, Robert Jenkins.

Yielding to Parliamentary pressure, Walpole launched the so-called "War of Jenkins' Ear," a predatory, but largely unsuccessful, attack against Spain's American empire. In 1740 British regulars failed to capture St. Augustine because South Carolina whites—still shaken by the Stono revolt—refused to commit militia units to the expedition. A year later a major British and American assault on the prosperous Spanish seaport of Cartagena (in present-day Colombia) likewise failed. Instead of enriching themselves with Spanish booty, hundreds of troops from the mainland colonies died of tropical diseases.

The War of Jenkins' Ear quickly became part of a general European conflict, the War of the Austrian Succession (1740–1749). Massive French armies battled British-subsidized German forces in Europe, and French naval forces roamed the West Indies, vainly trying to conquer a British sugar island. There was little fighting in North America until 1745, when 3,000 New England militiamen, supported by a British naval squadron, captured the powerful French naval fortress of Louisbourg at the entrance to the St. Lawrence River. To the dismay of New England Puritans, who feared invasion from Catholic Quebec, the Treaty of Aix-la-Chapelle (1748) returned Louisbourg to France. The treaty ensured British control over Georgia and reaffirmed its military superiority over Spain, but the New England colonists now understood that England would act in its own interests, not theirs.

The American Economic Challenge

During these years the Walpole ministry confronted an unexpected American threat to Britain's economic expansion. According to the mercantilist Navigation Acts, the colonies were to produce staple crops and to consume British manufactured goods. To enforce the manufacturing monopoly enjoyed by British firms, Parliament passed a series of acts prohibiting Americans from selling colonial-made textiles (1699), hats (1732), and iron products such as plows, axes, and skillets (1750). As staple exports from the mainland settlements grew by 400 percent between 1700 and 1750, Americans purchased increasing amounts of British textiles and iron goods.

However, the Navigation Acts had a major loophole because they allowed Americans to own ships and transport goods. Colonial merchants exploited those provisions to control 95 percent of the commerce between the mainland and the West Indies and 75 percent of the transatlantic trade in manufactures. Quite unintentionally, the mercantilist system had created a dynamic community of colonial merchants.

Moreover, by the 1720s the British sugar islands could not absorb all the flour, fish, and meat produced by the rapidly growing mainland settlements. Ignoring Britain's intense rivalry with France, colonial merchants sold this produce in the French West Indies. These supplies helped French planters produce low-cost sugar and outsell Britain in the European sugar market. When American rum distillers began to buy cheap molasses from the French islands, British planters petitioned Parliament for help. The resulting Molasses Act of 1733 permitted the mainland colonies to export fish and farm products to the French islands but—to give a price advantage to British molasses—placed a high tariff on imports of French molasses. American merchants and public officials protested that the act would cut farm exports, cripple the distilling industry, and make it more difficult for colonists to purchase British goods. When Parliament ignored their petitions, American merchants smuggled in French molasses by bribing customs officials. Luckily for the Americans, sugar prices rose sharply in the late 1730s and enriched planters in the British West Indies; so the act was not rigorously enforced.

The lack of adequate currency in the colonies led to another confrontation. American merchants sent most of the gold and silver coins and **bills of exchange** they earned in the West Indian trade to Britain to pay for manufactured goods and thereby drained the domestic supply of money. To remedy this problem, ten colonial assemblies established land banks that lent paper money to farmers, who used their land as collateral for the loans. Farmers used the paper money to buy tools or livestock or to pay their creditors, thereby stimulating trade. However, some assemblies, such as that of Rhode Island, issued large amounts of currency (which consequently fell in value) and required merchants to accept it as legal tender. English merchants and other creditors rightly complained that they were being forced to accept worthless money. So in 1751 Parliament passed the Currency Act, which barred the New England colonies from establishing new land banks and prohibited the use of public currency to pay private debts.

These economic conflicts and the assertiveness of the American assemblies angered a new generation of British political leaders, who believed that the colonies already had too much autonomy. In 1749 Charles Townshend of the Board of Trade charged that American legislatures had assumed many of the "ancient and established prerogatives wisely preserved in the Crown"; he vowed to replace salutary neglect with more rigorous imperial control.

The wheel of empire had come full circle. In the 1650s England had set out to build a colonial empire and, over the course of a century, achieved the economic part of that goal. Mercantilist legislation, commercial warfare against European rivals, and the forced labor of a million African slaves brought economic prosperity to Britain. However, because of the Glorious Revolution and the era of salutary neglect, the empire unexpectedly dissolved into a group of politically self-governing colonies. So in the late 1740s British officials vowed once again to create a politically centralized colonial system.

TIMELINE

1651	First Navigation Act	1720–1742	Sir Robert Walpole serves as chief minister
1660s	Virginia moves toward slave system		
1663	Charles II grants Carolina proprietorship	1720–1750	African American community forms
			Rice exports from Carolina soar
1664	English capture New Netherland, rename it New York		Planter aristocracy emerges
			Seaport cities expand
1681	William Penn founds Pennsylvania	1732	Parliament charters Georgia, challenging Spain
1686–1689	Dominion of New England		Hat Act
1688–1689	Glorious Revolution in England; William and Mary ascend throne	1733	Molasses Act
		1739	Stono Rebellion in South Carolina
	Revolts in Massachusetts, Maryland, and New York		War with Spain in the Caribbean
		1740	Veto of Massachusetts land bank
1689–1713	England, France, and Spain at war	1750	Iron Act restricts colonial iron manufactures
1696	Parliament creates Board of Trade		
1705	Virginia enacts slavery legislation	1751	Currency Act prohibits land banks and use of paper money as legal tender
1714–1750	British follow policy of "salutary neglect"		
	American assemblies gain power		

For Further Exploration

The best concise overview of England's empire is Michael Kammen, *Empire and Interest: The American Colonies and the Politics of Mercantilism* (1970), while Linda Colley, *Britons: Forging the Nation, 1707–1837* (1992), explores the impact of empire on Britain. A clearly written study of multicultural tensions in early New York is Joyce Goodfriend, *Before the Melting Pot: Society and Culture in Colonial New York City, 1664–1730.* Two fine portrayals of imperial military and political affairs in the eighteenth century are Fred Anderson, *A People's Army: Massachusetts Soldiers and Society in the Seven Years' War* (1984), a compelling picture of army life, and Richard Bushman, *King and People in Provincial Massachusetts* (1985), a nicely crafted story of the decline of British authority in New England.

Betty Wood, *Origins of American Slavery* (1998), offers a survey of this important topic. For a lucid discussion of the diversity and evolving character of African bondage, see Ira Berlin, *Many Thousands Gone: The First Two Centuries of Slavery in North America* (1999), and Philip D. Morgan, *Slave Counterpoint: Black Culture in the Eighteenth-Century Chesapeake and Low Country* (1998). Olaudah Equiano, *The Interesting Narrative of the Life of Olaudah*

Equiano (originally published 1789; Bedford/St. Martin's, 1995), provides a powerful first-person account of a child's life in Africa, his kidnapping and sale into slavery in America, and his odyssey toward freedom and fame. On Africa, consult Paul Bohannan and Philip Curtin, *Africa and the Africans* (3rd ed., 1988).

The PBS video *Africans in America*, "Part 1: Terrible Transformation, 1450–1750" (1.5 hours) covers the African American experience in the colonial period; the Web site at <http://www.pbs.org/wgbh/aia/part1/title.html> contains a wide variety of pictures, historical documents, and scholarly commentary. Excerpts from Slave Narratives, at <http://vi.uh.edu/pages/mintz/primary.htm>, present materials selected by Steven Mintz from forty-six accounts, arranged in eleven chronological and thematic categories. Jerome S. Handler and Michael L. Tuite Jr. present a comprehensive Visual Record of the Atlantic Slave Trade and Slave Life in the Americas at <http://hitchcock.itc.virginia.edu/Slavery/>.

For definitions of key terms boldfaced in this chapter, see the glossary at the end of the book.

To assess your mastery of the material covered in this chapter, see the Online Study Guide at **bedfordstmartins.com/henrettaconcise**.

For map resources and primary documents, see **bedfordstmartins.com/henrettaconcise**.

Chapter 4

GROWTH AND CRISIS IN COLONIAL SOCIETY
1720–1765

The thirst after Indian lands, is become almost universal.
SIR WILLIAM JOHNSON TO THE EARL OF SHELBURNE, 1766

I n 1736 Alexander MacAllister left the Highlands of Scotland for the backcountry of North Carolina, where his wife and three sisters soon joined him. Over the years MacAllister prospered as a landowner and mill proprietor and had only praise for his new home. Carolina was "the best poor man's country I have heard in this age," he wrote to his brother Hector, urging him to "advise all poor people . . . to take courage and come." In North Carolina there were no landlords to keep "the face of the poor . . . to the grinding stone," and so many Highlanders were arriving that "it will soon be a new Scotland." Here, on the far margins of the British empire, people could "breathe the air of liberty, and not want the necessarys of life." Tens of thousands of European migrants—Highland Scots, English, Scots-Irish, Germans—heeded such advice and helped to increase the population of Britain's North American settlements from 400,000 in 1720 to almost 2 million by 1765.

The rapid increase in the number of settlers—and slaves—transformed the character of life in every region of British America. Long-settled towns in New England became densely settled and then overcrowded. Antagonistic ethnic and religious communities jostled uneasily with one another in the Middle Atlantic region, and the influx of the MacAllisters and thousands of others into the backcountry of the South altered the dynamics of politics and social conflict there as well. Moreover, in every colony European intellectual and spiritual movements—the Enlightenment and Pietism—changed the tone of secular thought and religious life. Finally, and perhaps most important, as the immigrants and the landless children of long-settled families moved inland, they sparked warfare with the native peoples and with France and Spain, the other European powers contesting for North America. A generation of growth produced a decade of warfare.

Freehold Society in New England

In the 1630s the Puritans left a country where a handful of nobles and gentry owned 75 percent of the arable land and farmed it by using servants, leaseholding tenants, and wage laborers. In America the Puritans consciously created a yeoman society consisting primarily of independent farm families. However, by 1750 New England's rapidly growing population occupied most of the best farmland, challenging the future prospects of the freehold ideal.

Farm Families: Women's Place

The Puritans' commitment to family independence did not extend to gender relations. Puritan ideology celebrated the husband as head of the household and accorded him nearly complete control over his dependents. As the Reverend Benjamin Wadsworth of Boston advised women in *The Well-Ordered Family* (1712), being richer, more intelligent, or of higher social status than their husbands mattered little: "Since he is thy Husband, God has made him the head and set him above thee." Therefore, Wadsworth concluded, it was a woman's duty "to love and reverence him."

Throughout their lives women saw firsthand that their role was a subordinate one. Small girls watched their mothers defer to their fathers. As young women they saw the courts prosecute many women and very few men for the crime of fornication (having sexual union outside of marriage). And they learned that their marriage portions would be inferior in kind and size to those of their brothers; daughters usually received not highly prized land but rather livestock or household goods. Thus, Ebenezer Chittendon of Guilford, Connecticut, left all his land to his sons, decreeing that "Each Daughter have half so much as Each Son, one half in money and the other half in Cattle." Because English law had eliminated many customary restrictions over the disposition of wealth, fathers had nearly complete freedom to devise their property as they pleased.

In rural New England—indeed, throughout the colonies—women were raised to be dutiful helpmeets (helpmates) to their husbands. Farmwives spun thread and yarn from flax or wool and wove it into cloth for shirts and gowns. They knitted sweaters and stockings, made candles and soap, churned milk into butter and pressed curds into cheese, fermented malt for beer, preserved meats, and mastered dozens of other household tasks. The most exemplary or "notable" practitioners of these domestic arts won praise from the community because their physical labor was crucial to the rural household economy.

Bearing and rearing children were equally important tasks. Most women married in their early twenties and by their early forties had given birth to six or seven children, usually delivered with the assistance of midwives. These large families sapped the physical and emotional strength of most wives, and focused their attention on domestic activities for about twenty of their most active years.

The Character of Family Life: The Cheneys

Life in a large colonial-era family was very different from that in a small modern one.
Mrs. Cheney's face shows the rigors of having borne many children, a task that has occupied
her entire adult life (and may continue still, if the child she holds is her own). Her eldest daughter
has married the man standing at the rear and holds two of her own children, who are not much
younger than the last of her mother's brood. In such families, the lines between the generations
were blurred. National Gallery of Art, Washington, DC; gift of Edgar William and Bernice Chrysler Garbisch.

A Massachusetts mother explained that she had little room for religious activities
because "the care of my Babes takes up so large a portion of my time and attention."
Yet more women than men became full members of the Puritan congregations of
New England. As the revivalist Jonathan Edwards explained, many women joined
the church so "that their children may be baptized" and because they feared the dangers of childbirth.

As the size of farms shrank in long-settled communities, many couples chose to
have fewer children. After 1750, women in the typical farm village of Andover,
Massachusetts, bore an average of only four children and thus could pursue other
tasks. Farm women now made extra yarn, cloth, or cheese to exchange with neighbors or sell to shopkeepers and thereby enhanced their families' standard of living.
Or like Susan Huntington of Boston (the wife of a prosperous merchant), women
spent more time in "the care & culture of children, and the perusal of necessary
books, including the scriptures."

Yet women's lives remained tightly bound by a web of legal and cultural restrictions. While ministers often praised the women's piety, they excluded them from
an equal role in the church. When Hannah Heaton grew dissatisfied with her
Congregationalist minister, thinking him unconverted and a "blind guide," she

sought out Quaker and Baptist churches that welcomed questioning women and allowed them to become spiritual leaders. However, by the 1760s even evangelical Baptist congregations were stressing traditional male privileges. "The government of Church and State must be . . . family government" controlled by its "king," declared the Danbury (Connecticut) Baptist Association. Willingly or not, most New England women abided by the custom that, as the essayist Timothy Dwight put it, they should be "employed only in and about the house and in the proper business of the sex."

Farm Property: Inheritance

By contrast, European men who migrated to the colonies escaped many traditional constraints, including the curse of landlessness. "The hope of having land of their own & becoming independent of Landlords is what chiefly induces people into America," an official noted in the 1730s. For men who had been peasants in Europe, owning property was a key element of their social identity.

Indeed, property ownership and family authority were closely related. Most migrating Europeans wanted large farms that would provide sustenance for themselves and ample land for their children. Parents with small farms could not provide their offspring with farms and had to adopt different strategies. Many placed their sons and daughters as indentured servants in more prosperous households, where they would have enough to eat. When the indentures ended at age eighteen or twenty-one, their propertyless sons faced the daunting challenge of a ten-to-twenty-year climb up the agricultural ladder, from laborer to tenant and finally to freeholder.

Luckier sons and daughters in successful farm families received a marriage portion when they reached the age of twenty-three to twenty-five. The marriage portion—land, livestock, or farm equipment—repaid children for their past labor and allowed parents to choose their children's partners, which they did not hesitate to do. The parents' security during old age depended on a wise choice of a wife or husband. Normally, children could refuse an unacceptable match, but they did not have the luxury of "falling in love" with whomever they pleased.

Marriage under English common law was hardly a contract between equals. A bride relinquished to her husband the legal ownership of her land and personal property. After his death, she received her dower—the right to use (but not to sell) a third of the family's estate. The widow's death or remarriage canceled this use-right, and her portion was divided among the children. The widow's property rights were subordinate to those of the family "line," which stretched, through the children, across the generations.

Indeed, it was the father's cultural duty to provide inheritances for his children, and men who failed to do so lost status in the community. Some fathers willed the family farm to a single son and provided their other children with money, apprenticeship contracts, or uncleared frontier tracts (or they required the inheriting son to do so). Alternatively, yeomen moved their families to an unsettled region, where life was hard but land for the children was cheap and abundant. "The Squire's House stands on the Bank of the Susquehannah," the traveler Philip Fithian reported from the Pennsylvania backcountry in the early 1760s. "He tells me that he will be able to settle all his sons and his fair Daughter Betsy on the Fat of the Earth."

These farmers' historic accomplishment was the creation of whole communities composed of independent property owners. A French visitor noted the sense of personal dignity in this rural world, which contrasted sharply with European peasant life. Throughout the northern colonies, he found "men and women whose features are not marked by poverty, by lifelong deprivation of the necessities of life, or by a feeling that they are insignificant subjects and subservient members of society."

The Crisis of Freehold Society

How long would this happy circumstance last? Because of high rates of natural increase, New England's population doubled with each generation. The Puritan colonies had about 100,000 people in 1700, nearly 200,000 in 1725, and almost 400,000 in 1750. In long-settled areas many farms had been divided and then subdivided; now they consisted of fifty acres or less and many parents were unable to provide an adequate inheritance. In the 1740s the Reverend Samuel Chandler of Andover, Massachusetts, was "much distressed for land for his children," seven of whom were male. A decade later in the neighboring town of Concord, about 60 percent of the farmers owned less land than their fathers had.

Because parents had less to give their sons and daughters, they had less control over their children's lives. The system of arranged marriages broke down as young people engaged in premarital sex and used the urgency of pregnancy to win their fathers' permission to marry. Throughout New England the number of premarital conceptions rose spectacularly, from about 10 percent of firstborn children in the 1710s to 30 percent or more in the 1740s. Given another chance, young people "would do the same again," an Anglican minister observed, "because otherwise they could not obtain their parents' consent to marry."

New England families met the threat to the freeholder ideal through a variety of strategies. Many parents chose to have smaller families by using primitive methods of birth control. Others petitioned the provincial government for frontier land grants and hacked new farms out of the forests of central Massachusetts and western Connecticut—and eventually New Hampshire and the future Vermont. Still other farmers used their small plots more productively by replacing the traditional English crops of wheat and barley with high-yielding potatoes and Indian corn. Corn offered a hearty food for humans, and its leaves furnished feed for cattle and pigs, which in turn provided milk and meat. Gradually New England changed from a grain to a livestock economy and became the major supplier of salted and pickled meat to the slave plantations of the West Indies.

Finally, New England farmers survived on their smaller farms by exchanging goods and labor, developing the full potential of their household-based productive system. In this system, women and children joined other families in spinning yarn, sewing quilts, and shucking corn. Men lent each other tools, draft animals, and grazing land. Farmers plowed fields owned by artisans and shopkeepers, who repaid them with shoes, furniture, or store credit. Typically, no money changed hands; instead farmers, artisans, and shopkeepers recorded their debts and credits in personal account books and every few years "balanced" the books by transferring small amounts of cash to one another. The system of community exchange allowed households—and the entire economy—to achieve maximum output, thereby preserving the freehold ideal.

The Middle Atlantic: Toward a New Society, 1720–1765

The Middle Atlantic colonies of New York, New Jersey, and Pennsylvania became home to peoples of differing origins, languages, and religions. These settlers— Scots-Irish Presbyterians, English and Welsh Quakers, German Lutherans, Dutch Reformed Protestants, and others—created ethnic and religious communities that coexisted uneasily with one another.

Economic Growth and Social Inequality

Ample fertile land and a long growing season attracted migrants to the Middle Atlantic colonies, and profits from grain exports financed their rapid settlement. Between 1720 and 1770 a population explosion in western Europe increased the demand for wheat and doubled its price. By increasing their exports of wheat, corn, flour, and bread, Middle Atlantic farmers brought prosperity to the region and helped its population to surge from 120,000 in 1720 to 450,000 in 1765.

Even as the population rose, many migrants refused to settle in New York's fertile Hudson River Valley. There, the Van Rensselaers and other Dutch landlords presided over manors created by the Dutch West India Company in the 1620s and wealthy British families, such as the Clarkes and the Livingstons, dominated vast tracts granted by English governors between 1700 and 1714 (Map 4.1). Like the slave-owning Chesapeake planters, these landlords aspired to live like European gentry, but few migrants wanted to labor as poor and dependent peasants. Eventually the manorial lords were able to attract tenants but only by granting them long leases and the right to sell their improvements—their houses and barns—to the next tenant. The number of tenants on the vast Van Rensselaer estate rose slowly from 82 to 345 between 1714 and 1752 but then jumped to 700 by 1765.

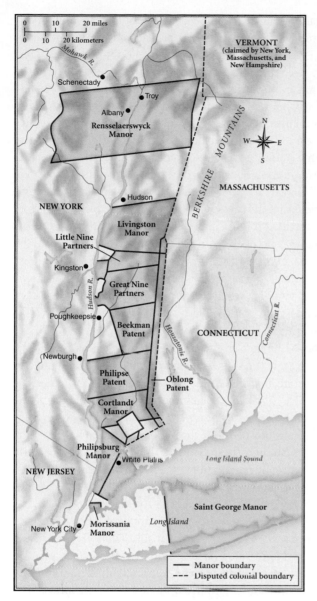

MAP 4.1 The Hudson River Manors

Dutch and English manorial lords dominated the fertile eastern shores of the Hudson River Valley, where they leased farms, on perpetual contracts, to German tenants and refused to sell land to freehold-seeking migrants from overcrowded New England. This powerful landed elite produced Patriot leaders, such as Gouverneur Morris and Robert Livingston, and leading American families, such as the Roosevelts.

Most tenant families hoped that with hard work and luck they could sell enough wheat to buy freehold farmsteads. However, preindustrial technology limited their output, especially during the crucial harvest season. As the wheat ripened, it had to be harvested quickly; any ripe uncut grain promptly sprouted and became useless. Yet a worker with a hand sickle could reap only half an acre a day, which limited the number of acres a family could harvest. The cradle scythe, an agricultural tool introduced during the 1750s, doubled or tripled the amount of grain a worker could cut. Even so, during the harvest season a family with two adult workers could reap only about twelve acres of grain—perhaps 150 to 180 bushels of wheat and rye. After family needs were met, the remaining grain might be worth £15—enough to buy salt and sugar, tools, and cloth but little else. The road to landownership was not an easy one.

Unlike New York, rural Pennsylvania and New Jersey were initially marked by relative economic equality. The original Quaker migrants arrived with approximately equal resources and lived simply in small houses with one or two rooms, a sleeping loft, a few benches or stools, some wooden trenchers (platters), and a few wooden noggins (cups). Only the wealthiest families ate off pewter or ceramic plates imported from England or Holland. However, the rise of the wheat trade and an influx of poor settlers created marked social divisions. By the 1760s some eastern Pennsylvania farmers used the labor of slaves and immigrant workers to grow wheat on large farms. Others bought up land and subdivided it into small tenancies, which they let out on profitable leases. Still others became successful commercial entrepreneurs by providing newly arrived settlers with farming equipment, sugar and rum from the West Indies, and financial services. Gradually a new class of agricultural capitalists—large-scale farmers, rural landlords, speculators, storekeepers, and gristmill operators—accumulated substantial estates and exhibited their wealth by buying mahogany tables, four-poster beds, table linen, and imported Dutch dinnerware.

By the 1760s, one-half of all white men in the Middle Atlantic region owned no property. Some propertyless men were the sons of farmers and would eventually inherit at least part of the family estate, but just as many were Scots-Irish "inmates"— single men or families "such as live in small cottages and have no taxable property, except a cow." In the predominantly German settlement of Lancaster, Pennsylvania, a merchant noted an "abundance of Poor people" who "maintain their Families with great difficulty by day Labour." Although these Scots-Irish and German migrants hoped to become tenants and eventually landowners, sharply rising land prices prevented many from realizing their dreams (see American Voices, "Runaway Servants and Slaves," p. 107).

Merchants and artisans took advantage of the ample supply of labor by organizing an outwork manufacturing system. They bought wool or flax from farmers and paid propertyless workers and land-poor farm families to spin it into yarn or weave it into cloth. In the 1760s an English traveler reported that hundreds of Pennsylvanians had turned "to manufacture, and live upon a small farm, as in many parts of England." Indeed, many eastern areas had become as crowded and socially divided as rural England, and farmers feared a return to the lowly status of the European peasant.

Cultural Diversity

The middle colonies were not a melting pot in which European cultures quickly blended into a homogeneous "American" society; rather, they consisted of a patchwork of ethnically and religiously diverse communities. In 1748 a traveler found no

AMERICAN VOICES

~

Runaway Servants and Slaves

*B*etween 1720 and 1775 tens of thousands of poor Europeans and English convicts came to the mainland colonies as indentured servants and redemptioners and were sold to the highest bidder. "They sell the servants here as they do their horses, and advertise them as they do their beef and oatmeal," wrote an astonished British officer. Many of these servants labored side by side with enslaved Africans, and as shown by these newspaper advertisements from the Pennsylvania Gazette, *the two groups found that they shared a passion for freedom.*

October 12, 1752

Run away from doctor Thomas Graeme's plantation, in Horsham township, Philadelphia county, a Molatto slave, named Will, about 29 years of age, approaching very near the Negroe complexion, being of a Negroe father, and Indian mother, about five feet eight inches high, of an open bold countenance, somewhat pitted with the small-pox, speaks both English and Dutch, and is a very cunning sensible fellow. There went with him, a labouring man, that work'd by the day or month, called Thomas Stillwell, a tall smooth fac'd fair complexion'd fellow, with pale strait hair. . . . The said Stillwell is supposed to countenance the escape of the Molatto, by assuming the character of his master, or some such false pretence.

May 21, 1761

FIVE POUNDS Reward

Run away from the Subscribers, living at Little-Elk, Caecil County, Maryland, a Servant Woman named Margaret Sliter (but probably will change her Name) about 28 Years old, fresh colour, darkish brown Hair, born in England; had on when she ran away, two Bed-Gowns, one blue and white, the other dark Brown, both Callicoe. . . . Also a Negroe Man, named Charles, a lusty able Fellow, about 29 Years of Age, pitted with the Small-Pox, speaks good English, talks fast, is apt to get drunk, and pretends to be married to the aforesaid Margaret Sliter; had on when he ran away, a Pair of Thickset Breeches . . . a light coloured Jacket, an old brown Body-coat. . . .

Virginia, Lancaster County, Sept. 22, 1752

RUN away from the subscriber . . . on the 4th of May, A convict servant woman, named Sarah Knox (alias Howard, alias Wilson) of a middle size, brown complexion, short notes, talks broad, and said she was born in Yorkshire . . . and is a very deceitful, bold, insinuating woman, and a great liar. . . . I find [in the *Gazette*] an extract of a letter from Chester, in Pennsylvania, mentioning a quack Doctor, by the name of Charles Hamilton . . . who turns out to be a woman in mens cloaths, and now assumes the name of Charlotte Hamilton. . . . If she talks broad, I have reason to believe that she is the very servant who belongs to me.

SOURCE: Billy G. Smith and Richard Wojtowicz, *Blacks Who Stole Themselves: Advertisements for Runaways in the* Pennsylvania Gazette, *1728–1790* (Philadelphia: University of Pennsylvania Press, 1989), pp. 35, 50, 164.

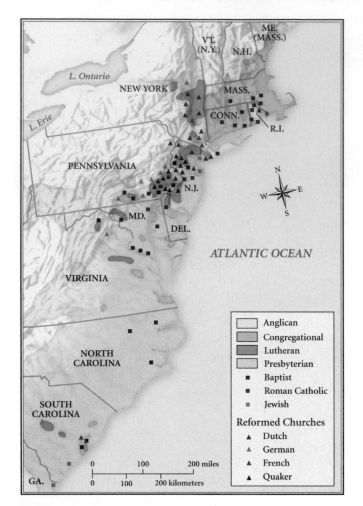

MAP 4.2 Religious Diversity in 1750

By 1750 religious diversity among European colonists was on the rise and not only in the ethnically disparate Middle Atlantic colonies. Baptists had increased their numbers in New England, long the stronghold of Congregationalism, and would soon be an important sect in Virginia. Already there were good-sized pockets of Presbyterians, Lutherans, and German Reformed in the South, where the Church of England (Anglicanism) was the established religion.

FOR MORE HELP ANALYZING THIS MAP, see the Online Study Guide at **bedfordstmartins.com/henrettaconcise**.

fewer than twelve religious denominations in Philadelphia, including Anglicans, Quakers, Swedish and German Lutherans, Scots-Irish Presbyterians, and even Roman Catholics (Map 4.2).

Migrants usually tried to preserve their cultural identities by marrying within their own ethnic groups or maintaining the customs of their native lands. The major exception was the Huguenots—Protestant Calvinists who were expelled from

Catholic France. They settled in New York and various seacoast cities and lost their French ethnic identity by intermarrying with other Protestants. More typical were the Welsh Quakers. Seventy percent of the children of the original Welsh migrants to Chester County, Pennsylvania, married other Welsh Quakers, as did 60 percent of the third generation.

Throughout Pennsylvania, Quakers became the dominant social group, at first because of their numbers and later because of their wealth and influence. Quakers controlled Pennsylvania's representative assembly until the 1750s and exercised considerable power in New Jersey as well. Because Quakers were pacifists, they dealt with Native Americans by negotiating treaties and buying land rather than seizing it. These conciliatory policies enabled Pennsylvania to avoid a major war with the Indian peoples until the 1750s. Some Quakers extended their religious values of equality and justice to African Americans. After 1750 many Quaker meetings condemned the institution of slavery, and some expelled members who continued to keep slaves.

The Quaker vision of a "peaceable kingdom" attracted German settlers who were fleeing their homelands because of war, religious persecution, and poverty. First to arrive, in 1683, was a group of religious dissenters—the Mennonites— attracted by the promise of religious freedom. In the 1720s religious upheaval and population growth in southwestern Germany and Switzerland brought a larger wave of migrants. "Wages were far better" in Pennsylvania, Heinrich Schneebeli reported to his friends in Zurich, and "one also enjoyed there a free unhindered exercise of religion." A third wave of Germans and Swiss—nearly 40,000 strong—landed in Philadelphia between 1749 and 1756. Some of these newcomers were redemptioners—a type of indentured servant—but many more were propertied farmers and artisans in search of ample land for their children.

Germans soon dominated many districts of eastern Pennsylvania, and thousands more moved down the Shenandoah Valley into the western parts of Maryland, Virginia, and the Carolinas. The migrants carefully guarded their language and cultural heritage. A minister in North Carolina admonished the young people in his congregation "not to contract any marriages with the English or Irish," explaining that "we owe it to our native country to do our part that German blood and the German language be preserved in America." Well beyond 1800 these settlers spoke German, read German-language newspapers, conducted church services in German, and preserved German farming practices, which sent women into the fields to plow and reap. English travelers remarked that German women were "always in the fields, meadows, stables, etc. and do not dislike any work whatsoever." Most German migrants were Protestants and lived easily as subjects of Britain's German-born and German-speaking monarchs, George I and George II. They engaged in politics only to protect their churches and cultural practices—insisting, for example, that as in Germany, married women should have the right to hold property and write wills.

German Farm in Western Maryland

Beginning in the 1730s, wheat became a major export crop in Maryland and Virginia. This engraving probably depicts a German farm because the harvesters are using oxen, not horses, and women are working in the field alongside men. Using "a new method of reaping" that is possibly of German origin, the harvesters cut only the grain-bearing tip and leave the wheat stalks in the fields, to be eaten by livestock. Library of Congress.

FOR MORE HELP ANALYZING THIS IMAGE, see the Online Study Guide at **bedfordstmartins.com/henrettaconcise**.

Migrants from Ireland formed the largest group of incoming Europeans, about 150,000 in number. Most were the descendants of the Presbyterian Scots who had been sent to Ireland by the English government during the seventeenth century to solidify its rule over Ireland's Catholic population. Once in Ireland, the Scots faced religious and economic discrimination from the English ruling classes. The Irish Test Act of 1704 excluded Presbyterians as well as Catholics from holding public office in Ireland; English mercantilist regulations placed heavy import duties on the woolens made by Scots-Irish weavers; and Scots-Irish farmers faced heavy taxes. "Read this letter, Rev. Baptist Boyd," a migrant to New York wrote back to his minister, "and tell all the poor folk of ye place that God has opened a door for their deliverance . . . all that a man works for is his own; there are no revenue hounds [tax collectors] to take it from us here." Lured by such reports, thousands of Scots-Irish sailed for Philadelphia beginning in the 1720s and then moved to central Pennsylvania and southward down the Shenandoah Valley into the backcountry of Maryland and Virginia. Like the Germans, the Scots-Irish retained their culture, holding firm to the Presbyterian faith.

Religious Identity and Political Conflict

In Western Europe the leaders of church and state condemned religious diversity, and some German ministers carried these sentiments to Pennsylvania. "The preachers do not have the power to punish anyone, or to force anyone to go to church," complained the minister Gottlieb Mittelberger. As a result, "Sunday is very badly kept. Many people plough, reap, thresh, hew or split wood and the like." Thus, Mittelberger concluded, "Liberty in Pennsylvania does more harm than good to many people, both in soul and body."

As Mittelberger noted, ministers in Pennsylvania could not invoke government authority to uphold religious values. However, the result was not social anarchy because religious sects in the colonies enforced moral behavior through communal self-discipline. Quaker families attended a weekly worship meeting and a monthly discipline meeting. Every three months, a committee from the monthly meeting reminded each family to provide their children with proper religious instruction and fathers acted accordingly. "If thou refuse to be obedient to God's teachings," Walter Faucit of Chester admonished his son, "thou will be a fool and a vagabond." The committee also supervised adult behavior; a Chester County meeting disciplined one of its members "to reclaim him from drinking to excess and keeping vain company." Significantly, Quaker meetings regulated marriages and granted permission only to couples with land and livestock sufficient to support a family. As a result, the children of well-to-do Friends usually married within the sect, while poor Quakers remained unmarried, wed at later ages, or married without permission—in which case they were often barred from Quaker meetings. These sanctions effectively sustained a self-contained and prosperous Quaker community.

In the 1750s Quaker dominance in Pennsylvania came under attack. Scots-Irish Presbyterians along the frontier challenged the pacifism of the Quaker-dominated assembly by demanding an aggressive Indian policy. New German migrants also opposed the Quakers because they were denied fair representation in the provincial assembly and laws that respected their inheritance customs. As a European visitor noted, Scots-Irish Presbyterians, German Baptists, and German Lutherans were trying to form "a general confederacy" against the Quakers; however, they could not unite because of "a mutual jealousy, for religious zeal is secretly burning."

These ethnic and religious passions embittered Middle Atlantic politics. In Pennsylvania Benjamin Franklin disparaged the "boorish" character and "swarthy complexion" of German migrants, while in New York a Dutchman declared that he "Valued English Law no more than a Turd." The region's experiment in cultural and religious diversity prefigured the passionate ethnic and social conflicts that would characterize much of American society in the centuries to come.

The Enlightenment and the Great Awakening, 1740–1765

Two great European cultural movements reached America between the 1720s and the 1760s: the Enlightenment and Pietism. The Enlightenment, which emphasized the power of human reason to understand and shape the world, appealed especially to well-educated men and women from merchant or planter families and to urban artisans. Pietism, an emotional, evangelical religious movement that stressed a Christian's personal relation to God, attracted even more adherents, primarily farmers and urban laborers. The two movements promoted independent thinking in different ways; together they transformed American intellectual and cultural life.

The Enlightenment in America

Many early Americans turned to folk wisdom to explain the workings of the natural world. Thus, Swedish settlers in Pennsylvania attributed medicinal powers to the great white mullein, a common wildflower, and treated fevers by tying its leaves around their feet and arms. Others relied on religion. Most Christians believed the earth stood at the center of the universe and that God (and Satan, by witchcraft and other means) intervened directly and continuously in human affairs. When a measles epidemic struck Boston in the 1710s, the Puritan minister Cotton Mather thought that only God could end it.

Colonists held to these beliefs despite the scientific revolution of the sixteenth and seventeenth centuries, which challenged both traditional Christian and folk worldviews. In the 1530s the astronomer Copernicus observed that the earth traveled around the sun rather than vice versa, implying a more modest place for humans in the universe than had previously been assumed. Eventually the English scientist Isaac Newton, in his *Principia Mathematica* (1687), used mathematics to explain the movement of the planets around the sun. Newton's laws of motion and concept of gravity described how the universe could operate without the constant intervention of a supernatural being, undermining traditional Christian explanations of the cosmos.

In the century between *Principia Mathematica* and the outbreak of the French Revolution in 1789, the philosophers of the European Enlightenment used empirical (experience- or fact-based) research and scientific reasoning to study all aspects of life, including social institutions and human behavior. Enlightenment thinkers advanced four fundamental principles: the lawlike order of the natural world, the power of human reason, the natural rights of individuals (including the right to self-government), and the progressive improvement of society.

In his *Essay Concerning Human Understanding* (1690), the English philosopher John Locke emphasized the impact of environment, experience, and reason on human behavior. He argued that the character of individuals and societies was not fixed but could be changed through education and purposeful action. Locke's *Two Treatises on Government* (1690) advanced the revolutionary theory that political authority was not given by God to monarchs (as kings such as James II had insisted). Rather, it derived from social compacts that people made to preserve their "natural rights" to life, liberty, and property. In Locke's view, a people should have the right to change government policies—or even the form of government—through the decision of a majority.

The ideas of Locke and other Enlightenment thinkers came to America through books, travelers, and educated migrants. As early as the 1710s the Reverend John Wise of Ipswich, Massachusetts, used Locke's political principles to defend the Puritans' practice of vesting power in ordinary church members. Wise argued that just as the social compact formed the basis of political society, the religious covenant made the congregation—not the bishops of the Church of England or even the ministers—the proper interpreter of religious truth. The Enlightenment influenced Cotton Mather as well. When a smallpox epidemic threatened Boston in the 1720s, Mather turned to a scientific rather than a religious remedy by joining with physician Nicholas Boyleston to publicize the new technique of inoculation.

Benjamin Franklin was the exemplar of the American Enlightenment. Born in Boston in 1706 to a devout Calvinist family and apprenticed to a printer as a youth, Franklin was a self-taught man. While working as a printer and journalist in Philadelphia, he formed "a club of mutual improvement" that met weekly to discuss "Morals, Politics, or Natural Philosophy." These discussions and Enlightenment literature, rather than the Bible, shaped Franklin's imagination. As Franklin explained in his *Autobiography*, written in 1771, "from the different books I read, I began to doubt of Revelation [God-revealed truth] itself."

Like many urban artisans, wealthy Virginia planters, and affluent seaport merchants, Franklin became a **deist**. Influenced by Enlightenment science, deists believed that God had created the world but allowed it to operate in accordance with the laws of nature. The deists' God was a divine "watchmaker" who did not intervene directly in history or in people's lives. Rejecting the authority of the Bible, deists relied on people's "natural reason" (their innate moral sense) to define right and wrong. A sometime slave owner himself, Franklin used his reason to question the moral legitimacy of racial bondage and repudiated it once he became a defender of American freedom from British political "slavery."

Franklin popularized the practical-minded outlook of the Enlightenment in *Poor Richard's Almanack* (1732–1757), an annual publication read by thousands. In 1743 he helped found the American Philosophical Society, an institution devoted to "the promotion of useful knowledge." Taking this message to heart, Franklin himself invented bifocal lenses for eyeglasses, the Franklin stove, and the lightning rod. His book on electricity, published in England in 1751, won praise as the greatest contribution to science since Newton. Inspired by Franklin's example, ambitious printers in the American seaport cities published newspapers and gentleman's magazines, the first significant nonreligious publications to appear in the colonies. Thus, the

European Enlightenment added a secular dimension to colonial intellectual life, preparing the way for the great American contributions to republican political theory by John Adams, James Madison, and other Patriots during the Revolutionary era.

American Pietism and the Great Awakening

As many educated Americans turned to deism, many other colonists embraced European Pietism, a Christian evangelical outlook. Pietists emphasized devout, or "pious," behavior, emotional church services, and a striving for a mystical union with God; they appealed to the heart, rather than the mind. In the 1720s German migrants carried this outlook to America, where they quickly sparked a religious revival. In Pennsylvania and New Jersey the Dutch minister Theodore Jacob Frelinghuysen moved from church to church, preaching rousing, emotional sermons to German settlers. In private prayer meetings he encouraged church members to spread the message of spiritual urgency. A decade later William Tennent and his son Gilbert copied Frelinghuysen's approach and led revivals among Scots-Irish Presbyterians throughout the Middle Atlantic region.

Simultaneously, an American-born Pietistic movement appeared in Puritan New England. The original Puritan settlers were emotionally intense, but over the decades since the 1630s, many congregations had lost their religious zeal. In the 1730s the minister Jonathan Edwards restored spiritual enthusiasm to the Congregational churches in the Connecticut River Valley. An accomplished philosopher as well as an effective preacher, Edwards urged his hearers—especially young men and women—to commit themselves to a life of piety and prayer.

George Whitefield, a young English evangelist, transformed these local revivals into a "Great Awakening" that spanned British North America. Whitefield had experienced conversion after reading German Pietistic tracts and became a follower of John Wesley, the founder of English Methodism. In 1739 Whitefield carried Wesley's fervent preaching style to America and over the next two years attracted huge crowds of "enthusiasts" from Georgia to Massachusetts. "Religion is become the Subject of most Conversations," the *Pennsylvania Gazette* reported. "No books are in Request but those of Piety and Devotion." The usually skeptical Benjamin Franklin was so impressed by Whitefield's oratory that when the preacher asked for contributions, Franklin emptied the coins in his pockets "wholly into the collector's dish, gold and all." When the evangelist reached Boston, the Reverend Benjamin Colman reported, the people were "ready to receive him as an angel of God."

Whitefield owed his appeal partly to his compelling personal presence. "He looked almost angelical; a young, slim, slender youth . . . cloathed with authority from the Great God," wrote a Connecticut farmer. Like most evangelical preachers, Whitefield did not read his sermons but spoke from memory. He preached as if inspired: gesturing eloquently, raising his voice for dramatic effect, using striking biblical metaphors, and even at times assuming a female persona—as a woman in labor struggling to deliver the word of God. When the young preacher told his

George Whitefield, c. 1742

No painting captured Whitefield's magical appeal, although this image conveys his open demeanor and religious intensity. When Whitefield spoke to a crowd near Philadelphia, an observer noted, his words were "sharper than a two-edged sword. . . . Some of the people were pale as death; others were wringing their hands . . . and most lifting their eyes to heaven and crying to God for mercy."

listeners they had all sinned and must seek salvation, hundreds of men and women suddenly felt the "new light" of God's grace within them. As "the power of god come down," Hannah Heaton recalled, "my knees smote together . . . it seemed to me I was a sinking down into hell . . . but then I resigned my distress and was perfectly easy quiet and calm . . . it seemed as if I had a new soul & body both." Strengthened and self-confident, these "New Lights" were eager to spread Whitefield's message throughout their communities.

Religious Upheaval in the North

Like all cultural explosions, the Great Awakening was controversial. Conservative (or "Old Light") ministers such as Charles Chauncy of Boston condemned the "cryings out, faintings and convulsions" produced by emotional preachers. Chauncy likewise attacked the New Lights' practice of allowing women to speak in public as "a plain breach of that commandment of the LORD, where it is said, Let your WOMEN keep silence in the churches." In Connecticut, the Old Lights persuaded the legislative assembly to prohibit evangelists from speaking to established congregations without the ministers' permission. When Whitefield returned to Connecticut in 1744, he found many pulpits closed to him. But the New Lights resisted attempts to silence them. Dozens of farmers, women, and artisans roamed the countryside, condemning the Old Lights as "unconverted" sinners and willingly accepting imprisonment: "I shall bring glory to God in my bonds," a dissident preacher wrote from jail.

As the Awakening proceeded, it undermined support for established churches and challenged their tax-supported status. In New England many New Lights left the legally established Congregational Church. By 1754 they had founded 125 "separatist" churches which supported their ministers through voluntary contributions. Other religious dissidents joined Baptist congregations, which also favored the separation of church and state. "God never allowed any civil state upon earth to impose religious taxes," declared the Baptist preacher Isaac Backus. In New York and New Jersey the Dutch Reformed Church split in two because New Lights resisted conservative church authorities in the Netherlands.

The Awakening challenged the authority of ministers, whose education and biblical knowledge had traditionally commanded respect. In an influential pamphlet, *The Dangers of an Unconverted Ministry* (1740), Gilbert Tennent asserted that the minister's authority came not from theological training but from the conversion experience. Reaffirming Martin Luther's belief in the priesthood of all Christians, Tennent suggested that anyone who had experienced the saving grace of God could speak with ministerial authority. Isaac Backus likewise celebrated this spiritual democracy, noting that "the common people now claim as good a right to judge and act in matters of religion as civil rulers or the learned clergy."

In many rural villages, revivalism reinforced the communal values of farm families by questioning the competitive and mercenary values of the marketplace. Suspicious of merchants and land speculators, Jonathan Edwards spoke for many rural colonists when he charged that a "private niggardly [miserly] spirit" was more suitable "for wolves and other beasts of prey, than for human beings." As Gilbert Tennent put it, "In any truly Christian society mutual love is the Band and Cement."

As religious enthusiasm spread, churches founded new colleges to educate their youth and train ministers. New Light Presbyterians established the College of New Jersey (Princeton) in 1746, and New York Anglicans founded King's College (Columbia) in 1754. Baptists set up the College of Rhode Island (Brown) while the

Dutch Reformed Church subsidized Queen's College (Rutgers) in New Jersey. The true intellectual legacy of the Awakening, however, was not education for the few but a new sense of authority among the many. As a European visitor to Philadelphia remarked in surprise, "the poorest day-laborer . . . holds it his right to advance his opinion, in religious as well as political matters, with as much freedom as the gentleman."

Social and Religious Conflict in the South

In the southern colonies religious enthusiasm also sparked social conflict. In Virginia the Church of England was legally established and supported by public taxes. However, Anglican ministers generally ignored the spiritual needs of African Americans (about 40 percent of the population), and landless whites (another 20 percent) attended irregularly. Middling white freeholders (35 percent of the residents) formed the core of most Anglican congregations. Prominent planters and their families (a mere 5 percent) held real power in the Church and used their control of parish finances to discipline Anglican ministers. One clergyman complained that dismissal awaited any minister who "had the courage to preach against any Vices taken into favor by the leading Men of his Parish."

The Great Awakening challenged both the dominance of the Church of England and the planter elite. In 1743 the bricklayer Samuel Morris, inspired by reading George Whitefield's sermons, led a group of Virginia Anglicans out of the Church. Seeking a more vital religious experience, Morris and his followers invited New Light Presbyterian ministers to lead their prayer meetings. Soon these Presbyterian revivals spread among Scots-Irish in the backcountry and English settlers in the Tidewater region, threatening the social authority of the Virginia gentry. Traditionally, planters and their well-dressed families arrived at Anglican services in elaborate carriages drawn by well-bred horses, and the men flaunted their power by marching in a body to their reserved front pews. Such potent reminders of the gentry's social superiority would vanish if freeholders attended New Light Presbyterian rather than Church of England services. Moreover, religious pluralism would threaten the tax-supported status of the Anglican Church.

To halt the spread of New Light doctrines, Virginia's governor denounced them as "false teachings," and Anglican justices of the peace closed down Presbyterian meetinghouses. This harassment kept most white yeomen families and poor tenants within the Church of England, as did the fact that most Presbyterian ministers were highly educated and sought converts mainly among skilled workers and propertied farmers.

Baptists succeeded where Presbyterians failed. The Baptists were a radical and widely persecuted Reformation sect that grew rapidly in number during and after the Great Awakening. The Baptists' central ritual was adult baptism, often involving complete immersion in water. Once men and women had experienced the infusion of grace—had been "born again"—they were baptized in an emotional public ceremony. The enthusiasm and democratic ways of the Baptist preachers who came to Virginia in the 1760s drew thousands of yeomen and tenant farm families into their congregations by offering them solace and emotional release in a troubled world.

Even slaves were welcome at Baptist revivals. In 1740 George Whitefield had condemned the brutality of slaveholders and urged that blacks be brought into the Christian fold. In South Carolina and Georgia a few New Light planters took up Whitefield's challenge, but white hostility and the commitment of Africans to their ancestral religions kept the number of converts low. The first significant conversion of slaves to Christianity came in Virginia in the 1760s, as second- and third-generation English-speaking African Americans responded positively to the Baptist message that all people were equal in God's eyes.

The ruling planters reacted violently to the Baptists, viewing them as a threat to hierarchical authority and their way of life. The Baptists emphasized spiritual equality by calling one another "brother" and "sister," and their preachers condemned the customary pleasures of Chesapeake planters—gambling, drinking, whoring, and cockfighting. Hearing Baptist Dutton Lane condemn "the vileness and danger" of drunkenness, planter John Giles took the charge personally: "I know who you mean! and by God I'll demolish you." In Caroline County, Virginia, an Anglican posse attacked a prayer meeting led by Brother John Waller; Waller, a fellow Baptist reported, "was violently jerked off the stage; they caught him by the back part of his neck, beat his head against the ground, and a gentleman gave him twenty lashes with his horsewhip."

Despite such attacks, Baptist congregations continued to multiply. By 1775 about 20 percent of Virginia's whites and hundreds of enslaved blacks had joined Baptist churches. To signify their state of grace, some Baptist men "cut off their hair, like Cromwell's round-headed chaplains." Many others refused to attend "a horse race or other unnecessary, unprofitable, sinful assemblies." Still others forged a new ethic of evangelical masculinity, "crying, weeping, lifting up the eyes, groaning" when touched by the Holy Spirit but defending themselves with vigor. "Not able to bear the insults" of heckler Robert Ashby, a group of Baptists "took Ashby by the neck and heels and threw him out of doors," sparking a bloody brawl.

However, the revival in the Chesapeake did not bring radical changes to the social order. Rejecting the requests of evangelical women, Baptist men kept church authority in the hands of "free born male members." Anglican slaveholders likewise retained power within the polity. Nonetheless, the Baptist insurgency gave spiritual meaning to the lives of the poor and empowered yeomen and tenants to defend their economic interests. Moreover, as Baptist ministers spread Christianity among slaves, the cultural gulf between blacks and whites shrank, undermining one justification for slavery and giving blacks a new religious identity. Within a generation African Americans would develop their own versions of Protestant Christianity.

The Midcentury Challenge: War, Trade, and Social Conflict, 1750–1765

Between 1750 and 1765 a series of events transformed colonial life. First, Britain embarked on the French and Indian War in America, which became a worldwide conflict — the Great War for Empire. Second, a surge in trade boosted colonial consumption but put Americans deeply in debt to British creditors. Third, a great westward migration sparked new battles with Indian peoples, armed conflicts between settlers and landowners, and frontier rebellions against eastern-controlled governments (Map 4.3).

The French and Indian War Becomes a War for Empire

In 1750 Indian peoples controlled the interior of eastern North America — the great valleys of the Ohio and Mississippi Rivers. Only a few Anglo-Americans had ventured across the Appalachian Mountains because there were few natural transportation routes and because of Indian resistance. The Iroquois in particular had firmly opposed white settlement and used their control of the fur trade to bargain for guns and subsidies from British and French officials.

However, the Iroquois strategy of playing off the French against the British was breaking down. The Europeans resented the rising cost of "gifts" of arms and money; equally important, Indian alliances began to crumble in the face of escalating Anglo-American demands for land. In the late 1740s the Mohawks rebuffed attempts by Sir William Johnson, a British Indian agent and land speculator, to settle Scottish migrants west of Albany. To the south, the Iroquois were infuriated when Governor Dinwiddie of Virginia and a group of prominent planters proposed "the Extension of His Majesties Dominions" into the upper Ohio River Valley, an area that the Iroquois controlled through alliances with the Delawares and the Shawnees. Supported by influential London merchants, the Virginia speculators formed the Ohio Company in 1749 and obtained a royal grant of 200,000 acres. "We don't know what you Christians, English and French intend," the outraged Iroquois complained, "we are so hemmed in by both, that we have hardly a hunting place left."

To maintain influence with the Iroquois Nations, the British Board of Trade called a great intercolonial meeting with the Indians at Albany, New York, in June 1754. At Albany the American delegates declared they had no designs on the lands of the Iroquois and sought their assistance against the French. To protect the British colonies from the French, Benjamin Franklin proposed a Plan of Union with a continental assembly that would manage all western affairs: trade, Indian policy, and defense. But neither Franklin's Albany Plan nor a proposal by the Board of Trade for a political "union between ye Royal, Proprietary, & Charter Governments" was in the cards. Both the provincial assemblies and British ministers feared that a consolidated American government would undermine their authority.

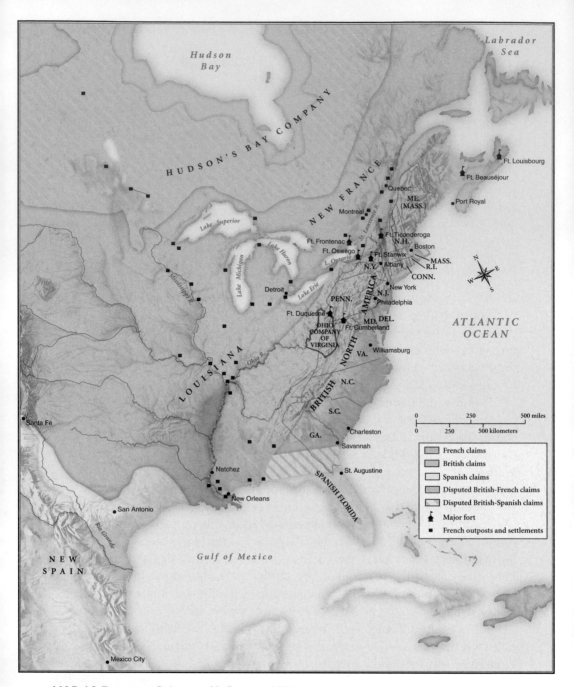

MAP 4.3 European Spheres of Influence, 1754

France and Spain laid claim to vast areas of North America and used their Indian allies to combat the numerical superiority of British settlers. For their part, Native Americans played off one European power against another. As a British official observed, "To preserve the Ballance between us and the French is the great ruling Principle of Modern Indian Politics." By expelling the French from North America, the Great War for Empire disrupted this balance and left the Indian peoples on their own to resist encroaching Anglo-American settlers.

The Ohio Company's land grant alarmed French authorities as well as the Iroquois. To counter it, they constructed a series of forts, including Fort Duquesne at the point where the Monongahela and Allegheny Rivers join to form the Ohio (present-day Pittsburgh). The confrontation escalated when Dinwiddie dispatched an expedition led by Colonel George Washington, a young Virginia planter and Ohio Company stockholder. In July 1754 French troops seized Washington and his men and expelled them from the Ohio Valley, prompting expansionists in Virginia and Britain to demand war. Henry Pelham, the British prime minister, urged calm: "There is such a load of debt, and such heavy taxes already laid upon the people, that nothing but an absolute necessity can justifie our engaging in a new War."

Pelham could not control the march of events. In Parliament William Pitt, a rising British statesman, and Lord Halifax, the new head of the Board of Trade, strongly advocated a policy of colonial expansion. They persuaded Pelham to dispatch military forces to America, where they joined with colonial militia in attacking French forts. In June 1755 British and New England troops captured Fort Beauséjour in Nova Scotia (Acadia). Subsequently, troops from Puritan Massachusetts seized nearly 10,000 French Catholic Acadians, permanently deported them to France, Louisiana, and the West Indies, and settled English and Scottish Protestants on their farms.

These Anglo-American successes were quickly offset by a stunning defeat. As 1,400 British regulars and Virginia militiamen advanced on Fort Duquesne in July 1755, they came under attack by a small force of French and a larger group of Delawares and Shawnees, who had allied with the French. In the ensuing battle the British commander, General Edward Braddock, lost his life and nearly two-thirds of his troops. "We have been beaten, most shamefully beaten, by a handfull of Men," Washington complained bitterly as he led the militiamen back to Virginia.

By 1756 the fighting in America had spread to Europe, where it arrayed France, Spain, and Austria against Britain and Prussia. When Britain mounted major offensives in India and West Africa as well as in North America, the conflict became a Great War for Empire (known as the Seven Years' War in Europe and the French and Indian War in the colonies). Since 1700 Britain had reaped unprecedented profits from its overseas trading empire and was determined to crush France, the main obstacle to its expansion.

William Pitt, the new secretary of state, was the grandson of the East Indies merchant "Diamond" Pitt, a committed expansionist, and an arrogant leader. "I know that I can save this country and that I alone can," he declared. Indeed, Pitt was a master of strategy, both commercial and military, and planned to cripple France by attacking its colonies. In designing the critical campaign against New France, Pitt exploited a demographic advantage: on the North American mainland, King George II's two million subjects outnumbered the French by 14 to 1. To mobilize the colonists, Pitt paid half the cost of their troops and supplied them with arms and equipment, an expenditure in America of nearly £1 million a year. Moreover, he committed a major British fleet and 30,000 British regulars to the American conflict.

Beginning in 1758 the powerful Anglo-American forces moved from one triumph to the next. They forced the French to abandon Fort Duquesne (which they renamed Fort Pitt) and then captured the major fortress of Louisbourg at the mouth of the St. Lawrence. In 1759 a force led by General James Wolfe sailed up the St. Lawrence and captured Quebec, the heart of France's American empire. Quebec's fall was the turning point of the war. The Royal Navy prevented French reinforcements from crossing the Atlantic, and in 1760 British forces captured Montreal and completed the conquest of Canada.

Elsewhere the British also went from success to success. Fulfilling Pitt's dream, the East India Company ousted French traders from India. British forces seized French Senegal in West Africa, the French sugar islands of Martinique and Guadeloupe, and the Spanish colonies of Cuba and the Philippine Islands. The Treaty of Paris of 1763 confirmed this triumph. It granted Britain sovereignty over half the continent of North America, including French Canada, all French territory east of the Mississippi River, and Spanish Florida. The French empire in North America was reduced to a handful of sugar islands in the West Indies and two rocky islands off the coast of Newfoundland.

Britain's victory alarmed Indian peoples from New York to Michigan, who feared an influx of Anglo-American settlers. Hoping that the French would return as a counterweight to British power, the Ottawa chief Pontiac declared, "I am French, and I want to die French." Neolin, a Delaware prophet, went further; he taught that the suffering of the Indian peoples stemmed from their dependence on the Europeans' goods, guns, and rum and called for the expulsion of all Europeans. Inspired by Neolin's vision and his own anti-British sentiments, in 1763 Pontiac led a group of loosely confederated tribes in a major uprising known as "Pontiac's rebellion." The Indian force seized nearly every British garrison west of Fort Niagara, besieged the fort at Detroit, and killed or captured over 2,000 frontier settlers. But the Indian alliance gradually weakened, and British military expeditions defeated the Delawares near Fort Pitt and broke the siege of Detroit. In the peace settlement, Pontiac and his allies accepted the British as their new political "fathers." In return, the British established the Proclamation Line of 1763 that closed the trans-Appalachian west to Anglo-American settlement.

British Economic Growth and the Consumer Revolution

Britain owed its military and diplomatic success to its unprecedented economic resources. Since 1700, when it had wrested control of many oceanic trade routes from the Dutch, Britain had been the dominant commercial power in the Atlantic and Indian Oceans. By 1750 it had also become the first country to use new manufacturing technology and work discipline. This combination of commerce and industry would soon make Britain the most powerful nation in the world.

Pipe of Peace

In 1760 the Ottawa chief Pontiac welcomed British troops to his territory, offering a pipe of peace to their commander, Major Robert Rogers. Three years later, Pontiac led a coordinated uprising against British troops, traders, and settlers, accusing them of cheating Native American peoples of their furs and lands. Library of Congress.

Mechanical power was a key ingredient of Britain's Industrial Revolution. British artisans designed and built mills and engines that efficiently used water and steam to power a wide array of other machines: lathes for shaping wood, jennies and looms for spinning and weaving textiles, and hammers for forging iron. The new power-driven machinery produced woolen and linen textiles, iron tools, furniture, and chinaware in greater quantities than traditional manufacturing methods— and at lower cost. Moreover, the entrepreneurs who ran the new workshops drove their employees hard, forcing them to keep pace with the machines and work long hours. To market the abundant products of these factories, English and Scottish merchants extended a full year's credit to colonial shopkeepers instead of the traditional six months. Americans were soon purchasing 20 percent of all British exports.

To pay for these goods, the colonists increased their exports of tobacco, rice, indigo, and wheat. In Virginia, farmers moved into the Piedmont, a region of plains and rolling hills just inland from the Tidewater counties. Using credit advanced by Scottish merchants, planters bought land, slaves, and equipment. The merchants took the planters' tobacco in payment and exported it to expanding markets in France and central Europe. In South Carolina planters supported their luxurious lifestyle by using British government subsidies to develop indigo plantations. By the 1760s they were exporting large quantities of the deep blue dye to English textile factories as well as selling 65 million pounds of rice a year to Holland and southern Europe. Simultaneously, New York, Pennsylvania, Maryland, and Virginia became the breadbasket of the Atlantic world by supplying Europe's exploding population with wheat at ever-increasing prices. In Philadelphia wheat prices jumped almost 50 percent between 1740 and 1765.

Americans used the profits of this trade to buy English manufactures in a "consumer revolution" that raised their standard of living. However, this first American spending binge, like most subsequent splurges, landed many consumers in debt. Even during the boom years of the 1750s, exports paid for only 80 percent of the imported British goods. The remaining 20 percent—millions of pounds—was financed from Britain by the extension of mercantile credit and by Pitt's military expenditures. When the end of military subsidies prompted an economic recession, colonial merchants looked anxiously at their overstocked warehouses and feared bankruptcy. "I think we have a gloomy prospect before us," a Philadelphia trader noted in 1765, "as there are of late some Persons failed, who were in no way suspected." The increase in transatlantic trade had raised living standards but also made Americans more dependent on overseas credit and international economic conditions.

The Struggle for Land in the East

In good times and bad, the colonial population continued to grow, intensifying the demand for arable land. The families who founded the town of Kent, Connecticut, in 1738 were descendants of the first settlers; like earlier generations, they had moved westward to establish new farms. Now they lived at the western boundary of the colony. To provide for the next generation, many Kent families joined to form the Susquehanna Company, a land-speculating venture created in 1749. Hoping to settle the Wyoming Valley in present-day northeastern Pennsylvania, the company asked the Connecticut legislature to assert its jurisdiction over that region on the basis of Connecticut's "sea-to-sea" royal charter of 1662. However, King Charles II had also granted the Wyoming Valley to William Penn, and the Penn family had issued its own land grants in the region. By the late 1750s settlers from the two colonies were asserting their claims by burning down their rivals' houses and barns.

Simultaneously, three distinct but related land disputes broke out in the Hudson River Valley. Wappinger Indians, Massachusetts migrants, and Dutch tenant farmers asserted ownership rights on lands long claimed by the Van Rensselaer, Livingston, and other manorial families. When the manorial lords turned to the legal system to uphold their claims, Dutch and English farmers in Westchester, Dutchess, and Albany Counties used mob violence to close the courts. At the behest of the royal governor, General Thomas Gage and two British regiments joined local sheriffs and manorial bailiffs to suppress the Dutch tenants, intimidate the Wappinger Indians, and evict the Massachusetts squatters.

Other land disputes erupted in New Jersey and the southern colonies, where resident landowners and English aristocrats successfully asserted legal claims based on long-dormant seventeenth-century charters. One court decision upheld the right of Lord Granville, an heir of one of the Carolina proprietors of 1660, to collect an annual tax on land in North Carolina; another decision awarded ownership of the entire northern neck of Virginia (along the Potomac River) to Lord Fairfax.

This revival of proprietary power stemmed from an expanding demand for land (and its increasing value) that prompted the landed gentry to reassert long-dormant claims. It also reflected the maturity of the colonial courts, which now had the authority to uphold many of these claims. These developments underscored the increasing resemblance between rural society in Europe and America. High-quality land on the Atlantic coastal plain was getting more expensive, and English aristocrats, manorial landlords, and wealthy speculators had control of much of it. Tenants and even yeomen farmers feared they soon might be reduced to the status of European peasants and looked westward for cheap freehold land near the Appalachian Mountains.

Western Uprisings and Regulator Movements

As farmers moved westward, they sparked new disputes over Indian policy, political representation, and debts. During the war with France, Delaware and Shawnee warriors had attacked frontier farms throughout central and western Pennsylvania, destroying property and killing and capturing hundreds of residents. Subsequently, Scots-Irish settlers demanded military action to expel all Indians, but Quaker leaders refused. In 1763 the Scots-Irish Paxton Boys took matters into their own hands and massacred twenty members of the peaceful Conestoga tribe. When Governor John Penn tried to bring the murderers to justice, about 250 armed Scots-Irish advanced on Philadelphia. Benjamin Franklin intercepted the angry mob at Lancaster and arranged a truce, narrowly averting a pitched battle with the militia. Prosecution of the Paxton Boys failed for lack of witnesses and the Scots-Irish dropped their demands, but the episode left a legacy of racial hatred and political resentment (Map 4.4).

Violence also broke out in the backcountry of South Carolina, where land-hungry Scottish and Anglo-American settlers clashed repeatedly with Cherokees during the war with France. When the war ended in 1763, a group of landowning vigilantes, the Regulators, tried to suppress outlaw bands of whites that were stealing cattle and other

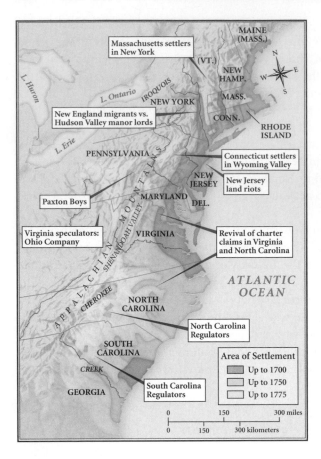

MAP 4.4 Westward Expansion and Land Conflicts, 1750–1775

Between 1750 and 1775 the mainland population doubled— from 1.2 million to 2.5 million— and spurred both westward migration and legal battles over land, which had become increasingly valuable. Violence broke out in eastern areas, as tenant farmers and smallholders contested landlord titles, and also in the backcountry, where migrating settlers fought with Indians, rival claimants, and the officials of eastern-dominated governments.

property (see American Voices, "Social Chaos on the Carolina Frontier," p. 127). The Regulators also wanted greater political rights and demanded that the eastern-controlled government provide their region with more courts, fairer taxes, and greater representation in the provincial assembly. Fearing slave revolts, the lowland rice planters who ran the South Carolina government chose to compromise with the Regulators rather than to fight them. In 1767 the assembly created locally controlled courts in the western counties and reduced the fees for legal documents. However, it refused to reapportion the assembly or lower western taxes. Like the Paxton Boys in Pennsylvania, the South Carolina Regulators attracted attention to western needs but ultimately failed to wrest power from the eastern elite.

In 1766 a more radical Regulator movement arose in the backcountry of North Carolina. The recession of the early 1760s caused a sharp fall in tobacco prices, and many farmers could not pay their debts. When creditors filed lawsuits, judges directed sheriffs to seize the indebted farmers' property and sell it to pay creditors and court costs. Backcountry farmers—including many German migrants—denounced the merchants' lawsuits, both because they generated high fees for lawyers and court

AMERICAN VOICES

~

Social Chaos on the Carolina Frontier

CHARLES WOODMASON

*T*o Charles Woodmason, a minister of the Church of England (the Anglican or Episcopal Church), the Carolina backcountry was a disorderly place. His journal contains vivid portraits of poor farming villages filled with immoral and violence-prone people—a chaotic mixture of ethnic and religious groups who had little respect for established authority. But a careful reading of his entries reveals a great deal of social and political cohesion, thanks to the influence of dissenting Protestant congregations led by affluent planters and politically astute lawyers.

[February 1767] I had appointed a [Church of England] Congregation to meet me at the Head of Hanging Rock Creek—Where I arriv'd on Tuesday Evening—Found the Houses filled with debauch'd licentious fellows, and Scot Presbyterians who had hir'd these lawless Ruffians to insult me, which they did with Impunity—Telling me, they wanted no D——d Black Gown Sons of Bitches among them—and threatening to lay me behind the Fire, which they assuredly would have done had not some travellers alighted very opportunely, and taken me under Protection—These Men sat up with, and guarded me all the Night. . . .

[June 1768] You must understand that all (or greatest Part) of this Part of the Province where I am, has been settled within these 5 years by Irish Presbyterians from Belfast, or Pennsylvania and they imagin'd that they could secure this large Tract of fine country to themselves and their Sect. Hereon, they built Meeting Houses, and got Pastors from Ireland, and Scotland. But with these there has also a Great Number of New Lights and Independants come here from New England, and many Baptists

To preserve their People from falling off to the Church established [Woodmason's Episcopal Church], . . . the [Presbyterian] Synods of Pensylvania and New England send out a Sett of Rambling fellows Yearly—who do no Good to the People, no Service to Religion—but turning of their Brains and picking up their Pockets of ev'ry Pistreen the Poor Wretches have. . . .

These Sects are eternally jarring among themselves—The Presbyterians hate the Baptists far more than they do the Episcopalians, and so of the Rest—but (as in England) they will unite altogether in a body to distress or injure the Church established. . . . Hence it is, that when any Bills have been presented to the Legislature to promote the Interests of Religion, these Sectaries have found Means to have them overruled, for the leading men of the House being all Lawyers, those People know how to grease Wheels as make them turn.

If Numbers were to be counted here, the Church People would have the Majority—but in Point of Interest, I judge that the Dissenters possess most Money—and thereby they can give a Bias to things at Pleasure.

SOURCE: *Blacks Who Stole Themselves: Advertisements for Runaways in the Pennsylvania Gazette 1728–1790* by Billy G. Smith and Richard Wojtwicz. Copyright © 1989 by Billy G. Smith. Reprinted by permission of the University of Pennsylvania Press.

OF TWELVE REGULATORS CONDEMNED AT
HILLSBORO, THE FOLLOWING SIX WERE EXECUTED
BY THE BRITISH GOVERNOR: JAMES PUGH, ROBERT
MATEAR, BENJAMIN MERRILL, CAPTAIN MESSER,
AND TWO OTHERS, WHOSE NAMES ARE NOW
UNKNOWN. "OUR BLOOD WILL BE AS GOOD SEED IN
GOOD GROUND THAT WILL SOON PRODUCE ONE
HUNDRED FOLD" — JAMES PUGH, UNDER THE GALLOWS
AT HILLSBORO, N.C., JUNE 19TH 1771.

History and Memory

This visually striking highway marker, erected by a government agency in North Carolina, offers an official—and only partially correct—view of the past. Rather than assail the Regulators as extra-legal vigilantes or outright lawbreakers (as many observers did at the time), the marker shrouds them in patriotism, as innocent victims of a vengeful British governor.

Alamance Battlefield, photo by Mike Mayse.

officials and because they violated rural customs, which allowed loans to remain un-paid for years.

To save their farms from grasping creditors and tax-hungry officials, North Carolina debtors joined together in a Regulator movement. Disciplined mobs of farmers intimidated judges, closed courts, and freed their comrades from jail. However, the Regulators also proposed a coherent set of reforms. They demanded legislation to lower legal fees and allow payment of taxes in the "produce of the country" rather than in cash. They also insisted on greater legislative representation and a fairer tax system, proposing that each person be taxed "in proportion to the profits arising from his estate." But it was all to no avail. In May 1771 royal governor William Tryon decided to suppress the Regulators. Mobilizing British troops and the eastern militia, Tryon defeated a large Regulator force at the Alamance River. When the fighting ended, thirty men lay dead and Tryon summarily executed seven insurgent leaders. Not since Leisler's regime in New York in 1689 (see Chapter 3) had a domestic political conflict caused so much bloodshed.

In 1771 as in 1689, colonial conflicts became intertwined with imperial politics. In Connecticut, the Reverend Ezra Stiles defended the North Carolina Regulators. "What shall an injured & oppressed people do," he asked, when faced with "Oppression and tyranny (under the name of Government)?" Stiles's remarks reflected growing resistance to British imperial control. America was still a dependent society closely tied to Britain by trade, culture, and politics, but it was also an increasingly complex society with the potential for an independent existence. British policies would determine the direction the maturing colonies would take.

T I M E L I N E

1700–1714	New Hudson River manors created	1743	Benjamin Franklin founds the American Philosophical Society
1710s–1730s	Enlightenment ideas spread from Europe to America Deists rely on "natural reason" to define a moral code	1749	Virginia speculators create the Ohio Company Connecticut farmers form the Susquehanna Company
1720s	Germans and Scots-Irish settle in the Middle Atlantic colonies Theodore Jacob Frelinghuysen preaches Pietism to German migrants	1750s	Industrial Revolution begins in England Consumer revolution increases American imports and debt
1730s	William and Gilbert Tennent lead Presbyterian revivals among Scots-Irish Jonathan Edwards preaches in New England	1754	French and Indian War begins Meeting of Iroquois and Americans at Albany; Plan of Union
1739	George Whitefield sparks the Great Awakening	1756	Britain begins the Great War for Empire
1740s–1760s	Growing shortage of farmland in New England Religious and ethnic pluralism in the Middle Atlantic colonies Rising grain and tobacco prices Increasing social inequality in rural areas	1759	Britain captures Quebec
		1760s	Land conflict along the border between New York and New England Regulator movements in the Carolinas suppress outlaw bands and seek power Baptist revivals in Virginia
1740s	Great Awakening sparks conflict between Old Lights and New Lights Colleges established by religious denominations	1763	Pontiac's uprising leads to the Proclamation of 1763 Treaty of Paris ends the Great War for Empire Scots-Irish Paxton Boys massacre Indians in Pennsylvania

For Further Exploration

The social history of eighteenth-century America comes alive in studies of individual lives. In *Good Wives: Image and Reality in the Lives of Women in Northern New England, 1650–1750* (1982), Laurel Thatcher Ulrich paints a vivid picture of the everyday lives of women as they assumed a variety of roles. Benjamin Franklin's *Autobiography* (available in many editions) provides an entertaining look at the bustling city of Philadelphia and demonstrates Franklin's Enlightenment sensibility and his pursuit of wealth and influence. A less successful quest for self-betterment is the subject of another autobiography, *The Infortunate: The Voyage and Adventures of William Moraley, an Indentured Servant*, edited by Susan E. Klepp and Billy G. Smith (1992). Harry S. Stout's *The Divine Dramatist: George Whitefield and the Rise of Modern Evangelicalism* (1991) shows how the charismatic preacher's flair for theatrics and self-promotion enabled him to preach effectively and fulfill his sense of duty to God.

Other well-written social histories are Rhys Isaac, *The Transformation of Virginia, 1740–1790* (1982); Patricia U. Bonomi, *A Factious People: Politics and Society in Colonial New York* (1971); and Fred Anderson, *A People's Army: Massachusetts Soldiers and Society in the Seven Years' War* (1984).

For insight into the day-to-day lives of women, see the PBS video *A Midwife's Tale* (1.5 hours), which tells the story of Martha Ballard, who lived at the end of the eighteenth century; additional materials on Ballard's experiences are available at <http://www.pbs.org/amex/midwife> and <http://www.DoHistory.org>. On day-to-day economic life, see the Colonial Currency and Colonial Coin site at <http://www.coins.nd.edu/ColCurrency/index.html>, which contains detailed essays as well as pictures of colonial money. Franklin's life and times are presented at The Electric Franklin, <http://www.ushistory.org/franklin/index.htm>. Jonathan Edwards On-Line, at <http://www.JonathanEdwards.com/>, provides access to the writings of the great philosopher and preacher, but note that this site uses Edwards's arguments to advance one side of a present-day theological debate. For a rich collection of documents and visual materials on the lives of migrant German sectarians, see the Bethlehem Digital History Project at <http://bdhp.moravian.edu/>.

For definitions of key terms boldfaced in this chapter, see the glossary at the end of the book.

To assess your mastery of the material covered in this chapter, see the Online Study Guide at **bedfordstmartins.com/henrettaconcise**.

For map resources and primary documents, see **bedfordstmartins.com/henrettaconcise**.

Chapter 5

TOWARD INDEPENDENCE: YEARS OF DECISION
1763–1775

The said [Stamp] act is contrary to the rights of mankind, and
subversive of the English Constitution.

TOWN MEETING OF LEICESTER, MASSACHUSETTS, 1765

A s the Great War for Empire ended in 1763, Seth Metcalf joined many
other American colonists celebrating the triumph of British arms. A Massachusetts
soldier during the war, Metcalf thanked "the Great Goodness of God" for the
"General Peace" that was so "percularly Advantageous to the English Nation." A
mere two years later, Metcalf saw God's dialogue with his chosen Puritan people
very differently. "God is angry with us of this land," the pious Puritan wrote in his
journal, "and is now Smiting [us] with his Rod Especially by the hands of our
[British] Rulers."

The rapid disintegration of the bonds uniting Britain and America—an event
that Metcalf could explain only in terms of Divine Providence—mystified many
Americans. How had it happened, the president of King's College in New York asked
in 1775, that such a "happily situated" people had armed themselves and were ready
to "hazard their Fortunes, their Lives, and their Souls, in a Rebellion"? Unlike other
colonial peoples of the time, white Americans lived in a prosperous society with a
strong tradition of self-government. They had little to gain and much to lose by re-
belling.

Or so it seemed in 1765, before the British government attempted to reform the
imperial system. These long overdue administrative reforms prompted a violent response, which began a downward spiral of ideological debate and political conflict.
"This year Came an act from England Called the Stamp Act . . . ," Metcalf reflected,
"which is thought will be very oppressive to the Inhabitants of North America."
"But," he added, "Mobbs keep it back." The course of events that ended finally in
civil war was far from inevitable. Careful statecraft and political compromise could
have saved the empire. Instead, inflexible responses by British ministers and passionate agitation by Patriot leaders brought about its demise.

The Imperial Reformers, 1763–1765

The Great War for Empire left a mixed legacy. Britain had driven the French out of Canada and now dominated eastern North America. But the cost was high: a mountain of debt that prompted the British ministry to impose new taxes on its American possessions. More fundamentally, the war spurred Parliament to redefine the character of the empire. The policy of salutary neglect, with its emphasis on trade and self-government, gave way to an emphasis on imperial power and direct Parliamentary rule.

The Legacy of War

The war changed the dimensions of the colonial relationship. During the fighting, colonial leaders and British generals disagreed sharply on military strategy. Moreover, the presence of 25,000 British troops revealed sharp cultural differences. The arrogance of British officers and their demands for deference shocked many Americans, including a Massachusetts militiaman who declared that British soldiers "are but little better than slaves to their officers." The disdain was mutual. British general James Wolfe complained that colonial troops were drawn from the dregs of society and that "there was no depending on them in action."

The war also exposed the weak authority of British royal governors. In theory, governors had extensive political powers, including command of the provincial militia; in reality, they had to share power with the colonial assemblies, which outraged British officials. In Massachusetts, complained the Board of Trade, "almost every act of executive and legislative power is ordered and directed by votes and resolves of the General Court." To enhance royal authority, British officials ordered a strict enforcement of the Navigation Acts. Before the war colonial merchants routinely bribed customs officials to avoid the duties imposed by the Molasses Act of 1733. To curb such corruption, in 1762 Parliament passed the Revenue Act, which tightened up the customs service. In addition, the ministry instructed the Royal Navy to seize vessels that were carrying goods between the mainland colonies and the French islands. It was absurd, declared an outraged British politician, that French armies which were attempting "to Destroy one English province, are actually supported by Bread raised in another."

Britain's victory over France provoked a fundamental shift in imperial military policy. In 1763 the ministry decided to deploy a peacetime army of ten thousand men in North America. The decision had many causes. King George III (r. 1760–1820) wanted patronage positions for his military friends, so he needed a large army, someplace to station it, and somebody to pay for it. His ministers worried about newly acquired colonies; they feared a rebellion by the 60,000 French residents of Canada or a Spanish invasion of Florida. Moreover, Pontiac's rebellion had nearly overwhelmed Britain's frontier forts and underscored the need for military garrisons to restrain the Indian peoples and to deter land-hungry whites from settling west of the Proclamation Line of 1763. Finally, some British politicians worried about the loyalty of the American settlers now that they no longer needed

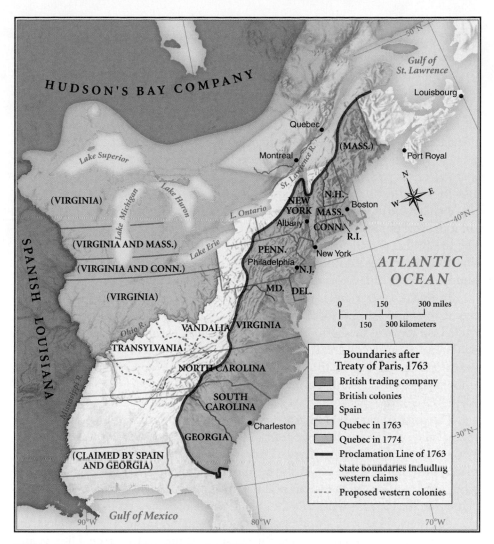

MAP 5.1 Britain's American Empire in 1763

Following the Great War for Empire and the Treaty of Paris of 1763, Britain held a dominant position in the West Indies and controlled all of eastern North America. British ministers dispatched troops to the conquered colonies of Florida and Quebec and, with the Proclamation Line of 1763, tried to prevent Anglo-American settlement west of the Appalachian Mountains.

protection from the French in Canada. As William Knox, a treasury official who had once served the crown in Georgia, put it: "The main purpose of Stationing a large Body of Troops in America is to secure the Dependence of the Colonys on Great Britain." By stationing an army in America, the British ministry was indicating its willingness to use force—whether against rebellious Indians, conquered Frenchmen, or dissident American colonists (Map 5.1).

Another significant result of the war was the growth of Britain's national debt, which soared from £75 million in 1754 to £133 million in 1763. The interest charges on the war debt now consumed 60 percent of the national budget and forced cutbacks in other government expenditures. To restore fiscal stability, Lord Bute, who became prime minister in 1760, needed to raise taxes. However, the Treasury Department opposed any increase in the British land tax, which was already at an all-time high and was paid by members of the propertied classes, who had great influence in Parliament. Therefore, Bute taxed the underrepresented poor and middling classes by imposing higher import duties on tobacco and sugar, which manufacturers passed on to consumers in the form of higher prices. The ministry also increased excise levies—essentially sales taxes—on goods such as salt, beer, and distilled spirits, once again passing on the costs of the war to the king's ordinary subjects. Left unresolved was the question of taxing the American colonists, who, like the British poor, had little influence in Parliament. However, ministers knew that free Americans contributed only about five shillings a year to the imperial budget, while British taxpayers paid nearly five times as much.

To collect existing taxes and duties, the British government doubled the size of the tax bureaucracy and increased its powers. Customs agents and informers patrolled the coasts of southern Britain, arresting smugglers and seizing tons of French wines and Flemish textiles. Convicted smugglers faced heavy penalties, including death or "transportation" to America as indentured servants. Despite protests by colonial assemblies, nearly fifty thousand English criminals had already been banished to America.

The price of empire had turned out to be debt and a more intrusive government, which confirmed the worst fears of the British opposition parties, the Radical Whigs and Country Party landlords. Both groups argued that the huge war debt had placed the treasury at the mercy of the "monied interest," the banks and financiers who were reaping millions of pounds in interest from government bonds. Moreover, the expansion of the tax bureaucracy had created thousands of patronage positions filled with "worthless pensioners and placemen." To reverse the growth of government power—and the consequent threats to personal liberty and property rights—reformers in Britain demanded that Parliament be made more representative of the property-owning classes. The Radical Whig John Wilkes called for an end to **rotten boroughs**—tiny districts whose voters were controlled by wealthy aristocrats and merchants. In domestic affairs as in colonial policy, the war had transformed British political life.

The Sugar Act and Colonial Rights

The active exercise of government power was particularly apparent in American affairs, thanks to the reforms implemented by a new generation of British officials. George Grenville, who became prime minister in 1763, launched the first initiatives. First Grenville won Parliamentary approval of the Currency Act of 1764, which

George Grenville, Architect of the Stamp Act

As prime minister from 1764 to 1766, Grenville assumed leadership of the movement for imperial reform and taxation. This portrait of 1763 suggests Grenville's energy and ambition. As events were to show, the new minister was determined to reform the imperial system and ensure that the colonists shared the cost of the empire. The Earl of Halifax, Garrowby, Yorkshire.

protected British merchants by banning the colonies from using paper money (which was often worth less than its face value) as legal tender. Now American merchants, planters, and ordinary farmers would have to pay their debts in gold or silver coin, which was always in short supply.

Then Grenville proposed a new Navigation Act, the Sugar Act of 1764, to replace the widely evaded Molasses Act of 1733. The new legislation was well designed. Treasury officials, who understood the pattern of colonial trade, convinced Grenville that the mainland settlers had to sell some of their wheat, fish, and lumber in the French islands. Without the molasses, sugar, and bills of exchange derived from those sales, the colonists would lack the funds to buy British manufactured goods. Grenville consequently resisted demands from British sugar planters for a duty of 6 pence per gallon, which would completely cut off colonial imports of

French molasses. Instead, he settled on a smaller duty of 3 pence per gallon, which would allow molasses from the British islands to compete with the cheaper French product.

This carefully crafted policy garnered little support in America because it threatened American merchants and distillers. Many New England merchants, such as John Hancock of Boston, had made their fortunes by smuggling French molasses and their profits would be cut severely if the new regulations were enforced. These merchants and New England distillers, who feared a rise in the price of molasses, claimed publicly that the Sugar Act would wipe out trade with the French islands. Privately, they vowed to evade the duty by smuggling or by bribing officials.

More important, the political allies of the merchants raised constitutional objections to the new legislation. The speaker of the Massachusetts House of Representatives argued that the duties constituted a tax, making the Sugar Act "contrary to a fundamental Principall of our Constitution: That all Taxes ought to originate with the people." The Sugar Act raised other constitutional issues as well. Merchants prosecuted under the act would be tried by **vice-admiralty courts**—maritime tribunals composed only of a British-appointed judge—and not by a friendly, local common-law jury. American legislatures had long opposed vice-admiralty courts and had found ways to curtail their legal powers so that merchants accused of violating the Navigation Acts were tried in common-law courts. The Sugar Act closed this legal loophole by extending the jurisdiction of vice-admiralty courts to all customs offenses.

The new powers given to the vice-admiralty courts revived old American fears. The influential Virginia planter Richard Bland reminded his fellow settlers that the colonies had long been subject to the Navigation Acts, which restricted their manufactures and commerce. But, he protested, the colonists "were not sent out to be the Slaves but to be the Equals of those that remained behind." John Adams, a young Massachusetts lawyer who was defending merchant John Hancock on a charge of smuggling, similarly condemned the new vice-admiralty courts, saying that they "degrade every American . . . below the rank of an Englishman."

While the logic of these arguments for equal treatment was compelling, some of the facts were wrong. The Navigation Acts certainly discriminated against the colonists in order to assist British-based merchants and manufacturers. However, the new vice-admiralty legislation was not discriminatory; similar rules had long been in force in Britain. The real issue was the new spirit of imperial reform and the growing administrative power of the British state. Having lived for decades under a policy of salutary neglect, Americans knew immediately that the new British policies challenged existing constitutional practices and understandings. As a committee of the Massachusetts House of Representatives put it, the Sugar Act and other British edicts "have a tendency to deprive the colonies of some of their most essential Rights as British subjects."

For their part, British officials insisted on the supremacy of Parliamentary laws and denied that the colonists enjoyed special privileges or even the traditional legal rights of Englishmen. When royal governor Francis Bernard heard that the Massachusetts House had objected to the Sugar Act, claiming no taxation without representation, he asserted that Americans did not have that constitutional right. "The rule that a British subject shall not be bound by laws or liable to taxes, but what he has consented to by his representatives," Bernard argued, "must be confined to the inhabitants of Great Britain only." In the eyes of most imperial officials and British reformers, the Americans were second-class subjects of the king, their rights limited by the Navigation Acts and the interests of the British state, as determined by Parliament.

An Open Challenge: The Stamp Act

Taxation sparked the first great imperial crisis. Grenville's plan was to follow the Sugar Act of 1764 with a stamp act in 1765. This new levy would cover part of the cost of keeping British troops in America—some £200,000 per year (about $50 million today). The tax would require stamps (or printed markings) on all court documents, land titles, contracts, playing cards, newspapers, and other printed items. A similar stamp tax in England was yielding £290,000 a year; Grenville hoped the American levy would raise at least £60,000. The prime minister knew that some Americans would object to the tax on constitutional grounds, so in 1764 he asked explicitly whether any member of the House of Commons doubted "the power and sovereignty of Parliament over every part of the British dominions, for the purpose of raising or collecting any tax." No one rose to object.

Confident of Parliament's support, Grenville vowed to impose a stamp tax unless the colonists would lay taxes for their own defense. The London merchants who served as agents and lobbyists for the colonial legislatures immediately protested that the Americans lacked a continent-wide body that could decide matters of taxation and defense. Representatives from the various colonies had met together officially only once, at the Albany Congress of 1754, and not a single assembly had accepted that body's proposals. Benjamin Franklin, who was in Britain as the agent of the Pennsylvania assembly, proposed another solution to Grenville's challenge: American representation in Parliament. "If you chuse to tax us," he suggested, "give us Members in your Legislature, and let us be one People."

With the exception of William Pitt, British politicians rejected Franklin's idea as too radical. They argued that the colonists were already **"virtually" represented** in Parliament by the members who were transatlantic merchants and West Indian sugar planters. Colonial leaders were equally skeptical. Americans were "situate at a great Distance from their Mother Country," the Connecticut assembly declared, and therefore "cannot participate in the general Legislature of the Nation." Influential Philadelphia merchants, perceiving that a handful of mainland delegates would be powerless in Parliament, warned Franklin "to beware of any measure that might extend to us seats in the Commons."

The way was clear for Grenville to introduce the Stamp Act. His goal was not only to raise revenue but also to assert a constitutional principle: "the Right of Parliament to lay an internal Tax upon the Colonies," as his chief assistant declared. The ministry's plan worked smoothly. The House of Commons ignored the American petitions opposing the act and passed the new legislation by an over-whelming vote of 205 to 49. At the request of General Thomas Gage, the British mil-itary commander in America, Parliament also passed the Quartering Act of 1765 directing colonial governments to provide barracks and food for the British troops. Finally, Parliament approved Grenville's proposal that violations of the Stamp Act be tried in vice-admiralty courts.

The design was complete. Using the doctrine of Parliamentary supremacy, Grenville had begun to fashion a genuinely imperial administrative system in America. As in Ireland, it would be run by British officials with little regard for the local assemblies. He thus provoked a constitutional confrontation not only on the specific issues of taxation, jury trials, and quartering of the military but also on the fundamental question of representative self-government.

The Dynamics of Rebellion, 1765–1766

Grenville had thrown down the gauntlet to the Americans. Although the colonists had often been forced to deal with unpopular laws and arrogant governors, they had faced an all-out attack on their institutions only once—in 1686 when James II had arbitrarily imposed the Dominion of New England. Now the danger was even greater, because the new reforms were backed not only by the king but also by the Parliament. However, the Patriots—as the defenders of American rights came to be called—met Grenville's challenge by organizing protests, encouraging riots, and ar-ticulating an ideology of resistance.

Politicians Protest and the Crowd Rebels

Addressing the Virginia House of Burgesses in May 1765, Patrick Henry attacked King George III for supporting Grenville's new legislation. Indeed, by comparing George III to the tyrannical Charles I, who had sparked the Puritan Revolution of the 1640s, Henry seemed to call for a new republican revolution. Although Henry's remarks bordered on treason and dismayed most Burgesses, they condemned the Stamp Act as "a manifest Tendency to Destroy American freedom." In Mas-sachusetts, James Otis, another republican-minded firebrand, persuaded the House of Representatives to call a meeting of all the colonies "to implore Relief" from the act.

Nine colonial assemblies sent delegates to the Stamp Act Congress, which met in New York City in October 1765. The Congress issued a set of Resolves challeng-ing the constitutionality of the Stamp and Sugar Acts and declaring that only the

The Intensity of Patrick Henry

This portrait, painted in 1795 when Henry was in his sixties, captures his lifelong seriousness and intensity. As an orator, Henry drew on evangelical Protestantism to create a new mode of political oratory. "His figures of speech . . . were often borrowed from the Scriptures," a contemporary noted, and the content of his speeches mirrored "the earnestness depicted in his own features." Mead Art Museum, Amherst College.

colonists' elected representatives could tax them. The Resolves also protested against the loss of American "rights and liberties," especially trial by jury. However, most delegates were moderate men who sought compromise, not confrontation. They concluded the Resolves by assuring Parliament that Americans "glory in being subjects of the best of Kings" and humbly petitioning for repeal of the Stamp Act. Other influential Americans advocated nonviolent resistance through a boycott of British goods.

Popular resentment was not so easily contained. When the law went into effect on November 1, disciplined mobs acted immediately. Led by men who called themselves the **Sons of Liberty**, the mobs demanded the resignation of stamp tax collectors, most of whom were native-born colonists. In Boston, the Sons of Liberty made an effigy of the collector Andrew Oliver, which they beheaded and burned; then they destroyed Oliver's new brick warehouse. Two weeks later Bostonians attacked the house of Lieutenant Governor Thomas Hutchinson, a defender of social privilege and imperial authority, breaking the furniture, looting the wine cellar, and burning the library.

The men who led the mobs on the streets were usually middling artisans and minor merchants. Behind them stood major merchants, such as John Hancock, and Patriot lawyers, such as Patrick Henry. "Spent the evening with the Sons of Liberty," lawyer John Adams wrote in his diary, "John Smith, the brazier [metalworker], Thomas Crafts, the painter, Edes, the printer, Stephen Cleverly, the brazier; Chase,

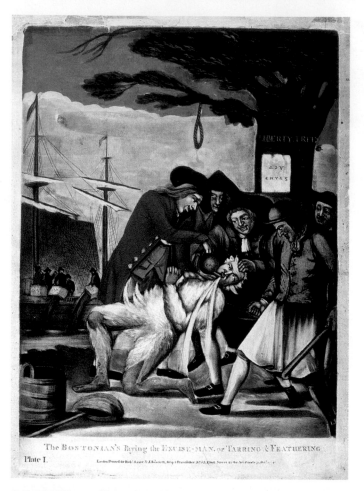

The BOSTONIAN'S Paying the EXCISE-MAN, or TARRING & FEATHERING.
Plate I.   London Printed for Rob.'t Sayer & J.Bennett, Map & Printseller N°53, Fleet Street, as the Act directs 31. oct.' 1774.

A British View of American Mobs

This satiric view of the Sons of Liberty attacks their brutal treatment of John Malcolm, the commissioner of customs in Boston, who was threatened with death (note the noose hanging from the tree) and then tarred and feathered and forced to drink huge quantities of tea. Note the men in the background, disregarding property rights by pouring tea into Boston Harbor. The presence of a "Liberty Tree" implicitly poses the question: Does liberty mean anarchy?

Courtesy, John Carter Brown Library at Brown University.

the distiller; [and] Joseph Field, Master of a vessel." These men knew each other through their work or as drinking buddies at the many taverns that dotted the streets of the major port cities and soon became centers of Patriot agitation.

However, resistance to the Stamp Act spread far beyond the port cities. In nearly every colony, crowds of angry people—the "rabble," as their detractors called them—intimidated royal officials. Near Wethersfield, Connecticut, five hundred farmers and artisans held tax collector Jared Ingersoll captive until he resigned his office. This was "the Cause of the People," shouted one rioter. In New York nearly three thousand shopkeepers, artisans, laborers, and seamen marched through the streets, breaking street lamps and windows and crying "Liberty!"

Such plebeian crowd actions were a fact of life in both Britain and America. Governments tolerated the mobs because, short of calling out the militia, they had no means to stop them and because they usually did little damage. Every November 5, Protestant mobs on both sides of the Atlantic burned effigies of the pope to celebrate Guy Fawkes Day, which commemorated the failure in 1605 of a plot by Fawkes and other English Catholics to blow up the Houses of Parliament. Likewise, colonial mobs regularly destroyed houses used as brothels and rioted to protest the impressment of merchant seamen by the Royal Navy.

If rioting was traditional, its political goals were new. In New York City the leaders of the Sons of Liberty were Radical Whigs who feared that reform of the imperial system would undermine political liberty. These men, minor merchants such as Isaac Sears and Alexander McDougall, tried to focus the raw energy of the crowd on the new taxes. However, mob members had their own agendas and goals. Some well-established artisans and their journeymen joined the crowds because imports of low-priced British shoes and other manufactured goods threatened their livelihoods, and they feared the additional burden of a stamp tax. Unlike "the Common people of England," a well-traveled colonist observed, "the people of America . . . never would submit to be taxed that a few may be loaded with palaces and Pensions . . . , while they themselves cannot support themselves and their needy offspring with Bread."

The religious passions of the Great Awakening motivated other members of the crowd. As evangelical Protestants who led disciplined, hardworking lives, they resented the arrogance of British military officers and the corruption of royal bureaucrats. In New England, where many people lived into their 60s and memories lived even longer, some protesters looked back to the Puritan Revolution and revived the antimonarchical sentiments of their great-grandparents. A letter to a Boston newspaper carrying the name of "Oliver Cromwell," the English republican revolutionary of the 1640s, promised to save "all the Freeborn Sons of America." Finally, the mobs in all areas included apprentices, journeymen, day laborers, and unemployed sailors—young men seeking excitement who, when fortified by drink, were ready to resort to violence.

Throughout the colonies popular resistance nullified the Stamp Act. Fearing a massive assault on Fort George on Guy Fawkes Day (November 5, 1765), New York lieutenant governor Cadwallader Colden called on General Gage to use his small military force to protect the stamps. Gage refused. "Fire from the Fort might disperse the Mob, but it would not quell them," he told Colden, and the result would be "an Insurrection, the Commencement of Civil War." Frightened collectors gave up their stamps, and angry Americans coerced officials into accepting legal documents without them. This popular insurrection gave a democratic cast to the emerging American Patriot movement and extended it far beyond the ranks of elected officials who called the Stamp Act Congress and even those merchants and lawyers, like Adams, who had helped to organize the Sons of Liberty. "Nothing is wanting but your own Resolution," declared a New York rioter, "for great is the Authority and Power of the People."

Slow communication across the Atlantic meant that the ministry's response to the Stamp Act Congress and the Liberty mobs would not be known until the spring of 1766. But royal officials in America knew already that they had lost the popular support that had ensured the empire's stability for three generations. As the collector of the customs in Philadelphia lamented, "What can a Governor do without the assistance of the Governed?"

Ideological Roots of Resistance

The American resistance movement emerged first in the seaport cities because British policies directly affected urban residents. The Stamp Act taxed the newspapers sold by printers and the contracts and court documents used by merchants and lawyers; the Sugar Act raised the cost of molasses to distillers; and the flood of British manufactures threatened the livelihood of urban artisans. Consequently, the first protests focused narrowly on these economic and political grievances. An official in Rhode Island reported that most colonists deemed the interests of Britain and the colonies "almost altogether incompatible in a Commercial View." A pamphleteer focused on taxes and complained that the colonists were being compelled to give the British "our money, as oft and in what quantity they please to demand it." Other writers alleged that the British had violated specific "liberties and privileges" embodied in colonial charters.

Initially the resistance movement had no acknowledged leaders, no organization, and no clear goals. However, men trained as lawyers gradually took the lead, partly because merchants hired them to protect their goods from seizure by customs officials. The lawyers' professional values provided another motive; as practitioners of the **common law** they opposed extension of vice-admiralty courts and favored trial by juries. Composing pamphlets of remarkable political sophistication, Patriot lawyers and publicists provided the resistance movement with an intellectual rationale, a political agenda, and a visible cadre of leaders.

Patriot publicists drew on three intellectual traditions. The first was English common law—the centuries-old body of legal rules and procedures that protected the lives and property of the king's subjects. In 1761 the Boston lawyer James Otis invoked English legal precedent in the famous Writs of Assistance case; in that instance Otis disputed the legitimacy of a general search warrant permitting customs officials to inspect any person's property and possessions. Similarly, in demanding a jury trial for John Hancock, John Adams appealed to the jury-trial provision in the "29th Chap. of Magna Charta," an ancient English document that "has for many Centuries been esteemed by Englishmen, as one of the . . . firmest Bulwarks of their Liberties." Other lawyers protested when the ministry changed the terms of appointment for colonial judges from "during good behavior" to "at the pleasure" of the royal governor because this change undermined the independence of the judiciary.

A second major intellectual resource for educated Americans was the rationalist thought of the Enlightenment. Unlike American common-law attorneys, who invoked legal precedents to criticize British measures, the Virginia planter Thomas Jefferson invoked Enlightenment philosophers, such as David Hume and Francis Hutcheson, who questioned past practices and relied on reason to correct social ills. Jefferson and other Patriot authors also drew on the Enlightenment political philosopher John Locke, who argued that all individuals possessed certain "natural rights," such as life, liberty, and property, which government must protect. And they celebrated the French theorist Montesquieu, who praised institutional arrangements, such as the separation of powers among government departments, which prevented arbitrary rule.

The republican and Whig strands of the English political tradition provided a third ideological source for American Patriots. Puritan New England had long venerated the Commonwealth era—the brief period between 1649 and 1660 when England was a republic. After the Glorious Revolution of 1688, colonists in all regions praised the constitutional restrictions placed on the monarchy by English Whigs, such as the ban on royally imposed taxes. Later, educated Americans such as Samuel Adams of Boston applauded when Radical Whigs denounced political corruption. This republican and Radical Whig outlook made many Americans suspicious of royal officials. Joseph Warren, a physician and Patriot, reported that many Bostonians believed the Stamp Act was intended "to force the colonies into rebellion," after which the ministry would use "military power to reduce them to servitude" (see American Voices, "An American View of the Stamp Act," p. 144).

This suspicion-minded Radical Whig outlook—swiftly disseminated in newspapers and pamphlets—convinced many Americans of the evil intentions of the British ministry and helped to turn a series of impromptu riots and tax protests into a coherent political movement.

Parliament Compromises, 1766

In Britain, Parliament was in turmoil. Although George III had dismissed Grenville as prime minister, his supporters continued to demand reform. When Benjamin Franklin declared that Americans would "never" pay a stamp tax "unless compelled by force of arms," Grenville's hard-line supporters demanded the dispatch of British soldiers to uphold the constitutional supremacy of Parliament and maintain its status as one of the few powerful representative bodies in eighteenth-century Europe. "The British legislature," declared Chief Justice Sir James Mansfield, "has authority to bind every part and every subject, whether such subjects have a right to vote or not."

AMERICAN VOICES

An American View of the Stamp Act

SAMUEL ADAMS

*T*hanks to his education at Harvard College, distiller Samuel Adams had impressive intellectual and literary skills. In this private letter to an English friend, Adams undertakes,
in reasoned prose, to refute the arguments used by British ministers to defend the new measures of imperial taxation and control.

To John Smith
December 19, 1765

Your acquaintance with this country . . . makes you an able advocate on her behalf, at a time
when her friends have everything to fear for her. . . . The [British] nation, it seems, groaning
under the pressure of a very heavy debt, has thought it reasonable & just that the colonies
should bear a part; and over & above the tribute which they have been continually pouring into
her lap, in the course of their trade, she now demands an internal tax. The colonists complain
that this is both burdensome & unconstitutional. They allege, that while the nation has been
contracting this debt solely for her own interest, they have [been] subduing & settling an uncultivated wilderness, & thereby increasing her power & wealth at their own expense. . . .

But it is said that this tax is to discharge the colonies' proportion of expense in carrying
on the [recent] war in America, which was for their defense. To this it is said, that it does
by no means appear that the war in America was carried on solely for the defense of the
colonies; . . . there was evidently a view of making conquests, [thereby] . . . advancing her
dominion & glory. . . .

There are other things which perhaps were not considered when the nation determined
this to be a proportionate tax upon the colonies. . . . The [British] nation constantly regu-
lates their trade, & lays it under what restrictions she pleases. The duties upon the goods
imported from her & consumed here . . . amount to a very great sum. . . .

There is another consideration which makes the Stamp Act obnoxious to the people
here, & that is, that it totally annihilates, as they apprehend, their essential rights as
Englishmen. The first settlers . . . solemnly recognized their allegiance to their sovereign in
England, & the Crown graciously acknowledged them, granted them charter privileges, &
declared them & their heirs forever entitled to all the liberties & immunities of free &
natural born subjects of the realm. . . .

The question then is, what the rights of free subjects of Britain are? . . . It is sufficient for
the present purpose to say, that the main pillars of the British Constitution are the right of
representation & trial by juries, both of which the Colonists lose by this act. Their property
may be tried . . . in a court of Admiralty, where there is no jury. [As for representation], if the
colonists are free subjects of Britain, which no one denies, it should seem that the Parliament
cannot tax them consistent with the Constitution, because they are not represented. . . .

SOURCE: Harry Alonzo Cushing, ed., *The Writings of Samuel Adams* (New York: G. P. Putnam, 1904),
78–79.

However, three other parliamentary factions advocated repeal of the Stamp Act. The Old Whigs, now led by Lord Rockingham, the new prime minister, favored repeal because they believed that America was more important for its "flourishing and increasing trade" than for its tax revenues. A second faction, composed of the supporters of British merchants and manufacturers, pointed out an American boycott of British goods cut deeply into their sales. A committee of "London Merchants trading to America" mobilized support for repeal, and in January 1766 the commercial centers of Liverpool, Bristol, and Glasgow deluged Parliament with petitions. "The Avenues of Trade are all shut up," complained a Bristol merchant. "We have no Remittances and are at our Witts End for want of Money to fulfill our Engagements with our Tradesmen." Finally, former prime minister William Pitt and his friends demanded that "the Stamp Act be repealed absolutely, totally, and immediately" as a failed policy. Pitt tried to draw a subtle distinction between taxation and legislation; he argued both that Parliament could not tax the colonies and that British authority over America was "sovereign and supreme, in every circumstance of government and legislation whatsoever." As Pitt's ambiguous—and perhaps contradictory—position indicated, the controversy had raised difficult constitutional questions to which there were few clear answers.

Rockingham played for time by arranging a compromise. To mollify colonial opinion and assist British merchants, he repealed the Stamp Act and modified the Sugar Act by reducing the duty on French molasses from 3 pence to 1 penny a gallon. Then Rockingham pacified imperial reformers and hard-liners with the Declaratory Act of 1766, which explicitly reaffirmed the British Parliament's "full power and authority to make laws and statutes . . . to bind the colonies and people of America . . . in all cases whatsoever."

Because the Stamp Act crisis ended swiftly, it might have been forgotten just as quickly. As of 1766 political positions had not yet hardened. Through compromise, leaders of goodwill could still hope to work out an imperial relationship acceptable both to British officials and American settlers.

The Growing Confrontation, 1767–1770

The compromise of 1766 was short lived. Within a year political rivalries in Britain sparked a more prolonged struggle with the American colonies and revived the passions of 1765. Increasing ideological rigidity among key British ministers and American Patriots dashed prospects for a quick political resolution.

The Townshend Initiatives

Often the course of history is changed by a small event—a leader's illness, a personal grudge, a chance remark. So it was in 1767, when Rockingham's ministry collapsed because of its domestic policies and George III named William Pitt to head the new government. Pitt, the master strategist of the Great War for Empire, was chronically ill with gout and frequently missed Parliamentary debates, leaving Chancellor of the Exchequer Charles Townshend in command. Pitt was sympathetic toward America; Townshend was not. As a member of the Board of Trade in the 1750s, Townshend strongly favored restrictions on the colonial assemblies, a view reinforced by his service on a parliamentary law-reform committee. So in 1767, when Grenville attacked the military budget and demanded that the colonists pay for the British troops in America, Townshend made an unplanned, fateful policy decision. Convinced of the necessity of imperial reform and eager to reduce the English land tax, he promised to find a new source of revenue in America.

The new tax legislation, the Townshend Act of 1767, had a political as well as a financial goal. The statute imposed duties on colonial imports of paper, paint, glass, and tea and would raise about £40,000 a year. To pacify Grenville, part of this sum would defray American military expenses. However, most of the revenue would create a colonial civil list—a fund to pay the salaries of royal governors, judges, and other imperial officials. Once freed from financial dependence on the American legislatures, royal officials would be able to enforce Parliamentary laws and the king's instructions. To increase royal power still further, Townshend devised the Revenue Act of 1767. This act created a Board of American Customs Commissioners in Boston and vice-admiralty courts in Halifax, Boston, Philadelphia, and Charleston. By using Parliamentary-imposed tax revenues to finance administrative and judicial innovations, Townshend directly threatened the autonomy and authority of American political institutions.

The full implications of Townshend's policies became clear in New York, where the assembly refused to comply with the Quartering Act of 1765. Fearing an unlimited drain on its treasury, the New York legislature first denied General Gage's requests for barracks and supplies for British troops and then limited its assistance. In response, the ministry demanded full compliance; if the assembly refused, some members of Parliament threatened to impose a special duty on New York's imports and exports. The earl of Shelburne, the new secretary of state, went even further. He proposed the appointment of a military governor with authority to seize funds from New York's treasury and "to act with Force or Gentleness as circumstances might make necessary." Townshend decided on a less provocative but equally coercive measure, the Restraining Act of 1767, which suspended the New York assembly until it submitted to the Quartering Act. Faced with the loss of self-government, New Yorkers reluctantly appropriated the required funds.

The Restraining Act raised the stakes of the contest. The British Privy Council had traditionally supervised the assemblies by invalidating unacceptable colonial laws (and, over the decades, voided about 5 percent of all colonial statutes, such as those establishing land banks). Townshend's Restraining Act went much further by declaring that New York's assembly (and, indeed, every American representative body) was completely dependent on the will of Parliament.

America Again Debates and Resists

The Townshend duties revived the constitutional debate over taxation. During the Stamp Act crisis some Americans, including Benjamin Franklin, had made a distinction between "external" and "internal" taxes. They suggested that "external" duties on trade, which Britain had long regulated through the Navigation Acts, were acceptable to Americans but that direct or "internal" taxes, which had not previously been levied, were not. Townshend thought this distinction between internal and external taxes "perfect nonsense," but he indulged the American argument and laid duties only on trade.

However, most colonial leaders refused to accept the legitimacy of Townshend's measures. They agreed with John Dickinson, author of *Letters from a Farmer in Pennsylvania* (1768), that the real issue was not whether the tax was internal or external but the intention of the legislation. These Americans argued that the Townshend duties were designed to raise revenue and therefore were taxes imposed without consent.

Townshend's measures turned American resistance into an organized movement. In February 1768 the Massachusetts House of Representatives sent a letter

WILLIAM JACKSON,

an *IMPORTER*; at the

BRAZEN HEAD,

North Side of the TOWN-HOUSE,

and *Oppoſite the Town-Pump, i*

Corn-hill, B O S T O N.

It is deſired that the SONS and DAUGHTERS of *LIBERTY*, would not buy any one thing of him, for in ſo doing they will bring Diſgrace upon *themſelves*, and their *Poſterity*, for *ever* and *ever*, AMEN.

A Nonimportation Broadside

To punish merchants who defied the boycott against the Townshend duties, Patriots in Boston and other seaports posted simply worded broadsides urging residents not to patronize their businesses. Some Sons and Daughters of Liberty resorted to more violent tactics, harassing the merchants' customers and vandalizing their buildings.
Massachusetts Historical Society.

condemning the Townshend Act to the other assemblies, and in the spring Boston and New York merchants began a new boycott of British goods. Philadelphia merchants, sailors, and dockworkers refused to join the boycott because they were heavily involved in direct trade with Britain and believed they had too much to lose. Nonetheless, public support for nonimportation quickly emerged in the smaller port cities of Salem, Newport, and Baltimore. Throughout Puritan New England, ministers and public officials discouraged the purchase of "foreign superfluities" and promoted the domestic manufacture of cloth and other necessities.

American women, ordinarily excluded from public affairs, became crucial to the nonimportation through their production of **homespun** textiles. During the Stamp Act boycott of English goods, the wives and daughters of Patriot leaders had increased their output of yarn and cloth. Resistance to the Townshend duties mobilized many more women, including pious farmwives who spun yarn at the homes of their ministers. Some gatherings were openly patriotic, such as one in Berwick, Maine, where "true Daughters of Liberty" celebrated American products by "drinking rye coffee and dining on bear venison." Other women's groups combined support for nonimportation with charitable work by spinning flax and wool to donate to the needy. Just as men followed tradition in joining crowd actions to attack imperial policy, so women's customary attention to the well-being of their communities guided their protest efforts.

Newspapers celebrated these "Daughters of Liberty." One Massachusetts town proudly claimed an annual output of thirty thousand yards of cloth; East Hartford, Connecticut, reported seventeen thousand yards. Although this surge in domestic production did not compensate for the loss of British imports, which had averaged about ten million yards of cloth each year, it inspired support for nonimportation by thousands of women in many communities.

Indeed, the boycott mobilized Americans, especially in the seaport cities, into an organized political action. The Sons of Liberty published the names of merchants who imported British goods, broke their store windows, and harassed their employees. By March 1769 most Philadelphia merchants finally responded to public pressure and joined the nonimportation movement. Two months later the members of the Virginia House of Burgesses vowed not to buy duties articles, luxury goods, or slaves imported by British merchants. "The whole continent from New England to Georgia seems firmly fixed," the *Massachusetts Gazette* proudly announced. "Like a strong, well-constructed arch, the more weight there is laid upon it, the firmer it stands; and thus with America, the more we are loaded, the more we are united." Reflecting colonial self-confidence, Benjamin Franklin called for a return to the pre-1763 mercantilist system and proposed a "plan of conciliation" that was really a demand for British capitulation: "repeal the laws, renounce the right, recall the troops, refund the money, and return to the old method of requisition."

American resistance only increased British determination. When the Massachusetts House's letter opposing the Townshend duties reached London, Lord

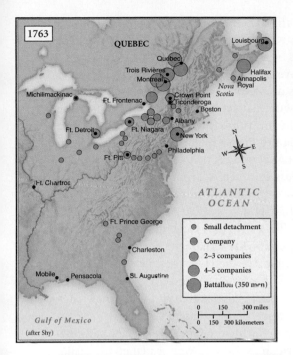

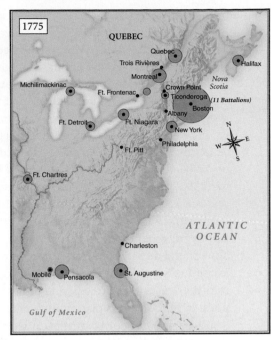

MAP 5.2 British Troop Deployments, 1763 and 1775

As the imperial crisis deepened, British military priorities changed. In 1763 most British battalions were stationed in Canada to deter Indian uprisings and French-Canadian revolts. After the Stamp Act riots of 1765, the British established large garrisons in New York and Philadelphia. By 1775 eleven battalions of British regulars occupied Boston, the center of the American Patriot movement.

Hillsborough, the secretary of state for American affairs, branded it as "unjustifiable opposition to the constitutional authority of Parliament." To strengthen the "Hand of Government" in Massachusetts and assist the customs commissioners there, Hillsborough dispatched four thousand British regular troops to Boston (Map 5.2). By the end of 1768, military coercion was a very real prospect. General Gage accused Massachusetts leaders of "Treasonable and desperate Resolves" and advised the ministry to "Quash this Spirit at a Blow." Parliament threatened to appoint a special commission to hear evidence of treason, and Hillsborough proposed to isolate Massachusetts from the other colonies and then use the army to bring the rebellious New Englanders to their knees. In 1765 American resistance to taxation had provoked a Parliamentary debate. In 1768 it produced a plan for military coercion.

Lord North Compromises, 1770

At this critical moment the British ministry's resolve faltered. A series of harsh winters and drought-ridden summers cut grain output and raised prices. In Scotland and northern England, thousands of tenants deserted their farms and boarded ships bound for America. Food riots spread across the English countryside and, in the highly publicized Massacre of Saint George Fields, troops killed seven protesters. The Radical Whig John Wilkes, supported by associations of merchants, tradesmen, and artisans, stepped up his attacks on government corruption and won election to Parliament. Overjoyed, American Patriots drank toasts to Wilkes and bought thousands of teapots and mugs emblazoned with his picture. Riots in Ireland over the growing military budget there added to the ministry's difficulties.

The American trade boycott also began to have a major impact on the British economy. Normally the colonies had an annual trade deficit with the home country of £500,000, but in 1768 they imported less from Great Britain, cutting the deficit to £230,000. By continuing to provide staple goods and shipping services to overseas markets while cutting imports of British goods, in 1769 Americans amassed a balance of payments surplus of £816,000. To revive their flagging sales to America, British merchants and manufacturers petitioned Parliament for repeal of the Townshend duties. British government revenues, which were heavily dependent on excise taxes and duties on imported goods, had also suffered. By late 1769 some ministers felt that the Townshend duties were a mistake, and the king no longer supported Hillsborough's plan to use military force against Massachusetts.

Early in 1770 Lord North became prime minister and arranged a new compromise. Arguing that it was foolish to tax British exports to America (thereby raising their price and decreasing consumption), North persuaded Parliament to repeal most of the Townshend duties. However, he retained the tax on tea as a symbol of Parliament's supremacy. Gratified by North's initiative, colonial merchants called off the boycott.

Even the outbreak of violence did not rupture the compromise. During the boycott New York artisans and workers had taunted British troops, mostly with words but occasionally with stones and fists. In retaliation the soldiers tore down a Liberty Pole (a Patriot flagpole), setting off a week of street fighting. In Boston friction between the residents and British soldiers over constitutional principles and everyday issues, such as competition for part-time jobs, sparked a violent conflict. In March 1770, a group of soldiers fired into a rowdy crowd of demonstrators, killing five men, including one of the leaders, Crispus Attucks, an escaped slave who was working as a seaman. Reviving fears of a ministerial conspiracy against liberty, Radical Whigs labeled the incident a "massacre" and filled the popular press with accusations that the British had deliberately planned it.

Although most Americans ignored such charges and remained loyal to the empire, five years of conflict over taxes and constitutional principles had taken their toll. In 1765 American leaders had accepted Parliament's authority; the Stamp Act Resolves had opposed only certain "unconstitutional" legislation. By 1770 the most outspoken Patriots—Benjamin Franklin in Pennsylvania, Patrick Henry in Virginia, and Samuel Adams in Massachusetts—had repudiated Parliamentary supremacy and claimed equality for the American assemblies within the empire. Perhaps thinking of various European "composite monarchies" (in which kings ruled far-distant provinces acquired by inheritance or conquest), Franklin suggested that the colonies were now "distinct and separate states" with the "the same Head, or Sovereign, the King."

Franklin's suggestion outraged Thomas Hutchinson, the American-born royal governor of Massachusetts. Hutchinson emphatically rejected the idea of "two independent legislatures in one and the same state"; in his mind, the British empire was a single whole, its sovereignty indivisible. "I know of no line," he told the Massachusetts assembly, "that can be drawn between the supreme authority of Parliament and the total independence of the colonies."

There the matter rested. The British had twice tried to impose taxes on the colonies, and American Patriots had twice forced a retreat. If Parliament insisted on exercising Britain's claim to sovereign power, at least some Americans were prepared to resist by force. Nor did they flinch when reminded that George III condemned their agitation. As the Massachusetts House told Hutchinson, "There is more reason to dread the consequences of absolute uncontrolled supreme power, whether of a nation or a monarch, than those of total independence." Fearful of civil war, the ministry hesitated to take the final, fateful step.

The Road to War, 1771–1775

The repeal of the Townshend duties in 1770 restored harmony to the British empire. Yet below the surface lay strong fears and passions and mutual distrust. Suddenly, in 1773 those undercurrents erupted, overwhelming any hope for compromise. In less than two years the Americans and the British stood on the brink of war.

The Compromise Ignored

Once roused, political passions are not easily quelled. In Boston, radical Patriots continued to warn Americans of the dangers of imperial domination. In November 1772 Samuel Adams persuaded the Boston town meeting to establish a Committee of Correspondence to urge Patriots in other towns "to state the Rights of the Colonists of this Province." Within a few months eighty Massachusetts towns had similar committees, all in communication with one another. Then smugglers burned the *Gaspée*, a customs vessel, in Rhode Island, and the British government set up a royal commission to investigate the incident. The commission's broad powers, particularly its authority to send Americans to Britain for trial, aroused the Virginia House of Burgesses to set up its own Committee of Correspondence "to communicate with the other colonies" about the situation in Rhode Island. By mid-1773 similar committees appeared in Connecticut, New Hampshire, and South Carolina.

These committees sprang into action when Parliament passed the Tea Act in May 1773. The act provided financial relief for the British East India Company, which was deeply in debt because of military expeditions that extended British trade and political influence in India. The Tea Act provided the company with a government loan and, more important, relieved the company of paying tariffs on the tea it imported into Britain or sent to the colonies. However, Lord North failed to realize how unpopular the Tea Act would be in America. Since 1768, when the Townshend Act had placed a duty of 3 pence a pound on tea, many Americans had bought smuggled tea provided by Dutch traders. By relieving the East India Company of English tariffs, the Tea Act gave its tea a competitive price advantage over that sold by Dutch merchants. Thus, the act encouraged Americans to drink East India tea—and in the process pay the Townshend duty that Lord North had continued.

Radical Patriots smelled a plot and accused the ministry of bribing Americans to give up their principled opposition to British taxation. As an anonymous woman wrote in the *Massachusetts Spy*, "the use of [British] tea is considered not as a private but as a public evil . . . a handle to introduce a variety of . . . oppressions amongst us." American merchants joined the protest because the East India Company planned to distribute its tea directly to shopkeepers, thereby excluding most colonial merchants from the profits of the trade. "The fear of an Introduction of a Monopoly in this Country," General Haldimand reported from New York, "has induced the mercantile part of the Inhabitants to be very industrious in opposing this Step and added Strength to a Spirit of Independence already too prevalent."

The newly formed Committees of Correspondence took the lead in organizing resistance to the Tea Act. They held public bonfires at which they persuaded their fellow citizens (sometimes gently, sometimes not) to consign British tea to the flames. The Sons of Liberty patrolled the wharves and prevented East India Company ships from landing new supplies. By forcing the company's captains to return the tea to Britain or store it in public warehouses, the Patriots effectively nullified the legislation.

However, Governor Thomas Hutchinson of Massachusetts hatched a scheme to land the tea and collect the tax. When a shipment of tea arrived on the *Dartmouth*, Hutchinson immediately passed the ship through customs so that it could dock in the harbor. If the Sons of Liberty blocked the tea from coming ashore, Hutchinson was prepared to order the British troops to unload the tea and supervise its sale by auction. Patriots foiled the governor's plan by raiding the *Dartmouth*: a group of artisans and laborers disguised as Indians boarded the ship, broke open the 342 chests of tea (valued at about £10,000, or roughly $800,000 today), and threw them into the harbor. "This destruction of the Tea is so bold and it must have so important Consequences," John Adams wrote in his diary, "that I cannot but consider it as an Epoch in History."

The British Privy Council was outraged, as was the king. "Concessions have made matters worse," George III declared. "The time has come for compulsion." Early in 1774 Parliament decisively rejected a proposal to repeal the duty on

American tea; instead, it enacted four Coercive Acts to force Massachusetts into submission. The Port Bill closed Boston Harbor until the East India Company was paid for its tea. The Government Act annulled the Massachusetts charter and prohibited most local town meetings. The new Quartering Act required the colony to build barracks or accommodate soldiers in private houses. Finally, to protect royal officials from Patriot-dominated juries in Massachusetts, the Justice Act allowed trials for capital crimes to be transferred to other colonies or to Britain.

Patriot leaders throughout the mainland branded these measures as "Intolerable" and rallied support for Massachusetts. In far-off Georgia, a Patriot warned the "Freemen of the Province" that "every privilege you at present claim as a birthright, may be wrested from you by the same authority that blockades the town of Boston." "The cause of Boston," George Washington declared from Virginia, "now is and ever will be considered as the cause of America." The activities of the Committees of Correspondence had created a firm sense of unity among Patriots.

In 1774 Parliament passed the Quebec Act, which heightened the sense of common danger among Americans of European Protestant descent. The law extended the boundaries of Quebec into the Ohio River Valley, thus restricting the western boundaries of Virginia and other coastal colonies and angering influential land speculators and politicians. The act also gave legal recognition in Quebec to Roman Catholicism. This humane concession to Quebec's predominantly Catholic population reignited religious passions in New England, where Puritans associated Catholicism with arbitrary royal government and popish superstition. Although the ministry had not intended the Quebec Act as a coercive measure, many colonial leaders saw it as another demonstration of Parliament's power to intervene in American domestic affairs (Map 5.3).

The Continental Congress Responds

Patriot leaders called a meeting of a new all-colony assembly, the Continental Congress. The newer mainland colonies—Florida, Quebec, Nova Scotia, and Newfoundland—did not attend, nor did Georgia, where the royal governor controlled the legislature. And the assemblies of the West Indian sugar islands, such as Barbados and Jamaica, fearful of revolts by their predominately African populations, reaffirmed their allegiance to the crown. However, delegates chosen by twelve mainland assemblies met in Philadelphia in September 1774 and addressed a set of controversial and divisive issues. Southern leaders, fearing a British plot "to overturn the constitution and introduce a system of arbitrary government," favored a new economic boycott. Bellicose representatives from New England advocated a political union and defensive military preparations. However, many delegates from the Middle Atlantic colonies wanted to seek a political compromise.

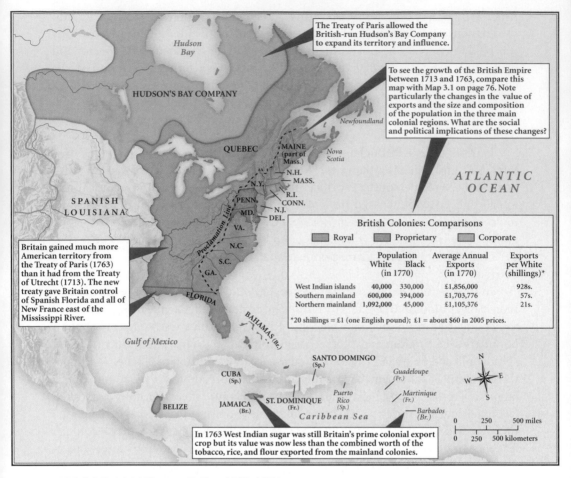

The Treaty of Paris allowed the British-run Hudson's Bay Company to expand its territory and influence.

To see the growth of the British Empire between 1713 and 1763, compare this map with Map 3.1 on page 76. Note particularly the changes in the value of exports and the size and composition of the population in the three main colonial regions. What are the social and political implications of these changes?

Britain gained much more American territory from the Treaty of Paris (1763) than it had from the Treaty of Utrecht (1713). The new treaty gave Britain control of Spanish Florida and all of New France east of the Mississippi River.

In 1763 West Indian sugar was still Britain's prime colonial export crop but its value was now less than the combined worth of the tobacco, rice, and flour exported from the mainland colonies.

British Colonies: Comparisons

■ Royal   ■ Proprietary   □ Corporate

	Population White (in 1770)	Black	Average Annual Exports (in 1770)	Exports per White (shillings)*
West Indian islands	40,000	330,000	£1,856,000	928s.
Southern mainland	600,000	394,000	£1,703,776	57s.
Northern mainland	1,092,000	45,000	£1,105,376	21s.

*20 shillings = £1 (one English pound); £1 = about $60 in 2005 prices.

MAP 5.3 British Western Policy, 1763–1774

Challenging the Proclamation Line of 1763, which restricted white settlement west of the Appalachian Mountains, Anglo-American settlers and land speculators proposed the new western colonies of Vandalia and Transylvania. However, the Quebec Act of 1774 designated most western lands as Indian reserves and, by vastly enlarging the boundaries of Quebec, eliminated the sea-to-sea land claims of many colonies along the Atlantic Coast. The Quebec Act also angered New England Protestants, who condemned its provisions allowing French residents to practice Catholicism, and colonial political leaders, who condemned its failure to provide a representative assembly.

FOR MORE HELP ANALYZING THIS MAP, see the Online Study Guide at **bedfordstmartins.com/henrettaconcise**.

Led by Joseph Galloway of Pennsylvania, these men of "loyal principles" outlined a new imperial system that resembled the Albany Plan of Union of 1754. Under Galloway's proposal, the king would appoint a president-general and the colonial assemblies would select a legislative council, which would have veto power over Parliamentary legislation that affected America. Despite this feature, delegates refused to endorse Galloway's plan. With British troops occupying Boston, the majority thought it was too conciliatory.

Instead, the First Continental Congress passed a Declaration of Rights and Grievances that condemned the Coercive Acts and demanded their repeal. It also repudiated the Declaratory Act of 1766, which had proclaimed Parliament's supremacy, and demanded that Britain restrict its control of American affairs to matters of external trade. Finally, the Congress approved a program of economic retaliation that would begin in December 1774 with a new nonimportation agreement. If Parliament did not repeal the Intolerable Acts by September 1775, the Congress vowed to cut off virtually all colonial exports to Britain, Ireland, and the British West Indies. Ten years of constitutional conflict had culminated in a threat of all-out commercial warfare.

Even at this late date a few British leaders hoped for compromise. In January 1775 William Pitt, now sitting in the House of Lords as the earl of Chatham, asked Parliament to renounce its power to tax the colonies and recognize the Continental Congress as a lawful body. In return for these concessions, he suggested, the Congress should acknowledge Parliamentary supremacy and grant a continuing revenue to help defray the British national debt.

The British ministry rejected Chatham's plan. Twice it had backed down in the face of colonial resistance; a third retreat was impossible. The honor of the nation was at stake. Branding the Continental Congress an illegal assembly, the ministry also ruled out Lord Dartmouth's proposal to send commissioners to America to negotiate a settlement. Instead, Lord North set stringent terms: Americans must pay for their own defense and administration and acknowledge Parliament's authority to tax them. To put teeth in these demands, North imposed a naval blockade on American trade with foreign nations and ordered General Gage to suppress dissent in Massachusetts. "Now the case seemed desperate," the prime minister told former Massachusetts governor Thomas Hutchinson, who had been forced into exile in London by Patriot agitators. "Parliament would not—could not—concede. For aught he could see it must come to violence."

The Rising of the Countryside

Ultimately, the success of the urban-led Patriot movement would depend on the large rural population. Traditionally, most farmers had little interest in imperial affairs. Their lives were deeply rooted in the soil, and their prime allegiance was to family and community. But imperial policy increasingly intruded into their isolated domestic worlds by taking their sons for military duty and raising their taxes. Before the outbreak of the French and Indian War in 1754, farmers in Newtown, Long Island, had paid an average of 10 shillings a year in taxes; by 1756 their taxes had jumped to 30 shillings. Peace brought only slight relief, because in 1771 the British-imposed Quartering Act kept taxes at the high rate of 20 shillings. Such levies angered rural Americans, though in fact they paid much lower taxes than did most Britons.

A SOCIETY of PATRIOTIC LADIES,
AT
EDENTON in NORTH CAROLINA.

Plate V.

Political Propaganda: The Empire Strikes Back

A British cartoon satirizes the women of Edenton, North Carolina, for supporting the boycott of British trade by hinting at their sexual lasciviousness and—by showing an enslaved black woman holding an inkstand for these supposed advocates of liberty—their moral hypocrisy. Library of Congress.

FOR MORE HELP ANALYZING THIS IMAGE, see the Online Study Guide at **bedfordstmartins.com/ henrettaconcise**.

The urban-led boycotts of 1765 and 1769 also raised the political consciousness of rural Americans. When the Continental Congress placed a new ban on British goods in 1774, it easily established a network of local Committees of Safety and Inspection to support it. Appealing to rural thriftiness, the Congress discouraged the wearing of expensive imported clothes to funerals, approving only "a black crape or ribbon on the arm or hat for gentlemen, and a black ribbon and necklace for ladies." In Concord, Massachusetts, 80 percent of the male heads of families and a number of single women signed a Solemn League and Covenant supporting nonimportation. In other towns men blacked their faces, disguised themselves in blankets "like Indians," and threatened violence against "those that trade in rum, molasses, & Sugar, &c." in violation of the boycott.

Patriots also appealed to the yeoman tradition of freehold ownership, which was everywhere under attack. In long-settled communities, arable land was now scarce and expensive, and in new communities merchants were seizing farmsteads for delinquent debts. Money was always in short supply among rural households, and the town meeting of Petersham, Massachusetts, complained that the new tax demands of the British government would further drain "this People of the Fruits of their Toil." "The duty on tea," warned a Patriot pamphlet, "was only a prelude to a window-tax, hearth-tax, land-tax, and poll-tax, and these were only paving the way for reducing the country to lordships." By the 1770s many northern yeomen felt personally threatened by British imperial policy.

Despite their higher standard of living, southern slave owners had similar fears. Many Virginia Patriots—including Patrick Henry, George Washington, and Thomas Jefferson—speculated in western lands and reacted angrily when first the Proclamation Line of 1763 and then the Quebec Act of 1774 invalidated their claims. Moreover, many Chesapeake planters were deeply in debt to British merchants; a debt of £1,000 had once been considered excessive, a planter observed in 1766, but "ten times that sum is now spoke of with indifference and thought no great burthen on Some Estates." Although extravagant spending threatened many planters with financial disaster, George Washington noted, they were determined to live "genteely and hospitably" and were "ashamed" to adopt frugal ways. Accustomed to being absolute masters on their slave-labor plantations, they resented their financial dependence on British merchants and dreaded the prospect of political subservience. Once Parliament used the Coercive Acts to subdue Massachusetts, the planters feared, it might seize control of the House of Burgesses and Virginia's county courts and assist British merchants to seize their debt-burdened property. Consequently, the Patriot gentry supported demands by yeomen planters to close the law courts so they could bargain with Scottish merchants over debts and tobacco prices without the threat of legal action. "The spark of liberty is not yet extinct among our people," one planter declared, "and if properly fanned by the Gentlemen of influence will, I make no doubt, burst out again into a flame."

While many wealthy planters and affluent merchants supported the Patriot cause, other prominent Americans worried that resistance to Britain would destroy respect for all political institutions and end in mob rule. Their fears increased when the Sons of Liberty used force to uphold nonimportation. As a well-to-do New Yorker complained, "No man can be in a more abject state of bondage than he whose Reputation, Property and Life are exposed to the discretionary violence . . . of the community." As the crisis continued, these men rallied to the support of the royal governors.

Other social groups likewise refused to support the Patriot movement. In Pennsylvania and New Jersey, many Quakers and Germans tried to remain neutral because of pacifist religious principles and fear of political change. In regions where many wealthy landowners became Patriots, such as the Hudson Valley of New York, tenant farmers supported the king because they hated their landlords. Similar social divisions prompted some Regulators in the North Carolina backcountry and many farmers on the eastern shore of Chesapeake Bay in Maryland to oppose the Patriots there. Enslaved blacks had even less reason to support the cause of their Patriot masters. In November 1774, James Madison reported that one group of Virginia slaves planned to flee from their Patriot owners "when the English troops should arrive."

To mobilize support for the king, prominent Americans of "loyal principles" denounced the Patriot leaders and accused them of seeking independence. These Loyalists—mostly royal officials, merchants with military contracts, clergy of the Church of England, and well-established lawyers—formed an articulate pro-British party, but one that remained small and ineffective. A Tory Association started by Governor Wentworth of New Hampshire enrolled just fifty-nine members, fourteen of whom were the governor's relatives. At this crucial juncture Americans who favored resistance to British rule commanded the allegiance—or at least the acquiescence—of the majority of white Americans.

The Failure of Compromise

When the Continental Congress met in September 1774, New England was already openly defying British authority. In August, the 150 delegates at an extra-legal Middlesex County Congress advised Patriots to close the royal courts of justice and transfer their political allegiance to the popularly elected House of Representatives. Following the congress, armed crowds harassed Loyalists and ensured Patriot rule in most of New England.

General Thomas Gage, the military governor of Massachusetts, tried desperately to maintain imperial power. In September 1774 he ordered British troops in Boston to seize Patriot armories and storehouses at Charlestown and Cambridge. In response, twenty thousand colonial militiamen mobilized to safeguard other military supply depots. The Concord town meeting voted to raise a defensive force, the famous **Minutemen**, to "Stand at a minutes warning in Case of alarm." Increasingly, Gage's authority was limited to Boston, where it rested primarily on the bayonets of his thirty-five hundred troops. Meanwhile, the Massachusetts House met on its own authority, collected taxes, bolstered the militia, and assumed the responsibilities of government.

In London, the colonial secretary, Lord Dartmouth, proclaimed Massachusetts to be in "open rebellion." Declaring that "force should be repelled by force," he ordered Gage to march quickly against the "rude rabble." On the night of April 18, 1775, Gage dispatched seven hundred soldiers to capture colonial leaders and supplies at Concord. But Paul Revere and two other Bostonians warned the Patriots, and at dawn local militiamen met the British troops first at Lexington and then at Concord. The skirmishes took a dozen lives. As the British retreated to Boston, militiamen from neighboring towns repeatedly ambushed them. By the end of the day, 73 British soldiers were dead, 174 wounded, and 26 missing. British fire had killed 49 American militiamen and wounded 39 (see Voices from Abroad, "A British View of Lexington and Concord," p. 159). Too much blood had now been spilled to allow another compromise. Twelve years of economic conflict and constitutional debate had ended in civil war.

VOICES FROM ABROAD

A British View of Lexington and Concord

LIEUTENANT COLONEL FRANCIS SMITH

*T*he past vanishes as soon as it occurs, and must be reconstructed by historians from documentary evidence. On April 26, 1775, a week after British troops marched on Lexington and Concord, the Patriot-controlled Massachusetts Provincial Congress issued what it called a "true, and authentic account" of the hostilities. The Congress alleged that at Lexington "the regulars rushed on with great violence and first began the hostilities" and that in the retreat of the British troops from Concord "houses on the road were plundered, . . . women in child-bed were driven by soldiery naked in the streets, [and] old men peaceably in their houses were shot dead." Four days earlier, in his official report to General Gage, British lieutenant colonel Francis Smith offered an account that presented British actions in a much more favorable light. Which version should the historian find more "true, and authentic"?

Sir,—In obedience to your Excellency's commands, I marched on the evening of the 18th inst. with the corps of grenadiers and light infantry for Concord, . . . to destroy all ammunition, artillery, tents &c. . . . Notwithstanding we marched with the utmost expedition and secrecy, we found the country had intelligence or strong suspicion of our coming. . . .

At Lexington . . . [we] found on a green close to the road a body of the country people drawn up in military order, with arms and accoutrements, and, as appeared afterward, loaded. . . . Our troops advanced towards them, without any intention of injuring them . . . ; but they in confusion went off, principally to the left, only one of them fired before he went off, and three or four more jumped over a wall and fired from behind it among the soldiers; on which the troops returned it, and killed several of them. They likewise fired on the soldiers from the Meeting[house] and dwelling-houses. . . .

While at Concord we saw vast numbers assembling in many parts; at one of the bridges they marched down, with a very considerable body, on the light infantry posted there. On their coming pretty near, one of our men fired on them, which they returned; on which an action ensued and some few were killed and wounded. In this affair, it appears that, after the bridge was quitted, they scalped and otherwise ill treated one or two of [our] men who were either killed or severely wounded. . . .

On our leaving Concord to return to Boston they began to fire on us from behind walls, ditches, trees, &c., which, as we marched, increased to a very great degree, and continued . . . for, I believe, upwards of eighteen miles; so that I can't think but it must have been a preconcerted scheme in them, to attack the King's troops the first favorable opportunity that offered; otherwise, I think they could not, in such a short a time from our marching out, have raised such a numerous body. . . .

SOURCE: *Proceedings of the Massachusetts Historical Society*, 1876 p. 350ff. Courtesy of the Massachusetts Historical Society.

TIMELINE

1754–1763	Great War for Empire British national debt doubles	**1766**	First compromise: Stamp Act repealed and Declaratory Act passed
1760	George III becomes king	**1767**	Townshend duties on certain colonial imports
1762	Revenue Act reforms customs service Royal Navy arrests smugglers		Restraining Act in New York temporarily suspends colonial assembly there Daughters of Liberty make "homespun" cloth
1763	Treaty of Paris ends war Proclamation Line restricts settlement west of Appalachians George Grenville becomes British prime minister John Wilkes demands political reform in England	**1768**	Second nonimportation movement British army occupies Boston
		1770	Second compromise: Townshend duties repealed Boston Massacre
1764	Currency Act protects British merchants Sugar Act places duty on imported French molasses Colonists oppose vice-admiralty courts	**1772**	Committees of Correspondence formed
		1773	Tea Act assists British East India Company Boston Tea Party
1765	Stamp Act imposes direct tax on colonists Quartering Act provides barracks for British troops Riots by Sons of Liberty Stamp Act Congress First nonimportation movement	**1774**	Coercive Acts punish Massachusetts Quebec Act offends Patriots First Continental Congress Third nonimportation movement Loyalists organize
		1775	General Thomas Gage marches to Lexington and Concord

For Further Exploration

Jack P. Greene and J. R. Pole, eds., *The Blackwell Encyclopedia of the American Revolution* (1991), illuminates both obscure and well-known aspects of the Revolutionary era, as do the personal testimonies in Barbara DeWolfe, *Discoveries of America: Personal Accounts of British Emigrants to North American during the Revolutionary Era* (1997). Edward Countryman, *The American Revolution* (1985), is a well-written scholarly overview, which tells the story through the lives of ordinary people. For a more journalistic account that focuses on leading men, see A. J. Langguth's *Patriots: The Men Who Started the American Revolution* (1988), a suspenseful story of such famous figures as George Washington, John Adams, Samuel Adams, and Patrick Henry. Edmund Morgan and Helen Morgan also use a biographical approach to tell the story of *The Stamp Act Crisis* (1953). Philip Lawson's *George Grenville* (1984) offers a sympathetic portrait of a reform-minded prime minister. The coming of the revolution is covered in three lucidly written and broadly conceived studies. Hiller B. Zobel's *The Boston Massacre* (1970) captures the social unrest and latent violence of these years, while Benjamin Labaree's *The Boston Tea Party* suggests how one "small" event altered the course of history and David Hackett Fischer explains the rise of the Radical Patriots and the outbreak of fighting in Massachusetts in *Paul Revere's Ride* (1994). For events in Virginia, see the probing study by Woody Holton, *Forced Founders: Indians, Debtors, Slaves, and the Making of the American Revolution in Virginia* (1999).

Liberty! The American Revolution (6 hours), a six-part video available through PBS, provides a coherent narrative of the movement for independence and has a fine companion Web site at <http://www.pbs.org/ktca/liberty/>. Two good collections of pamphlets, other political materials, and visual images pertaining to the Revolutionary era are available at Web sites at the University of Groningen in the Netherlands, <http://odur.let.rug.nl/~usa/D/index.htm> and at the University of Maryland, Baltimore County, <http://www.research.umbc.edu/~bouton/Revolution.links.htm>. The Web site of the National Gallery of Art, <http://www.nga.gov>, has an interesting section devoted to American paintings of the colonial and Revolutionary periods, including a detailed analysis of a work by Jonathan Copley. See its Index of American Design for a collection of eighteenth-century German American folk art.

For definitions of key terms boldfaced in this chapter, see the glossary at the end of the book.

To assess your mastery of the material covered in this chapter, see the Online Study Guide at **bedfordstmartins.com/henrettaconcise**.

For map resources and primary documents, see **bedfordstmartins.com/henrettaconcise**.

Part Two

THE NEW REPUBLIC

1775–1820

GOVERNMENT	DIPLOMACY	ECONOMY
Creating Republican Institutions	European Entanglements	Expanding Commerce and Manufacturing
1775 ▸ State constitutions devised and implemented Monarchy-friendly Loyalists depart	▸ Independence declared (1776) French alliance (1778)	▸ Wartime expansion of manufacturing Severe inflation threatens economy
1780 ▸ Articles of Confederation ratified (1781) Legislatures assert supremacy in states Philadelphia convention drafts U.S. Constitution (1787)	▸ Treaty of Paris (1783) Britain restricts U.S. trade with West Indies U.S. government signs treaties with Indian peoples	▸ Bank of North America founded (1781) Commercial recession (1783–1789) Western land speculation
1790 ▸ Conflict over Hamilton's economic policies First national parties: Federalists and Republicans	▸ Wars of the French Revolution Jay's and Pinckney's Treaties (1795) Undeclared war with France (1798)	▸ First Bank of the United States (1792–1812) States charter business corporations Outwork system grows
1800 ▸ Revolution of 1800 reduces activism of national government Chief Justice Marshall asserts judicial power	▸ Napoleonic Wars (1802–1815) Louisiana Purchase (1803) Embargo of 1807	▸ Cotton expands into Old Southwest Farm productivity improves Embargo encourages U.S. manufacturing
1810 ▸ Triumph of Republican Party and demise of Federalist Party State constitutions democratized	▸ War of 1812 Treaty of Ghent (1816) ends war Monroe Doctrine (1823)	▸ Second Bank of the United States (1816–1836) Supreme Court aids business Emergence of a national economy

SOCIETY	CULTURE
Defining Liberty and Equality	Pluralism and National Identity
▶ Emancipation of slaves in the North Judith Sargent Murray, *On the Equality of the Sexes* (1779)	▶ Thomas Paine's *Common Sense* calls for a republic
▶ Virginia Statute of Religious Freedom (1786) Idea of republican motherhood French Revolution sparks ideological debate	▶ State cessions and land ordinances create national domain in the West German settlers keep own language Noah Webster defines American English
▶ Bill of Rights ratified (1791) Sedition Act limits freedom of the press (1798)	▶ Indians form Western Confederacy Sectional divisions emerge between South and North
▶ Youth choose own marriage partners New Jersey decrees male-only suffrage (1807) Atlantic slave trade legally ended (1808)	▶ African Americans absorb Protestant Christianity Tenskwatawa and Tecumseh revive Indian identity
▶ Expansion of suffrage for white men New England abolishes established churches (1820s)	▶ War of 1812 tests national unity Second Great Awakening shapes American culture

"The American war is over," the Philadelphia Patriot Benjamin Rush declared in 1787, "but this is far from being the case with the American Revolution. On the contrary, nothing but the first act of the great drama is closed. It remains yet to establish and perfect our new forms of government." The job was even greater than Rush imagined, because the republican revolution of 1776 challenged nearly all the values and institutions of the colonial social order and forced changes not only in politics but also in economic, religious, and cultural life. By 1820 the new republic boasted activist state governments and vibrant movements for social reform and religious revival.

GOVERNMENT The first and most fundamental task was to create a republican system of government. But what precisely did that mean? In 1775, no one knew how the states should go about setting up republican institutions. Nor did American leaders know if there should be a permanent central authority along the lines of the Continental Congress. It would take time and experience to find out. It would take even longer to assimilate a new institution—the political party—into the workings of government. However, by 1820 difficult years of political compromise and constitutional revision had created state and national republican governments that commanded the allegiance of their citizens.

DIPLOMACY To create and preserve their new republic, Americans of European descent had to fight two wars against Great Britain, an undeclared war against France, and many battles with Indian peoples and confederations. The wars against Britain divided the country into bitter factions—Patriots against Loyalists in 1776, and prowar Republicans against antiwar Federalists in 1812—and expended much blood and treasure. Tragically, the extension of American sovereignty and settlement into the trans-Appalachian West brought cultural disaster to many Indian peoples, as their lives were cut short by European diseases and alcohol and their lands were seized by white settlers. Despite these external wars and internal conflicts, by 1820 the United States emerged as a strong independent state. Freed from a half century of entanglement in the wars and diplomacy of Europe, its people began to exploit the riches of the continent.

ECONOMY Already the expansion of markets and commerce had established the foundations for a strong national economy. Beginning in the 1780s northern merchants financed a banking system and organized a rural-based system of manufacturing, while state governments used charters and legal incentives to assist business entrepreneurs and provide improved roads, bridges, and waterways. Simultaneously, southern planters carried slavery westward to Alabama and

Mississippi and grew rich by exporting a new staple crop—cotton—to markets in Europe and the North. Some yeomen farm families migrated to the West to grow grain; those in the East turned to the production of raw materials such as leather and wool for the burgeoning manufacturing enterprises and worked part-time as handicraft workers. As a result of these activities, by 1820 the young American republic was on the verge of achieving economic as well as political independence.

SOCIETY As Americans undertook to create a republican society, they divided along lines of gender, race, religion, and class and disagreed over fundamental issues: legal equality for women, the status of slavery, the meaning of free speech and religious liberty, and the extent of public responsibility for social inequality. They resolved some disputes. Legislatures abolished slavery in the North, broadened religious liberty by allowing freedom of conscience, and (except in New England) ended the system of established churches. However, Americans continued to argue over social equality, in part because their republican creed placed authority in the family and society in the hands of men of property. This arrangement denied power not only to slaves but also to free blacks, women, and poor white men.

CULTURE The diversity of peoples and regions complicated efforts to define a distinct American culture and identity. Native Americans still lived in their own clans and nations, while black Americans, one-fifth of the enumerated population, were developing a new African American culture. The white inhabitants created vigorous regional cultures and preserved parts of their ancestral heritage—English, Scottish, Scots-Irish, German, and Dutch. Nevertheless, political institutions began to unite Americans, as did their increasing participation in the market economy and in evangelical Protestant churches. By 1820, to be an American meant, for many members of the dominant white population, to be a republican, a Protestant, and an enterprising individual in a capitalist-run market system.

Chapter 6

WAR AND REVOLUTION
1775–1783

A government of our own is our natural right. . . . 'TIS TIME
TO PART.

THOMAS PAINE, 1776

When the Patriots of Frederick County, Maryland, demanded allegiance to the American cause in 1776, Robert Gassaway would have none of it. "It was better for the poor people to lay down their arms and pay the duties and taxes laid upon them by King and Parliament," he told the local Council of Safety, "than to be brought into slavery and commanded and ordered about [by you]." The story was much the same in Farmington, Connecticut, where Patriot officials imprisoned Nathaniel Jones and seventeen other men for "remaining neutral" and not opposing a British raid. Everywhere, the logic of events was forcing families to choose sides between the Loyalists and the Patriots.

In this battle for the hearts and minds of ordinary men and women, the Patriots had an edge. Using their control of local governments, Patriot officials organized their neighbors into militia units and recruited volunteers for the Continental army. Gradually the American rebels forged an army that, despite its ragged appearance, held its own on the battlefield. "I admire the American troops tremendously!" exclaimed a French officer toward the end of the war. "It is incredible that soldiers composed of every age, even children of fifteen, of whites and blacks, almost naked, unpaid, and rather poorly fed, can march so well and withstand fire so steadfastly."

Military mobilization created political commitment. To encourage ordinary Americans to support the war—as soldiers, taxpayers, and hardworking citizens—the Patriot leadership prompted them to take an active role in the new republican governments. As the common people became the rulers rather than the ruled, the character of politics changed. "From subjects to citizens the difference is immense," remarked the South Carolina Patriot David Ramsay. "Each citizen of a free state contains . . . as much of the common sovereignty as another." By raising a democratic army and repudiating aristocratic and monarchical rule, the Patriots launched the age of republican revolutions first in Europe and then in Spain's American empire.

Toward Independence, 1775–1776

The Battle of Concord set the Patriots on the road to independence. During the following months Patriot legislators in the thirteen colonies stretching from New Hampshire to Georgia threw out their royal governors and created the two essentials for independence: a provisional government and a credible army.

The Second Continental Congress and Civil War

In May 1775 Patriot leaders gathered in Philadelphia for a Second Continental Congress. Soon after the Congress opened, more than 3,000 British troops attacked American fortifications on Breed's Hill and Bunker Hill overlooking Boston. After three assaults and 1,000 casualties, they finally dislodged the Patriot militia. Inspired by his countrymen's valor, John Adams exhorted the Congress to rise to the "defense of American liberty" by creating a Continental army and nominated George Washington of Virginia to lead it. After bitter debate Congress approved the proposals—but, Adams lamented, only "by bare majorities."

Despite the blood that had been shed, a majority in Congress still hoped for reconciliation with Britain. Led by John Dickinson of Pennsylvania, these moderates won approval of a petition that expressed loyalty to George III and requested repeal of oppressive Parliamentary legislation. But zealous Patriots such as Samuel Adams of Massachusetts and Patrick Henry of Virginia drummed up support for a Declaration of the Causes and Necessities of Taking Up Arms. Americans dreaded the "calamities of civil war," the declaration asserted, but were "resolved to die Freemen rather than to live [as] slaves." George III chose not to exploit these divisions among the Patriots; instead, in August 1775 he issued a Proclamation for Suppressing Rebellion and Sedition.

Even before the king's proclamation reached America, the radicals in Congress had won support for an invasion of Canada. Their goal was to unleash a popular French uprising and add a fourteenth colony to the rebellion. Patriot forces easily took Montreal, but in December 1775 they failed to capture Quebec City. Meanwhile, American merchants waged financial warfare by carrying out the promise of the First Continental Congress to cut off all exports to Britain and its West Indian sugar islands. With the tobacco and sugar trades in disarray, Parliament retaliated with the Prohibitory Act, which outlawed all trade with the rebellious colonies.

Skirmishes between Patriot and Loyalist forces broke out in many colonies. In Virginia the Patriot-dominated House of Burgesses forced the royal governor, Lord Dunmore, to take refuge on a British warship in Chesapeake Bay. Branding the Patriots as "traitors," the governor organized two military forces—one white, the Queen's Own Loyal Virginians, and one black, the Ethiopian Regiment, which enlisted about 1,000 slaves who had fled from their Patriot owners and were eager to fight for their liberty. In November 1775 Dunmore issued a controversial proclamation

George III, 1771

Like George Washington (b. 1732), King George III (b. 1738) was a young man when the American troubles began in 1765. In 1771, when Johann Zoffany painted this portrait of the king, George III was a headstrong monarch who was determined to impose his will on Parliament. Although he strongly supported Parliament's attempts to tax the colonies, his active involvement in the affairs of state sparked political confusion and contributed to the inept policy-making that led to the American rebellion.

The Royal Collection © (2005) Her Majesty Queen Elizabeth II.

promising freedom to slaves and indentured servants who joined the Loyalist cause. White planters denounced this "Diabolical scheme" as "pointing a dagger to their Throats." Faced with black unrest and pressed by yeoman and tenant farmers demanding independence, Patriot planters called for a final break with Britain.

In North Carolina, military clashes likewise prompted demands for independence. Early in 1776 Josiah Martin, North Carolina's royal governor, raised a Loyalist force of 1,500 Scottish Highlanders in the Carolina backcountry. In response, Patriots mobilized the low-country militia and in February defeated Martin's army at the Battle of Moore's Creek Bridge, capturing more than 800 Highlanders (see American Voices, "The Meaning of War," p. 169). Following this victory, radical Patriots turned the North Carolina assembly into an independent Provincial Congress, which instructed its representatives in Philadelphia "to concur with the Delegates of other Colonies in declaring Independence, and forming foreign alliances." In May, Virginia Patriots followed suit; led by James Madison, Edmund Pendleton, and Patrick Henry, they met in convention and resolved unanimously to support independence.

Common Sense

As the Patriots moved toward independence, many colonists retained a deep loyalty to the crown. Joyous crowds had toasted the health of George III when he ascended the throne in 1760 and when his ministers repealed the Stamp Act. Even as

AMERICAN VOICES

The Meaning of War

MARY HOOKS SLOCUMB

For sixteen-year-old Mary Hooks Slocumb, the outbreak of fighting in 1776 had a personal meaning. Already married and the mother of a young child, Slocumb so feared for the safety of her husband, a member of the North Carolina Light Horse Rangers, that, as she noted in a memoir written many years later, she threw caution to the wind, rushed to his side, and found herself in the role of a battlefield nurse.

The men all left on Sunday morning. More than eighty went from this house with my husband. . . . I kept thinking where they had got to—how far; where and how many of the regulars and tories they would meet. . . . [That night] I had a dream. . . . I saw distinctly a body wrapped in my husband's guard cloak—bloody—dead; and others dead and wounded on the ground around him. . . . If ever I felt fear it was at that moment. . . . I went to the stable, saddled my mare—as fleet and easy a nag as ever travelled; and in one minute we were tearing down the road at full speed. . . .

When day broke I was some thirty miles from home. . . . The blind path I had been following brought me into the Wilmington road leading to Moore's Creek Bridge. . . . [A] few yards from the road, under a cluster of trees were lying perhaps twenty men. . . . In an instant my whole soul was centered in one spot; for there, wrapped in his bloody guard-Cloak, was my husband's body! . . . I remember uncovering his head and seeing a face clothed with gore from a dreadful wound across the temple. I put my hand on the bloody face; 'twas warm; and an *unknown voice* begged for water. . . . I brought it; poured some in his mouth; washed his face; and behold—it was Frank Cogdell. He soon revived and could speak. I was washing the wound in his head. Said he, "It is not that; it is that hole in my leg that is killing me." A puddle of blood was standing on the ground around his feet. I took his knife, cut away his trousers and stocking, found the blood came from a shot-hole through and through the fleshy part of his leg. I looked about and could see nothing that looked as if it would do for dressing wounds but some heart-leaves. I gathered a handful and bound them tight to the holes; and the bleeding stopped. . . . I dressed the wounds of many a brave fellow who did good fighting long after that day! . . . . Just then I looked up, and my husband, as bloody as a butcher, and as muddy as a ditcher, stood before me.

"Why Mary," he exclaimed, "What are you doing there?" . . . I would not tell my husband what brought me there. . . . In the middle of the night I again mounted my mare and started for home. . . .What a happy ride I had back! and with what joy did I embrace my child as he ran to meet me!

SOURCE: *The Women of the American Revolution* by Elizabeth F. Ellet. © 1969 by Elizabeth F. Ellet. Reprinted by permission.

the imperial crisis worsened, Benjamin Franklin proposed that the king rule over autonomous American assemblies. This loyalty to the king stemmed in part from the character of social authority and family values. Every father was "a king, and governor in his family," according to the Stonington (Connecticut) Baptist Association. Just as the settlers submitted to male elders in their town meetings, churches, and families, so they should obey the king, their imperial "father." Denial of the king's legitimacy might threaten all paternal authority and disrupt the hierarchical social order.

Nonetheless, by 1775 many Americans had turned against the monarch. As the military conflict escalated, they accused George III of supporting oppressive legislation and ordering armed retaliation against them. Surprisingly, agitation became especially intense in Philadelphia, the largest—but hardly the most radical— seaport city. Many Philadelphia merchants harbored Loyalist sympathies and had been slow to join the boycott against the Townshend duties. However, artisans, who numbered about half the city's workers, had become a powerful force in the Patriot movement. Worried that British imports threatened their small-scale manufacturing enterprises, they organized a Mechanics Association to protect America's "just Rights and Privileges." By February 1776, forty artisans sat with forty-seven merchants on the Philadelphia Committee of Resistance, the extralegal body that enforced the latest trade boycott.

Many Scots-Irish artisans and laborers in Philadelphia became Patriots for cultural and religious reasons. They came from Presbyterian families who had fled from British-controlled Ireland to escape religious discrimination; moreover, many of them had embraced the egalitarian message preached by Gilbert Tennent and other New Light ministers. As pastor of Philadelphia's Second Presbyterian Church, Tennent had told his congregation that all men and women were equal before God. Applying that idea to politics, New Light Presbyterians shouted in street demonstrations that they had "no king but King Jesus." Republican ideas derived from the European Enlightenment also circulated freely in Pennsylvania. Well-educated scientists and political leaders such as Benjamin Franklin and Benjamin Rush questioned not only the wisdom of George III but also the idea of monarchy itself.

With popular sentiment in flux, a single pamphlet tipped the balance toward the Patriot side. In January 1776 Thomas Paine published *Common Sense*, a call for independence and a republican (nonmonarchical) form of government. Paine had served as a minor bureaucrat in the Customs Service in England and was fired for protesting low wages. He found his way to London, where he wangled a meeting with Benjamin Franklin. In 1774 Paine migrated to Philadelphia, where he met Benjamin Rush and other Patriots who shared his republican sentiments. In *Common Sense* Paine launched a direct assault on the traditional political order in rousing language that stirred popular emotions.

"Monarchy and hereditary succession have laid the world in blood and ashes," Paine proclaimed, leveling a personal attack against George III, "the hard hearted sullen Pharaoh of England." Mixing insults with biblical quotations, Paine blasted the British system of "mixed government" among the three estates of king, lords, and commoners. "That it was noble for the dark and slavish times in which it was created," Paine granted, but now this system of governance yielded only "monarchical tyranny in the person of the king" and "aristocratical tyranny in the persons of the peers."

Paine also made a compelling case for American independence. Turning the traditional metaphor of patriarchal authority on its head, he asked, "Is it the interest of a man to be a boy all his life?" Within six months *Common Sense* went through twenty-five editions and reached hundreds of thousands of people throughout the colonies. "There is great talk of independence," a worried New York Loyalist noted, "and the unthinking multitude are mad for it. . . . A pamphlet called Common Sense has carried off . . . thousands." Paine called on Americans to reject the king and Parliament and create independent republican states. "A government of our own is our natural right. . . . 'TIS TIME TO PART."

Independence Declared

Inspired by Paine's arguments and beset by armed Loyalists, Patriot conventions called urgently for a break from Britain. In June 1776 Richard Henry Lee presented the Virginia Convention's resolution to the Continental Congress: "That these United Colonies are, and of right ought to be, free and independent states . . . absolved from all allegiance to the British Crown." Faced with certain defeat, staunch Loyalists and anti-independence moderates withdrew from the Congress, and left committed Patriots to take the fateful step. On July 4, 1776, the Congress approved the Declaration of Independence (see Documents, p. D-1).

The main author of the Declaration was Thomas Jefferson, a young Virginia planter. As a member of the Virginia legislature, Jefferson had mobilized resistance to the Coercive Acts with the pamphlet *A Summary View of the Rights of British America*. To persuade Americans and foreign observers to support independence, Jefferson vilified George III: "He has plundered our seas, ravaged our coasts, burned our towns, and destroyed the lives of our people. . . . A prince, whose character is thus marked by every act which may define a tyrant," Jefferson concluded, conveniently ignoring his own actions as a slave owner, "is unfit to be the ruler of a free people."

Employing the ideas of the European Enlightenment (see Chapter 4), Jefferson justified **republicanism** by proclaiming a series of "self-evident" truths: "that all men are created equal"; that they possess the "unalienable rights" of "Life, Liberty, and the pursuit of Happiness"; that government derives its "just powers from the consent of the governed" and can rightly be overthrown if it "becomes destructive of these ends." By linking these doctrines of individual liberty, popular sovereignty, and a republican form of government with independence, Jefferson established them as defining values of the new nation.

For Jefferson, as for Paine, the pen proved mightier than the sword. In rural hamlets and seaport cities, crowds celebrated the Declaration by burning George III in effigy and toppling statues of the king. These acts of destruction broke the Patriots' psychological ties to the father-monarch and established the legitimacy of republican state governments. On July 8, 1776, in Easton, Pennsylvania, a "great number of spectators" heard a reading of the Declaration, "gave their hearty assent with three loud huzzahs, and cried out, 'May God long preserve and unite the Free and Independent States of America.'"

The Trials of War, 1776–1778

The Declaration of Independence coincided with a full-scale British military assault against the Patriots. For two years British forces won nearly every battle against the Continental army commanded by George Washington. A few inspiring American victories kept the rebellion alive, but during the winters of 1776 and 1777 the Patriot cause hung in the balance.

War in the North

When the British resorted to military force, few European observers gave the rebels a chance. Great Britain had 11 million people, compared with the colonies' 2.5 million, nearly 20 percent of whom were enslaved Africans. Economically, the British had an even greater advantage thanks to the immense wealth generated by the South Atlantic system and the emerging Industrial Revolution. Its financial resources paid for the most powerful navy in the world, a standing army of 48,000 men, and thousands of hired German soldiers. British military officers had experience in America during the Seven Years' War, and their soldiers were well armed. Finally, the imperial government had the support of thousands of American Loyalists and many Indian tribes. The Cherokees in the Carolinas were firmly committed to the British side, as were four of the six Iroquois Nations of New York—the Mohawks, Senecas, Cayugas, and Onondagas—who were led by the pro-British Mohawk chief Joseph Brant.

By contrast, the rebellious Americans were militarily weak. General Washington's army consisted of about 18,000 poorly trained, short-term recruits hastily assembled by state governments in Virginia and New England. The Patriots could field thousands more militiamen but only near their own farms. Although many American officers had fought during the French and Indian War, they had never commanded a large force or faced a disciplined European army.

To exploit this military advantage, Britain's prime minister, Lord North, assembled a large invasion force and selected General William Howe to lead it. North ordered Howe to capture New York City and seize control of the Hudson River, thereby isolating the radical Patriots in New England from the other colonies. As the Continental Congress was declaring independence in Philadelphia in July 1776, Howe landed 32,000 troops—British regulars and German mercenaries—outside New York City.

Joseph Brant

The Mohawk chief Thayendanegea, known to the whites as Joseph Brant, was a devout member of the Church of England who had helped to translate the Bible into the Iroquois language. An influential leader, Brant secured the support of four of the six Iroquois Nations for the British. In 1778 and 1779, he led Iroquois warriors and Tory Rangers in devastating attacks on American settlements in the Wyoming Valley of Pennsylvania and the Cherry Valley in New York. This portrait by Charles Willson Peale was painted in 1797. Independence National Historic Park.

FOR MORE HELP ANALYZING THIS IMAGE, see the Online Study Guide at **bedfordstmartins.com/henrettaconcise**

British superiority was immediately apparent. In August 1776 Howe attacked the Americans in the Battle of Long Island and forced their retreat to Manhattan Island. There Howe outflanked Washington's troops and nearly trapped them. Outgunned and outmaneuvered, the Continental army again retreated, first to Harlem Heights, then to White Plains, and finally across the Hudson River to New Jersey. By December, the British army had pushed the rebels out of New Jersey and across the Delaware River into Pennsylvania (Map 6.1).

From the Patriots' perspective winter came just in time. Following eighteenth-century military custom, the British halted their campaign for the cold months and allowed the Americans to catch them off guard. On Christmas night in 1776 Washington led his troops across the Delaware River and staged a surprise attack on Trenton, New Jersey, where he forced the surrender of 1,000 German soldiers. In early January 1777 the Continental army won another small victory at nearby Princeton. Bright stars in a dark night, these minor triumphs could not mask British military superiority. These are the times, wrote Tom Paine, that "try men's souls."

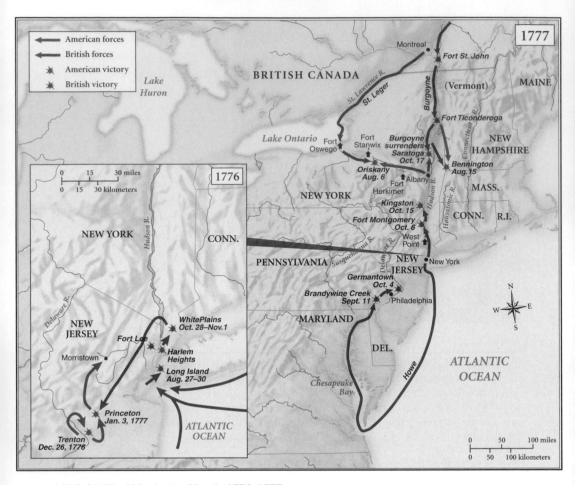

MAP 6.1 The War in the North, 1776–1777

In 1776 the British army drove Washington's forces across New Jersey into Pennsylvania. The Americans counterattacked successfully at Trenton and Princeton and then set up winter headquarters at Morristown. In 1777 British forces stayed on the offensive. General Howe attacked the Patriot capital of Philadelphia from the south, capturing it in early October. Meanwhile, General Burgoyne and Colonel St. Leger launched simultaneous invasions from Canada. Aided by thousands of New England militia, American troops commanded by General Horatio Gates defeated Burgoyne at Bennington, Vermont, and, in October 1777, at Saratoga, New York, the military turning point of the war.

Armies and Strategies

British superiority did not break the will of the Continental army and, thanks partly to General Howe's tactical decisions and mistakes, the rebellion continued. Howe had opposed the Coercive Acts of 1774, and he still hoped for a political compromise. Indeed, he had authority from Lord North to allow the rebels to surrender on honorable terms. Consequently, instead of ruthlessly pursuing the retreating American army, Howe was content to show his superior power and convince the Continental Congress that resistance was futile. Howe's tactics also reflected eighteenth-century military practices, which focused on winning the surrender of opposing forces rather than destroying them. Moreover, the British general knew that he could not afford a major defeat because he was 3,000 miles and many months away from reinforcements. Although Howe's prudent tactics were understandable, they cost the British the opportunity to nip the rebellion in the bud.

Howe's failure to win a decisive victory was paralleled by Washington's success in avoiding a major defeat. He too was cautious; as Washington advised Congress, "On our Side the War should be defensive." His strategy was to draw the British away from the seacoast, extend their lines of supply, and sap their morale while keeping the Continental army intact as a symbol and instrument of American resistance.

Congress had promised Washington a regular force of 75,000 men, but the Continental army never reached a third of that number. Yeomen farmers preferred to serve in the local militia so that they could continue to work their farms; consequently, many recruits in the regular army were propertyless farmers and laborers. The Continental soldiers recruited by the state of Maryland and commanded by General William Smallwood were either poor American-born youths or older foreign-born men—often British ex-convicts and former indentured servants. Such men enlisted not out of patriotism but for a bonus of $20 in cash (about $1,000 today) and the promise of 100 acres of land. Molding such recruits into a fighting force took time. Many men panicked in the face of a British artillery bombardment or flank attack; hundreds deserted, unwilling to submit to the discipline of military life. The soldiers who stayed resented the contemptuous way their officers treated the "camp followers," the women who fed and cared for the troops.

Such personal support was crucial, for the Continental army was poorly supplied and faintly praised. Radical Whig Patriots viewed a standing army as a threat to liberty and even in wartime preferred the militia to a professional force. General Philip Schuyler of New York complained that his troops were "weak in numbers, dispirited, naked, destitute of provisions, without camp equipage, with little ammunition, and not a single piece of cannon." Given these handicaps, Washington was fortunate to have escaped an overwhelming defeat.

Victory at Saratoga

Howe's failure to achieve a quick victory dismayed Lord North and his colonial secretary, Lord George Germain. Accepting the challenge of a long-term military commitment, the British leaders increased the land tax to finance the war and prepared to mount a major campaign in 1777.

The isolation of New England remained the primary British goal. To achieve it, Germain planned a three-pronged attack converging on Albany, New York. General John Burgoyne would lead a large contingent of British regulars from Quebec to Albany.

Colonel Barry St. Leger and a force of Iroquois warriors would attack from the west, and General Howe would dispatch a force northward from New York City (see Map 6.1).

Howe had a different scheme and it led to a disastrous result. Howe wanted to attack Philadelphia, the home of the Continental Congress, and end the rebellion with a single victory over Washington's army. With Germain's apparent approval, he set his plan in motion—but very slowly. Rather than march quickly through New Jersey, British troops sailed south from New York, then up the Chesapeake Bay to attack Philadelphia from the south. This strategy worked brilliantly, as Howe's troops easily outflanked the American positions along Brandywine Creek in Delaware and forced Washington to withdraw. On September 26 the British marched triumphantly into Philadelphia, expecting the capture of the rebels' capital would end the uprising. But the Continental Congress fled into the interior, determined to continue the struggle.

Moreover, Howe's slow attack against Philadelphia contributed directly to the defeat of Burgoyne's army. Initially Burgoyne's troops advanced quickly from Canada, crossing Lake Champlain, overwhelming the American defenses at Fort Ticonderoga and driving toward the upper reaches of the Hudson River. Then they stalled, for Burgoyne—"Gentleman Johnny," as he was called—fought with style and was slowed down by the extra weight of comfortable tents and ample stocks of food and wine. The American troops led by General Horatio Gates further impeded Burgoyne's progress by felling huge trees to delay his wagons and by raiding his long supply lines to Canada.

By the summer's end, Burgoyne's army of 6,000 British and German troops and 600 Loyalists and Indians was bogged down near Saratoga, New York. Desperate for food and horses, the British force staged a raid on nearby Bennington, Vermont, where 2,000 American militiamen repulsed them. Patriot forces in the Mohawk Valley likewise forced St. Leger and the Iroquois to retreat. To make matters worse, the British commander in New York City recalled the 4,000 troops he had sent toward Albany and dispatched them instead to bolster Howe's force in Philadelphia. While Burgoyne waited in vain for help, thousands of Patriot militiamen from Massachusetts, New Hampshire, and New York joined Gates's forces. They "swarmed around the army like birds of prey," reported an alarmed English sergeant, and in October 1777 forced Burgoyne to surrender.

The battle at Saratoga proved to be the turning point of the war. The Patriots captured more than 5,000 British troops and their equipment. Equally important, the victory ensured the success of American diplomats in Paris, who were seeking a military alliance with France.

Social and Financial Perils

As Patriots on the home front celebrated the triumph at Saratoga, their joy was muted by wartime difficulties. The fighting exposed tens of thousands of civilians to deprivation, displacement, and death. "An army, even a friendly one, are a dreadful scourge to any people," a Connecticut soldier wrote from Pennsylvania. "You cannot imagine what devastation and distress mark their steps." British and American armies marched back and forth across New Jersey, forcing Patriot and Loyalist families to flee their homes to escape arrest—or worse. Soldiers and partisans looted farms for food or political revenge. Wherever the armies went, disorderly troops harassed and raped women and girls. When British warships sailed up the Potomac River, women and children fled from Alexandria, Virginia, and "stowed themselves into every Hut they can get, out of the reach of the Enemys canon" and troops.

The war became a bloody partisan conflict. Patriots formed Committees of Safety that collected taxes, sent food and clothing to the Continental army, and imposed fines or jail sentences on those who failed to support the cause. In New England mobs of Patriot farmers beat suspected Tories and destroyed their property. "Every Body submitted to our Sovereign Lord the Mob," a Loyalist preacher lamented. In some areas of Maryland, the number of "nonassociators"—those who refused to join either side—was so large that they successfully defied Patriot organizers. "Stand off you dammed rebel sons of bitches," Robert Davis of Anne Arundel County shouted, "I will shoot you if you come any nearer."

Such defiance exposed the weakness of the new state governments, which teetered on the brink of bankruptcy. To feed, clothe, and pay their troops, state officials borrowed gold, silver, or British currency from wealthy individuals. When those funds ran out, Patriot officials were afraid to raise taxes. Instead, individual states printed paper money, issuing $260 million in currency. Because it was printed in huge quantities and was not backed by gold, tax revenues, or mortgages on land, many Americans refused

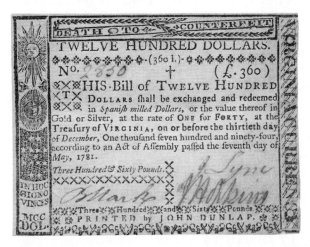

Paper Currency

To symbolize their independent status, the new state governments printed their own currency. Rejecting the English system of pounds and shillings, Virginia used the Spanish gold dollar as the basic unit of currency but included the equivalent in English pounds ($1,200 was £360, a ratio of 3.3 to 1). By 1781, Virginia had printed so much paper money to pay its soldiers and wartime expenses that the value of the currency had depreciated. It now took 40 Virginia paper dollars to buy the same amount of goods as one English pound (a 40-to-1 ratio). American Numismatic Society.

to accept the new currency at its face value. North Carolina's paper money came to be worth so little that even the tax collectors refused it.

The finances of the Continental Congress collapsed too, despite the efforts of the Philadelphia merchant Robert Morris, the government's chief treasury official. The Congress lacked the authority to impose taxes and so depended on funds requisitioned from the states, which frequently paid late or not at all. The Congress therefore borrowed gold from France and encouraged wealthy Americans to purchase Continental bonds. When those funds and other French and Dutch loans were exhausted, the Congress followed the lead of the states and printed $191 million in currency and bills of credit, which quickly declined in value. Unwilling to accept nearly worthless currency, farmers refused to sell their crops, even to the Continental army. Military morale crumbled, causing some Patriot leaders to doubt that the rebellion could succeed.

Fears reached their peak during the winter of 1777. While Howe's army partook of warm lodgings and ample food in Philadelphia, Washington's army retreated twenty miles to the west to Valley Forge, where about 12,000 soldiers and hundreds of camp followers suffered horribly. "The army . . . now begins to grow sickly," a surgeon confided to his diary. "Poor food—hard lodging—cold weather—fatigue— nasty clothes—nasty cookery. . . . Why are we sent here to starve and freeze?" Nearby farmers refused to help. Some were pacifists—Quakers and German sectarians—unwilling to support either side. Others looked out for their families, hoarding grain in hopes of higher prices or accepting only the gold and silver offered by British quartermasters. "Such a dearth of public spirit, and want of public virtue," Washington lamented, distressed that few Patriots were upholding republican ideas, but to no effect. By spring, 1,000 hungry soldiers had vanished into the countryside and another 3,000 had died from malnutrition and disease. One winter at Valley Forge took as many American lives as had two years of fighting.

In this dark hour Baron von Steuben raised the self-respect and readiness of the American army. A former Prussian military officer, von Steuben was one of a handful of republican-minded foreign aristocrats who aided the American cause. To counter falling morale, he instituted a system of drill and maneuver and encouraged officers to become more professional in their demeanor. Thanks to von Steuben, the smaller Continental army that emerged from Valley Forge in the spring of 1778 was a much tougher and better-disciplined force.

The Path to Victory, 1778–1783

Wars are often won by astute diplomacy and the War of Independence was no exception. The Patriots' prospects improved dramatically in 1778, when the United States formed a military alliance with France, the most powerful European nation. The alliance brought the Americans money, troops, and supplies and changed the conflict from a colonial rebellion to an international war.

The French Alliance

France and America were unlikely partners. France was Catholic and a monarchy; the United States was Protestant and a federation of republics. From 1689 to 1763 the two peoples had been military enemies, and New Englanders had recently forced the French population of Acadia (Nova Scotia) into exile. However, the Comte de Vergennes, the French foreign minister, was determined to avenge the loss of Canada to Britain. In 1776 he persuaded King Louis XVI to extend a secret loan to the rebellious colonies and supply them with much-needed gunpowder. Early in 1777 Vergennes opened negotiations with Benjamin Franklin and other American diplomats. When news of the American victory at Saratoga reached Paris in December 1777, Vergennes sought a formal alliance with the Continental Congress.

Franklin and his associates craftily exploited the rivalry between France and Britain to win an explicit commitment to American independence. The Treaty of Alliance of February 1778 specified that once France entered the war against Great Britain, neither partner would sign a separate peace before the "liberty, sovereignty, and independence" of the United States were ensured. In return, the American diplomats pledged that their government would recognize any French conquests in the West Indies. The alliance gave new life to the Patriots' cause. "There has been a great change in this state since the news from France," a Patriot soldier reported from Pennsylvania. Farmers—"mercenary wretches," he called them—"were as eager for Continental Money now as they were a few weeks ago for British gold."

The alliance bolstered the confidence of the Continental Congress. Acting now with purpose, the Congress addressed the demands of the officer corps. Most officers came from the upper ranks of society and had used their own funds to equip themselves and sometimes their men; in return they demanded lifetime military pensions at half pay. John Adams condemned the officers for "scrambling for rank and pay like apes for nuts," but General Washington urged Congress to grant the pensions, warning the lawmakers that "the salvation of the cause depends upon it." Congress reluctantly granted the officers half pay after the war, but only for seven years.

Meanwhile, the war was becoming increasingly unpopular in Britain. Radical agitators and republican-minded artisans supported American demands for greater rights and campaigned for domestic political reforms, such as the elimination of "rotten boroughs" (small voting districts controlled by wealthy men) and greater representation for cities in Parliament. The landed gentry protested increases in the land tax, and merchants condemned new levies on carriages, wine, and imported goods. "It seemed we were to be taxed and stamped ourselves instead of inflicting taxes and stamps on others," a British politician complained.

But George III still vowed to crush the rebellion. If America won independence, he warned Lord North, "the West Indies must follow them. Ireland would soon follow the same plan and be a separate state, then this island would be reduced to itself, and soon would be a poor island indeed." Following the British defeat at Saratoga, the king moderated his stance. To head off an American alliance with

France, he authorized North to seek a negotiated settlement. In February 1778 North persuaded Parliament to repeal the Tea and Prohibitory Acts and, in an amazing concession, to renounce its power to tax the colonies. Opening discussions with the Continental Congress, the prime minister proposed a return to the constitutional "condition of 1763," before the Sugar and Stamp Acts. The Patriots, now allied with France and seeking independence, rejected the overture.

War in the South

The French alliance expanded the war but did not bring it to a rapid conclusion. When France entered the conflict in June 1778, it sent its naval forces to the West Indies in hopes of capturing Barbados, Jamaica, or another rich sugar island. Spain, which joined the war against Britain in 1779, also had its own agenda: it wanted to regain Florida and Gibraltar. The Patriot cause was now caught up in a web of European territorial quarrels and diplomatic intrigue.

Beset by many enemies on many fronts, the British ministry revised its American strategy. It decided to use its army to recapture the rich tobacco- and rice-growing colonies of Virginia, the Carolinas, and Georgia and then rely on local Loyalists to hold them. The British could count on the allegiance of Scottish Highlanders in North Carolina and hoped to recruit other Loyalists from the ranks of the Regulators, the enemies of the low-country Patriot planters (see Chapter 4). The ministry also planned to exploit the racial divisions in the South. In 1776 over 1,000 slaves had fought for Lord Dunmore under the banner "Liberty to Slaves!"; a new British military offensive might prompt thousands more to flee from their Patriot owners or to rise in rebellion. South Carolina could not raise an army to defend itself, its representative told the Continental Congress, "by reason of the great proportion of citizens necessary to remain at home to prevent insurrection among the Negroes." When the Congress suggested that South Carolina raise 3,000 black troops, the state assembly overwhelmingly rejected the proposal.

Implementing Britain's southern military strategy became the responsibility of Sir Henry Clinton. After moving the main British army to secure quarters in New York City, Clinton launched a successful seaborne attack on Savannah, Georgia, in December 1778. Mobilizing hundreds of blacks to unload and transport supplies, Clinton moved inland and captured Augusta early in 1779. By the end of the year, Clinton's forces and local Loyalists controlled Georgia, and 10,000 troops were poised for an assault on South Carolina (Map 6.2).

During most of 1780 British forces marched from victory to victory. In May Clinton laid siege to Charleston, South Carolina, and forced the surrender of General Benjamin Lincoln and his garrison of 5,000 troops. Then Lord Cornwallis assumed control of the British forces and marched into the countryside. In August, at the battle of Camden, Cornwallis defeated an American force commanded by General Horatio Gates, the hero of Saratoga. Only 1,200 Patriot militiamen joined Gates at Camden— a fifth of the number at Saratoga—and many of them panicked. As Cornwallis took

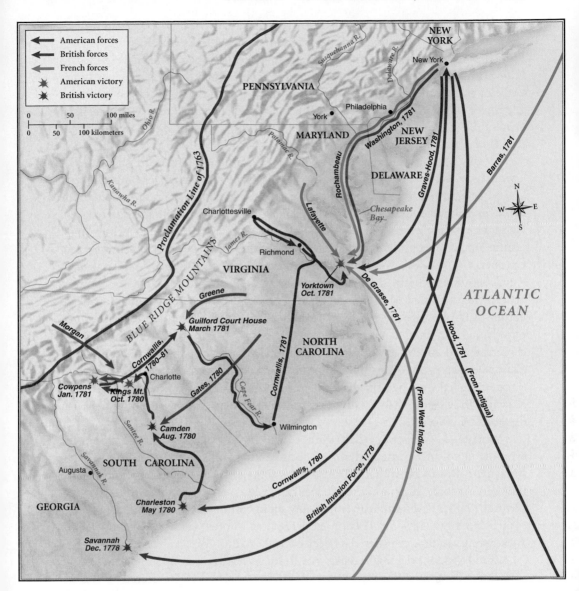

MAP 6.2 The War in the South, 1778–1781

The British ministry's southern strategy started well. British forces captured Savannah in December 1778, took control of Georgia during 1779, and vanquished Charleston in May 1780. Over the next eighteen months, brutal warfare conducted by small bands of irregular troops raged in the interior of the Carolinas and ended in a stalemate between British forces and their Loyalist supporters and the American army and militia. Hoping to break the deadlock, in 1781 British General Charles Cornwallis carried the battle into Virginia. A Franco-American army led by Washington and Lafayette, aided by the French fleet under Admiral de Grasse, surrounded Cornwallis's forces on the Yorktown peninsula and forced their surrender.

FOR MORE HELP ANALYZING THE MAP, see the Online Study Guide at **bedfordstmartins.com/henrettaconcise**.

control of South Carolina, hundreds of African Americans fled to freedom in British-controlled Florida, while hundreds more found refuge with the British army.

Then the tide of battle turned. The Dutch declared war against Britain, and France finally dispatched troops to America. The French decision was partly the work of the Marquis de Lafayette, a republican-minded aristocrat who had long supported the American cause. In 1780 Lafayette persuaded Louis XVI to send General Comte de Rochambeau and 5,500 men to Newport, Rhode Island, where they threatened British forces in New York City.

Meanwhile, Washington dispatched General Nathanael Greene to recapture the Carolinas. Greene faced a difficult task. His troops, he reported, "were almost naked and we subsist by daily collections and in a country that has been ravaged and plundered by both friends and enemies." To make use of local militiamen, who were "without discipline and addicted to plundering," Greene divided them into small groups under strong leaders and unleashed them on less-mobile British forces. In October 1780 a militia force of Patriot farmers defeated a regiment of Loyalists at King's Mountain, South Carolina, taking about 1,000 prisoners. Led by the "Swamp Fox," General Francis Marion, American guerrillas won a series of small but fierce battles in South Carolina. Then, in January 1781, General Daniel Morgan led another American force to a bloody victory at Cowpens, South Carolina. But Loyalist garrisons and militia units remained powerful, assisted by the well-organized Cherokees, who were determined to protect their lands from American settlers and troops. "We fight, get beaten, and fight again," General Greene declared doggedly. In March 1781, Greene's soldiers fought Cornwallis's seasoned army to a draw at North Carolina's Guilford Court House.

Weakened by this **war of attrition**, Cornwallis decided to concede the southernmost states to Greene and seek a decisive victory in Virginia. Aided by reinforcements from New York, the British general invaded the Tidewater region. There Benedict Arnold, the infamous Patriot traitor, led British troops in raids up and down the James River, where they met only slight resistance from an American force commanded by Lafayette. Then in May 1781, as the two armies sparred near the York Peninsula, France ordered its fleet from the West Indies to North America.

Emboldened by these French naval forces, Washington launched a well-coordinated attack. Feinting an assault on New York City, he secretly marched General Rochambeau's army from Rhode Island to Virginia, where it joined his Continental army. Simultaneously, the French fleet massed off the coast, establishing control of Chesapeake Bay. By the time the British discovered Washington's audacious plan, Cornwallis was surrounded, his 9,500-man army outnumbered two to one on land and cut off from reinforcement or retreat by sea. Abandoned by the British navy, Cornwallis surrendered at Yorktown in October 1781.

The Franco-American victory at Yorktown broke the resolve of the British government. "Oh God! It is all over!" Lord North exclaimed when he heard the news. Isolated diplomatically in Europe, stymied militarily in America, and lacking public support at home, the British ministry gave up active prosecution of the war.

The Patriot Advantage

Angry members of Parliament demanded an explanation. How could mighty Britain, victorious in the Great War for Empire, be defeated by a motley colonial army? The ministry blamed the military leadership, pointing with some justification to a series of blunders. Why had Howe not ruthlessly pursued Washington's army in 1776? How could Howe and Burgoyne have failed to coordinate the movement of their armies in 1777? Why didn't British generals make better use of the 55,000 Tories and thousands of Native American allies after 1778? Why had Cornwallis marched deep into the Patriot-dominated state of Virginia in 1781?

While criticizing these blunders, historians have emphasized the high odds against British success, given the broad support in America for the rebel cause. Although only a third of the white colonists were zealous Patriots, another third supported the war effort by paying taxes and joining the militia. Moreover, the Patriots had experienced politicians who commanded public support and, in George Washington, an inspired leader of the Continental army. An astute politician, Washington deferred to the civil authorities and thereby won respect and support from the Congress and the state governments. Confident of his own abilities, he recruited outstanding military officers to instill discipline in the fledgling Continental army and turn it into a respectable fighting force.

Finally, Washington also had a greater margin for error than the British generals did because Patriots controlled local governments. At crucial moments, they could mobilize the rural militia to assist his Continental army. Alone, the Patriot militia lacked the organization necessary to defeat the British army. However, in combination with the Continental forces, it proved potent, providing the margin of victory at Saratoga in 1777 and forcing Cornwallis from the Carolinas in 1781. In the end the American people decided the outcome. Preferring Patriot rule, they refused to support Loyalist forces or accept occupation by the British army. Consequently, while the British won many military victories, they achieved little. Once the rebels had the financial and military support of France, they could reasonably hope for a victory, such as that at Yorktown, that would end the conflict.

Diplomatic Triumph

After Yorktown diplomats took two years to conclude the war. Peace talks began in Paris in April 1782, but the French and Spanish stalled because they still hoped for a major naval victory or territorial conquest. Their delaying tactics infuriated the American diplomats—Benjamin Franklin, John Adams, and John Jay. Fearing that France might sacrifice American interests, the Patriot diplomats negotiated secretly with the British, prepared if necessary to sign a separate peace. The British ministry was also eager for a quick settlement because Parliament no longer supported the war and officials feared the loss of a rich West Indian sugar island.

Exploiting the rivalry between Britain and France, the American diplomats secured peace on very favorable terms. In the Treaty of Paris, signed in September 1783, Great Britain formally recognized the independence of its seaboard colonies. While retaining Canada, Britain also relinquished its claims to lands south of the Great Lakes and east of the Mississippi River and promised to withdraw British garrisons "with all convenient speed." Leaving the pro-British Indian peoples in the trans-Appalachian west to their fate, the British negotiators did not insist on a separate Indian territory. "In endeavouring to assist you," a Wea Indian complained to a British general, "it seems we have wrought our own ruin."

Other treaty provisions were equally favorable to the American side. They granted Americans fishing rights off Newfoundland and Nova Scotia, forbade the British from "carrying away any negroes or other property," and guaranteed freedom of navigation on the Mississippi to both British subjects and American citizens "forever." In return, the American government allowed British merchants to pursue legal claims for prewar debts and to encourage the state legislatures to return confiscated property to Loyalists and grant them citizenship.

In the Treaty of Versailles, signed at the same time as the Treaty of Paris, Britain made peace with France and Spain. Neither American ally gained very much. Spain reclaimed Florida from Britain but failed to regain the strategic fortress of Gibraltar, while France's only territorial gain was the Caribbean island of Tobago. Moreover, the war had quadrupled France's national debt, and six years later cries for tax relief and political liberty would spark the French Revolution. Only Americans profited handsomely from the treaties, which gave them independence from Britain and opened the trans-Appalachian west for settlement.

Republicanism Defined and Challenged

From the moment they became revolutionary republicans, Americans began to define their new social order. In the Declaration of Independence, Thomas Jefferson invoked John Locke, the philosopher of private liberty, in declaring a universal human right to "Life, Liberty, and the pursuit of Happiness." But Jefferson and many other Americans also lauded "republican virtue," an enlightened quest for the public good. As the New Hampshire constitution phrased it, "Government [was] instituted for the common benefits, protection, and security of the whole community." The tension between individual self-interest and the public interest would shape the future of the new nation.

Republican Ideals under Wartime Pressures

Simply put, a republic is a state with a representative system of government. For many Americans, republicanism also meant a community-oriented outlook. "The word republic" in Latin, wrote Thomas Paine, "means the public good," which all citizens have a duty to secure. "Every man in a republic is public property," asserted the Philadelphia Patriot Benjamin Rush, who eventually extended the notion to include women as well. "His time and talents—his youth—his manhood—his old age—nay more, life, all belong to his country." Reflecting this sense of community, members of the Continental Congress praised the militiamen who fought and fell at Lexington and Concord, Saratoga and Camden. And they applauded Henry Laurens of South Carolina when he condemned as a "total loss of virtue" the demand by Continental army officers for lifetime pensions. Raised as gentlemen, officers should be exemplars of virtue who gave freely to the republic.

However, the hardships of war undermined selfless idealism. Unruly Continental troops stationed at Morristown, New Jersey, in the winters of 1779 and 1780 mutinied, unwilling any longer to endure low pay and sparse rations. To restore military authority Washington ordered the execution of several mutineers but urged Congress to pacify the soldiers with back pay and new clothing. Later in the war, dissident officers at Newburgh, New York, talked of a military coup and Washington had to use his personal authority to thwart a dangerous challenge to Congress's authority.

Economic distress likewise tested the republican virtue of ordinary citizens. The British naval blockade cut supplies of European manufactures and disrupted the New England fishing industry. British occupation of Boston, New York, and Philadelphia trimmed domestic trade and manufacturing. As unemployed shipwrights, dock laborers, masons, coopers, and bakers deserted the cities and drifted into the countryside, New York City's population declined from 21,000 residents in 1774 to less than half that number by the war's end. In the Chesapeake, the British blockade deprived tobacco planters of European markets and forced them to cultivate grain, which could be sold to the contending armies. All across the land farmers and artisans adapted to a war economy.

Faced with a shortage of goods and constantly rising prices, government officials requisitioned military supplies directly from the people. In 1776 Connecticut officials called on the citizens of Hartford for 1,000 coats and 1,600 shirts and assessed smaller towns on a proportionate basis. In 1777 Connecticut officials again pressed the citizenry to provide shirts, stockings, and shoes for their Continental units. Soldiers added personal pleas. After losing "all the shirts except the one on my back" during the Battle of Long Island in 1776, Captain Edward Rogers told his wife that "the making of cloath . . . must go on. . . . I must have shirts and stockings & a jacket sent me as soon as possible & a blankit."

Patriot women responded to this challenge by increasing production of homespun cloth. One Massachusetts town produced 30,000 yards of homespun, while women in Elizabeth, New Jersey, promised "upwards of 100,000 yards of linnen and woolen cloth." Other women assumed the burdens of farm production while their men were away at war. Some went into the fields, plowing, harvesting, and loading grain, while others supervised hired laborers or slaves and acquired a taste for making decisions. "We have sow'd our oats as you desired," Sarah Cobb Paine wrote to her absent husband. "Had I been master I should have planted it to Corn." Taught

Mobilizing for War

This 1779 woodcut illustrated a poem by Molly Guttridge, a Daughter of Liberty in Marblehead, Massachusetts, and used a military image to symbolize the wartime contributions of American women. Although only a few Patriot women disguised themselves as men and fought in the war, hundreds more traveled with the Continental army and provided the troops with food and support. Most important, thousands of women ran farms in the absence of their soldier-husbands.

New-York Historical Society.

from childhood to value the welfare of their fathers, brothers, and husbands above their own, women were expected to act "virtuously" and often did so. Their wartime efforts not only maintained farm output but also boosted self-esteem and prompted some women to expect greater rights in the new republican society.

Despite the women's efforts, goods remained in short supply and prices rose sharply. Hard-pressed consumers decried merchants and traders as "enemies, extortioners, and monopolizers" and called for government regulation. But in 1777, when a convention of New England states imposed price ceilings, many farmers and artisans refused to sell their goods at the set prices. In the end, a government official admitted, consumers had to pay the higher market prices "or submit to starving."

The struggle over regulation came to a head in Philadelphia. Following the British withdrawal in 1778, artisans and laborers forced the municipal government to establish a Committee on Prices. Invoking the traditional concept of the "just price," the committee set rates for thirty-two commodities and urged citizens to act with "republican virtue." However, Patriot financier Robert Morris and most merchants condemned the price controls and espoused "classical liberal" ideas of free trade. They argued that regulation would encourage farmers to hoard their crops, whereas allowing prices to rise would bring more goods to market. As Benjamin Franklin put it, price controls were "contrary to the nature of commerce."

Nonetheless, most Philadelphians favored "fair" trade rather than "free" trade—at least in principle. At a town meeting in August 1779, over 2,000 Philadelphians voted for regulation, and fewer than 300 opposed it. In practice, however, many artisan-republicans—shoemakers, tanners, and bakers—found that they could not support their families on fixed prices and so refused to abide by them.

Spiraling inflation posed a severe challenge to all American families. By 1778 so much currency had been printed that a family needed $7 in Continental bills to buy goods worth $1 in gold or silver. As the ratio steadily escalated—to 42 to 1 in 1779, to 100 to 1 in 1780, and to 146 to 1 in 1781—it sparked social upheaval. In Boston a mob of women accused merchant Thomas Boyleston of hoarding goods, "seazd him by his Neck," and forced him to sell his wares at the traditional prices. In rural Ulster County, New York, women demanded that the Patriot Committee of Safety take steps to lower food prices; otherwise, they said, "their husbands and sons shall fight no more." To restore the value of Continental currency, the Congress asked the states to allow their citizens to pay taxes in depreciated Continental bills (with $40 in paper money counting as $1 in specie). This plan redeemed $120 million in Continental bills, but at the end of the war speculators still held $71 million in currency in the hope that the government would eventually redeem it at face value. "Private Interest seemed to predominate over the public weal," a leading Patriot complained.

Ultimately, this currency inflation transferred most of the costs of the war to ordinary Americans. Tens of thousands of farmers and artisans received Continental bills in return for supplies and thousands of soldiers took them as pay—only to find that the currency literally depreciated in their pockets. Every time they kept a paper dollar for a week, the money lost value and could buy less, thereby imposing a hidden "currency tax" on them. Each individual tax was small—a few pennies on each dollar they handled. But taken together—as millions of dollars changed hands multiple times—these currency taxes paid the huge cost of the war.

The Loyalist Exodus

As the war turned in favor of the Patriots, more than 100,000 Loyalists emigrated to the West Indies, Canada, and Britain. Relatively few of the more prominent refugees found happiness in exile in England; the majority complained of "their uneasy abode in this country of aliens." Many refugees suffered severe financial losses. John Tabor Kempe, the last royal attorney general of New York, sought £65,000 sterling (about $5 million today) in compensation from the British government but received only £5,000. The great mass of Loyalist refugees got nothing, and many lamented the loss of their old lives. Watching "sails disappear in the distance," an exiled Loyalist woman in Nova Scotia had "such a feeling of loneliness come over me that . . . I sat down on the damp moss with my baby on my lap and cried bitterly."

Some angry Patriots demanded that the state governments seize the property of wealthy Loyalists and distribute it to needy Americans. However, most Patriot leaders argued that confiscation would be contrary to individual rights and the republican principle of legal equality. In Massachusetts, officials cited the state's constitution of 1780, which declared that every citizen should be protected "in the enjoyment of his life, liberty, and property, according to the standing laws." Consequently, the new republican governments did not promote a social revolution. They confiscated only a small amount of Loyalist property and usually sold it to the highest bidder, who was often a wealthy Patriot rather than a yeoman or a propertyless foot soldier. In a few cases confiscation did produce a democratic result. In North Carolina about half the new owners of Loyalist lands were small-scale farmers. And on the former Philipse manor in New York many Patriot tenants used their hard-earned savings to buy the seized land. When Philipse tried to reclaim his land, former tenants told him they had "purchased it with the price of their best blood" and "will never become your vassals again." But in general the revolutionary upheaval did not drastically alter the structure of rural society.

Social turmoil was greater in the cities, as Patriot merchants replaced Tories at the top of the economic ladder. In Massachusetts the Lowell, Higginson, Jackson, and Cabot families moved their trading enterprises to Boston to fill the vacuum created by the departure of the Loyalist Hutchinson and Apthorp clans. In Philadelphia, small-scale Patriot traders stepped into the vacancies created by the collapse of Anglican and Quaker mercantile firms. The War of Independence replaced a tradition-oriented economic elite—one that invested its profits from trade in real estate and became landlords—with a group of entrepreneurial-minded republican merchants who promoted new trading ventures and domestic manufacturing.

The Problem of Slavery

Slavery revealed an enormous contradiction in the Patriots' republican ideology. "How is it that we hear the loudest yelps for liberty among the drivers of Negroes?" the British author Samuel Johnson chided the rebellious white Americans, a point some Patriots took to heart. "I wish most sincerely there was not a Slave in the province," Abigail Adams confessed to her husband, John. "It always appeared a most iniquitous Scheme to me—to fight ourselves for what we are daily robbing and plundering from those who have as good a right to freedom as we have."

In fact, the white Patriots' struggle for independence raised the prospect of freedom for enslaved Africans. As the war began, a black preacher in Georgia told his fellow slaves that King George III "came up with the Book [the Bible], and was about to alter the World, and set the Negroes free." Similar rumors circulated among slaves in Virginia and the Carolinas and prompted thousands of African Americans to flee behind British lines. Two neighbors of Richard Henry Lee, the Virginia Patriot, lost "every slave they had in the world," as did many other planters. When the British army evacuated Charleston, more than 6,000 former slaves went with them; another 4,000 left from Savannah. All told, some 30,000 blacks may have fled their owners. Hundreds of black Loyalists settled permanently in Canada. Over 1,000 others, poorly treated by British officials and settled on inferior land in Nova Scotia, sought a better life in the abolitionist settlement in Sierra Leone, West Africa.

Symbols of Slavery—and Freedom

The scar on the forehead of this black woman, who was widely known as "Mumbet," underlined the cruelty of slavery. Winning emancipation through a legal suit in Massachusetts, she chose a name befitting her new status: Elizabeth Freeman. This watercolor, by Susan Sedgwick, was painted in 1811. Massachusetts Historical Society.

Yet thousands of African Americans decided to serve the Patriot cause. Eager to raise their social status, free blacks in New England volunteered for military service in the First Rhode Island Company and the Massachusetts "Bucks." In Maryland a large number of slaves took up arms for the Patriot cause in return for a promise of freedom. Throughout the Chesapeake region slaves struck informal bargains with their Patriot masters by trading loyalty in wartime for a promise of eventual liberty. In 1782 the Virginia assembly passed an act allowing **manumission** (liberation); within a decade planters had freed 10,000 slaves.

The Quakers took the lead in condemning slavery. Beginning in the 1750s the Quaker evangelist John Woolman had urged Friends to free their slaves, and during the war many did so. Rapidly growing Christian evangelical churches, notably the Methodists and the Baptists, also advocated emancipation and admitted both enslaved and free blacks to their congregations. In 1784 a conference of Virginia Methodists declared that slavery was "contrary to the Golden Law of God on which hang all the Law and Prophets."

Enlightenment philosophy also worked to undermine slavery and racism. John Locke had argued that ideas were not innate but stemmed from a person's experiences in the world. Accordingly, Enlightenment thinkers suggested that the oppressive conditions of slavery, not inherent inferiority, accounted for the debased situation of

Africans in the Western Hemisphere. As one Enlightenment-influenced American put it, "A state of slavery has a mighty tendency to shrink and contract the minds of men." Anthony Benezet, a Quaker philanthropist who funded a school for blacks in Philadelphia, defied popular opinion in declaring that African Americans were "as capable of improvement as White People."

These new religious and intellectual currents sparked legal change. In 1784, judicial rulings abolished slavery in Massachusetts and, over the next twenty years, every state north of Delaware enacted legislation providing for the gradual end of slavery. However, these gradual emancipation laws compensated white owners by requiring more years—even decades—of servitude. For example, the New York Emancipation Act of 1799 granted freedom to slave children only when they reached the age of twenty-five. As late as 1810, almost 30,000 blacks in the northern states—nearly a fourth of their African American residents—were still enslaved. Emancipation came slowly because whites feared competition for jobs and the prospect of race melding. To keep the races separate, in 1786 Massachusetts reenacted an old law prohibiting whites from marrying blacks, Indians, or mulattos (see Voices from Abroad, "The Character of Northern Slavery," p. 191).

The tension between the republican values of liberty and property was greatest in the South, where slaves made up 30 to 60 percent of the population and represented a huge financial investment. Some Chesapeake tobacco planters, moved by religious principles or oversupplied with workers, allowed blacks to buy their freedom through paid work as artisans or laborers. Manumission and self-purchase gradually brought freedom to a third of the African American residents of Maryland. However, in 1792 the Virginia legislature made manumission more difficult. Following the lead of Thomas Jefferson, who owned more than 100 slaves, the Virginia legislators argued that slavery was a "necessary evil" required to maintain white supremacy and the luxurious planter lifestyle. Resistance to freedom for blacks was even greater in North Carolina, where the legislature condemned Quaker manumissions as "highly criminal and reprehensible." The rice-growing states of South Carolina and Georgia rejected emancipation out of hand (Map 6.3).

The debate over emancipation among southern whites ended in 1800, when Virginia authorities thwarted an uprising planned by the enslaved artisan Gabriel Prosser and hanged him and thirty of his followers. "Liberty and equality have brought the evil upon us," a letter to the *Virginia Herald* proclaimed, for such doctrines are "dangerous and extremely wicked in this country, where every white man is a master, and every black man is a slave." To preserve their privileged social position, southern whites redefined republicanism so that it applied only to the "master race."

A Republican Religious Order

The demand for greater liberty unleashed by the republican revolution of 1776 also forced Patriot lawmakers to devise new relationships between church and state. During the colonial era only the Quaker- and Baptist-controlled governments of

VOICES FROM ABROAD

The Character of Northern Slavery

ALEXANDER COVENTRY

W hen Alexander Coventry migrated from Scotland to New York in 1785, he began to record his daily experiences in a journal. The following selections provide insight into the condition of New York's rural African Americans, most of whom were slaves owned by farmers of Dutch descent. Coventry's comments suggest both the exploitation inherent in the system of slavery and the opportunities open to northern blacks to run away, form interracial liaisons, and bargain over the conditions of their work.

2 February 1787 Rode through the Cocksaxie settlement. . . . The houses are substantially built of Lime-stone, and are generally 1½ stories high; the barns are capacious. . . . Cocksaxie farmers are supposed to be the most opulent in the state. Their fertile soil, and its convenience to market, being much in their favor. The tact [area of land] is almost exclusively inhabited by the low Dutch . . . and each farmer has a number of Negro slaves . . . who did all the work on the farm, and in the house. . . . Although the blacks were slaves, yet I feel warranted in asserting that the laboring class in no country lived more easy, were better clothed and fed, or had more of life, than these slaves.

2 April 1787 [Went with] William Van Valkenburg to see his brother John, who has received a stab in his thigh about 5 inches deep. He received the wound from a negro, whom his former master and John went to take. The negro and his wench had run away, and escaped into Boston state (Massachusetts) where negroes are free.

9–11 April 1789 Van Curen's negro Cuff came here and wanted W.C. [William Coventry, Alexander's cousin] to buy him . . . but Van Curen and W.C. could not agree, therefore I told him if the negro would agree to live with me, I would buy him. He asked 77 pounds. I offered 76 pounds. We tossed up and he won. . . . I asked Cuff if he would live with me. He said he would; he helped to drive the cows home to fodder. . . . Cuff wanted two days next week to keep Paas [Easter Sunday]. I told him to return on Wednesday morning, which he said he would do.

4 April 1790 While foddering, Thursday, before sunrise, a man and woman passed, the man was black, and asked the road to Hudson. Heard since that it was a negro run off with a white woman.

21 December 1791 Went over to Jacobus Legat's to see whether he would sell his Wench, Cuff's wife. Legat offered her, with her youngest child for £45. I offered him £40 and so we parted [without a sale].

3 February 1792 Cornelius Van Curen here; wants to buy Cuff back again, but Cuff won't go to him again.

SOURCE: *Memoirs of an Emigrant: The Journal of Alexander Coventry, M.D.* Published by the Albany Institute of History and Art (1978). Reprinted by permission.

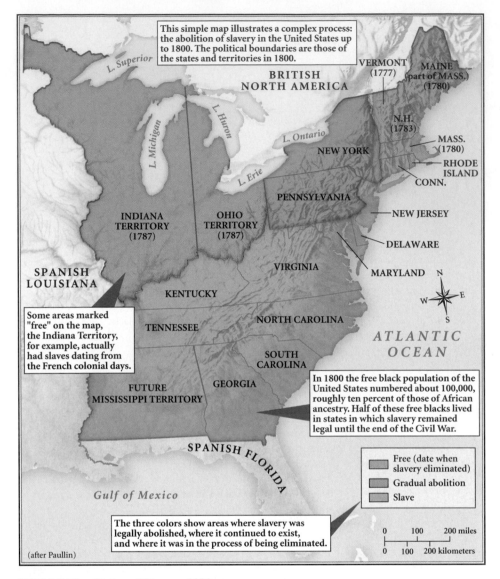

This simple map illustrates a complex process: the abolition of slavery in the United States up to 1800. The political boundaries are those of the states and territories in 1800.

L. Superior

BRITISH
NORTH AMERICA

VERMONT
(1777)

MAINE
(part of MASS.)
(1780)

L. Huron

L. Michigan

L. Ontario

N.H.
(1783)

MASS.
(1780)

NEW YORK

RHODE
ISLAND

L. Erie

CONN.

PENNSYLVANIA

NEW JERSEY

INDIANA
TERRITORY
(1787)

OHIO
TERRITORY
(1787)

DELAWARE

SPANISH
LOUISIANA

VIRGINIA

MARYLAND   N

KENTUCKY

W   E

Some areas marked "free" on the map, the Indiana Territory, for example, actually had slaves dating from the French colonial days.

TENNESSEE

NORTH CAROLINA

S

SOUTH
CAROLINA

ATLANTIC
OCEAN

FUTURE
MISSISSIPPI TERRITORY

GEORGIA

In 1800 the free black population of the United States numbered about 100,000, roughly ten percent of those of African ancestry. Half of these free blacks lived in states in which slavery remained legal until the end of the Civil War.

SPANISH FLORIDA

Free (date when slavery eliminated)

Gradual abolition

Slave

Gulf of Mexico

The three colors show areas where slavery was legally abolished, where it continued to exist, and where it was in the process of being eliminated.

0   100   200 miles

0   100   200 kilometers

(after Paullin)

MAP 6.3 The Status of Slavery, 1800

In 1775 racial slavery was legal in every British American colony. By the time the American states achieved their independence in 1783, most African Americans in New England had also become free. By 1800 nearly all of the states north of Maryland had provided for the gradual abolition of slavery, but the process was slow and not completed until the 1830s. After the Revolution, some slave owners in the Chesapeake region also manumitted their slaves, leaving only the whites of the Lower South firmly committed to racial bondage.

Pennsylvania and Rhode Island had repudiated the idea of an **established church**. Then in 1776 James Madison and George Mason used Enlightenment principles to undermine the traditional commitment to a state-supported church in Virginia. They persuaded the state's constitutional convention to issue a Declaration of Rights guaranteeing all Christians the "free exercise of religion." To win broad support for the war, the Virginia Anglican elite accepted the legitimacy of the dissenting Presbyterian and Baptist churches that they had previously persecuted. Indeed, in 1778 Virginia Anglicans launched their own revolution by severing ties with the hierarchy of the Church of England and creating the Protestant Episcopal Church of America.

After the Revolution an established church and compulsory religious taxes were no longer the norm in the United States. Baptists in particular opposed the use of taxes to support religion. In Virginia their political influence prompted lawmakers to reject a bill supported by George Washington and Patrick Henry, which would have imposed a general tax to fund all Christian churches. Instead, in 1786 the Virginia legislature enacted Thomas Jefferson's Bill for Establishing Religious Freedom, which made all churches equal before the law and granted direct financial support to none. In New York and New Jersey the sheer number of churches—Episcopalian, Presbyterian, Dutch Reformed, Lutheran, and Quaker, among others—prevented legislative agreement on an established church or compulsory religious taxes. In New England Congregationalism remained the official state church until the 1830s, but state laws allowed Baptists and Methodists to pay religious taxes to their own churches.

However, even in Virginia, the separation of church and state was never complete. Many Americans believed that firm connections between church and state were necessary to promote morality and respect for authority. "Pure religion and civil liberty are inseparable companions," a group of North Carolinians advised their minister. "It is your particular duty to enlighten mankind with the unerring principles of truth and justice, the main props of all civil government." Accepting this premise, most state governments provided churches with indirect aid by exempting their property and ministers from taxation.

Freedom of conscience proved equally difficult to achieve. In Virginia, Jefferson's Bill for Establishing Religious Freedom prohibited religious requirements for political and civil officeholding, but other states continued to deny full citizenship to those who dissented from the doctrines of Protestant Christianity. The North Carolina constitution of 1776 disqualified from public office any citizen "who shall deny the being of God, or the Truth of the Protestant Religion, or the Divine Authority of the Old or New Testament." New Hampshire's constitution contained a similar provision until 1868.

Americans influenced by the Enlightenment and by evangelical Protestantism condemned such religious restrictions but for different reasons. Leading American intellectuals, including Thomas Jefferson and Benjamin Franklin, argued that God had given humans the power of reason so that they could determine moral truths for themselves. To protect society from "ecclesiastical tyranny," they demanded complete freedom of conscience. Many evangelical Protestants also wanted religious liberty, but their goal was to protect their churches from the government. The New England minister Isaac Backus warned Baptists not to incorporate their churches or accept public funds because that might lead to state control. In Connecticut a devout Congregationalist welcomed voluntarism (the voluntary funding of churches by their members) because it allowed the laity to control the clergy, thereby furthering "the principles of republicanism."

In religion as in politics, independence provided American leaders with the opportunity to fashion a new institutional order. In both cases they repudiated the hierarchical ways of the past—monarchy and establishment—in favor of a republican alternative. These choices reflected the increased influence of ordinary citizens, who had fought and financed the long, difficult military struggle, and wanted a voice in the new republican political and religious institutions. As a wealthy Virginia planter had warned in April 1776, a successful revolt against British rule would assist yeomen to promote "their darling Democracy."

TIMELINE

1775	Battle of Concord (April 19)		Severe inflation of paper currency begins
	Second Continental Congress meets in Philadelphia (May)	**1778**	Franco-American alliance (February)
	Battle of Bunker Hill		Lord North seeks political settlement; Congress rejects negotiations
	Congress creates Continental army		
	Congressional moderates submit Olive Branch petition; king rejects it		British begin southern strategy; capture Savannah (December)
	Lord Dunmore's proclamation offers freedom to slaves and servants (November)	**1780**	Sir Henry Clinton seizes Charleston (May)
	American invasion of Canada		French army lands in Rhode Island
1776	Patriots and Loyalists skirmish in the South	**1781**	Lord Cornwallis invades Virginia (April); surrenders at Yorktown (October)
	Thomas Paine publishes *Common Sense* (January)		Large-scale Loyalist emigration
	Declaration of Independence (July 4)		Partial redemption of Continental currency at 40 to 1
	Howe forces Washington to retreat from New York and New Jersey	**1782**	Virginia passes law allowing slave manumission (reversed in 1792)
	Virginia Declaration of Rights		
1777	Patriot women become important in war economy	**1783**	Treaty of Paris (September 3) officially ends war
	Howe occupies Philadelphia (September)	**1786**	Virginia enacts Bill for Establishing Religious Freedom
	Gates defeats Burgoyne at Saratoga (October)	**1800**	Gabriel Prosser organizes slave rebellion in Virginia
	Continental army suffers at Valley Forge during winter		

For Further Exploration

In *Angel in the Whirlwind: The Triumph of the American Revolution* (1997), Benson Bobrick presents the break with England as a grand epic stretching from the French and Indian War to Washington's inauguration. Gordon Wood, *The Radicalism of the American Revolution* (1992), offers a more scholarly account of these years. A compelling fictional account of the life of Tom Paine is Howard Fast, *Citizen Tom Paine* (1943). Pauline Maier, *American Scripture: Making the Declaration of Independence* (1997), explains the background of the Declaration and shows how it has been redefined over the past two centuries. For some vivid firsthand accounts of the military conflict, see John C. Dann, ed., *The Revolution Remembered: Eyewitness Accounts of the War for Independence* (1980). James L. Stokesbury, *A Short History of the American Revolution* (1991), suggests parallels between the British defeat and the American failure in Vietnam. Colin G. Calloway, *The American Revolution in Indian Country: Crisis and Diversity in Native American Communities* (1995), traces the Revolution's impact on the native peoples, while Robin Blackburn, *The Overthrow of Colonial Slavery, 1776–1848* (1988), shows how it aided the decline of racial bondage in the Western Hemisphere. Sylvia R. Frey, *Water from the Rock: Black Resistance in a Revolutionary Age* (1991), traces the impact of the Revolution on African Americans and their adaptations of republican ideology and Christian beliefs. In *Liberty's Daughters: The Revolutionary Experience of American Women, 1750–1800* (1980), Mary Beth Norton portrays both the continuities and the changes in women's lives.

Liberty! *The American Revolution* (PBS video; 6 hours) and the companion Web site, at <http:/www.pbs.org/liberty>, cover the war and the making of the Constitution. The Virtual Marching Tour of the Philadelphia Campaign 1777, at <http://www.ushistory.org/brandywine/index.html>, offers an interesting multimedia view of Howe's attack on Philadelphia and subsequent events. A fine, data-rich source on the black experience is Africans in America: Revolution, at <http://www.pbs.org/wgbh/aia/part2/title.html>; other parts of this site cover the entire African American experience. To explore the political philosophy of Thomas Jefferson, log on to Thomas Jefferson: On Politics & Government, at <http://etext.virginia.edu/jefferson/quotations>, a site that is conveniently arranged by topic.

For definitions of key terms boldfaced in this chapter, see the glossary at the end of the book.

To assess your mastery of the material covered in this chapter, see the Online Study Guide at **bedfordstmartins.com/henrettaconcise**.

For map resources and primary documents, see **bedfordstmartins.com/henrettaconcise**.

Chapter 7

THE NEW POLITICAL ORDER
1776–1800

Idolatry to Monarchs, and servility to Aristocratical Pride, was never
so totally eradicated from so many minds in so short a time.

JOHN ADAMS, 1776

Like an earthquake, the American Revolution shook the foundations
of the European monarchical order, and its aftershocks were felt far into the nineteenth century. By "creating a new republic based on the rights of [the] individual, the North Americans introduced a new force into the world," the eminent German historian Leopold von Ranke bluntly advised the king of Bavaria in 1854. Indeed, the new ideology of republicanism might cost the monarch his throne:

> This was a revolution of principle. Up to this point, a king who ruled by the grace of God had been the center around which everything turned. Now the idea emerged that power should come from below [from the people]. . . .

Previous republican revolutions—such as that of the Puritan Commonwealth in England in the 1650s—had ended in political chaos and military rule, and many Europeans expected the new American states to experience the same fate. However, General George Washington stunned the political leaders of Europe in 1783 when he voluntarily left public life to return to his plantation. "Tis a Conduct so novel," the American painter John Trumbull reported from London, that it is "inconceivable to People [here]." Washington's voluntary retirement bolstered the authority of elected Patriot leaders, who were firmly committed to fashioning representative republican government.

This great task absorbed the energy and intellect of an entire generation. Between 1776 and 1800 Americans wrote new state and federal constitutions and devised a system of politics that was responsive to the popular will. Many political leaders worried that the result was too democratic. When a bill was introduced into a state legislature, grumbled conservative Ezra Stiles, every elected official "instantly thinks how it will affect his constituents" rather than its impact on the welfare of the entire public. What Stiles criticized as irresponsible self-interest, most ordinary Americans welcomed. For the first time the interests of middling citizens were represented in the halls of government, and the monarchs of Europe trembled.

Creating Republican Institutions, 1776–1787

Once independence became the goal, Patriots had to decide how to allocate political power among themselves. "Which of us shall be the rulers?" asked a Philadelphia newspaper. The question was complex: Where would power reside, in the national government or the states? Who would control the new republican institutions, traditional elites or average citizens?

The State Constitutions: How Much Democracy?

In May 1776 the Continental Congress urged Americans to suppress royal authority and establish new governing institutions. Most states quickly complied. Within six months Virginia, Maryland, North Carolina, New Jersey, Delaware, and Pennsylvania had written new constitutions, and Connecticut and Rhode Island had transformed their colonial charters into republican documents by deleting references to the king. "Constitutions employ every pen," an observer noted.

However, republicanism meant more than ousting the king. The Declaration of Independence had stated the principle of popular sovereignty: that governments derive "their just powers from the consent of the governed." In the heat of revolution many Patriots gave this clause a democratic twist. In North Carolina the backcountry farmers of Mecklenburg County instructed their delegates to the state's constitutional convention to "oppose everything that leans to aristocracy or power in the hands of the rich and chief men exercised to the oppression of the poor." In Virginia, voters elected a new assembly that, an observer remarked, "was composed of men not quite so well dressed, nor so politely educated, nor so highly born" as colonial era legislatures.

This democratic impulse received its fullest expression in Pennsylvania, thanks to a coalition of Scots-Irish farmers, Philadelphia artisans, and Enlightenment-influenced intellectuals. The Pennsylvania Constitution of 1776 abolished property owning as a test of citizenship and granted taxpaying men the right to vote and hold office. It also created a unicameral (one-house) legislature with complete power. There was no upper house, and no governor exercised veto power. Other constitutional provisions mandated an extensive system of elementary education and protected citizens from imprisonment for debt. Pennsylvania's democratic constitution alarmed many leading Patriots, who believed officeholding should be restricted to "men of learning, leisure and easy circumstances." From Boston John Adams denounced Pennsylvania's unicameral legislature as "so democratical that it must produce confusion and every evil work." "Remember," Adams continued, "democracy

The American Star

The portraits of kings and queens had traditionally served as icons or symbols of their monarchical nations. This idealized portrait of Washington, by the American artist John Coles Jr., follows this custom on the occasion of the death of the great American general and political leader. The Roman goddess Minerva, wise in the ways of peace and skilled in the arts of war, holds Washington's portrait, as a Revolutionary Era soldier and the American goddess Columbia lament his death.

The Metropolitan Museum of Art. Gift of Edgar William and Bernice Chrysler Garbisch, 1964 (64.309.6).

FOR MORE HELP ANALYZING THIS IMAGE, see the Online Study Guide at **bedfordstmartins. com/henrettaconcise.**

never lasts long. It soon wastes, exhausts, and murders itself." Along with other conservative Patriots, Adams feared that ordinary citizens would use their numerical advantage to tax the rich: "If you give [democrats] the command or preponderance in the . . . legislature, they will vote all property out of the hands of you aristocrats. . . ."

To counter the appeal of the Pennsylvania Constitution, Adams published his *Thoughts on Government* (1776). In his treatise Adams adapted the British Whig theory of mixed government (in which power was shared by the king, lords, and commons) to a republican society. To preserve liberty, his system dispersed authority by assigning the different functions of government—lawmaking, administering, and judging—to separate institutions. Legislatures would make the laws while the executive and the judiciary would enforce them. Adams also called for a bicameral (two-house) legislature in which the upper house would be composed of substantial property owners; its role would be to check the power of popular majorities in the lower house. As a further curb on democracy, he proposed an elected governor with the power to veto laws and an appointed—not elected—judiciary to review them.

Leading Patriots endorsed Adams's scheme for elected bicameral legislatures because it preserved representative government while restricting popular power.

However, they hesitated to give the veto power to governors because they recalled the arbitrary conduct of royal governors and had no wish to enhance the power of the executive. However, in line with Adams's suggestion, most states retained traditional property qualifications for voting. In New York 90 percent of white men could vote in elections for the assembly, but only 40 percent had enough property to vote for the governor and the upper house. The most flagrant use of property to maintain the power of the elite occurred in South Carolina, where the 1778 constitution required candidates for governor to have a debt-free estate of £10,000 (about $600,000 today), senators to be worth £2,000, and assemblymen to own property valued at £1,000. These provisions ruled out officeholding for about 90 percent of white men.

Nonetheless, post-Revolutionary politics had a distinctly democratic flavor. The legislature emerged as the dominant branch of government, and state constitutions apportioned seats on the basis of population, which gave farmers in rapidly growing western areas the fair representation they had long demanded. Indeed, backcountry pressure prompted some legislatures to move the state capital from merchant-dominated seaports such as New York City and Philadelphia to inland cities such as Albany and Harrisburg. Even conservative South Carolina moved its capital inland, from Charleston to Columbia.

Moreover, new sorts of political leaders now predominated in many state legislatures. Rather than electing their social "betters" to office, ordinary citizens increasingly chose men of "middling circumstances" who knew "the wants of the poor." By the mid-1780s middling farmers and urban artisans controlled the lower houses in most northern states and formed a sizable minority in southern assemblies. These middling men took the lead in opposing the collection of back taxes and other measures that tended "toward the oppression of the people."

The political legacy of the Revolution was complex. Only in Pennsylvania and Vermont were radical Patriots able to take power and create democratic institutions. Yet everywhere representative legislatures had more power, and the day-to-day politics of electioneering and interest-group bargaining became much more responsive to the demands of average citizens.

The extraordinary excitement of the Revolutionary era also tested the dictum that only men could engage in politics. While men continued to control all public institutions—legislatures, juries, government offices—upper-class women entered political debate and filled their letters and diaries (and undoubtedly their conversations) with opinions on public issues. "The men say we have no business [with politics]," Eliza Wilkinson of South Carolina complained in 1783. "They won't even allow us liberty of thought, and that is all I want." (See American Voices, "The Status of Women," p. 200.)

These American women did not insist on complete civic equality with men but on the elimination of certain restrictive customs and laws. Thus, Abigail Adams demanded equal legal rights for married women; she pointed out that under existing common law, wives could not own most forms of property and could not enter into contracts or initiate lawsuits without their husbands' action. "Men would be

AMERICAN VOICES

The Status of Women

ABIGAIL AND JOHN ADAMS

*M*ost American women of European descent accepted the subordinate status of their sex; it was the way life had always been and, many believed, the way God intended it to be. Yet, the rhetoric of liberty and equality prompted a few women, including Abigail Adams, the wife of the prominent Massachusetts Patriot John Adams, to challenge men's dominant position. However, as this exchange between the Adamses suggests, most of these challenges were very tentative and very brief.

March 31, 1776, Abigail Adams to John Adams

I long to hear that you have declared an independancy [from Britain]—and by the way in the new Code of Law . . . be more generous and favorable to [the Ladies] than your ancestors. Do not put such unlimited power into the hands of Husbands. Remember all Men would be tyrants if they could. If perticuliar care and attention is not paid to the Ladies we are determined to foment a Rebellion, and will not hold ourselves bound by any Laws in which we have no voice, or Representation. . . .

April 14, 1776, John Adams to Abigail Adams

As to your extraordinary Code of Laws, I cannot but laugh. We have been told that our Struggle [for independence] has loosened the bonds of Government every where. That Children and Apprentices were disobedient—that schools and Colledges were grown turbulent—that Indians slighted their Guardians and Negroes grew insolent to their Masters. But your letter was the first Intimation that another Tribe more numerous and powerful than all the rest were grown discontented. . . .

Depend on it, We know better than to repeal our Masculine System. Altho they are in full Force, . . . in Practice you know We are the subjects. We have only the Name of Masters, and rather than give up this, which would compleatly subject Us to the Despotism of the Peticoat, I hope General Washington, and all our brave Heroes would fight. . . .

May 7 and August 14, 1776, Abigail Adams to John Adams

Notwithstanding all your wise Laws and Maxims we have it in our power not only to free ourselves but to subdue our Masters, and without violence to throw both your natural and legal authority at our feet. . . .

I most sincerely wish that some more liberal plan might be laid or executed for the Benefit of the rising Generation, and that our new constitution may be distinguished for Learning and Virtue. If we mean to have Heroes, Statesmen and Philosophers, we should have learned women. The world would laugh at me, and accuse me of vanity, But you I know have a mind too enlarged and liberal. . . . If much depends as is allowed upon the early Education of youth and the first principles which are instilld take the deepest root, great benifit must arise from litirary accomplishmcnts in women.

SOURCE: *Adams Papers: Adams Family Correspondence, Volume I: December 1761—May 1776*, edited by L. H. Butterfield. The Belknap Press of Harvard University Press. Copyright © 1963 by the Massachusetts Historical Society. Reprinted by permission of the publisher.

tyrants" if they continued to hold such power over women, Adams declared to her husband, criticizing him and other Patriots for "emancipating all nations" from monarchical despotism while "retaining absolute power over Wives."

Most men paid little attention to women's requests, and most husbands remained patriarchs who dominated their households. Even young men who embraced the republican ideal of **"companionate" marriage** did not support reform of the common law or a public role for their wives and daughters. With the partial exception of New Jersey, which until 1807 granted the vote to unmarried and widowed women of property, women remained second-class citizens, unable to participate directly in American political life.

The republican quest for an educated citizenry allowed advances by some American women. In her 1779 essay "On the Equality of the Sexes," Judith Sargent Murray argued that men and women had an equal capacity for memory and that women had a superior imagination. She conceded that most women were inferior to men in judgment and reasoning, but only because of a lack of training: "We can only reason from what we know," Murray argued, and most women had been denied "the opportunity of acquiring knowledge." However, in the 1790s the attorney general of Massachusetts declared that girls had an equal right to schooling under the state constitution. With greater access to public elementary schools and

Judith Sargent (Murray), Age Nineteen

The well-educated daughter of a wealthy Massachusetts merchant, Judith Sargent enjoyed a privileged childhood. However, she endured a difficult seventeen-year marriage to John Stevens, who ultimately went bankrupt, fled from his creditors, and died in the West Indies. In 1788 she wed the Reverend John Murray, who became a leading American Universalist. Her portrait, painted around 1771 by the renowned artist John Singleton Copley, captures Sargent's skeptical view of the world, an outlook that enabled her to question customary gender roles.

Terra Museum of American Art, Chicago, Illinois. Daniel J. Terra Collection.

the rapid creation of girls' academies (private high schools), many young women became literate and knowledgeable. By 1850 as many women as men in the northeastern states would be able to read and write, and literate women would again challenge their subordinate legal and political status.

The Articles of Confederation

As the Patriots moved toward independence in 1776, they envisioned a central government with limited powers. Carter Braxton of Virginia thought the Continental Congress should have the power to "regulate the affairs of trade, war, peace, alliances, &c." but "should by no means have authority to interfere with the internal police [governance] or domestic concerns of any Colony."

This intensely state-oriented outlook informed the Articles of Confederation, passed by Congress in November 1777. The first national constitution, the Articles provided for a loose confederation in which "each state retains its sovereignty, freedom, and independence" as well as all powers and rights not "expressly delegated" to the United States. Still, the Articles gave the Confederation government considerable authority; it could declare war and peace, make treaties with foreign nations, adjudicate disputes between the states, borrow and print money, and requisition funds from the states "for the common defense or general welfare." These powers were exercised by a central legislature, Congress, in which each state had one vote regardless of its wealth or population. Important laws needed approval by at least nine of the thirteen states, and changes in the Articles required unanimous consent. In the Confederation government, there was no separate executive and no judiciary.

Because of disputes over western lands, some states did not ratify the Articles until 1781. States such as Virginia, Massachusetts, and Connecticut claimed that their royal charters gave them boundaries that stretched westward to the Pacific Ocean. States without western claims, such as Maryland and Pennsylvania, refused to accept the Articles until the land-rich states relinquished their claims to the Congress. Threatened by Cornwallis's army in 1781, Virginia finally agreed to give up its land claims, and Maryland, the last holdout, then ratified the Articles (Map 7.1).

This formal approval of the Articles was anticlimactic. During the previous four years Congress had exercised de facto constitutional authority as it raised the Continental army and negotiated with foreign nations. Nonetheless, the Confederation government had a major weakness because the state legislatures were slow to contribute to its support and it lacked the authority to impose taxes. By 1780 the Confederation was nearly bankrupt. Facing imminent disaster, General Washington called urgently for a national system of taxation, warning Patriot leaders that otherwise "our cause is lost."

In response, nationalist-minded members of Congress tried to expand the Confederation's authority. Robert Morris, who became superintendent of finance in 1781, persuaded Congress to charter the Bank of North America, a private institution in Philadelphia, in hopes that its notes could stabilize the inflated

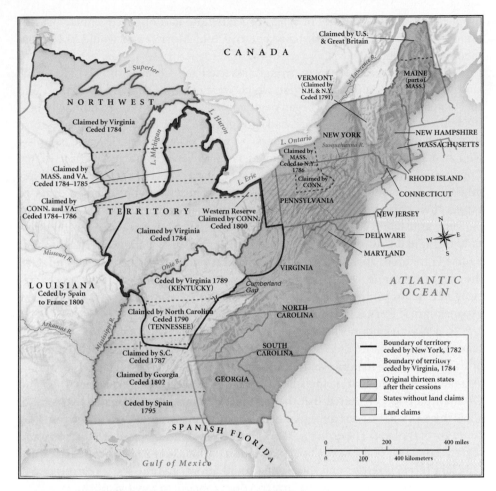

MAP 7.1 The Confederation and Western Land Claims

The Confederation Congress resolved the conflicting land claims of the states by creating a "national domain" west of the Appalachian Mountains. Between 1781 and 1802 all of the seaboard states with western land claims ceded them to the national government. In the Northwest Ordinances, the Confederation Congress divided the domain north of the Ohio River into territories, opened them to settlement by citizens from all the states, and set up democratic procedures by which they could join the Union.

FOR MORE HELP ANALYZING THIS MAP, see the Online Study Guide at **bedfordstmartins.com/henrettaconcise**.

Continental currency. Morris also developed a comprehensive financial system that handled army expenditures, apportioned war expenses among the states, and centralized the foreign debt. He hoped that the consciousness of a "national" debt would underline the Confederation's need for an import duty. But some state legislatures refused to increase the Confederation's powers, which required the unanimous consent of the states. Both Rhode Island and New York rejected Morris's proposal for an import duty of 5 percent. His state had opposed similar British-imposed duties, the New York representative told Morris, and would not accept them from Congress.

To raise revenue, Congress strongly asserted the Confederation's title to the lands of the trans-Appalachian West, which were much in demand by farmers and speculators. In 1783 Congress began negotiations with Indian tribes, hoping to persuade them that the Treaty of Paris had extinguished their land rights. Congress also sought payment from the white squatters— "white savages," John Jay called them— who had illegally settled on unoccupied land. Given the natural barrier of the Appalachian Mountains, many members of Congress feared that western settlers might set up separate republics and then ally themselves with Spain in order to export their crops via the Mississippi River and Spanish-controlled Louisiana. The danger was real: in 1784 settlers in what is now eastern Tennessee organized the new state of Franklin. To preserve its authority over the West, Congress refused to recognize Franklin or to admit it to the Confederation. Instead, the delegates directed the states of Virginia, North Carolina, and Georgia to administer the process of creating new states south of the Ohio River, a decision that indirectly encouraged the expansion of slavery into that vast region.

To deal with lands north of the Ohio River, Congress issued three important ordinances. The Ordinance of 1784, written by Thomas Jefferson, called for the division of the region into territories and the admission of a territory as a state as soon as its population equaled that of the smallest existing state. To deter squatters, the Land Ordinance of 1785 required that the regions be surveyed before settlement and, to allow this work to be done quickly, mandated a grid surveying system that ignored the contours of the land. The ordinance also specified a minimum price of $1 per acre and required that half of the townships be sold in single blocks of 23,040 acres each, which only large-scale investors and speculators could afford, and the rest in parcels of 640 acres each, which only well-to-do farmers could manage to buy (Map 7.2).

Finally, the Northwest Ordinance of 1787 provided for the creation of the territories that would eventually become the states of Ohio, Indiana, Illinois, Michigan, and Wisconsin. Reflecting the Enlightenment beliefs of Jefferson and other Patriots, the ordinance prohibited slavery in those territories and earmarked funds from land sales for the support of schools. It also specified that Congress would appoint a governor and judges to administer a new territory; once there were 5,000 free adult men in residence, they could elect a territorial legislature. When the population reached 60,000, the legislature could write a republican constitution and apply to join the Confederation on a basis of complete equality with the existing states.

The land ordinances of the 1780s were a great and enduring achievement. They provided for the orderly settlement of the West while reducing the prospect of secessionist movements and preventing the emergence of dependent "colonies." The ordinances also added a new "western" dimension to the national identity. The United States was no longer confined to thirteen governments on the eastern seaboard. It had space to expand.

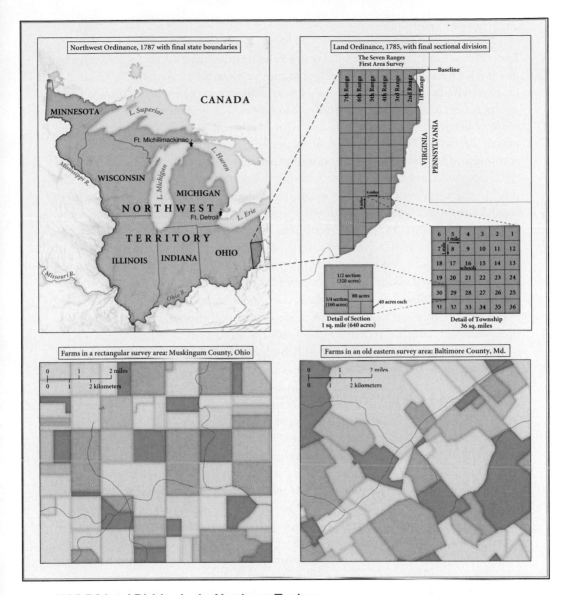

MAP 7.2 Land Division in the Northwest Territory

Throughout the Northwest Territory, government surveyors imposed a rectangular grid on the landscape, regardless of the local topography. The use of a grid reflected both the influence of Enlightenment conceptions of regularity and rationality and the desire to survey the land quickly to deter squatters from settling on it illegally. Congress specified that half of the townships be sold in huge blocks of 23,040 acres each, which ensured their purchase by land speculators, and the rest in substantial parcels of 640 acres each, which only well-to-do farmers could afford. The right-angled property lines in Muskingum County, Ohio (lower left), contrasted sharply with those in Baltimore County, Maryland (lower right), where—as in most of the eastern and southern states—boundaries followed the contours of the land.

Shays's Rebellion

However bright the future of the West, in the East postwar conditions were grim. Peace had brought a recession rather than a return to prosperity. The war had destroyed many American merchant ships and disrupted the export of tobacco, rice, and wheat. And now the British Navigation Acts, which had nurtured colonial commerce, barred Americans from trading with the British West Indies. Moreover, low-priced British manufactures flooded American markets and drove many urban artisans and wartime textile firms out of business.

State governments were equally fragile because they were saddled with large war debts. Speculators—mostly wealthy merchants and landowners—had purchased huge quantities of state debt certificates for far less than their face value. They demanded that the state governments redeem the bonds quickly and at full value, a policy that required high taxes. However, yeomen farmers and artisans, hard hit by the postwar recession, demanded tax relief, and most state legislatures followed their sentiments. To assist indebted yeomen, they printed more paper currency and passed laws allowing debtors to pay their creditors in installments. Although wealthy men deplored these stopgap measures as destructive of "the just rights of creditors," these laws probably prevented a major social upheaval.

In Massachusetts, the lack of such debtor-relief legislation provoked an armed uprising. Merchants and creditors persuaded the Massachusetts legislature to repay the state's war debt by imposing high taxes and to deter inflation by halting the issuance of paper currency. When cash-strapped farmers could not pay their private debts, creditors threatened them with court suits. Debtor Ephraim Wetmore heard that merchant Stephan Salisbury "would have my Body Dead or Alive in case I did not pay." In response, residents of central and western counties called extralegal meetings in 1786 to protest the taxes and property seizures and to demand the abolition of imprisonment for debt, the end of property qualifications for officeholding, and the elimination of the upper house of the state legislature. To back up these radical political demands, bands of angry farmers—including men of status and substance—closed the courts by force. "[I] had no Intensions to Destroy the Publick Government," declared Captain Adam Wheeler, a former town selectman; rather, he had rioted to prevent "Valuable and Industrious members of Society [being] dragged from their families to prison [because of their debts], to the great damage . . . [of] the Community at large." The resistance gradually grew into a full-scale revolt led by Captain Daniel Shays, a former Continental army officer.

As a struggle against taxes imposed by a distant government, Shays's Rebellion resembled colonial resistance to the British Stamp Act. To drive home that point, members of Shays's army placed twigs from pine trees in their hats, just as the Continental army had done. "The people have turned against their teachers the doctrines which were inculcated to effect the late revolution," complained the conservative Massachusetts political leader Fisher Ames. However, some men who were radical Patriots in 1776 also condemned the Shaysites. "Those Men, who . . . would lessen the

Weight of Government lawfully exercised must be Enemies to our happy Revolution and Common Liberty," charged onetime revolutionary Samuel Adams. To put down the rebellion, the Massachusetts legislature passed the Riot Act, outlawing illegal assembly. With financing from eastern merchants, Governor James Bowdoin equipped a formidable fighting force and called for additional troops from the Continental Congress. In the end, Shays's army fell victim to freezing weather and inadequate supplies during the winter of 1786–87, and Bowdoin's military force easily dispersed the rebels.

Shays's Rebellion provided graphic proof that the costs of war and the fruits of independence were not being shared evenly. Middling Patriot families who had endured wartime shortages and sacrifices felt they had exchanged one tyranny for another. Angry Massachusetts voters turned Governor Bowdoin out of office, and debt-ridden farmers in New York, northern Pennsylvania, Connecticut, and New Hampshire also closed courthouses and demanded economic relief. British officials in Canada predicted the imminent demise of the United States, and many Americans feared for the fate of their republican experiment. Events in Massachusetts, declared nationalist Henry Knox, formed "the strongest arguments possible" for the creation of "a strong general government."

The Constitution of 1787

From the moment of its creation, the Constitution was a controversial document, praised by advocates as a solution to the nation's economic woes and condemned by critics as a perversion of republicanism. Simply put, the issue was whether the institutions of self-government could function successfully only on the state level or could be adapted to govern a vast nation. This debate, begun in 1787, would not be finally resolved until the Civil War.

The Rise of a Nationalist Faction

Money questions—debts, taxes, and **tariffs**—dominated the postwar political agenda. Some men, mostly those who had served the Confederation government as military officers, diplomats, and officials, looked at these problems from a "national" perspective and became advocates of a stronger central government. Thus, General Washington, financier Robert Morris, and diplomats Benjamin Franklin, John Jay, and John Adams demanded that Congress be given the power to control foreign commerce and impose tariffs. However, key commercial states in the North—New York, Massachusetts, Pennsylvania—resisted national tariffs in order to protect local merchants and state-imposed levies on imported goods. Most southern planters also opposed tariffs because they wanted to import British textiles and ironware at the lowest possible prices.

Nonetheless, some southern planters joined the nationalist faction because they feared the financial policies of the state governments. Legislatures in Virginia and other southern states had responded to the economic hard times of the 1780s by lowering taxes. Such measures troubled wealthy creditors because they diminished public revenue and delayed the redemption of state debts. Taxpayers were being led to believe they would "never be compelled to pay" the public debt, lamented Charles Lee of Virginia, a wealthy bondholder. Private creditors had similar complaints against state governments that enacted laws that "stayed" (delayed) the payment of debts. "While men are madly accumulating enormous debts, their legislators are making provisions for their non-payment," complained a South Carolina creditor. To these nationalists, the democratic majorities in the state legislatures constituted a grave threat to republican government.

In 1786 James Madison and other nationalists persuaded the Virginia legislature to call a special commercial convention to discuss tariff and taxation policies. However, only five state governments sent delegates to the meeting in Annapolis, Maryland; undeterred by their small numbers, the twelve delegates called for another meeting in Philadelphia to undertake an even broader review of the Confederation government. Spurred on by Shays's Rebellion, nationalists in Congress secured a resolution supporting the Philadelphia convention and calling for a revision of the Articles of Confederation "adequate to the exigencies of government." "Nothing but the adoption of some efficient plan from the Convention," a fellow nationalist wrote to James Madison, "can prevent anarchy first & civil convulsions afterwards."

The Philadelphia Convention

In May 1787, fifty-five delegates arrived in Philadelphia, representing every state except Rhode Island, whose legislature opposed any increase in central authority. Most delegates were men of property: merchants, slaveholding planters, or "monied men." There were no artisans, backcountry settlers, or tenants, and only a single yeoman farmer.

Some delegates, such as Benjamin Franklin of Pennsylvania, had been early advocates of independence while others, including George Washington and Robert Morris, had risen to prominence during the war. Several important Patriots missed the convention. John Adams and Thomas Jefferson were abroad, as the American ministers to Britain and France, respectively. The Massachusetts legislature declined to send radical Samuel Adams, and his fellow firebrand from Virginia, Patrick Henry, refused to attend because he favored a strictly limited national government and "smelt a rat." Their absence allowed capable young nationalists to set the agenda of the convention. Arguing that decisions of the convention would "decide for ever the fate of Republican Government," James Madison insisted on an increase in national authority, while Alexander Hamilton demanded a strong central government that would protect the republic from "the imprudence of democracy."

The delegates elected Washington as the presiding officer and, to forestall popular opposition, decided to deliberate in secret. This secrecy encouraged the delegates to exceed their mandate to revise the Articles of Confederation and to consider the Virginia Plan, a scheme for a powerful national government devised by James Madison. Madison, just thirty-six years old, had arrived in Philadelphia determined to fashion a new political order run by men of high character. A graduate of Princeton, he had read classical and modern political theory and served in both the Confederation Congress and the Virginia assembly. Once an optimistic Patriot, Madison had grown increasingly discouraged as his experience in the Virginia legislature revealed the "narrow ambition" of many elected state officials.

Madison's Virginia Plan differed from the Articles of Confederation in three crucial respects. First, it rejected state sovereignty in favor of the "supremacy of national authority." The central government would have the power not only to "legislate in all cases to which the separate States are incompetent" but also to overturn state laws. Second, the plan called for a national government to draw authority directly from the entire people and to exercise direct power on them. As Madison explained, it would bypass the state governments, and operate directly "on the individuals composing them." Third, the plan created a three-tier national government in which the people would elect only the lower house of the legislature. The lower house would name the members of the upper house, and then both houses of the legislature would select the executive and judiciary.

From a political perspective Madison's plan had two fatal flaws. First, the provision allowing the national government to veto state laws raised the ire of state politicians and many ordinary citizens. Second, the great powers assigned to the lower house of the legislature, whose membership was based on population, greatly increased the influence of the large states. Delegates from small states immediately rejected this provision; as a Delaware delegate put it, Madison's scheme would allow the populous states to "crush the small ones whenever they stand in the way of their ambitious or interested views."

Delegates from the smaller states rallied behind a plan devised by William Paterson, a delegate from New Jersey. The New Jersey Plan, as it came to be called, strengthened the Confederation by giving it the power to raise revenue, control commerce, and make binding requisitions on the states. But it preserved the states' control over their own laws and guaranteed their equality: each state would have one vote in a unicameral legislature, as in the existing Confederation. Delegates from the populous states vigorously opposed this voting provision. Finally, after a month of debate, a bare majority of the states agreed to take Madison's Virginia Plan as the basis of discussion.

This decision raised the prospect of a dramatically new constitutional system and prompted two New York representatives— Robert Yates and John Lansing—to accuse the delegates of exceeding their mandate and to leave the convention. During the hot, humid summer of 1787 the remaining delegates met six days a week, debating high principles and discussing practical details. Experienced and realistic politicians, they knew that their plan had to be acceptable to existing political interests and powerful social groups. Pierce Butler of South Carolina invoked a classical Greek precedent: "We must follow the example of Solon, who gave the Athenians not the best government he could devise but the best they would receive."

Representation remained the central problem. To satisfy both large and small states the Connecticut delegates suggested that the upper house, the Senate, would always have two members from each state, while seats in the lower chamber, the House of Representatives, would be apportioned on the basis of population, as determined every ten years by a national census. After bitter debate, this "Great Compromise" was accepted, but only reluctantly; to some delegates from populous states it seemed less a compromise than a victory for the smaller states.

Other state-related issues were quickly settled by restricting (or leaving ambiguous) the extent of central authority. Some delegates opposed establishing national courts within the states, warning that "the states will revolt at such encroachments." The convention therefore defined the judicial power of the United States in broad terms, vesting it "in one supreme Court" and leaving the new national legislature to decide whether to establish lower courts within the states. The convention also refused to require voters in national elections to be landowners. "Eight or nine states have extended the right of **suffrage** beyond the freeholders [landowners]," George Mason of Virginia pointed out. "What will people there say if they should be disfranchised?" The convention also placed the selection of the president in an electoral college chosen on a state-by-state basis and specified that state legislatures, not the voters at large, would elect members of the U.S. Senate. By giving states an important role in the new constitutional system, the delegates encouraged their citizens to accept a reduction in state sovereignty.

Slavery hovered in the background of the delegates' debates, rarely discussed but always present. When the issue arose, speakers divided along regional lines. Speaking for many northerners Gouverneur Morris of New York condemned slavery as "a nefarious institution" and hoped for its eventual demise. Reflecting the outlook of Chesapeake planters, who already owned ample numbers of slaves, George Mason of Virginia called for an end to the Atlantic slave trade. However, rice-growing planters from South Carolina and Georgia insisted that slave imports must continue; otherwise their states "shall not be parties to the Union." At their insistence the delegates denied Congress the power to regulate immigration until 1808 (at which time Congress abolished the slave trade).

For the sake of national unity, the delegates likewise treated other slavery-related issues as political rather than moral questions. To protect the property of southern slave owners, they agreed to a "fugitive" clause that allowed masters to reclaim enslaved blacks (or white indentured servants) who took refuge in other states. To mollify antislavery sentiment in the northern states, the delegates did not give slavery national legal recognition by explicitly mentioning it in the Constitution (which spoke instead of citizens and "all other Persons"). They also refused southern demands to count slaves and citizens equally in determining states' representation in Congress. Instead, they counted a slave as three-fifths of a free person for purposes of representation and taxation.

Having allayed the concerns of small states and slave states, the delegates created a powerful procreditor national government. The finished document made the Constitution and all national legislation the "supreme" law of the land. It gave the national government broad powers over taxation, military defense, and external

Gouverneur Morris, Federalist Statesman

Morris almost became a Loyalist because he was a snob who liked privilege and feared the people. ("The mob begins to think and reason," he once noted with disdain.) He became a Federalist for similar reasons, helped to write the Philadelphia Constitution and, after 1793, strongly supported the Federalist Party.

National Portrait Gallery, Smithsonian Institution / Art Resource, NY.

commerce as well as the authority to make all laws "necessary and proper" to implement those and other provisions. To protect creditors and establish the fiscal integrity of the new government, the Constitution mandated that the United States honor the existing **national debt**. Finally, it restricted the ability of state governments to assist debtors by forbidding the states to issue money or enact "any Law impairing the Obligation of Contracts."

The proposed Constitution was not a "perfect production," Benjamin Franklin admitted on September 17, 1787, as he urged the forty-one delegates still present to sign it. Yet, the great diplomat confessed his astonishment at finding "this system approaching so near to perfection as it does." His colleagues apparently agreed; all but three signed the document.

The People Debate Ratification

The procedures for ratifying the new Constitution were as controversial as its contents. The delegates refused to submit the Constitution to the state legislatures for their unanimous consent, as required by the Articles of Confederation, because they knew that Rhode Island (and perhaps a few other states) would reject it. So they arbitrarily specified that the Constitution would go into effect when ratified by special conventions in nine of the thirteen states. Because of its nationalist sympathies, the Confederation Congress winked at this extralegal procedure; surprisingly, so too did most state legislatures, which promptly called the ratification conventions.

As the great constitutional debate began, the nationalists seized the initiative with two bold moves. First, they called themselves Federalists, suggesting that they favored a loose, decentralized system of government and obscuring their quest for a strong central authority. Second, they launched a coordinated pamphlet and newspaper campaign lauding the proposed Constitution.

The opponents of the Constitution, who became known as Antifederalists, had diverse backgrounds and motives. Some, like Governor George Clinton of New York, feared losing their power at the state level. Others were rural democrats who pointed out that the federal Constitution, unlike most state constitutions, lacked a declaration of individual rights. As smallholding farmers, they also worried that the powerful central government would be run by an aristocracy of wealth. "These lawyers and men of learning and monied men expect to be managers of this Constitution," worried a Massachusetts farmer, "and get all the power and all the money into their own hands and then they will swallow up all of us little folks . . . just as the whale swallowed up Jonah." Giving substance to these fears, Melancton Smith of New York argued that the large electoral districts prescribed by the Constitution would bring wealthy upper-class men into office, whereas the smaller districts used in state elections usually produced legislatures "composed principally of respectable yeomanry."

Well-educated Americans with a traditional republican outlook also opposed the new system. To keep government "close to the people," they wanted the nation to remain a collection of small sovereign republics tied together only for trade and defense—not the "United States" but the "States United." Citing the French political philosopher Montesquieu, these Antifederalists argued that republican institutions were best suited to cities or small states—a localist outlook that shaped American political thinking well into the twentieth century. "No extensive empire can be governed on republican principles," declared James Winthrop of Massachusetts. Patrick Henry predicted the Constitution would re-create the worst features of British rule: high taxes, an oppressive bureaucracy, a standing army, and a "great and mighty President . . . supported in extravagant munificence."

In New York, where ratification was hotly contested, James Madison, John Jay, and Alexander Hamilton countered these arguments in a series of eighty-five essays collectively called *The Federalist*. Although not widely read at the time outside of New York City (only a few of the essays were reprinted in newspapers elsewhere), *The Federalist* was subsequently recognized as a classic work of political theory. Its authors stressed the need for a strong government to conduct foreign affairs and denied that it would foster domestic tyranny. Citing Montesquieu's praise for mixed government (and drawing on John Adams's *Thoughts on Government*), Madison, Jay, and Hamilton pointed out that national authority would be divided among a president, a bicameral legislature, and a judiciary. Each branch of government would "check and balance" the others, thus preserving liberty.

Indeed, in *The Federalist*, No. 10, Madison made a significant contribution to political theory by denying that republicanism was suited only to small states. It was "sown in the nature of man," Madison wrote, that individuals would seek power and form factions to advance their interests. Indeed, "a landed interest, a manufacturing interest, a mercantile interest, a moneyed interest, with many lesser interests, grow up of necessity in civilized nations." He argued that a free society should not suppress those groups but rather prevent any one of them from becoming dominant—an end best achieved in a large republic. "Extend the sphere," Madison concluded, "and you take in a greater variety of parties and interests; you make it less probable that a majority of the whole will have a common motive to invade the rights of other citizens."

The delegates who debated these issues in the state ratification conventions included untutored farmers and middling artisans as well as educated gentlemen. Generally, backcountry representatives were Antifederalists; whereas those from the seacoast were Federalists. In Pennsylvania, Philadelphia merchants and artisans combined with Federalist-oriented commercial farmers to ratify the Constitution. Other early Federalist successes came in the less populous states of Delaware, New Jersey, Georgia, and Connecticut, where delegates hoped a strong national government would offset the power of large neighboring states (Map 7.3).

The Constitution's first real test came in January 1788 in Massachusetts, one of the most populous states and a hotbed of Antifederalist sentiment. Influential Patriots, including Samuel Adams and Governor John Hancock, opposed the new constitution, as did many former followers of Daniel Shays. But Boston artisans, who wanted tariff protection from British imports, supported ratification, and Federalist leaders assured delegates that the new government would consider a national bill of rights. By a close vote of 187 to 168, the Federalists carried the day.

Spring brought new Federalist victories in Maryland and South Carolina, and when New Hampshire narrowly ratified the Constitution in June, the required nine states had approved it. Still, the essential states of Virginia and New York had not yet acted, and it took the powerful arguments advanced in *The Federalist* and the promise of a national bill of rights to carry the day. The Constitution won ratification in Virginia, by 89 to 79, and that success carried the Federalists to victory in New York by the even smaller margin of 30 to 27. Suspicious of centralized power, the yeomen of North Carolina and Rhode Island ratified only in 1789 and 1790, respectively.

Ratification of the Constitution ended Antifederalist agitation and temporarily limited the resistance to centralized authority by the democratically and independently inclined state legislatures. "A decided majority" of the New Hampshire assembly had opposed the "new system," reported Joshua Atherton, but accepted the outcome, saying, "It is adopted, let us try it." In Virginia, Antifederalist firebrand Patrick Henry likewise vowed to "submit as a quiet citizen" and fight for amendments "in a constitutional way."

Working against great odds, the Federalists had created a national republic and partly restored an elitist system of political authority. To celebrate their victory Federalists organized great processions in the seaport cities. By marching in an orderly fashion—in conscious contrast to the riotous Revolutionary mobs—Federalist-minded citizens affirmed their allegiance to a self-governing republican community. To endow their regime with moral legitimacy, marching Federalists

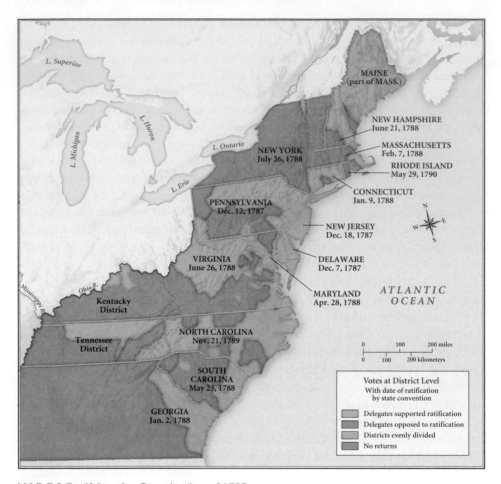

MAP 7.3 Ratifying the Constitution of 1787

In 1907 the geographer Owen Libby mapped the votes of members of the state conventions that ratified the Constitution. His map shows that most delegates from seaboard or commercial farming districts favored the Constitution, while those from backcountry areas opposed it. Subsequent research has confirmed Libby's socioeconomic interpretation of this voting pattern in North and South Carolina and Massachusetts; however, other factors influenced delegates in other states, such as Georgia, where the Constitution was ratified by delegates from all regions.

placed a copy of the Constitution on an "altar of liberty" float, using sacred symbolism to lay the foundations for a secular **"civil religion"** of American nationality.

The Federalists Implement the Constitution

The Constitution expanded the dimensions of American political life because voters could now elect national as well as local and state officials. The Federalists swept the election of 1788, placing forty-four supporters in the first House of

Representatives; only eight Antifederalists won election. As expected, members of the electoral college chose George Washington as president. John Adams received the second highest number of electoral votes and became vice president.

Washington, the military savior of his country, became its political father as well. At fifty-seven he was a man of great personal dignity and influence. Instinctively cautious, Washington generally followed the administrative practices of the Confederation and asked Congress to reestablish the existing executive departments: foreign affairs (state), finance (treasury), and war. However, he made one important innovation. The Constitution specified that the president could appoint major officials with the consent of the Senate, but Washington insisted that only he—and not the Senate—could remove them, thus ensuring the chief executive's control over the bureaucracy. To head the Department of State Washington chose Thomas Jefferson, a fellow Virginian and an experienced diplomat. For secretary of the treasury he turned to Alexander Hamilton, a lawyer and wartime military aide. The new president designated Jefferson, Hamilton, and Secretary of War Henry Knox as his cabinet, or advisory body.

The Constitution had created a Supreme Court but left the establishment of the rest of the national court system to Congress. Because the Federalists wanted national institutions to act directly on individual citizens, they enacted the Judiciary Act in 1789 that created a federal district court in each state. The act provided three circuit courts to hear appeals from the districts, with the Supreme Court having the final say. The Judiciary Act also permitted appeals to the Supreme Court of federal legal issues that arose in state-run courts, ensuring that national (and not state) judges would decide the meaning of the Constitution.

The Federalists kept their promise to add a declaration of rights to the Constitution. James Madison, who had been elected to the House of Representatives, submitted a list of nineteen amendments to the first Congress, and ten of them were approved by that Congress and ratified by the states in 1791. These ten amendments, which became known as the Bill of Rights, safeguarded certain fundamental personal liberties, such as freedom of speech and religion, and mandated various legal procedures that protected the individual, such as trial by jury. By addressing Antifederalists' concerns about the potentially oppressive power of the national government, the amendments secured the legitimacy of the new Constitution.

The Political Crisis of the 1790s

The final decade of the century brought fresh political challenges. The Federalists divided into two irreconcilable factions over financial policy, and this split widened further because of the ideological impact of the French Revolution. During these struggles, Alexander Hamilton and Thomas Jefferson offered contrasting visions of the American future. Would the United States remain, as Jefferson preferred, an agricultural nation in which local and state governments were predominant? Or, as Hamilton advised, would it use the authority of the national government to stimulate trade and industry?

Hamilton's Financial Program

One of George Washington's most important decisions was his choice of Alexander Hamilton as secretary of the treasury. An ambitious self-made man of great charm and intelligence, Hamilton had served as Washington's personal aide during the war. He married into the Schuyler family of rich and influential Hudson River Valley landowners, and during the 1780s became a leading lawyer in New York City. As a delegate to the Philadelphia convention, Hamilton condemned the "amazing violence and turbulence of the democratic spirit" and called for an authoritarian government headed by a president with nearly monarchical powers.

As treasury secretary Hamilton devised bold policies to enhance the national authority and favor wealthy financiers and seaport merchants. He outlined his plans in three path-breaking and interrelated reports to Congress: on public credit (January 1790), on a national bank (December 1790), and on manufactures (December 1791).

The financial and social implications of Hamilton's "Report on the Public Credit" made it instantly controversial. The report called for Congress to "redeem" at face value the millions of dollars in securities issued by the Confederation. Intended to bolster the government's credit, this plan also provided excessive profits to speculators. For example, the Massachusetts merchant firm of Burrell & Burrell had paid about $600 for Confederation notes with a face value of $2,500; their redemption at full value would bring an enormous profit of $1,900. Equally controversial, Hamilton proposed to pay the Burrells and other Confederation note holders with new government-issued, interest-bearing securities that could be bought and sold—thereby creating a permanent national debt.

Hamilton's plan for a permanent national debt owned by wealthy families reawakened Radical Whig and republican fears. Speaking for the Virginia House of Burgesses, Patrick Henry condemned this plan "to erect, and concentrate, and perpetuate a large monied interest" and warned that it would prove "fatal to the existence of American liberty." Challenging the morality of Hamilton's proposal, James Madison asked Congress to pay part of the redemption fee to the original owners—the thousands of shopkeepers, farmers, and soldiers who had accepted Confederation securities during the dark days of the war and who had then been forced by hard times to sell them to speculators. But finding the original owners would have been difficult, and nearly half the members of the House of Representatives owned Confederation securities and would personally profit from Hamilton's plan. Melding practicality with self-interest, the House rejected Madison's innovative proposal.

Hamilton then advanced a second proposal that favored wealthy creditors, a plan by which the national government would take over ("assume") the war debts of the states. Rumors of this plan unleashed a flurry of speculation and some governmental corruption. Before Hamilton's announcement, Assistant Secretary of the Treasury William Duer bought up the depreciated war bonds of southern states; if Congress approved the assumption plan, Duer and his speculator associates would reap an enormous profit. Concerned members of Congress condemned such speculation and pointed out that some state legislatures had already levied high taxes to pay off their war debts. Responding to that argument, Hamilton modified his plan to reimburse those states. Other representatives from Virginia and Maryland argued that assumption would further enhance the already excessive powers of the national government. To quiet their fears about a runaway central government, the treasury chief backed their bid to locate the permanent national capital along the banks of the Potomac—where they could easily watch its operations. Such astute political bargaining gave Hamilton the votes he needed in the House of Representatives to enact his assumption plan.

In December 1790 Hamilton issued a second report asking Congress to charter a national financial institution, the Bank of the United States. The bank would be jointly owned by private stockholders and the national government. Hamilton argued that the bank, by making loans to merchants, handling government funds, and issuing financial notes, would provide a respected currency for the specie-starved American economy and make the new national debt easier to fund. These benefits persuaded Congress to enact Hamilton's bank bill and send it to the president for approval.

At this critical juncture Secretary of State Thomas Jefferson joined ranks with Madison against Hamilton's financial initiatives. Jefferson had condemned the shady dealings in southern war bonds and the "corrupt squadron of paper dealers" who had arranged them. Now he charged that Hamilton's scheme for a national bank was unconstitutional. "The incorporation of a Bank," Jefferson told President Washington, was not a power "delegated to the United States by the Constitution." Giving a *strict* interpretation to the national charter, Jefferson maintained that the central government had only the limited powers explicitly assigned to it. In response, Hamilton articulated a *loose* interpretation, noting that Article 1, Section 8, empowered Congress to make "all Laws which shall be necessary and proper" to carry out the Constitution's provisions. Washington agreed with his treasury secretary and signed the legislation creating the bank.

Hamilton turned now to the final element of his financial system: a national revenue to pay the annual interest on the permanent debt. In 1792, at Hamilton's insistence, the Congress imposed a variety of domestic excise taxes, including a duty on whiskey distilled in the United States. But the revenue from those taxes was a mere $1 million a year. To raise another $4–5 million the treasury secretary proposed to raise tariffs on foreign imports. Although Hamilton's "Report on Manufactures" (1791) urged the nation to become self-sufficient in such goods, he did not ask Congress to impose high protective tariffs that would aid American

Two Visions of America

Thomas Jefferson and Alexander Hamilton confront each other in these portraits, as they did during the political battles of the 1790s. Jefferson was pro-French, Hamilton pro-British. Jefferson favored farmers and artisans; Hamilton supported merchants and financiers. Jefferson believed in democracy and rule by legislative majorities; Hamilton argued for a strong executive and for judicial review. But in 1800 Hamilton's support for Jefferson in his postelection struggle with Aaron Burr, whom Hamilton detested, secured the presidency for his longtime political foe.

Jefferson, by Rembrandt Peale, © White House Historical Association / Photo by National Geographic Society; Yale University Art Gallery, Mabel Brady Garven Collection.

manufacturers by excluding foreign products. Instead, Hamilton settled for a modest increase in customs duties, a revenue tariff that would allow trade and provide income for the national government.

Hamilton's scheme worked brilliantly. As American trade increased, customs revenue rose steadily (providing about 90 percent of the U.S. government's income from 1790 to 1820) and allowed the treasury to pay for the redemption and assumption programs. In less than two years Hamilton had devised a strikingly modern fiscal system that provided the new national government with financial stability.

Jefferson's Agrarian Vision

Hamilton paid a high price for this success. Even before Washington began his second four-year term in 1793, Hamilton's financial measures had split the Federalists who wrote and ratified the Constitution into two irreconcilable factions. Most northern Federalists adhered to the political alliance led by Hamilton and most southerners to a rival group headed by Madison and Jefferson. By the elections of 1794 the two factions had acquired names. Hamilton's supporters retained their original name: Federalists; Madison's and Jefferson's supporters called themselves Democratic-Republicans or simply Republicans.

The southern planters and western farmers who became Republicans rejected Hamilton's economic and social philosophy, and Thomas Jefferson spoke for them. Well read in architecture, natural history, scientific farming, and political theory, Jefferson embraced the optimistic spirit of the Enlightenment and believed in the "improvability of the human race." But he knew that progress was not inevitable and deplored both the long-standing speculative practices of merchants and financiers and the emerging social divisions of an industrial economy. Having seen the masses of propertyless laborers in the manufacturing regions in Britain, Jefferson had concluded that workers who depended on wages lacked the economic independence required to sustain a republic.

Consequently, Jefferson's vision of the American future was agrarian and democratic. Although he had grown up (and remained) a privileged slave owner, Jefferson pictured a West without slavery and settled by productive yeomen farm families. His vision took form in his *Notes on the State of Virginia* (1785): "Those who labor in the earth are the chosen people of God," he wrote. Their grain and meat would feed European nations, which "would manufacture and send us in exchange our clothes and other comforts" in an international division of labor similar to that proposed by the Scottish economist Adam Smith in *The Wealth of Nations* (1776).

Turmoil in Europe created new opportunities for American farmers and brought Jefferson's vision closer to reality. The French Revolution began in 1789, and four years later France's new republican government went to war against a British-led coalition of monarchical states. As warfare disrupted European farming, wheat prices leaped from 5 to 8 shillings a bushel and remained high for twenty years, bringing substantial profits to export-minded Chesapeake and Middle Atlantic farmers. Simultaneously, a boom in the export of raw cotton, fueled by the invention of the cotton gin and mechanization of cloth production in Britain (see Chapter 10), boosted the economy of Georgia and South Carolina. As Jefferson had hoped, European markets brought prosperity to American farmers and planters.

The French Revolution Divides Americans

American merchants profited even more handsomely from the European war. President Washington issued a Proclamation of Neutrality, which allowed U.S. citizens to trade with both sides. As neutral carriers, American ships claimed the right to pass through the British naval blockade along the French coastline and soon took over the lucrative sugar trade between France and its West Indian islands. The American merchant fleet increased dramatically from 355,000 tons in 1790 to more than 1.1 million tons in 1808. Commercial earnings rose spectacularly, averaging

$20 million annually in the 1790s—twice the value of cotton and tobacco exports. Northern shipowners provided work for thousands of shipwrights, sail makers, laborers, and seamen by investing in new vessels. Hundreds of carpenters, masons, and cabinetmakers in the major seaports of Boston, New York, and Philadelphia likewise found work building warehouses and fashionable "Federal-style" town houses for newly affluent merchants. In Philadelphia, a European visitor reported, "a great number of private houses have marble steps to the street door, and in other respects are finished in a style of elegance."

Even as they prospered from the European struggle, Americans argued passionately over its ideologies. Most Americans had welcomed the French Revolution of 1789 because it abolished feudalism and established a constitutional monarchy. But the creation of the democratic French republic in 1792 and the execution of King Louis XVI the following year divided public opinion. Many American artisans praised the egalitarianism of the radical French Jacobins and followed their example by addressing each other as "citizen" and by founding political clubs modeled on the radical democratic societies in Paris—the controversial Jacobin clubs. But Americans with strong religious beliefs condemned the new French regime for abandoning Christianity in favor of atheism. Wealthy Americans likewise denounced Robespierre and his radical republican followers for executing King Louis XVI, 3,000 of his aristocratic supporters, and 14,000 other citizens.

These ideological conflicts sharpened the debate over Hamilton's economic policies and even helped to foment a domestic insurrection. In 1794 farmers in western Pennsylvania mounted the Whiskey Rebellion to protest Hamilton's excise tax on spirits, which had raised the price—and thus cut the demand—for the corn whiskey they bartered for eastern manufactures. Like the Sons of Liberty of 1765 and the Shaysites of 1786, the whiskey rebels attacked both local tax collectors and the authority of a distant government. However, these protesters also waved banners proclaiming the French revolutionary slogan, "Liberty, Equality, and Fraternity!" To suppress these radical-minded dissenters, uphold national authority, and deter secessionist movements along the frontier, President Washington raised an army of 12,000 troops that soon dispersed the whiskey rebels.

Britain's maritime strategy also widened the growing political divisions in the United States. In November 1793 the Royal Navy began to prey on American ships bound for France from the West Indies and eventually seized more than 250 vessels and their cargoes of sugar. Seeking to resolve this controversy though diplomacy, President Washington dispatched John Jay to Britain. Jay returned in 1795 with a controversial treaty requiring the U.S. government to make "full and complete compensation" to British merchants for all pre–Revolutionary War debts owed by American citizens. The treaty also acknowledged Britain's right to remove French property from neutral ships, overturning the American merchants' claim that "free ships make free goods." In return, the agreement allowed American merchants to submit claims of illegal seizure to arbitration and, more importantly,

An Anti-French Cartoon

A five-headed monster, representing the leaders of France under the Directory, demands a bribe ("Money, Money, Money") from American diplomats. Federalists used the bribery incident—named the XYZ Affair for the three anonymous French agents who asked for the bribe—to whip up anti-French sentiment in the United States and to launch an undeclared naval war.
Huntington Library.

required the British to remove their military garrisons from the Northwest Territory and to end their aid to the Indians there. Jefferson and other Republicans attacked Jay's Treaty as too conciliatory, and the Senate ratified it only by the bare two-thirds majority required by the Constitution. However, as long as Hamilton and his Federalist allies were in power, the United States would have a pro-British foreign policy.

The Rise of Political Parties

The appearance of Federalists and Republicans marked a new stage in American politics. Although colonial legislatures had often divided into temporary factions based on family alliances, ethnicity, or region, they lacked well-organized parties.

The new state and national constitutions made no provision for organized political bodies; indeed, most Americans considered parties unnecessary and dangerous. Following classical republican principles, they wanted voters and legislators to act independently and in the interest of the entire public. Thus, Senator Pierce Butler of South Carolina criticized his congressional colleagues as "men scrambling for partial advantage, State interests, and in short, a train of narrow, impolitic measures."

Political parties appeared, however, because the financial and ideological conflicts of the 1790s divided the political elite and the revolutionary ideology of popular sovereignty drew average citizens into politics. The resulting contest for votes created a competitive—and divisive—party system. Most merchants, creditors, and urban artisans favored Federalist policies, as did wheat-exporting slaveholders in the Tidewater districts of the Chesapeake. The emerging Republican coalition was more diverse. It included not only southern tobacco and rice planters and debt-conscious western farmers but also Germans and Scots-Irish in the southern backcountry and subsistence-oriented eastern farmers.

Party identity crystallized during the election of 1796. To prepare for the election, Federalist and Republican leaders called legislative caucuses in Congress and conventions in the states to discuss policies and nominate candidates. To mobilize the citizenry the parties organized public festivals and processions, with the Federalists celebrating Washington's achievements and the Republicans invoking the egalitarian principles of the Declaration of Independence.

Federalist candidates triumphed in the 1796 election, winning a majority in Congress and electing John Adams as the new president. Adams continued Hamilton's pro-British foreign policy and reacted sharply when the French navy seized American merchant ships. When the French foreign minister Talleyrand solicited a loan and a bribe from American diplomats to stop the seizures, Adams charged that Talleyrand's agents, whom he dubbed X, Y, and Z, had insulted American honor. Responding to the "XYZ Affair," the Federalist-controlled Congress cut off trade with France in 1798 and authorized American privateers to seize French ships. Party conflict, which had begun over Hamilton's financial policies, now extended to foreign affairs.

Constitutional Crisis, 1798–1800

For the first time in American history (but not the last) a controversial foreign policy prompted domestic protest and governmental repression. As the United States fought an undeclared maritime war against France, pro-Republican and anti-British immigrants from Ireland vehemently attacked Adams's foreign policy. A Philadelphia Federalist pamphleteer responded in kind: "Were I president, I would hang them for otherwise they would murder me" (see Voices from Abroad, "Peter Porcupine Attacks Pro-French Americans," p. 223). To silence their critics, the Federalists enacted a series of coercive measures in 1798. The Naturalization Act

VOICES FROM ABROAD

Peter Porcupine Attacks Pro-French Americans

WILLIAM COBBETT

T *he Democratic-Republican followers of Thomas Jefferson declared that "he who is an*
enemy to the French Revolution, cannot be a firm republican." William Cobbett, a British
journalist who settled in Philadelphia and wrote under the pen name "Peter Porcupine," con-
tested this definition of republicanism. A strong supporter of the Federalist Party, Cobbett
attacked its opponents in caustic and widely read pamphlets and newspaper articles. Here he
evokes the horrors of the Terror in France, during which thousands of aristocrats and ordinary
citizens were executed, and warns that the triumph of Radical Republicanism would bring the
same fate to the United States.

France is a republic, and . . . this word outweighs, in the estimation of some persons (I wish
I could say they were few in number), all the horrors that have been and that can be committed in that country. One of these modern republicans will tell you that he does not deny
that hundreds of thousands of innocent persons have been murdered in France; that the
people have neither religion nor morals; . . . that its riches, along with millions of the best
of the people, are gone to enrich and aggrandize its enemies. . . . But at the end of all this,
he will tell you that it must be happy, because it is a republic. . . . Such a sentiment is characteristic of a mind locked up in a savage ignorance.

Shall we say that these things never can take place among us? . . . We are not what we
were before the French revolution. Political projectors from every corner of Europe, trou-
blers of society of every description, . . . have taken shelter in these States.

We have seen the guillotine toasted. . . . And what would the reader say, were I to tell him
of a Member of Congress, who wished to see one of these murderous machines employed
for lopping off the heads of the French, permanent in the State-house yard of the city of
Philadelphia?

If these men of blood had succeeded in plunging us into a war; if they had once got the
sword into their hands, they would have mowed us down like stubble. The word Aristocrat
would have been employed to as good account here, as ever it had been in France. We might,
ere this, have seen our places of worship turned into stables; we might have seen the banks
of the Delaware, like those of the Loire, covered with human carcasses, and its waters tinged
with blood. . . .

I know the reader will start back with horror. His heart will tell him that it is impossible.
But, once more, let him look at the example before us. The attacks on the character and conduct of the aged Washington, have been as bold, if not bolder, than those which led to the
downfall of the unfortunate French Monarch [Louis XVI, executed in 1793]. Can it then be
imagined, that, had they possessed the power, they wanted the will to dip their hands in his
blood?

SOURCE: William Cobbett, *Peter Porcupine in America*, ed., David A. Wilson (Ithaca: Cornell University
Press, 1994), 150–54.

lengthened the residency requirement for American citizenship from five to fourteen years; the Alien Act authorized the deportation of foreigners; and the Sedition Act prohibited the publication of ungrounded or malicious attacks on the president or Congress. "He that is not for us is against us," thundered the Federalist *Gazette of the United States*. Prosecutors arrested more than twenty Republican newspaper editors and politicians, accused them of sedition, and won convictions and jail sentences against some of them.

The Federalists' repressive actions created a constitutional crisis. Republicans charged that the Sedition Act violated the First Amendment's prohibition against "abridging the freedom of speech, or of the press." However, they did not appeal to the Supreme Court, both because the Court's power to review congressional legislation had not been established and because the Court was packed with Federalists. Instead, Madison and Jefferson looked to the state legislatures to remedy unconstitutional laws. At their urging, in 1798 the Kentucky and Virginia legislatures declared the Alien and Sedition Acts to be "unauthoritative, void, and of no force." The resolutions set forth a **"states' rights"** interpretation of the Constitution by arguing that the states had a "right to judge" the legitimacy of national laws.

The debate over the Sedition Act set the stage for the election of 1800. Jefferson, once opposed in principle to political parties, now saw them as a valuable way "to watch and relate to the people" the activities of an oppressive government. As Republicans strongly supported Jefferson's bid for the presidency, President Adams reevaluated his foreign policy. Adams was a complicated man who was easily offended but had great personal strength and determination. Rejecting Hamilton's advice to declare war against France (and benefit from an upsurge in patriotism), Adams put country ahead of party and entered into diplomatic negotiations that ended the fighting.

Nonetheless, the election of 1800 was the first "dirty" political campaign. The Federalists attacked Jefferson's character, branding him an irresponsible pro-French radical, "the arch-apostle of irreligion and free thought," and both parties changed state election laws to favor their candidates. A low Federalist turnout in Virginia and Pennsylvania and the three-fifths rule for slave representation (which boosted the electoral votes in the southern states) gave Jefferson a narrow 73 to 65 victory over Adams in the electoral college. But the Republican electors also gave seventy-three votes to Aaron Burr of New York, who was Jefferson's vice presidential running mate. Because both Republican candidates had the same number of votes, the Constitution specified that the House of Representatives would choose between them.

Ironically, the arch-Federalist aristocrat Alexander Hamilton ushered in a more democratic era. For thirty-five ballots, Federalists in the House of Representatives blocked Jefferson's election. Then Hamilton intervened. Calling Burr an "embryo Caesar" and the "most unfit man in the United States for the office of president," he persuaded key Federalists to permit Jefferson's selection. The Federalists' concern for political stability also played a role. As Senator James Bayard of Delaware explained, "It was admitted on all hands that we must risk the Constitution and a Civil War or take Mr. Jefferson."

Jefferson called the election the "Revolution of 1800," and so it was. The bloodless transfer of power demonstrated that governments elected by the people could be changed in an orderly way, even in times of bitter partisan conflict. In his inaugural address in 1801 Jefferson praised this achievement, declaring: "We are all Republicans, we are all Federalists." Defying the predictions of European conservatives, the new republican constitutional order of 1776 had survived a quarter century of economic and political turmoil.

T I M E L I N E

1776	Pennsylvania approves a democratic constitution	1789	George Washington inaugurated as first president
	John Adams, *Thoughts on Government*		Judiciary Act establishes federal court system
	Propertied women allowed to vote in New Jersey (retracted in 1807)		Outbreak of French Revolution
1777	Articles of Confederation (ratified 1781)	1790	Hamilton wins Congress's approval of redemption and assumption
1779	Judith Sargent Murray, "On the Equality of the Sexes" (published in 1790)	1791	Bill of Rights ratified
1780s	Postwar commercial recession increases creditor-debtor conflicts in the states	1792	Mary Wollstonecraft, *A Vindication of the Rights of Woman*
1781	Confederation Congress charters Bank of North America	1793	French create republic and execute King Louis XVI
1784– 1785	Political and Land Ordinances outline settlement policy for new states		Madison and Jefferson found Republican Party
1785	Thomas Jefferson, *Notes on the State of Virginia*		War between Britain and France; Washington's Proclamation of Neutrality
1786	Commercial convention in Annapolis, Maryland	1794	Whiskey Rebellion in western Pennsylvania
	Shays's Rebellion roils Massachusetts	1795	Jay's Treaty with Great Britain creates controversy
1787	Northwest Ordinance		
	Constitutional convention in Philadelphia	1798	Alien, Sedition, and Naturalization Acts
1787– 1788	States hold ratification conventions		Kentucky and Virginia Resolutions contest national authority
	John Jay, James Madison, and Alexander Hamilton write *The Federalist* essays	1800	Jefferson elected president in "Revolution of 1800"

For Further Exploration

For a lively, drama-filled retelling of the Constitutional Convention, see Catherine Drinker Bowen's *Miracle at Philadelphia: The Story of the Constitutional Convention, May to September 1787* (1966). Jack Rakove's *Original Meanings: Politics and Ideas in the Making of the Constitution* (1996) is a more complex analysis that shows the divergent perspectives of the framers and how they compromised their differences. A fine study of the opponents of the new constitution is Saul Cornell's *The Other Founders: The Antifederalists and the American Dissenting Tradition* (1999). Michael Kammen, *A Machine That Would Go by Itself: The Constitution in American Culture* (1986), explains the changing reputation of the founding document, while David Waldstreicher, *In the Midst of Perpetual Fetes: The Making of American Nationalism, 1776–1820* (1997), presents a fascinating analysis of the links between public celebrations and the emergence of an American national identity.

James Roger Sharp offers an engaging study of the near disintegration of the new nation in the 1790s in *American Politics in the Early Republic: The New Nation in Crisis* (1993). A detailed study of one of the major crises of these years, Thomas P. Slaughter's *The Whiskey Rebellion* (1986), shows how this uprising reflected the localistic, antitax outlook of the Revolutionary era. Rosemarie Zagarri suggests the impact of republicanism on women and provides a concise biography of an important Patriot in *A Woman's Dilemma: Mercy Otis Warren and the American Revolution* (1995). See also Linda Kerber, *No Constitutional Right to Be Ladies: Women and the Obligations of Citizenship* (1999).

The strong political and leadership abilities of the first president are a central theme of William Martin's fictionalized biography *Citizen Washington* (1999). William Martin also wrote the documentary *George Washington: The Man Who Wouldn't Be King* (PBS video, 1 hour). Additional material, including Washington's published correspondence, is available online at The Papers of George Washington, <http://www.virginia.edu/gwpapers/>. For more information on Thomas Jefferson consult the PBS Web site Thomas Jefferson, at <http://www.pbs.org/jefferson>, which contains information on the documentary (PBS video, 3 hours), transcripts of interviews with Jeffersonian scholars, and a good collection of documents relating to Jefferson's personal and public life.

For definitions of key terms boldfaced in this chapter, see the glossary at the end of the book.

To assess your mastery of the material covered in this chapter, see the Online Study Guide at **bedfordstmartins.com/henrettaconcise**.

For map resources and primary documents, see **bedfordstmartins.com/henrettaconcise**.

Chapter 8

THE DYNAMICS OF WESTERN SETTLEMENT AND EASTERN CAPITALISM
1790–1820

Once we became an independent people it was as much a law of nature that this [expansion to the west] should become our pretension as that the Mississippi should flow to the sea.

JOHN QUINCY ADAMS

"**I**t is a country in flux," a French aristocrat observed of the United States in 1799, and "that which is true today as regards its population, its establishments, its prices, its commerce will not be true six months from now." Indeed, by 1800, the American republic was poised to begin a period of dynamic westward expansion and eastern economic development that would soon change its very character. "If movement and the quick succession of sensations and ideas constitute life," another French observer wrote a few decades later, "here one lives a hundred fold more than elsewhere; here, all is circulation, motion, and boiling agitation."

Circulation and motion were especially evident along the western frontier. As early as 1766, a white observer had noted that "the thirst after Indian lands, is become almost universal." After 1783, when the Treaty of Paris gave Americans access to the trans-Appalachian West, hundreds of thousands of extraordinarily self-confident farmers trekked into the interior with little or no regard for Indian land rights. As western land speculator George Washington put it, the Sons of Liberty became "the lords and proprietors of a vast tract of continent." Unfortunately for Washington's Federalist Party, the votes of these western farmers bolstered the political ascendancy of Republican president Thomas Jefferson and his western-oriented policies. To provide even more land for American farmers, Jefferson doubled the country's size through the Louisiana Purchase in 1803. "[No] territory can be too large," declared Dr. David Ramsay of South Carolina, "for a people, who multiply with such unequalled rapidity."

As Republican policy in the West encouraged homesteading, state legislatures in the East promoted banking, manufacturing, and commercial expansion. This stimulus from state governments unleashed a cumulative process of capitalist-financed economic growth. "Experiment follows experiment; enterprise follows enterprise," a European traveler noted, and "riches and poverty follow." Of the two, riches were the more apparent. Beginning around 1800 per capita income in the United States increased by more than 1 percent per year—over 30 percent in a single generation. By the 1820s the nation was well on its way to becoming a republic that was continental in scope and **capitalist** in character.

Westward Expansion

Many generations past, Shawnee diplomats told American officials in 1803, their ancestors had gazed out into the Atlantic Ocean and seen a strange object. "At first they took it for a great bird, but they soon found it to be a monstrous canoe filled with . . . white people." Soon thereafter, the Indian emissaries continued, the white people robbed the Shawnees of their wisdom and then "usurped their land," purchasing it with goods that "were more the property of the Indians than the white people because the knowledge which enabled them to manufacture these goods actually belonged to the Shawnees."

Whatever the truth of this legend, by 1803 the expansionist-minded American republic clearly threatened the Shawnees and other native peoples. In 1790 the first national census counted only 200,000 Americans living west of the Appalachian Mountains, out of a total population of 3.9 million. Thirty years later, no fewer than 2 million slaves and citizens (of a total of 9.6 million) inhabited nine new states and three new territories west of the Appalachians. The country was moving west at an astonishing pace.

Native American Resistance

In the Treaty of Paris of 1783 Great Britain relinquished its claims to the trans-Appalachian region and, as one British statesman put it, left the Indian nations "to the care of their [American] neighbours." *Care* was hardly the right term, given that some influential Americans wanted to exterminate the native peoples. "Cut up every Indian Cornfield and burn every Indian town," proclaimed William Henry Drayton of South Carolina, so that their "nation be extirpated and the lands become the property of the public." Others, including Henry Knox, President Washington's first secretary of war, favored assimilating the Indians into American society. Knox proposed the division of commonly held tribal lands among individual Indian families, who would become citizens of the various states. Most Indians rejected these policies and continued to view themselves as members of a particular clan or tribe. A few Native American leaders raised the notion of a broader, pan-Indian identity, but without much success.

Treaty Negotiations at Greenville

In 1785 the Shawnee, Chipewyan, Ottawa, Miami, and other tribes formed the Western Confederacy to prevent white settlement north of the Ohio River. The American victory at the Battle of Fallen Timbers (1794) opened up the region for white farmers. However, the Treaty of Greenville (1795) recognized many Indian rights because, as the artist suggests, it was negotiated between relative equals. Note the height and stately bearing of the Indian leaders and their placement in the picture slightly in front of the American officers.

Unknown, *Treaty of Greenville*, n.d., Chicago Historical Society.

Not surprisingly, the major struggle between Indians and whites concerned land rights. Invoking the Paris treaty and viewing Britain's Indian allies as conquered peoples, the United States government asserted its ownership of the trans-Appalachian West. Native Americans rejected this claim and pointed out that they had not signed the treaty and had never been conquered. Brushing aside those arguments, U.S. commissioners used military threats to force pro-British Iroquois peoples—the Mohawks, Onondagas, Cayugas, and Senecas—to relinquish much of their land in New York and Pennsylvania in the Treaty of Fort Stanwix (1784). New York officials and land speculators used liquor and bribes to take title to millions of additional acres and confined the once-powerful Iroquois to relatively small reservations.

American negotiators employed similar tactics farther to the west. In 1785 they induced the Chipewyans, Delawares, Ottawas, and Wyandots to sign away most of the future state of Ohio. The tribes quickly repudiated the agreements, claiming—justifiably—that they were made under duress. Those peoples, along with the Shawnees, Miamis, and Potawatomis, formed the Western Confederacy to defend themselves. Led by Little Turtle, a Miami chief, they crushed American expeditionary forces commanded by General Harmar in 1790 and General St. Clair in 1791.

Fearing an alliance between the Western Confederacy and the British in Canada, President Washington doubled the size of the U.S. Army and ordered General "Mad Anthony" Wayne to lead a new expedition. In August 1794 Wayne defeated the Indians in the Battle of Fallen Timbers (near present-day Toledo, Ohio). Nevertheless, in 1795 the Western Confederacy forced a compromise peace in the Treaty of Greenville (Ohio). American negotiators acknowledged Indian ownership of the land, and the members of the confederacy agreed to place themselves "under the protection of the United States, and no other Power whatever." In practice, this agreement eventually brought the transfer of millions of acres of Indian land to the U.S. government. Indeed, during the Greenville negotiations the Indians ceded ownership of most of Ohio and various strategic areas along the Great Lakes, including Detroit and the future site of Chicago (Map 8.1). These American advances prompted Britain to reduce its trade with the Indian peoples and, in Jay's Treaty of 1795, to reaffirm its (still unfulfilled) obligation under the Treaty of Paris to remove its military garrisons from the region.

The Greenville Treaty sparked a wave of American migration. By 1805 the two-year-old state of Ohio had more than 100,000 residents. Thousands more farm families moved into the future states of Indiana and Illinois and sparked new conflicts with native peoples over land and hunting rights. As a Delaware Indian declared, "The Elks are our horses, the buffaloes are our cows, the deer are our sheep, & the whites shan't have them."

To alleviate these tensions the U.S. government encouraged Native Americans to become farmers and assimilate into white society. The goal, as one Kentucky Protestant minister put it, was to make the Indian "a farmer, a citizen of the United States, and a Christian." Some Indians embraced Christian teachings while retaining many ancestral values. To view themselves as individuals, as the Europeans demanded, meant repudiating the clan, the essence of Indian life. Consequently, most Native Americans resisted assimilation. As a Munsee prophet put it, "There are two ways to God, one for the whites and one for the Indians." To preserve their traditional cultures, many Indian peoples drove out white missionaries and forced Christianized Indians to participate in tribal rites. A few Indian leaders tried to find a middle path. Among the Senecas of New York the prophet Handsome Lake promoted traditional pagan ceremonies that gave thanks to the earth, plants, animals, water, and sun. But his teachings also included some Christian elements, such as a belief in heaven and hell, which he used to deter his followers from drinking alcohol, gambling, and practicing witchcraft. Handsome Lake's doctrines divided the tribe into hostile religious factions. More conservative Senecas, led by Chief Red Jacket, condemned Indians who accepted white

MAP 8.1 Indian Cessions and State Formation, to 1840

By virtue of the Treaty of Paris of 1783 with Britain, the United States claimed sovereignty over the entire trans-Appalachian West. The Western Indian Confederacy contested this claim, which the U.S. government upheld by military force. By 1840 Native American peoples had been forced by armed diplomacy to move west of the Mississippi River. White settlers occupied their lands, formed territorial governments, and eventually entered the Union as members of separate—and equal—states. Gradually, the trans-Appalachian region emerged as an important economic and political force.

ways, and they demanded a return to ancestral customs (see American Voices, "A Seneca Chief's Understanding of Religion," p. 232).

Most Indians also rejected the efforts of American missionaries to place agriculture in the hands of men. Among Eastern Woodland peoples, women had traditionally been responsible for growing staple foods; partly as a result, they controlled the inheritance

AMERICAN VOICES

A Seneca Chief's Understanding of Religion

RED JACKET

*T*he Seneca chief Red Jacket (c. 1758–1830) acquired his name during the Revolutionary War, when he fought for the British "redcoats" to protect his people from the threat posed by American settlers. Although reconciled to American rule, Red Jacket strongly adhered to Indian values and opposed attempts by missionaries to convert the Iroquois people to Christianity. In 1805 he explained why to a group of missionaries, whom he addressed as "Brother."

Brother: Continue to listen. You say that you are sent to instruct us how to worship the Great Spirit agreeably to his mind; and, if we do not take hold of the religion which you white people teach, we shall be unhappy hereafter. You say that you are right, and we are lost. How do we know this to be true? We understand that your religion is written in a book. If it was intended for us as well as you, why has not the Great Spirit given to us, and not only to us, but why did He not give to our forefathers, the knowledge of the book, with the means of understanding it rightly?

Brother: The Great Spirit has made us all, but he has made a great difference between his white and red children. He has given us different complexions and different customs. To you He has given the arts [i.e., manufacturing]. To these He has not opened our eyes. We know these things to be true. Since He has made a great difference between us in other things, why may we not conclude that He has given us different religion according to our understanding? The Great Spirit does right. He knows what is best for his children; we are satisfied.

SOURCE: David J. Rothman and Sheila Rothman, eds., *Sources of the American Social Tradition* (New York: Basic Books, 1975), 182.

of cultivation rights and exercised considerable political power. In fact, among the Shawnees, women "war chiefs" had the authority to dispatch war parties and order the torture of captives. Nor were Indian men interested in becoming farmers; when hunting was no longer possible, they turned to the grazing of cattle and sheep.

Migration and the Changing Farm Economy

Native American resistance did not halt the advance of white farmers and planters, who poured across the Appalachians and moved along the Atlantic coastal plain in search of fertile lands. This migratory upsurge brought financial rewards to many settlers and transformed the American farm economy.

Between 1790 and 1820 two great streams of migrants moved out of the southern states. One stream, composed primarily of white tenant farmers and struggling yeomen families, flocked through the Cumberland Gap into Kentucky and Tennessee. They were fleeing the depleted soils and planter elite of the Chesapeake region and hoped to prosper by growing cotton and hemp, which were in great demand. "Boundless settlements open a door for our citizens to run off and leave us," a worried eastern landlord lamented in the *Maryland Gazette*, "depreciating all our landed property and disabling us from paying taxes."

Many migrants to Kentucky and Tennessee were poor, without ready cash to buy land. To gain title to farmland, they invoked the "the ancient cultivation law" articulated earlier by the North Carolina Regulators (see Chapter 4). In their view, poor settlers had a customary right "from time out of Mind" to occupy "back waste vacant Lands" sufficient "to provide a subsistence for themselves and their posterity." The Virginia government, which administered the Kentucky Territory, had a more elitist and capitalist vision. Although it allowed poorer settlers to purchase up to 1,400 acres of land at reduced prices, it also sold or granted estates of 20,000 to 200,000 acres to scores of wealthy individuals and partnerships. Consequently, when Kentucky became a state in 1792, a handful of speculators owned one-fourth of the state, while half the adult white men owned no land and lived as squatters or tenant farmers.

Meanwhile, a second stream of southern migrants from the Carolinas, dominated by slave-owning planters and their enslaved African American workers, moved along the coastal plain of the Gulf of Mexico. At first, these planters set up new slave plantations in the interior of Georgia and South Carolina. Then they moved into the Old Southwest—the future states of Alabama, Mississippi, and Louisiana, taking some slaves with them and importing more from Africa. Between 1776 and 1808, when Congress cut off the Atlantic slave trade, these planters bought about 115,000 Africans. The American black population grew even more through reproduction and increased from half a million in 1775 to 1.8 million in 1820.

Although many African Americans still toiled in tobacco and rice fields of the Chesapeake and South Carolina, many more planted and picked a new crop: cotton. Beginning around 1750, technological innovations such as water-powered spinning jennies and weaving mules boosted European textile production and greatly increased the demand for raw wool and cotton. Responding to the demand for cotton, South Carolina and Georgia planters began growing the crop and American inventors—including Connecticut-born Eli Whitney—developed machines (called gins) that efficiently extracted the seeds from the strands of cotton. The cotton boom financed the rapid settlement of Alabama and Mississippi. In a single year a government land office in Huntsville, Alabama, sold $7 million of uncleared land, and the two states entered the Union in 1817 and 1819, respectively.

As southern whites and blacks moved into the trans-Appalachian West and the Gulf Coast, a third stream of migrants flowed out of the overcrowded communities of New England. Previous generations of yeomen farm families from Massachusetts and Connecticut had moved north and east, settling New Hampshire, Vermont, and Maine. Now farmers throughout New England were on the move, this time to the West. Seeking land for their children, thousands of parents packed their wagons

Slave Auction in Charleston, South Carolina, 1833

As one slave departs with his new master (far right), the auctioneer tries to interest the assembled planters in his next sale item, a black family. The artist, a British Canadian named Henry Byam Martin, showed his disdain for these proceedings in the sketch itself (compare the family's dignified bearing with the planters' slouching postures) and in its sarcastic title: *The Land of the Free and the Home of the Brave.* National Archives of Canada.

with tools and household goods and migrated into New York. By 1820 nearly 800,000 New England migrants lived in a string of settlements that stretched from Albany to Buffalo. Thousands more moved on to Ohio and Indiana.

This vast migration was organized not by governments or joint-stock companies but by the settlers themselves, who often moved in large groups linked by family and religion. As a traveler reported from central New York, "The town of Herkimer is entirely populated by families come from Connecticut. We stayed at Mr. Snow's who came from New London with about ten male and female cousins." When 176 residents of Granville, Massachusetts, moved to Ohio, they were led by the minister and elders of their Congregational church. Throughout this region— known as the Old Northwest—many "new" communities were actually old communities that had moved inland.

In New York, as in Kentucky, well-connected speculators snapped up much of the best land. In the 1780s the financier Robert Morris acquired 1.3 million acres in the Genesee region of central New York, where the Wadsworth family also bought thousands of acres and tried to set up a manorial regime like that in the Hudson Valley. To attract tenants, the Wadsworths leased farms rent-free for the first seven years, after which they charged rents. Many New England yeomen preferred to sign

agreements with the Holland Land Company, a Dutch-owned syndicate of speculators. Holland Land contracts allowed settlers to buy the land as they worked it, but
high interest rates and the lack of markets initially mired thousands of these aspiring freeholders in debt. As one pioneer recalled, "In the early years, there was none
but a home market and that was mostly barter—it was so many bushels of wheat
for a cow; so many bushels for a yoke of oxen."

As western farmers exported wheat to pay their debts, they forced changes in
eastern agriculture. Unable to compete against low-priced western grains, farmers
in New England switched to potatoes, which were high yielding and nutritious. To
compensate for the lost labor of sons and daughters, Middle Atlantic farmers
replaced metal-tipped wooden plows with cast-iron models that dug deeper and
required a single yoke of oxen instead of two or three. Such technological improvements allowed them to maintain production levels even with fewer laborers.

Easterners also took advantage of the progressive farming methods publicized
by wealthy British agricultural reformers. "Improvers" in Pennsylvania doubled the
average yield per acre by rotating their crops and planting nitrogen-rich clover to
offset nutrient-hungry crops of wheat and corn. Yeomen farmers diversified production by raising sheep and selling the wool to textile manufacturers. Many farmers adopted a year-round planting cycle, sowing wheat in the winter for market sale
and corn in the spring for animal fodder. Women and girls milked the family cows
and made butter and cheese for sale in the growing towns and cities.

In this new agricultural economy families worked harder and longer, but their
efforts were rewarded with higher output and a better standard of living. Whether
hacking fields out of western forests or carting manure to replenish eastern soils,
farm families increased their productivity. Westward migration had boosted the
entire American economy.

The Transportation Bottleneck

America's geography threatened to cut short this economic advance. Although water
transport was the quickest and cheapest way to get goods to market, no rivers cut
through the Appalachian Mountains. Improved inland trade therefore became a high
priority for the new state governments, which actively encouraged transportation ventures. Between 1793 and 1812 the Pennsylvania legislature granted fifty-five corporate
charters to private turnpike companies, and Massachusetts chartered over a hundred.
Turnpike companies built gravel roads that significantly reduced transport costs and
charged tolls for their use. State governments and private entrepreneurs constructed
even more cost-efficient waterways by dredging rivers to make them navigable and
constructing short canals to bypass waterfalls or rapids. By 1816 the United States
had about 100 miles of canals, but only three of these artificial waterways were more
than 2 miles long and none breached the great Appalachian barrier. Only after 1819,
when the Erie Canal connected the central counties of New York to the Hudson River,
could inland farmers easily sell their produce in eastern markets (see Chapter 10).

Hop Picking, by Lucy Sheldon, 1801

Work was nothing new for rural women and children, who had always labored about the farm. What was different after 1800 was the growing number of outworkers, landless or poor families who worked for shopkeepers and manufacturers. In this somewhat romanticized watercolor by a schoolgirl at the Litchfield Female Academy in Connecticut, a young couple and their children pick hops, which they will deliver to a storekeeper or local brewer to be made into beer. Litchfield Historical Society.

For western farmers the great streams that connected to the Mississippi River represented the great hope. Western settlers paid premium prices for land near the Ohio, Tennessee, and Mississippi Rivers, and speculators bought up property in growing towns along their banks: Cincinnati, Louisville, Chattanooga, and St. Louis. Western farmers and merchants built barges to float cotton, surplus grain, and meat down this great river system to the port of New Orleans, which by 1815 was handling about $5 million in agricultural products yearly.

However, many settlers in the trans-Appalachian West lacked access to these waterways and had to be self-sufficient. "A noble field of Indian corn stretched away into the forest on one side," an English visitor to an isolated Ohio farm noted,

> and immediately before the house was a small potato garden, with a few peach and apple trees. The woman told me that they spun and wove all the cotton and woollen garments of the family, and knit all the stockings; her husband, though not a shoemaker by trade, made all the shoes. She manufactured all the soap and candles they use.

Self-sufficiency meant a low standard of living. As late as 1840 per capita income in the Old Northwest was only 70 percent of the national average.

Despite these financial hardships and transportation bottlenecks, white Americans continued to migrate westward. They knew it would take a generation to clear land; build houses, barns, and roads; and plant orchards. Yet they were confident that their sacrifices and the expanding canal and road system would yield future security for themselves and their children. The humble achievements of thousands of yeomen and tenant families slowly transformed the landscape, turning forests into farms and crossroads villages into bustling communities.

The Republicans' Political Revolution

Agricultural expansion was a central policy of the Republican Party and accounted for much of its appeal. From 1801 to 1825 three Republicans from Virginia— Thomas Jefferson, James Madison, and James Monroe—served two terms each as president. Supported by voters in the new western states and strong majorities in Congress, this "Virginia Dynasty" completed what Jefferson called the Revolution of 1800 by reversing many Federalist policies and actively supporting a policy of westward expansion. The movement of American settlers onto lands claimed by Indian peoples, Spain, and Britain, together with maritime disputes in the Atlantic, precipitated the War of 1812.

The Jeffersonian Presidency

Thomas Jefferson was an accomplished statesman, an insightful political philosopher, and a superb politician. On assuming the presidency in 1801 Jefferson became the first chief executive to serve in the District of Columbia, the new national capital. However, his administration did not begin with a clean slate. A dozen years of Federalist presidents had filled the national judiciary with their appointees, including the formidable John Marshall of Virginia, who presided over the Supreme Court. To perpetuate Federalist power, the outgoing Congress passed a new Judiciary Act in 1801. The act created sixteen new judgeships and six additional circuit courts, which President Adams filled with "midnight appointments" just before he left office. The Federalists "have retired into the judiciary as a stronghold," Jefferson complained, "and from that battery all the works of Republicanism are to be beaten down and destroyed."

Jefferson's fears were quickly realized. In 1798, Republican-dominated legislatures in Kentucky and Virginia had repudiated the Alien and Sedition Acts and claimed the authority to determine the constitutionality of national laws (see Chapter 7). However, the Constitution stated that "the judicial Power shall extend to all Cases . . . arising under this Constitution [and] the Laws of the United States" and implied that the Supreme Court held the power of constitutional review. This important issue came to the fore when James Madison, the new secretary of state, refused to deliver the commission appointing William Marbury, one of Adams's midnight appointees, as a justice of the peace in the District of Columbia. Marbury petitioned the Supreme Court to compel delivery under the terms of the Judiciary Act of 1789. However, in *Marbury v. Madison* (1803), Chief Justice Marshall ruled that, while Marbury had a right to the commission, the Court did not have power under the Constitution to enforce that right. More important, in reaching this decision by voiding a section of the Judiciary Act of 1789, Marshall asserted the Court's power of **judicial review**. "It is emphatically the province and duty of the judicial department to say what the law is," Marshall declared, directly repudiating the Republican view that the state legislatures had that authority.

Despite this setback, Jefferson and the Republicans used their newfound national power to reverse many Federalist policies. Charging the Federalists with grossly expanding the national government's size and power, Jefferson mobilized the Republican Congress to shrink it back. When the Alien and Sedition Acts expired in 1801, the Congress branded the acts as politically motivated and unconstitutional and refused to reenact them. It also amended the Naturalization Act to permit resident aliens to become citizens after five years. But the new president governed tactfully. Although Jefferson secured repeal of the Judiciary Act, thereby ousting forty of Adams's "midnight appointees," he allowed competent Federalist bureaucrats to retain their jobs. Apart from the midnight appointees, he removed only 69 of 433 Federalist officeholders during his eight years as chief executive.

In foreign affairs Jefferson faced an immediate crisis. During the 1790s the Barbary States of North Africa had systematically raided merchant ships in the Mediterranean and, like many European states, Federalist officials had paid an annual bribe ("tribute") to protect American vessels. Initially Jefferson reversed this policy and refused to pay these bribes. When the Barbary "pirates" renewed their assaults, he ordered the U.S. Navy to retaliate. However, Jefferson wanted to avoid all-out war, which would increase taxes and the national debt, and so he negotiated a diplomatic settlement that reduced the tribute payment.

In domestic matters Jefferson set a clearly Republican course. He abolished all internal taxes, including the excise tax that had sparked the Whiskey Rebellion of 1794. Addressing his party's fears of a military coup, Jefferson reduced the size of the permanent army. He tolerated the economically important Bank of the United States (which he had condemned as unconstitutional in 1791) but chose as his secretary of the treasury Albert Gallatin, a fiscal conservative who believed that the national debt was "an evil of the first magnitude." By carefully controlling expenditures and using customs revenues to redeem government bonds, Gallatin reduced the debt from $83 million in 1801 to $45 million in 1808. With Jefferson and Gallatin at the helm, the nation was no longer run in the interests of northeastern creditors and merchants.

Jefferson and the West

Long before he became president, Jefferson championed the settlement of the West. He celebrated the yeoman farmer in *Notes on the State of Virginia* (1785), wrote one of the Confederation's western land ordinances, and strongly supported Pinckney's Treaty of 1795, which allowed settlers in the Mississippi River Valley to export crops through the Spanish-held port of New Orleans.

As president, Jefferson worked to increase the flow of settlers to the West. In 1796 a Federalist-dominated Congress had made it more difficult for migrating families to buy a farm in the national domain by doubling the minimum price to $2 per acre. To populate the West with yeomen farm families, the Republicans in Congress passed laws in 1800 and 1804 reducing the minimum allotment first to 320 and then to 160 acres. Eventually the Land Act of 1820 cut the minimum purchase to 80 acres and the price to $1.25 per acre, enabling a farmer with only $100 in cash to buy a western farm.

International events challenged Jefferson's vision of the West as a limitless source of land for American farmers. In 1799 Napoleon Bonaparte seized power in France and began an ambitious campaign to establish a French empire both in Europe and in America. In 1801 Napoleon coerced Spain into signing a secret treaty that returned to France its former colony of Louisiana. A year later he directed Spanish officials in Louisiana to restrict American access to New Orleans, thus violating the terms of Pinckney's Treaty. Meanwhile, Napoleon planned an invasion to restore French rule in Haiti (then called Saint-Domingue), a rich sugar island seized in 1793 by rebellious black slaves led by Toussaint L'Ouverture.

Napoleon's aggressive actions prompted Jefferson to question his party's pro-French foreign policy. "The day that France takes possession of New Orleans," the president warned, "we must marry ourselves to the British fleet and nation." To avoid hostilities with France Jefferson instructed Robert R. Livingston, the American minister in Paris, to negotiate the purchase of New Orleans. Simultaneously, Jefferson sent James Monroe to Britain to seek its assistance in case of war with France.

Jefferson's diplomacy yielded a magnificent prize: the entire territory of Louisiana. By 1802 the French invasion of Haiti was faltering in the face of disease and determined black resistance, a new war threatened in Europe, and Napoleon feared an American invasion of Louisiana. Acting with characteristic decisiveness, the French ruler offered to sell not only New Orleans but also the entire territory of Louisiana for $15 million (about $450 million today). "We have lived long," Livingston remarked to Monroe as they concluded the Louisiana Purchase, "but this is the noblest work of our lives."

The Louisiana Purchase forced the president to reconsider his "strict" interpretation of the Constitution. Jefferson had always maintained that the national government possessed only the powers "expressly" delegated to it in the Constitution. Because there was no constitutional provision for adding new territory, Jefferson pragmatically accepted a "loose" interpretation and used the treaty-making powers in the Constitution to complete the deal with France.

A scientist as well as a statesman, Jefferson wanted detailed information about the physical features of the new territory, its plant and animal life, and its native peoples. In 1804 he sent his personal secretary, Meriwether Lewis, to explore the region with William Clark, an army officer. Aided by Indian guides, Lewis and Clark and their group of American soldiers and frontiersmen traveled up the Missouri River, across the Rocky Mountains, and (venturing beyond the bounds of the Louisiana Purchase) down the Columbia River to the Pacific Ocean. After two years they returned with the first maps of the immense wilderness and vivid accounts of its natural resources and inhabitants.

Although the Louisiana Purchase was a stunning accomplishment that doubled the size of the nation, it brought a new threat. New England Federalists, fearing that western expansion would diminish the power of their states and their party, talked openly of leaving the Union. Because Alexander Hamilton refused to support their plan for a separate Northern Confederacy, the secessionists turned to Aaron Burr, the ambitious vice president. When Hamilton accused Burr of participating in a conspiracy to destroy the Union, Burr challenged him to a pistol duel. To uphold his aristocratic sense of "honor," Hamilton accepted the dare and died by gunshot in the illegal confrontation.

This tragic event propelled Burr into yet another secessionist scheme. As his vice presidential term ended in 1805, Burr moved west to avoid prosecution. There he conspired with General James Wilkinson, the military governor of the Louisiana Territory. Their plan remains a mystery, but it probably involved either the capture of territory in New Spain or a rebellion to establish Louisiana as a separate nation headed by Burr. However, Wilkinson betrayed Burr and arrested the former vice president as he led an armed force down the Ohio River. In a highly politicized trial presided over by Chief Justice John Marshall, the jury acquitted Burr of treason. The verdict was less important than the dangers to national unity that it revealed. The Republicans' policy of western expansion had increased party conflict and generated secessionist schemes in both New England and the West.

Conflict with Britain and France

As the Napoleonic Wars ravaged Europe between 1802 and 1815, they endangered American commerce because neither Britain nor France respected the neutrality of American merchant vessels. Napoleon imposed the "Continental System" on European ports controlled by France and ordered the seizure of neutral ships that had stopped in Britain. For its part, the British ministry set up a naval blockade that stopped ships carrying goods to Europe, including American vessels filled with sugar and molasses from the French West Indies. The British navy also searched American ships for British deserters and impressed (forced) them back into service in the Royal Navy. Between 1802 and 1811 British officers seized nearly eight thousand sailors, including many American citizens. In 1807 American resentment against impressment turned to outrage when a British warship attacked the U.S. Navy vessel *Chesapeake*, killing or wounding twenty-one men and seizing four alleged deserters. "Never since the battle of Lexington have I seen this country in such a state of exasperation as at present," Jefferson declared.

To protect American interests while avoiding war Jefferson pursued a policy of peaceful coercion. Working closely with Secretary of State James Madison, the president devised the Embargo Act of 1807, which prohibited American ships from leaving their home ports until Britain and France repealed their restrictions on U.S. trade. Though the embargo was a creative diplomatic measure—an economic weapon similar to the nonimportation movements of the 1760s—it overestimated the dependence of France and Britain on American shipping and underestimated resistance from New England merchants, who feared it would ruin them.

Indeed, the embargo was a disaster for the American economy. Exports plunged from $108 million in 1806 to $22 million in 1808, which hurt farmers as well as merchants and prompted Federalists to demand its repeal. "Would to God," exclaimed one Federalist, "that the Embargo had done as little evil to ourselves as it has done to foreign nations."

Despite discontent over the embargo, voters elected Republican James Madison to the presidency in 1808. As a powerful advocate for the Constitution, the architect of the Bill of Rights, and a prominent congressman and party leader, Madison had served the nation well. However, John Beckley, a loyal Republican, worried that Madison was "too timid and indecisive as a statesman" and events proved him correct. Acknowledging the embargo's failure, Madison replaced it with a series of new economic restrictions, none of which persuaded France and Britain to respect America's neutral rights. "The Devil himself could not tell which government, England or France, is the most wicked," an exasperated congressman declared.

Republican congressmen from the West—the future "war hawks" of 1812—thought Britain was the major offender and pointed in particular to its assistance to the Indians in the Ohio River Valley. Bolstered by British guns and supplies, in 1809 the Shawnee chief Tecumseh [ta-CUM-sa], assisted by his brother, the prophet Tenskwatawa [tens-QUA-ta-wa], revived the Western Confederacy. Their goal was to unite the Indian peoples and exclude whites from all lands west of the Appalachian Mountains. Republican expansionists in Congress condemned British support of Tecumseh and threatened to invade Canada. In 1811, following a series of clashes between settlers and the Western Confederacy, William Henry Harrison, the governor of the Indiana Territory, led an army against Tenskwatawa's village of Prophetstown (on the Wabash River in present-day Indiana). Fending off the confederacy's warriors at the Battle of Tippecanoe, Harrison burned the village to the ground.

Henry Clay of Kentucky, the new Speaker of the House of Representatives, and John C. Calhoun, a rising young congressman from South Carolina, pushed Madison toward war with Great Britain. Like other western Republicans, they favored the acquisition of new territory in British Canada and Spanish Florida. They also hoped that war would discredit the Federalists and their pro-British foreign policy. With national elections approaching, Madison demanded British respect for American sovereignty in the West and neutral rights on the Atlantic.

When the British did not respond quickly, Madison asked Congress for a declaration of war. In June 1812 a sharply divided Senate voted 19 to 13 for war, and the House of Representatives concurred, 79 to 49.

The underlying causes of the War of 1812 have been much debated. Officially, the United States went to war because of violations of its neutral rights: the seizure of merchant ships and the impressment of American sailors. But the Federalists who represented merchants' and seamen's interests in Congress voted against the war declaration, and in the election of 1812, voters in New England and the Middle Atlantic states cast their ballots (and 89 electoral votes) for the Federalist candidate for president, De Witt Clinton of New York. Madison amassed most of his 128 electoral votes in the South and West, where voters strongly supported the war. Because of this regional split, many historians argue that the conflict was actually "a western war with eastern labels."

The War of 1812

The War of 1812 was a near disaster for the United States, both militarily and politically. Predictions of an easy advance into British Canada ended quickly when an American invasion force had to beat a hasty retreat back to Detroit. But Americans stayed on the offensive in the West. Commodore Oliver Hazard Perry defeated a small British flotilla on Lake Erie, and in October 1813 General William Henry Harrison invaded Canada and triumphed over a combined British and Indian force at the Battle of the Thames, killing Tecumseh, who had become a general in the British army. Another American expedition burned York (present-day Toronto) and then quickly withdrew.

Political divisions prevented a major invasion of Canada in the East. New Englanders opposed the war and prohibited their militias from fighting outside their states. Boston merchants and banks declined to lend money to the federal government, making the war difficult to finance. In Congress Daniel Webster, a dynamic young representative from New Hampshire, led Federalist opposition to higher taxes and tariffs and to the national conscription of state militiamen.

Partly because of these domestic political conflicts, the tide of battle gradually turned in Britain's favor. Initially American privateers captured scores of British merchant vessels but the Royal Navy soon seized the initiative. By 1813 British shipping moved in relative safety and a flotilla of British warships harassed American shipping and threatened seaport cities along the Atlantic coast. In 1814 a British fleet sailed up Chesapeake Bay and British troops stormed ashore to attack Washington City, in the new federal district, where they burned U.S. government buildings. Then the troops advanced on Baltimore but were repulsed at Fort McHenry. After two years of warfare the United States was stalemated along the Canadian frontier and on the defensive in the Atlantic, with its new capital city in ruins. The only positive news came from the Southwest. There a rugged slave-owning planter named Andrew Jackson led an army of militiamen from Tennessee to victory over the British-supported Creek Indians in the Battle of Horseshoe Bend (1814) and forced the Indians to cede 23 million acres of land (Map 8.2).

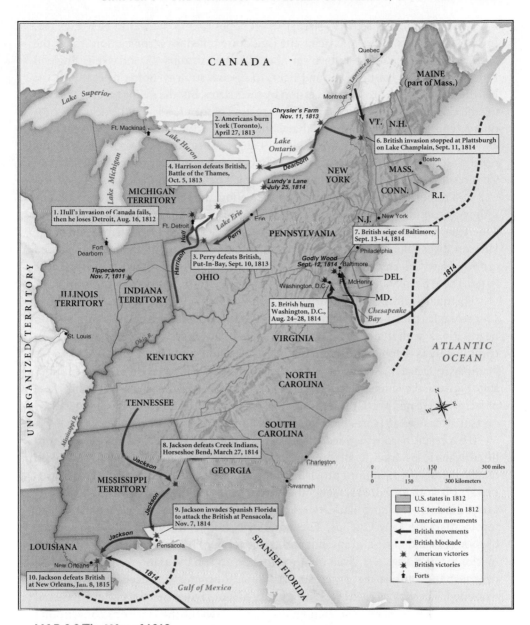

MAP 8.2 The War of 1812

Unlike the War for Independence, the War of 1812 had few large-scale military campaigns. In 1812 and 1813, most fighting took place along the Canadian border, as American armies and naval forces attacked British targets with mixed success (#1–4). The British took the offensive in 1814, launching a successful raid on Washington and Baltimore but suffering heavy losses when they invaded the United States along Lake Champlain (#5–7). Near the Gulf of Mexico, American forces moved from one success to another, as General Andrew Jackson defeated the pro-British Creek Indians at the Battle of Horseshoe Bend and, in the major battle of the war, routed an invading British army at New Orleans (#8–10).

American military setbacks strengthened opposition to the war in New England. In 1814 Federalists in the Massachusetts legislature called for a convention "to lay the foundation for a radical reform in the National Compact," and New England Federalists met in Hartford, Connecticut, to discuss strategy. Some delegates to the Hartford convention proposed secession by their states, but the majority favored revising the Constitution. To end Virginia's domination of the presidency, the delegates proposed a constitutional amendment that would limit the office to a single four-year term and rotate it among citizens from different states. They also suggested amendments restricting commercial embargoes to sixty days and requiring a two-thirds majority in Congress to declare war, prohibit trade, or admit a new state to the Union.

As a minority party in Congress and the nation, the Federalists could prevail only if the war continued to go badly—a very real prospect. In the late summer of 1814 an American naval victory on Lake Champlain narrowly averted a British invasion of the Hudson River Valley. A few months later, thousands of seasoned British troops landed outside New Orleans and threatened to cut American trade down the Mississippi River. The United States was under military pressure from both north and south.

Fortunately for the young American republic, Britain wanted peace. The twenty-year struggle against France had sapped its wealth and energy, and so it entered into negotiations with the United States in Ghent, Belgium. At first the American commissioners—John Quincy Adams, Albert Gallatin, and Henry Clay—demanded territory in Canada and Florida, and British diplomats insisted on an Indian buffer state between the United States and Canada. Ultimately, both sides realized that these objectives were not worth the costs of prolonged warfare. The Treaty of Ghent, signed on Christmas Eve 1814, restored the prewar borders of the United States.

This result hardly justified three years of fighting, but a final military victory lifted Americans' morale. Before news of the Treaty of Ghent reached the United States, newspaper headlines proclaimed an "ALMOST INCREDIBLE VICTORY!! GLORIOUS NEWS": on January 8, 1815, General Andrew Jackson's troops (including a contingent of French-speaking black Americans, the Corps d'Afrique) crushed the British forces attacking New Orleans. The Americans fought from carefully constructed breastworks and rained "grapeshot and cannister bombs" on the massed British formations. The British lost seven hundred men, with two thousand wounded or taken prisoner. By contrast the Americans sustained only thirteen dead and fifty-eight wounded. The victory made Jackson a national hero, redeemed the nation's battered pride, and, together with the coming of peace, undercut the Hartford convention's demands for a significant revision of the Constitution.

As Jackson emerged as a war hero, John Quincy Adams also rose to national prominence for his diplomatic efforts at Ghent and his successes as secretary of state under President James Monroe (1817–1825). The son of Federalist president John Adams, John Quincy had joined the Republican Party before the war. In 1817 Adams negotiated the Rush-Bagot Treaty with Great Britain, which limited both nations' naval forces on the Great Lakes; the following year he won an agreement setting the forty-ninth parallel as the border between the Louisiana Purchase and British Canada. Then in the Adams-Onís Treaty of 1819, he persuaded Spain to cede Florida to the United States. In return the American government took responsibility for its citizens' financial claims against Spain, renounced Jefferson's earlier claim that Spanish Texas was part of the Louisiana Purchase, and agreed on a compromise boundary between New Spain and the state of Louisiana, which had entered the Union in 1812 (Map 8.3). Finally, at Adams's behest in 1823, President Monroe warned Spain and other European powers not to interfere in the affairs of the former Spanish colonies in Latin America that had revolted and established independent republics. In announcing this new foreign policy (which thirty years later, became known as the Monroe Doctrine) the president declared that the American continents were not "subject for further colonization" by the nations of Europe. In return, he reiterated the policy of the United States "not to interfere in the internal concerns" of European nations. Thanks to Adams, the United States had taken a significant diplomatic initiative and gained undisputed possession of nearly all the land south of the forty-ninth parallel and east of the Rocky Mountains.

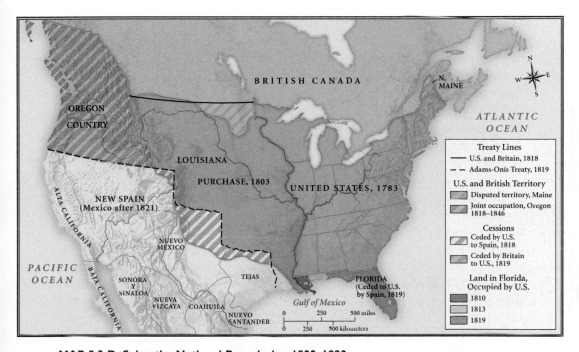

MAP 8.3 Defining the National Boundaries, 1800–1820

After the War of 1812 Secretary of State John Quincy Adams negotiated treaties with Great Britain and Spain that defined the boundaries of the Louisiana Purchase with British Canada to the north and New Spain (which in 1821 became the independent nation of Mexico) to the south and west. These treaties eliminated the threat of border wars with neighboring states for a generation, providing the United States with a much-needed period of peace and security.

FOR MORE HELP ANALYZING THIS MAP, see the Online Study Guide at **bedfordstmartins.com/henrettaconcise**.

The Capitalist Commonwealth

The increasing size of the American republic was matched by the growth of its economic institutions and wealth. Before 1790 the United States was an agricultural society that was dependent on Britain for markets, credit, and manufactured goods. Over the next generation the nation developed a more diverse economy as rural Americans became manufacturers, bankers supplied credit to expand trade, and merchants developed regional markets.

This new American economic order had an increasingly capitalist character. Some capitalist features, such as the private ownership of property and the development of a market economy, were legacies of the colonial era. However, after independence men who owned "capital"—landlords, bankers, and entrepreneurs—played an increasingly prominent role in political and financial life.

Banks, Manufacturing, and Markets

America was "a Nation of Merchants," a British visitor reported from Philadelphia in 1798, who were "keen in the pursuit of wealth in all the various modes of acquiring it." And acquire it they did by exploiting the opportunities for spectacular profits during the decades of warfare in Europe (1793–1815). Entrepreneurs such as the fur trader John Jacob Astor and the merchant Robert Oliver became the nation's first millionaires. Oliver started in Baltimore as an agent for Irish linen merchants and then opened his own mercantile firm. Exploiting the wartime shipping boom, he reaped enormous profits in the West Indian coffee and sugar trades. Migrating from Germany to New York in 1784, Astor became wealthy by carrying furs from the Pacific Northwest to markets in China.

To finance such mercantile enterprises Americans needed a banking system. Before 1776 ambitious colonists found it difficult to raise money. Farmers relied on government-sponsored land banks for loans, while merchants arranged partnerships, borrowed funds from other merchants, or obtained credit from British suppliers. Then in 1781 Philadelphia merchants persuaded the Confederation Congress to charter the Bank of North America to provide short-term commercial loans; in 1784 traders in Boston and New York founded similar institutions to finance their transactions. "Our monied capital has so much increased from the Introduction of Banks, & the Circulation of the Funds," the Philadelphia merchant William Bingham boasted in 1791, "that the Necessity of Soliciting Credits from England will no longer exist, & the Means will be provided for putting in Motion every Specie of Industry."

That same year Congress chartered the First Bank of the United States. The bank issued notes and made commercial loans, and its profits averaged a handsome 8 percent annually. Responding to the demand for commercial credit, by 1805 the bank had branches in eight major cities. Despite these successes, the bank did not survive. Jeffersonian Republicans, who were suspicious of corruption by monied men, accused the bank of encouraging "a consolidated, energetic government supported by public creditors, speculators, and other insidious men lacking in public spirit of any kind." When the bank's twenty-year charter expired in 1811, President Madison did not seek its renewal, and so merchants, artisans, and farmers petitioned their state legislatures to charter new banks. By 1816, there were 246 state-chartered banks with $68 million in banknotes in circulation.

However, many state banks were shady operations that issued notes without adequate specie reserves and made ill-advised loans to insiders. These banking policies were one cause of the Panic of 1819, a financial crisis sparked by a sharp drop in world agricultural prices. As farm prices and income abruptly dropped by 30 percent, many farmers could not pay their debts to local storekeepers, wholesale merchants, and state banks. The result was a massive wave of bankruptcies. By 1821, those state banks that were still solvent had only $45 million in circulation and court dockets were crowded with thousands of legal suits, as creditors tried to save their businesses by suing their debtors. The panic gave Americans their first taste of the **business cycle**—the periodic expansion and contraction of profits and employment that is an inherent part of a capitalist market economy.

The Panic of 1819 also revealed that artisans and yeomen as well as merchants now depended on regional or national markets. Before 1790 most artisans in New England and the Middle Atlantic region sold their handicrafts locally or bartered them with neighbors. For example, John Hoff of Lancaster, Pennsylvania, exchanged his fine wooden-cased clocks for a dining table, a bedstead, and labor on his small farm. But other artisans—shipbuilders in seacoast towns, iron smelters in Pennsylvania and Maryland, and shoemakers in Lynn, Massachusetts—sold their products in far-flung markets. Indeed, merchant-entrepreneurs had developed a rural-based manufacturing system similar to the European outwork, or putting-out, system (see Chapter 1). These enterprising merchants bought raw materials from farmers, hired workers in other farm families to manufacture goods, and then sold finished products in regional or national markets. When a French traveler visited central Massachusetts in 1795, he found "almost all these houses . . . inhabited by men who are both cultivators and artisans; one is a tanner, another a shoemaker, another sells goods, but all are farmers."

By the 1820s thousands of New England farm families made shoes, brooms, palm-leaf hats, and tinware—baking pans, cups, utensils, lanterns. Merchants shipped these products to cities and slave plantations, while New England peddlers, equipped "with a horse and a cart covered with a box or with a wagon," blanketed the South and acquired a reputation as crafty, hard-bargaining "Yankees."

This economic advance stemmed primarily from innovations in organization and marketing rather than in technology. Water-powered machines—the product of the Industrial Revolution in Britain—were adopted slowly in America. In the 1780s merchants built small textile mills along the waterways of New England and the Middle Atlantic states. They hired workers and installed water-powered machines that carded and combed wool—and later cotton—into long strands. Until 1820, the

The Yankee Peddler, c. 1830

Even in 1830 most Americans lived too far from market towns to go there regularly to buy needed goods. Instead, farm families, such as this relatively prosperous one depicted by an unknown artist, purchased most of their tinware, clocks, textiles, and other manufactures from peddlers, often from New England, who traveled far and wide in small horse-drawn vans such as that pictured in the doorway. Collection IBM Corporation, Armonk, NY.

FOR MORE HELP ANALYZING THIS IMAGE, see the Online Study Guide at **bedfordstmartins.com/henrettaconcise**.

outwork system handled the next steps in the textile manufacturing process. Wage-earning farm women and children spun the strands into yarn on foot-driven spinning wheels, and men in other households used foot-powered looms to weave the yarn into cloth. In his "Letter on Manufactures" (1810) Secretary of the Treasury Albert Gallatin estimated that there were 2,500 outwork weavers in New England. A decade later more than 12,000 household workers in the New England region wove woolen cloth, which was then pounded flat and given a smooth finish in water-powered fulling mills. Thus, even before textile production was centralized in factories, the nation had a profitable and expanding system of manufacturing (see Chapter 10).

The penetration of the market economy into rural areas motivated farmers to produce more goods. Ambitious farm families switched from growing crops to raising livestock; they sold meat to city markets, sent cattle hides to the booming shoe industry, and used the milk from dairy cows to make butter and cheese for market sale. "Along the whole road from Boston, we saw women engaged in making cheese," a Polish traveler reported from central Massachusetts in 1798. Hatmaking emerged as another new industry. "Straw hats and Bonnets are manufactured by many families," a Maine official commented, while another observer estimated that "probably 8,000 females" in the vicinity of Foxborough, Massachusetts, braided rye straw into hats for market sale. Other farm families raised sheep and sold raw wool to textile manufacturers. Processing these raw materials brought new businesses to many farming towns. In 1792 Concord, Massachusetts, had one slaughterhouse and five small tanneries; a decade later the town boasted eleven slaughterhouses and six large tanneries.

As the rural economy turned out more goods, it significantly altered the environment. Foul odors from stockyards and tanning pits now wafted over Concord and many other leather-producing towns, and each year tanners cut down thousands of acres of hemlock trees and used their bark in processing leather. The multiplication of livestock—dairy cows, cattle, and especially sheep—brought the destruction of even more trees as farmers created vast new pastures and meadows. By the mid-nineteenth century, most of the forests in southern New England and eastern New York were gone, leaving a barren visual landscape. "The hills had been stripped of their timber," the New York *Catskill Messenger* noted, "so as to present their huge, rocky projections." Scores of textile milldams now dotted New England's rivers, altering their flow and making it difficult for fish to reach their upriver spawning grounds. Even as the income of many farmers rose, the quality of their natural environment deteriorated.

The new capitalist-run market economy had other drawbacks. Rural parents and their children now worked longer and harder as they made yarn, hats, and brooms during the winter and carried on their regular farming chores during the warmer seasons. Perhaps more important, these farm families lost some of their economic independence. Instead of working solely for themselves, they toiled as part-time wage earners for merchants and manufacturers. Many families stopped making their own textiles and shoes and bought them with the cash or store credit they had earned. Thus, the new market system decreased the self-sufficiency of families and communities even as it made them more productive and prosperous. The tide of change was unstoppable.

Public Policy: The Commonwealth System

Throughout the nineteenth century state governments were the most important political institutions in the United States. They enacted legislation affecting all aspects of civil and criminal affairs, collected and spent most tax revenue, and oversaw county, city, and town officials. Consequently, state governments had a much greater impact on the day-to-day lives of Americans than did the national government.

Beginning in the 1790s state legislatures devised an American plan of mercantilism, known to historians as the commonwealth system (because its goal was to increase the "common wealth" of the society). Just as the British Parliament had promoted the imperial economy through the Navigation Acts, state legislatures enacted measures to stimulate commerce and economic development. In particular, they granted corporate charters to private businesses to build roads, bridges, and canals; they intended these enterprises to be "of great public utility," as the act establishing the Massachusetts Bank put it. Thus, in 1794 the Pennsylvania legislature chartered the Lancaster Turnpike Company to lay a graded gravel road between Lancaster and Philadelphia, a distance of sixty-five miles. The venture was expensive—nearly $500,000 (about $8 million today)—but the road made a modest profit for the investors and greatly enhanced the regional economy. "The turnpike is finished," a farm woman noted, "and we can now go to town at all times and in all weather." A boom in turnpike construction soon connected dozens of inland market centers to seaport cities.

By 1800 state governments had granted more than three hundred corporate charters. These charters often included a grant of limited liability that made it easier to attract investors; if the business failed, the personal assets of the shareholders could not be seized to pay the corporation's debts. Most transportation charters also included the power of eminent domain; this provision allowed turnpike, bridge, and canal corporations to force the sale of privately owned land along their routes at reasonable prices. State legislatures also aided capitalist flour millers and textile manufacturers whose dams flooded adjacent farmland. In Massachusetts, the Mill Dam Act of 1795 required farmers to accept "fair compensation" for their lost acreage.

To some critics such uses of state power by private companies ran contrary to republicanism, "which does not admit of granting peculiar privileges to any body of men." Charters not only violated the "equal rights" of all citizens, opponents argued, but also restricted the sovereignty of the people. As a Pennsylvanian put it, "Whatever power is given to a corporation, is just so much power taken from the State" and its citizens. Nonetheless, state courts consistently upheld corporate charters and routinely approved grants of eminent domain to private corporations. "The opening of good and easy internal communications is one of the highest duties of government," declared a New Jersey judge.

The state-based mercantilism of the commonwealth system soon encompassed much more than transportation. Following the embargo of 1807, which cut off goods and credit from Europe, New England states awarded charters to two hundred iron-mining, textile-manufacturing, and banking firms, and the Pennsylvania legislature granted more than eleven hundred. Thus by 1820 innovative state governments had created a new political economy: the commonwealth system that used state incentives to encourage business and improve the general welfare.

Federalist Law: John Marshall and the Supreme Court

Both Federalists and Republicans endorsed the commonwealth idea, but in different ways. Federalists supported Alexander Hamilton's program of national mercantilism: a funded debt, tariffs, and a central bank. Jeffersonian Republicans generally preferred the state-based commonwealth system. However, following the War of 1812 some Republicans advocated national economic initiatives. As Speaker of the House of Representatives in 1816, Republican Henry Clay of Kentucky won legislation creating the Second Bank of the United States and persuaded President Madison to sign it. In the following year Clay won passage of the Bonus Bill, sponsored by Representative John C. Calhoun of South Carolina, which would have established a national fund for roads and other internal improvements. But many Republicans believed that such internal improvements exceeded the powers delegated to the national government and welcomed Madison's veto of the Bonus Bill.

The difference between Federalist and Jeffersonian Republican conceptions of public policy emerged during John Marshall's tenure on the Supreme Court. Appointed chief justice by President John Adams in January 1801, Marshall was a committed Federalist who dominated the Court until 1822 and then upheld nationalist principles until his death in 1835. Marshall's success stemmed not from a mastery of legal principles and doctrines but from the power of his logic and the force of his personality. By winning the support of Joseph Story and other nationalist-minded Republican judges, Marshall shaped the evolution of the Constitution. Three principles formed the basis of his jurisprudence: a commitment to judicial authority, the supremacy of national over state legislation, and a traditional, static view of property rights.

John Marshall, by Chester Harding, c. 1830

Even at age seventy-five, John Marshall (1755–1835) had a commanding personal presence. Upon becoming chief justice of the U.S. Supreme Court in 1801, Marshall elevated the Court from a minor department of the national government to a major institution in American legal and political life. His decisions dealing with judicial review, contract rights, the regulation of commerce, and national banking permanently shaped the character of American constitutional law. Boston Athenaeum.

After Marshall proclaimed the power of judicial review in *Marbury v. Madison,* the doctrine evolved slowly. Before 1850 state courts voided relatively few laws and not until the *Dred Scott* decision in 1857 would the Supreme Court void another law passed by Congress (see Chapter 13).

However, the Marshall Court frequently overturned state laws that infringed on the national Constitution. Its jurisprudence on federal-state relations was most eloquently expressed in *McCulloch v. Maryland* (1819). When Congress created the Second Bank of the United States in 1816, it allowed the bank to set up branches in the various states. To preserve the competitive position of its state-chartered banks, the Maryland legislature imposed an annual tax of $15,000 on notes issued by the Baltimore branch office of the Second Bank. In response, the Second Bank contested the constitutionality of the Maryland law and claimed that it infringed on the powers of the national government. To make their case, lawyers for the state of Maryland invoked Jefferson's argument that Congress lacked the constitutional authority to charter a national bank. Even if such a bank could be created, the lawyers argued, Maryland had a right to tax its activities within the state.

Marshall and the nationalist-minded Republicans on the Court firmly rejected both arguments. The Second Bank was constitutional, said the chief justice, because it was "necessary and proper," given the national government's responsibility to control currency and credit. Like Alexander Hamilton, Marshall adopted a loose construction of the Constitution. If the goal of a law is "legitimate [and] . . . within the scope of the Constitution," he wrote, then "all means which are appropriate" to secure that goal are also constitutional, even if they are not explicitly mentioned. As for Maryland's right to tax the national bank, the chief justice stated that "the power to tax involves the power to destroy" and suggested that Maryland's bank tax would render the national government "dependent on the states"—an outcome that "was not intended by the American people" who ratified the Constitution.

The Marshall Court asserted the dominance of national statutes over state legislation again in *Gibbons v. Ogden* (1824). This decision struck down a monopoly that the New York legislature had granted to Aaron Ogden for steamboat passenger service across the Hudson River to New Jersey. Asserting that the Constitution gave the federal government the authority to regulate interstate commerce, the chief justice sided with Thomas Gibbons, who held a federal license to transport people and goods between the two states.

Marshall also used the Constitution to uphold his view of property rights. During the 1790s Thomas Jefferson and other Republicans had celebrated the primacy of statute (or "positive") law enacted by "the will of the supreme power, which is the will of THE PEOPLE." In response, Federalist judges and politicians warned that popular sovereignty would lead to "tyranny of the majority" if state legislatures enacted statutes that infringed on the property rights of wealthy citizens. To prevent this outcome, Federalist lawyers asserted that judges had the power to void laws that violated traditional common-law principles or were contrary to "natural law" or "natural rights" (see Chapter 4).

Marshall shared the goal of protecting individuals' property from the acts of popularly-elected legislatures and invoked the contract clause of the Constitution to do it. The contract clause (in Article 1, Section 10, on p. D-13) prohibits the states from passing any law "impairing the obligation of contracts." The delegates at the Philadelphia convention included the clause to overturn state legislation that prevented creditors from seizing the lands and goods of debtors. In *Fletcher v. Peck* (1810), Marshall expanded the clause to defend other property rights by broadly defining *contract* to include the grants and charters made by the state governments. The case involved a large grant of land made by the Georgia legislature to the Yazoo Land Company. When a new legislature canceled the grant, alleging fraud and bribery, speculators who had already purchased Yazoo lands appealed to the Supreme Court to uphold their titles. Marshall ruled that the legislative grant was a contract that could not subsequently be abridged. This far-reaching decision safeguarded "vested" property rights and, by protecting out-of-state investors, promoted the development of a national capitalist economy.

The Court extended its defense of vested property rights even further in *Dartmouth College v. Woodward* (1819). Dartmouth College was a private institution in New Hampshire established by a charter granted by King George III. In 1816 the Republican-dominated legislature enacted a statute that converted the college into a public university. The Dartmouth trustees opposed this legislation and engaged Daniel Webster to plead their case. A renowned constitutional lawyer as well as a leading Federalist politician, Webster cited the Court's decision in *Fletcher v. Peck* and argued that the royal charter constituted a contract that could not be altered by the New Hampshire legislature. The Supreme Court agreed and upheld the rights of the college. Marshall's triumph seemed complete. Important Federalist principles, such as judicial review and corporate property rights, had been permanently incorporated into the American legal system (see Voices from Abroad, "Law and Lawyers in the United States," p. 254).

Even as Marshall announced the *Dartmouth* and *McCulloch* decisions in 1819, the political fortunes of his Federalist Party were in severe decline. Nationalist-minded Republicans had won the allegiance of many Federalist voters in the East, while the pro-farmer policies of Jeffersonian Republicans commanded the support of most western settlers and southern planters. "No Federal character can run with success," Gouverneur Morris of New York lamented, and the election results of 1818 bore out his pessimism. Following the election Republicans outnumbered Federalists 37 to 7 in the Senate and 156 to 27 in the House of Representatives. Westward expansion and the transformation in American government begun by Jefferson's Revolution of 1800 had brought the demise of the Federalists and the end of the First Party System.

VOICES FROM ABROAD

Law and Lawyers in the United States

ALEXIS DE TOCQUEVILLE

A *French aristocrat and lawyer, Alexis de Tocqueville came to the United States to study its innovative prison system. Instead he wrote* Democracy in America *(1835), a comprehensive and astute analysis of the dynamic society and political system of the United States. Here Tocqueville argues that the raw vigor of American democracy was restrained by the ingrained conservatism of men of the law, who dominated the political system.*

The political activity that pervades the United States must be seen in order to be understood. No sooner do you set foot upon American ground than you are stunned by a kind of tumult . . . everything is in motion around you; here the people of one quarter of a town are met to decide upon the building of a church; there the election of a representative is going on. . . .

The political agitation of American legislative bodies, which is the only one that attracts the attention of foreigners, is a mere episode, or a sort of continuation, of that universal movement which originates in the lowest classes of the people and extends successively to all the ranks of society. . . .

In visiting the Americans and studying their laws, we perceive that the authority they have entrusted to the members of the legal profession, and the influence that these individuals exercise in the government, are the most powerful existing security against the excesses of democracy. . . . Men who have made a special study of the laws derive from [that] occupation certain habits of order, a taste for formalities, and a kind of instinctive regard for the regular connection of ideas, which naturally render them very hostile to the revolutionary spirit and the unreflecting passions of the multitude. . . .

[Moreover,] the government of democracy is favorable to the political power of lawyers; for when the wealthy, the noble, and the prince are excluded from the government, the lawyers take possession of it, in their own right, as it were, since they are the only men of information and sagacity, beyond the sphere of the people, who can be the object of popular choice. . . .

Lawyers belong to the people by birth and interest, and to the aristocracy by habit and taste; they may be looked upon as the connecting link between the two great classes of society. . . . When the American people are intoxicated by passion or carried away by the impetuosity of their ideas, they are checked and stopped by the almost invisible influence of their legal counselors.

As most public men are legal practitioners, they introduce the customs and technicalities of their profession into the management of public affairs. The jury extends this habit to all classes. The language of the law thus becomes, in some measure, a vulgar tongue . . . so that at last the whole people contract the habits and the tastes of the judicial magistrate.

The decline of the Federalists and of party politics prompted contemporary observers to dub James Monroe's two terms as president (1817–1825) the "Era of Good Feeling." Actually, political harmony was more apparent than real because the Republican Party was now divided into a National faction and a Jeffersonian (or state-oriented) faction. The two groups fought bitterly over the issue of federal support for internal improvement projects such as roads and canals. As the aging Jefferson himself complained about the National Republicans, "You see so many of these new republicans maintaining in Congress the rankest doctrines of the old federalists." This division in the ranks of the Republican Party would soon produce a Second Party System—in which national-minded Whigs faced off against state-focused Democrats (see Chapter 11). One cycle of American politics and economic debate had ended and another was about to begin.

TIMELINE

Year	Event	Year	Event
1783	Treaty of Paris gives Americans access to the trans-Appalachian West	1801–1807	Treasury Secretary Albert Gallatin reduces national debt
1787	Northwest Ordinance		Seizures of American ships by France and Britain
1790s	State mercantilism: states grant corporation charters	1803	Louisiana Purchase; Lewis and Clark expedition
	Entrepreneurs build turnpikes and short canals		Marshall asserts judicial review in *Marbury v. Madison*
	Merchants create a rural outwork system	1807	Embargo Act cripples American shipping
1790–1791	Little Turtle defeats American armies in Northwest Territory		Congress bans importation of slaves
		1809	Tecumseh and Tenskwatawa mobilize Indians
1791	First Bank of the United States founded; charter expires in 1811	1810	*Fletcher v. Peck* extends contract clause
1792	Kentucky joins Union; Tennessee follows (1796)	1810s	Expansion of slavery into Old Southwest
1794	Battle of Fallen Timbers	1811	Battle of Tippecanoe
1795	Treaty of Greenville recognizes Indian land rights	1812–1815	War of 1812
	Massachusetts Mill Dam Act promotes textile industry	1817–1825	Era of Good Feeling during Monroe's presidency
	Pinckney's Treaty with Spain allows U.S. use of Mississippi River	1819	Adams-Onís Treaty annexes Florida and defines Texas boundary
1801	Spain secretly restores Louisiana to France		*McCulloch v. Maryland* enhances power of national government
	John Marshall becomes chief justice of the Supreme Court		*Dartmouth College v. Woodward* protects property rights

For Further Exploration

Gregory Evans Dowd, *A Spirited Resistance: The North American Indian Struggle for Unity, 1745–1815* (1992), presents a fine survey of the Indian peoples, while Gregory Nobles, *American Frontiers: Cultural Encounters and Continental Conquest* (1997), traces the course of American expansion to the west. Two fine studies of cultural interaction are Theda Perdue, *Cherokee Women: Gender and Culture Change, 1700–1835* (1998) and William G. McLoughlin, *Cherokee Renascence in the New Republic* (1986).

Ralph Louis Ketcham's *Presidents above Party: The First American Presidency, 1789–1829* (1984) portrays the evolving political ideology of the early republic, while Gore Vidal's *Burr: A Novel* (1973) offers an entertaining narrative of the life and times of Aaron Burr. Donald R. Hickey, *The War of 1812: A Forgotten Conflict* (1989), places the conflict in an economic and diplomatic context. R. Kent Newmyer, *The Supreme Court under Marshall and Taney* (1968), concisely analyzes early constitutional development, and Jack Larkin, *The Reshaping of Everyday Life, 1790–1840* (1997), demonstrates the impact of economic change on material culture.

Lewis and Clark: The Journey of the Corps of Discovery (PBS video, 4 hours) tells the story of the initial exploration by white Americans of the Louisiana Purchase; the companion Web site, at <http://www.pbs.org/lewisandclark/>, contains a rich body of material on the explorers and the Indian peoples of the region. The Chickasaw Historical Research Page, at <http://home.flash.net/~kma/>, contains letters written by or about Chickasaw Indians between 1792 and 1849, the texts of more than thirty treaties, and other documents.

The Duel (PBS video, 1 hour) reenacts the confrontation between Alexander Hamilton and Aaron Burr, while A Century of Lawmaking for a New Nation, at <http://memory.loc.gov/ammem/amlaw/lawhome.html>, part of the Library of Congress's American Memory project, contains congressional documents and debates, including discussions of the Northwest Ordinance, the ban on slave imports, the embargo of 1807, and the decision for war in 1812. The site also contains information and maps of Indian land cessions from 1784 to 1894. For access to American Journeys: Eyewitness Accounts of Early American Exploration and Settlement, consult the documents and images compiled by the Wisconsin Historical Society at <http://www.americanjourneys.org/>.

For definitions of key terms boldfaced in this chapter, see the glossary at the end of the book.

To assess your mastery of the material covered in this chapter, see the Online Study Guide at **bedfordstmartins.com/henrettaconcise**.

For map resources and primary documents, see **bedfordstmartins.com/henrettaconcise**.

Chapter 9

THE QUEST FOR A REPUBLICAN SOCIETY
1790–1820

[Societies and] governments are republican only in proportion as they embody the will of their people.

THOMAS JEFFERSON, 1813

By the 1820s a sense of optimism pervaded white American society. "The temperate zone of North America already exhibits many signs that it is the promised land of civil liberty, and of institutions designed to liberate and exalt the human race," a Kentucky judge declared in a Fourth of July speech. Indeed, many Americans took it as a sign of divine favor that both John Adams and Thomas Jefferson died on July 4, 1826, the fiftieth anniversary of their experiment in republican government. Americans had good reason to feel fortunate. Despite periods of political conflict and economic turmoil, white Americans still lived in a self-governing society that was free from both arbitrary taxes and an oppressive church. Moreover, many citizens now considered themselves "republicans" not simply in their constitutional system of representative government but also in their political behavior, social outlook, and cultural habits.

Yet Americans defined republicanism in different ways. Many citizens in the North subscribed to "democratic republicanism." This ideology encouraged individuals to aspire to greater equality in politics and within the family, though they often fell short of this goal. In the South many whites shared these democratic aspirations, but their society was so sharply divided along the lines of class and race that such ideals were impossible to sustain. Consequently, southern leaders gradually devised an aristocratic-republican ideology that better described their hierarchical and deferential society. Yet a third vision of American republicanism appeared in the wake of the Second Great Awakening, the massive religious revival that swept through the nation during the first half of the nineteenth century. For the many Americans—white and black, southern and northern—who embraced this religious vision, the United States was both a great experiment in republican government and the seedbed of a new Christian civilization that would redeem the world.

Democratic Republicanism

After independence, leading Americans advocated a political system based on the principle of "ordered liberty," which in practice meant rule by the traditional elite. White men of modest means soon repudiated this elitist outlook and embraced a democratic republican outlook that celebrated political equality and social mobility. Many citizens also redefined the nature of the family and of education by seeking more egalitarian marriages and more affectionate ways of rearing and educating their children.

Social and Political Equality for White Men

Between 1780 and 1820 hundreds of well-educated Europeans visited the United States and declared, almost unanimously, that the American republic embodied a social order that was genuinely different and more just than that of their homelands. In his famous *Letters from an American Farmer* (1782), the French-born essayist St. Jean de Crèvecoeur wrote that European society was composed "of great lords who possess everything, and of a herd of people who have nothing." America, by contrast, had "no aristocratical families, no courts, no kings, no bishops."

The absence of a hereditary aristocracy encouraged Americans to condemn inherited social privilege and to extol the republican legal equality of all free men. "The law is the same for everyone both as it protects and as it punishes," noted one European traveler. Yet Americans willingly accepted social divisions based on personal achievement. As individuals used their "talents, integrity, and virtue" to amass wealth, they gained a higher social standing, a result that astounded some Europeans. "In Europe to say of someone that he rose from nothing is a disgrace and a reproach," remarked an aristocratic Polish visitor. "It is the opposite here. To be the architect of your own fortune is honorable. It is the highest recommendation."

Some Americans from long-distinguished families questioned the morality of a social order based on mobility and financial success. "The aristocracy of Kingston [New York] is more one of money than any village I have ever seen," complained Nathaniel Booth, whose family had once ruled Kingston but had lost its prominence. "Man is estimated by dollars," he lamented; "what he is worth determines his character and his position at once." For most white men such a system meant the opportunity to better themselves.

By the 1810s republicanism also meant voting rights for all free white men. As early as 1776 the state constitutions of Pennsylvania and Vermont allowed all taxpayers to vote. This provision opened up political participation to propertyless young men who paid a "poll" (or head) tax and artisans who did not own land but paid an occupational tax. By 1810 Maryland and South Carolina had extended the vote to all adult white men, and the new states of Indiana (1816), Illinois (1818),

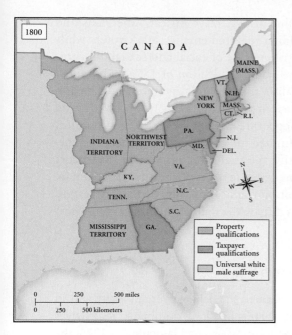

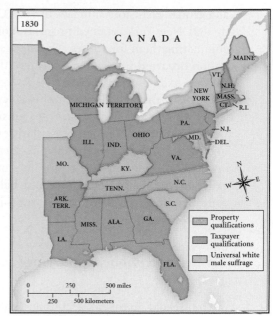

MAP 9.1 The Expansion of Voting Rights for White Men, 1800–1830

Between 1800 and 1830 the United States moved steadily toward political democracy for white men. Many existing states revised their constitutions, replacing property ownership with taxpaying or militia service as a qualification for voting. Some new states in the West extended suffrage to all adult white men. As parties sought votes from a broader electorate, the tone of politics became more open and competitive—swayed by the interests and values of ordinary people.

and Alabama (1819) provided for a broad male franchise in their constitutions. Within another decade fifteen states allowed all white male taxpayers to vote, and another seven instituted universal white manhood suffrage. Only three states retained property qualifications for voting (Map 9.1).

The expansion of suffrage changed the tone of politics. Most conservative politicians accepted popular rule but insisted that voters should elect men of high social status. As Samuel Stone put it, the Federalist ideal was "a speaking aristocracy in the face of a silent democracy." However, Americans increasingly refused to vote for politicians who flaunted their high social status by wearing "top boots, breeches, and shoe buckles," their hair in "powder and queues." Instead, voters elected men who dressed simply and endorsed democracy, even if those leaders favored policies that benefited those with substantial wealth.

As legislators eliminated property qualifications for voting by white men, they erected barriers for women and black men. During the colonial period, few white women or free blacks voted; regardless of their wealth, custom and prejudice ruled out their participation in public affairs. Now state officials wrote customary racial and gender exclusions into law. In 1802 Ohio disfranchised African Americans, and in 1821 New York retained property-holding requirements for black voters while eliminating them for whites. The most striking case of racial and sexual discrimination occurred in New Jersey, where the state constitution of 1776 had granted suffrage to all property holders. As Federalists and Republicans competed for votes after 1800, they challenged political custom by encouraging property-owning single women and widows to vote. Sensing a threat to the male-centered political world, in 1807 the New Jersey legislature limited full citizenship (and therefore voting rights) to white men only. To justify the exclusion of women, legislators invoked both biology and custom. As one letter to a newspaper put it, "Women, generally, are neither by nature, nor habit, nor education, nor by their necessary condition in society fitted to perform this duty with credit to themselves or advantage to the public."

Toward a Republican Marriage System

The controversy over gender in politics replicated the debate over authority within the household. European and American husbands had long dominated their wives and controlled the family's property. But as John Adams had lamented in 1776, the revolutionary doctrine of political equality had "spread where it was not intended" and encouraged some white women to speak out on public matters and to demand control of their finances. These women insisted that their subordinate social position was at odds with the republican ideology of equal natural rights. Patriarchy was not a "natural" rule but only a social contrivance, argued the Patriot author and historian Mercy Otis Warren; making men the heads of households was justified only "for the sake of order in families."

Economic and cultural changes also eroded customary paternal authority. Traditionally, landowning fathers had arranged their children's marriages to ensure the economic well-being of themselves and their wives during old age. As land holdings shrank in long-settled rural communities, yeomen fathers could no longer bequeath substantial farms and had less influence over their children's selection of spouses. Young men and women began to choose their own partners, influenced by the new cultural attitude of **sentimentalism**.

Sentimentalism originated in Europe as part of the Romantic movement of the late eighteenth century and spread quickly among all classes of American society. Sentimentalism celebrated the importance of "feeling"—that is, a physical, sensuous appreciation of God, nature, and other human beings. This new sensibility found many forms of expression. It dripped from the pages of German and English literary works, fell from the lips of actors in popular tear-jerking melodramas, and infused the emotional rhetoric of revivalist preachers.

As the passions of the heart overwhelmed the cool logic of the mind, a new marriage system appeared. Parents had always considered physical attraction and emotional compatibility as they arranged marriages for their children, but they were concerned primarily with the personal character and financial resources of a prospective son- or daughter-in-law. However, after 1800 magazines encouraged marriages "contracted from motives of affection, rather than of interest," and many young people sought a spouse who was, as Eliza Southgate of Maine put it, "calculated to promote my happiness."

As young people arranged their own marriages, fathers became paternalists who tried to protect the interests of their children. To guard against free-spending sons-in-law, wealthy fathers placed their daughters' inheritances in legal trusts— out of their husbands' control. As a Virginia planter wrote to his lawyer, "I rely on you to see the property settlement properly drawn before the marriage, for I by no means consent that Polly shall be left to the Vicissitudes of Life."

In theory, the new republican ideal of companionate marriage gave wives "true equality, both of rank and fortune," with their husbands, as one Boston man suggested. However, husbands continued to occupy a privileged position because of deeply ingrained cultural habits and because the legal system still gave them control of the family's property. The new marriage system also discouraged parents from becoming too involved in their children's married lives and made young wives more dependent on their husbands than their mothers had been. In addition, governments accepted no obligation to prevent domestic abuse; as a lawyer noted, women who would rather "starve than submit" to the orders of their husbands were left to their fate. The marriage contract "is so much more important in its consequences to females than to males," a young man at the Litchfield Law School in Connecticut astutely observed in 1820, "for besides leaving everything else to unite themselves to one man, they subject themselves to his authority. He is their all—their only relative—their only hope."

Young adults who chose partners unwisely were severely disappointed when their spouses failed as providers or faithful companions, and a few sought divorces. Before 1800 most petitioners for divorce charged their spouses with neglect, abandonment, or adultery—serious offenses against the moral order of society. After 1800 emotional grounds dominated divorce petitions. One woman complained that her husband had "ceased to cherish her," while a man grieved that his wife had "almost broke his heart." Reflecting these changed cultural values, some states expanded the legal grounds for divorce to include personal cruelty and drunkenness.

Republican Motherhood

In all societies, marriage has many purposes: it channels sexuality, facilitates the inheritance of property, and, by creating strong family and kinship ties, eases the rearing of children. Traditionally, most American women had focused their lives on family duties: working in the home or on the farm and bearing and nurturing children. However, by the 1790s the birthrate in the northern seaboard states was dropping dramatically. In the farm village of Sturbridge, Massachusetts, women who had married before 1750 gave birth on average to eight or nine children, whereas women who married around 1810 had only about six. In the growing seaport cities, native-born white women bore an average of only four children.

The United States was one of the first countries in the world to experience this sharp decline in the birthrate—what historians have termed the "demographic transition." There were several causes. Beginning in the 1790s thousands of young men migrated to the trans-Appalachian West; their departure left some women without partners for life and delayed marriage for many more. Women who married later in life had fewer children. In addition, thousands of white American couples in the middling classes of society deliberately limited the size of their families. Fathers favored smaller families so that they could provide each of their children with an adequate inheritance; mothers, affected by new ideas of individualism and self-achievement, were no longer willing to spend all of their active years bearing and rearing children. After having four or five children, such couples used birth control or abstained from sexual intercourse. Women's lives changed as well because of new currents in Christian social thought. Traditionally, most religious writers had viewed women as morally inferior to men—as sexual temptresses or witches—but by 1800, Protestant ministers were blaming men for sexual and social misconduct. This shift reflected both the numerical dominance of women in many churches (as men devoted their energies to business affairs) and new intellectual currents. Christian moralists now claimed that modesty and purity were inherent in women's nature and made them uniquely qualified to educate the spirit.

Reflecting this sentiment, political leaders called on women to become dedicated "republican wives" and "republican mothers" who would correctly shape the characters of American men. In his *Thoughts on Female Education* (1787), the Philadelphia physician Benjamin Rush argued that a young woman should receive intellectual training so that she would be "an agreeable companion for a sensible man" and ensure "his perseverance in the paths of rectitude." Rush also called for loyal "republican mothers" who would instruct "their sons in the principles of liberty and government."

Christian ministers readily embraced the idea of **republican motherhood**. "Preserving virtue and instructing the young are not the fancied, but the real 'Rights of Women,'" the Reverend Thomas Bernard told the Female Charitable Society of Salem, Massachusetts. He urged his audience to dismiss the public roles for women, such as voting and officeholding, advocated by English activist Mary Wollstonecraft and others. Instead, women should be content to care for their children, a responsibility that gave them "an extensive power over the fortunes of man in every generation." Although Bernard wanted women to remain in their traditional domestic sphere, he campaigned to enhance its value. A few ministers envisioned a public role for women based on their domestic virtues. As South Carolina minister Thomas Grimké asserted, "Give me a host of educated pious mothers and sisters and I will revolutionize a country, in moral and religious taste."

Republican Motherhood

Art often reveals the cultural values of the time. In this 1795 painting, the artist James Peale, brother of the famous portraitist Charles Willson Peale, depicts himself with his wife and children. The mother stands in the foreground, offering advice to her eldest daughter, while her husband stands to the rear, pointing to the other children. The father, previously the center of attention in family portraits during the colonial era (see p. 101), now gives pride of place to his wife and offspring. Pennsylvania Academy of the Fine Arts, Philadelphia.

Raising and Educating Republican Children

Republican social thought altered assumptions about inheritance and childrearing. Under English common law, property owned by a father who died without a will passed to his eldest son, a practice known as primogeniture. However, legislators in most American states enacted statutes that required such estates to be divided equally among all the offspring. Most American parents supported these statutes because they had already begun to treat their children as equals.

Foreign visitors believed that republican ideology encouraged American parents to relax parental discipline and give their children greater freedom. Because of the "general ideas of Liberty and Equality engraved on their hearts," suggested a Polish aristocrat who traveled around the United States in 1800, American children had "scant respect" for their parents. Several decades later a British traveler stood dumbfounded as an American father excused his son's "resolute disobedience" with a smile and the remark, "a sturdy republican, sir." The traveler guessed that American parents encouraged such independence to assist young people to "go their own way" in the world.

However, these relatively permissive childrearing habits were not universal. Foreign visitors interacted primarily with well-to-do Americans, who were often members of Episcopal or Presbyterian churches. These parents often followed the teachings of rationalist-minded religious writers influenced by John Locke and other Enlightenment thinkers. For such authors, children were "rational creatures" who should be encouraged to act correctly by means of praise, advice, and reasoned restraint. The parents' role was to develop the children's consciences and stress self-discipline so that young people would learn to control their own behavior and to think and act responsibly. This rationalist mode of childrearing became the preference among families in the rapidly expanding middle class.

By contrast, many yeomen and tenant farmers influenced by the Second Great Awakening (see p. 277) raised their children by following the precepts of authoritarian-minded ministers and authors. Many evangelical Baptists and Methodists believed that infants were "full of the stains and pollution of sin" and needed strict rules and harsh discipline. Fear was a "useful and necessary principle in family government," the minister John Abbott advised parents; a child "should submit to your authority, not to your arguments or persuasions." Abbott told parents to instill humility in children and to teach them to subordinate their personal desires to God's will.

The values transmitted within families were crucial because until the 1820s most education still took place within the household. In New England, locally funded public schools provided most boys and some girls with basic instruction in reading and writing. Among whites in other regions, about a quarter of the boys and perhaps 10 percent of the girls attended privately funded schools or had personal tutors. Even in New England only a small fraction of the men and almost no women went on to grammar (high) school. Only 1 percent of men graduated from college.

In the 1790s Bostonian Caleb Bingham, an influential textbook author, called for "an equal distribution of knowledge to make us emphatically a 'republic of letters.'" Thomas Jefferson and Benjamin Rush separately proposed ambitious schemes for a comprehensive system of primary and secondary schooling, followed by college attendance for young men. They also advocated the establishment of a university in which distinguished scholars would lecture on law, medicine, theology, and political economy.

To ordinary citizens such educational proposals smacked of elitism. Farmers, artisans, and laborers looked to schools for basic instruction in the "three Rs": reading, 'riting, and 'rithmetic. They supported public funding only for elementary education because their teenage children had to work and could not attend secondary schools or colleges. "Let anybody show what advantage the poor man receives from colleges," an anonymous "Old Soldier" wrote to the Maryland *Gazette*. "Why should they support them, unless it is to serve those who are in affluent circumstances, whose children can be spared from labor, and receive the benefits?"

Although many state constitutions encouraged legislatures to support education, few state governments acted until the 1820s. Then a new generation of reformers, led primarily by merchants and manufacturers, successfully campaigned to raise standards by certifying qualified teachers and appointing state superintendents of education. To encourage self-discipline and individual enterprise in the students, the reformers chose textbooks, such as *The Life of George Washington* by "Parson" Mason Weems, that praised honesty and hard work and condemned gambling, drinking, and laziness. Believing that patriotic instruction would foster shared cultural ideals, they also required the study of American history. As a New Hampshire schoolboy named Thomas Low recalled, "We were taught every day and in every way that ours was the freest, the happiest, and soon to be the greatest and most powerful country of the world."

The author Noah Webster championed the goal of American intellectual greatness. Asserting that "America must be as independent in *literature* as she is in politics," he called on his fellow citizens to detach themselves "from the dependence on foreign opinions and manners, which is fatal to the efforts of genius in this country." Webster's *Dissertation on the English Language* (1789) introduced American spelling (such as *labor* for the British *labour*) and defined words according to American usage. His "blue-backed speller," first published in 1783, sold 60 million copies over the next half century and helped give Americans of all backgrounds a common vocabulary and grammar. "None of us was 'lowed to see a book," an enslaved African American recalled, "but we gits hold of that Webster's old blue-back speller and we . . . studies [it]."

Despite Webster's efforts, a republican American literary culture was slow to develop. Ironically, the most accomplished and successful writer in the new republic was Washington Irving, an elitist-minded Federalist. His essays and histories, including *Salmagundi* (1807) and *Diedrich Knickerbocker's History of New York* (1809), had substantial American sales and won fame abroad. Impatient with the slow pace of American literary development, Irving lived in Europe for seventeen years, drawn to its aristocratic manners and intense intellectual life.

Apart from Irving, no American author was well known in Europe or, indeed, in the United States. "Literature is not yet a distinct profession with us," Thomas Jefferson told an English friend. "Now and then a strong mind arises, and at its intervals from business emits a flash of light. But the first object of young societies is bread and covering." Not until the 1830s and 1840s would American-born authors achieve a professional identity and, in the works of Ralph Waldo Emerson and novelists of the American Renaissance, make a significant contribution to the great literature of Western society (see Chapter 12).

Aristocratic Republicanism and Slavery

Both in theory and in practice, republicanism in the South differed significantly from that in the North. Republican authors had long identified political tyranny as a major threat to liberty, and southern planters, who feared governmental interference with their property in slaves, were especially aware of this danger. To prevent despotic rule by demagogues or radical-minded legislatures, they wanted authority to rest in the hands of incorruptible men of "virtue." Indeed, many affluent and well-educated planters saw themselves as the practical embodiment of this ideal. Some consciously cast themselves as republican aristocrats. "The planters here are essentially what the nobility are in other countries," declared James Henry Hammond of South Carolina. "They stand at the head of society & politics . . . [and form] an aristocracy of talents, of virtue, of generosity and courage."

The North and South Grow Apart

European visitors to the new American republic agreed that the South formed a distinct society but were much less positive than Hammond about its character. New England was home to religious "fanaticism," according to a British observer, but "the lower orders of citizens" there had "a better education, are more intelligent, and better informed" than those he met in the South. "The state of poverty in which a great number of white people live in Virginia" surprised the Marquis de Chastellux, and other visitors to the South commented on the rude manners, heavy drinking, and lack of a strong work ethic they found there. White tenant farmers and small freeholders seemed only to have a "passion for gaming at the billiard table, a cock-fight or cards," and many planters squandered their wealth in extravagant living while their slaves suffered bitter poverty.

Some southerners admitted that slavery corrupted their society and contributed to the ignorance and poverty of the mass of the white population. Thus, a South Carolina merchant linked slavery to a weak work ethic: "Where there are Negroes a White Man despises to work, saying what, will you have me a Slave and work like a Negroe?" For their part, wealthy planters wanted a compliant labor force that was content with the drudgery of agricultural work. Consequently, they trained most of their slaves as field hands (allowing only a few to learn the arts of the blacksmith, carpenter, or bricklayer), and did little to provide ordinary whites with elementary instruction in reading or arithmetic. In 1800 the political leaders of Essex County, Virginia, spent about twenty-five cents per person for local government, including schooling, while their counterparts in Acton, Massachusetts, expended about one dollar per person. This difference in support for education mattered: by the 1820s nearly all native-born men and women in New England could read and write, while over one-third of white southerners lacked these basic intellectual skills.

Slavery quickly found its way into national politics. At the Philadelphia convention in 1787 the delegates had accepted the existence of slavery and, to secure

The Internal Slave Trade

Mounted whites escort a convoy of slaves from Virginia to Tennessee in Lewis Miller's *Slave Trader, Sold to Tennessee* (1853). For white planters, the trade was a lucrative one because it pumped money into the declining Chesapeake economy and provided fresh workers for the expanding plantations of the cotton belt. For blacks it was a traumatic journey, a new Middle Passage, that broke up families and long-settled slave communities. Abby Aldrich Rockefeller Folk Art Center.

ratification of the constitution in the South, inserted clauses to deal with fugitive slaves and slave imports (see Chapter 7). Southerners immediately sought additional protection for slavery and won approval in the second session of the new national legislature of James Madison's resolution that "Congress have no authority to interfere in the emancipation of slaves, or in the treatment of them within any of the States."

Nonetheless, slavery remained a contested issue. Slave revolts in Haiti during the 1790s brought a flood of white refugees to the United States and prompted congressional debates about diplomatic relations with the island's new black government. Simultaneously, northern political leaders assailed the British impressment of American sailors as just "as oppressive and tyrannical as the slave trade" and demanded the end of both. When Congress prohibited legal American participation in the Atlantic slave trade in 1808, northern representatives called for the regulation of the interstate trade in slaves and the emancipation of illegally imported slaves. In response, southern leaders mounted a defense of their labor system. "A large majority of people in the Southern states do not consider slavery as even an evil," declared one congressman. And the South's political clout—especially its domination of the presidency and the Senate—ensured that the national government would continue to protect slavery.

Thus, American diplomats vigorously—and successfully—demanded compensation for slaves freed by the British during the War of 1812, and Congress enacted legislation upholding the property rights of slave owners in the District of Columbia.

Political conflict over slavery increased as the northern states gradually emancipated their African American laborers and the South expanded its slave-based agricultural economy into the lower Mississippi Valley. Antislavery advocates had hoped that African bondage would "die a natural death" following the demise of the Atlantic slave trade and the decline of the tobacco economy. But their hopes faded as the cotton boom increased the demand for slaves, and Louisiana (1812), Mississippi (1817), and Alabama (1819) joined the Union with state constitutions permitting slavery.

In 1817 the founders of the American Colonization Society, who included President James Monroe and Speaker of the House Henry Clay, acknowledged the baneful effects of the southern labor system. As Clay explained, racial bondage had placed his state of Kentucky "in the rear of our neighbors . . . in the state of agriculture, the progress of manufactures, the advance of improvement, and the general prosperity of society." Slavery had to end and, the colonization society argued, the freed slaves had to be sent back to Africa. Emancipation without removal, Clay predicted, "would be followed by instantaneous collisions between the two races, which would break out into a civil war that would end in the extermination or subjugation of the one race or the other." To prevent racial conflict, the society would encourage southern planters to emancipate their slaves—who now numbered nearly 1.5 million people—and would arrange for their resettlement in Africa.

The American Colonization Society was a dismal failure. Few planters freed their slaves and, despite appeals to wealthy individuals, churches, and state governments, the society was able to purchase freedom for only a few hundred slaves. Equally important, most free blacks rejected colonization. They agreed with Bishop Richard Allen of the African Methodist Episcopal Church that "this land which we have watered with our tears and our blood is now our mother country." Three thousand African Americans met in Philadelphia's Bethel Church to condemn colonization and to claim citizenship; their goal was to advance in American society using "those opportunities . . . which the Constitution and the laws allow to all." Lacking significant support from either blacks or whites, the society transported only 6,000 African Americans to Liberia, a colony it established on the west coast of Africa.

Toward a New Southern Social Order

Colonization failed in part because the South was changing in ways that encouraged the expansion of slavery. In 1780 the western boundary of the plantation system ran through the middle of Georgia; by 1820 the plantation frontier stretched through the middle of Louisiana. That advance of six hundred miles doubled the geographic area cultivated by slave labor. Moreover, many of the workers on the newly established cotton and sugar plantations were African-born slaves. Between 1780 and 1808 nearly 250,000 Africans were added to the southern workforce—a total that equaled the number of slaves imported into Britain's mainland settlements during the entire colonial period.

Despite this influx of new African workers, the demand for labor in the Southwest far exceeded the supply. "The Negro business is a great object with us," one merchant declared, because "the Planter will . . . sacrifice every thing to attain Negroes." To satisfy this demand, merchants and planters looked to the Chesapeake region, which now had a surplus of enslaved laborers. Between 1790 and 1820 whites relocated to the Southwest more than 150,000 African Americans from Maryland, Virginia, and parts of North and South Carolina. Some of these forced migrants—perhaps as many as one-half—moved with relatives and friends when their owners sold their old holdings and began new plantations on the fertile plains of Alabama, Mississippi, and Louisiana (Map 9.2).

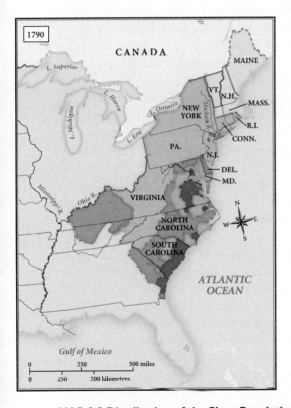
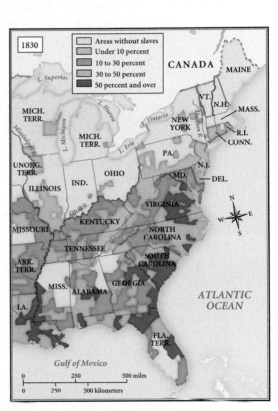

MAP 9.2 Distribution of the Slave Population in 1790 and 1830

The cotton boom prompted a great forced migration of enslaved African Americans from their eighteenth-century communities to the Old Southwest. In 1790, most slaves lived and worked on the tobacco plantations of the Chesapeake and in the rice and indigo areas of South Carolina. By 1830, tens of thousands of slaves were laboring on the cotton and sugar lands of the lower Mississippi Valley and on cotton plantations in Georgia and Florida.

FOR MORE HELP ANALYZING THIS MAP, see the Online Study Guide at **bedfordstmartins.com/henrettaconcise**.

However, many planters remained on their estates in Maryland, Virginia, the Carolinas, and Georgia and reaped impressive profits by selling their "surplus" workers to slave traders. For African American families, separation became a common experience. "I am Sold to a man by the name of Peterson a trader," lamented a Georgia slave. "My Dear wife for you and my Children my pen cannot Express the griffe I feel to be parted from you all." Some of these slaves lost touch with their families forever. "Dey sole [sold] my sister Kate," Anna Harris remembered decades later, ". . . and I ain't seed or heard of her since." The profits to be gained by planting cotton in the Southwest and selling enslaved laborers from the Southeast doomed both the colonization movement and many long-established African American communities.

Westward movement also changed the character of white society. Following the tobacco and rice revolutions around 1700 (see Chapter 3), a wealthy planter elite exercised considerable political power. However, in tobacco-growing areas, slave owning became broadly diffused. During the 1770s, about 60 percent of the white families in the Chesapeake region owned at least one African American worker and benefited directly from slavery. By 1820, however, a much smaller proportion of white southern families owned slaves, and the percentage continued to fall. In Alabama in 1830, only 30 percent of the voters owned slaves and most slaves were the property of wealthy men. Like the rice-growing plantations in South Carolina and Georgia, the cotton plantations in the lower Mississippi Valley were large-scale operations that used dozens of enslaved black workers. Their wealthy and influential owners dominated society and gave an aristocratic-republican definition to politics. In Alabama, a majority of the state's elected officials owned more than 20 African Americans, and one-quarter of the legislators held more than 50. "Inequality is the fundamental law of the universe," proclaimed one southern politician. "Slavery does indeed create an aristocracy."

As cotton production was consolidated in fewer and fewer hands, some white yeomen sold their land and became the tenants of wealthy planter-landlords. Other white families in plantation regions scraped by on small farms, growing foodstuffs for sustenance and a few bales of cotton for cash. Influenced by the patriarchal ideology of the planter class, the husbands in these households asserted traditional male authority over their wives and children and ruled their small worlds with a firm hand. Other yeomen families retreated into the backcountry near the Appalachian Mountains, where they struggled to maintain their economic independence and to control local county governments. Owning hilly farms of fifty to one hundred acres, these families grew some cotton but primarily raised corn and livestock, especially hogs. Their goal was modest: to preserve their holdings and secure enough new land to set up all of their children as small-scale farmers.

In the new southwestern economy, prosperity was limited primarily to the shrinking minority of the white population that owned plantations and slaves. The cotton revolution had undercut the democratic prospects of the Revolutionary era and powered the expansion of aristocratic-republican plantation society.

Slave Society and Culture

As wealthy planters solidified their rule over a class-divided society, African Americans created a distinct and increasingly homogeneous rural culture. A major cause of this homogeneity was the end of the transatlantic slave trade in 1808, which gradually created a slave population that was virtually all American born. Even in South Carolina—after 1776 a major point of entry for imported slaves—only 20 percent of the black inhabitants in 1820 had been born in Africa. The rapid movement of slavery into the Mississippi Valley also reduced cultural differences among slaves. Thus, the Gullah dialect spoken by migrants from the Carolina low country gradually died out on the cotton plantations of Alabama and Mississippi, replaced by the black English spoken by slaves from the Chesapeake.

Even as the black population became more homogeneous, African cultural influence remained important. At least one-third of the slaves who entered the United States between 1776 and 1809 were from the Congo region of west-central Africa, and they brought their culture with them. As the traveler Isaac Holmes reported in 1821, "In Louisiana, and the state of Mississippi, the slaves . . . dance for several hours during Sunday afternoon. The general movement is in what they call the Congo dance." Similar descriptions of blacks who "danced the Congo and sang a purely African song to the accompaniment of . . . a drum" appeared as late as 1890.

African Americans also continued to respect African incest taboos and shunned marriage between cousins. On the Good Hope plantation in South Carolina, nearly half of the slave children born between 1800 and 1857 were related by blood to one another, yet only one marriage had taken place between cousins. Because southern state legislatures and law courts prohibited legal marriages between slaves (so they could be sold without breaking a legal bond), African Americans devised their own rituals. Following African custom, many couples symbolized their married state by jumping over a broomstick together in a public ceremony. Christian slaves were often married by a white or black preacher, but these rites rarely ended with the customary phrase "until death do you part." Knowing that black marriages often ended through sale, one white minister blessed the couple "for so long as God keeps them together." To maintain their cultural identity, recently imported slaves often gave their children African names. Males born on Friday were often called Cuffee—the name of that day in several West African languages. Although most Chesapeake slaves chose names of British origin, they named sons after fathers, uncles, or grandfathers and daughters after grandmothers. Like incest rules and marriage rituals, this intergenerational sharing of names solidified kinship ties.

By forming stable families and strong communities, African Americans tried to create a sense of order in the harsh and arbitrary world of slavery. Some groups won substantial control over their lives. During the Revolutionary era, blacks in the rice-growing lowlands of South Carolina asserted the right to labor by the **task** rather than to work under constant supervision. Each day these task-workers had to complete a precisely defined job—for example, turn over a quarter acre of land, hoe half an acre, or pound seven mortars of rice. By working hard, many finished their tasks "by one or two o'clock in the afternoon," a Methodist preacher reported, and had "the rest of the day for themselves, which they spend in working their own private fields . . . planting rice, corn, potatoes, tobacco &c. for their own use and profit." These private efforts provided slaves with better clothes and food, but few African Americans enjoyed a comfortable standard of living (see American Voices, "A Child Learns the Meaning of Slavery," p. 273).

A few blacks, such as Gabriel and Martin Prosser in Virginia (1800), plotted mass uprisings and murders, and others, such as Denmark Vesey in South Carolina (1822), may have done so as well. But in most areas blacks numbered less than half the population, and everywhere they lacked the strong institutions—such as the communes of free peasants or serfs in Europe—needed to organize a successful rebellion. Moreover, whites were well armed, unified, and militant.

Escape was equally problematic. Blacks in the Lower South could seek freedom in Spanish Florida until 1819, when the United States annexed that territory. Even then, hundreds of blacks continued to flee to Florida, where they intermarried with the Seminole Indians. Elsewhere in the South small groups of escaped slaves eked out a meager existence in deserted marshy areas or in mountain valleys. Given these limited options, most slaves had no choice but to build the best possible lives for themselves on the plantations where they lived.

The Free Black Population

Between 1790 and 1820 the number of free blacks rose steadily from 8 percent of the African American population to about 13 percent, but few were truly free. One-third of all free blacks—some 50,000 in 1810—lived in the North, where they were treated as second-class citizens. In rural areas free blacks worked as farm laborers or tenant farmers; in towns and cities they toiled as domestic servants, laundresses, or day laborers. Only a small minority of free African Americans owned land. "You do not see one out of a hundred . . . that can make a comfortable living, own a cow, or a horse," a traveler in New Jersey noted. In addition, blacks were usually forbidden to vote, attend public schools, or sit next to whites in churches. Of the states admitted to the Union between 1790 and 1821, only Vermont and Maine extended the vote to free blacks, and they could testify against whites in court only in Massachusetts. The federal government did not allow free African Americans to work for the postal service, claim public lands, or hold a U.S. passport.

Nonetheless, a few African Americans were able to make full use of their talents, and some achieved great distinction. The mathematician and surveyor Benjamin Banneker published an almanac and helped lay out the new national capital in the District of Columbia. Joshua Johnston, a skilled painter, won praise for his portraiture, and merchant Robert Sheridan acquired a small fortune from his business enterprises. More impressive and enduring were the community institutions created by this first generation of free African Americans. Throughout the North they founded

AMERICAN VOICES

A Child Learns the Meaning of Slavery

JACOB STROYER

Jacob Stroyer, born into slavery in South Carolina, was emancipated and became a minis-ter in Salem, Massachusetts, and an abolitionist. In My Life in the South *(1885), he relates a dramatic incident that revealed his family's subordinate and powerless status as slaves.*

Father had a surname, Stroyer, which he could not use in public, as the surname Stroyer would be against the law; he was known only by the name of William Singleton, because that was his master's name.... Mother's name was Chloe. She belonged to Colonel M. R. Singleton too; she was a field hand, and was never sold, but her parents once were....

Father ... used to take care of horses and mules. I was around with him in the barnyard when but a small boy; of course that gave me an early relish for the occupation of hostler, and soon I made known my preference to Colonel Singleton, who was a sportsman and had fine horses.... Hence I was allowed to be numbered among those who took care of the fine horses, and learned to ride....

It was not long after I had entered my new work before they put me upon the back of a horse which threw me to the ground almost as soon as I reached his back.... When I got up there was a man standing near with a switch in hand, and he immediately began to beat me.... This was the first time I had been whipped by anyone except Mother and Father, so I cried out in a tone of voice as if I would say, this is the first and last whipping you will give me when Father gets hold of you.

When I got away from him I ran to Father with all my might, but soon my expectation was blasted, as Father very coolly said to me, "Go back to your work and be a good boy, for I cannot do anything for you." But that did not satisfy me, so I went on to Mother with my complaint and she came out to the man who whipped me. He was a groom, a white man whom master hired to train his horses ... [and] he took a whip and started for her, and she ran from him, talking all the time....

Then the idea first came to me that I, with my dear father and mother and the rest of my fellow Negroes, was doomed to cruel treatment through life and was defenseless....

One day, about two weeks after Boney Young and Mother had the conflict, he ... gave me a first-class flogging. That evening when I went home to Father and Mother, I said to them, "Mr. Young is whipping me too much now; I shall not stand it. I shall fight him." Father said to me, "You must not do that, because if you do he will say that your mother and I advised you to do it, and it will make it hard for your mother and me, as well as your-self. You must do as I told you my son.... I can do nothing more than pray to the Lord to hasten the time when these things shall be done away."

SOURCE: Linda R. Monk, ed., *Ordinary Americans: U.S. History through the Eyes of Everyday People* (Alexandria, VA: Close Up Publications, 1994), 71–72.

Captain Absalom Boston

Absalom Boston was born in 1785 on the island of Nantucket, the heart of the American whaling industry. A member of a community of free black whalers manumitted from slavery by their Quaker owners, Boston went to sea at age fifteen. By the age of thirty he had used his earnings to become the proprietor of a public inn. In 1822, Boston became the first black master with an all-black crew to undertake a whaling voyage from Nantucket. In later years he became an important leader of the island's black community, serving as a trustee of the African School. Nantucket Historical Association.

schools, mutual-benefit organizations, and fellowship groups, often with the title Free African Society. Discriminated against by white Protestants, they formed their own congregations and a new religious denomination—the African Methodist Episcopal (AME) Church, headed by Bishop Richard Allen. These institutions gave free African Americans a sense of cultural, if not political, autonomy.

Most free blacks who lived in slave states resided in the Upper South—some 110,000 in 1810. In Maryland a quarter of the black population was free; in Delaware free blacks outnumbered slaves by three to one. But their freedom was fragile. Free blacks accused of crimes were often denied a jury trial, and those charged with vagrancy were sometimes forced back into slavery. To prove their free status, African Americans had to carry manumission documents, which might not protect them from kidnapping and sale. Yet the shortage of skilled workers in southern cities created opportunities, and blacks became the backbone of the region's urban workforce. African American carpenters, blacksmiths, barbers, butchers, and shopkeepers played prominent roles in the economies of Baltimore, Richmond, Charleston, and New Orleans and in the social life of their black residents.

As a privileged group among African Americans, free blacks felt loyalty both to the welfare of their families, which often meant assimilating white culture, and to their race, which meant identifying with the great mass of enslaved African Americans. Some well-to-do free blacks, particularly the mulatto offspring of white masters and black women, drew apart from common black laborers and field hands and adopted the outlook of the planter class. In Charleston and New Orleans a few free African Americans even owned slaves.

However, most free African Americans acknowledged their unity with the enslaved population and saw blacks as one people. "We's different [from whites] in color, in talk and in 'ligion and beliefs," as one put it. Knowing their own liberty was not secure as long as slavery existed, free blacks sought freedom for all those of African ancestry. Free blacks in the South—who were often the offspring of white planters— aided fugitive slaves, while northern blacks supported the antislavery movement. In the rigid caste system of American race relations, free blacks stood as symbols of hope to enslaved African Americans and as omens of danger to the majority of whites.

The Missouri Crisis

The success of their campaign against the Atlantic slave trade encouraged northern reformers to rid American society of slave labor. In 1818 Congressman Nathaniel Macon of North Carolina warned southerners that radical-minded members of the "colonizing bible and peace societies" hoped to use the national government "to try the question of emancipation." In fact, a major national conflict over slavery came even more quickly than Macon had anticipated. When Missouri applied for admission to the Union as a slave state in 1819, Congressman James Tallmadge of New York proposed a ban on the importation of slaves into Missouri and the gradual emancipation of its black inhabitants. When Missouri whites rejected Tallmadge's proposals, the northern majority in the House of Representatives blocked the territory's admission to the Union.

Southerners were horrified. "It is believed by some, & feared by others," Alabama senator John Walker reported from Washington, that Tallmadge's amendment was "merely the entering wedge and that it points already to a total emancipation of the blacks." The outlook for the South was grim. "You conduct us to an awful precipice, and hold us over it," Mississippi congressman Christopher Rankin warned his northern colleagues. To underline their commitment to slavery, southerners used their power in the Senate (where they held half the seats) to withhold statehood from Maine, which was seeking to separate itself from Massachusetts.

In the ensuing debate, southerners advanced three constitutional arguments. First, raising the principle of "equal rights," they argued that Congress could not impose conditions on Missouri that it had not imposed on other territories seeking statehood. Second, they suggested that slavery was an internal affair that fell under the sovereignty of the state governments. Finally, they maintained that Congress had no authority to infringe on the property rights of individual slaveholders. Going beyond these constitutional issues, southern leaders abandoned their traditional argument that slavery was a "necessary evil" and now championed it as a "positive good." "Christ himself gave a sanction to slavery," declared Senator William Smith of South Carolina. "If it be offensive and sinful to own slaves," a prominent Mississippi Methodist added, "I wish someone would just put his finger on the place in Holy Writ."

Controversy raged for two years before Henry Clay of Kentucky put together a series of political agreements known collectively as the Missouri Compromise. The compromise allowed Maine to enter the Union as a free state in 1820 and Missouri to follow as a slave state in 1821. By admitting both states, the agreement preserved the existing balance in the Senate between North and South and set a precedent for future additions to the Union. To mollify antislavery sentiment in the House of Representatives, southern congressmen accepted legislation that prohibited slavery in the rest of the Louisiana Purchase north of latitude 36°30′, the southern boundary of Missouri (Map 9.3).

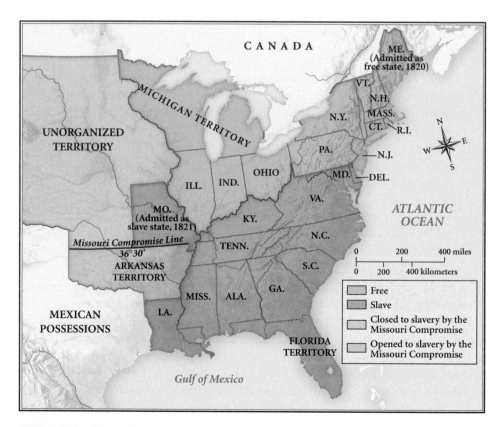

MAP 9.3 The Missouri Compromise, 1820–1821

The Missouri Compromise resolved for a generation the issue of slavery in the lands of the Louisiana Purchase. The agreement prohibited slavery north of the Missouri Compromise line (36°30′ north latitude), with the exception of the state of Missouri. To maintain an equal number of senators from free and slave states in the U.S. Congress, the compromise provided for the nearly simultaneous admission to the Union of Maine and Missouri.

As in the Constitutional Convention of 1787, white politicians had given first priority to the Union by devising ways to handle the perilous issue of slavery. But the task had become more difficult. The Philadelphia delegates had resolved sectional differences in two months. Congress took two years to work out the Missouri Compromise, and, because slavery had become an intensely debated political issue, there was no guarantee that it would work. The fate of the western lands, the Union, and the black race were now inextricably intertwined and raised the specter of civil war. As the aging Thomas Jefferson exclaimed during the Missouri crisis, "This momentous question, like a fire-bell in the night, awakened and filled me with terror."

Protestant Christianity as a Social Force

Throughout the colonial era, religion played a significant role in American life. However, beginning in 1790 a series of religious **revivals** planted the values of evangelical Protestant Christianity deep in the national character and gave a spiritual definition to American republicanism. The revivals also changed the lives of women and blacks. Thousands of African Americans absorbed the faith of white Baptists and Methodists and created a distinctive and powerful institution—the black Christian church. Evangelical Christianity likewise created new public roles for women, especially in the North, and set in motion a long-lasting movement for social reform.

The Second Great Awakening

The revivals that began around 1790 were much more complex than those of the First Great Awakening. In the 1740s most revivals had occurred in existing congregations; fifty years later they took place both in churches and frontier camp meetings and often led to the creation of new denominations.

In the new American republic, the churches that prospered were those that preached spiritual equality and governed themselves in a relatively democratic fashion. Because bishops and priests dominated the Roman Catholic Church, it attracted few converts among Protestants, who preferred Luther's doctrine of the priesthood of all believers. The unchurched—the great number of nonreligious Americans—likewise shunned Catholicism because they feared clerical power. Likewise, few ordinary native-born Americans joined the Episcopal Church (created by former members of the Church of England) because it had a hierarchical structure similar to that of Catholicism and was dominated by its wealthiest members. The Presbyterian Church was more popular, in part because its members elected laymen to the synods (congresses) which determined doctrine and practice. The Methodist and Baptist Churches attracted even more Americans because most of their preachers were fervent evangelists and promoted an egalitarian religious culture marked by communal singing and emotional services.

A continuous wave of revivalism fueled the expansion of Protestant Christianity. Beginning in the 1790s Baptists and Methodists evangelized the cities and the backcountry of New England. A new sect of Universalists, who repudiated the Calvinist doctrine of predestination and preached universal salvation, attracted thousands of converts, especially in Massachusetts and northern New England. After 1800 enthusiastic camp-meeting revivals swept the frontier regions of South Carolina, Kentucky, Tennessee, and Ohio.

When frontier preachers got together at a revival meeting, the atmosphere was electrifying. James McGready, a Scots-Irish Presbyterian preacher, "could so array hell before the wicked," an eyewitness reported, "that they would tremble and Quake, imagining a lake of fire and brimstone yawning to overwhelm them." James Finley described the Cane Ridge, Kentucky, revival of 1802:

> The noise was like the roar of Niagara. The vast sea of human beings seemed to be agitated as if by a storm. I counted seven ministers, all preaching at one time, some on stumps, others on wagons. . . . Some of the people were singing, others praying, some crying for mercy.

Through such revivals, Baptist and Methodist preachers reshaped the spiritual landscape of the South and the Old Southwest. Because of their emotional message and promise of religious fellowship, revivalists were particularly successful in attracting the unchurched and geographically mobile families who had few social ties in their new communities. With the assistance of black ministers, they began to implant evangelical Protestant Christianity among African Americans as well (see Voices from Abroad, "A Camp Meeting in Indiana," p. 279).

The Second Great Awakening changed the denominational makeup of American religion. The leading churches of the colonial period—the Congregationalists, Episcopalians, and Quakers—grew slowly through natural increase while Methodist and Baptist churches expanded in spectacular fashion by seeking converts and soon became the nation's largest religious denominations. In New England and the Middle Atlantic states, pious evangelical women supplemented the work of preachers and lay elders by holding prayer meetings and providing material aid and spiritual comfort to poorer members of congregations. In the South and West, Baptist and Methodist preachers traveled constantly. A Methodist minister followed a circuit, "riding a hardy pony or horse . . . with his Bible, hymn-book, and Discipline." These "circuit riders" established new churches by searching out devout families, bringing them together for worship, and then appointing lay elders to lead the congregation and enforce moral discipline until the circuit-riding preacher returned.

Evangelical ministers copied the "practical preaching" techniques of George Whitefield and other eighteenth-century revivalists. To attract converts, preachers adopted theatrical gestures and a flamboyant style, threw away their stodgy written sermons, and spoke in plain language. "Preach without papers" and emphasize piety

A Camp Meeting in Indiana

FRANCES TROLLOPE

*F*rances Trollope, the mother of the English novelist Anthony Trollope, lived during the late 1820s in Cincinnati, where she owned a bazaar that sold European goods. Unsuccessful as a storekeeper, she won great acclaim as the author of Domestic Manners of the Americans (1832), a critical study of life in the United States. Here she provides her readers with a vivid description of a revivalist meeting in Indiana around 1830.

We reached the ground about an hour before midnight. . . . The spot chosen was the verge of an unbroken forest, where a space of about twenty acres appeared to have been partially cleared for the purpose. Tents of different sizes were pitched very near together in a circle round the cleared space. . . .

Four high frames, constructed in the form of altars, were placed at the four corners of the inclosure; on these were supported layers of earth and sod, on which burned immense fires of blazing pine-wood. On one side a rude platform was erected to accommodate the preachers, fifteen of whom attended this meeting, and . . . preached in rotation, day and night, from Tuesday to Saturday.

When we arrived, the preachers were silent; but we heard issuing from nearly every tent mingled sounds of praying, preaching, singing, and lamentation. . . . [One of the tents contained a] . . . close-packed circle of men and women who knelt on the floor. Out of about thirty persons thus placed, perhaps half a dozen were men. One of these [was] a handsome-looking youth of eighteen or twenty. . . . His arm was encircling the neck of a young girl who knelt beside him, with her hair hanging dishevelled upon her shoulders, and her features working with the most violent agitation; soon after they both fell forward on the straw, as if unable to endure in any other attitude the burning eloquence of a tall grim figure in black, who, standing erect in the center, was uttering with incredible vehemence an oration that seemed to hover between praying and preaching. . . .

One tent was occupied exclusively by Negroes. They were all full-dressed, and looked exactly as if they were performing a scene on a stage. . . . The men were in snow white pantaloons, with gay colored linen jackets. One of these, a youth of coal-black comeliness, was preaching with the most violent gesticulations. . . .

At midnight, a horn sounded through the camp, which, we were told, was to call the people from private to public worship; and . . . about two thousand persons assembled.

One of the preachers began in a low nasal tone, and, like all other Methodist preachers, assured us of the enormous depravity of man. . . . Above a hundred persons, nearly all females, came forward, uttering howlings and groans so terrible that I shall never cease to shudder when I recall them. They appeared to drag each other forward, and on the word being given, "let us pray," they fell on their knees. . . .

SOURCE: Frances Trollope, *Domestic Manners of the Americans* (London: Whittaker, Treacher and Co., 1832), 139–42.

A Baptist Ceremony

Unlike many other Christian churches, which practiced infant baptism, Baptists reserved this sacred ceremony for adults who had been born again by the infusion of God's grace. Some Baptist congregations, such as the one depicted in this 1819 painting, required complete immersion in water, symbolizing the cleansing of all sins. Such communal practices, along with an egalitarian atmosphere and an intense religiosity, attracted tens of thousands of converts and quickly made the Baptists one of the largest American denominations. Chicago Historical Society.

FOR MORE HELP ANALYZING THIS IMAGE, see the Online Study Guide at **bedfordstmartins.com/henrettaconcise.**

rather than theology, advised one minister, "seem earnest & serious; & you will be listened to with Patience, & Wonder."

In the South evangelical religion was initially a disruptive force. By proclaiming the spiritual equality of all people—women and blacks as well as white men—it incurred the wrath of husbands and planters. In response Methodist and Baptist preachers adapted the social content of their religious message so that it upheld the authority of yeomen patriarchs and slave-owning planters. "We hold that a Christian slave must be submissive, faithful, and obedient," a Methodist conference proclaimed, while a Baptist minister declared that a man was naturally at "the head of the woman." Ultimately Christian republicanism in the South added a sacred dimension to the ideology of aristocratic republicanism.

But this was not the case among blacks. After the family, the religious community was the most important institution among slaves, and initially most blacks maintained the practices of their African homeland. "At the time I first went to Carolina," remembered Charles Ball, an escaped slave, "there were a great many African slaves in the country. . . . Many of them believed there were several gods [and] I knew several . . . Mohamedans [Muslims]."

When the First Great Awakening swept through the Upper South after 1750, only a few blacks joined Christian churches. The first major wave of African American conversions to Christianity occurred only in the mid-1780s along the James River in Virginia.

Subsequently, white evangelical Baptists and Methodists won the conversion of hundreds of slaves and free blacks, who adapted the teachings of the Protestant churches to their own needs. Black Christians generally envisioned God as a warrior who had liberated the Jews, his chosen people. Their "cause was similar to the Israelites'," Martin Prosser told his fellow slave conspirators as they plotted rebellion in Virginia in 1800. "I have read in my Bible where God says, if we worship him, . . . five of you shall conquer a hundred and a hundred of you a hundred thousand of our enemies." Confident of their special relationship with God, slaves prepared themselves spiritually for emancipation, the first step in their journey to the Promised Land.

Consequently, black Christians generally ignored the doctrines of original sin and predestination as well as biblical passages that encouraged unthinking obedience to authority. When a white minister urged slaves in Liberty County, Georgia, to obey their masters, "one half of my audience deliberately rose up and walked off." Slaves identified not only with the powerful Father-God but also with his persecuted Savior-Son, whose suffering helped them endure the manifest injustice of their own lives. Black Christianity thus developed as a complex mixture of stoical endurance and emotional fervor, and encouraged slaves to affirm their spiritual equality with whites.

Like African Americans, whites responded more positively to certain Christian doctrines than to others. The Calvinist preoccupation with human depravity and weakness had profoundly shaped the sensibilities of many colonial-era writers, teachers, and statesmen. By the early nineteenth century, most Protestant ministers placed greater stress on human ability and individual free will. In New England many educated and affluent Congregationalists, influenced by Enlightenment thought, placed increasing emphasis on the power of human reason. Rejecting the concept of the Trinity—Father, Son, and Holy Spirit—they worshiped an indivisible and "united" God; hence they took the name of Unitarians. "The ultimate reliance of a human being is, and must be, on his own mind," argued the famous Unitarian minister William Ellery Channing, "for the idea of God is the idea of our own spiritual nature, purified and enlarged to infinity."

Other New England Congregationalists likewise abandoned the Calvinist outlook of their Puritan ancestors. Although Lyman Beecher, the preeminent Congregationalist clergyman, continued to believe that humans had a natural tendency to sin, he affirmed the capacity of all men and women to choose God and to be saved. In emphasizing the free will of the believer and the possibility of universal salvation, Beecher testified to the growing confidence in the power of human action and the increasing democratic and capitalistic spirit of the age.

Reflecting this optimistic outlook, the minister Samuel Hopkins linked individual salvation to religious benevolence. Benevolence was the practice of disinterested virtue. According to the New York Presbyterian minister John Rodgers, fortunate individuals who had received God's grace had a duty "to dole out charity to their poorer brothers and sisters." Heeding this message, pious merchants founded the New York Humane Society and other charitable organizations. By the 1820s so many devout Protestant men and women had embraced benevolent reform that conservative church leaders warned against the pursuit of secular goals, such as the prevention of pauperism, to the neglect of spiritual matters. This criticism underlined a key element of the new religious outlook: its emphasis on improving society. It was her belief, the social reformer Lydia Maria Child later recalled, that "the only true church organization [is] when heads and hearts unite in working for the welfare of the human-race."

Unlike the First Great Awakening of the 1740s, which split churches into factions, the Second Great Awakening fostered cooperation among the denominations. Religious leaders founded five interdenominational societies between 1815 and 1826: the American Education Society (1815), the American Bible Society (1816), the American Sunday School Union (1824), the American Tract Society (1824), and the American Home Missionary Society (1826). Although based in eastern cities— New York, Boston, and Philadelphia—they ministered to a national congregation. Each year the societies dispatched hundreds of missionaries to small towns and rural villages and distributed tens of thousands of religious pamphlets.

The growing unity among Protestants had a galvanizing effect, as men and women scattered across the expanding nation saw themselves as part of a single religious movement that could change the course of history (Map 9.4). "I want to see our state evangelized," declared one pious layman who lived along the Erie Canal (where the fires of revivalism were so hot and so frequent that it was known as the "Burned-Over District"): "Suppose the great State of New York in all its physical, political, moral, commercial, and pecuniary resources should come over to the Lord's side. Why it would turn the scale and could convert the world. I shall have no rest until it is done."

Because the Second Awakening aroused such pious enthusiasm in thousands of Americans, religion became a central force in political life. On July 4, 1827, the Reverend Ezra Stiles Ely called on the members of the Seventh Presbyterian Church in Philadelphia to begin a "Christian party in politics." Ely's sermon, "The Duty of Christian Freemen to Elect Christian Rulers," proclaimed a religious goal for the American republic—an objective that Thomas Jefferson and John Adams would

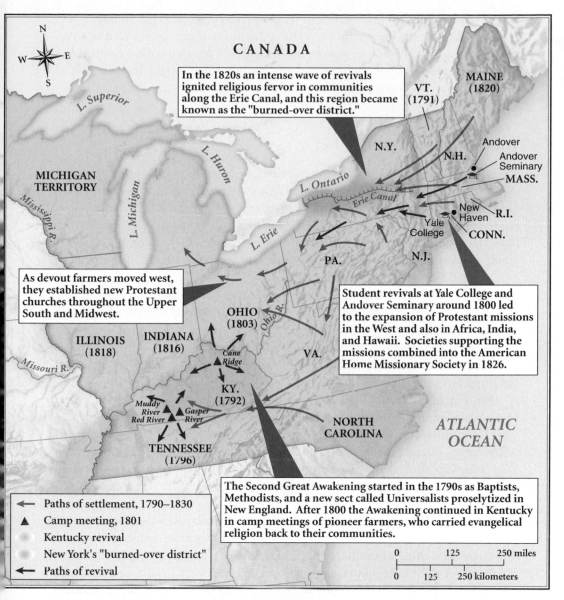

In the 1820s an intense wave of revivals ignited religious fervor in communities along the Erie Canal, and this region became known as the "burned-over district."

As devout farmers moved west, they established new Protestant churches throughout the Upper South and Midwest.

Student revivals at Yale College and Andover Seminary around 1800 led to the expansion of Protestant missions in the West and also in Africa, India, and Hawaii. Societies supporting the missions combined into the American Home Missionary Society in 1826.

The Second Great Awakening started in the 1790s as Baptists, Methodists, and a new sect called Universalists proselytized in New England. After 1800 the Awakening continued in Kentucky in camp meetings of pioneer farmers, who carried evangelical religion back to their communities.

← Paths of settlement, 1790–1830
▲ Camp meeting, 1801
⬤ Kentucky revival
⬤ New York's "burned-over district"
← Paths of revival

| 0 | 125 | 250 miles |
| 0 | 125 | 250 kilometers |

MAP 9.4 The Second Great Awakening, 1790–1860

The awakening lasted for decades and invigorated churches in every part of the nation. However, the revivals in Kentucky and in New York State were particularly intense and influential. As thousands of farm families migrated to the West, they carried with them the fervor generated by the Cane Ridge revival in Kentucky in 1802 and the religious wildfires that swept through the "Burned-Over District" along the Erie Canal in New York between 1825 and 1835.

have found strange if not troubling. The two recently deceased founders had believed that America's mission was to spread political republicanism. In contrast Ely urged the United States to become an evangelical Christian nation dedicated to religious conversion at home and abroad: "All our rulers ought in their official capacity to serve the Lord Jesus Christ."

Women's New Religious Roles

The upsurge in religious enthusiasm provided women with new opportunities to demonstrate their piety and even to found new sects. Mother Ann Lee organized the Shakers in Britain and in 1774 migrated to America, where she attracted numerous recruits; by the 1820s Shaker communities dotted the American countryside from New Hampshire to Kentucky and Indiana (see Chapter 12). Jemima Wilkinson, a young Quaker woman in Rhode Island, led a less successful religious movement. In 1776, stirred by reading the sermons of George Whitefield, Wilkinson had a vision that she had died and been reincarnated as Christ. Repudiating her birth name, Wilkinson declared herself to be the Publick Universal Friend and preached a new gospel, which blended the Calvinist warning of "a lost and guilty, gossiping, dying World" with Quaker-inspired plain dress, pacifism, and abolitionism. Wilkinson's charisma initially won scores of converts, but her radical personal lifestyle and teachings brought a rapid end to her sect.

Far more important than these religious experiments were the activities undertaken by women in mainstream churches. To give but a few examples, in New Hampshire women managed more than fifty local "cent" societies that raised funds for the Society for Promoting Christian Knowledge. Evangelical women in New York City founded the Society for the Relief of Poor Widows. And young Quaker women in Philadelphia ran the Society for the Free Instruction of African Females.

Women became active in religion and charitable work partly because they were excluded from other spheres of public life and partly because ministers relied increasingly on women to do the work of the church. After 1800 over 70 percent of the members of New England Congregational churches were female, and ministers acknowledged their numerical predominance by ending long-standing practices such as gender-segregated prayer meetings. Indeed, evangelical Methodist and Baptist preachers actively encouraged mixed praying. "Our prayer meetings have been one of the greatest means of the conversion of souls," a minister in central New York reported in the 1820s, "especially those in which brothers and sisters have prayed together."

Far from leading to sexual promiscuity, as critics feared, these new practices promoted greater moral self-discipline. Believing in female virtue, many young women and the men who courted them now postponed sexual intercourse until after marriage—a form of self-restraint uncommon in the eighteenth century. In Hingham,

Massachusetts, and many other New England towns, more than 30 percent of the women who married between 1750 and 1800 had borne a child within eight months of their wedding day. By the 1820s the proportion had dropped to 15 percent.

As women exercised their new spiritual authority, men scrutinized their behavior and tried to curb their power. Evangelical Baptist churches that had once stressed spiritual equality now denied women the right to vote on church affairs or to offer testimonies of faith before the congregation. Such activities, declared one layman, were "directly opposite to the apostolic command in Cor[inthians] xiv, 34, 35, 'Let your women learn to keep silence in the churches.'" "Women have a different *calling*," claimed another, "That they *be chaste, keepers at home* is the Apostle's direction." Seizing on that role, by the 1820s mothers throughout the United States had founded local maternal associations to encourage Christian childrearing. Newsletters such as *Mother's Magazine* were widely read in hundreds of small towns and villages and gave women a sense of shared purpose and identity.

Religious activism also advanced female education. Churches established scores of seminaries and academies where girls from the middling classes received sound intellectual and moral instruction. Emma Willard, the first American advocate of higher education for women, opened the Middlebury Female Seminary in Vermont in 1814 and later founded girls' schools in Waterford and Troy, New York.

TIMELINE

1782	St. Jean de Crèvecoeur publishes *Letters from an American Farmer*		Chesapeake blacks adopt Protestant beliefs
1787	Benjamin Rush writes *Thoughts on Female Education*	1807	New Jersey excludes propertied women from suffrage
1790s	Parents limit family size as farms shrink Second Great Awakening expands church membership Ministers encourage "republican motherhood"	1810s	Expansion of suffrage for men Spread of evangelical Baptists and Methodists Slavery defended as a "necessary evil" Growth of cotton South and domestic slave trade
1800	Gabriel Prosser plots a slave rebellion in Virginia		Five states join union: Louisiana (1812), Indiana (1816), Mississippi (1817), Illinois (1818), Alabama (1819)
1800s	Rise of sentimentalism and of companionate marriages Women's religious activism; founding of female academies Religious benevolence sparks social reform	1819–1821	Conflict over admission of Missouri as a slave state ends with Missouri Compromise
		1820s	Reform of public education Women become schoolteachers

Beginning in the 1820s women educated in these seminaries and academies displaced men as public-school teachers. Because educated women had few other opportunities for paid employment, they accepted lower pay than men would. Female schoolteachers earned from $12 to $14 per month with room and board—less than a farm laborer. However, as schoolteachers women had an acknowledged place in public life, a goal that had been beyond their reach in colonial and Revolutionary times.

Just as the ideology of democratic republicanism had expanded voting rights and the political influence of ordinary men in the North, so the values of Christian republicanism had bolstered the public authority of middling women. The Second Great Awakening made Americans a fervently Protestant people. Along with republican and capitalist values, this religious impulse—embodied in the shared experience of hundreds of thousands of Americans between the 1770s and the 1820s—formed the core of an emerging national identity, even as the citizens of the North and the South defined republicanism and economic progress in distinctly different ways.

For Further Exploration

For an intimate portrayal of family life on the Maine frontier, see Laurel Thatcher Ulrich, *A Midwife's Tale: The Life of Martha Ballard* (1990), which has also been made into a PBS dramatic documentary, *A Midwife's Tale* (1.5 hours). Additional materials on Ballard's experiences and women's lives are available on the Web at <http://www.pbs.org/amex/midwife> and <http://www.DoHistory.org>. Jan Lewis's *The Pursuit of Happiness: Family and Values in Jefferson's Virginia* (1983) explores the domestic and emotional lives of the paternalistic slave-owning gentry of the late eighteenth century in the Upper South, while Stephanie McCurry's *Masters of Small Worlds: Yeomen Households, Gender Relations, and the Political Culture of the Antebellum South Carolina Low Country* (1995) offers a brilliant analysis of yeomen families. Two recent studies of slave owners are William Kauffman Scarborough, *Masters of the Big House: Elite Slaveholders of the Mid-Nineteenth-Century South* (2003), and James David Miller, *South by Southwest: Planter Emigration and Identity in the Slave South* (2002).

Two stimulating analyses of the changing character of slavery and African American society are Ira Berlin, *Generations of Captivity: A History of African-American Slaves* (2003) and Peter Kolchin, *American Slavery, 1619–1877* (1993). Douglas R. Egerton, *Gabriel's Rebellion: The Virginia Slave Conspiracies of 1800 and 1802* (1995), traces the political and economic causes of Gabriel's movement and its near success. For primary documents that illustrate the ways in which African Americans acquired and transformed Protestant Christianity, log on to Documenting the American South: The Church in the Southern Black Community, at <http://docsouth.unc.edu/church/index.html>.

In *The Democratization of American Christianity* (1987) Nathan Hatch traces the impact of evangelical Protestantism on the life and politics of the early republic. Other fine overviews of American religion which offer dramatic portraits of revivalists, such as Charles

Grandison Finney, and explore the many links between religious enthusiasm and social reform are Mark A. Noll, *America's God: From Jonathan Edwards to Abraham Lincoln* (2003), and Bernard Weisberger, *They Gathered at the River* (1958). The Library of Congress offers a fine collection of material under Religion and the Founding of the American Republic at <http://www.loc.gov/exhibits/religion/>.

For definitions of key terms boldfaced in this chapter, see the glossary at the end of the book.

To assess your mastery of the material covered in this chapter, see the Online Study Guide at **bedfordstmartins.com/henrettaconcise**.

For map resources and primary documents, see **bedfordstmartins.com/henrettaconcise**.

Part Three

ECONOMIC REVOLUTION
AND SECTIONAL STRIFE

1820–1877

ECONOMY	SOCIETY	GOVERNMENT
The Economic Revolution Begins	A New Class Structure Emerges	Creating a Democratic Polity
1820 ▸ Waltham textile factory (1814) Erie Canal completed (1825); market economy expands	▸ Business class emerges Rural women and girls recruited as factory workers	▸ Spread of universal white male suffrage Rise of Jackson and Democratic Party
1830 ▸ Protective tariffs aid owners and workers Panic of 1837 U.S. textile makers outcompete British	▸ Mechanics form craft unions Depression shatters labor movement	▸ Anti-Masonic movement Whig Party formed (1834); Second Party System emerges
1840 ▸ Irish immigrants join labor force *Commonwealth v. Hunt* (1842) legalizes unions Manufacturing expands	▸ Working-class districts emerge in cities Irish and German immigration accelerates	▸ Log Cabin campaign mobilizes voters Antislavery parties: Liberty and Free-Soil
1850 ▸ Surge of cotton output in South and of railroads in the North and Midwest Panic of 1857	▸ Expansion of farm society into Midwest and Far West Free labor ideology justifies inequality	▸ Whig Party disintegrates; Republican Party founded (1854): Third Party System begins
1860 ▸ Republicans enact policy agenda: Homestead Act, railroad aid, high tariffs, national banking	▸ Emancipation Proclamation (1863) Free blacks struggle for control of land	▸ Thirteenth Amendment (1865) ends slavery Fourteenth Amendment (1868) extends legal and political rights
1870 ▸ Panic of 1873	▸ Rise of sharecropping in the South	▸ Fifteenth Amendment extends vote to black men (1870)

CULTURE	SECTIONALISM
Reforming People and Institutions	**From Compromise to Civil War and Reconstruction**
▶ American Colonization Society (1817) Benevolent reform movements Revivalist Charles Finney	▶ Missouri Compromise (1820) David Walker's *Appeal to the Colored Race* (1829)
▶ Joseph Smith founds Mormonism Female Moral Reform Society (1834) Temperance crusade expands	▶ Nullification crisis (1832) W. L. Garrison forms American Anti-Slavery Society (1833)
▶ Fourierist and other communal settlements founded Seneca Falls convention (1848)	▶ Texas annexation, Mexican War, and Wilmot Proviso (1846) increase sectional conflict
▶ Harriet Beecher Stowe's *Uncle Tom's Cabin* (1852) Anti-immigrant nativist movement	▶ Compromise of 1850 Kansas-Nebraska Act (1854) and Bleeding Kansas *Dred Scott* decision (1857)
▶ U.S. Sanitary Commission and American Red Cross founded	▶ South Carolina leads secession movement (1860) Confederate States of America (1861–1865)
▶ Freed African Americans create schools and churches	▶ Compromise of 1877 ends Reconstruction

I n America, a French visitor remarked in 1839, "all is circulation, motion, and boiling agitation. Enterprise follows enterprise [and] riches and poverty follow." Indeed, the society was changing in basic ways. In 1820 the United States was predominately an agricultural nation; by 1877 it boasted one of the world's most powerful manufacturing economies. This profound transformation affected every aspect of life in the northern and midwestern states and brought important changes to the agricultural states of the south as well. Indeed, the growing social and cultural differences among the regions was an important cause of the political divisions which led ultimately to the tragedy of the Civil War.

ECONOMY Two revolutions in industrial production and the market system transformed the nation's economy. Factory owners used high-speed machines and a new system of labor discipline to boost production, and enterprising merchants employed a recently built network of canals and railroads to create a vast national market. The manufacturing sector produced an ever-increasing share of the country's wealth: from less than 5 percent in 1820 to more than 30 percent in 1877.

SOCIETY The new economic system spurred the creation of a class-based society. A wealthy elite of merchants, manufacturers, bankers, and other entrepreneurs emerged at the top of the social order and tried to maintain social stability through a paternalistic program of benevolent reform. However, a rapidly growing urban middle class created a distinct material and religious culture and spearheaded movements for radical social reform. Equally striking, an increasing number of propertyless workers, many of them immigrants from Germany and Ireland, now labored for wages and lived at the edge of poverty in urban ghettos.

GOVERNMENT Economic expansion and social diversity combined with the growth of political parties to create a more open, democratic polity. Farmers, workers, and entrepreneurs turned increasingly to government to seek improved transportation, shorter workdays, and special corporate charters. Catholic immigrants from Ireland and Germany also entered the political arena in order to protect their religion and culture from attacks by nativists and reformers. Led by Andrew Jackson, the Democratic Party advanced the interests of southern planters, farmers, and urban workers. It carried through a democratic political and constitutional revolution that cut governmental aid to financiers, merchants, and business corporations. To contend with the Democrats, the Whig Party (and, beginning in the 1850s, the Republican Party) devised an interrelated program of economic development, moral reform, and individual social mobility. This party competition engaged the energies of the electorate and unified the fragmented social order.

CULTURE During these decades, a series of reform movements, many with religious roots and goals, swept across America. Dedicated men and women preached the gospel of temperance, observance of Sunday, prison reform, and dozens of other causes. Some Americans pursued their social dreams in utopian communities, but most reformers worked within society. Two interrelated groups—abolitionists and women's rights activists—demanded radical changes in the existing social order: the immediate end of slavery and the overthrow of the patriarchal legal and political order. As southern planters increasingly defended slavery as a "positive good," antislavery advocates turned to political action. During the 1840s and 1850s, they campaigned for free soil in the western territories and alleged that a "slave power conspiracy" threatened free labor and republican values throughout the nation.

SECTIONALISM These economic, political, and cultural changes sharpened sectional divisions: the North developed into an urbanizing and industrializing society based on free labor, whereas the South remained a rural, slaveholding society dependent on the production of cotton. Following the Mexican War (1846–1848), northern and southern politicians could not agree on the issue of permitting slavery in the vast territories seized from Mexico. The election of Republican Abraham Lincoln prompted the secession of the South from the Union and, thereafter, civil war. The conflict became a total war, a struggle between two societies as well as two armies. Because of new technology and the mass mobilization of armies, the two sides endured unprecedented casualties and costs before the North emerged victorious.

The fruits of victory were substantial. During Reconstruction, the Republican Party ended slavery, imposed its economic policies and constitutional doctrines on the nation, and began to extend full democratic rights to the former slaves. Faced by massive resistance from white Southerners, northern leaders lacked the will to undertake the fundamental transformation of the economic and political order of the South required to provide African Americans with the full benefits of freedom.

Chapter 10

THE ECONOMIC REVOLUTION
1820–1860

Ten years ago we had *nothing*—now we have *everything*.
THE CATSKILL (N.Y.) RECORDER, 1828

In 1804 life suddenly turned grim for eleven-year-old Chauncey Jerome of Connecticut. Following the death of his father, Jerome was hired out as an indentured servant to a farmer. Knowing that few farmers "would treat a poor boy like a human being," Jerome bought out his indenture by taking a job making dials for clocks and eventually ended up as a journeyman for clockmaker Eli Terry. A manufacturing wizard, Terry had designed an enormously popular desk-model clock with brass parts and turned Litchfield, Connecticut, into the clock-making center of the United States. Jerome followed in Terry's footsteps and in 1816 set up his own clock business. By organizing work more efficiently and using new machines that made interchangeable metal parts, Jerome drove down the price of a simple clock from $20 to $5 and then to less than $2. By the 1840s he was selling his clocks in England, the center of the Industrial Revolution; two decades later his workers were turning out two hundred thousand clocks a year, clear testimony to American enterprise. Together the Industrial Revolution and the Market Revolution created a new economy. By 1860 the United States was not only the world's leading exporter of cotton and wheat but also the third-ranked manufacturing nation behind Britain and France.

A European immigrant, Francis Grund, captured a key feature of Chauncey Jerome's experience and the American economic revolution. "Business is the very soul of an American: the fountain of all human felicity," Grund observed. "It is as if all America were but one gigantic workshop, over the entrance of which there is the blazing inscription, 'No admission here, except on business.'" Stimulated by the intensely work-oriented culture of early-nineteenth-century America, tens of thousands of artisan-inventors like Eli Terry and Chauncey Jerome propelled the country into a new economic era. As the editor of *Niles' Weekly Register* in Baltimore put it, there was an "almost universal ambition to get forward."

Not all Americans embraced the new ethic of enterprise, and many who did failed to share in the new prosperity. The spread of industry and commerce created a class-divided society that challenged the founders' vision of an agricultural republic with few distinctions of wealth. As the philosopher Ralph Waldo Emerson warned in 1839, "The invasion of Nature by Trade with its Money, its Credit, its Steam, [and] its Railroad threatens to . . . establish a new, universal Monarchy."

The Coming of Industry: Northeastern Manufacturing

Industrialization came to the United States around 1790, as merchants and manufacturers reorganized work routines and built new factories. The rapid construction of turnpikes, canals, and railroads by state governments and private entrepreneurs allowed these manufactures to be sold throughout the land. Thanks to these innovations in production and transportation, the average per capita wealth of Americans increased by nearly 1 percent per year—30 percent over the course of a generation. Goods that once had been luxury items became part of everyday life.

Division of Labor and the Factory

This impressive gain in living standards stemmed initially from changes in the organization of work. Consider the shoe industry. Traditionally, New England shoemakers worked in small wooden shacks called "ten-footers," where they turned leather hides into finished shoes and boots. During the 1820s and 1830s the merchants and manufacturers of Lynn, Massachusetts, took over the shoe industry by increasing output through an outwork system and a **division of labor**. The employers hired semiskilled journeymen and set them to work in large shops cutting the leather into soles and uppers. They sent out the upper sections to women shoe binders in dozens of Massachusetts towns who sewed in fabric linings. The manufacturers then had other journeymen assemble the shoes and return them to the central shop for inspection and packing. The new system turned an employer into a powerful "shoe boss" and eroded workers' control over their labor. "I guess you won't catch me to do that little thing again," vowed one woman shoe binder. Whatever the cost to workers, the division of labor dramatically increased the output of shoes and cut their price.

For products that were not suited to the outwork system, entrepreneurs created the modern factory, which concentrated production under one roof and divided the work into specialized tasks. For example, in the 1830s Cincinnati merchants built slaughterhouses that subdivided the process of butchering hogs into specific tasks. A simple system of overhead rails moved the hog carcasses past workers who split the animals, removed various organs, and trimmed the carcasses into pieces. Then packers stuffed the cuts of pork into barrels and pickled them to prevent spoilage. The Cincinnati system was so efficient and quick—sixty hogs per hour—that by the 1840s the city became known as "Porkopolis."

Pork Packing in Cincinnati

The only form of modern technology in this Cincinnati pork-packing plant was the overhead pulley system that carried hog carcasses past the workers. The plant's efficiency came from organization: a division of labor in which each worker performed a specific task. Such plants pioneered the design of the moving assembly lines that reached a high level of sophistication in the early twentieth-century automobile factories of Henry Ford. Cincinnati Historical Society.

Some factories boasted impressive new technology. The prolific Delaware inventor Oliver Evans built a highly automated flour mill driven by waterpower. His machinery lifted the grain to the top of the mill, cleaned the grain as it fell into hoppers, ground it into flour, conveyed the flour back to the top of the mill, and then cooled the flour during its descent into barrels. Evans's factory, remarked one observer, "was as full of machinery as the case of a watch." It needed only six men to mill one hundred thousand bushels of grain a year.

By the 1830s, factory owners used newly improved stationary steam engines to power their mills and manufactured new types of products. Previously, factories mainly processed agricultural goods—pork, leather, wool, and cotton; subsequently they fabricated metal goods and parts. Cyrus McCormick of Chicago used power-driven conveyor belts to assemble reaping machines, and Samuel Colt built an assembly line in Hartford, Connecticut, to produce his invention—the "six-shooter" revolver, as it became known. Such technological advances alarmed a team of British observers: "The contriving and making of machinery has become so common in this country, and so many heads and hands are at work with extraordinary energy, that . . . it is to be feared that American manufacturers will become exporters not only to foreign countries, but even to England."

The Textile Industry and British Competition

British textile manufacturers were particularly worried about American competition. To protect its industrial leadership, the British government prohibited the export of textile machinery and the emigration of **mechanics** who knew how to build it. However, lured by high wages or offers of partnerships, thousands of British mechanics disguised themselves as ordinary laborers and set sail for the United States. By 1812 there were more than 300 British mechanics at work in the Philadelphia area alone.

Samuel Slater was the most important of the immigrants. Slater came to America in 1789 after working for Richard Arkwright, the inventor of the most advanced British machinery for spinning cotton. He reproduced Arkwright's innovations in merchant Moses Brown's cotton mill in Providence, Rhode Island; its opening in 1790 marks the advent of the American Industrial Revolution.

In competing with British mills, American manufacturers had the advantage of an abundance of natural resources. The nation's farmers produced a wealth of cotton and wool, and its rivers provided a cheap source of energy. As rivers cascaded downhill from the Appalachian foothills to the Atlantic coastal plain, they were easily harnessed to run power machinery. From Massachusetts to Delaware, industrial villages and towns sprang up along these waterways, dominated by massive textile mills—some as large as 150 feet long, 40 feet wide, and four stories high.

Nevertheless, British textile producers easily undersold their American competitors. Thanks to cheap shipping and low interest rates in Britain, they could import raw cotton from the United States, manufacture it into cloth, and sell it in America at a bargain price. Moreover, the well-established British companies could engage in cutthroat competition by slashing prices sharply to drive the new American firms out of business. The most important British advantage was cheap labor. Britain had a larger population—about 12.6 million in 1810 compared with 7.3 million Americans—and thousands of landless laborers who were willing to take low-paying factory jobs.

To offset these British advantages American entrepreneurs won assistance from the federal government. In 1816 Congress passed a tariff that protected manufacturers from low-cost imports of cotton cloth. In 1824 a new tariff levied a tax of 35 percent on imported iron products, higher-grade woolen and cotton textiles, and various agricultural products, and the rate rose to 50 percent in 1828. But in 1833, under pressure from southern planters, western farmers, and urban consumers—who wanted inexpensive imports—Congress began to reduce tariffs (see Chapter 11) and some American textile firms went bankrupt.

American producers used two other strategies to compete with their British rivals. First, they improved on British technology. In 1811 Francis Cabot Lowell, a wealthy Boston merchant, toured British textile mills. A charming young man, he flattered his hosts by asking many questions and secretly made detailed drawings of power machinery. Paul Moody, an experienced American mechanic, then copied the machines and made improvements. In 1814 Lowell joined with merchants Nathan Appleton and Patrick Tracy Jackson to form the Boston Manufacturing Company. Raising the staggering sum of $400,000, they built a textile plant on the Charles River in Waltham, Massachusetts. The Waltham factory was the first in America to perform all the operations of cloth making under one roof. Thanks to Moody's improvements, Waltham's power looms operated at higher speeds than British looms and needed fewer workers.

The second American strategy was to find less expensive workers. In the 1820s the Boston Manufacturing Company pioneered a labor system that became known as the "Waltham plan." The company recruited thousands of farm girls and women to work as textile operatives and provided them with boardinghouses and cultural activities such as evening lectures. To reassure anxious parents, the mill owners enforced strict curfews, prohibited alcoholic beverages, and required regular church attendance. At Lowell (1822), Chicopee (1823), and other sites in Massachusetts and New Hampshire, the company built new cotton factories based on the Waltham plan; other Boston-owned firms quickly followed suit.

By the early 1830s more than 40,000 New England women worked in textile mills primarily because (an observer noted) the wages were "more than could be obtained by the hitherto ordinary occupation of housework." Lucy Larcom became a textile operative at the age of eleven so that she would not be "a trouble or burden or expense" to her widowed mother. Other women operatives used their wages to pay off their fathers' farm mortgages, send their brothers to school, or accumulate a dowry for themselves. A few just had a good time. Susan Brown, a Lowell weaver,

Mill Girl, c. 1850

This fine daguerreotype (an early form of photography) shows a neatly dressed textile worker about twelve years old. The harsh working conditions in the mill have taken a toll on her spirit and body: the young girl's eyes and mouth show little joy or life and her hands are rough and swollen. She probably worked either as a knotter, tying broken threads on spinning jennies, or a warper, straightening out the strands of cotton or wool as they entered the loom. Jack Naylor Collection.

spent half of her earnings on food and lodging and the rest on plays, concerts, lectures, and a two-day excursion to Boston. Like most textile operatives, Brown soon tired of the monotony and never-ending rigor of factory labor—twelve hours a day, six days a week. After eight months she quit, lived at home for a spell, and then moved to another mill. Whatever the hardships, waged work gave young women a new sense of freedom and autonomy. "Don't I feel independent!" a mill worker wrote to her sister. "The thought that I am living on no one is a happy one indeed to me" (see American Voices, "Early Days at Lowell," p. 298).

The owners of the Boston Manufacturing Company were even happier. By combining improved technology, female labor, and tariff protection, they could undersell their British rivals. Their textiles were also cheaper than those manufactured in New York and Pennsylvania, where farmworkers were better paid than in New England and textile wages consequently were higher. Manufacturers in those states remained in business by using advanced technology to produce higher-quality cloth. Even Thomas Jefferson, the great champion of yeoman farming, was impressed. "Our manufacturers are now very nearly on a footing with those of England," he noted in 1825.

American Mechanics and Technological Innovation

By the 1820s American-born craftsmen had replaced British immigrants at the cutting edge of technological innovation. Although few of these mechanics had a formal education, they now claimed respect as "men professing an ingenious art." In 1837 one such inventor, Richard Garsed, fashioned improvements that nearly doubled the speed of the power looms in his father's factory. By 1846 Garsed had patented a cam and harness device that allowed machines to weave fabrics such as damask (which contains elaborate designs).

In the Philadelphia region the most important inventors came from the remarkable Sellars family. Samuel Sellars Jr. invented a machine for twisting worsted woolen yarn. His son John devised more efficient ways of using waterpower to run the family's sawmills and built a machine to weave wire sieves. John's sons and grandsons built machine shops that turned out riveted leather fire hoses, paper-making equipment, and eventually locomotives. In 1824 the Sellars family and other mechanics founded the Franklin Institute in Philadelphia. Named after Benjamin Franklin, whom the mechanics admired for his scientific accomplishments and idealization of hard work, the Franklin Institute published a journal; provided high-school-level instruction in mechanics, chemistry, mathematics, and mechanical drawing; and organized annual fairs to exhibit new products. Craftsmen in Ohio and other states soon established their own mechanics' institutes, which disseminated technical knowledge and encouraged innovation. Around 1820 the United States Patent Office issued about two hundred patents on new inventions each year, mostly to gentlemen and merchants. By 1860 it was awarding four thousand patents annually, mostly to mechanics from modest backgrounds.

Early Days at Lowell

LUCY LARCOM

*L*ucy Larcom (1824–1893) went to work in a textile mill in Lowell, Massachusetts, when she was eleven years old and remained there for a decade. She then migrated to Illinois with her sisters and a great tide of other New Englanders. In later life Larcom became a teacher and a writer; in her autobiography she described the contradictory impact of industrial labor— confining and yet liberating—on the lives of young women from farms and rural villages.

I never cared much for machinery. The buzzing and hissing and whizzing of pulleys and rollers and spindles and flyers around me often grew tiresome. I could not see into their complications, or feel interested in them. But in a room below us we were sometimes allowed to peer in through a sort of blind door at the great waterwheel that carried the works of the whole mill. It was so huge we could only watch a few of its spokes at a time, and part of its dripping rim, moving with a slow, measured strength through the darkness that shut it in. It impressed me with something of the awe which comes to us in thinking of the great Power which keeps the mechanism of the universe in motion. . . .

We did not call ourselves ladies. We did not forget that we were working girls, wearing coarse aprons suitable to our work, and that there was some danger of our becoming drudges. I know that sometimes the confinement of the mill became very wearisome to me. In the sweet June weather I would lean far out of the window, and try not to hear the unceasing clash of sound inside. Looking away to the hills, my whole stifled being would cry out

Oh, that I had wings!

Still I was there from choice, and

The prison unto which we doom
ourselves,
No prison is.

I regard it as one of the privileges of my youth that I was permitted to grow up among these active, interesting girls, whose lives were not mere echoes of other lives, but had principle and purpose distinctly their own. Their vigor of character was a natural development. The New Hampshire girls who came to Lowell were descendants of the sturdy backwoodsmen who settled that State scarcely a hundred years before. Their grandmothers had suffered the hardships of frontier life. . . . Those young women did justice to their inheritance. They were earnest and capable; ready to undertake anything that was worth doing. My dreamy, indolent nature was shamed into activity among them. They gave me a larger, firmer ideal of womanhood. . . .

Country girls were naturally independent, and the feeling that at this new work the few hours they had of every-day leisure were entirely their own was a satisfaction to them. They preferred it to going out as "hired help." It was like a young man's pleasure in entering upon business for himself. Girls had never tried that experiment before, and they liked it. It brought out in them a dormant strength of character which the world did not previously see.

SOURCE: Lucy Larcom, *A New England Girlhood* (Boston: Houghton Mifflin, 1889), 153–55, 181–83, 196–200.

American craftsmen facilitated the rapid spread of the Industrial Revolution by pioneering the development of machine tools—machines for making other machines. Mechanics in the textile industry invented lathes, planers, and boring machines that turned out standardized parts for new spinning jennies and weaving looms. Moreover, the new jennies and looms were precise enough in design and construction to operate at higher speeds than British equipment.

Technological innovation swept through the rest of American manufacturing. In 1832 the mechanics employed by Samuel W. Collins in his Connecticut ax-making company built a vastly improved die-forging machine—a device that pressed and hammered hot metal into dies, or cutting forms. Using this machine, a worker could now make three hundred ax heads a day, as opposed to twelve using the old methods. In Richmond, Virginia, Welsh- and American-born mechanics made similar technical advances at the Tredegar Iron Works. The firearms industry witnessed major innovations. To produce thousands of guns for the federal government, Eli Whitney and his coworkers in Connecticut developed machine tools that produced interchangeable, precision-crafted parts. After Whitney's death his partner, John H. Hall, an engineer at the federal armory at Harpers Ferry, Virginia, built lathes to fashion gun stocks and an array of machine tools to work metal: turret lathes, milling machines, and precision grinders. Soon many manufacturers were using these machine tools to produce complicated manufacturing equipment with great speed, at low cost, and in large quantities.

With this expansion in the availability of machines, the American Industrial Revolution came of age. The sheer volume of output caused some products—Remington rifles, Singer sewing machines, and Yale locks—to become household names in the United States and abroad. After showing their machine-tooled goods at the Crystal Palace Exhibition in London in 1851 (the first major international display of industrial goods), Remington, Singer, and other American businesses built factories in Great Britain and soon dominated many European markets.

Wage Workers and the Labor Movement

As the Industrial Revolution gathered momentum, it changed the nature of work and of workers' lives. Each decade, more and more Americans took jobs as wage-earning workers who had little security of employment or control over their working conditions.

Some wageworkers labored as journeymen in one of the traditional artisan crafts. These carpenters, stonecutters, masons, and cabinetmakers had specialized skills and a strong sense of craft identity. Consequently, they were able to form unions and bargain with their master-artisan employers. The journeymen's main concern was the increasing length of the workday, which kept them from their families and from educational opportunities. During the eighteenth century the workday in the building trades had averaged about twelve hours, including breaks for meals. By the 1820s masters were demanding a longer day during the summer, when it stayed light longer, while paying journeymen the old daily rate. In response, 600 carpenters in Boston went on strike in 1825, demanding a ten-hour workday, 6 A.M. to 6 P.M., with an hour each for breakfast and lunch. Although the Boston protest failed, in 1827 journeymen carpenters in Philadelphia won a similar strike and then joined the Mechanics' Union of Trade Associations. This citywide organization of fifty unions and 10,000 Philadelphia wageworkers demanded "a just balance of power . . . between all the various classes." To secure this goal, in 1828 the Philadelphia artisans founded the Working Men's Party, which campaigned for the abolition of banks, equal taxation, and a universal system of public education. By the mid-1830s building-trades workers had won a ten-hour workday from many employers and from the federal government at the Philadelphia navy yard.

Artisans whose occupations were threatened by industrialization were less successful. As aggressive entrepreneurs and machine technology changed the nature of production, shoemakers, hatters, printers, furniture makers, and weavers faced declining incomes, unemployment, and loss of status. To avoid the regimentation of factory work some artisans in these trades moved to small towns or set up specialized shops. In New York City, 800 highly skilled cabinetmakers owned small shops that made fashionable or custom-made furniture. In status and income they outranked a much larger group of 3,200 semitrained workers—derogatively called "botches"—who labored for wages in large factories making cheap, mass-produced tables and chairs. The new industrial system had divided the traditional artisan class into two groups: self-employed craftsmen and wage-earning workers.

In many industries wage earners banded together to form unions and bargain for better pay and working conditions. However, under English and American common law, such organizations were illegal—"a government unto themselves," in the words of a Philadelphia judge—because they interfered with an employer's authority over his "servant" and prevented other workers from hiring out for whatever wages they wished. Despite such legal obstacles, unions sprang up. In 1830 in Lynn, Massachusetts, journeymen shoemakers founded a Mutual Benefit Society, which quickly spread to other shoemaking centers. "The division of society into the producing and nonproducing classes," the journeymen explained, had made workers like themselves into a mere "commodity" whose labor could be bought and sold without regard for their welfare. As another group of workers put it, "The capitalist has no other interest in us, than to get as much labor out of us as possible. We are hired men, and hired men, like hired horses, have no souls." In 1834 local unions from Boston to Philadelphia formed the National Trades' Union, the first regional union of different trades.

Union leaders criticized the new industrial order by articulating an artisan-republican ideology that celebrated the labor and autonomy of working people. Pointing out that wage earners were becoming "slaves to a monied aristocracy," they condemned the new outwork and factory systems in which "capital and labor stand opposed." To restore a just society in which workers could "live as comfortably as others," they proposed a **labor theory of value**. This theory stated that the price of a good should reflect the labor required to make it and that most of the money from its sale should go to the producer (and not merchants and factory owners). Appealing to the spirit of the American Revolution, which had destroyed the aristocracy of birth, they called for a new revolution to destroy the aristocracy of capital. Armed with this artisan-republican ideology, in 1836 union men organized nearly fifty strikes for higher wages.

Women textile operatives were equally active. Competition in the cotton textile industry was fierce because the output of textiles grew faster than demand and prices fell. As profits declined, employers reduced workers' wages and imposed more stringent work rules. In 1828 women mill workers in Dover, New Hampshire, struck against new rules and won some relief; six years later more than 800 Dover women walked out to protest wage cuts. In Lowell, Massachusetts, 2,000 women operatives backed a strike by withdrawing their savings from an employer-owned bank. "One of the leaders mounted a pump," the *Boston Transcript* reported, "and made a flaming . . . speech on the rights of women and the iniquities of the 'monied aristocracy.'" When conditions did not improve, young New England women refused to enter the mills, and impoverished Irish (and later French Canadian) immigrants took their places.

By the 1850s workers faced the threat of unemployment. As machines produced more goods, the supply of manufactures exceeded the demand for them and prompted employers to lay off workers. One episode of overproduction preceded the Panic of 1857—a financial crisis sparked by speculative investments in railroads that went bankrupt—and resulted in a major recession. Unemployment rose to 10 percent, reminding Americans of the social costs of the new—and otherwise very successful—system of industrial production.

The Market Revolution

As American factories and farms turned out more goods, merchants and legislators created faster and cheaper ways to get those products to consumers. Beginning in the 1820s they constructed a massive system of canals and roads that linked the Atlantic coast states with one another and with the new states in the trans-Appalachian West. This transportation system set in motion both a **Market Revolution** and a great migration of people. By 1860 nearly one-third of the nation's citizens lived in the Midwest (the five states carved out of the Northwest Territory—Ohio, Indiana, Illinois, Michigan, and Wisconsin—along with Missouri, Iowa, and Minnesota), where they created a complex society and economy that increasingly resembled that of the Northeast.

Migration to the Southwest and the Midwest

As vast numbers of men and women migrated to the West, they abandoned farms and homes in the countryside of the Carolinas, Vermont, and New Hampshire.

Some migrant families sought enough land to settle their children on nearby farms and re-create traditional rural communities. Others were more entrepreneurial and hoped for greater profits from the fertile soil of the western territories. By 1840 about 5 million people lived west of the Appalachians.

As in the past the new pioneers migrated in three great streams. In the South plantation owners met the voracious demand for raw cotton by expanding production into Louisiana, Mississippi, and Alabama. "The Alabama Feaver rages here with great violence," a North Carolina planter remarked, "and has carried off vast numbers of our Citizens." Subsequently, planters pushed on to Missouri (admitted in 1821) and Arkansas (1836).

Small-scale farmers from the Upper South, especially Virginia and Kentucky, formed another migrant stream as they crossed the Ohio River into the Northwest Territory. Some of these settlers were fleeing planter-dominated slave states. In a free community, thought Peter Cartwright, a Methodist lay preacher from southwestern Kentucky, "I would be entirely clear of the evil of slavery . . . [and] could raise my children to work where work was not thought a degradation." These southerners introduced corn and hog farming into Ohio, Indiana, and Illinois.

A third throng of migrants poured out of the overcrowded communities of New England. Thousands of settlers flowed first into upstate New York and then into the fertile farmlands of the Great Lakes basin, where they set up wheat farms in northern Ohio, northern Illinois, Michigan (admitted in 1837), Iowa (1846), and Wisconsin (1848) (Map 10.1).

To meet the demand for cheap farmsteads, in 1820 Congress reduced the price of federal land from $2.00 an acre to $1.25—just enough to cover the cost of the survey and sale. For $100 a farmer could buy eighty acres, the minimum required under federal law. By 1860 the population center of American society had shifted significantly to the west.

The Transportation Revolution Forges Regional Ties

To enhance the "common wealth" of their citizens, the federal and state governments chartered private companies to build toll-charging turnpikes in well-populated areas and subsidized road construction in the West. The most significant feat was the National Road, which started in Cumberland, Maryland, passed Wheeling (then in Virginia) in 1818, crossed the Ohio River in 1833, and reached Vandalia, Illinois, in 1839. The National Road and other interregional highways carried migrants and their heavily loaded wagons to the West and herds of livestock destined for eastern markets. However, such long-distance road travel was slow and expensive.

To carry wheat, corn, and manufactured goods to far-flung markets, Americans developed a water-borne transportation system of unprecedented size, complexity, and cost. When the New York legislature approved the building of the Erie Canal in 1817, no artificial waterway in the United States was longer than 28 miles—a reflection of the huge capital cost and the lack of American engineering expertise.

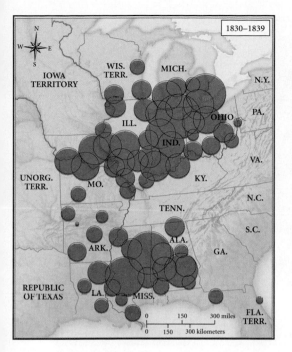
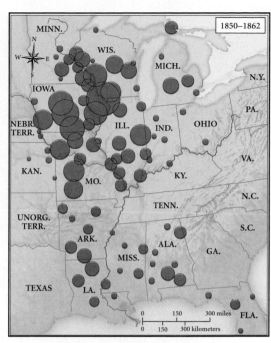

MAP 10.1 Western Land Sales, 1830–1839 and 1850–1862

The federal government set up offices to sell farmsteads to western settlers. During the 1830s the offices sold huge amounts of land in the corn and wheat belt of the Old Northwest (Ohio, Indiana, Illinois, and Michigan) and the cotton belt of the Old Southwest (especially Alabama and Mississippi). By the 1850s most government land sales were in the upper Mississippi River Valley (particularly Iowa and Wisconsin). Each circle centers on a government land office and depicts the relative amount of land sold at that office.

The New York project had three things in its favor: the vigorous support of New York City merchants, who wanted access to western markets; the backing of New York's governor, De Witt Clinton, who persuaded the legislature to finance the waterway from tax revenues, tolls, and bond sales to foreign investors; and the relative gentleness of the terrain west of Albany. Even so, the task was enormous. Workers—many of them Irish immigrants—had to dig out millions of cubic yards of soil, quarry thousands of tons of rock to build the huge locks that raised and lowered boats, and construct vast reservoirs to ensure a steady supply of water.

The first great engineering project in American history, the Erie Canal altered the ecology and the economy of an entire region. As towns and farming communities sprang up along the waterway, residents cut down millions of trees to provide wood for building, hemlock bark for tanning leather, and land for growing wheat and corn. Cows and sheep foraged on pastureland once occupied by forests, deer, and bears, and spring rains caused massive erosion of the denuded landscape. As one traveler noted, "the hills had been stripped of their timber so as to present their huge, rocky projections."

Building the Erie Canal

The success of the Erie Canal prompted the construction by 1860 of a vast canal system that was the precursor of the national railroad network of the late nineteenth century and the interstate highway system of the late twentieth century. Tens of thousands of workers—many of them Irish immigrants and free blacks—dug out thousands of miles of canals by hand and, with the aid of the simple hoists shown here, built hundreds of stone locks. The unknown artist who sketched this scene was more interested in the scale of the project than in the personalities of the faceless laborers who undertook this dangerous work. In the marshes near Syracuse, New York, a thousand workers fell ill with fever and many died.

Miriam and Ira D. Wallach Division of Art, Prints and Photographs. The New York Public Library. Astor, Lenox and Tilden Foundations.

The Erie Canal was an instant success. The first section, a stretch of 75 miles, opened in 1819 and immediately generated enough revenue to repay its cost. When the canal was completed in 1825, a 40-foot-wide ribbon of water stretched 364 miles from the Lake Erie port of Buffalo to Albany, where it joined the Hudson River for a 150-mile trip to New York City. After a trip on the canal, the novelist Nathaniel Hawthorne suggested that its water "must be the most fertilizing of all fluids, for it causes towns with their masses of brick and stone, their churches and theaters, their business and hubbub, their luxury and refinement, their gay dames and polished citizens, to spring up."

The Erie Canal brought prosperity to central and western New York by carrying wheat and meat to eastern cities and foreign markets. One-hundred-ton freight barges pulled by two horses moved along the canal at a steady 30 miles a day, cutting transportation costs and greatly accelerating the flow of goods. In 1818 the mills in Rochester had processed 26,000 barrels of flour; ten years later their output soared to 200,000 barrels and in 1840 to 500,000 barrels. Northeastern manufacturers used the canal to ship clothing, boots, and agricultural equipment to farm families throughout the Great Lakes basin and the Ohio Valley. In payment, the farmers sent grain, cattle, and hogs as well as raw materials (such as leather, wool, and hemp) to the East.

The spectacular benefits of the Erie Canal prompted a national canal boom. Civic and business leaders in Philadelphia and Baltimore proposed waterways to link their cities to the West. Copying New York's fiscal innovations, they persuaded their state governments to invest directly in canal companies or force state-chartered banks to do so. They also won state guarantees for canal bonds to encourage British and Dutch investors to buy them. Indeed, foreign investors provided almost three-quarters of the $400 million invested in canals by 1840. These waterways connected the Midwest with the great port cities of New York, Philadelphia, and Baltimore (via the Erie, Pennsylvania, and Chesapeake and Ohio Canals) and New Orleans (via the Ohio and Mississippi Rivers) (Map 10.2).

The steamboat, another product of the industrial age, ensured the success of the western transportation system. The engineer-inventor Robert Fulton had built the first American steamboat, the *Clermont,* which he navigated up the Hudson River in 1807. However, the first steamboats could not navigate shallow western rivers. During the 1820s engineers broadened the hulls of these boats, thereby enlarging their cargo capacity and giving them a shallower draft. The improved steamboats cut in half the cost of upstream river transport and, along with the canals, dramatically increased the flow of goods, people, and news into the interior. In 1830 a traveler or a letter from New York could go by water to Buffalo or Pittsburgh in less than a week and to Detroit or St. Louis in two weeks. Thirty years earlier the same journeys had taken twice as long.

The national government played a key role in the creation of this interregional system of transportation and communication. Following the passage of the Post Office Act of 1792, the mail network grew rapidly—to eight hundred post offices by 1800 and more than eight thousand by 1830—and safely carried thousands of letters and millions of dollars of banknotes from one end of the country to the other. The Supreme Court, headed by John Marshall, likewise encouraged interstate trade by striking down state restrictions on commerce. In the crucial case of *Gibbons v. Ogden* (1824) the Court voided a New York law that created a monopoly on steamboat travel into New York City and established the paramount authority of the federal government over interstate commerce (see Chapter 8). This decision meant that no local or state monopolies—or tariffs—would impede the flow of goods, services, and news across the nation.

Another product of industrial technology—the railroad—linked the Northeast and the Midwest. In 1852 canals carried twice the tonnage transported by railroads; within a decade, track mileage had increased dramatically and railroads became the main carriers of freight. Serviced by a vast network of locomotive and

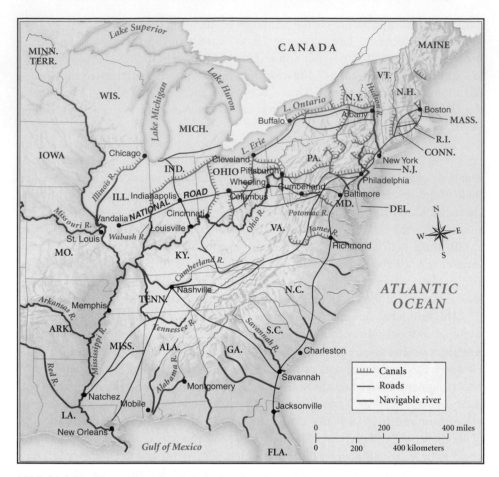

MAP 10.2 The Transportation Revolution: Roads and Canals, 1820–1850

By 1850 the United States had an efficient transportation system with three distinct parts. One system, composed of short canals and navigable rivers, carried cotton, tobacco, and other products from the up-country of the southern seaboard states into the Atlantic commercial system. A second system, centered on the Erie, Chesapeake and Ohio, and Pennsylvania Mainline Canals, linked the major seaport cities of the Northeast to the vast trans-Appalachian region. Finally, a set of regional canals in the Old Northwest connected most of the Great Lakes region to the Ohio and Mississippi Rivers and New Orleans.

FOR MORE HELP ANALYZING THIS MAP, see the Online Study Guide at **bedfordstmartins.com/henrettaconcise**.

freight-car repair shops, the Erie Railroad, the Pennsylvania Railroad, and other long-distance carriers connected the Atlantic ports—New York, Philadelphia, and Boston—with the Great Lakes cities of Cleveland and Chicago. As the railroad boom of the 1850s extended lines into the countryside and lowered the cost of

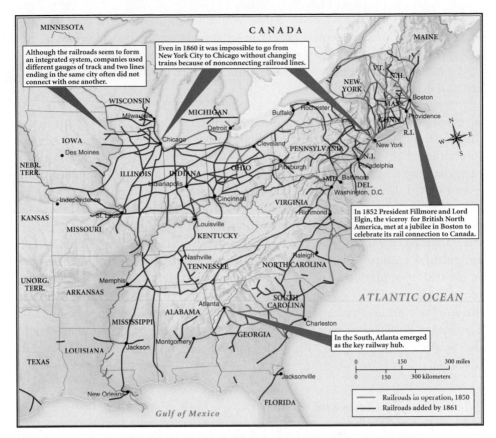

Although the railroads seem to form an integrated system, companies used different gauges of track and two lines ending in the same city often did not connect with one another.

Even in 1860 it was impossible to go from New York City to Chicago without changing trains because of nonconnecting railroad lines.

In 1852 President Fillmore and Lord Elgin, the viceroy for British North America, met at a jubilee in Boston to celebrate its rail connection to Canada.

In the South, Atlanta emerged as the key railway hub.

Railroads in operation, 1850
Railroads added by 1861

MAP 10.3 Railroads of the North and South, 1850–1860

In the decade before the Civil War, entrepreneurs in the Northeast and the Midwest laid thousands of miles of new railroad lines, which provided those regions with extensive and dense transportation systems that stimulated economic development. The South built a much simpler system. In all regions, railroad companies used different track gauges, which hindered the efficient flow of traffic.

shipping grain to market, settlers established 250,000 new farms (covering 19 million acres) on the prairie lands of the midwestern states (Map 10.3).

Many of the first migrants to the Midwest came from New England and relied on manufactured goods made in Britain or in the Northeast. They bought high-quality shovels and spades fabricated at the Delaware Iron Works, axes forged in Connecticut factories, and steel horseshoes manufactured in Troy, New York. By the 1830s midwestern entrepreneurs were producing these and other goods. As a blacksmith in Grand Detour, Illinois, John Deere made his first steel plow out of old saws in 1837; ten years later he opened a factory in Moline, Illinois, that used **mass-production** techniques. Deere's steel plows were stronger than the cast-iron models developed earlier in New York by Jethro Wood. Other midwestern companies—McCormick and Hussey—mass-produced self-raking reapers that allowed a farmer to harvest twelve acres of grain a day (rather than the two or three acres he could cut by hand) and vastly increased the amount of wheat available for export to eastern and European markets.

Extraregional trade also linked southern planters to northeastern textile plants and foreign markets. This commerce bolstered the wealth of the South but did not transform its economic and social order. Southern investors continued to commit their capital to land and slaves, which yielded high profits and also provided impressive increases in output. By the 1840s the South produced more than two-thirds of the world's cotton and accounted for almost two-thirds of American exports. However, except in Richmond, Virginia, and a few other places, planters did not invest their cotton profits in local manufacturing industries. Lacking cities, factories, and highly trained workers, the South remained an agricultural economy that provided high living standards only to the 25 percent of the white population who owned plantations and slaves. By 1860 the southern economy generated an average annual per capita income of $103, while the more productive economic system of the Northeast created an average income of $141. The national system of commerce left unchanged the agricultural character of the South even as it promoted a diversified economy in the Northeast and Midwest.

The Growth of Cities and Towns

The expansion of industry and trade led to a dramatic increase in the American urban population. In 1820 there were only 58 towns with more than 2,500 inhabitants; by 1840 there were 126 urban centers, located mostly in the Northeast and Midwest. During those two decades the total number of city dwellers grew fourfold, from 443,000 to 1,844,000.

The most rapid growth occurred in the new industrial towns that sprang up along the fall line (the point at which rivers began a rapid descent to the coastal plain). In 1822 the Boston Manufacturing Company built a complex of mills in the sleepy Merrimack River village of East Chelmsford, Massachusetts, and quickly transformed it into the bustling textile factory town of Lowell. Hartford, Connecticut; Trenton, New Jersey; and Wilmington, Delaware, also became urban centers, as mill owners exploited the waterpower of their rivers and recruited workers from the countryside.

Western commercial cities such as New Orleans, Pittsburgh, Cincinnati, and Louisville grew almost as rapidly. These cities expanded because of their location at points where goods were transferred from one mode of transport, such as canal boats or farmers' wagons, to another, such as steamboats or sailing vessels. As the midwestern population grew during the 1830s and 1840s, St. Louis and Detroit also emerged as dynamic centers of commerce. Their merchants and bankers developed the marketing, provisioning, and financial services that were essential to farmers and small-town merchants in the surrounding countryside.

Within a few decades these midwestern commercial hubs—joined by Buffalo, Cleveland, and Chicago—became manufacturing centers as well. Maximizing these cities' locations as key junctions for railroad lines and steamboats, entrepreneurs built docks, warehouses, flour mills, and packing plants and provided work for hundreds of artisans and factory laborers. In 1846 Cyrus McCormick moved his reaper factory from western Virginia to Chicago to be closer to his midwestern customers. St. Louis and Chicago were the fastest-growing boom towns and by 1860 had become the nation's third and fourth largest cities, respectively, after New York and Philadelphia.

The old Atlantic seaports—Boston, Philadelphia, Baltimore, Charleston, and especially New York City—remained important for their foreign commerce and, increasingly, as centers of finance and manufacturing. The New York metropolis grew at a phenomenal rate; between 1820 and 1860 its population quadrupled to more than 800,000 as tens of thousands of German and Irish immigrants poured into the city. Drawing on the abundant supply of labor, New York became a center of small-scale manufacturing and the ready-made clothing industry, which relied on the labor of thousands of low-paid seamstresses. "The wholesale clothing establishments are . . . absorbing the business of the country," a "Country Tailor" complained to the New York *Tribune*, "casting many an honest and hardworking man out of employment [and allowing] . . . the large cities to swallow up the small towns."

New York's growth stemmed primarily from its dominant position in foreign and domestic trade. It had the best harbor in the United States and, thanks to the Erie Canal, was the best gateway to the interior for manufactures and the best outlet for shipments of western grain. Exploiting the city's prime location, in 1818 four Quaker merchants founded the Black Ball Line, which carried cargo, people, and mail on a regular schedule between New York and the European ports of Liverpool, London, and Le Havre. New York merchants likewise dominated trade with the newly independent Latin American nations of Brazil, Peru, and Venezuela. New York–based traders took over the cotton trade by offering finance, insurance, and shipping to export merchants in southern ports. By 1840 the port of New York handled almost two-thirds of foreign imports into the United States, almost half of all foreign trade, and much of the immigrant traffic.

Changes in the Social Structure

The Industrial and Market Revolutions improved the material lives of many Americans by enabling them to live in larger houses, cook on iron stoves, and wear better-made clothes. But the new economic order created distinct social classes: a wealthy industrial and commercial elite, a substantial urban middle class, and a mass of propertyless wage earners. By creating a class-divided society, industrialization posed a momentous challenge to American republican ideals.

The Business Elite

Before industrialization, white Americans were members of various ranks, with "notable" families ruling over the "lower orders." However, in rural society the different ranks shared a common culture: gentlemen farmers talked easily with yeomen about crop yields, while their wives conversed about the art of quilting. In the South humble tenants and aristocratic slave owners shared the same amusements: gambling, cockfighting, and horse racing. Rich and poor attended the same Quaker meetinghouse or Presbyterian church. "Almost everyone eats, drinks, and dresses in the same way," a European visitor to Hartford, Connecticut, reported in 1798, "and one can see the most obvious inequality only in the dwellings."

The Industrial Revolution shattered this traditional order and created a fragmented society composed of distinct regions, classes, and cultures. Thus, the new economic system pulled many Americans into large cities, thereby accentuating the differences between rural and urban life. Moreover, it made a few city residents—the business elite of merchants, manufacturers, bankers, and landlords—very rich. In 1800 the top 10 percent of the nation's families owned about 40 percent of the wealth; by 1860 the wealthiest 10 percent owned nearly 70 percent. In large cities—New York, Chicago, Baltimore, New Orleans—the richest 1 percent of the population held more than 40 percent of all tangible property—such as land and buildings—and an even higher share of intangible property—such as stocks and bonds.

Government tax policies facilitated this accumulation of wealth. The U.S. Treasury raised most of its revenue from tariffs—taxes on imported goods such as textiles that were purchased mostly by ordinary citizens. State and local governments also favored the wealthier classes. They usually taxed real estate (farms, city lots, and buildings) and tangible personal property (such as furniture, tools, and machinery) but almost never taxed the stocks and bonds owned by the rich or the inheritances they passed on to their children.

Cities that were once relatively homogenous took on an increasingly fragmented character. Over time the wealthiest families consciously set themselves apart from the rest of the population. They dressed in well-tailored clothes, rode in fancy carriages, and lived in expensively furnished houses tended by butlers, cooks, and other servants. The women no longer socialized with those of lesser wealth, and the men no longer labored side by side with their journeymen. Instead, they became managers and directors and used trusted subordinates to issue orders to hundreds of factory operatives. Increasingly merchants, manufacturers, and bankers chose to live in separate residential areas, often at the edge of the city. The desire for greater privacy by privileged families and the massive flow of immigrants into other districts created cities that were divided geographically along the lines of class, race, and ethnicity.

The Middle Class

Standing between wealthy owners at one end of the urban social spectrum and non-propertied wage earners at the other was a growing middle class—the product of the Market Revolution. As a Boston printer explained, the bulk of the "middling class" was made up of "the farmers, the mechanics, the manufacturers, the traders, who carry on professionally the ordinary operations of buying, selling, and exchanging merchandize." Other members of the middle class came from various professional groups—building contractors, lawyers, and surveyors—who suddenly found their services in great demand and financially profitable. Middle-class business owners, employees, and professionals were most numerous in the Northeast, where in the 1840s they numbered about 30 percent of the population, but they could be found even in the agrarian South. In 1854 in the boom town of Oglethorpe, Georgia (population 2,500), there were no fewer than eighty "business houses" and eight hotels.

The growing size, wealth, and cultural influence of the middle class stemmed from a dramatic rise in urban prosperity. Between 1830 and the Panic of 1857, the per capita income of Americans increased by about 2.5 percent a year, a remarkable rate never since matched. This surge in income, along with the availability of inexpensive mass-produced goods, facilitated the creation of a distinct middle-class, urban culture. Middle-class husbands earned enough to support their families and saved about 15 percent of their income, which they used to buy a well-built house in a "respectable part of town." They purchased handsome clothes and drove about town in smart carriages. Relieved from the burden of labor, their wives became purveyors of culture as they bought books and pianos as well as commodious furniture for their front parlors. Rather than hiring servants to perform menial tasks, middle-class families turned to the new industrial technology. They outfitted their residences with furnaces that heated water for bathing and for radiators that warmed entire rooms; cooking stoves with ovens; and treadle-operated sewing machines. Urban families could keep their perishable food in iceboxes, which ice-company wagons filled periodically, and buy many varieties of packaged goods. As early as 1825 the Underwood Company of Boston was marketing well-preserved Atlantic salmon in jars.

If material comfort was one distinguishing mark of the middle class, moral and mental discipline was another. To pass on their status to their children, successful parents usually provided them with a high school education (in an era when most white children received only five years of schooling). Ambitious parents were equally concerned with their children's character and stressed discipline, morality, and hard work. Many American Protestants had long believed that diligent work in an earthly "calling" was a duty owed to God. Now the business elite and the middle class gave this idea a secular twist. They celebrated work as the key to a higher standard of living for the nation and social mobility for the individual.

Middle-Class Family Life, 1836

The family of Azariah Caverly boasted many of the amenities of middle-class life—handsome clothes, finely decorated furniture, and a striking floor covering. Underlining the social conventions of the time, the husband and his son hold a newspaper and a square, symbolizing the worlds of commerce and industry, while the wife and her daughter are pictured next to a Bible, indicating their domestic and moral vocations. New York State Historical Association, Cooperstown, NY.

FOR MORE HELP ANALYZING THIS IMAGE, see the Online Study Guide at **bedfordstmartins.com/henrettaconcise**.

Benjamin Franklin gave classical expression to the secular work ethic in his *Autobiography*, which was published in full in 1818 and immediately found a huge audience. Heeding Franklin's suggestion that an industrious man would become a rich one, tens of thousands of young American men worked hard, saved their money, adopted temperate habits, and practiced honesty in their business dealings. Countless magazines, children's books, self-help manuals, and novels taught the same lessons. The ideal of the **"self-made man"** became a central theme of American popular culture. Just as a rural-producer ethic had united the social ranks in pre-1800 America, this new goal of personal achievement tied together the upper and middle classes of the new industrializing society. Knowing that many affluent families had risen from modest beginnings, middle-class men and women took them as models and shunned the rapidly increasing numbers of working families who owned nothing and struggled just to survive.

Urban Workers and the Poor

As thoughtful business leaders surveyed their society, they concluded that the old yeoman ideal of independent producers no longer seemed possible. "Entire independence ought not to be wished for," Ithamar A. Beard, the paymaster of the Hamilton Manufacturing Company, told a mechanics' association in 1827. "In large manufacturing towns, many more must fill subordinate stations and must be under the immediate direction and control of a master or superintendent, than in the farming towns."

Beard had a point. In 1840 all of the nation's slaves and about half of its native-born free workers were laboring for others rather than for themselves. The bottom 10 percent of the white wage earners consisted of casual workers—those hired on a short-term basis for the most arduous jobs. Poor women washed clothes, while their husbands and sons carried lumber and bricks for construction projects, loaded ships, and dug out dirt and stones to build canals. When they could find work, these men earned "their dollar *per diem*," an "Old Inhabitant" wrote to the *Baltimore American*, but he cautioned that those workers could never save enough "to pay rent, buy fire wood and eatables" when the harbor froze up. During business depressions they bore the brunt of unemployment, and even in the best of times their jobs were temporary and dangerous.

Other laborers had greater security of employment, but few were prospering. In Massachusetts in 1825 the daily wage of an unskilled worker was about two-thirds that of a mechanic; two decades later it was less than half as much. The 18,000 native-born and immigrant women who made men's clothing in New York City in the 1850s earned less than $80 a year. Such meager wages barely paid for food and rent, so many wage earners were unable to take advantage of the rapidly falling prices of manufactured goods. Only the most fortunate working-class families could afford to educate their children, buy an apprenticeship for their sons, or accumulate small dowries so that their daughters could marry men with better prospects. Most families sent their children out to work, and the death of a parent often threw the survivors into dire poverty. As a charity worker noted, "What can a bereaved widow do, with 5 or 6 little children, destitute of every means of support but what her own hands can furnish (which in a general way does not amount to more than 25 cents a day)."

Over time, their poverty forced these urban workers to move into dilapidated housing or undesirable neighborhoods. Single men and women lived in crowded boardinghouses, while families jammed themselves into tiny apartments in the basements and attics of small houses. As immigrants poured into the nation after 1840, urban populations soared and developers squeezed more and more dwellings and foul-smelling outhouses onto a single lot. Venturing into the slums of New York City in the 1850s, shocked state legislators found gaunt, shivering people with "wild ghastly faces" living amid "hideous squalor and deadly effluvia, the dim, undrained courts oozing with pollution, the dark, narrow stairways, decayed with age, reeking with filth, overrun with vermin."

Living in such distressing conditions, many wage earners turned to the dubious solace of alcohol. Beer and rum had long been standard fare in many American rituals: patriotic ceremonies, work breaks, barn raisings, and games. But during the 1820s the consumption of intoxicating beverages and alcoholism throughout the population reached new heights. Heavy drinking killed Daniel Tomkins, vice president under James Monroe, and undermined Henry Clay's bid for the presidency. It had an equally devastating impact on urban wage earners. While Methodist artisans and ambitious craft workers "swore off" liquor to protect their work skills, health, and finances, other workers began to drink heavily on the job—and not just during the traditional 11 A.M. and 4 P.M. "refreshers." As a baker recalled, "One man was stationed at the window to watch, while the rest drank." Long before the arrival of spirit-drinking Irish and beer-drinking German immigrants, there were grogshops on almost every block in working-class districts. These saloons became focal points of disorder. Unrestrained drinking by young men led to fistfights, brawls, and robberies; the urban police forces, consisting of low-paid watchmen and untrained constables, were unable to contain the lawlessness.

The Benevolent Empire

The disorder among native-born urban wage earners sparked concern among well-to-do Americans. Inspired by the religious ideal of benevolence, they created a number of organizations that historians refer to collectively as the **"Benevolent Empire."** During the 1820s Congregational and Presbyterian ministers united with like-minded merchants and their wives to launch a program of social regulation. Their purpose, announced leading Presbyterian minister Lyman Beecher, was to restore "the moral government of God." The reformers introduced new forms of moral discipline into their own lives and tried to infuse them into the lives of working people as well. They would regulate popular behavior—by persuasion if possible, by law if necessary.

Although the Benevolent Empire targeted age-old evils such as drunkenness, prostitution, and crime, its methods were new. Instead of relying on church sermons and moral suasion by community leaders, the reformers set out to institutionalize charity and systematically combat evil. They established large-scale organizations, such as the Prison Discipline Society and the American Society for the Promotion of Temperance, among many others. Each organization had a managing staff, a network of hundreds of chapters and thousands of volunteer members, and a newspaper.

Often working in concert, these benevolent groups set out to improve society. First, they encouraged people to lead well-disciplined lives by campaigning for temperance and regular habits. They persuaded local governments to ban carnivals of drink and dancing, such as Negro Election Day (mock festivities in which African Americans symbolically took over the government), which had been enjoyed by whites as well as blacks. Second, they devised new institutions to assist dependent people and control those whom they considered threats to society. Reformers provided homes of refuge for abandoned children and asylums for insane individuals, who previously had been confined by their families in attics and cellars. They also campaigned to end corporal punishment and to rehabilitate criminals in new penitentiaries designed to modify antisocial behavior.

Women were an important part of the Benevolent Empire. Since the 1790s upper-class women had sponsored charitable organizations such as the Society for the Relief of Poor Widows with Small Children, founded in New York by Isabella Graham, a devout Presbyterian widow. Her daughter Joanna Bethune set up other charitable institutions, including the Orphan Asylum Society and the Society for the Promotion of Industry, which found jobs for hundreds of poor women as spinners and seamstresses.

Some reformers believed that the greatest threat to the "moral government of God" was the decline of the traditional Sabbath. As commerce increased, merchants and storekeepers conducted business on Sundays and urban saloons provided drink and entertainment. To halt such activities, in 1828 Lyman Beecher and other ministers formed the General Union for Promoting the Observance of the Christian Sabbath. General Union chapters—replete with women's auxiliaries— sprang up from Maine to the Ohio Valley. To rally Christians to their cause, the General Union demanded repeal of a law Congress had enacted in 1810 allowing mail to be transported—though not delivered—on Sunday. Its members also boycotted shipping companies that did business on the Sabbath and campaigned for municipal laws forbidding games and festivals on the Lord's day.

The program of the Benevolent Empire aroused controversy. Workers who labored twelve or fourteen hours a day for six days a week refused to spend their one day of leisure in meditation and prayer. Shipping company managers demanded that the Erie Canal provide lockkeepers on Sundays and joined those Americans who argued that using laws to enforce a particular set of moral beliefs was "contrary to the free spirit of our institutions." When some evangelical reformers proposed to teach Christianity to slaves, many white southerners were outraged. Such popular resistance or indifference limited the success of the Benevolent Empire.

Revivalism and Reform

The Presbyterian minister Charles Grandison Finney found a new way to propagate religious values among Americans. Finney was not part of the traditional religious elite. Born into a poor farming family in Connecticut, he hoped to join the new middle class as a lawyer. But in 1823 Finney underwent an intense conversion experience and decided to become a minister. Beginning in towns along the Erie Canal, the young minister conducted emotional revival meetings that stressed conversion rather than instruction and discipline. Repudiating traditional Calvinist beliefs, he maintained that God would welcome any sinner who submitted to the Holy Spirit. Finney's ministry drew on—and greatly accelerated—the Second Great Awakening, the wave of Protestant revivalism that had begun after the Revolution (see Chapter 9).

Charles Finney, Evangelist (1792–1875)

When this portrait was painted in 1834, Finney was forty-two years old and at the height of his career as an evangelist. Handsome and charismatic, Finney had just led a series of enormously successful revivals in Rochester, New York, and other cities along the Erie Canal. In 1835 he established a theology department at the newly founded Oberlin College in Ohio, where he helped train a genera- tion of ministers and served as its president from 1851 to 1866.

Oberlin College Archives.

Finney's message that "God has made man a moral free agent" who could choose salvation was particularly attractive to members of the new middle class, who had already chosen to improve their material lives. But he became famous for converting those at the ends of the social spectrum: the haughty rich, who had placed themselves above God, and the abject poor, who seemed lost to drink and sloth. Finney celebrated their common fellowship in Christ and identified them spiritually with pious middle-class respectability.

Finney's most spectacular triumph came in 1830, when he moved his revivals from small towns to Rochester, New York, now a major milling and commercial city on the Erie Canal. Preaching every day for six months and promoting group prayer meetings in family homes, he won over the influential merchants and manufactur- ers of Rochester, who pledged to reform their lives and those of their workers. They promised to attend church, give up intoxicating beverages, and work hard. To encourage their employees to follow suit, wealthy businessmen founded a Free Presbyterian church—"free" because members did not have to pay for pew space. Other evangelical Protestants founded similar churches to serve transient canal la- borers, and pious businessmen set up a savings bank to encourage thrift among the working classes. Meanwhile, Finney's wife, Lydia, and other pious middle-class women carried the Christian message to the wives of the unconverted, set up Sunday schools for poor children, and formed the Female Charitable Society to as- sist the unemployed.

Finney's efforts to create a harmonious community of morally disciplined Christians were not completely successful. Skilled workers who belonged to strong crafts organizations—boot makers, carpenters, stonemasons, and boat builders—argued that they needed higher wages and schools more urgently than sermons and prayers. And Finney's revival seldom attracted poor people, especially the Irish Catholic immigrants who had recently begun arriving in Rochester and other northeastern cities and who hated Protestants as religious heretics and as their political oppressors in Ireland.

Ignoring this resistance, revivalists from New England to the Midwest copied Finney's evangelical message and techniques. In New York City, the wealthy silk merchants Arthur and Lewis Tappan founded a magazine, *The Christian Evangelist*, which promoted Finney's ideas. The revival swept through Pennsylvania, North Carolina, Tennessee, and Indiana where, a convert reported, "you could not go upon the street and hear any conversation, except upon religion." The success of the revival "has been so general and thorough," concluded a Presbyterian general assembly, "that the whole customs of society have changed."

The **temperance movement** proved to be the most effective arena for evangelical social reform. In 1832 evangelicals gained control of the American Temperance Society; soon the society boasted two thousand chapters and more than 200,000 members. The society employed the methods that had worked so well in the revivals—group confession and prayer, a focus on the family and the spiritual role of women, and sudden, emotional conversion—and took them into every northern town and southern village. On one day in New York City in 1841, more than 4,000 people took the temperance "pledge." All across the land, the consumption of spirits fell dramatically, from five gallons per person in 1830 to two gallons in 1845 (see American Voices, "The Vice of Intemperance," p. 318).

Evangelical reformers celebrated religion as the moral foundation of the American work ethic. Laziness and drinking could not be cured by following Benjamin Franklin's method of self-discipline, they argued; rather, people had to experience the profound change of heart achieved through religious conversion. This evangelical message fostered individual enterprise and moral discipline not only among middle-class Americans but also among many wage earners. Thus, religion and the ideology of social mobility served as powerful cement that held society together in the face of the disarray created by the market economy, industrial enterprise, and cultural diversity.

Immigration and Cultural Conflict

Cultural diversity stemmed in part from a vast wave of immigrants. Between 1840 and 1860 about 2 million Irish, 1.5 million Germans, and 750,000 Britons poured into the United States. Most immigrants avoided the South because they opposed slavery, shunned blacks, or feared competition from enslaved workers. Many German migrants settled in the midwestern states of Wisconsin, Iowa, and Missouri. Other

AMERICAN VOICES

The Vice of Intemperance

JOHN GOUGH

J ohn Gough (1817–1886) was twelve years old when his impoverished English parents shipped him to New York City, where he found work as a bookbinder—and eventually turned to drink. In 1842, at age twenty-five, Gough converted to temperance. For the next four decades he used his eloquence as a lecturer—and his considerable talents as an actor—to command high fees and persuade thousands to join the temperance movement. The following selection is taken from his Autobiography *(1869).*

Will it be believed that I again sought refuge in rum? Yet so it was. Scarcely had I recovered from the fright, than I sent out, procured a pint of rum, and drank it all in less than an hour. And now came upon me many terrible sensations. Cramps attacked me in my limbs, which racked me with agony; and my temples throbbed as if they would burst. . . . Then came on the drunkard's remorseless torturer—delirium tremens, in all its terrors, attacked me. For three days I endured more agony than pen could describe, even were it guided by the mind of Dante. . . . I was at one time surrounded by millions of monstrous spiders, that crawled slowly over every limb, whilst the beaded drops of perspiration would start to my brow, and my limbs would shiver until the bed rattled. . . . All at once, whilst gazing at a frightful creation of my distempered mind, I seemed struck with sudden blindness. I knew a candle was burning in the room, but I could not see it—all was so pitchy dark. . . . And then the scene would change: I was falling—falling swiftly as an arrow—far down into some terrible abyss. . . .

By the mercy of God, I survived this awful seizure; and when I rose, a weak, broken-down man, and surveyed my ghastly features in the glass, I thought of my mother, and asked myself how I had obeyed the instructions received from her lips, and to what advantage I had turned the lessons she taught me. I remembered her countless prayers and tears. . . . Oh! how keen were my rebukes; and, in the excitement of the moment, I resolved to lead a better life, and abstain from the accursed cup.

For about a month, terrified by what I had suffered, I adhered to my resolution; then my wife came home, and, in my joy at her return, I flung my good resolutions to the wind, and, foolishly fancying that I could now restrain my appetite, which had a whole month remained in subjugation, I took a glass of brandy. That glass aroused the slumbering demon, who would not be satisfied by so tiny a libation. Another and another succeeded, until I was again far advanced in the career of intemperance. The night of my wife's return, I went to bed intoxicated.

SOURCE: *Antebellum American Culture: An Interpretive Anthology* by David Brion Davis, ed. Reprinted by permission of the author.

Germans and most of the Irish settled in the Northeast, where by 1860 they accounted for nearly one-third of white adults.

The immigrants were a diverse lot. The British were primarily Protestant and relatively prosperous; their ranks included many trained professionals, propertied farmers, and skilled workers. Many German immigrants also came from property-owning farming and artisan families and could afford to buy land in America. The poorest migrants were Irish peasants and laborers, who were fleeing a famine caused by severe overpopulation and a devastating blight on the potato crop. Arriving in dire poverty, the Irish settled in the cities of New England and New York and took low-paying jobs in factories and construction projects and as servants in private residences. Many Irish families lived in crowded tenements with primitive sanitation systems and were the first to die in epidemics. In the summer of 1849 a cholera epidemic took the lives of thousands of poor immigrants in St. Louis and New York City.

In times of hardship and sorrow, immigrants turned to their churches. Many Germans and virtually all the Irish were Catholics, and they fueled the growth of the Catholic Church. In 1840 there were sixteen Catholic dioceses and seven hundred churches in the United States; by 1860 the number had increased to forty-five dioceses and twenty-five hundred churches. Under the guidance of their priests and bishops, Catholics built an impressive network of institutions—charitable societies, orphanages, militia companies, parochial schools, and political organizations—that helped them maintain both their religion and their Irish or German identity.

Because of the Protestant religious fervor stirred up by the Second Great Awakening, Catholic immigrants met with widespread hostility. A rash of anti-Catholic publications greeted the first Irish immigrants in the 1830s. One of the most militant critics of Catholicism was the artist and inventor Samuel F. B. Morse (who would later make the first commercial adaptation of the telegraph). In 1834 Morse published *Foreign Conspiracy against the Liberties of the United States*, which warned of a Catholic threat to American republican institutions. Morse believed that Catholic immigrants would obey the dictates of Pope Pius IX, who had condemned republicanism as a false political ideology based on the sovereignty of the people rather than on the sovereignty of God. Republican-minded Protestants of many denominations shared Morse's fears, and *Foreign Conspiracy* became their textbook.

The social tensions stemming from industrialization also intensified anti-Catholic sentiment. Unemployed Protestant mechanics and factory workers joined mobs that attacked Catholics and accused them of taking jobs and driving down wages; other Protestants organized Native American Clubs, which called for limits on immigration, the restriction of public office to native-born citizens, and the exclusive use of the Protestant version of the Bible in public schools. Social reformers often supported the anti-Catholic movement for reasons of public policy—to prevent the diversion of tax resources to Catholic schools and to oppose rowdyism by drunken Irish men. These cultural conflicts hurt the labor movement because many Protestant wage earners felt they had more in common with their Protestant employers than with their Catholic coworkers.

In many northeastern cities, religious and cultural conflicts led to violence. In 1834 in Charlestown, Massachusetts, a quarrel between Catholic laborers repairing a convent owned by the Ursuline order of nuns and Protestant workers in a neighboring brickyard turned into a full-scale riot and the burning of the convent. In Philadelphia violence erupted in 1844 when the Catholic bishop persuaded public school officials to use both Catholic and Protestant versions of the Bible. Anti-Irish rioting incited by the city's Native American Clubs lasted for two months and escalated into open warfare between Protestants and the Pennsylvania militia.

Even as economic revolution brought prosperity to many Americans, it divided the society along class lines and, by encouraging the influx of immigrants, created new ethnic and religious tensions. Differences of class and culture now split the North in much the same way that race and class had long divided the South. To address these divisive economic and social issues, Americans looked increasingly to the political system, which was becoming increasingly democratic. Indeed, the resulting tension between social inequality and political democracy would soon become an enduring, and troubling, part of American life.

TIMELINE

1782	Oliver Evans develops automated flour mill	1824	Congress levies protective tariffs; increases rates in 1828
1790	Samuel Slater opens spinning mill in Providence, Rhode Island		*Gibbons v. Ogden* promotes interstate trade
1793	Eli Whitney manufactures cotton gins	1830s	Emergence of western commercial cities
1807	Robert Fulton launches the *Clermont*, the first American steamboat		Labor movement gains strength
			Class-segregated cities
			Growth of temperance movement
1810s	Cotton kingdom begins in Old Southwest		Creation of middle-class culture
		1830	Charles Grandison Finney begins Rochester revival
1814	Boston Manufacturing Company opens cotton mill in Waltham, Massachusetts	1837	Panic of 1837
1817	Erie Canal begun; completed in 1825		John Deere invents steel plow
1820	Minimum federal land price reduced to $1.25 per acre	1839	European financial crisis begins four-year depression in United States
1820s	New England women become textile operatives	1840s	Irish and German immigration; ethnic riots
	Building-trade workers seek ten-hour workday	1850s	Expansion of railroads in Northeast and Midwest
	Rise of Benevolent Empire		Rise of machine-tool industry
1821	End of Panic of 1819; fifteen-year boom begins	1857	Financial panic after fourteen-year boom

For Further Exploration

Stuart Weems Bruchey, *Enterprise: The Dynamic Economy of a Free People* (1990), offers a panoramic history of America's economy. An important study is Charles G. Sellers's, *The Market Revolution: Jacksonian America, 1815–1846* (1991), which focuses on social and cultural change and underlines the tensions between market capitalism and democratic politics. David Freeman Hawke, *Nuts and Bolts of the Past: A History of American Technology, 1776–1860* (1988), offers an entertaining account of eccentric inventors and technical progress. Sites that explore the impact of technology include The Eli Whitney Museum & Workshop at <http://www.eliwhitney.org/> and The City Transformed: Railroads and Their Influence on the Growth of Chicago in the 1850s at <http://hcs.harvard.edu/~dreyfus/history.html>.

Stephen Aron, *How the West Was Lost: The Transformation of Kentucky from Daniel Boone to Henry Clay* (1996), explores the drama of economic and political conflict in the trans-Appalachian West, while Peter Way, *Common Labor: Workers and the Digging of North American Canals, 1780–1860* (1993), describes the deprivation and anger experienced by the men who dug the western canals. For material on New York's Erie Canal, go to <http://www.canals.state.ny.us/culture/history/>.

The appearance of a new urban society forms the background of Stuart M. Blumin's study, *The Emergence of the Middle Class: Social Experience in the American City, 1760–1900* (1989). A fine study of urban disorder is David Grimsted's *American Mobbing* (1998). In *Home and Work: Housework, Wages, and the Ideology of Labor in the Early Republic* (1990), Jeanne Boydston takes a critical look at the impact of the Market Revolution and urban life on women's lives. For a woman textile operative's first-hand account of mill life, see <http://www.fordham.edu/halsall/mod/robinson-lowell.html>. W. J. Rorabaugh, *The Alcoholic Republic, an American Tradition* (1979), describes a society awash in liquor and the efforts of the temperance reformers to do something about it.

For more about the settlement of the Great Lakes region, log on to Pioneering the Upper Midwest: Books from Michigan, Minnesota, and Wisconsin, 1820–1910 at <http://memory.loc.gov/ammem/umhtml/umhome.html>, for the full text of first-person accounts, biographies, and promotional literature from the collections of the Library of Congress.

For definitions of key terms boldfaced in this chapter, see the glossary at the end of the book.

To assess your mastery of the material covered in this chapter, see the Online Study Guide at **bedfordstmartins.com/henrettaconcise**.

For map resources and primary documents, see **bedfordstmartins.com/henrettaconcise**.

Chapter 11

A DEMOCRATIC REVOLUTION
1820–1844

> Of the two great parties, ... I should say that one [the Democratic
> Party or the Democracy] has the best cause ... for free trade, for
> wide suffrage.... The other [the Whig Party] has the best men [but
> is] ... merely defensive of property. It vindicates no right, it aspires
> to no real good....
>
> RALPH WALDO EMERSON, "ESSAY ON POLITICS," 1844

If some Americans were critical of their political parties and republican institutions, they had strong allies among visiting Europeans. "The gentlemen spit, talk of elections and the price of produce, and spit again," Mrs. Frances Trollope reported in *Domestic Manners of the Americans* (1832). In her view American politics was the sport of party hacks who reeked of "whiskey and onions." Other European visitors likewise found little to celebrate. Harriet Martineau was "deeply disgusted" by the "clap-trap of praise and pathos" uttered by a leading Massachusetts politician, while Basil Hall could only shake his head in astonishment at the shallow arguments, the "conclusions in which nothing was concluded," that were advanced by the inept "farmers, shopkeepers, and country lawyers" who sat in the New York assembly.

The verdict was unanimous and negative. "The most able men in the United States are very rarely placed at the head of affairs," concluded the French aristocrat Alexis de Tocqueville in *Democracy in America* (1835), a result he ascribed to the character of democracy itself. Ordinary citizens ignored important issues of policy, refused to elect their intellectual superiors to office, and willingly assented to "the clamor of a mountebank [a charismatic fraud] who knows the secret of stimulating [their] tastes."

The European visitors were witnesses to the unfolding of the American democratic revolution. In the early years of the nation, the ruling ideology had been *republicanism*, rule by property-owning "men of TALENTS and VIRTUE." By the 1820s and 1830s, the watchword was *democracy*, which in practice meant rule by popularly elected party politicians. "That the majority should govern was a fundamental maxim in all free governments," declared Martin Van Buren, the most talented of the new breed of middle-class professional politicians who had taken over the halls of government. The new party politicians often pursued selfish goals, but by uniting ordinary Americans in "election fever" and party organizations, they held together a social order increasingly fragmented by the economic revolution.

The Rise of Popular Politics, 1820–1829

Expansion of the **franchise** was the most dramatic expression of the democratic revolution. As early as the 1810s some states ended property qualifications for voting and brought nearly every male farmer and wage earner into the political arena. Nowhere else in the world did ordinary men have so much power; in England, the Reform Bill of 1832 extended the vote to only 600,000 out of 6 million English men—a mere 10 percent.

The Decline of the Notables and the Rise of Parties

The American Revolution weakened the deferential society of the colonial era, but it did not overthrow it. Families in the low and middle ranks continued to accept the leadership of their social "betters," and wealthy notable men—northern landlords, slave-owning planters, and seaport merchants—dominated the political system. As former Supreme Court Justice John Jay put it in 1810, "Those who own the country are the most fit persons to participate in the government of it." Local notables managed elections by building up an "interest": lending money to small farmers, giving business to storekeepers, and treating their tenants to rum at election time. An outlay of $20 for refreshments, remarked one poll watcher, "may produce about 100 votes." Martin Van Buren, whose father was a tavern keeper, knew from personal experience that this gentry-dominated system excluded men without wealth and "powerful family connections" from running for office.

Smallholding farmers and ambitious laborers in the Midwest and Southwest launched the first challenges to the traditional political order. In Ohio, a traveler reported, "no white man or woman will bear being called a servant." Reflecting this social egalitarianism, the constitutions of the new states of Indiana (1816), Illinois (1818), and Alabama (1819) prescribed a broad male franchise and voters usually elected middling men to local and state offices. A well-to-do migrant in Illinois noted with surprise that the man who plowed his fields "was a colonel of militia, and a member of the legislature." Once in public office, men from modest backgrounds enacted laws that restricted imprisonment for debt, kept taxes low, and allowed farmers to claim "squatters' rights" to unoccupied land.

To deter migration to the West and unrest at home, the notables who ran state legislatures in the East grudgingly accepted a broader franchise. In 1810 in Maryland, reformers condemned property qualifications as a "tyranny" that endowed "one class of men with privileges which are denied to another" and won a broad franchise. By the mid-1820s only a few states—North Carolina, Virginia, Rhode Island—required the ownership of freehold property for voting. Many states had instituted universal white manhood suffrage, and others, such as Ohio and Louisiana, excluded only the relatively few men who did not pay taxes or serve in the militia. Moreover, between 1818 and 1821 Connecticut, Massachusetts, and New York wrote new constitutions that reapportioned legislative districts on the basis of population and made local governments more democratic by mandating the election (rather than the appointment) of judges and justices of the peace.

Democratic politics was contentious and often corrupt. Powerful entrepreneurs and speculators—both notables and self-made men—demanded government assistance for their business enterprises and paid bribes to legislators to get it. Bankers sought state charters and opposed limits on interest rates, while land speculators demanded the eviction of squatters and the building of roads and canals. Other Americans turned to politics to advance religious and cultural causes. In 1828 evangelical Presbyterians in Utica, New York, called for a town ordinance to restrict Sunday entertainment. In reply, a member of the local Universalist church (a free-thinking Protestant denomination) denounced such coercive reforms and called for "Religious Liberty."

The appearance of political parties encouraged debate on issues of government policy. Revolutionary era Americans had condemned political "factions" and "parties" as antirepublican and refused to give them constitutional status. But as the power of notables waned, political parties became more prominent. By the 1820s the parties were highly disciplined organizations managed by professional politicians, who were often middle-class lawyers and journalists. Some observers compared the parties to the mechanical innovations of the Industrial Revolution. Like a well-designed textile loom, they were "machines" that wove the diverse interests of social and economic groups into an elaborate tapestry—a coherent legislative program.

Martin Van Buren of New York was the chief architect of the emerging system of party government. Between 1817 and 1821 the "Little Magician" created the first statewide **political machine**, the Albany Regency; a decade later he organized the first nationwide political party, the Jacksonian Democrats. Van Buren repudiated the republican principle that political parties were dangerous to the common wealth and argued that the opposite was true: "All men of sense know that political parties are inseparable from free government" because they check the government's "disposition to abuse power . . . [and curb] the passions, the ambition, and the usurpations" of potential tyrants.

One key to Van Buren's success in New York was his systematic use of the *Albany Argus* and other party newspapers to promote a platform and drum up the vote. **Patronage** was even more important. The Albany Regency's control of the legislature gave Van Buren and his followers a greater "interest" than the notables—some six thousand appointments to New York's legal bureaucracy of judges, justices of the peace, sheriffs, deed commissioners, and coroners. Finally, Van Buren insisted on party discipline and required state legislators to follow the dictates of a party meeting, or caucus. On one crucial occasion, Van Buren persuaded seventeen legislators to "magnanimously sacrifice individual preferences for the general good" and honored them at a banquet where they were treated with "something approaching divine honors."

The Election of 1824

The advance of political democracy undermined the old system of national politics and the power of the leading notables who ran it. The aristocratic Federalist Party virtually disappeared, and the Republican Party broke up into competing factions. As the election of 1824 approached, no fewer than five candidates, all calling themselves Republicans, campaigned for the presidency. Three were veterans of President James Monroe's cabinet: Secretary of State John Quincy Adams, the son of former president John Adams; Secretary of War John C. Calhoun; and Secretary of the Treasury William H. Crawford. The fourth candidate was Henry Clay of Kentucky, the dynamic Speaker of the House of Representatives, and the fifth was General Andrew Jackson, now a senator from Tennessee. When a caucus of Republicans in Congress selected Crawford as the "official" nominee, the other candidates refused to accept that result.

Instead, they introduced democracy to national politics by seeking popular support. Because of democratic reforms, eighteen of the twenty-four states used popular elections (rather than a vote of the state legislature) to choose members of the electoral college. The battle was closely fought. Thanks to his diplomatic successes as secretary of state (see Chapter 8), John Quincy Adams enjoyed national recognition and, because of his Massachusetts origins, commanded the electoral votes of New England. Henry Clay framed his candidacy around domestic issues. As a congressman, Clay promoted the **American System**, an integrated program of national economic development that relied on the Second Bank of the United States to regulate state banks and advocated the use of tariff revenues to build roads and canals. Clay's nationalistic program was popular in the West, which needed transportation improvements, but sharply criticized in the South, which relied on rivers to carry its cotton to market and did not have manufacturing industries to protect. William Crawford of Georgia, an ideological heir of Thomas Jefferson, spoke for the South. Fearing the "consolidation" of political power in Washington, Crawford and other "Old Republicans" denounced the American System. Recognizing Crawford's appeal in the South, John C. Calhoun of South Carolina withdrew from the presidential race and endorsed Andrew Jackson.

As the hero of the Battle of New Orleans, Jackson benefited from the wave of nationalistic pride that flowed from the War of 1812. Born in the Carolina backcountry, Jackson had settled in Nashville, Tennessee, where he formed ties to influential families through marriage and his career as an attorney and slave-owning cotton planter. His rise from common origins fit the tenor of the new democratic age and his reputation as a "plain solid republican" attracted voters in all regions.

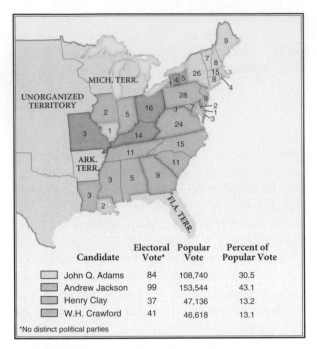

Candidate	Electoral Vote*	Popular Vote	Percent of Popular Vote
John Q. Adams	84	108,740	30.5
Andrew Jackson	99	153,544	43.1
Henry Clay	37	47,136	13.2
W.H. Crawford	41	46,618	13.1

*No distinct political parties

MAP 11.1 Presidential Election of 1824

Regional ties decided the presidential election of 1824. John Quincy Adams captured every electoral vote in New England and most of those in New York. Henry Clay carried Ohio and Kentucky, the most populous trans-Appalachian states, and William Crawford took the southern states of Virginia and Georgia. Only Andrew Jackson claimed a national constituency, winning Pennsylvania and New Jersey in the East, Indiana and Illinois in the Midwest, and most of the South. Only about 356,000 Americans voted, about 27 percent of the eligible adult white male electorate. In contrast, nearly 1.2 million American men cast ballots in 1828.

Still, Jackson's strong showing in the election surprised most political leaders. The Tennessee senator received 99 votes in the electoral college; Adams garnered 84 votes; Crawford, who suffered a stroke during the campaign, won 41; and Clay finished with 37 (Map 11.1). Since no candidate received an absolute majority, the Constitution specified that the House of Representatives would choose the president from among the three leading contenders. This procedure hurt Jackson because many congressmen rebelled at the thought of a rough-hewn "military chieftain" in the White House and worried he might become a political tyrant. Personally out of the race, Henry Clay used his influence as Speaker of the House to thwart Jackson's election. When the House met in February 1825, Clay had assembled a coalition of congressmen from New England and the Ohio Valley that voted Adams into the presidency. Adams showed his gratitude by appointing Clay as secretary of state, the traditional steppingstone to the presidency.

John Quincy Adams (1767–1848)

This famous daguerreotype of the former president, taken about 1843 by Philip Haas, conveys his rigid personality and high moral standards. These personal attributes hindered Adams's effectiveness as the nation's chief executive but contributed to his success as an antislavery congressman from Massachusetts in the 1830s and 1840s.

Metropolitan Museum of Art. Gift of I. N. Phelps Stokes, Edward S. Hawes, Alice Mary Hawes, Marion Augusta Hawes.

Clay's appointment was a politically fatal mistake for both men. John C. Calhoun accused Adams of using "the power and patronage of the Executive" to thwart the popular will. Jackson's many supporters likewise suspected that Clay had made a deal with Adams to become secretary of state. Condemning this "corrupt bargain," they vowed that Clay would never become president.

The Last Notable President: John Quincy Adams

As president, Adams called for bold national leadership. "The moral purpose of the Creator," he told Congress, was to use the president and every other public official to "improve the conditions of himself and his fellow men." Adams called for the establishment of a national university in Washington, extensive scientific explorations in the Far West, and a uniform standard of weights and measures. Most important of all, he embraced Henry Clay's American System of national economic development: (1) a protective tariff to stimulate manufacturing, (2) federally subsidized roads and canals to aid commerce, and (3) a national bank to control credit and provide a uniform currency.

Manufacturers, entrepreneurs, and market-oriented farmers in the Northeast and Midwest welcomed Adams's policies. However, they won little support among southern planters, who opposed protective tariffs, and smallholding farmers, who feared powerful banks. From his deathbed Thomas Jefferson condemned Adams for promoting "a single and splendid government of [a monied] aristocracy . . . riding and ruling over the plundered ploughman and beggared yeomanry."

Other politicians objected to the American System on constitutional grounds. In 1817 President Madison had vetoed a Bonus Bill that would have used the national government's income from the Second Bank of the United States to fund improvement projects in the various states. Such projects, Madison had argued, were the sole responsibilities of the states, a sentiment that was widely shared. Declaring his allegiance to the constitutional "doctrines of the Jefferson School," Martin Van Buren joined the Old Republicans in defeating most national subsidies for roads and canals. Congress approved only a few of Adams's proposals for internal improvements, such as a short extension of the National Road from Wheeling, Virginia, into Ohio.

The most far-reaching battle of the Adams administration came over tariffs. The Tariff of 1816 placed high duties on imports of cheap English cotton cloth, thereby allowing New England textile producers to dominate that market. In 1824 Adams and Clay supported a new tariff that protected manufacturers in New England and Pennsylvania against imports of more expensive woolen and cotton textiles as well as iron goods. When Van Buren and the Jacksonians took control of Congress in 1826, they wanted higher tariffs on imported raw materials, such as wool and hemp. Their goal was to win the support of farmers in New York, Ohio, and Kentucky for Jackson's presidential candidacy in 1828. The tariff had become a prisoner of politics. "I fear this tariff thing," remarked Thomas Cooper of South Carolina, "by some strange mechanical contrivance . . . it will be changed into a machine for manufacturing Presidents, instead of broadcloths, and bed blankets." Disregarding southern opposition, northern Jacksonians joined with the supporters of Adams and Clay to enact the Tariff of 1828, which raised duties on raw materials, textiles, and iron goods.

The new tariff enraged the South. As the world's cheapest producer of raw cotton, the South did not need a protective tariff. Moreover, by raising the price of British manufactures, the tariff cost southern planters about $100 million a year. Planters could either buy higher-cost American textiles and iron goods, thus enriching northeastern businesses and workers, or highly taxed British goods, thus paying the cost of the national government. The new tariff was "little less than legalized pillage" declared an Alabama legislator, a "Tariff of Abominations."

"The Democracy" and the Election of 1828

Ignoring the Jacksonians' support for the tariff, most southerners blamed President Adams for the new act. They also criticized Adams's Indian policy. A deeply moralistic man, the president had supported the land rights of Native Americans against expansionist-minded southern whites. In 1825 U.S. commissioners had secured a treaty from one Creek faction that ceded the tribe's lands in Georgia to the United States.

When the Creek National Council repudiated the treaty as fraudulent, Adams called for new negotiations. In response Governor George M. Troup attacked the president as a "public enemy . . . the unblushing ally of the savages" and persuaded Congress to pass legislation that extinguished the Creeks' land titles and forced most Creeks to leave the state.

Elsewhere in the nation Adams's primary weakness was his increasingly out-of-date political style. The last notable to serve in the White House, he acted the part: aloof, moralistic, paternalistic. When Congress rejected his activist economic policies, Adams questioned the wisdom of the people and advised elected officials not to be "palsied by the will of our constituents." Ignoring his waning popularity, the president did not use patronage to reward his supporters and allowed hostile federal officials to remain in office. Rather than "run" for reelection in 1828, Adams "stood" for it, telling supporters, "If my country wants my services, she must ask for them."

Martin Van Buren and the professional politicians handling Andrew Jackson's campaign had no reservations about "running" for the presidency. Now a U.S. senator from New York, Van Buren re-created the old Jeffersonian coalition by uniting northern farmers and artisans (the "plain Republicans of the North") with the southern slave owners and smallholding farmers who had voted for the Virginia Dynasty. John C. Calhoun, Jackson's vice-presidential running mate, brought his South Carolina allies into Van Buren's party, and Jackson's close friends in Tennessee rallied voters in the Old Southwest. At Van Buren's direction, state politicians orchestrated a massive newspaper campaign; in New York fifty newspapers declared their support for Jackson on the same day. Local Jacksonians organized mass meetings, torchlight parades, and barbecues to celebrate their candidate's frontier origins and his rise to fame. Old Hickory—the nickname came from the toughest American hardwood tree—was a "natural" aristocrat, a self-made man. "Jackson for ever!" was their cry.

Initially the Jacksonians called themselves Democratic Republicans, but as the campaign wore on, they became Democrats or "the Democracy." The name conveyed their message. As Jacksonian Thomas Morris told the Ohio legislature, the republic had been corrupted by legislative gifts of corporate charters that gave "a few individuals rights and privileges not enjoyed by the citizens at large." Morris promised that his party would destroy such "artificial distinction in society" and ensure rule by the majority—the Democracy. As Jackson himself declared, "Equality among the people in the rights conferred by government" was the "great radical principle of freedom."

Jackson's message of equal rights and popular rule appealed to many social groups. His hostility to business corporations and to Clay's American System won support among northeastern artisans and workers who felt threatened by industrialization. In the Southeast and the Midwest, Old Hickory's well-known animus toward Native Americans reassured white farmers who favored Indian removal. Although Jackson won votes from Pennsylvania ironworkers and New York farmers because of the controversial Tariff of Abominations, he remained popular in the South by declaring his personal preference for a "judicious" tariff.

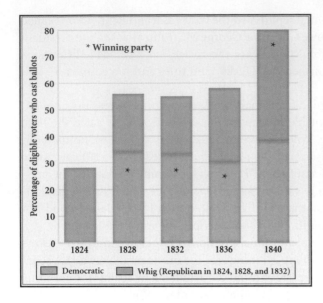

FIGURE 11.1 Changes in Voting Patterns, 1824–1840

Because of the return of two-party competition, voter participation soared in the critical presidential elections of 1828 and 1840.

The Democrats' commitment to popular democracy carried Jackson into office. In 1824 only about a fourth of the eligible electorate had voted; in 1828 more than half went to the polls, and they voted overwhelmingly for the senator from Tennessee (Figure 11.1). Jackson received 178 of 261 electoral votes and became the first president from a western state. As the president-elect traveled to Washington, an English visitor noted, he "wore his hair carelessly but not ungracefully arranged, and in spite of his harsh, gaunt features looked like a gentleman and a soldier." However, the massive outpouring of popular support for Jackson frightened men of wealth and influence. As the ex-Federalist and corporate lawyer Daniel Webster warned his clients, the new president would "bring a breeze with him. Which way it will blow, I cannot tell [but] . . . my fear is stronger than my hope." Watching an unruly crowd clamber over the elegant furniture in the White House to shake the hand of the newly inaugurated president, Supreme Court Justice Joseph Story could only lament that "the reign of King 'Mob' seemed triumphant" (see American Voices, "Republican Majesty and Mobs," p. 331).

The Jacksonian Presidency, 1829–1837

American-style political democracy—a broad franchise, a disciplined political party, and policies tailored to specific social groups—ushered Andrew Jackson into office. Subsequently, Jackson used his popular mandate to enhance the authority of the president over that of Congress, to destroy the nationalistic American System of Adams and Clay, and to ordain a new ideology for the Democracy. An Ohio supporter outlined Jackson's vision: "the Sovereignty of the People, the Rights of the States, and a Light and Simple Government."

AMERICAN VOICES

⁓

Republican Majesty and Mobs

MARGARET BAYARD SMITH

*W*hen Andrew Jackson ascended to the presidency in 1829, he threatened the established political system by questioning the legitimacy of a powerful central government and calling for democracy and "equal rights." Writing to her son, the Washington socialite Margaret Bayard Smith revealed a mixture of pride and anxiety about the new president and the coming of popular democracy.

The inauguration . . . was one grand whole—an imposing and majestic spectacle. . . . Thousands and thousands of people, without distinction of rank, collected in an immense mass around the Capitol, silent, orderly, and tranquil, with their eyes fixed on the front of the Capitol, waiting the appearance of the president. . . . The door from the Rotunda opens, preceded by the marshall surrounded by the judges of the Supreme Court, the old man [President Jackson] with his grey hair, that crown of glory, advances, bows to the people, who greet him with a shout that rends the air. The cannon, from the heights around from Alexandria and Fort Washington, proclaim the [oath of office] he has taken and all the hills around reverberate the sound. It was grand; it was sublime! An almost breathless silence succeeded and the multitude was still—listening to catch the sound of his voice. . . .

After reading his speech, the oath was administered to him by the chief justice. The marshall presented the Bible. The president took it from his hand, pressed his lips to it, laid it reverently down, then bowed again to the people. Yes, to the people in all their majesty— and had the spectacle closed here, even Europeans must have acknowledged that a free people, collected in their might, silent and tranquil, restrained solely by a moral power, without a shadow around of military force, was majesty, rising to sublimity, and far surpassing the majesty of kings and princes, surrounded with armies and glittering in gold. . . .

[But at the White House reception that followed,] what a scene did we witness!! The majesty of the people had disappeared, and a rabble, a mob . . . scrambling, fighting, romping . . . [crowded around] the president, [who,] after having literally been nearly pressed to death . . . escaped to his lodgings at Gadsby's. Cut glass and bone china to the amount of several thousand dollars had been broken in the struggle to get refreshments. . . .

God grant the people do not put down all rule and rulers. I fear . . . as they have been found in all ages and countries where they get power in their hands, that of all tyrants, they are the most ferocious, cruel, and despotic. The . . . rabble in the president's house brought to my mind descriptions I had read of the mobs in the Tuileries and at Versailles [during the French Revolution].

SOURCE: M. B. Smith to J. B. H. Smith, March 1829, Smith Family Correspondence, Library of Congress, in Linda R. Monk, ed., *Ordinary Americans: U.S. History through the Eyes of Ordinary People* (Alexandria, VA: Close Up Foundation, 1993), 49–50.

Jackson's Agenda: Patronage and Policy

To decide policy, Jackson relied primarily on an informal group of advisors, his so-called Kitchen Cabinet. Its most influential members were Francis Preston Blair of Kentucky, who edited the *Washington Globe*; Amos Kendall, also from Kentucky, who helped Jackson write his public addresses; Roger B. Taney of Maryland, who became attorney general, treasury secretary, and then chief justice of the United States; and, the most influential, Secretary of State Martin Van Buren.

Following Van Buren's example in New York, Jackson used patronage to create a loyal and disciplined national party. He insisted on rotation in office: when a new administration came to power, bureaucrats would have to leave government service and return "to making a living as other people do." Dismissing the argument that rotation would lessen expertise, Jackson suggested that most public duties were "so plain and simple that men of intelligence may readily qualify themselves for their performance." William L. Marcy, a New York Jacksonian, put it more bluntly: government jobs were like the spoils of war, and "to the victor belong the spoils of the enemy." Using the **spoils system**, Jackson dispensed government jobs to aid his friends and win support for his legislative program.

Jackson's main priority was to destroy the American System. As Henry Clay noted apprehensively, the new president wanted "to cry down old constructions of

President Andrew Jackson, 1830

The new president came to Washington with a well-deserved reputation as an aggressive Indian fighter and dangerous military chieftain. But in the "official" portrait of 1830 he appears "presidential"—his dress and posture (and the artist's composition) creating an image of a calm and deliberate statesman. Subsequent events would show that Jackson had not lost his hard-edged personality. Library of Congress.

the Constitution . . . to make all Jefferson's opinions the articles of faith of the new Church." Declaring that the "voice of the people" called for "economy in the expenditures of the Government," Jackson rejected national support for transportation projects, which he also opposed on constitutional grounds. In 1830 he vetoed four internal improvement bills, including an extension of the National Road, because they amounted to "an infringement of the reserved powers of states." Then Jackson turned his attention to two complex and equally controversial parts of the American System: protective tariffs and the national bank.

The Tariff and Nullification

The Tariff of 1828 had helped Jackson win the presidency, but it saddled him with a major political crisis. Fierce opposition to the tariff arose in South Carolina, where white planters suffered from chronic insecurity. South Carolina was the only state with an African American majority—56 percent of the population in 1830—and its slave owners, like the sugar planters in the West Indies, lived in fear of a black rebellion. They also worried about the legal abolition of slavery. The British Parliament had promised to end slavery in the West Indies (and did so in August 1833), and South Carolina planters worried that the U.S. government might do the same. "If the general government shall continue to stretch their powers," a southern congressman had warned as early as 1818, antislavery societies "will undoubtedly put them to try the question of emancipation." To sidetrack this possibility, South Carolina politicians tried to limit the power of the central government and chose the tariff as their target.

The crisis began in 1832 when high-tariff congressmen ignored southern warnings that they were "endangering the Union" and reenacted the Tariff of Abominations. In response, leading South Carolinians called a state convention in November, which boldly adopted an Ordinance of Nullification. The ordinance declared the tariffs of 1828 and 1832 null and void, forbade the collection of those duties in South Carolina after February 1, 1833, and threatened secession if federal bureaucrats tried to collect them.

South Carolina's act of **nullification** rested on the constitutional arguments developed in a tract of 1828, *The South Carolina Exposition and Protest*. Written anonymously by Vice President John C. Calhoun, the *Exposition* challenged the legitimacy of majority rule. "Constitutional government and the government of a majority are utterly incompatible," Calhoun wrote. "An unchecked majority is a despotism." To devise a mechanism to check the power of congressional majorities, Calhoun turned to the arguments advanced by Jefferson and Madison in the Kentucky and Virginia Resolutions of 1798. Developing a constitutional theory that states' rights advocates would use well into the twentieth century, Calhoun maintained that the U.S. Constitution had been ratified by citizens meeting in state conventions. Consequently, he argued, a state convention could decide if a congressional law was unconstitutional and declare it null and void within the state's borders.

Although Jackson wanted to limit the reach of the national government, he denounced this radical redefinition of the existing constitutional system: "Our Federal Union—it must be preserved," he declared in 1830. Two years later, the president's response to South Carolina's Nullification Ordinance was equally direct. Jackson declared that nullification violated the Constitution and was "unauthorized by its spirit . . . and destructive of the great object for which it was formed." "Disunion by armed force is treason," he warned. At Jackson's request, Congress passed a Force Bill early in 1833 that authorized the president to use military force to compel South Carolina to obey national laws. Simultaneously, Jackson addressed the South's objections to high import duties by winning passage of a Tariff Act that gradually reduced rates. By 1842, tariffs would revert to the modest rates of 1816, thereby eliminating another part of Clay's American System.

The compromise worked. Having won a gradual reduction in duties, the South Carolina convention rescinded its nullification of the tariff (while defiantly nullifying the Force Bill). Jackson was satisfied. He had upheld the principle that no state could nullify a law of the United States, a position that Abraham Lincoln would embrace in defense of the Union during the secession crisis of 1861.

The Bank War

In the middle of the tariff crisis, Jackson faced another major challenge from the political supporters of the Second Bank of the United States. Founded in Philadelphia in 1816, the bank was a privately managed institution that held a twenty-year charter from the federal government, which owned 20 percent of its stock. The bank's most important role was to stabilize the nation's money supply. Most American money consisted of notes and bills of credit—in effect, paper money—issued by state-chartered banks. The banks promised to redeem the notes on demand with "hard" money—that is, gold or silver coins (also known as specie). By collecting those notes and regularly demanding specie, the Second Bank kept the state banks from issuing too much paper money.

During the prosperous 1820s, the Second Bank had maintained monetary stability by closing reckless state banks and restraining expansion-minded bankers in the western states. This tight-money policy pleased bankers and entrepreneurs in Boston, New York, and Philadelphia, whose capital investments were underwriting economic development. However, most ordinary Americans did not understand the regulatory role of the Second Bank and feared its ability to force bank closures, which left them holding worthless paper notes. New York bankers also opposed the Second Bank because they resented the financial clout wielded by its arrogant president, Nicholas Biddle. "As to mere power," Biddle boasted, "I have been for years in the daily exercise of more personal authority than any President habitually enjoys." Fearing Biddle's influence, some state bankers wanted the specie owned by the federal government to be deposited in their institutions rather than in the Second Bank. Others, including friends of Jackson in Nashville, wanted to escape supervision by any central bank.

However, it was a political miscalculation by the Second Bank's political allies that brought about its downfall. In 1832 Jackson's opponents in Congress, led by Henry Clay and Daniel Webster, persuaded Biddle to seek an early extension of the bank's charter. They commanded enough votes in Congress to enact the required legislation and hoped to lure Jackson into a veto that would split the Democrats just before the 1832 elections.

Jackson turned the tables on Clay and Webster. He vetoed the bill that rechartered the bank and issued a masterful veto message that blended constitutional arguments with class rhetoric and patriotic fervor. Adopting Jefferson's position, Jackson declared that Congress had no constitutional authority to charter a national bank, which was "subversive of the rights of the States." Using the populist republican rhetoric of the American Revolution, he then attacked the Second Bank as "dangerous to the liberties of the people." Indeed, it was a nest of special privilege and monopoly power that promoted "the advancement of the few at the expense of . . . farmers, mechanics, and laborers." Finally, the president evoked national patriotism by pointing out that British aristocrats owned much of the bank's stock; any such powerful institution should be "purely American," he declared.

Jackson Destroys the Bank

In this political cartoon Jackson proudly orders the withdrawal of "Public Money" from the privately run Second Bank of the United States. Crushed by the subsequent collapse of the bank are its director Nicholas Biddle, depicted as the Devil, wealthy British and American investors, and the newspapers that supported Biddle during the bank war. Standing behind the president is "Major Jack Downing," the pseudonym for Seba Smith, a pro-Jackson humorist. Library of Congress.

FOR MORE HELP ANALYZING THIS IMAGE, see the Online Study Guide at **bedfordstmartins.com/henrettaconcise**.

Jackson's attack on the bank carried him to victory in the election of 1832. He jettisoned Calhoun as a running mate because of the South Carolinian's support for nullification and Calhoun's refusal to support Peggy Eaton, a cabinet wife accused of sexual improprieties. As his new vice president, Jackson chose his longtime political ally Martin Van Buren. Together Old Hickory and Little Van overwhelmed Henry Clay, who headed the National Republican ticket, by 219 to 49 electoral votes. Jackson's most fervent supporters were eastern workers and western farmers, whose lives had been disrupted by falling wages or price fluctuations and who blamed their fate on the Second Bank. "All the flourishing cities of the West are mortgaged to this money power," charged Jacksonian senator Thomas Hart Benton of Missouri. "They may be devoured by it at any moment." But just as many Jacksonians had prospered during a decade of strong economic growth. Along with thousands of middle-class Americans—lawyers, clerks, shopkeepers, artisans—they wanted equal opportunity to rise in the world and cheered Jackson's attacks on privileged corporations.

Early in 1833, Jackson called on Roger B. Taney, a strong opponent of corporate privilege, to launch a new assault on the Second Bank, which still had four years left on its original charter. Assuming control of the Treasury Department, Taney withdrew the government's gold and silver from the Second Bank and deposited it in state institutions, which critics called Jackson's "pet banks." To justify this abrupt (and probably illegal) act, Jackson claimed that his own reelection represented "the decision of the people against the bank" and gave him a mandate to destroy it. This was the first time a president had claimed that victory at the polls allowed him to act independently of Congress.

The "bank war" escalated into an all-out political battle. In March 1834 Jackson's opponents in the Senate passed Henry Clay's resolution censuring the president and warning of executive tyranny: "We are in the midst of a revolution, hitherto bloodless, but rapidly descending towards a total change of the pure republican character of the Government, and the concentration of all power in the hands of one man." Jackson was not deterred by widespread opposition in Congress. "The Bank is trying to kill me but I will kill it," he vowed to Van Buren. And so he did. When the Second Bank's national charter expired in 1836, Jackson prevented its renewal.

Jackson had destroyed both national banking—the creation of Alexander Hamilton—and the American System of protective tariffs and internal improvements favored by John Quincy Adams and Henry Clay. The result was a profound reduction in the purview and the powers of the national government. "All is gone," observed a Washington newspaper correspondent. "All is gone, which the General Government was instituted to create and preserve."

Indian Removal

The status of the Native American peoples posed an equally complex political problem. By the late 1820s white voices throughout the western states and territories were calling for the resettlement of Indians west of the Mississippi River. Many easterners who were sympathetic to the native peoples also favored resettlement.

Removal to the West seemed the only way to protect Indian societies from alcoholic degradation, economic sharp dealing, and cultural decline.

However, most Indians had no wish to leave their ancestral lands. The Old Southwest was home to the so-called Five Civilized Tribes: the Cherokees and Creeks in Georgia, Tennessee, and Alabama; the Chickasaws and Choctaws in Mississippi and Alabama; and the Seminoles in Florida. During the War of 1812 Andrew Jackson had forced the Creeks to relinquish millions of acres. But Indian peoples still controlled vast tracts and, led by the mixed-blood offspring of white traders and Indian women, strongly resisted removal. Growing up in a bicultural world, many mixed-bloods knew the political ways of whites and some emulated the lifestyle of southern planters. James Vann, a Georgia Cherokee, owned more than twenty black slaves, two trading posts, and a gristmill. Forty other Cherokee mixed-blood families owned a total of more than a thousand African American slaves. To protect their property and the lands of their people, the mixed-bloods promoted a strong Indian identity. Sequoyah, a mixed blood, developed a system of writing for the Cherokee language, and in 1827 mixed-blood Cherokees introduced a new charter of government modeled directly on the U.S. Constitution. Full-blooded Cherokees, who made up 90 percent of the population, resisted many of the mixed-bloods' cultural and political innovations but were equally determined to retain their ancestral lands. "We would not receive money for land in which our fathers and friends are buried," one chief declared. "We love our land; it is our mother."

The Cherokees' preferences carried no weight with the Georgia legislature. In 1802 Georgia had given up its western land claims in return for a federal promise to extinguish Indian landholdings in the state. Now it demanded the fulfillment of that promise. Having spent his military career fighting Indians and seizing their lands, Jackson gave full support to Georgia. On assuming the presidency, he withdrew the federal troops that had protected Indian enclaves there and in Alabama and Mississippi. The states, he declared, were sovereign within their borders.

Jackson then pushed through Congress the Indian Removal Act of 1830. The act granted money and lands in present-day Oklahoma and Kansas to Native American peoples who would give up their ancestral holdings (see American Voices, "A Sacred Reverence for Our Lands," p. 338). To persuade Indians to move, government officials promised that they could live on the new lands, "they and all their children, as long as grass grows and water runs." When Chief Black Hawk and his Sauk and Fox followers refused to move from rich farmland in western Illinois in 1832, Jackson sent troops to expel them. Rejecting Black Hawk's offer to surrender, the American army pursued him into the Wisconsin Territory and, in the brutal eight-hour Bad Axe Massacre, killed 850 of Black Hawk's 1,000 warriors. Over the next five years American diplomatic pressure and military power forced seventy Indian peoples to sign treaties and move west of the Mississippi (Map 11.2).

Meanwhile, the Cherokees had carried their case to the Supreme Court, where they claimed the status of a "foreign nation." In *Cherokee Nation v. Georgia* (1831)

AMERICAN VOICES

A Sacred Reverence for Our Lands

BLACK HAWK

B lack Hawk (1767–1838), or Makataimeshekiakiak in his native language, was a chief of the Sauk and Fox peoples. In 1833 he dictated his life story to a government interpreter, and a young newspaper editor published it. Here Black Hawk describes the coming of white settlers to his village, near present-day Rock Island, Illinois, and his decision to resist removal to lands west of the Mississippi River.

We had about eight hundred acres in cultivation. The land around our village . . . was covered with bluegrass, which made excellent pasture for our horses. . . . The rapids of Rock river furnished us with an abundance of excellent fish, and the land, being good, never failed to produce good crops of corn, beans, pumpkins, and squashes. We always had plenty—our children never cried with hunger, nor our people were never in want. Here our village had stood for more than a hundred years.

[In 1828] Nothing was now talked of but leaving our village. Ke-o-kuck [the principal chief] had been persuaded to consent to . . . remove to the west side of the Mississippi. . . . [I] raised the standard of opposition to Ke-o-kuck, with full determination not to leave my village. . . . I was of the opinion that the white people had plenty of land and would never take our village from us. . . .

During the [following] winter, I received information that three families of whites had arrived at our village and destroyed some of our lodges, and were making fences and dividing our corn-fields for their own use. . . . I requested them [to remove, but some weeks later] we came up to our village, and found that the whites had not left it— but that others had come, and that the greater part of our corn-fields had been enclosed. . . . Some of the whites permitted us to plant small patches in the fields they had fenced, keeping all the best ground for themselves. . . . The white people brought whiskey into our village, made people drunk, and cheated them out of their homes, guns, and [beaver] traps!

That fall [1829] I paid a visit to the agent, before we started to our hunting grounds. . . . He said that the land on which our village stood was now ordered to be sold to individuals; and that, when sold, our right to remain, by treaty, would be at an end, and that if we returned next spring, we would be forced to remove! I refused . . . to quit my village. It was here, that I was born—and here lie the bones of many friends and relatives. For this spot I felt a sacred reverence, and never could consent to leave it, without being forced therefrom.

SOURCE: David Jackson, ed., *Black Hawk: An Autobiography* (Urbana: University of Illinois Press, 1964), 88–90, 95–97, 111–13.

Black Hawk (1767–1838)

This portrait of Black Hawk, by Charles Bird King, shows the Indian leader as a young warrior, wearing a medal commemorating an early-nineteenth-century agreement with the U.S. government. Later, in 1830, when Congress approved Andrew Jackson's Indian Removal Act, Black Hawk mobilized Sauk and Fox warriors to protect ancestral lands in Illinois. "It was here, that I was born—and here lie the bones of many friends and relatives," the aging chief declared. "I . . . never could consent to leave it." Courtesy, Warner Collection of Gulf States Paper Corporation, Tuscaloosa, AL.

Chief Justice John Marshall denied their claim to an independent national existence. Speaking for a majority of the justices, Marshall declared that Indian peoples were "domestic dependent nations." However, in *Worcester v. Georgia* (1832) Marshall sided with the Cherokees against Georgia. Voiding Georgia's extension of state law over the Cherokee, he held that Indian nations were "distinct political communities, having territorial boundaries, within which their authority is exclusive . . . [and this is] guaranteed by the United States."

Rather than guaranteeing the Cherokees' territory, the U.S. government took it from them. After negotiating a removal treaty with a minority Cherokee faction, American officials insisted that all Cherokees abide by it. However, only 2,000 of the 17,000 Cherokees had departed by the deadline of May 1838, and Martin Van Buren, who had succeeded Jackson as president, ordered General Winfield Scott to enforce the treaty. Scott's army rounded up about 14,000 Cherokees and forcibly marched them 1,200 miles to the new Indian Territory, an arduous journey they remembered as the Trail of Tears. Along the way 3,000 Indians died of starvation and exposure. After the Creeks, Chickasaws, and Choctaws moved west of the Mississippi, the only remaining Indian people in the Old Southwest were the Seminoles. Aided by runaway slaves who had married into the tribe, the Seminoles fought a successful guerrilla war during the 1840s and retained their lands in Florida. They were the exceptions. The national government had forced the removal of most eastern Indian peoples.

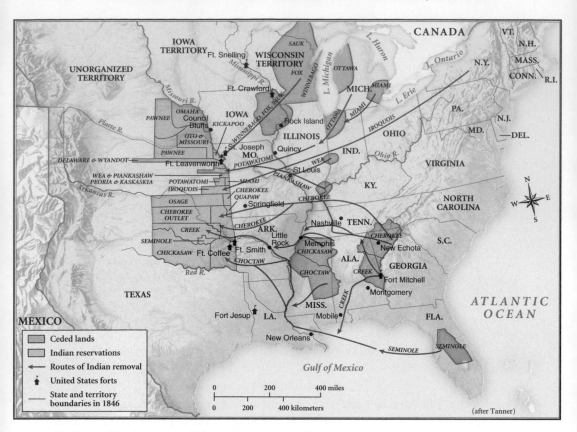

MAP 11.2 The Removal of Native Americans, 1820–1843

Beginning in the 1820s the U.S. government coerced scores of Native American peoples to sign treaties that exchanged Indian lands in the East for money and designated tracts in the West. During the 1830s the government used military force to expel the Cherokees, Chickasaws, Choctaws, Creeks, and many Seminoles from their ancestral homes in the Old Southeast and resettle them on reservations in the present-day states of Oklahoma and Kansas.

FOR MORE HELP ANALYZING THIS MAP, see the Online Study Guide at **bedfordstmartins.com/henrettaconcise**.

The Jacksonian Impact

Jackson's legacy, like that of every great president, was complex and rich. Thus, he permanently expanded the authority of the nation's chief executive. Using the rhetoric of popular sovereignty, Jackson asserted that "the President is the direct representative of the American people." Assuming that role during the nullification crisis, he upheld national authority by threatening the use of military force. At the same time, Jackson purposefully curbed the reach of national power. By undermining Clay's American System, he reinvigorated the Jeffersonian tradition of a limited and frugal central government.

As Jackson and his Democratic Party achieved political ascendancy, they infused many American institutions with their principles. Following John Marshall's death, Jackson appointed Roger B. Taney as chief justice of the Supreme Court. During his long tenure (1835–1864), Taney persuaded the Court to give constitutional legitimacy to Jackson's policies of antimonopoly and states' rights. In the landmark case *Charles River Bridge Co. v. Warren Bridge Co.* (1837), Taney declared that a legislative charter did not necessarily bestow a monopoly. Consequently, the legislature could promote the general welfare by chartering a competing bridge company. As Taney put it, "While the rights of private property are sacredly guarded, we must not forget that the community also has rights." This decision challenged John Marshall's interpretation of the contract clause of the Constitution in *Dartmouth College v. Woodward* (1819), which had emphasized the binding nature of public charters (see Chapter 8). By limiting the property claims of existing canal and turnpike companies, the decision opened the way for legislatures to charter railroads that would provide a cheaper and more efficient transportation system.

Other decisions by the Taney Court placed limits on Marshall's nationalistic interpretation of the commerce clause by enhancing the regulatory role of state governments. For example, in *Mayor of New York v. Miln* (1837) the Taney Court ruled that New York State could use its "police power" to inspect the health of arriving immigrants. The Jacksonian Court also restored to the states some of the economic powers they had exercised before 1787. In *Briscoe v. Bank of Kentucky* (1837) the Court ruled that issuance of currency by a bank owned and controlled by the state of Kentucky did not violate the provision of the U.S. Constitution (Article 1, Section 10, on p. D-13) that prohibits states from issuing "bills of credit."

Jacksonian Democrats in the various states mounted their own constitutional revolutions. Between 1830 and 1860 twenty states called conventions to revise their basic charters. Most states extended the vote to all white men and reapportioned their legislatures on the basis of population. The revised constitutions also brought government "near to the people" by mandating the election, rather than the appointment, of most public officials—including sheriffs, justices of the peace, and judges.

Just as Jackson had destroyed the American System and its program of national government subsidies, so his disciples in the states undermined the "commonwealth" philosophy of using chartered corporations and state funds to promote economic development. Most Jacksonian-era constitutions prohibited states from granting exclusive charters to corporations or extending loans and credit guarantees to private businesses. "If there is any danger to be feared in . . . government," declared a New Jersey Democrat, "it is the danger of associated wealth, with special privileges." The revised state constitutions also protected taxpayers by setting strict limits on state debts and encouraging judges to enforce them. As a New York reformer put it, "We will not trust the legislature with the power of creating indefinite mortgages on the people's property."

"The world is governed too much," the Jacksonians proclaimed, as they condemned government-granted special privileges and embraced a small-government, laissez-faire outlook. The first American "populists," they celebrated the power of ordinary people to make decisions in the marketplace and the voting booth.

Class, Culture, and the Second Party System

The rise of the Democracy and Jackson's tumultuous presidency sparked the creation in the mid-1830s of a second national party—the Whigs—and a new party system. For the next two decades Whigs and Democrats competed fiercely for votes. Many evangelical Protestants became Whigs, while most Catholics and nonevangelical Protestants joined the Democrats. By debating issues of economic policy, class power, and moral reform, party politicians offered Americans a clear choice between rival political ideologies and programs.

The Whig Worldview

The Whig Party began in 1834, when a group of congressmen banded together to oppose Andrew Jackson's policies and his high-handed, "kinglike" conduct. They took the name Whigs to identify themselves with the pre-Revolutionary American and British parties—also called Whigs—that had opposed the arbitrary actions of British monarchs. The Whigs accused "King Andrew I" of violating the Constitution by creating a "spoils system" and increasing presidential authority. Jackson's "executive usurpation," they charged, undermined government by elected legislators, who were the true representatives of the sovereign people.

Initially the Whigs were a diverse group, a "heterogeneous mass" drawn from various political factions and outlooks. However, led by Senators Webster of Massachusetts, Clay of Kentucky, and Calhoun of South Carolina, the Whigs gradually elaborated a distinct vision. Their goal, like that of the Federalists of the 1790s, was a political world dominated by men of ability and wealth; unlike the Federalists, the Whig elite would be chosen by talent, not birth.

The Whigs celebrated the role played by enterprising entrepreneurs. "This is a country of self-made men," they boasted, pointing to the relative absence of permanent distinctions of class and status among the white citizens of the United States. Embracing the Industrial Revolution, northern Whigs welcomed the investments of "moneyed capitalists" which provided the poor with jobs, "bread, clothing and homes." Whig congressman Edward Everett told a Fourth of July crowd in Lowell, Massachusetts, that there was a "holy alliance" among laborers, owners, and governments. Many workers agreed, especially those holding jobs in the New England textile factories and Pennsylvania iron mills that benefited from state subsidies and protective tariffs. To ensure continued economic progress, Everett and other northern Whigs called for a return to the American System of Henry Clay and John Quincy Adams.

BORN TO COMMAND.

OF VETO MEMORY.

HAD I BEEN CONSULTED.

KING ANDREW THE FIRST.

A Whig Cartoon

Attacking the president as "KING ANDREW THE FIRST," this political cartoon accuses Andrew Jackson of acting arbitrarily, like a monarch, and trampling on the principles of the Constitution. It emphasizes Jackson's contempt for Congress, expressed in his vetoes of legislation on banking and internal improvements. Seeking to turn democratic fervor and popular sovereignty to the advantage of the Whig Party, the caption asked: "Shall he reign over us, or shall the PEOPLE RULE?"
New-York Historical Society.

Support for the Whigs in the South rested on the appeal of specific policies rather than agreement with the Whigs' social vision. Some southern Whigs were wealthy planters who invested in railroads and banks or sold their cotton to New York merchants. The majority were yeomen whites who wanted to break the grip over state politics held by low-country planters, most of whom were Democrats. In addition, some states' rights Democrats in Virginia and South Carolina became Whigs because, like John C. Calhoun, they condemned Andrew Jackson's crusade against nullification.

Like Calhoun, most southern Whigs did not share their party's enthusiasm for high tariffs and social mobility. Indeed, Calhoun argued that the northern Whig ideal of equal opportunity was contradicted not only by slavery, which he considered a fundamental American institution, but also by the wage-labor system of industrial capitalism. "There is and always has been in an advanced state of wealth and civilization a conflict between labor and capital," Calhoun argued in 1837. He urged slave owners and factory owners to unite against their common foe: the working class composed of enslaved blacks and propertyless whites.

Most northern Whigs rejected Calhoun's class-conscious vision. "A clear and well-defined line between capital and labor" might fit the slave South or class-ridden European societies, Daniel Webster conceded, but in the North "this distinction grows less and less definite as commerce advances." Webster focused on the growing size and affluence of the northern middle class. Indeed, in the election of 1834 the Whigs won a majority in the House of Representatives by appealing to evangelical Protestants and upwardly mobile groups—the prosperous farmers, small-town merchants, and skilled industrial workers in New England, New York, and the new communities along the Great Lakes.

Many Whigs had previously supported the Anti-Masonic Party, a powerful but short-lived political movement of the late 1820s. As the name implies, Anti-Masons opposed the Order of Freemasonry, a secret deistic and republican organization that began in eighteenth-century Europe. The order spread rapidly in America and attracted political leaders—including George Washington, Henry Clay, and Andrew Jackson—and ambitious businessmen. By the mid-1820s there were 20,000 Masons in New York State alone, organized into 450 local lodges. Following the kidnapping and murder of William Morgan, a New York Mason who had threatened to reveal the order's secrets, the order fell into disrepute. Thurlow Weed, a Rochester newspaper editor, spearheaded an Anti-Masonic political party that attacked Masonry as a secret aristocratic fraternity and ousted its members from local and state offices.

The Whigs recruited Anti-Masons by endorsing their values of temperance, equality of opportunity, and evangelical moralism. Throughout the Northeast and Midwest, Whig politicians advocated legal curbs on the sale of alcohol and supported local bylaws that preserved Sunday as a day of worship. The Whigs also won congressional seats in the Ohio and Mississippi Valleys, where farmers, bankers, and shopkeepers favored Henry Clay's policies for governmental subsidies for roads, canals, and bridges.

In the election of 1836 the Whig Party faced Martin Van Buren, the architect of the Democratic Party and Jackson's handpicked successor. Van Buren denounced the American System and warned that its revival would undermine the rights of the states and create an oppressive system of "consolidated government." Positioning himself as a defender of individual rights, Van Buren likewise opposed the plans of Whigs and moral reformers to use governmental power to impose temperance and abolish slavery. "The government is best which governs least" became his motto.

To oppose Van Buren, the Whigs ran four regional candidates. Their plan was to garner enough electoral votes to throw the contest into the House of Representatives. However, the Whig tally—73 electoral votes collected by William Henry Harrison of Ohio, 26 by Hugh L. White of Tennessee, 14 by Daniel Webster of Massachusetts, and 11 by W. P. Mangum of Georgia—fell far short of Van Buren's 170 votes. Still, the size of the popular vote for the four Whig candidates—49 percent of the total—showed that the party's message of economic improvement and moral uplift appealed not only to middle-class Americans but also to farmers and workers with little or no property. For the next two decades, Whigs and Democrats dominated American political life.

Labor Politics and the Depression of 1837–1843

As the Democratic and Whig Parties battled for supremacy, they faced a challenge from the Working Men's Parties that had sprung up in fifteen states between 1827 and 1833. Rising prices and stagnant wages had lowered the standard of living of many urban artisans and wage earners. Increasingly aware of what they called "the glaring inequality of society," workers organized for political action. "Past experience teaches us that we have nothing to hope from the aristocratic orders of society," declared the New York Working Men's Party. It vowed "to send men of our own description, if we can, to the Legislature at Albany" and to pass laws that would put an end to private banks, chartered monopolies, and imprisonment for debt. In Philadelphia, the Working Men's Party demanded higher taxes on the wealthy and, in 1834, persuaded the Pennsylvania legislature to authorize free, tax-supported schools to assist workers' children to advance into the propertied classes.

Artisan republicanism—workers' independence—was the core ideology of Working Men's Parties. Their goal was a society in which (as the radical thinker Orestes Brownson put it) there would be no dependent wage earners and "all men will be independent proprietors, working on their own capitals, on their own farms, or in their own shops." This vision prompted many artisan-republicans to join Jacksonian Democrats in demanding equal rights and attacking chartered corporations. "The only safeguard against oppression," argued William Leggett, a leading member of the New York Loco-Foco (Equal Rights) Party, "is a system of legislation which leaves to all the free exercise of their talents and industry." At first the Working Men's Parties prospered at the polls, but divisions over policy and voter apathy soon took a toll. By the mid-1830s most politically active workers had joined the Democratic Party, which they urged to oppose protective tariffs and to tax the stocks and bonds of wealthy capitalists.

Even as they campaigned for a more egalitarian society, workers formed unions to bargain for higher wages for themselves. Employers responded by attacking the union movement. In 1836 clothing manufacturers in New York City agreed not to hire workers belonging to the Society of Journeymen Tailors and circulated a list—a so-called **blacklist**—of its members. The employers also brought lawsuits to overturn **closed-shop agreements** that required them to hire only union members. They argued that such contracts violated both the common law and legislative statutes that prohibited "conspiracies" in restraint of trade.

Judges usually agreed with the employers. In 1835 the New York Supreme Court found that a shoemakers' union in Geneva had illegally caused "an industrious man" to be "driven out of employment." "It is important to the best interests of society that the price of labor be left to regulate itself," the Court declared. When a court in New York City upheld a conspiracy verdict against a tailors' union, a crowd of 27,000 people demonstrated outside city hall, and tailors circulated handbills proclaiming that the "Freemen of the North are now on a level with the slaves of the South." In 1836, such popular demonstrations prompted juries to acquit shoemakers in Hudson, New York, carpet makers in Thompsonville, Connecticut, and plasterers in Philadelphia of similar conspiracy charges.

At this juncture the Panic of 1837 threw the American economy—and the union movement—into disarray. The panic began when the Bank of England, hoping to boost the faltering British economy, sharply curtailed the flow of money and credit to the United States. For the previous decade and a half, British manufacturers and investors had provided southern planters with credit to expand cotton production and had purchased millions of dollars of the canal bonds issued by northern states. Suddenly deprived of British funds, American planters, merchants, and canal corporations had to withdraw specie from domestic banks to pay their foreign loans and commercial debts. Moreover, because the Bank of England refused credit to brokers to buy cotton, the price of raw cotton in the South collapsed from 20 cents a pound to 10 cents or less.

Falling cotton prices and the drain of gold and silver set off a general financial crisis. On May 8 the Dry Dock Bank of New York City closed its doors. Panicked depositors quickly withdrew more than $2 million in gold and silver coins from other New York banks, which forced them to suspend all specie payments. Within two weeks every bank in the United States stopped trading specie and curtailed credit, which sent the economy into a steep decline. "This sudden overthrow of the commercial credit and honor of the nation" had a "stunning effect," observed Henry Fox, the British minister in Washington. "The conquest of the land by a foreign power could hardly have produced a more general sense of humiliation and grief."

A second, longer-lasting economic downturn began in 1839. Following the Panic of 1837, state governments increased their investments in canals and other transportation ventures. As more and more bonds to finance these ventures were sold in Europe, bond prices fell sharply and sparked a four-year-long international financial crisis. The crisis engulfed state governments, which were unable to meet the substantial interest payments on their bonds. Nine states defaulted on their obligations to foreign creditors, which undermined the confidence of European investors and cut the flow of capital to the United States. Bumper crops drove down cotton prices even further, bringing more bankruptcies.

The American economy fell into a deep depression. By 1843 canal construction had dropped 90 percent and prices nearly 50 percent. Unemployment reached almost 20 percent of the workforce in seaports and industrial centers. Minister Henry Ward Beecher described a land "filled with lamentation . . . its inhabitants wandering like bereaved citizens among the ruins of an earthquake, mourning for children, for houses crushed, and property buried forever."

By creating a surplus of unemployed workers, the depression devastated the labor movement. In 1837, six thousand masons, carpenters, and other building-trades workers lost their jobs in New York City, depleting union membership and destroying unions' bargaining power. By 1843 most local unions and all the national labor organizations had disappeared, along with their newspapers.

However, two events improved the long-term prospects of the labor movement. The first was a major legal success. In *Commonwealth v. Hunt* (1842), Massachusetts chief justice Lemuel Shaw upheld the rights of workers to form unions and enforce a closed shop. Shaw, one of the great jurists of the nineteenth century, overturned common-law precedents by ruling that a union was not an inherently illegal organization and could strike to enforce a closed shop. Courts in many states accepted Shaw's opinion, but judges (who were mostly Whigs) found other methods, such as **court injunctions**, to restrict strikes. Labor's second success was political. Continuing Jackson's effort to recruit workers to the Democratic Party, President Van Buren signed an executive order in 1840 setting a ten-hour day for federal employees. This victory showed that the outcome of workers' struggles—like conflicts over tariffs, banks, and internal improvements—depended not only on economic factors but also on political decisions.

"Tippecanoe and Tyler Too!"

The depression had a major impact on politics because many Americans blamed the Democrats for their economic woes. In particular, they derided Jackson for destroying the Second Bank and for issuing the Specie Circular of 1836, which required western settlers to use gold and silver coins to pay for land purchases. Not realizing that specie shipments to Britain (to pay off past debts) were the main cause of the financial panic, the Whigs blamed Jackson's policies.

The public turned its anger on Van Buren, who took office just as the panic began. Ignoring the pleas of influential bankers, the new president refused to revoke the Specie Circular or take other actions to reverse the downturn. Holding to his philosophy of limited government, Van Buren advised Congress that "the less government interferes with private pursuits the better for the general prosperity." As a major depression took hold in 1839, this laissez-faire outlook commanded less and less political support. Worse, Van Buren's major piece of economic legislation, the Independent Treasury Act of 1840, actually delayed recovery. The act pulled federal specie out of Jackson's "pet banks" (which had used it to back loans) and placed it in government vaults (where it did no economic good at all).

Determined to exploit Van Buren's weakness, the Whigs organized their first national convention in 1840 and nominated William Henry Harrison of Ohio for president and John Tyler of Virginia for vice president. A military hero of the Battle of Tippecanoe and the War of 1812, Harrison was well advanced in age (sixty-eight) and had little political experience. But the Whig leaders in Congress, Clay and Webster, simply wanted a president who would rubber-stamp their program for protective tariffs and a national bank. An unpretentious, amiable man, Harrison told voters that Whig policies were "the only means, under Heaven, by which a poor industrious man may become a rich man without bowing to colossal wealth."

Panic and depression stacked the political cards against Van Buren, but the contest turned as much on style as on substance. It became the great "log cabin"

The Log Cabin Campaign, 1840

During the Second Party System, politics became more responsive to the popular will as ordinary people voted for candidates who shared their values and lifestyles. The barrels of hard cider surrounding this homemade campaign banner evoke the drink of the common man, while the central image falsely portrays William Henry Harrison as a poor and simple frontier farmer.
New-York Historical Society.

campaign—the first occasion on which two well-organized parties competed for the loyalties of a mass electorate and created a new style of festive political celebrations. Whig pamphleteering, songfests, parades, and well-orchestrated mass meetings drew new voters into the political arena. Whig speakers assailed "Martin Van Ruin" as a manipulative politician with aristocratic tastes—a devotee of fancy wines and elegant clothes, as indeed he was. With less candor they praised Harrison, whose father was a wealthy planter who had signed the Declaration of Independence, as a self-made man who lived in a simple log cabin and enjoyed hard cider, a drink of the common people.

The Whigs boosted their electoral hopes by welcoming women to their festivities. Previously women had been excluded not only from voting and jury duty but also from marching in political parades. Jacksonian Democrats celebrated politics as a "manly" affair and denounced women who ventured into the political arena as "public" women—the prostitutes who plied their trade in theaters and other public places. However, the Whigs recognized that women from Yankee families, a core Whig constituency, had already entered American public life through religious revivalism, the temperance movement, and other benevolent activities. In October 1840 Daniel Webster addressed a mass meeting of 1,200 Whig women and praised their support for the Whig programs for moral reform. "This way of making politicians of their women is something new under the sun," noted one Democrat, worried that it would bring more Whig men to the polls. Indeed, more than 80 percent of the eligible male voters cast ballots in 1840 (up from less than 60 percent in 1832 and 1836). Heeding the Whig slogan "Tippecanoe and Tyler Too," they voted Harrison into the White House and gave the Whigs a majority in Congress.

The Whigs' joy was short-lived. One month after his inauguration Harrison died of pneumonia, and the nation got "Tyler Too." The new president, John Tyler of Virginia, had joined the Whigs to oppose Jackson's stance against nullification. On economic issues Tyler shared Jackson's hostility to the Second Bank and the American System. Consequently, he vetoed bills that would have raised tariffs and created a new national bank. Also like Jackson, Tyler favored the rapid settlement of the West. He approved the Preemption Act of 1841, which allowed cash-poor settlers to stake a free claim to 160 acres of federal land. By building a house and farming the land, they could buy the property later at a set price of $1.25 an acre.

The split between Tyler and the Whigs allowed the Democrats to regroup. The party vigorously recruited supporters among subsistence farmers in the North and smallholding planters in the South. It cultivated the votes of the urban working class and was particularly successful among Irish and German Catholic immigrants—whose numbers had increased rapidly during the 1830s—by supporting their demands for religious and cultural freedom. Thanks to these recruits, the Democrats remained the majority party in most parts of the nation. Their program of equal rights, states' rights, and cultural liberty was more attractive than the Whig platform of economic nationalism, moral reform, and individual mobility.

The continuing struggle between Whigs and Democrats, each claiming to speak for "the people," completed the democratic revolution that European visitors found so troubling. The new system perpetuated many problematic political customs—denying women, Indians, and most African Americans an effective voice in public life—and introduced a few more dubious practices, such as the spoils system and a coarser standard of public debate. Yet the United States now boasted universal suffrage for white men as well as a highly organized system of representative government that was responsive to ordinary citizens. In their scope and significance these political initiatives matched the economic advances of the Industrial and Market Revolutions.

TIMELINE

1810s	State constitutions revised to expand voting rights for white men	**1833**	Force Bill and compromise Tariff Act
	Martin Van Buren creates a disciplined party in New York	**1834**	Whig Party formed by Henry Clay, John C. Calhoun, and Daniel Webster
1825	John Quincy Adams elected president by House; advocates Henry Clay's American System	**1835**	Roger Taney named Supreme Court chief justice
		1837	*Charles River Bridge Co. v. Warren Bridge Co.* weakens legal position of chartered monopolies
1827	Philadelphia Working Men's Party organized		
1828	"Tariff of Abominations" raises duties on imported materials and manufactures		Panic of 1837 ends long period of economic expansion
	The South Carolina Exposition and Protest challenges legitimacy of national legislation and majority rule	**1838**	Trail of Tears: thousands of Cherokees die on forced march to new Indian Territory
1830	Andrew Jackson vetoes extension of National Road	**1839**	American borrowings spark international financial crisis and four-year economic depression
	Congress enacts Jackson's Indian Removal Act	**1840**	Van Buren finally wins Independent Treasury Act
1831	*Cherokee Nation v. Georgia* denies Indians' claim of national independence		Whig victory in "log cabin" campaign
1832	Expulsion of Sauk and Fox peoples; Bad Axe Massacre by American troops	**1841**	John Tyler succeeds William Henry Harrison as president
	Jackson vetoes the rechartering of the Second Bank		Preemption Act promotes purchase of federal land
	South Carolina asserts intention to nullify Tariffs of 1828 and 1832	**1842**	*Commonwealth v. Hunt* legitimates trade unions
	Worcester v. Georgia upholds political autonomy of Indian peoples		

For Further Exploration

George Dangerfield, *The Era of Good Feelings* (1952), is the classic study of American politics between 1815 and 1828. Two concise and well-written surveys of the Jacksonian era are Harry L. Watson, *Liberty and Power: The Politics of Jacksonian America* (1990), which emphasizes the importance of republican ideology and the Market Revolution, and Daniel Feller, *The Jacksonian Promise: America, 1815–1840* (1995), which underlines its tremendous optimism. In *The Idea of a Party System* (1969), Richard Hofstadter lucidly explains the traditional opposition to parties and their triumphant entry into American politics. The Internet Public Library has material on the election of 1824, the John Quincy Adams administration, and links to primary sources at <http://www.ipl.org/div/potus/jqadams.html>.

Robert V. Remini, *The Life of Andrew Jackson* (1988), highlights Jackson's triumphs without neglecting his shortcomings. The brutal impact of Jackson's Indian policy is brought to life in Robert J. Conley, *Mountain Windsong: A Novel of the Trail of Tears* (1992) and two studies by historians: Sean Michael O'Brien, *In Bitterness and in Tears: Andrew Jackson's Destruction of the Creeks and Seminoles* (2003) and John Buchanan, *Jackson's Way: Andrew Jackson and the People of the Western Waters* (2001). Major L. Wilson, *The Presidency of Martin Van Buren* (1984), provides a shrewd assessment of the man and his policies. The ideology and politics of the laboring population is the focus of Sean Wilentz, *Chants Democratic: New York City and the Rise of the American Working Class, 1788–1850* (1986).

Alexis de Tocqueville's classic, *Democracy in America* (1835), should be sampled for its insights into the character of American society and political institutions. The book is available online accompanied by an excellent exhibit and collection of essays at <http://xroads.virginia.edu/~hyper/detoc/home.html>. For a brief treatment of the life of Andrew Jackson and some of his important state papers, log on to the Revolution to Reconstruction site at the University of Groningen in the Netherlands at <http://odur.let.rug.nl/~usa/P/aj7/aj7.htm>. For material on the Cherokees, see the Web site prepared by Ken Martin, a tribal member of the Cherokee Nation of Oklahoma, <http://cherokeehistory.com/>, and also <http://www.rosecity.net/tears/>, which has links to articles, primary sources, and other Web sites.

For definitions of key terms boldfaced in this chapter, see the glossary at the end of the book.

To assess your mastery of the material covered in this chapter, see the Online Study Guide at **bedfordstmartins.com/henrettaconcise**.

For map resources and primary documents, see **bedfordstmartins.com/henrettaconcise**.

Chapter 12

RELIGION AND REFORM
1820–1860

A peaceable man can hardly venture to eat or drink, . . . to correct his child or kiss his wife, without obtaining the permission . . . of some moral or other reform society.

ORESTES BROWNSON, 1838

"The spirit of reform is in every place," the children of legal reformer David Dudley Field wrote in their handwritten monthly *Gazette* in 1842:

> The labourer with a family says "reform the common schools"; the merchant and the planter say, "reform the tariff"; the lawyer "reform the laws," the politician "reform the government," the abolitionist "reform the slave laws," the moralist "reform intemperance," . . . the ladies wish their legal privileges extended, and in short, the whole country is wanting reform.

Like many Americans, the young Field children sensed that the political whirlwind of the 1830s had transformed the way people thought about themselves as individuals and as a society. Suddenly, thousands of men and women, inspired by the optimistic enthusiasm of the Second Great Awakening and democratic spirit of the age, believed they could improve not just their personal lives but society as a whole. Some dedicated themselves to the cause of reform. Beginning as an antislavery advocate, William Lloyd Garrison went on to embrace women's rights, pacifism, and the abolition of prisons. Such individuals, the Unitarian minister Henry W. Bellows warned, were obsessed, pursuing "an object, which in its very nature is unattainable—the perpetual improvement of the outward condition."

Many obstacles stood in the way of the reformers' quest for a better society. The American social order was rigidly divided by race and gender as well as by wealth and religious belief. Moreover, recent social changes imposed new burdens on some individuals even as they enhanced the standard of living for many others. Most strikingly, the new market economy encouraged greater discipline, both at work and in family life. Planters forced enslaved African Americans to labor in organized gangs, and factory managers prescribed strict routines for factory operatives. Moreover, the first wave of American "social improvers," the benevolent reformers of the 1820s, celebrated the extension of discipline over all phases of life. To solve the nation's ills, they championed regular church attendance, temperance, and the strict moral codes of the evangelical churches.

Then in the 1830s and 1840s a more radical wave of reform spilled out of these conservative religious channels and threatened to submerge traditional values and institutions. The new reformers were mostly middle-class northerners and mid-westerners. They propounded a bewildering assortment of radical ideals—extreme individualism, common ownership of property, the immediate emancipation of slaves, and sexual equality—and demanded immediate action to satisfy their visions. Although they formed a small minority of the American population, the reformers launched intellectual and cultural debate that won the attention, if not the respect, of the majority. As a fearful southerner saw it, the goal of the reformers was a world in which there would be "No-Marriage, No-Religion, No-Private Property, No-Law and No-Government."

Individualism

The reform movement reflected the actual social conditions and intellectual currents of American life. In 1835 Alexis de Tocqueville coined a new word, *individualism*, to describe the lives of native-born white Americans. In his view, Americans were "no longer attached to each other by any tie of caste, class, association, or family" and so lived in a more solitary world than most Europeans did. Unlike Tocqueville, an aristocrat who feared the disintegration of society, the New England transcendentalist Ralph Waldo Emerson (1803–1882) celebrated this liberation of the individual from traditional social and institutional constraints. Emerson's vision of individual freedom—balanced by a sense of personal responsibility—influenced thousands of ordinary Americans and a generation of important artists and writers.

Emerson and Transcendentalism

Emerson was the leading spokesman for **transcendentalism**, an intellectual movement rooted in the religious soil of New England. Its first advocates were spiritually inclined young men, often Unitarian ministers from well-to-do New England families, who questioned the constraints of their Puritan heritage. For inspiration they turned to Europe and a new conception of self and society known as *Romanticism*. Romantic thinkers, such as the English poet Samuel Taylor Coleridge, rejected the ordered, rational world of the eighteenth-century Enlightenment. Instead they tried to capture the passionate aspects of the human spirit and gain deeper insights into the mysteries of existence. Drawing on the ideas of the German philosopher Immanuel Kant, English romantics and Unitarian radicals tried to go beyond rational thought and the world experienced through the senses of sight and sound

The Founder of Transcendentalism

As this painting of Ralph Waldo Emerson by an unknown artist indicates, the young New England philosopher was an attractive man, his face brimming with confidence and optimism. Because of his radiant personality and in-cisive intellect, Emerson deeply in-fluenced dozens of influential writers, artists, and scholars and enjoyed great success as a lecturer among the emerging middle class. The Metropolitan Museum of Art, bequest of Chester Dale, 1962 [64.97.4].

and touch. By tapping mysterious intuitive powers people could "transcend" the lim-its of ordinary existence and gain mystical knowledge of ultimate and eternal things.

As a Unitarian minister, Emerson already stood outside the mainstream of American Protestantism. Unlike most Christians, Unitarians held that God was a single being and not a trinity of Father, Son, and Holy Spirit. In 1832 Emerson took a more radical step by resigning his Boston pulpit and rejecting all organized reli-gion. Moving to Concord, Massachusetts, he gradually articulated the philosophy of transcendentalism. In a series of influential essays Emerson focused on what he called "the infinitude of the private man," the idea of the radically free individual.

The young philosopher saw people as being trapped in inherited customs and in-stitutions. They wore the ideas of earlier times—the tenets of New England Calvinism, for example—as a kind of "faded masquerade" and needed to shed those values and practices. "What is a man born for but to be a Reformer, a Remaker of what man has made?" he asked. For Emerson, an individual could be remade only by discovering his or her own "original relation with Nature," an insight that would produce a mystical union with the "currents of Universal Being." The ideal setting for such a transcendent discovery was solitude under an open sky, among nature's rocks and trees.

Emerson's genius lay in his capacity to translate such abstract ideas into ex-amples that made sense to ordinary middle-class Americans. His essays and lectures suggested that all nature was saturated with the presence of God—a pantheistic spiritual outlook that departed from traditional Christian doctrine. Emerson also warned his readers that the new market society was diverting the nation's spiritual energy into a preoccupation with work, profits, and the consumption of factory-made goods. "Things are in the saddle," Emerson wrote, "and ride mankind."

The transcendentalist message of self-realization reached hundreds of thousands of people, primarily through Emerson's writings and lectures. Public lectures had become a spectacularly successful way of spreading information and fostering discussion among the middle classes. Beginning in 1826 the American Lyceum promoted "the general diffusion of knowledge" by organizing lecture tours by hundreds of poets, preachers, scientists, and reformers. Named in honor of the place where the ancient Greek philosopher Aristotle taught, the Lyceum became an important cultural institution in the North and Midwest (but not in the South, where popular education had a lower priority and apologists for slavery discouraged the free discussion of ideas). In 1839, nearly 150 local Lyceums in Massachusetts invited lecturers to their towns to speak to more than 33,000 subscribers. The most popular lecturer on the Lyceum circuit, Emerson gave 1,500 lectures in more than 300 towns in twenty states.

Emerson's essays celebrated individuals who rejected traditional social restraints but acted as self-disciplined and responsible members of society. And, in fact, his writings spoke directly to the personal experience of many mid-nineteenth-century middle-class Americans, who had left the farms of their ancestors and made their own way in the urban world. Charles Grandison Finney's widely known account of his religious conversion underscored the appeal of Emerson's ideas and values. Finney pictured his conversion as a mystical union of an individual, alone in the woods, with God. And, like Emerson, Finney stressed the need to transcend the constraints and doctrines of the past. As the revivalist put it, "God has made man a moral free agent," endowing individuals with the ability—and the responsibility—to determine their spiritual fate.

Emerson's Literary Influence

Emerson took as one of his tasks the remaking of American literature. In an address entitled "The American Scholar" (1837) the philosopher issued a literary declaration of independence from the "courtly muse" of Old Europe. He urged American writers to celebrate democracy and individual freedom and find inspiration not in the lives of kings and aristocrats but in ordinary experiences: "the ballad in the street; the news of the boat; the glance of the eye; the form and gait of the body."

A young New England intellectual, Henry David Thoreau (1817–1862) heeded Emerson's call by turning to the American environment for inspiration. In 1845, depressed by his beloved brother's death, Thoreau turned away from society and embraced the natural world. He built a cabin at the edge of Walden Pond near Concord, Massachusetts, and lived alone there for two years. In 1854 he published *Walden, or Life in the Woods*, an account of his spiritual search for meaning beyond the artificiality of "civilized" life:

I went to the woods because I wished to live deliberately, to front only the essential facts of life, and see if I could not learn what it had to teach, and not, when I came to die, discover that I had not lived.

Although Thoreau's book had little impact during his lifetime, *Walden* has become an essential text of American literature and an inspiration to those who reject the dictates of society. Its most famous metaphor provides an enduring justification for independent thinking: "If a man does not keep pace with his companions, perhaps it is because he hears a different drummer." Beginning from this premise, Thoreau advocated social nonconformity and civil disobedience against unjust laws.

As Thoreau sought independence and self-realization for men, Margaret Fuller (1810–1850) explored the possibilities of freedom for women. Born into a wealthy Boston family, Fuller mastered six languages, read broadly in the classic works of literature, and educated her four siblings. While teaching in a school for girls, she became interested in Emerson's ideas and in 1839 began a transcendental "conversation," or discussion group, for educated Boston women. Soon Fuller was editing the leading transcendentalist journal, the *Dial*, and in 1844 she published *Woman in the Nineteenth Century*, which proclaimed that a "new era" was coming in the relations between men and women.

Fuller's philosophy began with the transcendental belief that women, like men, had a mystical relationship with God that gave them identity and dignity. Every woman therefore deserved psychological and social independence—the ability "to grow, as an intellect to discern, as a soul to live freely and unimpeded." "We would have every arbitrary barrier thrown down," she wrote, and "every path laid open to Woman as freely as to Man." Embracing that vision, Fuller became the literary critic of the New York *Tribune* and traveled to Italy to report on the Revolution of 1848. Her adventurous life led to an early death; returning to the United States, she drowned in a shipwreck. Nonetheless, Fuller's example and writings inspired a rising generation of women writers and reformers.

Another writer who responded to Emerson's call was the poet Walt Whitman (1819–1892). When Whitman first encountered Emerson, he had been "simmering, simmering." Then Emerson "brought me to a boil." Whitman worked as a teacher, a journalist, an editor of the *Brooklyn Eagle*, and an influential publicist for the Democratic Party. But poetry was the "direction of his dreams." In *Leaves of Grass*, first published in 1855 and constantly revised and expanded for almost four decades afterward, he recorded in verse his efforts to pass a number of "invisible boundaries": between solitude and community, between prose and poetry, and even between the living and the dead. A wild, exuberant poem in both form and content, *Leaves of Grass* self-consciously violated every poetic rule and every canon of respectable taste. At the center of *Leaves of Grass* is the individual—the figure of the poet, "I, Walt." He begins alone: "I celebrate myself, and sing myself." But because he has an Emersonian "original relation" with nature, Whitman claims not solitude but perfect communion with others: "For every atom belonging to me as good belongs to you." Whitman celebrates democracy as well as himself by seeking a profoundly intimate, mystical relationship with a mass audience. For Emerson, Thoreau, and Fuller, the individual had a divine spark. For Whitman the individual had expanded to become divine and democracy assumed a sacred character.

The transcendentalists were not naive optimists. Whitman wrote about human suffering with passion, and Emerson's accounts of transcendence were tinged with anxiety. "I am glad," he once said, "to the brink of fear." Thoreau had a gloomy judgment of everyday life: "The mass of men lead lives of quiet desperation." Still, such dark murmurings were muted in their work, overshadowed by triumphant and expansive assertions that nothing was impossible for an individual who could break free from tradition, law, and other social restraints.

Emerson's writings also influenced two great novelists, Nathaniel Hawthorne and Herman Melville, who had more pessimistic outlooks. Both sounded powerful warnings that unfettered egoism could destroy individuals and those around them. Hawthorne's most brilliant exploration of the theme of excessive individualism appeared in his novel *The Scarlet Letter* (1850). The two main characters, Hester Prynne and Arthur Dimmesdale, challenge their seventeenth-century New England community in the most blatant way—by committing adultery and producing a child. The result of their assertion of individual freedom from social discipline and responsibility is not liberation but degradation—a profound sense of personal guilt and condemnation by the community.

Herman Melville explored the limits of individualism in even more extreme and tragic terms and emerged as a scathing critic of transcendentalism. He made his most powerful statement in *Moby-Dick* (1851), the story of Captain Ahab's obsessive hunt for a mysterious white whale that ends in death not only for Ahab but also for all but one member of his crew. Here the quest for spiritual meaning in nature brings death, not transcendence, because Ahab, the liberated individual, lacks inner discipline and self-restraint.

Moby-Dick was a commercial failure. The middle-class audience that was the primary target of American publishers refused to follow Melville into the dark, dangerous realms of individualism gone mad. Readers also were unenthusiastic about Thoreau's advocacy of civil disobedience during the Mexican War and Whitman's boundless claims of a mystical union between the man of genius and the democratic masses. What American readers emphatically preferred were the more modest examples of individualism offered by Emerson and Finney—personal improvement through spiritual awareness and self-discipline.

Brook Farm

To escape the constraints of life in America's emerging market society, transcendentalists and other radical reformers created ideal communities, or utopias. They hoped that these planned societies, which organized life in new ways, would allow their members to realize their spiritual and moral potential. The most important transcendentalist communal experiment was Brook Farm, founded just outside Boston in 1841. By opting out of the competition and tension of urban society, its members hoped to develop their minds and souls and to inspire a new social order.

The intellectual life at Brook Farm was electric. Hawthorne lived there for a time and later used the setting for his novel *The Blithedale Romance* (1852). All the major transcendentalists, including Emerson, Thoreau, and Fuller, were residents or frequent visitors. A former member recalled that they "inspired the young with a passion for study, and the middle-aged with deference and admiration, while we all breathed the intellectual grace that pervaded the atmosphere." If Brook Farm provided intellectual bliss, it offered few economic rewards. To escape the unpredictable boom-and-bust cycle of a market economy, the Brook Farmers sought to become self-sufficient in food and to exchange their surplus milk, vegetables, and hay for nonagricultural goods. However, its first members were ministers, teachers, writers, and students who had few farming skills, and only the cash payments of intellectually inclined residents kept the enterprise afloat. Following a devastating fire in 1846, the organizers disbanded and sold the farm.

After the failure of Brook Farm, the Emersonians abandoned their quest for a new system of social organization. Most transcendentalists accepted the brute reality of the emergent industrial order and tried to reform it, especially through the education of workers. However, the passion of the transcendentalists for individual freedom and social progress lived on in the movement to abolish slavery, which many of them actively supported.

Communalism

Even as Brook Farm collapsed, thousands of Americans joined other communal settlements in the rural areas of the Northeast and Midwest (Map 12.1). Most communalists were ordinary farmers and artisans who were seeking refuge and security during the seven-year economic depression that began with the Panic of 1837. However, these rural utopias were also symbols of social protest and experimentation. By prescribing the common ownership of property and devising unconventional forms of marriage and family life, the communalist leaders challenged the legitimacy of acquisitive capitalist values and traditional gender roles.

The Shakers

The Shakers were the first successful American communal movement. In 1770 Ann Lee Stanley (Mother Ann), a young cook in Manchester, England, had a vision that she was an incarnation of Christ and that Adam and Eve had been banished from

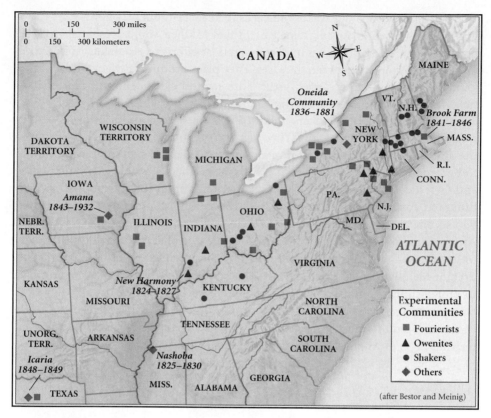

MAP 12.1 Major Communal Experiments before 1860

Some experimental communities settled along the frontier, but the vast majority chose relatively secluded areas in well-settled regions of the North and West. Because of their opposition to slavery, communalists avoided the South. Most secular experiments failed within a few decades, as the founders lost their reformist enthusiasm or died off; religious communities—such as the Shakers and the Mormons—were longer lived.

the Garden of Eden because of their sexual lust. Four years later she led a band of eight followers to America, where they established a church near Albany, New York. Because of the ecstatic dances that were part of their worship, the sect became known as "Shaking Quakers" or, more simply, "Shakers." After Mother Ann's death in 1784, the Shakers venerated her as the Second Coming of Christ, withdrew from the profane world, and formed strictly run religious communities. Members embraced the common ownership of property, accepted strict oversight by the church, and pledged to abstain from alcohol, tobacco, politics, and war. Shakers also repudiated marriage and sexual pleasure. Their commitment to celibacy followed Mother Ann's testimony against "the lustful gratifications of the flesh as the source and foundation of human corruption."

The Shakers' theology was as radical as their social thought. They held that God was "a dual person, male and female," and that Mother Ann represented God's female element. These doctrines underpinned their efforts to eliminate arbitrary distinctions of authority between the sexes. They placed community governance in the hands of both women and men—the eldresses and elders. However, in other respects Shakers maintained a traditional division of labor between the sexes.

Beginning in 1787 Shakers founded twenty communities, mostly in New England, New York, and Ohio. Their agriculture and crafts, especially furniture making, acquired a reputation for quality that enabled most of these communities to become self-sustaining and even comfortable. Thanks to this economic success and their ideology of sexual equality, Shaker communities attracted more than three thousand converts during the 1830s, with women outnumbering men more than two to one. They welcomed blacks as well as whites; to Rebecca Cox Jackson, an African American seamstress from Philadelphia, the Shakers seemed to be "loving to live forever." Because the Shakers disdained sexual intercourse and had no children of their own, they had to rely on converts and the adoption of young orphans to replenish their numbers. As these sources dried up in the 1840s and 1850s, the communities stopped growing and eventually began to decline. By the end of the nineteenth century most Shaker communities had disappeared, leaving as their material legacy a distinctive and much-imitated furniture style.

The Shaker Community at Poland Hill, Maine (detail)

Like all Shaker communities, the settlement at Poland Hill, Maine, painted by Joshua H. Bussell around 1850, was built on a regular gridlike plan. There was a large dwelling for communal living, surrounded by various workshops and farm buildings. The design of the architecture, like that of Shaker furniture, was plain and sparse.

Collection of the United Society of Shakers, Sabbathday Lake, ME.

FOR MORE HELP ANALYZING THIS IMAGE, see the Online Study Guide at **bedfordstmartins.com/ henrettaconcise**.

The Fourierist Phalanxes

One cause of the Shakers' decline was the rise during the 1840s of the American Fourierist movement. Charles Fourier (1777–1837) was a French utopian reformer who devised an eight-stage theory of social evolution that predicted the imminent decline of individualism and capitalism. As interpreted by Arthur Brisbane, Fourier's leading American disciple, Fourierism would allow the completion of "our great political movement of 1776" by eliminating the "menial and slavish system of Hired Labor or Labor for Wages." In the place of capitalist waged labor, men and women would work cooperatively in communities called phalanxes. The members of a phalanx would be its shareholders; they would own all its property in common, including stores and a bank as well as a school and a library.

Fourier and Brisbane saw the phalanx as a practical, more humane alternative to a society based on private property and capitalist values, and one that would liberate women as well as men. "In society as it is now constituted," Brisbane wrote, "Woman is subjected to unremitting and slavish domestic duties." In the "new Social Order . . . based upon Associated households" women's domestic labor would be shared with men.

Brisbane skillfully promoted Fourier's ideas in his influential book *The Social Destiny of Man* (1840), a regular column in Horace Greeley's New York *Tribune*, and hundreds of lectures, many of them in towns along the Erie Canal. Fourierist ideas found a receptive audience among educated farmers and craftsmen, who yearned for economic stability and communal solidarity in the wake of the Panic of 1837. During the 1840s Brisbane and his followers started nearly one hundred cooperative communities, mostly in western New York and the midwestern states of Ohio, Michigan, and Wisconsin. However, most of these communities quickly collapsed because of internal disputes over work responsibilities and social policies. Just as the rise of Fourierism underscored the social dislocation caused by the economic depression, so its collapse showed the difficulty of establishing a utopian community in the absence of charismatic leaders or a compelling religious vision.

John Humphrey Noyes and the Oneida Community

The radical minister John Humphrey Noyes (1811–1886) was both charismatic and deeply religious. He ascribed the Fourierists' failure to the absence of the strong religious ethic required for sustained altruism and cooperation and praised the Shakers as the true "pioneers of modern Socialism." The Shakers' marriageless society likewise appealed to Noyes and inspired him to create a community that defined sexuality and gender roles in radically new ways.

Noyes was a well-to-do graduate of Dartmouth College in New Hampshire who joined the ministry because of the inspired preaching of Charles Finney. Dismissed from his Congregational church for holding unorthodox beliefs, Noyes turned to perfectionism. Perfectionism was an evangelical movement that began in the 1830s and attracted thousands of religiously minded New Englanders who had moved to New York and Ohio. Perfectionists believed that the Second Coming of Christ had already occurred and that people could therefore aspire to sinless perfection in their earthly lives. Unlike most perfectionists (who lived conventional personal lives), Noyes believed that the major barrier to achieving this ideal state was marriage, which did not exist in heaven and should not exist on earth. "Exclusiveness, jealousy, quarreling have no place at the marriage supper of the Lamb," Noyes wrote. Like the Shakers, Noyes wanted to liberate individuals from sin by reforming relations between men and women. However, instead of Shaker celibacy, Noyes and his followers embraced complex marriage—all the members of his community were married to one another.

Noyes's marriage system reflected growing concern over the legal and cultural constraints on women's lives. He rejected monogamy partly because he wished to free women from being regarded as the property of their husbands, as they were by custom and by common law. To give women the time and energy to become full and equal participants in economic and social life, Noyes urged them to avoid multiple pregnancies. He asked men to assist this effort by avoiding orgasm during intercourse. To raise the children of his followers, Noyes set up communal nurseries that were run by both sexes. To symbolize sexual equality, Noyes's women followers cut their hair short and wore pantaloons under calf-length skirts.

In the late 1830s Noyes established a community based on complex marriage near his hometown of Putney, Vermont. When local opposition to his unorthodox sexual practices became intense, Noyes moved his followers to an isolated settlement in Oneida, New York. By the mid-1850s about two hundred people were living at Oneida, and it became financially successful when the inventor of a highly successful steel animal trap joined the community. With the profits acquired by selling those traps, Oneida diversified into the production of silverware. After Noyes fled to Canada in 1879 to avoid prosecution for adultery, the community abandoned complex marriage and founded a joint-stock silver manufacturing company, the Oneida Community, Ltd., which remained a well-known and prosperous enterprise well into the twentieth century.

As with the Shakers and Fourierists, the historical significance of Noyes and the Oneidians does not lie in their numbers, which were small, or in their fine crafts. Rather, these communities were important because, in a dramatically more radical fashion than Emerson and the transcendentalists, they questioned traditional customs and repudiated the class divisions and sexual norms of the emergent capitalist society. They stood as countercultural blueprints for a more egalitarian social order.

The Mormon Experience

The Shakers and the Oneidians challenged marriage and family life—two of the most deeply rooted institutions—but their small communities aroused little hostility. The

Mormons, members of the Church of Jesus Christ of Latter-day Saints, provoked much more animosity because of their different, but equally controversial, doctrines and their success in attracting thousands of members.

Like many social movements of the era, Mormonism emerged from the religious ferment among families of Puritan descent who lived along the Erie Canal. The founder of the Mormon Church was Joseph Smith (1805–1844), a vigorous, powerful individual. Born in Vermont to a poor farming and shopkeeping family, he moved at the age of ten to Palmyra in central New York. In a series of religious experiences that began in 1820, Smith came to believe that God had singled him out to receive a special revelation of divine truth. In 1830 he published *The Book of Mormon*, which he claimed to have translated from ancient hieroglyphics on gold plates shown to him by an angel named Moroni. *The Book of Mormon* told the story of ancient civilizations from the Middle East that had migrated to the Western Hemisphere and of the visit of Jesus Christ, soon after the Resurrection, to one of them.

Smith proceeded to organize the Church of Jesus Christ of Latter-day Saints. Seeing himself as a prophet to a sinful, excessively individualistic society, Smith revived traditional social doctrines, such as patriarchal authority within the family. Like many Protestant ministers, he also encouraged practices that were central to individual success in the age of capitalist markets and factories—frugality, hard work, and entrepreneurial enterprise. Unlike most other nineteenth-century ministers, Smith placed great emphasis on a communal framework that would protect the Mormon "New Jerusalem" from individualism and rival religious doctrines. His goal was a church-directed society that would inspire moral perfection.

Smith struggled for years to establish a secure home for his new religion. Facing persecution from anti-Mormons, Smith and his growing congregation trekked west, eventually settling in Nauvoo, Illinois, a town they founded on the Mississippi River (Map 12.2). By the early 1840s Nauvoo had become the largest utopian community in the United States, with 30,000 inhabitants. The rigid discipline and secret rituals of the Mormons—along with their prosperity, hostility to other sects, and bloc voting in Illinois elections—fueled resentment among their neighbors. This resentment turned to overt hostility when Smith refused to abide by any Illinois law that he did not approve, asked Congress to turn Nauvoo into a separate federal territory, and declared himself a candidate for president of the United States (see American Voices, "An Illinois 'Jeffersonian' Attacks the Mormons," p. 365).

Moreover, Smith claimed to have received a new revelation that justified polygamy—the practice of a man having more than one wife at one time. When a few leading Mormon men took several wives, they sparked a vigorous debate within the Mormon community and enraged Christians in neighboring towns and villages. In 1844 Illinois officials arrested Smith and charged him with treason for allegedly conspiring with foreign powers to create a Mormon colony in Mexican territory. An anti-Mormon mob stormed the jail in Carthage, Illinois, where Smith and his brother were being held, and murdered them.

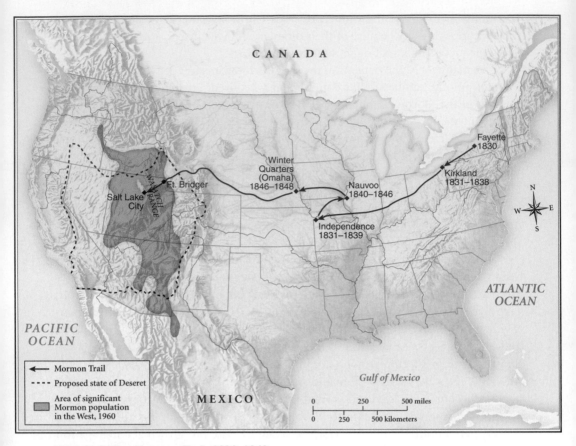

MAP 12.2 The Mormon Trek, 1830–1848

Because of their unorthodox religious views and communal solidarity, Mormons faced hostility first in New York and then in Missouri and Illinois. Following the murder of Joseph Smith, Brigham Young led the polygamist faction of Mormons into lands thinly populated by Native American peoples. From Omaha, the migrants followed the path of the Oregon Trail to Fort Bridger and then struck off to the Southwest, settling in Mexican territory along the Wasatch Range in the basin of the Great Salt Lake in present-day Utah.

Led by Brigham Young, a contingent of Mormons fled from these religious conflicts by leaving the United States. In 1846 Young guided more than 10,000 people across the Great Plains into Mexican territory, where they settled in the Great Salt Lake Valley in present-day Utah. Using communal labor and an elaborate irrigation system based on communal water rights, the Mormon pioneers transformed the region. They quickly spread planned agricultural communities along the base of the Wasatch mountain range. Many Mormons who rejected polygamy remained in the United States. Led by Smith's son, Joseph Smith III, they formed the Reorganized Church of Jesus Christ of Latter-day Saints and settled throughout the Midwest.

AMERICAN VOICES

_⁓_

An Illinois "Jeffersonian" Attacks the Mormons

_T_ _he corporate solidarity of the Mormons enraged many Illinois residents, who feared both the political power of Mormons' large and nearly independent city-state at Nauvoo and the military might of the two-thousand-strong "Legion" commanded by Joseph Smith. In 1844 a mob led by "respectable citizens" assassinated Smith and his brother, and some Illinois residents—such as the author of this letter to the_ Warsaw Signal, _a newspaper in a town near Nauvoo—called for the forcible expulsion of the Mormons._

Mr. Editor,

. . . It is a low pitiable contemptable kind of electioneering, that old Tom Jefferson would have been ashamed of—when a body of men acting under the garb of religion (as the Mormons themselves say they are) shall decide our elections and act together as a body politically, we might as well bid a final farewell to our liberties and the common rights of man.

Now Sir, under all these circumstances, it is high time that every individual should come out and clearly define the position that he occupies. I too am an Anti-Mormon both in principle and in practice. . . . Mr. Editor when I speak harshly of the Mormons, I wish it to be perfectly understood I do not mean every individual that advocates the Mormon cause. By no means; that there are some good, law-abiding peaceable citizens belonging to the Mormon profession I verily believe . . . but I am opposed to them because of the unprincipled manner in which the leaders of that fanatical sect, set at defiance the laws of the land . . . (as was the case in Missouri) claiming to be the chosen people of God; not subject to the laws of the state in any respect whatever, and receiving revelations direct from Heaven almost daily commanding them to take the property of the older citizens of the county and confiscate it to the use of the Mormon church. . . .

It was for the commission of such deeds together with deeds ten fold more dark and damning in their nature that finally led to their expulsion from that state, and one of the brightest pages in the history of Missouri is that, on which is written "Governor Boggs's exterminating order" directing that the lawless rabble should be driven beyond the limits of the state. . . .

Strange to tell, yet such is the fact, they have commenced nearly the same operation here that they did in Missouri . . . they have attempted to subsidize the press, thereby attempting to corrupt the very fountains of public virtue,—they have went [sic] into the legislative halls and attempted to bribe the representatives of the people . . . and made them their tools.

They have in short, by a long series of high handed outrages . . . forfeited all claims (if any they ever had) to confidence and respect, and ought justly to receive the condemnation of every individual, not only in this community, but in this nation.

SOURCE: _Antebellum America: An Interpretive Anthology_ by David Brion Davis, ed. Reprinted by permission of the author.

A Mormon Man and His Wives

During the 1840s various groups of Americans—including Shakers, Fourierists, and women's rights advocates—challenged traditional definitions of gender roles and of marriage. Generally, these groups sought to free women from restrictive customs and their husbands' authority. Conversely, the Mormons who migrated to Utah hoped to preserve traditional patriarchal authority and, through the practice of polygamy, to extend it. However, only a minority of Mormon men in Utah had more than one wife, and only a few had as many as this homesteader. Library of Congress.

When the United States acquired Mexico's northern territories in 1848 (see Chapter 13), the Salt Lake Mormons petitioned Congress to create a vast new state, Deseret, that stretched from present-day Utah to the Pacific coast (Map 12.2). Instead, Congress set up the much smaller Utah Territory in 1850 and named Brigham Young as territorial governor. In 1858 President James Buchanan responded to pressure from Protestant Christians to eliminate polygamy by removing Young from the governorship and sending a small army to Salt Lake City. However, the "Mormon War" proved bloodless. Fearing that the forced abolition of the "domestic institution" of polygamy would serve as a precedent for ending slavery, Buchanan pursued a prosouthern policy and withdrew the troops.

Mormons had succeeded where other social experiments and utopian communities had failed. By endorsing the private ownership of property and encouraging individualistic economic enterprise, they became prosperous contributors to the new market society. However, Mormon leaders resolutely used strict religious controls to create patriarchal families and disciplined communities, reaffirming traditional values inherited from the eighteenth century. This blend of economic innovation, social conservatism, and hierarchical leadership created a wealthy church with a strong missionary impulse.

Abolitionism

Abolitionism was more widespread than Mormonism and just as controversial. Abolitionists' demands for the immediate end to racial slavery led to fierce political debates, riots, and sectional conflict. Like other reform movements, abolitionism drew on the religious energy and ideas generated by the Second Great Awakening. Early-nineteenth-century reformers had criticized human bondage as contrary to republicanism and liberty. Now abolitionists condemned slavery as a sin and saw it as their moral duty to end this violation of God's law.

Uplift, Race-Equality, and Rebellion

During the first decades of the nineteenth century, leading African Americans in the North advocated policies of social uplift. They encouraged free blacks to "elevate" themselves through education, temperance, moral discipline, and hard work and, by securing "respectability," to assume a position of equality with the white citizenry. To promote that goal, black leaders such as James Forten, a Philadelphia sail maker; Prince Hall, a Boston barber; and ministers Hosea Easton and James Allen founded an array of churches, schools, and self-help associations. Capping off this effort in 1827, John Russwurm and Samuel D. Cornish of New York published the first African American newspaper, *Freedom's Journal*.

The black quest for respectability elicited a violent response from whites in Boston, Pittsburgh, and many other northern cities. Refusing to accept African Americans as their social equals, white mobs terrorized black communities. In Cincinnati, white mobs were so violent and destructive that they prompted several hundred African Americans to flee to Canada.

Responding to these attacks in 1829, David Walker published a stirring pamphlet: *An Appeal . . . to the Colored Citizens of the World*. Walker was a free black from North Carolina who had moved to Boston, where he sold secondhand clothes and *Freedom's Journal*. A self-educated man, Walker studied the speeches of Thomas Jefferson and, seeking to place racial slavery in a coherent historical context, devoured volumes of history. His *Appeal* ridiculed the religious pretensions of slaveholders, justified slave rebellion, and in biblical language warned white Americans that the slaves would revolt if justice was delayed. "We must and shall be free," he told white Americans. "And woe, woe, will be it to you if we have to obtain our freedom by fighting. . . . Your DESTRUCTION is at hand, and will be speedily consummated unless you REPENT." Within a year Walker's pamphlet had gone through three printings and, carried by black merchant seamen, had begun to reach free African Americans in the South.

In 1830 Walker and other African American activists called a national convention in Philadelphia. The delegates did not endorse Walker's radical call for revolt but made collective equality for all blacks—enslaved as well as free—their fundamental demand. This new generation of African American leaders focused on "race-equality" rather than individual uplift and respectability. They urged free blacks to use every legal means to break "the shackles of slavery" and improve the condition of their race.

As Walker was predicting violent black rebellion from Boston, Nat Turner, a slave in Southampton County, Virginia, staged a bloody slave revolt—a coincidence that had far-reaching consequences. As a child Turner had taught himself to read and had hoped to be emancipated, but a new master forced him into field work and another new master separated him from his wife. Turner became deeply spiritual and, in a religious vision, "the Spirit" told him that "Christ had laid down the yoke he had borne for the sins of men, and that I should take it on and fight against the Serpent, for the time was fast approaching when the first should be last and the last should be first." Taking an eclipse of the sun as an omen, Turner and a handful of relatives and close friends decided to meet the masters' terror with a terror of their own. In August 1831 Turner and his followers rose in rebellion and killed almost sixty whites. Turner hoped that a vast army of slaves would rally to his cause but he mustered only sixty men, and the white militia quickly dispersed his poorly armed force. Whites took their revenge. One company of cavalry killed forty blacks in two days and put the heads of fifteen on poles to warn "all those who should undertake a similar plot." After hiding for nearly two months Turner was captured and hanged, still identifying his mission with that of the Savior. "Was not Christ crucified?" he asked.

Deeply shaken by Nat Turner's Rebellion, the Virginia assembly debated a bill providing for gradual emancipation and colonization. When the representatives rejected the bill by a vote of 73 to 58, the possibility that southern planters would legislate an end to slavery faded forever. Instead, the southern states toughened their slave codes, limited the movement of blacks, and prohibited anyone from teaching slaves to read. They would meet Walker's radical *Appeal* with radical measures of their own.

Garrison and Evangelical Abolitionism

The prospect of a bloody racial revolution prompted a cadre of evangelical Christians in the North and Midwest to launch a moral crusade to abolish slavery. Many Quakers—and some pious Methodists and Baptists—had already freed their own slaves and advocated the gradual emancipation of all blacks. Beginning in 1831, radical Christian abolitionists demanded that southerners free their slaves immediately. The issue was absolute: if the slave owners did not allow slaves their God-given status as free moral agents, they faced revolution in this world and damnation in the next. "The conviction that SLAVERY IS A SIN is the Gibraltar of our cause," declared abolitionist Wendell Phillips.

The most uncompromising abolitionist leader was William Lloyd Garrison (1805–1879). A Massachusetts-born printer, Garrison had worked in Baltimore

William Lloyd Garrison, c. 1835

As this portrait suggests, William Lloyd Garrison was an intense and righteous man. In 1831 his hatred of slavery prompted Garrison to demand its immediate end, thereby beginning the abolitionist movement. Believing the U.S. Constitution upheld slavery, he publicly burned a copy, declaring, "So perish all compromises with tyranny." Garrison's attack on slavery led him eventually on a passionate quest to destroy all institutions and cultural practices that prevented individuals—whites as well as blacks, women as well as men—from discovering their full potential.

during the 1820s with Quaker Benjamin Lundy, the publisher of the *Genius of Universal Emancipation*. In 1830 Garrison went to jail, convicted of libeling a New England merchant engaged in the domestic slave trade. The following year Garrison moved to Boston, founded his own antislavery weekly, *The Liberator*, and spearheaded the formation of the New England Anti-Slavery Society.

From the outset *The Liberator* took a radical stance, demanding the immediate abolition of slavery without reimbursement to slaveholders. In pursuing this goal, Garrison declared, "I will not retreat a single inch—AND I WILL BE HEARD." He lived up to his word—winning attention as he accused the American Colonization Society of trying to perpetuate slavery and assailed the U.S. Constitution as "a covenant with death, an agreement with Hell," because of its implicit acceptance of racial bondage.

Theodore Dwight Weld, another leading abolitionist, came to the movement from the religious revivals of the 1830s. The son of a Congregationalist minister and inspired by Charles Finney, Weld advocated temperance and educational reform before turning to abolitionism. He told northern Presbyterians and Congregationalists that all Americans bore moral responsibility for slavery and encouraged students at Lane Theological Seminary in Cincinnati to form an antislavery society. Buttressed by the theological arguments he advanced in *The Bible against Slavery* (1837), Weld's crusade gathered force. Working closely with Weld were Angelina Grimké, whom he married in 1838, and her sister, Sarah. The Grimkés had left their father's South Carolina slave plantation, converted to Quakerism, and taken up the abolitionist cause in Philadelphia.

Weld and the Grimkés provided the abolitionist movement with a mass of evidence in *American Slavery as It Is: Testimony of a Thousand Witnesses* (1839). The book set out to answer a simple question—"What is the actual condition of the slaves in the United States?"—with evidence from southern newspapers and first-hand testimonies. In her testimonial, Angelina Grimké told of a treadmill that slave owners used for punishment: "One poor girl, [who was] sent there to be flogged, and who was accordingly stripped naked and whipped, showed me the deep gashes on her back—I might have laid my whole finger in them—large pieces of flesh had actually been cut out by the torturing lash." The book sold over 100,000 copies in its first year.

In 1833 Weld and Garrison met in Philadelphia with sixty abolitionists, black and white, and established the American Anti-Slavery Society. The society received financial support from Arthur and Lewis Tappan, wealthy silk merchants in New York City. Women abolitionists established separate organizations, such as the Philadelphia Female Anti-Slavery Society, founded by Lucretia Mott in 1833, and the Anti-Slavery Conventions of American Women, formed by a network of local societies in the late 1830s. The women's societies raised money for *The Liberator* and carried the movement to the farm villages and rural areas of the Midwest, where they distributed abolitionist literature and collected tens of thousands of signatures on antislavery petitions.

Abolitionist leaders developed a three-pronged plan of attack, beginning with an appeal to public opinion. To foster public opposition to slavery, they adopted the tactics of the religious revivalists: large rallies led by stirring speakers and home visits by local agents of the movement. The abolitionists also used the latest techniques of mass communication. Assisted by new steam-powered printing presses, the American Anti-Slavery Society distributed more than 100,000 pieces of literature in 1834. In 1835 the society launched its "great postal campaign," which flooded the nation, including the South, with a million abolitionist pamphlets.

The abolitionists' second tactic was to assist the African Americans who fled from slavery. Blacks who lived near a free state had the greatest chance of success, but fugitives from plantations deeper in the South received aid from the "underground railroad," an informal network of whites and free blacks in Richmond, Charleston, and other southern cities. In Baltimore, a free African American sailor lent his identification papers to the future abolitionist Frederick Douglass, who used them to escape to New York. Some escaped slaves, such as Harriet Tubman, returned repeatedly to the South, risking reenslavement or death to help others escape. As Tubman wrote, "I should fight for . . . liberty as long as my strength lasted, and when the time came for me to go, the Lord would let them take me." Thanks to the "railroad," by the 1840s about a thousand African Americans reached freedom in the North each year.

There they faced an uncertain future because whites did not favor civic equality for African Americans. In fact, six northern and midwestern states changed their constitutions to deny the franchise to free blacks. Moreover, the Fugitive Slave Law (1793) allowed masters and hired slave catchers to capture suspected fugitives and carry them back to bondage. To thwart these efforts, white abolitionists and free blacks in northern cities formed mobs that seized recaptured slaves and drove slave catchers out of town.

The third element of the abolitionists' program was to seek support among state and national legislators. In 1835 the American Anti-Slavery Society encouraged its members to bombard Congress with petitions demanding the abolition of slavery in the District of Columbia, an end to the domestic slave trade, and a ban on the admission of new slave states. By 1838 petitions with nearly 500,000 signatures had arrived in Washington.

This agitation drew thousands of deeply religious farmers and small-town proprietors to abolitionism. The number of local abolitionist societies grew from about two hundred in 1835 to nearly two thousand by 1840—when they had nearly 200,000 members, including many leading transcendentalists. Emerson condemned American society for tolerating slavery; Thoreau was even more assertive. Seeing the Mexican War (see Chapter 13) as an attempt to extend slavery, in 1846 he refused to pay his taxes and submitted to arrest. Two years later Thoreau published "Resistance to Civil Government," an essay urging individuals to resist the state and follow a higher moral law.

Opposition and Internal Conflict

Despite these successes, abolitionists remained a small minority. Perhaps 10 percent of northerners and midwesterners strongly supported the movement; another 20 percent were sympathetic to its goals. Its opponents were more numerous and equally aggressive. Men of wealth feared that the attack on slave property might become a general assault on all property rights; tradition-minded clergymen condemned the public roles assumed by abolitionist women; and northern merchants and textile manufacturers supported the southern planters who supplied them with cotton. Northern wage earners feared that freed slaves would work for subsistence wages and take their jobs. Finally, whites almost universally opposed the prospect of "amalgamation"—racial mixing and intermarriage—that Garrison seemed to support by encouraging meetings of black and white abolitionists of both sexes.

Motivated by such sentiments, northern antiabolitionists turned to violent mob actions, which were often led or instigated by "gentlemen of property and standing." In 1833 a mob of fifteen hundred New Yorkers stormed a church in search of Garrison and Arthur Tappan. Another white mob swept through

Philadelphia's African American neighborhoods, clubbing and stoning residents and destroying homes and churches. In 1835 in Utica, New York, a group of lawyers, merchants, and bankers broke up an abolitionist convention and beat several delegates. Two years later in Alton, Illinois, a mob shot and killed an abolitionist editor, Elijah P. Lovejoy. By pressing the issues of emancipation and equality, the abolitionists revealed the extent of racial prejudice in the North and the near impossibility of creating a biracial middle class of "respectable" whites and blacks. Indeed, their initiative had heightened race consciousness and encouraged whites—and blacks—to identify across class lines with those of their own race.

Racial solidarity was especially strong in the South, where whites reacted to abolitionism by banning the movement and demanding that northern states do the same. The Georgia legislature offered a $5,000 reward to anyone who would kidnap Garrison and bring him south to be tried for inciting rebellion. In Nashville, vigilantes whipped a northern college student for distributing abolitionist pamphlets, and in Charleston a mob attacked the post office and destroyed sacks of abolitionist mail. After 1835 southern postmasters simply refused to deliver mail suspected to be of abolitionist origin.

Politicians joined the fray. President Andrew Jackson was a longtime slave owner and a firm supporter of the southern social order. In 1835 he asked Congress to restrict the use of the mails by abolitionist groups. Congress did not comply, but in 1836 the House of Representatives adopted the so-called gag rule. Under this informal rule, which remained in force until 1844, antislavery petitions were automatically tabled when they were received so that they could not become the subjects of debate in the House (Map 12.3).

Assailed by racists from the outside, abolitionists were also divided among themselves over issues of gender. Many antislavery clergymen opposed an activist social role for women and condemned the Grimké sisters and other abolitionist women for lecturing to mixed-sex audiences. However, Garrison had broadened his reform agenda to include pacifism, the abolition of prisons, and women's rights. Arguing that "our object is universal emancipation, to redeem women as well as men from a servile to an equal condition," he demanded that the American Anti-Slavery Society support women's rights. At the society's convention in 1840 Garrison insisted on equal participation by women and precipitated a split with more conservative abolitionists. Women's rights advocates, such as Abby Kelley, Lucretia Mott, and Elizabeth Cady Stanton, remained with Garrison in the American Anti-Slavery Society, and proclaimed the common interests of enslaved blacks and free white women.

Garrison's opponents founded a new organization, the American and Foreign Anti-Slavery Society, which received financial backing from Lewis Tappan and focused its energies on ending slavery. Some of its members mobilized their churches to oppose racial bondage and others turned to electoral politics. In 1840 they established the Liberty Party, which nominated James G. Birney for president. Birney was a former Alabama slave owner who had been converted to abolitionism by Theodore Weld and

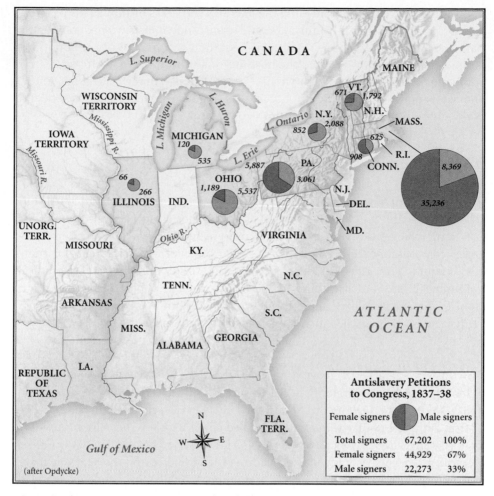

MAP 12.3 Women and Antislavery, 1837–1838

Beginning in the 1830s, abolitionists and antislavery advocates dispatched dozens of petitions to Congress, which, to avoid sectional conflict, refused to discuss them. Women made up two-thirds of the 67,000 people signing the petitions submitted in 1837–1838, which suggests not only their influence in the antislavery movement but also the extent of female organizations and social networks.

FOR MORE HELP ANALYZING THIS MAP, see the Online Study Guide at **bedfordstmartins.com/henrettaconcise**.

had founded an antislavery newspaper in Cincinnati. Birney and the Liberty Party argued that the Constitution did not recognize slavery and, consequently, that slaves became automatically free when they entered areas of federal authority, such as the District of Columbia and national territories. However, Birney won few votes in the election of 1840, and the future of political abolitionism appeared dim.

Coming hard on the heels of popular violence in the North and governmental suppression in the South, these schisms and electoral failures stunned the abolitionist movement. By melding the energies and ideas of thousands of evangelical Protestants, moral reformers, and transcendentalists, it had raised the banner of antislavery to new heights. Indeed, the very strength of the abolitionist movement had now aroused the hostility of a substantial majority of the nation's white population. "When we first unfurled the banner of *The Liberator*," Garrison admitted, ". . . it did not occur to us that nearly every religious sect, and every political party would side with the oppressor."

The Women's Rights Movement

The prominence of women among the abolitionists was the product of a broad shift in American culture. After 1800 women played an increasingly active role in public life, joining religious revivals and reform movements such as the temperance crusade. As a consequence of this activism, issues of gender—sexual behavior, marriage, family authority—suddenly became significant not only among radical communal groups but also among ordinary citizens. The public activities of abolitionist women crystallized these issues and made some reformers into women's rights activists, who argued for complete equality with men.

Origins of the Women's Movement

"Don't be afraid, not afraid, fight Satan; stand up for Christ; don't be afraid." So spoke Mary Walker Ostram on her deathbed in 1859. Her religious convictions were as firm at the age of fifty-eight as they had been in 1816, when she helped found the first Sabbath School in Utica, New York. Married to a lawyer-politician but childless, Ostram had devoted her life to evangelical Presbyterianism and the benevolent social reform that it helped to spawn. Her minister, Philemon Fowler, celebrated Ostram as a "living fountain" of faith, an exemplar of "Women's Sphere of Influence" in the world.

Such a public presence was hard won and still contested. Even as Reverend Fowler heaped praise on Ostram, he reiterated Revolutionary era precepts that women should limit their political role to that of "republican mothers" who would instruct "their sons in the principles of liberty and government." As Fowler put it, women inhabited a "**separate sphere**" and had no place in "the markets of trade, the scenes of politics and popular agitation, the courts of justice and the halls of legislation. Home is her peculiar sphere and members of her family her peculiar care."

But Ostram and many other middle-class women had transcended these rigid boundaries by joining in the Second Great Awakening. Such spiritual activities bolstered their authority within the household and gave them influence over many areas of family life, including the timing of pregnancies. Publications such as

Godey's Lady's Book and Catharine Beecher's *Treatise on Domestic Economy* (1841) taught women how to make their homes more efficient and alerted them to threats to their lives of middle-class domesticity. To protect their homes and husbands from the dangers of alcoholic excess, many farm women joined the Independent Order of Good Templars, a temperance organization that granted them full membership and sought to safeguard family life.

Some women used their newfound religious authority to increase their public activities, especially in the area of moral reform. In 1834 a group of middle-class New York women founded the Female Moral Reform Society and elected Lydia Finney, the wife of the evangelical minister Charles Finney, as its president. Its goals were to end prostitution, redeem fallen women, and protect single women from moral corruption. Rejecting the sexual double standard, the society demanded chastity for men as well as for women. By 1840 it had grown into a national association, with 555 chapters and 40,000 members throughout the North and Midwest. Employing only women as its agents, the society provided moral guidance for factory girls, seamstresses, and female servants who lived away from their families. Society members visited brothels, where they sang hymns, offered prayers, searched for runaway girls, and noted the names of clients. They also founded homes of refuge for prostitutes and won the passage of laws in Massachusetts and New York regulating men's sexual behavior and making seduction a crime.

Other women turned their energies to the improvement of almshouses, asylums, hospitals, and jails, all of which grew in number in the 1830s and 1840s. The Massachusetts reformer Dorothea Dix led these efforts and persuaded many state legislatures to expand state-run hospitals to accommodate mentally ill women rather than jail them with criminals. Other female reformers likewise solicited governmental support for their endeavors. In New York in 1849 the Female Guardian Society secured legal authority to take charge of the children of "dissipated and vicious parents" and to supervise their upbringing and education.

Both as reformers and as teachers, northern women transformed public education. From Maine to Wisconsin women vigorously supported the movement led by Horace Mann to increase the number of elementary schools and improve their quality. As secretary of the newly created Massachusetts Board of Education from 1837 to 1848, Mann lengthened the school year; established teaching standards in reading, writing, and arithmetic; and improved instruction by recruiting well-educated women as teachers. The intellectual leader of the new corps of women educators was Catharine Beecher, who founded academies for young women in Hartford and Cincinnati. In widely read publications Beecher argued that "energetic and benevolent women" were better qualified than men to impart moral and intellectual instruction to the young. By the 1850s most teachers were women both because local school boards heeded Beecher's arguments and because women could be paid less than men could.

Abolitionism and Women

Women had long played an active part in the antislavery movement (Map 12.3). During the Revolutionary era, Quaker women in Philadelphia established schools for freed slaves, and Baptist and Methodist women in the Upper South endorsed religious arguments against slavery. One of the first abolitionists recruited by William Lloyd Garrison was Maria W. Stewart, an African American, who spoke to mixed audiences of men and women in Boston in the early 1830s. As the abolitionist movement mushroomed, scores of white women delivered lectures condemning slavery and thousands more conducted home "visitations" to win converts to their cause.

Women abolitionists were acutely aware of the special horrors of slavery for their sex. In her autobiography, *Incidents in the Life of a Slave Girl*, the black abolitionist Harriet Jacobs described forced sexual relations with her white owner: "I cannot tell how much I suffered in the presence of these wrongs." As Jacobs and other female slaves testified, such sexual assaults were compounded by cruel treatment at the hands of their masters' wives, who were enraged by their husbands' promiscuity. In her best-selling novel, *Uncle Tom's Cabin* (1852), Harriet Beecher Stowe charged that among the greatest moral failings of slavery was the degradation of slave women.

As abolitionist women assailed slavery and sexual oppression, many men challenged their right to participate in public debate. In response, activist women rejected the subordinate status of their sex. The most famous were Angelina and Sarah Grimké, who had become antislavery lecturers. When some Congregationalist clergymen demanded in 1836 that they cease lecturing to mixed male and female audiences, Sarah Grimké turned to the Christian Bible for justification: "The Lord Jesus defines the duties of his followers in his Sermon on the Mount . . . without any reference to sex or condition," she wrote. "Men and women are CREATED EQUAL! They are both moral and accountable beings and whatever is right for man to do is right for woman." In a debate with Catharine Beecher (who wanted women to exercise power primarily as wives, mothers, and schoolteachers), Angelina Grimké pushed the argument beyond religion by invoking Enlightenment principles to claim equal civic rights for women:

> It is a woman's right to have a voice in all the laws and regulations by which she is governed, whether in Church or State. . . . The present arrangements of society, on these points are a violation of human rights, a rank usurpation of power, a violent seizure and confiscation of what is sacredly and inalienably hers.

By 1840 female abolitionists were asserting that traditional gender roles amounted to the "domestic slavery" of women. "How can we endure our present marriage relations," asked Elizabeth Cady Stanton, since they give woman "no charter of rights, no individuality of her own?" As another female reformer put it, "the radical difficulty . . . is that women are considered as *belonging* to men" (see American Voices, "A Farm Woman Defends the Grimké Sisters," p. 377). Drawn into

AMERICAN VOICES

A Farm Woman Defends the Grimké Sisters

KEZIAH KENDALL

T he Grimké sisters' lecture tour of New England on behalf of abolitionism sparked a huge outcry from orthodox ministers and social conservatives, who questioned the propriety of women assuming public roles and speaking to "mixed" audiences of men and women. In a lecture titled "The Legal Rights of Women," Simon Greenleaf, Royall Professor of Law at Harvard College, added his voice to those advocating a restricted role for women. Replying to Greenleaf, Keziah Kendall—possibly the fictional creation of a contemporary women's rights advocate— sent the following letter to her local newspaper.

My name is Keziah Kendall. I live not many miles from Cambridge, on a farm with two sisters, one older, one younger than myself. I am thirty two. Our parents and only brother are dead—we have a good estate—comfortable house—nice barn, garden, orchard &c and money in the bank besides. . . . Under these circumstances the whole responsibility of our property, not less than twenty five thousand dollars rest upon me.

Well—our milkman brought word when he came from market that you were a going to lecture on the legal rights of women, and so I thought I would go and learn. Now I hope you wont think me bold when I say, I did not like that lecture much . . . [because] there was nothing in it but what every body knows. . . .

What I wanted to know, was good reasons for some of those laws that I cant account for. . . . One Lyceum lecture that I heard in C[ambridge] stated that the Americans went to war with the British, because they were taxed without being represented in Parliament. Now we [women] are taxed every year to the full amount of every dollar we possess— town, county, state taxes—taxes for land, for movable [property], for money and all. Now I don't want to [become a legislative] representative . . . any more than I do to be a "constable or a sheriff," but I have no voice about public improvements, and I don't see the justice of being taxed any more than the "revolutionary heroes" did.

Nor do I think we are treated as Christian women ought to be, according to the Bible rule of doing to others as you would others should do unto you. . . . Another thing . . . women have joined the Antislavery societies, and why? Women are kept for slaves as well as men—it is a common cause, deny the justice of it, who can! To be sure I do not wish to go about lecturing like the Misses Grimkie, but I have not the knowledge they have, and I verily believe that if I had been brought up among slaves as they were . . . I should run the venture of your displeasure, and that of a good many others like you.

SOURCE: Dianne Avery and Alfred S. Konefsky, "The Daughters of Job: Property Rights and Women's Lives in Mid-Nineteenth-Century Massachusetts," *Law and History Review* 10 (Fall 1992): 323–56.

public life by abolitionism, thousands of northern women had become firm advocates of greater rights not only for enslaved African Americans but also for themselves.

The Program of Seneca Falls and Beyond

During the 1840s women's rights activists devised a pragmatic program of reform. While championing full civil equality for women, they did not challenge the institution of marriage or even the conventional division of labor within the family. Rather, they tried to strengthen the legal rights of married women, especially with respect to property. This initiative won crucial support from affluent men, who wanted to protect their wives' assets in case their own businesses went into bankruptcy in the volatile economy of mid-nineteenth-century America. By giving property rights to their married daughters, fathers also hoped to protect them (and their inheritances) from irresponsible, spendthrift sons-in-law. Such considerations prompted legislatures in three states—Mississippi, Maine, and Massachusetts—to enact Married Women's Property Acts between 1839 and 1845. In New York, women activists won a more comprehensive statute (1848), which gave a woman full legal control over the property she brought to a marriage and became the model for similar laws in fourteen other states.

To advance the nascent women's movement, Elizabeth Cady Stanton and Lucretia Mott, who had become friends at the World Anti-Slavery Convention in London in 1840, organized a gathering in the small town of Seneca Falls in central New York in 1848. Seventy women activists and thirty men attended the meeting, which devised a rousing manifesto for women's equality. Taking the republican ideology of the Declaration of Independence as a starting point, the attendees declared that "all men and women are created equal." "The history of mankind is a history of repeated injuries and usurpations on the part of man toward woman," their Declaration of Sentiments continued, "having in direct object the establishment of an absolute tyranny over her." To persuade Americans to right this long-standing wrong, the activists resolved to "use every instrumentality within our power . . . [to] employ agents, circulate tracts, petition the State and National legislatures, and endeavor to enlist the pulpit and the press on our behalf." By staking out claims for equality for women in public life, the Seneca Falls reformers repudiated the idea that "separate spheres" for men and women was the natural order of society.

Most men dismissed the Seneca Falls Declaration as nonsense, and many women repudiated the activists and their message. Writing in her diary, one small-town mother and housewife lashed out at the female reformer who "aping mannish manners . . . wears absurd and barbarous attire, who talks of her wrongs in harsh tone, who struts and strides, and thinks that she proves herself superior to the rest of her sex."

Nonetheless, the women's rights movement attracted a growing number of supporters. In 1850 the activists convened the first national women's rights convention in Worcester, Massachusetts, and hammered out a program of action. Local and state conventions of women called on churches to revise concepts of female inferiority in their theology. Addressing state legislatures, they proposed laws that would guarantee the custody rights of mothers in the event of divorce or the husband's death, and ensure that married women could institute lawsuits and testify in court. Finally, and above all else, they began a concerted campaign to win the vote for women. The national women's rights convention of 1851 declared that suffrage was "the corner-stone of this enterprise, since we do not seek to protect woman, but rather to place her in a position to protect herself."

The struggle for legislation required leaders who had talents as organizers and lobbyists. The most prominent political operative was Susan B. Anthony (1820–1906). Anthony came from a Quaker family and as a young woman had been active in temperance and antislavery efforts. Her experience in those movements,

Sojourner Truth

Few women had as interesting a life as Sojourner Truth. Born as "Isabella" in Dutch-speaking rural New York about 1797, she labored as a slave until 1827. Following a religious vision, Isabella moved to New York City, learned English, and worked for deeply religious—and ultimately fanatical—Christian merchants. In 1843, seeking further spiritual enlightenment, she took the name "Sojourner Truth" and left New York. After briefly joining the Millerites (who believed the world would end in 1844), Truth became famous as a forceful speaker on behalf of abolitionism and women's rights. This illustration, showing Truth addressing an antislavery meeting, suggests her powerful personal presence. Miriam and Ira D. Wallach Division of Art, Prints and Photographs, the New York Public Library.

Anthony explained, had taught her "the great evil of woman's utter dependence on man." In 1851 she joined the movement for women's rights. Working closely with Elizabeth Cady Stanton, Anthony created a network of political "captains," all women, who relentlessly lobbied the legislature in New York and other states. In 1860 her efforts culminated in a New York law granting women the right to collect and spend their own wages (which fathers or husbands previously could insist on controlling), to bring suit in court, and, if widowed, to acquire full control of the property they had brought to the marriage. Such successes laid the basis for more aggressive reform attempts after the Civil War.

The attack by women's rights activists against the traditional legal and social prerogatives of husbands, like the abolitionists' assault on the power and property of southern slaveholders, prompted many Americans to fear that social reform might not perfect their society but destroy it instead. The various movements for reform, begun with such confidence and religious zeal, had raised legal and political issues that threatened the fabric of society and the unity of the nation.

TIMELINE

Year	Event	Year	Event
1829	David Walker's *Appeal . . . to the Colored Citizens* encourages slave rebellion	1841	Transcendentalists found Brook Farm, a utopian community
1830	Joseph Smith publishes *The Book of Mormon*		Dorothea Dix promotes hospitals for the insane
1831	William Lloyd Garrison founds *The Liberator*	1844	Margaret Fuller publishes *Woman in the Nineteenth Century*
	Nat Turner's uprising in Virginia	1845	Henry David Thoreau withdraws to Walden Pond
1832	Ralph Waldo Emerson rejects organized religion and embraces transcendentalism	1846	Mormon followers of Brigham Young trek to Salt Lake
1833	American Anti-Slavery Society founded	1848	John Humphrey Noyes founds Oneida Community
1834	New York Female Moral Reform Society created		Seneca Falls convention proposes women's equality
1835	Abolitionists launch mail campaign; antiabolitionists riot against them	1850	Nathaniel Hawthorne publishes *The Scarlet Letter*
1836	House of Representatives adopts gag rule on antislavery petitions	1851	Herman Melville's *Moby-Dick*
	Grimké sisters defend public roles for women	1852	Harriet Beecher Stowe writes *Uncle Tom's Cabin*
1840	Liberty Party runs James G. Birney for president		Walt Whitman issues first edition of *Leaves of Grass*
1840s	Fourierist communities founded in Midwest	1858	The "Mormon War" over polygamy

For Further Exploration

Ronald Walters, *American Reformers, 1815–1860* (1978), offers a succinct discussion of the major antebellum reform movements. Robert H. Abzug, *Cosmos Crumbling: American Reform and the Religious Imagination* (1994), demonstrates the religious roots of the reform impulse. David S. Reynolds, *Walt Whitman's America: A Cultural Biography* (1995), is a comprehensive study of the poet and nineteenth-century society. Charles Capper, *Margaret Fuller: An American Romantic Life* (1992), illuminates Fuller's intellectual milieu. Fuller inspired the character of Zenobia in Nathaniel Hawthorne's *The Blithedale Romance* (1852), which reflects his life at Brook Farm and touches on many issues (and fads) of the day, including communalism and mesmerism. For a fine Web site on transcendentalism, log on to <http://www.vcu.edu/engweb/transcendentalism/>. A provocative study of religious utopianism gone mad is Paul E. Johnson and Sean Wilentz, *The Kingdom of Matthias: A Story of Sex and Salvation in Nineteenth-Century America* (1995).

James B. Stewart, *Holy Warriors: The Abolitionists and American Slavery* (1976), places the Garrisonian movement in a broad social context. See also Mark Perry, *Lift Up Thy Voice: The Grimké Family's Journey from Slaveholders to Civil Rights Leaders* (2001). Stephen B. Oates, *The Fires of Jubilee: Nat Turner's Fierce Rebellion* (1975), explores the life of the insurrectionist, while materials including *The Confessions of Nat Turner* are available at <http://docsouth.unc.edu/turner/menu.html>. *The Narrative of the Life of Frederick Douglass, An American Slave, Written by Himself* (1845) is a literary masterpiece. For antiabolitionism, see the probing studies by Leonard L. Richards, *"Gentlemen of Property and Standing": Anti-Abolition Mobs in Jacksonian America* (1970), and David Roediger, *The Wages of Whiteness* (1995). For many resources on slavery and abolition, see the PBS Africans in America site: <http://www.pbs.org/wgbh/aia/part4/>.

Mary Ryan, *Women in Public: Between Banners and Ballots, 1825–1880* (1990), explores the limits on women's civic activities, and Eleanor Flexner, *Century of Struggle* (1959), narrates the history of the women's movement. The PBS video directed by Ken Burns, *Not for Ourselves Alone: The Story of Elizabeth Cady Stanton and Susan B. Anthony* (3 hours), offers insight into the first generation of activists. See also the National Park Service Web site for Seneca Falls: <http://www.nps.gov/wori/>.

For definitions of key terms boldfaced in this chapter, see the glossary at the end of the book.

To assess your mastery of the material covered In this chapter, see the Online Study Guide at **bedfordstmartins.com/henrettaconcise**.

For map resources and primary documents, see **bedfordstmartins.com/henrettaconcise**.

Chapter 13

THE CRISIS OF THE UNION
1844–1860

This government was made by our fathers, by white men for the benefit of white men and their posterity forever.

STEPHEN DOUGLAS, 1858

$\mathbf{D}$uring the 1850s crusaders for temperance and antislavery faced off against defenders of traditional rights. The resulting struggle was especially intense in South Carolina. When temperance activists demanded a "Maine law" to prohibit the sale of intoxicants, Randolph Turner was outraged: any such "legislation upon Liquor would cast a shade on my character which as a Caucassian [sic] and a white man, I am not willing to bear." A candidate for the South Carolina assembly, Turner vowed to shoulder his musket and, along with "hundreds of men in this district, . . . fight for individual rights, as well as State Rights."

In Washington, South Carolina congressman Preston Brooks battled for "Southern Rights." In an inflammatory speech in 1856, Senator Charles Sumner of Massachusetts denounced the South and accused Senator Andrew P. Butler of South Carolina of having taken "the harlot slavery" as his mistress. Outraged by Sumner's verbal attack on his uncle, Brooks accosted the Massachusetts senator at his desk and beat him unconscious with a walking cane. As these events unfolded in Washington, Axalla Hoole of South Carolina and other proslavery migrants in the Kansas Territory leveled their guns at an armed force of abolitionist settlers. Passion and violence had replaced political compromise as the hallmark of American public life.

The immediate cause of the political violence of the 1850s was the geographic expansion that began with the admission of Texas to the Union in 1845 and the acquisition of vast territories from Mexico in 1848. The ultimate causes were more complex and stemmed from the growing economic and cultural differences between the northern and southern states. By midcentury these sectional disparities were keenly felt, especially in the South. White southerners feared the North's increasing wealth, political power, and moral righteousness, John C. Calhoun explained in 1850, especially its "long-continued agitation of the slavery question."

A massive surge of population to the West accentuated the importance of those divisions. To many Americans it was the nation's "manifest destiny" to extend republican institutions to the Pacific Ocean. But whose republican institutions: the aristocratic traditions and practices of the slaveholding South or the more democratic customs and culture of the reform-minded North and Midwest? The answer to this question would determine the future of the nation.

Manifest Destiny

Shaken by the crisis over Missouri (see Chapter 9), the two major political parties shunned policies that would spark another confrontation over slavery. This policy worked as long as the geographic boundaries of the United States remained unchanged, but by the 1840s the people of the nation were again on the move.

The Mature Cotton Economy, 1820–1860

Between 1820 and 1860 the white planters in the South grew rich and powerful as they developed a cotton economy. By 1840 the American South produced over two-thirds of the world's supply of raw cotton—1.5 million bales (at 500 pounds per bale) each year. Smallholding white families accounted for hundreds of thousands of bales of the prized fiber, but most cotton came from large plantations employing slave labor. As *Hunt's Merchants' Magazine* noted in 1855, "The whole Commerce of the world turns upon the product of slave labor." To increase output, profit-conscious slave owners in the upland regions of South Carolina and Georgia and the fertile plains of Alabama and Mississippi devised a new **gang-labor system**. Previously planters had either supervised their workers sporadically or assigned a daily quota and let them work at their own pace. Now masters with twenty or more slaves organized disciplined teams, or "gangs," supervised by black "drivers" or white overseers. They instructed drivers and overseers to use the lash to work the gangs at a steady pace, clearing and plowing the land or hoeing and picking cotton. A traveler glimpsed two gangs returning from work in Mississippi:

> First came, led by an old driver carrying a whip, forty of the largest and strongest women I ever saw together; they were all in a simple uniform dress of a bluish check stuff, the skirts reaching little below the knee; . . . they carried themselves loftily, each having a hoe over the shoulder, and walking with a free, powerful swing.

Next marched the plow hands with their mules, "the cavalry, thirty strong, mostly men, but a few of them women." Finally, "a lean and vigilant white overseer, on a brisk pony, brought up the rear." By 1860 nearly two million enslaved African Americans were laboring along an arc of fertile land—the "black belt"—sweeping from Mississippi through Georgia, and the South's annual cotton output had surged dramatically to 4 million bales.

The slaveholding elite who owned great plantations and scores of slaves thought of themselves as aristocrats and acted accordingly. They married their children to one another, and their sons and daughters became commercial and cultural leaders—the men working as planters, merchants, lawyers, newspaper editors, and ministers and the women hosting plantation balls and church bazaars. To confirm their status, leading planters lived extravagantly. John Henry Hammond, a leading South Carolina politician, built a Greek Revival mansion with a center hall fifty-three feet by twenty feet, its floor embellished with stylish Belgian tiles and expensive Brussels carpets. "Once a year, like a great feudal landlord," a guest recounted, Hammond "gave a fete or grand dinner to all the country people."

The planters justified their rule in moral terms. Ignoring the old defense of slavery as a "necessary evil," southern apologists now argued that slavery was a "positive good" that allowed a civilized lifestyle for leading whites and provided tutelage for genetically inferior Africans. Southern ministers pointed out that the Hebrews, God's chosen people, had owned slaves and that Jesus Christ had never condemned slavery. As Hammond told a British abolitionist in 1845: "What God ordains and Christ sanctifies should surely command the respect and toleration of man." Some defenders of slavery depicted planters and their wives as aristocratic models of "disinterested benevolence," who provided food and housing for their workers and cared for them in old age (see American Voices, "A Slaveholding Woman's Diary," p. 385).

Although elite planters encouraged ambitious men to buy slaves and grow rich, southern politics and society remained deeply divided along the lines of class and geography. Wealthy planters used their political influence to exempt slave property from taxation and to shift the tax burden to backcountry yeomen farmers, by imposing land taxes by acreage rather than by value. Planters also enacted laws that forced yeomen to "fence in" their livestock and spared themselves the cost of building fences around their fields. Finally, planter-dominated legislatures forced all white men—whether they owned slaves or not—to serve in the patrols and militias that deterred black uprisings. Defending such onerous regulations, John Henry Hammond told his poor white neighbors that "in a slave country every freeman is an aristocrat."

Planters worried constantly that enslaved African Americans—a majority of the population throughout the "black belt"—would rise in rebellion. In theory, a master had virtually unlimited power over his slaves, who were subject to his discipline and could be bought and sold as if they were horses. As Justice Thomas Ruffin of the North Carolina Supreme Court wrote in a decision in 1829, "The power of the master must be absolute to render the submission of the slave perfect."

However, in practice, African American resistance limited the masters' power. Slaves slowed the pace of work by feigning illness and losing or breaking tools. Some blacks challenged their owners' authority by insisting that people be sold "in families." One Maryland slave, faced with transport to Mississippi and separation from his wife,

AMERICAN VOICES

A Slaveholding Woman's Diary

MARY BOYKIN CHESNUT

*I*n response to Harriet Beecher Stowe's Uncle Tom's Cabin *(1852) and Republican celebrations of free labor, proslavery advocate George Fitzhugh wrote* Sociology for the South; or, the Failure of Free Society *(1857). Fitzhugh depicted slavery as a benevolent institution and contrasted the planters' concern for their workers with the factory owners' indifference toward their wage laborers. Mary Boykin Chesnut (1823–1886), wife of South Carolina senator James Chesnut, held a more complex view of slavery. While Chesnut believed that blacks were innately inferior and that southern women were benevolent, she hated slavery because it oppressed the women of both races. During the Civil War Chesnut recorded her views in notes and later revised them into a beautifully written diary.*

March 18, 1861 ... I wonder if it be a sin to think slavery a curse to any land. [Massachusetts senator Charles] Sumner said not one word of this hated institution which is not true. Men and women are punished when their masters and mistresses are brutes and not when they do wrong—and then we live surrounded by prostitutes. ... God forgive us, but ours is a monstrous system and wrong. ... Like the patriarchs of old our men live all in one house with their wives and their concubines, and the mulattoes one sees in every family exactly resemble the white children—and every lady tells you who is the father of all the mulatto children in everybody's household, but those in her own she seems to think drop from the clouds, or pretends so to think. Good women we have ... the purest women God ever made. Thank God for my countrywomen—alas for the men! ...

November 27, 1861 ... Now what I have seen of my mother's life, my grandmother's, my mother-in-law's: These people were educated at Northern schools mostly—read the same books as their Northern condemners, the same daily newspapers, the same Bible—have the same ideas of right and wrong—are highbred, lovely, good, pious—doing their duty as they conceive it. They live in negro villages. They do not preach and teach hate as a gospel and the sacred duty of murder and insurrection, but they strive to ameliorate the condition of these Africans in every particular. ... These women are more troubled by their duty to negroes, have less chance to live their own lives in peace than if they were African missionaries. They have a swarm of blacks about them as children under their care—not as Mrs. Stowe's fancy paints them, but the hard, unpleasant, unromantic, undeveloped savage Africans. And they hate slavery worse than Mrs. Stowe. ...

We are human beings of the nineteenth century—and slavery has to go, of course. All that has been gained by it goes to the North and to negroes. The slave-owners, when they are good men and women, are the martyrs. And as far as I have seen, the people here are quite as good as anywhere else. I hate slavery.

"neither yields consent to accompany my people, or to be exchanged or sold," his owner reported. Masters ignored such resistance at their peril because the slave (or his relatives) might retaliate by setting fire to houses and barns, poisoning his food, or destroying crops or equipment. Such worries, as well as critical scrutiny by abolitionists, prompted many masters to resort less frequently to the lash and to use positive incentives of food and other privileges to manage their laborers. Slavery was never a regime of equality, but over the first half of the nineteenth century, masters and their now-American-born slaves devised rules and rituals that reduced the extent of day-to-day violence. Even as slavery evolved, it remained central to the southern social order, and white planters and politicians wanted to extend its sway across the continent.

The Independence of Texas

By the 1830s settlers from the Ohio Valley and the South had carried both yeoman farming and plantation slavery into Arkansas and Missouri. Between those states and the Rocky Mountains stretched the semiarid lands of the Great Plains, which an army explorer, Major Stephen H. Long, described as the Great American Desert, "almost wholly unfit for cultivation." Consequently, settlers looking for land turned south toward the Mexican province of Texas.

Texas had long been occupied primarily by Indian peoples. The Spanish government in Mexico had used Texas as a buffer zone against the French prior to the Louisiana Purchase of 1803; afterward the province became a shield against the United States. Although some American adventurers settled in Texas, the Adams-Onís Treaty of 1819 guaranteed Spanish sovereignty over the region.

After winning independence from Spain in 1821, the Mexican government used lavish land grants to encourage both Mexicans and Americans to move to Texas. One early grantee was American Moses Austin, who created an aristocratic-like landed estate occupied by tenants and smallholders: "one great family who are under my care." His son, Stephen F. Austin, later acquired about 180,000 acres, which he sold to incoming Americans. By 1835 about 27,000 white Americans and their 3,000 African American slaves were raising cotton and cattle in eastern and central Texas; they far outnumbered the 3,000 Mexican residents, most of whom lived in the southwestern towns of Goliad and San Antonio (Map 13.1).

As the Mexican government asserted greater political control over Texas in the mid-1830s, the Americans split into two groups. A "peace party," led by Stephen Austin and other longtime settlers, sought more autonomy for the province, while the "war party," led by recent migrants from Georgia, demanded independence. Austin won significant concessions from Mexican authorities, but the new national-minded president, General Antonio López de Santa Anna, nullified these measures. When Santa Anna appointed a military commandant for Texas, the war party provoked a rebellion that most of the American settlers ultimately supported. On March 2, 1836, the American rebels proclaimed the independence of Texas and adopted a constitution legalizing slavery.

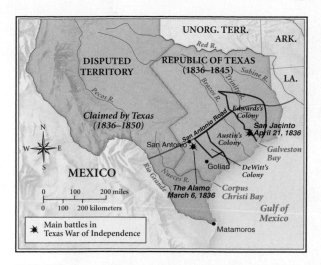

MAP 13.1 American Settlements in Texas, 1821–1836

During the 1820s Mexican authorities granted huge tracts of land in the province of Texas to Stephen F. Austin and other American *empresarios* (land entrepreneurs who were expected to encourage immigration). By 1835 Austin had issued land titles to more than 1,000 families, who grew cotton and exported it from Galveston and other Gulf ports. By the mid-1830s, there were nearly 30,000 Americans in Texas. They far outnumbered Mexican settlers, who lived primarily in the town of Goliad and areas to the south.

Santa Anna vowed to put down the rebellion. On March 6 his army wiped out the rebel garrison defending the Alamo in San Antonio and then took control of Goliad. Santa Anna thought he had crushed the rebellion, but New Orleans and New York newspapers romanticized the heroism of the Texans and the deaths at the Alamo of folk heroes Davy Crockett and Jim Bowie. Drawing on anti-Catholic rhetoric, the newspapers described the Mexicans as tyrannical butchers in the service of the pope. Hundreds of American adventurers, lured by offers of land grants, flocked to Texas to join the rebel army. Led by General Sam Houston, the Texas rebels routed the Mexicans in the Battle of San Jacinto in April 1836. Thereafter, the Mexican government abandoned efforts to reconquer Texas but refused to accept its status as an independent republic.

The Texans quickly voted by plebiscite for annexation by the United States, but Presidents Andrew Jackson and Martin Van Buren refused to act. They knew that adding Texas as a slave state would divide the Democratic Party and the nation and almost certainly lead to war with Mexico.

The Push to the Pacific: Oregon and California

The annexation of Texas became a more pressing issue in the 1840s, as American expansionists developed continental ambitions. The term **Manifest Destiny** captured those dreams. As John L. O'Sullivan, the editor of the *Democratic Review* who coined

SIEGE OF THE ALAMO.

Assault on the Alamo

After a thirteen-day siege, on March 6, 1836, a Mexican army of 4,000 stormed the small mission in San Antonio, Texas. "The first to climb were thrown down by bayonets . . . or by pistol fire," reported a Mexican officer. Only a half hour of continuous assaults gave the attackers control of the wall. This contemporary woodcut shows the fierceness of the battle, which took the lives of all 250 American defenders; the Mexicans suffered 1,500 dead or wounded. Archives Division, Texas State Library.

FOR MORE HELP ANALYZING THIS IMAGE, see the Online Study Guide at **bedfordstmartins.com/henrettaconcise**.

the term in 1845, put it, "Our manifest destiny is to overspread the continent allotted by Providence for the free development of our yearly multiplying millions." Underlying the rhetoric of Manifest Destiny was a sense of American cultural and racial superiority; "inferior" peoples—Native Americans and Mexicans—were to be brought under American dominion, taught republicanism, and converted to Protestantism.

Already many residents of the Ohio River Valley were casting their eyes westward to the fertile valleys of the Oregon Country. This region stretched along the Pacific Coast from the border with Mexican California to the border with Russian Alaska. Since 1818 a British-American convention had allowed both British and Americans to settle anywhere in the disputed region. The British-run Hudson's Bay Company developed a lucrative fur trade north of the Columbia River, while several hundred Americans settled to the south, mostly in the Willamette Valley. On the basis of this settlement, the United States claimed the zone between California and the Columbia River.

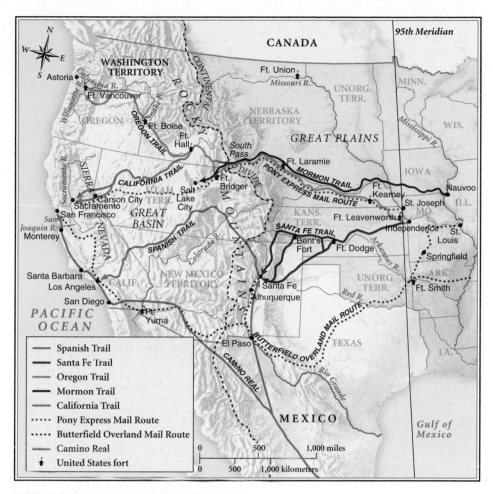

MAP 13.2 Routes to the West, 1835–1860

By the 1840s a variety of trails spanned the arid zone between the ninety-fifth meridian and the Pacific Coast. From the south, El Camino Real linked Mexico City to the California coast, Santa Fe, and the breakaway province of Texas. From the east, the Santa Fe, Oregon, California, and Mormon Trails carried tens of thousands of Americans from departure points on the Mississippi and Missouri Rivers to new communities in Utah and along the Pacific Coast. By the 1860s both the Pony Express and the Butterfield Overland Mail provided reliable communication between the eastern states and California.

In 1842 American interest in Oregon increased dramatically. The U.S. Navy published a glowing report of fine harbors in the Puget Sound, which was welcome news to New England merchants plying the China trade. In the same year a party of a hundred settlers journeyed along the Oregon Trail that fur traders and explorers had blazed through the Great Plains and the Rocky Mountains. Their reports from Oregon told of a mild climate and fertile soil (Map 13.2).

"Oregon fever" suddenly raged. In May 1843 a thousand men, women, and children—with more than a hundred wagons and five thousand oxen and cattle—gathered in Independence, Missouri, for the six-month trek to Oregon. The migrants were mostly farming and trading families from Missouri, Kentucky, and Tennessee. Overcoming flooding streams, dust storms, dying livestock, and encounters with Indians, they reached the Willamette Valley, after a journey of 2,000 miles. During the next two years another 5,000 people reached Oregon, and the numbers continued to grow.

By 1860 about 350,000 Americans had braved the Oregon Trail. More than 34,000 of them died in the effort, mostly from disease and exposure; only 400 deaths came from Indian attacks. The walking migrants wore three-foot-deep paths and their wagons carved five-foot-deep ruts across sandstone formations in southern Wyoming—tracks that are visible today. Women found the trail especially difficult because it exaggerated the authority of their husbands and added the labor of driving wagons and animals to their traditional chores.

Some pioneers ended up in the Mexican province of California. They left the Oregon Trail at the Snake River, trudged down the California Trail, and settled in the interior along the Sacramento River. Lying at the northern edge of Spain's American empire, California had been settled by the Spanish only in the 1770s, when they built a chain of religious missions and forts (presidios) along the coast (see Chapter 8). To promote California's development, the Mexican government took over the Franciscan-run missions and liberated the 20,000 Indians who worked on them. Some mission Indians rejoined their Native American tribes but many intermarried with mestizos (Mexicans of mixed Spanish and Indian ancestry) and worked as laborers and cowboys on large cattle ranches.

The rise of cattle ranching linked California to the United States. New England merchants dispatched dozens of agents to buy leather and tallow for use in the booming Massachusetts boot and shoe industry. Many of those resident agents married into the families of the elite Mexicans—the Californios—and adopted their dress, manners, outlook, and Catholic religion. A crucial exception was Thomas Oliver Larkin, the most successful merchant in the coastal town of Monterey. Larkin worked closely with Mexican ranchers, but he remained an American citizen and plotted for the peaceful annexation of California to the United States. Like Larkin, American migrants in the Sacramento Valley had no desire to assimilate into Mexican society. Many were squatters or held land grants of dubious legality and hoped for eventual annexation by the United States. However, these settlers numbered only about 700 in the early 1840s, compared with the coastal population of 7,000 Mexicans and 300 American traders.

The Fateful Election of 1844

The election of 1844 determined the American government's western policy. Since 1836 some southern leaders had advocated the territorial expansion of slavery, but their plans had been thwarted by cautious party politicians and northern abolitionists. Now southerners sensed a British threat to their ambitions. There were rumors that Britain wanted the Mexican government to cede California in payment for large debts owed to British investors. Southern leaders also believed that Britain was encouraging Texas to remain independent and had designs on Spanish Cuba, which some southerners wanted to annex. To thwart such British schemes, southern expansionists demanded the immediate annexation of Texas.

At this crucial moment "Oregon fever" and Manifest Destiny altered the political and diplomatic landscape in the North. In 1843 Americans in the Ohio Valley and the Great Lakes states organized "Oregon conventions" that called for an end to joint occupation of the region. In July, Democrat and Whig politicians met in a bipartisan national convention and demanded that the United States seize Oregon all the way to 54°40′ north latitude, the southern limit of Russian Alaska.

With northern Democrats demanding expansion in Oregon, southern Democrats could champion the annexation of Texas. Moreover, they had the support of President John Tyler. Disowned by the Whigs because of his opposition to Henry Clay's nationalist economic program, Tyler hoped to win reelection in 1844 as a Democrat. To curry favor among expansionists, Tyler proposed to annex Texas and seize all of Oregon. In April 1844 Tyler and John C. Calhoun, his new secretary of state, sent to the Senate a treaty to annex Texas. Two rival presidential candidates, Democrat Martin Van Buren and Whig Henry Clay, quickly declared their opposition. Knowing that annexation would raise the issue of slavery and divide the nation, they persuaded the Senate to defeat the treaty.

Texas and Oregon became the central issues in the election of 1844. The Democrats passed over Tyler, whom they did not trust, and Van Buren, whom southerners despised for his opposition to annexation. They selected Governor James K. Polk of Tennessee, a slave owner who favored annexation. Unimpressive in appearance, Polk was a man of iron will and boundless ambition for the nation. "Fifty-four forty or fight!" became the patriotic cry of his expansionist campaign.

The Whigs nominated Henry Clay, who again championed his American System of internal improvements, high tariffs, and national banking. Clay initially dodged the issue of Texas but ultimately indicated support for annexation. His evasive position disappointed thousands of northern Whigs and Democrats who opposed any expansion of slavery. Rather than vote for Clay, they voted for James G. Birney of the Liberty Party. Birney garnered less than 3 percent of the national vote but won enough support among Whigs in New York to cause Clay to lose that state. By taking New York's 36 electoral votes, Polk won the presidency by a margin of 170 to 105 in the electoral college.

Following Polk's victory, Democrats in Congress called for the immediate annexation of Texas. Unable to secure the needed two-thirds majority in the Senate to ratify a treaty with the Republic of Texas, they approved annexation by a joint resolution of Congress, which required only a majority vote in each house. Polk's strategy of linking Texas and Oregon had put him in the White House and Texas in the Union.

War, Expansion, and Slavery, 1846–1850

Texas was just the beginning. Polk wanted American control over all Mexican territory between Texas and the Pacific Ocean and was prepared to go to war to get it. What he consciously ignored was the major crisis over slavery that would be unleashed by his expansionist dreams.

The War with Mexico, 1846–1848

Since gaining independence, Mexico had not prospered. Its stagnant economy yielded few surpluses and modest tax revenues, which were quickly devoured by interest payments on foreign debts and a bloated government bureaucracy. The distant northern provinces of California and New Mexico contributed little to the national economy and, with a Spanish-speaking population of only 75,000 in 1840, remained sparsely settled. Nonetheless, Mexican officials vowed to preserve their nation's historical territories; when the breakaway Republic of Texas entered the American Union on July 4, 1845, Mexico broke off diplomatic relations with the United States.

Nonetheless, President Polk set into motion his plans to acquire Mexico's far northern provinces. To intimidate the Mexican government, he ordered General Zachary Taylor and an American army of 2,000 soldiers to occupy disputed lands between the Nueces River (the historical southern boundary of Texas) and the Rio Grande, which the Republic of Texas had claimed as its border with Mexico (see Map 13.1). Simultaneously Polk launched a secret diplomatic initiative. He sent John Slidell to Mexico City with instructions to win acceptance of the Rio Grande boundary and buy the Mexican provinces of New Mexico and California, paying as much as $30 million. When Slidell arrived in December 1845, Mexican officials refused to see him.

Anticipating the failure of Slidell's mission, Polk had already embarked on an alternative plan. He hoped to foment a revolution in California that, as in Texas, would lead to an independent republic and a request for annexation. In October 1845 Secretary of State James Buchanan told merchant Thomas O. Larkin, now the U.S. consul in the port of Monterey, to encourage influential Mexican residents to declare independence and support peaceful annexation. To add military muscle, Polk ordered American naval commanders to seize San Francisco Bay and California's coastal towns in case of war with Mexico. The president also had the War Department dispatch Captain John C. Frémont and an "exploring" party of heavily armed soldiers into Mexican territory. By December 1845 Frémont had reached California's Sacramento Valley.

Events now moved quickly toward war. Polk ordered General Taylor toward the Rio Grande to incite an armed response by Mexico. "We were sent to provoke a fight," an American officer recalled, "but it was essential that Mexico should commence it." When the armies clashed near the Rio Grande in May 1846, Polk called for war. Taking liberties with the truth, the president declared that Mexico "has passed the boundary of the United States, has invaded our territory, and shed American blood upon the American soil." Ignoring Whig pleas for a negotiated settlement, the Democratic majority in Congress voted for war, a decision that was greeted with great popular acclaim. To avoid a simultaneous conflict with Britain, Polk retreated from his campaign pledge of "fifty-four forty or fight" and accepted a British proposal to divide the Oregon Country at the forty-ninth parallel.

American forces in Texas quickly established their military superiority. Zachary Taylor's army crossed the Rio Grande, occupied Matamoros, and after a fierce six-day battle in September 1846, took the interior Mexican town of Monterrey. Two months later a U.S. naval squadron in the Gulf of Mexico seized Tampico, Mexico's second most important port. By the end of 1846 the United States controlled much of northeastern Mexico (Map 13.3).

Fighting had also broken out in California. In June 1846 naval commander John Sloat landed 250 marines in Monterey and declared that California "henceforward will be a portion of the United States." Almost simultaneously American settlers in the interior staged a revolt and, supported by Frémont's forces, captured the town of Sonoma. To cement these victories, Polk ordered army units to capture Santa Fe in New Mexico and then march to California. Despite stiff Mexican resistance, American forces secured control of California early in 1847.

Polk expected that these American victories would end the war, but he had underrated the Mexicans' national pride and the determination of President Santa Anna. Santa Anna took the offensive and attacked the depleted units of Zachary Taylor at Buena Vista in February 1847. Only superior artillery enabled Taylor to hold the American line in northeastern Mexico.

To bring Santa Anna to terms, Polk accepted General Winfield Scott's plan to strike deep into the heart of Mexico. In March 1847 Scott captured the port of Veracruz and began the 260-mile march to Mexico City. Leading Scott's 14,000 troops was a cadre of talented West Point officers who would become famous in the Civil War: Robert E. Lee, George Meade, and P. G. T. Beauregard. Scott's troops crushed Santa Anna's forces at Cerro Gordo and Churubusco and seized Mexico City in September 1847. A new Mexican government agreed to make peace with the United States.

A Divisive Victory

Initially many Americans viewed the war with Mexico as a noble struggle to extend American republican institutions, but the conflict soon divided the nation. A few Whigs, such as Charles Francis Adams of Massachusetts (the son of President John Quincy Adams) and Joshua Giddings of Ohio, opposed the war from the beginning on moral grounds. Known as "conscience Whigs," they warned of a southern conspiracy to add new slave states in the West, undermine the Jeffersonian ideal of a yeoman freeholder society, and ensure permanent control of the federal government by slaveholding Democrats. These antislavery Whigs grew bolder after the elections of 1846 gave their party control of Congress.

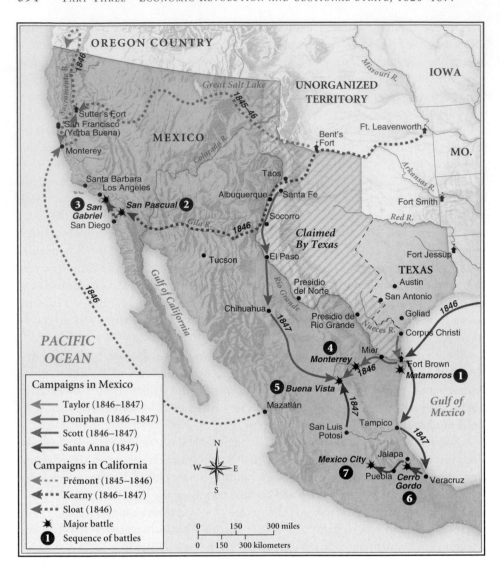

MAP 13.3 The Mexican War, 1846–1848

Departing from Fort Leavenworth in present-day Kansas, American forces commanded by Captain John C. Frémont and General Stephen Kearney defeated Mexican armies in California in 1846 and early 1847. Simultaneously U.S. armies under General Zachary Taylor and Colonel Alfred A. Doniphan won victories over General Santa Anna's forces far to the south of the Rio Grande. Then in mid-1847 General Winfield Scott mounted a successful attack on Mexico City, ending the war.

Polk's expansionist policy also split the Democrats into sectional factions. As early as 1839 Democratic senator Thomas Morris of Ohio had warned that "the power of slavery is aiming to govern the country, its Constitutions and laws." In August 1846 David Wilmot, a Democratic congressman from Pennsylvania, took up that refrain. To limit the spread of slavery, Wilmot proposed to prohibit the institution in any territories acquired from Mexico. This measure, known as the Wilmot Proviso, rallied antislavery northerners. In the House of Representatives, the northern Democratic allies of Martin Van Buren joined forces with antislavery Whigs to pass the proviso. The Senate, dominated by southerners and proslavery northern Democrats, killed it.

Fervent Democratic expansionists became even more aggressive. Polk, Secretary of State Buchanan, and Senators Stephen A. Douglas of Illinois and Jefferson Davis of Mississippi called for the United States to take Mexican territory south of the Rio Grande. However, to avoid a longer war and the assimilation of a huge number of Mexicans, John C. Calhoun and other southern leaders insisted that the United States should acquire only California and New Mexico, the most sparsely populated areas of Mexico.

To reunify the Democratic Party, Polk accepted Calhoun's policy. In February 1848 Polk signed the Treaty of Guadalupe Hidalgo, in which the United States agreed to pay Mexico $15 million in return for more than one-third of its territory: Texas, New Mexico, and California. The Senate ratified the treaty in March 1848.

The passions aroused by the war dominated the election of 1848. The Senate's rejection of the Wilmot Proviso prompted antislavery advocates to revive Thomas Morris's charge of a massive "Slave Power" conspiracy. To thwart any such plan, thousands of ordinary northerners joined a new "**free-soil**" movement. "The curse of slavery," Abijah Beckwith of Herkimer County in New York told his grandson, "threatens the general and equal distribution of our lands into convenient family farms." For Beckwith and other yeomen farmers, slavery was an institution of "aristocratic men" and a threat to the liberties of "the great mass of the people."

The free-soilers abandoned the Liberty Party's focus on the sinfulness of slavery and the natural rights of African Americans. Like Beckwith, they depicted slavery as a threat to republican institutions and white yeoman farming. This shift in emphasis led the radical abolitionist William Lloyd Garrison to denounce free-soil doctrine as racist "whitemanism." However, Frederick Douglass, the foremost black abolitionist, endorsed the movement as the best means of confronting the South and overthrowing slavery. Indeed, the Wilmot Proviso's call for free soil was the first antislavery proposal to attract broad popular support. Hundreds of women in the Great Lakes states joined female free-soil organizations formed by the American and Foreign Anti-Slavery Society.

The conflict over slavery took a toll on Polk and the Democratic Party. Opposed by free-soilers and exhausted by his rigorous dawn-to-midnight work regime, Polk declined to run for a second term and died three months after leaving office. In his place the Democrats nominated Senator Lewis Cass of Michigan, an avid expansionist who had advocated buying Cuba, annexing Mexico's Yucatán Peninsula, and taking all of Oregon. To maintain party unity, Cass was deliberately vague on the question of slavery in the West. He promoted a new idea—squatter sovereignty—that would allow settlers in each territory to determine its status as free or slave. Cass's political ingenuity failed to hold the party together. Demanding unambiguous opposition to the expansion of slavery, some northern Democrats joined the newly formed Free-Soil Party, which nominated Martin Van Buren for president. To attract Whig votes, the Free-Soil Party chose conscience Whig Charles Francis Adams as its candidate for vice president.

To keep their party intact, the Whigs nominated General Zachary Taylor. Taylor was a Louisiana slave owner, but he had not taken a position on the charged issue of slavery in the territories. Equally important, the general's military exploits had made him a popular hero. Known as "Old Rough and Ready," Taylor possessed a common touch that had won him the affection of his troops. "Our Commander on the Rio Grande," wrote Walt Whitman, "emulates the Great Commander of our revolution"—George Washington.

In 1848, as in 1840, running a military hero worked for the Whigs. Taylor took 47 percent of the popular vote against 42 percent for Cass. However, he won a majority in the electoral college (163 to 127) only because the Free-Soil ticket of Van Buren and Adams deprived the Democrats of enough votes in New York to cost Cass that state and the presidency. The bitter debate over the Wilmot Proviso had fractured the Democratic Party in the North and changed the dynamics of American politics.

1850: Crisis and Compromise

Even before President Zachary Taylor took office, events in California sparked a major political crisis. In January 1848 workmen building a mill for John A. Sutter in the Sierra Nevada foothills in northern California discovered flakes of gold. Sutter was a Swiss immigrant who arrived in California in 1839, became a Mexican citizen, and established an estate in the Sacramento Valley. He tried to keep the discovery a secret, but by May Americans who had already migrated to Monterey and San Francisco were pouring into the foothills. When President Polk confirmed the discovery in December, the gold rush was on. By January 1849 sixty-one crowded ships had left from northeastern ports to sail around Cape Horn to San Francisco, and by May, twelve thousand wagons had crossed the Missouri River, also bound for the gold fields. In 1849 alone more than 80,000 migrants—the "forty-niners"—arrived in California.

The rapid influx of settlers revived the national debate over free soil. The forty-niners, who lived in crowded, chaotic towns and mining camps, demanded the formation of a territorial government to protect their lives and property. To avoid an extended debate over slavery, President Taylor advised the Californians to apply for statehood immediately, and in November 1849 they ratified a state constitution that prohibited slavery. Taylor wanted to attract Free-Soilers and northern Democrats into the Whig Party and urged Congress to admit California as a free state.

The swift victory of the antislavery forces in California alarmed southern politicians. The admission of California as a free state would prevent the expansion of slavery to the Pacific and raise the number of free states in the Senate to sixteen, as opposed to fifteen slave states. Fearing that the South would be placed at a permanent disadvantage in Congress, southerners decided to block California's admission unless the federal government guaranteed the future of slavery.

California Gold Prospectors

Beginning in 1849, thousands of fortune seekers from all parts of the world converged on the California gold fields. By 1852 the state had 200,000 residents, including 25,000 Chinese, many of whom toiled in the gold fields as wage laborers. Working at the head of the Auburn Ravine in 1852, these prospectors are using a primitive technique—panning—to separate gold from sand and gravel. California State Library.

The resulting political impasse produced passionate debates in Congress and four distinct positions with respect to slavery in the territories. On the verge of death, John C. Calhoun took his usual extreme stance. He asserted the right of states to secede from the Union and proposed a constitutional amendment that would permanently balance the political power of the North and the South. Calhoun also advanced the radical doctrine that Congress had no constitutional authority to regulate slavery in the territories. This argument ran counter to a half century of practice. In 1787 Congress had prohibited slavery in the Northwest Territory, and in the Missouri Compromise of 1820 it had extended this ban to most of the Louisiana Purchase.

Calhoun's assertion that the territories were open to slavery won support in the Deep South, but many southerners favored a second—more moderate—position: an extension of the Missouri Compromise line to the Pacific Ocean. Such an extension would guarantee slave owners access to some western territory, including a separate state in southern California. Some northern Democrats, including former secretary of state James Buchanan, also favored this means of resolving the crisis.

A third alternative was squatter sovereignty, the idea advanced by Lewis Cass in 1848 and now championed by Democratic senator Stephen Douglas of Illinois. Douglas called his plan "**popular sovereignty**" to emphasize its roots in republican ideology, and it had considerable appeal. Popular sovereignty would place decisions about slavery in the hands of local settlers and their territorial governments and remove the explosive issue from national politics. However, popular sovereignty was a vague and slippery concept. Could residents accept or ban slavery when a territory was first organized or only when a territory had enough people to frame a constitution and apply for statehood?

Moreover, antislavery advocates were unwilling to accept any plan for California that might involve the expansion of slavery in the territories. Senator Salmon P. Chase of Ohio, elected by a Democratic–Free-Soil coalition, and Senator William H. Seward, a New York Whig, urged federal authorities to restrict slavery within its existing boundaries and then extinguish it completely. Condemning slavery as "morally unjust, politically unwise, and socially pernicious" and invoking "a higher law than the Constitution," Seward demanded bold action to protect freedom, "the common heritage of mankind."

Standing on the brink of disaster, senior politicians desperately sought a compromise. Assisted by Millard Fillmore, who became president in 1850 on the death of Zachary Taylor, Whig leaders Henry Clay and Daniel Webster and Democrat Stephen A. Douglas devised a package of six laws known collectively as the Compromise of 1850. To mollify the South, the Compromise included a new Fugitive Slave Act that enlisted federal magistrates in the task of returning runaway slaves. To satisfy the North, the legislation admitted California as a free state, resolved a boundary dispute between New Mexico and Texas in favor of New Mexico, and abolished the slave trade (but not slavery) in the District of Columbia. Finally, the Compromise organized the rest of the lands acquired from Mexico into the territories of New Mexico and Utah on the basis of popular sovereignty (Map 13.4).

The Compromise averted a secession crisis in 1850—but only barely. At one point the governor of South Carolina declared that there was not "the slightest doubt" that his state would secede from the Union. He and other "fire-eaters" in Georgia, Mississippi, and Alabama organized special conventions to ensure "Southern Rights" through secession. To persuade these conventions to support the Compromise, moderate southern politicians agreed to support secession in the future if Congress abolished slavery anywhere or refused to grant statehood to a territory with a proslavery constitution. Political wizardry had solved the immediate constitutional crisis but not the underlying issue of slavery.

The End of the Second Party System, 1850–1858

The architects of the Compromise of 1850 hoped it would last for at least a generation, but their optimism was quickly dashed. Demanding freedom for fugitive slaves and free soil in the West, antislavery northerners refused to accept the Compromise, and expansionist-minded southerners plotted to extend slavery into the West and the Caribbean. The resulting disputes destroyed the Second Party System and deepened the crisis of the Union.

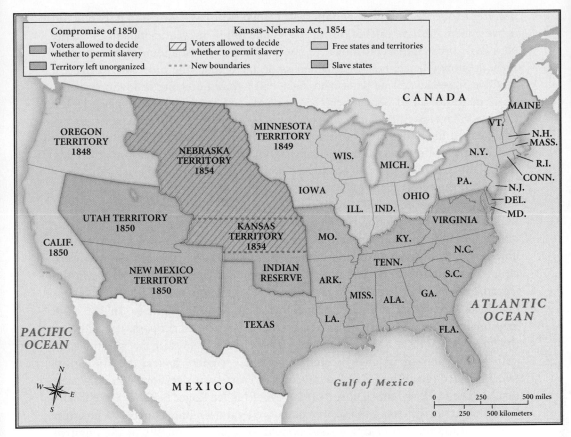

MAP 13.4 The Compromise of 1850 and the Kansas-Nebraska Act of 1854

Vast territories were at stake in the contest over the extension of slavery. The Compromise of 1850 resolved the status of lands in the Far West: California would be a free state, and the settlers of the Utah and New Mexico Territories would vote for or against slavery (the doctrine of popular sovereignty). The decision in 1854 to use popular sovereignty to decide the fate of slavery in the Kansas and Nebraska Territories sparked a bitter local war and revealed a fatal flaw in the doctrine.

FOR MORE HELP ANALYZING THIS MAP, see the Online Study Guide at **bedfordstmartins.com/henrettaconcise**.

Resistance to the Fugitive Slave Act

The Fugitive Slave Act proved the most controversial element of the Compromise. Under its terms federal magistrates in the northern states determined the status of alleged runaway slaves. The law denied accused blacks jury trials and even the right to testify. Using its provisions, southern owners reenslaved about two hundred fugitives (as well as some free northern blacks).

The plight of runaways and the appearance of slave catchers in the North and Midwest aroused popular hostility, and free blacks and abolitionists defied the new law. In October 1850 Boston abolitionists helped two slaves escape to freedom and drove a Georgia slave catcher out of town. The following year rioters in Syracuse, New York, broke into a courthouse to free a fugitive slave. Abandoning his commitment to nonviolence, Frederick Douglass declared that "the only way to make a Fugitive Slave Law a dead letter is to make half a dozen or more dead kidnappers." As if in response, in September 1851 a deadly confrontation took place in the Quaker village of Christiana, Pennsylvania. About twenty African Americans exchanged gunfire with a group of slave catchers from Maryland, killing two of them. Federal authorities indicted thirty-six blacks and four whites for treason for defying the law. But a Pennsylvania jury acquitted one defendant, and northern public opinion forced the government to drop charges against the rest.

Harriet Beecher Stowe's abolitionist novel *Uncle Tom's Cabin* (1852) magnified northern opposition to the Fugitive Slave Act. By translating the moral principles of abolitionism into heartrending personal situations, Stowe's novel evoked empathy and outrage throughout the North. Northern state legislatures were equally incensed that the act allowed the federal government to intervene in the internal affairs of their states. In response, they enacted personal-liberty laws that extended legal rights to their citizens, including accused fugitives. In 1857 the Wisconsin Supreme Court went even further. In *Ableman v. Booth*, it ruled that the Fugitive Slave Act was void in Wisconsin as contrary to state law and the constitutional rights of its citizens. Taking a "states' rights" stance, the Wisconsin court rejected the authority of federal courts to review its decision. When the case reached the U.S. Supreme Court in 1859, Chief Justice Roger B. Taney led a unanimous Court in affirming the supremacy of federal over state courts—a position that has stood the test of time—and upheld the constitutionality of the Fugitive Slave Act. By that time popular opposition in the North had made it nearly impossible to catch fugitive blacks. As Frederick Douglass had hoped, the act had become a "dead letter."

The Political System in Decline

The conflict over slavery split both major political parties along sectional lines and stymied creative political leadership. The Whigs, weakened by the death of Henry Clay, chose General Winfield Scott, another hero of the war with Mexico, as their presidential candidate in 1852. However, many southern Whigs refused to support Scott because northern Whigs refused to support slavery. The Democrats were equally divided. Southerners wanted a candidate who would support Calhoun's position that all territories should be open to slavery. But northern and midwestern Democrats advocated popular sovereignty, as did the three leading candidates—Lewis Cass of Michigan, Stephen Douglas of Illinois, and James Buchanan of Pennsylvania. Ultimately, the party settled on a compromise nominee, Franklin Pierce of New Hampshire, a congenial man reputed to be sympathetic to the South.

The Democrats' cautious strategy paid off, and they swept the election. Pleased by the admission of California as a free state, Martin Van Buren and many other Free-Soilers voted for Pierce, reuniting the Democratic Party. Conversely, the election fragmented the Whig Party into sectional wings; it would never again wage a national campaign.

As president, Pierce pursued an expansionist foreign policy. To assist northern merchants, he sent a mission to Japan to negotiate a commercial treaty. To mollify southern expansionists, he revived Polk's plan to annex extensive Mexican territories south of the Rio Grande. When Mexico rejected this initiative, Pierce settled for the purchase of a narrow slice of land that would assist his negotiator, James Gadsden, to build a southern-based transcontinental rail line.

Pierce's most dramatic, and most ill-fated, foreign policy initiative came in the Caribbean. Southern expansionists had previously funded three clandestine military expeditions to Cuba, where they hoped to prod sugar-producing slave owners to declare independence from Spain and join the United States. In 1853, Pierce covertly supported a new Cuban expedition and, to assist this venture, threatened war with Spain over the seizure of an American ship. When northern Democrats in Congress refused to support this aggressive diplomacy, Pierce and Secretary of State William L. Marcy had to back down. Still determined to seize Cuba, Marcy tried to buy the island from Spain. When that scheme also failed, Marcy arranged for American diplomats in Europe to inform Pierce, in the so-called Ostend Manifesto of 1854, that the United States would be justified "by every law, human and Divine" in seizing Cuba. Leaked to the press by antiexpansionists, the publication of the Ostend Manifesto revived northern fears of a "Slave Power" conspiracy and halted planter dreams of carving out an empire for slavery in the Caribbean.

The Kansas-Nebraska Act and the Rise of New Parties

In 1854 a new struggle over westward expansion inflamed sectional divisions. Because the Missouri Compromise prohibited new slave states in the Louisiana Purchase north of 36°30′, southern senators had delayed the political organization of that area. But westward-looking residents of the Ohio River Valley and the Upper South demanded its settlement. Senator Stephen A. Douglas of Illinois became their spokesman, partly because he supported the construction of a transcontinental railroad linking Chicago to California. In 1854 Douglas introduced a bill to extinguish Native American rights on the central Great Plains and organize a large free territory to be called Nebraska.

Douglas's bill conflicted with the plans of southern politicians who wanted to extend slavery throughout the Louisiana Purchase and wanted a southern city— New Orleans, Memphis, or St. Louis—to serve as the eastern terminus of a transcontinental railroad. To win southern support for the organization of Nebraska, Douglas made two major concessions. First, he amended his bill so that it explicitly repealed the Missouri Compromise and organized the region on the basis of popular sovereignty. Second, Douglas agreed to the formation of two new territories, Nebraska and

Kansas. This provision would give southern planters the opportunity to settle Kansas and, using popular sovereignty, eventually make it a slave state (see Map 13.4). To win support of this scheme by northern congressmen, Douglas argued that Kansas was not suited to plantation agriculture and would become a free state. After weeks of bitter debate, the Senate enacted the Kansas-Nebraska Act. When sixty-six northern Democrats in the House of Representatives defied party policy to vote against the act, Pierce used patronage and persuasion to get twenty-two members to change their votes, and the measure squeaked through.

The Kansas-Nebraska Act had disastrous consequences for the American political system because it destroyed the Whig Party and nearly wrecked the Democratic Party. Denouncing the act as "part of a great scheme for extending and perpetuating supremacy of the slave power," northern Whigs and "anti-Nebraska" Democrats abandoned their respective parties. They joined with Free-Soilers and abolitionists in a new Republican Party, which vowed to ban slavery from the territories. Although the Republican Party was a coalition of diverse groups, its founders shared a common philosophy. They opposed slavery because it degraded manual labor by enslaving blacks and driving down the wages and working conditions of free whites. And they celebrated the moral virtues of a society based on "the middling classes who own the soil and work it with their own hands." Abraham Lincoln, an Illinois Whig who became a Republican, articulated the party's vision of social mobility. "There is no permanent class of hired laborers among us," he argued, and every man had a chance to become a property owner. In the face of increasing class divisions in the industrializing North and Midwest, Lincoln and his fellow Republicans asserted the values of republican freedom and individual enterprise.

The Republicans faced severe competition from another new party, the American, or "Know-Nothing," Party. The American Party had its origins in the anti-immigrant and anti-Catholic organizations of the 1840s (see Chapter 10). In 1850 these secret societies banded together as the Order of the Star-Spangled Banner, and the following year they formed the American Party. The secrecy-conscious members often replied "I know nothing" to outsiders' questions, thus giving the party its nickname, but its program was far from secret. Know-Nothings hoped to unite native-born Protestants against the "alien menace" of Irish and German Catholics, prohibit further immigration, and institute literacy tests for voting. In 1854 the Know-Nothings gained control of the state governments of Massachusetts and Pennsylvania and, allied with the Whigs, commanded a majority in the U.S. House of Representatives. The emergence of a major party led by nativists suddenly became a real possibility.

Moreover, the Kansas-Nebraska Act had created yet another political crisis. In 1854 thousands of settlers rushed into the Kansas Territory, putting Douglas's theory of popular sovereignty to the test. On the side of slavery, Senator David R. Atchison of Missouri organized residents to cross into Kansas and vote in crucial elections there. Opposing him was the abolitionist New England Emigrant Aid Society, which dispatched hundreds of free-soilers to Kansas. In March 1855 the Pierce administration stepped into the fray by accepting the legitimacy of the territorial legislature sitting in

Lecompton, Kansas, which had been elected primarily by border-crossing Missourians and had adopted proslavery legislation. However, the majority of Kansas residents favored free soil and refused allegiance to the Lecompton government.

In May 1856 both sides turned to violence. A proslavery gang, seven hundred strong, sacked the free-soil town of Lawrence, destroying two newspaper offices, looting stores, and burning down buildings (see American Voices, "'Bleeding Kansas': A Southern View," p. 404). The attack enraged John Brown, a fifty-six-year-old abolitionist from New York and Ohio, whose free-state militia force arrived too late to save the town. Brown was a complex man with a checkered financial past. Despite a long record of failed businesses, Brown had an intelligence and a moral intensity that won the trust of influential people. Taking vengeance for the sack of Lawrence, he and a few followers murdered and mutilated five proslavery settlers. We must "strike terror in the hearts of the proslavery people," Brown declared. The southerners' sack of Lawrence and the "Pottawatomie massacre," as Brown's killings became known, began a guerrilla war in Kansas that took about two hundred lives.

The Election of 1856 and Dred Scott

The violence in Kansas dominated the presidential election of 1856. The two-year-old Republican Party counted on anger over "Bleeding Kansas" to boost its fortunes. The party's platform denounced the Kansas-Nebraska Act and, alleging a "Slave Power" conspiracy, insisted that the federal government prohibit slavery in all the territories. Its platform also called for federal subsidies for transcontinental railroads, reviving an element of the Whig economic program that was popular among midwestern Democrats. For president the Republicans nominated Colonel John C. Frémont, a Free-Soiler famous for his role in the conquest of California.

The American Party also entered the election with high hopes, but it quickly split into sectional factions over Kansas. The southern faction of the American Party nominated former Whig president Millard Fillmore. The Republicans cleverly maneuvered the northern faction of the American Party into endorsing Frémont, and they won the votes of Know-Nothing workingmen by emphasizing anti-Catholic nativism and high tariffs on foreign manufactures. As a Pennsylvania Republican put it, "Let our motto be, protection to everything American, against everything foreign." In New York, Republicans assumed the mantle of reform by shaping their policies "to cement into a harmonious mass . . . all of the Anti-Slavery, Anti-Popery and Anti-Whiskey" voters.

The Democrats reaffirmed their support for popular sovereignty and the Kansas-Nebraska Act and nominated James Buchanan of Pennsylvania. A tall, dignified figure of sixty-four, Buchanan was an experienced but unimaginative politician. Drawing upon his party's organizational strength and the loyalty of Democratic voters, Buchanan won the three-way race, amassing 174 votes in the electoral college and winning the popular vote—1.8 million votes (45 percent) to 1.3 million (33 percent) for Frémont. However, Buchanan took only five free states

AMERICAN VOICES

"Bleeding Kansas": A Southern View

AXALLA JOHN HOOLE

*E*arly in 1856 Axalla John Hoole and his bride left South Carolina to build a new life in the Kansas Territory (K.T.). These letters from Hoole to his family show that things did not go well from the start and gradually got worse; after eighteen months the Hooles returned to South Carolina. A Confederate militia captain during the Civil War, Axalla Hoole died in the Battle of Chickamauga in September 1863.

Kansas City, Missouri, Apl. 3d., 1856. The Missourians . . . are very sanguine about Kansas being a slave state & I have heard some of them say it shall be . . . but generally speaking, I have not met with the reception which I expected. Everyone seems bent on the Almighty Dollar, and as a general thing that seems to be their only thought. . . . [T]he supper bell has rung and I must close. Give my love to [the family] and all the Negroes. . . .

Lecompton, K.T., Sept. 12, 1856. I have been unwell ever since the 9th of July. . . . I thought of going to work in a few days, when the Abolitionists broke out and I have had to stand guard of nights when I ought to have been in bed, took cold which . . . caused diarrhea. . . . Betsie is well. . . . I am now in Lecompton, almost all of the Proslavery party between this place and Lawrence are here. We brought our families here, as we thought that we would be better able to defend ourselves. . . .

Lane [and a force of abolitionists] came against us last Friday (a week ago to-day). As it happened we had about 400 men with two cannon—we marched out to meet him, though we were under the impression at the time that we had 1,000 men. We came in gunshot of each other, but the regular [U.S. Army] soldiers came and interfered, but not before our party had shot some dozen guns, by which it is reported that five of the Abolitionists had been killed or wounded. We had strict orders . . . not to fire until they made the attack, but some of our boys would not be restrained. I was a rifleman and one of the skirmishers, but did all that I could to restrain our men though I itched all over to shoot myself. . . .

July the 5th., 1857. I fear, Sister, that [our] coming here will do no good at last, as I begin to think that this will be made a Free State at last. 'Tis true we have elected Proslavery men to draft a state constitution, but I feel pretty certain, if it is put to a vote of the people, it will be rejected, as I feel pretty confident that they have a majority here at this time. The South has ceased all efforts, while the North is redoubling her exertions. We nominated a candidate for Congress last Friday—Ex-Gov. Ransom of Michigan. I must confess I have not much faith in him, tho he professes to hate the abolitionists bitterly. . . . If we had nominated a Southern man, he would have been sure to have been beaten. . . .

SOURCE: "A Southerner's Viewpoint of the Kansas Situation, 1856–1857" from *Kansas Historical Quarterly* 3 (1934) edited by William Stanley Hoole. Reprinted by permission of the publisher.

(as opposed to eleven for Frémont), and a small shift of the popular vote to Frémont in Illinois and Pennsylvania would have given him the presidency. Fillmore, the candidate of the southern faction of the American Party, won 21 percent of the national vote but only 8 electoral votes.

The dramatic restructuring of parties was now apparent (Map 13.5). With the splintering of the Know-Nothings, the Republicans had replaced the Whigs as the second major party. Moreover, because they had no support in the South, a Republican victory in the next presidential election might prompt the southern states to withdraw from the Union. The fate of the republic hinged on the ability of President Buchanan to defuse the passions of the past decade and devise a way of protecting free soil in the West and slavery in the South.

Events—and his own values and weaknesses—conspired against Buchanan. During the election, the Supreme Court considered the case of *Dred Scott v. Sandford*, which raised the controversial issue of Congress's constitutional authority to regulate slavery in the territories. Scott was an enslaved African American who had lived for a time with his owner, an army surgeon, in the free state of Illinois and at Fort Snelling, then in the Wisconsin Territory, where the Northwest Ordinance (1787) prohibited slavery. In his suit Scott claimed that his residence in a free state and a free territory had made him free. Partly as result of Buchanan's pressure on several northern justices, seven of the nine members of the Court agreed that Scott

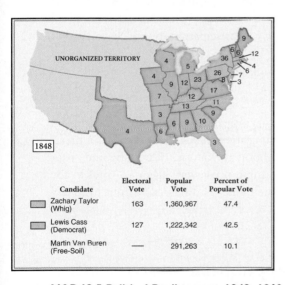

Candidate	Electoral Vote	Popular Vote	Percent of Popular Vote
Zachary Taylor (Whig)	163	1,360,967	47.4
Lewis Cass (Democrat)	127	1,222,342	42.5
Martin Van Buren (Free-Soil)	—	291,263	10.1

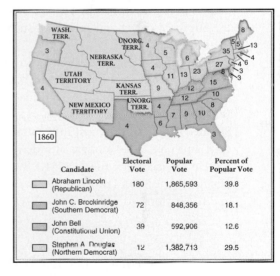

Candidate	Electoral Vote	Popular Vote	Percent of Popular Vote
Abraham Lincoln (Republican)	180	1,865,593	39.8
John C. Brockinridge (Southern Democrat)	72	848,356	18.1
John Bell (Constitutional Union)	39	592,906	12.6
Stephen A. Douglas (Northern Democrat)	12	1,382,713	29.5

MAP 13.5 Political Realignment, 1848–1860

In the presidential election of 1848, both Whigs and Democrats won electoral votes in most parts of the nation. Then the political conflict over slavery and the Compromise of 1850 destroyed the Whig Party in the South. As the only nationwide party, the Democrats won easily over the Whigs in 1852 and, because of the split between Republicans and Know-Nothings, in 1856 as well. However, by 1860 a new regionally based party system had taken shape and would persist for the next seventy years, with Democrats dominant in the South and Republicans in the Northeast and Midwest.

remained a slave. But the judges were unable to agree on the legal issues, and each justice wrote a separate opinion.

Chief Justice Roger B. Taney of Maryland composed the most influential opinion. He declared that Negroes, whether enslaved or free, could not be citizens of the United States, and that Scott therefore had no right to sue in federal court. That argument was controversial enough, since free blacks could be citizens of a state, which presumably gave them access to the federal courts. But Taney proceeded to make two even more controversial points. First, he endorsed John C. Calhoun's argument regarding the Fifth Amendment. Because the amendment prohibited "takings" of property without due process of law, Taney ruled that Congress could not deny southern citizens the right to take their slave property into the territories and own it there. Consequently, the chief justice concluded, the provisions of the Northwest Ordinance and the Missouri Compromise that prohibited slavery had never been constitutional. Second, Taney declared that Congress could not give to territorial governments any powers that Congress itself did not possess. Since Congress had no authority to prohibit slavery in a territory, neither did a territorial government. Taney thereby endorsed Calhoun's interpretation of popular sovereignty: only when settlers wrote a constitution and requested statehood could they prohibit slavery.

In a single stroke a Democrat-dominated Supreme Court had declared the Republicans' antislavery platform to be unconstitutional, a decision the Republicans could never accept. Led by Senator William H. Seward of New York, they accused the Supreme Court and President Buchanan of participating in the "Slave Power" conspiracy.

Buchanan then added new fuel to the raging constitutional fire. In early 1858 he recommended the admission of Kansas as a slave state under the Lecompton constitution, although its legitimacy was widely questioned. Angered that Buchanan would not permit a referendum on the Lecompton constitution, Stephen Douglas, the most influential Democratic senator, broke with the president and persuaded Congress to deny statehood to Kansas. (Kansas would enter the Union as a free state in 1861.) By pursuing a proslavery agenda—first in the *Dred Scott* decision and then in Kansas—Buchanan had helped to split his party and the nation.

Abraham Lincoln and the Republican Triumph, 1858–1860

The crisis of the Union intensified as the Democratic Party fragmented and the Republicans gained support in the North. Abraham Lincoln emerged as the pivotal figure in American politics, the only Republican leader whose policies and temperament might have saved the Union. But few southerners trusted Lincoln, and the prospect of his election to the presidency gave new life to the southern secessionists who had threatened to leave the Union since 1850.

Lincoln's Political Career

The middle-class world of storekeepers, lawyers, and entrepreneurs in the small towns of the Ohio River Valley shaped Lincoln's early career. He came from an impoverished yeoman farm family that had moved from Kentucky, where Lincoln was born in 1809, to Indiana and then to Illinois. In 1831 Lincoln rejected his father's life as a subsistence farmer and became a store clerk in New Salem, Illinois. Socially ambitious, Lincoln sought entry into the middle class by joining the New Salem Debating Society, reading Shakespeare, and studying law.

Lincoln's ambition was "a little engine that knew no rest," his closest associate remarked. Admitted to the bar in 1837, Lincoln moved to Springfield, the new state capital. There he met Mary Todd, the cultured daughter of a Kentucky banker; they married in 1842. The couple was a picture in contrasts. Her tastes were aristocratic; his were humble. She was volatile in temperament; he had an easygoing manner but suffered bouts of depression that tried her patience and tested his character. Entering political life, Lincoln served four terms as a Whig in the Illinois assembly, where he promoted education, state banking, and canals and railroads.

In 1846 the rising lawyer-politician won election to Congress, which was bitterly divided over the Wilmot Proviso. Lincoln had long felt that human bondage was unjust but did not believe that the federal government had the constitutional authority to tamper with slavery in the South. To exclude slavery from the territories, he voted for the Wilmot Proviso. Lincoln also proposed that Congress enact legislation for the gradual (and therefore compensated) emancipation of slaves in the District of Columbia. He argued that such measures—firm opposition to the expansion of slavery, gradual emancipation, and the colonization of freed slaves in Africa—was the only practical way to address the issue. However, both abolitionists and proslavery activists derided these pragmatic policies and Lincoln lost his bid for reelection. Dismayed, he withdrew from politics and developed a lucrative legal practice representing railroads and manufacturers.

Lincoln returned to the political fray after the passage of Stephen Douglas's Kansas-Nebraska Act. Attacking Douglas's doctrine of popular sovereignty, Lincoln reaffirmed his position on slavery. He would not threaten the institution in the states where it existed but would use national authority to exclude it from the territories. Confronting the moral issue, Lincoln declared that if the nation was to uphold its republican ideals, then it must eventually cut out slavery like a "cancer."

Abandoning the Whig Party in favor of the Republicans, Lincoln quickly emerged as their leader in Illinois. Campaigning for the U.S. Senate against Stephen Douglas in 1858, Lincoln alerted his audiences to the dangers of the "Slave Power." He warned that the proslavery Supreme Court might soon declare that the Constitution "does not permit a state to exclude slavery from its limits," just as it had decided (in *Dred Scott*) that "neither Congress nor the territorial legislature can do it." In that event, he continued, "we shall awake to the reality . . . that the Supreme Court has made Illinois a slave state." The prospect of slavery spreading into the North informed Lincoln's famous "House Divided" speech. Quoting from the Bible, "A house divided against itself cannot stand," he predicted a crisis: "I believe this government cannot endure permanently half slave and half free. . . . It will become all one thing, or all the other."

The contest in Illinois attracted national interest because of Douglas's prominence and Lincoln's reputation as a formidable speaker. During a series of seven debates, Douglas declared his support for white supremacy and attacked Lincoln for supporting "negro equality." Put on the defensive by Douglas's racial tactics, Lincoln advocated economic opportunity for blacks but not equal political rights. He asked how Douglas could accept the *Dred Scott* decision (which protected slave owners' property in the territories) and yet advocate popular sovereignty (which asserted settlers' power to exclude slavery). Douglas responded with the so-called Freeport Doctrine, which suggested that the residents could exclude slavery simply by not adopting a law to protect it. Although Douglas's Freeport statement pleased neither proslavery advocates nor abolitionists, the Democrats won a narrow victory over the Republicans in Illinois, and the state legislature reelected Douglas to the U.S. Senate.

Abraham Lincoln and Stephen Douglas, 1860

When Douglas and Lincoln squared off in the presidential election of 1860, they distributed thousands of silk campaign ribbons bearing their portraits and signatures. The well-known photographer Matthew Brady took their pictures and retouched the images to make them more flattering—smoothing out Lincoln's gaunt and well-lined face and slimming down Douglas's ample cheeks.

Collection of Janice L. and David J. Frent.

The Party System Fragments

The debates with Douglas gave Lincoln a national reputation, while the election of 1858 gave the Republican Party control of the House of Representatives. In the wake of these Republican gains, southern Democrats divided into two groups. Moderates, such as Senator Jefferson Davis of Mississippi, who were known as Southern Rights Democrats, continued to seek political commitments to protect slavery. However, radical southern leaders, such as Robert Barnwell Rhett of South Carolina and William Lowndes Yancey of Alabama, repudiated the Union and actively promoted secession. Radical antislavery northerners played into their hands. Senator William Seward of New York declared that freedom and slavery were locked in "an irrepressible conflict" and the militant abolitionist John Brown suggested what that might mean. In October 1859, Brown led eighteen heavily armed black and white men in a raid on the federal arsenal at Harpers Ferry, Virginia. Brown hoped to secure arms, lead a slave rebellion, and establish a separate African American state in the South.

Republican leaders disavowed Brown's unsuccessful raid, but Democrats called his plot "a natural, logical, inevitable result of the doctrines and teachings of the Republican party." Brown was charged with treason, sentenced to death, and hanged—only to be praised by reformer Henry David Thoreau as "an angel of light." Horrified by northern admiration of Brown, southerners looked to the future with fear. "The aim of the present black republican organization is the destruction of the social system of the Southern States, without regard to consequences," warned one newspaper.

Nor could the South count on the Democratic Party to protect its interests. At the party convention in April 1860, northern Democrats rejected Jefferson Davis's program to protect slavery in the territories, so the delegates from eight southern states quit the meeting. At a second Democratic convention in Baltimore, northern and western delegates nominated Stephen Douglas for president; meeting separately, southern Democrats nominated John C. Breckinridge of Kentucky.

With the Democrats divided, the Republicans sensed victory. They courted white voters by opposing both slavery and racial equality: "Missouri for white men and white men for Missouri," declared that state's Republican platform. The national Republican convention chose Lincoln as its presidential candidate because his position on slavery was more moderate than that of the best-known Republicans, Senator William H. Seward of New York and Salmon P. Chase of Ohio, who demanded its abolition. Lincoln also conveyed a compelling egalitarian image that appealed to smallholding farmers and wage earners. And Lincoln's home territory—the rapidly growing Midwest—was crucial in the competition between Democrats and Republicans.

The Republican strategy succeeded. Lincoln received only 40 percent of the popular vote but won a majority in the electoral college by carrying every northern and western state except New Jersey. Douglas took 30 percent of the total vote, but won electoral votes only in Missouri and New Jersey. Breckinridge captured every state in the Deep South as well as Delaware, Maryland, and North Carolina, while John Bell, a former Tennessee Whig who was the nominee of the compromise-seeking Constitutional Union Party, carried the Upper South states where the Whigs had been strongest: Kentucky, Tennessee, and Virginia.

The Republicans had united the Northeast, the Midwest, and the Far West behind free soil and had seized national power. A revolution was in the making. Slavery had permeated the American federal republic for so long and so thoroughly that southerners had come to see it as part of the constitutional order—an order now under siege. To many southerners it seemed time to think carefully about the meaning of Lincoln's words of 1858 that the Union must "become all one thing, or all the other."

TIMELINE

1820s	Expansion of cattle raising in Mexican California		California, New Mexico, and Texas to the United States
1821	Mexico wins independence from Spain	1850	Compromise of 1850 seeks to preserve the Union
1836	Texas proclaims independence from Mexico		Fugitive Slave Act rejected by northern abolitionists
1842	Overland migration to Oregon begins	1851	American (Know-Nothing) Party formed
1844	Policy toward Texas and Oregon dominates presidential election	1852	Harriet Beecher Stowe publishes *Uncle Tom's Cabin*
1845	John O'Sullivan coins term *Manifest Destiny*	1854	Ostend Manifesto seeks to expand slavery by acquiring Cuba
	Texas admitted to Union as a slave state		Kansas-Nebraska Act tests policy of popular sovereignty
	John Slidell's diplomatic mission to Mexico fails		Republican Party formed
1846	United States declares war on Mexico	1856	"Bleeding Kansas" undermines popular sovereignty
	Treaty with Britain divides Oregon Country at forty-ninth parallel		
	Wilmot Proviso prohibiting slavery in newly acquired territories approved by House but not by Senate	1857	*Dred Scott v. Sandford* allows slavery in the territories
1847	American troops under General Winfield Scott capture Mexico City	1858	James Buchanan backs Lecompton constitution
			Lincoln-Douglas debates
1848	Gold discovered in California	1860	Abraham Lincoln elected president in four-way contest
	Free-Soil Party organized		
	In Treaty of Guadalupe Hidalgo Mexico cedes its provinces of		

For Further Exploration

Patricia Nelson Limerick, *The Legacy of Conquest: The Unbroken Past of the American West* (1989), provides a sharply written interpretation of the struggle among individuals, groups, and nations for control of the West. First-Person Narratives of California's Early Years, 1849–1900 are available through the Library of Congress at <http://lcweb2.loc.gov/ammem/cbhtml/cbhome.html>. A fine video documentary, *The West* (6 hours), by Ken Burns and Stephen Ives has a useful Web site—New Perspectives on the West, at <http://www.pbs.org/thewest>—that includes a good collection of maps, biographical essays, original documents, and images. For the early history of Texas, see <http://www.tsl.state.tx.us/treasures/>. The PBS documentary *The U.S.-Mexican War* (4 hours) and its Web site, at <http://www.pbs.org/usmexicanwar>, view the war both from the American and the Mexican perspectives and draw on the expertise of historians from each country.

David Potter, *The Impending Crisis, 1848–1861* (1976), presents a lucid account of the political history of the pre–Civil War years. Two recent works, John Patrick Daly, *When Slavery Was Called Freedom: Evangelicalism, Proslavery, and the Causes of the Civil War* (2002), and Leonard L. Richards, *The Slave Power: The Free North and Southern Domination, 1780–1860* (2000), offer a broad cultural analysis of the sectional conflict.

For an eloquent discussion of the ideology and politics of the Republican Party, see Eric Foner, *Free Soil, Free Labor, Free Men* (1970). Michael Holt's *The Political Crisis of the 1850s* (1978) shows how the loss of morale among voters and the collapse of the Second Party System allowed sectional rivalries to engulf the nation in war. For an incisive treatment of Lincoln's personal and political life, see Stephen Oates, *With Malice Toward None: A Life of Abraham Lincoln* (1977). For Lincoln's speech on the *Dred Scott* decision, refer to <http://www.usconstitution.com/AbrahamLincolnonDredScottDecision.htm>; the justices' opinions in the case can be read at <http://odur.let.rug.nl/~usa/D/1851-1875/dredscott/dredxx.htm>. Uncle Tom's Cabin and American Culture: A Multi-Media Archive, at <http://jefferson.village.virginia.edu/utc/>, is an extremely rich Web site that explores the literary and cultural context of the time through essays, original documents, and recordings of minstrel music.

For definitions of key terms boldfaced in this chapter, see the glossary at the end of the book.

To assess your mastery of the material covered in this chapter, see the Online Study Guide at **bedfordstmartins.com/henrettaconcise**.

For map resources and primary documents, see **bedfordstmartins.com/henrettaconcise**.

Chapter 14

TWO SOCIETIES AT WAR
1861–1865

Our fathers made this country, we their children are to save it.
ENLISTEE, TWELFTH OHIO REGIMENT, UNION ARMY, 1861

"What a scene it was," the Union soldier Elisha Hunt Rhodes wrote in his diary in July 1863 as the battle of Gettysburg ended. "Oh the dead and the dying on this bloody field." The passions kindled by southern rights and northern reformism had already inspired thousands of men to die in battle, and the slaughter would continue for two more years. "What is this all about?" asked Confederate lieutenant R. M. Collins at the end of another gruesome battle. "Why is it that 200,000 men of one blood and tongue . . . [should be] seeking one another's lives? We could settle our differences by compromising and all be at home in ten days." But there was no compromise—not in 1863 nor even in 1865.

To explain why Southerners seceded and then fought the war to the bitter end is not simple, but racial slavery is an important part of the answer. For political leaders in the South, the Republican victory in 1860 presented a clear and immediate danger to the slave-owning republic that had existed since 1776. Lincoln was elected without a single electoral vote from the South, and Southerners knew that his Republican Party would prevent the extension of slavery into the territories.

Moreover, they did not believe Lincoln when he promised not "directly or indirectly, to interfere with the institution of slavery in the States where it exists." "The mission of the Republican party," a southern newspaper declared, was "to meddle with everything—to meddle with the domestic institutions of other States, and to meddle with family arrangements in their own states—to overthrow Democracy, Catholicism and Slavery." Soon, a southern senator warned, "cohorts of Federal office-holders, Abolitionists, may be sent into [our] midst" to mobilize the African American population. The result would be bloody slave revolts and racial intermixture—by which was meant relations between black men and white women, as white owners had already fathered untold numbers of children by their black women slaves. "Better, far better! [to] endure all horrors of civil war," insisted a Confederate recruit from Virginia, "than to see the dusky sons of Ham leading the fair daughters of the South to the altar." To preserve black slavery and the supremacy of white men, radical southern leaders embarked on the dangerous journey of secession.

Lincoln and the North would not let them go in peace. Living in a world still ruled by kings and princes, northern leaders believed that the failure of the American Union might destroy for all time the prospect of a republican government based on constitutional procedures, majority rule, and democratic elections. "We cannot escape history," the new president eloquently declared. "We shall nobly save, or meanly lose, the last best hope of earth." A young Union army recruit from Ohio put the issue more simply: "If our institutions prove a failure . . . of what value will be house, family, or friends?"

And so came the Civil War. Called the "War between the States" by Southerners and the "War of the Rebellion" by Northerners, the struggle continued until the great issues of the Union and slavery had been finally resolved. The cost was incredibly high: more lives lost than in all the nation's subsequent wars and a century-long legacy of bitterness between the triumphant North and the vanquished South.

Secession and Military Stalemate, 1861–1862

Following Lincoln's election in November 1860, secessionist fervor swept through the Deep South, and the future of the Union appeared dim. Henry Clay and Daniel Webster, architects of the great sectional agreements of the past, had died and lesser men now sat in Congress. Nonetheless, veteran Washington politicians did not give up. In the four months before Lincoln's election, they struggled to forge a new compromise that (like those of 1787, 1821, and 1850) would preserve the Union.

Choosing Sides

The movement toward secession was most rapid in South Carolina—the home of John C. Calhoun, nullification, and the Southern Radical movement. Robert Barnwell Rhett and other "fire-eaters" had called for secession ever since the crisis of 1850 and, with Lincoln's election, their goal was suddenly within reach. On December 20 a special state convention voted unanimously to dissolve "the union now subsisting between South Carolina and other States."

Moving quickly, fire-eaters elsewhere in the Deep South called similar conventions and mobilized vigilante groups and militia units to suppress local Unionists and prepare for war. In early January, amid an atmosphere of public celebration, Mississippi enacted a secession ordinance. Within a month Florida, Alabama, Georgia, Louisiana, and Texas had also left the Union (Map 14.1). In early February the jubilant secessionists met in Montgomery, Alabama, to proclaim a new nation—the Confederate States of America. Adopting a provisional constitution, the delegates named Jefferson Davis of Mississippi, a former U.S. senator and secretary of war, as its interim president.

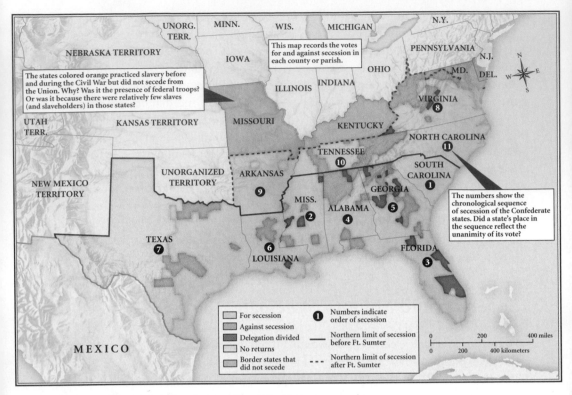

MAP 14.1 The Process of Secession, 1860–1861

The states of the Lower South, which had the highest concentration of slaves, led the secessionist movement. After the attack on Fort Sumter, the states of the Upper South joined the Confederacy. Yeoman farmers in Tennessee and the backcountry of Alabama, Georgia, and Virginia opposed secession but, except in the future state of West Virginia, initially rallied to the Confederate cause. Consequently, the South entered the Civil War with a relatively united white population.

Secessionist fervor was less intense in the eight slave states of the Upper South (Virginia, Delaware, Maryland, North Carolina, Kentucky, Tennessee, Missouri, and Arkansas), where there were fewer slaves and yeomen farmers had greater political power. Yeomen had long resented the authority claimed by the slave-owning gentry, and some actively opposed it. In the 1850s, Hinton Helper of North Carolina roused the "Non-slaveowners of the South! farmers, mechanics and workingmen," and warned them that "the slaveholders, the arrogant demagogues whom you have elected to offices of honor and profit, have hoodwinked you." Influenced partly by such sentiments, in January 1861 the legislatures of Virginia and Tennessee refused to join the secessionist movement. Seeking a compromise, Upper South leaders proposed federal guarantees for slavery in the states where it existed.

Meanwhile, the Union government floundered. In his final message to Congress in December 1860, President Buchanan declared secession illegal but denied that the federal government had the authority to restore the Union by force. South Carolina viewed Buchanan's message as an implicit recognition of its independence and demanded the surrender of Fort Sumter, a federal garrison in Charleston harbor. To test the secessionists' resolve, Buchanan ordered the resupply of the fort by an unarmed merchant ship. When the South Carolinians fired on the ship, Buchanan showed his own lack of resolve by refusing to order the navy to escort it into the harbor.

Instead, Buchanan urged Congress to find a compromise. The scheme proposed by Senator John J. Crittenden of Kentucky, an aging follower of Henry Clay, received the most support. Crittenden's plan had two parts. The first part, which won congressional approval, called for a constitutional amendment that would permanently protect slavery from federal interference in any state where it already existed. Crittenden's second provision called for the westward extension of the Missouri Compromise line (36°30′ north latitude) to the California border. Slavery would be barred north of the line and protected to the south, including any territories "hereafter acquired."

On Lincoln's instructions, congressional Republicans rejected this part of Crittenden's plan. The president-elect was firmly committed to the doctrine of free soil and feared this compromise would simply encourage the South to embark on new imperialist adventures in the Caribbean and Latin America. Crittenden's plan, Lincoln charged, would be "a perpetual covenant of war against every people, tribe, and State owning a foot of land between here and Tierra del Fuego [the southern tip of South America]."

In his inaugural address in March 1861, Lincoln carefully balanced a call for reconciliation with a firm commitment to the Union. He promised to safeguard slavery where it existed and to ensure free soil in the territories. Most important, Lincoln stated that the Union was "perpetual"; consequently, the secession of the Confederate states was illegal and acts of violence in support of their action constituted insurrection. He clearly declared his intention to enforce federal law throughout the Union and—of particular relevance to Fort Sumter—to continue to "hold, occupy, and possess" federal property in the seceded states and "to collect duties and imposts" there. If force was necessary to preserve the Union, Lincoln—like Andrew Jackson during the nullification crisis—promised to use it. The choice was the South's: return to the Union or face war.

The South's decision came quickly. The garrison at Fort Sumter urgently needed food and medicine. Upholding his promise to defend federal property, Lincoln dispatched a relief expedition and assured the Confederate government of its peaceful mission. However, Jefferson Davis and associates wanted a military confrontation to turn the wavering Upper South against the North and win foreign support for the Confederate cause. Davis demanded the surrender of the fort and, when Major Robert Anderson refused, the Confederate forces opened fire and forced a capitulation on April 14. The next day Lincoln called 75,000 state militiamen into federal service for ninety days to put down an insurrection "too powerful to be suppressed by the ordinary course of judicial proceedings." All talk of compromise was past.

Northerners responded to Lincoln's call to arms with wild enthusiasm. Asked to provide thirteen regiments of volunteers, Republican governor William Dennison of Ohio sent twenty. Many northern Democrats declared their support for the Union cause. "Every man must be for the United States or against it," Stephen Douglas declared. "There can be no neutrals in this war, only patriots—or traitors."

The white residents of the Upper South now had to choose between the Union and the Confederacy, and their decision was crucial. Those eight states accounted for two-thirds of the South's white population, more than three-fourths of its industrial production, and well over half of its food and fuel. They were home to many of the nation's best military leaders, including Colonel Robert E. Lee of Virginia, a career officer whom veteran general Winfield Scott recommended to Lincoln to lead the new Union army. And they were geographically strategic. Kentucky, with its 500-mile border on the Ohio River, was essential to the movement of troops and supplies. Maryland was vital to the Union's security because it surrounded the nation's capital on the north.

The weight of history decided the outcome in Virginia, the original home of American slavery. Three days after the fall of Fort Sumter, a Virginia convention voted to secede by a margin of 88 to 55, with the dissenters drawn mainly from the yeoman-dominated northwestern counties. Elsewhere, Virginia whites rallied to the Confederate cause. "The North was the aggressor," declared lawyer William Poague as he enlisted in an artillery unit. "The South resisted her invaders." Refusing Scott's offer of the Union command, Robert E. Lee resigned from the army. "Save in defense of my native state," Lee told Scott, "I never desire again to draw my sword." Arkansas, Tennessee, and North Carolina quickly joined Virginia in the Confederacy.

Lincoln moved aggressively to hold the rest of the Upper South. In May he ordered General George B. McClellan to take control of northwestern Virginia to secure the railway line between Washington and the Ohio Valley. In October, voters in that yeoman region overwhelmingly approved the formation of a breakaway territory, West Virginia, which was admitted to the Union in 1863. Unionists easily carried the day in Delaware but not in Maryland, where slavery was well entrenched. A pro-Confederate mob attacked Massachusetts troops marching between railroad stations in Baltimore, causing the war's first combat deaths: four soldiers and twelve civilians. When secessionists destroyed railroad bridges and telegraph lines, Lincoln ordered the military occupation of Maryland and the arrest of Confederate sympathizers, including state legislators. He released them only in November 1861, after Unionists gained control of the Maryland government.

In the west, Lincoln was equally energetic and resourceful. To win Missouri (and control of trade and communications along the Missouri and upper Mississippi Rivers), Lincoln mobilized the German American militia; in July, it defeated a force of Confederate sympathizers commanded by the governor. Despite continuing raids by Confederate guerrilla bands, the Union retained control of the state (see Voices from Abroad, "German Immigrants and the Civil War within Missouri," p. 417). In Kentucky, secessionist and Unionist sentiment was evenly balanced, so Lincoln moved cautiously. When Unionists took control of the state government in August, Lincoln ordered federal troops to halt Kentucky's thriving trade

VOICES FROM ABROAD

German Immigrants and the Civil War within Missouri

ERNEST DUVEYIER DE HAURANNE

*T*ens *of thousands of Germans migrated to Missouri and other midwestern states after 1840, and as the following letter by the Frenchman Ernest Duveyier de Hauranne indicates, most of them supported the Union cause. Hauranne traveled widely, and his letters home offer an intelligent commentary on American politics and society during the Civil War.*

St. Louis, September 12, 1864

Missouri is to all intents and purposes a rebel state, an occupied territory where the Federal forces are really nothing but a garrison under siege. . . . Party quarrels here are poisoned by class hatreds. . . . The old Anglo-French families, attached to Southern institutions, harbor a primitive, superstitious prejudice in favor of slavery. Conquered now, but full of repressed rage, they exhibit the implacable anger peculiar to the defenders of lost causes. . . .

The more recent German population is strongly abolitionist. They have brought to the New World the instincts of European democracy, together with its radical attitudes and all-or-nothing doctrines. Ancient precedents and worn-out laws matter little to them. They have not studied history and have no respect for hallowed injustices; but they do have, to the highest degree, that sense of moral principle which is more or less lacking in American democracy. They aren't afraid of revolution: to destroy a barbarous institution they would, if necessary, take an axe to the foundations of society.

Furthermore, their interests coincide with their principles. . . . The immigrant arrives poor and lives by his work. A newcomer, having nothing to lose and caring little for the interests of established property owners, sees that the subjection of free labor to the ruinous competition of slave labor must be ended. At the same time, his pride rebels against the prejudice attached to work in a land of slavery; he wants to reestablish its value. . . .

There is no mistaking the hatred the two parties, not to say the two peoples, have for each other. . . . The Federal government sent General [John C.] Frémont here as army commander and dictator. . . . An abolitionist and a self-made man, he put himself firmly at the head of the German party, determined to crush the friends of slavery. He formed an army of Germans who are completely devoted to their chief. . . .

[However,] bands of guerrillas hold the countryside, where they raid as much as they please; politics serves as a fine pretext for looting. Their leaders are officers from the army of the South who receive their orders from the Confederate government. . . . These "bushwackers," who ordinarily rob indiscriminately, maintain their standing as political raiders by occasionally killing some poor, inoffensive person. . . . You can see what emotions are still boiling in this region that is supposed to be pacified.

SOURCE: Ernest Duveyier de Hauranne, *A Frenchman in Lincoln's America* (Chicago: Lakende Press, 1974), 305–9.

with the Confederacy and to defend the state. In September, Illinois volunteers under the command of the relatively unknown Brigadier General Ulysses S. Grant crossed the Ohio River and drove out an invading Confederate force. Of the eight states of the Upper South, Lincoln had kept four (Delaware, Maryland, Kentucky, and Missouri) and a portion of a fifth (western Virginia) in the Union.

Setting War Aims and Devising Strategies

At his inauguration in February 1861, Jefferson Davis called on the people of the Confederacy to defend its independence. He identified the Confederates' cause with that of the American revolutionaries: like their grandfathers, white Southerners were fighting against tyranny and for the "sacred right of self-government." As Davis put it, the Confederacy sought "no conquest, no aggrandizement . . . ; all we ask is to be let alone." The decision to focus on the defense of the Confederacy and not to seek western territories gave the South a strategic advantage: it needed only a military stalemate to guarantee independence. Ignoring opposition to slavery among potential European allies, the Confederate constitution explicitly stated that "No . . . law denying or impairing the right of property in negro slaves shall be passed," and vice president Alexander Stephens ruled out any plan for gradual emancipation. In Stephens's view, the Confederacy's "cornerstone rests upon the great truth that the Negro is not equal to the white man, that slavery—subordination to the superior race—is his natural or normal condition."

Lincoln made his first major statement on Union goals and strategy in a speech to Congress on July 4, 1861. He portrayed secession as an attack on popular government, which was America's great contribution to world history, and tested "whether a constitutional republic, or a democracy . . . [can] maintain its territorial integrity against its domestic foe." Convinced that the Union had to crush the rebellion, Lincoln rejected General Winfield Scott's plan to use economic sanctions and a naval blockade to persuade the Confederates to return to the Union. Instead, the president insisted on an aggressive military strategy and a policy of unconditional surrender.

The president hoped that a quick strike against the Confederate capital of Richmond, Virginia, would end the rebellion. He therefore dispatched General Irvin McDowell and an army of 30,000 men to attack P. G. T. Beauregard's force of 20,000 troops at Manassas, a rail junction thirty miles southwest of Washington. In July, McDowell launched a strong assault near Manassas Creek (also called Bull Run), but panic swept through his troops during a Confederate counterattack. For the first time Union soldiers heard the hair-raising rebel yell. "The peculiar corkscrew sensation that it sends down your backbone under these circumstances can never be told," one Union veteran wrote. "You have to feel it." McDowell's troops retreated in disarray to Washington, along with the many civilians who had come to observe the battle.

The rout of the Union army at Bull Run made it clear that the rebellion would not be easily crushed. Lincoln replaced McDowell with General George B. McClellan and enlisted an additional million men, who would serve for three years in the newly created Army of the Potomac. A cautious military engineer, McClellan spent the winter of 1861 training the recruits, and early in 1862 he launched a major offensive. With great logistical skill, the Union general transported 100,000 troops by boat down the Potomac River and put them ashore on the peninsula between the York and James Rivers (Map 14.2). Ignoring Lincoln's advice to "strike a blow" quickly, McClellan

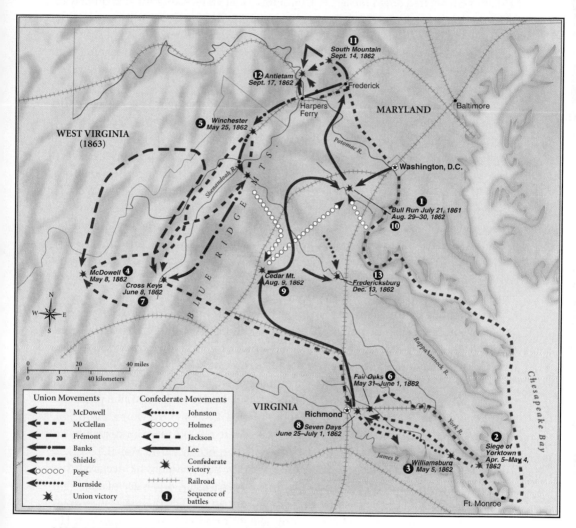

MAP 14.2 The Eastern Campaigns of 1862

Many of the great battles of the Civil War took place in the 125 miles between the Union capital of Washington and the Confederate capital of Richmond. During 1862, Confederate generals Robert J. "Stonewall" Jackson and Robert E. Lee secured defensive victories that safeguarded the Confederate capital (# 3, 6, 8 and 13) and launched offensive strikes against Union forces that guarded Washington (# 1, 4, 5, 7, 9, and 10). They also suffered a defeat—at Antietam, in Maryland—that was almost fatal (#12). As was often the case in the Civil War, the victors in these battles were either too bloodied or too timid to exploit their advantage.

advanced slowly toward the South's capital. His deliberate tactics allowed the Confederates to mount a counterstroke. To relieve the pressure on Richmond, a Confederate army under Thomas J. ("Stonewall") Jackson marched rapidly north up the Shenandoah Valley in western Virginia and threatened Washington. Lincoln recalled 30,000 troops from McClellan's army to protect the Union's capital, but Jackson, a brilliant general, tied down the larger Union forces. Then Jackson returned quickly to Richmond and the main Confederate army commanded by General Robert E. Lee. Lee launched a ferocious attack that lasted for seven days (June 25–July 1), suffering 20,000 casualties to the Union's 10,000. When McClellan failed to exploit the Confederates' weakness and requested fresh troops, Lincoln ordered the withdrawal of the Army of the Potomac, and Richmond remained secure.

Seeking victories that would humiliate Lincoln's government, Lee went on the offensive. Joining with Jackson in northern Virginia, he routed Union troops in the Second Battle of Bull Run (August 1862) and then struck north through western Maryland, where he met with near disaster. When Lee divided his force—sending Jackson to capture Harpers Ferry in West Virginia—a copy of his orders fell into McClellan's hands. The Union general again failed to exploit his advantage. He delayed his attack against Lee's depleted army, thereby allowing it to occupy a strong defensive position behind Antietam Creek, near Sharpsburg, Maryland. Outnumbered 87,000 to 50,000, Lee desperately fought off McClellan's attacks. Just as Union regiments were about to overwhelm his right flank, Jackson's troops arrived, saving the Confederates from a major defeat. Appalled by the number of Union casualties, McClellan let Lee retreat to Virginia.

The fighting at Antietam was savage. A Wisconsin officer described his men as "loading and firing with demoniacal fury and shouting and laughing hysterically." At a critical point in the battle, a sunken road—nicknamed Bloody Lane—was filled with Confederate bodies two and three deep, and the attacking Union troops knelt on "this ghastly flooring" to shoot at the retreating Confederates. The battle at Antietam on September 17, 1862, remains the bloodiest single day in U.S. military history. Together, the Confederate and Union dead numbered 4,800 and the wounded 18,500, of whom 3,000 soon died. (In comparison, there were 6,000 American casualties on D-Day, which began the invasion of Nazi-occupied France in World War II.)

In public, Lincoln declared Antietam a victory, but privately he declared that McClellan should have fought Lee to the finish. A masterful organizer of men and supplies, McClellan lacked the stomach for an all-out attack. Dismissing McClellan as his main commander, Lincoln began a long search for an effective replacement. His first choice was Ambrose E. Burnside, who proved to be more daring but less competent than his predecessor. In December, after heavy losses in futile attacks against well-entrenched Confederate forces at Fredericksburg, Virginia, Burnside resigned his command and Lincoln replaced him with Joseph ("Fighting Joe") Hooker. As 1862 ended, the Confederates had reason to be content: the war in the East was stalemated.

In the West, Union commanders had been more successful (Map 14.3). Their goal was to control the Ohio, Mississippi, and Missouri Rivers, and thereby divide the

Fields of Death

Fought with mass armies and new weapons, the Civil War took a huge toll in human lives. This grisly photograph depicts a thin slice of the battlefield at Antietam, Maryland, where, in September 1862, nearly 8,000 Union and Confederate soldiers lost their lives and another 15,000 suffered wounds. Library of Congress.

FOR MORE HELP ANALYZING THIS IMAGE, see the Online Study Guide at **bedfordstmartins.com/henrettaconcise**.

Confederacy and reduce the mobility of its armies. Thanks to Kentucky's refusal to join the rebellion, the Union already dominated the Ohio River Valley. In 1862, the Union army launched a series of highly innovative land and water operations to gain control of the Tennessee and Mississippi Rivers as well. In the North, General Ulysses S. Grant used riverboats clad with iron plates to take Fort Henry on the Tennessee River and Fort Donelson on the Cumberland. Grant then moved south along the Tennessee to seize critical railroad lines. On April 6, a Confederate army led by Albert Sidney Johnston and P. G. T. Beauregard caught Grant by surprise near a small log church named Shiloh. In the ensuing battle, Grant relentlessly committed troops (and took huge casualties) until he forced a Confederate withdrawal. As the fighting ended, Grant looked out over a large field "so covered with dead that it would have been possible to walk over the clearing in any direction, stepping on dead bodies, without a foot touching the ground." The cost in lives was high, but Lincoln was pleased. "What I want . . . is generals who will fight battles and win victories."

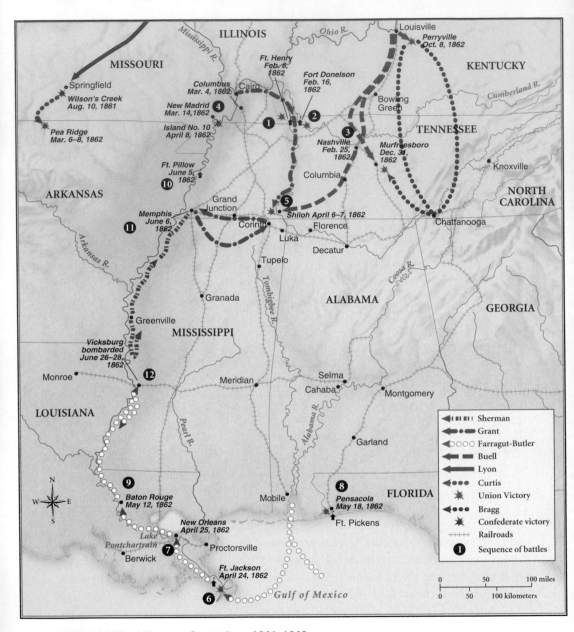

MAP 14.3 The Western Campaigns, 1861–1862

As the Civil War intensified in 1862, Union and Confederate military and naval forces fought to control the great valleys of the Ohio, Tennessee, and Mississippi Rivers. From February through April of 1862, Union armies moved south through western Tennessee (#1, 2, 3, and 5). By the end of June, Union naval forces controlled the Mississippi River north of Memphis (#4, 10, and 11) and from the Gulf of Mexico to Vicksburg (#6, 7, 9, and 12). These military and naval victories gave the Union control of crucial transportation routes, kept Missouri in the Union, and carried the war to the borders of the states of the Deep South.

Three weeks later Union naval forces commanded by David G. Farragut struck the Confederacy from the Gulf of Mexico and captured New Orleans. The Union now held the South's financial center and largest city as well as a major base for future naval operations. Union victories in the West had significantly undermined Confederate strength in the Mississippi Valley.

Toward Total War

The military carnage in 1862 made it clear that the war would be long and costly. After Shiloh, Grant later noted, he "gave up all idea of saving the Union except by complete conquest." The conflict became a **total war**—arraying the entire resources of the two societies against each other. Aided by the Republican Party and a talented cabinet, Lincoln skillfully organized an effective central government. Jefferson Davis was less successful in harnessing the resources of the South because the eleven states of the Confederacy remained deeply suspicious of centralized rule.

Mobilizing Armies and Civilians

Initially, patriotic fervor filled both armies with eager volunteers. The widowed mother of nineteen-year-old Elisha Hunt Rhodes of Pawtuxet, Rhode Island, sent her son to war, saying, "My son, other mothers must make sacrifices and why should not I?" The call for soldiers was especially successful in the South, which had a strong military tradition, an ample supply of trained officers, and a culture that stressed duty and honor. "Would you, My Darling, . . . be willing to leave your Children under such a [despotic Union] government?" James B. Griffin of Edgefield, South Carolina, asked his wife. "No—I know you would sacrifice every comfort on earth, rather than submit to it." However, enlistments fell off as potential recruits learned of the realities of mass warfare: heavy losses to epidemic diseases in the camps and wholesale death on the battlefields. Both governments soon faced the necessity of forced enlistment.

The Confederacy was the first to act. In April 1862, after the bloody battle at Shiloh, the Confederate Congress imposed the first legally binding draft in American history. One law extended existing enlistments for the duration of the war; another required three years of military service from men between the ages of eighteen and thirty-five. In September, after the heavy casualties at Antietam, the age limit was raised to forty-five. The Confederate draft had two loopholes, both controversial. First, it exempted one white man—the planter, a son, or an overseer—for each twenty slaves and so allowed some whites on large plantations to avoid military service. Second, drafted men could hire substitutes. Before this provision was repealed in 1864, the price for a substitute had risen to $300 in gold, about three times the annual wages of a skilled worker. Laborers and yeomen farmers angrily complained that it was "a rich man's war and a poor man's fight."

Consequently, some Southerners refused to serve. Because the Confederate constitution vested sovereignty in the individual states, the Confederate government lacked the power to compel military service. Strong governors such as Joseph Brown of Georgia and Zebulon Vance of North Carolina simply ignored Davis's first draft call in early 1862. Elsewhere state judges issued writs of **habeas corpus** (a legal process designed to protect people from arbitrary arrest) and ordered the Confederate army to release protesting draftees. However, the Confederate Congress overrode the judges' authority to free conscripted men and enabled the government to keep substantial armies in the field well into 1864.

The Union government acted more ruthlessly toward potential foes and reluctant citizens. To prevent sabotage and resistance to the war effort, Lincoln suspended habeas corpus and over the course of the war imprisoned about 15,000 Confederate sympathizers without trial. The president also extended martial law to civilians, which subjected them to military courts rather than local juries if they discouraged enlistments or resisted the draft. These firm policies had the desired effect. When the Militia Act of 1862 set local recruitment quotas, states and towns enticed volunteers with cash bounties and eventually signed up nearly a million men. As in the South, wealthy men could avoid military service by providing a substitute or paying a $300 commutation, or exemption, fee.

The Enrollment Act of 1863 raised quotas and was strongly opposed by recent immigrants from Germany and Ireland, who protested that it was not their war. Northern Democrats seized upon this issue. They accused Lincoln of drafting poor whites to win freedom for blacks, who would flood into the cities and take their jobs. In July 1863, the immigrants' hostility to the draft and to African Americans brought violence to the streets of New York City. For five days Irish and German workers ran rampant, burning draft offices, sacking the homes of influential Republicans, and attacking the police. The rioters lynched and mutilated a dozen African Americans, drove hundreds of black families from their homes, and burned down the Colored Orphan Asylum. Lincoln rushed in Union troops, fresh from the battle of Gettysburg, who killed over a hundred rioters and suppressed the insurrection.

The Union government's commitment to total war won greater support among native-born, middle-class citizens. In 1861, prominent New Yorkers established the United States Sanitary Commission to provide medical services and prevent the spread of epidemic diseases. Through its network of 7,000 local auxiliaries, the sanitary commission collected clothing, food, and medicine and recruited battlefield nurses and doctors for the Union Army Medical Bureau. Despite such measures, dysentery, typhoid, and malaria spread through the camps, as did childhood viruses such as mumps and measles, to which many rural men had not developed immunity. Diseases and infections killed about 250,000 Union soldiers, about twice the number who died in combat. Still, better sanitation and high-quality food kept the mortality rate among Union troops significantly below that of soldiers in nineteenth-century European wars. Confederate soldiers were less fortunate. Thousands of women volunteered as nurses,

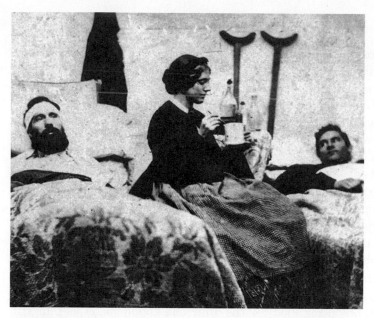

Hospital Nursing

Working as nurses in battlefront hospitals, thousands of Union and Confederate women gained firsthand experience of the horrors of war. A sense of calm prevails in this behind-the-lines Union hospital in Nashville, Tennessee, as nurse Anne Belle tends to the needs of soldiers recovering from their wounds. Most Civil War nurses served as unpaid volunteers and spent time cooking and cleaning for their patients as well as tending their injuries. U.S. Army Military History Institute.

but the Confederate health system was poorly organized. Thousands of southern soldiers contracted scurvy because of the lack of vitamin C in their diets, and they died from camp diseases at higher rates than did Union soldiers.

Women took a leading role in the sanitary commission and other wartime agencies. As superintendent of female nurses, Dorothea Dix became the first woman to receive a major federal appointment. Dix successfully combated the prejudice against women providing medical treatment to men and thereby opened a new occupation to women. Thousands of educated Union women joined the war effort as clerks in the expanding government bureaucracy, while in the South women staffed the efficient Confederate postal service. Indeed, in both sections millions of women assumed new economic responsibilities and worked with far greater intensity. They took over many farm tasks previously done by men and filled jobs not only in schools and offices but also in textile, clothing, and shoe factories. A number of women even took on military duties as spies, scouts, and (disguising themselves as men) soldiers. As the nurse Clara Barton, who later founded the American Red Cross, recalled, "At the war's end, woman was at least fifty years in advance of the normal position which continued peace would have assigned her."

Mobilizing Resources

Wars are usually won by the side with superior resources and economic organization, and in this regard the Union entered the war with a distinct advantage. With nearly two-thirds of the population of the nation, two-thirds of the railroad mileage, and almost 90 percent of the industrial output, the North's economy was far superior to the South's. The North had an especially great advantage in the manufacture of cannon and rifles because many of its arms factories were equipped for mass production.

However, the Confederate position was far from weak. Virginia, North Carolina, and Tennessee had substantial industrial capacity. Richmond, with its Tredegar Iron Works, was an important manufacturing center, and in 1861 the Confederacy transported the gun-making machinery from the U.S. armory at Harpers Ferry to Richmond. The production of the Richmond armory, the purchase of Enfield rifles from Britain, and the capture of 100,000 Union guns enabled the Confederacy to provide every infantryman with a modern rifle-musket by 1863.

Moreover, with 9 million people, the Confederacy could mobilize enormous armies. Although more than one-third of that number were slaves, their masters kept them in the fields, producing food for the army and cotton for export. In fact, Confederate leaders counted on "King Cotton" to provide the revenue to purchase clothes, boots, blankets, and weapons from abroad. They also counted on cotton as a diplomatic weapon that would persuade Britain, which depended on the South to supply its textile factories, to grant diplomatic recognition and provide military aid. However, British manufacturers had stockpiled raw cotton, and when those stocks ran out, they found new sources in Egypt and India. Nonetheless, the South's hope was partially fulfilled. Although the British government never recognized the independence of the Confederacy, it recognized the rebel government as a belligerent power with the right under international law to borrow money and purchase weapons. Thus, the odds did not necessarily favor the Union, despite its superior resources.

To mobilize the resources of the North, Lincoln and the Republicans enacted a program of government-assisted national economic development that far surpassed the American System advocated by Henry Clay and the Whig Party. First, the Republicans raised tariffs to win the political support of northeastern manufacturers and laborers, who feared competition from cheaper foreign goods. Then Secretary of the Treasury Salmon P. Chase secured national banking legislation that forced thousands of local banks to accept federal charters and regulations. This integrated banking system was far more effective in raising capital and controlling inflation than earlier efforts by the First and Second Banks of the United States had been. Finally, the Lincoln administration implemented Clay's program for a nationally financed system of internal improvements. In 1862 the Republican Congress chartered the Union Pacific and Central Pacific companies to build a transcontinental railroad line and assisted them with lavish subsidies. In addition the Republicans provided northern farmers with "free land" in the West. The Homestead Act of 1862 gave heads of families or individuals age twenty-one or older the title to 160 acres of public land after five years of residence. This economic program won the allegiance of many Northerners to the Republican Party and bolstered the Union's ability to fight the war.

The Confederate government had a much less coherent economic policy. True to its states' rights philosophy, the Confederacy initially left most economic matters in the hands of the state governments. As the realities of total war became clear, the Davis administration took some extraordinary measures: it built and operated shipyards, armories, foundries, and textile mills; commandeered food and scarce raw materials such as coal, iron, copper, and lead; requisitioned slaves to work on fortifications; and exercised direct control over foreign trade. Ordinary southern citizens increasingly resented and resisted these governmental measures. To sustain the war effort, the Confederacy increasingly counted on white solidarity: Jefferson Davis warned whites that a Union victory would destroy slavery "and reduce the whites to the degraded position of the African race."

For both sides, the cost of fighting a total war was enormous. In the Union, government spending shot up from less than 2 percent of gross national product to about 15 percent. To meet those expenses, the Republicans established a powerful modern state that raised money in three ways. First, the government increased tariffs on consumer goods and imposed direct taxes on business corporations, large inheritances, and incomes. These levies paid for about 20 percent of the cost of the war. The sale of treasury bonds financed another 65 percent. Led by Jay Cooke, a Philadelphia banker, the treasury used newspaper advertisements and 2,500 subagents to persuade nearly a million northern families to buy war bonds. In addition the National Banking Acts of 1863 and 1864 forced most banks to purchase treasury bonds.

The Union paid the remaining cost of the war by printing paper money. The Legal Tender Act of 1862 authorized the issue of $150 million in treasury notes—which soon became known as greenbacks—and required the public to accept them as legal tender. As with the "Continentals" issued during the War of Independence, these treasury notes were not backed by specie; unlike the Continentals, this paper was printed in relatively limited amounts and so did not depreciate disastrously in value. By imposing broad-based taxes, borrowing from the middle classes, and creating a national monetary system, the Union government had created the financial foundations of a modern nation-state.

The financial demands on the South were just as great, but it lacked a powerful central government that could tax and borrow. The Confederate Congress fiercely opposed taxes on cotton exports and slaves, the most valuable property of wealthy planters, and urban middle-class and yeomen farm families often refused to pay their taxes. Consequently, the Confederacy covered less than 5 percent of its expenditures through taxation. The government paid for another 35 percent by borrowing, although wealthy planters and foreign bankers were increasingly wary of investing in Confederate bonds that might never be redeemed.

Thus, the Confederacy had to finance about 60 percent of its expenses with unbacked paper money. The flood of currency created a spectacular inflation; by 1865 prices had risen to ninety-two times their 1861 level. As the vast supply of money (and shortages of goods) caused food prices to soar, riots broke out in more than a dozen southern cities and towns. In Richmond several hundred women broke into bakeries, crying, "Our children are starving while the rich roll in wealth." As inflation rose, Southerners increasingly refused to accept Confederate money, sometimes with serious consequences. When South Carolina store clerk Jim Harris rejected the Confederate notes presented by a group of soldiers, they raided his storehouse and "robbed it of about five thousand dollars worth of goods." Army supply officers did the same and offered payment in worthless IOUs. Fearing a strong government and high taxation, the Confederacy ended up violating the property rights of its citizens to sustain the war effort.

The Turning Point: 1863

By 1863 the Lincoln administration had created a complex war machine and a coherent financial system. "Little by little," the young diplomat Henry Adams noted at his post in London, "one began to feel that, behind the chaos in Washington power was taking shape; that it was massed and guided as it had not been before." Slowly but surely, the tide of the struggle shifted toward the Union.

Emancipation

From the beginning of the conflict, antislavery Republicans demanded their party make abolition—as well as restoration of the Union—a central goal. Because slave-grown crops sustained the Confederacy, they argued for abolition on military as well as moral grounds. As Frederick Douglass put it, "Arrest that hoe in the hands of the Negro, and you smite the rebellion in the very seat of its life." Initially, Lincoln downplayed these demands for black freedom: "[I]f I could save the Union without freeing any slave, I would do it," he told Horace Greeley of the New York *Tribune*. However, as war casualties mounted, Lincoln and some Republican leaders began to redefine the conflict as a struggle against slavery—the cornerstone of southern society.

Nonetheless, it was enslaved African Americans who forced the issue by seizing freedom for themselves. Exploiting the disorder of wartime, tens of thousands of slaves left their plantations and sought refuge behind Union lines. When three slaves reached the camp of General Benjamin Butler in Virginia in May 1861, he labeled them "contraband of war" and refused to return them. His term stuck, and within a few months a thousand "contrabands" were camping with Butler's army. To define their status and undermine the Confederate war effort, in August 1861 Congress passed a Confiscation Act, which authorized the seizure of all property—including slaves—used to support the rebellion.

Radical Republicans—Treasury Secretary Salmon Chase, Senator Charles Sumner of Massachusetts, and Representative Thaddeus Stevens of Pennsylvania—now saw a way to use wartime legislation to end slavery. A longtime congressman and an uncompromising foe of slavery, Stevens was a masterful politician who was adept at fashioning legislation that could win majority support. In April 1862 Stevens and his Radical allies persuaded Congress to end slavery in the District of Columbia by providing compensation for owners. In June, Congress outlawed slavery in the federal territories (finally enacting the Wilmot Proviso of 1846) and in July passed a second Confiscation Act. This far-reaching legislation overrode the property rights of Confederate slave owners, declaring "forever free" all fugitive slaves and all slaves captured by the Union army. Emancipation had become an instrument of war.

Lincoln built upon the Radicals' initiative. In July 1862 he prepared a general proclamation of emancipation and, viewing the battle of Antietam as "an indication of the Divine Will," issued it on September 22, 1862. Invoking the president's responsibility as commander in chief to suppress the rebellion, the proclamation abolished slavery in all states that still remained out of the Union on January 1, 1863. The rebel states had a hundred days in which to preserve slavery by renouncing secession. None chose to do so.

The proclamation was politically astute. Because Lincoln wanted to avoid hostility from slave owners in the Union-controlled border states, such as Maryland and Missouri, and because he had only limited power as commander in chief over areas not in the rebellion, the proclamation left slavery intact in those states. It also left slavery untouched in the areas occupied by Union armies—western and central Tennessee, western Virginia, and southern Louisiana, including New Orleans. Consequently, the Emancipation Proclamation did not actually free a single slave. Yet, as the abolitionist Wendell Phillips perceived, Lincoln's proclamation had moved the institution of slavery to "the edge of Niagara," where it would soon be swept over the brink. Indeed, advancing Union troops became agents of liberation. "I became free in 1863, in the summer, when the yankees come by and said I could go work for myself," Jackson Daniel of Maysville, Alabama, recalled. "I was farming after that [and also] . . . making shoes." The conflict was no longer simply a struggle to preserve the Union but, as Lincoln put it, a war of "subjugation" in which "the old South is to be destroyed and replaced by new propositions and ideas."

As a war aim, emancipation was controversial. In the Confederacy, Jefferson Davis labeled it the "most execrable measure recorded in the history of guilty man," while in the North it produced a backlash among white voters. During the congressional election of 1862, the Democrats denounced emancipation as unconstitutional, warned of slave uprisings, and claimed that a "black flood" would wash away the jobs of northern workers. Democrat Horatio Seymour won the governorship of New York by declaring that if abolition was a goal of the war, the South should not be conquered. Other Democrats swept to victory in Pennsylvania, Ohio, and Illinois, and the party gained thirty-four seats in Congress. However, the Republicans still held a twenty-five-seat majority in the House and had gained five seats in the Senate. Lincoln refused to retreat. On New Year's Day 1863 he signed the Emancipation Proclamation. To reassure Northerners, Lincoln urged slaves to "abstain from all violence" and justified emancipation as an "act of justice." "If my name ever goes into history," he said, "it was for this act."

Vicksburg and Gettysburg

The fate of the proclamation would depend on the success of Union armies and the Republican Party. The outlook was not encouraging. Not only had Democrats registered gains in the election of 1862 but there was also increased popular support for a negotiated peace. Two brilliant victories by Lee, whose army defeated Hooker's forces at Fredericksburg (December 1862) and Chancellorsville, Virginia (May 1863), caused further erosion of northern support for the war.

At this critical juncture General Grant mounted a major offensive in the West designed to split the Confederacy in two. Grant drove south along the west bank of the Mississippi and then moved his troops across the river near Vicksburg, Mississippi, where he defeated two Confederate armies and laid siege to the city. After repelling Union assaults for six weeks, the exhausted and starving Vicksburg garrison surrendered on July 4, 1863. Five days later Union forces took Port Hudson, Louisiana, and established Union control of the Mississippi River. Grant had taken 31,000 prisoners, cut off Louisiana, Arkansas, and Texas from the rest of the Confederacy, and prompted hundreds of slaves to desert their plantations.

Grant's initial advance down the Mississippi prompted an argument over strategy among Confederate leaders. Jefferson Davis and other politicians wanted to send reinforcements to Vicksburg and dispatch troops to Tennessee to draw Grant out of Mississippi. But General Robert E. Lee, buoyed by his recent victories over Hooker, favored a new invasion of the North, which might draw Union armies to the east, thereby relieving the pressure on Vicksburg, or give the Confederacy a major victory that would undermine northern support for the war.

Lee won out. In June 1863 he maneuvered his army north through Maryland into Pennsylvania. The Union's Army of the Potomac moved along with him, positioning itself between Lee and the federal capital of Washington. Early in July the two great armies met by accident at Gettysburg, Pennsylvania, in what became a decisive confrontation (Map 14.4). On the first day of battle, July 1, Lee drove the Union's advance guard to the south of town. General George G. Meade, who had just taken over command of the Union forces from Hooker, placed his troops in well-defended hilltop positions and called up reinforcements. By the morning of the second day Meade had 90,000 troops to Lee's 75,000. Aware that he was outnumbered but bent on victory, Lee ordered assaults on both of Meade's flanks but failed to turn them. General Richard B. Ewell, assigned to attack the Union right, was unwilling to risk his men in an all-out assault, and General Longstreet, on the Union left, could not dislodge Meade's forces from a hill known as Little Round Top.

On July 3, Lee decided on a frontal assault against the center of the Union lines. He recognized the danger of this tactic but he had enormous confidence in his troops and thought they could inflict a crushing defeat on the North. After the heaviest

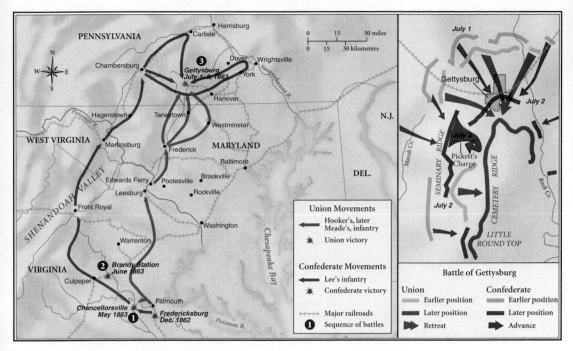

MAP 14.4 Lee Invades the North, 1863

After Lee's victory at Chancellorsville and Brandy Station in May and June of 1863 (#1 and 2), the Confederate forces moved northward, constantly shadowed by the Union army. In early July the two armies met accidentally near Gettysburg, Pennsylvania. In the ensuing battle (#3), the Union army, commanded by General George Meade, emerged victorious, primarily because it was much larger than the Confederate force and held well-fortified positions along Cemetery Ridge, which gave its units a major tactical advantage.

artillery barrage of the war, Lee ordered 14,000 men under General George E. Pickett to take Cemetery Ridge. Anticipating this attack, Meade had reinforced the center of his line with artillery and his best troops. When Pickett's men charged across a mile of open terrain, they were met by massive fire from artillery and rifle-muskets; thousands were killed, wounded, or captured. As the three-day battle ended, Lee had suffered 28,000 casualties, one-third of the Army of Northern Virginia, while 23,000 of Meade's soldiers lay killed or wounded. Shocked by the bloodletting, Meade allowed the remaining Confederate soldiers to escape. "As it is," Lincoln brooded, "the war will be prolonged indefinitely."

Nonetheless, Gettysburg was a great Union victory and, in combination with the triumph at Vicksburg, represented a major turning point in the conflict. Never again would a southern army invade the North. In the fall of 1863, Republicans reaped the political gains by sweeping state and local elections in Pennsylvania, Ohio, and New York. In the South the military setbacks accentuated war weariness. The Confederate elections of 1863 went sharply against the politicians who supported Jefferson Davis.

A few members of the new Confederate Congress and many ordinary citizens criticized the ineffectiveness of the war effort.

Vicksburg and Gettysburg also transformed the balance of diplomatic power and ended the Confederacy's chances of winning foreign recognition and acquiring advanced weapons. In 1862 British shipbuilders had supplied the Confederacy with an ironclad cruiser, the *Alabama*, which had sunk or captured more than a hundred Union merchant ships, and the delivery of two more ironclad cruisers was imminent. News of the Union victories changed everything, and Charles Francis Adams, the American minister, persuaded the British government to impound the ships. Britain did not want to risk Canada or its merchant marine by provoking the military might of the United States. Such concerns, along with Britain's increasing reliance on cheap wheat from the North and the strong opposition to slavery by British workers and reformers, deterred the government from supporting the Confederacy.

The Union Victorious, 1864–1865

While the Union victories of 1863 meant that the South could not achieve a decisive military triumph, the Confederacy could still realistically hope for a stalemate on the battlefield and a negotiated peace. Lincoln faced the daunting alternative of winning an overwhelming victory or losing the support of the northern voters.

Soldiers and Strategy

Two developments allowed the Union to prosecute the war with continued vigor and eventually to prevail: the enlistment of African American soldiers and the emergence of capable and determined generals.

As early as 1861, free African Americans and fugitive slaves had tried to enlist in the Union army, and the black abolitionist Frederick Douglass had embraced their cause: "Once let the black man get upon his person the brass letters, 'U.S.' . . . a musket on his shoulder and bullets in his pockets, and there is no power on earth which can deny that he has earned the right to citizenship in the United States." The prospect of citizenship for blacks frightened many northern whites, and most Union generals doubted that former slaves would make good soldiers. Consequently, the Lincoln administration initially refused to consider blacks for military service. Nonetheless, by 1862 free and contraband blacks had formed regiments in South Carolina, Louisiana, and Kansas and were eager to join the fighting.

The Emancipation Proclamation changed popular thinking and military policy. If blacks were to benefit from a Union victory, some northern whites argued, they should share in the fighting and dying. The valor exhibited by the first African American regiments also influenced northern opinion. In January 1863 Thomas Wentworth Higginson, the white abolitionist commander of the black First South Carolina Volunteers, wrote a glowing newspaper account of its military prowess: "No officer in this regiment now doubts that the key to the successful prosecution of the

Black Soldiers in the Union Army

Determined to end racial slavery, tens of thousands of African Americans volunteered for service in the Union army in 1864 and 1865, boosting the northern war effort at a critical time. These proud soldiers were members of the 107th Colored Infantry, stationed at Fort Corcoran near Washington, D.C. In January 1865 their regiment participated in the daring capture of Fort Fisher, which protected Wilmington, North Carolina, the last Confederate port open to blockade-runners. Library of Congress.

war lies in the unlimited employment of black troops." In July the heroic, but costly, attack on Fort Wagner, South Carolina, by another black regiment, the Fifty-fourth Massachusetts Infantry, convinced many Union officers of the value of black soldiers. The War Department authorized their enlistment, and as white resistance to conscription increased, the Lincoln administration recruited as many African Americans as it could. Without black soldiers, the president suggested in the autumn of 1864, "we would be compelled to abandon the war in three weeks." By the spring of 1865, there were nearly 200,000 African American soldiers and sailors.

Military service did not end racial discrimination. Black soldiers served under white officers in segregated regiments and were used primarily to build fortifications, garrison forts, and guard supply lines. At first they were paid less than white soldiers ($10 versus $13 per month) and won equal pay only by threatening to lay down their arms. Despite such treatment African Americans volunteered for military service in disproportionate numbers and diligently served the Union cause. They knew they were fighting for freedom and the possibility of a new social order. "Hello, Massa," said one black soldier to his former master, who had been taken prisoner. "Bottom rail on top dis time." The worst fears of the secessionists had come true: through the agency of the Union army, blacks had risen in a great rebellion against slavery.

As African Americans joined the army's ranks, Lincoln finally found a capable commanding general. In March 1864 Lincoln placed General Ulysses S. Grant in charge of all the Union armies and created a unified structure of command. From then on, the president would determine general strategy and Grant would decide how best to implement it. Lincoln directed Grant to advance simultaneously against all the major Confederate forces, a strategy Grant had long favored. Both the general and the president wanted a decisive victory before the election of 1864.

As the successful western campaigns of mid-1863 showed, Grant understood how to fight a modern war—a war relying on industrial technology and directed at an entire society. At Vicksburg he had besieged an entire city and forced its surrender. Then, in November 1863, he had used railroad transport to charge to the rescue of a Union army near Chattanooga, Tennessee, and drive back an invading Confederate army. Moreover, Grant was willing to accept heavy casualties in assaults on strongly defended positions. The attempts of earlier Union commanders "to conserve life" through cautious tactics had prolonged the war, Grant argued. Such aggressive methods earned Grant a reputation as a butcher both of his own men and of enemy armies, which he pursued relentlessly.

In May 1864 Grant ordered major new offensives on two fronts. Personally taking charge of the 115,000-strong Army of the Potomac, he set out to destroy Lee's force of 75,000 troops in Virginia. Simultaneously he instructed General William Tecumseh Sherman, who shared his views on warfare, to invade Georgia and take Atlanta. As Sherman prepared for battle, he wrote that "all that has gone before is mere skirmish. The war now begins."

Grant advanced toward Richmond, hoping to force Lee to fight in open fields, where the Union's superior manpower and artillery could prevail. Remembering his tactical errors at Gettysburg, Lee remained in strong defensive positions and attacked only when he held an advantage. The Confederate general seized such opportunities twice and won narrow victories in early May at the battles of the Wilderness and Spotsylvania Court House. Despite heavy losses at Cold Harbor, Grant drove on. His attacks severely eroded Lee's forces, which suffered 31,000 casualties, but Union losses were even higher at 55,000 men (Map 14.5).

The fighting took a heavy psychological toll. "Many a man has gone crazy since this campaign began from the terrible pressure on mind and body," observed a Union captain. As the morale and health of the soldiers declined, many deserted. In June Grant laid siege to Petersburg, an important railroad center near Richmond. Protracted trench warfare, which foreshadowed that of World War I, made the spade as important as the sword. Union and Confederate soldiers built complex networks of trenches, tunnels, and artillery emplacements for almost fifty miles around Richmond and Petersburg. Invoking the intense imagery of the Bible, an officer described the continuous artillery firing and sniping as "living night and day within the 'valley of the shadow of death.'" The stress was especially great for the outnumbered Confederate troops, who spent months in the muddy, sickening trenches without rotation to the rear.

As time passed, Lincoln and Grant felt pressures of their own. The enormous casualties and continued military stalemate threatened Lincoln with defeat in the November election. The outlook for the Republicans worsened in July 1864, when

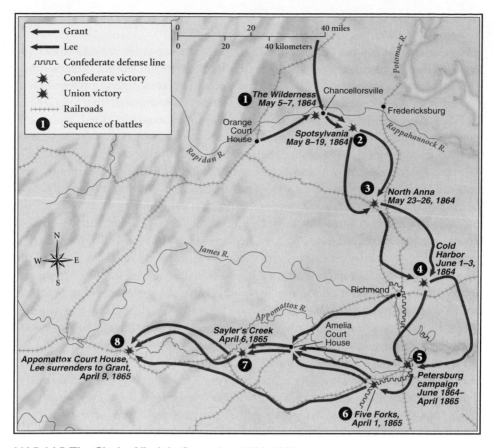

MAP 14.5 The Closing Virginia Campaign, 1864–1865

Beginning in May 1864, General Ulysses Grant launched an all-out campaign against Richmond. By threatening General Robert E. Lee's lines of supply from Richmond, Grant attempted to lure him into open battle. Lee avoided a major test of strength. Instead, he retreated to defensive positions and inflicted heavy casualties on the Union attackers at the Wilderness, Spotsylvania, North Anna, and Cold Harbor (#1–4). From June 1864 to April 1865, the two armies faced each other across defensive fortifications outside Petersburg (#5), a protracted siege broken finally by Grant's flanking maneuver at Five Forks (#6). Lee's surrender followed shortly.

a raid near Washington by Jubal Early's cavalry forced Grant to divert his best troops from the Petersburg campaign. To punish farmers in the Shenandoah Valley, who had provided a base for Early and food for Lee's army, Grant ordered General Philip H. Sheridan to turn the region into "a barren waste." Sheridan's troops conducted a scorched-earth campaign and destroyed grain supplies, barns, farming implements, and gristmills. Such terrorism went beyond the military norms of the day; most officers regarded civilians as noncombatants and feared that punishing them would erode military discipline. However, Grant's practice of carrying the war to Confederate civilians was changing the definition of conventional warfare.

The Election of 1864 and Sherman's March to the Sea

As the siege at Petersburg dragged on, the president's hopes for reelection increasingly depended on General William Tecumseh Sherman in Georgia. Sherman had gradually penetrated to within about thirty miles of Atlanta, a great railway hub at the heart of the Confederacy. Although his army outnumbered that of General Joseph E. Johnston by 90,000 to 60,000 men, Sherman avoided a direct attack and slowly pried the Confederates out of one defensive position after another. Finally, on June 27 at Kennesaw Mountain, Sherman engaged Johnston in a set battle, only to suffer 3,000 casualties while inflicting about 600. By late July the Union general had laid siege to Atlanta on the north, but the next month brought little gain. Like Grant, Sherman seemed bogged down in a hopeless campaign.

Meanwhile, the presidential campaign of 1864 was well under way. In June a Republican convention attended by both Republicans and Unionist Democrats resisted the attempt of dissidents to prevent Lincoln's renomination. They endorsed the president's war strategy, demanded the unconditional surrender of the Confederacy, and called for a constitutional amendment to abolish slavery. Attempting to attract border-state voters to their party, Lincoln and the Republican leadership gave it a new name, the National Union Party, and chose as Lincoln's vice presidential running mate Andrew Johnson, a slave owner and a Unionist Democrat from Tennessee.

The Democratic convention met in late August and nominated General George B. McClellan, whom Lincoln had twice removed from military commands— first for an excess of caution and then for his opposition to emancipation. Like McClellan, the Democratic delegates rejected freedom for blacks and condemned Lincoln's uncompromising repression of domestic dissent. However, they split into two camps over the issue of continuing the war. By threatening to leave the convention, the "Peace Democrats" forced through a platform calling for "a cessation of hostilities" and a constitutional convention to restore peace. Although personally a "War Democrat," McClellan promised if elected to recommend an immediate armistice and a peace convention. Rejoicing in "the first ray of real light I have seen since the war began," Confederate vice president Alexander Stephens declared that if Atlanta and Richmond held out, then Lincoln could be defeated and northern Democrats persuaded to accept an independent Confederacy.

However, on September 2, 1864, Atlanta fell to Sherman's army. In a stunning move, the Union general pulled his troops from the trenches and swept around the city and destroyed its rail links to the rest of the Confederacy. Fearing that Sherman would be able to trap his army, Hood abandoned the city. "Atlanta is ours, and fairly won," Sherman telegraphed Lincoln, sparking 100-gun salutes and wild Republican celebrations in northern cities. A deep pessimism settled over the Confederacy. In her diary Mary Chesnut, a slave-owning plantation mistress, confessed that she "felt as if all were dead within me, forever" and foresaw the end of the Confederacy: "We are going to be wiped off the earth." Acknowledging the dramatically changed military situation, McClellan repudiated the Democratic peace platform, and dissident

Republicans abandoned efforts to dump Lincoln. Instead, the Republican Party went on the offensive. Its newspapers charged that McClellan was still a peace candidate and that Peace Democrats were "copperheads" (poisonous snakes) who were hatching treasonous plots.

Sherman's success in Georgia gave Lincoln a clear-cut victory in November. The president received 55 percent of the popular vote and won 212 of 233 electoral votes. Republicans captured 145 of the 185 seats in the House of Representatives and increased their Senate majority to 42 of 52 seats. Many of those victories came from the votes of Union troops, most of whom wanted the war to continue until the Confederacy met every Union demand, including emancipation.

Legal emancipation was already under way at the edges of the South. In 1864 Maryland and Missouri amended their constitutions to free their slaves, and the three occupied states of Tennessee, Arkansas, and Louisiana followed suit. Abolitionists still worried that the Emancipation Proclamation, which was based on the president's wartime powers, would lose its force at the end of the war and that some states would reestablish slavery. Urged on by Lincoln, the Republican-dominated Congress took a major step to guarantee black freedom. On January 31, 1865, it approved the Thirteenth Amendment, which prohibited slavery throughout the United States, and sent it to the states for ratification. Slavery was nearly dead.

Thanks to William Tecumseh Sherman, the Confederacy was nearly dead as well. After the capture of Atlanta, Sherman decided on a bold strategy. Rather than follow the retreating Confederate army northward into Tennessee, he proposed to move south and "cut a swath through to the sea." To persuade Lincoln and Grant to approve his unconventional plan to cut his supply links and live off the land, Sherman pointed out that his march would devastate Georgia and score a major psychological victory. It would be "a demonstration to the world, foreign and domestic, that we have a power [Jefferson] Davis cannot resist" (Map 14.6).

Sherman carried out the concept of "hard war" that he and Sheridan had pioneered: destruction of the enemy's economic resources and will to resist. "We are not only fighting hostile armies," Sherman wrote, "but a hostile people, and must make old and young, rich and poor, feel the hard hand of war." He left Atlanta in flames and, during his three-hundred-mile march to the sea, consumed or demolished everything in his path. A Union veteran wrote that "[we] destroyed all we could not eat, stole their niggers, burned their cotton & gins, spilled their sorghum, burned & twisted their R.Roads and raised Hell generally." The havoc so demoralized Confederate soldiers that many deserted their units and fled home to protect their farms and families (see American Voices, "Sherman's March through Georgia," p. 439). When Sherman reached Savannah, Georgia, in mid-December, the 10,000 Confederate defenders left without a fight.

In February 1865 Sherman invaded South Carolina, both to link up with Grant at Petersburg and punish the state where secession had begun. His troops cut a comparatively narrow swath across the state but completely ravaged the countryside. After capturing South Carolina's capital, Columbia, they burned the business district, most churches, and the wealthiest residential neighborhoods. "This disappointment to me

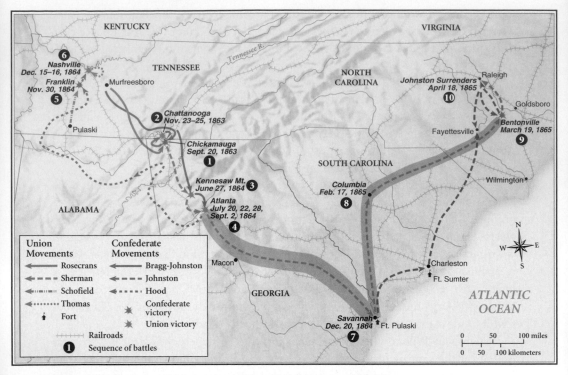

MAP 14.6 Sherman's March through the Confederacy, 1864–1865

The Union victory (#2) in November 1863 at Chattanooga, Tennessee, was almost as critical as the victories in July at Gettysburg and Vicksburg because it opened up a route of attack into the heart of the Confederacy. In mid-1864 General William Tecumseh Sherman advanced on the railway hub of Atlanta (#3 and 4). After finally taking the city in September 1864, Sherman relied on other Union armies to repulse General John B. Hood's invasion of Tennessee (#5 and 6). Sherman swept on to Savannah in a devastating "March to the Sea" (#7) and then in 1865 cut a swath through the Carolinas (#8, 9, and 10).

FOR MORE HELP ANALYZING THIS MAP, see the Online Study Guide at **bedfordstmartins.com/henrettaconcise**.

is extremely bitter," lamented Jefferson Davis. By March Sherman had reached North Carolina and was on the verge of linking up with Grant and crushing Lee's army.

Grant's war of attrition had already exposed an internal Confederate weakness: rising class resentment on the part of poor whites. Long angered by the "twenty-negro" exemption from military service given to slave owners and fearing that the Confederacy was doomed, ordinary southern farmers resisted military service. "It is no longer a reproach to be known as a deserter," a Confederate officer in South Carolina complained as early as 1863. "I am now going to work instead of to the war," declared David Harris, a backcountry farmer. "I think I will like it the best." By early 1865 the Confederacy had so few new recruits that its leaders decided to take an extreme measure: arming the slaves. Urged on by Lee, the Confederate Congress voted to enlist black soldiers and Davis issued an executive order granting freedom

AMERICAN VOICES

~

Sherman's March through Georgia

DOLLY SUMNER LUNT

"We must make old and young, rich and poor, feel the hard hand of war," General William Tecumseh Sherman wrote to General Grant late in 1864, as he signaled his intention to carry the war to the civilian population of the South. A few weeks later Dolly Sumner Lunt of Covington, Georgia, found out what Sherman meant. Born in Maine in 1817, Dolly Sumner came south to teach school, married a slave owner, and following his death, ran the family's plantation. Her wartime journal describes its destruction by Sherman's army.

November 19, 1864

Slept in my clothes last night, as I heard that the Yankees went to neighbor Montgomery's on Thursday night at one o'clock, searched his house, drank his wine, and took his money and valuables. As we were not disturbed, I walked after breakfast . . . up to Mr. Joe Perry's, my nearest neighbor, where the Yankees were yesterday. Saw Mrs. Laura [Perry] in the road surrounded by her children . . . looking for her husband. . . . Before we were done talking, up came Joe and Jim Perry from their hiding-place. Jim was very much excited. Happening to turn and look behind, as we stood there, I saw some blue-coats coming down the hill. Jim immediately raised his gun, swearing he should kill them anyhow.

"No, don't" said I, and ran home as fast as I could.

I could hear them cry "Halt! Halt!" and their guns went off in quick succession. Oh God, the time of trial has come. . . .

I hastened back to my frightened servants [slaves] and told them they had better hide, and then went back to the gate to claim protection and a guard. But like demons they [Sherman's troops] rushed in! . . . The thousand pounds of meat in my smokehouse is gone in a twinkling, my flour, my meat, my lard, butter, eggs . . . all gone. My eighteen fat turkeys, hens, chickens . . . are shot down in my yard and hunted as if they were rebels themselves. Utterly powerless I ran out and appealed to the guard.

"I cannot help you, Madam; it is orders." . . .

Sherman himself and a greater portion of his army passed my house that day . . . ; they tore down my garden palings, made a road through my back-yard and lot field . . . desolating my home—wantonly doing it when there was no necessity for it.

Such a day, if I live to the age of Methuselah, may God spare me from ever seeing again!

As night drew its sable curtains around us, the heavens from every point were lit up with flames from burning buildings.

SOURCE: *Eyewitnesses and Others: Readings in American History* (New York: Holt, Rinehart and Winston, 1995), 1: 413–17.

to all blacks who served in the Confederate army. But the war ended too soon to reveal whether any slaves would have fought for the Confederacy.

The symbolic end of the war took place in Virginia. In April 1865 Grant finally gained control of the crucial railroad junction at Petersburg and cut off Lee's supplies. Lee abandoned Richmond and moved west to join Confederate forces in North Carolina. While Lincoln visited the ruins of the Confederate capital, mobbed by joyful ex-slaves, Grant cut off Lee's escape route. On April 9, almost precisely four years after the attack on Fort Sumter, Lee surrendered to Grant at Appomattox Court House, Virginia. By late May, all the Confederate generals had ceased to fight, and the Confederate army and government simply dissolved.

The armies of the Union had destroyed the Confederacy and much of its economy. The South's factories, warehouses, and railroads were in ruins, as were many of its farms and some of its most important cities. Almost 260,000 Confederate soldiers had paid for secession with their lives. The military struggle had preserved the Union and destroyed slavery. But the cost of victory was enormous in money, resources, and lives, with 360,000 Union soldiers dead and hundreds of thousands maimed. The hard and bitter war was over, and a reunited nation turned to the tasks of peace. These were to be equally hard and bitter.

TIMELINE

1861	Confederate States of America formed (February 4)	**1863**	Lincoln signs Emancipation Proclamation (January 1)
	Abraham Lincoln inaugurated (March 4)		Union victories at battles of Gettysburg (July 1–3) and Vicksburg (July 4)
	Confederates fire on Fort Sumter (April 12)		
	Virginia leads Upper South out of Union (April 17)		Enrollment Act begins draft in North; riots in New York City (July)
	General Benjamin Butler declares runaway slaves "contraband of war" (May)	**1864**	Ulysses S. Grant given command of all Union armies (March)
	Confederates rout Union forces at first Battle of Bull Run (July 21)		Grant advances on Richmond (May)
			William T. Sherman takes Atlanta (September 2)
1862	Congress begins to print greenbacks		Lincoln reelected (November)
	Homestead Act provides free land to settlers		Sherman marches through Georgia (November and December)
	Congress gives federal subsidies to transcontinental railroads	**1865**	Congress approves Thirteenth Amendment, which outlaws slavery (January)
	Battle of Shiloh advances Union cause in West (April 6–7)		
	Confederacy introduces first draft		Robert E. Lee surrenders at Appomattox Court House, Virginia (April 9)
	Union halts Confederate offensive at Antietam, Maryland (September 17)		
	Lincoln issues preliminary Emancipation Proclamation (September 22)		Ratification of Thirteenth Amendment

For Further Exploration

Charles P. Roland, *An American Iliad: The Story of the Civil War* (1991), is an excellent brief survey, while James M. McPherson, *The Battle Cry of Freedom* (1988), offers a fine synthesis. For a lucid description of the complex mixture of goals, personalities, and circumstances that precipitated the conflict, read Richard Current, *Lincoln and the First Shot* (1963). John Hope Franklin, *The Emancipation Proclamation* (1963), explains the background of Lincoln's edict and its impact.

Nancy Scott Anderson and Dwight Anderson, *The Generals: Ulysses S. Grant and Robert E. Lee* (1988), is a vivid, popular account of their personal histories and military exploits. For scholarly analyses of military matters, consult Mark Grimsley, *The Hard Hand of War: Union Military Policy toward Southern Civilians, 1861–1865* (1995), and Gary W. Gallagher, *The Confederate War: How Popular Will, Nationalism, and Military Strategy Could Not Stave Off Defeat* (1997).

James M. McPherson, *For Cause and Comrades: Why Men Fought in the Civil War* (1997), uses the letters of ordinary soldiers to explain their extraordinary commitment to the cause of the Union and the Confederacy. For experiences of black soldiers told in their own words, see Ira Berlin et al., eds., *Freedom's Soldiers: The Black Military Experience in the Civil War* (1998). Earl J. Hess, *The Union Soldier in Battle: Enduring the Ordeal of Combat* (1997), presents a vivid account of the heat, smell, sounds, and feel of battle, as does Michael Shaara's *Killer Angels* (1974), a masterful novel of the battle of Gettysburg. *Mary Chesnut's Civil War* (1981), edited by C. Vann Woodward, is the diary of a planter's wife that provides an incisive view of southern society.

Civil War photographs from the New-York Historical Society and the Matthew Brady Collection are available at the American Memory project: <http://memory.loc.gov/ammem/ndlpcoop/nhihtml/cwnyhshome.html> and <http://memory.loc.gov/ammem/cwphtml/cwphome.html>. Two award-winning Web sites are "The Valley of the Shadow" at <http://jefferson.village.virginia.edu/vshadow2/>, which traces the history of a northern and a southern community using a multitude of hyperlinked sources—including newspaper, letters, diaries, photographs, and maps—and The Freedmen and Southern Society Project at <http://www.history.umd.edu/Freedmen/home.html>, which captures the drama of war and emancipation in the words of liberated slaves and defeated masters, common folk and political leaders.

For definitions of key terms boldfaced in this chapter, see the glossary at the end of the book.

To assess your mastery of the material covered in this chapter, see the Online Study Guide at **bedfordstmartins.com/henrettaconcise**.

For map resources and primary documents, see **bedfordstmartins.com/henrettaconcise**.

Chapter 15

RECONSTRUCTION
1865–1877

> I felt like a bird out of a cage. Amen. Amen. Amen. I could hardly ask to feel better than I did on that day.
>
> HOUSTON H. HOLLOWAY, A FORMER SLAVE RECALLING
>
> HIS EMANCIPATION IN 1865

In his second inaugural address, President Lincoln spoke of the need to "bind up the nation's wounds." No one knew better than Lincoln how daunting a task that would be. Slavery was finished. That much was certain. But what system of labor should replace plantation slavery? What rights should the freedmen be accorded beyond emancipation? How far should the federal government go to settle these questions? And, most immediately pressing, on what terms should the rebellious states be restored to the Union?

The last speech Lincoln delivered, on April 11, 1865, demonstrated his grasp of these issues. Reconstruction, he said, had to be regarded as a practical, not a theoretical, problem. It could be solved only if Republicans remained united, even if that meant compromising on principled differences dividing them, and only if the defeated South gave its consent, even if that meant forgiveness of the South's transgressions. The speech showed, above all, Lincoln's sense of the fluidity of events, of policy toward the South as an evolving, not a fixed, position.

What course Reconstruction might have taken had Lincoln lived is one of the unanswerable questions of American history. On April 14, 1865—five days after Lee's surrender at Appomattox—Lincoln was shot in the head at Ford's Theatre in Washington by a fanatic actor named John Wilkes Booth. Ironically, Lincoln might have been spared if the war had dragged on longer, for Booth and his Confederate associates had originally plotted to kidnap the president to force a negotiated settlement. After Lee's surrender, Booth became bent on revenge. Without regaining consciousness, Lincoln died on April 15, 1865.

With one stroke John Wilkes Booth had sent Lincoln to martyrdom, hardened many Northerners against the South, and handed the presidency to a man utterly lacking in Lincoln's moral sense and political judgment, Vice President Andrew Johnson.

Presidential Reconstruction

The problem of Reconstruction—how to restore rebellious states to the Union—was not addressed by the Founding Fathers. The Constitution does not say which branch of government handles the readmission of rebellious states or, for that matter, even contemplates the possibility of secession. It was an open question whether, upon seceding, the Confederate states had legally left the Union. If so, their reentry surely required legislative action by Congress. If not, if even in defeat they retained their constitutional status, then the terms for restoring them to the Union might be defined as an administrative matter best left to the president. The ensuing battle between the White House and Capitol Hill was one of the fault lines in Reconstruction's stormy history.

Lincoln's Approach

Lincoln, as wartime president, had taken the initiative, offering in December 1863 a general amnesty to all but high-ranking Confederates willing to pledge loyalty to the Union. When 10 percent of a state's 1860 voters had taken this oath, the state would be restored to the Union, provided that it abolished slavery. The Confederate states (save those like Louisiana and Tennessee that were under Union control) rebuffed Lincoln's generous offer, ensuring that the war would have to be fought to the bitter end.

What the Ten Percent Plan also revealed was the rocky road that lay ahead for Reconstruction. In Louisiana, for example, the Unionist government restored under Lincoln's offer employed curfew laws to restrict the movements of the freed slaves and vagrancy regulations to force them back to work. But the Louisiana freedmen fought back. Led by the free blacks of New Orleans, they began to agitate for political rights. No less than their former masters, ex-slaves intended to be actors in the savage drama of Reconstruction.

With the struggle in Louisiana in mind, congressional Republicans proposed a stricter substitute for Lincoln's Ten Percent Plan. The initiative came from the Radical wing of the party—those bent on a stern peace and full rights for the freedmen—but with broad support among more moderate Republicans. The Wade-Davis Bill, passed on July 2, 1864, laid down, as conditions for the restoration of the rebellious states to the Union, an oath of allegiance by a majority of each state's adult white men, new state governments formed only by those who had never carried arms against the Union, and permanent disfranchisement of Confederate leaders. The Wade-Davis Bill served notice that the congressional Republicans were not about to hand over Reconstruction policy to the president.

Rather than openly challenging Congress, Lincoln executed a **pocket veto** of the Wade-Davis Bill by not signing it before Congress adjourned. At the same time he initiated informal talks with congressional leaders aimed at finding common ground. Lincoln's successor, however, had no such inclinations. Andrew Johnson held the view that Reconstruction was the president's prerogative, and by an accident of timing he was free to act on his convictions. Under leisurely rules that went back to the early republic, the 39th Congress elected back in November 1864 was not scheduled to convene until December 1865.

Johnson Seizes the Initiative

Andrew Johnson was a self-made man from the hills of eastern Tennessee. A Jacksonian Democrat, he saw himself as the champion of the common man. He hated what he called the "bloated, corrupt aristocracy" of the Northeast and was equally disdainful of the southern planters, whom he blamed for the poverty of the South's small farmers. It was the poor whites that he championed, however. Johnson, a slave owner himself, had little sympathy for the enslaved blacks. Johnson's political career had taken him to the U.S. Senate, where he remained when the war broke out, loyal to the Union. After federal forces captured Nashville, Johnson became Tennessee's military governor. The Republicans nominated him for vice president in 1864 in an effort to promote wartime unity and to court the support of southern Unionists.

In May 1865, just a month after Lincoln's death, Johnson launched his own Reconstruction plan. He offered amnesty to all Southerners who took an oath of allegiance to the Constitution, except for high-ranking Confederate officials and wealthy planters. This elite, whom Johnson blamed for secession, could be pardoned only by him. Johnson appointed provisional governors for the southern states and,

Andrew Johnson

The president was not an easy man. This photograph of Andrew Johnson (1808–1875) conveys some of the prickly qualities that contributed so centrally to his failure to reach an agreement with Republicans on a moderate Reconstruction program.

Library of Congress.

as conditions for their restoration, required only that they revoke their ordinances of secession, repudiate their Confederate debts, and ratify the Thirteenth Amendment, which abolished slavery. Within months all the former Confederate states had met Johnson's terms and enjoyed functioning, elected governments.

At first Republicans responded favorably. The moderates among them were sympathetic to Johnson's argument that it was up to the states, not the federal government, to define the civil and political rights of the freedmen. Even the Radicals held their fire. They liked the stern treatment of Confederate leaders, and they hoped that the new southern governments would show good faith by generous treatment of the freed slaves.

Nothing of the sort happened. The South lay in ruins. But Southerners held fast to the old order. The newly seated legislatures moved to restore slavery in all but name. They enacted laws—known as **Black Codes**—designed to drive the former slaves back to the plantations. The new governments had mostly been formed by southern Unionists, but when it came to racial attitudes, little distinguished these loyalists from the Confederates. The latter, moreover, soon filtered back into the corridors of power. Despite his hard words against them, Johnson forgave ex-Confederate leaders easily, so long as he got the satisfaction of humbling them when they appealed for pardons.

His perceived indulgence of their efforts to restore white supremacy emboldened the ex-Confederates. They packed the delegations to the new Congress with old comrades—nine members of the Confederate Congress, seven former officials of Confederate state governments, four generals and four colonels, and even the vice president of the Confederacy, Alexander Stephens. This was the last straw for the Republicans.

Under the Constitution, Congress is "the judge of the Elections, Returns and Qualifications of its own Members" (Article 1, Section 5). With this power the Republican majorities in both houses refused to admit the southern delegations when Congress convened in early December 1865, effectively blocking Johnson's Reconstruction program. In response, the southern states backed away from the most flagrant of the Black Codes, replacing them with regulatory ordinances silent on race yet, in practice, applied only to blacks, not to whites. On top of that, a wave of violence erupted across the South against the freedmen. In Tennessee a Nashville paper reported that white gangs "are riding about whipping, maiming and killing all negroes who do not obey the orders of their former masters, just as if slavery existed." Listening to the testimony of officials, observers, and victims, Republicans concluded that the South had embarked on a concerted effort to circumvent the Thirteenth Amendment. The only possible response was for the federal government to intervene.

Back in March 1865, before adjourning, the 38th Congress had established the Freedmen's Bureau to provide emergency aid to ex-slaves during the transition from war to peace. Now in early 1866, under the leadership of the moderate Republican senator Lyman Trumbull, Congress voted to extend the Freedmen's

Bureau's life, gave it direct funding for the first time, and authorized its agents to investigate mistreatment of blacks.

More extraordinary was Trumbull's civil rights bill, declaring all persons born in the United States to be citizens and granting them—without regard to race—equal rights of contract, access to the courts, and protection of person and property. Trumbull's bill nullified all state laws denying citizens equal protection, authorized U.S. attorneys to bring enforcement suits in the federal courts, and provided for fines and imprisonment for violators, including public officials. Provoked by an unrepentant South, even the most moderate Republicans demanded that the federal government assume responsibility for securing the civil rights of the freedmen.

Acting on Freedom

While Congress debated, emancipated slaves acted on their own ideas about freedom. News that their bondage was over left them exultant and hopeful (see American Voices, "Relishing Freedom," p. 447). Freedom meant many things—the end of punishment by the lash, the ability to move around, the reuniting of families, the opportunity to begin schools, to form churches and social clubs, and, not least, to engage in politics. Across the South blacks held mass meetings, paraded, and formed organizations. Topmost among their demands were equality before the law and the right to vote—"an essential and inseparable element of self-government."

First of all, however, came ownership of land, which emancipated blacks believed was the basis for true freedom. In the chaotic final months of the war, as plantation owners fled Union forces, freedmen seized control of plantations where they could. Most famously, General William T. Sherman reserved large coastal tracts in Georgia and South Carolina for liberated slaves and settled them on forty-acre plots. Sherman just didn't want to be bothered with the refugees as his army drove across the Lower South, but the freedmen assumed that Sherman's order meant that the land would be theirs. When the war ended, resettlement became the responsibility of the Freedmen's Bureau, which was charged with feeding and clothing war refugees, distributing confiscated land to "loyal refugees and freedmen," and regulating labor contracts between freedmen and planters. Many black families stayed on their old plantations, awaiting redistribution of the land to them after the war. When the South Carolina planter Thomas Pinckney returned home, his freed slaves told him: "We ain't going nowhere. We are going to work right here on the land where we were born and what belongs to us."

Johnson's amnesty plan, entitling pardoned Confederates to recover property seized during the war, shattered these hopes. In October 1865 Johnson ordered General Oliver O. Howard, head of the Freedmen's Bureau, to restore the plantations on the Sea Islands off the South Carolina coast to their white owners. When Howard reluctantly obeyed, the dispossessed blacks protested: "Why do you take away our lands? You take them from us who have always been true, always true to the Government! You give them to our all-time enemies! That is not right!"

Relishing Freedom

JOURDON ANDERSON

*F*olklorists have recorded the sly ways that slaves found, even in bondage, for "puttin' down" their masters. But only in freedom—and beyond reach in a northern state at that—could Anderson's sarcasm be expressed so openly, with the jest that his family might consider returning if they first received the wages due them, calculated to the dollar, for all those years in slavery. Yet, intermixed with the bitterness and the pride in personal dignity is an admission of affection for "the dear old home" that helps explain why, even after the horror of bondage, ex-slaves often chose to remain in familiar surroundings and even work for their former masters. Anderson's letter, although probably written or edited by a white friend in Dayton, surely is faithful to what the ex-slave wanted to say.

Dayton, Ohio. August 7, 1865.
To My Old Master, Colonel P. H. Anderson, Big Spring, Tennessee.
Sir:

I got your letter, and was glad to find that you had not forgotten Jourdon, and that you wanted me to come back and live with you again, promising to do better for me than anybody else can. I have often felt uneasy about you. I thought the Yankees would have hung you long before this, for harboring Rebs they found at your house. I suppose they never heard about your going to Colonel Martin's to kill the Union soldier that was left by his company in their stable. Although you shot at me twice before I left you, I did not want to hear of your being hurt, and am glad you are still living. It would do me good to go back to the dear old home again, and see Miss Mary and Miss Martha and Allen, Esther, Green, and Lee. Give my love to them all, and tell them I hope we will meet in the better world, if not in this. . . .

I want to know particularly what the good chance is you propose to give me. I am doing tolerably well here. I get twenty-five dollars a month, with victuals and clothing; have a comfortable home for Mandy,—the folks call her Mrs. Anderson,—and the children—Milly, Jane, and Grundy—go to school and are learning well. . . . We are kindly treated. Sometimes we overhear others saying, "Them colored people were slaves" down in Tennessee. The children feel hurt when they hear such remarks; but I tell them it was no disgrace in Tennessee to belong to Colonel Anderson. Many darkeys would have been proud, as I used to be, to call you master. Now if you will write and say what wages you will give me, I will be better able to decide whether it would be to my advantage to move back again. . . .

In answering this letter, please state if there would be any safety for my Milly and Jane, who are now grown up, and both good-looking girls. You know how it was with poor Matilda and Catherine. I would rather stay here and starve—and die, if it come to that—than have my girls brought to shame by the violence and wickedness of their young masters. You will also please state if there has been any schools opened for the colored children in your neighborhood. The great desire of my life now is to give my children an education, and have them form virtuous habits.

Say howdy to George Carter, and thank him for taking the pistol from you when you were shooting at me.

From your old servant,
Jourdon Anderson

SOURCE: *Looking for America* 2nd edition, Volume I by Stanley I. Kutler. Copyright © 1979, 1976 by Stanley I. Kutler. Used by permission of W. W. Norton & Company, Inc.

In the Sea Islands and elsewhere, former slaves resisted efforts to evict them. Led by black veterans of the Union army, they fought pitched battles with plantation owners and bands of ex-Confederate soldiers. Landowners struck back hard. One black veteran wrote from Maryland: "The returned colard Solgers are in Many cases beten, and their guns taken from them, we darcent walk out of an evening. . . . They beat us badly and Sumtime Shoot us." Often aided by federal troops, the local whites generally prevailed in this land war.

As planters prepared for a new growing season, a great battle took shape over the labor system that would replace slavery. Convinced that blacks needed supervision, planters wanted to retain the gang labor of the past, only now with wages replacing the food, clothing, and shelter their slaves had once received. The Freedmen's Bureau, although watchful against exploitative labor contracts, sided with the planters. The main thing, its designers had always felt, was that the bureau not encourage dependency "in the guise of guardianship." Rely upon your "own efforts and exertions," an agent told a large crowd of freedmen in North Carolina, "make contracts with the planters" and "respect the rights of property."

Wage Labor of Former Slaves

This photograph, taken in South Carolina shortly after the Civil War, shows former slaves leaving the cotton fields. Ex-slaves were organized into work crews probably not that different from earlier slave gangs, although they now labored for wages and their plug-hatted boss bore little resemblance to the slave drivers of the past. New-York Historical Society.

This was advice given with little regard for the world in which those North Carolina freedmen lived. It was not only their unequal bargaining power they worried about or even that their ex-masters' real desire was to reenslave them under the guise of "free" contracts. In their eyes the condition of wage labor was itself, by definition, debasing. The rural South was not like the North, where working for wages was the norm and qualified a man as independent. In the South, selling one's labor to another—and in particular, selling one's labor to work another's land—implied not freedom, but dependency. "I mean to own my own manhood," responded one South Carolina freedman to an offer of wage work. "I'm going to own my own land."

So the wage issue cut to the very core of the former slaves' struggle for freedom. Nothing had been more horrifying than that as slaves their persons had been the property of others. When a master cast his eye on a slave woman, her husband had no recourse, nor, for that matter, was rape of a slave a crime. In a famous oration celebrating the anniversary of emancipation, the Reverend Henry M. Turner spoke bitterly of the time when his people had "no security for domestic happiness," when "our wives were sold and husbands bought, children were begotten and enslaved by their fathers," and "we therefore were polygamists by virtue of our condition." That was why formalizing marriage was so urgent a matter after emancipation and why, when hard-pressed planters demanded that freedwomen go back into the fields, they resisted so resolutely. If the ex-slaves were to be free as white folk, then their wives could not, any more than white wives, labor for others. "I seen on some plantations," one freedman recounted, "where the white men would . . . tell colored men that their wives and children could not live on their places unless they work in the fields. The colored men [answered that] whenever they wanted their wives to work they would tell them themselves; and if he could not rule his own domestic affairs on that place he would leave it and go someplace else."

The reader will see the irony in this definition of freedom: it assumed the wife's subordinate role and designated her labor the husband's property. But if that was the price of freedom, freedwomen were prepared to pay it. Far better to take a chance with their own men than with their ex-masters.

Many former slaves voted with their feet, abandoning their old plantations and seeking better lives and more freedom in the towns and cities of the South. Those who remained in the countryside refused to work the cotton fields under the hated gang-labor system or negotiated tenaciously over the terms of their labor contracts. Whatever system of labor finally might emerge, it was clear that the freedmen would never settle for anything resembling the old plantation system.

The efforts of former slaves to control their own lives challenged deeply entrenched white attitudes. "The destiny of the black race," asserted one Texan, could be summarized "in one sentence—subordination to the white race." Southern whites, a Freedmen's Bureau official observed, could not "conceive of the negro having any rights at all." And when freedmen resisted, white retribution was swift and often terrible. In Pine Bluff, Arkansas, "after some kind of dispute with some freedmen," whites set fire to their cabins and hanged twenty-four of the inhabitants—men, women, and children. The toll of murdered and beaten blacks mounted into untold thousands. The governments established under Johnson's plan only put the stamp of legality on the pervasive efforts to enforce white supremacy. Blacks "would be *just as well* off with no law at all or no Government," concluded a Freedmen's Bureau agent, as with the justice they got under the restored white rule.

In this unequal struggle, blacks turned to Washington. "We stood by the government when it wanted help," a black Mississippian wrote President Johnson. "Now . . . will it stand by us?"

Congress versus President

Andrew Johnson was not the man to ask. In February 1866 he vetoed the Freedmen's Bureau bill. The bureau, Johnson charged, was an "immense patronage," showering benefits on blacks never granted to "our own people." Republicans could not muster enough votes to override his veto. A month later, further rebuffing his critics, Johnson vetoed Trumbull's civil rights bill, arguing that federal protection of black civil rights constituted "a stride toward centralization." His racism, hitherto muted, now blazed forth: "This is a country for white men, and by God, as long as I am president, it shall be government for white men."

Galvanized by Johnson's attack on the civil rights bill, the Republicans went into action. In early April they got the necessary two-thirds majorities in both houses and enacted it into law. Passage of the Civil Rights Act was a truly historic event, the first time Congress had prevailed over a presidential veto on a major piece of legislation. Republican resolve was reinforced by news of mounting violence in the South, culminating in three days of rioting in Memphis. Forty-six blacks and two whites were left dead, and hundreds of black homes, churches, and schools were looted and burned. In July an angry Congress renewed the Freedmen's Bureau over a second Johnson veto.

Anxious to consolidate their gains, Republicans moved to enshrine black civil rights in an amendment to the Constitution. The heart of the Fourteenth Amendment was Section 1, which declared that "all persons born or naturalized in the United States" were citizens. No state could abridge "the privileges or immunities of citizens of the United States," deprive "any person of life, liberty, or property, without due process of law," or deny anyone "the equal protection of the laws." These phrases were vague, intentionally so, but they established the constitutionality of the Civil Rights Act and, more important, the basis on which the courts and Congress could erect an enforceable national standard of equality before the law in the states.

For the moment, however, the Fourteenth Amendment was most important for its impact on national politics. With the 1866 congressional elections approaching, Johnson somehow figured he had a winning issue in the Fourteenth Amendment. He urged the states not to ratify it. Months earlier, Johnson had begun to maneuver politically against the Republicans, aiming to build a coalition of white Southerners, northern Democrats, and conservative Republicans under the banner of a new party, National Union. Any hope of launching it, however, was shattered by Johnson's intemperate behavior and by escalating violence in the South. A dissension-ridden National Union convention in July ended inconclusively, and Johnson's campaign against the Fourteenth Amendment became, effectively, a campaign for the Democratic Party.

Republicans responded furiously, unveiling a practice that would become known as "waving the bloody shirt." The Democrats were traitors, charged Indiana governor Oliver Morton, and their party was "a common sewer and loathsome receptacle, into which is emptied every element of treason North and South." In late August Johnson embarked on a disastrous "swing around the circle"—a railroad tour from Washington to Chicago and St. Louis and back—that violated the custom that presidents not campaign personally. Johnson made matters worse by engaging in shouting matches with hecklers and insulting the hostile crowds.

The 1866 congressional elections inflicted a humiliating defeat on Johnson. The Republicans won a three-to-one majority in Congress, so that, to begin with, the Republicans considered themselves "masters of the situation," free to proceed "entirely regardless of [Johnson's] opinions or wishes." As a referendum on the Fourteenth Amendment, moreover, the election registered overwhelming popular support for the civil rights of the former slaves. The Republican Party emerged with a new sense of unity—a unity coalescing not at the center, but on the left, around the unbending program of the Radical minority.

The Radicals represented the abolitionist strain within the Republican Party. Most of them hailed from New England or from the area of the upper Midwest settled by New Englanders. In the Senate they were led by Charles Sumner of Massachusetts and in the House by Thaddeus Stevens of Pennsylvania. For them Reconstruction was never primarily about restoring the Union but about remaking southern society. "The foundations of their institutions . . . must be broken up and relaid," declared Stevens, "or all our blood and treasure will have been spent in vain."

Only a handful went as far as Stevens in demanding that the plantations be treated as "forfeited estates of the enemy" and broken up into small farms for the former slaves. About the need to guarantee the freedmen's civil and political rights, however, there was agreement. In this endeavor Radicals had no qualms about expanding the powers of the national government. "The power of the great landed aristocracy in those regions, if unrestrained by power from without, would inevitably reassert itself," warned Congressman George W. Julian of Indiana. Radicals were aggressively partisan. They regarded the Republican Party as the instrument of God for the regeneration of the South.

At first, in the months after Appomattox, few but the Radicals themselves imagined that so extreme a program had any chance of enactment. Black **suffrage** especially seemed beyond reach, since the northern states themselves (excepting in New England) denied blacks the vote. And yet, as fury mounted against the intransigent South, Republicans became ever more radicalized until, in the wake of the smashing victory of 1866, they embraced the Radicals' vision of a reconstructed South.

Radical Reconstruction

Afterward, thoughtful Southerners admitted that the South had brought radical Reconstruction on itself. "We had, in 1865, a white man's government in Alabama," remarked the man who had been Johnson's provisional governor, "but we lost it." The state's "great blunder" was not to "have at once taken the negro right under the protection of the laws." Remarkably, the South remained defiant even after the

Resistance in the South

This engraving, entitled "If He Is a Union Man or Freedman: Verdict, Hang the D——Yankee and Nigger," appeared in *Harper's Weekly* on March 23, 1867, just as the Reconstruction Act was being adopted. Thomas Nast's cartoon encapsulated the outrage at the South's murderous intransigence that led even moderate Republicans to support radical Reconstruction. Library of Congress.

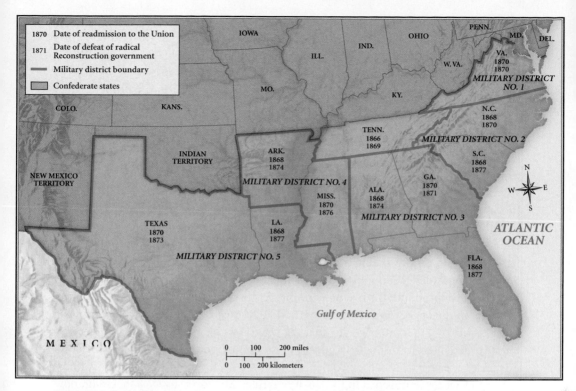

MAP 15.1 Reconstruction

The federal government organized the Confederate states into five military districts during radical Reconstruction. For each state the first date indicates when that state was readmitted to the Union; the second date shows when radical Republicans lost control of the state government. All the ex-Confederate states rejoined the Union from 1868 to 1870, but the periods of radical rule varied widely. Republicans lasted only a few months in Virginia; they held on until the end of Reconstruction in Louisiana, Florida, and South Carolina.

FOR MORE HELP ANALYZING THIS MAP, see the Online Study Guide at **bedfordstmartins.com/henrettaconcise**.

1866 elections. Every state legislature but Tennessee's rejected the Fourteenth Amendment, mostly by virtual acclamation. It was as if they could not imagine that governments installed under the presidential imprimatur and fully functioning might be swept away. But that, in fact, is just what the Republicans intended to do.

Congress Takes Command

The Reconstruction Act of 1867, enacted in March by the Republican Congress, organized the South as a conquered land, dividing it into five military districts, each under the command of a Union general (Map 15.1). The price for reentering the Union was granting the vote to the freedmen and disfranchising those of the South's prewar leadership class who had participated in the rebellion. Each military commander was ordered to register all eligible adult males (black as well as white), supervise the election of state conventions, and make certain that the new constitutions contained guarantees of black suffrage. Congress would readmit a state to the Union if its voters ratified the constitution, if that document proved acceptable to Congress, and if the new state legislature approved the Fourteenth Amendment (thus insuring the needed ratification by three-fourths of the states). Johnson vetoed the Reconstruction Act, but Congress overrode the veto (Table 15.1).

The Tenure of Office Act, a companion to the Reconstruction Act, required Senate consent for the removal of any official whose appointment had required Senate confirmation. Congress chiefly wanted to protect Secretary of War Edwin M. Stanton, a Lincoln holdover and the only member of Johnson's cabinet who favored radical Reconstruction. In his position Stanton could do much to frustrate Johnson's anticipated efforts to undermine Reconstruction. The law also required the president to issue all orders to the army through its commanding general, Ulysses S. Grant. In effect, Congress was attempting to reconstruct the presidency as well as the South.

Seemingly defeated, Johnson appointed generals recommended by Stanton and Grant to command the five military districts in the South. But he was just biding his time. In August 1867, after Congress had adjourned, he "suspended" Stanton and replaced him with Grant, believing that the general would act like a good soldier and follow orders. Next Johnson replaced four of the commanding generals. Johnson, however, had misjudged Grant, who publicly objected to the president's machinations. When the Senate reconvened in the fall, it overruled Stanton's suspension. Grant, now an open enemy of Johnson's, resigned so that Stanton could resume his office.

On February 21, 1868, Johnson formally dismissed Stanton. The feisty secretary of war, however, barricaded the door of his office and refused to admit Johnson's appointee. Three days later, for the first time in United States history, House Republicans introduced articles of **impeachment** against a sitting president, employing the power granted the House of Representatives by the Constitution to charge high federal officials with "Treason, Bribery, or other high Crimes and Misdemeanors." The House overwhelmingly approved eleven counts of presidential misconduct, nine of them violations of the Tenure of Office Act.

The case went to the Senate, which acts as the court in impeachment cases, with Chief Justice Salmon P. Chase presiding. After an eleven-week trial, thirty-five senators on May 15 voted for conviction, one vote short of the two-thirds majority required. Seven moderate Republicans broke ranks, voting for acquittal along with twelve Democrats. The dissenting Republicans felt that the Tenure of Office Act was of dubious validity (in fact, the Supreme Court subsequently declared it unconstitutional) and that removing a president for defying Congress was too extreme, too damaging to the constitutional system of checks and balances, even for the sake of punishing Johnson. Despite his acquittal, however, Johnson had been defanged. For the remainder of his term he was powerless to alter the course of Reconstruction.

The impeachment controversy made Grant, already the North's war hero, a Republican hero as well, and he easily won the party's presidential nomination in

TABLE 15.1 Primary Reconstruction Laws and Constitutional Amendments

Law (Date of Congressional Passage)	Key Provisions
Thirteenth Amendment (January 1865*)	Prohibited slavery
Civil Rights Act of 1866 (April 1866)	Defined citizenship rights of freedmen
	Authorized federal authorities to bring suit against those who violated those rights
Fourteenth Amendment (June 1866†)	Established national citizenship for persons born or naturalized in the United States
	Prohibited the states from depriving citizens of their civil rights or equal protection under the law
	Reduced state representation in House of Representatives by the percentage of adult male citizens denied the vote
Reconstruction Act of 1867 (March 1867)	Divided the South into five military districts, each under the command of a Union general
	Established requirements for readmission of ex-Confederate states to the Union
Tenure of Office Act (March 1867)	Required Senate consent for removal of any federal official whose appointment had required Senate confirmation
Fifteenth Amendment (February 1869‡)	Forbade states to deny citizens the right to vote on the grounds of race, color, or "previous condition of servitude"
Ku Klux Klan Act (April 1871)	Authorized the president to use federal prosecutions and military force to suppress conspiracies to deprive citizens of the right to vote and enjoy the equal protection of the law

*Ratified by three-fourths of all states in December 1865.
†Ratified by three-fourths of all states in July 1868.
‡Ratified by three-fourths of all states in March 1870.

1868. In the fall campaign he supported radical Reconstruction, but he also urged reconciliation between the sections. His Democratic opponent, Horatio Seymour, a former governor of New York, almost declined the nomination because he doubted that the Democrats could overcome the stain of disloyalty.

As Seymour feared, the Republicans "waved the bloody shirt," stirring up old wartime emotions against the Democrats to great effect. Grant won about the same share of the northern vote (55 percent) that Lincoln had won in 1864 and received 214 of 294 electoral votes. The Republicans also retained two-thirds majorities in both houses of Congress.

In the wake of their smashing victory, the Republicans quickly produced the last major piece of Reconstruction legislation—the Fifteenth Amendment, which forbade either the federal government or the states from denying citizens the right to vote on the basis of race, color, or "previous condition of servitude." The amendment left room for **poll taxes** and property requirements or literacy tests that might be used to discourage blacks from voting, a necessary concession to northern and western states that already relied on such provisions to keep immigrants and the "unworthy" poor from the polls. A California senator warned that in his state, with its rabidly anti-Chinese sentiment (see Chapter 16), any restriction on that power would "kill our party as dead as a stone."

Despite grumbling by Radical Republicans, the amendment passed without modification in February 1869. Congress required the states still under federal control—Virginia, Mississippi, Texas, and Georgia—to ratify it as a condition for being readmitted to the Union. A year later the Fifteenth Amendment became part of the Constitution.

Woman Suffrage Denied

If the Fifteenth Amendment troubled some proponents of black suffrage, this was nothing compared to the outrage felt by women's rights advocates. They had fought the good fight for the abolition of slavery for so many years, only to be abandoned when the chance finally came to get the vote for women. All it would have taken was one more word in the Fifteenth Amendment so that the protected categories for voting would have read "race, color, *sex*, or previous condition." Leading suffragists such as Susan B. Anthony and Elizabeth Cady Stanton did not want to hear from Radical Republicans that this was "the Negro's hour" and that women would have to wait for another day. How could suffrage be granted to former slaves, Stanton demanded, but not to them?

In a decisive debate in May 1869 at the Equal Rights Association, the champion of universal suffrage, the black abolitionist Frederick Douglass pleaded for understanding. "When women, because they are women, are hunted down . . . dragged from their homes and hung upon lamp posts . . . when their children are not allowed to enter schools; then they will have an urgency to obtain the ballot equal to our own." Not even all his black sisters agreed. "If colored men get their rights, and not colored women theirs," protested Sojourner Truth, "you see the colored men will be masters over the women, and it will be just as bad as it was before." As for white women in the audience, remarked Frances Harper in support of Douglass, they "all go for sex, letting race occupy a minor position," or worse. In her despair, Elizabeth Cady Stanton lashed out in ugly racist terms against "Patrick and Sambo and Hans and Ung Tung," who were entitled to vote in ignorance even of the Declaration of Independence while the most accomplished of American women remained voteless. Douglass's resolution in support of the Fifteenth Amendment failed, and the Equal Rights convention broke up in acrimony.

At this searing moment a rift opened in the ranks of the women's movement. The majority, led by Lucy Stone and Julia Ward Howe, reconciled themselves to disappointment and accepted the priority of black suffrage. Organized into the American Woman Suffrage Association, these moderates remained allied to the Republican Party, in hopes that once Reconstruction had been settled it would be time for the woman's vote. The Stanton-Anthony group, however, struck out in a new direction. The embittered Stanton declared that woman "must not put her trust in man" in fighting for her rights. The new organization she headed, the New York–based National Woman Suffrage Association, accepted only women, focused exclusively on women's rights, and resolutely took up the battle for a federal woman suffrage amendment.

The fracturing of the women's movement obscured the common ground the two sides shared. Both began to appeal to constituencies beyond the narrow confines of abolitionism and evangelical reform. Both elevated suffrage into the preeminent women's issue. And both were energized for the battles that lay ahead. "If I were to give vent to all my pent-up wrath concerning the subordination of woman," Lydia Maria Child wrote the Republican warhorse Charles Sumner in 1872, "I might frighten *you*. Suffice it, therefore, to say, either the theory of our government is *false*, or women have a right to vote." If radical Reconstruction seemed a barren time for women's rights, in fact it had planted the seeds of the modern feminist movement.

Republican Rule in the South

Between 1868 and 1871 all the southern states met the congressional stipulations and rejoined the Union. Protected by federal troops and encouraged by northern party leaders, state Republican organizations took hold across the South and won control of the newly established Reconstruction governments. These Republican administrations remained in power for periods ranging from a few months in Virginia to nine years in South Carolina, Louisiana, and Florida. Their core support came from African Americans, who constituted a majority of registered voters in Alabama, Florida, South Carolina, and Mississippi.

Southern white Republicans faced the scorn of Democratic ex-Confederates, who mocked them as **scalawags**—an ancient Scots-Irish term for runty, worthless animals. Whites who had come from the North they denounced as **carpetbaggers**— self-seeking interlopers who carried all their property in cheap suitcases called carpetbags. Such labels glossed over the actual diversity of these white Republicans.

Some carpetbaggers, while motivated by personal profit, also brought capital and skills. Others were Union army veterans taken with the South—its climate, people, and economic opportunities. And interspersed with the self-seekers were many idealists anxious to advance the cause of emancipation.

The scalawags were even more diverse. Some were former slave owners, ex-Whigs and even ex-Democrats, drawn to Republicanism as the best way to attract northern capital to southern railroads, mines, and factories. But most were yeomen farmers from the backcountry districts who wanted to rid the South of its slaveholding aristocracy. They had generally fought against, or at least refused to support, the Confederacy, believing that slavery had victimized whites as well as blacks. "Now is the time," a Georgia scalawag wrote, "for every man to come out and speak his principles publickly [sic] and vote for liberty as we have been in bondage long enough."

The Democrats' scorn for black political leaders as ignorant field hands was just as false as stereotypes about white Republicans. The first African American leaders in the South came from an elite of free blacks. They were joined by northern blacks who moved south when radical Reconstruction offered the prospect of meaningful freedom. Like their white allies, many were Union army veterans. Some had participated in the antislavery crusade; a number were employed by the Freedmen's Bureau or northern missionary societies. Others had escaped from slavery and were returning home. One of these was Blanche K. Bruce, who had been tutored on the Virginia plantation of his white father. During the war Bruce escaped and established a school for ex-slaves in Missouri. In 1869 he moved to Mississippi, became active in politics, and in 1874 became Mississippi's second black U.S. senator.

As the reconstructed Republican governments of 1867 began to function, this diverse group of ministers, artisans, shopkeepers, and former soldiers reached out to the freedmen. African American speakers, some financed by the Republican Party, fanned out into the old plantation districts and recruited ex-slaves for political roles. Still, few of the new leaders were field hands; most had been preachers or artisans. The literacy of one ex-slave, Thomas Allen, who was a Baptist minister and shoemaker, helped him win election to the Georgia legislature. "In my county," he recalled, "the colored people came to me for instructions, and I gave them the best instructions I could. I took the *New York Tribune* and other papers, and in that way I found out a great deal, and I told them whatever I thought was right."

Although never proportionate to their numbers in the population, black officeholders were prominent across the South. In South Carolina African Americans constituted a majority in the lower house of the legislature in 1868. Three were elected to Congress; another joined the state supreme court. Over the entire course of Reconstruction, twenty African Americans served in state administrations as governor, lieutenant governor, secretary of state, treasurer, or superintendent of education; more than six hundred served as state legislators; and sixteen were congressmen.

The Republicans who took office had ambitious plans for a reconstructed South. They wanted to end its dependence on cotton agriculture and build an entrepreneurial

THE FIRST COLORED SENATOR AND REPRESENTATIVES,

In the 41st and 42nd Congress of the United States.

African American Congressional Delegation, 1872

This Currier and Ives lithograph celebrates one of the notable achievements of radical Reconstruction—the representation that ex-slaves won, however briefly, in the U.S. Congress. Hiram Revels of Mississippi, the Senate's first African American member, is seated at the extreme left. Granger Collection.

economy like the North's. They fell far short of achieving this vision but accomplished more than their critics gave them credit for.

The Republicans modernized state constitutions, eliminated property qualification for the vote, and swept out the Black Codes that coerced the freedmen back to the plantation and limited their mobility. Women also benefited from the Republican defense of personal liberty. The new constitutions expanded the rights of married women, enabling them to hold property and earnings independent of their husbands—"a wonderful reform," a Georgia woman wrote, for "the cause of Women's Rights." Republican social programs called for the establishment of hospitals, more humane penitentiaries, and asylums for orphans and the insane. Republican governments built roads in areas where roads had never existed. They poured money into rebuilding the region's railroad network.

To pay for their ambitious programs the Republican governments copied taxes that Jacksonian reformers had earlier introduced in the North—in particular, general property taxes on both real estate and personal wealth. The goal was to make planters pay their fair share and to broaden the tax base. In many plantation counties, former slaves served as tax assessors and collectors, administering the taxation of their one-time owners.

Higher tax revenues never managed to overtake the huge obligations assumed by the Reconstruction governments. State debts mounted rapidly and, as interest payments on bonds fell behind, public credit collapsed. On top of that, much of the spending was wasted or ended up in the pockets of state officials. Corruption was ingrained in American politics, present in the southern states before the Republicans came on the scene, and rampant everywhere in this era, not least in the Grant administration itself. Still, in the free-spending atmosphere of the southern Republican regimes, corruption was especially luxuriant and damaging to the cause of radical Reconstruction.

Nothing, however, could dim the achievement in public education. Here the South had lagged woefully; only Tennessee had a system of public schooling before the Civil War. Republican state governments vowed to make up for lost time, viewing education as the foundation for a democratic order. African Americans of all ages rushed to attend the newly established schools, even when they had to pay tuition. An elderly man in Mississippi explained his hunger for education: "Ole missus used to read the good book [the Bible] to us . . . on Sunday evenin's, but she mostly read dem places where it says, 'Servants obey your masters.' . . . Now we is free, there's heaps of tings in that old book we is just suffering to learn."

The building of schools was part of a larger effort by African Americans to fortify the institutions that had sustained their spirit in the shadow of slavery. Religious belief had struck deep roots in nineteenth-century slave society. Now, in freedom, the African Americans left the white-dominated congregations, where they had been relegated to segregated balconies and denied any voice in church governance, and built churches of their own. These churches joined together to form African American versions of the Southern Methodist and Southern Baptist denominations, including, most prominently, the National Baptist Convention and the African Methodist Episcopal Church. Everywhere the black churches served not only as places of worship but as schools, social centers, and political meeting halls.

Black clerics were community leaders and often political leaders as well. As Charles H. Pearce, a Methodist minister in Florida, declared, "A man in this State cannot do his whole duty as a minister except he looks out for the political interests of his people." Calling forth the special destiny of the ex-slaves as the new "Children of Israel," black ministers provided a powerful religious underpinning for the Republican politics of their congregations.

The Quest for Land

In the meantime the freedmen were locked in a great economic struggle with their former owners. In 1869 the Republican government of South Carolina had established a land commission empowered to buy property and resell it on easy terms to the landless. In this way about 14,000 black families acquired farms. South

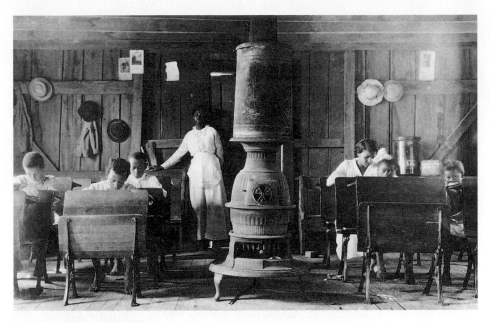

Freedmen's School, c. 1870

This rare photograph shows the interior of one of the 3,000 freedmen's schools established across the South after the Civil War. Although many of these schools were staffed by white missionaries, a main objective of northern educators was to prepare blacks to take over the classrooms. The teacher shown here is surely one of the first. Library of Congress.

For more help analyzing this image, see the Online Study Guide at **bedfordstmartins.com/henrettaconcise**.

Carolina's land distribution plan showed what was possible, but it was the exception and not the rule. Despite a lot of rhetoric, Republican regimes elsewhere did little to help the freedmen fulfill their dreams of becoming independent farmers. Federal efforts proved equally feeble. The Southern Homestead Act of 1866 offered eighty-acre grants to settlers, limited for the first year to freedmen and southern Unionists. The advantage was mostly symbolic, however, since the public land made available to homesteaders was off the beaten track in swampy, infertile parts of the Lower South. Only about a thousand families succeeded.

There was no reversing President Johnson's order restoring confiscated lands to ex-Confederates. Property rights, it seemed, trumped everything else, even for most Radical Republicans. The Freedman's Bureau, which had earlier championed the land claims of the ex-slaves, now devoted itself to teaching them how to be good agricultural laborers.

While they yearned for farms of their own, most freedmen started out landless and with no option but to work for their former owners. But not, they vowed, under the conditions of slavery—no gang work, no overseers, no fines or punishments, no regulation of their private lives. In certain parts of the agricultural South wage work became the norm—for example, on the great sugar plantations of Louisiana taken over after the war by northern investors. The problem was that cotton planters lacked the money to pay wages, at least not until the crop came in, and sometimes, in lieu of a straight wage, they offered a share of the crop. As a wage, this was a bad deal for the freedmen, but if they could be paid in shares for their work, why could they not pay in shares to rent the land they worked?

This form of land tenantry was already familiar in parts of the white South, and the freedmen now seized on it for the independence it offered them. Planters resisted, believing, as one wrote, that "wages are the only successful system of controlling hands." But, in a battle of wills that broke out all across the cotton South, the planters yielded to "the inveterate prejudices of the freedmen, who desire to be masters of their own time."

Thus there sprang up the distinctive laboring system of cotton agriculture— **sharecropping**, in which the freedmen worked as renters, exchanging their labor for the use of land, house, implements, sometimes seed and fertilizer, typically turning over half to two-thirds of their crops to the landlord (Map 15.2). The sharecropping system joined laborers and the owners of land and capital in a common sharing of risks and returns. But it was a very unequal relationship, given the force of southern law and custom on the white landowner's side and the sharecroppers' dire economic circumstances. Starting out penniless, they had no way of making it through the first growing season without borrowing for food and supplies.

Country storekeepers stepped in. Bankrolled by their northern suppliers, they "furnished" the sharecropper and took as collateral a **lien** on the crop, effectively assuming ownership of the cropper's share and leaving him only the proceeds that remained after his debts had been paid. Once indebted at one store, the sharecropper was no longer free to shop around and became an easy target for exorbitant prices, unfair interest rates, and crooked bookkeeping. As cotton prices declined during the 1870s, more and more sharecroppers failed to settle accounts and fell into permanent debt. And if the merchant was also the landowner, or conspired with the landowner, the debt became a pretext for forced labor, or **peonage**, although evidence now suggests that sharecroppers generally managed to pull up stakes and move on once things became hopeless. Sharecroppers always thought twice about moving, however, because part of their "capital" was being known and well reputed in their home communities. Freedmen who lacked that local standing generally found sharecropping hard going and ended up in the ranks of agricultural laborers.

In the face of so much adversity, black families struggled to better themselves. That it enabled family struggle was, in truth, the saving advantage of sharecropping because it mobilized husbands and wives in common enterprise while shielding both from personal subordination to whites. The wives were doubly blessed. Neither field hands for their ex-masters nor dependent housewives, they became partners laboring side by side with their husbands. The trouble with sharecropping, one planter grumbled, was that "it makes the laborer too independent; he becomes a partner, and has to be consulted." By the end of Reconstruction, about one-quarter of sharecropping families had managed to save enough to rent with cash payments, and eventually black farmers owned about a third of the land they cultivated.

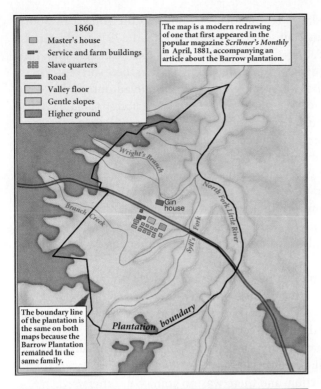

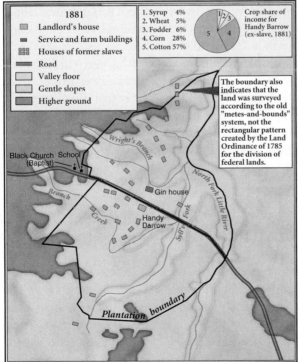

MAP 15.2 The Barrow Plantation, 1860 and 1881

Comparing the 1860 map of this central Georgia plantation with the 1881 map reveals the impact of sharecropping on patterns of black residence. In 1860 the slave quarters were clustered near the planter's house. By 1881 the sharecroppers had scattered across the plantation's 2,000 acres, building cabins on the ridges of land between the low-lying streams. The name Barrow was common among the share-cropping families, which means almost certainly that they had been slaves on the Barrow plantation and that, years after emancipation, they still had not moved on. For all the sharecrop-pers, freedom surely meant hav-ing not only their individual lots and cabins but also the school and church shown on the map.

The battle over the land was by no means unique to the American South. Whenever slavery ended—in Haiti after the slave revolt of 1791, in the British Caribbean by abolition in 1833, in Cuba and Brazil by gradual emancipation during the 1880s—a fierce struggle ensued between planters bent on restoring a gang-labor system and ex-slaves bent on gaining economic autonomy. The outcome of this universal conflict depended on the ex-slaves' access to land. Where vacant land existed, as in British Guiana, or where plantations could be seized, as in Haiti, the ex-slaves became subsistence farmers, and insofar as the Caribbean plantation economy survived without the ex-slaves, it did so by the importation of indentured servants from India and China. Where land could not be had, as in British Barbados or Antigua, the ex-slaves returned to plantation labor as wageworkers, although often in some combination with customary rights to housing and garden plots. The cotton South fit neither of these broad patterns. The freedmen did not get the land, but neither did the planters get field hands. What both got was sharecropping.

The reason for this exceptional outcome was ultimately political. Elsewhere, emancipation almost never meant civil or political equality for the freed slaves. Even in the British islands, where substantial self-government existed, high property qualifications effectively disfranchised the ex-slaves. In the United States, however, hard on the heels of emancipation came civil rights, manhood suffrage, and, for a brief era, a real measure of political power for the freedmen. Sharecropping took shape during Reconstruction, and there was no going back afterward.

For the freedmen sharecropping was not the worst choice; it certainly beat laboring for their former owners. But for southern agriculture the costs were devastating. Sharecropping committed the South inflexibly to cotton because, as a market crop, it alone generated the cash required by landlords and furnishing merchants. Neither soil depletion nor low prices ever enabled sharecroppers to shift away from cotton. And with farms leased year-to-year, neither tenant nor owner had much incentive to improve the property. The crop-lien system lined merchants' pockets with unearned profits that might otherwise have gone into agricultural improvement. The result was a stagnant farm economy, blighting the South's future and condemning it to economic backwardness—a kind of retribution, in fact, for the fresh injustices visited on the people it had once enslaved.

The Undoing of Reconstruction

Ex-Confederates were blind to the accomplishments of radical Reconstruction. Indeed, no amount of achievement could have persuaded them that it was anything but an abomination, undertaken without their consent and denying them their rightful place in southern society. Led by the planters, ex-Confederates staged a massive counterrevolution—one designed to "redeem" the South and restore them to political power under the banner of the Democratic Party. But the Redeemers could not have succeeded on their own. They needed the complicity of the North. The undoing of Reconstruction is as much about northern acquiescence as it is about southern resistance.

Counterrevolution

Insofar as they could win at the ballot box, southern Democrats took that route. They worked hard to get ex-Confederates restored to the voting rolls, they appealed to southern patriotism, and they campaigned against black rule as a threat to white supremacy. But force was equally acceptable. Throughout the Deep South, especially where black voters were heavily concentrated, ex-Confederate planters and their supporters organized secret societies and waged campaigns of terror against blacks and their white allies.

Most fearsome was the Ku Klux Klan, which first appeared in 1866 in Tennessee as a paramilitary force under the aegis of Nathan Bedford Forrest, the Confederacy's most decorated cavalry general. By 1870 the Klan was operating almost everywhere in the South as a terrorist organization. The Klan murdered and whipped Republican politicians, burned black schools and churches, and attacked party gatherings (see American Voices, "The Intimidation of Black Voters," p. 466). Such terrorist tactics enabled the Democrats to seize power in Georgia and North Carolina in 1870 and make substantial gains elsewhere.

Congress responded by passing legislation, including the Ku Klux Klan Act of 1871, authorizing federal prosecutions, military force, and martial law to suppress conspiracies to deprive citizens of their political rights and equal protection of the law. In South Carolina, where the Klan was most deeply entrenched, federal troops occupied nine counties, made hundreds of arrests, and drove as many as 2,000 Klansmen from the state.

The Grant administration's assault on the Klan raised the spirits of southern Republicans, but it also emphasized how dependent they were on the federal government. The potency of the Ku Klux Klan Act, a Mississippi Republican wrote, "derived alone from its source" in the federal government. "No such law could be enforced by state authority, the local power being too weak." If they were to prevail over anti-black terrorism, Republicans needed what one carpetbagger described as "steady, unswerving power from without."

But northern Republicans were growing weary of Reconstruction and the endless bloodshed it seemed to produce. Prosecuting Klansmen was an uphill battle. U.S. attorneys usually faced all-white juries and lacked the resources to handle the cases. After 1872 prosecutions began to drop off; many Klansmen received hasty pardons.

In a kind of self-fulfilling prophecy, the unwillingness of the Grant administration to shore up Reconstruction guaranteed that it would fail. Republican governments that were denied federal help found themselves overwhelmed by the massive resistance of their ex-Confederate enemies. Democrats overthrew Republican governments in Texas in 1873, in Alabama and Arkansas in 1874, and in Mississippi in 1875.

The Intimidation of Black Voters

HARRIET HERNANDES

T he following testimony was given in 1871 by Harriet Hernandes, a black resident of Spartanburg, South Carolina, to the Joint Congressional Select Committee investigating conditions in the South. The terrorizing of black women through rape and other forms of physical violence was among the means of oppression used by the Ku Klux Klan.

Question: How old are you?
Answer: Going on thirty-four years. . . .
Q: Are you married or single?
A: Married.
Q: Did the Ku-Klux come to your house at any time?
A: Yes, sir; twice. . . .
Q: Go on to the second time. . . .
A: They came in; I was lying in bed. Says he, "Come out here, sir; come out here, sir!" They took me out of bed; they would not let me get out, but they took me up in their arms and toted me out — me and my daughter Lucy. He struck me on the forehead with a pistol, and here is the scar above my eye now. Says he, "Damn you, fall." I fell. Says he, "Damn you, get up." I got up. Says he, "Damn you, get over this fence!" and he kicked me over when I went to get over; and then he went on to a brush pile, and they laid us right down there, both together. They laid us down twenty yards apart, I reckon. They had dragged and beat us along. They struck me right on top of my head, and I thought they had killed me; and I said, "Lord o'mercy, don't, don't kill my child!" He gave me a lick on the head, and it liked to have killed me; I saw stars. He threw my arm over my head so I could not do anything with it for three weeks, and there are great knots on my wrist now.
Q: What did they say this was for?
A: They said, "You can tell your husband that when we see him we are going to kill him. . . ."
Q: Did they say why they wanted to kill him?
A: They said, "He voted the radical ticket [slate of candidates], didn't he?" I said, "Yes," that very way. . . .
Q: When did [your husband] get back home after this whipping? He was not at home, was he?
A: He was lying out; he couldn't stay at home, bless your soul! . . .
Q: Has he been afraid for any length of time?
A: He has been afraid ever since last October. He has been lying out. He has not laid in the house ten nights since October.
Q: Is that the situation of the colored people down there to any extent?
A: That is the way they all have to do — men and women both.
Q: What are they afraid of?
A: Of being killed or whipped to death.
Q: What has made them afraid?
A: Because men that voted radical tickets they took the spite out on the women when they could get at them.
Q: How many colored people have been whipped in that neighborhood?
A: It is all of them, mighty near.

SOURCE: Report of the Joint Congressional Select Committee to Inquire into the Condition of Affairs in the Late Insurrectionary States, House Report, 42nd Cong., 2nd sess. (Washington, DC: U.S. Government Printing Office, 1872), vol. 5, South Carolina, December 19, 1871.

Klan Portrait

Two armed Klansmen pose in their disguises, which they donned not only to hide their identities but also to intimidate their black neighbors. Northern audiences saw a lithograph based on this photograph in *Harper's Weekly* on December 28, 1868.

Rutherford B. Hayes Presidential Center.

The Mississippi campaign showed all too clearly what the Republicans were up against. As elections neared in 1875, paramilitary groups such as the Rifle Clubs and Red Shirts operated openly. Often local Democrats paraded armed, as if they were militia companies. They identified black leaders in assassination lists called "dead books," broke up Republican meetings, provoked rioting that left hundreds of African Americans dead, and threatened voters. Mississippi's Republican governor, Adelbert Ames, a Congressional Medal of Honor winner from Maine, appealed to President Grant for federal troops, but Grant refused. Ames then contemplated organizing a state militia but ultimately decided against it, believing that only blacks would join and that the state would be plunged into racial war. Brandishing their guns and stuffing the ballot boxes, the Redeemers swept the 1875 elections and took control of Mississippi. Facing impeachment by the new Democratic legislature, Governor Ames resigned his office and returned to the North.

By 1876 Republican governments, backed by token U.S. military units, remained in only three states—Louisiana, South Carolina, and Florida. Elsewhere, the former Confederates were back in power.

The Acquiescent North

The faltering of Reconstruction stemmed from more than discouragement about prosecuting the Klan, however. Sympathy for the freedman began to wane. The North was flooded with one-sided, often racist reports, such as James M. Pike's *The Prostrate State* (1873), describing extravagant, corrupt Republican rule and South Carolina in the grip of "a mass of black barbarism." The impact of this propaganda could be seen in the fate of the civil rights bill, which Charles Sumner introduced in 1870 at the height of radical Reconstruction. Sumner's bill was a remarkable application of federal power against discrimination in the country, guaranteeing citizens equal access to public accommodation, schools, and jury service. By the time the bill passed in 1875, it had been stripped of its key provisions and was of little account as a weapon against discriminatory treatment of African Americans. The Supreme Court finished the demolition job when it declared the remnant Civil Rights Act unconstitutional in 1883.

The political cynicism that overtook the Civil Rights Act signaled the Republican Party's reversion to the practical politics of earlier days. In many states a second generation took over the party—men like Roscoe Conkling of New York, who treated the Manhattan Customs House, with its regiment of political appointees, as an auxiliary of his organization. Conkling and similarly minded politicos had little enthusiasm for Reconstruction, except as it benefited the Republican Party. As the party lost headway in the South, they abandoned any interest in the battle for black rights. In Washington President Grant presided benignly over this transformation of his party, turning a blind eye on corruption even as it began to lap against the White House.

Grant won a second term overwhelmingly in 1872, capturing 56 percent of the popular vote and every electoral vote against a hapless Horace Greeley, longtime editor of the *New York Tribune* and a warhorse of American reform. But thereafter charges of Republican corruption began to be heard, coming to a head in 1875. The scandal involved the Whiskey Ring, a network of liquor distillers and treasury agents who defrauded the government of millions of dollars of excise taxes on whiskey. The ringleader was a Grant appointee, and Grant's own private secretary, Orville Babcock, had a hand in the thievery. The others went to prison, but Grant stood by Babcock, possibly perjuring himself to save his secretary from jail. The stench of scandal, however, had engulfed the White House.

On top of this the economy had fallen into a severe depression, which was triggered in 1873 by the bankruptcy of the Northern Pacific Railroad and its main investor, Jay Cooke. Both Cooke's privileged role as financier of the Civil War and the generous federal subsidies to the Northern Pacific suggested to many economically pressed Americans that Republican financial manipulation had caused the depression. Grant's administration responded ineffectually, rebuffing the pleas of debtors for relief by increasing the money supply (see Chapter 19).

Among the casualties of the bad economy was the Freedman's Savings and Trust Company, which held the small deposits of thousands of ex-slaves. When the bank failed in 1874, Congress refused to compensate the depositors, and many lost their life savings. In denying their pathetic pleas, Congress was signaling also that Reconstruction had lost its moral claim on the country. National politics had moved on; not the South, but rather concerns about the economy and political fraud absorbed the northern voter as another presidential election approached in 1876.

The Political Crisis of 1877

Abandoning Grant, the Republicans nominated Rutherford B. Hayes, governor of Ohio, a colorless figure but untainted by corruption or by strong convictions—in a word, a safe man. His Democratic opponent was Samuel J. Tilden, governor of New York, a wealthy lawyer with ties to Wall Street and a reform reputation for his role in cleaning up New York City politics. The Democrat Tilden, of course, favored **home rule** for the South but so, more discreetly, did the Republican Hayes. Reconstruction actually did not figure prominently in the campaign and was mostly subsumed under broader Democratic charges of "corrupt centralism" and "incapacity, waste, and fraud." By now Republicans had essentially written off the South. Not a lot was said about the states still ruled by Reconstruction governments— Florida, South Carolina, and Louisiana.

Once the returns started coming in on election night, however, those three states began to loom very large indeed. Tilden led in the popular vote and, victorious in key northern states, he seemed headed for the White House until sleepless politicians at Republican headquarters realized that if they kept Florida, South Carolina, and Louisiana, Hayes would win by a single electoral vote. Republicans still controlled the state election machinery and, citing Democratic fraud and intimidation, they certified Republican victories. The audacious announcement came forth from Republican headquarters: Hayes had carried Florida, South Carolina, and Louisiana and won the election. Newly elected Democratic officials also sent in electoral votes for Tilden, and, when Congress met in early 1877, it faced two sets of electoral votes from those states.

The Constitution does not provide for this contingency. All it says is that the president of the Senate (in 1877, a Republican) opens the electoral certificates before the House (Democratic) and the Senate (Republican) and that "the Votes shall then be counted" (Article 2, Section 1). Suspense gripped the country. There was talk of inside deals, of a new election, even of a violent coup. Just in case, the commander of the army, General William T. Sherman, deployed four artillery companies in Washington. Finally, Congress appointed an electoral commission to settle the question. The commission included seven Republicans, seven Democrats, and, as the deciding member, David Davis, a Supreme Court justice not known to have fixed party loyalties. Davis, however, disqualified himself by accepting an Illinois seat in the Senate. He was replaced by Republican justice Joseph P. Bradley, and by 8 to 7 the commission awarded the disputed votes to Hayes.

Outraged Democrats had one more trick up their sleeves. They controlled the House, and they stalled a final count of the electoral votes so as to prevent Hayes's inauguration on March 4. But a week before, secret Washington talks had begun between southern Democrats and Ohio Republicans representing Hayes. Everything turned on South Carolina and Louisiana, where rival governments were encamped at the state capitols, with federal soldiers holding the Democrats at bay. Exactly what deal was struck or how involved Hayes himself was will probably never be known, but on March 1 the House Democrats suddenly ended their delaying tactics, the ceremonial counting of votes went forward, and Hayes was inaugurated on schedule. He soon ordered the Union troops back to their barracks, the Republican governors in South Carolina and Louisiana fled the unprotected statehouses, and Democratic claimants took control. Reconstruction had ended.

In 1877 political leaders on all sides seemed ready to say that what Lincoln had called "the work" was complete. But for the former slaves, the work had only begun. Reconstruction turned out to have been a magnificent aberration, a leap beyond what most white Americans actually felt was due their black fellow citizens. Still, something real had been achieved—three rights-defining amendments to the Constitution, some elbow room to advance economically, and, not least, a stubborn confidence among blacks that, by their own efforts, they could lift themselves up. Things would, in fact, get worse before they got better, but the work of Reconstruction was imperishable and could never be erased.

T I M E L I N E

1863	Lincoln announces his Ten Percent Plan	1868	Impeachment crisis
1864	Wade-Davis Bill passed by Congress		Fourteenth Amendment ratified
	Lincoln "pocket" vetoes Wade-Davis Bill		Ulysses S. Grant elected president
1865	Freedmen's Bureau established	1870	Ku Klux Klan at peak of power
	Lincoln assassinated; Andrew Johnson succeeds as president		Fifteenth Amendment ratified
	Johnson implements his restoration plan	1872	Grant's reelection
1866	Civil Rights Act passes over Johnson's veto	1873	Panic of 1873 ushers in depression of 1873–1877
	Memphis riots		
	Johnson makes disastrous "swing around the circle"; Democrats defeated in congressional elections	1875	Whiskey Ring scandal undermines Grant administration
1867	Reconstruction Act	1877	Compromise of 1877; Rutherford B. Hayes becomes president
	Tenure of Office Act		Reconstruction ends

For Further Exploration

The best current book on Reconstruction is Eric Foner's major synthesis, *Reconstruction: America's Unfinished Revolution, 1863–1877* (1988), available also in a shorter version. *Black Reconstruction in America* (1935), by the African American activist and scholar W. E. B. Du Bois, deserves attention as the first book to challenge traditional racist interpretations of Reconstruction and stress the role of blacks in their own emancipation. For the presidential phase of Reconstruction, see Dan T. Carter, *When the War Was Over: The Failure of Self-Reconstruction in the South, 1865–1867* (1985). On the freedmen, Leon F. Litwack, *Been in the Storm So Long: The Aftermath of Slavery* (1979), provides a stirring account. More recent emancipation studies emphasize slavery as a labor system: Julie Saville, *The Work of Reconstruction: From Slave to Wage Laborer in South Carolina, 1860–1870* (1994), and Amy Dru Stanley, *From Bondage to Contract* (1999), which expands the discussion to show what the onset of wage labor meant for freedwomen. Eric Foner, *Nothing But Freedom: Emancipation and Its Legacy* (1983), helpfully places emancipation in a comparative context. William S. McFeely, *Grant: A Biography* (1981), deftly explains the politics of Reconstruction. The emergence of the sharecropping system is explored in Gavin Wright, *Old South, New South* (1986), and Edward Royce, *The Origins of Southern Sharecropping* (1993). On the Compromise of 1877, see C. Vann Woodward's classic *Reunion and Reaction* (1956). Two informative Web sites are <http://womhis.binghampton.edu/intro.htm>, which deals with northern women who assisted the freedpeople, and <http://lcweb2.loc.gov/ammen/aaohtml/aollist.html>, which provides Library of Congress documents and illustrations on African Americans during Reconstruction.

For definitions of key terms boldfaced in this chapter, see the glossary at the end of the book.

To assess your mastery of the material covered in this chapter, see the Online Study Guide at **bedfordstmartins.com/henrettaconcise**.

For map resources and primary documents, see **bedfordstmartins.com/henrettaconcise**.

Part Four

A MATURING INDUSTRIAL SOCIETY

1877–1914

	ECONOMY	SOCIETY	CULTURE
	The Triumph of Industrialization	**The West**	**The Rise of the City**
1877	▶ Andrew Carnegie launches modern steel industry Knights of Labor becomes national movement (1878)	▶ Nomadic Indian life ends	▶ National League founded (1876) Dwight L. Moody pioneers urban revivalism
1880	▶ Gustavus Swift pioneers vertically integrated firm American Federation of Labor (1886)	▶ Chinese Exclusion Act (1882) Dawes Act divides tribal lands (1887)	▶ Electrification transforms city life First *Social Register* defines high society (1888)
1890	▶ United States surpasses Britain in iron and steel output Economic depression (1893–1897) Industrial-merger movement begins	▶ U.S. Census declares westward movement over Wounded Knee massacre marks end of armed Indian resistance Preservationists win establishment of California's national parks	▶ Immigration from southeastern Europe rises sharply Settlement houses spread progressive ideas to cities William Randolph Hearst pioneers yellow journalism
1900	▶ Immigrants dominate factory work Industrial Workers of the World (1905)	▶ California farmers rely on Japanese workers Replacement of Japanese by Mexicans after "Gentlemen's Agreement" (1908) reveals durability of western migratory labor system	▶ Muckraking journalism Movies begin to overtake vaudeville
1910	▶ Henry Ford builds first automobile assembly line	▶ Women gain vote in western states U.S. government approves Hetch Hetchy reservoir	▶ Urban liberalism World War I halts European migration

POLITICS	DIPLOMACY
From Inaction to Progressive Reform	**An Emerging World Power**
▶ Election of Rutherford B. Hayes ends Reconstruction	▶ United States becomes net exporter
▶ Ethnocultural issues dominate state and local politics Civil service reform (1883)	▶ Diplomacy of inaction Naval buildup begins
▶ Black disfranchisement in the South William McKinley wins presidency; defeats Bryan's free-silver crusade (1896)	▶ Social Darwinism and Anglo-Saxonism promote expansion Spanish-American War (1898–1899); conquest of the Philippines
▶ McKinley assassinated (1901); Theodore Roosevelt inaugurates progressivism in national politics Hepburn Act regulates railroads (1906)	▶ Panama cedes Canal Zone to United States (1903) Roosevelt Corollary to Monroe Doctrine (1904)
▶ NAACP (1910) Woodrow Wilson elected (1912) New Freedom legislation creates Federal Reserve, FTC	▶ Taft's diplomacy promotes U.S. business Wilson proclaims U.S. neutrality in World War I

T he year 1876 marked the hundredth anniversary of the Declaration of Independence. In celebration the nation mounted a Centennial Exposition where it all began, in Philadelphia. Observing the hectic preparations, the German journalist Ernst Otto Hopp anticipated that this grand world's fair would come as a revelation to his compatriots. "Foreigners will be astounded at the vision of American production. . . . The pits of Nevada will display their enormous stores of silver, Michigan its copper, California its gold and quicksilver, Missouri its lead and tin, Pennsylvania its coal and iron. . . . And from a thousand factories will come the evidences of the wonders of American mechanical skill." Herr Hopp got it right. As it prepared to celebrate its hundredth birthday, Hopp's "young giant" was on the cusp of becoming, for better or worse, the economic powerhouse of the world.

THE WEST The final surge of settlement across the Great Plains and Far West was under way, largely driven by the pressures of an industrializing economy. Cities demanded new sources of food, and factories needed the West's mineral resources. Defending their way of life, western Indians were ultimately defeated not so much by army rifles as by the unceasing encroachment of railroads, mines, ranches, and proliferating farms. These same forces disrupted the long-established Hispanic communities of the Southwest and spurred Asian, Mexican, and European migrations that made for a multiethnic western society.

ECONOMY Equally momentous as the completion of the westward movement was the fact that for the first time, as the decade of the 1870s passed, farmers no longer constituted a majority of working Americans. Henceforth, America's future would be linked to its development as an industrial society. In the manufacturing sector, production became increasingly mechanized and largely directed at making the capital goods that undergirded economic growth. As the railroad system was completed, vertically integrated national firms began to dominate American enterprise. The labor movement became firmly established, and as immigration surged, the foreign born and their children became America's workers. What had been partial and limited now became general and widespread as America turned into a land of factories, corporate enterprise, and industrial workers.

THE CITY Industrial development also transformed the nation's urban life. By 1900 one in five Americans lived in cities. That was where the jobs were—as workers in the factories; as clerks and salespeople; as members of a new salaried middle class of managers, engineers, and professionals; and at the apex, as a wealthy elite of investors and entrepreneurs. The city was more than just a place to make a living, however. It provided a setting for an urban style of life unlike anything seen before in America.

POLITICS The unfettered, booming economy of the Gilded Age tended at first to marginalize political life. The major parties remained robust, not because they stood for much programmatically but because they exploited a culture of popular participation and embraced the ethnocultural interests of their constituencies. The depression of the 1890s triggered a major challenge to the political status quo by the agrarian Populist Party, with its demand for free silver. The election of 1896 turned back that challenge and established the Republicans as the dominant national party. Still unresolved, however, was the threat that corporate power posed to the marketplace and democratic politics. How to curb the trusts dominated national debate during the Progressive Era. In those years, too, the country took a critical look at its institutions and began to address its social ills. From different angles political reformers, women progressives, and urban liberals went about the business of cleaning up machine politics and making life better for America's urban masses. African Americans, victimized by disfranchisement and segregation, found allies among white progressives and launched a new drive for racial equality.

DIPLOMACY Finally, the dynamism of America's economic development decisively altered the country's foreign relations. In the decades after the Civil War, America had been inward looking, neglectful of its navy and inactive diplomatically. The business crisis of the 1890s, however, brought home the need for a more aggressive foreign policy that would advance the nation's overseas economic interests. In short order the United States went to war with Spain, acquired an overseas empire, and became actively engaged in Latin America and Asia. There was no mistaking America's standing as a Great Power, and as World War I approached, no evading the responsibilities and entanglements that came with that status.

Chapter 16

THE AMERICAN WEST

Who are to go there? The territory consists of mountains almost inaccessible, and low lands . . . where rain never falls, except during spring. . . . Why sir, sir, of what use will this be for agricultural purposes? I would not, for that purpose, give a pinch of snuff for the whole territory.

SENATOR GEORGE MCDUFFIE SPEAKING IN CONGRESS
ABOUT ACQUIRING CALIFORNIA FROM MEXICO, 1843

D uring the last decades of the nineteenth century, America seemed like two nations. One was an advanced industrial society—the America of factories and sprawling cities. But another America remained frontier country, with pioneers streaming onto the Great Plains, repeating the old dramas of "settlement" they had been performing ever since Europeans had first set foot on the continent. Not until 1890 did the U.S. census declare that a "frontier of settlement" no longer existed: the country's "unsettled area has been so broken into . . . that there can hardly be said to be a frontier line."

Eighteen-ninety also marked the year the country surpassed Great Britain in the production of iron and steel. Newspapers carried reports of Indian wars and industrial strikes in the same edition. The last tragic episode in the suppression of the Plains Indians, the massacre at Wounded Knee, South Dakota, occurred only eighteen months before the great Homestead steel strike of 1892. This alignment of events from the distant worlds of factory and frontier was not accidental. The final surge of settlement across the Great Plains and the Far West was powered primarily by the energy of American industrialism.

The Great Plains

During the 1860s agricultural settlement reached the western margins of the tall-grass prairie. Beyond, roughly at the ninety-eighth meridian (Map 16.1), stretched a vast, dry country, uninviting to farmers accustomed to woodlands and ample

476

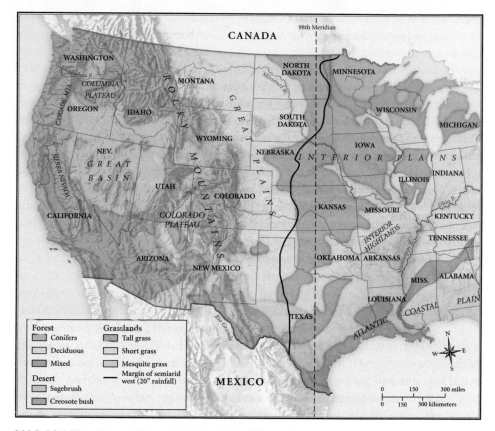

MAP 16.1 The Natural Environment of the West, 1860s

As settlers pushed into the Great Plains and beyond the line of semiaridity, they sensed the overwhelming power of the natural environment. In a landscape without trees for fences and barns and without adequate rainfall, ranchers and farmers had to relearn their business. The Native Americans peopling the plains and mountains had in time learned to live in this environment, but this knowledge counted for little against the ruthless pressure of the settlers to domesticate the West.

rainfall. They saw it much as did the New York publisher Horace Greeley on his way to California in 1859: "a land of starvation," "a treeless desert," baking in heat in the daytime and "chill and piercing" cold at night.

Greeley was describing the Great Plains. The geologic event creating the Great Plains occurred sixty million years ago when the Rocky Mountains arose out of the ocean covering western North America. With no outlet, the shallow inland sea to the east dried up, forming a hard pan on which sediment washing down from the mountains built up a loose, featureless surface. The climate was dry because the moisture-laden winds from the Pacific spent themselves on the western slopes of the Sierras. Only vegetation capable of withstanding the periodic cycles of drought could take hold on the plains. The short grama grass, the linchpin of this fragile ecosystem, matted the easily blown soil into place and sustained a rich wildlife dominated by grazing antelope and buffalo. What the dry short-grass country had not sustained, until the past few centuries, was human settlement.

Indians of the Great Plains

Probably 100,000 Native Americans lived on the Great Plains in the mid-nineteenth century. They were a diverse people, divided into six linguistic families and at least thirty tribal groupings. On the eastern margins and along the Missouri River, the Mandans, Arikaras, and Pawnees planted corn and beans and lived in permanent villages. Smallpox and measles introduced by Europeans ravaged these settled tribes. Less vulnerable to epidemics because they were dispersed were the hunting tribes that had first arrived on the Great Plains in the seventeenth century: Kiowas and Comanches in the southwest; Arapahos and Cheyennes on the central plains; and, to the north, Blackfeet, Crows, and the great Sioux nation.

Originally the Sioux had been eastern prairie people, occupying settlements in the lake country of northern Minnesota. With fish and game dwindling, some tribes drifted westward and around 1760 began to cross the Missouri River. These Sioux, or Lakota (meaning "allies"), became nomadic, living in portable skin tepees and hunting the buffalo. From tribes to the southwest, they acquired horses. Once mounted, the Sioux became splendid hunters and formidable fighters, claiming the entire Great Plains north of the Arkansas River as their hunting grounds and driving out or subjugating longer-settled tribes.

A society that celebrates the heroic virtues of hunting and war is likely to define gender roles sharply. But before the Sioux had horses, buffalo hunting could not be an exclusively male enterprise. It took the efforts of both men and women to construct the "pounds," into which, beating the brush side by side, they endeavored to stampede the herds. Once on horseback, however, the men rode off to the hunt while the women stayed behind to prepare the mounting piles of buffalo skins. Subordination to the men was not how Sioux women understood their unrelenting labor; this was their allotted share in a partnership on which the proud, nomadic life of the Sioux depended.

Living so close to nature, depending on its bounty for survival, the Sioux saw sacred meaning in every manifestation of the natural world. Unlike Europeans, they conceived of God not as a supreme being but, in the words of the pioneering ethnologist Clark Wissler, as a "series of powers pervading the universe"—Wi, the sun; Skan, the sky; Maka, the earth; Inyan, the rock. Below these came the moon, wind, and buffalo down through a hierarchy embodying the entire natural order. By prayer and fasting Sioux prepared themselves to commune with these mysterious powers. Medicine men provided instruction, but the religious experience was personal and open to both sexes. The vision, when a supplicant achieved it, attached itself to some object—a feather, an animal skin, or a shell—that was tied into a sacred bundle and became the person's lifelong talisman. In the Sun Dance the entire tribe celebrated the rites of coming of age, fertility, the hunt, and combat, followed by fasting and dancing in supplication to Wi, the sun.

The world of the Lakota Sioux was not self-contained. From their earliest days as nomadic hunters, they had exchanged pelts and buffalo robes for the produce of agriculturalist Pawnees and Mandans. When white traders appeared on the upper Missouri River during the eighteenth century, the Sioux began to trade with them. Although the buffalo remained their staff of life, the Sioux came to rely as well on the traders' kettles, blankets, knives, and guns. The trade system they entered was linked to the Euro-American market economy, yet it was also integrated into the Sioux way of life. Everything depended on the survival of the Great Plains as the Sioux had found it—wild grassland on which the antelope and buffalo ranged free.

Wagon Trains, Railroads, and Ranchers

On first encountering the Great Plains, Euro-Americans thought these unforested lands best left to the Indians. After exploring a drought-stricken stretch in 1820, Major Stephen H. Long declared it "almost wholly unfit for cultivation, and of course uninhabitable by a people depending upon agriculture for their subsistence."

For years thereafter maps marked the plains as the Great American Desert. With that notion in mind Congress formally designated the Great Plains in 1834 as permanent Indian country. The army wanted the border forts, stretching from Lake Superior to Fort Worth, Texas, constructed of stone because they would be there forever. Trade with the Indians would continue but now closely supervised and licensed by the federal government, with the Indian country otherwise off limits to whites.

Events swiftly overtook the nation's solemn commitment as Americans began to eye Oregon and California; Indian country became a bridge to the Pacific. The first wagon train headed west for Oregon from Missouri in 1842. Soon thousands of emigrants traveled the Oregon Trail to the Willamette Valley or cut south beyond Fort Hall into California. Approaching Fort Hall in 1859, Horace Greeley thought "the white coverings of the many emigrant and transport wagons dott[ing] the landscape" gave "the trail the appearance of a river running through great meadows, with many ships sailing on its bosom." Only these "ships" left behind not a trailing wake of foam but a rutted landscape littered with abandoned wagons and rotting garbage.

Talk about the need for a railroad to the Pacific soon surfaced in Washington. How else could the Pacific territories acquired from Mexico and Britain in 1848 (see Chapter 13) be linked to the Union or the ordeal of the overland journey by wagon train be alleviated? The project languished while North and South argued over the terminus for the route. Meanwhile, the Indian country was crisscrossed by overland freight lines, and Pony Express riders delivered mail between Missouri and California. In 1861 telegraph lines brought San Francisco into instant communication with the East. The next year, with the South in rebellion, the federal government finally moved forward with the transcontinental rail project.

No private company could be expected to foot the bill by itself. The construction costs were staggering, and in the short run not much traffic could be expected along the thinly populated route. So the federal government awarded generous land grants plus millions of dollars in loans to the two companies that undertook the transcontinental project.

The Union Pacific, building westward from Omaha, made little headway until the Civil War ended but then advanced rapidly across Indian country, reaching Cheyenne, Wyoming, in November 1867. It took the Central Pacific nearly that long moving eastward from Sacramento, California, to cross the crest of the Sierra Nevada. Both then worked furiously—since the government subsidy was based on miles of track laid—until, to great fanfare, the tracks met at Promontory, Utah, in 1869. None of the other railroads following other westward routes made it as far as the Rockies before Jay Cooke's Northern Pacific failed, triggering the Panic of 1873 and bringing work on all the western roads to an abrupt halt.

By then, however, railroad tycoons had changed their minds about the Great Plains. No longer did they see it through the eyes of the Oregon-bound settlers— as a place to be gotten through en route to the Pacific. They realized that railroads were laying the basis for the economic exploitation of the Great Plains. With economic recovery in 1878, construction soared. During the 1880s, 40,000 miles of track were laid west of the Mississippi, including links from southern California, via the Southern Pacific to New Orleans and via the Santa Fe to Kansas City, and from the Northwest, via the Northern Pacific to St. Paul, Minnesota (see Map 17.2 on p. 511).

Of all the opportunities beckoning, the most obvious was cattle raising. Grazing buffalo made it easy to imagine the plains as cow country. But first the buffalo had to go. All that it would take was the right commercial incentives. A small market for buffalo robes had existed for years, and hunters like William F. "Buffalo Bill" Cody made a good living provisioning army posts and leading sporting parties. Then in the early 1870s eastern tanneries discovered how to cure the hides, sparking a huge demand by shoe and harness manufacturers. Parties of professional hunters with high-powered rifles began a systematic slaughter of the buffalo. Already diminished by disease and shrinking pasturage, the great herds almost vanished within ten years. Many people spoke out against this mass killing, but no way existed to stop people bent on making a quick dollar. Besides, as General Philip H. Sheridan pointed out, exterminating the buffalo would starve the Indians into submission.

In south Texas about five million head of longhorn cattle already grazed on Anglo ranches, hardly worth bothering about because they could not be profitably marketed. In 1865, however, the Missouri Pacific Railroad reached Sedalia, Missouri, far enough west to be accessible to Texas ranchers and their herds. At the Sedalia terminus, a longhorn worth $3 in Texas might command $40. With this incentive Texas ranchers inaugurated the famous Long Drive, hiring cowboys to herd the longhorn cattle hundreds of miles north to the railroads that were pushing west across Kansas.

At Abilene, Ellsworth, and Dodge City, ranchers sold their cattle and trail-weary cowboys went on a binge. These cattle towns captured the nation's imagination as symbols of the Wild West. The reality was much more ordinary. The cowboys, many

Cowboys on the Open Range

In open-range ranching, cattle from different ranches grazed together. At the roundup, cowboys separated the cattle by owner and branded the calves. Cowboys, celebrated in dime novels, were really farmhands on horseback, with the skills to work on the range. An ethnically diverse group, including blacks and Hispanics, they earned $25 a month, plus meals and a bed in the bunkhouse, in return for long hours of grueling, lonesome work. Library of Congress

of them African Americans and Hispanics, were in fact farmhands on horseback who worked long hours under harsh conditions for small pay. Colorful though it seemed, the Long Drive was actually a makeshift method of bridging a gap in the developing transportation system. As soon as railroads reached the Texas range country during the 1870s, ranchers abandoned the Long Drive.

The Texas ranchers owned or leased the land they used, sometimes in huge tracts. North of Texas, where the land was in the public domain, cattlemen simply helped themselves. Hopeful ranchers would spot a likely area along a creek and claim as much land as they could qualify for as settlers under federal homesteading laws, plus what might be added by the fraudulent claims taken out by one or two ranch hands. By a common usage that quickly became established, ranchers had a "range right" to all the adjacent land rising up to the divide—the point where the land sloped down to the next creek.

News of easy money traveled fast. Calves cost $5; steers sold for maybe $60 on the Chicago market. Rail connections were in place or coming in. The grass was free. The rush was on, drawing from as far away as Europe both hardheaded investors and romantics (like the recent Harvard graduate Teddy Roosevelt) eager for a taste of the Wild West. By the early 1880s the plains overflowed with cattle—as many as 7.5 million head ravaging the grass and trampling the water holes.

A cycle of good weather only postponed the inevitable disaster. When it came—a hard winter in 1885, a severe drought the following summer, then record blizzards and bitter cold—cattle died by the hundreds of thousands. An awful scene of rotting carcasses greeted the cowhands riding out onto the range the following spring. Beef prices plunged when hard-pressed ranchers dumped the surviving cattle on the market. The boom collapsed and investors fled, leaving behind a more enduring ecological catastrophe: the destruction of native grasses from the relentless overgrazing by the cattle herds.

Open-range ranching came to an end. Ranchers fenced their land and planted hay. No longer would cattle be left to fend for themselves over the winters. Hispanic shepherds from New Mexico brought sheep in to feed on the mesquite and prickly pear that supplanted the native grasses. Sheep raising, previously scorned by ranchers as unmanly and resisted as a threat to cattle, became a major enterprise in the sparser high country. Some ranchers even sold out to the despised "nesters"—those who wanted to try farming the Great Plains.

Homesteaders

Potential settlers, of course, needed first to be persuaded that crops would grow in that dry country. Powerful interests worked hard to overcome the popular notion that the plains were the Great American Desert. Foremost were the railroads, eager to sell off the public land they had been granted—180 million acres of it—and to develop traffic for their routes. They aggressively advertised, offered cut-rate tickets, and sold off their land at bargain prices. Land speculators, transatlantic steamship lines, and the western states and territories did all they could to encourage settlers. And so did the federal government, which offered 160 acres of public land to all comers under the Homestead Act (1862).

"Why emigrate to Kansas?" asked a testimonial in *Western Trail*, the Rock Island Railroad's gazette. "Because it is the garden spot of the world. Because it will grow anything that any other country will grow, and with less work. Because it rains here more than any other place, and at just the right time."

As if to confirm the optimists, an exceptionally wet cycle occurred between 1878 and 1886. Some settlers attributed the increased rainfall to soil cultivation and tree planting. Others credited God. As a settler on the southern plains remarked, "The Lord just knowed we needed more land an' He's gone and changed the climate."

No amount of optimism, however, could dispel the pain of migration. "That last separating word of *Farewell!* sinks deeply into the heart," one pioneer woman recorded in her diary, thinking of family and friends left behind. But then came the treeless plains. "Such an air of desolation," wrote a Nebraska-bound woman; from another woman in Texas, "such a lonely country." To an emigrant like Ida Lindgren (see American Voices, "Swedish Emigrant in Frontier Kansas," p. 483) no place could have seemed farther from home or more alien.

~

Swedish Emigrant in Frontier Kansas

IDA LINDGREN

L *ike many emigrants, Ida Lindgren did not find it easy to adjust to the harsh new life on the frontier. Her diary entries and letters home show that the adjustment for the first generation was never complete.*

May 15, 1870 [Lake Sibley, Nebraska]

What shall I say? Why has the lord brought us here? Oh, I feel so oppressed, so unhappy! Two whole days it took us to get here and they were not the least trying part of our travels. We sat on boards in the work-wagon packed in so tightly that we could not move a foot, and we drove across endless, endless prairies, on narrow roads; no, no, not roads, tracks like those in the fields at home when they harvested grain. No forest but only a few trees which grow along the rivers and creeks. And then here and there you see a homestead and pass a little settlement. The Indians are not so far away from here, I can understand, and all the men you see coming by, riding or driving wagons, are armed with revolvers and long carbines, and look like highway robbers.

No date [probably written July 1870]

Claus and his wife lost their youngest child at Lake Sibley and it was very sad in many ways. There was no real cemetery but out on the prairie stood a large, solitary tree, and around it they bury their dead, without tolling of bells, without a pastor, and sometimes without any coffin. A coffin was made here for their child, it was not painted black, but we lined it with flowers and one of the men read the funeral service, and then there was a hymn, and that was all.

August 25, 1874 [Manhattan, Kansas]

It has been a long time since I have written, hasn't it? . . . When one never has anything fun to write about, it is no fun to write. . . . We have not had rain since the beginning of June, and then with this heat and often strong winds as well, you can imagine how everything has dried out. There has also been a general lamentation and fear for the coming year. We are glad we have the oats (for many don't have any and must feed wheat to the stock) and had hoped to have the corn leaves to add to the fodder. But then one fine day there came millions, trillions of grasshoppers in great clouds, hiding the sun, and coming down into the fields, eating up everything that was still there, the leaves on the trees, peaches, grapes, cucumbers, onions, cabbage, everything, everything. Only the peach stones still hung on the trees, showing what had once been there.

July 1, 1877 [Manhattan, Kansas]

. . . It seems so strange to me when I think that more than seven years have passed since I have seen you all. . . . I can see so clearly that last glimpse I had of Mamma, standing alone amid all the tracks of Eslov station. Oliva I last saw sitting on her sofa in her red and black dress, holding little Brita, one month old, on her lap. And Wilhelm I last saw in Lund at the station, as he rolled away with the train, waving his last farewell to me. . . .

Some women were liberated by this hard experience. Prescribed gender roles broke down as women shouldered men's work on new farms and became self-reliant in the face of danger and hardship. When husbands died or gave up, wives operated farms on their own. Under the Homestead Act, which accorded widows and single women the same rights as men, women filed 10 percent of the claims. Even with a man around, women contributed crucially to the farm enterprise. Farming might be thought of as a dual economy in which men's labor brought in the big wage at harvest time, while women provisioned the family day by day and produced a steady bit of money for groceries by selling eggs or butter. If the crop failed, it was women's labor that carried the family through. No wonder farming placed a high premium on marriage: a mere 2.4 percent of Nebraska women in 1900 had never married.

Male or female, the vision of new land beckoned people onto the plains. By the 1870s the older agricultural states had filled up, and farmers looked hungrily westward. "Hardly anything else was talked about," recalled the short-story writer Hamlin Garland about his Iowa neighbors. "Every man who could sell out had gone west or was going. . . . Farmer after farmer joined the march to Kansas, Nebraska, and Dakota. . . . The movement . . . had . . . become an exodus, a stampede."

The same excitement took hold in northern Europe, as Norwegians and Swedes for the first time joined the older German migration. At the peak of the "American fever" in 1882, over 105,000 Scandinavians emigrated to the United States. Swedish and Norwegian became the primary languages in parts of Minnesota and the Dakotas. Roughly a third of the farmers on the northern plains were foreign-born.

Buffalo Chips

With no trees around for firewood, settlers on the plains had to make do with dried cow and buffalo droppings. Gathering the "buffalo chips" must have been a regular chore for Ada McColl and her daughter on her homestead near Lakin, Kansas, in 1893.

Kansas State Historical Society

FOR MORE HELP ANALYZING THIS IMAGE, see the Online Study Guide at **bedfordstmartins.com/henrettaconcise**.

The motivation for most settlers, American or European, was to better themselves economically. But for some southern blacks, Kansas briefly represented something more precious—the Promised Land of racial freedom. In the spring of 1879, with Reconstruction over and federal protection withdrawn, black communities fearful of white vengeance were swept by enthusiasm for Kansas. Within a month or so, some 6,000 blacks left Mississippi and Louisiana, most of them with nothing more than the clothes on their backs and faith in the Lord. They called themselves Exodusters, participants in the exodus to the dry prairie. How many of them remained is hard to say, but the 1880 census reported 40,000 blacks in Kansas—by far the largest African American concentration in the West aside from Texas—whose expanding cotton frontier attracted hundreds of thousands of black migrants during the 1870s and 1880s.

No matter where they came from, homesteaders found the plains an alien place. A cloud of grasshoppers might descend and destroy a crop in a day; a brush fire or hailstorm could do the job in an hour. What forested land had always provided—ample water, lumber for cabins and fencing, firewood—was absent. For shelter, settlers often cut dugouts into hillsides and after a season or two erected houses made of turf cut from the ground.

The absence of trees, on the other hand, meant an easier time clearing the land. New technology overcame obstacles once thought insurmountable. Steel plows enabled homesteaders to break the tightly matted ground, and barbed wire provided cheap, effective fencing against roaming cattle. Strains of hard-kernel wheat tolerant of the extreme temperatures of the plains came in from Europe. Homesteaders had good crops while the wet cycle held and began to anticipate the wood-frame house, deep well, and full coal bin that might make life tolerable on the plains.

In the mid-1880s the dry years came and wrecked those hopeful calculations. "From day to day," reported the budding novelist Stephen Crane from Nebraska, "a wind hot as an oven's fury . . . raged like a pestilence," destroying the crops and leaving farmers "helpless, with no weapon against this terrible and inscrutable wrath of nature." Land only recently settled emptied out as homesteaders fled in defeat. The Dakotas lost 50,000 settlers between 1885 and 1890, and comparable departures occurred up and down the drought-stricken plains.

Other settlers held on grimly. Stripped of the illusion that rain followed the plow, the survivors came to terms with the semiarid climate prevailing west of the ninety-eighth meridian. Mormons around the Great Salt Lake had demonstrated how irrigation could turn a wasteland into a garden. But the Great Plains generally lacked the water reserves needed for irrigation. The answer lay in dry-farming methods, which involved deep planting to bring subsoil moisture to the roots and quick harrowing after rainfalls to turn over a dry mulch that slowed evaporation. Dry farming developed most fully on the huge corporate farms in the Red River Valley of North Dakota. But even family farms, the norm elsewhere, could not survive on less than 300 acres of grain crops, plus machinery for plowing, planting, and harvesting. Dry farming was not for the unequipped homesteader.

By the turn of the century, the Great Plains had fully submitted to agricultural development. About half the nation's cattle and sheep, a third of its cereal crops, and nearly three-fifths of its wheat came from the newly settled lands. In this process there was little of the "pioneering" that Americans associated with the westward movement. The railroads came before the settlers, eastern capital financed the ranching bonanza, and dry farming depended on sophisticated techniques and modern machinery.

The economic capital of the Great Plains was far eastward in Chicago. There, at the hub of the nation's rail system, the wheat pit traded western grain and consigned it to world markets; the great packing houses slaughtered western livestock and supplied the nation with sausage, bacon, and sides of beef. In return western ranchers and farmers received lumber, barbed wire, McCormick reapers, and Sears, Roebuck catalogues. Chicago was truly "nature's metropolis."

The Fate of the Indians

What of the Native Americans who inhabited the Great Plains? Basically, their history has been told in the foregoing account of western settlement. "The white children have surrounded me and have left me nothing but an island," lamented the great Sioux chief Red Cloud in 1870, the year after the completion of the transcontinental railroad. "When we first had all this land we were strong; now we are all melting like snow on a hillside, while you are grown like spring grass."

Settlement occurred despite the provisions for a permanent Indian country that had been written into federal law and ratified by treaties with various tribes. As incursions into their lands increased from the late 1850s onward, the Indians resisted as best they could, striking back all along the frontier: the Apaches in the Southwest, the Cheyennes and Arapahos in Colorado, and the Sioux in the Wyoming and Dakota Territories. The Indians hoped that, if they resisted stubbornly enough, the whites would tire of the struggle and leave them in peace. This reasoning seemed not altogether fanciful given the country's exhaustion after the Civil War. But the federal government did not give up; instead it formulated a new policy for dealing with the western Indians.

Few whites questioned the necessity of moving the Native Americans out of the path of settlement and into reservations. That, indeed, had been the fate of the eastern and southern tribes. Now, however, Indian removal included something new: a strategy for undermining the Indians' tribal way of life. The first step was a peace commission appointed in 1867 to negotiate an end to the fighting and sign treaties by which the western Indians would cede their lands and move to reservations. There, under the tutelage of the Office of Indian Affairs, they would be wards of the government until they learned "to walk on the white man's road."

The government set aside two extensive areas, allocating the southwestern quarter of the Dakota Territory—present-day South Dakota west of the Missouri River— to the Lakota Sioux tribes and assigned what is now Oklahoma to the southern Plains

Indians, along with the major southern tribes—the Choctaw, Cherokee, Chickasaw, Creek, and Seminole—and eastern Indians who had been removed there thirty years before. Scattered reservations went to the Apaches, Navajos, and Utes in the Southwest and to the mountain Indians in the Rockies and beyond.

That the Plains Indians would resist was inevitable. "You might as well expect the rivers to run backward as that any man who was born a free man should be contented when penned up and denied liberty to go where he pleases," said Chief Joseph of the Nez Percé, who led his people in 1877, including women and children, on an epic 1,500-mile march from eastern Oregon to escape confinement in a small reservation. In a series of heroic engagements, the Nez Percé fought off the pursuing U.S. Army until, after four months of extraordinary hardship, the remnants of the tribe were finally cornered and forced to surrender in Montana near the Canadian border.

The U.S. Army was thinly spread, having been cut back after the Civil War to a total force of 27,000. But these were veteran troops, including 2,000 black cavalrymen of the Ninth and Tenth Regiments, whom Indians called, with grim respect, "buffalo soldiers." Technology also favored the army. Telegraph communications and railroads enabled the troops to be quickly concentrated; repeating rifles and Gatling machine guns increased their firepower. As fighting intensified in the mid-1870s, a reluctant Congress appropriated funds for more western troops. Because of tribal rivalries, the army could always find Indian allies. Worst of all, however, beyond the U.S. Army or the Indians' disunity, was the overwhelming impact of white settlement.

Resisting the reservation solution, the Indians fought on for years—in Kansas in 1868 and 1869, in the Red River Valley of Texas in 1874, and sporadically among the fierce Apaches, who made life miserable for white settlers in the Southwest until their wily chief Geronimo was finally captured in 1886. On the northern plains the crisis came in 1875, when the Office of Indian Affairs—despite an 1868 treaty—ordered the Sioux to vacate their Powder River hunting grounds and withdraw to the reservation.

Led by Sitting Bull, Sioux and Cheyenne warriors gathered on the Little Big Horn River west of the Powder River country. In a typical concentrating maneuver, army columns from widely separated forts converged on the Little Big Horn. The Seventh Cavalry, commanded by famous Civil War hero George A. Custer, came upon the Sioux encampment on June 25, 1876. Disregarding orders, the reckless Custer sought out battle on his own. He attacked from three sides, hoping to capitalize on the element of surprise. But his forces were spread too thin. The other two contingents fell back with heavy losses to defensive positions, but Custer's own force of 256 men was surrounded and annihilated by Crazy Horse's warriors. It was a great victory but not a decisive one. The day of reckoning was merely postponed.

Pursued by the military, physically exhausted Sioux bands one by one gave up and moved to the reservation. Last to come in were Sitting Bull's followers. They had retreated to Canada, but in 1881 after five hard years they recrossed the border and surrendered at Fort Buford, Montana.

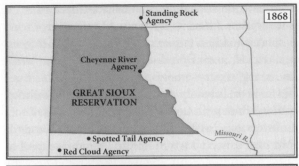

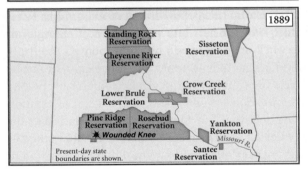

MAP 16.2 The Sioux Reservations in South Dakota, 1868–1889

In 1868, when they bent to the demand that they move onto the reservation, the Sioux thought they had gained secure rights to a substantial part of their ancestral hunting grounds. But as they learned to their sorrow, fixed boundary lines only increased their vulnerability to the land hunger of the whites and sped up the process of expropriation.

Not Indian resistance, but white greed wrecked the reservation solution. In the mid-1870s prospectors began to dig for gold in the Black Hills, land sacred to the Sioux and entirely inside their Dakota reservation. Unable to hold back the prospectors or to buy out the Sioux, the government opened up the Black Hills to gold seekers at their own risk. In 1877, after Sioux resistance had crumbled, federal agents forced the tribes to cede the western third of their Dakota reservation (Map 16.2).

The Indian Territory of Oklahoma met a similar fate. Two million acres in the heart of the territory had not been assigned, and white homesteaders coveted that fertile land. The "boomer" movement, stirred up initially by railroads operating in the Indian Territory, agitated for an opening of this so-called Oklahoma District to settlers. In 1889 the government reluctantly placed the Oklahoma District under the Homestead Act. On April 22, 1889, a horde of claimants rushed in and staked out the

Indian School

In this photograph taken at the Riverside Indian School in Anadarko, Oklahoma Territory, the pupils have been shorn of their braids and dressed in laced shoes, Mother Hubbard dresses, and shirts and trousers—one step on the journey into the mainstream of white American society. Children as young as five were separated from their families and sent to Indian schools like this one that taught them new skills while encouraging them to abandon traditional Indian ways.

University of Oklahoma, Western History Collections

entire district within a few hours. Two tent cities—Guthrie with 15,000 people and Oklahoma City with 10,000—were in full swing by nightfall.

In the meantime the campaign to move the Indians onto "the white man's road" relentlessly went forward. During the 1870s the Office of Indian Affairs developed a program to train Indian children for farm work and prepare them for citizenship. Some attended reservation schools, while the less lucky were sent to distant boarding schools. Mother Hubbard dresses and shirts and trousers visibly demonstrated that these bewildered children were being inducted into white society.

And not a moment too soon, believed many avowed friends of the Native Americans. The Indians had never lacked sympathizers—especially in the East, where reformers created the Indian Rights Association after the Civil War. The movement got a boost from Helen Hunt Jackson's influential book *A Century of Dishonor* (1881), which told the story of the unjust treatment of the Indians. What would save them, the reformers believed, was assimilation into white society, starting with the children. The reformers also favored efforts by the Office of Indian Affairs to undermine tribal authority. Above all, they esteemed private property as a "civilizing force" and hence advocated the division of reservation lands into individually owned parcels.

The result was the Dawes Act of 1887, authorizing the president to carve up tribal lands, with each family head receiving an allotment of 160 acres and individuals receiving smaller parcels. The land would be held in trust by the government for twenty-five years, and the Indians would become U.S. citizens. Remaining reservation lands would be sold off, with the proceeds placed in an Indian education fund.

The Sioux were among the first to bear the brunt of the Dawes Act. The federal government, announcing it had gained tribal approval, opened their "surplus" land to white settlement on February 10, 1890. But no surveys had been made nor had any provision been made for land allotments for the Indians living in the ceded areas. On top of these signs of bad faith, drought wiped out the Indians' crops that summer. It seemed beyond endurance. They had lost their ancestral lands. They faced a future as farmers, which was alien to their traditions. And immediately confronting them was a winter of starvation.

But news of salvation had also come. An Indian messiah, a holy man who called himself Wovoka, was preaching a new religion on a Paiute reservation in Nevada. In a vision Wovoka had gone to heaven and received God's word that the world would be regenerated. The whites would disappear, all the Indians of past generations would return to earth, and life on the Great Plains would be as it was before the white man appeared. All this would come to pass in the spring of 1891. Awaiting that great day the Indians should practice the Ghost Dance, a day-long ritual that sent the spirits of the dancers rising to heaven. As the frenzy of the Ghost Dance swept through some Sioux encampments in the fall of 1890, resident whites became alarmed and called for army intervention.

Wovoka had an especially fervent following among the Minneconjous, where the medicine man Yellow Bird held sway. But their chief, Big Foot, had fallen desperately ill with pneumonia, and the Minneconjous agreed to come in under military escort to an encampment at Wounded Knee Creek on December 28. The next morning, when the soldiers attempted to disarm the Indians, a battle exploded in the encampment. Among the U.S. troopers 25 died; among the Indians 146 men, women, and children perished, many of them shot down as they fled.

Wounded Knee was the final episode in the war against the Plains Indians but not the end of their story. The division of tribal lands now proceeded without hindrance. The Lakota Sioux fared relatively well, and many of the younger generation settled down as small farmers and stock grazers. Ironically, the more fortunate tribes were probably those occupying infertile land unattractive to white settlement and thus spared the allotment process. The flood of whites into South Dakota and Oklahoma, on the other hand, left the Indians as small minorities in lands once wholly theirs—20,000 Sioux in a South Dakotan population of 400,000 in 1900; 70,000 of various tribes in a population of a million when Oklahoma became a state in 1907.

The Far West

On the western edge of the Great Plains, the Rocky Mountains rise up to form a great barrier between the mostly flat eastern two-thirds of the country and the rugged Far West. Beyond the Rockies lie two vast highlands: in the north the Columbia plateau, extending into eastern Oregon and Washington, and, flanking the southern Rockies, the Colorado plateau. Where the plateaus break off, the desert-like Great Basin begins, covering western Utah and all of Nevada. Separating this arid interior from the Pacific Ocean are two great mountain ranges—the Sierra Nevada and, to the north, the Cascades—beyond which lies a coastal region that is cool and rainy in the north but increasingly dry southward, until in southern California rainfall becomes almost as sparse as in the interior.

What most impressed white Americans was the sheer inhospitability of this land. The transmountain West could not be occupied in standard American fashion—that is, by a multitude of settlers moving westward along a broad front and, home-stead by homestead, bringing it under cultivation. The wagon trains moving to Oregon's Willamette Valley adopted an entirely different strategy of occupation — the planting of an island of settlement in a vast, mostly barren landscape.

New Spain had pioneered this strategy when in 1598 it had sent the first wagon trains 700 miles northward from Mexico into the upper Rio Grande Valley. When the United States seized the Southwest 250 years later, major Hispanic settlements existed in New Mexico and California, with lesser settlements scattered along the borderlands into south Texas. At that time, aside from Oregon, the only significant Anglo settlement was around the Great Salt Lake in Utah, where Mormons had moved to escape persecution and plant a New Zion. Fewer than 100,000 Euro-Americans—roughly 25,000 of them Anglo, the rest Hispanic—lived in the entire Far West when it became U.S. territory in 1848.

The Mining Frontier

More emigrants would be coming, certainly, but the Far West seemed unlikely to be much of a magnet. California was "hilly and mountainous," noted a U.S. naval officer in 1849, too dry for farming and surely not "susceptible of supporting a very large population." He had not taken account of the recent discovery of gold in the Sierra foothills, however. California would indeed support a very large population, drawn not by arable land but by dreams of gold.

Extraction of mineral wealth became the basis for the Far West's develop-ment (Map 16.3). By 1860, when the Great Plains was still Indian country, California was a booming state with 300,000 residents. There was also a burst of city building. Overnight San Francisco became a bustling metropolis—it had 57,000 residents in 1860—and was the hub of a mining empire that stretched to the Rockies.

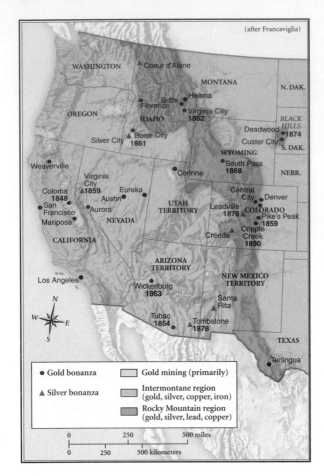

(after Francaviglia)

MAP 16.3 The Mining Frontier, 1848–1890

The Far West was America's gold country because of its geological history. Veins of gold and silver form when molten material from the earth's core is forced up into fissures caused by the tectonic movements that create mountain ranges, such as the ones that dominate the far western landscape. It was these veins, the product of mountain-forming activity many thousands of years earlier, that prospectors began to discover after 1848 and furiously exploit. Although widely dispersed across the Far West, the lodes that they found followed the mountain ranges bisecting the region and bypassing the great plateaus not shaped by the ancient tectonic activity.

FOR MORE HELP ANALYZING THIS MAP, see the Online Study Guide at **bedfordstmartins.com/ henrettaconcise**.

In its swift urbanization the Far West resembled Australia, whose gold rush began in 1851, much more than it resembled the American Midwest. Like San Francisco, Melbourne was a city incongruously grand amid the empty spaces and rough mining camps of the Australian "outback." The distinctive pattern of isolated settlement persisted in the Far West, driven now, however, by a proliferation of mining sites and by people moving not east to west but west to east, coming mainly from California.

By the mid-1850s, as easy pickings in the California gold country diminished, prospectors began to pull out and spread across the West in hopes of striking it rich elsewhere. Gold was discovered on the Nevada side of the Sierra Nevada, in the Colorado Rockies, and along the Fraser River in British Columbia. New strikes occurred in Montana and Wyoming during the 1860s, a decade later in the Black Hills of South Dakota, and in the Coeur d'Alene region of Idaho during the 1880s.

As the news of each gold strike spread, a wild, remote area turned almost overnight into a mob scene of prospectors, traders, gamblers, prostitutes, and saloon keepers (see Voices from Abroad, "A Western Boom Town," p. 493). At least

A Western Boom Town

BARON JOSEPH ALEXANDER VON HÜBNER

During a leisurely trip around the world in 1871 Baron von Hübner, a distinguished Austrian diplomat, traveled across the United States, taking advantage of the newly completed transcontinental railroad to see the Wild West. After observing Mormon life in Salt Lake City, he went northward to Corinne, Utah, near the juncture where the Central and Union Pacific railroads met. He was struck not only by the crudeness of Corinne (see Map 16.3) but also by the tough "rowdies" inhabiting the place.

Corinne has only existed for four years. Sprung out of the earth as if by enchantment, this town now contains upwards of 2,000 inhabitants, and every day increases in importance. It is a victualing center for the advanced posts of the [miners] in Idaho and Montana. A coach runs twice a week to Virginia City and to Helena, 350 and 500 miles to the north. Despite the serious dangers and the terrible fatigue of the journeys, these diligences are always full of passengers. Various articles of consumption and dry goods of all sorts are sent in wagons. The "high road" is but a rough track in the soil left by the wheels of the previous vehicles.

The streets of Corinne are full of white men armed to the teeth, miserable looking Indians dressed in the ragged shirts and trousers furnished by the federal government, and yellow Chinese with a business-like air and hard, intelligent faces. No town in the Far West gave me so good an idea as this little place of what is meant by "border life," the struggle between civilization and savage men and things. . . .

All commercial business centers in Main Street. The houses on both sides are nothing but boarded huts. I have seen some with only canvas partitions. . . . The lanes alongside of the huts, which are generally the resort of Chinese women of bad character, lead into the desert, which begins at the doors of the last houses. . . .

To have on your conscience a number of man-slaughters committed in full day, under the eyes of your fellow citizens; to have escaped the reach of justice by craft, audacity, or bribery; to have earned a reputation for being "sharp," that is, for knowing how to cheat all the world without being caught—those are the attributes of the true rowdy in the Far West. . . . Endowed as they often are with really fine qualities—courage, energy, and intellectual and physical strength—they might in another sphere and with the moral sense which they now lack, have become valuable members of society. But such as they are, these adventurers have a reason for being, a providential mission to fulfill. The qualities needed to struggle with and conquer savage nature have naturally their corresponding defects. Look back, and you will see the cradles of all civilization surrounded with giants of Herculean strength ready to run every risk and to shrink from neither danger nor crime to attain their ends. It is only by the peculiar temper of the time and place that we can distinguish them from the backwoodsman and rowdy of the United States.

SOURCE: *This Was America* by Oscar Handlin, ed. Reprinted by permission.

100,000 fortune seekers flocked to the Pike's Peak area of Colorado in the spring of 1859. Trespassers on government or Indian land, the prospectors made their own law. The mining codes devised at community meetings limited the size of a mining claim to what a person could reasonably work. This kind of informal lawmaking also became an instrument for excluding or discriminating against Mexicans, Chinese, and African Americans in the gold fields. It turned into hangman's justice for the many outlaws who infested the mining camps.

The heyday of the prospectors was always brief. They were equipped only to skim gold from the surface outcroppings and stream beds. Extracting the metal locked in underground lodes required mine shafts and crushing mills—hence capital, technology, and business organization. The original claim holders quickly sold out when a generous bidder came along. At every gold-rush site the prospector soon gave way to entrepreneurial development and large-scale mining. Rough mining camps turned into big towns.

Nevada's Virginia City started out as a bawdy, ramshackle mining camp, but with the opening of the Comstock silver lode in 1859 it soon boasted a stock exchange, mansions for the mining kings, fancy hotels, and even Shakespearean theater. Virginia City remained a rough boomtown nonetheless. It was a magnet for job seekers of both sexes: the men laboring as miners below ground for $4 a day, many of the wage-earning women becoming dance-hall entertainers and prostitutes because that was the best they could do in Virginia City. In 1870 a hundred saloons operated day and night, brothels lined D Street, and men outnumbered women two to one.

In its final stage the mining frontier entered the industrial world. At some sites gold and silver proved less important than the more common metals—copper, lead, and zinc—for which there was a huge demand by eastern manufacturing. Entrepreneurs raised capital, built rail connections, financed the technology for treating the lower-grade copper deposits, constructed smelting facilities, and recruited a labor force. Like other workers, western miners organized trade unions (see Chapter 17). As elsewhere in corporate America, the western mining industries went through a process of consolidation, culminating by the turn of the century in near-monopoly control of western copper and lead production.

But for its mineral wealth the Far West's history would certainly have been very different. Before the discovery of gold at Sutter's Mill in 1848, Oregon's Willamette Valley, not dry California, mostly attracted westward-bound settlers. And, but for the gold rush, California would likely have remained like the Willamette Valley—an agricultural backwater with no markets for its products and a slow-growing population. In 1860, although already a state, Oregon had scarcely 25,000 inhabitants, and its principal city, Portland, was little more than a village. Booming California and its tributary mining country pulled Oregon from the doldrums by creating a market for the state's produce and timber. During the 1880s Oregon and Washington (which became a state in 1889) grew prodigiously. Where scarcely 100,000 settlers had lived twenty years earlier, there were nearly 750,000 by 1890 (Map 16.4). Portland and, even more dramatically,

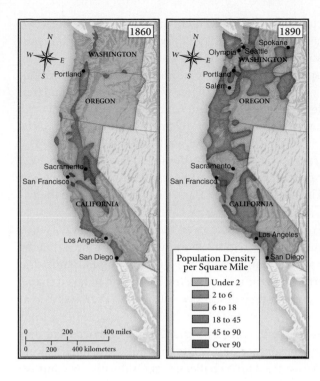

MAP 16.4 The Settlement of the Pacific Slope, 1860–1890

In 1860 the settlement of the Pacific slope was remarkably uneven—fully underway in northern California and scarcely begun anywhere else. By 1890 a new pattern had begun to emerge, with the swift growth of southern California foreshadowed and the settlement of the Pacific Northwest well launched.

Seattle blossomed into important commercial centers, both prospering from a mixed economy of farming, ranching, logging, and fishing.

At a certain point, especially as railroads opened up eastern markets, this diversified growth became self-sustaining. But what had triggered it—what had provided the first markets and underwritten the economic infrastructure—was the bonanza mining economy, at the hub of which stood San Francisco, the metropolis for the entire Far West.

Hispanics, Chinese, Anglos

California was the anchor of two distinct far western regions. First, it joined with Oregon and Washington to form the Pacific slope. Second, by climate and Hispanic heritage, California was linked to the Southwest, which today includes Arizona, New Mexico, and Texas.

The first Europeans to enter the Far West—two centuries before the earliest Anglos—were Hispanics moving northward out of Mexico. There, along a 1,500-mile borderland, outposts had been planted over many years by the viceroys of New Spain. Most populous were the settlements along New Mexico's upper Rio Grande Valley; the main town, Santa Fe, was over 200 years old and contained 4,635 residents in 1860. Farther down the Rio Grande was El Paso, nearly as old but much smaller, and, to the west in present-day Arizona, Tucson, an old presidio, or garrison, town. At the western end of this Hispanic crescent, in California, a Spanish-speaking population was spread thinly in the old presidio towns along the coast and on a patchwork of great ranches.

The economy of this Hispanic crescent was pastoral, consisting primarily of cattle and sheep ranching. In south Texas there were family-run ranches. Everywhere else the social order was highly stratified. At the top stood an elite—the dons occupying royal land grants—who were proudly Spanish and devoted to the traditional life of a landed aristocracy. Below them, with little in between, was a laboring class of servants, artisans, vaqueros (cowboys), and farm hands. New Mexico also contained a large mestizo population—people of mixed Hispanic and Indian blood, a Spanish-speaking and Catholic peasantry but still faithful to the village life and farming methods of their Pueblo heritage.

Pueblo Indians, although their dominance over the Rio Grande Valley had long passed, still occupied much of the region, living in the old ways in adobe villages, rendering the New Mexico countryside a patchwork of Hispanic and Pueblo settlements. To the north a vibrant new tribe, the Navajos, had taken shape, warriors like the Apaches from whom they descended but who were also skilled at crafts and sheep raising.

New Mexico was one place where European and Native American cultures managed a successful, if uneasy, coexistence and where the Indian inhabitants were equipped to hold their own against the Anglo challenge. In California, by contrast, the Hispanic occupation had been harder on the indigenous hunter-gatherer peoples, undermining their tribal structure, reducing them to forced labor, and making them easy prey for the aggressive Anglo miners and settlers, who, in short order, nearly wiped out California's once numerous Indian population.

The fate of the Hispanic Southwest after its incorporation into the United States in 1848 depended on the rate of Anglo immigration. In New Mexico, which remained off the beaten track even after the arrival of railroads in the 1880s, the Santa Fe elite more than held its own, incorporating the Anglo newcomers into Hispanic society through intermarriage and business partnerships. In California, however, expropriation of the great ranches was relentless, even though the 1848 treaty with Mexico had recognized the property rights of the Californios and had made them U.S. citizens. Around San Francisco the great ranches disappeared almost in a puff of smoke. Farther south, where Anglos were slow to arrive, the dons held on longer, but by the 1880s just a handful of the original Hispanic families still retained their Mexican land grants.

The New Mexico peasants found themselves equally embattled. Crucial to their livelihood was the grazing of livestock on communal lands. But these were customary rights that could not withstand legal challenge when Anglo ranchers established title and began putting up fences. The peasants responded as best they could. Their subsistence economy relied on a division of labor that gave women a productive role in the village economy. Women tended the small gardens, engaged in village bartering, and maintained the households. With the loss of the communal lands, the men began migrating seasonally to railway work or the Colorado mines and sugar-beet fields, earning dollars while leaving the village economy in their wives' hands.

Elsewhere, hard-pressed Hispanics struck back for what they considered rightfully theirs. When Anglo ranchers began to fence in communal lands in San Miguel County, the New Mexicans long settled there, *los pobres* (the poor ones), organized themselves into masked night-riding raiders and in 1889 mounted an effective campaign of harassment against the interlopers. After 1900, when Anglo farmers swarmed into south Texas bent on exploiting new irrigation methods, the displaced Tejanos responded with sporadic but persistent night-riding attacks. Much of the raiding by Mexican "bandits" from across the border in the years before World War I was really more in the nature of a civil war by embittered Hispanics who had lived north of the Rio Grande for generations.

But they, like the New Mexico villagers who became seasonal wage laborers, could not avoid being driven into the ranks of a Mexican American working class as the Anglo economy developed. This same development also began to attract increasing numbers of immigrants from Mexico itself.

All along the Southwest borderlands, economic activity picked up in the late nineteenth century. Railroads were being built, copper mines opening in Arizona, cotton and vegetable agriculture spreading in south Texas, and orchards being planted in southern California. In Texas the Hispanic population increased from about 20,000 in 1850 to 165,000 in 1900. Some came as contract workers for railway gangs and harvest crews; virtually all were relegated to the lowest-paying and most back-breaking work; and everywhere they were discriminated against by Anglo workers.

The galloping economic development that drew Mexican migrants also accounted for the exceptionally high number of European immigrants in the West. One-third of California's population was foreign-born, more than twice the level for the country as a whole. Most numerous were the Irish, followed by the Germans and British. But there was another group unique to the West — the Chinese.

First attracted by the California gold rush, 200,000 Chinese came to the United States between 1850 and 1880. In those years they constituted a considerable minority of California's population — around 9 percent — and because virtually all were actively employed, they represented a much larger proportion of the state's labor force — probably a quarter. Elsewhere in the West, at the crest of mining activity, their numbers could surge remarkably, to over 25 percent of Idaho's population in 1870, for example.

The arrival of the Chinese in North America was part of a worldwide Asian migration that had begun in the mid-nineteenth century. Driven by poverty, the Chinese went to Australia, Hawaii, and Latin America; Indians to Fiji and South Africa; and Javanese to Dutch colonies in the Caribbean. Most of these Asians migrated as indentured servants, which in effect made them the property of others. In America, however, indentured servitude was no longer lawful — by the 1820s state courts were banning it as involuntary servitude — so the Chinese came as free workers, going into debt for their passage money but not surrendering their personal freedom or the right to choose their employers.

Once in America, Chinese immigrants normally entered the orbit of the Six Companies, a powerful confederation of Chinese merchants in San Francisco's Chinatown. Most of the arrivals were young men eager to earn a stake and return to their native Cantonese villages. The Six Companies not only steered new arrivals to jobs but also provided the social and commercial services needed to survive in an alien world. The few Chinese women—the male-female ratio was thirteen to one—worked mostly as servants and prostitutes, sad victims of the desperate poverty that drove the Chinese to America. Some were sold by impoverished parents; others were enticed or kidnapped by procurers and transported to America.

Until the early 1860s, when surface mining played out, Chinese men labored mainly in the California gold fields—as prospectors where white miners permitted it and as laborers and cooks where they did not. Then, when construction began on the transcontinental railroad, the Central Pacific hired Chinese workers. Eventually they constituted four-fifths of the railroad's labor force, doing most of the pick-and-shovel work laying the track across the Sierra Nevada. Many were recruited by labor agents and worked in labor gangs run by "China bosses," who not only supervised but fed, housed, paid, and often cheated them.

When the transcontinental railroad was completed in 1869, the Chinese scattered. Some stayed in railroad construction gangs, while others labored on swamp-drainage

Building the Central Pacific

Chinese laborers, in 1867, are hard at work on the great trestle spanning the canyon at Secrettown in the Sierra Nevada.
University of California at Berkeley, Bancroft Library

and irrigation projects in California's Central Valley or as agricultural workers and, if they were lucky, became small farmers and orchardists. The mining districts of Idaho, Montana, and Colorado also attracted large numbers of Chinese, but according to the 1880 census, nearly three-quarters remained in California. "Wherever we put them, we found them good," remarked Charles Crocker, one of the promoters of the Central Pacific. "Their orderly and industrious habits make them a very desirable class of immigrants."

White workers, however, did not share Crocker's enthusiasm. In other parts of the country, racism was directed against African Americans; in California, where there were few blacks, it found a target in the Chinese. "They practice all the unnameable vices of the East," wrote the young journalist Henry George. "They are utter heathens, treacherous, sensual, cowardly and cruel." Sadly, this vicious racism was intertwined with labor's republican ideals. The Chinese, argued George, would "make nabobs and princes of our capitalists, and crush our working classes into the dust . . . substitut[ing] . . . a population of serfs and their masters for that population of intelligent freemen who are our glory and our strength."

The anti-Chinese frenzy climaxed in San Francisco in the late 1870s when mobs ruled the streets, at one point threatening to burn the docks of the Pacific Mail Steamship Company where the Chinese immigrants debarked. The fiercest agitator, an Irish teamster named Denis Kearney, quickly became a dominant figure in the California labor movement. Under the slogan "The Chinese Must Go!" Kearney led a Working Men's Party against the state's major parties. Democrats and Republicans jumped on the bandwagon, joining together in 1879 to write a new state constitution replete with anti-Chinese provisions and pressuring Washington to take up the issue. In 1882 Congress passed the Chinese Exclusion Act, which barred further entry of Chinese laborers into the country.

The injustice of this law—no other nationality was similarly targeted—rankled the Chinese. Why us, protested one woman to a federal agent, and not the Irish, "who were always drunk and fighting?" Merchants and American-born Chinese, who were free to come and go, routinely registered a newly born son after each trip, enabling many an unrelated "paper son" to enter the country. Even so, resourceful as the Chinese were at evading the exclusion law, the flow of immigrants slowed to a trickle.

But the job opportunities that had attracted the Chinese to America did not subside. If anything, the West's agricultural development intensified the demand for cheap labor, especially in California, which was shifting from wheat, the state's first great cash crop, to fruits and vegetables. Such intensive agriculture required lots of workers: stoop labor, meagerly paid and mostly seasonal. This was not, as one San Francisco journalist put it, "white men's work." That ugly phrase serves as a touchstone for California agricultural labor as it would thereafter develop—a kind of caste labor system, always drawing some downtrodden, footloose whites, yet basically defined along color lines.

But if not the Chinese, then who? First to arrive were Japanese immigrants, who came in increasing numbers and by the early twentieth century constituted half of the state's agricultural labor force. Then, when anti-Japanese agitation closed off that population flow in 1908, Mexico became the next, essentially permanent, source of migratory workers for California's booming commercial agriculture.

The irony of the state's social evolution is painful to behold. Here was California, a land of limitless opportunity, boastful of its democratic egalitarianism, and yet simultaneously, and from its very birth, a racially torn society, at once exploiting and despising the Hispanic and Asian minorities whose hard labor helped make California the enviable land it was.

Golden California

Life in California contained all that the modern world of 1890 had to offer— cosmopolitan San Francisco, comfortable travel, a high living standard, colleges and universities, even resident painters and writers. Yet California was still remote from the rest of America, a long journey away and, of course, differently and spectacularly endowed by nature. Location, environment, and history all conspired to set California somewhat apart from the American nation. In certain ways so did the Californians.

What Californians yearned for was a cultural tradition of their own. Closest to hand was the bonanza era of the forty-niners, captured on paper by Samuel Clemens. Clemens left his native Missouri for Nevada in 1861. He did a bit of prospecting, worked as a reporter, and adopted the pen name Mark Twain. In 1864 he arrived in San Francisco, where he became a newspaper columnist writing about what he pronounced "the livest, heartiest community on our continent."

Listening to the old miners in Angel's Camp in 1865, Twain jotted down one tale in his notebook, as follows:

> Coleman with his jumping frog—bet stranger $50—stranger had no frog, and
> C. got him one:—in the meantime stranger filled C's frog full of shot and he
> couldn't jump. The stranger's frog won.

In Twain's hands, this fragment was transformed into a tall tale that caught the imagination of the country and made his reputation as a humorist. "The Celebrated Jumping Frog of Calaveras County" somehow encapsulated the entire world of make-or-break optimism in the mining camps.

In such short stories as "The Luck of Roaring Camp" and "The Outcasts of Poker Flat," Twain's fellow San Franciscan Bret Harte developed this theme in a more literary fashion and firmly implanted it in California's memory. But this past was too raw, too suggestive of the tattered beginnings of so many of the state's leading citizens—in short too disreputable—for an up-and-coming society.

Then in 1884 Helen Hunt Jackson published her novel *Ramona*. In this story of a half-Indian girl caught between two cultures, Jackson intended to advance the cause of the Native Americans, but she placed her tale in the evocative context of early California and that rang a bell. By then the chain of missions planted by the Catholic

Church had been long abandoned. The padres were wholly forgotten, their Indian converts scattered and in dire poverty. Now that lost world of "sun, silence and adobe" became all the rage. Sentimental novels and histories appeared in abundance. There was a movement to restore the missions. Many communities began to stage Spanish fiestas, and the mission style of architecture enjoyed a great vogue among developers.

In its Spanish past California found the cultural traditions it needed. The same kind of discovery was taking place elsewhere in the Southwest, although in the case of Santa Fe and Taos there really were live Hispanic roots to celebrate.

All this enthusiasm was strongly tinged with commercialism. And so was a second distinctive feature of California's development—the exploitation of its climate. While northern California boomed, the southern part of the state remained thinly populated, too dry for anything but grazing and some chancy wheat growing. What it did have, however, was an abundance of sunshine. At the beginning of the 1880s there burst upon the country amazing news of the charms of southern California. "There is not any malaria, hay fever, loss of appetite, or languor in the air; nor any thunder, lightning, mad dogs . . . or cold snaps." This publicity was mostly the work of the Southern Pacific Railroad, which had reached Los Angeles in 1876 and was eager for business.

When the Santa Fe Railroad arrived in 1885, a furious rate war broke out. One-way fares from Chicago or St. Louis to Los Angeles dropped to $25 or less. Thousands of people, mostly Midwesterners, poured in. A dizzying real estate boom developed, along with the frantic building of such resort hotels as San Diego's opulent Hotel del Coronado. Los Angeles County, which had less than 3 percent of the state's population in 1870, had 12 percent by 1900. By then southern California had firmly established itself as the land of sunshine and orange groves. It had found a way to translate climate into riches.

That California was specially favored by nature some Californians knew even as the great stands of redwoods and sugar pine were being hacked down, the streams polluted, and the hills torn apart by reckless mining techniques. Back in 1864 influential Americans who had seen it prevailed on Congress to grant to the state of California "the Cleft, or Gorge in the granite peak of the Sierra Nevada Mountain, known as Yosemite Valley," which would be reserved "for public pleasuring, resort, and recreation." When the young naturalist John Muir arrived in California four years later, he headed straight for Yosemite. Its "grandeur . . . comes as an endless revelation," he wrote. Muir and others like him became devoted to studying the High Sierra and protecting the area from "despoiling gain-seekers . . . eagerly trying to make everything immediately and selfishly commercial." One result was the creation of California's national parks in 1890—Yosemite, Sequoia, and General Grant (later part of King's Canyon). Another was the formation in 1892 of the Sierra Club, which became a powerful voice for the defenders of California's wilderness.

They won some and lost some. Advocates of water-resource development insisted that California's irrigated agriculture and thirsty cities could not grow without tapping the abundant snow pack of the Sierra Nevada. By the turn of the century, Los Angeles faced a water crisis that threatened its growth. The answer was a

Kitty Tatch and Friend on Glacier Point, Yosemite

From the time the Yosemite Valley was set aside in 1864 as a place "for public pleasuring, resort, and recreation," it attracted a stream of tourists eager to experience the grandeur of the American West. As is suggested by this photograph taken sometime in the 1890s, the magic of Yosemite was enough to set even staid young ladies dancing. The Yosemite Museum

238-mile aqueduct to the Owens River in the southern Sierra. A bitter controversy blew up over this immense project, driven by the resistance of local residents to the flooding of the beautiful Owens Valley. More painful for John Muir and his preservationist allies was their failure to save the Hetch Hetchy gorge north of Yosemite National Park. After years of controversy the federal government in 1913 approved the damming of Hetch Hetchy to serve the water needs of San Francisco.

When the stakes became high enough, nature lovers like John Muir generally came out on the short end. Even so, something original and distinctive had been added to California's heritage—the linking of a society's well-being with the preservation of its natural environment. This realization, in turn, said something important about the nation's relationship to the West. If the urge to conquer and exploit persisted, at least it was now tempered by a sense that nature's bounty was not limitless. And this, more than any announcement by the U.S. census that a "frontier line" no longer existed, registered the country's acceptance that the age of heedless westward expansion had ended.

T I M E L I N E

1849	California gold rush	**1876**	Battle of Little Big Horn
	Chinese migration begins	**1877**	San Francisco anti-Chinese riots
1862	Homestead Act	**1879**	Exoduster migration to Kansas
1864	Yosemite Valley reserved as public park	**1882**	Chinese Exclusion Act
1865	Long Drive of Texas longhorns begins	**1884**	Helen Hunt Jackson's novel *Ramona*
1867	U.S. government adopts reservation policy for Plains Indians	**1886**	Dry cycle begins on the Great Plains
1868	Indian treaty confirms Sioux rights to Powder River hunting grounds	**1887**	Dawes Act
1869	Union Pacific–Central Pacific transcontinental railroad completed	**1889**	Oklahoma opened to white settlement
1875	Sioux ordered to vacate Powder River hunting grounds; war breaks out	**1890**	Indian massacre at Wounded Knee, South Dakota
			U.S. census declares end of the frontier

For Further Exploration

The starting point for western history is Frederick Jackson Turner's famous essay, "The Significance of the Frontier in American History" (1893). In recent years there has been a reaction against Turnerian scholarship for being Eurocentric—for seeing western history only through the eyes of frontiersmen and settlers—and for masking the rapacious and environmentally destructive underside of western settlement. Patricia N. Limerick's skillfully argued *The Legacy of Conquest* (1987) opened the debate. Richard White, *"It's Your Misfortune and None of My Own": A New History of the American West* (1991), provides the fullest synthesis. For some of the most debated issues, see the essays in Clyde A. Milner, ed., *A New Significance: Re-Envisioning the History of the American West* (1996). On women's experiences—a primary concern of the new scholarship—a useful introduction is Susan Armitage and Elizabeth Jameson, eds., *The Women's West* (1987). On the Plains Indians a lively account is Robert M. Utley, *The Indian Frontier of the American West* (1984). The ecological impact of plains settlement is subtly probed in Frieda Knobloch, *The Culture of Wilderness: Agriculture as Colonization in the American West* (1996). One facet of this subject is reconsidered in Andrew C. Isenberg, *The Destruction of the Bison: An Environmental History* (2000). On the integration of the plains economy with the wider world, an especially rich book is William Cronon, *Nature's Metropolis: Chicago and the Great West* (1991). Sarah Deutsch, *No Separate Refuge* (1987), offers an imaginative treatment of the New Mexican peasantry. On the Asian migration to America the best introduction is Ron Takaki, *Strangers from a Different Shore* (1989). Kevin Starr, *California and the American Dream, 1850–1915* (1973), provides a full account of the emergence of a distinctive California culture. A comprehensive Web site with many links is <http://americanwest.com/>.

For definitions of key terms boldfaced in this chapter, see the glossary at the end of the book.

To assess your mastery of the material covered in this chapter, see the Online Study Guide at **bedfordstmartins.com/henrettaconcise**.

For map resources and primary documents, see **bedfordstmartins.com/henrettaconcise**.

Chapter 17

CAPITAL AND LABOR
IN THE AGE OF ENTERPRISE
1877–1900

An almost total revolution has taken place, and is yet in progress, in every branch and in every relation of the world's industrial and commercial system.

DAVID A. WELLS, *RECENT ECONOMIC CHANGES*, 1899

The year that Reconstruction ended, 1877, also marked the end of the first great crisis of American industrial capitalism. In 1873, four years earlier, a severe depression had set in. Railroad building ground to a halt. Orders for industrial goods disappeared. Hundreds of thousands of workers lost their jobs, and suffering was widespread. Before long the foundations of the social order began to shake.

On July 16, 1877, railroad workers went on strike to protest a wage cut at the Baltimore and Ohio Railroad. In towns along the B&O tracks, crowds cheered as the strikers attacked company property and prevented trains from running. The strike rippled across the country. The Pennsylvania Railroad's roundhouse in Pittsburgh went up in flames on July 21, and at many rail centers rioters and looters roamed freely. Only the arrival of federal troops restored order. On August 15 President Rutherford B. Hayes wrote in his diary, "The strikers have been put down *by force.*" The Great Strike of 1877 had been crushed but only after raising the specter of social revolution.

And then recovery came. Within months the economy was booming again. In the next fifteen years, the output of manufactured goods increased by over 150 percent. Confidence in the nation's industrial future rebounded. "Upon [material progress] is founded all other progress," asserted a railroad president in 1888. "Can there be any doubt that cheapening the cost of necessaries and conveniences of life is the most powerful agent of civilization and progress?"

The rail magnate's boast represents the confident face of America's industrial revolution. President Hayes's anxious diary entries suggest a darker side. After 1877 armories appeared in cities across the country. They were fortresses designed to withstand assault by strikers and rioters. It was a paradox of the nation's industrial history that an economy celebrated for its dynamism and inventiveness was also brutally indifferent to the many who fell by the wayside and hence an economy never secure, never free of social conflict.

Industrial Capitalism Triumphant

Economic historians speak of the late nineteenth century as the age of the Great Deflation, an era when, worldwide, prices fell steadily. Falling prices normally signal economic stagnation; there is not enough demand for available goods and services. In England, a mature industrial power, the Great Deflation did indeed signal economic decline. But not in the United States. Indeed, industrial expansion there went into high gear during the Great Deflation. Increasing manufacturing efficiencies enabled American firms to cut prices and yet earn profits and afford still better equipment. Real income for Americans went up dramatically, increasing by nearly 50 percent (from $388 to $573) between 1877 and 1900. The industrializing economy was a wealth-creating machine beyond anything the world had ever seen (Figure 17.1).

The Age of Steel

By the 1870s factories were a familiar sight in America. But the goods they produced—textiles, shoes, paper, and furniture—only replaced articles made at home or by individual artisans. Early manufacturing was really an extension of the agricultural economy. Gradually, however, a different kind of demand developed as the country's economy surged. Railroads needed locomotives; new factories needed

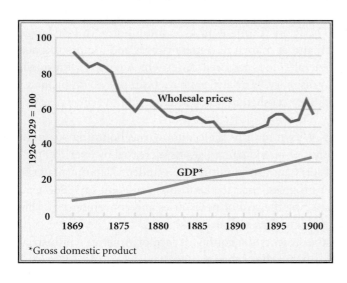

FIGURE 17.1 Business Activity and Wholesale Prices, 1869–1900

This graph shows the key feature of the performance of the late-nineteenth-century economy: while output was booming, the price of goods was falling.

machinery; cities needed trolley lines, sanitation systems, and commercial buildings. Railroad equipment, machinery, and construction materials were *capital goods*, that is, goods that added to the nation's productive capacity. It was this activity, the manufacture of capital goods, that now drove America's industrial economy.

Central to the capital-goods sector was a technological revolution in steel making. The country was already a big producer of wrought iron, a malleable metal easily worked by blacksmiths and farmers. But wrought iron was ill suited for industrial uses; in particular, it did not stand up under heavy use as railway track. And wrought iron was expensive because it could only be produced in small batches by skilled metal workers. In 1856 the British inventor Henry Bessemer designed a furnace— the Bessemer converter—that refined raw pig iron into an essentially new product: steel, a metal harder and more durable than wrought iron. Bessemer's invention attracted many users, but it was Andrew Carnegie who fully exploited its potential.

An iron maker and former railroad manager, Carnegie in 1872 erected a massive steel mill outside Pittsburgh, with the Bessemer converter as its centerpiece. The converter broke a bottleneck at the refining stage and enabled Carnegie's engineers to design a mill that functioned on the basis of continuous operation. Iron ore entered the blast furnaces at one end and emerged at the other end as finished steel rails. Named after Carnegie's admired boss at the Pennsylvania Railroad, the Edgar Thompson Works became a model for the modern steel industry. Giant integrated steel plants swiftly replaced the iron mills that had once dotted western Pennsylvania.

The technological breakthrough in steel spurred the intensive exploitation of the country's rich mineral resources. Once iron ore began to be shipped down the Great Lakes from the rich Mesabi Range in northern Minnesota, the industry was assured of an ample supply of its primary raw material. The other key ingredient, coal, came from the great Appalachian field that stretched from Pennsylvania to Alabama (Map. 17.1). A minor enterprise before the Civil War, coal production doubled every decade after 1870, exceeding 400 million tons a year by 1910.

As steam engines became the nation's energy workhorse, prodigious amounts of coal began to be consumed by railroads and factories. Industries previously dependent on waterpower rapidly converted to steam. The turbine, utilizing continuous rotation rather than the steam engine's back-and-forth piston motion, marked another major advance during the 1880s. With the coupling of the steam turbine to the electric generator, the nation's energy revolution was completed, and after 1900 America's factories began a massive conversion to electric power.

The Railroad Boom

Although moving goods by water satisfied the country's transportation needs at the time, it was love at first sight when locomotives arrived from Britain in the early 1830s. Americans were impatient for the year-round, on-time service that canal

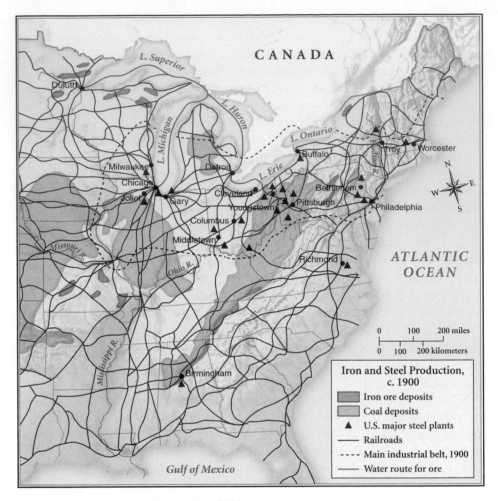

MAP 17.1 Iron and Steel Production, 1900

Before the Civil War the iron industry was concentrated in eastern Pennsylvania and northern New Jersey. With the shift to steel and the westward movement of population and industry, production moved first to western Pennsylvania and then to Ohio, Indiana, Illinois, and southward into Alabama. The specific locations—Pittsburgh, Youngstown, Chicago, and Birmingham—were dictated by the rail network, new sources of coal and iron ore, and markets for steel.

For more help analyzing this map, see the Online Study Guide at **bedfordstmartins.com/henrettaconcise**.

barges and riverboats could not provide. By 1860, with a network of tracks already crisscrossing the country east of the Mississippi, the railroad clearly was on the way to being industrial America's mode of transportation.

The question was, who would pay for it? Railroads could be state enterprises, like the canals, or they could be financed by private investors. Unlike most European countries, the United States chose free enterprise. Even so, government played a big role, helping to underwrite the cost of railroad construction with land grants and

The Corliss Engine

The symbol of the Philadelphia Centennial in 1876 was the great Corliss engine, which towered over Machinery Hall and powered all the equipment on exhibit there. Yet the Corliss engine also signified the incomplete nature of American industrialism at that time; it soon became obsolete. Westinghouse turbines generating electricity would be the power source for the nation's next World's Fair in Chicago in 1893.

Culver Pictures.

financial aid. The most important boost, however, was not money or land but a legal form of organization—the corporation—that enabled private capital to be raised in prodigious amounts. Investors who bought stock in the railroads enjoyed *limited liability*: they risked only the money they had invested and were not personally liable for the railroad's debts. A corporation could also borrow money by issuing interest-bearing bonds, which was how the railroads actually raised most of the money they needed.

Railroad building generally was handed over to construction companies, which, despite the name, were primarily financial structures. Hiring contractors and suppliers often involved persuading them to accept the railroad's bonds as payment and, when that failed, wheeling and dealing to raise cash by selling or borrowing on the bonds. The construction companies were notoriously corrupt. In the worst case, the Union Pacific's Credit Mobilier, probably half the construction funds ended up in the pockets of the promoters.

The railroad business was not for the faint of heart. Most successful were promoters with the best access to capital, such as John Murray Forbes, a great Boston merchant in the China trade who developed the Chicago, Burlington, and Quincy Railroad in the Midwest; or Cornelius Vanderbilt, who started with the fortune he had made in the steamboat business. Vanderbilt was primarily a consolidator, linking previously independent lines and ultimately, via his New York Central, providing unified railroad service between New York City and Chicago. James J. Hill, who without federal subsidy made the Great Northern into the best of the transcontinental railroads, was certainly the nation's champion railroad builder. In contrast Jay Gould, at various times owner of the Erie, Wabash, Union Pacific, and Missouri Pacific systems, always remained a stock-market speculator at heart.

Railroad development in the United States was often sordid, fiercely competitive, and subject to boom and bust. Yet promoters raised vast sums of capital and built a network bigger than that of the rest of the world combined. By 1900 virtually no corner of the country lacked rail service.

Along with this prodigious growth came increasing efficiency. The early railroads, built by competing local companies, had been a jumble of discontinuous segments. Gauges of track—the width between the rails—varied widely and at terminal points railroads were not connected. As late as 1880, goods could not be shipped through from Massachusetts to South Carolina. Eight times along the way, freight cars had to be emptied and their contents transferred to other cars across a river or at a different terminal.

In 1883 the railroads rebelled against the jumble of local times that made scheduling a nightmare and, acting on their own, divided the country into the four standard time zones still in use (Map 17.2). By the end of the 1880s, a standard track gauge (4 feet, 8½ inches) had been adopted everywhere. Fast-freight firms and standard accounting procedures enabled shippers to move goods without breaks in transit, transfers between cars, or the other delays that had once bedeviled them.

At the same time railroad technology was advancing. Durable steel rails permitted heavier traffic. Locomotives became more powerful and capable of pulling more freight cars. To control the greater mass being hauled, the inventor George Westinghouse perfected the automatic coupler, the air brake, and the friction gear for starting and stopping a long line of cars. Costs per ton-mile fell by 50 percent between 1870 and 1890, resulting in a steady drop in freight rates for shippers.

The railroads more than met the transportation needs of the maturing industrial economy. For investors, however, the costs of freewheeling competition and unrestrained growth were painfully high. On the many routes served by too many railroads, competitors fought for the available traffic by cutting rates to the bone. Many were saddled with huge debts from the extravagant construction era; about a fifth of railroad bonds failed to pay interest even in a good year like 1889. When the economy turned bad, as it did in 1893, a third of the industry went into bankruptcy.

Out of the rubble came a major railroad reorganization. This was primarily the handiwork of Wall Street investment banks such as J. P. Morgan & Co. and Kuhn Loeb & Co., whose main role had been to market railroad stocks and bonds. When railroads failed, the investment bankers stepped in to pick up the pieces. They persuaded investors to accept lower interest rates or put up more money. They eased competitive pressures by consolidating rivals. By the early twentieth century, half a dozen great regional systems had emerged, and the nerve center of American railroading had shifted to Wall Street.

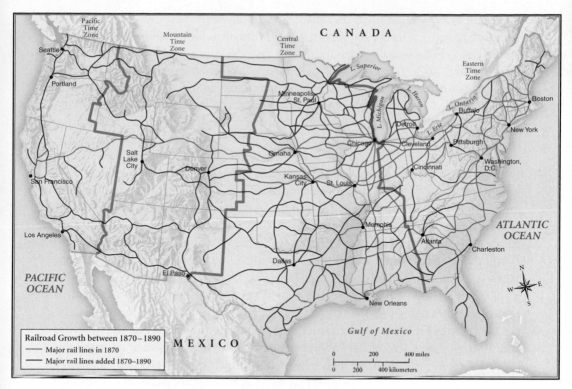

MAP 17.2 The Expansion of the Railroad System, 1870–1890

In 1870 the nation had 53,000 miles of rail track; in 1890 it had 167,000 miles. That burst of construction essentially completed the nation's rail network, although there would be additional expansion for the next two decades. The main areas of growth were in the South and west of the Mississippi. The time zones introduced in 1883 are marked by the thick gray lines.

Large-Scale Enterprise

Until well into the industrial age, all but a few manufacturers operated on a small scale and mostly for nearby markets. After the Civil War the scale of their activities began to change. "Combinations of capital on a scale hitherto wholly unprecedented constitute one of the remarkable features of modern business methods," the economist David A. Wells wrote in 1889. He could see "no other way in which the work of production and distribution can be prosecuted." What was there about the nation's economy that led to Wells's sense that big business was inevitable?

Most of all, the American market. Unlike Europe, the United States was not carved up by national borders that impeded the flow of goods. The population, swelled by immigration and a high birth rate, jumped from 40 million in 1870 to over 60 million in 1890. People flocked to the cities and the railroads brought these expanding markets within the reach of distant producers. Americans were ready consumers of standardized, mass-marketed goods. Their geographic mobility tended to erase the preference for distinctively local products that shaped European tastes. Moreover, social class in America, though by no means absent, was blurred at the edges and did not, for example, call for class-specific ways of dressing. Foreign visitors often noted that ready-made clothing made it difficult to tell salesgirls from debutantes on city streets. Nowhere else did manufacturers have so vast and receptive a market for standardized products.

How they seized that opportunity is perhaps best revealed in the meatpacking industry. With the opening of the Union Stock Yards in 1865, Chicago became the cattle market for the country. Livestock came in by rail from the Great Plains, was auctioned off at the Chicago stockyards, then shipped to eastern cities, where, as in the past, the cattle were slaughtered in local "butchertowns." Such an arrangement—a national livestock market but localized processing—adequately met the needs of an exploding urban population and could have done so indefinitely.

Gustavus F. Swift, a shrewd Chicago cattle dealer from Massachusetts, saw the future differently. He recognized that livestock lost weight en route to the East and that local slaughterhouses lacked the scale to utilize waste by-products or cut labor costs. If it could be kept fresh in transit, however, dressed beef could be processed in bulk at the Chicago stockyards. Once his engineers developed an effective cooling system, Swift invested in a fleet of refrigerator cars and constructed a central beef-packing plant next to the Chicago stockyards. This was only the beginning of Swift's innovations. No refrigerated warehouses existed in the cities that received his chilled beef, so Swift built his own network of branch houses. Next he acquired a fleet of wagons to distribute his products to retail butcher shops. Swift constructed additional facilities to process the fertilizer, chemicals, and other usable by-products from his slaughtering operations. As demand grew, Swift built more packing houses in other stockyard centers, including Kansas City, Fort Worth, and Omaha.

Step by step Swift created a new kind of enterprise—a *vertically integrated firm* capable of handling within its own structure all the functions of an industry. Swift's lead was followed by several big Chicago packers already operating plants that preserved pork products. By 1900 five firms, all of them nationally organized and vertically integrated, produced nearly 90 percent of the meat shipped in interstate commerce.

In most fields no single innovation was as decisive as Swift's refrigerator car. But other entrepreneurs did share Swift's insight that the essential step was to identify a mass market and then develop a national enterprise capable of serving it. In the petroleum industry John D. Rockefeller built the Standard Oil Company partly by taking over rival firms, but he also built a distribution system to reach the enormous market for kerosene for lighting and heating homes. The Singer Sewing Machine Company formed its own sales organization, using both retail stores and door-to-door salesmen. Through such distribution systems manufacturers also were able to provide technical information, credit, and repair facilities.

To gain the benefits of mass distribution, retail business went through comparable changes. Montgomery Ward and Sears, Roebuck developed into national mail-order houses for rural consumers. From Vermont to California, farm families selected identical goods from catalogues and became part of a nationwide consumer market.

The department store, pioneered by John Wanamaker in Philadelphia in 1875, soon became a fixture in downtowns across the country. Alternatively, a retailer could reach consumers efficiently by opening a chain of stores, which was the strategy of the Great Atlantic and Pacific Tea Company (A&P) and F. W. Woolworth's five-and-dimes.

It was not always smooth going for these innovative firms. Shop owners put up stiff resistance, appealing to local pride and sometimes agitating for ordinances that might keep Swift and A&P at bay. Nor were standardized goods universally welcomed. Many people were leery, for example, of Swift's Chicago beef. How could it be wholesome weeks later in Boston or Philadelphia? Cheap prices helped, but advertising mattered more. Modern advertising was born in the late nineteenth century, bringing brand names and a billboard-cluttered urban landscape. By 1900 companies were spending over $90 million a year for space in newspapers and magazines. Advertisements urged readers to bathe with Pears' soap, eat Uneeda biscuits, sew on a Singer machine, and snap pictures with a Kodak camera. The active molding of demand became a major function of the managers of vertically integrated firms.

Kellogg's Toasted Corn Flakes

Like crackers, sugar, and other nonperishable products, cereal had been traditionally sold in bulk from barrels. In the 1880s the Quaker Oats Company hit on the idea of selling oatmeal in boxes of standard size and weight. A further wrinkle was to process the cereal so that it could be consumed right from the box (with milk) for breakfast. And lo and behold: Kellogg's Corn Flakes! This is one of Kellogg's earliest advertisements.

Picture Research Consultants & Archives.

FOR MORE HELP ANALYZING THIS IMAGE, see the Online Study Guide at **bedfordstmartins.com/ henrettaconcise**.

And so, even more urgently, did the task of controlling these far-flung enterprises. Nothing in the world of small business from which they sprang prepared Swift and other industrial pioneers for this challenge. Fortunately for them, railroaders had already paved the way. A managerial crisis had overtaken the trunk lines as they thrust westward before the Civil War. On a 50-mile road, remarked the Erie executive Daniel C. McCallum in a classic statement of the problem, the superintendent could personally attend to every detail, "and any system, however imperfect, may prove comparatively successful." But 500-mile trunk lines were too big for even the most energetic superintendent to oversee directly. It was in "the want of a system" that lay "the true secret of their failure." Acknowledging that he was working in the dark—"we have no precedent or experience upon which we can fully rely"—McCallum urged that the railroads begin devising the structures, the *system*, that would enable them to control their widespread activities. Step by step, always under the prod of necessity, the trunk lines separated overall management from day-to-day operations, departmentalized operations by function (maintenance of way, rolling stock, traffic), defined lines of communication, and perfected cost-accounting methods enabling managers to assess performance of operating units. By the end of the 1870s, the railroads' managerial crisis had been resolved.

Just in time for emerging industrial firms like Swift's, which, sometimes quite directly, drew on the railroad management model. With few exceptions, vertically integrated firms followed a centralized, functionally departmentalized plan, with a main office housing top executives and departments covering specific areas of activity—purchasing, auditing, production, transportation, or sales. These functionally defined departments provided "middle management," something not seen before in American industry. Although managers of operating units functioned much like earlier factory owners, middle managers undertook entirely new tasks, directing the flow of goods and information through the integrated enterprise. They were key innovators, equivalent in matters of business practice to engineers in improving technology.

By the turn of the century, the hundred largest companies controlled roughly a third of the nation's total productive capacity. The day of small manufacturers had not passed. They still flourished, or at least survived, in many fields. Indeed, places like Philadelphia were hubs of small-scale, diversified industry—textiles, leather goods, machine tools—that excelled in what economic historians have called "flexible specialization." But the dominant form of industrial organization had become, and would long remain, large-scale enterprise.

The World of Work

In a free-enterprise system, profit drives the entrepreneur. But the industrial order is not populated only by profit makers. It includes—in vastly larger numbers—wage earners. Economic change always affects working people but rarely so drastically as it did in the late nineteenth century.

Labor Recruits

Industrialization invariably set people in motion. Farm folk migrated to cities. Artisans entered factories. An industrial labor force emerged. This happened in the United States as it did in Europe, but with a difference. In the late nineteenth century rural Americans, although highly mobile and frequently city-bound, mostly rejected factory work. They lacked the industrial skills for the higher-paid jobs as puddlers, rollers, molders, and machinists, but they did have skills—language, basic literacy, a cultural ease—that made them employable in the multiplying white-collar jobs in offices and retail stores.

So the United States could not rely primarily on its own rural population for a supply of workers, except in the South. There a low-wage industrial sector emerged after Reconstruction as local boosters tried to build a "New South" and catch up with the North. The textile mills that sprang up in the Piedmont country of the Carolinas and Georgia recruited workers from the surrounding hill farms, where people struggled to make ends meet (Map 17.3). To attract them mill wages had to exceed farm earnings, but not by much. Paying rock-bottom wages, the new mills had a competitive advantage over the long-established New England industry—as much as 40 percent lower labor costs in 1897.

The labor system that evolved was based on hiring whole families. "Papa decided he would come because he didn't have nothing much but girls and they had to get out and work like men," recalled one woman. It was not Papa, in fact, but his girls whom the mills wanted to work as spinners and loom tenders. Only they could not be recruited individually: no right-thinking parent would have permitted that. Hiring by families, on the other hand, was already familiar; after all, everyone had been expected to work on the farm. So the family system of mill labor developed, with a labor force that was half female and very young. In the 1880s a quarter of all southern textile workers were under fifteen years of age. In the mill villages workers built close-knit, supportive communities, but for whites only. Although blacks sometimes worked as day laborers and janitors, they hardly ever got jobs as operatives in the cotton mills. The same was true in James B. Duke's tobacco factories, where machine tending was restricted to white women.

In natural resources, the South's other growth sector, employers recruited with little regard for race. Logging in the vast pine forests, for example, was racially integrated, with a labor force evenly divided between blacks and whites. There was a similar influx of racially mixed rural Southerners into Alabama's booming iron industry, which by 1890 was producing nearly a million tons of metal annually.

What distinguished the southern labor market was that it was insulated from the rest of the country. Why so few Southerners, black or white, left for the higher-wage North is puzzling. At its core the explanation is that the South was a place apart, with social and racial mores that discouraged all but the most resourceful from seeking opportunity elsewhere. Modest numbers of blacks did migrate out of the South—roughly 80,000 between 1870 and 1890 and another 200,000 between

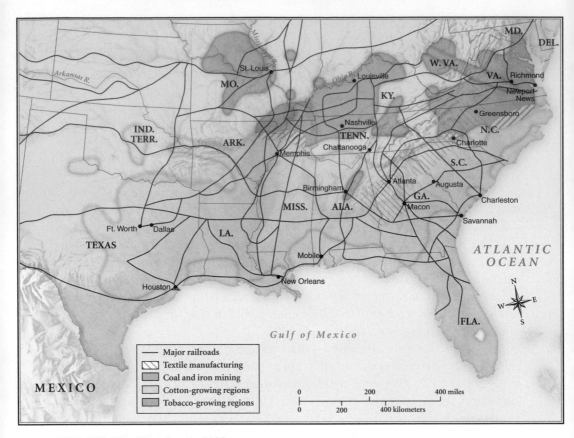

MAP 17.3 The New South, 1900

The economy of the Old South focused on raising staple crops, especially cotton and tobacco. In the New South staple agriculture continued to dominate, but there was marked industrial development as well. Industrial regions evolved, producing textiles, coal and iron, and wood products. By 1900 the South's industrial pattern was well defined.

1890 and 1910. Most of them settled where industrial work was available, but not for them. Employers turned black applicants away from the factory gates—and away from their one best chance for a fair shake at American opportunity—because immigrant workers already supplied companies with as much cheap labor as they needed.

The great migration from the Old World had started in the 1840s, when over a million Irish fled the potato famine. In the following years, as European agriculture became increasingly commercialized, the peasant economies began to fail, first in Germany and Scandinavia and then, later in the nineteenth century, across Austria-Hungary, Russia, Italy, and the Balkans. Europe's industrial districts also sent many seasoned workers, some of them—like hand-loom weavers—displaced by new technologies, others lured by higher American wages.

Ethnic origin largely determined the work the immigrants took in America. Seeking to use skills they already had, the Welsh labored as tin-plate workers, the English as miners, the Germans as machinists and traditional artisans (for example, bakers and carpenters), the Belgians as glass workers, and Scandinavians as seamen on Great Lakes boats. For common labor employers had long counted on the brawn of Irish rural immigrants, although all emigrating groups contributed to the pool of unskilled workers.

As mechanization advanced, the demand for ordinary labor skyrocketed. The sources of immigration began to shift, and by the early twentieth century arrivals from southern and eastern Europe far outstripped immigrants from western Europe (Figure 17.2). Italian and Slavic immigrants without industrial skills flooded into American factories. Heavy, low-paid labor became the domain of the recent immigrants (see Voices from Abroad, "Pittsburgh Inferno," p. 518). Blast-furnace jobs, a job-seeking investigator heard, were "Hunky work," not suitable for him or any other American. The derogatory term *Hunky*, although referring to Hungarian workers, was applied indiscriminately to Poles, Slovaks, and all other ethnic Slavs arriving in America's industrial districts and, for all these groups, was tinged with racism. In the steel districts, it was commonly said that Hunky work was not for "white" men.

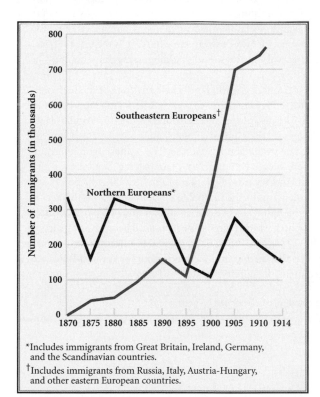

FIGURE 17.2 American Immigration, 1870–1914

This graph shows the surge of European immigration in the late nineteenth century. While northern Europe continued to send substantial numbers, it was overshadowed after 1895 by southern Europeans pouring into America to work in mines and factories.

*Includes immigrants from Great Britain, Ireland, Germany, and the Scandinavian countries.

†Includes immigrants from Russia, Italy, Austria-Hungary, and other eastern European countries.

VOICES FROM ABROAD

Pittsburgh Inferno

COUNT VAY DE VAYA UND LUSKOD

*C*ount Vay de Vaya und Luskod, a Hungarian nobleman and high functionary in the Catholic Church, crossed the United States several times between 1903 and 1906 en route to his post as the Vatican's representative to Asia. In a book about his travels, he expresses his distress at the plight of his countrymen laboring in the mills of the Pittsburgh steel district.

The bells are tolling for a funeral. The modest train of mourners is just setting out for the little churchyard on the hill. Everything is shrouded in gloom, even the coffin lying upon the bier and the people who stand on each side in threadbare clothes and with heads bent. Such is my sad reception at the Hungarian workingmen's colony at McKeesport. Everyone who has been in the United States has heard of this famous town, and of Pittsburgh, its close neighbor. . . .

Fourteen-thousand tall chimneys are silhouetted against the sky . . . discharg[ing] their burning sparks and smok[ing] incessantly. The realms of Vulcan could not be more somber or filthy than this valley of the Monongahela. On every hand are burning fires and spurting flames. Nothing is visible save the forging of iron and the smelting of metal. . . . And this fearful place affects us very closely, for thousands of immigrants wander here from year to year. Here they fondly seek the realization of their cherished hopes, and here they suffer till they are swallowed up by the inferno. He whom we are now burying is the latest victim. Yesterday he was in full vigor and at work at the foundry, toiling, struggling, hoping—a chain broke, and he was killed. . . .

This is scarcely work for mankind. Americans will hardly take anything of the sort; only [the immigrant] rendered desperate by circumstances . . . and thus he is at the mercy of the tyrannous Trust, which gathers him into its clutches and transforms him into a regular slave.

This is one of the saddest features of the Hungarian emigration. In making a tour of these prisons, wherever the heat is most insupportable, the flames most scorching, the smoke and soot most choking, there we are certain to find compatriots bent and wasted with toil. Their thin, wrinkled, wan faces seem to show that in America the newcomers are of no use except to help fill the moneybags of the insatiable millionaires. . . . In this realm of Mammon and Moloch everything has a value—except human life. . . . Why? Because human life is a commodity the supply of which exceeds the demand. There are always fresh recruits to supply the place of those who have fallen in battle; and the steamships are constantly arriving at the neighboring ports, discharging their living human cargo still further to swell the phalanx of the instruments of cupidity.

SOURCE: *This Was America* by Oscar Handlin, ed. Reprinted by permission.

Not only skill determined where immigrants ended up in American industry. The newcomers, although generally not traveling in groups, moved within well-defined networks, following relatives or fellow villagers already in America and relying on them to land a job. A high degree of ethnic clustering resulted, even within a single factory. At the Jones and Laughlin steel works in Pittsburgh, for example, the carpentry shop was German, the hammer shop Polish, and the blooming mill Serbian. Immigrants also had different job preferences. Men from Italy, for instance, liked outdoor work, often laboring in gangs under a *padrone* (boss), much as they had in Italy.

Immigrants entered a modern industrial order, but it was not a world they wanted. They were peasants, displaced by the breakdown of traditional rural economies. Many had lost their land and fallen into the class of dependent, propertyless servants. In Europe job-seeking peasants commonly tried seasonal agricultural labor or temporary work in nearby cities. America represented merely a larger leap, made possible by cheap and speedy steamships across the Atlantic. The peasant immigrants, most of them young and male, regarded their stay in America as temporary, although, once there, many changed their minds. About half did return, departing in great numbers during depression years. No one knows how many left because they had saved enough and how many left for lack of work. For their American employers it scarcely mattered. What did matter was that the immigrants took the worst jobs and were always available when they were wanted. For the new industrial order, they made an ideal labor supply.

Working Women and the Family Economy

Over four million women worked for wages in 1900. They made up a quarter of the nonfarm labor force and played a vital part in the industrial economy. The opportunities they found were shaped by gender—by the fact that they were women. Contemporary beliefs about womanhood largely determined which women took jobs and how they were treated once they became wage earners.

Traditionally, wives were not supposed to work outside the home; in fact, fewer than 5 percent did so in 1890. Only among African Americans did many married women—above 30 percent—work for wages. Among whites the typical working woman was under twenty-four and unmarried. When older women worked, remarked one observer, it "was usually a sign that something had gone wrong"—their husbands had died, deserted them, or lost their jobs.

Since women were held to be inherently different from men, it followed that they not be permitted to do "men's work." Nor, regardless of her skill, could a woman be paid a man's wage because, as one investigator reported, "it is expected that she has men to support her." The ideal at the time was not equal pay for equal work, but a "family wage" for men that would render wives' employment outside the home unnecessary.

At the turn of the century, women's work fell into three categories. A third worked as domestic servants. Another third held "female" white-collar jobs in teaching, nursing, sales, and office work. The remaining third worked in industry, mostly

Switchboard Operators

Telephone work offers a prime historical example of sex typing in American employment. When the first telephone exchange was set up in Boston in 1878, the lines were operated by teenage boys, following the practice set in the telegraph industry. During the 1880s, however, young women increasingly replaced the boys, and by 1900 switchboard operation was defined as women's work. In this photograph of a telephone exchange in Columbus, Ohio, in 1907, the older woman at left has risen to the position of supervisor, but it is the two men in the picture who are clearly in charge. The other major occupations in this new industry—telephone installation and line maintenance— were just as strictly male as switchboard operation was female but of course on a higher pay scale.
© Bettmann / Corbis.

in the garment trades and textile mills, but also in many other industries as inspectors, packers, assemblers, and other "light" occupations. Few worked as supervisors, fewer in the skilled crafts, and nearly none as day laborers.

Just how jobs came to be defined as male or female—in sociological terms, the *sex typing* of occupations—is not easy to explain. Jobs as telephone operators and store clerks, originally male, had by the 1890s become female. Once women dominated an occupation, people came to think of it as having feminine attributes, even though very similar or even identical work elsewhere was done by men. Jobs identified as women's work became unsuitable for men. There were no male telephone operators by 1900.

Sex typing was justified by the sentimental view of women as the weaker sex, but powerful interests also played a role. Craft workers protected their male domain, and employers profited from cut-rate work. Wherever they worked women earned less than the lowest paid males. At the turn of the century, the wage for women factory workers came to roughly $7 a week, $3 less than that of unskilled men and $5 below the average of all industrial workers.

As with male workers, ethnicity and race played a big part in the distribution of women's jobs. Exclusion from all but the most menial jobs applied as rigidly to black women as it did to black men. White-collar jobs were reserved for native-born women, which in the cities increasingly included the second-generation daughters of immigrants. And as with men, ethnicity created clustering patterns in women's jobs or, in the case of Italians, restricted daughters to tasks that could be done in the safety of the home.

Disapproval of wives taking paying jobs, though expressed in sentimental and moral terms, was based on solid necessity. Cooking, cleaning, and tending the children were not income producing or reckoned in terms of money. But everyone knew that the family household could not function without the wife's contribution. Therefore, her place was in the home.

Working-class families, however, found the going hard on a single income. Talk of a "family wage" was mostly just that—the talk of speech makers. Only among highly skilled workers, wrote one investigator, "was it possible for the husband unaided to support his family." The rockiest period came during the child-bearing years, when there were many mouths to feed and only the earnings of the father to provide the food. Thereafter, as the children grew old enough to work, the family income began to increase. Not only unmarried sons and daughters but also the younger children contributed their share. In 1900 one of every five children under sixteen worked. "When the people own houses," remarked a printer from Fall River, Massachusetts, "you will generally find that it is a large family all working together."

Autonomous Labor

No one supervised the nineteenth-century coal miner. He was a tonnage worker, paid for the amount of coal he produced. He provided his own tools, worked at his own pace, and knocked off early when he chose. Such autonomous craft workers—almost all of them men—flourished in many branches of nineteenth-century industry. They were mule spinners in cotton mills; puddlers and rollers in iron works; molders in stove making; and machinists, glass blowers, and skilled workers in many other industries.

In the shop they abided by the *stint*, a self-imposed limit on how much they would produce each day. This informal system of restricting output infuriated efficiency-minded engineers. But to the worker it signified personal dignity and "unselfish brotherhood" with fellow employees. The male craft worker took pride in a "manly" bearing, toward both his fellows and the boss. One day a shop in Lowell, Massachusetts, posted regulations requiring all employees to be at their posts in

Breaker Boys

In the anthracite districts of eastern Pennsylvania, giant machines called "breakers" processed the coal as it came out of the mines, crushing it and sorting it by size for sale as domestic fuel. The boys shown in this photograph had the job of picking out the stones as the processed coal came down the chutes, working long hours in a constant cloud of coal dust for less than a dollar a day. Breaker boy was the first job, often begun before the age of ten, in a lifetime in the mines. The photograph does not show any old men, but sick and disabled miners often ended their careers as breaker boys—hence the saying among coal diggers, "Twice a boy and once a man is the poor miner's life."

Library of Congress.

work clothes at the opening bell and to remain, with the shop door locked, until the dismissal bell. A machinist promptly packed his tools, declaring that he had not "been brought up under such a system of slavery."

Underlying this ethical code was a keen sense of the craft, each with its own history and customs. Hat finishers—masters of the art of applying fur felting to top hats and bowlers—had a language of their own. When a hatter was hired, he was "shopped"; if fired, he was "bagged"; when he quit work, he "cried off"; and when he took an apprentice, the boy was "under teach." The hatters, most of whom worked in Danbury, Connecticut, or Orange, New Jersey, formed a distinctive, self-contained community.

Women workers found much the same kind of social meaning in their jobs. Department-store clerks, for example, developed a work culture and language just as robust as that of any male craft group. The most important fact about wage-earning women, however, was their youth. For many their first job was a chance to be independent, to form friendships with other young women, and to experience, however briefly, a fun-loving time of nice clothes, dancing, and other "cheap amusements." Young male workers, by contrast, underwent a process of job socialization presided over by seasoned, older coworkers. Being young mattered to male workers, certainly, but did not define work experience for them as it did for women.

To some degree their youthful preoccupations made it easier for working women to accept the miserable terms under which they labored. But this did not mean that they lacked a sense of solidarity or self-respect. A pretty dress might appear frivolous to the casual observer but also conveyed the message that the working girl considered herself as good as anyone. Rebellious youth culture sometimes united with job grievances to produce astonishing strike movements, as demonstrated, for example, after the turn of the century by the Jewish garment workers of New York and the Irish American telephone operators of Boston.

Rarely, however, did women workers wield the kind of craft power that the skilled male worker commonly enjoyed. He hired his own helpers, supervised their work, and paid them from his earnings. In the late nineteenth century, when increasingly sophisticated production called for closer shop-floor supervision, many factory managers deliberately shifted this responsibility to craft workers. In metal-fabricating firms that did precise machining and complex assembling, a system of inside contracting developed in which skilled employees bid for a production run, taking full responsibility for the operation, paying their crew and pocketing the profits.

Dispersal of authority was characteristic of nineteenth-century industry. The aristocracy of the workers—the craftsmen, inside contractors, and foremen—enjoyed a high degree of autonomy. However, their subordinates often paid dearly for that independence. Any worker who paid his helpers from his own pocket might be tempted to exploit them. In the Pittsburgh area foremen were known as "pushers," notorious for driving their gangs mercilessly. On the other hand industrial labor in the nineteenth century remained on a human scale. People dealt with each other face to face, often developing cohesive ties within the shop. Striking craft workers commonly received the support of helpers and laborers, and labor gangs sometimes walked out on behalf of a popular foreman.

Systems of Control

As technology advanced, workers increasingly lost the proud independence characteristic of nineteenth-century craft work. One cause of this de-skilling process was a new system of manufacture—Henry Ford called it "mass production"—that lent itself to mechanization. Agricultural implements, typewriters, bicycles, and, after 1900, automobiles were assembled from standardized parts. The **machine tools** that cut, drilled, and ground these metal parts were originally operated by skilled machinists. But because they produced long runs of a single item, these machine tools became more specialized; they became *dedicated* machines—machines set up to do the same job over and over without the need for skilled operatives. In the manufacture of sewing machines, one machinist complained in 1883, "the trade is so subdivided that a man is not considered a machinist at all. One man may make just a particular part of a machine and may not know anything whatever about another part of the same machine." Such a worker, noted an observer, "cannot be master of a craft, but only master of a fragment."

Employers were attracted to automatic machinery because it increased output. Mechanization also made it easier to control workers, but that was only an incidental benefit. Gradually, however, the idea took hold that focusing on workers—getting them to work harder or more efficiently—might itself be a way to reduce the cost of production.

The pioneer in this field was Frederick W. Taylor. An expert on metal-cutting methods, Taylor believed that the engineer's approach might be applied to managing workers, hence the name for his method: **scientific management**. To get the maximum work from the individual worker, Taylor suggested two basic reforms. First, eliminate the brain work from manual labor. Managers would assume "the burden of gathering together all of the traditional knowledge which in the past has been possessed by the workmen and then of classifying, tabulating, and reducing this knowledge to rules, laws, and formulae." Second, deprive workers of the authority they had exercised on the shop floor. Workers would "do what they are told promptly and without asking questions or making suggestions. . . . The duty of enforcing . . . rests with the management alone."

Once managers had the knowledge and the power, they would put labor on a "scientific" basis. This meant subjecting each task to *time-and-motion study* by an engineer who would analyze and time each job with a stopwatch. Workers would be paid at a differential rate—that is, a certain amount if they met the stopwatch standard and a higher rate for additional output. Taylor claimed that his techniques would guarantee optimum worker efficiency. His assumption was that only money mattered to workers and that they would automatically respond to the lure of higher earnings.

Scientific management was not, in practice, a great success. Implementing it proved to be very expensive, and workers stubbornly resisted the job-analysis method. "It looks to me like slavery to have a man stand over you with a stopwatch," complained one iron molder. A union leader insisted that "this system is wrong, because we want our heads left on us." Far from solving the labor problem, as Taylor claimed it would, scientific management embittered relations on the shop floor.

Yet Taylor achieved something of fundamental importance. He was a brilliant publicist, and his teachings spread throughout American industry. Taylor's disciples moved beyond his simplistic economic psychology, creating the new fields of personnel work and industrial psychology, whose practitioners purported to know how to extract more and better labor from workers. A threshold had been crossed into the modern era of labor management.

So the circle closed on American workers. With each advance the quest for efficiency eroded their cherished autonomy, diminishing them and cutting them down to fit the industrial system. The process occurred unevenly. For textile workers the loss had come early. Miners and ironworkers felt it much more slowly. Others, such as construction workers, escaped almost entirely. But increasing numbers of workers found themselves in an environment that crushed any sense of mastery or even understanding.

The Labor Movement

Wherever industrialization took hold, workers organized and formed labor unions. The movements they built, however, varied from one industrial society to another. In the United States workers were especially uncertain about the best path. Only in the 1880s did the American labor movement settle onto a steady course.

Reformers and Unionists

Thomas B. McGuire, a New York wagon driver, was ambitious. He had saved $300 from his wages "so that I might become something of a capitalist eventually." But his venture as a cab driver in the early 1880s soon failed:

> Corporations usually take that business themselves. They can manage to get men, at starvation wages, and put them on a hack, and put a livery on them with a gold band and brass buttons, to show that they are slaves—I beg pardon; I did not intend to use the word slaves; there are no slaves in this country now—to show that they are merely servants.

Slave or liveried servant, the symbolic meaning was the same to McGuire. He was speaking of the crushed aspirations of the independent American worker.

What would satisfy the Thomas McGuires of the nineteenth century? Only the establishment of an egalitarian society, one in which every citizen might hope to become economically independent. This republican goal did not mean returning to the agrarian past, but rather replacing the existing wage system with a more just order that did not distinguish between capitalists and workers. All would be "producers," laboring together in what was commonly called the "cooperative commonwealth." This was the ideal that inspired the Noble and Holy Order of the Knights of Labor.

Founded in 1869 as a secret society of garment workers in Philadelphia, the Knights of Labor spread to other cities and by 1878 emerged as a national movement. The Knights boasted an elaborate ritual calculated to appeal to the fraternal spirit of nineteenth-century workers. The local assemblies of the Knights engendered a spirit of comradeship very much like that offered by the Masons or Odd Fellows. For the Knights, however, fraternalism was harnessed to labor reform. The goal was to "give voice to that grand undercurrent of mighty thought, which is today [1880] crystallizing in the hearts of men, and urging them on to perfect organization through which to gain the power to make labor emancipation possible."

But how was "emancipation" to be achieved? Through cooperation, the Knights argued. They intended to set up factories and shops that would be owned and run by the employees. As these cooperatives flourished, American society would be transformed into a cooperative commonwealth. But little was actually done. Instead the Knights devoted themselves to "education." Their leader, Grand Master Workman Terence V. Powderly, regarded the organization as a vast labor college open to all but lawyers and saloonkeepers. The cooperative commonwealth would arrive in some mysterious way as more and more "producers" became members and learned the group's message from lectures, discussions, and publications. Social evil would not end in a day but "must await the gradual development of educational enlightenment."

The labor reformers, exemplified by the Knights, expressed the grander aspirations of American workers. Another kind of organization—the trade union—tended to their everyday needs. Ever since they first appeared early in the century, unions had been at the center of the lives of craft workers. Apprenticeship rules regulated entry into a trade, and the **closed shop**—reserving all jobs for union members—kept out lower-wage and incompetent workers. Union rules specified the terms of work, sometimes in minute detail. Above all, trade unionism defended the craft worker's traditional skills and rights.

The trade union also expressed the craft's social identity. Hatters took pride in their alcohol consumption, an on-the-job privilege that was jealously guarded. More often craft unions had an uplifting character. A Birmingham iron puddler claimed that his union's "main object was to educate mechanics up to a standard of morality and temperance, and good workmanship." Some unions emphasized mutual aid. Because operating trains was a high-risk occupation, the railroad brotherhoods provided accident and death benefits and encouraged members to assist one another. On and off the job, the unions played a big part in the lives of craft workers.

The earliest unions were local craft organizations, sometimes, especially among German workers, limited to a single ethnic group. As expanding markets intruded, breaking down their ability to control local conditions, unions began to form national organizations. The first was the International Typographical Union in 1852. By the 1870s molders, ironworkers, bricklayers, and about thirty other trades had done likewise. The national union, uniting local unions of the same trade, was becoming the dominant organizational form in America.

The practical job interests that trade unions espoused might have seemed a far cry from the idealism of the Knights of Labor. But both kinds of motives arose from a single workers' culture. Seeing no conflict, many workers carried membership cards in both the Knights and a trade union. And because the Knights, once established in a town or city, tended to become politically active and field independent slates of candidates, that too became a magnet attracting trade unionists interested in local politics.

Trade unions generally barred women, and so did the Knights until 1881, when women shoe workers in Philadelphia struck in support of their male coworkers and won the right to form their own local assembly. By 1886 probably 50,000 women belonged to the Knights of Labor. Their courage on the picket line prompted Powderly's rueful remark that women "are the best men in the Order." For a handful of women, such as the hosiery worker Leonora M. Barry, the Knights provided a rare chance to take up leadership roles as organizers and officials.

Similarly, the Knights of Labor grudgingly opened the door for black workers, out of the need for solidarity and, just as important, in deference to the Order's egalitarian principles. The Knights could rightly boast that their "great work has been to organize labor which was previously unorganized."

The Triumph of "Pure and Simple" Unionism

In the early 1880s the Knights began to act more and more like trade unions. Boycott campaigns against the products of "unfair" employers achieved impressive results. With the economy booming and workers in short supply, the Knights began to win strikes, including a major victory against Jay Gould's Southwestern railway system in 1885. Workers flocked to the organization, and its membership jumped from 100,000 to perhaps 700,000. For a brief time the Knights stood poised as a potential industrial-union movement capable of bringing all workers into its fold.

The rapid growth of the Knights frightened the national trade unions. They began to insist on a clear separation of roles, with the Knights confined to labor reform. This was partly a battle over turf, but it reflected also a deepening divergence of labor philosophies.

Samuel Gompers, a cigar maker from New York City, led the ideological assault on the Knights, hammering out the philosophical position that would become known as "pure and simple" unionism. His starting point was that grand theories and schemes like those that excited the labor reformers should be strictly avoided. Unions, Gompers thought, should focus on concrete, achievable gains, and they should organize workers not as an undifferentiated mass of "producers" but by craft and occupation. The battleground should be at the workplace, where workers could best mobilize their power, not in the quicksands of politics (see American Voices, "Trade Unionist," p. 529). "No matter how just," said Gompers, "unless the cause is backed up with power to enforce it, it is going to be crushed and annihilated."

The struggle for the eight-hour day crystallized the conflict between the rival movements. Both, of course, favored a shorter workday, but for different reasons. For the Knights more leisure was desirable because workers had duties "to perform as American citizens and members of society." Trade unionists took a more hard-boiled view: the eight-hour day would spread the available jobs among more workers, protect them against overwork, and give them an easier life. When the trade unions set May 1, 1886, as the deadline for achieving the eight-hour day, the leadership of the Knights objected. But workers everywhere responded enthusiastically, and as the deadline approached, a wave of strikes and demonstrations broke out across the country.

At one such eight-hour-day strike, at the McCormick reaper works in Chicago, a battle erupted on May 3, leaving four strikers dead. Chicago was a hotbed of **anarchism**—the revolutionary advocacy of a stateless society—and local anarchists, most of them German immigrants, called a protest meeting the next evening at Haymarket Square. When police began to disperse the crowd, someone threw a bomb that killed and wounded several of the police, who responded with wild

Samuel Gompers

This is a photograph of the labor leader in his forties taken when he was visiting striking miners in West Virginia, an area where mine operators resisted unions with special fierceness. The photograph was taken by a company detective.

George Meany Memorial Archives.

gunfire. Most of the casualties, including some policemen, came from police bullets. Despite no evidence of their involvement, the anarchists were found guilty of murder and criminal conspiracy. Four were executed, one committed suicide, and the others received long prison sentences. They were victims of one of the great miscarriages of American justice.

Seizing on the antiunion hysteria set off by the Haymarket affair, employers took the offensive. They broke strikes violently, compiled blacklists of strikers, and forced workers to sign **yellow-dog contracts**, in which, as a condition of employment, they pledged not to join a labor organization. If trade unionists needed any confirmation of the tough world in which they lived, they found it in Haymarket and its aftermath.

In December 1886, having failed to persuade the Knights of Labor to desist from union activity, the national trade unions formed the American Federation of Labor (AFL), with Samuel Gompers as president. The AFL in effect locked into place the trade-union structure as it had evolved by the 1880s. Underlying this structure was the conviction that workers had to take the world as it was, not as

AMERICAN VOICES

Trade Unionist

ROSE SCHNEIDERMAN

*R*ose Schneiderman (1882–1972) typified the young Jewish garment workers who became
the firebrands of their Manhattan industry. Schneiderman went on to an illustrious career as a labor organizer and social reformer. At the time of her initiation, recorded below, she
was twenty-one years old.

We had no idea that there was a union in our industry and that women could join it. Nor
did we have a full realization of the hardships we were needlessly undergoing. There was
the necessity of owning a sewing machine before you could work. Then you had to buy
your own thread. But the worst of it was the incredibly inefficient way in which work was
distributed. Because we were all pieceworkers, any time lost during the season was a real
hardship. . . .

We formed a committee composed of my friend Bessie Mannis, who worked with me,
myself, and a third girl. Bravely we ventured into the office of the United Cloth Hat and
Cap Makers Union. . . . We were told that we would have to have at least twenty-five
women. . . . We waited at the doors of factories and, as the girls were leaving for the day, we
would approach them and speak our piece. . . . Within days we had the necessary number,
and in January 1903 we were chartered as Local 23, and I was elected secretary. . . .

The only cloud in the picture was mother's attitude toward my becoming a trade unionist. She kept saying I'd never get married because I was so busy—a prophecy which came
true. . . .

That June we decided to put our strength to the test. . . . On Saturdays . . . we women
had to hang around until three or four o'clock before getting our pay. I headed a committee which informed Mr. Fox that we wanted to be paid at the same time as the men.

. . . He didn't say outright that he agreed; he wouldn't give us that much satisfaction. But
on the first Saturday in July, when we went for our pay at twelve noon, there it was ready
for us.

SOURCE: Rose Schneiderman, *All for One* (1967), reprinted in Irving Howe and Kenneth Libo, eds., *How
We Lived* (New York: New American Library, 1979), pp. 139–41.

they dreamed it might be. At this point the American movement swung away from
its European counterparts, for Gompers's AFL was in opposition to a political
party for workers.

The Knights of Labor never recovered from Haymarket. Powderly retreated to
the rhetoric of labor reform, but wage earners had lost interest. By the mid-1890s the
Knights of Labor had faded away. In the meantime the AFL took firm root, justify-
ing Gompers's confidence that he had found the correct formula for the American
labor movement.

Industrial War

American trade unions were conservative. They accepted the economic order. All they wanted was a larger share for working people. But it was precisely that claim against company earnings that made American employers so opposed to **collective bargaining**. In the 1890s they unleashed a fierce counterattack on the trade-union movement.

In Homestead, Pennsylvania, the site of one of Carnegie's steel mills, the skilled workers thought themselves safe from that threat. They earned good wages, lived comfortably, and generally owned their own homes. They elected fellow workers to public office and considered the town very much their community. And they had faith in Andrew Carnegie—for had not Good Old Andy said in a famous magazine article that workers had as sacred a right to combine as did capitalists and that workers had a moral claim on their jobs that forbade the use of strikebreakers by employers?

Espousing high-toned principles made Carnegie feel good, but a healthy profit made him feel even better. He decided that collective bargaining had become too expensive, and he was confident that his skilled workers could be replaced by the advanced machinery he was installing. Lacking the stomach for the hard battle, Carnegie fled to a remote estate in Scotland, leaving behind a second-in-command well qualified to do the dirty work. This was Henry Clay Frick, a former coal baron and a veteran of labor wars in the coal fields.

After a brief pretense at bargaining, Frick announced that effective July 1, 1892, the company would no longer deal with the Amalgamated Association of Iron and Steel Workers. If the employees wanted to work, they would have to come back on an individual basis. The mill had already been fortified so that strikebreakers could be brought in to resume operations. At stake for Carnegie's employees now were not just wage cuts but the defense of a way of life. The town mayor, a union man, turned away the county sheriff when he tried to take possession of the plant. The entire community mobilized in defense of the union.

At dawn on July 6 barges were seen approaching Homestead up the Monongahela River. On board were armed guards hired by the Pinkerton Detective Agency to take possession of the steel works. Behind hastily erected barricades the strikers opened fire, and a bloody battle ensued. When the Pinkertons surrendered they were mercilessly pummeled by the enraged women of Homestead as they retreated to the railway station. Frick appealed to the governor of Pennsylvania, who called out the state militia and placed Homestead under martial law. The great steel works was taken over and opened to strikebreakers, while union leaders and town officials were arrested on charges of riot, murder, and treason.

The defeat at Homestead marked the beginning of the end for trade unions in the steel industry. Ended too were any lingering illusions about the sanctity of workers' communities like Homestead. "Men talk like anarchists or lunatics when they insist that the workmen of Homestead have done right," asserted one conservative journal. Nothing could be permitted to interfere with Carnegie's property rights or threaten law and order.

The Homestead strike ushered in a decade of strife that pitted working people against the formidable power of corporate industry and the even more formidable power of their own government. That hard reality was driven home to workers at a place that seemed an even less likely site for class warfare than Homestead.

Pullman, Illinois, was a model factory town, famous for the beauty of its landscaping and city plan. Built in 1880, the town was named for its creator, George M. Pullman, inventor of the sleeping car that brought comfort and luxury to railway travel. When business fell off during the economic depression in 1893, Pullman cut wages but not the rents for company housing. When a workers' committee complained in May 1894, Pullman denied that there was any connection between his roles as employer and landlord. He then fired the workers' committee.

The strike that ensued would have warranted only a footnote in American labor history but for the fact that the Pullman workers belonged to the American Railway Union (ARU), a rapidly growing, new union of railroad workers. Its leader, Eugene V. Debs, directed ARU members not to handle Pullman sleeping cars, which, although operated by the railroads, were owned and serviced by the Pullman Company. This was a *secondary labor boycott*: force was applied on a second party (the railroads) to bring pressure on the primary target (Pullman). Since the railroads insisted on running the Pullman cars, a far-flung strike soon spread across the country, threatening the entire economy.

The railroads maneuvered quietly to bring the federal government into the dispute. Their hook was the U.S. mail cars, which they attached to every train hauling Pullman cars. When strikers stopped these trains, the railroads appealed to President Cleveland to protect the U.S. mail and halt the growing violence. Richard Olney, Cleveland's attorney general, was a former railroad lawyer who unabashedly sided with his former employers. When federal troops failed to get the trains running again, Olney obtained court injunctions prohibiting the ARU leaders from conducting the strike. Debs and his associates refused to obey, were charged with contempt of court, and jailed. Now leaderless and uncoordinated, the strike quickly disintegrated.

No one could doubt why the great Pullman boycott had failed: it had been crushed by the naked use of government power on behalf of the railroad companies.

American Radicalism in the Making

Oppression does not radicalize every victim, but some it does radicalize. And when social injustice is most painfully felt, when the underlying power realities stand openly revealed, the process of radicalization speeds up. Such was the case during the depression of the 1890s. Out of the industrial strife of that decade emerged the main forces of twentieth-century American radicalism.

Very little in Eugene Debs's background would have suggested that he would one day become the nation's leading socialist. A native of Terre Haute, Indiana, a prosperous railroad town, Debs grew up believing in the essential goodness of American society. A popular young man-about-town, Debs considered a career in politics or business but instead became involved in the local labor movement. In 1880, at the age of twenty-five, he was elected national secretary-treasurer of the Brotherhood of Locomotive Firemen, one of the craft unions that represented the skilled operating trades on the railroads.

Troubled by his union's indifference to the low-paid track and yard laborers, Debs unexpectedly resigned from his comfortable post to devote himself to a new organization, the American Railway Union, that would organize all railroad workers irrespective of skill—that is, an *industrial union*.

The Pullman strike visibly changed Debs. Sentenced to six months in a federal prison on what he regarded as trumped-up charges, Debs emerged an avowed radical, committed to a lifelong struggle against a system that enabled employers to enlist the powers of government to beat down working people. Initially, Debs identified himself as a Populist (see Chapter 19), but he quickly gravitated to the Socialist camp.

German refugees had brought the ideas of Karl Marx, the radical German theorist, to America after the failed revolutions of 1848 in Europe. Marx postulated a class struggle between capitalists and workers, ending in a revolution that would abolish private ownership of the means of production and bring about a classless society. Little noticed by most Americans, Marxist socialism struck deep roots in the German American communities of Chicago and New York. With the formation of the Socialist Labor Party in 1877, Marxist socialism established itself as a permanent, if narrowly based, presence in American politics.

When Eugene Debs appeared in their midst in 1897, the Socialists were in disarray. American capitalism had just gone through its worst crisis, yet they had failed to make much headway. Many blamed the party head, Daniel De Leon, who considered ideological purity more important than winning elections. Debs joined in the revolt against the dogmatic De Leon and helped launch the rival Socialist Party of America in 1901.

A spellbinding campaigner, Debs talked socialism in an American idiom, making Marxism understandable and persuasive to many ordinary citizens. Under him the new party began to break out of its immigrant base and attract American-born voters. In Texas, Oklahoma, and Minnesota, socialism exerted a powerful appeal among distressed farmers. The party was also highly successful at attracting women activists. Inside of a decade, with a national network of branches and state organizations, the Socialist Party had become a force to be reckoned with in American politics.

Farther west a different brand of American radicalism was taking shape. After many years of mostly friendly relations, the atmosphere in the western mining camps turned ugly during the 1890s. The powerful new corporations that were taking over wanted to be rid of the miners' union, the Western Federation of Miners (WFM). Moreover, silver and copper prices began to drop, bringing pressure to cut miners' wages. When strikes resulted, they took an especially violent turn.

In 1892 at Coeur d'Alene, a silver-mining district in northern Idaho, striking miners engaged in gun battles with company guards, sent a car of explosive powder careering into the Frisco mine, and threatened to blow up the smelters. Martial law was declared, the strikers were imprisoned in stockades, and the strike was broken. In subsequent miners' strikes, government intervention was equally naked and unrestrained. This was partly because of labor's violence, but also because of the politics of the lightly settled western states: either the miners would dominate—as they did in coalition with the Populists in Colorado in the mid-1890s—or, as was increasingly true, the mine owners would dominate, with disastrous consequences for the miners. By 1897 the WFM president, Ed Boyce, was calling on all union members to arm themselves, and his rhetoric—he called the wage system "slavery in its worst form"—developed a hard edge.

Led by the fiery Boyce and "Big Bill" Haywood, the Western Federation of Miners joined in 1905 with left-wing Socialists to create a new movement, the Industrial Workers of the World (IWW). The Wobblies, as IWW members were called, fervently supported the Marxist class struggle—but at the workplace rather than in politics. By resistance at the point of production and ultimately by means of a **general strike**, they believed that the workers would bring about a revolution. A new society would emerge, run directly by the workers through their industrial unions. The term *syndicalism* describes this brand of workers' radicalism.

In both its major forms—politically oriented Socialism and the syndicalist IWW—American radicalism flourished after the crisis of the 1890s, but only on a limited basis and never with the possibility of seizing national power. Nevertheless, Socialists and Wobblies served a larger purpose. American radicalism, by its sheer vitality, bore witness to what was exploitative and unjust in the new industrial order.

T I M E L I N E

1869	Knights of Labor founded in Philadelphia	1892	Homestead steel strike crushed
			Wave of western miners' strikes begins
1872	Andrew Carnegie starts construction of Edgar Thomson steelworks	1893	Panic of 1893 leads to national depression
1873	Panic of 1873 ushers in economic depression		Surge of railroad bankruptcies; reorganization by investment bankers begins
		1894	President Cleveland sends troops to break Pullman boycott
1875	John Wanamaker establishes first department store in Philadelphia		
		1895	Southeastern European immigration exceeds northern European immigration for first time
1877	Baltimore and Ohio workers trigger nationwide railroad strike		
			Frederick W. Taylor formulates scientific management
1878	Gustavus Swift introduces refrigerator car		
1883	Railroads establish national time zones	1901	Eugene V. Debs helps found Socialist Party of America
1886	Haymarket Square bombing in Chicago American Federation of Labor (AFL) founded	1905	Industrial Workers of the World (IWW) launched

For Further Exploration

For students new to economic history, biography offers an accessible entry point into what can be a dauntingly technical subject. The biographical literature is especially rich in American history because of this country's fascination with its great magnates and because of a long-standing debate among historians over what contribution, if any, the business moguls made to America's industrializing economy. The initiating book is Matthew Josephson's classic, *The Robber Barons* (1934), which, as the title implies, argues that America's great fortunes were built on the wealth that others had created. The contrary view is taken by the financial historian Julius Grodinsky, whose *Jay Gould: His Business Career, 1867–1892* (1957) explains masterfully how this railroad buccaneer helped shape the transportation system. Since then, there have been superb, mostly sympathetic, business biographies, including Joseph F. Wall, *Andrew Carnegie* (1970); Ron Chernow, *Titan: The Life of John D. Rockefeller* (1998), Jean Strause, *Morgan: American Financier* (1999), and for the man who revolutionized the newspaper business, David Nasaw, *The Chief: The Life of William Randolph Hearst* (2002). The founder of scientific management has also recently been the subject of a robust biography: Robert Kanigel, *The One Best Way: Frederick W. Taylor and the Enigma of Efficiency* (1997).

On labor's side, the biographical literature is nearly as rich. The founder of the AFL is the subject of a lively brief biography by Harold Livesay, *Samuel Gompers and Organized Labor in America* (1978); Gompers's autobiography, *Seventy Years of Life and Labor* (2 vols., 1925), also makes rewarding reading. His main critic is treated with great insight in Nick Salvatore, *Eugene V. Debs: Citizen and Socialist* (1982). The IWW leader William D. Haywood left a colorful autobiography, *Bill Haywood's Book* (1929), and Haywood is also the subject of Peter Carlson's biography, *Roughneck* (1982). Biography, of course, tends to overlook the foot soldiers of history, but social historians have striven mightily in recent years to tell their story. An excellent example is Paul Krause, *The Battle for Homestead, 1880–1892* (1992), which rescues from obscurity the working people who led that decisive steel strike. There is an excellent Web site on Andrew Carnegie at <pbs.org/wgbh/amex/pandeoi.html> and a site on the Bessemer converter that established his dominance in steel at <anglia.co.uk/angmulti/indrev/steel5.html>.

For definitions of key terms boldfaced in this chapter, see the glossary at the end of the book.

To assess your mastery of the material covered in this chapter, see the Online Study Guide at **bedfordstmartins.com/henrettaconcise**.

For map resources and primary documents, see **bedfordstmartins.com/henrettaconcise**.

Chapter 18

THE RISE OF THE CITY

> These vast aggregations of humanity, where he who seeks isolation
> may find it more truly than in a desert; where wealth and poverty
> touch and jostle; where one revels and another starves within a few
> feet of each other—they are the centers and types of our
> civilization.
>
> HENRY GEORGE, 1883

Visiting his fiancée's Missouri homestead in 1894, Theodore Dreiser was struck by "the spirit of rural America, its idealism, its dreams." But this was an "American tradition in which I, alas, could not share." Said Dreiser, "I had seen Pittsburgh. I had seen Lithuanians and Hungarians in their [alleys] and hovels. I had seen the girls of the city—walking the streets at night." Only twenty-three at the time, Dreiser would go on to write one of the great American urban novels, *Sister Carrie* (1900), about one young woman in the army of small-town Americans flocking to the Big City. But Dreiser, part of that army, already knew that between rural America and Pittsburgh an unbridgeable chasm had opened up.

In 1820, after two hundred years of settlement, fewer than one in twenty Americans lived in a city of 10,000 people or more. After that, decade by decade, the urban population swelled until, by 1900, one of every five Americans was a city dweller. Nearly 6.5 million inhabited just three great cities: New York, Chicago, and Philadelphia (Table 18.1).

The city was the arena of the nation's vibrant economic life. Here the factories went up, and here the new immigrants settled, constituting in 1900 a third of the residents of the major American cities. Here, too, lived the millionaires and a growing white-collar middle class. For all these people the city was more than a place to make a living. It provided the setting for an urban culture unlike anything seen before in the United States. City people, although differing vastly among themselves, became distinctively and recognizably urban.

TABLE 18.1 Ten Largest Cities by Population, 1870 and 1900

1870		1900	
City	*Population*	*City*	*Population*
1. New York	942,292	New York	3,437,202
2. Philadelphia	674,022	Chicago	1,698,575
3. Brooklyn*	419,921	Philadelphia	1,293,697
4. St. Louis	310,864	St. Louis	575,238
5. Chicago	298,977	Boston	560,892
6. Baltimore	267,354	Baltimore	508,957
7. Boston	250,526	Cleveland	381,768
8. Cincinnati	216,239	Buffalo, N.Y.	352,387
9. New Orleans	191,418	San Francisco	342,782
10. San Francisco	149,473	Cincinnati	325,902

*Brooklyn was consolidated with New York in 1898.
Source: U.S. Census data.

Urbanization

The march to the cities seemed irresistible to nineteenth-century Americans. "The greater part of our population must live in cities," declared the Congregational minister Josiah Strong. And from another writer: "There was no resisting the trend." Urbanization became inevitable because of another inevitability of American life—industrialism.

Until the Civil War, cities lived on commerce, not industry. They were the places where goods were bought and sold for distribution into the interior or out to world markets. Early industry, on the other hand, sprang up mostly in the countryside, where factories had access to water power from streams, nearby fuel and raw materials, and workers recruited from farms and villages.

As industrialization proceeded, city and factory began to merge. Once steam engines came along, mill operators no longer depended on water-driven power. Railroads freed entrepreneurs to locate their factories at places best situated in relation to suppliers and markets. Iron makers gravitated to Pittsburgh because of its superior access to coal and ore fields. Chicago, midway between western livestock suppliers and eastern markets, became a great meatpacking center. Geographic concentration of industry meant urban growth. And so did the rising scale of production. A plant that employed thousands of workers instantly created a small city in its vicinity, sometimes in the form of a company town like Aliquippa, Pennsylvania, which became body and soul the property of the Jones and Laughlin Steel Company. Other firms built big plants at the edge of large cities so that they could draw on the available labor supply and transportation facilities.

Older commercial cities meanwhile became more industrial. Warehouse districts could readily be converted to small-scale manufacturing; a distribution network was right at hand. In addition, as gateways for immigrants, port cities offered abundant cheap labor. Boston, Philadelphia, Baltimore, and San Francisco became hives of small-scale, labor-intensive industrial activity. New York's enormous pool of immigrant workers made that city a magnet for the garment trades, cigar making, and diversified light industry. Preeminent as a city of trade and finance, New York also ranked as the nation's largest manufacturing center.

City Innovation

Cities grew larger under the impact of industrialism. In so doing, they encountered staggering problems. How would so many people move around, communicate, have their physical meets met? The city demanded innovation no less than did industry itself and, in the end, compiled just as impressive a record of technological achievement.

The older commercial cities had been compact places, densely settled around harbors or riverfronts. As late as 1850, when it had 565,000 people, Philadelphia covered only ten square miles. From the foot of Chestnut Street on the Delaware River, a person could walk almost anywhere in the city within forty-five minutes. Thereafter, as it developed, Philadelphia spilled out and, like American cities everywhere, engulfed the surrounding countryside.

A downtown area emerged, usually on the site of the original commercial city. Downtown in turn broke up into shopping, financial, warehousing, manufacturing, hotel and entertainment, and red-light districts. Moving out from the center, industrial development tended to follow the arteries of transportation—railroads, canals, and rivers—and, at the city's outskirts, to create concentrations of heavy industry.

"The only trouble about this town," wrote Mark Twain on arriving in New York in 1867, "is that it is too large. You cannot accomplish anything in the way of business, you cannot even pay a friendly call without devoting a whole day to it. . . . [The] distances are too great." Moving nearly a million New Yorkers around was not as hopeless as Twain thought, but it did challenge the ingenuity of city builders.

The first innovation, dating back to the 1820s, was the omnibus, an elongated version of the horse-drawn carriage. More efficient was the horsecar, whose key advantage was that it ran on iron tracks so that the horses could pull more passengers at a faster clip through congested city streets. The chief objection to tracks was resolved by a modest but crucial refinement in 1852—a grooved rail that was flush with the pavement. Then came the electric trolley car, the brainchild primarily of Frank J. Sprague, an engineer once employed by the great inventor Thomas A. Edison. In 1887 Sprague designed an electric-driven system for Richmond, Virginia: a "trolley" carriage running along an overhead power line was attached by cable to streetcars equipped with an electric motor—hence the name "trolley car." After Sprague's success, the trolley swiftly displaced the horsecar and became the primary mode of transportation in most American cities.

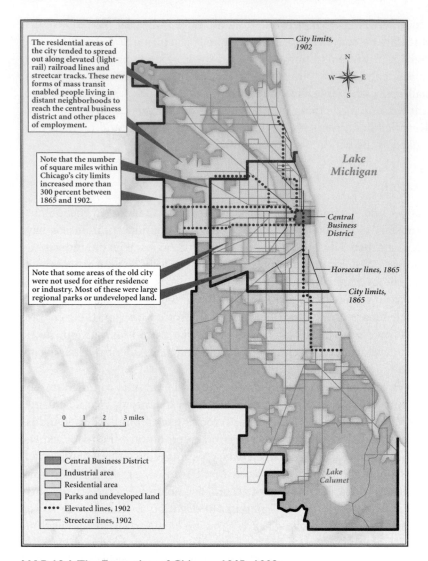

The residential areas of the city tended to spread out along elevated (light-rail) railroad lines and streetcar tracks. These new forms of mass transit enabled people living in distant neighborhoods to reach the central business district and other places of employment.

Note that the number of square miles within Chicago's city limits increased more than 300 percent between 1865 and 1902.

Note that some areas of the old city were not used for either residence or industry. Most of these were large regional parks or undeveloped land.

City limits, 1902

Lake Michigan

Central Business District

Horsecar lines, 1865

City limits, 1865

0   1   2   3 miles

Lake Calumet

- Central Business District
- Industrial area
- Residential area
- Parks and undeveloped land
- •••• Elevated lines, 1902
- — Streetcar lines, 1902

MAP 18.1 The Expansion of Chicago, 1865–1902

In 1865 Chicagoans depended on horsecar lines to get around town. By 1900 the city limits had expanded enormously and so had the streetcar service, which was by then electrified. Elevated trains eased the congestion on downtown streets. And the continuing extension of the streetcar lines, some beyond the city limits, assured that suburban development would be continuing as well.

FOR MORE HELP ANALYZING THIS MAP, see the Online Study Guide at **bedfordstmartins.com/henrettaconcise**.

In the great metropolitan centers, however, congestion led to demands that transit lines be moved off the streets. In 1879 the first elevated railroads went into operation on Sixth and Ninth Avenues in New York City. Powered at first by steam engines, the "els" converted to electricity following Sprague's success with the trolley. Chicago developed elevated transit most fully (Map 18.1). Others looked below ground.

Boston opened a short underground line in 1897, but it was the completion in 1904 of a subway running the length of Manhattan that demonstrated the full potential of the high-speed underground train. Mass transit had become *rapid* transit.

Equally remarkable was the architectural revolution sweeping metropolitan business districts. With steel girders, durable plate glass, and the passenger elevator available by the 1880s, a wholly new way of construction opened up. A steel skeleton supported the building, while the walls, previously weight bearing, served as curtains enclosing the structure. The sky, so to speak, became the limit.

The first "skyscraper" to be built on this principle was William Jenney's ten-story Home Insurance Building (1885) in Chicago. Although unremarkable in appearance—it looked just like the other downtown buildings—the steel-girder technology Jenney's building contained liberated the aesthetic perceptions of American architects. A Chicago school sprang up, dedicated to the design of buildings whose form expressed, rather than masked, their structure and function. Chicago pioneered skyscraper construction, but New York, with its unrelenting need for prime downtown space, took the lead after the mid-1890s. The fifty-five story Woolworth Building, completed in 1913, marked the beginning of the modern Manhattan skyline.

For ordinary citizens the electric lights that dispelled the gloom at night offered the most dramatic evidence that times had changed. Gaslight—illuminated gas produced from coal—had been in use since the early nineteenth century but, at 12 candlepower, the lamps were too dim to brighten the city's downtown streets and public spaces. The first use of electricity, once generating technology made it commercially feasible in the 1870s, was for better city lighting. Charles F. Brush's electric arc lamps, installed in Wanamaker's department store in Philadelphia in 1878, threw a brilliant light and soon replaced gaslight on city streets across the country. Electric lighting then entered the American home, thanks to Thomas Edison's invention of a serviceable incandescent bulb in 1879. Edison's motto—"Let there be light!"—truly described the experience of the modern city.

Before it had any significant effect on industry, electricity gave the city its modern tempo, lifting elevators, powering streetcars and subway trains, turning night into day. Meanwhile, Alexander Graham Bell's telephone (1876) sped communication beyond anything imagined previously. Twain's complaint of 1867, that it was impossible to carry on business in New York, had been answered: all he needed to do was pick up the phone.

Private City, Public City

City building was very much an exercise in private enterprise. The lure of profit spurred the great innovations—the trolley car, electric lighting, the skyscraper, the elevator, the telephone—and drove urban real estate development. The investment opportunities looked so tempting that new cities sprang up almost overnight from the ruins of the Chicago fire of 1871 and the San Francisco earthquake of 1906. Real estate interests, eager to develop subdivisions, often were instrumental in pushing streetcar lines outward from the central districts of cities.

America gave birth to what one urban historian has called the "private city"—shaped primarily by the actions of many individuals, all pursuing their own goals and bent on making money. The prevailing belief was that the sum of such private activity would far exceed what the community could accomplish through public effort.

Yet constitutionally it was up to city governments to draw the line between public and private. New York City was entirely within its rights to operate a municipally owned subway, the State Supreme Court ruled in 1897. Even the use of private land was subject to whatever regulations the city might impose. Thus the skylines of Chicago and Boston did not resemble Manhattan's because of the limits those cities imposed on the heights of buildings. Moreover, city governance improved impressively in the late nineteenth century. Though by no means free of the corruption of earlier days, municipal agencies became far better organized and staffed and, above all, more expansive in the functions they undertook. Nowhere in the world, indeed, were there more massive public projects—aqueducts, sewage systems, bridges, and spacious parks.

In the space between public and private, however, was an environmental no-man's land. City streets were often filthy and poorly maintained. "Three or four days of warm spring weather," remarked a New York journalist, would turn Manhattan's garbage-strewn, snow-clogged streets into "veritable mud rivers." Air quality likewise suffered. A visitor to Pittsburgh noted "the heavy pall of smoke which constantly overhangs her . . . until the very sun looks coppery through the sooty haze." As for the lovely hills rising from the rivers, "they have been leveled down, cut into, sliced off, and ruthlessly marred and mutilated." Pittsburgh presented "all that is unsightly and forbidding in appearance, the original beauties of nature having been ruthlessly sacrificed to utility."

Hardest hit by urban growth were the poor. In earlier times they had mainly lived in makeshift wooden structures in alleys and back streets and then, as more prosperous families moved away, in the subdivided homes left behind. As land values climbed after the Civil War, speculators tore down these houses and began to erect buildings specifically designed for the urban masses. In New York City the dreadful result was five- or six-story *tenements*, structures housing twenty or more families in cramped, airless apartments. In New York's Eleventh Ward, an average of 986 persons occupied each acre, a density only to be exceeded in Bombay, India.

Reformers recognized the problem but seemed unable to solve it. Some favored model tenements financed by public-spirited citizens willing to accept a limited return on their investment. When private philanthropy failed to make much of a dent, cities turned to housing codes. The most advanced code was New York's Tenement House Law of 1901, which required interior courts, indoor toilets, and fire safeguards for new structures, but did little for existing housing stock. Commercial development had pushed up land values in downtown areas. Only high-density, cheaply built housing could earn a sufficient profit for the landlords of the poor. This economic fact defied nineteenth-century solutions.

It was not that America lacked an urban vision. On the contrary, an abiding **rural ideal** had influenced American cities for many years. Frederick Law Olmsted, who designed New York City's Central Park, wanted cities that exposed people to the beauties of nature. One of Olmsted's projects, the Chicago Columbian Exposition of 1893, gave rise to the influential "City Beautiful" movement. The results included larger park systems, broad boulevards and parkways, and after the turn of the century, zoning laws and planned suburbs.

Cities usually heeded urban planners too little and too late. "Fifteen or twenty years ago a plan might have been adopted that would have made this one of the most beautiful cities in the world," Kansas City's park commissioners reported in 1893. At that time "such a policy could not be fully appreciated." Nor, even if Kansas City had foreseen its future, would it have shouldered the "heavy burden" of trying to shape its development. The American city had placed its faith in the dynamics of the marketplace, not the restraints of a planned future. The pluses and minuses are perhaps best revealed by the following comparison.

A Balance Sheet: Chicago and Berlin

Chicago and Berlin, Germany, had virtually equal populations in 1900. But they had very different histories. Seventy years earlier, when Chicago had been a muddy frontier outpost, Berlin was already a city of 250,000 and the royal seat of the Hohenzollerns of Prussia.

With German unification in 1871, the imperial authorities rebuilt Berlin on a grander scale. "A capital city is essential for the state, to act as a pivot for its culture," proclaimed the Prussian historian Heinrich von Treitschke. Berlin served that national purpose—"a center where Germany's political, intellectual, and material life is concentrated, and its people can feel united." Chicago had no such pretensions. It was strictly a place of business, made great by virtue of its strategic grip on the commerce of America's heartland. Nothing in Chicago evoked the grandeur of Berlin's boulevards or its monumental palaces and public buildings, nor were Chicagoans witness to the pomp and ceremony of the imperial parades up broad, tree-lined Unter den Linden to the national cathedral.

Yet as a functioning city, Chicago was in many ways superior to Berlin. Chicago's waterworks pumped 500 million gallons of water a day, or 139 gallons of water per person, while Berliners had to make do with 18 gallons. Flush toilets, a rarity in Berlin in 1900, could be found in 60 percent of Chicago's homes. Chicago's streets were lit by electricity, while Berlin still relied mostly on gaslight. Chicago had a much bigger streetcar system, twice as much acreage devoted to parks, and a public library containing many more volumes. And Chicago had just completed an amazing sanitation project that reversed the course of the Chicago River so that its waters—and the city's sewage—would flow away from Lake Michigan and southward down into the Illinois and Mississippi Rivers.

Giant sanitation projects were one thing; an inspiring urban environment was something else. For well-traveled Americans admiring of things European, the sense of inferiority was palpable. "We are enormously rich," admitted the journalist

Edwin L. Godkin, "but . . . what have we got to show? Almost nothing. Ugliness from an artistic point of view is the mark of all our cities." Thus the urban balance sheet: a utilitarian infrastructure that was superb by nineteenth-century standards, but "no municipal splendors of any description, nothing but population and hotels."

Upper Class/Middle Class

In the compact city of the early republic, class distinctions had been embedded in the way men and women dressed and by the deference they demanded from or granted others. As the industrial city grew, these marks of class faltered. In the anonymity of a big city, recognition and deference no longer served as mechanisms for conferring status. Instead, people began to rely on conspicuous display of wealth, membership in exclusive clubs, and above all, residence in exclusive neighborhoods.

For the poor, place of residence depended, as always, on being close to their jobs. But for higher-income urbanites, where to live became a matter of personal means and social preference.

The Urban Elite

As early as the 1840s, Boston merchants had taken advantage of the new railway service to escape the congested city. Fine rural estates appeared in Milton, Newton, and other outlying towns. By 1848 roughly 20 percent of Boston's businessmen were making the trip by train to their downtown offices. Ferries that plied the harbor between Manhattan and Brooklyn or New Jersey served the same purpose for New Yorkers.

As commercial development engulfed downtown residential areas, the exodus by the well-to-do quickened. In Cincinnati, wealthy families settled on the scenic hills rimming the crowded, humid tableland that ran down to the Ohio River. On those hillsides, a traveler noted in 1883, "the homes of Cincinnati's merchant princes and millionaires are found . . . elegant cottages, tasteful villas, and substantial mansions, surrounded by a paradise of grass, gardens, lawns, and tree-shaded roads."

Despite the attractions of country life, many of the very richest preferred the heart of the city. Chicago boasted its Gold Coast; San Francisco, Nob Hill; Denver, Quality Hill; and Manhattan, Fifth Avenue. New York novelist Edith Wharton recalled how the comfortable mid-century brownstones gave way to the "'new' millionaire houses," which spread northward on Fifth Avenue along Central Park. Great mansions, emulating the aristocratic houses of Europe, lined Fifth Avenue at the turn of the century.

But great wealth did not automatically confer social standing. An established elite dominated the social heights, even in such relatively raw cities as San Francisco and Denver. It had taken only a generation—sometimes less—for money made in commerce or real estate to shed its tarnish and become "old" and genteel. In long-settled Boston, wealth passed intact through several generations, creating a closely knit tribe of elite families that kept moneyed newcomers at bay. Elsewhere urban elites tended to be more open, but only to the socially ambitious who were prepared to make visible and energetic use of their money.

New York City became the home of a national elite as the most ambitious gravitated to this preeminent capital of American finance and culture. Manhattan's extraordinary vitality in turn kept the city's high society fluid and relatively open. In Theodore Dreiser's novel *The Titan* (1914), the tycoon Frank Cowperwood reassures his unhappy wife that if Chicago society will not accept them, "there are other cities. Money will arrange matters in New York—that I know. We can build a real place there, and go in on equal terms, if we have money enough." New York thus came to be a magnet for millionaires. The city attracted them not only because of its importance as a business center but for the opportunities it offered for display and social recognition.

This infusion of wealth shattered the older elite society of New York. Seeking to be assimilated into the upper class, the flood of moneyed newcomers simply overwhelmed it. There followed a curious process of reconstruction, a deliberate effort to define the rules of conduct and identify those who properly "belonged" in New York society.

The key figure was Ward McAllister, a southern-born lawyer who had made a quick fortune in gold-rush San Francisco and then took up a second career as the arbiter of New York society. In 1888 McAllister compiled the first *Social Register*, which announced that it would serve as a "record of society, comprising an accurate and careful list" of all those deemed eligible for New York society. McAllister instructed the socially ambitious on how to select guests, set a proper table, arrange a party, and launch a young lady into society. He presided over a round of assemblies, balls, and dinners that defined the boundaries of an elite society. At the apex stood "The Four Hundred"—the true cream of New York society. McAllister's list corresponded to those invited to Mrs. William Astor's gala ball of February 1, 1892.

From Manhattan an extravagant life of leisure radiated out to such favored resorts as Saratoga Springs, New York, and Palm Beach, Florida. In Rhode Island, Newport featured a grand array of summer "cottages," crowned by the Vanderbilts' Marble House and The Breakers. Visitors arrived via private railway car or aboard yachts and amused themselves at the races and gambling casinos. In the city, the rich dined extravagantly at Sherry's and Delmonico's, on one famous occasion while mounted on horseback. The underside to this excess—scandalous affairs, rowdy feasts that ended in police court, the fabulous costume ball thrown at the Waldorf-Astoria by the Bradley Martins at the peak of economic depression in 1897—was avidly followed in the press and awarded the celebrity we now accord to rock singers and Hollywood stars.

Americans were adept at making money, remarked the journalist Edwin L. Godkin in 1896, but they lacked the aristocratic traditions of Europe for spending it. "Great wealth has not yet entered our manners," Godkin remarked. In their struggle to find the rules and establish the manners, the moneyed elite made an indelible mark on urban life. If there was magnificence in the American city, that was mainly their handiwork. And if there was conspicuous waste and display, that too was their doing.

The Suburban World

The middle class left a smaller imprint on the public face of urban society. Many of its members, unlike the rich, preferred privacy and retreated into the domesticity of suburban comfort and family life.

Since colonial times the American economy had spawned a robust middle class of mostly self-employed lawyers, doctors, merchants, and proprietors. This older middle class remained important, but it was joined by a new salaried middle class brought forth by industrialism. Corporate organizations required managers, accountants, and clerks. The new technology called for engineers, chemists, and designers, while the distribution system needed salesmen, advertising executives, and store managers. These salaried ranks increased sevenfold between 1870 and 1910—much faster than any other occupational group. Nearly 9 million people held white-collar jobs in 1910, more than a fourth of all employed Americans.

Some members of this salaried class lived in the row houses of Baltimore and Boston or the comfortable apartment buildings of New York City. More preferred to escape the clamor and congestion of the city. They were attracted by a persisting rural ideal, agreeing with the landscape architect Andrew Jackson Downing that "nature and domestic life are better than the society and manners of town." As trolley service expanded out from the city center, middle-class Americans followed the wealthy into the countryside. All sought what one Chicago developer promised for his North Shore subdivision in 1875—"qualities of which the city is in a large degree bereft, namely, its pure air, peacefulness, quietude, and natural scenery."

No major American city escaped *suburbanization* during the late nineteenth century. City limits everywhere expanded rapidly, but even so, much of the suburban growth took place beyond city limits. By 1900 more than half of Boston's people lived in "streetcar suburbs" outside Boston proper; nationwide, according to the 1910 census, about 25 percent of the urban population lived in such autonomous suburbs.

The geography of the suburbs was truly a map of class structure because where a family lived told where it ranked socially. The farther out from the city center, the finer the houses and the larger the lots. Affluent businessmen and professionals had the time and flexibility to travel a long distance into town. People closer in wanted transit lines that went straight into the city center and carried them quickly between home and office. Lower-income commuters were likely to have more than one wage earner in the family, less secure employment, and jobs requiring movement around the city. It was better for them to be closer to the city center because crosstown lines afforded the mobility they needed for their work.

Suburban boundaries shifted constantly, as working-class city residents who wanted to better their lives moved to the cheapest suburbs, prompting an exodus of older residents who in turn pushed the next higher group farther out in search of space and greenery. Suburbanization was the sum of countless individual decisions. Each family's move represented an advance in living standards—not only more light, air, and quiet but better accommodation than the city afforded. Suburban

Middle-Class Domesticity

For middle-class Americans the home was a place of nurture, a refuge from the world of competitive commerce. Perhaps that explains why their residences were so heavily draped and cluttered with bric-a-brac. All of it emphasized privacy and pride of possession. Culver Pictures.

houses were typically larger for the same money and came equipped with flush toilets, hot water, central heating, and, by the turn of the century, electricity.

The small towns of rural America had fostered community life. Not so the suburbs. The grid street pattern, while efficient for laying out lots, offered no natural focus for group life, nor did the shops and services that lay scattered along the trolley-car streets. Suburban development conformed to the economics of real estate and transportation, and so did the thinking of middle-class home seekers entering the suburbs. They wanted a house that gave them good value and convenience to the trolley line.

The need for community had lost some of its force for middle-class Americans. Two other attachments assumed greater importance: one was work; the other, family.

Middle-Class Families

In the preindustrial economy there was little separation between work and family life. Farmers, merchants, and artisans generally worked at home. The family included not only blood relatives but everyone living and working in the household.

As industrialism progressed, the middle-class family became separated from economic activity. The father departed every morning for the office, and children spent more years in school. Clothing was bought ready made; food came increasingly in cans and packages. Middle-class families became smaller, excluding all but nuclear members and consisting typically by 1900 of husband, wife, and three children.

Within this family circle relationships became intense and affectionate. "Home was the most expressive experience in life," recalled the literary critic Henry Seidel Canby of his growing up in the 1890s. "Though the family might quarrel and nag, the home held them all, protecting them against the outside world." The suburb provided a fit setting for such middle-class families. The quiet, tree-lined streets created a domestic space insulated from the hurly-burly of commerce and enterprise.

The burdens of this domesticity fell heavily on the wife. It was nearly unheard of for her to seek an outside career—that was her husband's role. Her job was to manage the household. "The woman who could not make a home, like the man who could not support one, was condemned," Canby remembered. As the physical burdens of household work eased, higher-quality homemaking became the new ideal—a message propagated by Catharine Beecher's best-selling book *The American Woman's Home* (1869) and by such magazines as the *Ladies' Home Journal* and *Good Housekeeping*, which first appeared during the 1880s. This advice literature instructed wives that, in addition to their domestic duties, they were responsible for bringing sensibility, beauty, and love to the household. "We owe to women the charm and beauty of life," wrote one educator. "For the love that rests, strengthens and inspires, we look to women." In this idealized view the wife made the home a refuge for her husband and a place of nurture for their children.

Womanly virtue, even if much glorified, by no means put wives on equal terms with their husbands. Although the legal status of married women—their right to own property, control separate earnings, make contracts, and get a divorce—improved markedly during the nineteenth century, law and custom still dictated a wife's submission to her husband. She relied on his ability as the family breadwinner, and despite her superior virtues and graces she was thought below him in vigor and intellect. Her mind could be employed "but little and in trivial matters," wrote one prominent physician, and her proper place was as "the companion or ornamental appendage to man" (see American Voices, "We Did Not Know . . . Whether Women's Health Could Stand the Strain of College Education," p. 547).

Not surprisingly, many bright, independent-minded women rebelled against marriage. The marriage rate fell to its lowest point during the last forty years of the nineteenth century. More than 10 percent of women of marriageable age remained single, and the rate was much higher among college graduates and professionals. "I know that something perhaps, humanly speaking, supremely precious has passed me by," remarked the writer Vida Scudder. "But how much it would have

AMERICAN VOICES

"We Did Not Know . . . Whether Women's Health Could Stand the Strain of College Education"

M. CAREY THOMAS

*P*resident of Bryn Mawr College for many years, M. Carey Thomas (1857–1935) recalls in a retrospective essay her dreams of college as a girl growing up in Baltimore in the 1870s.

The passionate desire of women of my generation for higher education was accompanied thruout its course by the awful doubt, felt by women themselves as well as by men, as to whether women as a sex were physically and mentally fit for it. . . . I was always wondering whether it could be really true, as everyone always said, that boys were cleverer than girls. . . . I often remember praying about it, and begging God that if it were true that because I was a girl I could not successfully master Greek and go to college and understand things to kill me at once, as I could not bear to live in such an unjust world. When I was a little older I read the Bible entirely thru with passionate eagerness because I had heard it said that it proved that women were inferior to men. . . . To this day I can never read many parts of the Pauline epistles without feeling again the sinking of the heart with which I used to hurry over the verses referring to women's keeping silence in the churches and asking their husbands at home. . . .

It was not to be wondered at that we were uncertain in those old days as to the ultimate result of women's education. We did not know when we began whether women's health could stand the strain of college education. We were haunted in those early days by the clanging chains of that gloomy little specter, Dr. Edward H. Clarke's *Sex in Education*. With trepidation of spirit I made my mother read it, and was much cheered by her remark that, as neither she, nor any of the women she knew, had ever seen girls or women of the kind described in Dr. Clarke's book, we might as well act as if they did not exist. Still, we did not know whether college might not produce a crop of just such invalids. . . .

Before I myself went to college I had never seen but one college woman. I had heard that such a woman was staying at the house of an acquaintance. I went to see her with fear. Even if she had appeared in hoofs and horns I was determined to go to college all the same. But it was a relief to find this Vassar graduate tall and handsome and dressed like other women. When, five years later, I went to Leipzig to study after graduating from Cornell, my mother used to write me that my name was never mentioned to her by the women of her acquaintance. I was thought by them to be as much a disgrace to my family as if I had eloped with the coachman. . . .

We are now [1908] living in the midst of great and, I believe on the whole beneficent, social changes which are preparing the way for the coming economic independence of women. . . . The passionate desire of the women of my generation for a college education seems, as we study it now in the light of coming events, to have been part of this greater movement.

SOURCE: Linda K. Kerber and Jane De Hart-Mathews, eds., *Women's America: Refocusing the Past*, 2nd ed. (New York: Oxford University Press, 1987), 263–65.

excluded!" Married life "looks to me often as I watch it terribly impoverished, for women."

If fewer women were marrying, of course, so were fewer men. One historian has labeled the late nineteenth century the Age of the Bachelor, a time when being an unattached male lost its social stigma and, especially in large cities, became a happy alternative for many men of marriageable age. A bachelor's counterpart to Vida Scudder's dim view of marriage was this ditty making the rounds in the early 1880s:

> No wife to scold me
> No children to squall
> God bless the happy man
> Who keeps bachelor's hall.

With its residential hotels, restaurants, and abundant personal services, the urban scene afforded bachelors all the comforts of home and, doubtless more important, an ample array of men's clubs, saloons, and sporting events on which to erect a robust male subculture.

The appeal of the manly life was not, however, confined to confirmed bachelors. American males inherited a pride in independence—achieved above all by being one's own boss—but the salaried jobs they increasingly held left them distinctly not their own bosses. Nor, once work and household had been severed, could they enjoy the patriarchal hold over family life that had empowered their fathers and grandfathers. A palpable anxiety arose that the American male was becoming, as one magazine editor warned, "weak, effeminate, decaying." There was a telling shift in language. While people had once spoken of *manhood*, which meant leaving *childhood* behind, they now spoke of *masculinity*, the opposite of *femininity*: being a man meant surmounting the feminizing influences of modern life.

And how was this to be accomplished? By engaging in competitive sports like football, which became hugely popular in this era. By working out and becoming fit because, as the psychologist G. Stanley Hall put it, "you can't have a firm will without firm muscles." By resorting to the great outdoors—preferably out West—and engaging in Theodore Roosevelt's "strenuous life." Or vicariously, by reading Owen Wister's best-selling cowboy novel, *The Virginian* (1902), or that celebration of primitive man, Edgar Rice Burroughs's *Tarzan of the Apes* (1912). The surging popularity of westerns and adventure novels was surely a marker of the fears by urban dwellers that theirs was not a life for real men.

Women perhaps had an easier time of it. Around 1890 the glimmerings of a sexual revolution appeared in the middle-class family. Experts abandoned the notion, put forth by one popular medical text, that "the majority of women (happily for society) are not very much troubled by sexual feeling of any kind." In succeeding editions of his book *Plain Home Talk on Love, Marriage, and Parentage*, physician Edward Bliss Foote began to favor a healthy sexuality that gave pleasure to women as well as men.

During the 1890s the artist Charles Dana Gibson created the image of the "new woman." In his drawings the *Gibson girl* was tall, spirited, athletic, and chastely sexual. She rejected bustles, hoop skirts, and tightly laced corsets, preferring shirtwaists and other natural styles that did not disguise her female form. In the city, women's sphere began to take on a more public character. Among the new urban institutions catering to women, the most important was the department store, which became a temple for their emerging role as consumers.

The offspring of the middle class experienced their own revolution. In the past children had been regarded as an economic asset—added hands for the family farm, shop, or countinghouse. Especially for the urban middle class, this no longer held true. Parents stopped expecting their children to be working members of the family. In the old days Ralph Waldo Emerson remarked in 1880, "children had been repressed and kept in the background; now they are considered, cosseted, and pampered." There was such a thing as "the juvenile mind," lectured Jacob Abbott in his book *Gentle Measures in the Management and Training of the Young* (1871). The family was responsible for providing a nurturing environment in which the young personality could grow and mature.

Preparation for adulthood became increasingly linked to formal education. School enrollment went up 150 percent between 1870 and 1900. As the years before adulthood began to stretch out, a new stage of life—adolescence—emerged. While rooted in longer years of family dependency, adolescence shifted much of the socializing role from parents to peer group. The impact was most marked on the daughters of the middle class, who, freed from the chores of housework, were now encouraged to devote themselves to self-development, which meant for many the new opportunity to attend high school. The liberating consequences surely went beyond their parents' expectations. In a revealing shift in terminology, "young lady" gave way to "school girl" (with the added benefit that "girl" no longer applied so comfortably to women servants, of all ages), and the daughterly submissiveness of earlier times gave way to self-expressive independence. On achieving adulthood, it was not so big a step for the daughters of the middle class to become Gibson's "new women."

City Life

With its soaring skyscrapers, jostling traffic, and hum of business, the city symbolized energy and enterprise. When the budding writer Hamlin Garland and his brother arrived in Chicago from Iowa in 1881, they knew immediately that they had entered a new world: "Everything interested us. . . . Nothing was commonplace, nothing was ugly to us." In one way or another, every city-bound migrant, whether from the American countryside or from a foreign land, experienced something of this sense of wonder.

But with the boundless variety came disorder and uncertainty. The city was utterly unlike the rural world. In the countryside every person had been known to

The New Woman

John Singer Sargent's painting *Mr. and Mrs. Isaac Newton Phelps Stokes* (1897) captures on canvas the essence of the "new woman" of the 1890s. Nothing about Mrs. Phelps Stokes, neither how she is dressed nor how she presents herself, suggests physical weakness or demure passivity. She confidently occupies center stage, a fit partner for her husband, who is relegated to the shadows of the picture.

The Metropolitan Museum of Art. Bequest of Edith Minturn Phelps Stokes (Mrs. I. N.), 1938 (38.104). Photo © 1992 The Metropolitan Museum of Art.

his or her neighbors. Mark Twain found New York "a splendid desert, where a stranger is lonely in the midst of a million of his race. . . . Every man rushes, rushes, rushes, and never has time to be companionable [or] to fool away on matters which do not involve dollars and duty and business."

Rural people could never re-create in the city the communities they had left behind. But they found ways to gain a sense of belonging, they built a multitude of new institutions, and they learned how to function in an impersonal, heterogeneous environment. An urban culture emerged, and through it there developed a new breed of American who was entirely at home in the modern city.

Mulberry Street, New York City, c. 1900

The influx of southern and eastern Europeans created teeming ghettos in the heart of New York City and other major American cities. The view is of Mulberry Street, with its pushcarts, street peddlers, and bustling traffic. The inhabitants are mostly Italians, and some of them, noticing the photographer preparing his camera, have gathered to be in the picture. Library of Congress.

FOR MORE HELP ANALYZING THIS IMAGE, see the Online Study Guide at **bedfordstmartins.com/henrettaconcise**.

Newcomers

The explosive growth of America's big-city population—the numbers living in places of 100,000 people or more jumped from about 6 million to 14 million between 1880 and 1900—meant that the cities were very much a world of newcomers. Many came from the nation's countryside; half of rural families on the move in these years were city bound. But it was those newcomers further marked off by skin color or ethnicity who found entry into city life most daunting. At the turn of the century, upwards of 30 percent of the residents of New York, Chicago, Boston, Cleveland, Minneapolis, and San Francisco were foreign-born. The biggest ethnic group in Boston was Irish; in Minneapolis, Swedish; in most other northern cities, German. But by 1910 the influx from southern and eastern Europe had changed the ethnic complexion of many of these cities. In Chicago, Poles took the lead; in New York, eastern European Jews; in San Francisco, Italians.

As the earlier "walking cities" disappeared, so did the opportunities for inter-mingling with the older populations. The later arrivals from southern and eastern Europe had little choice about where they lived; they needed to find cheap housing near their jobs. Some gravitated to the outlying factory districts; others settled in the congested downtown ghettos. In New York Italians crowded into the Irish neigh-borhoods west of Broadway, and Russian and Polish Jews pushed the Germans out of the Lower East Side (Map 18.2). A colony of Hungarians lived around Houston Street, and Bohemians occupied the poorer stretches of the Upper East Side between Fiftieth and Seventy-sixth Streets.

Capitalizing on fellow feeling, institutions of many kinds sprang up to meet the immigrants' needs. Newspapers appeared wherever substantial numbers lived. In 1911 the 20,000 Poles in Buffalo, New York, supported two Polish-language daily papers. Immigrants throughout the country avidly read *Il Progresso Italo-Americano* and the Yiddish-language *Jewish Daily Forward*, both published in New York City (see American Voices, "Bintel Brief," p. 554). Companionship could always be found on street corners, in barbershops and club rooms, and in saloons. Italians marched in saint's day parades, Bohemians gathered in singing societies, and New York Jews patronized a lively Yiddish theater. To provide help in times of sickness and death, the immigrants organized mutual-aid societies. The Italians of Chicago had sixty-six of these organizations in 1903, mostly composed of people from particular provinces or towns. Immigrants built a rich and functional institutional life in urban America to an extent unimagined in their native places.

The great African American migration from the rural South to northern cities was just beginning at the turn of the century. The black population of New York in-creased by 30,000 between 1900 and 1910, making New York second only to Washington, D.C., as a black urban center, but the 91,000 African Americans in New York in 1910 represented fewer than 2 percent of the population, and that was true of Chicago and Cleveland as well.

Urban blacks retreated from the scattered neighborhoods of older times into concentrated ghettos—Chicago's Black Belt on the South Side, for example, or the early outlines of New York's Harlem. Race prejudice cut down job opportunities. Twenty-six percent of Cleveland's blacks had been skilled workers in 1870, but only 12 percent were skilled by 1890; entire occupations such as barbering (except for a black clientele) became exclusively white. Two-thirds of Cleveland's blacks in 1910 worked as domestics and day laborers, with little hope of moving up the job ladder.

In the face of pervasive discrimination, urban blacks built their own commu-nities. They created a flourishing press, fraternal orders, a vast array of women's organizations, and a middle class of doctors, lawyers, and small entrepreneurs. Above all, there were the black churches—twenty-five in Chicago in 1905, mainly Methodist and Baptist. More than any other institution, remarked one scholar in

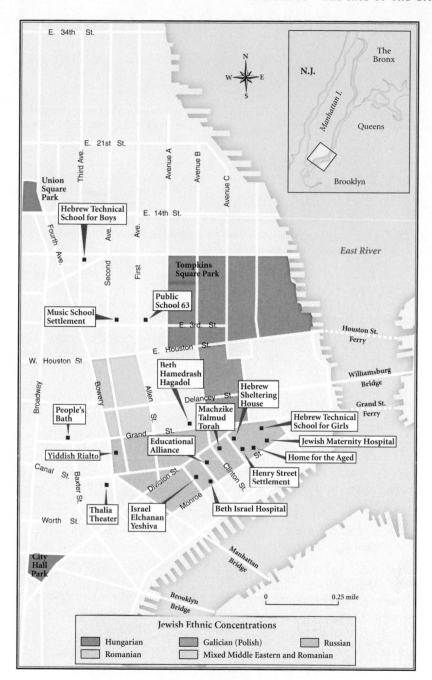

MAP 18.2 The Lower East Side, New York City, 1900

As this map shows, the Jewish immigrants dominating Manhattan's Lower East Side preferred living in neighborhoods populated by those from their home regions of eastern Europe. Their sense of a common identity made for a remarkable flowering of educational, cultural, and social institutions on the Jewish East Side.

Bintel Brief

ANONYMOUS

I n Yiddish bintel brief *means "bundle of letters." That was the name of the famous section of the Jewish Daily Forward devoted to letters from immigrant readers about their trials and tribulations in America.*

I am a girl sixteen years old. I live together with my parents and my two older sisters. Last year I met a young man. We love one another. He is a very respectable man, and makes a fine living. My sisters have no fiancés. I know that should I marry they will never talk to me. My parents are also strongly against it since I am the youngest child. I do not want to lose my parents' love, and neither do I want to lose my lover because that would break my heart. Give me some advice, dear Editor!

I was born in a small town in Russia, and until I was sixteen I studied in *Talmud Torahs* and *yeshivas*, but when I came to America I developed spiritually and became a freethinker. Yet every year when the time of *Rosh Hashana* and *Yom Kippur* comes around I become very gloomy. . . . So strong are my feelings that I enter the synagogue, not in order to pray to God but to heal and refresh my aching soul by sitting among *landsleit* [countrymen] and listening to the cantor's sweet melodies. The members of my Progressive Society don't understand. They say I am a hypocrite. . . . What do you think? *Answer.* No one can tell another what to do with himself on *Yom Kippur*.

To a man everything is permissible, to a woman nothing. A man is king over us and may do his will. When I argue that morality is more demanding on women, my husband gets angry and denies it with all his might. There is no such thing as a man with a bad name, but just let one spot fall upon a woman. . . . Why?!

I am in favor of giving women full rights, but most of my friends are against it. They argue that the woman would then no longer be the housewife, the mother to her children, the wife to her husband—in a word, everything would be destroyed. I do not agree because a woman is a human being just like a man, and if women are recognized as human beings, they must be granted all the rights of human beings. *Answer.* Justice can reign among people only when they all have equal rights.

Why do the police favor the clothing stores on Canal Street which remain open seven days a week? . . . Where else in the world do people sell their lives to make a living with no holidays and no rest? I am one of the corpses who works seven days a week in one of those electric-lit graves on Canal Street.

I am a young man of twenty-five, and I recently met a fine girl. She has a flaw, however—a dimple in her chin. It is said that people who have this lose their first husband or wife. I love her very much. But I'm afraid to marry her lest I die because of the dimple. *Answer.* The tragedy is not that the girl has a dimple in her chin but that some people have a screw loose in their heads.

SOURCE: Irving Howe and Kenneth Libo, eds., *How We Lived* (New York: New American Library, 1979), 88–90.

The Cherry Family, 1906

Wiley and Fannie Cherry migrated in 1893 from North Carolina to Chicago, settling in the small African American community on the West Side. The Cherrys apparently prospered and by 1906, when this family portrait was taken, had entered the black middle class. When migration intensified after 1900, longer-settled urban blacks like the Cherrys became uncomfortable, and relations with the needy rural newcomers were often tense.

Courtesy, Lorraine Heflin, Chicago Historical Society.

1913, it was the church "which the Negro may call his own. . . . A new church may be built . . . and . . . all the machinery set in motion without ever consulting any white person. . . . [Religion] more than anything else represents the real life of the race." As in the southern countryside, the church was the central institution for city blacks, and the preacher was the most important local citizen. Manhattan's Union Baptist Church, housed like many others in a storefront, attracted the "very recent residents of this new, disturbing city" and, ringing with spirituals and fervent prayer, made Christianity come "alive Sunday mornings."

Ward Politics

Race and ethnicity tended to divide newcomers. Politics, by contrast, integrated them into the wider urban society. Every migrant to an American city automatically became a *ward* resident and acquired a spokesman at city hall in the form of the local alderman. He could arrange for streets to be paved, or water mains extended, or permits granted—so that, for example, in 1888 Vito Fortounescere could "place and keep a stand for the sale of fruit, inside the stoop-line, in front of the northeast corner of Twenty-eighth Street and Fourth Avenue" in Manhattan, or the parish-ioners of Saint Maria of Mount Carmel could set off fireworks at their Fourth of July picnic.

These favors came via a system of boss control that, although present at every level of party politics, flourished most luxuriantly in the big cities. Urban **political machines** like Tammany Hall in New York depended on a loyal grassroots con-stituency, so each ward was divided into a precinct of a few blocks. The precinct cap-tain reported to the ward leader, who was likely also to be the alderman. The main job of these functionaries was to be accessible and, as best they could, serve the needs of the party faithful.

The machine acted as a rough-and-ready social service agency, providing jobs for the jobless, a helping hand for a bereaved family, and intercession against an un-feeling city bureaucracy. The Tammany ward boss George Washington Plunkitt had a "regular system" when fires broke out in his district. He arranged for housing for burned-out families, "fix[ing] them up till they get things runnin' again. It's philan-thropy, but it's politics, too—mighty good politics."

The business community was similarly served. Contractors sought city business; gas companies and streetcar lines wanted licenses; manufacturers needed services and not-too-nosy inspectors; and the liquor trade and numbers rackets relied on a tolerant police force. All of them turned to the machine boss and his lieutenants.

Of course, the machine exacted a price for these services. The tenement dweller gave his vote. The businessman wrote a check. Naturally, some of the money that changed hands leaked into the pockets of machine politicians. This "boodle" could be blatantly corrupt—kickbacks by contractors; protection money from gamblers, saloonkeepers, and prostitutes; payoffs from gas and trolley companies. In the 1860s boss William Marcy Tweed had made Tammany a byword for corruption, until his extravagant graft in the building of a lavish city courthouse led to his arrest in 1871, and a decline thereafter in the more blatant forms of machine corruption. The turn-of-the-century Tammanyite George Plunkitt declared that he had no need for kickbacks and bribes. He favored what he called "honest graft," the easy profits that came to savvy insiders. Plunkitt made most of his money building wharves on Manhattan's waterfront. One way or another, legally or otherwise, machine politics rewarded its supporters.

Plunkitt was an Irishman, and so were most of the machine politicians con-trolling Tammany Hall. But by the 1890s Plunkitt's Fifteenth District was filling up with Italians and eastern European Jews. In general the Irish had no love for these newer immigrants, but Plunkitt played no favorites. On any given day (as recorded in a diary) he might attend an Italian funeral in the afternoon and a Jewish wedding in the evening, and at each he probably paid his respects with a few Italian words or a choice bit of Yiddish.

In an era when so many forces acted to isolate ghetto communities, politics served an *integrating* function, cutting across ethnic lines and giving immigrants and blacks a stake in the larger urban order.

Religion in the City

For African Americans, as we have seen, the church was a central institution of urban life. So it was for many other city dwellers. But the city was difficult ground for religious practice. All the great faiths present at the time—Judaism, Catholicism, and Protestantism—had to scramble to reconcile religious belief with the secular urban world.

About 250,000 Jews, mostly of German origin, were living in America when the eastern European Jews began arriving in the 1880s. Well established and prosperous, the German Jews had embraced Reform Judaism, abandoning religious practices—from keeping a kosher kitchen to conducting services in Hebrew—"not adapted to the views and habits of modern civilization." This was not the way of the Yiddish-speaking Jews from eastern Europe. Eager to preserve their traditional piety, they founded their own Orthodox synagogues, often in vacant stores and ramshackle buildings, and practiced Judaism as they had at home.

In the villages of eastern Europe, however, Judaism had involved not only worship but an entire way of life. Insular though it might be, ghetto life in the American city could not re-create the communal environment on which strict religious observance depended. "The very clothes I wore and the very food I ate had a fatal effect on my religious habits," confessed the hero of Abraham Cahan's novel *The Rise of David Levinsky* (1917). "If you . . . attempt to bend your religion to the spirit of your surroundings, it breaks. It falls to pieces." Levinsky shaved off his beard and plunged into the Manhattan clothing business. Orthodox Judaism survived this shattering of faith but only by reducing its claims on the lives of the faithful.

Catholics faced much the same problem. The issue, defined within the Roman Catholic Church as "Americanism," turned on the degree to which its congregants should adapt to American society. Should Catholic children attend parochial or public schools? Should they intermarry with non-Catholics? Should the traditional education for the clergy be changed? Bishop John Ireland of St. Paul, Minnesota, felt that "the principles of the Church are in harmony with the interests of the Republic." But traditionalists, led by Archbishop Michael A. Corrigan of New York, denied the possibility of such harmony and argued for insulating the Church from the pluralistic American environment.

Immigrant Catholics generally supported the Church's conservative wing because they wanted to preserve what they had known in Europe. But they also desired that church life express their ethnic identities. Newly arrived Catholics wanted their own parishes where they could celebrate their customs, speak their languages, and establish their own parochial schools. When they became numerous enough, they also demanded their own bishops. The Catholic hierarchy, which was dominated by Irish Catholics, felt that the integrity of the Church itself was at stake. The demand for ethnic parishes implied local control of Church property. And if there were

Immaculate Heart of Mary Church, 1908

In crowded immigrant neighborhoods the church rose from undistinguished surroundings to assert the centrality of religious belief in the life of the community. This photograph is a view of Immaculate Heart of Mary Church, taken from Polish Hill in Pittsburgh in 1908.

Pittsburgh City Photographer Collection, Archives Service Center, University of Pittsburgh.

bishops for specific ethnic groups, this would mean disrupting the diocesan structure that unified the Church.

With some strain, the Church managed to satisfy the immigrant faithful. It met the demand for representation in the hierarchy by appointing immigrant priests as auxiliary bishops within existing dioceses. Ethnic parishes also flourished. Before World War I American Catholics worshiped in more than two thousand foreign-language churches, and many others were bilingual. Not without strain the Catholic Church made itself a central institution for the expression of ethnic identity in urban America.

For the Protestant churches the city posed different but not easier challenges. Every major city retained great downtown churches where wealthy Protestants worshiped. Some of these churches, richly endowed, took pride in nationally prominent pastors, such as Henry Ward Beecher of Plymouth Congregational Church in Brooklyn or Phillips Brooks of Trinity Episcopal Church in Boston. But the eminence of these churches, with their fashionable congregations and imposing edifices, could not disguise the growing remoteness of traditional Protestantism from much of its urban constituency. "Where is the city in which the Sabbath day is not losing ground?" lamented a minister in 1887. The families of businessmen, lawyers, and doctors could be seen in any church on Sunday morning, he noted, "but the workingmen and their families are not there."

To counter this decline the Protestant churches responded by evangelizing among the unchurched and indifferent. Starting in the 1880s they also began providing reading rooms, day nurseries, clubhouses, vocational classes, and other services. The Salvation Army, which arrived from Great Britain in 1879, spread the gospel of repentance among the urban poor and built an assistance program that ranged from soup kitchens to shelters for former prostitutes. When all else failed the down-and-outers of American cities knew they could count on the Salvation Army.

For single people, there were the Young Men's and Women's Christian Associations, which had arrived from Britain before the Civil War. Housing for single women was an especially important mission of the YWCAs. The gymnasiums that made the YMCAs synonymous with "muscular Christianity" were equally important for young men. No other organizations so effectively combined activities for young people with an evangelizing appeal through Bible classes, nondenominational worship, and a religious atmosphere.

The social meaning that people sought in religion explained the enormous popularity of a book called *In His Steps* (1896). The author, a Congregational minister named Charles M. Sheldon, told the story of a congregation that resolved to live by Christ's precepts for one year. "If the church members were all doing as Jesus would do," Sheldon asked, "could it remain true that armies of men would walk the streets for jobs, and hundreds of them curse the church, and thousands of them find in the saloon their best friend?"

The most potent form of urban evangelism—revivalism—said little about social uplift. From their origins in the eighteenth century, revival movements had steadfastly focused on individual redemption. The resolution of earthly problems, revivalists believed, would follow the conversion of the people to Christ. Beginning in the mid-1870s, revival meetings swept through the cities.

The pioneering figure was Dwight L. Moody, a former Chicago shoe salesman and YMCA official. After preaching in Britain for two years, Moody returned to America in 1875 and began staging revival meetings that drew thousands. He preached an optimistic, uncomplicated, nondenominational message. Eternal life could be had for the asking, Moody shouted as he held up his Bible. His listeners needed only "to come forward and take, TAKE!"

Many other preachers followed in Moody's path. The most colorful was Billy Sunday, a hard-drinking former outfielder for the Chicago White Stockings who mended his ways and found religion. Like Moody and other city revivalists, Sunday was a farm boy. His rip-snorting attacks on fashionable ministers and the "booze traffic" carried the ring of rustic America. By realizing that many people remained villagers at heart, revivalists found a key for bringing city dwellers back to the church.

City Amusements

City people compartmentalized life's activities, setting workplace apart from home and working time apart from free time. "Going out" became a necessity, demanded not only as solace for a hard day's work but proof that life was better in the New World than in the Old. "He who can enjoy and does not enjoy commits a sin," a Yiddish-language paper told its readers. And enjoyment now meant buying a ticket and being entertained.

Music halls attracted huge audiences. Chicago had six vaudeville houses in 1896, twenty-two in 1910. Evolving from tawdry variety and minstrel shows, vaudeville cleaned up its routines, making them suitable for the entire family, and turned into thoroughly professional entertainment handled by national booking agencies. With its standard program of nine singing, dancing, and comedy acts, vaudeville attained enormous popularity just as the movies arrived. The first primitive films, a minute or so of humor or glimpses of famous people, appeared in 1896 in penny arcades and as filler in vaudeville shows. Within a decade, millions of city people were watching films of increasing length and artistry at *nickelodeons* (named after the five-cent admission charge) across the country.

For young unmarried workers the cheap amusements of the city created a new social space. "I want a good time," a New York clothing operator told an investigator. "And there is no . . . way a girl can get it on $8 a week. I guess if anyone wants to take me to a dance he won't have to ask me twice." Hence the widespread ritual among the urban working class of "treating." The girls spent what money they had dressing up; their boyfriends were expected to pay for the fun. Parental control over courtship broke down, and amid the bright lights and lively music of the dance hall and amusement park, working-class youth forged a more easygoing culture of sexual interaction and pleasure seeking.

The geography of the big city carved out ample space for commercialized sex. Prostitution was not new to urban life, but in the late nineteenth century it became more open and more intermingled with other forms of public entertainment. Opium and cocaine were widely available and not yet illegal. In New York the red-light district was the Tenderloin, running northward from Twenty-third Street between Fifth and Eighth Avenues.

The Tenderloin and the Bowery farther downtown were also the sites of a robust gay subculture. The long-held notion that homosexual life was covert, in the closet, in late-nineteenth-century America appears not to be true, at least not in the country's premier city. In certain corners of the city, a gay world flourished, with a full array of saloons, meeting places, and drag balls, which were widely known and patronized by uptown "slummers."

Of all forms of (mostly) male diversion, none was more specific to the city, or so spectacularly successful, as professional baseball. The game's promoters decreed that baseball had been created in 1839 by Abner Doubleday in the village of Cooperstown, New York. Actually, baseball was neither of American origin—it developed from the British game of rounders—nor a product of rural life. The game apparently first appeared in the early 1840s in New York City, where a group of gentlemen enthusiasts competed on an empty lot. Over the next twenty years, clubs sprang up across the country and intercity competition developed on a scheduled basis. In 1868 baseball became openly professional, following the lead of the Cincinnati Red Stockings in signing players to contracts for the season.

Big-time baseball came into its own with the launching of the National League in 1876. The team owners were profit-minded businessmen who shaped the sport to please the fans. Wooden grandstands gave way to the concrete and steel stadiums of the early twentieth century, such as Fenway Park in Boston, Forbes Field in Pittsburgh, and Shibe Park in Philadelphia. For the urban multitudes baseball grew into something more than an afternoon at the ballpark. By rooting for the home team, fans found a way of identifying with the city in which they lived. Amid the diversity and anonymity of urban life, the common experience and language of baseball acted as a bridge among strangers.

Most efficient at this task, however, was the newspaper. James Gordon Bennett, founder of the *New York Herald* in 1835, wanted "to record the facts . . . for the great masses of the community." The news was whatever interested city readers, starting with crime, scandal, and sensational events. After the Civil War the *New York Sun* added the human-interest story, which made news of ordinary happenings. Newspapers also targeted specific audiences. A women's page offered recipes and fashion news, separate sections covered sports and high society, and the Sunday supplement helped fill the weekend hours.

The competition for readers became fierce when Joseph Pulitzer, the owner of the *St. Louis Post-Dispatch*, invaded New York in 1883 by buying the *New York World*. Pulitzer was in turn challenged by William Randolph Hearst, who arrived from San Francisco in 1895 prepared to beat the *New York World* at its own game. Hearst's sensationalist style of newspaper reporting became known as **yellow journalism.** The term, linked to the first comic strip to appear in color, *The Yellow Kid* (1895), meant a type of reporting in which accuracy came second to eliciting a "Gee Whiz!" feeling in the reader.

"He who is without a newspaper," said the great showman P. T. Barnum, "is cut off from his species." Barnum was speaking of city people and their hunger for information. By meeting this need, newspapers revealed their sensitivity to the public they served (Table 18.2).

The Higher Culture

In the midst of this popular ferment, new institutions of higher culture were taking shape in America's cities. A desire for the cultivated life was not, of course, specifically urban. Before the Civil War the lyceum movement had sent lecturers to the remotest towns, bearing messages of culture and learning. Chautauqua, founded in upstate New York in 1874, carried on this work of cultural

TABLE 18.2 Newspaper Circulation, 1870–1909	
Year	*Total Circulation*
1870	2,602,000
1880	3,566,000
1890	8,387,000
1900	15,102,000
1909	24,212,000

Source: Historical Statistics of the United States (1975), 2: 810.

dissemination. However, great institutions such as museums, public libraries, opera companies, and symphony orchestras could flourish only in metropolitan centers.

The nation's first major art museum, the Corcoran Gallery of Art, opened in Washington, D.C., in 1869. New York's Metropolitan Museum of Art started in rented quarters two years later, then moved in 1880 to its permanent site in Central Park and launched an ambitious program of art acquisition. When financier J. P. Morgan became chairman of the board in 1905, the Metropolitan's preeminence was assured. The Boston Museum of Fine Arts was founded in 1876 and Chicago's Art Institute in 1879.

Symphony orchestras also appeared, first in New York under the conductors Theodore Thomas and Leopold Damrosch in the 1870s and then in Boston and Chicago during the next decade. National tours by these leading orchestras planted the seeds for orchestral societies in many other cities. Public libraries grew from modest collections (in 1870 only seven had as many as fifty thousand books) into major urban institutions. The greatest library benefactor was Andrew Carnegie, who announced in 1881 that he would build a library in any town or city that was prepared to maintain it. By 1907 Carnegie had spent more than $32.7 million to establish about a thousand libraries throughout the country.

The late nineteenth century was the great age not only of moneymaking, but also of money *giving*. Generous with their surplus wealth, new millionaires patronized the arts partly as a civic duty, partly to promote themselves socially, but also out of a sense of national pride.

"In America there is no culture," pronounced the English critic G. Lowes Dickinson in 1909. Science and the practical arts, yes— "every possible application of life to purposes and ends"—but "no life for life's sake." Such condescending remarks received a respectful American hearing out of a sense of cultural inferiority to the Old World. In 1873 Mark Twain and Charles Dudley Warner published a novel, *The Gilded Age*, satirizing America as a land of money grubbers and speculators. This enormously popular book touched a nerve in the American psyche.

Its title has since been appropriated by historians to characterize the late nineteenth century—America's "Gilded Age"—as an era of materialism and cultural shallowness.

Some members of the upper class, such as the novelist Henry James, despaired of the country and moved to Europe. But the more common response was to try to raise the nation's cultural level. The newly rich had a hard time of it. They did not have much opportunity to cultivate a taste for art, and a great deal of what they collected was junk. On the other hand George W. Vanderbilt, grandson of the rough-hewn Cornelius Vanderbilt, championed French Impressionism, and the coal and steel baron Henry Clay Frick built a brilliant art collection that is still housed as a public museum in his mansion in New York City. The enthusiasm of moneyed Americans largely fueled the great cultural institutions that sprang up during the Gilded Age.

A deeply conservative idea of culture sustained this generous patronage. The aim was to embellish life, not to probe or reveal its meaning. "Art," says the hero of the Reverend Henry Ward Beecher's sentimental novel *Norwood* (1867), "attempts to work out its end solely by the use of the beautiful, and the artist is to select out only such things as are beautiful." The idea of culture also took on an elitist cast: Shakespeare, once a staple of popular entertainment (in various bowd-lerized versions), was appropriated into the domain of "serious" theater. And simultaneously the world of culture became feminized. "Husbands or sons rarely share those interests," noted one observer. In American life, remarked the clergy-man Horace Bushnell, men represented the "force principle," women the "beauty principle."

The depiction of life, the eminent editor and novelist William Dean Howells wrote, "must be tinged with sufficient idealism to make it all of a truly uplifting character. We cannot admit stories which deal with false or immoral relations. . . . The finer side of things—the idealistic—is the answer for us." The "genteel tradition," as this literary school came to be known, dominated the nation's purveyors of elite culture—its universities and publishers—from the 1860s onward.

But the urban world could not finally be kept at bay. Howells himself resigned in 1881 as editor of the *Atlantic Monthly*, a stronghold of the genteel tradition, and called for a literature that sought "to picture the daily life in the most exact terms possible." In a series of realistic novels—*A Modern Instance* (1882), *The Rise of Silas Lapham* (1885), and *A Hazard of New Fortunes* (1890)—Howells captured the urban middle class. Stephen Crane's *Maggie: Girl of the Streets* (1893), privately printed because no publisher would touch it, unflinchingly described the destruction of a slum girl.

The city had entered the American imagination and become, by the early 1900s, a main theme of American art and literature. And because it challenged so many assumptions of an older, republican America, the city also became an overriding concern of reformers and a main theater in the drama of the Progressive Era.

TIMELINE

1869	Corcoran Gallery of Art, nation's first major art museum, opens in Washington, D.C.	1885	William Jenney builds first steel-framed structure, Chicago's Home Insurance Building
1873	Mark Twain and Charles Dudley Warner publish *The Gilded Age*	1887	First electric trolley line constructed in Richmond, Virginia
1875	Dwight L. Moody launches urban revivalist movement	1893	Chicago Columbian Exposition "City Beautiful" movement
1876	Alexander Graham Bell patents telephone	1895	William Randolph Hearst enters New York journalism
	National Baseball League founded	1897	Boston builds first American subway
1879	Thomas Edison invents lightbulb	1900	Theodore Dreiser publishes *Sister Carrie*
	Salvation Army arrives from Britain		
1881	Andrew Carnegie offers to build a library for every American city	1901	New York Tenement House Law
		1904	New York subway system opens
1883	New York City's Metropolitan Opera founded	1906	San Francisco earthquake
	Joseph Pulitzer purchases *New York World*	1913	Fifty-five-story Woolworth Building opens in New York City

For Further Exploration

The starting point for modern urban historiography is Sam Bass Warner's pioneering book on Boston, *Streetcar Suburbs, 1870–1900* (1962). In a subsequent work, *The Private City: Philadelphia in Three Periods* (1968), Warner broadened his analysis to show how private decision making shaped the character of the American city. Innovations in urban construction are treated in Carl Condit, *Rise of the New York Skyscraper, 1865–1913* (1996); Alan Trachtenberg, *The Brooklyn Bridge* (1965); and Harold L. Platt, *The Electric City: Energy and the Growth of the Chicago Area, 1880–1930* (1991).

On the social elite, see Frederic C. Jaher, *The Urban Establishment* (1982), and Sven Beckert, *The Moneyed Metropolis: New York City and the Consolidation of the American Bourgeoisie, 1850–1896* (2001). Aspects of middle-class life are revealed in Margaret Marsh, *Suburban Lives* (1990); Michael A. Ebner, *Creating Chicago's North Shore: A Suburban History* (1988); Jane Hunter, *How Young Ladies Became Girls: The Victorian Origins of American Girlhood* (2003); Howard B. Chudacoff, *The Age of the Bachelor: Creating an American Subculture* (1999); and, on the entry of immigrants into the middle class, Andrew R. Heinze, *Adapting to Abundance* (1990).

On urban life, see especially Gunther Barth, *City People: The Rise of Modern City Culture* (1982); John F. Kasson, *Amusing the Million: Coney Island at the Turn of the Century* (1978); Timothy J. Gilfoyle, *City of Eros: New York City, Prostitution and the Commercialization of Sex,*

1790–1920 (1991); Kathy Peiss, *Cheap Amusements: Working Women and Leisure in Turn-of-the-Century New York* (1986). The best introduction to Gilded Age intellectual currents is Alan Trachtenberg, *The Incorporation of America: Culture and Society, 1865–1893* (1983).

On the Columbian Exposition of 1893, an excellent Web site is The World's Columbian Exposition: Idea, Experience, Aftermath at <http://xroads.virginia.edu/~ma96/wce/title>, which includes detailed guides to every site at the fair and an analysis of its lasting impact. On the Lower East Side, at <http://acad.smumn.edu/history/contents.html>, offers a collection of first-rate articles and documents written at the turn of the century about life on New York's Lower East Side, from housing and child labor to ethnic communities and pushcarts.

For definitions of key terms boldfaced in this chapter, see the glossary at the end of the book.

To assess your mastery of the material covered in this chapter, see the Online Study Guide at **bedfordstmartins.com/henrettaconcise**.

For map resources and primary documents, see **bedfordstmartins.com/henrettaconcise**.

Chapter 19

POLITICS IN THE AGE OF ENTERPRISE
1877–1896

> Politics has now become a gainful profession, like advocacy, stockbroking, [or] the dry goods trade.... People go into it to make a living.
>
> JAMES BRYCE, *THE AMERICAN COMMONWEALTH*, 1888

Ever since the founding of the republic, foreign visitors had been coming to America to witness the political goings-on of a democratic society. Most celebrated was the French aristocrat Alexis de Tocqueville, the author of *Democracy in America* (1832). When an equally brilliant visitor, the Englishman James Bryce, sat down to write his own account fifty years later, he decided that Tocqueville's great book could not be his model. For Tocqueville, Bryce noted, "America was primarily a democracy, the ideal democracy, fraught with lessons for Europe." In his own book, *The American Commonwealth* (1888), Bryce was much less rhapsodic. Tocqueville's robust democracy had devolved into the barren politics of post–Civil War America, whose practitioners, as Bryce complains in this chapter's epigraph, had lost sight of the higher purpose of public service.

Bryce was anxious, however, not to be misunderstood. Europeans would find in his book "much that is sordid, much that will provoke unfavorable comment." But they needed to be aware of "a reserve of force and patriotism more than sufficient to sweep away all the evils now tolerated, and to make a politics of the country worthy of its material grandeur and of the private virtues of its inhabitants." Bryce was ultimately an optimist: "A hundred times in writing this book have I been disheartened by the facts I was stating; a hundred times has the recollection of the abounding strength and vitality of the nation chased away these tremors."

What it was that Bryce found so disheartening in the practice of American politics is this chapter's first subject; the second is the underlying vitality that Bryce sensed, and how it reemerged and reinvigorated the nation's politics by the century's end.

The Politics of the Status Quo, 1877–1893

In times of national ferment, as a rule, public life becomes magnified. Leaders emerge. Great issues are debated. The powers of government expand. All this had been true of the Civil War era, when the crises of Union and Reconstruction had severely tested the nation's political structure, not least by the contested presidential election of 1876. In 1877, with Rutherford B. Hayes safely settled in the White House, the era of sectional strife finally ended.

Political life went on, but drained of its earlier drama. The 1880s heralded no Lincolns, no great national debates. An irreducible core of public functions remained and even, as on the question of railroad regulation, grudging acceptance of new federal responsibilities. But the dominant rhetoric celebrated that government which governed least, and as compared to the Civil War era, American government did govern less.

The National Scene

There were five presidents from 1877 to 1893: Rutherford B. Hayes (Republican, 1877–1881), James A. Garfield (Republican, 1881), Chester A. Arthur (Republican, 1881–1885), Grover Cleveland (Democrat, 1885–1889), and Benjamin Harrison (Republican, 1889–1893). All were estimable men. Hayes had served effectively as governor of Ohio for three terms, and Garfield had done well as a congressional leader. Arthur, despite his reputation as a hack politician, had shown fine administrative skills as head of the New York customs house. Cleveland enjoyed an enviable reputation as reform mayor of Buffalo and governor of New York. None was a charismatic leader, but circumstances, more than personal qualities, explain why these presidents did not make a larger mark on history.

The president's most demanding task was dispensing **patronage** to the faithful. Under the **spoils system**, government appointments were treated as rewards for those who had served the victorious party. Reform of this practice became urgent after President Garfield was shot and killed in 1881 by Charles Guiteau. Although Guiteau's motives were murky, advocates of civil service reform blamed the poisonous atmosphere of a spoils system that left many disappointed in the scramble for office. The resulting Pendleton Act (1883) directed that federal jobs henceforth be filled by examination under a nonpartisan Civil Service Commission. The original list covered only 10 percent of the jobs, however, and the White House still staggered (as Cleveland grumbled) under the "damned, everlasting clatter for office." Though standards of public administration did rise, there was no American counterpart to the professional civil services taking shape in Britain and Germany in these years.

The duties of the executive branch were, in any event, modest. Its biggest job was delivering the mail; of 100,000 federal employees in 1880, 56 percent worked

PUCK.

"WHERE IS HE?"

Where Is He?

This *Puck* cartoon, which appeared two weeks after Benjamin Harrison's defeat for reelection at Grover Cleveland's hands in 1892, is a commentary on Harrison's insignificance as president. The hat in Uncle Sam's hands belonged to Benjamin Harrison's grandfather, President William Henry Harrison. *Puck* started using the hat as a trademark for Benjamin Harrison after he had been elected in 1888. As his term progressed, the hat grew increasingly larger and the president successively smaller. By the time of his defeat, just the hat was left and Harrison had disappeared altogether.

Bancroft Library, University of California at Berkeley. *Puck*, November 16, 1892.

FOR MORE HELP ANALYZING THIS IMAGE, see the Online Study Guide at **bedfordstmartins.com/ henrettaconcise**.

for the Post Office. Even the important cabinet offices—Treasury, State, War, Navy, Interior—were sleepy places carrying on largely routine duties. Virtually all federal funding came from customs duties and excise taxes on liquor and tobacco. These sources produced more money than the government spent. How to reduce the federal surplus ranked as one of the most nettlesome issues of the 1880s.

As for setting a national agenda, this was—unlike in Lincoln's day—not to be looked for from the White House. "The office of President is essentially executive in nature," Cleveland insisted. On matters of national policy, the presidents took a back seat to Capitol Hill.

But Congress functioned badly. It was regularly bogged down by procedural rules and by unruly members resistant to party discipline. Nor did either party have a strong agenda. Historically, the Democrats favored states' rights, while the Republicans were heirs to the Whig enthusiasm for federally assisted economic development. After Reconstruction, however, the Republicans backed away from state interventionism and, in truth, party differences became muddy. On most leading issues of the day—civil service reform, the currency, regulation of the railroads— the divisions occurred within the parties and not between them.

Only the **tariff** remained a fighting issue. From Lincoln's administration on- ward, high duties had protected American industry from imported goods. It was an article of Republican faith, as President Harrison said in 1892, that "the protec- tive system . . . has been a mighty instrument for the development of the national wealth." The Democrats, free traders by tradition, regularly attacked Republican protectionism. Yet, in practice, the tariff was a negotiable issue like any other. Congressmen voted their constituents' interests regardless of party rhetoric. As a result, every tariff bill was a patchwork of bargains among special interests.

Issues were treated gingerly partly because the parties were so equally balanced. The Democrats, in retreat immediately after the Civil War, quickly regrouped and by the end of Reconstruction stood on virtually equal terms with the Republi- cans. Every presidential election from 1876 to 1892 was decided by a thin margin (Map 19.1), and neither party gained permanent command of Congress. Political caution seemed best; any false move on national issues might tip the scales to the other side. "Neither party has any principles, any distinctive tenets," grumbled James Bryce. "All has been lost, except office or the hope of it."

The decline of principled politics was evident in the Republicans' retreat from their Civil War legacy. The major unfinished business after 1877 involved the plight of the former slaves. The Republican agenda called for federal funding to combat il- literacy and, even more contentious, federal protection for black voters in southern elections. Neither measure managed to make it through Congress. With little mileage left in Reconstruction politics, the Republicans backpedaled on the race issue and abandoned the blacks to their fate.

That did not stop Republican orators from "waving the bloody shirt" against the Democrats. Service in the Union army gave candidates a strong claim to public office, and veterans' benefits always stood high on the Republican agenda. The Democrats played the same patriotic card in the South as defenders of the Lost Cause. Bryce rightly criticized American politicians for "clinging too long to out- worn issues and neglecting the problems . . . which now perplex the country."

Alternatively, campaigns could descend into comedy. In the hard-fought elec- tion of 1884, for example, the Democrat Cleveland burst on the scene as a reformer, fresh from his victories over corrupt machine politics in New York State. But years earlier Cleveland, a bachelor, had fathered an illegitimate child, and throughout the campaign he was dogged by the ditty, "Maw, Maw, where's my Paw?" (After election day Cleveland's supporters gleefully responded, "He's in the White House, haw- haw-haw.") Cleveland's opponent, James G. Blaine, already on the defensive for tak- ing favors from the railroads, was weakened by the unthinking charge of a too ardent Republican supporter that the Democrats were the party of "Rum, Romanism and Rebellion." In a twinkling he had insulted Catholic voters and

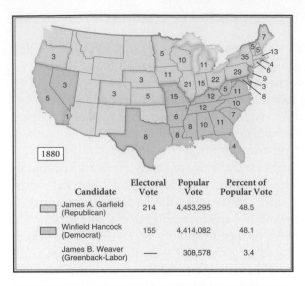

Candidate	Electoral Vote	Popular Vote	Percent of Popular Vote
James A. Garfield (Republican)	214	4,453,295	48.5
Winfield Hancock (Democrat)	155	4,414,082	48.1
James B. Weaver (Greenback-Labor)	—	308,578	3.4

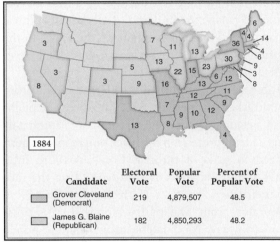

Candidate	Electoral Vote	Popular Vote	Percent of Popular Vote
Grover Cleveland (Democrat)	219	4,879,507	48.5
James G. Blaine (Republican)	182	4,850,293	48.2

MAP 19.1 Presidential Elections of 1880, 1884, and 1888

The anatomy of political stalemate is evident in this trio of electoral maps of the 1880s. First, note the equal division of the popular vote between Republicans and Democrats. Second, note the remarkable persistence in the pattern of electoral votes, in which overwhelmingly states went to the same party in all three elections. Finally, we can identify who determined the outcomes—the two "swing" states, New York and Indiana, whose vote shifted every four years and always in favor of the winning candidate.

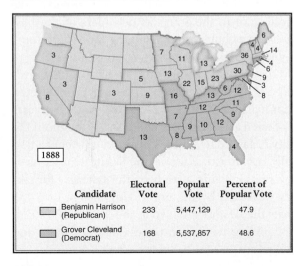

Candidate	Electoral Vote	Popular Vote	Percent of Popular Vote
Benjamin Harrison (Republican)	233	5,447,129	47.9
Grover Cleveland (Democrat)	168	5,537,857	48.6

possibly lost the election for Blaine. In the midst of all the mudslinging, the issues got lost.

The Ideology of Individualism

The characteristics of public life in the 1880s—the passivity of the federal government, the evasiveness of the political parties, the absorption in politics for its own sake—derived ultimately from the conviction that little was at stake in public affairs. In 1887 Cleveland vetoed a small appropriation for drought-stricken Texas farmers with the remark that "though the people support the Government, the Government should not support the people." Governmental activity was itself considered a bad thing. All the state could do, said Republican senator Roscoe Conkling, was "to clear the way of impediments and dangers, and leave every class and every individual free and safe in the exertions and pursuits of life." Conkling was expressing the political corollary to the economic doctrine of **laissez-faire**—the belief that the less government did, the better.

A flood of popular writings trumpeted the creed of individualism, from the rags-to-riches tales of Horatio Alger to innumerable success manuals with such titles as *Thoughts for the Young Men of America, or a Few Practical Words of Advice to Those Born in Poverty and Destined to be Reared in Orphanages* (1871). Self-made men such as Andrew Carnegie became cultural heroes. A best-seller was Carnegie's *Triumphant Democracy* (1886), which paid homage to a country that enabled a penniless Scottish child to rise from bobbin boy to steel magnate.

From the pulpit came the assurances of the Episcopal bishop William Lawrence of Massachusetts that "Godliness is in league with riches." Bishop Lawrence was voicing a familiar theme of American Protestantism: success in one's earthly calling revealed the promise of eternal salvation. It was all too easy for a conservative ministry to bless the furious acquisitiveness of industrial America. "To secure wealth is an honorable ambition," intoned the Baptist minister Russell H. Conwell in his lecture "Acres of Diamonds."

The celebration of American acquisitiveness drew strong support from social theorizing drawn from science. In *On the Origin of Species* (1859), British naturalist Charles Darwin had developed a bold hypothesis to explain the evolution of plants and animals. In nature, Darwin wrote, all living things struggle to survive. Individual members of a species are born with genetic mutations that better fit them for their particular environment—camouflage coloring for a bird, for example, or resistance to thirst in a camel. These survival characteristics, since they are genetically transmissible, become dominant in future generations, and the species evolves. This mechanism, which Darwin called *natural selection*, put evolution on a firm intellectual basis and revolutionized biological science.

Drawing on Darwin, the British philosopher Herbert Spencer spun out an elaborate analysis of how human society had evolved through competition and "survival of the fittest." **Social Darwinism**, as Spencer's ideas became known, was

Facing the World

The cover of this Horatio Alger novel (1893) captures the American myth of opportunity. Our hero, Harry Vane, is a poor but earnest lad, ready to make his way in the world and, despite the many obstacles thrown in his path, sure to succeed. In some 135 books Horatio Alger repeated this story, with minor variations, for an eager reading public that numbered in the millions.

Frank and Marie-Therese Wood Print Collections, Alexandria, VA.

championed in America by William Graham Sumner, a sociology professor at Yale. Competition, said Sumner, is a law of nature that "can no more be done away with than gravitation." And who are the fittest? "The millionaires. . . . They may fairly be regarded as the naturally selected agents of society. They get high wages and live in luxury, but the bargain is a good one for society."

Social Darwinists regarded with horror any interference with social processes. "The great stream of time and earthly things will sweep on just the same in spite of us," Sumner wrote in a famous essay, "The Absurd Attempt to Make the World Over" (1894). As for the government, it had "at bottom . . . two chief things . . . with which to deal. They are the property of men and the honor of women. These it has to defend against crime."

The Supremacy of the Courts

Suspicion of government not only paralyzed political initiative; it also shifted power away from the executive and legislative branches. "The task of constitutional government," declared Sumner, "is to devise institutions which shall come into play at critical periods to prevent the abusive control of the powers of a state by the controlling classes in it." Sumner meant the judiciary. From the 1870s onward the courts increasingly accepted the role that he assigned to them, becoming the guardians of the rights of private property against the grasping tentacles of government.

The main target of the courts was not Washington, but state activism. This was because, under the federal system as it was understood in the late nineteenth century, the residual powers—those not delegated by the Constitution to the federal government—left the states with primary authority over social welfare and economic regulation through the use of police powers. The great question in American law was how to strike a balance between the regulatory power to advance the general welfare and the liberty of individuals to pursue their private interests. Most states, caught up in the conservative ethos of the day, were cutting back on expenditures and public services. Even so, there were more than enough state initiatives to alarm vigilant judges. Thus, in the landmark case *In Re Jacobs* (1885), the New York Supreme Court struck down a state law prohibiting cigar manufacturing in tenements on the grounds that such regulation exceeded the police powers of the state.

As the federal courts took up the battle against state activism, they found their strongest weapon in the Fourteenth Amendment (1868), which prohibited the states from depriving "any person of life, liberty, or property, without due process of law." The due process clause had been adopted during Reconstruction to protect the civil rights of the former slaves. But due process protected the property rights and contractual liberty of any "person," and legally, corporations counted as persons. So interpreted, the Fourteenth Amendment became by the turn of the century a powerful restraint on the states in the use of their police powers to regulate private business.

The Supreme Court similarly hamstrung the federal government. In 1895 the Court ruled that the federal power to regulate interstate commerce did not cover manufacturing and struck down a federal income tax law. And in areas where federal power was undeniable—such as the regulation of railroads—the Supreme Court scrutinized every measure for undue interference with the rights of property.

The preeminent jurist of the day, Stephen J. Field, made no bones about the dangers he saw in the nation's headlong industrial development. "As the inequalities in the conditions of men become more and more marked and . . . angry menaces against order find vent in loud denunciations—it becomes more and more the imperative duty of the court to enforce with a firm hand every guarantee of the Constitution."

Power conferred status. The law, not politics, attracted the ablest people and held the public's esteem. A Wisconsin judge boasted, "The bench symbolizes on earth the throne of divine justice. . . . Law in its highest sense is the will of God." Judicial supremacy revealed how entrenched the ideology of individualism had become in industrial America and also how low American politicians had fallen in the esteem of their countrymen.

Politics and the People

The country may have felt, as Kansas editor William Allen White wrote, "sick with politics" and "nauseated at all politicians," but somehow this did not curb the popular appetite for politics. Proportionately more voters turned out in presidential elections from 1876 to 1892 than at any other time in American history. People voted Democratic or Republican loyally for a lifetime. National conventions attracted huge crowds. "The excitement, the mental and physical strains," remarked an Indiana Republican after the 1888 convention, "are surpassed only by prolonged battle in actual warfare, as I have been told by officers of the Civil War who latter engaged in convention struggles." The convention he described had nominated the colorless Benjamin Harrison on a routine platform. What was all the excitement about?

Cultural Politics: Party, Religion, and Ethnicity

In the late nineteenth century, politics was a vibrant part of the nation's culture. America "is a land of conventions and assemblies," a journalist noted, "where it is the most natural thing in the world for people to get together in meetings, where almost every event is the occasion for speechmaking." During the election season the party faithful marched in torchlight parades. Party paraphernalia flooded the country—handkerchiefs, mugs, posters, and buttons emblazoned with the Democratic donkey or the Republican elephant, symbols that had been adopted in the 1870s. In the 1888 campaign the candidates were featured on cards, like baseball players, tucked into packets of Honest Long Cut tobacco. In an age before movies and radio, politics ranked as one of the great American forms of entertainment.

Party loyalty was a deadly serious matter, however. Long after the killing ended, Civil War emotions ran high. Among family friends in Cleveland, recalled the urban reformer Brand Whitlock, the Republican Party was "a synonym for patriotism, another name for the nation. It was inconceivable that any self-respecting person should be a Democrat"—or, among ex-Confederates in the South, that any self-respecting person could be a Republican.

Beyond these sectional differences the most important determinants of party loyalty were religion and ethnicity (Figure 19.1). Statistically, northern Democrats tended to be foreign-born and Catholic, while Republicans tended to be native-born and Protestant. Among Protestants, the more *pietistic* a person's faith—that is, the more personal and direct the believer's relationship to God—the more likely he or she was to be a Republican and to favor using the powers of the state to uphold social values and regulate personal behavior.

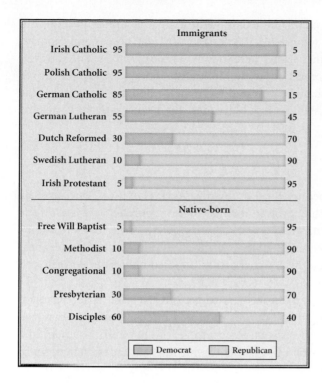

Immigrants

Irish Catholic	95	5
Polish Catholic	95	5
German Catholic	85	15
German Lutheran	55	45
Dutch Reformed	30	70
Swedish Lutheran	10	90
Irish Protestant	5	95

Native-born

Free Will Baptist	5	95
Methodist	10	90
Congregational	10	90
Presbyterian	30	70
Disciples	60	40

☐ Democrat   ☐ Republican

FIGURE 19.1 Voting Patterns in the Midwest, 1870–1892

These figures demonstrate how voting patterns among Midwesterners reflected ethnicity and religion in the late nineteenth century. Especially striking is the overwhelming preference by immigrant Catholics for the Democratic Party. Among Protestants there was an equally strong preference for the Republican Party by certain groups of immigrants (Swedish Lutherans and Irish Protestants) and native born (Free Will Baptists, Methodists, and Congregationalists), but other Protestant groups were more evenly divided in their party preferences.

During the 1880s, as ethnic tensions built up in many cities, education became an arena of bitter conflict. One issue was whether instruction in the public schools should be in English. Immigrant groups often wanted their children taught in their own languages. In St. Louis, a heavily German city, the long-standing policy of teaching German to all students was overturned after a heated campaign. Religion was an even more explosive educational issue. Catholics fought a losing battle over public aid for parochial schools, which by 1900 was prohibited by twenty-three states. In Boston a furious controversy broke out in 1888 over the use of an anti-Catholic history textbook. When the school board withdrew the offending book, angry Protestants elected a new board and returned the text to the curriculum.

Then there was the regulation of public morals. In many states so-called *blue laws* restricted activity on Sundays. When Nebraska banned Sunday baseball, the state supreme court approved the law as a blow struck in "the contest between Christianity and wrong." But German and Irish Catholics, who saw nothing evil in a bit of fun on Sunday, considered blue laws a violation of their personal freedom. **Ethnocultural** conflict also flared over the liquor question. Many states adopted strict licensing and local-option laws governing the sale of alcoholic beverages. Indiana permitted drinking but only joylessly in rooms containing "no devices for amusement or music . . . of any kind."

Because the hottest social issues of the day—education, the liquor question, and observance of the Sabbath—were also party issues, they lent deep significance to party affiliation. And because these issues were fought out mostly at the state and local levels, they hit very close to home. Crusading Methodists thought of Republicans as the party of morality. For embattled Irish and German Catholics, who favored "the largest individual liberty consistent with public order," the Democratic Party was the defender of their freedoms.

Organizational Politics

Politics was also important because of the organizational activity it generated. By the 1870s both major parties had evolved formal, well-organized structures. At the base lay the precinct or ward, where party meetings were open to all members (see Chapter 18). County, state, and national committees ran the ongoing business of the parties. Conventions determined party rules, adopted platforms, and selected the party's candidates.

At election time the party's main job was to get out the vote. Wherever elections were close and hard fought, the parties mounted intensive efforts organized down to the individual voter. In Indiana, for example, the Republicans appointed ten thousand "district men," each responsible for turning out a designated group of voters.

Party governance seemed, on its face, highly democratic, since in theory all power derived from the party members. In practice, however, the parties were run by unofficial internal organizations—**political machines**—which consisted of insiders willing to do party work in exchange for public jobs or the sundry advantages of being connected. Although most evident in city politics, the machine system was integral to party activity at every level, right up to the national organizations.

The machines tended toward one-man rule, although the "boss" ruled more by the consent of the secondary leaders than by his own absolute power. Absorbed in the tasks of power brokerage, party bosses treated public issues as somewhat irrelevant. The high stakes of money, jobs, and influence made for intense factionalism. After Ulysses S. Grant left the White House in 1877, the Republican Party divided into two warring factions—the Stalwarts, led by Senator Roscoe Conkling of New York, and the Halfbreeds, led by James G. Blaine of Maine. The split was sparked by a personal feud between Conkling and Blaine, but it persisted because of a furious struggle over patronage. The Halfbreeds represented a newer Republican generation more favorably disposed than the Stalwarts to political reform and less committed to shopworn Civil War issues. But issues were secondary in the strife between Stalwarts and Halfbreeds. They were really fighting over the spoils of party politics.

Yet the record of machine politics was not wholly negative. In certain ways the standards of governance got better. Disciplined professionals, veterans of machine politics, proved effective as state legislators and congressmen because they were more experienced in the give-and-take of politics. More important, party machines filled a void in the nation's public life. They did informally much of what the governmental system left undone, especially in the cities (see Chapter 18).

But machine politics never managed to win the respect of the general public. Many of the nation's social elite—intellectuals, well-to-do businessmen, and old-line families—resented a politics that excluded people like themselves, the "best men." There was, too, a genuine clash of values. Political reformers called for "dis-interestedness" and "independence"—the opposite of the self-serving careerism and party regularity fostered by the machine system. Many of these critics had earned their spurs as Liberal Republicans who had broken from the party and fought President Grant's reelection in 1872.

In 1884 Carl Schurz, Edwin L. Godkin, and Charles Francis Adams Jr. again left the Republican Party because they could not stomach its presidential candidate, James G. Blaine, whom they associated with corrupt politics. Mainly from New York and Massachusetts, these Republicans became known as Mugwumps—a derisive bit of contemporary slang, supposedly of Indian origin, referring to pompous or self-important persons. The Mugwumps threw their support to Democrat Grover Cleveland and may have ensured his election by giving him the winning margin in New York State.

After the 1884 election the enthusiasm for reform spilled over into local politics, spawning good-government campaigns across the country. Although they won some municipal victories, the Mugwumps were more adept at molding public opinion than at running government. Controlling the newspapers and journals read by the educated middle class, the Mugwumps defined the terms of political debate, denying the machine system legitimacy and injecting an elitist bias into political opinion.

Mark Twain was not alone in proclaiming "an honest and saving loathing for universal suffrage." This democratic triumph of the early republic—a beacon for other nations to follow—now went into reverse, as northern states began to impose **literacy tests** and limit the voting rights of immigrants. The secret ballot, an import from Australia widely adopted around 1890, abetted the Mugwump campaign. Traditionally, voters had submitted party-supplied tickets in public view at the polling place. With the Australian reform, citizens cast their ballots in the privacy of the voting booth, freed from party surveillance, but—for the uneducated and foreign-speaking—burdened by the need to navigate an official ballot. Additional opportunities for discouraging those the Mugwumps considered unfit for suffrage were amply available in the voter registration procedures accompanying the Australian ballot.

The Mugwumps were reformers, but not on behalf of social justice. The travails of working people meant little to them, while keeping the state out of the welfare business meant a great deal. As far as the Mugwumps were concerned, the government that was best was the government that governed least. Theirs was the brand of "reform" perfectly in keeping with the conservative ethos of the time. In this respect, they were not different from conservative judges and party leaders who disdained the term "reformer."

Women's Political Culture

The young Theodore Roosevelt, an up-and-coming Republican state politician in 1884, referred to the Mugwumps contemptuously as "man-milliners" (makers of ladies' hats). The sexual slur was not accidental. In attacking organizational politics, the Mugwumps were challenging a bastion of male society. At party meetings and conventions, men carried on not only the business of politics but also the rituals of male sociability amid cigar smoke and whiskey. Politics was identified with manliness. It was competitive. It dealt in the commerce of power. It was frankly self-aggrandizing. Party politics, in short, was no place for a woman.

So, naturally, the woman suffrage movement met fierce opposition. Acknowledging the uphill battle that lay ahead, suffragists overcame the bitter divisions of the Reconstruction era (see Chapter 15), reuniting in 1890 in the National American Woman Suffrage Association. In that same spirit of realism, suffragists abandoned efforts to get a constitutional amendment and concentrated on state campaigns. Except out West—in Wyoming, Idaho, Colorado, and Utah—the most they could win was the right to vote for school boards or on tax issues. "Men are ordained to govern in all forceful and material things, because they are men," asserted an antisuffrage resolution, "while women, by the same decree of God and nature, are equally fitted to bear rule in a higher and more spiritual realm, where the strong frame and the weighty brain count for less"—that is to say, not in politics.

Yet this invocation of the doctrine of "**separate spheres**"—that men and women had different natures, and that women's nature fitted them for "a higher and more spiritual realm"—did open a channel for women to enter public life. "Women's place is Home," acknowledged the journalist Retha Childe Dorr. "But Home is not contained within the four walls of an individual house. Home is the community. The city full of people is the Family. . . . And badly do the Home and Family need their mother." Indeed, women had since the early nineteenth century engaged in uplifting activities—fighting prostitution, assisting the poor, agitating for prison reform, and demanding better educational and job opportunities. Since many of these goals required state involvement, women's organizations of necessity became politically active. They stressed that partisan politics was not their game. Quite the contrary: women were bent on creating their own political sphere.

No issue joined home and politics more poignantly than the liquor question. Just before Christmas in 1873 the women of Hillsboro, Ohio, began to hold vigils in front of the town's saloons, pleading with the owners to close and end the misery of families of hard-drinking fathers. Thus began a spontaneous uprising of women that spread across the country. From this agitation came the Women's Christian Temperance Union (WCTU), which after its formation in 1874 rapidly blossomed into the largest women's organization in the country.

Because it excluded men, the WCTU was the spawning ground for a new generation of women leaders. Under the guidance of Frances Willard, who became

The Levi P. Morton Association

The top-hatted gentlemen in this photograph constituted the local Republican Party organization of Newport, Rhode Island, named in honor of Levi P. Morton, Republican leader and vice president during the Benjamin Harrison administration (1889–1893). The maleness of party politics leaps from the photograph and asserts more clearly than a thousand words why the suffragist demand for the right to vote was met with ridicule and disbelief. Newport Historical Society.

president in 1879, the WCTU moved beyond temperance and adopted a "Do-Everything" policy. Women recognized that alcoholism was not simply a personal failing; it stemmed from larger social problems in American society. Willard also wanted to attract women who had no particular interest in the liquor question. Local affiliates were encouraged to undertake causes that were important in their own communities. By 1889 the WCTU had thirty-nine departments concerned with labor, prostitution, health, international peace, and other issues.

Most important, the WCTU was drawn to woman suffrage. This was necessary, Willard argued, "because the liquor traffic is entrenched in law, and law grows out of the will of majorities, and majorities of women are against the liquor traffic." The WCTU began by stressing moral suasion and personal discipline—hence the word "temperance" in its name—but broadened its attack on liquor to include prohibition by law. Women needed the vote, said Willard, to fulfill their social responsibilities *as women* (see American Voices, "The Case for Women's Political Rights," p. 580). This was very different from the claim made by the suffragists—that the ballot was an inherent right of all citizens *as individuals*—and was less threatening to masculine pride.

Not much changed in the short run. The WCTU, divided on the suffrage issue, did not become a major participant in later struggles for women's right to vote. But

The Case for Women's Political Rights

HELEN POTTER

*I*n 1883 Helen Potter, a New York educator, testified before the Senate Committee on Education and Labor. She meant to speak about the sanitary conditions of the poor in New York City, but in the course of her testimony she delivered a powerful indictment of the unequal treatment of women that spoke volumes about the evolving women's political culture of the late nineteenth century.

The Witness. It is really an important question—this of the condition of women in our community. When I was a young girl I had some ambition, and when I heard a good speaker, or when I read something written by a good writer, I had an ambition to do something of that kind myself. I was exceedingly anxious to preach, but the churches would not have me; why, they said that a woman must not be heard. . . .

Question. I suppose you have an idea that women might abolish some of the tricks of the politician's trade?

Answer. Well, sir, it would take them a long time to learn to dare to do those things that men do in the way of politics—to sell and buy votes. . . .

Q. Why do you think that the suffrage is not extended to women by men—what is the true reason, the radical reason, why men do not give up one half their political power to women?

A. Well, it may arise from a false notion of gallantry. I think most men feel like taking care of, and protecting the ladies. . . . It would be all very well, perhaps, if all women had representatives, and if all had a generous, straightforward honorable man to represent them. But take the case of a good woman who has a drunken husband; how can he represent her? He votes for liquor and for everything he may happen to want, even though it may ruin her and turn her out of doors, and even though it may ruin her children. If the husband is a bad man would it not be better for that woman to represent herself?

Q. What effect do you think the extension of the suffrage to women would have upon their material condition, their wage-earning power and the like?

A. They would get equal pay for equal work of equal value. I do not think a woman ought to be paid the price of an expert, when she is not herself an expert, but I believe there would be a stimulus for a woman to fit herself for the very best work. What stimulus is there for woman to fit herself properly, if she never can attain the highest pay, no matter what sort of work she does? If women had a vote I think larger avenues of livelihood would be opened for them and they would be more respected by the governmental powers.

SOURCE: U.S. Senate, Committee on Education and Labor, Report upon Relations between Labor and Capital, II (1885), 627, 629–32.

by linking women's social concerns to women's political participation, the WCTU helped lay the groundwork for a fresh attack on male electoral politics in the early twentieth century. In the meantime, even without the vote, the WCTU demonstrated how potent a voice women could find in the public arena and how vibrant a political culture they could build.

Race and Politics in the New South

When Reconstruction ended in 1877, so did the hopes of African Americans that they would enjoy the equal rights of citizenship promised them by the Fourteenth and Fifteenth Amendments. Southern schools were strictly segregated. Access to jobs, the courts, and social services was racially determined and unequal. However, public accommodations were not yet legally segregated, and practices varied a good deal across the South. Only on the railroads, as rail travel became more common, did whites demand that blacks be excluded from first-class cars, with the result that southern railroads became, after 1887, the first public accommodation subject to segregation laws.

In politics the situation was still more fluid. Blacks had not been driven out of politics. On the contrary, their turnout at elections in the post-Reconstruction years was not far behind the turnout by whites. But blacks did not participate on equal terms with whites. In the black belt areas, where African Americans sometimes outnumbered whites, voting districts were designed to ensure that, while blacks got some offices, political control remained in white hands. Blacks were routinely intimidated during political campaigns. Even so, an impressive majority remained staunchly Republican, refusing, as the last black congressman from Mississippi told his House colleagues in 1882, "to surrender their honest convictions, even upon the altar of their personal necessities."

Whatever hopes blacks entertained for better days, however, faded during the 1880s and then, in the next decade, expired in a terrible burst of racial terrorism.

Biracial Politics

No democratic society can survive if it does not enable competing economic and social interests to be heard. In the United States the two-party system performs that role. The Civil War crisis severely tested the two-party system because, in both North and South, political opposition came to be seen as treasonable. In the victorious North, despite the best efforts of the Republicans, the Democrats shed their disgrace after the war and reclaimed their status as a major party. In the defeated South, however, the scars of war cut deep, and Reconstruction cut even deeper. The struggle for "home rule" empowered southern Democrats. They had "redeemed" the South from Republican domination—hence the name they adopted: Redeemers. Cloaked in the mantle of the Lost Cause, the Redeemers claimed a monopoly on political legitimacy.

The Republican Party in the South did not fold up, however. On the contrary, it soldiered on, sustained by tenacious black loyalty, by a hard core of white support, by patronage from Republican national administrations, and by a key Democratic vulnerability. This was the gap between the universality the Democrats claimed as the party of Redemption and its actual domination by a single interest—the South's economic elite.

Class antagonism, though masked by sectional patriotism, was never absent from southern society. The Civil War had brought out long-smoldering differences between planters and hill-country farmers, who felt called on to shed blood for a slaveholding system in which they had no interest. Afterward, class tensions were exacerbated by the spread of farm tenancy and by an emergent class of low-wage industrial workers. Unable to make their grievances heard, economically distressed Southerners broke with the Democratic Party in the early 1880s and mounted insurgent movements across the region. Most notable were the Readjusters, who briefly gained power in Virginia over the issue of speculation in Reconstruction debt: they opposed repayment that would have rewarded bondholding speculators while leaving the state destitute. After subsiding briefly, this agrarian discontent revived with a vengeance in the late 1880s, as tenant farmers sought political power through farmers' alliances and the newly evolving Populist Party.

As this insurgency against the Democrats accelerated, the question of black participation became critical. Racism cut through southern society and, so some thought, most infected the lowest rungs. "The white laboring classes here," wrote an Alabamian in 1886, "are separated from the Negroes, working all day side by side with them, by an innate consciousness of race superiority," which "excites a sentiment of sympathy and equality with the classes above them." Yet when times got bad enough, hard-pressed whites could also see blacks as fellow victims. "They are in the ditch just like we are," asserted one white Texan. Southern Populists never fully reconciled these contradictory impulses. They did not question the racist conventions of social inequality. Nor were the interests of white farmers and black tenants and laborers always in concert. But once agrarian protest turned political, the logic of interracial solidarity became hard to deny.

In the meantime, black farmers had developed a political structure of their own. The Colored Farmers' Alliance operated much less openly than its white counterparts—it could be worth a black man's life to make too open a show of his independence—but nevertheless made black voters a factor in the political calculations of southern Populists. The demands of partisan politics, once the break with the Democrats came, clinched the argument for interracial unity. Where the Populists fused with the Republican Party, as in North Carolina and Tennessee, they automatically became allies of black leaders. Where the Populists fielded separate third-party tickets, they needed to appeal directly to black voters. "The accident of color can make no difference in the interest of farmers, croppers, and laborers," argued the Georgian Tom Watson. "You are kept apart that you may be separately fleeced of your earnings" (see American Voices, "The Case for Interracial Unity," p. 583). By making

The Case for Interracial Unity

TOM WATSON

*I*n the post-Reconstruction South, racial animosities dividing poor whites from poor blacks
enabled a conservative elite to maintain its grip on political power. Recognizing this, the
fiery Georgia Populist Tom Watson appealed to whites and blacks to look to their class inter-
ests, most memorably in the following statement made in advance of the 1892 election. In the
bitter aftermath Watson reversed course and rebuilt his career as a race-baiting politician ex-
ploiting the very hatreds that he had once so strenuously resisted.

The white tenant lives adjoining the colored tenant. Their houses are almost equally destitute
of comforts. Their living is confined to bare necessities.... They pay the same enormous prices
for farm supplies. Christmas finds them both without any satisfactory return for a year's toil.
Dull and heavy and unhappy, they both start the plows again when "New Year's" passes.

Now the People's Party says to these two men, "You are kept apart that you may be separately fleeced of your earnings. You are made to hate each other because upon that hatred
is rested the keystone of the arch of financial despotism which enslaves you both. You are
deceived and blinded that you may not see how this race antagonism perpetuates a monetary system which beggars both."

This is so obviously true it is no wonder both these unhappy laborers stop to listen. No
wonder they begin to realize that no change of law can benefit the white tenant which does
not benefit the black one likewise; that no system which now does injustice to one of them
can fail to injure both. Their every material interest is identical. The moment this becomes
a conviction, mere selfishness, the mere desire to better their conditions, escape onerous
taxes, avoid usurious charges, lighten their rents, or change their precarious tenements into
smiling, happy homes, will drive these two men together, just as their mutual inflamed
prejudices now drive them apart.

... Why should the colored man always be taught that the white man of his neighborhood hates him, while a Northern man, who taxes every rag on his back, loves him? Why
should not my tenant come to regard me as his friend rather than the manufacturer who
plunders us both? Why should we perpetuate a policy which drives the black man into the
arms of the Northern politician?

... To the emasculated individual who cries "Negro supremacy!" there is little to be said....
Not being prepared to make any such admission in favor of any race the sun ever shone on, I
have no words which can portray my contempt for the white men, Anglo-Saxons, who can
knock their knees together, and through their chattering teeth and pale lips admit they are afraid
the Negroes will "dominate us." The question of social equality does not enter into the calculation at all. That is a thing each citizen decides for himself....

The conclusion, then, seems to me this: They will become political allies, and neither can
injure the one without weakening both. It will be in the interest of both that each should
have justice. And on these broad lines of mutual interest, mutual forbearance, and mutual
support the present will be made the stepping-stone to future peace and prosperity.

SOURCE: Paul F. Boller and Ronald Story, eds., *A More Perfect Union: Documents in U.S. History* (Boston:
Houghton Mifflin, 1984), 2: 83–85.

this interracial appeal, even if not always wholeheartedly, the Populists put at risk the foundations of conservative southern politics.

One-Party Rule Triumphant

The Democrats struck back with all their might. They played the race card to the hilt, parading as the "white man's party" while denouncing the Populists for promoting "Negro rule." Yet they shamelessly competed for the black vote. In this they had many advantages: money, control of the local power structures, and a paternalistic relationship to the black community. When all else failed, mischief at the polls enabled the Democrats to beat back the Populists. Across the South in the 1892 elections, the Democrats snatched victory from defeat by a miraculous vote count of the blacks—including many long dead or gone. Thus the Mississippian Frank Burkitt's bitter attack on the conservatives: they were "a class of corrupt office-seekers" who had "hypocritically raised the howl of white supremacy while they debauched the ballot boxes . . . disregarded the rights of the blacks . . . and actually dominated the will of the white people through the instrumentality of the stolen negro vote."

In the midst of these deadly struggles, the Democrats decided to settle matters once and for all. The movement to disfranchise the blacks, hitherto tentative, swiftly gathered steam (Map 19.2). In 1890 Mississippi adopted a literacy test that effectively drove the state's blacks out of politics. The motives behind it were cynical, but the literacy test could be dressed up as a reform for white Mississippians tired of electoral fraud and violence. Their children and grandchildren, argued one influential figure, should not be left "with shotguns in their hands, a lie in their mouths and perjury on their lips in order to defeat the negroes." Better, a Mississippi journalist wrote, to devise "some legal defensible substitute for the abhorrent and evil methods on which white supremacy lies." This logic even persuaded some weary Populists: Frank Burkitt, for example, was arguing *for* the Mississippi literacy test in the words quoted in the previous paragraph.

The race issue helped bring down the Populists; now it helped reconcile them to defeat. Embittered whites, deeply ambivalent all along about interracial cooperation, turned their fury on the blacks. Insofar as disfranchising measures asserted militant white supremacy, poor whites approved. Of course, it was important that their own vulnerability—their own lack of education—be partially offset by lenient enforcement of the literacy test. Thus—to take a blatant instance—Louisiana's grandfather clause exempted from the test those entitled to vote on January 1, 1867 (before the Fifteenth Amendment gave freedmen that right), together with their sons and grandsons. But poor whites were not protected from property and **poll-tax** requirements, and many stopped voting.

Poor whites might have objected more had their spokesmen not been conceded a voice in southern politics. A new brand of demagogic politician came forward to speak for them, appealing not to their economic interests but to their racial prejudices.

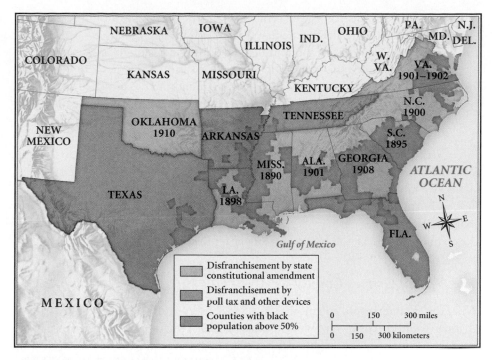

MAP 19.2 Disfranchisement in the New South

In the midst of the Populist challenge to Democratic one-party rule in the South, a movement to deprive blacks of the right to vote spread from Mississippi across the South. By 1910 every state in the region except Tennessee, Arkansas, Texas, and Florida had made constitutional changes designed to prevent blacks from voting, and these four states accomplished much the same result through poll taxes and other exclusionary methods. For the next half century, the political process in the South would be for whites only.

FOR MORE HELP ANALYZING THIS MAP, see the Online Study Guide at **bedfordstmartins.com/henrettaconcise**.

Tom Watson, the Georgia Populist, rebuilt his political career as a spellbinding practitioner of race baiting. In South Carolina "Pitchfork" Ben Tillman, more of a mainstream Democratic politician, was adept at manipulating images of white manhood. What bound Southerners together, no matter their class, was their sturdy independence, their defense of the virtue of white womanhood, and their resistance to outside meddling in southern affairs. A U.S. senator for many years, Tillman was as fiery as Tom Watson at condemning blacks as "an ignorant and debased and debauched race."

A brand of white supremacy emerged that was more virulent than anything blacks had faced since Reconstruction. The color line, hitherto incomplete, became rigid and comprehensive. Segregated seating in trains, first adopted in the late 1880s, provided a precedent for the legal separation of the races. The enforcing legislation, known as **Jim Crow** laws, soon applied to every type of public facility—

restaurants, hotels, streetcars, even cemeteries. In the 1890s the South became a region fully segregated by law for the first time.

The U.S. Supreme Court soon ratified the South's decision. In *Plessy v. Ferguson* (1896), the Court ruled that segregation was not discriminatory—that is, it did not violate black civil rights under the Fourteenth Amendment—provided that blacks received accommodations equal to those of whites. The "separate but equal" doctrine ignored the realities of southern life: segregated facilities were rarely if ever "equal" in any material sense, and segregation was itself intended to underscore the inferiority of blacks. With a similar disregard for reality, the Supreme Court in *Williams v. Mississippi* (1898) validated the disfranchising devices of the southern states: so long as race was not a specified criterion for disfranchisement, the Fifteenth Amendment was not being violated even though the practical effect was that blacks no longer participated in politics in the South and, more fundamentally, the symbolic effect that they were no longer truly citizens of the republic.

The Case of Grimes County

What this counterrevolution meant is perhaps best captured locally, by the events in Grimes County, a cotton-growing area in east Texas, where African Americans composed more than half of the population. They kept the local Republican Party going after Reconstruction and regularly sent black representatives to the Texas legislature during the 1870s and 1880s. More remarkably, the local Populist Party that appeared among white farmers proved immune to Democrats' taunts of "black rule." A Populist-Republican coalition swept the county elections in 1896 and 1898, a surprising remnant of the southern Populist movement.

In 1899, defeated Democratic candidates and prominent citizens organized the secret White Man's Union. Blacks were forcibly prevented from voting in town elections that year. The two most important black leaders were shot down in cold blood. Night riders terrorized both white Populists and black Republicans. When the Populist sheriff proved incapable of enforcing the law, the game was up. Reconstituted as the White Man's Party, the Union became the local Democratic Party in a new guise. The Democrats carried Grimes County by an overwhelming vote in 1900. The day after the election, gunmen laid siege to the sheriff's office. They killed his brother and a friend and drove him, badly wounded, out of the county forever.

The White Man's Party ruled Grimes County for the next fifty years. The whole episode was the handiwork of the county's "best citizens," suggesting how respectable terror had become in the service of white supremacy. Grimes County, as a leading citizen grimly said, intended to "force the African to keep his place." After Populism was crushed in that corner of Texas, blacks could survive only if they stayed out of politics and avoided trouble with whites.

Like the blacks of Grimes County, southern blacks in many places resisted as best they could. When Georgia adopted the first Jim Crow law applying to streetcars in 1891, Atlanta blacks declared a boycott, and over the next fifteen years blacks

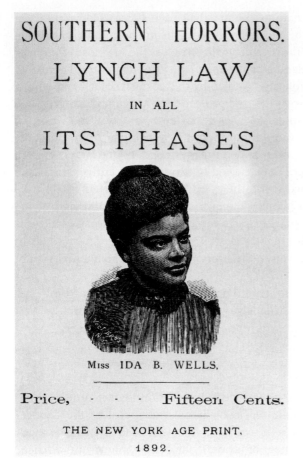

SOUTHERN HORRORS.

LYNCH LAW

IN ALL

ITS PHASES

MISS IDA B. WELLS.

Price, · · · Fifteen Cents.

THE NEW YORK AGE PRINT,
1892.

Miss Ida B. Wells

In 1887 Ida Wells (Wells-Barnett after she married in 1895) was thrown bodily from a train in Tennessee for refusing to vacate her seat in a section reserved for whites, launching her into a lifelong crusade for racial justice. Her mission was to expose the evil of lynching in the South. This portrait is from the title page of a pamphlet she published in 1892 entitled, "Southern Horrors. Lynch Law in All Its Phases."

Miriam and Ira D. Wallach Division of Art, Prints and Photographs, The New York Public Library. Astor, Lenox and Tilden Foundations.

boycotted segregated streetcars in at least twenty-five cities. "Do not trample on our pride by being 'jim crowed,'" the Savannah *Tribune* urged its readers: "Walk!" Ida Wells-Barnett emerged as the most outspoken black crusader against lynching, so enraging the Memphis white community by the editorials in her newspaper, *Free Speech*, that she was forced in 1892 to leave the city.

Some blacks were drawn to the Back-to-Africa movement, abandoning all hope that they would ever find justice in America. But emigration was not a real choice, and African Americans had to bend to the raging forces of racism and find a way to survive.

The Crisis of American Politics: The 1890s

Populism was a catalyst for political crisis not only in the South but across the entire nation. But while in the South the result was preservation of one-party rule, in national politics the result was a revitalized two-party system.

Ever since Reconstruction, national politics had been stalemated by the even balance between the parties. In the late 1880s the equilibrium began to break down. Benjamin Harrison's election to the presidency in 1888 was the last close election of the era (Democrat Grover Cleveland actually got a larger popular vote). Thereafter, the tide turned against the Republicans, saddled by the lackluster Harrison administration and by Democratic charges that the protectionist McKinley Tariff of 1890 was a giveaway to the business interests. That year Democrats took the House of Representatives decisively and won a number of governorships in normally Republican states. In 1892 Cleveland regained the presidency by the largest margin in twenty years (the only president to be elected to two nonconsecutive terms).

Had everything else remained equal, the events of 1890 and 1892 might have initiated an era of Democratic supremacy. But everything else did not remain equal. By the time of Cleveland's inauguration, farm foreclosures and railroad bankruptcies signaled economic trouble. On May 3, 1893, the stock market crashed. In Chicago 100,000 jobless workers walked the streets; nationwide the unemployment rate soared above 20 percent.

As depression set in, which party would prevail—and on what platform—became an open question. The first challenge to the status quo arrived from the West and South, where falling grain and cotton prices were devastating farmers.

The Populist Revolt

Farmers were of necessity joiners. They needed organization to overcome their social isolation and provide economic services—hence the appeal of the Granger movement, which had spread across the Midwest after 1867, and after the Grange's decline, the appeal of a new movement of farmers' alliances in many rural districts. From diffuse organizational beginnings, two dominant organizations emerged. One was the Farmers' Alliance of the Northwest, which was confined mainly to the midwestern states. More dynamic was the National (or Southern) Farmers' Alliance, which in the mid-1880s spread rapidly from Texas onto the Great Plains and eastward into the cotton South as "traveling lecturers" extolled the virtues of cooperative activity and reminded farmers of "their obligation to stand as a great conservative body against the encroachments of monopolies and . . . the growing corruption of wealth and power."

The Texas Alliance established a huge cooperative, the Texas Exchange, that marketed the crops of cotton farmers and provided them with cheap loans. When cotton prices fell sharply in 1891, the Texas Exchange failed. The Texas Alliance then proposed a new scheme—a **"subtreasury" system**, which would enable farmers to borrow against their unsold crops from a public fund until the cotton could be marketed profitably. The credit and marketing functions would be as in the defunct Texas Exchange but with a crucial difference: they would be underwritten by the federal government. When the subtreasury plan was rejected by the Democratic Party as too radical, the Texas Alliance decided to strike out in politics independently.

En Route to a Populist Rally, Dickinson County, Kansas

Farm people traveled miles to rallies and meetings for the chance to voice their grievances and socialize with like-minded folks. This tradition infused Populism with a special fervor. Gatherings such as the one these Kansans were heading to testified visibly to the meaning of Populism—a movement of the "people." Kansas State Historical Society.

These events in Texas revealed, with special clarity, a process of politicization that rippled through the Alliance movement. Rebuffed by the established parties, alliance men more or less reluctantly abandoned their Democratic and Republican allegiances, and as state alliances grew stronger and more impatient, they began to field independent slates. The confidence gained at the state level led to the formation of the national People's (Populist) Party in 1892. In the elections that year, with the veteran antimonopoly campaigner James B. Weaver as their presidential candidate, the Populists captured a million votes and carried four western states. For the first time agrarian protest truly challenged the national two-party system.

Populism was distinguished by the many women in the movement. In established parties the grassroots political clubs were for men only. Populism, on the other hand, arose from a network of local alliances that had formed for largely social purposes and that welcomed women. Although they participated actively and served prominently as speakers and lecturers, few women became leaders of the alliance movement, and their role diminished with the shift into politics. In deference to the southern wing, the Populist platform was silent on woman suffrage. Still, neither Democrats nor Republicans would have countenanced a spokeswoman such as the fiery Mary Elizabeth Lease, who became famous for calling on farmers "to raise less corn and more hell." The profanity might have been a reporter's invention, but the sentiment was all hers. Mrs. Lease insisted just as strenuously on Populism's "grand and holy mission . . . to place the mothers of this nation on an equality with the fathers."

Populism developed a robust class ideology. "There are but two sides," proclaimed a Populist manifesto. "On the one side are the allied hosts of monopolies, the money power, great trusts and railroad corporations. . . . On the other are the farmers, laborers, merchants and all the people who produce wealth. . . . Between these two there is no middle ground." By this reasoning farmers and workers formed a single producer class. The claim was not merely rhetorical. Texas railroad workers and Colorado miners cooperated with the farmers' alliances, got their support in strikes, and actively participated in forming state Populist parties. The national platform contained strong labor planks, and party leaders earnestly sought union support. In its explicit class appeal—in recognizing that "the irrepressible conflict between capital and labor is upon us"—Populism parted company from the two mainstream parties.

In an age dominated by laissez-faire doctrine, what most distinguished Populism was its positive attitude toward the state. In the words of the Populist platform: "We believe that the power of government—in other words, of the people—should be expanded as rapidly and as far as the good sense of an intelligent people and the teachings of experience shall justify, to the end that oppression, injustice and poverty should eventually cease in the land." Spokesmen such as Lorenzo Dow Lewelling, Populist governor of Kansas, considered it to be "the business of the government to make it possible to live and sustain the life of my family."

At the founding Omaha convention in 1892, Populists called for nationalization of the railroads and communications; protection of the land, including natural resources, from monopoly and foreign ownership; a graduated income tax; the Texas Alliance's subtreasury plan; and the free and unlimited coinage of silver. From this array of issues, the last—free silver—emerged as the cardinal demand of the Populist Party.

In the early 1890s, reeling from rock-bottom prices, embattled farmers gravitated to free silver because they hoped that an increase in the money supply would raise farm prices and give them some relief. In addition the party's slim resources would be fattened by hefty contributions from silver-mining interests who, scornful though they might be of Populist radicalism, yearned for the day when the government would buy at a premium all the silver they could produce.

Free silver triggered a debate for the soul of the Populist Party. Social democrats such as Henry Demarest Lloyd of Chicago argued that free silver, if it became the defining party issue, would undercut the broader Populist program and alienate wage earners, who had no enthusiasm for inflationary measures. Any chance of a farmer-labor alliance that might transform Populism into an American version of the social-democratic parties of Europe would be doomed. The bread-and-butter appeal of free silver, however, was simply too great.

In making that choice, however, Populists fatally compromised their party's identity as an independent movement. For free silver was not an issue over which the Populists held a monopoly but, on the contrary, a question at the very center of mainstream American politics.

Money and Politics

In a rapidly developing economy, the money supply is bound to be a hotly contested issue. If money does not increase rapidly enough, economic growth will be stifled. How fast the money supply should grow, however, is a divisive question. Debtors, commodity producers, and new businesses want a larger money supply: more money in circulation inflates prices and reduces the real cost of borrowing. The "sound-money" people—creditors, individuals on fixed incomes, those in the slower-growing sectors of the economy—have an opposite interest.

Before the Civil War the main source of the nation's money supply had been state-chartered banks, several thousand of them, all issuing banknotes to borrowers that then circulated as money. The economy's need for money was amply met by the state banks, although the soundness of the banknotes—the ability of the issuing banks to stand behind their notes and redeem them at face value—was always uncertain. This freewheeling activity was sharply curtailed by the U.S. Banking Act of 1863. However, because the Lincoln administration itself was printing paper money—*greenbacks*, so-called—to finance the Civil War, the economic impact of the Banking Act was not immediately felt.

After the war the sound money interests lobbied for a return to the traditional national policy, which based the federal currency on the amount of *specie*—gold and silver—held by the U.S. Treasury. The issue was hotly contested for a decade, but in 1875 the sound money interests prevailed, and the circulation of greenbacks as legal tender—that is, backed by nothing more than the good faith of the federal government—came to an end. With state banknotes also in short supply, the country entered an era of chronic **deflation** and tight credit.

This was the context out of which the silver question emerged. The country had always operated on a bimetallic standard, but the supply of silver had gradually tightened, and as they became more valuable as metal than as money, silver coins disappeared from circulation. In 1873 silver was officially dropped as a medium of exchange. Soon afterward western mines began producing silver in abundance; silver prices plummeted. Inflationists began to agitate for a resumption of the bimetallic policy. If the government resumed buying at the fixed ratio prevailing before 1873—16 ounces of silver equaling 1 ounce of gold—silver would flow into the treasury and greatly expand the money in circulation.

With so much at stake for so many people, the currency question became one of the staples of post-Reconstruction politics. Twice the prosilver coalition in Congress won modest victories. First, the Bland-Allison Act of 1878 required the U.S. Treasury to purchase and coin between $2 million and $4 million worth of silver each month. Then, in the more sweeping Sherman Silver Purchase Act of 1890, an additional 4.5 million ounces of silver bullion was to be purchased monthly, to serve as the basis for new issues of U.S. Treasury notes.

These legislative battles, although hard fought, cut across the parties in the familiar fashion of post-Reconstruction politics. But when the crash of 1893 hit, silver suddenly became a burning issue that divided politics along party lines.

Climax: The Election of 1896

As the party in power, the Democrats bore the brunt of responsibility for the economic crisis. Any Democratic president would have been hard pressed, but the man who actually held the job, Grover Cleveland, could hardly have made a bigger hash of it. When jobless marchers—the so-called Coxey's army—arrived in Washington in 1894 to demand federal relief, Cleveland dispersed them forcibly and arrested their leader, Jacob S. Coxey, for trespassing on the Capitol grounds. Cleveland's brutal handling of the Pullman strike further alienated the labor vote (see Chapter 17). Nor did he live up to his reputation as a tariff reformer. Cleveland lost control of the battle when the protectionist McKinley Tariff of 1890 came up for revision in Congress. The resulting Wilson-Gorman Tariff of 1894, which Cleveland allowed to pass into law without his signature, caved in to special interests and left many important rates unchanged.

Most disastrous, however, was Cleveland's stand on the silver question. Cleveland was a committed sound-money man. Nothing that happened after the depression set in—not collapsing prices, not the suffering of farmers, not the groundswell of support for free silver within his own party—budged Cleveland. Economic pressures, in fact, soon forced him to abandon a silver-based currency altogether. With the government's gold reserves dwindling, Cleveland persuaded Congress in 1893 to repeal the Sherman Silver Purchase Act, in effect sacrificing the country's painfully crafted program for maintaining a limited bimetallic standard. Then, as his administration's problems deepened, Cleveland turned in 1895 to a syndicate of private bankers led by J. P. Morgan to arrange the gold purchases needed to replenish the treasury's depleted reserves. The administration's secret negotiations with Wall Street, once discovered, enraged Democrats and completed Cleveland's isolation from his party.

At their Chicago convention in 1896, the Democrats repudiated Cleveland and turned left. The leader of the triumphant silver Democrats was William Jennings Bryan of Nebraska. Bryan was a political phenomenon. Only thirty-six years old, he had already served two terms in Congress and had become a passionate advocate of free silver. Bryan, remarked the journalist Frederic Howe, was "preeminently an evangelist," whose zeal sprang from "the Western self-righteous missionary mind." With biblical fervor Bryan swept up his audiences when he joined the debate on free silver at the Democratic convention. He locked up the presidential nomination with a stirring attack on the gold standard: "You shall not press down upon the brow of labor this crown of thorns, you shall not crucify mankind on a cross of gold."

Bryan's nomination meant that the Democrats had become the party of free silver; his "cross of gold" speech meant that the money question would be a national crusade. No one could be neutral on this defining issue. Silver Republicans bolted their party; gold Democrats went for a splinter Democratic ticket or supported the Republican Party. The Populists, meeting after the Democratic convention, accepted Bryan as their candidate. The free-silver issue had become so vital that they could not do otherwise. Although they nominated their own vice presidential candidate, Tom Watson of Georgia, the Populists found themselves for all practical purposes absorbed into the Democratic silver campaign.

The Republicans took up the challenge. Their party leader was the wealthy Cleveland iron maker Mark Hanna, a brilliant political manager and an exponent of the new industrial capitalism. Hanna orchestrated an unprecedented money-raising campaign among America's corporate interests. His candidate, William McKinley of Ohio, personified the virtues of Republicanism, standing solidly for high tariffs, sound money, and prosperity. While Bryan broke with tradition and crisscrossed the country by railroad in a furious whistle-stop campaign, the dignified McKinley received delegations at his home in Canton, Ohio. Bryan orated with moral fervor; McKinley talked of economic progress and a full dinner pail.

Not since 1860 had the United States witnessed so hard fought an election over such high stakes. For the middle class, sound money stood symbolically for the soundness of the social order. With jobless workers tramping the streets and bankrupt farmers up in arms, Bryan's fervent assault on the gold standard struck fear in many hearts. Republicans denounced the Democratic platform as "revolutionary and anarchistic" and Bryan's supporters as "social misfits who have almost nothing in common but opposition to the existing order and institutions."

Though little noticed at the time, ethnocultural issues figured strongly in the campaign. The Republicans, the party of morality, beat a strategic retreat from temperance and Sunday laws. McKinley had represented an ethnically mixed district of northeastern Ohio in Congress. In appealing to his working-class constituents, he had learned the art of easy tolerance, expressed in his words, "live and let live." Of the two candidates, the prairie orator Bryan, with his biblical language and moral righteousness, presented the more alien image to traditional Democratic voters in the big cities.

McKinley won handily, with 271 electoral votes to Bryan's 176. He kept the ground Republicans had regained in the 1894 midterm elections and pushed into Democratic strongholds, especially in the cities. Boston, New York, Chicago, and Minneapolis, all taken by Cleveland in 1892, went for McKinley in 1896. Bryan ran strongly only in the South, in silver-mining states, and in the Populist West (Map 19.3). But the gains his evangelical style brought him in some Republican rural areas did not compensate for his losses in traditionally Democratic urban districts.

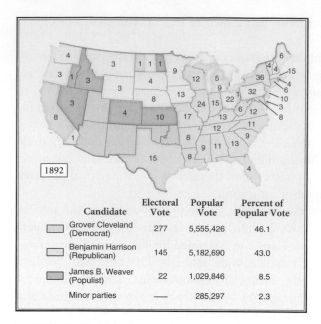

Candidate	Electoral Vote	Popular Vote	Percent of Popular Vote
Grover Cleveland (Democrat)	277	5,555,426	46.1
Benjamin Harrison (Republican)	145	5,182,690	43.0
James B. Weaver (Populist)	22	1,029,846	8.5
Minor parties	—	285,297	2.3

MAP 19.3 Presidential Elections of 1892 and 1896

In the 1890s the age of political stalemate came to an end. Students should compare the 1892 map with Map 19.1 (p. 570) and note especially Cleveland's breakthrough in the normally Republican states of the upper Midwest. In 1896 the pendulum swung in the opposite direction, with McKinley's consolidation of Republican control over the Northeast and Midwest far overbalancing the Democratic advances in the thinly populated western states. The 1896 election marked the beginning of forty years of Republican dominance in national politics.

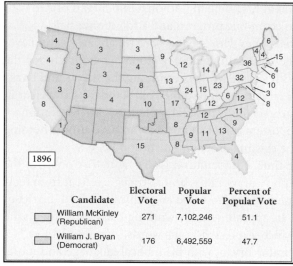

Candidate	Electoral Vote	Popular Vote	Percent of Popular Vote
William McKinley (Republican)	271	7,102,246	51.1
William J. Bryan (Democrat)	176	6,492,559	47.7

The paralyzing equilibrium in American politics ended in 1896. The Republicans skillfully turned both economic and cultural challenges to their advantage. They persuaded the nation that they were the party of prosperity, and they persuaded many traditionally Democratic urban voters that they were sympathetic to ethnic diversity. In so doing the Republicans became the nation's majority party. In 1896, too, electoral politics regained its place as an arena for national debate, setting the stage for the reform politics of the Progressive Era.

T I M E L I N E

1877	Rutherford B. Hayes inaugurated president, marking end of Reconstruction
1881	President James A. Garfield assassinated
1883	Pendleton Civil Service Act
1884	Mugwump reformers leave Republican Party to support Grover Cleveland, first Democrat elected president since 1856
1887	Florida adopts first law segregating railroad travel
1888	James Bryce's *The American Commonwealth*
1890	McKinley Tariff
	Democrats sweep congressional elections, inaugurating brief era of Democratic Party dominance
	Mississippi becomes first state to adopt literacy test to disfranchise blacks

1892	People's (Populist) Party founded
1893	National depression begins
	Repeal of Sherman Silver Purchase Act (1890)
1894	Coxey's army of unemployed fails to win federal relief
1896	Election of Republican president William McKinley; free-silver campaign crushed
	Plessy v. Ferguson upholds constitutionality of "separate but equal" facilities
1897	Economic depression ends; era of agricultural prosperity begins
1898	*Williams v. Mississippi* rules that disfranchising devices did not violate Fifteenth Amendment

For Further Exploration

Late-nineteenth-century politics is a topic on which historians have had a field day. On the ideological underpinnings, an older book by Robert G. McCloskey, *American Conservatism in the Age of Enterprise* (1951), still retains its freshness. The mass appeal of Gilded Age politics is incisively explored in Michael E. McGerr, *The Decline of Popular Politics: The American North, 1865–1928* (1986). Alexander Keyssar, *The Right to Vote: The Contested History of Democracy in the United States* (2000) is illuminating on the conservative assault on voting rights in the late nineteenth century. Kathryn Kish Sklar, *Florence Kelley and the Nation's Work* (1995), traces the emergence of women's political culture through the life of a leading reformer. On southern politics the seminal book is C. Vann Woodward, *Origins of the New South, 1877–1913* (1951), which still defines the terms of discussion among historians. The most far-reaching revision is Edward L. Ayers, *The Promise of the New South* (1992). The process of sectional reconciliation is imaginatively treated in David W. Blight, *Race and Reunion: The Civil War in American Memory* (2001). The most recent treatment of disfranchisement is Michael Perman, *Struggle for Mastery: Disfranchisement in the South, 1888–1908* (2001). Richard D. Hofstadter, *The Age of Reform* (1955), stresses the darker side of Populism, in which intolerance and paranoia figure heavily. Hofstadter's thesis, which once dominated debate among historians, has given way to a much more positive assessment. The key book here is Lawrence Goodwyn, *Democratic Promise: The Populist Moment* (1976), which argues that Populism was a broadly based response to industrial capitalism. Peter H. Argesinger, *The Limits of Agrarian Radicalism* (1995), stresses the capacity of the political status quo to frustrate western Populism. Michael Kazin, *The Populist Persuasion* (1995), describes how the language of Populism entered the discourse of mainstream American politics. Much information on the Gilded Age presidents can be found at the Web site <americanpresident.org/presidentialresources.htm>.

For definitions of key terms boldfaced in this chapter, see the glossary at the end of the book.

To assess your mastery of the material covered in this chapter, see the Online Study Guide at **bedfordstmartins.com/henrettaconcise**.

For map resources and primary documents, see **bedfordstmartins.com/henrettaconcise**.

Chapter 20

THE PROGRESSIVE ERA

Society is looking itself over, in our day, from top to bottom. . . . We
are in a temper to reconstruct economic society.

WOODROW WILSON, 1913

O n the face of it, the political tumult of the 1890s ended with William
McKinley's election in 1896. After the bitter struggle over free silver, the victorious
Republicans had no stomach for crusades. The main thing, as party chief Mark
Hanna said, was to "stand pat and continue Republican prosperity."

Yet beneath the surface a deep unease had set in. Hard times had unveiled truths
not acknowledged in better days—that a frightening chasm, for example, had
opened between America's social classes. In Richard Olney's view the great
Pullman strike of 1894 had brought the country "to the ragged edge of anarchy." As
Cleveland's attorney general, it had been Olney's job to crush the strike (see Chapter
17). But he took little joy from his success. He asked himself, rather, how such
repressive actions might be avoided in the future. His answer was that the government
should regulate labor relations on the railroads so that crippling rail strikes would
not happen. As a first step toward Olney's goal, Congress adopted the Erdman
Mediation Act in 1898. In such ways did the crisis of the 1890s turn the nation's
thinking to reform.

The problems themselves, however, were of much older origin. For many
decades Americans had been absorbed in building the world's most advanced
industrial economy. At the beginning of the twentieth century, they paused, looked
around, and began to add up the costs—a frightening concentration of corporate
power, a rebellious working class, misery in the cities, and the corruption of machine
politics.

Now, with the strife-torn 1890s behind them, reform became an absorbing concern of many Americans. It was as if social awareness reached a critical mass around
1900 and set reform activity going as a major, self-sustaining phenomenon. For this
reason the years from 1900 to World War I have come to be known as the
Progressive Era.

The Course of Reform

Historians have sometimes spoken of a progressive "movement." But progressivism was not a movement in any meaningful sense. There was no single progressive constituency, no agreed-upon agenda, no unifying organization. Both the Republican and Democratic parties had progressive elements. At different times and places, different social groups became active. People who were reformers on one issue might be conservative on another. The term *progressivism* embraces a widespread, many-sided effort after 1900 to build a better society. Progressive reformers shared only this objective, plus an intellectual style that can be called "progressive."

Progressive Ideas

If the facts could be known, everything else was possible. That was the starting point for progressive thinking. Hence the burst of enthusiasm for scientific investigation—statistical studies by the federal government of immigration, child labor, and economic practices; social research by privately funded foundations delving into industrial conditions; vice commissions in many cities looking into prostitution, gambling, and other moral ills of an urban society. Progressives likewise placed great faith in academic expertise. In Wisconsin the state university became a key resource for Governor Robert La Follette's reform administration—the reason, one supporter boasted, for "the democracy, the thoroughness, and the accuracy of the state in its legislation."

Similarly, progressives were strongly attracted to scientific management, which had originally been intended to rationalize work in factories (see Chapter 17). But its founder, Frederick W. Taylor, argued that his basic approach—the "scientific" analysis of human activity—offered solutions to waste and inefficiency in municipal government, schools and hospitals, even at home. Scientific management, said Taylor, could solve all the social ills that arise from "such of our acts as are blundering, ill-directed, or inefficient."

Scientific management was an American invention, but progressives also felt themselves part of a transatlantic world. Ideas flowed in both directions, with the Americans, in fact, very much on the receiving end. Since the 1870s, they had flocked to German universities, absorbing the economics and political science that became key tools of progressive reform. On many fronts, social politics overseas seemed far in advance of the United States. The sense of having fallen behind—that "the tables are turned," as the young progressive Walter Weyl wrote, and "America no longer teaches democracy to an expectant world, but herself goes to school in Europe and Australia"—was a spur to action.

The main thing was to resist ways of thinking that discouraged purposeful action. Social Darwinists who had so dominated Gilded Age thought (see Chapter 19) were wrong in their belief that society developed according to fixed and unchanging laws. "It is folly," pronounced the Harvard philosopher William James, "to speak of the 'laws of history,' as of something inevitable, which science only has to discover, and which anyone can then foretell and observe, but do nothing to alter or avert." James denied the existence of absolute truths and advocated instead a philosophy he called **pragmatism**, which judged ideas by their consequences. Philosophy should be concerned with solving problems, James insisted, and not with contemplating ultimate ends.

Progressives prided themselves on being tough-minded, on being expert at making things happen. But they were not indifferent to the moral grounds for reform. Progressives were, in truth, unabashed idealists. The progressive cause, proclaimed Theodore Roosevelt, "is based on the eternal principles of righteousness."

Protestant churches, long troubled by the plight of the urban poor, now translated that concern into a major theological doctrine—the Social Gospel. Its leading exponent was the Baptist cleric Walter Rauschenbush, whose ideas had been forged by his ministry in the squalid Hell's Kitchen section of New York City. The churches must not wall themselves off from the misery and despair in their midst, he concluded. They had to embrace the "social aims of Jesus." The Kingdom of God on Earth would be achieved not by striving for personal salvation but in the cause of social justice.

Progressive leaders characteristically grew up in homes imbued with evangelical piety. Many went through a religious crisis, ultimately settling on a career in social work, education, or politics where religious striving might be translated into secular action. Jane Addams, for example, had taken up settlement-house work believing that by uplifting the poor, she would herself be uplifted: she would experience "the joy of finding Christ" by acting "in fellowship" with the needy.

The progressive mode of thought—idealistic in intent, tough-minded in practice—nurtured a new kind of reform journalism. During the 1890s bright new magazines like *Collier's* and *McClure's* began to find an urban audience for lively, fact-filled reporting. Almost by accident, editors discovered that what most interested readers was the exposure of mischief in American life. Investigative reporters fanned out on the trail of evildoers.

Lincoln Steffens's article "Tweed Days in St. Louis" in the October 1902 issue of *McClure's* is credited with starting the trend. In a riveting series Steffens wrote about "the shame of the cities"—the corrupt ties between business and political machines. Ida M. Tarbell attacked the Standard Oil monopoly, and David Graham Phillips told how money controlled the Senate. William Hard exposed industrial accidents in "Making Steel and Killing Men" (1907) and child labor in "De Kid Wot Works at Night" (1908). Hardly a sordid corner of American life escaped the scrutiny of these tireless reporters.

Theodore Roosevelt, among many others, thought they went too far. In a 1906 speech, he compared them to the man with a muckrake in *Pilgrim's Progress* (by the seventeenth-century English preacher John Bunyan) who was too absorbed with raking the filth on the floor to look up and accept a celestial crown. Thus the term **muckraker** became attached to journalists who exposed the underside of American life. Their efforts were in fact health giving. More than any other group, the muckrakers called the people to arms.

Ida Tarbell Takes on Rockefeller

A popular biographer of Napoleon and Lincoln in the 1890s, Ida Tarbell turned her journalistic talents to muckraking. Her first installment of "The History of the Standard Oil Company" appeared in *McClure's* in November 1902. John D. Rockefeller, she wrote, "was willing to strain every nerve to obtain for himself special and illegal privileges from the railroads which were bound to ruin every man in the oil business not sharing them with him." As Tarbell built her case, criticism rained down on Rockefeller. A more sympathetic cartoon in *Judge* magazine pleads with Rockefeller's critics: "Boys, don't you think you have bothered the old man just about enough?"

Courtesy of The Ida Tarbell Collection, Pelletier Library, Allegheny College / Culver Pictures.

Women Progressives

Among the first to respond were middle-class women who, in their well-established role as "social housekeepers," had long shouldered the burden of humanitarian work in American cities. They were the foot soldiers for charity organizations, visiting needy families, assessing their problems, and referring them to relief agencies.

After many years of such dedicated labor, Josephine Shaw Lowell of New York City concluded that giving assistance to the poor was not enough. "If the working people had all they ought to have, we should not have the paupers and criminals," she declared. "It is better to save them before they go under, than to spend your life fishing them out afterward." Lowell founded the New York Consumers' League in 1890. Her goal was to improve the wages and working conditions of female clerks in the city's stores by issuing a "White List"—a very short list at first—of cooperating shops.

From these modest beginnings the league spread to other cities and blossomed into the National Consumers' League in 1899. By then the women at its head had lost faith in voluntary action; only the state had the resources to rescue poor families. Under the crusading leadership of Florence Kelley, formerly a chief factory inspector in Illinois, the Consumers' League became a powerful lobby for protective legislation for women and children.

Among its achievements, none was more important than the Supreme Court's *Muller v. Oregon* decision in 1908, which upheld an Oregon law limiting the workday for women to ten hours. The Consumers' League recruited the brilliant Boston lawyer Louis D. Brandeis, whose brief before the Court devoted a scant two pages to the narrow constitutional issue—whether, under its police powers, Oregon had the right to regulate women's working hours. Instead, Brandeis rested his case on social data gathered by the Consumers' League describing the toll that long hours took on women. The *Muller* decision, by approving an expansive welfare role for the states, cleared the way for a mighty lobbying effort by women's organizations, whose victories included the first law providing public assistance for mothers with dependent children in Illinois in 1911; the first minimum wage law for women in Massachusetts in 1912; more effective child-labor laws in many states; and at the federal level, the Children's and Women's bureaus in the Labor Department in 1912 and 1920, respectively. The **welfare state**, insofar as it arrived in America in these years, was what women progressives had made of it; they erected a "maternalist" welfare system.

A parallel path for women's reform, the settlement-house movement, was blazed by Hull House, which Jane Addams and Ellen Gates Starr established in 1889 on Chicago's West Side after visiting Toynbee Hall in the London slums. During the progressive years, scores of settlement houses sprang up in the ghettos of the nation's cities, serving as community centers and spark plugs for neighborhood reform. Jane Addams led battles for garbage removal, playgrounds, better street lighting, and police protection.

In a famous essay, Addams spoke of the "subjective necessity" of the settlement house. She meant that it was as much for resident young men and women eager to serve, as it was a response to the needs of slum dwellers. Addams herself was a case in point. Born in 1860 in Cedarville, Illinois, she grew up in comfortable circumstances and graduated from Rockford College. Then Addams faced an empty future—an ornamental wife if she married, a sheltered spinster if she did not. Hull House became her salvation, enabling her to "begin with however small a group to accomplish and to live."

Women activists like Jane Addams and Florence Kelley breathed new life into the suffrage movement. Why, they asked, should a woman who was capable of running a settlement house or lobbying a bill be denied the right to vote? And by encouraging working-class women to help themselves, women progressives got a whole new class interested in fighting for suffrage.

In 1903 social reformers founded the National Women's Trade Union League. Financed and led by wealthy supporters, the league organized women workers, played a considerable role in their strikes, and trained working-class leaders. One such leader was Rose Schneiderman, who became a union organizer among New York's garment workers; another was Agnes Nestor, who led Illinois glove workers. Although they often resented the patronizing ways of their well-to-do patrons, such trade union women identified their cause with the broader struggle for women's rights.

Around 1910, suffrage activity began to quicken, and tactics shifted. In Britain suffragists had begun to picket Parliament, assault politicians, and stage hunger strikes while in jail. Inspired by their example, Alice Paul, a young Quaker once a resident of Britain, applied similar confrontational tactics to the American struggle. Although woman suffrage had been won in six western states since 1910, Paul rejected the state-by-state route as too slow (Map 20.1). She advocated a constitutional amendment that in one stroke would grant women everywhere the right to vote. In 1916 Paul organized the militant National Woman's Party.

The mainstream National American Woman Suffrage Association (NAWSA), from which Paul had split off, was also rejuvenated. Carrie Chapman Catt, a skilled organizer from the New York movement, took over as national leader in 1915. Under her guidance NAWSA brought a broad-based organization to the campaign for a federal amendment.

In the midst of this suffrage struggle, something new and more fundamental began to happen. A younger generation—college-educated, self-supporting women—refused to be hemmed in by the social constraints of women's "separate sphere." "Breaking into the Human Race" was the aspiration they proclaimed at a mass meeting in New York in 1914. "We intend simply to be ourselves," declared the chair Marie Jenny Howe, "not just our little female selves, but our whole big human selves."

The women at this meeting called themselves **feminists**, a term that was just coming into use. In this, its first incarnation, feminism meant freedom for full personal development. Thus did Charlotte Perkins Gilman, famous for her advocacy of communal kitchens as a means of liberating women from homemaking, imagine the new woman: "Here she comes, running, out of prison and off the pedestal; chains off, crown off, halo off, just a live woman."

Feminists were militantly prosuffrage, but unlike their more traditional suffragist sisters, uninterested in arguing that women would uplift American politics. Rather, they demanded the right to vote because they considered themselves just as good as men. At the moment the reviving suffrage movement was about to triumph,

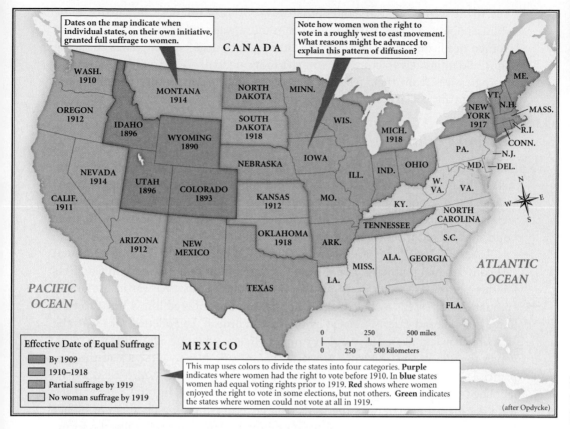

Dates on the map indicate when individual states, on their own initiative, granted full suffrage to women.

Note how women won the right to vote in a roughly west to east movement. What reasons might be advanced to explain this pattern of diffusion?

Effective Date of Equal Suffrage
- By 1909
- 1910–1918
- Partial suffrage by 1919
- No woman suffrage by 1919

This map uses colors to divide the states into four categories. **Purple** indicates where women had the right to vote before 1910. In **blue** states women had equal voting rights prior to 1919. **Red** shows where women enjoyed the right to vote in some elections, but not others. **Green** indicates the states where women could not vote at all in 1919.

(after Opdycke)

MAP 20.1 Woman Suffrage, 1890–1919

By 1909, after more than sixty years of agitation, only four lightly populated western states had granted women full voting rights. A number of other states offered partial suffrage, limited mostly to voting for school boards and such issues as taxes. Between 1910 and 1918, as the effort shifted to the struggle for a constitutional amendment, eleven states joined the list granting full suffrage. The most stubborn resistance was in the South.

FOR MORE HELP ANALYZING THIS MAP, see the Online Study Guide at **bedfordstmartins.com/henrettaconcise**.

it was overtaken by a larger revolution that redefined the struggle for women's rights as a battle against all the constraints that prevented women from achieving their potential as human beings.

This feminist revolution also challenged women's social progressivism, which was premised on the argument that women were the weaker sex. It was just this argument, at the very heart of Brandeis's brief in the landmark *Muller* case, that rang true with the Supreme Court. "The two sexes differ in structure of body, in the functions to be performed by each, in the amount of physical strength," the Court agreed. "This difference justifies . . . legislation . . . designed to compensate for some of the burdens which rest upon her." But feminists wanted no such compensation.

Thus, to the surprise of Maryland's progressive governor Charles J. Bonaparte, some feminists objected to his 1914 women's minimum wage bill because it implied that "women need some special care, protection and privilege." A wedge was surfacing that would ultimately fracture the women's movement, dividing an older generation of progressives from their feminist successors who prized gender equality more highly than any social benefit.

Reforming Politics

Like the Mugwumps of the Gilded Age (see Chapter 19), progressive reformers attacked the boss rule of the party system, but more adeptly and more aggressively. Indeed, because politics was about power, in this realm the motives of progressives were always mixed. Their ideals of civic betterment elbowed uneasily with their politician's drive for self-aggrandizement.

Robert M. La Follette of Wisconsin led the way. Born in 1855, La Follette started as a conventional politician, rising from the Republican ranks to serve in Congress for three terms. He was a party regular, never doubting that he was in honorable company until, by his own account, a Republican boss offered him a bribe to fix a judge in a railroad case. Awakened by this "awful ordeal," La Follette broke with the Wisconsin machine in 1891 and became a tireless advocate of political reform, which for him meant restoring America's democratic ideals. "Go back to the first principles of democracy; go back to the people," he told his audience when he launched his campaign against the state Republican machine. In 1900, after battling for a decade, La Follette won the Wisconsin governorship on a platform of higher taxes for corporations, stricter utility and railroad regulation, and political reform.

The key to party reform, La Follette felt, was to deny bosses the power to choose the party's candidates. This could be achieved by state legislation requiring that nominations be decided not in party conventions but by popular vote. Enacted in 1903, the **direct primary** expressed La Follette's democratic idealism, but it also suited his particular political talents. The party regulars opposing him were insiders, more comfortable in the caucus room than out on the stump. But that was where La Follette, a superb campaigner, excelled. The direct primary gave La Follette an iron grip on Republican politics in Wisconsin that lasted until his death twenty-five years later.

What was true of La Follette was more or less true of all successful progressive politicians. They typically described their work as political restoration, frequently confessing that they had converted to reform after discovering how far party politics had drifted from the ideals of representative government. Like La Follette, Albert B. Cummins of Iowa, William S. U'Ren of Oregon, and Hiram Johnson of California all espoused democratic ideals, and all skillfully used the direct primary as the stepping stone to political power. They practiced a new kind of popular politics, which in a reform age could be a more effective way to power than the backroom techniques of the old-fashioned machine politicians.

Even the most democratizing of reforms espoused by the progressives—the initiative and recall—were really exercises in power politics. The *initiative* enabled citizens to have issues placed on the ballot; *recall* empowered them to remove officeholders who had lost the public's confidence. It soon became clear, however, that direct democracy did not supplant organized politics. Initiative and recall campaigns required organization, money, and expertise, and these were attributes not of the people at large but of well-financed interests. Like the direct primary, the initiative and recall had as much to do with power relations as with political reform.

Racism and Reform

The direct primary was the flagship of progressive politics—the crucial reform, as La Follette said, for defeating the party bosses and returning politics to "the people." The primary originated not in Wisconsin, however, but in the South, and by the time La Follette got his primary law in 1903, primaries were already operating in seven southern states. In the South, however, the primary was a *white* primary. Since by 1900 the Democratic nomination in the South was tantamount to election, barring African Americans from the party primary effectively barred them from political participation.

How could this exercise in white supremacy be justified as democratic reform? By the racism that pervaded even the progressive ranks. In a 1902 book on Reconstruction, Professor John W. Burgess of Columbia University pronounced the Fifteenth Amendment "a monstrous thing" for granting blacks the vote after the Civil War. Burgess was southern born, but he was confident that his northern audience saw the "vast differences in political capacity" between blacks and whites. Even the Republican Party offered no rebuttal. Indeed, as president-elect in 1908, William Howard Taft applauded southern disfranchising laws as necessary to "prevent entirely the possibility of domination by . . . an ignorant electorate." Taft assured southerners that "the federal government has nothing to do with social equality." Taft's successor, Woodrow Wilson, was prepared to go even further, signaling after he entered the White House in 1913 that he favored segregation of the U.S. civil service.

The black leader of the day was Booker T. Washington, who in a famous speech in Atlanta in 1895 had retreated from the defiant stand of an older generation of black abolitionists like Frederick Douglass. Conciliatory toward the South, Washington considered "the agitation of the question of social equality the extremest folly." The Atlanta Compromise, as his stance became known, was "accommodationist," in the sense that it gave up on political protest and avoided a direct assault on white supremacy. Despite the humble face he put on before white audiences, however, Washington did not concede the struggle. Behind the scenes he lobbied hard against Jim Crow laws and disfranchisement. In an age of severe racial oppression, no black dealt more skillfully with the elite of white America or wielded greater influence inside the Republican Party.

What Booker T. Washington banked on was black economic progress. He sought to capitalize on a southern dilemma. Racist dogma dictated that blacks be kept down and conform to their image as lazy, shiftless workers. But southern prosperity required an efficient labor force. Washington made this need the target of his efforts. Founder of the Tuskegee Institute in Alabama in 1881, Washington advocated industrial education—manual and agricultural training. He preached the virtues of thrift, hard work, and property ownership. Washington regarded members of the white southern elite as crucial allies because only they had the power to change the South. When it was in their economic interest, when they had grown dependent on black labor and black enterprise, white men of property would recognize the justice of black rights. As Washington put it, "There is little race prejudice in the American dollar."

Black leaders knew Washington as a hard taskmaster, jealous of his authority and not disposed to regard opposition kindly. Even so, opposition surfaced, especially among younger, educated blacks. They thought Washington was conceding too much. He instilled black pride, but of a narrowly middle-class and utilitarian kind. What about the special genius of blacks that W. E. B. Du Bois, a Harvard-educated African American sociologist, celebrated in his collection of essays, *The Souls of Black Folk* (1903)? And what of the "talented tenth" of the black population, whose promise could only be stifled by manual education? Moreover, the situation for blacks was deteriorating, even in the North. Over 200,000 blacks migrated from the South between 1900 and 1910, sparking white resentment in northern cities. Attacks on blacks became widespread, capped by a bloody race riot in Springfield, Illinois, in 1908. In the face of all this, many black activists lost patience with Booker T. Washington's silence.

The key figure was William Monroe Trotter, the pugnacious editor of the *Boston Guardian*. "The policy of compromise has failed," Trotter argued. "The policy of resistance and aggression deserves a trial." In 1906, after breaking with Washington, Trotter and Du Bois called a meeting at Niagara Falls—but on the Canadian side because no hotel on the U.S. side would admit blacks. The Niagara Movement that resulted had an impact far beyond the scattering of members and local bodies it organized. The principles it affirmed would define the struggle for the rights of African Americans: first, encouragement of black pride; second, an uncompromising demand for full political and civil equality; and above all, the resolute denial "that the Negro-American assents to inferiority, is submissive under oppression and apologetic before insults."

Going against the grain, a handful of white reformers rallied to the African American cause. Among the most devoted was Mary White Ovington, who grew up in an abolitionist family. Like Jane Addams, Ovington became a settlement-house worker, but among urban blacks in New York rather than in immigrant Chicago. News of the Springfield race riot of 1908 changed her life. Convinced that her duty was to fight racism, Ovington called a meeting of sympathetic white progressives, which led to the formation of the National Association for the Advancement of Colored People (NAACP) in 1909. Most of the members of the strife-torn Niagara Movement moved over to the NAACP. The organization's national leadership was dominated by whites, with one crucial exception. Du Bois became the editor of the NAACP's journal, *The Crisis*. With a passion that only a black voice could provide, Du Bois used that platform

W. E. B. Du Bois

No activity undertaken by the NAACP in the early years was more important than the publication of its journal, *The Crisis*, which under the brilliant editorship of W. E. B. Du Bois became the strongest voice for equal rights and black pride in the country. In this photograph Du Bois is pictured at his desk at the magazine's editorial office.

Schomburg Center for Research in Black Culture, New York Public Library.

to demand equal rights. The NAACP scored its first success in helping beat back the Wilson administration's effort at segregating the federal civil service.

On social welfare the National Urban League took the lead, uniting in 1911 the many agencies serving black migrants arriving in northern cities. Like the NAACP, the Urban League was interracial, including both white reformers such as Ovington and black welfare activists such as William Lewis Bulkley, a New York school principal who was the league's main architect. In the South welfare work was very much the province of black women, who to some extent filled the vacuum left by black disfranchisement. Mostly working in the churches and schools, they also utilized the southern branches of the National Association of Colored Women's Clubs, which had started in 1896. And because their activities seemed unthreatening to white supremacy, black women were able to reach across the color line and find allies among white southern women.

Progressivism was a house of many chambers. Most were infected by the racism of the age, but not all. A saving remnant of white progressives rallied to the cause of racial justice. National institutions—the NAACP, Urban League, and such black organizations as the National Association of Colored Women's Clubs—took shape in the Progressive Era that would lead the black struggle for a better life over the next half century.

Urban Liberalism

When the Republican Hiram Johnson ran for California governor in 1910, he was the reform candidate of the state's middle class. Famous as prosecutor of the corrupt San Francisco boss Abe Ruef, Johnson pledged to purify California politics and curb the Southern Pacific Railroad—the dominating economic power in the state. By his second term, Johnson was championing social and labor legislation. His original base in the middle class had eroded, and he had become the champion of California's working class.

Johnson's career reflected a shift in the center of gravity of progressivism, which had begun as a movement of the middle class but then took on board America's working people. A new strain of progressive reform emerged that historians have labeled urban liberalism. To understand this phenomenon, we have to begin with city machine politics.

Thirty minutes before quitting time on Saturday afternoon, March 25, 1911, fire broke out at the Triangle Shirtwaist Company in downtown New York. The flames trapped the workers, who were mostly young immigrant women. Forty-seven leapt to their deaths; another ninety-nine never reached the windows.

In the wake of the tragedy, the New York State Factory Commission developed a remarkable program of labor reform: fifty-six laws dealing with fire hazards, unsafe machines, industrial homework, and wages and hours for women and children. The chairman of the commission was Robert F. Wagner; the vice chairman was Alfred E. Smith. Both were Tammany Hall politicians, serving at the time as leaders in the state legislature. They established the commission, participated fully in its work, and marshaled the party regulars to pass the proposals into law—all with the approval of the Tammany machine.

Tammany's response to the Triangle fire meant that it was conceding that social problems had outgrown the capacity of party machines. Only the state could bar industrial firetraps or alleviate sweatshop work and slum life. And if that meant weakening rank-and-file loyalty to Tammany, so be it. Al Smith and Robert Wagner absorbed the lessons of the Triangle investigation. They formed durable ties with such progressives as the social worker Frances Perkins, who sat on the commission as the representative of the New York Consumers' League, and became urban liberals—advocates of active intervention by the state in uplifting the laboring masses of America's cities.

It was not only altruism that converted seasoned politicians like Smith and Wagner. The city machines faced strong competition from a new breed of middle-class progressive, skilled urban reformers such as Mayor Brand Whitlock of Toledo, Ohio, whose administration not only attacked city-hall corruption but also provided better

Triangle Shirtwaist Factory Fire

The doors were the problem. Most were locked (to keep the working girls from leaving early); the few that were open became jammed by bodies as the flames spread. When the fire trucks finally came, the ladders were too short. Compared with those caught inside, the girls who leapt to their deaths were the lucky ones. "As I looked up I saw a love affair in the midst of all the horror," a reporter wrote. A young man was helping girls leap from a window. The fourth "put her arms about him and kiss[ed] him. Then he held her out into space and dropped her." He immediately followed. "Thud—dead, Thud—dead . . . I saw his face before they covered it. . . . He was a real man. He had done his best." New York *Tribune*, March 26, 1911.

schools, cleaner streets, and more social services for Toledo's needy. Like La Follette, Whitlock placed his faith in the people, believing "that the cure for the ills of democracy was not less democracy . . . but more democracy." Combining campaign magic and popular programs, Whitlock and similarly progressive mayors in Cleveland, Jersey City, and elsewhere won over the urban masses and challenged the rule of the machines.

Also confronting the bosses was a challenge from the left. The Socialist Party was making headway in the cities, electing Milwaukee's Victor Berger as the nation's first Socialist congressman in 1910 and winning municipal elections across the country. The political universe of the urban machines had changed, and they had to pay closer attention to opinion in the precincts.

City machines, always pragmatic, adopted urban liberalism without much ideological struggle. The same could not be said of the trade unions, the other institution that spoke for American working people. In its early years the American Federation of Labor (AFL) had strongly opposed state interference in labor's affairs. Samuel Gompers preached that workers should not seek from government what they could accomplish by their own economic power and self-help. **Voluntarism**, as trade unionists called this doctrine, did not die out, but it weakened substantially during the progressive years.

One reason was that the labor movement came under severe attack by the courts. In the *Danbury Hatters* case (1908), the Supreme Court declared a boycott by the Hatters' Union against the antiunion D. E. Loewe & Company to be a conspiracy in restraint of trade under the Sherman Act, awarding triple damages to the company and signaling the vulnerability of trade unions to crushing antitrust suits. Hundreds of members of the Hatters' Union stood to lose their homes and savings until the labor movement raised the money to pay the fines.

Even worse was the willingness of judges to grant **injunctions**—court orders—prohibiting unions from carrying on strikes or boycotts. The justification was to prevent "irreparable damage" to an employer while the court was considering the legality of the union's actions. But the effect of this "temporary" measure was invariably to immobilize and defeat the union.

Only a political response could blunt these assaults on labor's economic weapons. In its "Bill of Grievances" of 1906, the AFL demanded that Congress grant unions immunity from antitrust suits and injunctions. Rebuffed, the unions became more politically active, entering campaigns and supporting candidates who favored their program.

Once into politics, the labor movement had difficulty denying the case for social legislation. The AFL, after all, claimed to speak for the entire working class. When muckrakers exposed exploitation of workers and middle-class progressives came forward with solutions, how could the labor movement fail to respond? Thus began a retreat from labor's commitment to voluntarism. In state after state, organized labor joined the battle for progressive legislation and increasingly became its strongest advocate, including most particularly workers' compensation for industrial accidents.

Industrial hazards took an awful toll at the workplace (see American Voices, "Tracking Down Lead Poisoning," p. 612). Two thousand coal miners were killed every year, dying from cave-ins and explosions at a rate 50 percent higher than in German mines. Liability rules, based on **common law**, so heavily favored employers that victims of industrial accidents rarely got more than token compensation. The tide turned quickly once the labor movement got on board; between 1910 and 1917 all the industrial states enacted insurance laws covering on-the-job accidents.

The United States hesitated, however, to broaden the attack on the hazards of modern industrial life. Health insurance and unemployment compensation, although popular in Europe, scarcely made it onto the American political agenda. Old-age pensions, which Britain adopted in 1908, got a serious hearing, only to come up against an odd barrier: the United States already had a pension system of a kind, for Civil War veterans. Easy access—as many as half of all native-born men over sixty-four or their survivors were collecting veterans' benefits in the early twentieth century—reinforced fears of state-induced dependency. Clarence J. Hicks, an industrial-relations expert, recalled Civil War pensioners idling away the hours around the wood stove in the grocery store in his Wisconsin town. They had decided "that the country owed them a living," lost their initiative, and "retreated from the battle of life."

Not until a later generation experienced the Great Depression would the country be ready for social insurance. A secure old age, unemployment payments, health benefits—these human needs of a modern industrial order were beyond the reach of urban liberals in the Progressive Era.

Progressivism and National Politics

The gathering forces of progressivism reached the national scene slowly. Reformers had been spurred by immediate and visible problems, far from Washington. But in 1906 Robert La Follette left Wisconsin for the U.S. Senate. Other seasoned progressives, also ambitious for a wider stage, followed. By 1910 a vocal progressive bloc was making itself heard in both houses of Congress.

Progressivism arrived on the national scene not via Congress, however, but by way of the presidency. This was partly because the White House provided a "bully pulpit"—to use Theodore Roosevelt's phrase. But just as important was the twist of fate that brought Roosevelt to the White House on September 14, 1901.

The Making of a Progressive President

Like many other budding progressives, Theodore Roosevelt was motivated by a high-minded, Christian upbringing. Born in 1858, he always identified himself—loudly—with the cause of righteousness. But Roosevelt did not scorn power and its uses. To the amazement of his socially prominent family, he plunged into Republican politics after Harvard and maneuvered himself into the New York State legislature.

Tracking Down Lead Poisoning

DR. ALICE HAMILTON

*A*lice Hamilton (1869–1970) studied medicine over the objections of her socially prominent family in Fort Wayne, Indiana. When she finally landed a job teaching pathology in
Chicago in 1897, Dr. Hamilton at last had her chance to fulfill a girlhood dream of living at
Jane Addams's Hull House. That experience launched her on an illustrious career as a pioneer
in industrial medicine—one of the many paths to social reform opened up by settlement-house
work.

When I look back on the Chicago of 1897 I can see why life in a settlement seemed so great
an adventure. It was all so new, this exploring of the poor quarters of a big city. The thirst
to know how the other half lives had just begun to send people pioneering in the unknown
parts of American life.... To settle down to live in the slums of a great city was a piece of
daring as great as trekking across the prairie in a covered wagon....

It was also my experience at Hull House that aroused my interest in industrial diseases.
Living in a working-class quarter, coming in contact with laborers and their wives, I could
not fail to hear tales of the dangers that working men faced, of cases of carbon-monoxide
poisoning in the great steel mills, of painters disabled by lead palsy, of pneumonia and
rheumatism among the men in the stockyards. Illinois then had no legislation providing
compensation for accident or disease caused by occupation.

At the time I am speaking of [1910] Professor Charles Henderson . . . persuaded [the
governor] to appoint an Occupational Disease Commission, the first time a state had ever
undertaken such a survey.... We were staggered by the complexity of the problem we faced

Contemptuous of the gentlemen Mugwumps, he much preferred the company of
party professionals. Roosevelt rose in the New York party because he skillfully
developed broad popular support and thus forced himself on reluctant state
Republican bosses.

Safely back from the Spanish-American War as the hero of San Juan Hill (see
Chapter 21), Roosevelt won the New York governorship in 1898. During his term in office he signaled his progressivism by pushing through civil service reform and a tax on
corporations. He discharged the corrupt superintendent of insurance over the
Republican Party's objections and asserted his confidence in the government's capacity
to improve the life of the people.

Hoping to neutralize him, the party chieftains chose Roosevelt in 1900 for what
seemed a dead-end job: William McKinley's running mate. Roosevelt accepted
reluctantly. But on September 6, 1901, an anarchist named Leon F. Czolgosz shot
the president. When McKinley died eight days later, Roosevelt became president, to the
dismay of party regulars.

and we soon decided to limit our field almost entirely to the occupational poisons, for at least we knew what their action was, while the action of various kinds of dust, and of temperature extremes and heavy exertion, was only vaguely understood at the time. The only poisons we had to cover were lead, arsenic, brass, carbon monoxide, the cyanides, and turpentine. Nowadays [1943], the list involved in a survey of the painters' trade alone is many times as long as that.

But to us it seemed far from a simple task. We could not even discover what were the poisonous occupations in Illinois. The Factory Inspector's Office was blissfully ignorant, yet that was the only governmental body concerned with working conditions. There was nothing to do but begin with trades we knew were dangerous and hoped that as we studied them, we would discover others less well known. My field was to be lead. . . .

One case, of colic and double wristdrop,* which was discovered in the Alexian Brothers' Hospital, took me on a pretty chase. The man, a Pole, said he had worked in a sanitary-ware factory, putting enamel on bathtubs. I had not come across this work in the English or German authorities on lead poisoning, and had no idea it was a lead trade. . . . The management assured me that no lead was used in the coatings and invited me to inspect the workrooms. . . . Completely puzzled, I made a journey to the Polish quarter to see the palsied man and heard from him I had not even been in the enameling works, only the one for final touching up. The real one was far out on the Northwest Side. I found it and discovered that enameling means sprinkling a finely ground enamel over a red hot tub where it melts and flows over the surface. I learned that the air is thick with enamel dust . . . rich in red oxide of lead. A specimen . . . proved to contain as much as 20 per cent soluble lead— that is, lead that dissolves into solution in the stomach. Thus I nailed down the fact that sanitary-ware enameling is a dangerous lead trade.

*Paralysis of the wrist muscles, causing the hand to droop.
SOURCE: *Exploring the Dangerous Trades: The Autobiography of Alice Hamilton* (Boston: Little, Brown and Co., 1943).

Roosevelt in fact moved cautiously, attending first to politics. Anxious to rein in the formidable conservative bloc in Congress, he adroitly used the patronage powers of his office to gain control of the Republican Party. But Roosevelt was also uncertain about how to proceed. At first the new president might have been described as a progressive without a cause.

Even so, Roosevelt displayed his activist bent. An ardent outdoorsman, his first annual message to Congress emphasized conservation. Unlike John Muir (see Chapter 16), Roosevelt was not a wilderness **preservationist**. Rather, he wanted to *conserve* the country's natural resources, balancing private development against the public interest. In 1902 he backed the Newlands Reclamation Act, which designated the proceeds from public land sales for irrigation in arid regions. His administration expanded the national forests, upgraded land management, and to the chagrin of some Republicans, energetically prosecuted violators of federal land laws. In the cause of **conservation**, Roosevelt showed his disdain for those who sought profit "by betraying the public" (Map 20.2).

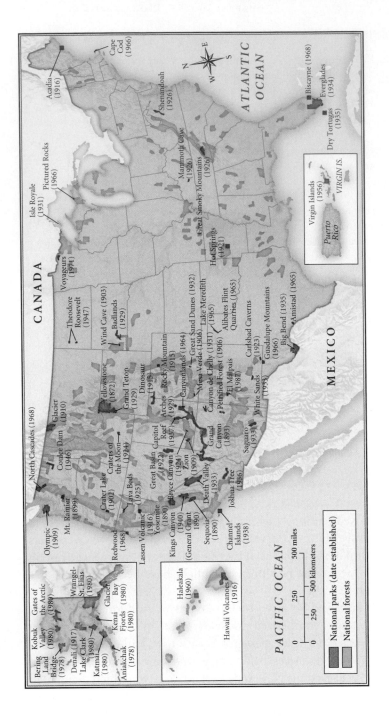

MAP 20.2 National Parks and Forests, 1872–1980

Close inspection of this map reveals that the national park system did not begin with the Progressive Era. Indeed, Yellowstone, the first park, dates from 1872. In 1893, the federal government began the protection of national forests. Without Roosevelt, however, the national forest program might have languished, and during his presidency he added 125 million acres to the forest system plus six national parks. More importantly, Roosevelt endowed these systems with a progressive, public-spirited stamp that has remained a principal resource of environmentalists striving to preserve the nation's natural heritage from overdevelopment and destructive exploitation. In the list of progressive triumphs, a robust national-park and forest system is one of the most enduring.

That same energetic bent prompted Roosevelt's intervention in the miners' strike of 1902. Anthracite (hard coal) was the main fuel for home heating in those days. As winter approached, settling the strike became urgent. The United Mine Workers, led by John Mitchell, was willing to submit to arbitration, but the coal operators would not talk to the union. Although lacking legal grounds for intervening, the president called both sides to a White House conference on October 1, 1902. When the operators balked, Roosevelt threatened a government takeover of the mines. He also persuaded the financier J. P. Morgan to use his considerable influence. At that point the coal operators caved in. The strike ended with the appointment by Roosevelt of an arbitration commission—another unprecedented step. While not especially sympathetic to organized labor, Roosevelt blamed the crisis on the "arrogant stupidity" of the mine owners.

"Of all the forms of tyranny the least attractive and the most vulgar is the tyranny of mere wealth," Roosevelt wrote in his autobiography. He was prepared to deploy all his presidential authority against the "tyranny" of irresponsible business.

Regulating the Marketplace

The economic issue that most troubled Roosevelt was the threat posed by big business to competitive markets. The drift toward large-scale enterprise was itself not new; for many years industrialists had been expanding their operations because of the efficiencies that vertical integration offered (see Chapter 17). But the bigger the business, the greater also was the power to control markets. And when, in the aftermath of the depression of the 1890s, promoters scrambled to merge rival firms, the primary motive was not lower costs but the elimination of competition. These mergers—**trusts**, as they were called—greatly increased business concentration. By 1910, 1 percent of the nation's manufacturers accounted for 44 percent of the nation's industrial output (see Voices from Abroad, "America in 1905: 'Business Is King,'" p. 616).

As early as his first annual message, Roosevelt acknowledged the nation's uneasiness with the "real and grave evils" of economic concentration. But what weapons could the president use in response?

The legal principles upholding free competition were already firmly established under common law: anyone injured by monopoly or illegal restraint of trade could sue for damages. With the passage of the Sherman Antitrust Act of 1890, these common-law rights entered the U.S. statute books and could be enforced by the federal government where offenses involved interstate commerce. Neither President Cleveland nor President McKinley showed much interest, but the Sherman Act was there waiting to be used. In the right hands the Sherman Act could be a mighty weapon against the abuse of economic power.

Roosevelt's opening move was to create a Bureau of Corporations (1903) empowered to investigate business practices and bolster the Justice Department's capacity to mount antitrust suits. The department had already filed such a suit against the Northern Securities Company, a combine of the railroad systems of the Northwest. In a landmark decision the Supreme Court ordered Northern Securities dissolved in 1904.

VOICES FROM ABROAD

America in 1905: "Business Is King"

JAMES BRYCE

J *ames Bryce, British author of* The American Commonwealth *(1888), a great treatise on American politics, visited the United States regularly over many years. In an essay published in 1905, Lord Bryce took stock of the changes he had seen during the previous quarter century. What most impressed him, beyond the sheer growth of material wealth, was the loss of individualism and the intensifying concentration of corporate power. In this he was at one with his old friend Theodore Roosevelt, who at that very time was gearing up to do battle with the trusts.*

That which most strikes the visitor to America today is its prodigious material development. Industrial growth, swift thirty or forty years ago, advances more swiftly now. The rural districts are being studded with villages, the villages are growing into cities, the cities are stretching out long arms of suburbs, which follow the lines of road and railway in every direction. The increase of wealth, even more remarkable than the increase of population, impresses the European more than ever before because the contrast with Europe is greater. The huge fortunes, the fortunes of those whose income reaches or exceeds a million dollars a year, are of course far more numerous than in any other country. . . . With this extraordinary material development it is natural that in the United States, business, that is to say, industry, commerce, and finance, should have more and more come to overshadow and dwarf all other interests, all other occupations. . . . Business is king.

That year Roosevelt handily defeated a weak conservative Democratic candidate, Judge Alton B. Parker. Now president in his own right, Roosevelt stepped up the attack on the trusts. He took on many of the nation's giant firms, including Standard Oil, American Tobacco, and DuPont. His rhetoric rising, Roosevelt became the nation's trust-buster, a crusader against "predatory wealth."

But Roosevelt was not antibusiness. He regarded large-scale enterprise as a natural tendency of modern industrialism. Only firms that abused their power deserved punishment. But how to identify those companies? Under the Sherman Act, following common-law practice, the courts decided whether an act in restraint of trade was "unreasonable"—that is, harmful of the public interest—on a case-by-case basis. In the *Trans-Missouri* decision (1897), however, the Supreme Court abandoned this discretionary "rule of reason," holding now that actions that restrained or monopolized trade, regardless of the public impact, automatically violated the Sherman Act.

Little noticed at first, *Trans-Missouri* placed Roosevelt in a quandary. He had no desire to hamstring legitimate business activity, but he could not rely on the courts to distinguish between "good" and "bad" trusts. So Roosevelt assumed this task

Commerce and industry themselves have developed new features. Twenty-two years ago there were no trusts. . . . Even then, however, corporations had covered a larger proportion of the whole field of industry and commerce in America than in Europe, and their structure was more flexible and efficient. Today this is still more the case; while as for trusts, they have become one of the most salient phenomena of the country. They fix the attention, they excite the alarm of economists and politicians as well as of traders in the Old World, while they exercise and baffle the ingenuity of American legislators. Workingmen follow, though hitherto with unequal steps, the efforts at combination which the lords of production and distribution have been making. The consumer stands, if not with folded hands, yet so far with no clear view of the steps he may make for his own protection. Perhaps his prosperity—for he is prosperous—helps him to be quiescent.

The example of the United States, the land in which individualism has been most conspicuously vigorous, may seem to suggest that the world is passing out of the stage of individualism and returning to that earlier stage in which groups of men formed the units of society. The bond of association was, in those early days, kinship, real or supposed, and a servile or quasi-servile dependence of the weak upon the strong. Now it is the power of wealth which enables the few to combine so as to gain command of the sources of wealth. . . . Is it a paradox to observe that it is because the Americans have been the most individualistic of peoples that they are now the people among whom the art of combination has reached its maximum? The amazing keenness and energy, which were stimulated by the commercial conditions of the country, have evoked and ripened a brilliant talent for organization. This talent has applied new methods to production and distribution and has enabled wealth, gathered into a small number of hands, to dominate even the enormous market of America.

SOURCE: *America through British Eyes*, edited by Allan Nevins. Copyright © 1968 by Allan Nevins. Reprinted by permission of Peter Smith Publisher, Gloucester, MA.

himself, which he could do because as chief executive it was up to him to approve antitrust prosecutions in the first place. It was his negative power that counted here: he could also choose not to prosecute a trust.

In November 1904, with an antitrust suit looming, the United States Steel Corporation's chairman Elbert H. Gary approached Roosevelt with a deal— cooperation in exchange for preferential treatment. The company would open its books to the Bureau of Corporations; if it found evidence of wrongdoing, the company would be warned privately and given a chance to set matters right. Roosevelt accepted this "gentlemen's agreement" because it met his interest in accommodating the modern industrial order while maintaining his public image as slayer of the trusts.

The railroads posed a different problem. As quasi-public enterprises, they had never been free of oversight by the states; in 1887 they became subject to federal regulation by the Interstate Commerce Commission (ICC). As with the Sherman Act, this assertion of federal authority was mostly symbolic at first. Then Roosevelt got started, pushing through in 1903 the Elkins Act that prohibited discriminatory railway rates unfairly favoring preferred or powerful customers. With the 1904

Jack and the Wall Street Giants

In this vivid cartoon from the humor magazine *Puck*, Jack (Theodore Roosevelt) has come to slay the giants of Wall Street. To the country, trust-busting took on the mythic qualities of the fairy tale — with about the same amount of awe for the fearsome Wall Street giants and hope in the prowess of the intrepid Roosevelt. J. P. Morgan is the giant leering at front right. Library of Congress.

FOR MORE HELP ANALYZING THIS IMAGE, see the Online Study Guide at **bedfordstmartins.com/ henrettaconcise.**

election behind him, Roosevelt launched a drive for real railroad regulation. In 1906, after nearly two years of wrangling, Congress passed the Hepburn Railway Act, which empowered the ICC to set maximum shipping rates and prescribe uniform methods of bookkeeping. As a concession to the conservative Republican bloc, however, the courts retained broad powers to review the ICC's rate decisions.

Passage of the Hepburn Act was a triumph of Roosevelt's skills as a political operator. Despite grumbling by Senate progressives, Roosevelt was satisfied. He had achieved a landmark expansion of the government's regulatory powers over business.

The protection of consumers, another signature issue for progressives, was very much the handiwork of muckraking journalism. What sparked the issue was a riveting series of articles in *Collier's* by Samuel Hopkins Adams exposing the patent-medicine business as "undiluted fraud," dangerous to the nation's health.

Then, in 1906, Upton Sinclair's novel *The Jungle* appeared. Sinclair thought he was writing about the exploitation of workers in Chicago meatpacking plants, but what caught the nation's attention were his descriptions of rotten meat and filthy conditions. President Roosevelt, weighing into the legislative battle, authorized a federal investigation of the stockyards. Within months the Pure Food and Drug and the Meat Inspection Acts passed, and another administrative agency joined the expanding federal bureaucracy—the Food and Drug Administration.

During the 1904 presidential campaign, Roosevelt had taken to calling his program the Square Deal. This kind of labeling was new and would become a hallmark of American politics in the twentieth century, emblematic of a political style that dramatized issues, mobilized public opinion, and asserted leadership. But the label meant something of substance as well. After many years of passivity and weakness, the federal government was reclaiming the role it had abandoned after the Civil War. Now, however, the target was the business economy. When companies abused their corporate power, the government would intercede to assure ordinary Americans a "square deal."

Roosevelt was well aware, however, that his Square Deal was built on nineteenth-century foundations. In particular, antitrust doctrine seemed inadequate when the economy's tendency was toward industrial concentration. Better, Roosevelt felt, for the federal government to regulate big business than try to break it up. In his final presidential speeches, Roosevelt dwelled on the need for a reform agenda for the twentieth century. Having chosen to retire after two terms, this was the task he bequeathed to his chosen successor, William Howard Taft.

Campaigning for the Square Deal

When William McKinley ran for president in 1896, he sat on his front porch in Canton, Ohio, and received delegations of voters. That was not Theodore Roosevelt's way. He considered the presidency a "bully pulpit," and he used the office brilliantly to mobilize public opinion and to assert his leadership. The preeminence of the presidency in American public life begins with Roosevelt's administration. Here, at the height of his crusading power, Roosevelt stumps for the Square Deal in the 1904 election. Library of Congress.

The Fracturing of Republican Progressivism

William Howard Taft was an estimable man in many ways. An able jurist and a su-perb administrator, he had served Roosevelt loyally as governor-general of the Philippines and as secretary of war. He was an avowed Square Dealer. But he was not by nature a progressive politician. He disliked the give-and-take of politics, he dis-trusted power, and he revered the processes of law. He could not, for example, have imagined intruding into the 1902 anthracite strike, as Roosevelt had done, or taken so flexible a view of the Sherman Act. He was, in fundamental ways, a conservative.

Taft's Democratic opponent in the 1908 campaign was William Jennings Bryan. This was Bryan's last hurrah, his third attempt at the presidency, and he made the most of it. Eloquent as ever, Bryan attacked the Republicans as the party of the "plutocrats" and outdid them in urging tougher antitrust legislation, stricter railway regulation, and advanced labor legislation. Almost single-handedly, Bryan moved the Democratic Party into the mainstream of national progressive politics. But his robust campaign was not enough to offset Taft's advantages as Roosevelt's candi-date. Taft won comfortably, entering the White House with a mandate to pick up where Roosevelt left off. That, however, was not to be.

By 1909 reform politics had unsettled the Republican Party. On the right the conservatives were girding themselves against further losses. Led by the formidable Senator Nelson W. Aldrich of Rhode Island, they were still a force to be reckoned with. On the left, progressive Republicans were rebellious. They had broad popular support—especially in the Midwest—and in Robert La Follette, a fiery leader. The progressives felt that Roosevelt had been too easy on business, and with him gone from the White House, they intended to make up for lost time. Reconciling these conflicting forces within the Republican Party would have been a daunting task for the most accomplished politician. For Taft it spelled disaster.

First there was the tariff. Progressives considered protective tariffs a major rea-son why competition had declined and the trusts had taken hold. Although Taft had campaigned for tariff reform, he was won over by the conservative Republican bloc and ended up approving the protectionist Payne-Aldrich Tariff Act of 1909, which critics charged sheltered eastern industry from foreign competition.

Next came the Pinchot-Ballinger affair. U.S. Chief Forester Gifford Pinchot, an ardent conservationist and a chum of Roosevelt's, accused Secretary of the Interior Richard A. Ballinger of conspiring to transfer Alaskan public land to a private busi-ness group. When Pinchot aired these charges, Taft fired him for insubordination. Despite Taft's strong conservationist credentials, in the eyes of the progressives the Pinchot-Ballinger affair marked him as a friend of the "interests" bent on plunder-ing the nation's resources.

Taft found himself propelled into the conservative Republican camp, an ally of "Uncle Joe" Cannon, the dictatorial Speaker of the House of Representatives. When a House revolt finally broke Cannon's power in 1910, it was regarded as a defeat for the president as well. Galvanized by Taft's defection, the reformers in the Republican

Party became a dissident faction, calling themselves "Progressives," or in more belligerent moments, "Insurgents."

Home from a year-long safari in Africa, Roosevelt yearned to reenter the political fray. Taft's dispute with the Progressives gave Roosevelt the cause he needed. But Roosevelt was a loyal party man and too astute a politician not to recognize that a party split would benefit the Democrats. He could be spurred into rebellion only by a true clash of principles. On the question of the trusts, just such a clash materialized.

Taft's legalistic mind rebelled at Roosevelt's practice of choosing among trusts when it came to antitrust prosecutions. The Sherman Act was on the books. "We are going to enforce that law or die in the attempt," Taft promised grimly. But he was held back until the Supreme Court reasserted the rule of reason in the *Standard Oil* decision (1911), which meant that, once again, the courts themselves would distinguish between good and bad trusts. With that burden lifted from the executive branch, Taft's attorney general George W. Wickersham stepped up the pace of antitrust actions, immediately targeting the United States Steel Corporation. One of the charges was that the steel trust had acted illegally by acquiring the Tennessee Coal and Iron Company in 1907. Roosevelt had personally approved the acquisition, believing it was necessary—so U.S. Steel representatives had told him—to prevent a financial collapse on Wall Street. Taft's suit against U.S. Steel thus amounted to an attack on Roosevelt that he could not, without dishonor, ignore.

Ever since leaving the White House, Roosevelt had been pondering the trust problem. Between breaking up big business and submitting to corporate rule lay another alternative. The federal government could be empowered to oversee the nation's industrial corporations to make sure they acted in the public interest. They would be regulated by a federal trade commission as if they were natural monopolies or public utilities.

In a speech in Osawatomie, Kansas, in August 1910, Roosevelt made the case for what he called the New Nationalism. The central issue, he argued, was human welfare versus property rights. In modern society, property had to be controlled "to whatever degree the public welfare may require it." The government would become "the steward of the public welfare."

This formulation unleashed Roosevelt's reformist bent. He took up the cause of social justice, adding to his program a federal child labor law, regulation of labor relations, and a national minimum wage for women. Most radical, perhaps, was Roosevelt's attack on the legal system. Insisting that the courts stood in the way of reform, Roosevelt proposed sharp curbs on their powers, even raising the possibility of popular recall of court decisions.

Early in 1912 Roosevelt announced his candidacy for the presidency, immediately sweeping the Progressive Republicans into his camp. A bitter party battle ensued. Roosevelt won the states that held primary elections, but Taft controlled the party caucuses elsewhere. Dominated by party regulars, the Republican convention chose Taft. Considering himself cheated out of the nomination, Roosevelt led his followers into a new Progressive Party, soon nicknamed the "Bull Moose" Party. In a crusading campaign Roosevelt offered the New Nationalism to the people.

Woodrow Wilson and the New Freedom

While the Republicans battled among themselves, the Democrats were on the move. The scars caused by the free-silver campaign of 1896 had faded, and in the 1908 campaign William Jennings Bryan established the party's progressive credentials. The Democrats made dramatic gains in 1910, taking over the House of Representatives for the first time since 1892 and capturing a number of traditionally Republican governorships. After fourteen years as the party's standard-bearer, Bryan made way for a new generation of leaders.

The ablest was Woodrow Wilson of New Jersey, a noted political scientist who, as university president, had brought Princeton into the front rank of American universities. In 1910, with no political experience, he accepted the Democratic nomination for governor of New Jersey and won. Wilson compiled a sterling reform record, including the direct primary, workers' compensation, and utility regulation. Wilson went on to win the Democratic presidential nomination in 1912 in a bruising battle.

Wilson possessed, to a fault, the moral certainty that was common among progressive leaders. The product of a family of Presbyterian clerics, he instinctively assumed the mantle of righteousness. Only gradually, however, did Wilson hammer out, in reaction to Roosevelt's New Nationalism, a coherent reform program, which he called the New Freedom. As he warmed to the debate, Wilson cast his differences with Roosevelt in fundamental terms of slavery and freedom. "This is a struggle for emancipation," he proclaimed in October 1912. "If America is not to have free enterprise, then she can have freedom of no sort whatever." Wilson also scorned Roosevelt's social program. Welfare might be benevolent, he declared, but it also would be paternalistic and contrary to the traditions of a free people. The New Nationalism represented a future of collectivism, Wilson warned, whereas the New Freedom would preserve political and economic liberty.

Wilson actually had much in common with Roosevelt. "The old time of individual competition is probably gone by," Wilson admitted. Like Roosevelt, he opposed not bigness but the abuse of economic power. Wilson even agreed that preventing the abuse of power required a strong federal government. He parted company from Roosevelt over *how* government should restrain private power.

Despite all the rhetoric, the 1912 election fell short as a referendum on the New Nationalism versus the New Freedom. The outcome turned on a more humdrum reality: Wilson won because he kept the traditional Democratic vote, while the Republicans split between Roosevelt and Taft. Despite a landslide in the electoral college, Wilson received only 42 percent of the popular vote. At best the 1912 election signified that the American public was in the mood for reform. Only 23 percent, after all, had voted for the one candidate who stood for the status quo, President Taft, and as a marker of the public mood, the Socialist candidate Eugene V. Debs got a record 6 percent of the vote (Map 20.3). Wilson's own program, however, had received no clear mandate from the people.

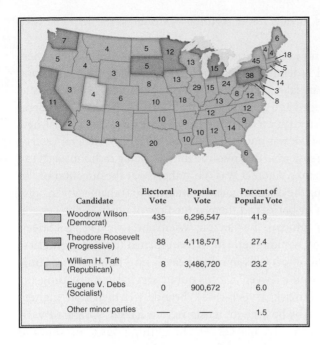

Candidate	Electoral Vote	Popular Vote	Percent of Popular Vote
Woodrow Wilson (Democrat)	435	6,296,547	41.9
Theodore Roosevelt (Progressive)	88	4,118,571	27.4
William H. Taft (Republican)	8	3,486,720	23.2
Eugene V. Debs (Socialist)	0	900,672	6.0
Other minor parties	—	—	1.5

MAP 20.3 Presidential Election of 1912

The 1912 election reveals why the two-party system is so strongly rooted in American politics. The Democrats, though a minority party, won an electoral landslide because the Republicans divided their vote between Roosevelt and Taft. This result indicates what is at stake when major parties splinter. The Socialists, despite a record vote of 900,000, received no electoral votes. To vote Socialist in 1912 meant in effect to throw away one's vote.

Yet the 1912 election proved a turning point for economic reform. The debate between Roosevelt and Wilson had brought forth, in the New Freedom, a program capable of finally resolving the crisis over corporate power that had gripped the nation for a decade. Just as important, the election created a rare legislative opportunity in Washington. With Congress in Democratic hands, the time was ripe to act on the New Freedom.

Long out of power, the Democrats were hungry for tariff reform. From the prevailing average of 40 percent, the Underwood Tariff Act of 1913 pared rates down to 25 percent. Targeting especially the trust-dominated industries, Democrats confidently expected the Underwood Tariff to spur competition and reduce prices for consumers.

Wilson's administration then turned to the nation's banking system, whose key weakness was the absence of a central bank, or federal reserve. The main function of central banks at that time was to regulate commercial banks and back them up in case they could not meet their obligations to depositors. In the past this backup role had been assumed by the great New York banks that handled the accounts of outlying banks. If the New York banks weakened, the entire system could collapse. This had nearly happened in 1907, when the Knickerbocker Trust Company failed and panic swept the nation's financial markets.

But if the need for a central bank was clear, the form it should take was hotly disputed. Wall Street wanted a unified system run by the bankers. Rural Democrats and their spokesman, Senator Carter Glass of Virginia, preferred a decentralized network of reserve banks. Progressives in both parties demanded strong public control. The New York bankers, already under scrutiny by Congress for their collusive practices, were on the defensive.

President Wilson, initially no expert, learned quickly and reconciled the reformers and bankers. The monumental Federal Reserve Act of 1913 gave the nation a banking system that was resistant to financial panic. The act delegated operational functions to twelve district reserve banks funded and controlled by their member banks. The Federal Reserve Board imposed public regulation on this regional structure. One crucial new power granted the Federal Reserve was authority to issue currency—federal reserve notes based on assets within the system—that resolved the paralyzing cash shortages experienced during runs on the banks. Another was the authority, at the direction of the Federal Reserve Board, for setting the discount rate (the interest rate) charged by the district reserve banks to the member banks and thereby the flow of credit to the general public. In one stroke the act strengthened the banking system and reined in Wall Street.

Having dealt with tariff and banking reform, Wilson turned to the big question of how to curb the trusts. In this effort Wilson relied heavily on a new advisor, Louis D. Brandeis, famous as the "people's lawyer" for his public service in many progressive causes (including the landmark *Muller* case). Brandeis denied that bigness meant efficiency. On the contrary, he argued, trusts were wasteful compared with firms that vigorously competed in a free market. The main thing was to prevent the trusts from unfairly using their power to curb free competition.

This could be done by strengthening the Sherman Act, but the obvious course—defining with precision what constituted anticompetitive practices—proved hard to implement. Was it feasible to say exactly when interlocking directorates, discriminatory pricing, or exclusive contracts became illegal? Brandeis decided that it was not, and Wilson assented. In the Clayton Antitrust Act of 1914, amending the Sherman Act, the definition of illegal practices was left flexible, subject to the test of whether an action "substantially lessen[ed] competition or tend[ed] to create a monopoly."

This retreat from a definitive antitrust prescription meant that a federal trade commission would be needed to back up the Sherman and Clayton acts. Wilson was understandably hesitant, given his principled opposition to Roosevelt's powerful trade commission in the campaign. At first Wilson favored an advisory, information-gathering agency. But ultimately, under the 1914 law establishing it, the Federal Trade Commission (FTC) received broad powers to investigate companies and issue "cease and desist" orders against unfair trade practices that violated antitrust law.

Despite a good deal of commotion, this arduous legislative process was actually an exercise in consensus building. Wilson opened the debate in a conciliatory way. "The antagonism between business and government is over," he said, and the time ripe for a program representing the "best business judgment in America." Afterward, Wilson felt he had brought the long controversy over corporate power to a successful conclusion, and in fact he had. Steering a course between Taft's conservatism and Roosevelt's radicalism, Wilson had carved out a middle way that brought to bear the powers of government without threatening the constitutional order and curbed abuse of corporate power without threatening the capitalist system.

What few Americans recognized, in the midst of this protracted struggle, was how very odd it seemed from a European standpoint. Neither Britain nor Germany, America's industrial rivals, made such a fuss over competitive markets. It was true that the fundamental concept—restraint of trade—originated in English common law, but the British, free traders and big exporters, lacked the opportunity to engage in market-controlling behavior and hence had no need for antitrust legislation. Germany, by contrast, was a veritable hotbed of conspiracies in restraint of trade, only they were called "cartels"—business groups that divided the market and set prices, operating with the approval of the imperial government. In this respect, American progressivism was a distinctly homemade product.

On social policy, as with antitrust policy, Wilson charted a middle way. Having denounced Roosevelt's paternalism, he was at first unreceptive to what he saw as special-interest demands by labor and farm organizations. On the leading issue—that they be exempted from antitrust prosecution—the most Wilson was willing to accept was cosmetic language in the Clayton Act that did not grant them the immunity they sought.

The labor vote had grown increasingly important to the Democratic Party, however. Wilson's tenure in the White House, moreover, coincided with a burst of industrial conflict, including dramatic strikes by textile workers, mostly immigrant women, in Lawrence, Massachusetts, in 1912, and Paterson, New Jersey, in 1913, and a violent coal miners' strike in 1914 in Colorado, which climaxed with the torching of a tent city at Ludlow by state militia. The resulting asphyxiation of strikers' wives and children hiding in the tents horrified the nation and made Ludlow the focus of a wide-ranging investigation into the troubled industrial relations of the country. The "labor question" was suddenly prominent on the progressive agenda.

As his second presidential campaign drew near, Wilson lost some of his scruples about pro-labor legislation. In 1915 and 1916 he championed a host of bills beneficial to American workers: a federal child-labor law, the Adamson eight-hour law for railroad workers, and the landmark Seamen's Act, which eliminated age-old abuses of sailors aboard ship. Likewise, after earlier resistance, Wilson approved in 1916 the Federal Farm Loan Act, which provided the low-interest rural credit system long demanded by farmers. Nor was it lost on observers that, his New Freedom rhetoric notwithstanding, Wilson presided over an ever more active federal government and an ever-expanding federal bureaucracy.

Wilson encountered the same dilemma that confronted all successful progressives—the clash of moral principle against the unyielding realities of political life. Progressives were high-minded but not radical. They saw evils in the system, but they did not consider the system itself to be evil. They also prided themselves on being realists as well as moralists. So it stood to reason that Wilson, like other progressives who achieved power, would find his place at the center.

But it would be wrong to underestimate their achievement. Progressives made presidential leadership important again, they brought government back into the nation's life, they laid the foundation for twentieth-century social and economic policy. And, as we shall see, they put an enduring stamp on America's self-definition as a world power.

TIMELINE

1889	Jane Addams and Ellen Gates Starr found Hull House	1908	*Muller v. Oregon* upholds regulation of working hours for women
1895	Booker T. Washington sets out Atlanta Compromise		William Howard Taft elected president
1899	National Consumers' League founded	1909	NAACP formed
1900	Robert M. La Follette elected Wisconsin governor	1910	Roosevelt announces the New Nationalism
			Woman suffrage movement revives
1901	President McKinley assassinated; Theodore Roosevelt succeeds him	1911	*Standard Oil* decision restores "rule of reason"
1902	President Roosevelt settles national anthracite strike		Triangle Shirtwaist fire
		1912	Progressive Party formed
1903	National Women's Trade Union League founded		Woodrow Wilson elected president
1904	Supreme Court dissolves the Northern Securities Company	1913	Federal Reserve Act
			Underwood Tariff Act
1906	Upton Sinclair's *The Jungle*	1914	Clayton Antitrust Act
	Hepburn Railway Act		
	AFL adopts "Bill of Grievances"		

For Further Exploration

The historical literature on the Progressive Era offers an embarrassment of riches. A good entry point is John Milton Cooper, *Pivotal Decades: 1900–1920* (1990). Richard Hofstadter, *Age of Reform* (1955), is an elegantly written interpretation that remains worth reading despite its disputed central arguments. The following books are a sampling of the best that has been written about progressivism: Robert M. Crunden, *Ministers of Reform, 1889–1920* (1982), on the religious underpinnings; Nancy S. Dye, *As Equals and Sisters* (1980), on working women in the movement; David P. Thelen, *The New Citizenship* (1972), on La Follette and Wisconsin progressivism; John D. Buenker, *Urban Liberalism and Progressive Reform* (1973), on the politics of urban liberalism; Nancy F. Cott, *The Grounding of Modern Feminism* (1987); Naomi Lamoreaux, *The Great Merger Movement in American Business, 1895–1904* (1985); Martin J. Sklar, *The Corporate Reconstruction of American Capitalism, 1890–1916* (1988), on the progressive struggle to fashion a regulatory policy for big business.

Among the stimulating recent books, see Nancy Cohen, *The Reconstruction of American Liberalism, 1865–1914* (2002), on the intellectual origins of progressivism; Daniel T. Rodgers, *Atlantic Crossings: Social Democracy in a Progressive Age* (1998), a brilliant exploration of progressivism as an international phenomenon; Linda Gordon, *Pitied but Not Entitled: Single Mothers and the History of Welfare, 1890–1935* (1994), which uses the modern debate over welfare reform as a lens for probing the tangled origins of the American welfare system; Sara Hunter Graham, *Woman Suffrage and the New Democracy* (1996), which treats the battle for the vote as a precocious exercise in modern single-issue politics; Elizabeth Lasch-Quinn, *Black Neighbors* (1993), on the racial conservatism of settlement-house progressives; Julie Greene, *Pure and Simple Politics: The AF of L, 1881–1915* (1997), on labor's increasing engagement in partisan politics; and Leon Fink, *Progressive Intellectuals and the Dilemmas of Democratic Commitment* (1997). The following biographies offer another rewarding avenue into progressivism: John Milton Cooper, *The Warrior and the Priest* (1983), a joint biography of Roosevelt and Wilson; Allen F. Davis, *American Heroine: Jane Addams* (1973); Kathryn Kish Sklar, *Florence Kelley and the Nation's Work* (1995); Louis B. Harlan, *Booker T. Washington: Wizard of Tuskegee* (1983); David Levering Lewis, *W. E. B. Du Bois: Biography of a Race, 1868–1919* (1993).

Votes for Women: NAWSA, 1848–1921, at <http://lcweb2.loc.gov/ammem/naw/nawshome.html>, is a searchable archive of over 160 documents from the NAWSA collection. Theodore Roosevelt: Icon of the American Century, at <http://www.npg.si.edu/exh/roosevelt.htm>, presents pictures from the National Portrait Gallery, a biographical narrative, and information on Roosevelt's family and friends. The Evolution of the Conservation Movement, at <http://memory.loc.gov/ammem/amrvhtml/conshome.html>, offers a time line and archive of materials on the development of the conservation movement from 1850 to 1920.

For definitions of key terms boldfaced in this chapter, see the glossary at the end of the book.

To assess your mastery of the material covered in this chapter, see the Online Study Guide at **bedfordstmartins.com/henrettaconcise**.

For map resources and primary documents, see **bedfordstmartins.com/henrettaconcise**.

Chapter 21

AN EMERGING WORLD POWER
1877–1914

God has marked the American people as His chosen nation to finally
lead in the regeneration of the world. This is the divine mission of
America, and it holds for us all the profit, all the glory, all the
happiness possible to man.

SENATOR ALBERT J. BEVERIDGE, ARGUING FOR U.S. ACQUISITION
OF THE PHILIPPINES, 1900

In 1881 Great Britain sent a new envoy to Washington. He was Sir
Lionel Sackville-West, son of an earl and brother-in-law of the Tory leader Lord
Denby, but otherwise distinguished only as the lover of a celebrated Spanish dancer.
His well-connected friends wanted to park Sir Lionel somewhere comfortable, but
out of harm's way. So they made him minister to the United States.

Twenty years later such an appointment would have been unthinkable. All the
European powers staffed their missions in Washington with top-of-the-line ambas-
sadors. And they treated the United States, without question, as a fellow Great
Power.

In Sir Lionel's day the United States scarcely cast a shadow on world affairs.
America's army was smaller than Bulgaria's; its navy ranked thirteenth in the
world and was a threat mainly to the crews manning its rickety ships. By 1900,
however, the United States was flexing its muscles. It had just made short work
of Spain in a brief but decisive war and acquired an empire stretching from
Puerto Rico to the Philippines. America's standing as a rising naval power was
manifest, and so was its muscular assertion of national interest in the Caribbean
and the Pacific.

The Europeans could not be sure what America's role would be, since the
United States retained its traditional policy against entangling alliances. But foreign
offices across the Continent acknowledged the importance of the United States and
carefully assessed its likely response to every event.

The Roots of Expansion

With 50 million people in 1880, the United States by population already ranked with the great European powers. In industrial production the nation stood second only to Britain and was rapidly closing the gap. Anyone who doubted the military prowess of Americans needed only to recall the ferocity with which they had fought one another in the Civil War. The great campaigns of Lee, Sherman, and Grant had entered the military textbooks and were closely studied by army strategists everywhere, as was evident in the skirmishing lines and massed charges employed by the German infantry against the French in the Franco-Prussian War of 1870.

And when vital interests were at stake, the United States had not shown itself lacking in diplomatic vigor. The Civil War had put the United States at odds with both France and Britain. The dispute with France involved the establishment in Mexico of a French-sponsored regime under Archduke Maximilian in 1863. With the seizure of the Southwest from Mexico in 1848 still a recent event, the United States regarded this development as a threat to its regional security and waited only until its hands were freed by the end of the Civil War to respond. In 1867, as American troops under General Philip Sheridan massed on the Mexican border, the French military withdrew, abandoning Maximilian to a Mexican firing squad.

With Britain, the thorny issue involved damages to Union shipping by the *Alabama* and other Confederate sea raiders operating from English ports. American hopes of taking Canada as compensation were dashed by Britain's grant of dominion status to Canada in 1867. But four years later, after lengthy negotiations, Britain expressed regret for its unneutral acts and agreed to the arbitration of the *Alabama* claims, settling to America's satisfaction the last outstanding diplomatic issue of the Civil War.

Diplomacy in the Gilded Age

In the years that followed, the United States lapsed into diplomatic inactivity, not out of weakness but for lack of any clear national purpose in world affairs. The business of building the nation's industrial economy absorbed Americans and turned their attention inward. And while telegraphic cables provided the country with swift overseas communication after the 1860s, wide oceans still kept the world at a distance and gave Americans a sense of isolation and security.

European affairs, which centered on Franco-German rivalry and on bewildering Balkan enmities, hardly concerned the United States. As far as President Cleveland's secretary of state, Thomas F. Bayard, was concerned, "we have not the slightest share or interest [in] the small politics and backstage intrigues of Europe."

In these circumstances, why maintain a big navy? After the Civil War, the fleet gradually deteriorated. Of the 125 ships on the navy's active list, only about 25 were seaworthy at any one time, mainly sailing ships and obsolete ironclads modeled on the *Monitor* of Civil War fame. The administration of Chester A. Arthur (1881–1885) began a modest upgrading program, commissioning new ships, raising the standards for the officer corps, and founding the Naval War College. But the fleet remained small, without a unified naval command, and had little more to do than maintain coastal defenses.

The conduct of diplomacy was likewise of little account. Appointment to the foreign service was mostly through the spoils system. American envoys and consular officers were a mixed lot, with many idlers and drunkards among the hardworking and competent. For its part the State Department tended to be inactive, exerting little control over either policy or its missions abroad. In distant places the American presence was likely to be Christian missionaries proselytizing among the native populations of Asia, Africa, and the Pacific islands.

In the Caribbean the expansionist enthusiasms of the Civil War era subsided. William H. Seward, Lincoln and Andrew Johnson's secretary of state, had dreamed of an American empire extending from the Caribbean across Mexico to Hawaii. Nothing came of his grandiose plans, nor of President Grant's efforts to purchase Santo Domingo (the future Dominican Republic) in 1870, and the Senate regularly blocked later moves to acquire bases in Haiti, Cuba, and Venezuela. The long-cherished interest in a canal across Central America also faded. Despite its claims of exclusive rights, the United States stood by when a French company headed by the builder of the Suez Canal, Ferdinand de Lesseps, started to dig across the Panama isthmus in 1880. That project failed after a decade, but because of bankruptcy, not American opposition.

Diplomatic activity quickened when the energetic James G. Blaine became secretary of state in 1881. He got involved in a border dispute between Mexico and Guatemala, tried to settle a war Chile was waging against Peru and Bolivia, and called the first Pan-American conference. Blaine's interventions in Latin American disputes went badly, however, and his successor canceled the Pan-American conference after Blaine left office in late 1881. This was a characteristic example of Gilded Age diplomacy, driven largely by partisan politics and carried out without any clear sense of national purpose.

Pan-Americanism—the notion of a community of states of the Western Hemisphere—took root, however, and Blaine, returning in 1889 for a second stint at the State Department, approved the plans of the outgoing Cleveland administration for a new Pan-American conference. But little came of it, except for an agency in Washington that became the Pan-American Union. Any South American goodwill won by Blaine's efforts was soon blasted by the humiliation the United States visited upon Chile because of a riot against American sailors in the port of Valparaiso in 1891. Threatened with war, Chile was forced to apologize to the United States and pay an indemnity of $75,000.

In the Pacific, American interest centered on Hawaii, where sugarcane had attracted a horde of American planters and investors. Nominally an independent nation, Hawaii fell under American dominance. An 1875 treaty gave Hawaiian sugar duty-free

Sugarcane Plantation, Hawaii

Over 300,000 Asians from China, Japan, Korea, and the Philippines came to work in the Hawaiian cane fields between 1850 and 1920. The hardships they endured are reflected in plantation work songs, such as this one by Japanese laborers:

But when I came what I saw was Hell
The boss was Satan
The lunas [overseers] his helpers.

George Bacon Collection, Hawaii State Archives.

entry into the American market and declared the islands off limits to other powers. A second treaty in 1887 granted the United States naval rights at Pearl Harbor.

When Hawaii's favored access to the American market was abruptly canceled by the McKinley Tariff of 1890, sugar planters began to plot an American takeover of the islands. They organized a revolt in January 1893 against Queen Liliuokalani and quickly negotiated a treaty of annexation with the Harrison administration. Before the Senate could approve it, however, Grover Cleveland returned to the presidency and withdrew the treaty. To annex Hawaii, he declared, would violate America's "honor and morality" and an "unbroken tradition" against acquiring territory far from the nation's shores.

Meanwhile, the American presence elsewhere in the Pacific was growing. The purchase of Alaska from imperial Russia in 1867 gave the United States not only a huge territory with vast natural resources but an unlooked-for presence stretching across the northern Pacific. And far to the south, in the Samoan islands, the United States secured rights in 1878 to a coaling station for its steamships at Pago Pago harbor—a key link on the route to Australia—and established an informal protectorate there. In 1889, after some jostling with Germany and Britain, the rivalry over Samoa ended in a tripartite protectorate, with America retaining its rights in Pago Pago.

American diplomacy in these years has been characterized as a series of incidents, not the pursuit of a foreign policy. Many things happened, but intermittently and without any well-founded conception of national objectives. This was possible because, as the Englishman James Bryce remarked in 1888, America still sailed "upon a summer sea." In the stormier waters that lay ahead, a different kind of diplomacy would be required.

The Economy of Expansionism

"A policy of isolation did well enough when we were an embryo nation," remarked Senator Orville Platt of Connecticut in 1893. "But today things are different. . . . We are 65 million people, the most advanced and powerful on earth, and regard to our future welfare demands an abandonment of the doctrines of isolation." What especially demanded that Americans look outward was their prodigious economy.

America's gross domestic product—the total value of goods and services—quadrupled between 1870 and 1900. But were American markets big enough to absorb this multiplying output? Over 90 percent was consumed at home. Even so, foreign markets mattered. Roughly a fifth of the nation's agricultural output was exported, and as the industrial economy expanded, so did manufactured goods, whose share of total exports jumped from 15 percent to over 30 percent between 1880 and 1900.

American firms began to plant themselves overseas. As early as 1868 the Singer Sewing Machine Company established a factory in Glasgow, Scotland. The giant among American firms doing business abroad was Rockefeller's Standard Oil, with European branches operating tankers and marketing kerosene across the Continent. In Asia, Standard Oil cans, converted into utensils and roofing tin, became a visible sign of American market penetration.

Foreign trade was important partly for reasons of international finance. As a developing economy the United States attracted a lot of foreign capital. The result was a heavy outflow of dollars to pay interest and dividends to foreign investors. To balance this account, the United States needed to export more goods than it imported. In fact, a favorable import-export balance was achieved in 1876 (Figure 21.1). But because of its dependence on foreign capital, America had to be constantly vigilant about its export trade.

Even more important, however, was the relationship that many Americans perceived between foreign markets and the nation's social stability. Hard times always sparked agrarian unrest and labor strife. The problem, many thought, was that the

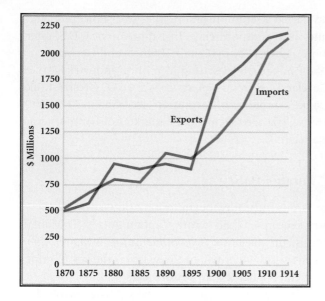

FIGURE 21.1 Balance of U.S. Imports, 1870–1914

By 1876 the United States had become a net exporting nation. The brief reversal after 1888 aroused fears that the United States was losing its foreign markets and helped fuel the expansionist drive of the 1890s.

nation's capacity to produce was outrunning its capacity to consume. When the economy slowed, cutbacks in domestic demand drove down farm prices and caused layoffs across the country. The answer was to make sure there would always be enough buyers for America's surplus products, and this meant buyers in foreign markets.

How did these concerns about overseas trade relate to America's foreign policy? The bulk of American exports in the late nineteenth century—over 80 percent— went to Europe and Canada. In these countries the normal practice of diplomacy sufficed to protect the nation's economic interests. But Asia, Latin America, and other regions that Americans considered "backward" demanded a tougher brand of intervention because there the United States was competing with other industrial powers.

Asia and Latin America represented only a modest part of America's export trade. Still, this trade was growing—it was worth $200 million in 1900—and parts of it mattered a great deal to specific industries—for example, the Chinese market for American textiles. The real importance of these non-Western markets, however, was not so much their current value as their future promise. China especially exerted a powerful grip on the American mercantile imagination. Many felt that the China trade, although quite small at the time, would one day be the key to American prosperity. Therefore, China and other beckoning markets must not be closed to the United States.

In the mid-1880s the pace of European imperialism picked up. After the Berlin Conference of 1884, Africa was rapidly carved up by the European powers. In a burst of modernizing energy, Japan transformed itself into a major power and began to challenge China's claims to Korea. In the Sino-Japanese War (1894–1895),

Japan won an easy victory and started a scramble among the Great Powers, including Russia, to divide China into spheres of influence. In Latin America, U.S. interests began to be challenged more aggressively by Britain, France, and Germany.

On top of all this came the Panic of 1893, setting in motion industrial strikes and agrarian protests that Cleveland's secretary of state, Walter Q. Gresham, like many other Americans, took to be "symptoms of revolution" (see Chapter 17). With the nation's social stability seemingly at risk, securing the markets of Latin America and Asia became an urgent matter.

The Making of a "Large" Foreign Policy

"Whether they will or no, Americans must now begin to look outward. The growing production of the country requires it." So wrote Captain Alfred T. Mahan, America's leading naval strategist, in his book *The Influence of Seapower upon History* (1890). Mahan's argument was that control of the seas was the key to imperial power, and from this insight emerged an expansionist strategy.

The United States should regard the oceans not as barriers, Mahan wrote, but as "a great highway . . . over which men pass in all directions." Traversing that highway required a robust merchant marine (America's had fallen on hard times since its heyday in the 1850s), a powerful navy to protect American commerce, and overseas bases. Having converted from sail to steam, navies required coaling stations far from home. Without such stations, Mahan warned, warships were "like land birds, unable to fly far from their own shores."

Mahan advocated the construction of a canal across Central America connecting the Atlantic and Pacific Oceans. Such a canal would enable the eastern United States to "compete with Europe, on equal terms as to distance, for the markets of East Asia." The canal's approaches would need to be guarded by bases in the Caribbean Sea. Hawaii would have to be annexed to extend American power into the Pacific. What Mahan envisioned was a form of colonialism different from Europe's—not rule over territories and populations but control over strategic points around the globe in defense of America's trading interests.

Other enthusiasts of a powerful America flocked to Mahan, including such up-and-coming politicians as Theodore Roosevelt and Henry Cabot Lodge. The influence of these men, few in number but well connected, increased during the 1890s, with Lodge entering the Senate and Roosevelt high up in the Navy Department under McKinley. They pushed steadily for what Lodge called a "large policy."

Mahan proposed a battleship fleet capable of striking a decisive blow against an enemy far from America's shores. In 1890 Congress appropriated funds for three battleships as the first installment on a two-ocean navy. Battleships might be expensive, said Benjamin F. Tracy, Harrison's ambitious secretary of the navy, but they were "the premium paid by the United States for the insurance of its acquired wealth and its growing industries." The battleship took on a special aura for those—like the young Roosevelt—who had grand dreams for the United States. "Oh, Lord!

if only the people who are ignorant about our Navy could see those great warships in all their majesty and beauty, and could realize how [well fitted they are] to uphold the honor of America!"

The incoming Cleveland administration was less spread-eagled and, by canceling Harrison's scheme for annexing Hawaii, established its antiexpansionist credentials. But after hesitating briefly Cleveland picked up the naval program of his Republican predecessor, pressing Congress just as forcefully for more battleships (five were authorized) and making the same basic argument. The nation's commercial vitality— "free access to all markets," in the words of Cleveland's second secretary of state, Richard Olney—depended on its naval power.

While rejecting the territorial aspects of Mahan's thinking, Cleveland absorbed the underlying strategic arguments about where America's vital interests lay. This explains the remarkable crisis that suddenly blew up in 1895 over Venezuela.

For years Venezuela had disputed its boundary with British Guiana. Now the United States demanded that the issue be resolved. The European powers were carving up Africa and Asia. How could the United States be sure that Europe did not have similar designs on Latin America? Secretary of State Olney made that point in a bristling note to London on July 25, 1895, insisting that Britain accept arbitration or face the consequences. Invoking the Monroe Doctrine, Olney warned that the United States would brook no challenge to its vital interests in the Caribbean. These vital interests were America's, not Venezuela's; Venezuela was not consulted during the entire dispute.

Once the British realized that Cleveland meant business, they backed off and agreed to arbitration of the boundary dispute. Afterward, Olney remarked with satisfaction that, as a great industrial nation, the United States needed "to accept [a] commanding position" and take its place "among the Powers of the earth." Other countries would have to accommodate America's need for access to "more markets and larger markets for the consumption and products of the industry and inventive genius of the American people."

The Ideology of Expansionism

As policymakers hammered out a new foreign policy, a sustaining ideology took shape. One source of expansionist dogma was the Social Darwinist theory that dominated the political thought of this era (see Chapter 18). If, as Charles Darwin had shown, animals and plants evolved through the survival of the fittest, so did nations. "Nothing under the sun is stationary," warned the American social theorist Brooks Adams in *The Law of Civilization and Decay* (1895). "Not to advance is to recede." By this criterion the United States had no choice; if it wanted to survive, it had to expand.

Linked to Social Darwinism was a spreading belief in the inherent superiority of the Anglo-Saxon "race." In the late nineteenth century, Great Britain basked in the glory of its representative institutions, industrial prosperity, and far-flung empire— all ascribed to the supposed racial superiority of its people and, by extension, of their

American cousins as well. On both sides of the Atlantic, **Anglo-Saxonism** was in vogue. Thus did John Fiske, an American philosopher and historian, lecture the nation on its future responsibilities: "The work which the English race began when it colonized North America is destined to go on until every land on the earth's surface that is not already the seat of an old civilization shall become English in its language, in its religion, in its political habits, and to a predominant extent in the blood of its people."

Fiske titled his lecture "Manifest Destiny." A half century earlier this term had expressed the sense of national mission—America's "manifest destiny"—to sweep aside the Native American peoples and occupy the continent. In his widely read book *The Winning of the West* (1896), Theodore Roosevelt drew a parallel between the expansionism of his own time and the suppression of the Indians. To Roosevelt, what happened to "backward peoples" mattered little because their conquest was "for the benefit of civilization and in the interests of mankind." More than historical parallels, however, linked the **Manifest Destiny** of past and present.

In 1890 the U.S. Census reported the end of the continental movement westward: there was no longer a frontier beyond which land remained to be conquered (see Chapter 16). The psychological impact of that news was profound, spawning among other things a new historical interpretation that said the nation's character was shaped by the frontier. In a landmark essay setting out this thesis—"The Significance of the Frontier in American History" (1893)—the young historian Frederick Jackson Turner suggested a link between the closing of the frontier and overseas expansion. "He would be a rash prophet who should assert that the expansive character of American life has now entirely ceased," Turner wrote. "Movement has been its dominant fact, and, unless this training has no effect upon a people, the American energy will continually demand a wider field for its exercise." As Turner predicted, Manifest Destiny did turn outward.

Thus a strong current of ideas, deeply rooted in American experience and traditions, justified the new diplomacy of expansionism. The United States was eager to step onto the world stage. All it needed was the right occasion.

An American Empire

Ever since the early nineteenth century, when Spain had lost its South American empire, Cubans yearned to join their mainland brothers and sisters in freedom. In February 1895 Cuban patriots rebelled and began a guerrilla war. A standoff developed; the Spaniards controlled the towns, the insurgents much of the countryside. In early 1896 the newly appointed Spanish commander, Valeriano Weyler, adopted a harsh policy of *reconcentration*, forcing entire populations into guarded camps. Because no aggressive pursuit followed, this ruthless strategy only inconvenienced the guerrilla fighters. The toll on civilians, however, was devastating. Out of a population of 1,600,000, as many as 200,000 died of starvation, exposure, or dysentery.

The Cuban Crisis

Rebel leaders shrewdly saw that they could tip the balance by drawing the United States into their struggle. A key group of exiles, the Junta, set up shop in New York to make the case for *Cuba Libre*. By itself, their cause might not have attracted much interest. The Spaniards were behaving no more dishonorably than any other colonial power; nor were atrocities in short supply elsewhere in the world. The Cuban exiles, however, arrived at a lucky moment. William Randolph Hearst had just purchased the *New York Journal*, and he was in a hurry to build readership. Cuba was ideal for Hearst's purposes. Locked in a circulation war with Joseph Pulitzer's *New York World*, Hearst elevated Cuba's agony into flaming front-page headlines.

Across the country powerful sentiments stirred: humanitarian concern for the suffering Cubans, sympathy with their aspirations for freedom, and as anger against Spain rose, a fiery patriotism soon tagged **jingoism**. These sentiments were often entwined with American anxieties over the perceived effeminacy of modern life (see Chapter 18). A gendered language infused much of the debate, with rebels portrayed as chivalric defenders of Cuban women against the "lustful bondage" of the Spaniards. It would be good for the nation's character, jingoists argued, for Americans to ride to the rescue. The government should not pass up this opportunity, said Senator Albert J. Beveridge, to "manufacture manhood." In this superheated atmosphere, Congress began calling for Cuban independence.

Grover Cleveland, still in office when the rebellion broke out, took a cooler view of the situation. His concern was with America's vital interests, which, he told Congress, were "by no means of a wholly sentimental or philanthropic character." The Cuban civil war was disrupting trade and destroying American property, especially Cuban sugar plantations. Cleveland also was worried that Spain's troubles might draw in other European powers. A chronically unstable Cuba was incompatible with America's strategic interests, in particular, the planned interoceanic canal whose Caribbean approaches would have to be safeguarded. If Spain could put down the rebellion, that was fine with Cleveland. But there was a limit, he felt, to how long the United States could tolerate Spain's impotence.

The McKinley administration, on taking office in March 1897, adopted much the same pragmatic line. Like Cleveland, McKinley was motivated by vital interests he felt the United States had in the Caribbean. McKinley, however, was inclined to be tougher on the Spaniards. He was upset by their "uncivilized and inhumane conduct" in Cuba. And he had to contend with rising jingoism in the Senate. But the notion, long held by historians, that McKinley was swept along against his better judgment by popular opinion and by congressional war hawks was incorrect. McKinley was very much his own man—a skilled politician and a canny, if undramatic, president. In particular, McKinley was sensitive to business fears of any rash action that might disrupt an economy just recovering from depression.

On September 18, 1897, the American minister in Madrid informed the Spanish government that it was time to "put a stop to this destructive war." Either ensure an "early and certain peace" or the United States would step in. At first America's hard line seemed to work. The conservative regime fell, and a liberal government, upon taking office in October 1897, moderated its Cuban policy. Spain recalled General Weyler, backed away from reconcentration, and offered Cuba a degree of self-rule but not independence. Madrid's incapacity soon became clear, however. In January 1898 Spanish loyalists in Havana rioted against the offer of autonomy. The Cuban rebels, encouraged by the prospect of American intervention, demanded full independence.

On February 9, 1898, Hearst's *New York Journal* published a private letter by Dupuy de Lôme, the Spanish minister to the United States. In it de Lôme called President McKinley "weak" and "a bidder for the admiration of the crowd." Worse, his letter suggested that the Spanish government was not taking the American demands seriously. De Lôme immediately resigned, but the damage had been done.

A week later the U.S. battle cruiser *Maine* blew up and sank in Havana harbor, with the loss of 260 seamen. "Whole Country Thrills with the War Fever," proclaimed the *New York Journal*. From that moment onward popular passions against Spain became a major factor in the march toward war.

McKinley kept his head. He assumed that the sinking had been accidental. A naval board of inquiry, however, issued a damaging report. Disagreeing with a Spanish investigation, the American board concluded improbably that the sinking had been caused by a mine. (A 1976 naval inquiry faulted the ship's design, in particular, explosive magazines too close to coal bunkers that were prone to spontaneous fires.) No evidence linked the Spanish to the purported mine. But if a mine did sink the ship, then the Spanish were responsible for not protecting a peaceful American vessel within their jurisdiction.

President McKinley had no stomach for the martial spirit engulfing the country. He was not swept along by the calls for blood to avenge the *Maine*. But he could not ignore an aroused public opinion. Hesitant business leaders now also became impatient for the dispute with Spain to end. War was preferable to the unresolved Cuban crisis. McKinley cabled to Madrid what was in effect an ultimatum: an immediate armistice for six months, abandonment of the practice of reconcentration, and, with the United States as mediator, peace negotiations with the rebels leading to Cuban independence. Spain categorically rejected these humiliating demands.

On April 11, McKinley asked Congress for authority to intervene in Cuba. His motives were as he described them: "In the name of humanity, in the name of civilization, in behalf of endangered American interests which give us the right and the duty to speak and to act, the war in Cuba must stop." The war hawks in Congress chafed under McKinley's cautious progress. But the president did not lose control, and he defeated their demand for recognition of the rebel republican government, which would have reduced the administration's freedom of action in dealing with Spain.

The resolutions authorizing intervention in Cuba contained an amendment by Senator Henry M. Teller of Colorado disclaiming any intention by the United States to take possession of Cuba. No European government should say that "when we go out to make battle for the liberty and freedom of Cuban patriots, that we are doing it for the purpose of aggrandizement." This had to be made clear with regard to Cuba, "whatever," Senator Teller added, "we may do as to some other islands."

Did McKinley have in mind "some other islands"? Was this really a war of aggression, secretly motivated by a desire to seize strategic territory from Spain? In a strict sense almost certainly no. It was not *because* of expansionist ambitions that McKinley forced Spain into a corner. But once war came McKinley saw it as an opportunity. As he wrote privately after hostilities began: "While we are conducting war and until its conclusion, we must keep all we get; when the war is over we must keep what we want." Precisely what would be forthcoming, of course, depended on the fortunes of battle.

The Spoils of War

Hostilities formally began when Spain declared war on the United States on April 24, 1898. Across the country regiments began to form. Theodore Roosevelt immediately resigned as assistant secretary of the navy, ordered a fancy uniform, and accepted a commission as lieutenant colonel of a volunteer cavalry regiment soon to become famous as the Rough Riders. Raw recruits poured into makeshift bases around Tampa, Florida. Confusion reigned. Tropical uniforms did not arrive; the food was bad, the sanitation worse; and rifles were in short supply. No provision had been made for getting the troops to Cuba; the government hastily began to collect a miscellaneous fleet of yachts, lake steamers, and commercial boats. Fortunately, the small regular army was a disciplined, highly professional force: its 28,000 seasoned troops provided a nucleus for the 200,000 civilians who had to be turned into soldiers inside of a few weeks.

The navy was in better shape. Spain had nothing to match America's seven battleships and armored cruisers, and the ships it did have were undermanned and ill-prepared for battle. The Spanish admiral, Pascual Cervera, gloomily expected that his fleet would "like Don Quixote go out to fight windmills and come back with a broken head."

On April 23, acting on plans already drawn up, Commodore George Dewey's small Pacific fleet set sail from Hong Kong for the Philippines. Here, at this Spanish possession in the far Pacific, not in Cuba, the decisive engagement of the war took place. On May 1 American ships cornered the Spanish fleet in Manila Bay and destroyed it. The victory produced euphoria in the United States. Immediately, part of the army being trained for the Cuban campaign was diverted to the Philippines. Manila, the Philippine capital, fell on August 13, 1898.

Battle of Santiago de Cuba, 1898

James G. Tyler's dramatic painting of the final sea battle of the Spanish-American War showcased America's newest weapon of war, the battleship. Franklin D. Roosevelt Library.

With Dewey's naval victory, American strategic thinking clicked into place. "We hold the other side of the Pacific and the value to this country is almost beyond imagination," declared Senator Lodge. "We must on no account let the [Philippine] Islands go." President McKinley agreed, and so did his key advisors. Naval strategists had long coveted an anchor in the western Pacific. At this time, too, the Great Powers were carving up China into spheres of influence. If American merchants wanted a crack at that glittering market, the United States would have to project its power into Asia.

Once the decision for a Philippine base had been made, other decisions followed almost automatically. The question of Hawaii was quickly resolved. After stalling the previous year, Hawaiian annexation went through Congress by joint resolution in July 1898. Hawaii had suddenly acquired a crucial strategic value: it was a halfway station on the way to the Philippines. The navy pressed for a coaling base in the central Pacific; that meant Guam, a Spanish island in the Marianas. There was need also for a strategically located base in the Caribbean; that meant Puerto Rico. By July, before the assault on Cuba, the full scope of McKinley's war aims had crystallized.

The campaign in Cuba was somewhat anticlimactic. The Spanish forces, already depleted by the long guerrilla war, always had to protect their rear while

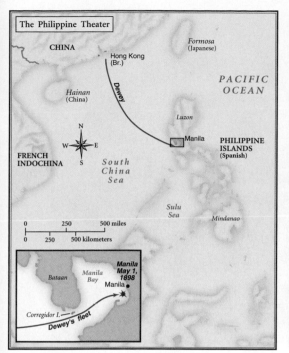

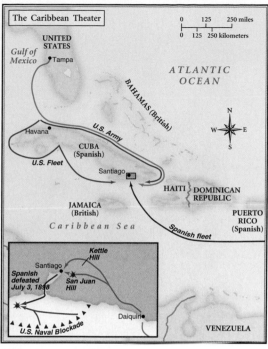

MAP 21.1 The Spanish-American War of 1898

The swift American victory in the Spanish-American War resulted from overwhelming naval superiority. Dewey's destruction of the Spanish fleet in Manila harbor doomed the Spaniards in the Philippines. In Cuba, American ground forces won a hard victory on San Juan Hill, for they were ill equipped and poorly supplied. With the United States in control of the seas, the Spaniards saw no choice but to give up the battle for Cuba.

FOR MORE HELP ANALYZING THIS MAP, see the Online Study Guide at **bedfordstmartins.com/henrettaconcise**.

confronting the arriving Americans. That the landings at Daiquiri went uncontested had something to do with the effective work of the rebels. Santiago, where the Spanish fleet was anchored, became the key to the military campaign (Map 21.1). Half-trained and ill-equipped, the American forces moving on the city might have been checked by a determined opponent. The Spaniards fought to maintain their honor, but they had no stomach for a real war against the Americans.

The main battle, on July 1, occurred near Santiago on the heights commanded by San Juan Hill. Roosevelt's dismounted Rough Riders (there had been no room for horses on the transports) seized Kettle Hill. Then the frontal assault against the San Juan heights began. Four black regiments took the brunt of the fighting. White observers grudgingly credited much of the victory to the "superb gallantry" of the black soldiers (see American Voices, "Black Soldiers in a White Man's War," p. 643). In fact it was not quite a victory. The Spaniards, driven from their forward positions, retreated to a well-fortified second line. The exhausted Americans had

The Battle of San Juan Hill

On July 1, 1898, the key battle for Cuba took place on heights overlooking Santiago. African American troops bore the brunt of the fighting. Although generally overlooked, the black role in the San Juan battle is done justice in this contemporary lithograph, without the demeaning stereotypes by which blacks were normally depicted in an age of intensifying racism. Even so, the racial hierarchy is maintained. The blacks are the foot soldiers; their officers are white. Library of Congress.

FOR MORE HELP ANALYZING THIS IMAGE, see the Online Study Guide at **bedfordstmartins.com/henrettaconcise**.

suffered heavy casualties; whether they could have mounted a second assault was questionable. They were spared this test, however, by the Spanish. On July 3 Cervera's fleet in Santiago harbor made a daylight attempt to run the American blockade and was destroyed. A few days later, convinced that Santiago could not be saved, the Spanish forces surrendered.

The two nations signed an armistice in which Spain agreed to liberate Cuba and cede Puerto Rico and Guam to the United States. American forces occupied Manila pending a peace treaty.

The Imperial Experiment

The big question was the Philippines, an archipelago of 7,000 islands populated—as William R. Day, McKinley's secretary of state, put it in the racist language of that era—by "eight or nine millions of absolutely ignorant and many degraded people." Not even avid American expansionists had advocated colonial

AMERICAN VOICES

Black Soldiers in a White Man's War

GEORGE W. PRIOLEAU

*T*he chaplain of the Ninth Cavalry regiment expresses his bitterness toward the racism experienced by black troopers in the South on their way to battle in Cuba.

Hon. H. C. Smith
Editor, *Gazette*
Dear Sir:
All the way from northwest Nebraska this regiment was greeted with cheers and hurrahs. At places where we stopped the people assembled by the thousands. While the Ninth Cavalry band would play some national air the people would raise their hats, men, women and children would wave their handkerchiefs, and the heavens would resound with their hearty cheers. The white hand shaking the black hand. The hearty "goodbyes," "God bless you," and other expressions aroused the patriotism of our boys. . . . These demonstrations, so enthusiastically given, greeted us all the way until we reached Nashville. . . . From there until we reached Chattanooga there was not a cheer given us. . . .

The prejudice against the Negro soldier and the Negro was great, but it was of heavenly origin to what it is in this part of Florida. . . . The southerners have made their laws and the Negroes know and obey them. They never stop to ask a white man a question. He (Negro) never thinks of disobeying. You talk about freedom, liberty, etc. Why sir, the Negro of this country is a freeman and yet a slave. Talk about fighting and freeing poor Cuba and of Spain's brutality; of Cuba's murdered thousands, and starving reconcentradoes. Is America any better than Spain? Has she not subjects in her very midst who are murdered daily without a trial of judge or jury? Has she not subjects in her own borders whose children are half-fed and half-clothed, because their father's skin is black. . . . Yet the Negro is loyal to his country's flag. . . .

The four Negro regiments are going to help free Cuba, and they will return to their homes, some then mustered out and begin again to fight the battle of American prejudice. . . .
Yours truly,
Geo. W. Prioleau
Chaplain, Ninth Cavalry

SOURCE: *Smoked Yankees and the Struggle for Empire* 1898–1902 by Willard Gatewood. Copyright 1987 by the Board of Trustees of the University of Arkansas. Reprinted by permission of the University of Arkansas Press.

rule over subject peoples—that was European-style imperialism, not the strategic bases that Mahan and his followers had in mind. Mahan and Lodge initially advocated keeping only Manila. It gradually became clear, however, that Manila was not defensible without the whole of Luzon, the large island on which the city was located.

McKinley and his advisors surveyed the options. One possibility was to return most of the islands to Spain, but the reputed evils of Spanish rule made that a "cowardly and dishonorable" solution. Another possibility was to partition the Philippines with one or more of the Great Powers. But as McKinley observed, to turn over valuable territory to "our commercial rivals in the Orient—that would have been bad business and discreditable."

Most plausible was the option of Philippine independence. As in Cuba, Spanish rule had already stirred up a rebellion, led by the ardent patriot Emilio Aguinaldo. An arrangement might have been possible like the one being negotiated with the Cubans over Guantanamo Bay: the lease of a naval base to the Americans as the price of freedom. But after some hesitation McKinley was persuaded that "we could not leave [the Filipinos] to themselves—they were unfit for self-rule—and they would soon have anarchy and misrule over there worse than Spain's was."

As for the Spaniards, they had little choice against what they considered "the immoderate demands of a conqueror." In the Treaty of Paris they ceded the Philippines to the United States for a payment of $20 million. The treaty encountered harder going at home and was ratified by the Senate (requiring a two-thirds majority) on February 6, 1899, with only a single vote to spare.

The administration's narrow margin signaled the revival of an antiexpansionist tradition that had been briefly silenced by the passions of a nation at war. In the

Emilio Aguinaldo

At the start of the war with Spain, U.S. military leaders brought the Filipino patriot Emilio Aguinaldo back from Singapore because they thought he would stir up a popular uprising that would help defeat the Spaniards. Aguinaldo came because he thought the Americans favored an independent Philippines. These differing intentions—it has remained a matter of dispute what assurances Aguinaldo received—were the root cause of the Filipino insurrection that proved far costlier in American and Filipino lives than the war with Spain that preceded it. Brown Brothers.

Senate opponents of the treaty invoked the country's republican principles. Under the Constitution, argued the conservative Republican George F. Hoar, "no power is given to the Federal Government to acquire territory to be held and governed permanently as colonies." The alternative—making 8 million Filipinos American citizens—was equally unpalatable to the anti-imperialists, who were no more champions of "these savage people" than were the expansionists.

Leading citizens enlisted in the anti-imperialist cause, including the steel king Andrew Carnegie, who offered a check for $20 million to purchase the independence of the Philippines; the labor leader Samuel Gompers, who feared the competition of cheap Filipino labor; and Jane Addams, who believed that women should stand for peace. The key group, however, was a social elite of old-line Mugwump reformers such as Carl Schurz, Charles Eliot Norton, and Charles Francis Adams. In November 1898 a Boston group formed the first of the Anti-Imperialist Leagues that began to spring up around the country.

Although skillful at publicizing their cause, the anti-imperialists never became a popular movement. They shared little but their anti-imperialism and, within the Mugwump core, lacked the common touch. Moreover the Democrats, their natural allies, waffled on the issue. Although an outspoken anti-imperialist, William Jennings Bryan, the Democratic standard-bearer, confounded his friends by favoring ratification of the treaty and afterward hesitated to stake his party's future on a crusade against a national policy he privately believed to be irreversible. Still, if it was an accomplished fact, Philippine annexation lost the moral high ground because of the grim events that began to unfold on those islands.

On February 4, 1899, two days before the Senate ratified the treaty, fighting broke out between American and Filipino patrols on the edge of Manila. Confronted by American annexation, Aguinaldo asserted his nation's independence and turned his guns on the occupying American forces.

The ensuing conflict far exceeded in ferocity the war just concluded with Spain. Fighting tenacious guerrillas, the U.S. Army resorted to the same tactics the Spaniards had employed in Cuba, moving people into towns, carrying out indiscriminate attacks beyond the perimeters, and burning crops and villages. Atrocities became commonplace on both sides. In three years of warfare, 4,200 Americans and many thousands of Filipinos died. The fighting ended in 1902, and William Howard Taft, who had been appointed governor-general, set up a civilian administration. He intended to make the Philippines a model of American road-building and sanitary engineering.

McKinley's convincing victory over William Jennings Bryan in the 1900 election, though by no means a referendum on American expansionism, suggested popular satisfaction with America's overseas adventure. Yet a strong undercurrent of misgivings was evident. Americans had not anticipated the brutal methods needed to subdue the Filipino guerrillas. "We are destroying these islanders by the thousands, their villages and cities," protested the philosopher William James. "No life shall you have, we say, except as a gift from our philanthropy after your unconditional surrender to our will. . . . Could there be any more damning indictment of that whole bloated ideal termed 'modern civilization'?"

There were, moreover, disturbing constitutional issues to be resolved. Did the Constitution extend to the acquired territories? Did their inhabitants automatically become U.S. citizens? In 1901 the Supreme Court said no on both counts; these were matters for Congress to decide. A special commission appointed by McKinley recommended independence for the islands after an indefinite period of U.S. rule, during which the Filipinos would be prepared for self-government. In 1916 the Jones Act committed the United States to granting Philippine independence but set no date (the Philippines formally achieved independence in 1946).

The brutal war in the Philippines rubbed off some of the moralizing gloss but left undeflected America's global aspirations. In a few years the United States had assembled an overseas empire: Hawaii, Puerto Rico, Guam, the Philippines, and finally, in 1900, several of the Samoan islands that had been jointly administered with Germany and Britain. The United States, remarked the legal scholar John Bassett Moore in 1899, had moved "from a position of comparative freedom from entanglements into a position of what is commonly called a world power."

Onto the World Stage

In Europe the flexing of America's muscles against Spain caused a certain amount of consternation. The major powers had tried before war broke out to intercede on Spain's behalf—but tentatively, because no one was looking for trouble with the Americans. President McKinley had listened politely to their envoys and then proceeded with his war.

The decisive outcome confirmed what the Europeans already suspected. After Dewey's naval victory, the semiofficial French paper *Le Temps* observed that "what passes before our eyes is the appearance of a new power of the first order." And the *London Times* concluded: "This war must . . . effect a profound change in the whole attitude and policy of the United States. In the future America will play a part in the general affairs of the world such as she has never played before" (see Voices from Abroad, "American Goliath," p. 648).

A Power among Powers

The politician most ardently agreeing with the *London Times*'s vision of America's future was the man who, with the assassination of William McKinley, became president on September 14, 1901. Unlike his predecessors in the White House, Theodore Roosevelt was an avid student of world affairs, widely traveled and acquainted with many European leaders. He had no doubt about America's role in the world.

It was important, first of all, to uphold the country's honor in the community of nations. The country should never shrink from righteous battle. "All the great masterful races have been fighting races," Roosevelt declared. But when he spoke of war, Roosevelt had in mind actions by the "civilized" nations against "backward peoples." Roosevelt felt "it incumbent on all the civilized and orderly powers to insist on the proper policing of the world." That was why Roosevelt sympathized with European imperialism and how he justified American dominance in the Caribbean.

As for the "civilized and orderly" policemen of the world, the worst thing that could happen was for them to fall to fighting among themselves. Roosevelt had an acute sense of the fragility of world peace, and he was farsighted about the likelihood—in this he was truly exceptional among Americans—of a catastrophic world war. He believed in American responsibility for helping to maintain the balance of power.

The cornerstone of Roosevelt's thinking was Anglo-American friendship. The British, increasingly isolated in world affairs, eagerly reciprocated. In the Hay-Pauncefote Agreement (1901), Britain gave up its treaty rights to participate in any Central American canal project, clearing the way for a canal under exclusive U.S. control. And two years later the last of the vexing U.S.-Canadian border disputes—this one involving British Columbia and Alaska—was settled, again to American satisfaction.

No formal alliance was forthcoming, but Anglo-American friendship had been placed on such a firm basis that after 1901 the British admiralty designed its war plans on the assumption that America was "a kindred state with whom we shall never have a parricidal war."

Among nations, however, what counted was strength, not merely goodwill. Roosevelt wanted "to make all foreign powers understand that when we have adopted a line of policy we have adopted it definitely, and with the intention of backing it up with deeds as well as words." As Roosevelt famously said, "Speak softly and carry a big stick." By a "big stick" he meant, above all, naval power.

The battleship program went on apace under Roosevelt. In 1904 the U.S. Navy stood fifth in the world; by 1907 it was third. At the top of Roosevelt's agenda, however, was a canal across Central America. The Spanish-American War had graphically demonstrated the strategic need: the entire country had waited anxiously while the battleship *Oregon* steamed at full speed from the Pacific around the tip of South America to join the final action against the Spanish fleet in Cuba.

Freed now by Britain's consent to proceed independently, Roosevelt turned to the delicate task of leasing from Colombia the needed strip of land across Panama, a Colombian province. Furious when the Colombian legislature voted down the proposed treaty, Roosevelt contemplated outright seizure of Panama but settled on a more devious solution. With an independence movement brewing in Panama, the United States lent covert assistance that ensured the success of a bloodless revolution against Colombia. On November 6, 1903, the United States recognized Panama and two weeks later got a perpetually renewable lease on a canal zone. Roosevelt never regretted the victimization of Colombia, although the United States, as a kind of conscience money, paid Colombia $25 million in 1922.

Building the canal, one of the heroic engineering feats of the century, involved a vast swamp-clearing project, the construction of a series of great locks,

VOICES FROM ABROAD

American Goliath

JEAN HESS, ÉMILE ZOLA, AND RUBEN DARIO

A merica's emergence as an imperial power provoked much anxious comment abroad. Not surprisingly, the commentary tended to mirror the concerns of the commentators. What was unexpected, as the following excerpts suggest, was that they took seriously America's high estimate of itself. If its actions violated professed ideals, foreign critics were not averse to calling the United States to account.

Jean Hess, a Frenchman well traveled in East Asia, questioned American motives for intervening in the Philippines (1899).

Nowhere, in my opinion, better than in the Philippines, has it been shown that modern wars are simply "deals." The American intervention in the struggle engaged in by the revolutionary Tagals against the Spanish government has turned out to be nothing but a speculation of "business men," and not the generous effort of a people paying a debt in procuring for others the liberty that it concedes belongs to all. . . . Back of all these battles, this devastation and mourning . . . there was only, there is only, what the people of the Bourse [stock market] call a deal.

Émile Zola, the great French novelist, feared that America's military adventurism was dealing a blow to the cause of world peace (1900).

Nations which till now seem to have held aloof from the contagion, to have escaped this madness so prevalent in Europe, now appear to be attacked. Thus, since the Spanish war,

and the excavation of 240 million cubic yards of earth. It took the U.S. Army Corps of Engineers and the digging by thousands of hired laborers eight years to finish the huge project. When the Panama Canal opened in 1914, it gave the United States a commanding commercial and strategic position in the Western Hemisphere.

Next came the task of making the Caribbean basin secure. The countries there, said Secretary of State Elihu Root, had been placed "in the front yard of the United States" by the Panama Canal. Therefore, as Roosevelt put it, they had to "behave themselves."

In the case of Cuba, good behavior was readily managed by the settlement following the Spanish-American War. Before withdrawing in 1902 the United States reorganized Cuban public finances and concluded a swamp-clearing program that eliminated yellow fever, a disease that had ravaged Cuba for many years. As a condition for gaining independence, Cuba accepted a proviso in its constitution called the Platt Amendment, which gave the United States the right to intervene if Cuban independence was threatened or if internal order broke down. Cuba also granted the United States seems to have become a victim of the war fever. . . . I can see in that great nation a dangerous inclination toward war. I can detect the generation of vague ideas of future conquest. Until the present time that country wisely occupied itself with its domestic affairs and let Europe severely alone, but now it is donning plumes and epaulets, and will be dreaming of possible campaigns and be carried away with the idea of military glory. . . .

In 1905, a year after the promulgation of the Roosevelt Corollary, the acclaimed Nicaraguan poet Ruben Dario issued an impassioned challenge from a small Central American country under the shadow of the Goliath, addressing his poem "To Roosevelt."

The United States is grand and powerful . . .
a wealthy country. . . .
But our own America . . .
has lived, since the earliest moments of its life,
in light, in fire, in fragrance, and in love—
the America of Moctezuma and Atahuelpa. . . .
O men with Saxon eyes and barbarous souls,
our America lives. And dreams. And loves.
And it is the daughter of the Sun. Be Careful.
Long live Spanish America!

SOURCES: *Selected Poems of Ruben Dario* by Ruben Dario, translated by Lysander Kemp. Copyright © 1965, renewed 1993. By permission of the University of Texas Press.

the United States a lease on Guantanamo Bay (which is still in effect), where the U.S. Navy built a large base.

Claiming that instability in the Caribbean invited the intervention of European powers, Roosevelt announced in 1904 that the United States would act as "policeman" of the region, stepping in, "however reluctantly, in flagrant cases . . . of wrongdoing or impotence" (Map 21.2). This so-called Roosevelt Corollary to the Monroe Doctrine transformed its broad principle against European interference in Latin America into an unrestricted American right to regulate Caribbean affairs. The Roosevelt Corollary was not a treaty with other states; it was a unilateral declaration sanctioned only by American power and national interest.

Citing the Roosevelt Corollary, the United States intervened regularly in the internal affairs of Caribbean states. In 1905 American personnel took over the customs and debt management of the Dominican Republic and, similarly, the finances of Nicaragua in 1911 and Haiti in 1916. When domestic order broke down, the U.S. Marines occupied Cuba in 1906, Nicaragua in 1909, and Haiti and the Dominican Republic in later years.

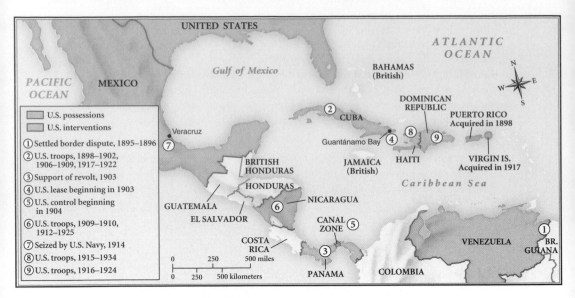

MAP 21.2 Policeman of the Caribbean

After the Spanish-American War, the United States vigorously asserted its interest in the affairs of its neighbors to the south. As the record of interventions shows, the United States truly became the "policeman" of the Caribbean.

The Open Door in Asia

Commercial interest dominated American policy in East Asia, especially the prospect of the huge China market. By the late 1890s Japan, Russia, Germany, France, and Britain had all carved out spheres of influence in China. Fearful of being frozen out, U.S. Secretary of State John Hay in 1899 sent them an Open Door note claiming the right of equal trade access—an open door—for all nations that wanted to do business in China. Despite its Philippine bases, the United States lacked real leverage in East Asia and elicited only noncommittal responses from the occupying powers. But Hay chose to interpret them as accepting the American open-door position.

When a secret society of Chinese nationalists, the Boxers, rebelled against the foreigners in 1900, the United States sent 5,000 troops from the Philippines and joined the multinational campaign to break the Boxers' siege of the diplomatic missions in Peking (Beijing). America took this opportunity to assert a second principle of the Open Door: that China would be preserved as a "territorial and administrative entity." As long as the legal fiction of an independent China survived, so would American claims to equal access to the China market.

The European powers had acceded to American dominance in the Caribbean. But Britain, Germany, France, and Russia were strongly entrenched in East Asia and not inclined to defer to American interests (Map 21.3). The United States also confronted a powerful Asian nation—Japan—that had its own vital interests. Although

MAP 21.3 The Great Powers in East Asia, 1898–1910

The pattern of foreign dominance over China was via "treaty ports," where the powers based their naval forces, and "spheres of influence" extending from the ports into the hinterland. This map reveals why the United States had a weak hand; it lacked a presence on this colonized terrain. The Boxer Rebellion, by bringing an American expeditionary force to Peking, gave the United States a chance to insert itself onto the Chinese mainland, and American diplomats made the most of the opportunity to defend U.S. commercial interest in China.

the **open-door policy** was important to him, Roosevelt sensed that there were higher stakes at risk in the Pacific.

Japan had unveiled its military strength in the Sino-Japanese War of 1894–1895, which began the division of China into spheres of influence—not colonies, but regions marked off by the Great Powers over which they asserted informal dominance. A decade later, provoked by Russian rivalry in Manchuria and Korea, Japan suddenly attacked the tsar's fleet at Port Arthur, Russia's leased port in China. In a series of brilliant victories, the Japanese smashed the Russian forces in Asia. Anxious to restore a balance of power, Roosevelt mediated a settlement of the Russo-Japanese War at Portsmouth, New Hampshire, in 1905. Japan emerged as the dominant power in East Asia.

Contemptuous of other Asian nations, Roosevelt respected the Japanese—"a wonderful and civilized people . . . entitled to stand in absolute equality with all the other peoples of the civilized world." He conceded that Japan had "a paramount interest in what surrounds the Yellow Sea, just as the United States has a paramount interest in what surrounds the Caribbean." But American strategic and commercial interests in the Pacific had to be accommodated. The United States approved of Japan's protectorate over Korea in 1905, and then of its declaration of full sovereignty six years later. However, a surge of anti-Asian feeling in California complicated Roosevelt's efforts. In 1906 San Francisco's school board placed all Asian students in a segregated school, infuriating Japan. The "Gentlemen's Agreement" of 1907, in which Japan agreed to restrict immigration to the United States, smoothed matters over, but periodic racist slights by Americans made for continuing tensions with the Japanese.

Roosevelt meanwhile moved to balance Japan's military power by increasing American naval strength in the Pacific. American battleships visited Japan in 1908 on a global tour that impressively displayed U.S. sea power. Late that year, near the end of his administration, Roosevelt achieved a formal accommodation with Japan. The Root-Takahira Agreement confirmed the status quo in the Pacific, as well as the principles of free oceanic commerce and equal trade opportunity in China.

William Howard Taft, however, entered the White House in 1909 convinced that the United States had been short-changed. He pressed for a larger role for American investors, especially in the railroad construction going on in China. An exponent of **dollar diplomacy**—the aggressive coupling of American political and economic interests abroad—Taft hoped that American capital would counterbalance Japanese power and pave the way for increased commercial opportunities. When the Chinese Revolution of 1911 toppled the ruling Manchu dynasty, Taft supported the victorious Chinese Nationalists, who wanted to modernize their country and liberate it from Japanese domination. The United States thus entered a long-term rivalry with Japan that would end in war thirty years later.

The United States had become embroiled in a distant struggle, heavy with future liabilities but few of the fabulous profits that had lured Americans to Asia.

Wilson and Mexico

When Woodrow Wilson became president in 1913, he was bent on reform in American foreign policy no less than in domestic politics. Wilson did not really differ with his predecessors on the importance of America's economic interests overseas. He applauded the "tides of commerce" that would arise from the Panama Canal. But he opposed dollar diplomacy, which he believed bullied weaker countries financially and gave undue advantage to American business. It seemed to Wilson "a very perilous thing to determine the foreign policy of a nation in terms of material interest."

The United States, Wilson insisted, should conduct its foreign policy in conformity with its democratic principles. In a major foreign-policy speech in 1913, Wilson promised Latin America that the United States would "never again seek one additional foot of territory by conquest." He was committed to advancing "human rights, national integrity, and opportunity" abroad. To do otherwise would make "ourselves untrue to our own traditions."

Mexico became the primary object of Wilson's ministrations. A cycle of revolution had begun there in 1911. The dictator Porfirio Díaz, who had seized power in 1876, was overthrown by Francisco Madero, who spoke much as Wilson did about liberty and constitutionalism. But before Madero got very far with his reforms, he was deposed and murdered in February 1913 by one of his generals, Victoriano Huerta. Other powers recognized Huerta's provisional government but not the United States, despite a long-standing tradition of granting quick recognition to new governments. Wilson abhorred Huerta, called him a murderer, and pledged "to force him out."

By intervening in this way, Wilson insisted, "we act in the interest of Mexico alone. . . . We are seeking to counsel Mexico for its own good." Wilson meant that he intended to put the Mexican Revolution back on the constitutional path started by Madero. Wilson was not deterred by the fact that American business interests, with big investments in Mexico, favored Huerta.

The emergence of armed opposition in northern Mexico under Venustiano Carranza strengthened Wilson's hand. But Carranza's Constitutionalist movement was ardently nationalist and had no desire for American intervention. Carranza angrily rebuffed Wilson's efforts to bring about elections by means of a compromise with the Huerta regime. He also vowed to fight any intrusion of U.S. troops in his country. All he wanted from Wilson, Carranza asserted, was recognition of the Constitutionalists' belligerent status, so that they could purchase arms in the United States. In exchange for vague promises to respect property rights and "fair" foreign concessions, Carranza finally got his way in 1914. American weapons began to flow to his troops.

When it became clear that Huerta was not about to fall, the United States threw its own forces into the conflict. On the pretext of a minor insult to the U.S. Navy at Tampico, Wilson ordered the occupation of the port of Veracruz on April 21, 1914, at the cost of 19 American and 126 Mexican lives. At that point the Huerta regime began to crumble. Carranza nevertheless condemned the United States, and his forces came close to engaging the Americans. When he entered Mexico City in triumph in August 1914, Carranza had some cause to thank the Yankees. But if any sense of gratitude existed, it was overshadowed by the anti-Americanism inspired by Wilson's insensitivity to Mexican pride and revolutionary zeal.

No sooner had the Constitutionalists triumphed than Carranza was challenged by his northern general, Pancho Villa, with some encouragement by American interests in Mexico. Defeated and driven northward, Villa began to stir up trouble along the border, killing sixteen American civilians taken from a train in January 1916 and two months later raiding the town of Columbus, New Mexico. Wilson sent

In Pursuit of Pancho Villa

Pancho Villa's attack on American citizens prompted General Pershing's punitive expedition into Mexico in 1916. U.S. troops captured some of Villa's followers, but he and his main force escaped. It was an early lesson about the difficulties Great Powers have when pitted against a guerrilla foe who is able to melt away into a larger civilian society. © Bettmann / Corbis.

11,000 troops under General John J. Pershing across the border after the elusive Villa. Soon Pershing's force resembled an army of occupation more than a punitive expedition. Mexican public opinion demanded that Pershing withdraw, and armed clashes with Mexican troops began. At the brink of war, the two governments backed off, and U.S. forces began to withdraw in early 1917. Soon after, with a new constitution ratified and elections completed, the Carranza government finally received official recognition from Washington.

The Gathering Storm in Europe

In the meantime Europe had begun a drift toward war. There were two main sources of tension. One was the rivalry between Germany, the new superpower of Europe, and the European states threatened by its might—above all France, which had been humiliated in the Franco-Prussian War of 1870. The second danger zone was the Balkans, where the Ottoman Empire was disintegrating and where, in the midst of explosive ethnic rivalries, Austria-Hungary and Russia were maneuvering for dominance. Out of these conflicts an alliance system had emerged, with Germany, Austria-Hungary, and Italy (the Triple Alliance) on one side and France and Russia (the Dual Alliance) on the other.

The tensions in Europe were partially released by European imperial adventures, especially by France in Africa and by Russia in Asia. These activities made France and Russia rivals of imperial Britain, effectively excluding Britain from the European alliance system. Fearful of Germany, however, Britain in 1904 resolved her differences with France, and the two countries reached a friendly understanding, or *entente*. When Britain came to a similar understanding with Russia in 1907, the basis was laid for the Triple Entente. A deadly confrontation between two great European power blocs became possible.

In these European quarrels Americans had no obvious stake nor any inclination, in the words of a cautionary Senate resolution, "to depart from the traditional American foreign policy which forbids participation . . . [in] political questions which are entirely European in scope." But on becoming president, Theodore Roosevelt took a lively interest in European affairs and was eager, as the head of a Great Power, to make a contribution to the cause of peace there. In 1905 he got his chance.

The Anglo-French entente of the previous year was based partly on an agreement over territory in North Africa: the Sudan went to Britain, Morocco to France. Then Germany suddenly challenged France over Morocco—a disastrous move, conflicting with Germany's self-interest in keeping France's attention diverted from Europe. The German ruler, Kaiser Wilhelm II, turned to Roosevelt for help. Roosevelt arranged an international conference, which was held in January 1906 at Algeciras, Spain. With U.S. diplomats playing a key role, the crisis was defused. Germany got a few token concessions, but France's dominance over Morocco was sustained.

Algeciras marked an ominous turning point—the first time the power blocs fated to come to blows in 1914 squared off against one another. But in 1906 the outcome of the conference seemed a diplomatic triumph. Roosevelt's secretary of state, Elihu Root, boasted of America's success in "preserv[ing] world peace because of the power of our detachment."

Root's words prefigured how the United States would define its role among the Great Powers. It would be the apostle of peace, distinguished by its "detachment," by its lack of selfish interest in European affairs. Opposing this internationalist impulse, however, was America's traditional isolationism.

Americans had applauded the international peace movement launched by the Hague Peace Conference of 1899. The Permanent Court of Arbitration that resulted offered new hope for the peaceful settlement of international disputes. Both the Roosevelt and Taft administrations negotiated arbitration treaties with other countries, pledging to submit their disputes to the Hague Court, only to have the treaties emasculated by a Senate unwilling to permit any erosion of the nation's sovereignty. Nor was there any sequel to Roosevelt's initiative at Algeciras. It was coolly received in the Senate and by the nation's press.

When Wilson became president, he chose William Jennings Bryan to be secretary of state. An apostle of world peace, Bryan devoted himself to negotiating a series of "cooling off" treaties with other countries—so called because the parties agreed to wait for one year while disputed issues were submitted to a conciliation process. Although admirable, these bilateral agreements had no bearing on the explosive power politics of Europe. As tensions there reached the breaking point in 1914, the United States remained effectively on the sidelines.

Yet at Algeciras Roosevelt had correctly anticipated what the future would demand of America. So did the French journalist Andre Tardieu, who remarked in 1908:

> The United States is . . . a world power. . . . Its power creates for it . . . a duty— to pronounce upon all those questions that hitherto have been arranged by agreement only among European powers. . . . The United States intervenes thus in the affairs of the universe. . . . It is seated at the table where the great game is played, and it cannot leave it.

TIMELINE

Year	Event	Year	Event
1875	Treaty brings Hawaii within U.S. orbit	1901	Theodore Roosevelt becomes president; diplomacy of the "big stick"
1876	United States achieves favorable balance of trade		Hay-Pauncefote Agreement
1881	Secretary of State James G. Blaine inaugurates Pan-Americanism	1902	United States withdraws from Cuba; Platt Amendment gives United States right of intervention
1889	Tripartite agreement on Samoa; U.S. rights to Pago Pago secured	1903	United States recognizes Panama and receives grant of Canal Zone
1890	Alfred Thayer Mahan's *The Influence of Seapower upon History*	1904	Roosevelt Corollary
1893	Annexation of Hawaii fails	1906	United States mediates Franco-German crisis over Morocco at Algeciras
	Frederick Jackson Turner's "The Significance of the Frontier in American History"	1907	Gentlemen's Agreement with Japan
		1908	Root-Takahira Agreement
1894	Sino-Japanese War begins breakup of China into spheres of influence	1913	Wilson asserts new principles for American diplomacy
1895	Venezuela crisis		Intervention in the Mexican Revolution
	Cuban civil war		
1898	Spanish-American War	1914	Panama Canal opens
	Hawaii annexed		World War I begins
	Anti-imperialist movement launched		
1899	Treaty of Paris		
	Guerrilla war in the Philippines		
	Open-door policy in China		

For Further Exploration

Walter LaFeber, *The American Search for Opportunity, 1865–1913* (1993), is an excellent, up-to-date synthesis. LaFeber emphasizes economic interest—the need for overseas markets—as the source of American expansionism. His immensely influential *The New Empire, 1860–1898* (1963) initiated the scholarly debate on this issue. A robust counterpoint is Fareed Zakaria's *From Wealth to Power* (1998), which asks why the United States was so slow (compared to other imperial nations) to translate its economic power into international muscle. The debate can be explored at greater depth in Thomas J. McCormick, *China Market: America's Quest for Informal Empire, 1893–1901* (1967); Michael Hunt, *Ideology and U.S. Foreign Policy* (1987); and Mark R. Shulman, *Navalism and the Emergence of American Sea Power, 1882–1893* (1995). On the war with Spain the liveliest narrative is still Frank Freidel, *A Splendid Little War* (1958). Ivan Musicant, *Empire by Default* (1998), offers a fuller, up-to-date treatment. The overlooked role of the Cuban rebels is brought to light in Louis S. Perez, *The War of 1898: The United States and Cuba in History and Historiography* (1998). Lewis Gould, *The Spanish-American War and President McKinley* (1982), emphasizes McKinley's strong leadership. Ernest R. May, *Imperial Democracy: The Emergence of America as a Great Power* (1961), exemplifies the earlier view that McKinley was a weak figure driven to war by jingoistic pressures. One source of the raging jingoism of this era is uncovered in Kristin L. Hoganson, *Fighting for American Manhood: How Gender Politics Provoked the Spanish-American and Philippine-American Wars* (1998). David Healy, *Drive to Hegemony: The United States in the Caribbean, 1898–1917* (1988), is the starting point for that phase of American expansionism. On the Mexican involvement see John S. D. Eisenhower, *Intervention! The United States and the Mexican Revolution* (1993). The revolution as experienced by the Mexicans is brilliantly depicted in John Womack, *Zapata and the Mexican Revolution* (1968).

The Library of Congress maintains an excellent Web site, The Spanish-American War, at <lcweb.loc.gov/rr/hispanic/1898/>, with separate sections on the war in Cuba, the Philippines, Puerto Rico, and Spain. American Imperialism, at <http://boondocksnet.com>, includes an extensive collection of stereoscopic images, political cartoons, maps, photographs, and documents from the period.

For definitions of key terms boldfaced in this chapter, see the glossary at the end of the book.

To assess your mastery of the material covered in this chapter, see the Online Study Guide at **bedfordstmartins.com/henrettaconcise**.

For map resources and primary documents, see **bedfordstmartins.com/henrettaconcise**.

Part Five

THE MODERN STATE AND SOCIETY

1914–1945

	GOVERNMENT	DIPLOMACY	ECONOMY
	The Rise of the State	**From Isolation to World Leadership**	**Prosperity, Depression, and War**
1914	▸ Wartime agencies expand power of federal government	▸ United States enters World War I (1917) Wilson's Fourteen Points (1918)	▸ Shift from debtor to creditor nation Agricultural glut
1920	▸ Republican ascendancy Prohibition (1920–1933) Business-government partnership Nineteenth Amendment gives women the vote	▸ Treaty of Versailles rejected by U.S. Senate (1920) Washington Conference sets naval limits (1922)	▸ Economic recession (1920–1921) Booming prosperity (1922–1929) Rise of welfare capitalism
1930	▸ Franklin D. Roosevelt becomes president (1933) The New Deal: unprecedented government intervention in economy, social welfare, arts	▸ Roosevelt's Good Neighbor Policy toward Latin America (1933) Abraham Lincoln Brigade fights in Spanish Civil War U.S. neutrality proclaimed (1939)	▸ Great Depression (1929–1941) Rise of labor movement Married women increasingly participate in workforce
1940	▸ Government mobilizes industry for war production and rationing	▸ United States enters World War II (1941) Allies defeat Axis powers; bombing of Hiroshima (1945)	▸ War mobilization ends depression

SOCIETY	CULTURE
Nativism, Migration, and Social Change	**The Emergence of a Mass National Culture**
▶ Southern blacks begin migration to northern cities	▶ Silent screen; Hollywood becomes movie capital of the world
▶ Rise of nativism National Origins Act (1924) Mexican American immigration increases	▶ Consumer culture—advertising, radio, magazines, movies—flourishes Consumer culture promotes image of emancipated womanhood, the flapper
▶ Farming families migrate from dust bowl states to California and the West Indian New Deal	▶ Documentary impulse Federal patronage of the arts
▶ Rural whites and blacks migrate to war jobs in cities Civil rights movement revitalized	▶ Film industry enlisted to aid war effort

I n the 1930s journalist Mark Sullivan described World War I as a "fundamental alteration, from which we would never go back." Sullivan was correct in viewing the war as a pivotal point in world history, but many of the important factors that were transforming America were in place before the war. By 1914 industrialization, economic expansion abroad, massive immigration, and the growth of a vibrant urban culture had set the foundations for a distinctly modern American society. In all facets of politics, the economy, and daily life, American society was becoming more organized, more bureaucratic, and more complex. By 1945, after having fought in two world wars and weathering a dozen years of economic depression, the edifice of the new society was largely complete.

GOVERNMENT An essential building block of modern American society was the strong national state. This state came late to America compared with the industrialized countries of Western Europe. American participation in World War I called forth an unprecedented mobilization of the domestic economy, but policymakers quickly dismantled the centralized wartime bureaucracies in 1919. During the 1920s the Harding and Coolidge administrations embraced a philosophy of business-government partnership, believing that unrestricted corporate capitalism would benefit the American people. The Great Depression, with its countless business failures and devastating unemployment, overthrew that assumption. Franklin D. Roosevelt's New Deal dramatically expanded federal responsibility for the economy and the welfare of ordinary citizens. An even greater expansion of the national state resulted from the massive mobilization necessary to fight World War II. Unlike the experience after World War I, the new state apparatus remained in place when the war ended.

DIPLOMACY America was drawn into a position of world leadership, which it continues to hold today. Before 1914 the world had been dominated by Europe, but after World War I the United States increasingly influenced the world. In 1918 American troops provided the margin of victory for the Allies, and President Wilson helped to shape the treaties that ended the war. Even though the United States refused to join the League of Nations, its dominant economic position guaranteed it an active role in world affairs in the 1920s and 1930s. The globalization of America accelerated in 1941, when the nation threw all its energies into a second world war that had its roots in the imperfect settlement of the first one. Of all the powers that participated in World War II, only mainland America emerged physically unscathed. It was also the only nation to possess a dangerous new weapon—the atomic bomb. Within wartime decisions and strategies lay the roots of the Cold War that followed.

ECONOMY Modern America developed a strong domestic economy, becoming—between 1914 and 1945—the most productive nation in the world. Even the Great Depression, which hit the United States harder than any other industrialized nation, did not permanently affect America's global economic standing. Indeed, American businesses successfully competed in world markets, and American financial institutions played the leading role in international economic affairs. Large-scale corporate organizations replaced smaller family-run businesses. The automobile industry pioneered mass-production techniques. Many workers shared in the general prosperity but also bore the brunt of economic downturns. These uncertainties fueled the dramatic growth of the labor movement in the 1930s.

SOCIETY The nation was transformed by the great wave of immigration and the movement from farms to cities. Metropolitan areas grew dramatically, and increased mobility broke down regional differences. Viewing these changes with alarm, in 1924 old-stock, white nativists succeeded in all but eliminating immigration except from within the Western Hemisphere, where migration across the border from Mexico continued to shape the West and Southwest. As African Americans moved north and west to take factory jobs and dust bowl farmers in the 1930s moved to the West to find better livelihoods, internal migration further changed the face of the nation. World War II accelerated these migration patterns even more.

CULTURE Modern America saw the emergence of a mass national culture. By the 1920s Americans were increasingly drawn into a web of interlocking cultural experiences. Advertising and the new entertainment media—movies, radio, and magazines—disseminated the new values of consumerism; the movies exported this vision of the American experience worldwide. Not even the Great Depression could divert Americans from their desire for leisure, self-fulfillment, and consumer goods. The emphasis on consumption and a quest for a rising standard of living would define the American experience for the rest of the twentieth century.

Chapter 22

WAR AND THE AMERICAN STATE
1914–1920

It is not the army we must shape and train for war, it is a nation.

WOODROW WILSON, 1917

"It's Up to You—Protect the Nation's Honor—Enlist Now." "Rivets Are Bayonets—Drive Them Home!" "Women! Help America's Sons Win the War: Buy U.S. Government Bonds." "Food Is Ammunition—Don't Waste It." At every turn during the eighteen months of U.S. participation in the Great War—at the movies, in schools and libraries, in shop windows and post offices, at train stations and factories—Americans encountered dramatic posters urging them to do their share. More than the colorful reminders of a bygone era they seem today, these **propaganda** tools were meant to unify the American people in voluntary, self-sacrificing service to the nation. They suggest not only that the federal government had increased its presence in the lives of Americans but also that in modern war victory demanded more than armies. On the home front, businessmen, workers, farmers, housewives, and even children had important roles to play.

Although the United States' participation in the conflict was of short duration, the war would have a lasting impact on the nation's domestic life as well as on its international position. The American decision to enter the conflict in 1917 confirmed one of the most important shifts of power in the twentieth century. Before the outbreak of the Great War in 1914, the world had been controlled by Europe; the postwar world was increasingly dominated by the United States as it spread its political, economic, and cultural influence across the globe. Related changes that shaped the country for the rest of the twentieth century also emerged at home. New federal bureaucracies had to be created to coordinate the war effort—a process that hastened the emergence of a national administrative state. War meant new opportunities, albeit temporary, for white women and for members of ethnic minorities. It also meant new divisions among Americans and new hatreds, first of Germans and Austrians and then of "Bolshevik" Reds. When the war ended, the United States was forced to confront the deep class, racial, and ethnic divisions that had surfaced during wartime mobilization.

662

The Great War, 1914–1918

When war erupted in August 1914, most Americans saw no reason to involve themselves in the struggle among Europe's imperialistic powers. No vital U.S. interests were at stake. Indeed the United States had a good relationship with both sides, and its industries benefited from providing war material for the combatants. Many Americans placed their faith in what historians call *U.S. exceptionalism*—the belief that their superior democratic values and institutions made their country immune from the corruption and chaos of other nations. Horrified by the carnage and sympathetic to the suffering, Americans nevertheless expected that they would be able to follow their president's dictum to be neutral in their attitude toward the belligerents.

War in Europe

Almost from the moment France, Russia, and Britain formed the Triple Entente in 1907 to counter the Triple Alliance of Germany, Austria-Hungary, and Italy (see Chapter 21), European leaders began to prepare for what they saw as an inevitable conflict. The spark that ignited the war came in Europe's perennial tinderbox, the Balkans, where Austria-Hungary and Russia had begun competing for power and influence after the decline of the Ottoman Empire made the region unstable. Austria's seizure of the provinces of Bosnia and Herzegovina in 1908 had enraged Russia and its client, the independent state of Serbia. Serbian terrorists responded by recruiting Bosnians to agitate against Austrian rule. On June 28, 1914, a nineteen-year-old Bosnian student, Gavrilo Princip, assassinated Franz Ferdinand, the heir to the Austro-Hungarian throne, and his wife, the Duchess of Hohenberg, in the town of Sarajevo.

After the assassination the complex European alliance system, which had for years maintained a fragile peace, drew all the major powers into war. Austria-Hungary, blaming Serbia for the assassination, declared war on Serbia on July 28. Russia, which had a secret treaty with Serbia, mobilized its armies; Germany responded by declaring war on Russia and its ally, France, and by invading neutral Belgium. The brutality of the invasion, and Britain's commitment to Belgian neutrality, prompted Great Britain to declare war on Germany on August 4. Within a few days all the major European powers had formally entered the conflict.

The combatants were divided into two rival blocs. The Allied Powers—Great Britain, France, Japan, Russia, and, in 1915, Italy—were pitted against the Central Powers—Germany, Austria-Hungary, Turkey, and, in 1915, Bulgaria (Map 22.1). Two fronts emerged. The British and French (and later the Americans) battled on the Western Front against the Central Powers, while the Eastern Front pitted the Russians against the Central Powers. Because the alliance system encompassed competing imperial powers, however, the conflict spread to parts of the world far beyond

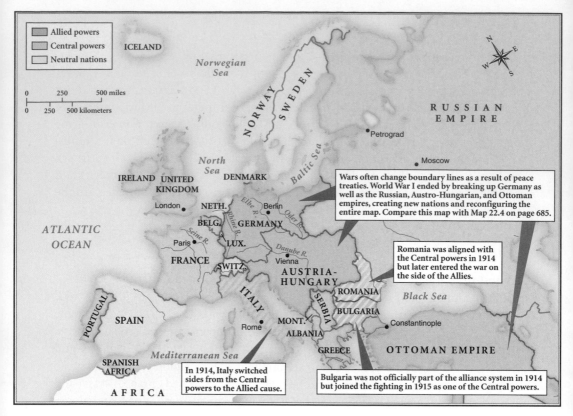

In the map:

Allied powers
Central powers
Neutral nations

ICELAND

Norwegian Sea

NORWAY SWEDEN

RUSSIAN EMPIRE

• Petrograd

North Sea

Baltic Sea

• Moscow

IRELAND UNITED KINGDOM DENMARK

London • NETH. Berlin •

Elbe R. *Oder R.*

BELG. GERMANY

Rhine R.

ATLANTIC OCEAN

Paris • LUX.

Seine R.

FRANCE SWITZ. *Danube R.*

Vienna •

AUSTRIA-HUNGARY

ROMANIA *Black Sea*

ITALY SERBIA BULGARIA

PORTUGAL SPAIN

Rome • MONT.

Constantinople •

ALBANIA

Mediterranean Sea GREECE OTTOMAN EMPIRE

SPANISH AFRICA

AFRICA

0 250 500 miles
0 250 500 kilometers

> Wars often change boundary lines as a result of peace treaties. World War I ended by breaking up Germany as well as the Russian, Austro-Hungarian, and Ottoman empires, creating new nations and reconfiguring the entire map. Compare this map with Map 22.4 on page 685.

> Romania was aligned with the Central powers in 1914 but later entered the war on the side of the Allies.

> In 1914, Italy switched sides from the Central powers to the Allied cause.

> Bulgaria was not officially part of the alliance system in 1914 but joined the fighting in 1915 as one of the Central powers.

MAP 22.1 European Alliances in 1914

In early August 1914 a complex set of interlocking alliances drew the major European powers into war. At first the United States avoided the conflict. Not until April 1917 did America enter the war on the Allied side.

Europe, including the Middle East, Africa, and China. Its worldwide scope gave it the name the Great War, or later, World War I.

The term *Great War* also suggested the terrible devastation the conflict produced. It was the first modern war in which extensive harm was done to civilian populations. New military technology, much of it from the United States, made armies more deadly than ever before. Soldiers carried long-range, high-velocity rifles that could hit a target at 1,000 yards—a vast technical improvement over the 300-yard range of the rifle-musket used in the American Civil War. Another innovation was the machine gun, whose American-born inventor, Hiram Maxim, moved to Great Britain in the 1880s to follow a friend's advice: "If you want to make your fortune, invent something which will allow those fool Europeans to kill each other more quickly."

For four bloody years, between 1914 and 1918, the Western Front, a narrow swath of territory in Belgium and northern France crisscrossed by 25,000 miles of heavily fortified ditches, was the scene of deadly trench warfare that produced

Soldiers at the Front

This 1918 photograph of World War I soldiers in France captures a moment of peace and barely hints at the carnage of trench warfare that profoundly scarred so many men by causing "gas neurosis," "burial-alive neurosis," and "soldier's heart"—all symptoms of shell shock.

Imperial War Museum, London.

FOR MORE HELP ANALYZING THIS IMAGE, see the Online Study Guide at **bedfordstmartins .com/henrettaconcise**.

unprecedented numbers of casualties. If one side tried to break the stalemate by venturing into the "no man's land" between the trenches, its soldiers, caught in a sea of deadly barbed wire, were mowed down by artillery fire or poison gas, first used by the Germans at Ypres in April 1915. Between February and December 1916, the French suffered 550,000 casualties and the Germans 450,000, as Germany tried to break through the French lines at Verdun. The front did not move (see American Voices, "Trench Warfare," p. 666).

The Perils of Neutrality

As the stalemate continued, the United States grappled with its role in the international conflagration. Two weeks after the outbreak of war in Europe, President Woodrow Wilson had made the American position clear. The president called on Americans to be "neutral in fact as well as in name, impartial in thought as well as in action." Wilson wanted to keep the nation out of the war partly because he believed that if America kept aloof from the quarrel, he could arbitrate—and influence—its ultimate settlement.

The nation's divided loyalties also influenced Wilson's policy. Many Americans, including Wilson, felt deep cultural ties to the Allies, especially Britain and France.

AMERICAN VOICES

Trench Warfare

HARRY CURTIN

B efore the United States entered the Great War, many young American men, eager to get
*into the fight, enlisted in the British forces. In February 1918 Californian Harry Curtin
wrote letters describing trench warfare in France that vividly captured the ravaged landscape
and the pervasive tension as men waited fearfully for the next shell to hit.*

Picture to yourself a scene of utter desolation and loneliness. A rolling plain of moist, black, sticky mud, so pitted by shell holes that they overlap—shell holes all the way from three feet wide to twenty, and ranging from four to fifteen feet deep. These holes are filled with mud, riled up by continuous shell fire into the consistency of syrup, so that if one had the misfortune to slip into one, he is in a quagmire and dies a miserable death, unless his comrades drag him out. . . .

Amidst this scene of ruin and death is a trench. It is one of many, but as it is the one I am in, it intimately concerns me and I will describe it.

This trench is about six feet deep, the excavated earth being thrown up in front to form a parapet which makes it apparently seven and a half feet. It ranges in width from eighteen inches at the bottom to three feet at the top and is about eighteen feet in length. About seven feet of this is roofed over with scantling and pieces of rubber sheeting, an outer covering of about eighteen inches of dirt being added. This portion is divided from the rest of the trench by walls made of rubber sheeting, and in it all cooking and sleeping is done. In this trench is a machine gun and its crew, of which I am one. There are others, but we are all segregated so as to minimize casualties. . . .

Although the ground throbs with the concussion of heavy guns and shells, both our own and the enemy's, one experiences a sense of security and aloofness in these places which is peculiar. The talk ranges over a variety of subjects. Everything is discussed except the war, which is taboo.

Somebody looks at his watch and the next . . . guard listens to assure himself that there are no aeroplanes about, opens the flap and goes out, carefully tucking it down after him so that no gleam of light can escape. The man he relieves comes in a little later and casually remarks that "Fritz is throwing some ironmongery [shells] over." And he is!

Out of the black heavens outside is coming a rain of shells from 5.9 up to 9-inch, high explosives, which throw columns of dirt sixty feet high and make holes in the ground from eight feet in diameter to fifteen and ten feet deep. . . . I said that no one ever spoke about the war—with an exception, however. Whenever the concussion of a bursting shell puts the light out and a shower of dirt and stones patters into the trench, the discussion closes abruptly; someone says: "That was pretty close"—and we wait.

SOURCE: Bulletin (Los Angeles Consistory, Scottish Rite, December 1918), 68.

Yet most Irish Americans resented Britain's centuries-long occupation of their home-land and the cancellation of Home Rule in 1914. Pro-German sentiments drew strength from America's 10 million immigrants from Germany and Austria-Hungary. Indeed, German Americans made up one of the largest and best-established ethnic groups in the United States. Wilson could not easily have rallied the nation to the Allied side in 1914.

Many Americans had no strong sympathy for either side. Some progressive re-formers vehemently opposed American participation in the European conflict. Virtually the entire political left, led principally by Eugene Debs and the Socialist Party, condemned the war as imperialistic. African American leaders such as A. Philip Randolph viewed it as a conflict of the white race only. Newly formed pacifist groups, among them the American Union against Militarism and the Women's Peace Party, both founded in 1915, also mobilized popular opposition. And some prominent industrialists bankrolled antiwar activities. In December 1915 Henry Ford spent almost half a million dollars to send more than a hundred men and women to Europe on a "peace ship" in an attempt to negotiate an end to the war.

These factors might have kept the nation neutral if the conflict had not spread to the high seas. Here the United States wished to assert its neutrality rights—freedom to trade with nations on both sides of a conflict. But the warring nations would not long grant America this luxury. By the end of August 1914, the British had imposed a naval blockade on the Central Powers, hoping to cut off military supplies and starve the German people into submission. But their actions also prevented neutral nations like the United States from trading with Germany and its allies. The United States chafed at the infringement of its neutral rights but chose to do little besides complain, largely because the war had produced a spectacular increase in trade with the Allies that more than made up for the lost commerce with the Central Powers. American trade with Britain and France grew from $824 million in 1914 to $3.2 billion in 1916. By 1917 U.S. banks had lent the Allies $2.5 billion. In contrast, American trade with and loans to Germany totaled only $29 million and $27 million, respectively, by 1917. This trade imbalance translated into closer U.S. ties with the Allies, despite the nation's official posture of neutrality.

To challenge British control of the seas, the German navy launched a devastat-ing new weapon, the U-boat (submarine). In April 1915 the German embassy in the United States had issued a warning to civilians that all ships flying the flags of Britain or its allies were liable to destruction. A few weeks later, a German U-boat off the coast of Ireland torpedoed the British luxury liner *Lusitania*, killing 1,198 people, 128 of them Americans. The attack on the unarmed passenger vessel (which was later revealed to have been carrying munitions) incensed Americans—newspapers branded it a "mass murder"—and prompted President Wilson to send a series of strongly worded protests to Germany. Mounting tension between the two nations temporarily subsided in September 1915, when Germany announced its U-boats would no longer attack passenger ships without warning.

The *Lusitania* crisis was one factor that prompted Wilson to rethink his opposition to preparedness. He was further discouraged by the failure of his repeated attempts in 1915 and 1916 to mediate an end to the European conflict through his aide, Colonel Edward House. With neither side apparently interested in serious peace negotiations, Wilson worried that the potential for the United States to be drawn into the conflict was deepening. In the fall of 1915, he endorsed a $1 billion buildup of the army and the navy, and by 1916 armament was well under way.

Nevertheless, public opinion still ran against entering the war, a factor that profoundly shaped the election of 1916. The Republican Party passed over the belligerently prowar Theodore Roosevelt in favor of Supreme Court Justice Charles Evans Hughes, a former governor of New York. The Democrats renominated Wilson, whose campaign emphasized his progressive reform record (see Chapter 20) but whose telling campaign slogan was "He kept us out of war." Wilson won reelection by only 600,000 popular votes and by 23 votes in the electoral college, a slim margin that limited his options in mobilizing the nation for war.

The events of early 1917 diminished Wilson's lingering hopes of staying out of the conflict. On January 31 Germany announced the resumption of unrestricted submarine warfare, a decision dictated by the impasse in the land war. In response Wilson broke off diplomatic relations with Germany on February 3. A few weeks later, newspapers published an intercepted communication from Germany's foreign secretary, Arthur Zimmermann, to the German minister in Mexico City, in which Zimmermann urged Mexico to join the Central Powers in the war. In return Germany promised to help Mexico recover "the lost territory of Texas, New Mexico, and Arizona." This threat to the territorial integrity of the United States jolted both congressional and public opinion, especially in the West, where opposition to entering the war was strong. Combined with the resumption of unrestricted submarine warfare, the Zimmermann telegram inflamed anti-German sentiment. Although the likelihood of Mexico's reconquering the border states was small, the continued instability there in the final phases of the Mexican Revolution had led to border raids conducted by Pancho Villa that killed sixteen U.S. citizens in January 1916 (see Chapter 21) and made American policymakers take the German threat seriously.

Throughout March, U-boats attacked American ships without warning, sinking three on March 18 alone. On April 2, 1917, Wilson appeared before a special session of Congress to ask for a declaration of war. The rights of the nation had been trampled, and its trade and citizens' lives imperiled, he charged. But while U.S. self-interest shaped the decision to go to war, Americans' long-standing sense of their exceptionalism, coupled with Progressive Era zeal to right social injustices, also played a part. Believing that the United States, in contrast to other nations, was uniquely high-minded in the conduct of its international affairs, many Americans accepted Wilson's claim that America had no selfish aims: "We desire no conquest, no dominion. We seek no indemnities for ourselves, no material compensation for the sacrifices we shall freely make. We are but one of the champions of the rights of mankind." In a memorable phrase intended to ennoble the nation's role, Wilson proposed that U.S. participation in the war would make the world "safe for democracy."

Four days after Wilson's speech, on April 6, 1917, the United States declared war on Germany. Reflecting the divided feelings of the country as a whole, the vote was far from unanimous. Six senators and fifty members of the House voted against the action, including Representative Jeannette Rankin of Montana, the first woman elected to Congress. "I want to stand by my country," she declared, "but I cannot vote for war."

"Over There"

To native-born Americans, Europe seemed a great distance away—literally "over there," as the lyrics of George M. Cohan's popular song described it. After the declaration of war, many citizens were surprised to learn that the United States planned to send troops to Europe, optimistically having assumed that the nation's participation could be limited to military and economic aid. In May 1917 General John J. Pershing traveled to London and Paris to determine how the United States could best support the war effort. The answer, as Marshal Joseph Joffre of France put it, was clear: "Men, men, and more men."

The problem was that the United States had never maintained a large standing army in peacetime. To field a fighting force strong enough to enter a global war, the government turned to conscription (military draft). The passage of the Selective Service Act in May 1917 demonstrated the increasing impact of the state on ordinary citizens. Though draft resistance had been common during the Civil War, no major riots occurred in 1917. The Selective Service system worked in part because it combined central direction from Washington with local administration and civilian control and thus did not tread on the nation's tradition of individual freedom and local autonomy. Draft registration also demonstrated the potential bureaucratic capacity of the American state. On a single day, June 5, 1917, more than 9.5 million men between the ages of twenty-one and thirty were processed for military service in their local voting precincts. By the end of the war almost 4 million men, popularly known as doughboys, plus a few thousand female navy clerks and army nurses, were in uniform. Another 300,000 men, called slackers, evaded the draft, and 4,000 were classified as conscientious objectors.

Wilson chose Pershing to head the American Expeditionary Force (AEF). But the newly raised army did not have an immediate impact on the fighting. The fresh recruits had to be trained and outfitted and then wait for transport across the submarine-infested Atlantic. The nation's first significant contribution was to secure the safety of the seas. Aiming for safety in numbers in the face of mounting German submarine activity, the government began sending armed convoys across the Atlantic. The plan worked: no American soldiers were killed on the way to Europe, and Allied shipping losses were cut dramatically.

Meanwhile, trench warfare on the Western Front continued its deadly grind. Allied commanders pleaded for American reinforcements, but Pershing was reluctant to put his soldiers under foreign commanders, preferring to delay introducing American troops until the AEF could be brought up to full strength. Thus, until May 1918, the brunt of the fighting continued to fall on the French and British. Their burden increased when the Eastern Front collapsed after the Russian Revolution in November 1917. Under the Treaty of Brest-Litovsk, the new **Bolshevik** regime under Vladimir Ilych Lenin surrendered about one-third of Russia's territories, including Russian Poland, Ukraine, and the Baltic provinces, in return for an end to hostilities. (Following a protracted civil war, the Soviet Union would be established under Communist rule in 1924.)

When the war with Russia ended, the Germans launched a major offensive against the Allies on the Western Front on March 21, 1918. By May the German army had advanced to within 50 miles of Paris and was bombarding the city. When Allied leaders intensified their calls for American troops, Pershing committed about 60,000 Americans to help the French repel the Germans in the battles of Château-Thierry and Belleau Wood (Map 22.2). American reinforcements now began to arrive in large numbers. Augmented by American troops, the Allied forces brought the German offensive to a halt in mid-July. By mid-September 1918 American and French troops led by General Pershing had forced the Germans to retreat at St. Mihiel. The last major assault of the war began on September 26, when Pershing pitted over a million American soldiers against vastly outnumbered and exhausted German troops. The Meuse-Argonne campaign pushed the enemy back across the Selle River near Verdun and broke the German defenses, at a cost of over 26,000 American lives.

World War I ended on November 11, 1918, when German and Allied representatives signed an armistice in the railway car of Marshal Ferdinand Foch of France. The flood of American troops and supplies during the last six months of the war had helped secure the Allied victory. The nation's decisive contribution signaled a shift in international power as European diplomatic and economic dominance declined, and the United States emerged as a world leader.

About 2 million American soldiers were in France at the war's end. Two-thirds of them had seen action at least briefly on the Western Front, but most Americans had escaped the horrors of sustained trench warfare that sapped the morale of Allied and German troops. During the eighteen months in which the United States fought, 48,000 American servicemen were killed in action or died from wounds. Another 27,000 died from other causes, mainly the influenza epidemic that swept the world in 1918 and 1919. But the nation's casualties were minimal compared with the 8 million soldiers lost by the Allies and the Central Powers.

American soldiers who served in the "Great War" reflected the heterogeneity of the nation's population. Approximately 12,000, or 25 percent, of the adult male Native American population served in the military. About one-fifth of the American soldiers had been born in another country, leading some people to call the AEF the

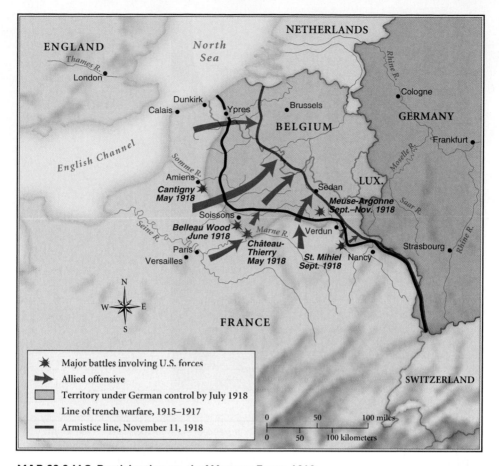

MAP 22.2 U.S. Participation on the Western Front, 1918

When American troops reached the European front in significant numbers in 1918, the Allied and Central Powers had been grinding each other down in a war of attrition for almost four years. The influx of American troops and supplies broke the stalemate. Successful offensive maneuvers by the American Expeditionary Force included those at Belleau Wood and Château-Thierry and the Meuse-Argonne campaign.

American Foreign Legion. Army censors had to be able to read forty-nine languages to check letters written home by American servicemen. Although the diversity of the military worried some observers, most predicted that service in the armed forces would promote the Americanization of the nation's immigrants.

The "Americanization" of the army remained imperfect at best, with African American soldiers receiving the worst treatment. Over 400,000 black men served in the military, accounting for 13 percent of the armed forces; 92 percent were draftees, a far higher rate than that of whites. Blacks were organized into rigidly segregated units, almost always under the control of white officers. In addition blacks were assigned to the most menial tasks, such as kitchen and clean-up detail. Although the

World War I Veteran Fred Fast Horse

In contrast to the segregation African Americans experienced, Native Americans served in integrated combat units in the military. Ironically, racial stereotypes about their natural abilities as warriors, their adroit tactics, sense of strategy, and feats of camouflage both enhanced the reputation of Native Americans' military ability and meant that officers gave them hazardous duties as advance scouts, messengers, and snipers. Casualties were high. Roughly 5 percent died, compared to 1 percent for the military as a whole. Fred Fast Horse, a Rosebud Sioux, pictured here, was partially paralyzed in the Meuse-Argonne campaign. William Hammond Mathers Museum, Indiana University.

policy of segregation minimized contact between black and white recruits, racial violence erupted at several camps. The worst incident occurred in Houston in August 1917, when black members of the Twenty-fourth Infantry's Third Battalion killed fifteen white soldiers and police officers in retaliation for a string of racial incidents, including the beating of a black woman by a white police officer. Sixty-four soldiers were tried in military courts, and nineteen were hanged. The army quickly disbanded the battalion, but the legacy of racial mistrust lingered throughout the rest of the war.

After the armistice, American troops came home to begin the process of readjusting to civilian life. But the war lived on in the minds of the men and women who had gone "over there." Spared the trauma of sustained battle, many members of the AEF had experienced the war more as tourists than as soldiers. Before joining

Fighting the Flu

The influenza epidemic of 1918 to 1919 traversed the globe, making it a pandemic that killed between 20 and 40 million people. In the United States, one-fifth of the population was infected and
more than 600,000 died—ten times the number who died in the war. The speed with which the
disease spread led Surgeon General Vaughan to warn that "If the epidemic continues its mathemat-
ical rate of acceleration, civilization could easily disappear from the face of the earth within a few
weeks." In October 1918 alone, 200,000 died. The epidemic strained the resources of a public-
health system already fully mobilized for the war effort. Here doctors, army officers, and reporters
don surgical masks and gowns before touring hospitals that treat influenza patients. Note the patriotic poster entreating citizens to buy bonds on the wall behind them. Corbis-Bettmann.

the army most recruits had barely traveled beyond their hometowns, and for
them the journey across the ocean to Europe was a once-in-a-lifetime event. In
1919 a group of former AEF officers formed the American Legion "to preserve the
memories and incidents of our association in the great war." The word *legion* perfectly captured the romantic, almost chivalric memories that many veterans held
of their wartime service. Only later did disillusionment set in over the contested
legacy of World War I.

War on the Home Front

Fighting World War I required extraordinary economic mobilization on the home front in which corporations, workers, and the general public cooperated. Although the federal government did expand its power and presence during the emergency, the watchword was voluntarism. The government avoided compulsion as much as possible. Ambivalence about expanding state power, coupled with the pressures of wartime mobilization, severely damaged the impetus for progressive reforms that had characterized the prewar era. Yet even in the context of international crisis, some reformers expected that the war could serve the cause of improving American society.

Mobilizing Industry and the Economy

The continuing impact of the prewar progressive reform movement was evident in the financing of the war, the cost of which would eventually mount to $33 billion. The government paid for the war in part by using the Federal Reserve System established in 1913 (see Chapter 20) to expand the money supply, making it easier to borrow money. Two-thirds of the funds came from loans, especially the popular liberty bonds. To augment the funds raised by bonds, Treasury Secretary William McAdoo increased the federal income tax. Income taxes had been instituted by Congress after the passage of the Sixteenth Amendment to the Constitution in 1913. Now the War Revenue Bills of 1917 and 1918 transformed the tax into the foremost method of federal fund-raising. The Wilson administration took a progressive approach, rejecting a tax on all wages and salaries in favor of a tax on corporations and prosperous individuals. The excess-profits tax signaled a direct and unprecedented intrusion of the state into the workings of corporate capitalism. By 1918 U.S. corporations were paying over $2.5 billion in excess-profits taxes per year—more than half of all federal taxes.

The revenue bills should not mask the fact that the federal government for the most part took a collaborative, rather than a coercive, approach to big business during the war. To the dismay of many progressives who had hoped that the war emergency would increase federal regulation of business, the government suspended antitrust laws to encourage cooperation and promote efficiency. For economic expertise the administration turned to business executives who flocked to Washington, where they served with federal officials on a series of boards and agencies that sought a middle ground between total state control of the economy and total freedom for business.

The central agency for mobilizing wartime industry was the War Industries Board (WIB), established in July 1917. In March 1918, after a fumbling start that showed the limits of voluntarism in a national emergency, the Wilson administration reorganized the board under the direction of Bernard Baruch, a Wall Street financier. The WIB produced an unparalleled expansion of the federal government's economic powers: it allocated scarce resources, gathered economic data and statistics, controlled the flow of raw materials, ordered the conversion from peacetime to war production, set prices, imposed efficiency and standardization procedures, and coordinated purchasing. Though the board had the authority to compel compliance, Baruch preferred to win voluntary cooperation from industry, often through personal intervention. Business generally supported this governmental oversight because it coincided with its own interests in improving efficiency and productivity. Despite higher taxes corporate profits soared, producing an economic boom that continued without interruption until 1920.

In some instances new federal agencies took dramatic, decisive action. In the face of the severe winter of 1917 to 1918, which led to coal shortages in northeastern cities and industries, the Fuel Administration ordered all factories east of the Mississippi River to shut down for four days. An even more striking example of the temporary use of federal power came in December 1917. When a massive railroad traffic snarl interfered with the transport of troops, the Railroad War Board, which coordinated the nation's sprawling transportation system, took over the railroads. Guaranteeing railroad owners a "standard return" equal to their average earnings between 1915 and 1917, the board promised that the carriers would regain private control no later than twenty-one months after the end of the war. Although reformers hoped to continue this experiment in federal control on behalf of labor and consumers, the government fulfilled its pledge.

Reliance on voluntary compliance in mobilizing for war was best exemplified in the Food Administration, created in August 1917 and led by Stanford-trained engineer Herbert Hoover, who proposed to "mobilize the spirit of self-denial and self-sacrifice in this country." Using the slogan "Food will win the war," Hoover encouraged farmers to expand production of wheat and other grains from 45 million acres in 1917 to 75 million in 1919. Although the Food Administration issued reams of rules and regulations for producers and retailers, at no time did the government contemplate domestic food rationing. Rather, Hoover sent women volunteers from door to door to secure housewives' cooperation in observing "wheatless" Mondays, "meatless" Tuesdays, and "porkless" Thursdays and Saturdays—a campaign that resulted in substantial voluntary conservation of food resources. Hoover emerged from the war as one of the nation's most admired public figures.

With the signing of the armistice in November 1918, the United States scrambled to dismantle wartime controls. Wilson, determined to "take the harness off," disbanded the WIB on January 1, 1919, resisting suggestions that the board would help stabilize the economy during demobilization. Like most Americans, Wilson could tolerate government planning power during an emergency but not as a permanent feature of the economy.

Although the nation's participation in the war lasted just eighteen months, it left an enduring legacy: the modern bureaucratic state. Entire industries were organized as never before, linked to a maze of government agencies and executive departments. A modern system of income taxation was established, with the potential for vastly increasing federal reserves. Finally, the collaboration between business and government was mutually beneficial, teaching both partners a lesson they would put to use in state building in the 1920s and afterward.

Mobilizing American Workers

Modern wars are never won solely by armies and business and government leaders. Farmers, factory workers, and other civilians play crucial roles, ones that the federal government constantly promoted in its propaganda posters and other means of exhorting citizens "to do their bit for Uncle Sam." One result was that organized labor's position improved during the war, although it remained a junior partner to business and government. Acute labor shortages, caused by the demands of the draft, the abrupt decline in European immigration, and the urgency of war production, had enhanced workers' bargaining power. The National War Labor Board (NWLB), formed in April 1918, also helped to improve labor's position. Composed of representatives of labor, management, and the public, the NWLB established an eight-hour day for war workers, with time and a half for overtime, and endorsed equal pay for women workers. Workers were not allowed to disrupt war production through strikes or other disturbances. In return the NWLB supported the workers' right to organize unions, required employers to deal with shop committees, and arbitrated labor disputes.

After years of federal hostility toward labor, the NWLB's actions brought a welcome change in labor's status and power. From 1916 to 1919 AFL membership grew by almost 1 million workers, reaching over 3 million at the end of the war. Few of the wartime gains lasted, however. Like other agencies, the NWLB was quickly disbanded. Wartime inflation ate up most of the wage hikes, and a virulent postwar antiunion movement caused a rapid decline in union membership that lasted into the 1930s.

While the war emergency benefited labor in general, it had a special effect on workers who were traditionally excluded from many industrial jobs. For the first time northern factories actively recruited African Americans, spawning the "Great Migration" (Map 22.3). Over 400,000 African Americans from the South moved northward to cities such as St. Louis, Chicago, New York, and Detroit during the war. The lure of decent jobs was potent. As one Mississippi man said in anticipation of working in northern meatpacking houses: "You could not rest in your bed at night for thoughts of Chicago." African Americans encountered discrimination in the North—in jobs, housing, and education—but most were able to better their circumstances as they found new opportunities and an escape from the repressive southern agricultural system (see American Voices, "Southern Migrants," p. 678).

Mexican Americans in California, Texas, New Mexico, and Arizona also found new opportunities. Wartime labor shortages prompted many Mexican Americans to leave farm labor for industrial jobs in rapidly growing southwestern cities. Continuing political instability in Mexico following the revolution encouraged many

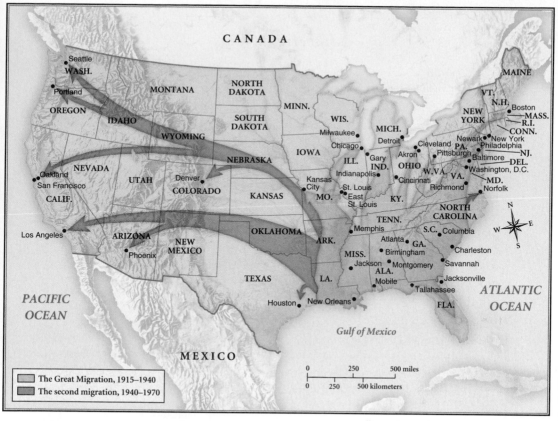

MAP 22.3 The Great Migration and Beyond

This map indicates broad migration patterns, but does not reveal the complex process of circuitous routes and back-and-forth migration by which many individuals and families moved away from the South. Employment opportunities that opened up during World War I and World War II served as catalysts for "great migrations" out of the rural South. In the first migration that began in 1915, African Americans headed primarily to industrial cities of the North and Midwest, such as Chicago, New York, and Pittsburgh. With the Second World War, their destinations expanded to include the West, especially Los Angeles, the San Francisco Bay area, and Seattle.

FOR MORE HELP ANALYZING THIS MAP, see the Online Study Guide at **bedfordstmartins.com/henrettaconcise**.

Mexicans to relocate, temporarily or permanently, across the border, a process facilitated by newly opened railroad lines. At least 100,000 Mexicans entered the United States between 1917 and 1920, often settling in segregated neighborhoods (barrios) in urban areas, meeting discrimination similar to that faced by African Americans.

Women were the largest group to take advantage of new wartime opportunities. White women and, to a lesser degree, black and Mexican American women found that factory jobs usually reserved for men had been opened to them. About 1 million women joined the labor force for the first time, while many of the 8 million women

◊

Southern Migrants

*T*he Great Migration of southern African Americans to the cities of the North disrupted communities and families, but the migrants kept in touch with friends and kin through letters and visits. Cities like Chicago offered new opportunities and experiences, as these letters suggest, and migrants eagerly promoted their promise to the folks back home.

CHICAGO, ILLINOIS.

My dear Sister: I was agreeably surprised to hear from you and to hear from home. I am well and thankful to say I am doing well. The weather and everything else was a surprise to me when I came. I got here in time to attend one of the greatest revivals in the history of my life—over 500 people joined the church. We had a Holy Ghost shower. You know I like to have run wild. It was snowing some nights and if you didnt hurry you could not get standing room. Please remember me kindly to any who ask of me. The people are rushing here by the thousands and I know if you come and rent a big house you can get all the roomers you want. You write me exactly when you are coming. I am not keeping house yet I am living with my brother and his wife. My son is in California but will be home soon. He spends his winter in California. I can get a nice place for you to stop until you can look around and see what you want. I am quite busy. I work in Swifts packing Co. in the sausage department. My daughter and I work for the same company—We get $1.50 a day and we pack so many sausages we dont have much time to play but it is a matter of a dollar with me and I feel that God made the path and I am walking therein.

Tell your husband work is plentiful here and he wont have to loaf if he want to work. . . . Well goodbye from your sister in Christ.

CHICAGO, ILLINOIS, 11/13/17.

Mr. H————
Hattiesburg, Miss.
Dear M————: Yours received sometime ago and found all well and doing well. Hope you and family are well.

I got my things alright the other day and they were in good condition. I am all fixed now and living well. I certainly appreciate what you done for us and I will remember you in the near future.

M, old boy, I was promoted on the first of the month I was made first assistant to the head carpenter when he is out of the place I take everything in charge and was raised to $95. a month. You know I know my stuff.

Whats the news generally around H'burg? I should have been here 20 years ago. I just begin to feel like a man. It's a great deal of pleasure in knowing that you have got some privilege. My children are going to the same school with the whites and I dont have to umble to no one. I have registered—Will vote the next election and there isnt any "yes sir" and "no sir"—its all yes and no and Sam and Bill.

Florine says hello and would like very much to see you.

All joins me in sending love to you and family. How is times there now? Answer soon, from your friend and bro.

SOURCE: *Journal of Negro History* 4, no. 4 (1919): 457, 458–59.

Wartime Opportunities

Women took on new jobs during the war, working as mail carriers, police officers, drill-press operators, and farm laborers attached to the Women's Land Army. These women are riveters at the Puget Sound Navy Yard in Washington. Black women in particular, who customarily were limited to employment as domestic servants or agricultural laborers, found that the war opened up new opportunities and better wages in industry. When the war ended, black and white women alike usually lost jobs deemed to be men's work. National Archives.

who already held jobs switched from low-paying fields like domestic service to higher-paying industrial work. Americans soon got used to the sight of female streetcar conductors, train engineers, and defense workers. But everyone   including most working women—believed that those jobs would return to men after the war.

Wartime Reform: Woman Suffrage and Prohibition

Of the many progressive reformers who anticipated that mobilization for war could usher in a wide range of social reforms, none were more optimistic than the supporters of woman suffrage who hoped that the war would reinvigorate their cause. The National American Woman Suffrage Association (NAWSA) continued to lobby for the proposed woman suffrage amendment to the Constitution. It also threw the support of its 2 million members behind the Wilson administration, encouraging women to do their part to win the war. Women in communities all over the country labored exhaustively to promote food conservation, to protect children and women workers, and to distribute emergency relief through organizations like the Red Cross. Many agreed with Carrie Chapman Catt, president of NAWSA, that women's patriotic service could advance the cause of woman suffrage.

Alice Paul and the National Woman's Party (NWP) took a more militant tack. To the dismay of NAWSA leaders, NWP militants began picketing the White House in July 1917 to protest their lack of the vote. Arrested and sentenced to seven months in jail, Paul and other women prisoners went on a hunger strike, which prison authorities met with forced feeding. Public shock at the women's treatment made them martyrs, drawing attention to the issue of woman suffrage.

The combination of NWP militance and NAWSA's policy of patient persuasion finally brought results. In January 1918 Woodrow Wilson withdrew his opposition to a federal woman suffrage amendment. The constitutional amendment quickly passed the House but took eighteen months to get through the Senate. Then came another year of hard work for ratification by the states. Finally, on August 26, 1920, Tennessee gave the Nineteenth Amendment the last vote it needed. The goal that had first been declared publicly at the Seneca Falls convention in 1848 was finally achieved seventy-two years later, in large part because of women's contributions to the war effort.

Other activists also saw the war as an opportunity to further their long-standing goals. Moral reformers concerned with vice and prostitution found that their agenda meshed with the military's interest in army efficiency. With the slogan "Keeping fit to fight," the federal government launched an ambitious campaign against sexually transmitted diseases, forcing the shutdown of "red-light" districts in cities with military training camps. With the cooperation of the YMCA and the YWCA, the government undertook a far-reaching sex education program, designed to enlighten both men and women about the dangers of sexual activity and the value of "social purity."

While some reformers worried about soldiers' physical and moral welfare, others acted to protect the families they left behind. Responding to concerns about familial disruption and deprivation among working-class families, Congress enacted the War Risk Insurance Act in 1917, which required that enlisted men and noncommissioned officers allot $15 monthly from their military pay to their dependents, who also received allowances from the federal government, which disbursed almost $570 million for the program between 1917 and its end in 1921. The funds gave women some degree of financial security and even independence, but the program also reinforced expectations that women's proper role was in the home and men's was as the family breadwinner. This unprecedented expansion of the federal government into the private lives of families, although short-lived, would shape the welfare programs established in the New Deal era (see Chapter 25).

A more dramatic enlargement of federal power resulted from the efforts of **prohibitionists** who viewed alcoholic beverages as the nation's key social evil. In the early twentieth century, many Americans viewed the legal prohibition of alcohol as a progressive reform and not a denial of individual freedom. Urban reformers, concerned about good government, poverty, and public morality, supported a nationwide ban on drinking. The drive for Prohibition also had substantial backing in rural communities. Many people equated liquor with all the sins of the city: prostitution, crime, immigration, machine politics, and public disorder. The churches with the greatest strength in rural areas, including the Methodists, the Baptists, and the Mormons, also strongly condemned drinking. Protestants from rural areas dominated the membership of the Anti-Saloon League, which supplanted the Women's Christian Temperance Union as the leading proponent of Prohibition early in the century.

Temperance advocates were right in identifying cities as the sites of resistance to Prohibition. Alcoholic beverages, especially beer and whiskey, played an important role in the social life of certain ethnic cultures in the nation's heavily urbanized areas, especially those of German Americans and Irish Americans. Most saloons were in working-class neighborhoods and served as gathering places for workers. Machine politicians indeed conducted much of their business in bars. Thus many immigrants and working-class people opposed Prohibition, not only as an attack on drinking but as an attempt to impose middle-class cultural values on them.

Numerous states—mostly those in the South and Midwest without a significant immigrant presence—already had Prohibition laws, but World War I offered the impetus for national action. Because several major breweries had German names (Pabst and Busch, for example), beer drinking became unpatriotic in many people's minds. To conserve food Congress prohibited the use of foodstuffs such as hops and barley in breweries and distilleries. Finally, in December 1917, Congress passed the Eighteenth Amendment, which prohibited the "manufacture, sale, or transportation of intoxicating liquors." Ratified in 1919 and effective on January 16, 1920, the Eighteenth Amendment demonstrated the widening influence of the state in matters of personal behavior.

The Eighteenth Amendment was also an example of how progressive reform efforts could benefit from the climate of war. But despite the stimulus the Great War gave to some types of reform, for the most part it blocked rather than furthered change. Though many progressives had anticipated that the stronger federal presence in wartime would lead to stronger economic controls and corporate regulation, federal agencies were quickly disbanded once the war was over, reflecting the unease most Americans felt about a strong bureaucratic state. The wartime collaboration between government and business gave corporate leaders more influence in shaping the economy and government policy, not less.

Promoting National Unity

For the liberal reformers convinced that the war for democracy could promote a more just society at home, perhaps the most discouraging development was the campaign to promote "One Hundred Percent Americanism," which meant an insistence on conformity and an intolerance of dissent. It was Woodrow Wilson who had predicted what came to pass: "Once lead this people into war, and they'll forget there ever was such a thing as tolerance." The president recognized the need to manufacture support for the war, but ironically his efforts encouraged a repressive spirit hostile to reform.

In April 1917 Wilson formed the Committee on Public Information (CPI) to promote public support for the war. This government propaganda agency, headed by the journalist George Creel, quickly attracted progressive reformers and muck-raking journalists. Professing lofty-sounding goals—such as educating citizens about democracy, promoting national unity, assimilating immigrants, and breaking down the isolation of rural life—the committee also acted as a nationalizing force by promoting the development of a common ideology.

During the war the CPI touched the lives of practically every American. It distributed 75 million pieces of patriotic literature and sponsored speeches at local movie theaters, reaching cumulative audiences estimated at more than 300 million—three times the population of the United States at the time. In its zeal the committee often ventured into hatemongering. In early 1918, for example, it encouraged speakers to use inflammatory stories of alleged German atrocities to build support for the war effort.

As a spirit of conformity pervaded the home front, many Americans found themselves targets of suspicion. Local businesses paid for newspaper and magazine ads that asked citizens to report to the Justice Department "the man who spreads pessimistic stories, cries for peace, or belittles our efforts to win the war." Posters encouraged Americans to be on the lookout for German spies. And quasi-vigilante groups such as the American Protective League mobilized about 250,000 self-appointed agents, furnished with badges issued by the Justice Department, to spy on neighbors and coworkers.

The CPI also urged ethnic groups to give up their Old World customs in the spirit of One Hundred Percent Americanism. German Americans bore the brunt of this campaign. In an orgy of hostility generated by propaganda about German militarism and outrages, everything associated with Germany became suspect. German music, especially opera, was banished from the concert halls. Publishers removed pro-German references from textbooks, and many communities banned the teaching of the German language. Sauerkraut was renamed "liberty cabbage," and hamburgers were transformed into "liberty sandwiches." Though anti-German hysteria dissipated when the war ended, hostility toward the "hyphenated" American survived into the 1920s.

In law enforcement, officials tolerated little criticism of established values and institutions. The main legal tools for curbing dissent were the Espionage Act of 1917 and the Sedition Act of 1918. The Sedition Act focused on disloyal speech, writing, and behavior that might "incite, provoke, or encourage resistance to the United States, or to promote the cause of its enemies." The Espionage Act imposed stiff penalties for antiwar activities and allowed the federal government to ban treasonous materials from the mails. The postmaster general revoked the mailing privileges of groups considered to be radical, virtually shutting down their publications.

Individuals suffered as well. Because these acts defined treason and sedition loosely, they led to the conviction of more than a thousand people. The Justice Department focused particularly on Socialists, who criticized the war and the draft, and on radicals like the Industrial Workers of the World (see Chapter 17), whose attacks on militarism threatened to disrupt war production in the western lumber and copper industries. Socialist Party leader Eugene Debs was sentenced to ten years in jail for stating that the master classes declared war while the subject classes fought the battles. Victor Berger, a Milwaukee Socialist who had been jailed under the Espionage Act, was twice prevented from taking the seat to which he had been elected in the U.S. House of Representatives.

The courts rarely resisted these wartime excesses. In *Schenck v. United States* (1919), the Supreme Court upheld the conviction of the general secretary of the Socialist Party, Charles T. Schenck, who had been convicted of mailing pamphlets urging draftees to resist induction. In a unanimous decision Justice Oliver Wendell Holmes ruled that an act of speech uttered under circumstances that would "create a clear and present danger to the safety of the country" could be constitutionally restricted. Because of the national war emergency, then, the Court upheld limits on freedom of speech that would not have been acceptable in peacetime. In wartime, the drive for conformity reigned, dashing reformers' optimistic hopes that war could be what philosopher John Dewey had called a "plastic juncture," in which the country would be more open to progressive ideas.

An Unsettled Peace, 1919–1920

The war's end did not bring the tranquility Americans had hoped for. Demobilization proceeded with little planning, in part because Wilson was so preoccupied with the peacemaking process and his efforts to promote a league of nations. Spending only ten days in the United States between December 1918 and June 1919, for more than six months he was virtually an absentee president. Unfortunately, many urgent domestic issues demanded strong leadership that never emerged. In particular, racial, ethnic, and class tensions racked the nation as it attempted to adjust to a postwar order.

The Treaty of Versailles

President Wilson brought to the 1919 peace negotiations in France an almost missionary zeal. Confident in his own vision for a new world order, he believed that if necessary, "I can reach the peoples of Europe over the heads of their rulers," a belief encouraged by the wildly enthusiastic popular reception he received during his European tour. He scored an early victory when the Allies accepted his **Fourteen Points** as the basis for the peace negotiations that began in January 1919. In this blueprint for the postwar world, the president called for open diplomacy, "absolute freedom of navigation upon the seas," arms reduction, the removal of trade barriers, and an international commitment to **national self-determination**. Essential to Wilson's vision was the creation of a multinational organization "for the purpose of affording mutual guarantees of political independence and territorial integrity to great and small States alike." The League of Nations became Wilson's obsession.

The Fourteen Points were imbued with the spirit of progressivism. Widely distributed as propaganda during the final months of the war, Wilson's plan proposed to extend the ideals of America—democracy, freedom, and peaceful economic expansion—to the rest of the world. The League of Nations, acting as a kind of international Federal Trade Commission, would supervise disarmament and—according to the crucial Article X of its covenant—curb aggressor nations through collective military action. More grandiosely, Wilson anticipated that the league would mediate disputes between nations, preventing future wars, and thus ensuring that the Great War would be "the war to end all wars." By emphasizing these lofty goals, Wilson set the stage for disappointment: his ideals for world reformation proved too far-reaching to be practical or attainable.

Twenty-seven countries sent representatives to the peace conference in Versailles, near Paris. Distrustful of the new Bolshevik regime in Russia and its call for proletarian revolution against capitalism and imperialism, the Allies deliberately excluded its representatives. Nor was Germany invited. The Big Four—Wilson, Prime Minister David Lloyd George of Great Britain, Premier Georges Clemenceau of France, and Prime Minister Vittorio Orlando of Italy—did most of the negotiating. The three European leaders sought a peace that differed radically from Wilson's plan. They wanted to punish Germany and treat themselves to the spoils of war by demanding heavy reparations. In fact, before the war ended, Britain, France, and Italy had already made secret agreements to divide up the German colonies.

It is a tribute to Wilson that he managed to influence the peace settlement as much as he did. He was able to soften some of the harshest demands for reprisal against Germany. National self-determination, a fundamental principle of Wilson's Fourteen Points, bore fruit in the creation of the independent states of Austria, Hungary, Poland, Yugoslavia, and Czechoslovakia from the defeated empires of the Central Powers (Map 22.4). The establishment of the new nations of Finland, Estonia, Lithuania, and Latvia not only upheld the principle of self-determination but also served Wilson's (and the Allies') desire to isolate Soviet Russia from the rest of Europe.

Wilson had less success in achieving other goals. He won only limited concessions regarding the colonial empires of the defeated powers. The Central Powers' colonial empires in Africa, Asia, and the Middle East were dismantled, but instead of becoming independent countries the colonies were assigned to victorious Allied nations to administer as mandates, a far cry from Wilson's ideal of national self-determination. From these unstable and ultimately ungovernable regions, states like Iraq appeared, and Britain's Palestine Mandate, combined with the Balfour Declaration promising a "national home" for the Jews, would later reveal how difficult implementing self-determination could be. The Allies' refusal to consider a Japanese treaty provision vaguely affirming racial equality meant that the Japanese,

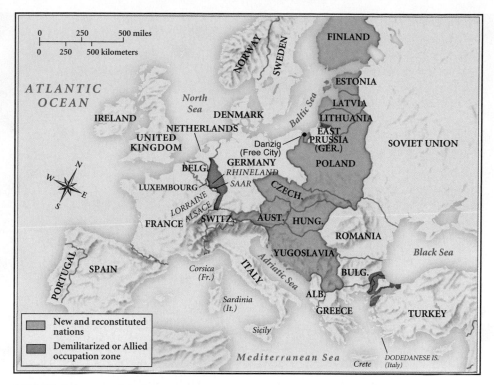

MAP 22.4 Europe after World War I

World War I and its aftermath dramatically altered the landscape of Europe, most notably with the reunification of countries such as Poland, Yugoslavia, and Czechoslovakia from territory of the defeated powers of Germany and Russia. Twenty years later, these new countries were the battlegrounds of the next world war.

like the Italians (disappointed not to receive some of the territories that became Yugoslavia), left the peace conference disappointed and ready to join Germany when war began again two decades later. Ho Chi Minh, the future revolutionary leader of Vietnam, also attended the conference in an attempt to secure the independence of his country from France, but he was not given an audience. Seemingly insignificant at the time, this would have grave consequences for France and the United States in the second half of the twentieth century (see Chapter 29). Certain topics, such as freedom of the seas and free trade, never even appeared on the agenda because of Allied resistance. Finally, Wilson had only partial success in scaling back French and British demands for reparations from Germany, which eventually were set at $33 billion.

In the face of these disappointments, Wilson consoled himself with the negotiators' commitment to his proposed League of Nations. He acknowledged that the peace treaty had defects but expressed confidence that they could be resolved by a permanent international organization dedicated to the peaceful resolution of disputes.

The Peace at Versailles

This painting by Sir William Orpen of the signing of the peace treaty in the Hall of Mirrors at
Versailles in June 1919 captures the solemnity of the occasion and the grandeur of the surroundings.
Wilson was justifiably proud of his role in the peace negotiations, but he faced strong opposition in
the Senate. Imperial War Museum, London.

On June 28, 1919, representatives gathered in the Hall of Mirrors at the Palace
of Versailles to sign the peace treaty. Wilson sailed home to a public enthusiastic
about a league of nations in principle. Major newspapers and the Federal Council
of Churches of Christ of America supported the treaty, and even an enemy of the
proposed league, Senator Henry Cabot Lodge of Massachusetts, acknowledged that
"[T]he people of the country are very naturally fascinated by the idea of eternal
preservation of the world's peace."

But by the time Wilson presented the agreement to the Senate on July 10, it was
clear that the treaty was in trouble, with support in the Senate being far short of the
two-thirds vote necessary for ratification. Wilson had not paid much attention to
the political realities of building support for the League of Nations and the treaty
in the Senate. He had failed to include a prominent Republican in the American
commission that represented the United States at Versailles. Stubbornly convinced
of his own rectitude and ability, he had kept the negotiations firmly in his own
hands. When the Senate balked at the treaty, Wilson adamantly refused to compromise.

"I shall consent to nothing," he told the French ambassador. "The Senate must take its medicine."

The Senate, however, did not oblige. And despite the president's attempt to make the 1918 congressional elections a referendum for his peace plans, Americans returned a Republican majority to Congress. Wilson and the league faced stiff opposition in the Senate. Some progressive senators, who endorsed the idea of American internationalism, felt that the peace agreement was too conservative, that it served to "validate existing empires" of the victorious Allies. The "irreconcilables," including progressive senators William E. Borah of Idaho, Hiram W. Johnson of California, and Robert M. La Follette of Wisconsin, disagreed fundamentally with the premise of permanent U.S. participation in European affairs. More influential was a group of Republicans led by Lodge. They proposed a list of amendments that focused on Article X, the section of the league covenant that called for **collective security** measures when a member nation was attacked. This provision, they argued, would restrict Congress's constitutional authority to declare war and would limit the freedom of the United States to pursue a unilateral foreign policy.

Wilson refused to budge, especially not to placate Lodge, his hated political rival. Hoping to mobilize support for the treaty, in September 1919 the president launched an extensive speaking tour during which he brought large audiences to tears with his impassioned defense of the treaty. But the strain proved too much, and the ailing sixty-two-year-old president collapsed in Pueblo, Colorado, late in September. One week later, in Washington, Wilson suffered a severe stroke that paralyzed one side of his body. While his wife, Edith Bolling Galt Wilson, his physician, and the various cabinet heads oversaw the routine business of government, Wilson slowly recovered, but he was never the same again.

From his sickbed Wilson remained inflexible in his refusal to compromise, ordering Democratic senators to vote against all Republican amendments. The treaty came up for a vote in November 1919 but was not ratified. When another attempt in March 1920 fell seven votes short, the issue was dead. Wilson died in 1924 "as much a victim of the war," David Lloyd George noted, "as any soldier who died in the trenches."

The United States never ratified the Versailles treaty or joined the League of Nations. Many wartime issues were only partially resolved, notably Germany's future, the fate of the colonial empires, and rising demands worldwide for national self-determination. These unsolved problems played a major role in the coming of World War II; some, like the competing ethnic nationalisms in the Balkans, remain unresolved today (see Chapters 26 and 31).

Racial Strife, Labor Unrest, and the Red Scare

Shortly after the end of the war, an author in the popular periodical *World's Work* observed that "the World War has accentuated all our differences. It has not created those differences, but it has revealed and emphasized them." These differences virtually exploded in the aftermath of war. Race riots exposed white resistance to the rising expectations of African Americans. Thousands of strikes signified class tensions, and a witch hunt for foreign radicals reflected anxieties about social order and the nation's ethnic pluralism.

Many African Americans emerged from the war determined to stand up for their rights, and they contributed to a spirit of black militancy that characterized the early 1920s. The volatile mix of black migration and raised expectations of blacks as a result of service in World War I combined to exacerbate white racism. In the South the number of lynchings rose from forty-eight in 1917 to seventy-eight in 1919. Several African American men were lynched while wearing military uniforms. In the North race riots broke out in more than twenty-five cities, with one of the first and most deadly occurring in 1917 in East St. Louis, Illinois, where nine whites and more than forty blacks died in a conflict sparked by competition over jobs at a defense plant.

By the summer of 1919, the death toll from racial violence had reached 120. One of the worst race riots in American history took place in Chicago in July, where five days of rioting left twenty-three blacks and fifteen whites dead. A variety of tensions were at work in cities where violence erupted. Black voters often determined the winners of close elections, thereby enraging white racists who resented black political influence. Blacks also competed with whites for jobs and scarce housing. Even before the July riot, blacks in Chicago had suffered the bombing of their homes and other forms of harassment. They did not sit meekly by as whites destroyed their neighborhoods: they fought back in self-defense and for their rights as citizens. Wilson's rhetoric about democracy and self-determination had raised their expectations, too.

Workers of all races harbored similar hopes for a better life after the war. The war years had brought them higher pay, shorter hours, and better working conditions. Yet many native-born Americans continued to identify unions with radicalism and foreigners, and soon after the armistice many employers resumed their attacks on union activity. In addition rapidly rising inflation—in 1919 the cost of living was 77 percent higher than its prewar level—threatened to wipe out workers' wage increases. Nevertheless, workers hoped to hold onto and perhaps even expand their wartime gains.

The result of workers' determination—and employers' resistance—was a dramatic wave of strikes. More than four million workers—one in every five—went on strike in 1919, a proportion never since equaled. The year began with a walkout by shipyard workers in Seattle, a strong union town. Their action spread into a general strike that crippled the city. Another hard-fought strike disrupted the steel industry when 350,000 steel workers demanded union recognition and an end to twelve-hour shifts and the seven-day workweek. And in the fall the Boston police force shocked many Americans by going on strike. Governor Calvin Coolidge of Massachusetts propelled himself into the political spotlight by declaring, "There is no right to strike against the public safety by anybody, anywhere, any time." Coolidge fired the entire police force, and the strike failed. The public supported this harsh reprisal, and Coolidge was rewarded with the Republican vice presidential nomination in 1920.

A crucial factor in organized labor's failure to win many of its strikes in the postwar period was the pervasive fear of radicalism. This concern coincided with mainstream Americans' long-standing anxiety about unassimilated immigrants—an anxiety the war had made worse. The Russian Revolution of 1917 so alarmed the Allies that Wilson sent several thousand troops to Russia in the summer of 1918 in hopes of weakening the Bolshevik regime. When the Bolsheviks founded the Third International (or Comintern) in 1919 to export Communist doctrine throughout the world, American fears deepened. As domestic labor unrest increased, Americans began to see radicals everywhere. Hatred of the German "Huns" was quickly replaced by hostility toward the Bolshevik Reds.

Ironically, as public concern about domestic Bolshevism increased, radicals were rapidly losing members and political power. No more than 70,000 Americans belonged to either the fledgling U.S. Communist Party or the Communist Labor Party in 1919. Both the IWW and the Socialist Party had been weakened by wartime repression and internal dissent. Yet the public and the press continued to blame almost every disturbance, especially labor conflicts, on alien radicals. "REDS DIRECTING SEATTLE STRIKE—TO TEST CHANCE FOR REVOLUTION," warned a typical newspaper headline.

Tensions mounted with a series of bombings in the early spring. "The word 'radical' in 1919," as one historian observed, "automatically carried with it the implication of dynamite." In June a bomb detonated outside the Washington townhouse of the recently appointed attorney general, A. Mitchell Palmer. His family escaped unharmed, but the bomber was blown to bits. Angling for the presidential nomination, Palmer capitalized on the event, fanning fears of domestic radicalism.

In November 1919, on the second anniversary of the Russian Revolution, the attorney general staged the first of what became known as "Palmer raids." Federal agents stormed the headquarters of radical organizations, capturing supposedly revolutionary booty such as a set of blueprints for a phonograph (at first thought to be sketches for a bomb). The dragnet pulled in thousands of aliens who had committed no crime but were suspect because of their anarchist or revolutionary beliefs or their immigrant backgrounds. Lacking the protection of U.S. citizenship, they faced deportation without formal trial or indictment. In December 1919 the USS *Buford*, nicknamed the "Soviet Ark," embarked for Finland and the Soviet state with a cargo of 294 deported radicals.

The peak of Palmer's power came with his New Year's raids in January 1920. In one night, with the greatest possible publicity, federal agents rounded up 6,000 radicals, invading private homes, union headquarters, and meeting halls, arresting citizens and aliens alike. Palmer was riding high in his ambitions for the presidency, but then he overstepped himself. He predicted that on May Day 1920 an unnamed conspiracy would attempt to overthrow the U.S. government. State militia units and police went on twenty-four-hour alert to guard the nation against the threat of revolutionary violence, but not a single incident occurred. As the summer of 1920 passed without major labor strikes or renewed bombings, the hysteria of the Red Scare began to abate.

The wartime legacy of antiradicalism and anti-immigrant sentiment, however, persisted well into the next decade. In May 1920, at the height of the Red Scare, Nicola Sacco, a shoemaker, and Bartolomeo Vanzetti, a fish peddler, were arrested for the robbery and murder of a shoe company's paymaster in South Braintree, Massachusetts. The two men, self-proclaimed anarchists and alien draft evaders, were both armed at the time of their arrest. Convicted in 1921, Sacco and Vanzetti sat on death row for six years while supporters appealed their verdicts. Although new evidence suggesting their innocence surfaced, Judge Webster Thayer denied a motion for a new trial. Scholars still debate the question of their guilt, but most agree that the two anarchists did not receive a fair trial. The verdict stemmed as much from their status as radicals and immigrants as it did from evidence. As future Supreme Court jurist Felix Frankfurter said at the time, "The District Attorney invoked against them a riot of political passion and patriotic sentiment."

The war—with its nationalistic emphasis on conformity—left racial, ethnic, and class tensions in its wake. But there were other legacies as well. World War I did not have the catastrophic effect on the United States that it did on European countries. With relatively few casualties and no physical destruction at home, America emerged from the conflict stronger than ever before. Consolidating developments that had begun with the Spanish-American War, the United States became a major international power, both economically and politically. Increased efficiency and technological advancements fostered exceptional industrial productivity, making the United States the envy of the rest of the world in the postwar decade.

T I M E L I N E

1914	Outbreak of war in Europe	1918	Wilson proposes Fourteen Points peace plan
	United States declares neutrality		Meuse-Argonne campaign
1915	German submarine sinks *Lusitania*		Eugene Debs imprisoned under Sedition Act
			Armistice ends war
1916	Woodrow Wilson reelected president		U.S. troops intervene in Russia
	Revenue Act of 1916	1919	Treaty of Versailles
	National Defense Act		Chicago race riot
1916– 1919	Height of "Great Migration" of blacks		Steel strike
			Red Scare and Palmer raids
1917	United States enters World War I		*Schenck v. United States*
	Selective Service Act		American Legion founded
	War Risk Insurance Act		League of Nations defeated in Senate
	War Industries Board established		Eighteenth Amendment (Prohibition) ratified
	Suffrage militancy		War Industries Board disbanded
	East St. Louis race riot	1920	Nineteenth Amendment (woman suffrage)
	Espionage Act		
	Bolshevik Revolution		Sacco and Vanzetti arrested
	Committee on Public Information established	1924	Woodrow Wilson dies

For Further Exploration

Meirion Harries and Susie Harries, *The Last Days of Innocence: America at War, 1917–1918* (1997), is a recent overview that admirably captures America's war experience at home and abroad. Jennifer D. Keene, *The United States and the First World War* (2000) provides an overview and a useful set of documents. Frank Freidel, *Over There: The Story of America's First Great Overseas Crusade* (1990), offers soldiers' vivid firsthand accounts of the war. William M. Tuttle Jr., *Race Riot: Chicago in the Red Summer of 1919* (1970), provides a moving and thoughtful analysis of that devastating riot, as well as a good summary of the "Great Migration" of African Americans. For the war in fiction begin with William March, *Company K* (1993), and Ernest Hemingway's *In Our Time* (1925) and *A Farewell to Arms* (1929). *Pale Horse, Pale Rider* (1939) by Katherine Anne Porter offers insight to the war on the home front.

The Library of Congress Web site, American Leaders Speak: Recordings from World War I and the 1920 Election, at <http://memory.loc.gov/ammem/nfhtml/>, offers voice recordings of General John J. Pershing and other key figures of the World War I era. The Diary of Bugler Benjamin Edgar Cruzan, Battery F, 341st Field Artillery, Eighty-ninth Division, Third Army, in which an ordinary soldier poignantly discusses his battle experiences, friendships, and the peace negotiations, is provided at <http://www2.mo-net.com/~mcruzan/diary.htm>.

The South Texas Border, 1900–1920, available through the Library of Congress Web site, offers the Robert Runyon Photograph Collection of the South Texas Border Area, which is a collection of over 8,000 items pertaining to the lower Rio Grande Valley in the early part of the twentieth century. Of particular relevance to this chapter is the material on the border in the years surrounding World War I. Access it at <http://memory.loc.gov/ammem/award97/txuhtml/runhome.html>. World War I Documents Archive, at <http://www.lib.byu.edu/~rdh/wwi>, provides extensive primary documents as well as a series of World War I links. The Public Broadcasting Service's The Great War and the Shaping of the Twentieth Century, at <http://www.pbs.org/greatwar/index.html>, is a companion to the documentary series. Its rich offerings, which emphasize the European context of the war, include bibliographies and maps.

For definitions of key terms boldfaced in this chapter, see the glossary at the end of the book.

To assess your mastery of the material covered in this chapter, see the Online Study Guide at **bedfordstmartins.com/henrettaconcise**.

For map resources and primary documents, see **bedfordstmartins.com/henrettaconcise**.

Chapter 23

MODERN TIMES: THE 1920s

> Modern life is everywhere complicated, but especially so in the
> United States. . . . The tendency to seize upon new types of machines,
> rich natural resources and vast driving power, have hurried us dizzily
> away from the days of the frontier into a whirl of modernisms which
> almost passes belief.
>
> Report of the President's Commission
on Recent Social Trends, 1933

In 1924 sociologists Robert Lynd and Helen Merrell Lynd arrived in Muncie, Indiana, to study the life of a small American city. They observed how the citizens of Middletown (the fictional name they gave the city) made a living, maintained a home, educated their young, practiced their religion, organized community activities, and spent their leisure time. As the Lynds' fieldwork proceeded, they were struck by how much had changed over the past thirty-five years—the lifetime of a middle-aged Middletown resident—and decided to contrast the Muncie of the 1890s with the Muncie of the 1920s. When *Middletown* was published in 1929, this "study in modern American culture" became an unexpected best-seller. Its success spoke to Americans' desire to understand the forces that were transforming their society.

This transformation began with World War I. The United States emerged from the war as a powerful modern state and a major player in the world economy. The 1920s, however, rather than World War I were the watershed in the development of a mass national culture. Only then did the Protestant work ethic and the old values of self-denial and frugality begin to give way to the fascination with consumption, leisure, and self-realization that is the essence of modern American culture. At the same time, Americans also grappled with other "modern" issues, especially the implications of racial, ethnic, and religious pluralism. In economic organization, political outlook, and cultural values, the 1920s had more in common with the United States today than with the industrializing America of the late nineteenth century.

Business-Government Partnership of the 1920s

The business-government partnership fostered by World War I continued on an informal basis throughout the 1920s. As the *Wall Street Journal* enthusiastically proclaimed, "Never before, here or anywhere else, has a government been so completely fused with business." While the *Journal* exaggerated the fusion, it did convey the way in which business interests powerfully influenced public policy. From 1922 to 1929 the nation's prosperity seemed to confirm the economy's ability to regulate itself with minimal government intervention. Gone, or at least submerged, was the reform impulse of the Progressive Era, and business leaders were no longer considered villains, at least in the growing national media, but were respected public figures.

Politics in the Republican "New Era"

Except for Woodrow Wilson's two terms, the Republican Party had controlled the presidency since 1896. When Wilson's progressive coalition floundered in 1918, the Republicans seized their chance to regain the White House. With the ailing Wilson out of the picture, in the 1920 election the Democrats nominated Governor James M. Cox of Ohio for president and Assistant Secretary of the Navy Franklin D. Roosevelt as vice president. The Democratic platform called for U.S. participation in the League of Nations and a continuation of Wilson's progressivism. The Republicans, led by Warren G. Harding and Calvin Coolidge, promised a return to "normalcy," which meant a strong probusiness stance and conservative cultural values. Reflecting many Americans' desire to put the war and the stresses of 1919 behind them, voters rejected the party in power. Harding and Coolidge won in a landslide, marking the solidification of a Republican dominance that would last until 1932.

Central to what Republicans termed the "New Era" was business-government cooperation. Although Republican administrations generally opposed expanding state power to promote progressive reforms, they had no qualms about using federal power to assist corporations. Thus Harding's secretary of the treasury, financier Andrew W. Mellon, engineered a tax cut that undermined the wartime Revenue Acts, thereby benefiting wealthy individuals and corporations. The Republican-dominated Federal Trade Commission (FTC) generally ignored the Progressive Era antitrust laws rather than use federal power to police industry.

Perhaps the best example of government-business cooperation emerged in the Department of Commerce, headed by Herbert Hoover. Hoover thought that with the offer of government assistance, businessmen would voluntarily run their enterprises in ways that would benefit the public interest, thereby helping the entire country. Under Hoover the Commerce Department expanded dramatically, offering new services like the compilation and distribution of trade and production statistics to American business. It also assisted private trade associations in their efforts to rationalize and make more efficient major sectors of industry and commerce by using such tools as product standardization and wage and price controls.

Unfortunately, not all government-business cooperation was as high-minded as Hoover had anticipated. Many of Harding's political associates turned out to be dishonest and corrupt. When Harding died suddenly of a heart attack in San Francisco in August 1923, evidence of widespread fraud and corruption in his administration had just come to light. In 1924 a particularly damaging scandal concerned the secret leasing of government oil reserves in Teapot Dome, Wyoming, and in Elk Hills, California, without competitive bidding. Secretary of the Interior Albert Fall was eventually convicted of taking $300,000 in bribes; he became the first cabinet officer in American history to serve a prison sentence.

After Harding's death, the taciturn vice president, Calvin Coolidge, moved into the White House. In contrast to his predecessor's political cronyism and outgoing style, Coolidge personified an austere rectitude. As vice president "Silent Cal" often sat through official functions without uttering a word. A dinner partner once challenged him by saying, "Mr. Coolidge, I've made a rather sizable bet with my friends that I can get you to speak three words this evening." Responded Coolidge icily, "You lose." Although Coolidge was quiet and unimaginative, his image of unimpeachable integrity reassured voters, and he soon announced his candidacy for the presidency in 1924.

When the Democrats gathered that July in the sweltering heat of New York City, they faced a divided party that drew its support mainly from the South and from northern urban political machines like Tammany Hall in New York. These two constituencies often collided. They disagreed mightily over Prohibition, immigration restriction, and most seriously, the mounting power of the resurgent racist and anti-immigrant Ku Klux Klan (Map 23.1). The resolutions committee remained deadlocked for days over whether the party should condemn the Klan, eventually reaching a weak compromise that affirmed its general opposition to "any effort to arouse religious or racial dissension."

With this contentious background, the convention took 103 ballots to nominate John W. Davis, a Wall Street lawyer, for the presidency. To attract rural voters the Democrats chose as their vice presidential candidate Governor Charles W. Bryan of Nebraska, William Jennings Bryan's brother. But the Democrats could not mount an effective challenge to their more popular and better-financed Republican rivals, whose strength came chiefly from the native-born Protestant middle class, augmented by small-business people, skilled workers, farmers, northern blacks, and wealthy industrialists.

The 1924 campaign also featured a third-party challenge by Senator Robert M. La Follette of Wisconsin, who ran on the Progressive Party ticket. La Follette's candidacy mobilized reformers and labor leaders as well as disgruntled farmers in an effort to reinvigorate the reform movement both major parties had abandoned. Their platform called for nationalization of railroads, public ownership of utilities, and the right of Congress to overrule Supreme Court decisions. It also favored the direct election of the president by the voters rather than by indirect election through the electoral college.

In an impressive Republican victory, Coolidge received 15.7 million popular votes to Davis's 8.4 million and won a decisive margin in the electoral college. La Follette chalked up almost 5 million popular votes, but he carried only Wisconsin in the electoral college. Perhaps the most significant aspect of the election was the low voter turnout. Only 52 percent of the electorate cast their ballots in 1924, compared to more than 70 percent in presidential elections of the late nineteenth century.

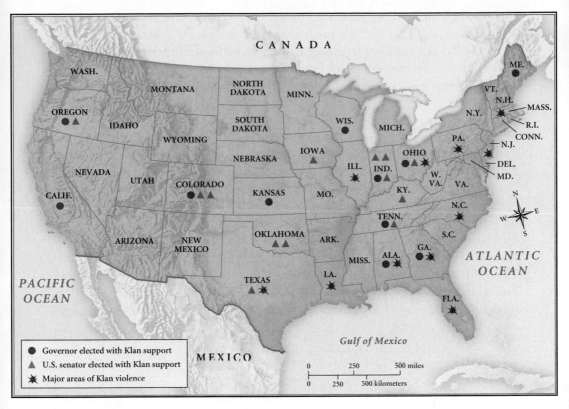

MAP 23.1 Ku Klux Klan Politics and Violence in the 1920s

Unlike the Reconstruction-era Klan, the Klan of the 1920s was geographically dispersed, achieving substantial strength in the West and Midwest. Although the Klan is often thought of as a rural movement, some of its strongest "klaverns" were in such cities as Chicago, Los Angeles, Atlanta, and Detroit. The organization's violence included vigilante acts, but small Klan riots also erupted in many communities where ethnic tensions led to confrontations between Klansmen and their opponents.

Newly enfranchised women voters were not to blame, however; a long-term drop in voting by men, rather than apathy among women, caused the decline.

After their suffrage victory, women activists continued their political involvement. In the 1920s African American women struggled for voting rights in the Jim Crow South and pushed unsuccessfully for a federal antilynching law. Many women tried to break into party politics, but Democrats and Republicans granted them only token positions on party committees. Women were more influential as lobbyists. The Women's Joint Congressional Committee, a Washington-based coalition of ten major white women's organizations, including the newly formed League of Women Voters, lobbied actively for reform legislation. Its major accomplishment was the passage in 1921 of the Sheppard-Towner Federal Maternity and Infancy Act, which appropriated $1.25 million for well-baby clinics, educational programs, and visiting nurse projects. Such major reform legislation was rare in the 1920s, however, and its success was short-lived. The Sheppard-Towner Act had passed in part because politicians feared that if it did not go through, women would vote them out of office. Once politicians realized that women did not vote as a bloc, they stopped listening to the women's lobby, and in 1929 Congress cut off the act's funding.

The roadblocks women activists faced were part of a broader public antipathy to ambitious reforms. Although some states—such as New York, where an urban liberalism was coalescing under leaders like Al Smith—did enact a flurry of legislation that promoted workmen's compensation, public-health programs, and conservation measures, on the national level reforms that would strengthen federal power made little headway. After years of progressive reforms and an expanded federal presence in World War I, Americans were unenthusiastic about increased taxation or more governmental bureaucracy. The Red Scare had given ammunition to opponents of reform by making it easy to claim that legislation calling for governmental activism was the first step toward Bolshevism. The general prosperity of the 1920s further hampered the reform spirit. With a strong economy, the Republican policy of an informal partnership between business and government seemed to work and made reforms regulating corporations and the economy seem unnecessary and even harmful.

The Economy

Although prosperity and the 1920s appear synonymous, the decade got off to a bumpy start in the transition from a wartime to a peacetime economy. In the immediate postwar years, the nation suffered rampant inflation: prices jumped by a third in 1919, accompanied by feverish business activity. Then in 1920 and 1921, the United States experienced a recession that was the sharpest short-term downturn the United States had ever faced. Unemployment reached 10 percent. Foreign trade dropped by almost half as European nations resumed production after the disruptions of war. Prices fell dramatically—more than 20 percent—and reversed much of the wartime inflation.

In 1922, stimulated by an abundance of consumer products, particularly automobiles, the economy began a recovery that continued with only brief interruptions through 1929. Between 1922 and 1929 the gross domestic product (GDP) grew from $74.1 billion to $103.1 billion, approximately 40 percent. Per capita income rose from $641 in 1921 to $847 in 1929. Soon the federal government was recording a budget surplus. This economic expansion provided the backdrop for the partnership between business and government.

As industries churned out an abundance of new consumer products—cars, appliances, chemicals, electricity, radios, aircraft, and movies—manufacturing output expanded 64 percent. Behind the growth lay new techniques of management and mass production, which brought a 40 percent increase in workers' productivity. The demand for goods and services kept unemployment low in most industries throughout the decade. High employment rates combined with low inflation enhanced the spending power of many Americans, especially skilled workers and the middle class.

The economy had some weaknesses, however. Income distribution reflected significant disparity: 5 percent of the nation's families received one-third of all income. In addition a number of industries were unhealthy. Agriculture never fully recovered from the 1920 and 1921 recession. During the inflationary period of 1914 to 1920, farmers had borrowed heavily to finance mortgages and equipment in response to government incentives, increased demand, and rising prices. When the war ended, European countries resumed agricultural production, glutting the world market and slashing the prices of agricultural products. Farmers were not the only ones whose incomes plunged. Certain "sick industries," such as coal and textiles, had also expanded in response to wartime demand, which dropped sharply at war's end. Their troubles foreshadowed the Great Depression of the 1930s.

But for the most part, despite these ominous signs, the nation was in a confident mood about the economy and the corporations that shaped it. Throughout the decade business leaders enjoyed enormous popularity and respect; their reputations often surpassed those of the era's lackluster politicians. The most revered businessman of the decade was Henry Ford, whose rise from poor farm boy to corporate giant embodied both the traditional value of individualism and the triumph of mass production. Success stories like Ford's prompted President Calvin Coolidge to declare solemnly, "The man who builds a factory builds a temple. The man who works there worships there."

This apotheosis of big business was accompanied by a vigorous trend toward consolidation. There were more mergers in the 1920s than at any time since the flourishing of business combinations in the 1880s and 1890s, with the largest number occurring in rapidly growing industries such as chemical, electrical appliance, and automobile manufacturing. By 1930 the 200 largest corporations controlled almost half the nonbanking corporate wealth in the United States. Rarely did any single corporation monopolize an entire industry; instead, oligopolies, in which a few large producers controlled an industry, became the norm, as in auto manufacturing, oil, and steel. The nation's financial institutions expanded and consolidated along with its corporations. In 1929 almost half the nation's banking resources were controlled by 1 percent of American banks, a mere 250 depositories.

Most Americans benefited from corporate success in the 1920s. Although unskilled African Americans and immigrants participated far less fully in the prosperity of the decade, many members of the working class enjoyed higher wages and a better standard of living. A shorter workweek (five full days and a half day on Saturday) and paid vacations gave many more leisure time. But in the workplace itself, labor had less power (see Voices from Abroad, "The Ford Miracle: 'Slaves' to the Assembly Line," p. 698). Scientific management techniques, first introduced in 1895 by Frederick W. Taylor but widely implemented only in the 1920s, reduced workers' control over their labor.

VOICES FROM ABROAD

The Ford Miracle: "Slaves" to the Assembly Line

During the 1920s many foreign observers came to the United States to witness firsthand the drama of mass production industries, particularly the Ford plant at Rouge River and what was often termed "the Ford miracle." While most observers commented approvingly on the impressive advances Americans had made in manufacturing, some were critical. Australian journalist Hugh Grant Adams, traveling with a delegation of trade unionists from his own country, offered a scathing attack on American mass production industries for the way in which they undermined the skill and power of workers. In this passage from An Australian Looks at America, *he paints a depressing picture of work on the motorcar assembly line.*

At 8 A.M. the worker takes his place at the side of a narrow platform down the centre of which runs a great chain moving at the rate of a foot a minute. His tool is an electrically-driven riveter. As he stands, riveter poised, the half-built framework of the car passes slowly in front of him. On the opposite side of the chain, one foot farther up the line, a workman with a long pair of tongs has slipped two red-hot bolts through two holes that seem to be just always there. Once, twice, he plunges the riveter down upon the hot metal . . . once, twice . . . once, twice. . . . And so on for six, eight or ten hours, whatever the rule of the factory may be, day after day, year after year—if he can keep the job.

There is not a job on the mass-production chain more complicated technically than that. The chain never stops. The pace never varies. The man is part of the chain, the feeder and the slave of it. He must keep going—always the same action and always at the same speed—or the chain would jam, and he would be execrated all along the line; for each man is paid not according to what he himself does, but according to the progress of the chain. If one man holds up the chain every man in the line loses wages. . . .

What a happy circumstance for industry! Here we find the manufacture of the most ingenious products of human skill demanding no skill in the making, able to continue, and able to develop indefinitely without asking or paying for more than the mere ability to lift a hammer or turn a screw or drive a nail. Out of every hundred workers in these industries, ninety are denied the opportunity to give more than that—and this in a country that, having practically closed its doors against fresh supplies of raw labour, is preaching and teaching individualism, the ambition to push ahead, and the shame of staying the rut.

America cannot have it both ways. . . .

SOURCE: Hugh Grant Adams, *An Australian Looks at America: Are Wages Really Higher?* (Sydney, Australia: Cornstalk Publishing Co, 1927), 21–23.

The 1920s were also the heyday of **welfare capitalism**, a system of labor relations that stressed management's responsibility for employees' well-being. At a time when unemployment compensation and government-sponsored pensions did not exist, large corporations offered workers stock plans, health insurance, and old-age pension plans. Employee security was not, however, the primary aim of these programs.

Deterring the formation of unions was. The approach reflected the conservative values of the 1920s, which placed the responsibility for economic welfare in the private sector to avoid government interference on the side of labor. Coupled with an aggressive drive for what corporate leaders called the American Plan (or an open, nonunion shop) and with Supreme Court decisions that limited workers' ability to strike, welfare capitalism helped to erode the unions' strength. Membership dropped from 5.1 million in 1920 to 3.6 million in 1929—about 10 percent of the nonagricultural workforce—and the number of strikes also fell dramatically from the level in 1919. Technology and management had combined to undermine workers' power, and unions would find it increasingly difficult to secure a foothold in American industry.

Economic Expansion Abroad

The power of American corporations emerged also in the international arena. During the 1920s the United States was the most productive country in the world, with an enormous capacity to compete in foreign markets that eagerly desired American consumer products such as radios, telephones, automobiles, and sewing machines. The demand for U.S. capital was just as great. American investment abroad more than doubled between 1919 and 1930: by the end of the 1920s, American corporations had invested $15.2 billion in foreign countries. Soon the United States became the world's largest creditor nation, reversing its pre–World War I status as a debtor and causing a dramatic shift of power in the world's capital markets.

American power abroad was also evident in the country's new role as a creditor nation. European countries, particularly Germany, needed American capital to finance their economic recovery following World War I. Germany had to rebuild its economy and pay reparations to the Allies; Britain and France had to repay wartime loans. As late as 1930 the Allies still owed the United States $4.3 billion. American political leaders, responding to voters' disenchantment with the cost of the war, rigidly demanded payment. "They hired the money, didn't they?" President Coolidge scoffed.

European countries had difficulty repaying their debts because the United States was maintaining high protective tariffs against foreign-made goods. The Fordney-McCumber Tariff of 1922 and the Hawley-Smoot Tariff of 1930 advanced the long-standing Republican policy of protectionism and economic nationalism. Most American manufacturers favored high tariffs because they feared foreign competition would reduce their profits. But the difficulty of selling goods in the United States hindered European nations' efforts to pay off their debts in dollars.

In 1924, at the prodding of the United States, the nations of France, Great Britain, and Germany joined with the United States in a plan to promote European financial stability. The Dawes Plan (named for Charles G. Dawes, the Chicago banker who negotiated the agreement) offered Germany substantial loans from American banks and a reduction in the amount of reparations owed to the Allies.

Bananas

... a good mixer
with every fruit that grows

Oranges, apples, grapefruit, pineapples, pears, melons, grapes—all these and many others—blend perfectly with bananas. The distinctive flavor of the banana, when added to a fruit cup, a fruit salad, or any fruit combination, brings out the flavor of the other fruits and makes them taste better.

"Ripe bananas are good for little children."

"EAT plenty of fresh fruits" is now an accepted principle of diet—and the mere sight of mellow, luscious bananas is an invitation to serve many delicious and nourishing fruit combinations.

All year round from the tropics ... Easter, Fourth of July, Thanksgiving, Christmas—every season, every day—bananas are available. Thanks to the nearness and all-year-round productiveness of the tropics, they always can be had at your grocery or fruit store.

Children crave the temptingly flavored banana instinctively. And it is well that they do, for bananas are one of the most important energy-producing foods. Doctors and dietitians consider the banana not only one of the most valuable foods, but also one of the most easily digested ... as beneficial for grown-ups as for children.

Serve bananas with other fruits, with cereals, with milk or cream ... or serve them plain. But always be sure they are fully ripe (generously flecked with brown spots). If they are not at the proper stage of ripeness when you buy them, let them ripen at room temperature. Never place them in the ice-box.

UNIFRUIT   BANANAS
Reg. U. S. Pat. Off.
A United Fruit Company Product
Imported and Distributed by Fruit Dispatch Company
17 Battery Place, New York, N. Y.

American Companies Abroad

United Fruit was one of the many American companies that found opportunities for investment in South America in the 1920s and as a result introduced "new" foods to the United States. Bananas were such an exotic fruit that advertisements had to tell consumers such facts as how to tell when bananas were ripe and never to put them in the icebox. Duke University Library, Special Collections.

But the Dawes Plan did not provide a permanent solution because the international economic system was inherently unstable. It depended on the flow of American capital to Germany, reparations payments from Germany to the Allies, and the repayment of the Allies' debts to the United States. If the outflow of capital from the United States were to slow or stop, the international financial structure could collapse.

American efforts to shore up the international economy belie the common view of U.S. foreign affairs as **isolationist** in the interwar period—as representing a time when the United States, disillusioned after World War I, willfully retreated from involvement in the rest of the world. In fact the United States played an active role in world affairs during this period. Expansion into new markets was fundamental to the prosperity of the 1920s. U.S. officials ardently sought a stable international order to facilitate American investments in Latin American, European, and Asian markets.

A wide variety of American companies aggressively sought investment opportunities abroad. General Electric built plants in Latin America, China, Japan, and Australia; Ford had major facilities throughout the British empire. The United Fruit Company developed plantations in Costa Rica, Honduras, and Guatemala. American capital ran sugar plantations in Cuba and rubber plantations in the Philippines, Sumatra, and Malaya. Standard Oil of New Jersey led American oil companies in acquiring petroleum reserves in Mexico and Venezuela.

The United States continued the quest for peaceful ways to dominate the Western Hemisphere both economically and diplomatically. Policy retreated slightly from the military intervention in Latin America that had become common in the early twentieth century, when the United States stepped in to quell civil unrest and to deter European interference in the region. U.S. troops occupied the Dominican Republic between 1916 and 1924 and remained in Nicaragua almost continuously from 1912 to 1933 and in Haiti from 1915 to 1934. Relations with Mexico remained tense, a legacy of U.S. intervention during the Mexican Revolution (see Chapter 21) and of U.S. resentment over the Mexican government's efforts to wrest control of its oil and mineral deposits away from foreign owners, a policy that particularly alarmed American petroleum companies.

There was little popular or political support, however, for formal diplomatic commitments to allies, European or otherwise. The United States never joined the League of Nations or the Court of International Justice (the World Court). International cooperation came through other forums, such as the 1921 Washington Naval Arms Conference. At that meeting the leading naval powers—Britain, the United States, Japan, Italy, and France—agreed to halt construction of large battleships for ten years and to limit their future shipbuilding to a set ratio among the five nations. By placing limits on naval expansion, policymakers hoped to encourage stability in areas like the Far East and to protect the fragile postwar economy from an expensive arms race. A thinly veiled agenda was to contain Japan, whose expansionist tendencies in Asia were alarming other nations.

Seven years later, in a similar spirit of international cooperation, the United States joined the world community in condemning militarism through the Kellogg-Briand Peace Pact. Fifteen nations signed the pact in Paris in 1928; forty-eight more approved it later. The signatories agreed to "condemn recourse to war for the solution of international controversies, and renounce it as an instrument of national policy." U.S. peace groups—such as the Women's International League for Peace and Freedom—enthusiastically supported the pact, and the U.S. Senate ratified it eighty-five to one. Yet critics complained that it lacked mechanisms for enforcement, calling it nothing more than an "international kiss."

In the end, fervent hopes and pious declarations were no cure for the massive economic, political, and territorial problems created by World War I. U.S. policy-makers vacillated, as they would in the 1930s, between wanting to play a larger role in world events and fearing that treaties and responsibilities would limit their ability to act unilaterally. Their diplomatic efforts ultimately proved inadequate to the mounting crises that followed in the wake of the war.

A New National Culture

The 1920s represented an important watershed in the development of a mass national culture. A new emphasis on leisure, consumption, and amusement characterized the era. Automobiles, paved roads, the parcel post service, movies, radios, telephones, mass-circulation magazines, brand names, chain stores—all linked mill towns in the southern Piedmont, rural outposts on the Oklahoma plains, and ethnic enclaves on the coasts in an expanding web of national experience. In fact, with the exportation of automobiles, radios, and movies to consumers throughout the world, American culture became a global model.

A Consumer Culture

In homes across the country, Americans sat down to a breakfast of Kellogg's corn flakes and toast from a General Electric toaster. Then they got into a Ford Model T to go about their business, perhaps shopping at one of the chain stores that had sprung up across the country, such as Safeway or A&P. In the evening the family gathered to listen to radio programs like *Great Moments in History* or to read the latest issue of the *Saturday Evening Post*; on weekends they might go to see the newest Charlie Chaplin film at the local theater. Millions of Americans, in other words, now shared similar daily experiences.

Yet participation in commercial mass culture was not universal, nor did it necessarily mean total conversion to mainstream values, as is often assumed. The historian Lizabeth Cohen concluded that "Chicago's ethnic workers were not transformed into more Americanized, middle-class people by the objects they consumed. Buying an electric vacuum cleaner did not turn Josef Dobrowolski into *True Story*'s Jim Smith." What is more, the unequal distribution of income limited many consumers' ability to buy the enticing new products. At the height of the nation's prosperity in the 1920s, about 65 percent of families had incomes of less than $2,000 a year, which barely supported a decent standard of living. Poor minority families in particular were isolated from the new consumerism. Many Americans stretched their incomes by buying on the newly devised installment plan that allowed people to purchase such items as cars, radios, refrigerators, and sewing machines "on time." "A dollar down and a dollar forever," a cynic remarked.

Many of the new products were household appliances made feasible by the rapid electrification that had reached 85 percent of American nonfarm households by 1930. Such technological advances had a dramatic impact on women's lives, especially prosperous white women. Despite enfranchisement and participation in the workforce, the primary role for most women remained that of housewife. Electric appliances made housewives' chores less arduous, but paradoxically, the new products did not dramatically increase women's leisure time. Instead, more middle-class housewives began to do their own housework and laundry, replacing human servants with electric ones. The new gadgets also raised standards of cleanliness, encouraging women to spend more time doing household chores.

Few of the new consumer products could be considered necessities, so the advertising industry spent billions of dollars to entice consumers to buy their products. Increasingly sophisticated advertisements appealed to people's social aspirations by projecting images of successful and elegant sophisticates who smoked a certain brand of cigarettes or drove a recognizable make of car. Ad writers also sold products by preying on people's insecurities, coming up with a variety of socially unacceptable "diseases," such as the dreaded "B.O." (body odor).

Yet consumers were not merely passive victims. Recognizing that the buying public made choices, advertisers struggled to offer messages that appealed to their targeted audiences. In the process they made consumption a cultural ideal for most of the middle class. Character, religion, and social standing, once the main criteria for judging self-worth, became less important than the gratification of personal desires through the acquisition of more and better possessions.

No possession typified the new consumer culture better than the automobile. "Why on earth do you need to study what's changing this country?" a Muncie, Indiana, resident asked sociologists Robert and Helen Lynd. "I can tell you what's happening in just four letters: A-U-T-O!" The showpiece of modern capitalism, the automobile revolutionized the way Americans spent their money and leisure time. In the wake of the automobile, the isolation of rural life broke down. Cars touched so many aspects of American life that the word *automobility* was coined to describe their impact on production methods, the landscape, and American values.

Mass production of cars stimulated the prosperity of the 1920s. Before the introduction of the moving assembly line in 1913, Ford workers took twelve and a half hours to put together an auto; on an assembly line they took only ninety-three minutes. By 1927 Ford was producing a car every twenty-four seconds. Auto sales climbed from 1.5 million in 1921 to 5 million in 1929, a year in which Americans spent $2.58 billion on cars. By the end of the decade, Americans owned about 80 percent of the world's automobiles—an average of one car for every five people.

The success of the auto industry had a ripple effect on the American economy. In 1929, 3.7 million workers owed their jobs to the automobile, either directly or indirectly. Auto production stimulated the steel, petroleum, chemical, rubber, and glass industries. Highway construction became a billion-dollar-a-year enterprise, financed by federal subsidies and state gasoline taxes. Car ownership also spurred the growth of suburbs, contributed to real estate speculation, and in 1924 spawned the first shopping center, Country Club Plaza in Kansas City.

The auto also changed the way Americans spent their leisure time. They took to the roads, becoming a nation of tourists. The American Automobile Association, founded in 1902, reported that in 1929 about 45 million people—almost a third of the population—took vacations by automobile, patronizing the "autocamps" and tourist cabins that were the forerunners of motels. And like movies and other products of the new mass culture, cars changed the dating patterns of young Americans. Contrary to many parents' views, premarital sex was not invented in the backseat of a Ford, but a Model T offered more privacy and comfort than did the family living room or the front porch and contributed to increased sexual experimentation among the young.

Mass Media and New Patterns of Leisure

Equal in importance to the automobile in transforming American culture were the increasingly significant mass media. The movie industry probably did more than anything else to disseminate common values and attitudes. American movies had their roots in the turn-of-the-century nickelodeons, where for a nickel the mostly working-class audience could see a one-reel silent film. Because the films, mostly comedies and melodramas, were silent, they could be understood by immigrants who did not speak English. Both democratic and highly lucrative, the new medium quickly became popular. By 1910 the moviemaking industry had concentrated in southern California, which had cheap land, plenty of sunshine, and varied scenery—mountains, deserts, cities, and the Pacific Ocean—within easy reach. Another attraction was Los Angeles's reputation as an antiunion town. By World War I's end the United States was producing 90 percent of the world's films.

As directors turned to feature films and began exhibiting them in large, ornate theaters, movies quickly outgrew their working-class audiences and began to appeal to the middle class. Early movie stars, including Buster Keaton, Charlie Chaplin, Mary Pickford, and Douglas Fairbanks, became idols who helped to set national trends in clothing and hairstyles. Then a new cultural icon, the flapper, burst on the scene to represent emancipated womanhood. Clara Bow was Hollywood's favorite flapper, a bobbed-hair "jazz baby" who rose to stardom almost overnight. Decked out in short skirt and rolled-down silk stockings, the flapper wore makeup (once assumed to be a sign of sexual availability in lower-class women), smoked, and danced to jazz, flaunting her liberated lifestyle. Like so many cultural icons, the flapper represented only a tiny minority of women. Yet the movies, along with advertising, mass marketed this symbol of women's emancipation, suggesting it was the norm.

Movies became even more powerful cultural influences with the advent of the "talkies." Warner Brothers' *The Jazz Singer* (1927), starring Al Jolson, was the first feature-length film to offer sound. Two years later all the major studios had made the transition to "talkies." By the end of the 1920s, the nation had almost 23,000 movie theaters, including elaborate picture palaces built by the studios in major cities. Movie attendance rose from 60 million in 1927 to 90 million in 1930. In two short decades movies had become thoroughly entrenched as the most popular— and probably the most influential—form of urban-based mass media.

That the first talkie was *The Jazz Singer* was perhaps no coincidence. Jazz was such an important part of the new mass culture that the 1920s are often referred to as the Jazz Age. An improvisational style whose notes were (and are) rarely written down, jazz originated in the dance halls and bordellos of New Orleans around the turn of the century. A synthesis of African American music forms, such as ragtime and the blues, it also drew on African and European styles. Most of the early jazz musicians were blacks who brought music that originated in the South to Chicago, New York, and other northern cities. Some of the best-known performers were composer-pianist Ferdinand "Jelly Roll" Morton, trumpeter Louis Armstrong, composer-bandleader Edward "Duke" Ellington, and singer Bessie Smith.

Although Smith was known as the "Empress of the Blues," numerous other women—Ida Cox, Ma Rainey, Mamie Smith, and Ethel Waters among them—also made a name for themselves singing the blues and bringing a modern form of this rural music to a broader audience. While many of their songs described a woman lamenting the man "who done her wrong," others, like "Young Woman's Blues," exuberantly expressed women's enjoyment of sexuality as well as their resilience and desire for personal autonomy in the face of harsh circumstances. As they performed in urban clubs or makeshift rural honky-tonks, showing off elaborate gowns as well as their musical talent, blues women offered a glamorous image of successful black womanhood that belied the difficult lives that many of them experienced.

Phonograph records increased the appeal of jazz and the blues by capturing its spontaneity and distributing it to a wide audience; jazz, in turn, boosted the infant recording industry. Soon this uniquely American art form had caught on in Europe, especially in France. That jazz, which often expressed black dissent in the face of mainstream white values, also appealed to white audiences signifies the role that African Americans played in shaping the contours of American popular culture— a role that would continue to increase in the twentieth century.

Other forms of mass media also helped to establish national standards of taste and behavior. In 1922 ten magazines claimed a circulation of at least 2.5 million, including the *Saturday Evening Post*, the *Ladies' Home Journal*, and *Good Housekeeping*. Tabloid newspapers, which were half the size of standard papers and highlighted crime, sports, comics, and scandals, also became part of the national scene. Thanks to syndicated newspaper columns and features, people across the United States could read the same articles. They could also read the same books, preselected by a board of expert judges for the Book-of-the-Month Club, founded in 1926.

The newest instrument of mass culture, professional radio broadcasting, took off on November 2, 1920, when station KDKA in Pittsburgh carried the presidential

CRAZY BLUES

By PERRY BRADFORD

Get this number for your phonograph on Okeh Record No. 4169

PUBLISHED BY
PERRY BRADFORD
MUSIC PUB. CO.
1547 BROADWAY, N. Y. C.

All That Jazz

The phonograph dramatically expanded the popularity and market for jazz recordings like this one by Mamie Smith and her Jazz Hounds. The success of "Crazy Blues" convinced record companies that there was a market to be tapped in black communities for what were called "race records," and Mamie Smith skyrocketed to fame with this 1920 recording.

Division of Political History, Smithsonian Institution, Washington, DC.

election returns. By 1929 about 40 percent of the nation's households owned a radio. More than 800 stations, most affiliated with the Columbia Broadcasting Service (CBS) or the National Broadcasting Company (NBC), were on the air. Unlike European networks, which were government monopolies, American radio stations operated for profit. Though the federal government licensed the stations, their revenue came primarily from advertisers and corporate sponsors.

The automobile and new forms of entertainment like movies and radio pointed to a new emphasis on leisure. As the workweek shrank and some workers won the right to paid vacations, Americans had more time and energy to spend on recreation. Like so much else in the 1920s, leisure became increasingly tied to consumption and mass culture. Public recreation flourished as cities and suburbs built baseball diamonds, tennis courts, swimming pools, and golf courses. Americans not only played sports but had the time and money to watch professional athletes perform in increasingly commercialized enterprises. They could see a game in a comfortable stadium, listen to it on the radio, or catch highlights in the newsreel at the local movie theater.

Americans reveled vicariously in the accomplishments of the superb athletes of the 1920s. Baseball continued to be the national pastime, drawing as many as 10 million fans a year. Tarnished in 1919 by the "Black Sox" scandal, in which some Chicago White Sox players took bribes to throw the World Series, baseball bounced back with the rise of stars like Babe Ruth of the New York Yankees. African Americans, however, had different heroes from whites. Excluded from the white teams, black athletes like Satchel Paige played in Negro leagues formed in the 1920s.

Thanks to media attention, the popularity of sports figures rivaled that of movie stars. In football Red Grange of the University of Illinois was a major star, while Jack Dempsey and Gene Tunney attracted a loyal following in boxing and Bobby Jones helped to popularize golf. Bill Tilden dominated men's tennis, while Helen Wills and Suzanne Lenglen reigned in the women's game. The decade's best-known swimmer was Gertrude Ederle, who crossed the English Channel in 1926 in just over fourteen hours.

The decade's most popular hero, however, was neither an athlete nor a movie star. On May 20, 1927, aviator Charles Lindbergh, flying the small plane *The Spirit of St. Louis*, made the first successful nonstop solo flight between New York and Paris, a distance of 3,610 miles, in 33 1/2 hours. Returning home to tickertape parades and effusive celebrations, he became *Time* magazine's first Man of the Year in 1928. Lindbergh captivated the nation by combining his mastery of the new technology (the airplane) with the pioneer virtues of individualism, self-reliance, and hard work. He symbolized Americans' desire to enjoy the benefits of modern industrialism without renouncing their traditional values.

Dissenting Values and Cultural Conflict

As movies, radio, advertising, and mass-production industries helped to transform the country into a modern, cosmopolitan nation, many Americans welcomed them as exciting evidence of progress. But others were uneasy. Flappers dancing to jazz, youthful sexual experimentation in the back of Ford Model Ts, hints of a decline in religious values: these harbingers of a new era worried more tradition-minded folk. In the nation's cities the powerful presence of immigrants and African Americans suggested the waning of white Protestant cultural dominance. Beneath the clichés

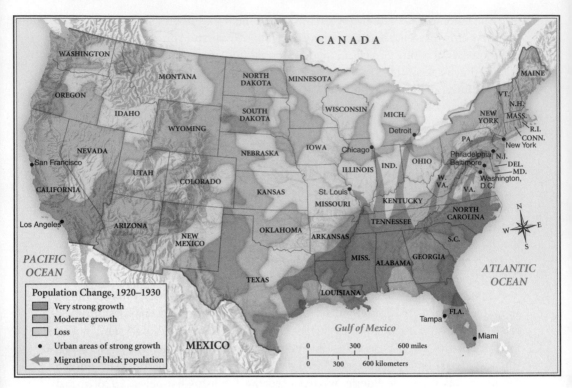

MAP 23.2 The Shift from Rural to Urban Population, 1920–1930

Despite the increasingly urban tone of modern America after 1920, regional patterns of population growth and decline were far from uniform. Cities in the South and West grew most dramatically as southern farmers moved to more promising areas with familiar climates. An important factor in the growth of northern cities, such as New York and Chicago, was the migration of southern blacks set in motion by World War I (see Map 22.3).

FOR MORE HELP ANALYZING THIS MAP, see the Online Study Guide at **bedfordstmartins.com/henrettaconcise**.

of the Roaring Twenties were deeply felt tensions that surfaced in conflicts over immigration, religion, Prohibition, and race relations.

The Rise of Nativism

Tensions between the fast-paced city and the traditional, small-town values of the country partially explain the decade's conflicts. As farmers struggled with severe economic problems, rural communities lost residents to the cities at an alarming rate. The 1920 census revealed that for the first time in the nation's history city people outnumbered rural people: 52 percent of the population lived in urban areas, compared with just 28 percent in 1870. Though the census exaggerated the extent of urbanization—its guidelines classified towns with only 2,500 people as cities—there was no mistaking the trend (Map 23.2). By 1929 ninety-three cities had populations over 100,000. The mass media generally reflected the cosmopolitan values of these urban centers, and many old-stock Americans worried that the cities and the immigrants who clustered there would soon dominate the culture.

Yet the polarities between city and country should not be overstated. Rural and small-town people were affected by the same forces that influenced urban residents. Much of the new technology—especially automobiles—enhanced rural life. Country people, like their urban counterparts, were tempted by the materialistic new values proclaimed on the radio, in magazines, and in movies. Moreover, many urban residents—immigrant Catholics, for example—were just as alarmed about declining moral standards as rural Protestants were. A simplified urban-rural dichotomy misrepresents the complexity of the decade's cultural and ethnic conflicts.

These conflicts often centered on the question of growing racial and ethnic pluralism. When native-born white Protestants—both rural and city dwellers— looked at their communities in 1920, they saw a nation that had changed dramatically in only forty years. During that time more than 23 million immigrants had come to America, many of them Jews or Catholics, most of peasant stock. Senator William Bruce of Maryland branded them "indigestible lumps" in the "national stomach," implying that mainstream society could not absorb their large numbers and foreign customs. This sentiment, termed **nativism**, was widely shared.

Nativist animosity fueled a new drive against immigration. The Chinese had been excluded in 1882, and Theodore Roosevelt had negotiated a "gentleman's agreement" to limit Japanese immigration in 1907 (see Chapter 21). Yet efforts to restrict European immigration did not meet with much success until after World War I, which had heightened suspicion of "hyphenated" Americans. During the Red Scare, nativists had played up the supposed association of the immigrants with radicalism and labor unrest, charging that southern and eastern European Catholics and Jews were incapable of becoming true Americans.

In response Congress passed an emergency bill in 1921, limiting the number of immigrants to 3 percent of the foreign born from each national group as represented in the 1910 census. In 1924 a more restrictive measure, the National Origins Act, reduced immigration until 1927 to 2 percent of each nationality's representation in the 1890 census—which had included relatively small numbers of people from southeastern Europe and Russia. After 1927 (later postponed to 1929) the law set a cap of 150,000 immigrants per year and continued to tie admission into the United States to the quota system. Japanese immigrants were excluded entirely. While limiting all immigration, the act clearly privileged older immigrant groups whose "national origins" were northern and western European at the expense of more recent southern and eastern Europeans. By placing Japanese immigrants outside the quota system, the act also drew sharp racial lines as to who was welcome to American shores (see American Voices, "A Foreigner in America," p. 710).

One remaining loophole in immigration law permitted unrestricted immigration from countries in the Western Hemisphere. This source became increasingly significant over the years, as Mexicans and Central and South Americans crossed the

AMERICAN VOICES

A Foreigner in America

KAZUO KAWAI

*B*efore the 1920s the laws regulating immigration from Asia contained more loopholes for the Japanese than the Chinese. As a result there were approximately 110,000 Japanese living in the United States in 1920. Asian immigrants' experience of prejudice was much sharper than that of Europeans; in California, for example, the Alien Land Law of 1913 barred foreign-born Japanese from purchasing land or leasing it for more than three years. At the same time the experiences of Japanese immigrants such as Kazuo Kawai echoed the problems that many young ethnic Americans faced in the 1920s as they recognized that they did not belong in the old country but were not accepted as "One Hundred Percent Americans."

Then, for the first time, I began to think about my trip to Japan. I found myself wondering if I could prepare myself for some work there. . . . I began to feel that no matter for what position I prepared myself for in America, I would be unrecognized and handicapped. I would be able to go just so high and no higher. But thinking of my trip to Japan, I realized that there was a nation, complete in itself, great, wonderful, with a glorious future, where every position from the bottom to the top was filled by Japanese. There, I would meet no cool unrecognition. If I had the ability, I could go to the top, and set the limit myself. . . . For the first time, I felt myself becoming identified with Japan, and began to realize that I was a Japanese. But there was another side. Was I a Japanese? What could I be able to do in Japan? I couldn't read or write Japanese. I didn't know any of the customs or traditions of Japan. How could I do anything there? I realized with a shock that I was not a Japanese. Thus, at the same time that I came to realize that I was a Japanese, I came to realize also that I was not a Japanese. Where did I belong? I realized with a pang that I was a "man without a country." . . . [I]t hurt because I couldn't say: "This is my own, my native land." What was my native land? Japan? True, I was born there. But it had seemed a queer, foreign land to me when I visited it. America? I had, until now, thought so. I had even told my father once that even in case of war between Japan and America, I would consider America as my country. In language, in thought, in ideals, in custom, in everything, I was American. But America wouldn't have me. She wouldn't recognize me in high school. She put the pictures of those of my race at the tail end of the year book. (I was a commencement speaker, so they had to put my picture near the front.) She won't let me play tennis on the courts in the city parks of Los Angeles, by city ordinance. She won't give me service when I go to a barber's shop. She won't let me own a house to live in. She won't give me a job, unless it is a menial one that no American wants. I thought I was American, but America wouldn't have me. Once I was American, but America made a foreigner out of me—not a Japanese, but a foreigner—a foreigner to any country, for I am just as much a foreigner to Japan as to America.

SOURCE: *Stanford Survey of Race Relations* (Stanford, CA: Stanford University, 1924), Hoover Institute Archives.

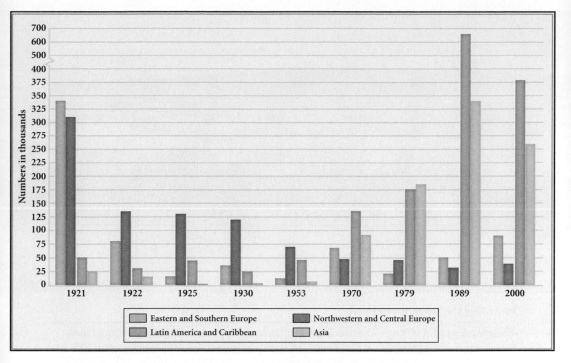

FIGURE 23.1 American Immigration after World War I

Legislation reflecting nativism slowed the influx of immigrants after 1920, as did the dislocations brought on by depression and war in the 1930s and 1940s. Note the higher rate of non-European immigration since the 1970s, a reflection of changes in immigration laws that began in 1965 (see Chapters 28 and 31).

border to fill jobs made available by the cutoff of immigration from Europe and Asia (Figure 23.1). Over 1 million Mexicans entered the United States between 1900 and 1930, including a wave who crossed the border after the Mexican Revolution of 1910 and another who entered during the labor shortages of World War I. Nativists and representatives of organized labor, who viewed Mexican immigrants as unwanted competition, lobbied Congress to close the loophole but were unsuccessful until the 1930s, when the economic devastation of the Great Depression minimized the need for immigrant labor.

Another expression of nativism in the 1920s was the revival of the Ku Klux Klan (see Chapter 15). Shortly after the premiere of *Birth of a Nation* in 1915, a popular film glorifying the Reconstruction-era Ku Klux Klan, a group of southerners gathered on Stone Mountain outside Atlanta to revive the racist organization. Taking as its motto "Native, white, Protestant supremacy," the modern Klan appealed to both urban and rural folk, though its largest "klaverns" were in urban areas. Spreading out from its southern base, the group found significant support

Patrolling the Texas Border

These border patrol officers in Laredo, Texas, in 1926 were deputized to stop illegal immigration from Mexico. Their guns, military uniforms, and stern expressions did not present a warm welcome to immigrants arriving from south of the border. University of Texas at Austin.

in the Far West, the Southwest, and the Midwest, especially Oregon, Indiana, and Oklahoma. Unlike the Klan that was founded after the Civil War, the Klan of the 1920s did not limit its harassment to blacks; Catholics and Jews were just as likely to be its targets. Many of its tactics, however, were the same: arson, physical intimidation, and economic boycotts (see Map 23.1). The new Klan also turned to politics, succeeding in electing hundreds of Klansmen to public office and controlling numerous state legislatures. In Oregon, the Klan was behind a 1922 state initiative to outlaw private schools, a measure aimed at Catholic parochial schools. Although the voters passed the initiative, the Supreme Court later ruled the measure unconstitutional. At the height of its power in 1925, the Klan had over 3 million members—including a strong contingent of women who pursued a political agenda that combined racism, nativism, and equal rights for white Protestant women.

After 1925 the Klan declined rapidly. Internal rivalries and the disclosure of rampant corruption hurt the group's image. Especially damaging was the revelation that Grand Dragon David Stephenson, the Klan's national leader, had kidnapped and sexually assaulted his former secretary, driving her to suicide. And the passage of the National Origins Act in 1924 reduced the nativist fervor, robbing the Klan of its most potent issue.

Ku Klux Klan Women Parade in Washington, D.C.

The Ku Klux Klan was so well integrated into the daily life of some white Protestants that one woman from rural Indiana remembered her time in the KKK in the 1920s as "Just a celebration . . . a way of growing up." Perhaps as many as 500,000 women joined the Women of the Ku Klux Klan (WKKK) in the 1920s, including these women who paraded down Pennsylvania Avenue in Washington, D.C., in 1928. National Archives at College Park, MD.

FOR MORE HELP ANALYZING THIS IMAGE, see the Online Study Guide at **bedfordstmartins.com/henrettaconcise**.

Legislating Values: The Scopes Trial and Prohibition

Other cultural tensions erupted over religion. The debate between modernist and fundamentalist Protestants, which had been simmering since the 1890s (see Chapter 18), came to a boil in the 1920s. Modernists, or liberal Protestants, tried to reconcile their religion with Charles Darwin's theory of evolution and recent technological and scientific discoveries. In response, **fundamentalists** insisted upon a literal interpretation of the Bible. Most major Protestant denominations experienced heated internal conflicts over these issues, but the most conspicuous evangelical figures came from outside mainstream denominations. Popular preachers like

Billy Sunday used revivals and storefront churches to popularize their own blends of charismatic fundamentalism and traditional values.

In Los Angeles, Sister Aimee McPherson founded the Foursquare Gospel Church, her distinct version of Pentecostalism, and built the enormous Angeles Temple that drew immense crowds to witness her Sunday services, which were elaborate theatrical productions rather than conventional sermons. Like other popular ministers of the time, she also brilliantly used the radio to spread, as she put it, "on the winged feet of the winds, the story of hope, the words of joy, of comfort, of salvation."

Religious controversy soon entered the political arena when fundamentalists, worried about increasing secularism and declining morality, turned to the law to shore up their vision of a righteous Protestant nation. Some states enacted legislation to block the teaching of evolution in the schools. In 1925, for instance, Tennessee passed a law declaring that "it shall be unlawful . . . to teach any theory that denies the story of the Divine creation of man as taught in the Bible, and to teach instead that man has descended from a lower order of animals." In a test case involving John T. Scopes, a high school biology teacher in Dayton, Tennessee, the fledgling American Civil Liberties Union (ACLU) challenged the constitutionality of that law. Clarence Darrow, the famous criminal lawyer, defended Scopes; the spellbinding orator William Jennings Bryan, three-time presidential candidate and ardent fundamentalist, was the most prominent member of the prosecution's team.

The press quickly dubbed the *Scopes* trial the "monkey trial," referring both to Darwin's theory that human beings and primates share a common ancestor and to the circus atmosphere in the courtroom. In July 1925 more than 100 journalists crowded the sweltering courthouse in Dayton, Tennessee, giving massive publicity to the knotty questions of faith and scientific theory that the trial addressed. The jury took only eight minutes to deliver its verdict: guilty. Though the Tennessee Supreme Court later overturned the conviction on a technicality, the reversal prevented further appeals of the case, and the controversial law remained on the books for more than thirty years. Historically, the trial symbolizes the conflict between the two competing value systems, cosmopolitan and traditional, that clashed in the 1920s. It suggests that despite the period's image as a frivolous and decadent time, traditional religious values of spirituality and morality continued to matter deeply to many Americans.

Like the dispute over evolution, Prohibition involved the power of the state to enforce social values. Americans did drink less overall after passage of the Eighteenth Amendment, which took effect in January of 1920 (see Chapter 22). Yet more than any other issue, Prohibition gave the decade its reputation as the Roaring Twenties. In major cities, whose ethnic populations had always opposed Prohibition, noncompliance was widespread. People imitated rural moonshiners by distilling "bathtub gin." Illegal saloons called speakeasies sprang up everywhere—more than 30,000 of them in New York City alone. Liquor smugglers operated with ease along borders and coastlines. Organized crime, already a presence in major cities, supplied a ready-made distribution network for the bootleg liquor, using the "noble experiment," as Prohibition was called, to entrench itself more deeply in city politics.

Ignoring Prohibition

Despite their popularity, speakeasies were rarely drawn or photographed; after all, they were supposed to be private clubs tucked away beyond the reach of the law. Fancy hotels were unable to compete with speakeasies once their bars were shut down, and many went out of business in the 1920s. But John Sloan's 1928 painting shows the rich enjoying themselves at New York's posh Lafayette Hotel. It is likely that these gentlemen and ladies had flasks concealed somewhere in their evening finery.

John Sloan, *The Lafayette*, 1928, Metropolitan Museum of Art, New York. Gift of Friends of John Sloan, 1929 (28.18).

By the middle of the decade, Prohibition was clearly failing. Government appropriations for its enforcement were woefully inadequate; the few highly publicized raids hardly made a dent in the liquor trade. Forces for repeal—the "wets," as opposed to the "drys," who continued to support the Eighteenth Amendment—began the long process to obtain the necessary votes in Congress and state legislatures to amend the Constitution once more. The wets argued that Prohibition had undermined respect for the law and had seriously impinged on individuals' liberty.

The onset of the Great Depression hastened the repeal process, as politicians began to see alcohol production as a way to create jobs and prop up the faltering economy. On December 5, 1933, the Eighteenth Amendment was repealed. Ironically, drinking became more socially acceptable, though not necessarily more widespread, than it had been before the experiment began.

Intellectual Crosscurrents

The most articulate and embittered dissenters of the 1920s were writers and intellectuals disillusioned by the horrors of World War I and the crass materialism of the new consumer culture. Some artists were so repelled by what they saw as the complacent, moralistic, and anti-intellectual tone of American life that they settled in Europe—some temporarily, like the novelists Ernest Hemingway and F. Scott Fitzgerald, others permanently, like writer Gertrude Stein. Prominent African American artists, such as dancer Josephine Baker and writer Langston Hughes, sought temporary escape from racism in France. The poet T. S. Eliot, who left the United States before the war, ultimately became a British citizen. His despairing poem *The Waste Land* (1922), with its images of a fragmented civilization in ruins after the war, influenced a generation of writers.

Other writers also made powerful statements against war and contemporary culture, including John Dos Passos, whose first novel, *The Three Soldiers* (1921), was inspired by the war, and whose *1919* (1932), the second volume in his USA trilogy, railed against the obscenity of "Mr. Wilson's war." Ernest Hemingway's novels *In Our Time* (1924), *The Sun Also Rises* (1926), and *A Farewell to Arms* (1929) also powerfully described the dehumanizing consequences and the futility of war. In 1925 F. Scott Fitzgerald published *The Great Gatsby*, which showed the corrosive consequences of the mindless pursuit of wealth.

But the artists and writers who migrated to Europe, particularly Paris, were not simply a "lost generation" fleeing America. They were also drawn to Paris as the cultural and artistic capital of the world and a beacon of modernism. Paris, as Gertrude Stein put it, was "where the twentieth century was happening." Indeed, the **modernist movement**, which was marked by skepticism and technical experimentation in literature, art, and music, invigorated American writing both abroad and at home. Many American writers, whether they settled in Paris or remained in the United States, joined the movement, which had begun before the war as intellectuals reacted with excitement to the cultural and social changes that science, industrialization, and urbanization had brought.

The literature of the 1920s was rich and varied. Poetry enjoyed a renaissance in the works of Robert Frost, Wallace Stevens, Marianne Moore, and William Carlos Williams. Edith Wharton won a Pulitzer Prize—the first woman so honored—for *The Age of Innocence* (1920). Influenced by Freudian psychology, William Faulkner achieved his first critical success with *The Sound and the Fury* (1929), set in the fictional Mississippi county of Yoknapatawpha, where inhabitants clung to the values of the old agrarian South as they struggled to adjust to modern industrial capitalism. Playwright Eugene O'Neill showed the influence of Freudian psychology in his experimental plays, including *The Hairy Ape* (1922) and *Desire Under the Elms* (1924). Although both Faulkner and O'Neill went on to produce additional major works in the 1930s, on the whole the creative energy of the literary renaissance of the 1920s did not survive into the 1930s. The Great Depression, social and ideological unrest, and the rise of totalitarianism would reshape the intellectual landscape.

A different kind of cultural affirmation took place in the African American community of Harlem in the 1920s. In the words of the Reverend Adam Clayton Powell Sr., pastor of the influential Abyssinian Baptist Church, Harlem loomed as "the symbol of liberty and the Promised Land to Negroes everywhere." The migration of African Americans out of the South and into the cities during the war years had continued into the 1920s, helping to make Harlem in particular a vital place that attracted talented artists and writers. Here they created the Harlem Renaissance, which broke with older genteel traditions of black literature to reclaim a cultural identity with African roots. Alain Locke, editor of the anthology *The New Negro* (1926), summed up the movement when he stated that, through art, "Negro life is seizing its first chances for group expression and self-determination."

The Harlem Renaissance championed racial pride and cultural identity in the midst of white society. The poet Langston Hughes, who became a leading exponent of the Harlem Renaissance, captured its affirmative spirit when he asserted, "I am a Negro—and beautiful." Authors such as Claude McKay, Jean Toomer, Jessie Fauset, and Zora Neale Hurston explored the black experience and represented the "New Negro" in fiction. Countee Cullen and Langston Hughes turned to poetry, and Augusta Savage used sculpture to draw attention to black accomplishments. Their production of creative work showed the ongoing African American struggle to find a way, as W. E. B. Du Bois put it, "to be both a Negro and an American."

The artistic outpouring encouraged a wide range of creative expression. Jean Toomer, a writer passionately committed to black self-expression, wrote the influential novel *Cane* in 1923. With its poems, sketches, and stories about a northern black's discovery of the rural black South, it inspired other African American artists and writers. Langston Hughes drew on the black artistic forms of blues and jazz in *The Weary Blues* (1926), a groundbreaking collection of poems. Considered the most original black poet and the most representative African American writer of the time, Hughes also wrote novels, plays, and essays. Zora Neale Hurston, born in Florida to a family of poor tenant farmers, attended Howard University in Washington, D.C., and won a scholarship to study anthropology at Barnard College in New York City. She spent a decade collecting folklore in the South and the Caribbean and incorporated that material into her short stories and novels. Her genius for storytelling won her acclaim.

The vitality of the Harlem Renaissance was short-lived. Although the NAACP's magazine *The Crisis* was a forum for the Harlem writers, the black middle class and the intellectual elite in Harlem were relatively small and could not support the group's efforts. Its main audience consisted of white intellectuals and philanthropists, and many writers were ambivalent about depending on white patronage as they struggled to attain an authentic voice in their fiction. Langston Hughes became disillusioned with his white patron when she withdrew support as he began to write about common black people in Kansas and New York rather than keeping with African themes.

During the Jazz Age, when Harlem was in vogue, the publishing industry courted its writers, but the stock market crash of 1929 brought that interest to a sudden end. The movement waned in the 1930s as the depression deepened. Nonetheless, the writers of the Harlem Renaissance would influence a future generation of black writers when their works were rediscovered by black intellectuals during the civil rights movement of the 1960s.

Although the Harlem Renaissance had little direct impact on the masses of African Americans, the Universal Negro Improvement Association (UNIA) was the black working class's first mass movement. Under the leadership of the Jamaican-born Marcus Garvey, the UNIA built racial pride; challenged white political and cultural **hegemony**; and championed black separatism. At its height, the Harlem-based organization claimed 4 million followers, many of whom were recent migrants to northern cities. Like several nineteenth-century reformers, Marcus Garvey urged blacks to return to Africa because, he reasoned, blacks would never be treated justly in countries ruled by whites. Although he did not anticipate a massive migration, he did envision a strong black Africa that could use its power to protect blacks everywhere. Garvey's wife, Amy Jacques Garvey, appealed to black women by combining black nationalism with an emphasis on women's contributions to culture and politics.

The UNIA grew rapidly in the early 1920s. It published a newspaper called *Negro World* and undertook extensive business ventures to support black enterprise. The most ambitious project, the Black Star Line steamship company, was supposed to ferry cargo between the West Indies and the United States and take African Americans back to Africa. Irregularities in fund-raising for the project, however, led to Garvey's conviction for mail fraud in 1925, and he was sentenced to five years in prison. President Coolidge commuted his sentence in 1927, but Garvey was deported to Jamaica. Without his charismatic leadership, the movement collapsed.

Cultural Clash in the Election of 1928

The works of the lost generation and the Harlem Renaissance touched only a small minority of Americans in the 1920s, but emotionally charged issues like Prohibition, fundamentalism, and nativism eventually spilled over into national politics. The Democratic Party, which attracted both rural Protestants in the South and the West and ethnic minorities in northern cities, was especially vulnerable to the cultural conflicts of the time. The 1924 Democratic National Convention had revealed an intensely polarized party, split between the urban machines and the rural wing.

In 1928 the urban wing held sway and succeeded in nominating New York's Governor Alfred E. Smith, a descendant of Irish immigrants and a product of Tammany Hall. Proud of his background, Smith adopted "The Sidewalks of New York" as his campaign song. His candidacy troubled many voters, however. His heavy New York accent, his brown derby, and his colorful style highlighted his urban, ethnic, working-class origins, and his early career in Tammany Hall suggested incorrectly that he was little more than a cog in the machine. Smith's stand on Prohibition—although he promised to enforce it, he wanted it repealed—alienated even more voters.

An equally serious handicap, however, was his religion. In 1928 most Protestants were not ready for a Catholic president. Although Smith insisted that his religion would not interfere with his duties as president, his perceived allegiance to Rome cost him the support of Democrats and Republicans alike. Protestant clergymen, who already opposed Smith because he supported the repeal of Prohibition, led the drive against him. "No Governor can kiss the papal ring and get within gunshot of the White House," declared one Methodist bishop.

Smith's candidacy met with much opposition, but for his supporters he embodied a new America. Throughout the decade, attacks on immigrants, Catholics, and Jews had repeatedly labeled them as unwelcome outsiders. Ethnic and religious leaders and communities had vehemently countered these criticisms by offering a more inclusive vision of citizenship. One Catholic bishop summed it up neatly in 1921, stating that "National aspirations constitute Americanism. We are the blend of all the peoples of the world, and I think we are much the better for that. Americanism is not a matter of birth, Americanism is a matter of faith, of consecration to the ideals of America." That Al Smith, a man of Catholic immigrant stock, could be the Democratic Party's nominee for president suggested to many in 1928 that the country might yet embrace a more pluralistic conception of American identity.

Just as Smith was a new kind of presidential candidate for the Democrats, so was Herbert Hoover for the Republicans. As a professional administrator and engineer who had never before been elected to political office, Hoover embodied the new managerial and technological elite that was restructuring the nation's economic order. During his campaign, in which he gave only seven speeches, Hoover asserted that his vision of individualism and cooperative endeavor would banish poverty from the United States. That rhetoric, as well as his reputation for organizing a drive for humanitarian relief during the war, caused many voters to see him as more progressive than Smith. Hoover won a stunning victory, receiving 58 percent of the popular vote to Smith's 41 percent and 444 electoral votes to Smith's 87. The election suggested important underlying political changes. Despite the overwhelming loss, the Democrats' turnout increased substantially in urban areas with significant concentrations of ethnic voters. Smith also won the industrialized states of Massachusetts and Rhode Island. The Democrats were on their way to fashioning a new identity as the party of the urban masses, a reorientation the New Deal would complete in the 1930s.

It is unlikely that any Democratic candidate, let alone a Catholic, could have won the presidency in 1928. With a prosperous economy, national consensus on foreign policy, and strong support from the business community, the Republicans proved unbeatable (Map 23.3). Ironically, Herbert Hoover's victory would put him in the unenviable position of leading the United States when the Great Depression struck in 1929. Having claimed credit for the prosperity of the 1920s, the Republicans could not escape blame for the depression; twenty-four years would pass before a Republican won the presidency again.

But as Hoover began his presidency in early 1929, most Americans expected progress and prosperity to continue. The New Era the Republicans had touted meant more than Republican ascendancy in politics, more than business-government cooperation, and more than a decline in the progressive reform movement. To most Americans the New Era embodied the industrial productivity and technological advances that made consumer goods widely available and movies and radio exciting parts of American life. At home and abroad the nation seemed unprecedentedly vigorous and powerful. Despite disruptive cultural conflicts and a changing workplace that undermined workers' power, despite inequities in the racial order and in the distribution of income, the general tone was one of optimism, of faith in the modern society the country had become.

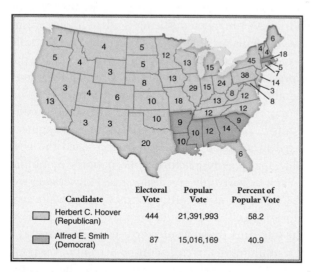

Candidate	Electoral Vote	Popular Vote	Percent of Popular Vote
Herbert C. Hoover (Republican)	444	21,391,993	58.2
Alfred E. Smith (Democrat)	87	15,016,169	40.9

MAP 23.3 Presidential Election of 1928

Historians still debate the extent to which 1928 was a critical election—an election that produced a significant realignment in voting behavior. Although the Republican Herbert Hoover swept the electoral college, Democrats were heartened by the fact that Alfred E. Smith won the heavily industrialized states of Rhode Island and Massachusetts. Not evident on this map is that Democratic turnout increased substantially in urban areas with a significant concentration of ethnic voters, a trend that would eventually lead to a new identity for the Democrats as the party of the urban masses.

TIMELINE

1920	Eighteenth Amendment outlawing alcohol takes effect		Teapot Dome scandal
	First commercial radio broadcast		U.S. troops withdraw from Dominican Republic
	Warren G. Harding elected president		National Origins Act further limits immigration
	Census reveals shift in population from farms to cities		
	Edith Wharton, *The Age of Innocence*	**1925**	F. Scott Fitzgerald, *The Great Gatsby*
1920–1921	National economic recession		Height of Ku Klux Klan's power
			Scopes ("monkey") trial
1921	Sheppard-Towner Act	**1926**	Alain Locke, *The New Negro*
	Immigration Act limits immigration		The Book-of-the-Month Club is founded
	Washington Conference supports naval disarmament	**1927**	First "talkies"
			Charles Lindbergh's solo flight
1922	T. S. Eliot, *The Waste Land*		Ford's Model A car
1922–1929	Record economic expansion	**1928**	Herbert Hoover elected president
			Kellogg-Briand Pact condemning militarism signed
1923	Harding dies in office; succeeded by Calvin Coolidge as president	**1929**	*Middletown* published
	Time magazine founded		Ernest Hemingway, *A Farewell to Arms*
	Jean Toomer, *Cane*		William Faulkner, *The Sound and the Fury*
1924	Dawes Plan reduces German reparation payments		

For Further Exploration

An overview of the decade that pays extensive attention to racial, religious, and ethnic pluralism is Lynn Dumenil, *The Modern Temper: American Culture and Society in the 1920s* (1995). Invaluable collections of primary documents include Alain Locke, ed., *The New Negro* (1925), which features authors of the Harlem Renaissance; and Loren Baritz, ed., *The Culture of the Twenties* (1970), which covers such diverse topics as the lost generation and the Ku Klux Klan. For fiction, in addition to the titles offered in the text, see Sinclair Lewis's two classic midwestern novels, *Babbitt* (1922) and *Main Street* (1920); Sherwood Anderson's dark stories in *Winesburg, Ohio* (1919); and Nella Larsen's novel *Quicksand* (1928), about an African American woman's conflicted identity.

The State University of New York at Binghamton's Web page Women and Social Movements in the United States, 1830–1930, at <http://womhist.binghamton.edu/>, is especially rich on the 1920s, with material on conflicts between African American and white women activists, women in the peace movement, and women's participation in partisan politics. The Library of

Congress's American Memory Collection, Prosperity and Thrift: The Coolidge Era and the Consumer Economy, 1921–1929, at <http://memory.loc.gov/ammem/coolhtml/coolhome.html>, is an extensive site with original documents, film footage, and scholarly insights on a variety of topics dealing with the 1920s.

Greatest Films of the 1920s, at <http://www.filmsite.org/20sintro.html>, is an informative site that provides summaries and reviews of such significant movies as *King of Kings* (1927) and *The Sheik* (1921). Ad Access, <http://scriptorium.lib.duke.edu/adaccess/>, provides images of U.S. advertisements between 1911 and 1955 culled from the J. Walter Thompson Company Competitive Advertisements Collection of the John W. Hartman Center for Sales, Advertising, and Marketing History at Duke University. The user may search in five categories: radio, television, transportation, beauty and hygiene, and World War II. *Marcus Garvey: Look for Me in the Whirlwind* is a Public Broadcasting Service *American Experience* documentary. Its companion Web site, <http://www.pbs.org/wgbh/amex/garvey/>, includes images, a voice recording by Marcus Garvey, a timeline of his life, material on other African American leaders of the era, and an online forum on race relations.

For definitions of key terms boldfaced in this chapter, see the glossary at the end of the book.

To assess your mastery of the material covered in this chapter, see the Online Study Guide at **bedfordstmartins.com/henrettaconcise**.

For map resources and primary documents, see **bedfordstmartins.com/henrettaconcise**.

Chapter 24

THE GREAT DEPRESSION

> Mass unemployment is both a statistic and an empty feeling in the stomach. To fully comprehend it, you have to both see the figures and feel the emptiness.
>
> CABELL PHILLIPS

O ur images of the 1920s and the decade that followed are polar opposites. Flappers and movie stars, admen and stockbrokers, caught up in what F. Scott Fitzgerald called the "world's most expensive orgy"—these are our conceptions of the Jazz Age. The 1930s are remembered in terms of breadlines and hobos, dust bowl devastation and hapless migrants piled into dilapidated jalopies. Almost all of our impressions of that decade are black and white, in part because widely distributed photographs taken by Farm Security Administration photographers etched this dark visual image of depression-era America on the popular consciousness.

But this contrast between the flush times of the 1920s and the hard times of the 1930s is too stark. The vaunted prosperity of the 1920s was never as widespread or as deeply rooted as many believed. Though America's mass-consumption economy was the envy of the world, many people lived on its margins. Not all Americans were devastated by the depression, but few could escape its wide-ranging social, political, and cultural effects. Whatever their personal situations were, Americans understood that the nation was deeply scarred by the pervasive struggle to survive and overcome "hard times."

The Coming of the Great Depression

Booms and busts are a permanent feature of the **business cycle** in capitalist economies. Since the beginning of the Industrial Revolution early in the nineteenth century, the United States had experienced recessions or panics at least once every twenty years. But none was as severe as the Great Depression of the 1930s. The country would not recover from the depression until World War II put American factories and people back to work.

723

Causes of the Depression

The economic downturn began slowly and almost imperceptibly. After 1927 consumer spending declined and housing construction slowed. Soon inventories piled up; in 1928 manufacturers began to cut back production and lay off workers, reducing incomes and buying power and reinforcing the slowdown. By the summer of 1929, the economy was clearly in recession.

Yet stock market activity continued unabated. By 1929 the stock market had become the symbol of the nation's prosperity, an icon of American business culture. In a *Ladies' Home Journal* article titled "Everyone Ought to Be Rich," financier John J. Raskob advised that $15 a month invested in sound common stocks would grow to $80,000 in twenty years. Not everyone was playing the market, however. Only about 4 million Americans, or roughly 10 percent of the nation's households, owned stock in 1929.

Stock prices had been rising steadily since 1921, but in 1928 and 1929 they surged forward, rising on average over 40 percent. At the time market activity was essentially unregulated. **Margin buying**, in particular, proceeded at a feverish pace, as customers were encouraged to buy stocks with a small down payment and finance the rest with a broker loan. But then on "Black Thursday," October 24, 1929, and again on "Black Tuesday," October 29, the bubble burst. On those two bleak days, more than 28 million shares changed hands in frantic trading. Overextended investors, suddenly finding themselves heavily in debt, began to sell their portfolios. Waves of panic selling ensued. Practically overnight stock values fell from a peak of $87 billion (at least on paper) to $55 billion.

The impact of what became known as the Great Crash was felt far beyond the trading floors of Wall Street. Commercial banks had invested heavily in corporate stock. Speculators who had borrowed from banks to buy their stocks could not repay their loans because they could not sell their shares. Throughout the nation bank failures multiplied. Since bank deposits were uninsured, a bank collapse meant that depositors lost all their money. The sudden loss of their life savings was a tremendous shock to members of the middle class, many of whom had no other resources to cope with the crisis. More symbolically, the crash destroyed the faith of those who viewed the stock market as the crowning symbol of American prosperity, precipitating a crisis of confidence that prolonged the depression.

Although the stock market crash triggered the Great Depression, long-standing weaknesses in the economy accounted for its length and severity. Agriculture, in particular, had never recovered from the recession of 1920 and 1921. Farmers faced high fixed costs for equipment and mortgages, which they had incurred during the inflationary war years. When prices fell because of overproduction, many farmers defaulted on their mortgage payments, risking foreclosure. Because farmers accounted for about a fourth of the nation's gainfully employed workers in 1929, their difficulties weakened the general economic structure.

Certain basic industries also had economic setbacks during the prosperous 1920s. Textile manufacturing, faced a steady decline after the war and suffered from decreased demand and overproduction. Mining and lumbering, which had expanded in response to wartime demand, confronted the same problems. Railroads, damaged by stiff competition from the emerging trucking industry, faced shrinking passenger revenues and stagnant freight levels, worsened by inefficient management. While these older sectors of the economy faltered, newer and more successful consumer-based industries—such as chemicals, appliances, and food processing—proved not yet strong enough to lead the way to recovery.

The unequal distribution of the nation's wealth was another underlying weakness of the economy. During the 1920s the share of national income going to families in the upper- and middle-income brackets increased. The tax policies of Secretary of the Treasury Andrew Mellon contributed to a concentration of wealth by lowering personal income-tax rates, eliminating the wartime excess-profits tax, and increasing deductions that favored corporations and the affluent. In 1929 the lowest 40 percent of the population received only 12.5 percent of aggregate family income, while the top 5 percent of the population received 30 percent. Once the depression began, this skewed income distribution left the majority of people unable to spend the amount of money that was needed to revive the economy.

The Great Depression became self-perpetuating. The more the economy contracted, the longer people expected the depression to last. The longer they expected it to last, the more afraid they became to spend or invest their money, if they had any—and spending and investment was exactly what was needed to stimulate economic recovery. The economy showed some improvement in the summer of 1931, when low prices encouraged consumption, but plunged again late that fall.

The nation's banks, already weakened by the stock market crash, continued to collapse. The wave of bank failures frightened depositors, who withdrew their savings, deepening the crisis. In 1931 a change in the nation's monetary policy compounded the banks' problems. In the first phase of the depression, the Federal Reserve System had reacted cautiously. But in October 1931 the Federal Reserve Bank of New York significantly increased the discount rate—the interest rate charged on loans to member banks—and reduced the amount of money placed in circulation through the purchase of government securities. This miscalculation squeezed the money supply, forcing prices down and depriving businesses of funds for investment. In the face of the money shortage, the American people could have pulled the country out of the depression only by spending faster. But because of falling prices, rising unemployment, and a troubled banking system, Americans preferred to keep their dollars, stashing them under the mattress rather than depositing them in the bank, further limiting the amount of money in circulation. Economic stagnation solidified.

The Worldwide Depression

President Hoover later blamed the severity of the depression on the international economic situation. Although domestic factors far outweighed international causes of America's protracted decline, Hoover was correct in surmising that economic problems in the rest of the world affected the United States and vice versa. Indeed, the international economic system had been out of kilter since World War I. It functioned only as long as American banks exported enough capital to allow European countries to repay their debts and to buy U.S. manufactured goods and foodstuffs. By the late 1920s European economies were staggering under the weight of huge debts and trade imbalances with the United States, which effectively undercut their recovery from the war. By 1931 most European economies had collapsed.

In an interdependent world the economic downturn in America had enormous repercussions. When U.S. companies cut back production, they also cut their purchases of raw materials and supplies abroad, devastating many foreign economies. When American financiers sharply reduced their foreign investment and consumers bought fewer European goods, debt repayment became even more difficult, straining the **gold standard**, the foundation of international commerce in the interwar period. As European economic conditions worsened, demand for American exports fell drastically. Finally, when the Hawley-Smoot Tariff of 1930 went into effect, raising rates to all-time highs, foreign governments retaliated by imposing their own trade restrictions, further limiting the market for American goods and intensifying the worldwide depression.

No other nation was as hard hit as the United States. From the height of its prosperity before the stock market crash in 1929 to the depths of the depression in 1932 and 1933, the U.S. gross domestic product (GDP) was cut almost in half, declining from $103.1 billion to $58 billion in 1932. Consumption expenditures dropped by 18 percent, construction by 78 percent; private investment plummeted 88 percent, and farm income, already low, was more than halved. In this period 9,000 banks went bankrupt or closed their doors and 100,000 businesses failed. The consumer price index (CPI) declined by 25 percent, and corporate profits fell from $10 billion to $1 billion.

Most tellingly, unemployment rose from 3.2 percent to 24.9 percent, affecting approximately 12 million workers. Statistical measures at the time were fairly crude, so the figures were probably understated. At least one in four workers was out of a job, and even those who had jobs faced wage cuts, work for which they were overqualified, or layoffs. Their stories put a human face on the almost incomprehensible dimensions of the economic downturn.

Hard Times

"We didn't go hungry, but we lived lean." That statement sums up the experiences of many families during the Great Depression. For most the depression did not mean losing thousands of dollars in the stock market or pulling children out of boarding school, nor did it mean going on relief or living in a shantytown. In a typical family in the 1930s, the husband still had a job and the wife was still a homemaker. Families usually managed to "make do." But many families suffered enormously and for others life was far from easy; most Americans worried about an uncertain future that might bring even harder times into their lives.

The Breadline

Some of the most vivid images from the depression were breadlines and men selling apples on street corners. Note that all the people in this breadline are men. Women rarely appeared in breadlines, often preferring to endure private deprivation rather than violate standards of respectable behavior by appearing in public to ask for help.

Franklin D. Roosevelt Library, Hyde Park, NY.

Many variables—race, ethnicity, age, class, and gender—influenced how Americans experienced the depression. Blacks, Mexican Americans, and others already on the economic margins saw their opportunities shrink further. Often the last hired, they were the first fired. Hard times weighed heavily on the nation's senior citizens of all races, many of whom faced destitution. Many white middle-class Americans experienced downward mobility for the first time. Strong believers in the Horatio Alger ethic of upward mobility through hard work, they suddenly found themselves floundering in a society that did not reward them for that work as they had expected. Thus the depression challenged basic American tenets of individualism and success. Yet even in the midst of pervasive unemployment, many people blamed themselves for their misfortune. This sense of damaged pride pervaded letters written to President Franklin D. Roosevelt and his wife Eleanor, summed up succinctly in one woman's plea for assistance: "Please don't think me unworthy."

After exhausting their savings and credit, many families found the traditional path of turning to relatives, neighbors, church, and mutual-aid societies in time of need blocked. Private charities and benefit societies were overwhelmed by the needy, and individuals often had too few resources to share. For many the only alternative was the humiliation of going on relief—seeking aid from state or local governments, which offered only limited help. In New York State, where benefits were among the highest in the nation, a family on relief received only $2.39 a week. Such hardships left a deep wound, an "invisible scar." And the scar branded more than those who were forced onto the relief rolls. For the majority of Americans, the fear of losing control over their lives was the crux of the Great Depression.

Families Face the Depression

Sociologists who studied family life during the 1930s found that the depression usually intensified existing behavior. If a family had been stable and cohesive before the depression, then members pulled together to overcome the new obstacles. But if a family had shown signs of disintegration, the depression made the situation worse. On the whole far more families hung together than broke apart.

Men and women experienced the Great Depression differently, partly because of the gender roles that governed male and female behavior in the 1930s. From childhood men had been trained to be breadwinners; they considered themselves failures if they could no longer support their families (see American Voices, "A Working-Class Family Encounters the Great Depression," p. 729). But while millions of men lost their jobs, few of the nation's 28 million homemakers lost their positions in the home. In contrast to men, women's sense of self-importance increased as they struggled to keep their families afloat. Sociologists Robert and Helen Lynd noticed this phenomenon in their follow-up study of *Middletown* (Muncie, Indiana), published in 1937: "The men, cut adrift from their usual routine, lost much of their sense of time and dawdled helplessly and dully about the streets;

A Working-Class Family Encounters the Great Depression

LARRY VAN DUSEN

Although many families endured the privations of the Great Depression with equanimity, others, like Larry Van Dusen's, experienced tremendous strains. In this passage from his oral account to journalist Studs Terkel, he describes the pressures on male wage earners and their children.

One of the most common things—and it certainly happened to me—was this feeling of your father's failure. . . . Sure things were tough, but why should I be the kid who had to put a piece of cardboard into the sole of my shoe to go to school? It was not a thing coupled with resentment against my father. It was simply this feeling of regret, that somehow he hadn't done better, that he hadn't gotten the breaks. . . .

He would get jobs he considered beneath his status during this period. Something would happen: he'd quarrel with the foreman, he'd have a fight with the boss. He was a carpenter. He couldn't be happy fixing a roadbed or driving a cab or something like that. He was a skilled tradesman and this whole thing had him beat. I think it bugged the family a lot.

Remember, too, the shock, the confusion, the hurt that many kids felt about their fathers not being able to provide for them. This reflected itself very often in bitter quarrels between father and son. I recall I had one. I was the oldest of six children. I think there was a special feeling between the father and the oldest son. . . .

My father led a rough life: he drank. During the Depression, he drank more. There was more conflict in the home. A lot of fathers—mine, among them—had a habit of taking off. They'd go to Chicago to look for work. To Topeka. This left the family at home, waiting and hoping that the old man would find something. And there was always the Saturday night ordeal as to whether or not the old man would get home with his paycheck. Everything was sharpened and hurt more by the Depression.

Heaven would break out once in a while, and the old man would get a week's work. I remember he'd come home at night, and he'd come down the path through the trees. He always rode a bicycle. He'd stop and sometimes say hello, or give me a hug. And that smell of fresh sawdust on those carpenter overalls, and the fact that Dad was home, and there was a week's wages—well, this is something you remember, too. That's the good you remember.

And then there was always the bad part. That's when you'd see your father coming home with the toolbox on his shoulder. Or carrying it. That meant the job was over. The tools were home now, and we were back on the treadmill again.

I remember coming back home, many years afterwards. Things were better. It was after the Depression, after the war. . . . My father turned into an angel. They weren't wealthy, but they were making it. They didn't have the acid and the recriminations and the bitterness that I had felt as a child.

SOURCE: *Hard Times* by Studs Terkel. Copyright © 1986 by Studs Terkel. Reprinted by permission of Donadio & Olson, Inc.

while in the homes the women's world remained largely intact and the round of cooking, housecleaning, and mending became if anything more absorbing."

Even if a wife took a job when her husband lost his, she retained almost total responsibility for housework and child care. To economize women sewed their own clothes and canned fruits and vegetables. They bought day-old bread and heated several dishes in the oven at once to save fuel. Women who had once employed servants did their own housework. Eleanor Roosevelt described the stressful effects of the depression on these women's lives: "It means endless little economies and constant anxiety for fear of some catastrophe such as accident or illness which may completely swamp the family budget." Housewives' ability to watch every penny often made the difference in a family's survival.

Another measure of the impact of the depression on family life was the change in demographic trends. The marriage rate fell from 10.14 per thousand persons in 1929 to 7.87 per thousand in 1932. The divorce rate decreased as well because couples could not afford the legal expense of dissolving failed unions. And between 1930 and 1933, the birthrate, which had fallen steadily since 1800, dropped from 21.3 live births per thousand to 18.4, a dramatic 14 percent decrease. The new level would have produced a decline in population if maintained. Though it rose slightly after 1934, by the end of the decade it was still only 18.8. (In contrast, at the height of the baby boom following World War II, the birthrate was 25 per thousand.)

The drop in the birthrate during the Great Depression could not have happened without increased access to effective contraception. In 1936, in *United States v. One Package of Japanese Pessaries*, a federal court struck down all federal restrictions on the dissemination of contraceptive information. The decision gave doctors wide discretion in prescribing birth control for married couples, making it legal everywhere except the heavily Catholic states of Massachusetts and Connecticut. While abortion remained illegal, the number of women who underwent the procedure increased. Because many abortionists operated under unsafe or unsanitary conditions, between 8,000 and 10,000 women died each year from the illegal operations.

Margaret Sanger played a major role in encouraging the availability and popular acceptance of birth control. Sanger began her career as a public-health nurse in the 1910s in the slums of New York City. At first she joined forces with Socialists trying to help working-class families to control their fertility. In the 1920s and 1930s, however, she appealed to the middle class for support, identifying those families as the key to the movement's success. Sanger also courted the medical profession, pioneering the establishment of professionally staffed birth control clinics and winning the American Medical Association's endorsement of contraception in 1937. As a result of Sanger's efforts, birth control became less a feminist issue and more a medical question. And in the context of the depression it became an economic issue as well, as financially pressed couples sought to delay or limit their childbearing while they weathered hard times.

One way for families to make ends meet was to send an additional member of the household to work. Whereas in African American families that role already often fell to a married woman by the turn of the century, it was not until the 1930s that married

FEBRUARY, 1932   On sale the second Friday of every month   10 Cents

LADIES' HOME
JOURNAL

IT'S UP
TO
THE
WOMEN

IN THIS ISSUE—
Booth Tarkington
H. G. Wells
Bess Streeter Aldrich
Dorothy Dix
Mary Roberts Rinehart

It's Up to the Women

Ironically, as women struggled to cope with their own unemployment or to help their families weather the hard times, advertisers relentlessly urged middle-class women to maintain their consumption patterns as a means of stimulating the economy and bringing about recovery. This 1932 cover for *Ladies' Home Journal* not only emphasizes the perception of women's pivotal role as consumers but also evokes the patriotism of the Great War through use of the icon of Uncle Sam, so familiar in World War I posters. The analogy between fighting a war and fighting the depression was a common theme throughout the decade.

Ladies' Home Journal, February 1932. Collection of Picture Research Consultants & Archives.

white women expanded their presence in the labor market, too; the total number of married women employed outside the home rose 50 percent. Working women, especially white married women, encountered sharp resentment and outright discrimination in the workplace. When asked in a 1936 Gallup poll whether wives should work when their husbands had jobs, 82 percent of those interviewed said no. Such public disapproval encouraged restrictions on women's right to work. From 1932 to 1937 the federal government would not allow a husband and a wife to hold government jobs at the same time. Many states adopted laws that prohibited married women from working.

Married or not, most women worked because of necessity. A sizable minority were the sole support of their families because their husbands had left home or lost their jobs. Single, divorced, deserted, or widowed women had no husbands to support them. This was especially true of poor black women. A survey of Chicago revealed that two-fifths of adult black women in the city were single. These working women rarely took jobs away from men. "Few of the people who oppose married women's employment," observed one feminist in 1940, "seem to realize that a coal miner or steel worker cannot very well fill the jobs of nursemaids, cleaning women, or the factory and clerical jobs now filled by women." Custom made gender crossovers from one field to another rare.

The division of the workforce by gender gave white women a small edge during the depression. Many fields where they had concentrated—including clerical, sales, and service and trade occupations—reinforced the traditional stereotypes of female work but suffered less from economic contraction than heavy industry, which employed men almost exclusively. As a result unemployment rates for white women, although extremely high, were somewhat lower than those for their male counterparts. This small bonus came at a high price, however. When the depression ended, women were even more concentrated in low-paying, dead-end jobs than when it began. White women also benefited at the expense of minority women. To make ends meet white women willingly sought jobs usually held by blacks or other minority workers—domestic service jobs, for example—and employers were quick to act on their preference for white workers.

White men also took jobs once held by minority males. Contemporary observers' concerns about the crisis of the male breadwinner or married women in the workforce rarely extended to blacks. Most commentators paid scant attention to the impact of the depression on the black family, focusing instead on the perceived threats to the stability of white households. As one historian explains it, few leaders worried "over the baneful effects of economic independence on the male ego when the ego in question was that of a black husband."

During the Great Depression there were few feminist demands for equal rights, at home or on the job. On an individual basis, women's self-esteem probably rose because of the importance of their work to family survival. Most men and women, however, continued to believe that the two sexes should have fundamentally different roles and responsibilities and that a woman's life cycle should be shaped by marriage and her husband's career.

The depression hit another segment of the family—the nation's 21 million young people—especially hard. Though small children often escaped the sense of bitterness and failure that gripped their elders, hard times made children grow up fast. About 250,000 young people became so demoralized that they took to the road as hobos and "sisters of the road," as female tramps were called. Others chose to stay in school longer: public schools were free, and they were warm in the winter. In 1930 less than half the nation's youth attended high school, compared with three-fourths in 1940, toward the end of the depression. College, however, remained the privilege of a distinct minority. About 1.2 million young people, or 7.5 percent of the population between eighteen and twenty-four, attended college in the 1930s. Forty percent of them were women. After 1935 college became slightly more affordable when the National Youth Administration (NYA) gave part-time employment to more than 2 million college and high school students. The government agency also provided work for 2.6 million out-of-school youths.

College students worked hard in the 1930s; financial sacrifice encouraged seriousness of purpose. Interest in fraternities and sororities declined as many students became involved in political movements. Fueled by disillusionment with World War I, thousands of youth took the "Oxford Pledge" never to support U.S. involvement in a war. In 1936 the Student Strike against War drew support from several hundred thousand students across the country.

Although many youths enjoyed more education in the 1930s, the depression damaged their future prospects. Studies of social mobility confirm that young men who entered their twenties during the depression era had less successful careers than those who came before or after. Having conducted extensive interviews with these youths all over the nation, the writer Maxine Davis described them as "runners, delayed at the gun," adding, "The depression years have left us with a generation robbed of time and opportunity just as the Great War left the world its heritage of a lost generation."

Popular Culture Views the Depression

Americans turned to popular culture to alleviate some of the trauma of the Great Depression. In June 1935 a Chicago radio listener wrote station WLS, "I feel your music and songs are what pulled me through this winter." She explained that "Half the time we were blue and broke. One year during the depression and no work. Kept from going on relief but lost everything we possessed doing so. So thanks for the songs, for they make life seem more like living." Mass culture flourished in the 1930s, offering not just entertainment but commentary on the problems that beset the nation. Movies and radio served as a forum for criticizing the system—especially politicians and bankers—as well as vehicles for reaffirming traditional ideals.

Despite the closing of one-third of the country's theaters by 1933, the movie industry and its studio system flourished. Sixty percent of Americans—some 60 to 75 million people—embraced this low-cost entertainment and flocked to the cinema each week, seeking solace from the pain of the depression. In the early thirties moviegoers might be titillated or scandalized by Mae West, who was known for her sexual innuendos: "I used to be Snow White, but I drifted." But in response to public outcry against immorality in the movies, especially from the Protestant and Catholic churches, the industry established a means of self-censorship, the Production Code Administration. After 1934 somewhat racy films were supplanted by sophisticated, fast-paced, screwball comedies like *It Happened One Night*, which swept the Oscars in 1934. The musical comedies of Fred Astaire and Ginger Rogers, including *Top Hat* (1935) and *The Gay Divorcee* (1934), in which the two dancers seemed to glide effortlessly through opulent sets, provided a stark contrast with most moviegoers' own lives.

But Hollywood, which produced 5,000 films during the decade, offered much more than what on the surface might seem to be escapist entertainment. Many of its movies contained complex messages that reflected a real sense of the societal crisis that engulfed the nation. Depression-era films repeatedly portrayed politicians as cynical and corrupt. In *Washington Merry-Go-Round* (1932), lobbyists manipulated weak congressmen to undermine democratic rule. The Marx Brothers' irreverent comedies, like *Animal Crackers* (1930), *Duck Soup* (1933), and *A Night at the Opera* (1935), more humorously criticized authority—and most everything else. Even if they did not deal specifically with the economic or political crisis, many films reaffirmed traditional values like democracy, individualism, and egalitarianism. They also contained criticisms—suggestions that the system was not working or that law and

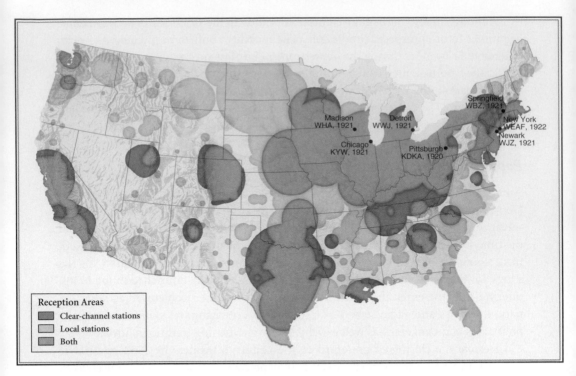

Reception Areas
■ Clear-channel stations
□ Local stations
■ Both

MAP 24.1 The Spread of Radio, to 1939

In 1938 more than 26 million American households, or about three-quarters of the population, had a radio. Four national networks dominated the field, broadcasting news and entertainment across the country. Powerful clear-channel stations reached listeners hundreds of miles away. By 1939 only sparsely populated areas were beyond radio's reach.

order had broken down. Thus popular gangster movies—such as *Public Enemy* (1931), with James Cagney, or *Little Caesar* (1930), starring Edward G. Robinson— could be seen as perverse Horatio Alger tales, in which the main character struggled to succeed in a harsh environment. Often these movies suggested that incompetent or corrupt politicians, police, and businessmen were as much to blame for organized crime as the gangsters themselves.

Few filmmakers left more of a mark on the decade than Frank Capra. An Italian immigrant who personified the possibilities for success that the United States offered, Capra made films that spoke to Americans' idealism. In movies like *Mr. Deeds Goes to Town* (1936) and *Mr. Smith Goes to Washington* (1939), he pitted the virtuous small-town hero against corrupt urban shysters—businessmen, politicians, lobbyists, and newspaper publishers—whose machinations subverted the nation's ideals. Though the hero usually prevailed, Capra was realistic enough to suggest that the victory was not necessarily permanent and that the problems the nation faced were serious.

Radio occupied an increasingly important place in popular culture during the 1930s (Map 24.1). At the beginning of the decade, about 13 million households had radios; by the end 27.5 million owned them. Listeners tuned in to daytime serials like *Ma Perkins*, picked up useful household hints on *The Betty Crocker Hour*, or enjoyed the Big Band "swing" of Benny Goodman, Duke Ellington, and Tommy Dorsey. Weekly variety shows featured Jack Benny; George Burns and Gracie Allen; and the ventriloquist Edgar Bergen and his impudent dummy, Charlie McCarthy. And millions of listeners followed the adventures of the Lone Ranger, Superman, and Dick Tracy.

Americans did not spend all their leisure time in commercial entertainment. In a resurgence of traditionalism, attendance at religious services rose and the home again became a center for pleasurable pastimes. Amateur photography and stamp collecting enjoyed tremendous vogues, as did the new board game Monopoly, invented in 1934 by an unemployed Germantown, Pennsylvania, man. Reading aloud from books borrowed from the public library was another affordable diversion. But Americans bought books, too. Taking advantage of new manufacturing processes that made books cheaper, they made best-sellers of Margaret Mitchell's *Gone with the Wind* (1936), James Hilton's *Lost Horizon* (1933), and Pearl Buck's *The Good Earth* (1932).

Harder Times for the Down and Out

Much writing about the 1930s has focused on white working-class or middle-class families caught suddenly in a downward spiral. For African Americans, farmers, Mexican Americans, and Asian Americans, times had always been hard; during the 1930s they got much harder. As the poet Langston Hughes noted, "The depression brought everybody down a peg or two. And the Negroes had but few pegs to fall."

African Americans in the Depression

The African American worker had always known discrimination and limited opportunities and thus viewed the depression differently from most whites. "The novelist and poet Maya Angelou, who grew up in Stamps, Arkansas, recalled, "The country had been in the throes of the Depression for two years before the Negroes in Stamps knew it. I think that everyone thought the Depression, like everything else, was for the white folks."

Despite the black migration to northern cities, which had begun before World War I, as late as 1940 more than 75 percent of African Americans still lived in the South. Nearly all black farmers lived in the South, their condition scarcely better than it had been at the end of Reconstruction. Only 20 percent of black farmers owned their land; the rest toiled at the bottom of the South's exploitative agricultural system as tenant farmers, farm hands, and sharecroppers. African Americans rarely earned more than $200 a year, less than a quarter of the average annual wages of a factory worker. In one Louisiana parish black women averaged only $41.67 a year picking cotton.

Throughout the 1920s southern agriculture had suffered from falling prices and overproduction. The depression made an already desperate situation worse. Some black farmers tried to protect themselves by joining the Southern Tenant Farmers Union (STFU), which was founded in 1934. The STFU was one of the few southern groups that welcomed both blacks and whites. "The same chain that holds you hold my people, too," an elderly black farmer reminded whites on the organizing committee. Landowners, however, had a stake in keeping sharecroppers from organizing, and they countered the union's efforts with repression and harassment. In the end the STFU could do little to reform an agricultural system based on such deep economic and racial inequities.

All blacks faced harsh social and political discrimination throughout the South. In a celebrated 1931 case in Scottsboro, Alabama, two white women who had been riding a freight train claimed to have been raped by nine black youths, all under twenty years old. The two women's stories contained many inconsistencies, and one woman later recanted. But in the South when a white woman claimed to have been raped by a black, she was taken at her word and the accused man's guilt was taken for granted. Two weeks later juries composed entirely of white men found all nine defendants guilty of rape; eight were sentenced to death. (One defendant escaped the death penalty because he was a minor.) Though the U.S. Supreme Court overturned the sentences in 1932 and ordered new trials on grounds that the defendants had been denied adequate legal counsel, five of the men eventually were again convicted and sentenced to long prison terms. The Scottsboro case received wide coverage in black communities across the country. Along with an increase in lynching in the early 1930s (twenty blacks were lynched in 1930, twenty-four in 1933), it gave black Americans a strong incentive to head for the North and the Midwest.

Harlem, one of their main destinations, was already strained by the enormous influx of African Americans in the 1920s. The depression only aggravated the housing shortage. Residential segregation kept blacks from moving elsewhere, so they paid excessive rents to live in deteriorating buildings where crowded living conditions fostered disease and premature death. As whites clamored for jobs traditionally held by blacks—as waiters, domestic servants, elevator operators, and garbage collectors—unemployment in Harlem rose to 50 percent, twice the national rate. At the height of the depression, shelters and soup kitchens staffed by the Divine Peace Mission, under the leadership of the charismatic black religious leader Father Divine, provided 3,000 meals a day for Harlem's destitute.

In March 1935 Harlem exploded in the only major race riot of the decade. Anger about the lack of jobs, a slowdown in relief services, and economic exploitation of the black community had been building for years. Although white-owned stores were entirely dependent on black trade, store owners would not employ blacks. The arrest of a black shoplifter, followed by rumors that he had been severely beaten by white police, triggered the riot. Four blacks were killed, and $2 million worth of property was damaged.

There were some signs of hope for African Americans in the 1930s. Partly in response to the 1935 riot but mainly in return for growing black allegiance to the

Scottsboro Defendants

The 1931 trial in Scottsboro, Alabama, of nine black youths accused of raping two white women became a symbol to blacks of the injustices they faced in the South's legal system. Denied access to an attorney, the defendants were all found guilty and eight were sentenced to death. When the U.S. Supreme Court overturned their convictions in 1932, the International Labor Defense organization hired the noted criminal attorney, Samuel Leibowitz, for their new trial. This photograph, taken in a Decatur jail, shows from left to right standing Olen Montgomery, Clarence Norris, Willie Roberson (front), Andrew Wright, Ozie Powell, Eugene Williams, Charley Weems, and Roy Wright. Seated at right is Haywood Patterson; at left is Samuel Leibowitz. Brown Brothers.

Democratic Party (see Chapter 25), the New Deal would channel significant amounts of relief money toward blacks outside the South. And the National Association for the Advancement of Colored People (NAACP) continued to challenge the status quo of race relations. Though calls for racial justice went largely unheeded during the depression, World War II and its aftermath would further the struggle for black equality.

Dust Bowl Migrations

A distressed agricultural sector had been one of the causes of the Great Depression. In the 1930s conditions only got worse, especially for farmers on the Great Plains. In the semiarid states of Oklahoma, Texas, New Mexico, Colorado, Arkansas, and Kansas,

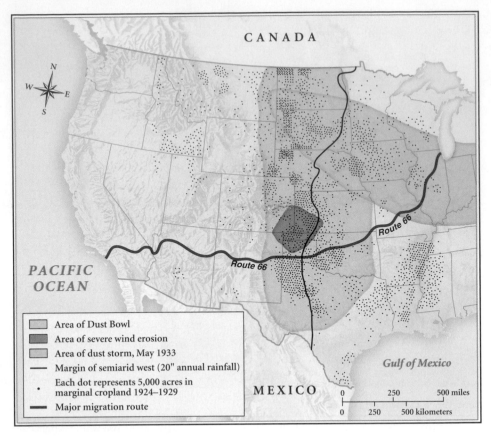

MAP 24.2 The Dust Bowl, 1930–1941

A U.S. Weather Bureau scientist called the drought of the 1930s "the worst in the climatological history of the country." Conditions were especially severe in the southern plains, where the dramatic increases in farming on marginal land had strained production even before the drought struck. Many farm families saw no choice but to follow Route 66, the highway that went west through Missouri, Oklahoma, and north Texas to California, the promised land.

FOR MORE HELP ANALYZING THIS MAP, see the Online Study Guide at **bedfordstmartins.com/henrettaconcise**.

farmers had always risked the ravages of drought (see Chapter 16), but the years 1930 to 1941 witnessed the worst drought in the country's history. Low rainfall alone did not create the Dust Bowl, however. National and international market forces, like the rising demand for wheat during World War I, had caused farmers to push the farming frontier beyond its natural limits. To capture a profit they had stripped the land of its native vegetation, destroying the delicate ecological balance of the plains (Map 24.2). When the rains dried up and the winds came, nothing remained to hold the soil. Huge clouds of dust rolled over the plains, causing streetlights to blink on as if night had fallen. Dust seeped into houses and "blackened the pillow around one's head, the dinner plates on the table, the bread dough on the back of the stove."

Drought Refugees

Like the Joad family in John Steinbeck's powerful novel *The Grapes of Wrath* (1939), many thousands of poor people hit hard by the drought, dust, and debt of farm life in the Great Plains loaded all their possessions in a pickup truck and set out for a new start in the West. In this 1937 photograph of Missouri drought refugees on Highway 99 near Tracy, California, photographer Dorothea Lange vividly captures the migrants' bleak circumstances. Library of Congress.

FOR MORE HELP ANALYZING THIS IMAGE, see the Online Study Guide at **bedfordstmartins.com/henrettaconcise**.

The ecological disaster prompted a mass exodus from the plains. Their crops ruined, their lands barren and dry, their homes foreclosed for debts they could not pay, at least 350,000 "Okies" (so called whether or not they were from Oklahoma) loaded their belongings into beat-up Fords and headed west, encouraged by handbills distributed by growers that promised good jobs in California. Some went to metropolitan areas, but about half settled in rural areas where they worked for low wages as migratory farm laborers. John Steinbeck's novel *The Grapes of Wrath* (1939) immortalized them and their journey. In the novel the Joads abandon their land not only because of drought but also as a result of the economic transformation of American agriculture that had begun during World War I. By the 1930s large-scale commercialized farming had spread to the plains, where family farmers still used draft animals. In Steinbeck's novel, after the bank forecloses on the Joads' farm, a gasoline-engine tractor, the symbol of mechanized farming, plows under their crops and demolishes their home. Though it was a powerful novel, *The Grapes of Wrath* did not convey the diversity of the westward migration. Not all Okies were destitute dirt farmers; perhaps one in six was a professional, a business proprietor, or a white-collar worker. For most the drive west was fairly easy. Route 66 was a paved two-lane road; in a decent car the journey from Oklahoma or Texas to California took only three to four days.

Before the 1930s Californians had developed a different type of agriculture from that practiced in the Southwest and Midwest. Basically industrial in nature, California agriculture was large-scale, intensive, and diversified, ironically requiring a massive irrigation system that would lay the groundwork for serious future environmental problems. The key crops were specialty foods—citruses, grapes, potatoes—whose staggered harvests required a great deal of transient labor during short picking seasons. A steady supply of cheap migrant labor provided by Chinese, Mexicans, Okies, Filipinos, and, briefly, East Indians made this type of farming economically feasible.

The migrants had a lasting impact on California culture. At first they met outright hostility from old-time Californians—a demoralizing experience for white native-born Protestants, who were ashamed of the Okie stereotype. But they stayed, filling important roles in California's expanding economy. Soon some communities in the San Joaquin Valley—Bakersfield, Fresno, Merced, Modesto, and Stockton—took on a distinctly Okie cast, identifiable by southern-influenced evangelical religion and the growing popularity of country music.

Mexican American Communities

As Okies arrived in California, many Mexican Americans were leaving. In the depths of the depression, with fear of competition from foreign workers at a peak, perhaps a third of the Mexican American population, most of them immigrants, returned to Mexico. A federal deportation policy—fostered by racism and made possible by the proximity of Mexico—was partly responsible for the exodus, but many more Mexicans left voluntarily when work ran out and local relief agencies refused to assist them. Los Angeles lost approximately one-third of its Mexican community of 150,000—the largest concentration of Mexicans outside Mexico—during the deportations, which separated families, disrupted children's education, and caused extreme financial hardship during the worst years of the depression. They also created a leadership vacuum in Mexican American community and labor organizations, as leaders of these groups returned—sometimes involuntarily—to Mexico.

A Bitter Harvest

In the early 1930s California was rocked by strikes, and one of the largest was the cotton-pickers' strike of 1933. Demanding higher wages and better working conditions, the predominantly Mexican American workforce set up camps for the duration of the strike. As usual, it was the women who bore most of the responsibility for cooking, cleaning, and child care.

Bancroft Library, University of California, Berkeley.

Although forced repatriation slowed after 1932, for those who remained in America deportation was still a constant threat, an unmistakable reminder of their fragile status in the United States.

Discrimination and exploitation were omnipresent in the Mexican community. The harsh experiences of migrant workers influenced a young Mexican American named César Chávez, who would become one of the twentieth century's most influential labor organizers. In the mid-1930s Chávez's father became involved in several bitter labor struggles in California's Imperial Valley. Thirty-seven major agricultural strikes occurred in California in 1933 alone, including one in the San Joaquin Valley that mobilized 18,000 cotton pickers—the largest agricultural strike to date. All these strikes failed, but they gave the young Chávez a background in labor organizing, which he would use to found the National Farmworkers Association (later the United Farm Workers union) in 1962.

Not all Mexican Americans were migrant farmworkers. A significant number lived in urban areas and held industrial jobs, especially in steel mills, meatpacking plants, and refineries, where they established a strong tradition of labor activism. Mexican American smelter and refinery workers joined the International Union of Mine, Mill and Smelter Workers (known colloquially as "Mine-Mill") in large numbers and became key leaders. Bert Corona launched his career as a labor organizer with the International Longshoremen's and Warehousemen's Union in Los Angeles. In California, Mexican Americans also found employment in fruit- and vegetable-processing plants. Young single women especially preferred the higher-paying cannery work to domestic service, needlework, and farm labor. In plants owned by corporate giants like Del Monte, McNeill, and Libby, Mexican American women earned around $2.50 a day, while their male counterparts received $3.50 to $4.50. Labor unions came to the canneries in 1939 with the formation of the United Cannery, Agricultural, Packing, and Allied Workers of America, an unusually democratic union in which women, the majority of the rank-and-file workers, played a leading role.

Activism in the fields and factories demonstrated how a second generation of Mexican Americans, born in the United States, had turned increasingly to the struggle for political and economic justice in the United States rather than retaining primary allegiance to Mexico. Joining American labor unions and becoming more involved in American politics (see Chapter 25) were important steps in the creation of a distinct Mexican American ethnic identity.

Asian Americans Face the Depression

Men and women of Asian descent—mostly from China, Japan, and the Philippines—constituted a tiny minority that concentrated primarily in the western states. Their experiences during the depression were as diverse as the people themselves, although all were subject to a pervasive anti-Asian racism. Second-generation Japanese Americans, for example, had eagerly pursued higher education, finishing an average of two years of college during the period of 1925 to 1935, but relatively few professional jobs were open to them as white firms refused to hire them. They and their families concentrated in farming and small ethnic enterprises, often linked to agriculture, such as fruit and vegetable vending. They had carved out a modest success by the time of the depression, despite a 1913 California law, strengthened in 1920, that prohibited Japanese immigrants from owning land. Having circumvented the laws by various devices—including putting land titles in the names of their citizen children—during the depression, most Japanese farmers managed to hold on to their land, and the amount of acreage owned actually increased. But times were hard, and many farm families barely eked out a decent subsistence. Twenty-two percent of the immigrant population—presumably the poorest—returned to Japan during the depression. And toward the end of the decade, economic anxieties were compounded by renewed anti-Japanese sentiment, stemming from mounting tensions between the United States and Japan over the latter's aggression in Asia (see Chapter 26).

Chinese Americans as a rule had not prospered as much as the Japanese. For example statistics show that as late as 1940, only around 3 percent of Chinese Americans were engaged in professional and technical occupations. But ironically the discrimination that had kept them isolated from the mainstream economy may have proved somewhat beneficial as they weathered the 1930s. In San Francisco, where Chinese were excluded from most industrial jobs, they clustered in ethnic enterprises in the city's Chinatown. Like the rest of the nation's small enterprises, Chinatown's businesses and their employees suffered during the depression, but they bounced back much more quickly. And similar to the experience of white working women, Chinese women found that the labor market that had limited them to a handful of low-paid job categories in light industry and service work in good times worked to their advantage in hard times. They were far less likely to be unemployed than Chinese men. Despite these factors that may have meliorated the hardships of the depression, most Chinese immigrants and their families were on the margins economically. In hard times they turned inward to the community, getting assistance from traditional Chinese social organizations such as *huiguan* (district associations) and kin networks until San Francisco finally extended relief assistance to them. Approximately one-sixth of the city's Chinese population was on public assistance in 1931. The New Deal aided them as well, although many programs were limited to citizens and thus barred Chinese immigrants who were "aliens ineligible for citizenship" until the repeal of the Chinese Exclusion Act in 1943.

Filipinos differed from the Japanese and Chinese in that they alone were not affected by the ban on Asian immigration passed in 1924 (see Chapter 23) because the Philippines was a U.S. territory. Consequently, their numbers swelled during the 1920s, and by 1930 over 45,000 had emigrated, concentrating mostly along the Pacific Coast. Relegated primarily to menial labor, 60 percent found jobs in agriculture, where they were preferred for the arduous stoop labor for which growers believed they were exceptionally well suited. When the depression struck, Filipinos were among the most militant of the agricultural workers who organized to try to extract decent pay from their employers. Although their first major strike in 1933 was broken, in part by the use of Mexican, Japanese, and East Indian strikebreakers, they later enjoyed some success in extracting wage concessions. In 1936 Filipinos and Mexican workers came together in a Field Workers Union chartered by the American Federation of Labor.

Just as the depression focused attention on Mexican immigration, hard times also led to demands that Filipino immigration be restricted. Racial hostility, as well as a concern about Filipinos as competitors for jobs and public relief, fueled the drive to bring about immigration exclusion by making the Philippines an independent nation. In 1934 Congress passed the Tydings-McDuffie Act, which granted independence, classified all Filipinos in the United States as aliens, and restricted immigration to fifty persons per year. By the time the act passed, immigration had slowed to a trickle, but their new status as aliens ineligible for citizenship—or most New Deal assistance programs—had a powerful impact on the Filipinos who remained as unwelcome interlopers.

Herbert Hoover and the Great Depression

Had Herbert Hoover been elected in 1920 instead of 1928, he probably would have been a popular president. As the director of successful food conservation programs at home and charitable food relief abroad during World War I, he was respected as an intelligent and able administrator. Although Hoover's name frequently emerged as a possible candidate in 1920, he did not run for president until the end of the decade. Timing was against him. Although his optimistic predictions in the 1928 campaign—that "the poorhouse is vanishing from among us" and that America was "nearer to the final triumph over poverty than ever before in the history of any land"—reflected beliefs that many Americans shared, that prosperity and Hoover's reputation were soon to be dramatically undermined. When the stock market crashed in 1929, Hoover stubbornly insisted that the downturn was only temporary. In June 1930 he greeted a business delegation with the words, "Gentlemen, you have come sixty days too late. The Depression is over." As the country hit rock bottom in 1931 and 1932, the president finally acted, but by then it was too little, too late.

Hoover Responds

Hoover's approach to the Great Depression was shaped by his priorities as secretary of commerce. Hoping to avoid coercive measures on the part of the federal government, he turned to the business community for leadership in overcoming the economic downturn. Hoover asked business executives to maintain wages and production levels voluntarily and to work with the government to build people's confidence in the economic system.

Hoover did not rely solely on public pronouncements, however; he also used public funds and federal action to encourage recovery. Soon after the stock market crash, he cut federal taxes and called on state and local governments to increase their expenditures on public construction projects. He signed the 1929 Agricultural Marketing Act, which gave the federal government an unprecedented role in stabilizing agriculture. In 1930 and the first half of 1931, Hoover raised the federal budget for public works to $423 million, a dramatic increase in expenditures not traditionally considered to be the federal government's responsibility. Hoover also eased the international crisis by declaring a moratorium on the payment of Allied debts and reparations early in the summer of 1931. The depression continued, however. When the president, alarmed about the federal deficit, asked Congress for a 33 percent tax increase to balance the budget, the ill-advised move choked investment and, to a lesser extent, consumption, contributing significantly to the continuation of the depression.

Not all the steps taken by the Hoover administration were so ill conceived. The president pushed Congress to create a system of government home-loan banks in 1932 and supported the Glass-Steagall Banking Act of 1932, which made government securities available to guarantee Federal Reserve notes and thus temporarily propped up the ailing banking system. The federal government under Hoover also spent $700 million—an unprecedented sum for the time—on public works.

Hoover's most innovative program to aid the economy—one the New Deal would later draw on—was the Reconstruction Finance Corporation (RFC), approved by Congress in January 1932. Modeled on the War Finance Corporation of World War I and developed in collaboration with the business and banking communities, the RFC was the first federal institution created to intervene directly in the economy during peacetime. To alleviate the credit crunch for business, the RFC would provide federal loans to railroads, financial institutions, banks, and insurance companies in a strategy that has been called **pump priming**. In theory, money lent at the top of the economic structure would stimulate production, creating new jobs and increasing consumer spending. These benefits would eventually "trickle down" to the rest of the economy.

Unfortunately, the RFC lent its funds too cautiously to make a significant difference. Nonetheless, it represents a watershed in American political history and the growth of the federal government: when voluntary cooperation failed, the president turned to federal action to stimulate the economy. Yet Hoover's break with the past had clear limits. In many ways his support of the RFC was just another attempt to encourage business confidence. Compared with previous chief executives—and in contrast to his popular image as a "do-nothing" president—Hoover responded to the national emergency on an unprecedented scale. But the nation's needs were also unprecedented, and Hoover's programs failed to meet them (see American Voices, "Public Assistance Fails a Southern Farm Family," p. 746).

In particular, federal programs fell short of helping the growing ranks of the unemployed. Hoover remained adamant in his refusal to consider any plan for direct federal relief to those out of work. Throughout his career he had believed that privately organized charities were sufficient to meet the nation's social welfare needs. During World War I he had headed the Commission for Relief of Belgium, a private group that distributed 5 million tons of food to Europe's suffering civilian population. And in 1927 he had coordinated a rescue and cleanup operation after a devastating flood of the Mississippi River left 16.5 million acres of land under water in seven states. The success of these and other predominantly voluntary responses to public emergencies had confirmed Hoover's belief that private charity, not federal aid, was the "American way" of solving social problems. He would not undermine the country's hallowed faith in individualism, even in the face of evidence that charities and state and local relief agencies could not meet the needs of a growing unemployed population.

Rising Discontent

As the country entered the fourth year of depression, signs of rising discontent and rebellion emerged. Farmers were among the most vocal protesters, banding together to harass the bank agents and government officers who enforced evictions and

AMERICAN VOICES

~

Public Assistance Fails a Southern Farm Family

W*hen times were tough, even public assistance could be bad for a family in dire straits. Here the letter of a young mother living in the farming community of Commerce, Georgia, relates how relief efforts ironically proved to be a burden to her family of eight. She also indicates the strains that "making do" put on poor women.*

I've just met with a problem I cannot solve alone. I am a Mother of six children the oldest is only 11 years old the youngest 18 months and I'm expecting another in March. We couldn't get any crop for 1936 because we could neither furnish ourselves or had any stock. So here we are having made out on a little work once in a while all summer. And then in Aug I had to have a serious operation and now I'm not able to feed & clothe our six children as my husband couldnt find anything at all to do was compelled to get on relief job at $1.28 a day 16 days a month. Well you take 8 meals 3 times a day out of $1.28 and what will you have left is 24 meals and what kind of meals do you have? We have to buy everything we eat. We have nothing except what we buy. Our bedclothes are threadbare our clothes the same. No shoes and no money to buy yet the relief say that cant help us as he is working. Can he work naked. Can he sleep cold. I don't know of any one at all that can help me and I know we cant go on like this.

We have four children in school and they cant go on unless thay [*sic*] have some warm clothes when cold weather sets in. . . . Do you know of any people in Atlanta that have any used clothes they would give in exchange for piecing quilts or quilting. Id be glad to do anything I can in exchange for clothes to keep our children in school.

I hate to be like this but can a person that is willing to work for a living and that honest and disable to help themselves sit idle and see their small children suffer day after day without enough food or clothes to keep their bodies warm when there are thousands of people with plenty to give if they knew your need.

How it hurts to know that you are almost starving in the land of plenty.

SOURCE: Julia Kirk Blackwelder, "Letters from the Great Depression," in *Southern Exposure* 6, no. 3 (Fall 1978): 77.

foreclosures and to protest the low prices they received for their crops. Midwestern farmers had watched the price of wheat fall from $3 a bushel in 1920 to barely 30 cents in 1932. Now they formed the Farm Holiday Association, barricaded local roads, and dumped milk, vegetables, and other farm produce in the dirt rather than accept prices that would not cover their costs. Nothing better captured the cruel irony of maldistribution than farmers destroying food at a time when thousands were going hungry.

Protest was not confined to rural America, however. Bitter labor strikes occurred in the depths of the depression, despite the threat that strikers would lose their jobs. In Harlan County, Kentucky, in 1931 miners struck over a 10 percent wage cut. Their

Hoovervilles

By 1930 shantytowns had sprung up in most of the nation's cities. In New York City squatters camped out along the Hudson River railroad tracks, built makeshift homes in Central Park, or lived in the city dump. This scene from the old reservoir in Central Park looks east toward the fancy apartment buildings of Fifth Avenue and the Metropolitan Museum of Art, at left.
© Bettmann / Corbis.

union was crushed by mine owners and the National Guard. In 1932 at Ford's River Rouge factory outside Detroit, a demonstration provoked violence from police and Ford security forces; three demonstrators were killed, and fifty more were seriously injured. Later some 40,000 people viewed the coffins under a banner charging that "Ford Gave Bullets for Bread."

In 1931 and 1932 violence broke out in the nation's cities. Groups of the unemployed battled local authorities over inadequate relief, staging rent riots and hunger marches. Some of these actions, such as "unemployment councils" that agitated for jobs and food and a hunger march on Washington, D.C., in 1931, were organized by the Communist Party—still a tiny organization with only 12,000 members—as a challenge to the capitalist system. Though the marches were well attended and often got results from local and federal authorities, they did not necessarily win converts to communism.

Not radicals but veterans staged the most publicized—and most tragic—protest. In the summer of 1932, the "Bonus Army," a ragtag group of about 15,000 unemployed World War I veterans, hitchhiked to Washington to demand immediate payment of their bonuses, originally scheduled for distribution in 1945. While their leaders lobbied Congress, the Bonus Army camped out in the capital. "We were heroes in 1917, but we're bums now," one veteran complained bitterly. When the marchers refused to leave their Anacostia Flats camp, Hoover called out riot troops to clear the area. Led by General Douglas MacArthur, and assisted by Major Dwight D. Eisenhower and Major George S. Patton, the troops burned the encampment to the ground. In the fight that followed, more than a hundred marchers were injured. Newsreel footage captured the deeply disturbing spectacle of the U.S. Army moving against its own veterans, and Hoover's popularity plunged even lower.

The 1932 Election: A New Order

Despite the evidence of discontent, the nation overall was not in a revolutionary mood as it approached the 1932 election. Having internalized Horatio Alger's ideal of the **self-made man**, many Americans initially blamed themselves rather than the system for their hardship. Despair and apathy, not anger, was their mood. The Republicans, who could find no credible way to dump an incumbent president, unenthusiastically renominated Hoover. The Democrats turned to Governor Franklin Delano Roosevelt of New York, who won the nomination by capitalizing on that state's reputation for innovative relief and unemployment programs.

Roosevelt, born into a wealthy New York family in 1882 (a fifth cousin to former president Theodore Roosevelt), had attended Harvard College and Columbia Law School. He had served in the New York State legislature and as assistant secretary of the navy in the Wilson administration, a post that had earned him the vice presidential nomination on the Democratic ticket in 1920. Roosevelt's rise to the presidency was interrupted in 1921 by an attack of polio that left both his legs paralyzed for life. But he fought back from illness, emerging from the ordeal a stronger, more resilient man. "If you had spent two years in bed trying to wiggle your toe, after that anything would seem easy," he explained. His wife, Eleanor, strongly supported his return to public life and helped to mastermind his successful campaign for the governorship of New York in 1928.

The 1932 campaign for the presidency foreshadowed little of the New Deal. Roosevelt hinted only vaguely at new approaches to alleviating the depression: "The country needs and, unless I mistake its temper, the country demands bold, persistent experimentation." He won easily, receiving 22.8 million votes to Hoover's 15.7 million. Despite the nation's economic collapse, Americans remained firmly committed to the two-party system. The Socialist Party candidate, Norman Thomas, got fewer than a million votes, and the Communist candidate, party leader William Z. Foster, drew only 100,000 votes (Map 24.3).

The 1932 election marked a turning point in American politics—the emergence of a Democratic coalition that would help to shape national politics for the next

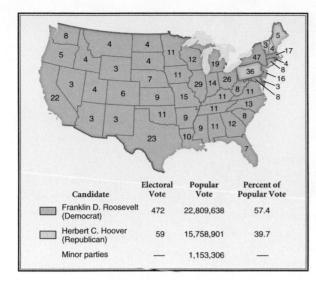

MAP 24.3 Presidential Election of 1932

Franklin Roosevelt's convincing electoral victory over Herbert Hoover in 1932 resulted from a political realignment and dissatisfaction with the incumbent president. Even in the midst of the gravest crisis capitalism ever faced, candidates of the Communist and Socialist Parties received fewer than 1 million votes out of almost 40 million cast.

Candidate	Electoral Vote	Popular Vote	Percent of Popular Vote
Franklin D. Roosevelt (Democrat)	472	22,809,638	57.4
Herbert C. Hoover (Republican)	59	15,758,901	39.7
Minor parties	—	1,153,306	—

four decades. Roosevelt won the support of the **Solid South**, which returned to the Democratic fold after defecting in 1928 because of Al Smith's Catholicism and his views on Prohibition. Roosevelt drew substantial support in the West and in the cities, continuing a trend first noticed in 1928, when the Democrats appealed successfully to recent immigrants and urban ethnic groups. However, Roosevelt's election was hardly a mandate to reshape American political and economic institutions. Many people voted as much against Hoover as for Roosevelt.

Having spoken, the voters had to wait until Roosevelt's inauguration in March 1933 to see him put his ideas into action. (The four month interval between the election and the inauguration was shortened by the Twentieth Amendment in 1933.) In the worst winter of the depression, Americans could do little but hope that things would get better. According to the most conservative estimates, unemployment stood at 20 to 25 percent nationwide. The rate was 50 percent in Cleveland, 60 percent in Akron, and 80 percent in Toledo—cities dependent on manufacturing jobs in industries that had essentially shut down. The nation's banking system was so close to collapse that many state governors closed banks temporarily to avoid further panic.

By the winter of 1932–33, the depression had totally overwhelmed public-welfare institutions. Private charity and public relief, both of whose expenditures had risen dramatically, still reached only a fraction of the needy. Hunger haunted cities and rural areas alike. When a teacher tried to send a coal miner's daughter home from school because she was weak from hunger, the girl replied, "It won't do any good . . . because this is sister's day to eat." In New York City hospitals reported ninety-five deaths from starvation. This was the America that Roosevelt inherited when he took the oath of office on March 4, 1933.

TIMELINE

1929	Stock market crash	**1933**	Unemployment rises to highest level
	Agricultural Marketing Act to stabilize agriculture		Franklin Delano Roosevelt becomes president
1930	Midwestern drought begins		Birthrate drops to lowest level due to depression
	Hawley-Smoot Tariff		The Marx Brothers in *Duck Soup*
1931	Scottsboro case	**1934**	Southern Tenant Farmers Union founded
	Hoover declares moratorium on Allied war debts		*It Happened One Night* sweeps Oscars
	Miners strike in Harlan County, Kentucky		Tydings-McDuffie Act grants Philippine independence and curtails immigration
1932	Reconstruction Finance Corporation created	**1935**	National Youth Administration created
	Bonus Army rebuffed in Washington		Harlem race riot
	Height of deportation of Mexican migrant workers	**1936**	Student Strike against War
	Farm Holiday Association dumps produce		Margaret Mitchell, *Gone with the Wind*
	Strike at Ford's River Rouge plant in Michigan		Birth control legalized
	Communist-led hunger marches	**1939**	John Steinbeck, *The Grapes of Wrath*
			Frank Capra, *Mr. Smith Goes to Washington*

For Further Exploration

The 1930s are particularly richly documented by collections of oral histories and other primary sources. Robert S. McElvaine's *Down and Out in the Great Depression* (1983) offers poignant letters written by ordinary people to the Roosevelts, Herbert Hoover, and other government officials. Studs Terkel's *Hard Times: An Oral History of the Great Depression* (1970) is an invaluable collection, as are Ann Banks, ed., *First-Person America* (1980), and Tom E. E. Terrill and Jerrold Hirsch, eds., *Such as Us: Southern Voices of the Thirties* (1978). James Agee and Walker Evans's *Let Us Now Praise Famous Men* (1941) is a powerful book on southern poverty, illustrated with haunting photographs by Evans. For a memoir of a depression-era childhood, see Russell Baker's *Growing Up* (1982). Similarly, there is much to choose from in the literature of the decade. The most familiar novel is John Steinbeck's *The Grapes of Wrath* (1939), but see also the radical novel *Pity Is Not Enough* (1933) by Josephine Herbst and Richard Wright's *Native Son* (1940), his classic novel about Bigger Thomas, a young African American man in Chicago mired in a life of poverty and violence. For a collection of poetry, fiction, and nonfiction writing, see Harvey Swados, *The American Writer and the Great Depression* (1966).

The University of Virginia's America in the 1930s is a comprehensive Web site. See especially On the Air, which offers audio clips of radio programs at <http://xroads.virginia. edu/~1930s/home_1.html>. Much valuable material can be found on the University of

Utrecht's American Culture in the 1930s site at <http://www.let.uu.nl/ams/xroads/ 1930proj.htm>, which in turn points to other sites dealing with literature, film, and other aspects of American culture during the depression. The Library of Congress's American Memory collection has extensive material on the depression, including the multimedia presentation Voices from the Dust Bowl: The Charles L. Todd and Robert Sonkin Migrant Worker Collection, 1940–41, at <http://memory.loc.gov/ammem/afctshtml/tshome.html>. Riding the Rails, a site connected to a PBS documentary, includes tales from teenage hobos, recordings of hobo songs, discussion of the increased problems faced by African American hobos, a timeline, and maps of the railway systems the hobos traveled. Find it at <http://www.pbs.org/wgbh/amex/rails/sfeature/ index.html>. "The Scottsboro Boys" Trials 1931–1937 is part of the Famous American Trials site created by University of Missouri–Kansas City law professor Douglas O. Linder. The site, <http://www.law.umkc.edu/faculty/projects/ FTrials/scottsboro/scottsb.htm>, offers a rich collection, including images, biographies, and details of the trials.

For definitions of key terms boldfaced in this chapter, see the glossary at the end of the book.

To assess your mastery of the material covered in this chapter, see the Online Study Guide at **bedfordstmartins.com/henrettaconcise**.

For map resources and primary documents, see **bedfordstmartins.com/henrettaconcise**.

Chapter 25

THE NEW DEAL
1933–1939

> I have been seeing people who, according to almost any standard, have practically nothing to look forward to or hope for. But there is hope; confidence, something intangible and real: the president won't forget us.
>
> WPA REPORTER MARTHA GELLHORN, GASTON COUNTY,
> NORTH CAROLINA, 1934

In his bold inaugural address on March 4, 1933, President Franklin Delano Roosevelt told a despondent, impoverished nation, "The only thing we have to fear is fear itself." That memorable phrase rallied a nation that had already endured almost four years of the worst economic contraction in its history, with no end in sight. His demeanor grim and purposeful, Roosevelt preached his first inaugural address like a sermon. Issuing ringing declarations of his vision of governmental activism—"This Nation asks for action, and action now"—he repeatedly compared combating the Great Depression to fighting a war. The new president was willing to ask Congress for "broad Executive power to wage a war against the emergency, as great as the power that would be given to me if we were in fact invaded by a foreign foe."

To wage this war Roosevelt proposed the *New Deal*, a term that he first used in his acceptance speech at the Democratic National Convention in 1932 and that eventually came to stand for his administration's complex set of responses to the nation's economic collapse. The New Deal was never a definitive plan of action but rather evolved and expanded over the course of Roosevelt's presidency. In a time of major crisis, it was meant to relieve suffering yet conserve the nation's political and economic institutions through unprecedented activity on the part of the national government. Its legacy would be an expanded federal presence in the economy and in the lives of ordinary citizens.

The New Deal Takes Over, 1933–1935

The Great Depression destroyed Herbert Hoover's political reputation and helped to make Roosevelt's. Although some Americans—especially wealthy conservatives— hated Roosevelt, he was immensely popular and beloved by many. Ironically, the

FDR

Franklin Delano Roosevelt was a consummate politician who loved the adulation of a crowd, such as this one greeting him in Elm Grove, West Virginia, as he campaigned for the presidency in 1932. Here he is pictured with coal miner Zeno Santanella. On his lap is a baby named Ruth Ann Dell.
Courtesy of the Franklin D. Roosevelt Library.

ideological differences between Hoover and Roosevelt were not that vast. Both were committed to maintaining the nation's basic institutional structure. Both believed in the basic morality of a balanced budget and extolled the values of hard work, cooperation, and sacrifice. But Roosevelt's personal charm, his political savvy, and his willingness to experiment made all the difference. Above all, his New Deal programs put people to work, instilling hope and restoring the nation's confidence.

The Roosevelt Style of Leadership

Roosevelt established an unusually close rapport with the American people. "Mr. Roosevelt is the only man we ever had in the White House who would understand that my boss is a son of a bitch," remarked one worker. Many ordinary citizens credited Roosevelt with the positive changes in their lives, saying, "He gave me a job" or "He saved my home." Roosevelt's masterful use of the new medium of radio, typified by the "fireside chats" he broadcast during his first two terms, fostered this personal identification (see American Voices, "Americans Respond to the Fireside Chats," p. 755). In the week after the inauguration, more than 450,000 letters, many of which addressed Roosevelt as a friend or a member of the family, poured into the White House. Whereas one person had handled public correspondence during the Hoover administration, a staff of fifty was required under Roosevelt.

Roosevelt's charisma allowed him to continue the expansion of presidential power begun in the administrations of Theodore Roosevelt and Woodrow Wilson. From the beginning he dramatically enlarged the role of the executive branch in initiating policy, thereby helping to create the modern presidency. For policy formulation he turned to his cabinet, which included Secretary of the Interior Harold Ickes, Frances Perkins at Labor, and Henry A. Wallace at Agriculture. When searching for new ideas, Roosevelt was just as likely to turn to advisors and administrators scattered throughout the New Deal bureaucracy. Eager young people flocked to Washington to join the New Deal. Lawyers in their mid-twenties and fresh out of Harvard found themselves drafting legislation or being called to the White House for strategy sessions with the president. Many young New Dealers who went on to distinguished careers in government or public service later recalled that nothing could match the excitement of the early New Deal.

The Hundred Days

The first problem the new president confronted was the banking crisis, which, far more than the stock market crash, had brought the depression home to the middle class. Since the onset of the depression, about 9 million people had lost their savings. On the eve of his inauguration, thirty-eight states had closed their banks. On March 5, the day after the inauguration, the president declared a national "bank holiday"—a euphemism for closing all the banks—and called Congress into special session. Four days later Congress passed Roosevelt's proposed emergency banking bill, which permitted banks to reopen beginning on March 13 but only if a Treasury Department inspection showed they had sufficient cash reserves. The House approved the plan quickly, as it would almost all early New Deal legislation, after only thirty-eight minutes of debate.

The Emergency Banking Act, which Roosevelt developed in consultation with banking leaders, was a conservative document that mirrored Herbert Hoover's proposals. The difference was the public's reaction. On the Sunday evening before the banks reopened, Roosevelt broadcast his first fireside chat to a radio audience estimated at 60 million. In simple terms he reassured citizens that the banks were safe, and Americans believed him. When the banks reopened on Monday morning, deposits exceeded withdrawals. "Capitalism was saved in eight days," observed Raymond Moley, who had served as Roosevelt's speechwriter in the 1932 campaign. By using the federal government to investigate the nation's banks and restore confidence in the system, the banking act did its job. Though more than 4,000 banks failed in 1933—the majority in the months before the law was passed—only 61 closed their doors in 1934.

Americans Respond to the Fireside Chats

*O**ver the course of his presidency, Franklin D. Roosevelt delivered thirty-one of his famous "fireside chats," in which he explained his policies, encouraged Americans to be optimistic about the future, and called upon them to support his programs. Roosevelt proved a master of the medium, and radio was one of the factors that gave so many Americans a sense of close connection to their president. The chats provoked floods of letters to the White House, many laudatory, others critical. The following were sent to Roosevelt after his first broadcast on March 12, 1933, when he explained how the New Deal would tackle the banking crisis and urged his listeners, "You people must have faith; you must not be stampeded by rumors or guesses. Let us unite in Banishing fear."*

My dear Mr. President,

Several neighbors . . . happened to be spending Sunday evening . . . when it was announced over the radio that you were to talk on the banking situation in the United States at ten o'clock.

There was silence for a moment and then the discussion began. There seemed to be a wide divergence of opinion as to whether or not you were going to make good and whether or not you had the confidence of the people. They were unanimous, however, in agreeing that your Inaugural address was a masterpiece, and that your message to Congress shot straight from the shoulder. Yet some were frantic and expressed the hope that your message would be such as to allow them to withdraw their life savings from some of the local banks.

When your radio talk began everyone seemed to become hypnotized, because there wasn't a word spoken by anyone until you had finished and then as if one voice were speaking all spoke in unison "we are saved." The frantic individuals of a few moments before declared that they would leave their money in the banks and that they were not afraid of the future. This little episode convinces me more than ever that you have the confidence of the people, that you are the man of the hour, and that with the united support of all its people, you are going to rehabilitate this great nation.

Sincerely,

Frank J. Cregg

Justice of the New York Supreme Court

Syracuse, N.Y.

Dear Sir:

While listening to your broadcast Sunday night, our little home seemed a church, our radio the pulpit—and you the preacher.

Thank you for the courage and faith you have given us.

May God bless and keep you to carry on the fight and we, the American people, will help you win.

Respectfully yours,

(Mrs.) Louise Hill

Chicago, Illinois

SOURCE: *The People and the President* by Lawrence W. Levine. Copyright © 2002 by Lawrence W. Levine and Cornelia Roettcher Levine. Reprinted by permission of Beacon Press, Boston.

The banking act was the first of fifteen pieces of major legislation enacted by Congress in the opening months of the Roosevelt administration, in what became known as the "Hundred Days." Congress created the Home Owners Loan Corporation to refinance home mortgages threatened by foreclosure. A second banking law, the Glass-Steagall Act, created the Federal Deposit Insurance Corporation (FDIC), which insured deposits up to $2,500. Another act established the Civilian Conservation Corps (CCC), which sent 250,000 young men to do reforestation and conservation work. The Tennessee Valley Authority (TVA) received legislative approval for its innovative plan of government-sponsored regional development and public energy. And in a move that lifted public spirits immeasurably, Roosevelt legalized beer in April. Full repeal of Prohibition came eight months later in December 1933.

To speed economic recovery the Roosevelt administration targeted three pressing problems: agricultural overproduction, business failures, and unemployment relief. Roosevelt considered a healthy farming sector crucial to the nation's economic well-being. As he put it in 1929, "If farmers starve today, we will all starve tomorrow." Thus he viewed the Agricultural Adjustment Act (AAA) as a key step toward the nation's recovery. The AAA established a system for seven major commodities (wheat, cotton, corn, hogs, rice, tobacco, and dairy products) that provided cash subsidies to farmers who cut production—a policy that continues to the present day. New Deal planners hoped prices would rise in response to the federally subsidized scarcity, spurring a general recovery.

Though the AAA stabilized the agricultural sector, its benefits were distributed unevenly. Subsidies for reducing production went primarily to the owners of large- and medium-size farms, who often cut production by reducing their renters' and share-croppers' acreage rather than their own. In the South, where many sharecroppers were black and the landowners and government administrators were white, that strategy had racial overtones. As many as 200,000 black tenant farmers were displaced from their land by the AAA. Thus New Deal agricultural policies fostered the migration of marginal farmers in the South and Midwest to northern cities and California, while they consolidated the economic and political clout of larger landholders.

The New Deal's major response to the problem of economic recovery, the National Industrial Recovery Act, launched the National Recovery Administration (NRA). The NRA, which drew on the World War I experience of Bernard Baruch's War Industries Board, established a system of industrial self-government to handle the problems of overproduction, cutthroat competition, and price instability that had caused business failures. Each industry—ranging from large concerns such as coal, cotton, and steel to small ones such as dog food and costume jewelry—hammered out a code of prices and production quotas, similar to those for farm products. In effect, these legally enforceable agreements suspended the antitrust laws. The codes also established minimum wages and maximum hours and outlawed child labor. One of the most far-reaching provisions, Section 7(a), guaranteed workers the right to organize and bargain collectively, "through representatives of their own choosing." These union rights dramatically spurred the growth of the labor movement in the

1930s. Yet trade associations, controlled by large companies, tended to dominate the code-drafting process, thus solidifying the power of large businesses at the expense of smaller enterprises. Labor had little input, and consumer interests almost none.

The early New Deal also addressed the critical problem of unemployment. In the fourth year of the depression, the total exhaustion of private and local sources of charity made some form of federal relief essential. Reluctantly, Roosevelt moved toward federal assumption of responsibility for the unemployed. The Federal Emergency Relief Administration (FERA), set up in May 1933 under the direction of Harry Hopkins, a social worker from New York, offered federal money to the states for relief programs. FERA was designed to keep people from starving until other recovery measures took hold. In his first two hours in office, Hopkins distributed $5 million. Over the program's two-year existence, FERA spent $1 billion.

Roosevelt and his advisors maintained a strong distaste for the dole. As Hopkins worried, "I don't think anybody can go year after year, month after month, accepting relief without affecting his character in some ways unfavorably. It is probably going to undermine the independence of hundreds of thousands of families." Whenever possible New Deal administrators promoted work relief over cash subsidies, and they consistently favored jobs that would not compete directly with the private sector. When the Public Works Administration (PWA), under Secretary of the Interior Harold L. Ickes, received a $3.3 billion appropriation in 1933, Ickes's cautiousness in initiating public works projects limited the agency's effectiveness. But in November 1933 Roosevelt established the Civil Works Administration (CWA) and named Harry Hopkins its head. Within thirty days the CWA had put 2.6 million men and women to work; at its peak in January 1934, it employed 4 million in jobs such as repairing bridges, building highways, constructing public buildings, and setting up community projects. The CWA, regarded as a stopgap measure to get the country through the winter of 1933–34, lapsed the next spring after spending all its funds.

Many of these early emergency measures were deliberately inflationary. They were designed to trigger price increases, which were thought necessary to stimulate recovery and halt the steep deflation. Another element of this strategy was Roosevelt's executive order of April 18, 1933, to abandon the international gold standard and allow gold to rise in value like any other commodity. As the price of gold rose, administrators hoped, so too would the prices of manufactured and agricultural goods. Though removing the country from the gold standard did not accomplish much toward economic recovery, it did provide the Federal Reserve System freedom to attempt to promote stable prices and full employment without being tied to the value of gold on the international market. Now it could manipulate the value of the dollar in response to fluctuating economic conditions.

After the Hundred Days, with no end to the depression in sight, Roosevelt and Congress continued to pass legislation to promote recovery and restore confidence. Much of it focused on reforming business practices to prevent future depressions. In 1934 Congress established the Securities and Exchange Commission (SEC) to regulate the stock market. The commission had the power to regulate the purchase

"Gulliver's Travels"

So many new agencies flooded out of Washington in the 1930s that one almost needed a scorecard to keep them straight. Here a July 1935 *Vanity Fair* cartoon by William Gropper substitutes Uncle Sam for Captain Lemuel Gulliver, tied to the ground by Lilliputians, in a parody of Jonathan Swift's *Gulliver's Travels*. Courtesy, *Vanity Fair*. © 1935 (renewed 1963) by The Conde Nast Publications, Inc.

of stocks on credit, or margin buying, and to restrict speculation by those with inside information on corporate plans. The Banking Act of 1935 authorized the president to appoint a new Board of Governors of the Federal Reserve System, placing control of interest rates and other money-market policies at the federal level rather than with regional banks. By requiring all large state banks to join the Federal Reserve System by 1942 to take advantage of the federal deposit insurance system, the law further encouraged centralization of the nation's banking system.

The New Deal under Attack

As Congress and the president consolidated the New Deal, their work came under attack from several quarters. Although Roosevelt billed himself as the savior of capitalism, noting that "to preserve we had to reform," his actions provoked strong hostility from many Americans who charged that he was undermining capitalism. To the wealthy Roosevelt became simply "that man," a traitor to his class. Business leaders and conservative Democrats formed the Liberty League in 1934 to lobby against the New Deal and its "reckless spending" and "socialist" reforms.

The conservative majority on the Supreme Court also disagreed with the direction of the New Deal. On "Black Monday," May 27, 1935, the Supreme Court struck down the National Industrial Recovery Act in *Schechter v. United States*, ruling unanimously that the NIRA represented an unconstitutional delegation of legislative power to the executive. The so-called sick-chicken case concerned a Brooklyn, New York, firm convicted of violating NRA codes by selling diseased poultry. The Court found in favor of the poultry firm, stating in its decision that the NRA illegally regulated commerce within states, while the Constitution limited federal regulation to interstate commerce.

Many citizens thought the New Deal had not gone far enough. Francis Townsend, a Long Beach, California, doctor, spoke for the nation's elderly who feared poverty because few had pension plans and many had lost their life savings in bank failures. In 1933 Townsend proposed the Old Age Revolving Pension Plan, which would give $200 a month—a considerable sum at the time—to citizens over the age of sixty. To receive payments the elderly would have to retire from their jobs, thus opening their positions to others, and would also have to agree to spend the money within a month. Townsend Clubs soon sprang up across the country, particularly in the Far West, and mobilized mass support for old-age pensions that would eventually help secure the passage of the far less ambitious plan created by the Social Security Act of 1935.

Father Charles Coughlin also challenged Roosevelt's leadership, attracting a large following, especially in the Midwest. A parish priest in Detroit, Coughlin had turned to the radio in the mid-1920s to enlarge his pastorate. In 1933 about 40 million Americans listened regularly to the Radio Priest's broadcasts. At first Coughlin supported the New Deal, but he soon broke with Roosevelt over the president's refusal to support the nationalization of the banking system and the expansion of the money supply. Although Coughlin offered varying solutions to the economic crisis, he tended to rely heavily on inflationary schemes that harked back to the Populist era (see Chapter 18). In 1935 he organized the National Union for Social Justice to promote his views, billing them as an alternative to those of "Franklin Double-Crossing Roosevelt." Because he was Canadian born and a priest, Coughlin was not likely to make a run for president, but his rapidly growing constituency threatened to complicate the 1936 election.

The most direct threat to Roosevelt came from Senator Huey Long. As governor of Louisiana, the flamboyant Long had achieved stunning popularity. He had increased the share of state taxes paid by corporations and had embarked on a program of public works that included construction of new highways, bridges, hospitals, and schools. But Long's accomplishments came at a price: to push through his reforms he had seized almost dictatorial control of the state government. He maintained power

The Kingfish

Huey Long, the Louisiana governor and senator, called himself "the Kingfish" because, he said, "I'm a small fish here in Washington. But I'm the Kingfish to the folks down in Louisiana." An exceptionally charismatic man and a brilliant campaigner, he attracted a significant following with his "Share Our Wealth" plan, which aimed to redistribute the nation's wealth. Democrats worried that he might run for president in 1936 on a third-party ticket, thus threatening Franklin Roosevelt's reelection, but his assassination in 1935 at the hands of a Louisiana doctor put an end to his political agenda. Long is seen here on the right, hat in hand. Louisiana State Museum.

over Louisiana's political machine even after his election to the U.S. Senate in 1930. Though he supported Roosevelt in 1932, he made no secret of his own presidential ambitions.

In 1934 Senator Long broke with the New Deal, arguing that its programs did not go far enough. Like Coughlin he established his own national movement, the Share Our Wealth Society, which boasted over 4 million followers by 1935. Arguing that the unequal distribution of wealth in the United States was the fundamental cause of the depression, Long advocated taxing 100 percent of all incomes over $1 million and all inheritances over $5 million, distributing the money to the rest of the population. He knew his plan was unworkable but confided privately, "When they figure that out, I'll have something new for them."

Like Coughlin, Long offered quick-fix solutions to the nation's economic ills that only addressed part of the complex problems that fueled the continuing depression. Their extreme proposals alarmed liberals, as both men showed little regard for the niceties of representative government. Coughlin had actually promised to dictate if necessary to preserve democracy. And the demagogic Long had dismissed complaints about his unconstitutional interference with the Louisiana legislative process by announcing, "I'm the Constitution around here." Coughlin's rhetoric, furthermore, often had disturbingly anti-Semitic overtones. Long and Coughlin's ideas and their rapid rise in popularity suggested strong currents of public dissatisfaction with the Roosevelt administration. The president's strategists feared that Long might join forces with Coughlin and Townsend to form a third party, enabling the Republicans to win the 1936 election.

The Second New Deal, 1935–1938

As the depression continued and attacks on the New Deal mounted, Roosevelt and his advisors embarked on a new course, which historians have labeled the Second New Deal. By 1935, frustrated by his inability to win the support of big business, Roosevelt began to openly criticize the "money classes," proudly stating of his administration that "We have earned the hatred of entrenched greed." Pushed to the left by the popularity of movements like Long's as well as by signs of militancy among workers, Roosevelt, always an astute politician, began to construct a new coalition and broaden the scope of his response to the depression.

Legislative Accomplishments

The first beneficiary of Roosevelt's change in direction was the labor movement. The rising number of strikes in 1934—about 1,800 involving a total of 1.5 million workers—reflected the dramatic growth of rank-and-file militancy. After the Supreme Court declared the NRA unconstitutional in 1935, invalidating Section 7(a), labor representatives demanded effective legislation that would protect the right to organize and bargain collectively. Named for its sponsor, Senator Robert F. Wagner of New York, the Wagner Act (1935) offered a degree of protection to labor. It upheld the right of industrial workers to join a union (farmworkers were not covered) and outlawed many unfair labor practices used to squelch organizing, such as firing workers for union activities. The act also established the nonpartisan National Labor Relations Board (NLRB) to protect workers from employer coercion, supervise elections for union representation, and guarantee the process of collective bargaining.

The Social Security Act signed by Roosevelt on August 14, 1935, was partly a response to the political mobilization of the nation's elderly through the Townsend and Long movements. But it also reflected prodding from social reformers like Grace Abbott, head of the Children's Bureau, and Secretary of Labor Frances Perkins. The Social Security Act provided pensions for most workers in the private sector, although originally agricultural workers and domestics were not covered, a limitation that disproportionately disadvantaged poor blacks, especially women. Pensions were to be financed by a federal tax that both employers and employees would pay. The act also established a joint federal-state system of unemployment compensation, funded by a tax on employers.

The Social Security Act was a milestone in the creation of the modern **welfare state**. Now the United States followed the path of industrialized countries like Great Britain and Germany in providing old-age pensions and unemployment compensation to citizens. (The Roosevelt administration chose not to push for national health insurance, even though most other industrialized nations offered such protection.) The act also mandated categorical assistance to the blind, deaf, and disabled and to dependent children—the so-called deserving poor, who clearly could not support themselves.

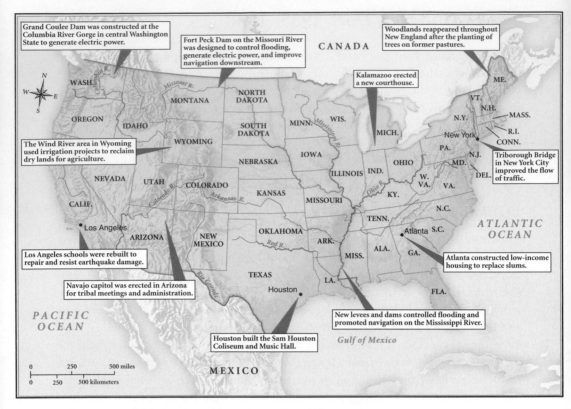

MAP 25.1 Public Works in the New Deal: The PWA in Action, 1933–1939

Between 1933 and 1939, the New Deal agencies of the Civilian Conservation Corps (CCC), the Works Progress Administration (WPA), and the Public Works Administration (PWA) created public works projects designed to put unemployed Americans to work and prime the economy with federal dollars, while simultaneously making lasting contributions to the nation's communities. The PWA, established in 1933 and directed by Harold Ickes, was the first federal agency to undertake extensive public works that ranged from courthouses to swimming pools, airports to aircraft carriers, the Triborough Bridge to the Grand Coulee Dam, as this map of selected projects indicates.

Roosevelt was never enthusiastic about large expenditures for social welfare programs. But in the sixth year of the depression, 10 million Americans were still out of work, creating a pressing moral and political issue for FDR and the Democrats. Under Harry Hopkins the Works Progress Administration (WPA) became the main federal relief agency for the rest of the depression. While FERA had supplied grants to state relief programs, the WPA put relief workers directly onto the federal payroll. Between 1935 and 1943 the WPA employed 8.5 million Americans, spending $10.5 billion. The agency's employees constructed 651,087 miles of roads, 125,110 public buildings, 8,192 parks, and 853 airports and built or repaired 124,087 bridges (Map 25.1). Though the WPA was an extravagant operation by the standards of the 1930s, it never reached more than a third of the nation's unemployed. Wages were kept low—on average $55 a month—so as not to compete with private-sector jobs, and thus workers on the WPA roles could barely eke out a living.

The Revenue Act of 1935, a tax-reform bill that increased estate and corporate taxes and instituted higher personal income-tax rates in the top brackets, showed Roosevelt's willingness to push for reforms that were considered too controversial earlier in his presidency. Much of the business community had already turned violently against Roosevelt in reaction to the NRA, the Social Security Act, and the Wagner Act. Now wealthy conservatives quickly labeled the Revenue Act an attempt to "soak the rich." Roosevelt, seeking to defuse the popularity of Huey Long's Share Our Wealth plan, was just as interested in the political mileage of the tax bill as in its actual results, which increased federal revenue by only $250 million a year.

As the 1936 election approached, the broad range of New Deal programs brought new voters into the Democratic coalition. Many had been personally helped by federal programs. Others benefited because their interests had found new support in the federal expansion: Roosevelt could count on a potent coalition of urban-based workers, organized labor, northern blacks, farmers, white ethnic groups, Catholics, Jews, liberals, intellectuals, progressive Republicans, and middle-class families concerned about unemployment and old-age dependence. The Democrats also held on, though with some difficulty, to their traditional constituency of white southerners.

The Republicans realized that they could not directly oppose Roosevelt and the New Deal. To run against the president, they chose the progressive governor of Kansas, Alfred M. Landon, who accepted the general precepts of the New Deal. Landon and the Republicans concentrated on criticizing the inefficiency and expense of many New Deal programs, stridently accusing FDR of harboring dictatorial ambitions.

Roosevelt's victory in 1936 was one of the biggest landslides in American history. The assassination of Huey Long in September 1935 had deflated the threat of a serious third-party challenge; the candidate of the combined Long-Townsend-Coughlin camp, Congressman William Lemke of North Dakota, garnered fewer than 900,000 votes (1.9 percent) for the Union Party ticket. Roosevelt received 60.8 percent of the popular vote and carried every state except Maine and Vermont. The New Deal was at high tide.

Stalemate

From this high point the New Deal soon slid into retrenchment, controversy, and stalemate. The first setback came when Roosevelt stunned Congress and the nation by asking for fundamental changes in the structure of the Supreme Court. Shortly after finding the NRA unconstitutional in *Schechter v. United States*, the Court had struck down the Agricultural Adjustment Act, a coal conservation act, and New York State's minimum wage law. With the Wagner Act, the TVA, and Social Security coming up on appeal, the future of New Deal reform measures seemed in doubt.

Roosevelt responded by proposing the addition of one new justice for each sitting justice over the age of seventy—a scheme that would have increased the number of justices from nine to fifteen. Roosevelt's opponents quickly protested that he
was trying to "pack" the Court with justices who favored the New Deal. The president's proposal was also regarded as an assault on the principle of the separation of
powers. Congress blocked the proposal, but Roosevelt ultimately achieved some
part of what he wanted, as the Supreme Court upheld several key pieces of New
Deal legislation, and a series of resignations created vacancies on the Court. Within
four years, retirements allowed Roosevelt to reshape the Supreme Court to suit his
liberal philosophy through seven new appointments, including Hugo Black, Felix
Frankfurter, and William O. Douglas.

Congressional conservatives had long opposed the direction of the New Deal,
but the court-packing episode galvanized them by demonstrating that Roosevelt
was no longer politically invincible. Throughout Roosevelt's second term a conservative coalition composed mainly of southern Democrats and Republicans from
rural areas blocked or impeded social legislation. Two pieces of reform legislation
that did win passage were the National Housing Act of 1937, which mandated the
construction of low-cost public housing, and the Fair Labor Standards Act of 1938,
which made permanent the minimum wage, maximum hours, and anti–child labor
provisions in the NRA codes.

The "Roosevelt recession" of 1937 to 1938 dealt the most devastating blow to
the president's political effectiveness in his second term. Until that point the economy had made steady progress. From 1933 to 1937 the gross domestic product had
grown at a yearly rate of about 10 percent, and by 1937 industrial output and real
income had finally returned to 1929 levels. Unemployment had declined from 25 percent to 14 percent. The steady improvement of the economy cheered Roosevelt, who
had never been comfortable with large federal expenditures. Accordingly, Roosevelt
slashed the federal budget in 1937. Between January and August Congress cut the
WPA's funding in half, causing layoffs of about 1.5 million workers. Fearing inflation,
the Federal Reserve tightened credit, creating a sharp drop in the stock market.
Unemployment soared to 19 percent, which translated into more than 10 million
workers without jobs. Roosevelt soon found himself in the same situation that had
confounded Hoover. Having taken credit for the recovery between 1933 and 1937,
he had to take the blame for the recession.

Shifting gears, Roosevelt spent his way out of the downturn. Large WPA appropriations and a resumption of public works projects poured enough money
into the economy to lift it out of the recession by early 1938. Roosevelt and his economic advisors were groping their way toward the general theory advanced by
John Maynard Keynes, a British economist who proposed that governments use
deficit spending (the spending of public funds obtained by borrowing rather than
through taxation) to stimulate the economy when private spending proves insuffi-
cient. But **Keynesian economics** would not be widely accepted until a dramatic increase in defense spending for World War II finally ended the Great Depression.

Still struggling with attacks on the New Deal, Roosevelt decided to "purge" the Democratic Party of some of his most conservative opponents as the 1938 election approached. In the spring primaries he campaigned against members of his own party who had been hostile or unsympathetic to New Deal initiatives. The purge failed abysmally and widened the liberal-conservative rift in the party. In the general election of 1938, Republicans capitalized on the "Roosevelt recession" and the backlash against the court-packing attempt: they picked up eight seats in the Senate and eighty-one in the House. The Republicans also gained thirteen governorships.

Even without these political reversals, the reform impetus of the New Deal probably would not have continued. Roosevelt had always set clear limits on how far he was willing to go. His instincts were basically conservative, not revolutionary; he had wanted only to save the capitalist economic system by reforming it. The new activism of the Second New Deal was a major step beyond the informal, one-sided business-government partnership of the preceding decade, but it was a step Roosevelt took only because the emergency of the depression had pushed him in that direction.

The New Deal's Impact on Society

Despite the limits of the New Deal, it had a tremendous impact on the nation and fundamentally altered Americans' relationship to their government. With an optimistic faith in using government for social purposes, New Dealers sponsored programs in the arts. They created vast projects to conserve the country's natural beauty and resources and to make them more accessible to its citizens. The New Deal also brought the voices of more citizens—women, blacks, labor, Mexican Americans—into the public arena, helping to promote the view that Roosevelt and his party represented and mediated for the common people.

New Deal Constituencies and the Broker State

The New Deal accelerated the expansion of the federal bureaucracy that had been under way since the turn of the century. In a decade the number of civilian government employees increased 80 percent, exceeding a million by 1940. The number of federal employees who worked in Washington grew at an even faster rate, doubling between 1929 and 1940. Power was increasingly centered in the nation's capital and not in the states.

The growth of the federal government increased the potential impact of its decisions (and spending) on various constituencies. During the 1930s the federal government operated as a **broker state**, mediating between contending pressure groups seeking power and benefits. Democrats recognized the importance of satisfying certain blocs of voters to cement their allegiance to the party. Even before the depression they had begun to build a coalition based on urban political machines and white ethnic voters. In the 1930s organized labor, women, African Americans, and other groups joined that coalition, receiving increased attention from the Democrats and the federal government they controlled.

During the 1930s, after decades of federal hostility or inattention to the rights of workers, labor relations became a legitimate arena for federal action and intervention, and organized labor claimed a place in national political life. Labor's dramatic growth in the 1930s represented one of the most important social and economic changes of the decade, an enormous contrast to its demoralized state at the end of the 1920s. Several factors encouraged the growth of the labor movement: the inadequacy of welfare capitalism in the face of the depression, New Deal legislation like the Wagner Act, the rise of the Congress of Industrial Organizations (CIO), and the growing militancy of rank-and-file workers. By the end of the decade, the number of unionized workers had tripled to almost 9 million, or 23 percent of the nonfarm workforce. Organized labor won the battle not only for union recognition but for higher wages, seniority systems, and grievance procedures.

The CIO served as the cutting edge of the union movement by promoting "industrial unionism"—that is, organizing all the workers in an industry, both skilled and unskilled, into one union. John L. Lewis, leader of the United Mine Workers (UMW) and the foremost exponent of industrial unionism, broke with the American Federation of Labor, which favored organizing workers on a craft-by-craft basis, and in 1935 helped to found the CIO. The CIO achieved some of its momentum through the presence in its ranks of members of the Communist Party. The rise of **fascism** in Europe had prompted the Soviet Union to mobilize support in democratic countries. In Europe and the United States, Communist parties called for a "popular front," welcoming the cooperation of any group concerned about the threat of fascism to civil rights, organized labor, and world peace. Under the popular front Communists softened their revolutionary rhetoric and concentrated on becoming active leaders in many CIO unions. While few workers actually joined the Communist Party, its influence in labor organizing in the thirties was far greater than its numbers, which in 1936 reached 40,000.

The CIO's success also stemmed from the recognition that unions must be more inclusive in order to succeed. The CIO worked deliberately to attract new groups to the labor movement. Mexican Americans and African Americans found the CIO's commitment to racial justice a strong contrast to the AFL's long-established patterns of exclusion and segregation. And about 800,000 women workers also found a limited welcome in the CIO. Few blacks, Mexican Americans, or women held leadership positions, however.

The CIO scored its first major victory in the automobile industry. On December 31, 1936, General Motors workers in Flint, Michigan, staged a sit-down strike, vowing to stay at their machines until management agreed to collective bargaining. The workers lived in the factories and machine shops for forty-four days before General Motors recognized their union, the United Automobile Workers (UAW). Shortly thereafter the CIO won another major victory, at the U.S. Steel Corporation. Despite a long history of bitter opposition to unionization, as demonstrated in the 1919 steel strike (see Chapter 22), Big Steel executives capitulated without a fight and recognized the Steel Workers Organizing Committee (SWOC) on March 2, 1937.

The 1930s constituted one of the most active periods of labor solidarity in American history. The sit-down tactic spread rapidly. In March 1937 a total of 167,210 workers staged 170 sit-down strikes. Labor unions called for nearly 5,000 strikes that year and won favorable terms in 80 percent of them. Yet large numbers of middle-class Americans felt alienated by sit-down strikes, which they considered attacks on private property. The Supreme Court agreed and in 1939 upheld a law that banned the practice.

Labor's new vitality spilled over into political action. The AFL generally had stood aloof from partisan politics, but the CIO quickly allied itself with the Democratic Party, hoping to use its influence to elect candidates sympathetic to labor and social justice. Establishing a group it rather misleadingly called Labor's Nonpartisan League, the CIO gave $770,000 to Democratic campaigns in 1936. Labor also provided solid support for Roosevelt's plan to reorganize the Supreme Court.

Despite the breakthroughs of the New Deal, the labor movement never developed into a dominant force in American life. Roosevelt never made the growth of the labor movement a high priority, and many workers remained indifferent or even hostile to unionization. And although the Wagner Act guaranteed unions a permanent place in American industrial relations, it did not revolutionize working conditions. The right to collective bargaining, rather than redistributing power in American industry, merely granted labor a measure of legitimacy. Management even found that unions could be used as a buffer against rank-and-file militancy. New Deal social welfare programs also tended to diffuse some of the pre-1937 radical spirit by channeling economic benefits to workers whether or not they belonged to unions. The road to union power, even with New Deal protection, continued to be a rocky and uncertain one.

Like organized workers white women achieved new influence in the experimental climate of the New Deal, as unprecedented numbers of them were offered positions in the Roosevelt administration. Frances Perkins, the first woman named to a cabinet post, served as secretary of labor throughout Roosevelt's presidency. Molly Dewson, a social reformer turned politician, headed the Women's Division of the Democratic National Committee, where she pushed an issue-oriented program that supported New Deal reforms. Roosevelt's women appointees also included the first female director of the mint, the head of a major WPA division, and a judge on a circuit court of appeals. Many of those women were close friends as well as professional colleagues and cooperated in an informal network to advance feminist and reform causes.

Eleanor Roosevelt exemplified the growing prominence of women in public life. In the 1920s she had worked closely with other reformers to increase women's power in political parties, labor unions, and education. The experience proved an invaluable apprenticeship for her White House years, when her marriage to FDR developed into one of the most successful political partnerships of all time. He was the pragmatic politician, always aware of what could be done; she was the idealist, the gadfly, always pushing him—and the New Deal—to do more. Eleanor Roosevelt served as the conscience of the New Deal.

Despite the advocacy by a female political network for equal opportunity for women, grave flaws still marred New Deal programs. A fourth of the NRA codes set a lower minimum wage for women than for men performing the same jobs. New Deal agencies like the Civil Works Administration and the Public Works Administration gave jobs almost exclusively to men: only 7 percent of CWA workers were female. And the CCC excluded women entirely, prompting critics to ask, "Where is the 'she-she-she'?"

When they did hire women, New Deal programs tended to reinforce the broader society's gender and racial attitudes. Program administrators resisted placing women in nontraditional jobs, and under the WPA, sewing rooms became a sort of dumping ground for unemployed women. African American and Mexican American women, if they had access to work relief at all, often found themselves shunted into training as domestics, whose work was not covered by the Social Security and Fair Labor Standards Acts. For the most part, progress for women did not come from specific attempts to recognize them as a group but occurred as part of a broader effort to improve the economic security of all Americans.

Just as the New Deal did not seriously challenge gender inequities, it did relatively little to battle racial discrimination. In the 1930s the majority of the American people did not regard civil rights as a legitimate area for federal intervention. Indeed many New Deal programs reflected prevailing racist attitudes. CCC camps segregated blacks and whites, and many NRA codes did not protect black workers. Most tellingly, Franklin Roosevelt repeatedly refused to support legislation to make lynching a federal crime, claiming it would antagonize southern members of Congress whose support he needed to pass New Deal measures.

Nevertheless, blacks did receive significant benefits from those New Deal relief programs that were directed toward the poor regardless of their race or ethnic background. Blacks made up about 18 percent of the WPA's recipients, although they constituted only 10 percent of the population. The Resettlement Administration, established in 1935 to help small farmers buy land and to resettle sharecroppers and tenant farmers on more productive land, fought for the rights of black tenant farmers in the South, until angry southerners in Congress drastically cut its appropriations. Still, many blacks reasoned that the tangible aid from Washington outweighed the discrimination that marred many federal programs.

African Americans were also pleased to see blacks appointed to federal office. Mary McLeod Bethune, an educator who ran the Office of Minority Affairs of the National Youth Administration, headed the "black cabinet." This informal network worked for fairer treatment of blacks by New Deal agencies in the same way the white women's network advocated feminist causes. Both groups benefited greatly from the support of Eleanor Roosevelt. The first lady's promotion of equal treatment for blacks ranks as one of her greatest legacies.

Eleanor Roosevelt and Civil Rights

One of Eleanor Roosevelt's greatest legacies was her commitment to civil rights. For example, she publicly resigned from the Daughters of the American Revolution (DAR) in 1939 when the group refused to let the black opera singer Marian Anderson perform at Constitution Hall. Roosevelt developed an especially close working relationship with Mary McLeod Bethune of the National Youth Administration, shown here at a conference in 1939.

AP/ Wide World Photos, Inc.

Help from the WPA and other New Deal programs and a belief that the White House—or at least Eleanor Roosevelt—cared about their plight, caused a dramatic change in African Americans' voting behavior. Since the Civil War, blacks had voted Republican, a loyalty based on Abraham Lincoln's freeing of the slaves. As late as 1932 black voters in northern cities overwhelmingly supported Republican candidates. But in 1936 black Americans outside the South (where blacks were still largely prevented from voting) gave Roosevelt 71 percent of their votes. In Harlem, where relief dollars increased dramatically in the wake of the 1935 riot (see Chapter 24), their support for Roosevelt was an extraordinary 81.3 percent. Black voters have remained overwhelmingly Democratic ever since.

The election of Franklin Roosevelt also had an immediate effect on Mexican American communities, demoralized by the depression and the deportations of the Hoover years. In cities like Los Angeles and El Paso, Mexican Americans qualified for relief more easily under New Deal guidelines, and there was more relief to go around (see American Voices, "A Chicana Youth Gets New Deal Work," p. 770). Even though New Deal regulations prohibited discrimination based on an immigrant's legal status, the new climate encouraged a marked rise in requests for naturalization papers. Mexican Americans also benefited from New Deal labor policies; joining the CIO was an important stage for many in becoming Americans. Inspired by New Deal rhetoric about economic recovery and social progress through cooperation, Mexican Americans increasingly identified with the United States rather than with Mexico.

Participating in the political system increasingly became part of Mexican American life. Los Angeles activist Beatrice Griffith noted, "Franklin D. Roosevelt's name was the spark that started thousands of Spanish-speaking persons to the polls." In 1939 El Congreso Nacional del Pueblo de Habla Español, the first national civil

AMERICAN VOICES

~

A Chicana Youth Gets New Deal Work

SUSANA ARCHULETA

A lthough African Americans and Chicanos often experienced discrimination in New Deal
programs, many did find opportunities in agencies like the Civilian Conservation Corps,
the National Youth Administration, and the Works Progress Administration. And they attributed
the help they received directly to Franklin Delano Roosevelt's election, as Susana Archuleta's
reminiscence of life in Wyoming suggests.

I was born in New Mexico, on a farm up North in Mora County. I was the fifth of eight
children. When I was very little, my dad moved us all to Wyoming. You see, he heard that
they had free textbooks in Wyoming, while here in New Mexico the parents had to pay for
the books. Daddy didn't have much money, and he felt that we all needed an opportunity
for education. We left the farm—the animals, the machinery, everything—and he went to
work in the mines up in Rock Springs, Wyoming. . . .

During the Depression, things got bad. My dad passed away when I was about twelve,
leaving my mother with eight children and no means of support. There wasn't any welfare.
My mother took in washings to make a living, and our job was to pick up the washings on
the way home from school. We'd pick up clothes from the schoolteachers, the attorney, and
what-have-you. Then, at night, we'd help iron them and fold them. . . .

When I was a teenager, the Depression began to take a turn. Franklin Roosevelt was
elected, and the works projects started. The boys and young men who'd been laid off at the
mines went to the CCC camps, and the girls joined the NYA. When school was over, we'd
go and work right there in the school building. We'd help out in the office, do filing and
other things. Actually, we didn't do much work—it was our first job. But we learned a lot.
It was good experience.

They paid us about twenty-one dollars a month. Out of that we got five and the other
sixteen was directly issued to our parents. The same was true of the boys working in the
camps. They got about thirty dollars a month. They were allowed to keep five of it. The rest
was sent to their families. All of us were hired according to our family income. If a man
with a lot of children was unemployed, he was given preference over someone who had less
children. They also had projects for women who were widows. They made quilts and mattresses. Those programs were great. Everybody got a chance to work. I think there should
be more training programs like that, instead of giveaway programs like welfare.

SOURCE: *Las Mujeres: Conversations from a Hispanic Community* by Nan Elasser. Copyright © 1980 by
Susana Archuleta. Reprinted by permission of the Feminist Press at the City University of New York.
www.feministpress.org.

rights conference for Spanish-speaking peoples, called on its members to become American citizens and vote. The Democrats made it clear that they welcomed Mexican American voters and considered them an important part of the New Deal coalition. This politicization provided additional spurs to political activism after World War II.

But what about groups that did not mobilize politically or were not recognized as key participants in the New Deal coalition? Native Americans were one of the nation's most disadvantaged and powerless minorities. The average annual income of a Native American in 1934 was only $48; the unemployment rate among Native Americans was three times the national average. Concerned New Deal administrators like Secretary of the Interior Harold Ickes and Commissioner of the Bureau of Indian Affairs John Collier tried to correct some of those inequities. The Indian Section of the Civilian Conservation Corps brought needed money and projects to reservations throughout the West. Indians also received benefits from FERA and CWA work relief projects.

More ambitious was the Indian Reorganization Act of 1934, sometimes called the "Indian New Deal." That law reversed the Dawes Act of 1887 by promoting more extensive self-government through tribal councils and constitutions. The government also abandoned the attempt to force Native Americans to assimilate into mainstream society in favor of promoting **cultural pluralism**. The New Deal pledged to help preserve Indian languages, arts, and traditions and to restore some lands lost in the allotment program (see Chapter 16).

Despite the intention to redress some of the ills produced by earlier government policies, the Indian New Deal was profoundly flawed. Reflecting Collier's paternalistic approach, it tended to treat all tribes as identical, with the same needs and structures. Ironically, its imposition of U.S.–style democracy did not always mesh with Native

A New Deal for Indians

John Collier, the New Deal's commissioner for Indian affairs, was a former social worker who had become interested in Native American tribal cultures in the 1920s. Here, Collier speaks with Chief Richard of the Blackfoot Nation, one of the Indian leaders attending the Four Nation celebration at historic Old Fort Niagara, New York, in 1934. © Bettmann / Corbis.

Americans' consensus technique of decision making. The Seneca, for example, argued that the Indian Reorganization Act violated their treaty rights and the system of self-government they had adopted in 1848. A majority—174 nations—accepted the reorganization policy, while 78 refused to participate. While some native groups may have benefited from the Indian New Deal, the problems of Native Americans were so severe that these changes in federal policy did little to improve their lives or reinvigorate tribal communities.

The New Deal and the Land

Concern for the land was one of the dominant motifs of the New Deal, and the shaping of the public landscape was among its most visible legacies. During the 1920s conservation supporters allied themselves with business interests and focused primarily on the commercial benefits of responsible use of natural resources. The expansion of federal responsibilities in the 1930s created a climate conducive to a broader vision of conservation efforts, as did public concern heightened by the dramatic images of drought and devastation in the Dust Bowl. Roosevelt's own strong commitment to what he called "the gospel of conservation" helped to bring a more public-oriented, while still practical, approach to the fore. Although the long-term success of New Deal resources policy was mixed, it innovatively stressed scientific management of the land, conservation instead of commercial development, and the aggressive use of public authority to safeguard both private and public holdings.

The most extensive New Deal environmental undertaking was the Tennessee Valley Authority (Map 25.2). Since World War I, experts had recognized the need for dams to control flooding and erosion in the Tennessee River Basin, a seven-state area with some of the country's heaviest rainfall, and in the 1920s a small group of progressive reformers had hoped to create a model of publicly owned power in the region. But not until 1933 was the Tennessee Valley Authority established to develop the region's resources under public control. The TVA was the ultimate watershed demonstration area, integrating flood control, reforestation, and agricultural and industrial development, including the production of chemical fertilizers. A hydro-electric grid provided cheap electric power for the valley's residents.

The Dust Bowl helped to focus attention on land management and ecological balance. Agents from the Soil Conservation Service in the Department of Agriculture taught farmers the improved techniques for tilling hillsides. Government agronomists also tried to remove marginal land from cultivation and to prevent soil erosion through better agricultural practices. One of their most widely publicized programs was the creation of the Shelterbelts, which involved the planting of 220 million trees running along roughly the ninety-ninth meridian from Abilene, Texas, to the Canadian border. Planted as a windbreak, the trees also prevented soil erosion. Another priority of the Roosevelt administration was helping rural Americans to stay on the land. The Rural Electrification Administration, established in 1935, brought power to farms in an attempt to improve the quality of rural life.

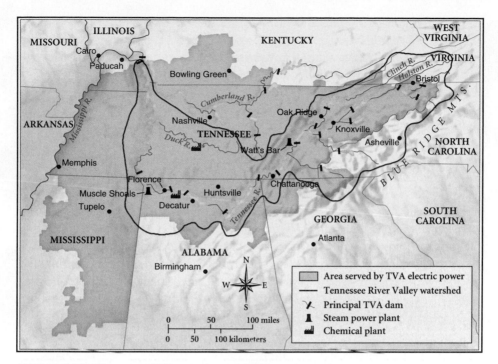

MAP 25.2 The Tennessee Valley Authority, 1933–1952

The Tennessee Valley Authority was one of the New Deal's most far-reaching environmental projects. Between 1933 and 1952, the TVA built twenty dams and improved five others. The cheap hydroelectric power generated by the dams brought electricity to hundreds of thousands of area residents.

FOR MORE HELP ANALYZING THIS MAP, see the Online Study Guide at **bedfordstmartins.com/henrettaconcise.**

Today New Deal projects affecting the environment can be seen throughout the country. CCC and WPA workers built the Blue Ridge Parkway, which connects the Shenandoah National Park in Virginia with the Great Smoky Mountain National Park in North Carolina. In the West government workers built the San Francisco Zoo, Berkeley's Tilden Park, and the canals of San Antonio. The CCC helped to complete the East Coast's Appalachian Trail and the West Coast's Pacific Crest Trail through the Sierra Nevada. In state parks across the country, cabins, shelters, picnic areas, lodges, and observation towers, built in a style that has been called "government rustic," are witness to the New Deal ethos of recreation coexisting with conservation.

The New Deal and the Arts

The depression dried up traditional sources of patronage for the arts, and like many Americans, creative artists had nowhere to turn but Washington. A WPA project known as "Federal One" put unemployed artists, actors, and writers to work, but its

The Promise of the New Deal

This 1936 mural by noted artist Ben Shahn depicts the beginnings of Roosevelt, New Jersey, originally called "Jersey Homesteads." The product of a New Deal planning initiative, the town included
a cooperative consisting of retail stores, a factory, and a farm, and was designed for poor immigrants from New York City. While the mural includes the intended beneficiaries of the new community in the background and acknowledges the powerful presence of Franklin D. Roosevelt with
the image on the wall, it focuses on the New Deal planners themselves, capturing some of the faith
in experts and social planning of the New Deal era. Roosevelt Arts Project.

FOR MORE HELP ANALYZING THIS IMAGE, see the Online Study Guide at **bedfordstmartins.com/henrettaconcise**.

spirit and purpose extended far beyond relief. New Deal administrators wanted to
redefine the relationship between artists and the community so that art would no
longer be the exclusive province of the elite. "Art for the millions" became a popular New Deal slogan.

The Federal Art Project (FAP) gave work to many who would become the twentieth century's leading painters, muralists, and sculptors at a point in their careers
when the lack of private patronage might have prevented them from continuing their
artistic production. Under the direction of Holger Cahill, an expert on American folk
art, the FAP commissioned murals for public buildings and post offices across the
country. Jackson Pollock, Alice Neel, Willem de Kooning, and Louise Nevelson all
received support from the FAP.

The Federal Music Project employed 15,000 musicians under the direction of
Nicholas Sokoloff, the conductor of the Cleveland Symphony Orchestra. Government-
sponsored orchestras toured the country, presenting free concerts of both classical and

popular music. Like many New Deal programs, the Music Project emphasized American themes. The composer Aaron Copland wrote his ballets *Billy the Kid* (1938) and *Rodeo* (1942) for the WPA, basing the compositions on western folk motifs. The distinctive "American" sound and athletic dance style of these works made them immensely appealing to audiences. The federal government also employed the musicologist Charles Seeger and his wife, the composer Ruth Crawford Seeger, to catalog hundreds of American folk songs.

The former journalist Henry Alsberg headed the Federal Writers' Project (FWP), which at its height employed about 5,000 writers. Young FWP employees who later achieved fame included Saul Bellow, Ralph Ellison, Tillie Olsen, and John Cheever. The black folklorist and novelist Zora Neale Hurston finished three novels while in the Florida FWP, among them *Their Eyes Were Watching God* (1937). And Richard Wright won the 1938 *Story* magazine prize for the best tale by a WPA writer. Wright used his spare time to complete his novel *Native Son* (1940).

Of all the New Deal arts programs, the Federal Theatre Project (FTP) was the most ambitious. American drama thrived in the 1930s, the only time during which the United States had a federally supported national theater. Under the gifted direction of Hallie Flanagan, former head of Vassar College's Experimental Theater, the FTP reached an audience of 25 to 30 million people in the four years of its existence. Talented directors, actors, and playwrights, including Orson Welles, John Houseman, and Arthur Miller, offered their services. The tendency to take a hard and critical look at social problems, however, made the program vulnerable to **red-baiting**. After a series of investigations as to alleged Communist influence, Congress terminated the FTP in 1939. Director Flanagan wryly remarked, "I could see why certain powers would not want even 10 percent of the Federal Theatre plays to be the sort to make people in our democracy think. Such forces might well be afraid of thinking people."

The WPA arts projects were influenced by a broad artistic trend called the "documentary impulse." Combining social relevance with distinctively American themes, this approach, which presented actual facts and events in a way that aroused the interest and emotions of the audience, characterized the artistic expression of the 1930s. The documentary, probably the decade's most distinctive genre, influenced practically every aspect of American culture—literature, photography, art, music, film, dance, theater, and radio. It is evident in John Steinbeck's fiction (see Chapter 24) and in John Dos Passos's *USA* trilogy, which used actual newspaper clippings, dispatches, and headlines in its fictional story. *The March of Time* newsreels, which movie audiences saw before feature films, presented the news of the world for the pretelevision age. The filmmaker Pare Lorentz commissioned the composer Virgil Thompson to create music that set the mood for documentary movies such as *The Plow That Broke the Plains* (1936) and *The River* (1936). The new photojournalism magazines, including *Life* and *Look*, also reflected this documentary approach. And the New Deal institutionalized the trend by sending investigators like the journalist Lorena Hickok and the writer Martha Gellhorn into the field to report on the conditions of people on relief.

Finally, the federal government played a leading role in compiling the photographic record of the 1930s. The Historical Section of the Resettlement Administration had a mandate to document and photograph the American scene for the government. Through their haunting images of sharecroppers, dust bowl migrants, and the urban homeless, photographers Dorothea Lange, Walker Evans, Ben Shahn, and Margaret Bourke-White permanently shaped the image of the Great Depression. The government hired photographers solely for their professional skills, not to provide them relief, as in Federal One projects. Their photographs, collected by the Historical Section, which in 1937 became part of the newly created Farm Security Administration (FSA), rank as the best visual representation of life in the United States during the depression years.

The Legacies of the New Deal

The New Deal set in motion far-reaching changes, notably the growth of a modern state of significant size. For the first time people experienced the federal government as a concrete part of everyday life. During the 1930s more than a third of the population received direct government assistance from new federal programs, including Social Security payments, farm loans, relief work, and mortgage guarantees. Furthermore, the government had made a commitment to intervene in the economy when the private sector could not guarantee economic stability. New legislation regulated the stock market, reformed the Federal Reserve System by placing more power in the hands of Washington policymakers, and brought many practices of modern corporate life under federal regulation. Thus the New Deal accelerated the pattern begun during the Progressive Era of using federal regulation to bring order and regularity to economic life, a pattern that would persist for the rest of the twentieth century, despite recurring criticism about the increased presence of the state in American life.

One particularly important arena of expansion was the development of America's welfare state—that is, the federal government's acceptance of greater responsibility for the individual and collective welfare of the people. Although the New Deal offered more benefits to American citizens than they had ever received before, its safety net had many holes, especially in comparison with the far more extensive welfare systems of Western Europe. The Social Security Act did not include national health care. Another serious defect of the emerging welfare system was its failure to reach a significant minority of American workers, including domestics and farmworkers, for many years. Since state governments administered the programs, benefits varied widely, with southern states consistently providing the lowest amounts.

Another shortcoming of the welfare system stemmed from male and female New Dealers' gendered conceptions of the "family wage," an ideal that assumed men were workers and women were homemakers. The old-age pensions and unemployment compensation provisions in the Social Security Act, which were designed primarily with men in mind and with the hope of maintaining the dignity of the male breadwinner, tended to be more generous and applied universally, regardless of need. Moreover, Social Security policies discriminated against married women until the 1970s. The programs for dependent children of poor women, usually referred to as simply "welfare," by contrast, applied means and morals tests and provided funds to keep women out of the workforce and in their proper place in the home. Denying the growing presence of women in the workforce, welfare made no provisions for helping poor working women sustain their families. A highly stigmatized program, welfare rarely offered enough for a decent standard of living or a means for poor women to get out of poverty.

To its credit the New Deal recognized that poverty was an economic problem and not a matter of personal failure. However, it did not come up with the perfect economic solution. Reformers assumed that once the depression was over, full employment and an active economy would take care of the nation's welfare needs and poverty would wither away. It did not. When later administrations confronted the persistence of inequality and unemployment, they grafted welfare programs onto the jerry-built structure left over from the New Deal rather than reimagining the system. Thus the American welfare system would always be marked by its birth during the crisis atmosphere of the Great Depression.

Even if the depression-era welfare system had some serious flaws, it was brilliant politics. The Democratic Party courted the allegiance of citizens who benefited from New Deal programs. Organized labor aligned itself with the administration that had made it a legitimate force in modern industrial life. Blacks voted Democratic in direct relation to the economic benefits that poured into their communities. At the grassroots level the Women's Division of the Democratic National Committee mobilized 80,000 women who recognized what the New Deal had done for their communities. The unemployed also looked kindly on the Roosevelt administration. According to one of the earliest Gallup polls, 84 percent of those on relief voted the Democratic ticket in 1936.

But the Democratic Party did not attract only the down-and-out. Roosevelt's magnetic personality and the dispersal of New Deal benefits to families throughout the social structure brought middle-class voters, many of them first- or second-generation immigrants, into the Democratic fold. Thus the New Deal completed the transformation of the Democratic Party that had begun in the 1920s toward a coalition of ethnic groups, city dwellers, organized labor, blacks, and a broad cross section of the middle class. Those voters would form the backbone of the Democratic coalition for decades to come and would provide support for liberal reforms that extended the promise of the New Deal.

But the New Deal coalition also contained potentially fatal contradictions involving mainly the issue of race. Because Roosevelt depended on the support of southern white Democrats to pass New Deal legislation, he was unwilling to challenge the economic and political marginalization of blacks in the South. At the same time New Deal programs were changing the face of southern agriculture by undermining the sharecropping system and encouraging the migration of southern blacks to northern and western cities. Outside the South blacks were not prevented from voting, guaranteeing that civil rights would enter the national agenda. The resulting fissures would eventually weaken the coalition that seemed so invincible at the height of Roosevelt's power.

With all its shortcomings the New Deal nonetheless had a profound impact on the nation, all the more remarkable in light of its short duration—most of its legislation passed between 1933 and 1936. While the Supreme Court–packing scheme, the "Roosevelt recession," and the political successes of Republicans in 1938 helped to bring an end to the New Deal, the darkening international scene also played a part. As Europe moved toward war and Japan flexed its muscles in the Far East, Roosevelt became increasingly preoccupied with international relations and pushed domestic reform further and further into the background.

TIMELINE

1933	FDR's inaugural address and first fireside chat		Social Security Act
			Works Progress Administration (WPA)
	Emergency Banking Act begins the Hundred Days		Huey Long assassinated
			Rural Electrification Administration (REA)
	Glass-Steagall Act establishes Federal Deposit Insurance Corporation (FDIC)		Supreme Court finds Agricultural Adjustment Act unconstitutional
	Civilian Conservation Corps (CCC)		Congress of Industrial Organizations (CIO) formed
	Agricultural Adjustment Act (AAA)		
	National Industrial Recovery Act (NIRA)		
	Tennessee Valley Authority (TVA)	**1935–1939**	Communist Party at height of influence
	United States abandons gold standard		
	Townsend Clubs promote Old Age Revolving Pension Plan	**1936**	General Motors sit-down strike
			Landslide reelection of FDR marks peak of New Deal power
	Twenty-First Amendment repeals Prohibition		*The Plow That Broke the Plains* and *The River*, documentary movies by Pare Lorentz
1934	Securities and Exchange Commission (SEC)		
	Indian Reorganization Act	**1937**	FDR's attempted Supreme Court reorganization fails
	Share Our Wealth Society established by Senator Huey Long		
		1937–1938	"Roosevelt recession"
1935	Supreme Court finds the NRA unconstitutional in *Schechter v. United States*		
		1938	Aaron Copland's *Billy the Kid*
	National Union for Social Justice (Father Charles Coughlin)		Fair Labor Standards Act (FLSA)
	National Labor Relations (Wagner) Act	**1939**	Federal Theatre Project terminated

For Further Exploration

A valuable synthesis of the New Deal is Robert S. McElvaine, *The Great Depression* (1984). An older but still engaging account of FDR is James MacGregor Burns, *Roosevelt* (1956). Insights into Eleanor Roosevelt's life are compellingly offered in Blanche Wiesen Cook's two-volume biography, *Eleanor Roosevelt* (vol. 1, 1992; vol. 2, 1999). For other New Dealers, see Katie Loucheim, ed., *The Making of the New Deal: The Insiders Speak* (1983). For contemporary material from the Federal Writers' Project, see *These Are Our Lives* (1939). Photography of the New Deal era is presented and analyzed in Carl Fleischhauer, ed., *Documenting America, 1935–1943* (1988). Responses to Roosevelt's fireside chats may be found in Lawrence W. Levine and Cornelia R. Levine, eds., *The People and the President* (2002).

The New Deal Network, sponsored by the Franklin and Eleanor Roosevelt Institute and the Institute for Learning Technologies, has an impressive Web site at <http://www.newdeal. feri.org/>, with extensive images, features such as Work-Study-Live: The Resident Youth Centers of the NYA, and links to other New Deal sites. The Library of Congress provides over 55,000 photographs from the Farm Security Administration and Office of War Information Collection at <http://www.nara.gov/exhall/newdeal/newdeal.html>. Another invaluable Library of Congress collection is By the People, For the People: Posters from the WPA 1936–1943, which offers more than 900 of the Works Project Administration posters. Log on at <http://memory.loc.gov/ammem/wpaposters/wpahome.html>.

The National Archives' site at <http://www.archives.gov/exhibit_hall/new_deal_for_ the_arts/index.html> contains A New Deal for the Arts, which covers folklore, music, writing, photography, film, and painting sponsored by New Deal agencies.

Remembering the Flint Sit-Down Strike, a site hosted by Michigan State University, is part of their Historical Voices collection. It offers audio recordings of the strikers and other participants' reminiscences. Transcripts of the interviews are also provided, as well as images, a timeline, and a bibliography. Access the site at <http://www.historicalvoices.org/flint/>.

A number of sites offer resources for local and state history. An excellent example is the Michigan State History Museum's The Great Depression, with material on the Flint sit-down strike and New Deal relief programs, at <http://www.sos.state.mi.us/history/museum/ explore/museums/hismus/hismus.html>.

For definitions of key terms boldfaced in this chapter, see the glossary at the end of the book.

To assess your mastery of the material covered in this chapter, see the Online Study Guide at **bedfordstmartins.com/henrettaconcise**.

For map resources and primary documents, see **bedfordstmartins.com/henrettaconcise**.

Chapter 26

THE WORLD AT WAR
1939–1945

> The great majority of the American people understand very well that this war is not a war only, but an end and a beginning—an end to things known and a beginning of things unknown.
>
> ARCHIBALD MACLEISH, *ATLANTIC*, 1943

Times Square in New York City on August 15, 1945, was awash with people celebrating V-J (Victory over Japan) Day. World War II was over. Civilians and soldiers "jived in the streets and the crowd was so large that traffic was halted and sprinkler trucks were used to disperse pedestrians." The spontaneous street party seemed a fitting end to what had been the country's most popular war. For many Americans World War II had been what one man described to journalist Studs Terkel as "an unreal period for us here at home. Those who lost nobody at the front had a pretty good time."

Americans had many reasons to view World War II as the "good war." Shocked by the Japanese attack on Pearl Harbor on December 7, 1941, they united in their determination to fight German and Japanese totalitarianism in defense of their way of life. When evidence of the grim reality of the Jewish Holocaust came to light, U.S. participation in the war seemed even more just. And despite their sacrifices, many people found the war a positive experience because it ended the devastating Great Depression, bringing full employment and prosperity. The unambiguous nature of the victory and the subsequent emergence of the United States as an unprecedentedly powerful nation further contributed to the sense of the war as one worth fighting.

But the good war had other sides. The period brought significant social disruption, accompanied by widespread anxiety about women's presence in the workforce and a rise in juvenile delinquency. In a massive violation of civil liberties, over 100,000 people of Japanese ancestry were incarcerated in internment camps, victims of racially based hysteria. African Americans served in a segregated military and, with Chicanos, faced discrimination and violence at home. The war also fostered the rise of a **military-industrial complex** and unleashed the terrible potential of the atomic bomb. Perhaps the most significant legacy of World War II emerged out of the unresolved issues of the wartime alliance: the debilitating Cold War, which would dominate American foreign policy for decades to come.

The Road to War

While Americans focused on getting through the Great Depression, trouble was massing overseas. The right wing antidemocratic **totalitarian** movement known as fascism had begun to emerge in Europe in the 1920s, and by the 1930s Fascist states had developed, characterized by strong dictators backed by the military, such as Adolf Hitler in Nazi Germany, Benito Mussolini in Italy, and Francisco Franco in Spain. When the League of Nations proved too weak to deal with the crises evoked by their aggression, President Roosevelt recognized that the United States might be pulled into the conflict. An internationalist at heart, he wanted the United States to play a prominent role in world affairs to foster the long-term prosperity necessary for a lasting peace. Hampered at first by the pervasive isolationist sentiment in the country, by 1939 he was leading the nation toward war.

The Rise of Fascism

As early as 1936, President Roosevelt had foreseen the possibility of U.S. participation in another European war, but he was determined to stay in line with public opinion. Gallup polls showed that two-thirds of the American people believed the United States had made a mistake in entering World War I. However, the aggressive actions of Germany, Italy, and Japan, all determined to expand their borders and their influence, challenged American neutrality repeatedly.

The first crisis was precipitated by Japan, a country whose militaristic regime was intent on dominating the Pacific basin. In 1931 Japan occupied Manchuria, the northernmost province of China; then in 1937 it launched a full-scale invasion of China. In both instances the League of Nations condemned Japan's action but was helpless to stop the aggression. Japan simply served the required one-year notice of withdrawal from the league.

Japan's defiance of the league encouraged a Fascist dictator half a world away. Italy's Benito Mussolini had long been unhappy with the Versailles treaty, which had not awarded Italy any formerly German or Turkish colonies. In 1935 Italy invaded Ethiopia, one of the few independent countries left in Africa. The Ethiopian emperor, Haile Selassie, appealed to the League of Nations, which condemned the invasion and imposed sanctions but to little effect. By 1936 the Italian subjugation of Ethiopia was complete.

But it was Germany, not Italy, that presented the gravest threat to the world order in the 1930s. There, huge World War I reparation payments, economic depression, fear of communism, labor unrest, and rising unemployment fueled the rise of Adolf Hitler and his National Socialist (Nazi) Party. In 1933 Hitler became chancellor of Germany and assumed dictatorial powers. Aiming at nothing short of world domination, as he made clear in his book *Mein Kampf* (My Struggle), Hitler sought to overturn the territorial settlements of the Versailles treaty, to "restore" all the Germans of central and eastern Europe to a single greater German fatherland, and to annex large areas of eastern Europe. In his warped vision, "inferior races" such as Jews, Gypsies, and Slavs, as well as "undesirables" such as homosexuals and the mentally impaired, would have to make way for the "master race." In 1933 Hitler established the first concentration camp at Dachau and opened a campaign of persecution against Jews, which expanded to a campaign of extermination when the war began.

Hitler's strategy for gaining territory through the use of troops and intimidation provoked a series of crises that made Britain and France decide to let him have his way rather than to risk war, a policy that became known as **appeasement**. Germany withdrew from the League of Nations in 1933; two years later Hitler announced that he planned to rearm the nation in violation of the Versailles treaty. No one stopped him. In 1936 Germany reoccupied the Rhineland, a region that had been declared a demilitarized zone under the treaty. Once again, France and Britain took no action. Later that year, Hitler and Mussolini joined forces in the Rome-Berlin Axis, a political and military alliance. When the Spanish civil war broke out, Germany and Italy armed the Spanish Fascists. The same year, Germany and Japan signed the Anti-Comintern Pact, a precursor to the military alliance between Japan and the Axis that was formalized in 1940.

Depression-Era Isolationism

During the early years of the New Deal, America's involvement in international affairs, especially those in Europe, remained limited. One of Roosevelt's few diplomatic initiatives had been the formal recognition of the Soviet Union in November 1933. A second significant development was the Good Neighbor Policy, under which the United States voluntarily renounced the use of military force and armed intervention in the Western Hemisphere. This policy recognized that the friendship of Latin American countries was essential to the security of the United States. One practical outcome came in 1934 when Congress repealed the Platt Amendment, a relic of the Spanish-American War, which asserted the U.S. right to intervene in Cuba's affairs (see Chapter 21). Indicating the limits to the Good Neighbor Policy, the U.S. Navy kept (and still maintains) a major base at Cuba's Guantanamo Bay and continued to meddle in Cuban politics. And in numerous Latin American countries, U.S. diplomats frequently resorted to economic pressure to solidify the influence of the United States and benefit its international corporations.

Roosevelt and his secretary of state, Cordell Hull, might have hoped to pursue more far-reaching diplomatic initiatives. But isolationism had been building in both Congress and the nation throughout the 1920s, a product in part of disillusionment with American participation in World War I. In 1934 Gerald P. Nye, a

Republican senator from North Dakota, began a congressional investigation into the profits of munitions makers during World War I and then widened the investigation to determine the influence of economic interests on America's decision to declare war. Nye's committee concluded that war profiteers, whom it called "merchants of death," had maneuvered the nation into World War I for financial gain.

Though most of the committee's charges were dubious or simplistic, they gave momentum to the isolationist movement, contributing to the passage of the Neutrality Act of 1935. Designed explicitly to prevent a recurrence of the events that had pulled the United States into World War I, the act imposed an embargo on arms trading with countries at war and declared that American citizens traveled on the ships of belligerent nations at their own risk. In 1936 Congress expanded the Neutrality Act to ban loans to belligerents, and in 1937 it adopted a "cash-and-carry" provision: if a country at war wanted to purchase nonmilitary goods from the United States, it had to pay for them in cash and pick them up in its own ships.

The same year, Congress explicitly reinforced earlier bans on sales of arms to Spain, when the bloody civil war erupted there in 1936. Francisco Franco, strongly supported by the Fascist regimes in Germany and Italy, was leading a rebellion against the democratically elected Republican government. Backed officially only by the Soviet Union and Mexico, the Republicans, or Loyalists, relied heavily on individual volunteers from other countries, including the American Lincoln Brigade, which fought courageously and sustained heavy losses throughout the war. The governments of the United States, Great Britain, and France, despite their Loyalist sympathies, remained neutral—a policy that virtually ensured a Fascist victory.

In 1938 Hitler's aggression expanded: he sent troops to annex Austria, while simultaneously scheming to seize part of Czechoslovakia. Because Czechoslovakia had an alliance with France, war seemed imminent. But at the Munich Conference in September 1938, Britain and France capitulated, agreeing to let Germany annex the Sudetenland—the German-speaking border areas of Czechoslovakia—in return for Hitler's pledge to seek no more territory.

Within six months, however, Hitler's forces had overrun the rest of Czechoslovakia and were threatening to march into Poland. Britain and France realized that their policy of appeasement had been disastrous and prepared to take a stand. Then in August 1939 Hitler signed the Nonaggression Pact with the Soviet Union, which assured Germany it would not have to wage war on two fronts at once. On September 1, 1939, German troops attacked Poland; two days later Britain and France declared war on Germany. World War II had begun.

Retreat from Isolationism

Because the United States had become a major world power, its response would affect the course of the European conflict. Two days after the war started, the United States officially declared its neutrality. Roosevelt made no secret of his sympathies, however. He pointedly rephrased Woodrow Wilson's declaration of 1914: "This nation will remain a neutral nation, but I cannot ask that every American remain neutral in thought as well." The overwhelming majority of Americans supported the Allies (Britain and France) over the Nazis, but most Americans did not want to be drawn into another world war.

At first the need for American intervention seemed remote. After the German conquest of Poland in September 1939, a false calm settled over Europe. But then on April 9, 1940, Nazi tanks overran Denmark. Norway fell to the Nazi *blitzkrieg* (lightning war) next, then the Netherlands, Belgium, and Luxembourg. Finally, on June 22, 1940, France fell. Britain stood alone against Hitler's plans for world domination.

In America the developments in Europe stirred debate over neutrality. The journalist William Allen White and his Committee to Defend America by Aiding the Allies led the interventionists. Isolationists, including the aviator Charles Lindbergh, formed the America First Committee to keep the nation out of the war; they attracted the support of the *Chicago Tribune*, the Hearst newspapers, and other conservative publications.

Despite the isolationist pressure, in 1940 the United States moved closer to involvement in the war. In May Roosevelt began putting the economy and the government on a defense footing by creating the National Defense Advisory Commission and the Council of National Defense. During the summer he traded fifty World War I destroyers to Great Britain in exchange for the right to build military bases on British possessions in the Atlantic, thus circumventing the nation's neutrality law by executive order. In October Congress approved a large increase in defense spending and instituted the first peacetime draft registration and conscription in American history.

While the war expanded in Europe and throughout the colonial world, spreading across Asia, North Africa, and the Middle East, the United States was preparing for the 1940 presidential election. The conflict had convinced Roosevelt that he should seek an unprecedented third term. Despite some conservative opposition, Roosevelt chose the liberal secretary of agriculture Henry A. Wallace as his running mate. The Republicans nominated Wendell Willkie of Indiana, a former Democrat who supported many New Deal policies. The two parties' platforms differed only slightly. Both pledged aid to the Allies but stopped short of calling for American participation in the war. Though Willkie's spirited campaign resulted in a closer election than those of 1932 or 1936, Roosevelt and the Democrats won 55 percent of the popular vote and a lopsided total in the electoral college.

With the election behind him, Roosevelt concentrated on persuading the American people to increase aid to Britain, whose survival he viewed as the key to American security. In November 1939 FDR had won a bitter battle in Congress to amend the Neutrality Act of 1937 to allow the Allies to buy weapons from the United States—but only on the cash-and-carry basis the act had established for nonmilitary goods. In March 1941, with German submarines sinking British ships faster than they could be replaced and Britain no longer able to afford to pay cash for arms, Roosevelt convinced Congress to pass the Lend-Lease Act. The legislation authorized the president to "lease, lend, or otherwise dispose of" arms and other equipment to any country whose defense was considered vital to the security of the United States. After Germany invaded the Soviet Union in June 1941 (abandoning the Nazi-Soviet Nonaggression Pact of two years earlier), the United States extended lend-lease to the Soviet Union, which became part of the Allied coalition. The implementation of lend-lease marked the unofficial entrance of the United States into the European war.

The United States became even more involved in August 1941, when Roosevelt and Winston Churchill, who had become British prime minister in 1940, conferred secretly to discuss goals and military strategy. Their joint press release, which became known as the Atlantic Charter, provided the ideological foundation of the Western cause and of the peace to follow. Like Wilson's Fourteen Points, the charter called for economic collaboration and guarantees of political stability after the war ended to ensure that "all men in all the lands may live out their lives in freedom from fear and want." The charter also supported free trade, national self-determination, and the principle of collective security.

As in World War I, when Americans started supplying the Allies, Germany attacked U.S. and Allied ships. By September 1941 Nazi submarines and American vessels were fighting an undeclared naval war in the Atlantic, unknown to the American public (Map 26.1). Without a dramatic enemy attack, however, and with the public reluctant to enter the conflict, Roosevelt hesitated to ask Congress for a declaration of war.

The Attack on Pearl Harbor

The final provocation came not from Germany but from Japan. Throughout the 1930s, Japanese military advances in China had upset the balance of political and economic power in the Pacific, where the United States had long enjoyed the benefits of the open-door policy (see Chapter 21). After the Japanese invasion of China in 1937, Roosevelt denounced "the present reign of terror and international lawlessness," suggesting that aggressors such as Japan be "quarantined" by peace-loving nations. Despite such rhetoric, however, the United States avoided taking a stand. During the brutal sack of Nanking in 1937, the Japanese sunk an American gunboat, the *Panay*, in the Yangtze River. The crisis was smoothed over, though, when the United States accepted Japan's apology and more than $2 million in damages.

Japan soon became more expansionist in its intentions, signing the Tri-Partite Pact with Germany and Italy in 1940. In the fall of 1940, Japanese troops occupied the northern part of French Indochina and declared a Greater East Asia Co-Prosperity Sphere. The United States retaliated by restricting trade with Japan and placing an embargo on aviation-grade gasoline and scrap metal. Despite mounting tensions, Roosevelt hoped to avoid war with Japan. But in July 1941 Japanese troops occupied the rest of Indochina. Roosevelt responded by freezing Japanese assets in

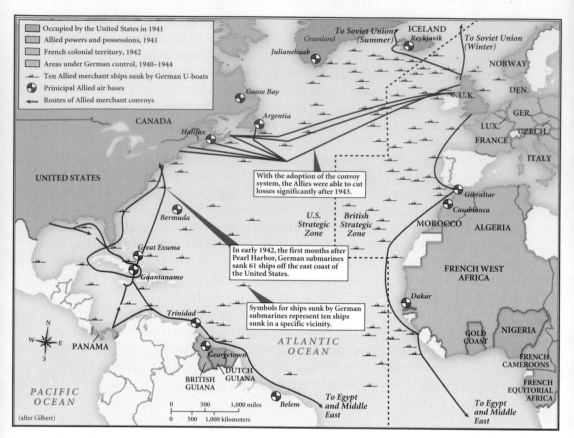

MAP 26.1 World War II in the North Atlantic, 1939–1943

After the start of the war in Europe in September 1939, Germany escalated its attacks on Allied and American merchant shipping in the Atlantic, spurring Congress to pass the Lend-Lease Act in March 1941 and President Roosevelt and Prime Minister Churchill to issue the Atlantic Charter in August. A pivotal factor in the Allied victory in Europe would be countering the German submarine threat in the Atlantic so that U.S. troops and materiel could be transported safely overseas. With the establishment of the convoy system—the protection of merchant vessels with destroyers—the Atlantic shipping lanes became safer, and the numbers of boats sunk after 1943 declined.

the United States and instituting an embargo on all trade with Japan, including vital oil shipments that accounted for almost 80 percent of Japanese consumption.

In September 1941 the government of Prime Minister Hideki Tojo began secret preparations for war against the United States. By November American military intelligence knew that Japan was planning an attack but did not know where. Early on Sunday morning, December 7, 1941, Japanese bombers attacked Pearl Harbor in Hawaii, killing more than 2,400 Americans. Eight battleships, three cruisers, three destroyers, and almost two hundred airplanes were annihilated or heavily damaged.

Although the attack was devastating, it infused the American people with a determination to fight. Pearl Harbor Day is still etched in the memories of millions of

Americans who remember precisely what they were doing when they heard about the attack. The next day Roosevelt went before Congress. Calling December 7 "a date which will live in infamy," he asked for a declaration of war against Japan. The Senate voted unanimously for war, and the House concurred by a vote of 388 to 1. The lone dissenter was Jeannette Rankin of Montana, who had also opposed American entry into World War I. Three days later Germany and Italy declared war on the United States, and the United States in turn declared war on those nations.

Organizing for Victory

The task of fighting a global war accelerated the growing influence of the state on all aspects of American life. A dramatic expansion of power occurred at the presidential level when Congress passed the War Powers Act of December 18, 1941, giving Roosevelt unprecedented authority over all aspects of the conduct of the war. Coordinating the changeover from civilian to war production, raising an army, and assembling the necessary workforce taxed government agencies to the limit. Mobilization on such a scale demanded close cooperation between business executives and political leaders in Washington, solidifying a partnership that had been growing since World War I.

Defense Mobilization

Defense mobilization had a powerful impact on the federal government's role in the economy. During the war the federal budget expanded by a factor of ten, and the national debt grew sixfold, peaking at $258.6 billion in 1945. At the same time, the national government became more closely tied to its citizens' pocketbooks. The Revenue Act of 1942 continued the income-tax reform that had begun during World War I by taxing not just wealthy individuals and corporations but average citizens as well. Tax collections rose from $2.2 billion to $35.1 billion, facilitated by payroll deductions and tax withholding instituted in 1943. This system of mass taxation, a revolutionary change in the financing of the modern state, was sold to the taxpayers as a way to express their patriotism.

The war also brought significant changes in the federal bureaucracy. The number of civilians employed by the government increased almost fourfold, to 3.8 million—a far more dramatic growth than the New Deal period had witnessed. Leadership of federal agencies also changed as the Roosevelt administration turned to business executives to replace the reformers who had staffed New Deal relief agencies in the 1930s. The executives became known as "dollar-a-year men" because they volunteered for government service while remaining on the corporate payroll.

Many wartime agencies extended the power of the federal government. One of the most important was the War Production Board (WPB), which awarded defense contracts, evaluated military and civilian requests for scarce resources, and oversaw the conversion of industry to military production. The WPB used the carrot more often than the stick. To encourage businesses to convert to war production, the board granted generous tax write-offs for plant construction and approved contracts with cost-plus provisions that guaranteed a profit and promised that businesses could keep the new factories after the war. As Secretary of War Henry Stimson put it, in capitalist countries at war "you had better let business make money out of the process or business won't work."

In the interest of efficiency and maximum production, the WPB preferred to deal with major corporations rather than with small businesses. The fifty-six largest corporations received three-fourths of the war contracts; the top ten received a third. Together business and government produced an astonishing number of military goods. By 1945 the United States had turned out 86,000 tanks, 296,000 airplanes, 15 million rifles and machine guns, 64,000 landing craft, and 6,500 ships. Mobilization on this gigantic scale gave a tremendous boost to the economy, causing it to more than double, rising from a gross domestic product in 1940 of $99.7 billion to $211 billion by the end of the war. After years of depression, Americans' faith in the capitalist system was restored. But it was a transformed system that relied heavily on the federal government's participation in the economy, and would lay the basis for the military-industrial complex of the postwar years, which linked the federal government, corporations, and the military in an interdependent partnership (see Chapter 27).

An expanded state presence was also evident in the government's mobilization of a fighting force. By the end of World War II, the armed forces of the United States numbered more than 15 million men and women. Draft boards had registered about 31 million men between the ages of eighteen and forty-four. More than half the men failed to meet the physical standards: many were rejected because of defective teeth or poor vision. The military also tried to screen out homosexuals, but its attempts were ineffectual. Once in the service homosexuals found opportunities to participate in a gay subculture more extensive than that in civilian life, where they were often channeled into marriage and heterosexual societal roles.

Racial discrimination prevailed in the armed forces, directed mainly against the approximately 700,000 blacks who fought in all branches of the military in segregated units. Though the National Association for the Advancement of Colored People (NAACP) and other civil rights groups chided the government with reminders such as "A Jim Crow army cannot fight for a free world," the military continued to segregate African Americans and to assign them the most menial duties. In contrast Mexican Americans were never officially segregated. Unlike blacks they were welcomed into combat units, and seventeen Mexican Americans won the Congressional Medal of Honor. Native Americans also served in nonsegregated combat, and some, like the Navajo Code Talkers, played a unique role in circumventing Japanese codebreaking efforts by using their native language to send military messages.

Approximately 350,000 American women enlisted in the armed services and achieved permanent status in the military, serving in agencies such as the army

WAACS (Women's Auxilliary Army Corps) and naval WAVES (Women Accepted for Volunteer Emergency Service). One-third of the nation's registered nurses, almost 75,000 overall, volunteered for military duty. In addition about 1,000 WASPs (Women's Airforce Service Pilots) ferried planes and supplies in noncombat areas. The armed forces limited the types of duty assigned to women, as it did with blacks. Women were barred from combat, although nurses and medical personnel sometimes served close to the front lines, risking capture or death. Most of the jobs women did—clerical work, communications, and health care—reflected stereotypes of women's roles in civilian life.

Workers and the War Effort

When millions of citizens entered military service, the United States faced a critical labor shortage which the War Manpower Commission sought to remedy. Well-organized government propaganda stressed patriotism as it urged women into the workforce. "Longing won't bring him back sooner . . . GET A WAR JOB!" one poster beckoned, while the artist Norman Rockwell's famous "Rosie the Riveter" appealed to women from the cover of the *Saturday Evening Post*. Although the government directed its propaganda at housewives, women who were already employed gladly abandoned low paying "women's" jobs as domestic servants or file clerks for higher-paying jobs in the defense industry. Suddenly the nation's factories were full of women working as riveters, welders, and drill-press operators. Women made up 36 percent of the labor force in 1945, compared with 24 percent at the beginning of the war. Despite their new opportunities, women war workers faced much discrimination, including sexual harassment, on the job. In shipyards women with the most seniority and responsibility earned $6.95 a day, whereas the top men made as much as $22.

When the men came home from war, and the nation's plants returned to peacetime operations, Rosie the Riveter was out of a job. But many women refused to put on aprons and stay home. Though women's participation in the labor force dropped temporarily when the war ended, it rebounded steadily for the rest of the 1940s, especially among married women (see Chapter 27).

Wartime mobilization also opened up opportunities to advance the labor movement. Organized labor responded to the war with an initial burst of patriotic unity. On December 23, 1941, representatives of the major unions made a "no-strike" pledge—though it was nonbinding—for the duration of the war. In January 1942 Roosevelt set up the National War Labor Board (NWLB), composed of representatives of labor, management, and the public. The NWLB established wages, hours, and working conditions and had the authority to order government seizure of plants that did not comply. Forty plants were seized during the war.

During its tenure the NWLB handled 17,650 disputes affecting 12 million workers. It resolved the controversial issue of union membership through a compromise. New hires did not have to join a union, but those who already belonged had to maintain their membership over the life of a contract. Agitation for wage increases caused a more serious disagreement. Because managers wanted to keep production running smoothly and profitably, they were willing to pay higher wages. However, pay raises would conflict with the government's efforts to combat inflation, which drove up prices dramatically in the early war years. Incomes rose as much as 70 percent during the war because workers earned overtime pay, which was not covered by wage ceilings.

Despite high incomes, many union members felt cheated as they watched corporate profits soar in relation to wages. Dissatisfaction peaked in 1943. That year a nationwide railroad strike was narrowly averted. Then John L. Lewis led more than half a million United Mine Workers out on strike, demanding an increase in wages over that recommended by the NWLB. Though Lewis won concessions, he alienated Congress, and because he had defied the government, he became one of the most disliked public figures of the 1940s.

Congress countered Lewis's action by overriding Roosevelt's veto of the Smith-Connally Labor Act of 1943, which required a thirty-day cooling-off period before a strike and prohibited entirely strikes in defense industries. Nevertheless, about 15,000 walkouts occurred during the war. Though less than one-tenth of 1 percent of working hours were lost to labor disputes, the public perceived the disruptions to be far more extensive. Although union membership increased dramatically during the war, from 9 million to almost 15 million workers—a third of the nonagricultural workforce—the labor movement also evoked significant public and congressional hostility that would hamper it in the postwar years.

Just as labor sought to benefit from the war, African Americans manifested a new mood of militancy. "A wind is rising throughout the world of free men everywhere," Eleanor Roosevelt wrote during the war, "and they will not be kept in bondage." Black leaders pointed out parallels between anti-Semitism in Germany and racial discrimination in America and pledged themselves to a "Double V" campaign: victory over Nazism abroad and victory over racism and inequality at home.

Even before Pearl Harbor, black activism was on the rise. In 1940 only 240 of the nation's 100,000 aircraft workers were black, and most of them were janitors. Black leaders demanded that the government require defense contractors to integrate their workforces. When the government took no action, A. Philip Randolph, head of the Brotherhood of Sleeping Car Porters, the largest black union, announced plans for a "March on Washington" in the summer of 1941. Though Roosevelt was not a strong supporter of civil rights, he feared the embarrassment of a massive public protest. Even more, he worried about a disruption of the nation's war preparations.

In June 1941, in exchange for Randolph's cancellation of the march, Roosevelt issued Executive Order 8802, declaring, "there shall be no discrimination in the employment of workers in defense industries or government because of race, creed, color, or national origin," and established the Fair Employment Practices Commission (FEPC). Though this federal commitment to minority employment rights was unprecedented,

Fighting for Freedom at Home and Abroad

This protester from the Negro Labor Relations League pointedly drew the parallel between blacks serving in the armed forces and a 1941 labor discrimination dispute at a Chicago dairy.

Library of Congress.

For more help analyzing this image, see the Online Study Guide at **bedfordstmartins.com/ henrettaconcise.**

it was limited in scope; for instance, it did not affect **segregation** in the armed forces. Moreover, the FEPC could not require compliance with its orders and often found that the needs of defense production often took precedence over fair employment practices. The committee nonetheless resolved about a third of the more than 8,000 complaints it received.

Encouraged by the ideological climate of the war years and the establishment of the FEPC, civil rights organizations increased their pressure for reform. The League of United Latin American Citizens (LULAC) built on their community's patriotic contributions to national defense and the armed services to challenge long-standing patterns of discrimination and exclusion. In Texas, where it was still common to see signs reading, "No Dogs or Mexicans Allowed," the organization protested segregation

VOICES FROM ABROAD

American Race Relations

GERMAN POWs

*D*uring World War II Nazi prisoners of war were assigned to various army camps throughout the United States, where their labor was often contracted out to help with the acute shortage of workers caused by war mobilization. German prisoners thus had a unique opportunity to observe American life. Here are some of their observations, mainly centered on the issue of race.

We picked cotton the length of the Mississippi. I'm an agriculturalist, and I know how to handle hard work, but there it was truly very, very hard. It was terribly hot, and we had to bend over all day. We had nothing to drink. . . . There were a great number of Blacks on the plantation. They required us to gather 100 lbs. of cotton a day; but of the Blacks, they demanded two or three times more. . . . For them it was worse than for us. And you have to see how they lived. Their farms: very ugly, very primitive. These people were so exploited. . . .

Me, I was in peas; picking and the canning factory. The farmers liked me, and wanted me to stay after the war, but I wasn't sure. . . . I met some old people of German origin one day, and these poor old people told me: "We feel alone here. It's sad. It's too big. If we could, we would walk back to Germany on foot. . . ." And the Blacks! They were always saying: "We are just like you: Prisoners; Oppressed; Second-class men. . . ."

There was a plumber who came to work in the camp. His name was Gutierrez, and he was Mexican. . . . He was a very nice guy. When he went to the barbershop, he stood in the corner, he did not move, and, as he was "colored," he had to wait until all the Whites were done. You know, things like that upset us very much. . . .

I was in a camp near Miami in Florida. I was one of the scavenger commandos; every morning we went to gather the garbage in the city. . . . People of German origin were the least nice to us. . . . Those who helped us the most, on the contrary, were the Jews. . . . Ah, the Jews and the Blacks.

SOURCE: *Nazi Prisoners of War in America* by Arnold Krammer. Copyright © 1979 by Arnold Krammer. Reprinted by permission of the author.

in schools and public facilities. African American groups also flourished. The NAACP grew ninefold to 450,000 by 1945, and in Chicago James Farmer helped to found the Congress of Racial Equality (CORE), a group that became known nationwide for its use of direct action like demonstrations and sit-ins. These wartime developments—both federal intervention in the form of the FEPC and resurgent African American militancy—laid the groundwork for the civil rights revolution of the 1950s and 1960s (see Voices from Abroad, "American Race Relations," above).

Politics in Wartime

During the early years of the war, Roosevelt rarely pressed for social and economic change, in part because he was preoccupied with the war but also because he wanted to counteract Republican political gains. Republicans had picked up ten seats in the Senate and forty-seven seats in the House in the 1942 elections, thus bolstering conservatives in Congress who sought to roll back New Deal measures. With little protest Roosevelt agreed to drop several popular New Deal programs, including the Civilian Conservation Corps and the National Youth Administration, which were less necessary once war mobilization brought full employment.

Later in the war Roosevelt began to promise new social welfare measures. In his State of the Union address in 1944, he called for a second bill of rights, which would serve as "a new basis of security and prosperity." This extension of the New Deal identified jobs, adequate food and clothing, decent homes, medical care, and education as basic rights. But the president's commitment to them remained largely rhetorical; congressional support for this vast extension of the welfare state did not exist in 1944. Some of those rights, however, did become realities for veterans, a group that was popularly considered to have "earned" benefits for their service. The Servicemen's Readjustment Act (1944), known as the GI Bill of Rights, provided education, job training, medical care, pensions, and mortgage loans for men and women who had served in the armed forces during the war. An extraordinarily influential program, particularly in making higher education more widely available, it distributed almost four billion dollars' worth of benefits to nine million veterans between 1944 and 1949 and in the 1950s would be extended to veterans of the Korean War era.

Roosevelt's renewed call for social legislation was part of a plan to woo Democratic voters after the congressional setbacks of the 1942 elections. The Democrats realized they would have to work hard to maintain their strong coalition in 1944. Once again Roosevelt headed the ticket, reasoning that the continuation of the war made a fourth term necessary. Democrats, concerned about Roosevelt's health and the need for a successor, dropped Vice President Henry Wallace, whose outspoken support for labor, civil rights, and domestic reform was too extreme for many party leaders. In his place they chose Senator Harry S Truman of Missouri, known for heading a Senate investigation of government efficiency in awarding wartime defense contracts.

The Republicans nominated Governor Thomas E. Dewey of New York. Only forty-two years old, Dewey had won fame fighting organized crime as a U.S. attorney. He accepted the broad outlines of the welfare state and was among those Republicans who rejected isolationism in favor of an internationalist stance. The 1944 election was the closest since 1916: Roosevelt received only 53.5 percent of the popular vote. The party's margin of victory came from the cities: in urban areas of more than 100,000 people the president drew 60 percent of the vote, reflecting in part ethnic minorities' loyalty to the Democratic Party. A significant segment of this urban support came from organized labor. The CIO's Political Action Committee made substantial contributions to the party, canvassed door to door, and conducted voter registration campaigns—a role organized labor would continue to play after the war.

Life on the Home Front

Although the United States did not suffer the physical devastation that ravaged much of Europe and the Pacific, the war affected the lives of those who stayed behind. Every time relatives of a loved one overseas saw the Western Union boy on his bicycle, they feared a telegram from the War Department saying that their son, husband, or father would not be coming home. All Americans tolerated small deprivations daily. "Don't you know there's a war on?" became the standard reply to any request that could not be fulfilled. People accepted the fact that their lives would be different "for the duration." They also accepted, however grudgingly, the increased role of the federal government in shaping their daily lives.

"For the Duration"

Just like the soldiers in uniform, people on the home front had a job to do. They worked on civilian defense committees, collected old newspapers and scrap material, and served on local rationing and draft boards. About 20 million home "Victory gardens" produced 40 percent of the nation's vegetables. All these endeavors were encouraged by various federal agencies, especially the Office of War Information (OWI), which strove to disseminate information and promote patriotism. Working closely with advertising agencies, the OWI urged them to link their clients' products to the "four freedoms," explaining that patriotic ads would not only sell goods but would "invigorate, instruct and inspire [the citizen] as a functioning unit in his country's greatest effort."

Popular culture, especially the movies, reinforced the connections between the home front and troops serving overseas. Average weekly movie attendance soared to over 100 million during the war. Demand was so high that many theaters operated around the clock to accommodate defense workers on the swing and night shifts. Many movies, encouraged in part by the OWI, had patriotic themes; stars such as John Wayne, Anthony Quinn, and Spencer Tracy portrayed the heroism of American fighting men in films like *Back to Bataan* (1945), *Guadalcanal Diary* (1943), and *Thirty Seconds over Tokyo* (1945). Other movies, such as *Watch on the Rhine* (1943), warned of the danger of fascism at home and abroad, while the Academy Award–winning *Casablanca* (1943) demonstrated the heroism and patriotism of ordinary citizens. *Since You Went Away* (1943), starring Claudette Colbert as a wife who took a defense job after her husband left for war, was one of many films that portrayed struggles on the home front. Newsreels accompanying the feature films kept the public up-to-date on the war, as did on-the-spot radio broadcasts by commentators such as Edward R. Murrow. Thus popular culture reflected America's new international involvement at the same time that it built morale on the home front.

Perhaps the major source of Americans' high morale was wartime prosperity. Federal defense spending had ended the depression; unemployment had disappeared, and per capita income had risen from $691 in 1939 to $1,515 in 1945. Despite geographical dislocations and shortages of many items, about 70 percent of Americans admitted midway through the war that they had personally experienced "no real sacrifices." A Red Cross worker put it bluntly: "The war was fun for America. I'm not talking about the poor souls who lost sons and daughters. But for the rest of us, the war was a hell of a good time."

For many Americans the major inconveniences of the war were the limitations placed on their consumption. In contrast to the largely voluntaristic approach used during World War I, federal agencies such as the Office of Price Administration subjected almost everything Americans ate, wore, or used during World War II to rationing or regulation. In response to depleted domestic gasoline supplies and a shortage of rubber—the Japanese had conquered Malaysia and Netherlands Indies, the source of 97 percent of American rubber—the government restricted the sale of tires, rationed gas, and imposed a nationwide speed limit of 35 miles per hour, which cut highway deaths dramatically. By 1943 the amount of meat, butter, sugar, and other foods Americans could buy was also regulated. Most people cooperated with the complicated system of restrictions, but almost a fourth occasionally bought items on the black market, especially meat, gasoline, and cigarettes.

The war and the government affected not only what people ate, drank, and wore, but also where they lived. When men entered the armed services, their families often followed them to training bases or points of debarkation. About 15 million Americans changed residence during the war years, half of them moving to another state.

As a major center of defense production, California was affected by wartime migration more than any other state. The state welcomed nearly 3 million new residents during the war, a 53 percent growth in population. "The Second Gold Rush Hits the West," headlined the San Francisco Chronicle in 1943. During the war one-tenth of all federal dollars went to California, and the state turned out one-sixth of the total war production. People went where the defense jobs were—to Los Angeles, San Diego, and the San Francisco Bay area. Some towns grew practically overnight: just two years after the Kaiser Corporation opened a shipyard in Richmond, California, the population had quadrupled.

The growth of war industries prompted the migration of more than a million African Americans to defense centers in California, Illinois, Michigan, Ohio, and Pennsylvania (see Map 22.3). The migrants' need for jobs and housing led to racial conflict in several cities. Early in 1942 black families encountered resistance and intimidation when they tried to move into the Sojourner Truth housing project in the Polish community of Hamtramck near Detroit, the new home of a large number of southern migrants, both black and white. In June 1943 similar tensions erupted in Detroit, where a major race riot left thirty-four people dead. Racial conflicts broke out in forty-seven cities across the country during 1943.

Other Americans also experienced racial violence. In Los Angeles male Latinos who belonged to pachuco (youth) gangs dressed in "zoot suits"—broad-brimmed felt hats, pegged trousers, and clunky shoes—wore their long hair slicked down, and carried pocket knives on gold chains. The young women they kept company with favored long coats, huarache sandals, and pompadour hairdos. Blacks and some working-class white teenagers in Los Angeles, Detroit, New York, and Philadelphia also wore zoot suits as a symbol of alienation and self-assertion. To adults and to many Anglos, however, the zoot suit symbolized wartime juvenile delinquency.

In Los Angeles white hostility toward Mexican Americans had been smoldering for some time, and zoot-suiters soon became the targets. In July 1943 rumors that a pachuco gang had beaten a white sailor set off a four-day riot, during which white servicemen entered Mexican American neighborhoods and attacked zoot-suiters, taking special pleasure in slashing their pegged pants. The attacks occurred in full view of white police officers, who did nothing to stop the violence.

Although racial confrontations and zoot-suit riots recalled the widespread racial tensions of World War I, the mood on the home front was generally calm in the 1940s. German Americans generally did not experience the intense prejudice of World War I nor did Italian Americans, though some aliens in both groups were interned. Leftists and Communists faced little repression, mainly because after Pearl Harbor the Soviet Union became an ally of the United States.

Japanese Internment

The internment of Japanese Americans on the West Coast was a glaring exception to this record of tolerance, a reminder of the fragility of civil liberties in wartime. California had a long history of antagonism toward both Japanese and Chinese immigrants (see Chapters 16, 21, and 24). The Japanese Americans, who clustered together in highly visible communities, were a small, politically impotent minority, numbering only about 112,000 in the three coastal states. But unlike German and Italian Americans, the Japanese stood out. "A Jap's a Jap," snapped General John DeWitt. "It makes no difference whether he is an American citizen or not." This sort of sentiment, coupled with fears of the West Coast's vulnerability to attack and the inflammatory rhetoric of newspapers and local politicians, fueled mounting demands that the region be rid of supposed Japanese spies.

In early 1942 Roosevelt issued Executive Order 9066, which gave the War Department the authority it needed for its plan to evacuate Japanese Americans from the West Coast and intern them in relocation camps for the rest of the war. Despite the lack of any evidence of their disloyalty or sedition—no Japanese American was ever charged with espionage—few public leaders opposed the plan.

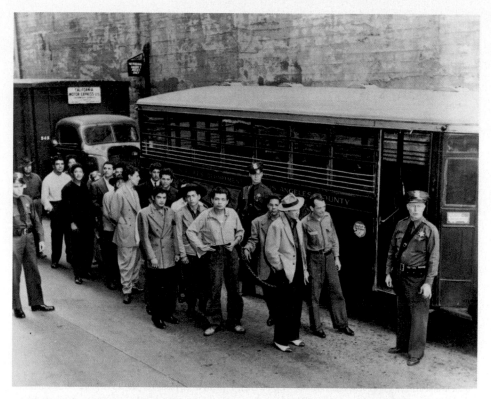

Zoot Suit Youth in Los Angeles

During a four-day riot in June 1943 servicemen in Los Angeles attacked young Latino men wearing distinctive "zoot suits," which were widely viewed as emblems of a delinquent youth culture. The police response was to arrest scores of zoot-suiters. Here, a group of young men are about to board a Los Angeles County Sheriff's bus in order to make a court appearance. Note the wide-legged pants that taper at the ankle. Library of Congress.

The announcement shocked Japanese Americans, more than two-thirds of whom were native-born American citizens. (They were Nisei, children of the foreign-born Issei.) Most had to sell their property and possessions at cut rate prices and were then rounded up in temporary assembly centers and sent by the War Relocation Authority to internment camps located in desolate areas in California, Arizona, Utah, Colorado, Wyoming, Idaho, and Arkansas (Map 26.2).

Almost every Japanese American in California, Oregon, and Washington was involuntarily detained for some period during World War II. Ironically, the Japanese Americans who made up one-third of the population of Hawaii, and presumably posed a greater threat because of their numbers and proximity to Japan, were not interned. Less vulnerable to suspicion because of the islands' multiracial heritage, the Japanese also provided much of the unskilled labor in the island territory. The Hawaiian economy simply could not function without them.

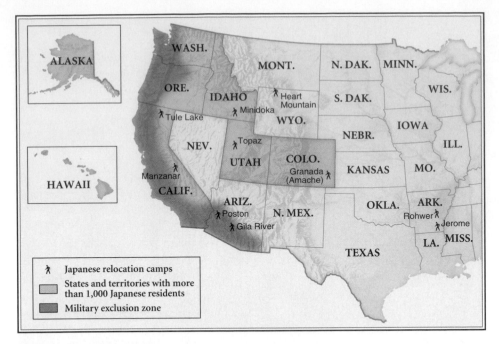

MAP 26.2 Japanese Relocation Camps

In 1942 the government ordered 112,000 Japanese Americans living on the West Coast into internment camps in the nation's interior because of their supposed threat to public safety. Some of the
camps were as far away as Arkansas. The federal government had rescinded the mass evacuation
order in December 1944, but when the war ended in August 1945, 44,000 people still remained in
the camps.

Cracks soon appeared in the relocation policy. A labor shortage in farming led
the government to furlough seasonal agricultural workers from the camps as early
as 1942. About 4,300 young people who had been in college when they were interned were allowed to return to school if they would transfer out of the West Coast
military zone. Another route out of the camps was enlistment in the armed services.
The 442nd Regimental Combat Team, a segregated unit composed almost entirely
of Nisei volunteers, served in Europe and became one of the most decorated units
in the armed forces.

In a series of three cases dealing with curfews and other discriminatory treatment of the Japanese related to the relocation process—*United States v. Minoru
Yasui* (1943), *Hirabayashi v. United States* (1943), and *Korematsu v. United States*
(1944)—the Supreme Court legitimated internment, while not expressly ruling on
its constitutionality. In 1944 it held in *Ex Parte Endo* that U.S. citizens who could be
proved to be loyal could not be detained, but it was not until 1988 that Congress
decided to issue a public apology and to give $20,000 in cash to each of the 80,000
surviving internees.

Fighting and Winning the War

World War II, noted military historian John Keegan, was "the largest single event in human history." Fought on six continents at a cost of 50 million lives, it was far more global than World War I. At least 405,000 Americans were killed and 671,000 wounded in the worldwide fighting—less than half of 1 percent of the U.S. population. In contrast the Soviets lost as many as 21 million soldiers and civilians during the war, or about 8 percent of their population.

Wartime Aims and Strategies

The Allied coalition was composed mainly of Great Britain, the United States, and the Soviet Union; other nations, notably China and France, played lesser roles. President Franklin Roosevelt, Prime Minister Winston Churchill of Britain, and Premier Joseph Stalin of the Soviet Union took the lead in setting overall strategy. The Atlantic Charter, which Churchill and Roosevelt had drafted in August 1941, formed the basis of the Allies' vision of the postwar international order. But Stalin had not been part of that agreement, a fact that would later cause disagreements over its goals.

But before the postwar world could be planned, the Germans and Japanese needed to be defeated on the battlefield. One way to wear down the Germans would have been to open a second front on the European continent, preferably in France. The Russians argued strongly for this strategy because it would draw German troops away from Russian soil. In 1941 the German army had reached the outskirts of Leningrad and Moscow, but the Russians had pushed them back from Moscow in the winter of 1941–42. Though Roosevelt assured Stalin informally that the Allies would open a second front in 1942, British opposition and the need first to raise American war production to full capacity stalled the effort. At a conference in Tehran, Iran, in late November 1943, Churchill and Roosevelt agreed to open a second front within six months in return for Stalin's promise to join the fight against Japan after the war in Europe ended. Both sides kept their promises. However, the long delay in creating a second front meant that for most of the war the Soviet Union bore the brunt of the land battle against Germany. Roosevelt and Churchill's foot-dragging angered Stalin, who was suspicious about American and British intentions. His mistrust and bitterness carried over into the Cold War that followed the Allied victory.

The War in Europe

During the first seven months of 1942, the military news was so bad that it threatened to swamp the Allies. They suffered severe defeats on land and sea in both Europe and Asia. German armies pushed deeper into Soviet territory, into the Ukraine and the oil-rich Caucasus, moving toward Stalingrad. Simultaneously the Germans began an offensive in North Africa aimed at seizing the Suez Canal. At sea German submarines were crippling Allied convoys carrying vital supplies to Britain and the Soviet Union.

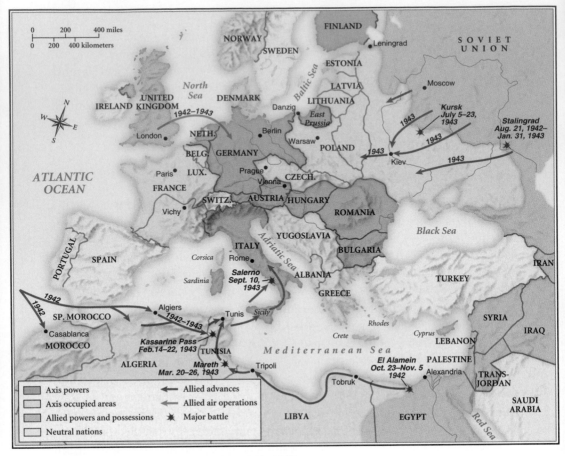

MAP 26.3 World War II in Europe, 1941–1943

Hitler's Germany reached its greatest extent in 1942, when Nazi forces stalled at Leningrad and Stalingrad. The tide of battle turned in the fall, when the Soviet army launched a massive counter-attack at Stalingrad and Allied forces began to drive the Germans from North Africa. In 1943 the Allies invaded Sicily and the Italian mainland.

FOR MORE HELP ANALYZING THIS MAP, see the Online Study Guide at **bedfordstmartins.com/henrettaconcise**.

The major turning point of the war in Europe occurred in the winter of 1942–43, when the Soviets halted the German advance in the Battle of Stalingrad (Map 26.3). By 1944 Stalin's forces had driven the German army out of the Soviet Union. Meanwhile, the Allies launched a major offensive in North Africa, Churchill's substitute for a second front in France. Between November 1942 and May 1943, Allied troops under the leadership of General Dwight D. Eisenhower and General George S. Patton defeated Germany's *Afrika Korps*, led by General Erwin Rommel.

From Africa, the Allied command moved to attack the Axis through what Churchill called its "soft underbelly": Sicily and the Italian peninsula. In July 1943

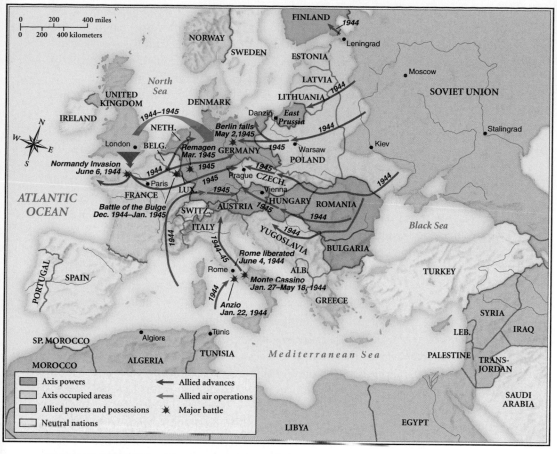

MAP 26.4 World War II in Europe, 1944–1945

On June 6, 1944 (D-Day), the Allies finally invaded France. It took almost a year for the Allied forces to close in on Berlin—the Soviets from the east and the Americans, British, and French from the west. Germany surrendered on May 8, 1945.

FOR MORE HELP ANALYZING THIS MAP, see the Online Study Guide at **bedfordstmartins.com/henrettaconcise**.

after Benito Mussolini's Fascist regime fell and Mussolini was executed, Italy's new government joined the Allies. The Allied forces fought bitter battles against the German army during the Italian campaign, finally entering Rome in June 1944 (Map 26.4), although the last German forces in Italy did not surrender until May 1945.

The long-promised invasion of France came on "D-Day," June 6, 1944. That morning, after an agonizing delay caused by bad weather, the largest armada ever assembled moved across the English Channel. Over the next few days, under the command of General Dwight Eisenhower, more than 1.5 million American, British, and Canadian soldiers crossed the channel. The beaches of Normandy, where the Allies landed—code-named Utah, Omaha, Juno, Gold, and Sword—soon became household words in the United States, sites of great and quiet bravery as well as terrible casualties and death. In August Allied troops helped to liberate Paris; by September they had driven the Germans out of most of France and Belgium.

The Germans were not yet ready to give up, however. In December 1944 their forces in Belgium mounted an attack that began the Battle of the Bulge, so called because their advance made a large balloon in the Allied line on war maps. After ten days of heavy fighting in what was to be the final German offensive of the war, the Allies regained their momentum and pushed the Germans back across the Rhine River. American and British troops led the drive from the west toward Berlin, while Soviet troops advanced from the east through Poland, arriving in Berlin first. On April 30, with much of Berlin in rubble from intense Allied bombing, Hitler committed suicide in his bunker. Germany surrendered to the Soviets on May 8, 1945, the date that became known as V-E (Victory in Europe) Day.

When Allied troops advanced into Germany in the spring of 1945, they came face to face with Hitler's "final solution of the Jewish question": the extermination camps where 6 million Jews had been put to death, along with another 6 million Poles, Slavs, Gypsies, homosexuals, and other "undesirables." Photographs of the Nazi death camps at Buchenwald, Dachau, and Auschwitz, showing bodies stacked like cordwood and survivors so emaciated they were barely alive, horrified the American public.

The Roosevelt administration had reliable information about the death camps as early as November 1942. Even if it aggressively sought a means to rescue the inmates, the obstacles of negotiating with Hitler's regime made it unlikely that many could have been saved once incarcerated. But the United States can be criticized for its failure to respond to the desperate circumstances of Jews seeking to flee Europe. As early as 1935, when the Germans instituted the Nuremberg Laws, which drastically curtailed their social and political freedoms, Jews were seeking to leave Germany. So few Jews escaped the Holocaust because the United States and the rest of the world would not take them in. During the war State Department policies allowed only 21,000 refugees to enter the United States. The War Refugee Board, established in 1944 with little support from the Roosevelt administration, eventually helped to save about 200,000 Jews, who were placed in refugee camps in countries such as Morocco and Switzerland. Several factors combined to inhibit U.S. action: anti-Semitism; fears of economic competition from a flood of refugees into a country just recovering from the depression; the failure of the media to grasp the magnitude of the story and to publicize it accordingly; and the failure of religious and political leaders, Jews and non-Jews alike, to speak out.

The War in the Pacific

After the victory in Europe, the Allies still had to defeat Japan. American forces bore the brunt of the fighting in the Pacific, just as the Russians had done in the land war

AMERICAN VOICES

An Army Nurse in Bataan

Juanita Redmond

*A*rmy nurse Juanita Redmond recounts her experience as one of the last nurses to remain in Bataan in the Philippines as the Japanese advanced. She was evacuated shortly before the Americans surrendered on May 6, 1942. Her description reveals both the horror of warfare and the extraordinary service performed by military nurses.

[The bomb] landed at the hospital entrance and blew up an ammunition truck that was passing. The concussion threw me to the floor. There was a spattering of shrapnel and pebbles and earth on the tin roof. Then silence for a few minutes.

I heard the corpsmen rushing out with litters, and I pulled myself to my feet. Precious medicines were dripping to the ground from the shattered dressing carts, and I tried to salvage as much as possible.

The first casualties came in. The boys in the ammunition truck had been killed, but the two guards at the hospital gate had jumped into their foxholes. By the time they were extricated from the debris that filled up the holes they were both shell-shock cases.

There were plenty of others. . . .

Only one small section of my ward remained standing. Part of the roof had been blown into the jungle. There were mangled bodies under the ruins; a blood-stained hand stuck up through a pile of scrap; arms and legs had been ripped off and flung among the rubbish. Some of the mangled torsos were almost impossible to identify. One of the few corpsmen who had survived unhurt climbed a tree to bring down a body blown into the top branches. Blankets, mattresses, pajama tops hung in the shattered trees.

We worked wildly to get to the men who might be buried, still alive, under the mass of wreckage, tearing apart the smashed beds to reach the wounded and the dead. These men were our patients, our responsibility; I think we were all tortured by an instinctive, irrational feeling that we had failed them.

SOURCE: Judy Barrett Litoff and David C. Smith, eds., *American Women in a World at War: Contemporary Accounts from World War II* (Wilmington, DE: Scholarly Resource Books, 1997), 85–86. Reprinted from Juanita Redmond, *I Served on Bataan* (Philadelphia: Lippincott, 1943), 106–22.

in Europe. In early 1942 the news from the Pacific was uniformly grim. In the wake of Pearl Harbor, Japan had scored quickly with seaborne invasions of Hong Kong, Wake Island, and Guam. Japanese forces soon conquered much of Burma, Malaya, and the Solomon Islands and began to threaten Australia and India. The U.S. surrender in the Philippines on May 6, 1942, and the horrific Bataan "death march," in which between 5,000 and 11,000 prisoners of war perished, were particularly demoralizing for Americans (see American Voices, "An Army Nurse in Bataan," above).

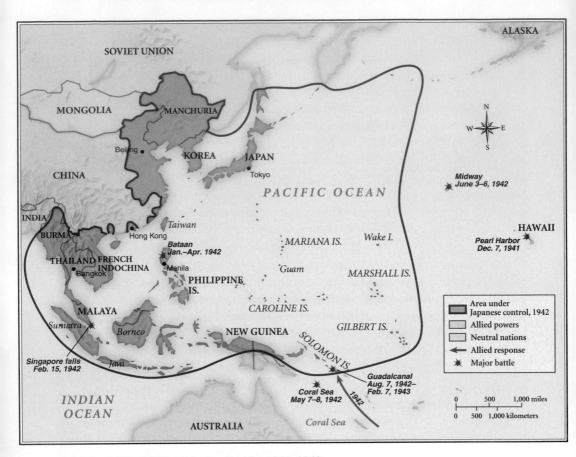

MAP 26.5 World War II in the Pacific, 1941–1942

After the attacks on Pearl Harbor in December 1941, the Japanese rapidly extended their domination in the Pacific. The Japanese flag soon flew as far east as the Marshall and Gilbert Islands and as far south as the Solomon Islands and parts of New Guinea. Japan also controlled the Philippines, much of Southeast Asia, and parts of China, including Hong Kong. American naval victories at the Coral Sea and Midway stopped further Japanese expansion.

But on May 7 and 8, 1942, in the Battle of the Coral Sea near southern New Guinea, American naval forces halted the Japanese offensive against Australia. In June, at the island of Midway, the Americans inflicted crucial damage on the Japanese fleet. With that success the American military command, led by General Douglas MacArthur and Admiral Chester W. Nimitz, took the offensive in the Pacific (Map 26.5). For the next eighteen months, American forces advanced arduously from one island to the next. In October 1944 the reconquest of the Philippines began with a victory in the Battle of Leyte Gulf, a massive naval encounter in which the Japanese lost practically their entire fleet, whereas the Americans suffered only minimal losses (Map 26.6).

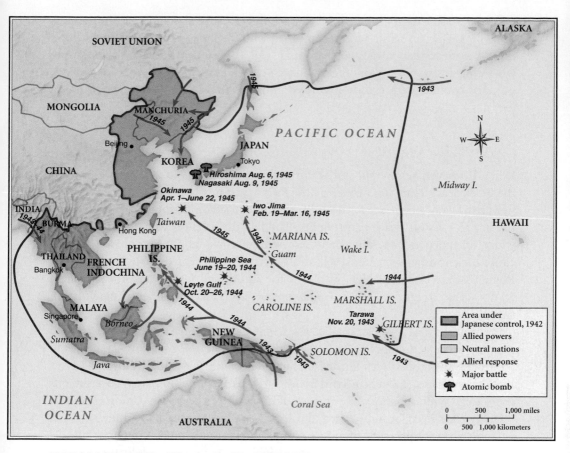

MAP 26.6 World War II in the Pacific, 1943–1945

Allied forces retook the islands in the central Pacific in 1943 and 1944 and the Philippines early in 1945. The capture of Iwo Jima and Okinawa put bombers in position to attack Japan itself. At Yalta, Stalin pledged that following Germany's defeat, the Soviet Union would join the Allies fighting in the Pacific. Before the Soviets could act, the Japanese offered to surrender on August 10, after the United States dropped atomic bombs on Hiroshima and Nagasaki.

By early 1945 victory over Japan was in sight. The campaign in the Pacific moved slowly toward what military leaders anticipated would be a massive and costly invasion of Japan. In some of the fiercest fighting of the war, the marines sustained more than 20,000 casualties at Iwo Jima, including 6,000 dead; at Okinawa the toll reached 7,600 dead and 32,000 wounded. The closer U.S. forces got to the Japanese home islands, the more fiercely the Japanese fought. On Iwo Jima almost all of the 21,000 Japanese soldiers died.

By mid-1945 Japan's army, navy, and air force had suffered devastating losses. American bombing of the mainland had killed about 330,000 civilians and crippled the Japanese economy. In a last-ditch effort to stem the tide, Japanese pilots began suicidal kamikaze missions, crashing their planes and boats into American ships. This desperate action, combined with the Japanese military leadership's refusal to surrender, suggested that Japan would keep up the fight despite overwhelming losses. Based on the fighting at Okinawa and Iwo Jima, American military commanders grimly predicted millions of casualties in the upcoming invasion.

Planning the Postwar World

When Roosevelt, Churchill, and Stalin met in February 1945 at Yalta, a resort on the Black Sea, victory in Europe and the Pacific was in sight, but no agreement had been reached on the peace to come. Roosevelt focused on maintaining Allied unity, the key to postwar peace and stability. The fate of British colonies such as India, where an independence movement led by Mahatma Gandhi had already begun, caused friction between Roosevelt and Churchill. Some of the tensions with the Russians were resolved when, in return for additional possessions in the Pacific, Stalin agreed to enter the war against Japan within three months of the German surrender.

A more serious source of conflict was Stalin's desire for a band of Soviet-controlled satellite states to protect the Soviet Union's western border. With Soviet armies in control of much of Eastern Europe, Stalin had become increasingly inflexible about that region, insisting that he needed friendly (that is, Soviet-dominated) governments there to provide a buffer zone that would guarantee the Soviet Union's national security. Roosevelt acknowledged the legitimacy of that demand but, with the Atlantic Charter's principle of self-determination in mind, hoped for democratically elected governments in Poland and the neighboring countries. Unfortunately, the two goals proved mutually exclusive.

At Yalta Roosevelt and Churchill agreed in principle on the idea of a Soviet sphere of influence in Eastern Europe but deliberately left its dimensions vague. Stalin in return pledged to hold "free and unfettered elections" at an unspecified time. (Those elections never took place.) The compromise reached by the three leaders at Yalta was open to multiple interpretations. Admiral William D. Leahy, Roosevelt's chief military aide, described the agreement as "so elastic that the Russians can stretch it all the way from Yalta to Washington without ever technically breaking it."

The three leaders proceeded with plans to divide Germany into four zones to be controlled by the United States, Great Britain, France, and the Soviet Union. The capital city, Berlin, which lay in the middle of the Soviet zone, would also be partitioned among the four powers. The issue of German reparations remained unsettled.

The Big Three made further progress toward the establishment of an international organization in the form of the United Nations. They agreed that the Security Council of the United Nations would include the five major Allied powers—the United States, Britain, France, China, and the Soviet Union—plus six other

The Big Three at Yalta

With victory in Europe at hand, Roosevelt journeyed in 1945 to Yalta, on the Black Sea, to meet one last time with Churchill and Stalin. It was here that they discussed the problems of peace settlements. The Yalta agreement mirrored a new balance of power and set the stage for the Cold War. Franklin D. Roosevelt Library.

nations elected on a rotating basis. They also decided that the permanent members of the Security Council should have veto power over decisions of the General Assembly, in which all nations would be represented. Roosevelt, Churchill, and Stalin announced that the United Nations would convene in San Francisco on April 25, 1945.

Roosevelt returned to the United States in February, visibly exhausted by his 14,000-mile trip. He neglected to inform the American public of the concessions he had made to maintain the increasingly fragile wartime alliance. When he reported to Congress on the Yalta agreements, he made an unusual acknowledgment of his physical infirmity. Referring to the heavy steel braces he wore on his legs, he asked Congress to excuse him for giving his speech while sitting down. The sixty-three-year-old president was a sick man, suffering from heart failure and high blood pressure. On April 12, 1945, during a short visit to his vacation home in Warm Springs, Georgia, Roosevelt suffered a cerebral hemorrhage and died.

Hiroshima

This aerial view of Hiroshima after the dropping of an atomic bomb on August 6, 1945, shows the terrible devastation of the city. A U.S. Army report prepared in 1946 describes the bomb exploding "with a blinding flash in the sky, and a great rush of air and a loud rumble of noise extended for many miles around the city; the first blast was soon followed by the sounds of falling buildings and of growing fires, and a great cloud of dust and smoke began to cast a pall of darkness over the city." With the exception of around 50 concrete-reinforced buildings designed to withstand earthquakes, every structure within one mile of the center of the bomb blast was reduced to rubble. The physical destruction was second to the human cost: with a population estimated at between 300,000 and 400,000 people, Hiroshima lost 100,000 in the initial explosion and many thousands more died slowly of radiation poisoning. U.S. Air Force.

When Harry S Truman assumed the presidency, he learned about the top-secret Manhattan Project, charged with developing a new weapon—an atomic bomb. The project, which cost $2 billion and employed 120,000 people, culminated in Los Alamos, New Mexico, where the country's top physicists assembled the first bomb. Not until the first test—at Alamogordo, New Mexico, on July 16, 1945—did scientists know that the bomb would work. A month later Truman ordered the dropping of atomic bombs on two Japanese cities, Hiroshima on August 6 and Nagasaki on August 9.

TIMELINE

1933	Adolf Hitler becomes chancellor of Germany	**1942**	Allies suffer severe defeats in Europe and Asia
1935	Italy invades Ethiopia		Executive Order 9066 leads to Japanese internment camps
1935–1937	U.S. Neutrality Acts		Battles of Coral Sea and Midway halt Japanese advance
1936	Germany reoccupies Rhineland demilitarized zone		Women recruited for war industries
	Rome-Berlin Axis established	**1942–1945**	Rationing
	Japan and Germany sign Anti-Comintern Pact	**1943**	Race riots in Detroit and Los Angeles
1937	Japan invades China		Fascism falls in Italy
1938	Munich agreement between Germany, Britain, and France	**1944**	D-Day
			GI Bill of Rights
1939	Nazi-Soviet Nonaggression Pact	**1945**	Yalta Conference
	Germany invades Poland		Battles of Iwo Jima and Okinawa
	Britain and France declare war on Germany		Germany surrenders
1940	American conscription reinstated		Harry S Truman becomes president after Roosevelt's death
	Germany, Italy, and Japan sign Tri-Partite Pact		United Nations convenes
1941	Roosevelt promulgates Four Freedoms		Atomic bombs dropped on Hiroshima and Nagasaki
	Germany invades Soviet Union		Japan surrenders
	Lend-Lease Act passed		
	Fair Employment Practices Commission		
	Atlantic Charter		
	Japanese attack Pearl Harbor		

Many later questioned why the United States did not warn Japan about the attack or choose a target that would produce fewer civilian casualties; the rationale for dropping the second bomb was even less clear. Some historians have argued that American policymakers, already worried about potential conflicts with the Soviets over the postwar order, used the bomb to intimidate them. Others have suggested that the fact that the Japanese were a nonwhite race facilitated the momentous decision to use the new, alarming weapon. At the time, however, the belief that Japan's military leaders would never surrender unless their country was utterly devastated convinced policymakers that they had to deploy the atom bomb. Moreover, by 1945, the unprecedented numbers of dead and wounded as a result of the war had created a sense of callousness on all sides, and the Truman administration did not debate the morality of using the bomb. One hundred thousand people died at Hiroshima and sixty thousand at Nagasaki; tens of thousands more died slowly of radiation poisoning. Japan offered to surrender on August 10 and signed a formal treaty of surrender on September 2, 1945.

Franklin Roosevelt's death and the dropping of the atomic bomb came at a critical juncture in world affairs. Many issues had been left deliberately unresolved, in hopes of keeping the wartime alliance intact through the transition to peace. But once the common enemies had been defeated, the wartime alliance became strained and then began to split apart in fundamental ways. World War II had a tremendous long-term impact on Americans' domestic life, especially in the realms of the economy, demographic changes, and civil rights. The greatly expanded presence of the federal government, with its growing bureaucracy and escalating budget was a particularly striking result of the war years and would contribute in the postwar era to what observers called the military-industrial complex, the close linkage between the federal government and the nation's defense industries. That partnership grew out of perhaps the most far-reaching legacy of World War II: the Cold War that would follow.

For Further Exploration

An engaging overview of war on the home front that emphasizes social and cultural conflicts embodied in the war effort is John Morton Blum, *V Was for Victory* (1976). An anthology that focuses on popular culture—including an analysis of glamorous movie icons like Betty Grable—as a means to understanding the wartime experience is Lewis A. Erenberg and Susan E. Hirsch, eds., *The War in American Culture* (1996). Stephen J. Ambrose offers insight into military life from the ordinary man's point of view with *Citizen Soldiers* (1997). Two oral history collections are indispensable. Studs Terkel, *The Good War* (1984), examines the notion that, in contrast to America's more recent war in Vietnam, World War II is largely remembered in positive terms. Sherna B. Gluck, *Rosie the Riveter Revisited* (1988), offers compelling accounts by women war workers. Powerful novels inspired by the war include James Jones, *From Here to Eternity* (1951), Norman Mailer, *The Naked and the Dead* (1948), and John Hersey, *Bell for Adano* (1944).

The National Archives Administration, at <http://www.archives.gov/exhibit_hall/index.html>, has two World War II sites. A People at War offers a number of documents, including a letter about the Navajo Code Talkers. Powers of Persuasion: Poster Art from World War II contains thirty-three color posters and a sound file of the song "Any Bonds Today." The Library of Congress Web site at <http://lcweb.loc.gov/exhibits/wcf/wcf0001.html> has an online exhibit, Women Come to the Front: Journalists, Photographers, and Broadcasters During World War II, that features articles, biographies, and photographs of eight women who covered the war. See also Rosie Pictures: Select Images Relating to American Women Workers During World War II at <http://lcweb.loc.gov/rr/print/126_rosi.html>. There are many sites on Japanese internment. The University of Washington provides a particularly interesting one at <http://www.lib.washington.edu/exhibits/harmony/default.htm>, on the experiences of the Seattle Japanese American community's incarceration at the Puyallup Assembly Center; it includes letters, photographs, and other documents. The Rutgers Oral History Archive of World War II, at <http://fas-history.rutgers.edu/oralhistory/orlhom .htm>, offers over one hundred oral histories that cover not just the interviewees' war experiences but their life histories as well, providing valuable insights into community life in depression-era and wartime New Jersey.

For definitions of key terms boldfaced in this chapter, see the glossary at the end of the book.

To assess your mastery of the material covered in this chapter, see the Online Study Guide at **bedfordstmartins.com/henrettaconcise**.

For map resources and primary documents, see **bedfordstmartins.com/henrettaconcise**.

Part Six

AMERICA AND THE WORLD

1945 TO THE PRESENT

	DIPLOMACY	GOVERNMENT	ECONOMY
	The Cold War and After	**Redefining the Role of the State**	**Ups and Downs of U.S. Economic Dominance**
1945	▶ Truman Doctrine (1947) Marshall Plan (1948) NATO founded (1949)	▶ Truman's Fair Deal liberalism Taft-Hartley Act (1947)	▶ Bretton Woods system established: World Bank, IMF, GATT
1950	▶ Permanent mobilization: NSC-68 (1950) Korean War (1950–1953)	▶ Eisenhower's modern Republicanism Warren Court activism	▶ Rise of military-industrial complex Service sector expands
1960	▶ Cuban missile crisis (1962) Vietnam War escalates (1965)	▶ Great Society, War on Poverty Nixon ushers in conservative era	▶ Kennedy-Johnson tax cut, military expenditures fuel economic growth
1970	▶ Nixon visits China (1972) SALT initiates détente (1972) Paris Peace Accords (1973)	▶ Watergate scandal; Nixon resigns (1974) Weak presidencies of Ford and Carter	▶ Arab oil embargo (1973–1974); inflation surges Unemployment rises while income stagnates
1980	▶ Reagan begins arms buildup INF Treaty (1988) Berlin Wall falls (1989)	▶ Reagan Revolution Supreme Court conservatism	▶ Reaganomics Budget and trade deficits soar
1990–2004	▶ War in the Persian Gulf (1990) USSR collapses; Cold War ends U.S. peacekeeping forces in Bosnia Radical Muslim terrorist attacks on New York and the Pentagon (2001) United States and allies invade Iraq (2003)	▶ Bill Clinton impeached and acquitted (1998–1999) Republican Congress shifts federal government tasks to states George W. Bush narrowly elected president (2000) USA PATRIOT Act passed (2002)	▶ Corporate downsizing: boom of the mid-1990s gives way to weakening economy Globalization intensifies Bush tax cut of 2001 attempts to stimulate recovery

SOCIETY	CULTURE
Social Movements and Demographic Diversity	**Consumer Culture and the Information Revolution**
▸ Migration to cities accelerates Armed forces desegregated (1948)	▸ End of wartime rationing Rise of television
▸ *Brown v. Board of Education* (1954) Montgomery bus boycott (1955)	▸ Growth of suburbia Baby boom
▸ Student activism Civil rights legislation (1964, 1965) Revival of feminism	▸ Shopping malls spread Baby boomers swell college enrollment Youth counterculture
▸ *Roe v. Wade* (1973) New right urges conservative agenda	▸ Rise of consumer and environmental protection movements Gasoline shortages Apple introduces first personal computer (1977)
▸ New Latino and Asian immigration AIDS epidemic	▸ Cable News Network (CNN) founded (1980) Compact discs and cell phones invented
▸ Los Angeles riots (1992) "Culture wars" over affirmative action, feminism, and gay rights Welfare reform	▸ Health-care crisis Dramatic growth of the Internet and World Wide Web Biotech revolution Gay marriages performed in many states

I n 1945, journalist Walter Lippmann proclaimed that "What Rome was to the ancient world, what Great Britain has been to the modern world, America is to be for the world of tomorrow." Lippmann aptly recognized that the United States emerged from World War II with unprecedented international political and economic power. For the next sixty years, far more than in previous eras, the U.S. position in the world profoundly influenced the nation's domestic economy, political affairs, and social and cultural trends.

DIPLOMACY The United States took a leading role in global diplomatic and military affairs. When the Soviet Union challenged America's vision of postwar Europe, the Truman administration responded by crafting the policies and alliances that came to define the Cold War. That struggle lasted for more than forty years, spawned two "hot" wars in Korea and Vietnam, and fueled a terrifying nuclear arms race. The Cold War continued until the collapse of the Soviet Union in 1991. Nonetheless, international conflicts persisted, arising from regional, religious, and ethnic differences. In 1990 the United States fought the Gulf War against Iraq and ten years later sent peacekeeping troops to war-torn Bosnia. America and its allies' invasion of Iraq in 2003 that toppled the regime of Saddam Hussein further signaled the nation's willingness to exercise its military power. At the same time Americans grappled with the growing menace of international terrorism, shockingly symbolized by the devastating attacks on New York's World Trade Center and the Pentagon in September 2001.

GOVERNMENT America's global commitments had dramatic consequences for the U.S. government; its leaders kept the nation in a state of permanent mobilization with a large military establishment. The end of the Cold War brought modest cutbacks, but with new diplomatic challenges, military expenditures remained a high priority and competed with spending for domestic needs. In the 1960s Lyndon B. Johnson's "Great Society" erected an extensive federal and state apparatus to provide for social welfare. In subsequent years, particularly under the presidency of Ronald Reagan in the 1980s and the Republican-controlled Congress in the mid-1990s, conservatives cut back on many major social programs and tried to delegate federal powers to the states.

ECONOMY Thanks to the growth of a military-industrial complex and the expansion of consumer culture, the quarter century after 1945 represented the heyday of American capitalism and unparalleled domestic affluence. In the early 1970s, however, other countries began to challenge America's economic supremacy, and for the next two decades, many American workers experienced high unemployment, declining real wages, and stagnant incomes. Following this period of global economic restructuring, the U.S. economy rebounded in the mid-1990s, reclaiming a position of undisputed dominance and playing an increasing role in "globalization," the integration of the world's economies. By 2001, however, American prosperity was undercut by a weakening economy and a volatile stock market as well as concerns that disparities in wealth and opportunity were growing.

SOCIETY The victory over fascism in World War II led to renewed calls for America to make good on its promise of liberty and equality for all. In great waves of protests in the 1950s and 1960s, African Americans—and then women, Latinos, and other groups—challenged the political status quo. The resulting hard-won reforms brought concrete gains for many Americans, but since the late 1970s, conservatives have challenged many of these initiatives. At the beginning of the twenty-first century, the promise of true equality remained unfulfilled.

CULTURE American economic power in the postwar era accelerated the development of a consumer society based on suburbanization and technology. As millions of Americans migrated to new suburban developments after World War II, growing baby-boom families provided an expanded market for household products of all types. Among the most significant were new technological devices, such as televisions and personal computers, that helped break down the isolation of suburban and rural living. In the 1990s the popularization of the Internet initiated an "information revolution" that expanded and challenged the power of corporate-sponsored consumer culture.

Today, more than a half century after the end of World War II, Americans are living in an interwoven network of national and international forces. Outside events shape ordinary lives in ways that were inconceivable a century ago. With the Cold War fading into history, the United States is the world's sole military superpower and is extraordinarily wealthy, but its ability to achieve its foreign-policy aims and meet the needs of all its citizens remains elusive.

Chapter 27

COLD WAR AMERICA
1945–1960

We have been in the process of fighting monsters without stop for a generation and a half, looking all that time into the nuclear abyss. And the abyss has looked back into us.

DANIEL ELLSBERG, 1971

$\mathbf{W}$hen Harry Truman arrived at the White House on April 12, 1945, after Franklin Roosevelt died, he asked the president's widow, "Is there anything I can do for you?" Eleanor Roosevelt responded, "Is there anything we can do for you? For you are the one in trouble now." Truman inherited the presidency at one of the most perilous times in modern history. Unscathed by bombs and battles on the home front, U.S. industry and agriculture had grown rapidly during World War II. The nation wielded enormous military power as the sole possessor of the atomic bomb. The most powerful country in the world, the United States had become a preeminent force in the international arena. Only the Soviet Union represented an obstacle to American hegemony, or dominance, in global affairs. Soon the two superpowers were locked in a Cold War of economic, political, and military rivalry but without direct engagement on the battlefield.

Soviet-American confrontations during the postwar years had important domestic repercussions. The Cold War boosted military expenditures, fueling a growing **arms race**. It fostered a climate of fear and suspicion of "subversives" in government, education, and the media who might undermine American democratic institutions. It both constrained and assisted the emerging civil rights movement. The economic benefits of internationalism also gave rise to a period of unprecedented affluence and prosperity during which the United States enjoyed the highest standard of living in the world (see Chapter 28). That prosperity helped to continue and in some cases to expand federal power, perpetuating the New Deal state in the postwar era.

Protect Them

The Cold War and nuclear arms race pervaded American culture in the post–World War II years. The government's Civil Defense Agency, founded in 1950, mounted an extensive campaign to alert the nation to the need for civil defense plans, including the construction of public shelters and the development of emergency evacuation strategies. This Teaneck, New Jersey, poster not only reminded Americans of the potential for attack, but also, by picturing a mother and children in need of protection, reinforced the era's emphasis on family and traditional gender roles. Collection of Janice L. and David J. Frent.

FOR MORE HELP ANALYZING THIS IMAGE, see the Online Study Guide at **bedfordstmartins.com/henrettaconcise.**

The Cold War Abroad

The defeat of Germany and Japan did not bring stability to the world. Six years of devastating warfare had destroyed prewar governments and national boundaries, creating new power relationships that helped to dissolve colonial empires. Even before the war ended, the United States and the Soviet Union were struggling for advantage in those unstable areas; after the war they engaged in a protracted global conflict. Hailed as a battle between communism and capitalism, the Cold War was in reality a more complex power struggle covering a range of economic, strategic, and ideological issues. As each side tried to protect its own national security and way of life, its actions aroused fear in the other, contributing to a cycle of distrust and animosity that would shape U.S.-Soviet relations until the collapse of the USSR in 1991.

Descent into Cold War, 1945–1946

During the war Franklin Roosevelt worked effectively with Soviet leader Joseph Stalin and was determined to continue good relations with the Soviet Union in peacetime. In particular he hoped that the United Nations would provide a forum for resolving postwar conflicts. Avoiding the disagreements that had doomed American membership in the League of Nations after World War I, the Senate approved America's participation in the United Nations in December 1945. Coming eight months after Roosevelt's death, the vote was in part a memorial to the late president's hopes for peace.

Shortly before his death, however, Roosevelt had been disturbed by Soviet actions in Eastern Europe. As the Soviet army drove the Germans out of Russia and back through Eastern Europe, the Soviet Union sponsored provisional governments in the occupied countries. Since the Soviet Union had been a victim of German aggression in both world wars, Stalin was determined to prevent the rebuilding and rearming of its traditional foe, and he insisted on a security zone of friendly governments in Eastern Europe for further protection. At the Yalta Conference in February 1945, both America and Britain had agreed to recognize this Soviet "sphere of influence," with the proviso that "free and unfettered elections" would be held as soon as possible. But in succeeding months the Soviets made no move to hold elections and rebuffed Western attempts to reorganize the Soviet-installed governments.

When Truman assumed the presidency after Roosevelt's death, he had little experience with foreign affairs and was not privy to Roosevelt's plans for the postwar world. He immediately took a belligerent stance toward the Soviet Union. Recalling Britain's disastrous appeasement of Hitler in 1938, he decided that the United States had to take a hard line against Soviet expansion. At a meeting held shortly after he took office, the new president berated the Soviet foreign minister, V. M. Molotov, over the Soviets' failure to honor their Yalta agreement to support free elections in Poland. Truman used what he called "tough methods" that July at the Potsdam Conference, which brought together the United States, Britain, and the Soviet Union. After learning of the successful test of America's atomic bomb, Truman "told the Russians just where they got off and generally bossed the whole meeting," recalled British prime minister Winston Churchill. Negotiations on critical postwar issues deadlocked, revealing serious cracks in the Grand Alliance.

One issue tentatively resolved at Potsdam was the fate of occupied Germany. At Yalta the Allies had divided the defeated German state into four zones of occupation, controlled by the United States, France, Britain, and the Soviet Union. At Potsdam the Allies agreed to disarm the country, dismantle its military production facilities, and permit the occupying powers to extract reparations from the zones they controlled. Plans for future reunification stalled, however, as the United States and the Soviet Union each worried that a united Germany would fall into the other's sphere. The foundation was thus laid for what would become the political division into East and West Germany four years later (Map 27.1).

As tensions over Europe divided the former Allies, hopes of international cooperation in the control of atomic weapons faded as well. In the Baruch Plan, submitted to the United Nations in 1946, the United States proposed a system of international control that relied on mandatory inspection and supervision but

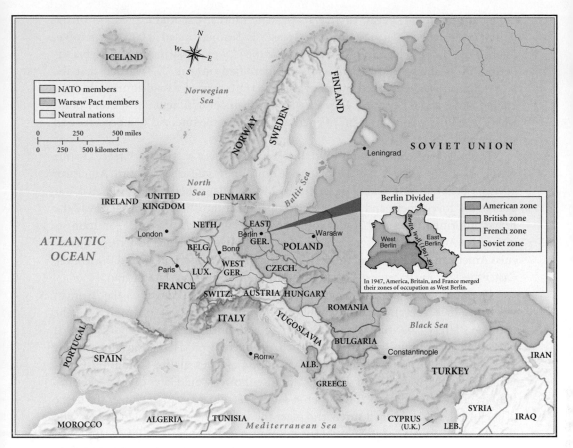

MAP 27.1 Cold War in Europe, 1955

In 1949 the United States sponsored the creation of the North Atlantic Treaty Organization (NATO)—an alliance of ten European nations, the United States, and Canada. West Germany was formally admitted to NATO in May 1955. A few days later the Soviet Union and seven other Communist nations established a rival alliance, the Warsaw Pact. The divided city of Berlin, with West Berlin located deep in Communist East Germany, was a major flash point in Cold War controversies.

preserved American nuclear monopoly. The Soviets, rejecting the plan, worked hard to complete their own bomb. Meanwhile, the Truman administration pursued projects to develop nuclear energy and weapons further. Thus the failure of the Baruch Plan signaled the hardening of tensions and the beginning of a frenzied nuclear arms race between the two superpowers.

The Truman Doctrine and Containment

As tensions mounted between the superpowers, the United States increasingly perceived Soviet expansionism as a threat to its own interests, and a new American policy, **containment**, began to take shape. The most influential expression of the policy came in February 1946 from George F. Kennan in an 8,000-word cable, dubbed the "Long Telegram," from his post at the U.S. embassy in Moscow to his superiors in Washington. Kennan, who was identified only as "X," warned that the Soviet Union was embarked on an aggressive trajectory of expansionism that the United States should counter with a policy of "firm containment . . . at every point where [the Russians] show signs of encroaching upon the interests of a peaceful and stable world."

The policy of containment crystallized in 1947 over a crisis in Greece. In the spring of 1946, several thousand local Communist guerrillas, whom American advisors believed were taking orders from Moscow, launched a full-scale civil war against the government and the British occupation authorities. In February 1947 the British informed Truman that they could no longer afford to assist anti-Communists in Greece. American policymakers worried that Soviet influence in Greece threatened American and European interests in the eastern Mediterranean and the Middle East, especially in strategically located Turkey and the oil-rich state of Iran.

In response the president announced what would be known as the Truman Doctrine. In a speech to the Republican-controlled Congress on March 12, he requested large-scale military and economic assistance for Greece and Turkey. If Greece fell to communism, Truman warned, the effects would be serious not only for Turkey but for the entire Middle East. This notion of an escalating Communist contagion was an early version of what Dwight Eisenhower would later call the "**domino theory**." Truman declared, "If we falter in our leadership, we may endanger the peace of the world," and "we shall surely endanger the welfare of our own nation." Despite the open-endedness of this military commitment, Congress quickly approved Truman's request for $300 million in aid to Greece and $100 million for Turkey. The appropriation reversed the postwar trend toward sharp cuts in foreign spending and marked a new level of commitment to the emerging Cold War.

During this period Secretary of State George Marshall proposed a plan to provide economic as well as military aid to Europe. By bolstering European economies devastated by war, Marshall and Truman believed, the United States could forestall severe economic dislocation, which might give rise to communism. American economic self-interest was also a contributing factor; the legislation required that foreign-aid dollars be spent on U.S. goods and services. A revitalized Europe centered on a strong West German economy would provide a better market for U.S. goods.

Truman's pledge of financial aid to European economies, however, met with significant opposition in Congress. Republicans castigated the Marshall Plan as a huge "international W.P.A." But in the midst of the congressional stalemate, on February 25, 1948, came a Communist coup in Czechoslovakia. A stark reminder of the menace of Soviet expansion in Europe, the coup rallied congressional support for the Marshall Plan. In March 1948 Congress voted overwhelmingly to approve funds for the program. Like most other foreign-policy initiatives of the 1940s and 1950s, the Marshall Plan won bipartisan support.

Over the next four years, the United States contributed nearly $13 billion to a highly successful recovery effort. Western European economies revived, and industrial production increased 64 percent, opening new opportunities for international trade (see Voices from Abroad, "Truman's Generous Proposal," p. 822). The Marshall Plan did not specifically exclude Eastern Europe or the Soviet Union, but it required that all participating nations exchange economic information and work toward the elimination of tariffs and other trade barriers. Denouncing those conditions as attempts to draw Eastern Europe into the American orbit, Soviet leaders forbade its satellite states of Czechoslovakia, Poland, and Hungary to participate.

The Marshall Plan accelerated American and European efforts to rebuild and unify the West German economy. In June 1948, after agreeing to fuse their zones of occupation, the United States, France, and Britain initiated a program of economic reform in West Berlin. This attention to Berlin, located deep within the Soviet zone of occupation, alarmed the Soviets, who feared a resurgent Germany aligned with the West, and they imposed a blockade on all highway, rail, and river traffic to West Berlin. Truman countered with an airlift: for nearly a year American and British pilots, who had been dropping bombs on Berlin only four years earlier, flew in 2.5 million tons of food and fuel—nearly a ton for each resident. On May 12, 1949, Stalin lifted the blockade, which had made West Berlin a symbol of resistance to communism.

The coup in Czechoslovakia and the crisis in Berlin convinced U.S. policymakers of the need for a collective security pact. In April 1949, for the first time since the end of the American Revolution, the United States entered into a peacetime military alliance, the North Atlantic Treaty Organization (NATO). Truman asked Congress for $1.3 billion in military assistance to NATO and authorized the basing of four U.S. Army divisions in Western Europe. Under the NATO pact, twelve nations— the United States, Canada, Britain, France, Italy, Belgium, the Netherlands, Luxembourg, Denmark, Norway, Portugal, and Iceland—agreed that "an armed attack against one or more of them in Europe or North America shall be considered an attack against them all." In May 1949 those nations also agreed to the creation of the Federal Republic of Germany (West Germany), which joined NATO in 1955.

In October 1949, in response to the creation of NATO, the Soviet Union tightened its grip on Eastern Europe by creating a separate government for East Germany, which became the German Democratic Republic. The Soviets also organized an economic association, the Council for Mutual Economic Assistance (COMECON) in 1949, and a military alliance for Eastern Europe, the Warsaw Pact, in 1955. The postwar division of Europe was nearly complete.

New impetus for the policy of containment came in September 1949, when American military intelligence detected a rise in radioactivity in the atmosphere— proof that the Soviet Union had detonated an atomic bomb. The American atomic monopoly, which some military and political advisors had argued would last for decades, had ended in just four years, forcing a major reassessment of the nation's foreign policy.

Truman's Generous Proposal

JEAN MONNET

*J*ean Monnet was an eminent French statesman and a tireless promoter of postwar European union. As head of a French postwar planning commission, he helped oversee the dispersal of Marshall Plan funds, the importance of which he describes in his memoirs.

So we had at last concerted our efforts to halt France's economic decline; but now, once more, everything seemed to be at risk. Two years earlier [1947], we thought that we had plumbed the depths of material poverty. Now we were threatened with the loss of even basic essentials. . . . Our dollar resources were melting away at an alarming rate, because we were having to buy American wheat to replace the crops we had lost during the winter. . . . A further American loan was soon exhausted.

Nor was this grim situation confined to France. Britain too had come to the end of her resources. In February 1947 she had abruptly cancelled her aid to Greece and Turkey, whose burdens she had seemed able to assume in 1945. Overnight, this abrupt abdication gave the United States direct responsibility for part of Europe. Truman did not hesitate for a moment: with the decisiveness that was to mark his actions as President, he at once asked for credits and arms for both Turkey and Greece. . . . [Soon after], he announced the Truman Doctrine of March 12, 1947. Its significance was general: it meant that the United States would prevent Europe from becoming a depressed area at the mercy of Communist advance. On the very same day, the Four-Power Conference began in Moscow. There, for a whole month, George Marshall, Ernest Bevin, and Georges Bidault argued with Vyacheslav Molotov about all the problems of the peace, and above all about Germany.

When Marshall returned to Washington, he knew that for a long time there would be no further genuine dialogue with Stalin's Russia. The "Cold War," as it was soon to be known, had begun. . . . Information from a number of sources convinced Marshall and his Under-Secretary Dean Acheson that once again, as in 1941, the United States had a great historic duty. And once again there took place what I had witnessed in Washington a few years earlier: a small group of men brought to rapid maturity an idea which, when the Executive gave the word, turned into vigorous action. This time, it was done by five or six people, in total secrecy and at lightning speed. Marshall, Acheson, Clayton, Averell Harriman, and George Kennan worked out a proposal of unprecedented scope and generosity. It took us all by surprise when we read the speech that George Marshall made at Harvard on June 5, 1947. Chance had led him to choose the University's Commencement Day to launch something new in international relations: helping others to help themselves.

SOURCE: *Memoirs* by Jean Monnet, Introduction by George W. Ball. Translated by Richard Mayne. Copyright © 1978 by Doubleday, a division of Bantam, Doubleday, Dell Publishing Group, Inc. Used by permission of Doubleday, a division of Random House, Inc.

To devise a new diplomatic and military blueprint, Truman turned to the National Security Council (NSC), an advisory body established by the National Security Act of 1947 that also created the Department of Defense and the Central Intelligence Agency (CIA), to set defense and military priorities. In April 1950 the NSC delivered its report, known as "NSC-68," to the president. Filled with alarmist rhetoric and exaggerated assessments of Soviet capabilities, the document made several specific recommendations, including the development of a hydrogen bomb, an advanced weapon a thousand times more destructive than the atomic bombs that had destroyed Hiroshima and Nagasaki. (The United States would explode its first hydrogen bomb in November 1952 and the Soviet Union its first in 1953.) NSC-68 also supported increases in U.S. conventional forces and the establishment of a strong system of alliances. Most important, it called for increased taxes to finance "a bold and massive program of rebuilding the West's defensive potential to surpass that of the Soviet world."

Though Truman was an aggressive anti-Communist, he was reluctant to commit to a major defense buildup, fearing that it would overburden the budget. But the Korean War, which began just two months after NSC 68 was completed, helped to transform the report's recommendations into reality, as the Cold War spawned a hot war.

Containment in Asia and the Korean War

As mutual suspicion deepened between the United States and the Soviet Union, Cold War doctrines began to influence the American position in Asia as well. American policy there was based on Asia's importance to the world economy as much as on the desire to contain communism. At first American plans for the region centered on a revitalized China, but political instability there shifted the focus to Japan. After dismantling Japan's military forces and weaponry, American occupation forces under General Douglas MacArthur drafted a democratic constitution and oversaw the rebuilding of the economy, paving the way for the restoration of Japanese sovereignty in 1951.

In China the situation was more precarious. Since the 1930s a civil war had been raging, as Communist forces led by Mao Zedong (Mao Tse-tung) and Zhou Enlai (Chou En-lai) contended for power with conservative Nationalist forces under Jiang Jieshi (Chiang Kai-shek). Although dissatisfied with the corrupt and inefficient Jiang regime, officials for the Truman administration did not see Mao as a good alternative, and they resigned themselves to working with the Nationalists. Between 1945 and 1949 the United States provided more than $2 billion to Jiang's forces, but in August 1949 the Truman administration cut off aid to the Nationalists when reform did not occur, sealing their fate. The People's Republic of China was formally established under Mao on October 1, 1949, and what was left of Jiang's government fled to Taiwan.

Although nothing less than a massive U.S. military commitment could have stopped the Chinese Communists, many Americans viewed Mao's success as a defeat for the United States. A pro-Nationalist "China lobby," supported by the powerful publisher Henry R. Luce and by Republican senators Karl Mundt of South Dakota and William S. Knowland of California, protested that under Truman's newly appointed secretary of state, Dean Acheson, the State Department was responsible for the "loss of China." The China lobby's influence blocked the U.S. recognition of what it called "Red China"; instead, the nation recognized the exiled Nationalist government in Taiwan. The United States also prevented China's admission to the United Nations. For almost twenty years U.S. administrations treated mainland China, the world's most populous country, as a diplomatic nonentity.

In Korea, as in China, Cold War confrontation grew out of World War II roots. Both the United States and the Soviet Union had troops in Korea at the end of the war and had agreed to occupy the nation jointly. They divided Korea into competing spheres of influence at the thirty-eighth parallel. The Soviets supported a Communist government, led by Kim Il Sung, in North Korea; the United States backed a long-time Korean nationalist, Syngman Rhee, in South Korea. Soon sporadic fighting broke out along the thirty-eighth parallel, and a civil war began.

On June 25, 1950, the North Koreans launched a surprise attack across the thirty-eighth parallel (Map 27.2). The attack was part of an initiative for Korean reunification that came from Kim Il Sung, with Stalin's support (although the extent of Soviet involvement was unknown at the time). Soviet and North Korean leaders may have expected Truman to ignore this armed challenge, but the president felt that the United States must take a firm stance against the spread of communism. Truman immediately asked the U.N. Security Council to authorize a "police action" against the invaders. Because the Soviet Union was temporarily boycotting the Security Council to protest the exclusion of the People's Republic of China from the United Nations, it could not veto Truman's request. Three days after the Security Council voted to send what was called a "peacekeeping force," Truman ordered U.S. troops to Korea.

Though fourteen other non-Communist nations sent troops, the rapidly assembled U.N. army in Korea was overwhelmingly American. At the request of the Security Council, President Truman named General Douglas MacArthur to head the U.N. forces. At first the North Koreans held an overwhelming advantage, controlling practically the entire peninsula except for the area around Pusan. But on September 15, 1950, MacArthur launched a surprise amphibious attack at Inchon, far behind the North Korean front line, while U.N. forces staged a breakout from Pusan. Within two weeks the U.N. forces controlled Seoul, the South Korean capital, and almost all the territory up to the thirty-eighth parallel. Encouraged by this success, MacArthur sought the authority to lead his forces across the thirty-eighth parallel and into North Korea. Though the Chinese government in Beijing threatened repeatedly that such a move would provoke retaliation, American officials ignored the warnings. MacArthur's troops crossed the thirty-eighth parallel on October 9, reaching the Chinese border at the Yalu River by the end of the month.

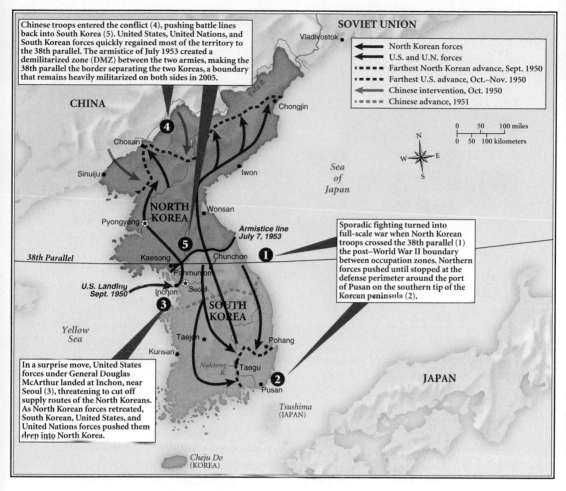

Chinese troops entered the conflict (4), pushing battle lines back into South Korea (5). United States, United Nations, and South Korean forces quickly regained most of the territory to the 38th parallel. The armistice of July 1953 created a demilitarized zone (DMZ) between the two armies, making the 38th parallel the border separating the two Koreas, a boundary that remains heavily militarized on both sides in 2005.

SOVIET UNION

Vladivostok

→ North Korean forces
→ U.S. and U.N. forces
▪▪▪▪ Farthest North Korean advance, Sept. 1950
▪▪▪▪ Farthest U.S. advance, Oct.–Nov. 1950
→ Chinese intervention, Oct. 1950
▪▪▪▪ Chinese advance, 1951

CHINA

Chongjin

0   50   100 miles
0   50   100 kilometers

Chosan

④

Sinuiju   Iwon

Sea of Japan

N
W   E
S

NORTH KOREA   Wonsan

Pyongyang

Armistice line July 7, 1953

Sporadic fighting turned into full-scale war when North Korean troops crossed the 38th parallel (1) the post–World War II boundary between occupation zones. Northern forces pushed until stopped at the defense perimeter around the port of Pusan on the southern tip of the Korean peninsula (2).

38th Parallel   Kaesong   Chunchon   ①

⑤

U.S. Landing Sept. 1950   Inchon   Panmunjom   Seoul

③

SOUTH KOREA

Yellow Sea

Taejon   Pohang

Kunsan

Naktong R.   Taegu

②

Pusan

Tsushima (JAPAN)

JAPAN

In a surprise move, United States forces under General Douglas MacArthur landed at Inchon, near Seoul (3), threatening to cut off supply routes of the North Koreans. As North Korean forces retreated, South Korean, United States, and United Nations forces pushed them deep into North Korea.

Cheju Do (KOREA)

MAP 27.2 The Korean War, 1950–1953

The Korean War, which the United Nations officially deemed a "police action," lasted three years and cost the lives of over 36,000 U.S. troops. South and North Korean deaths were estimated at over 900,000. Although hostilities ceased in 1953, the U.S. military and the North Korean army faced each other across the Demilitarized Zone for the next fifty years.

FOR MORE HELP ANALYZING THIS MAP, see the Online Study Guide at **bedfordstmartins.com/henrettaconcise**.

Just after Thanksgiving a massive Chinese counterattack of almost 300,000 troops forced MacArthur to retreat south of the thirty-eighth parallel. Then on January 4, 1951, Communist troops reoccupied Seoul.

Two months later American forces and their allies counterattacked, regained Seoul, and pushed back to the thirty-eighth parallel. Then stalemate set in. Public support in the United States had dropped after Chinese intervention increased the likelihood of a long war. Given domestic opinions and the deadlock in Korea,

The Korean War

As a result of Harry Truman's 1948 executive order, the Korean War marked the first time in the nation's history that all troops, such as the men of the Second Infantry Battalion, shown here in Korea in 1950, served in racially integrated combat units. National Archives.

Truman and his advisors decided to work for a negotiated peace. They did not want to tie down large numbers of U.S. troops in Asia, far from what were considered more strategically important trouble spots in Europe and the Middle East.

MacArthur disagreed. Headstrong, arrogant, and brilliant, the general fervently believed that the nation's future lay in Asia, not Europe. Disregarding Truman's instructions, MacArthur traveled to Taiwan and urged the Nationalists to join in an attack on mainland China. He pleaded for permission to use the atomic bomb against China. In an inflammatory letter to the House minority leader, Republican Joseph J. Martin of Massachusetts, he denounced the Korean stalemate, declaring that "There is no substitute for victory." Martin released MacArthur's letter on April 6, 1951, as part of a concerted Republican campaign to challenge Truman's conduct of the war. The strategy backfired. On April 11 Truman relieved MacArthur of his command in Korea and Japan, accusing him of insubordination—a decision the Joint Chiefs of Staff supported. Truman's decision was highly unpopular, but he had the last word. After failing to win the Republican presidential nomination in 1952, MacArthur faded from public view.

The war dragged on for more than two years after MacArthur's dismissal. Truce talks began in Korea in July 1951, but an armistice was not signed until July 1953. Approximately 45 percent of American casualties were sustained during this period.

The settlement left Korea divided very near the original post–World War II border at the thirty-eighth parallel, with a demilitarized zone between the two countries. North Korea remained firmly allied with the Soviet Union; South Korea signed a mutual defense treaty with the United States in 1954.

The Korean War had a lasting impact on the conduct of American foreign policy. Truman's decision to commit troops to Korea without congressional approval set a precedent for future undeclared wars. The war also expanded American involvement in Asia, transforming containment into a truly global policy. During and after the war, the United States stationed large numbers of troops in South Korea and increased military aid to French forces fighting Communist insurgents in Indochina (see Chapter 29). Such commitments were costly. Overall defense expenditures grew from $13 billion in 1950, roughly one-third of the federal budget, to $50 billion in 1953, nearly two-thirds of the budget. Although military expenditures dropped briefly after the Korean War, defense spending remained at over $35 billion annually throughout the 1950s. American foreign policy had become more global, more militarized, and more expensive. Even in times of peace, the United States now functioned in a state of permanent mobilization.

Eisenhower and the "New Look" of Foreign Policy

The election of 1952 brought Republican Dwight D. Eisenhower to the White House. Despite his lack of political experience, Eisenhower's military reputation — he had been Supreme Commander of Allied forces in Europe — engendered confidence in his leadership. Although Eisenhower shared many of Truman's and the Democrats' assumptions about the Cold War, his administration's policies were distinctive. Eisenhower's "New Look" in foreign policy continued the nation's commitment to containment but sought less expensive ways of implementing the nation's predominance in the Cold War struggle against international communism.

One of Eisenhower's first acts as president was to use his negotiating skills to bring an end to the Korean War. With the armistice signed, he turned his attention to Europe and the Soviet Union. Stalin's death in March 1953 precipitated an intraparty struggle in the Soviet Union, which lasted until 1956, when Nikita S. Khrushchev emerged as Stalin's successor. Although Khrushchev surprised westerners by calling for "peaceful coexistence" between Communist and capitalist societies, he made certain that the Soviet Union's Eastern European satellites did not deviate too far from the Soviet path. When nationalists revolted in Hungary in 1956 and moved to take the country out of the Warsaw Pact, Soviet tanks moved rapidly into Budapest — an action the United States could condemn but could not realistically resist. Soviet repression of the Hungarian revolt showed that American policymakers had few, if any, options for rolling back Soviet power in Eastern Europe, short of going to war with the Soviet Union.

Although Eisenhower strongly opposed communism, he hoped to keep the cost of containment at a manageable level. Under his "New Look" defense policy,

Eisenhower and Secretary of State John Foster Dulles decided to economize by developing a massive nuclear arsenal as an alternative to more expensive conventional forces. Nuclear weapons delivered "more bang for the buck," explained Defense Secretary Charles E. Wilson. To that end the Eisenhower administration expanded its commitment to the hydrogen bomb, approving extensive atmospheric testing in the South Pacific and in western states such as Nevada, Colorado, and Utah. To improve the nation's defenses against an air attack from the Soviet Union, the administration made a commitment to develop the long-range bombing capabilities of the Strategic Air Command and installed the Distant Early Warning line of radar stations in Alaska and Canada in 1958.

Those measures did little to improve the nation's security, however, as the Soviets matched the United States weapon for weapon in an escalating arms race. The Soviet Union carried out its own atmospheric tests of hydrogen bombs between 1953 and 1958 and developed a fleet of long-range bombers. By 1958 both nations had intercontinental ballistic missiles (ICBMs). When an American nuclear submarine launched an atomic-tipped Polaris missile in 1960, Soviet engineers raced to produce an equivalent weapon. While the arms race boosted the military-industrial sectors of both nations, it debilitated their social welfare programs by funneling immense resources into soon-to-be-obsolete weapons systems.

The New Look policy also extended collective security agreements between the United States and its allies. To complement the NATO alliance in Europe, for example, Secretary of State Dulles orchestrated the creation of the Southeast Asia Treaty Organization (SEATO), which in 1954 linked America and its major European allies with Australia, Pakistan, Thailand, New Zealand, and the Philippines. This extensive system of defense tied the United States to more than forty other countries (Map 27.3).

U.S. policymakers tended to support stable governments, no matter how repressive, as long as they were overtly anti-Communist. Some of America's staunchest allies—the Philippines, Iran, Cuba, South Vietnam, and Nicaragua—were governed by dictatorships or repressive right-wing regimes that lacked broad-based popular support. In fact, Dulles often resorted to **covert interventions** against governments that were, in his opinion, too closely aligned with communism.

For such tasks he used the newly formed Central Intelligence Agency (CIA), which had moved beyond its original mandate of intelligence gathering into active, albeit covert, involvement in the internal affairs of foreign countries, even to the extent of overthrowing several governments. When Iran's nationalist premier, Muhammad Mossadegh, seized British oil properties in 1953, CIA agents helped the young shah of Iran, Muhammad Reza Pahlavi, depose him. In 1954 the CIA engineered a coup in Guatemala against the popularly elected Jacobo Arbenz Guzman, who had expropriated but offered to pay fair market prices for 250,000 uncultivated acres held by the American-owned United Fruit Company and accepted arms from the Communist government of Czechoslovakia. Eisenhower specifically approved those CIA efforts. "Our traditional ideas of international sportsmanship," he wrote privately in 1955, "are scarcely applicable in the morass in which the world now flounders."

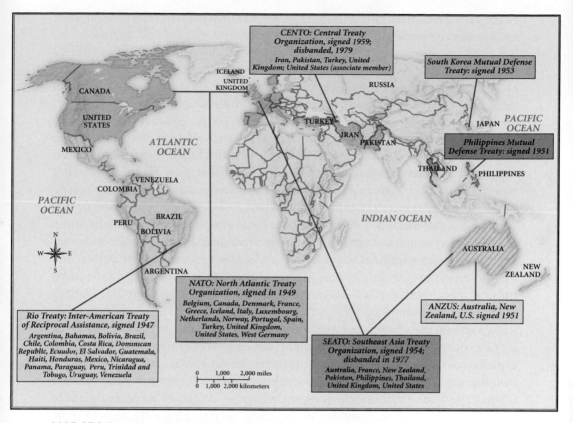

MAP 27.3 American Global Defense Treaties in the Cold War Era

The experience of World War II and the advent of the Cold War led to a major shift in American foreign policy—the signing of mutual defense treaties. Dating back to George Washington's call "to steer clear of permanent alliances with any portion of the foreign world," the United States had remained officially neutral in conflicts between other nations. As late as 1919, the U.S. Senate had rejected the principle of "collective security," the centerpiece of the League of Nations established by the Treaty of Versailles that ended World War I. In response to fears of Soviet expansion globally, in the late 1940s and 1950s, the United States pledged to defend much of the non-Communist world. As illustrated by the map, major treaty organizations to which the United States belonged included NATO, SEATO, CENTO, ANZUS, and the Rio Treaty.

The Cold War in the Middle East

American leaders had devised the containment policy in response to Soviet expansion in Eastern Europe, but they soon extended it to the new nations that were emerging in the **Third World**. Before World War II, nationalism, socialism, and religion had inspired powerful anticolonial movements; in the 1940s and 1950s those forces intensified and spread, especially in the Middle East, Africa, and Asia. Between 1947 and 1962 the British, French, Dutch, and Belgian empires all but disintegrated. Seeking to draw the newly created countries into an American-led world system, U.S. policymakers encouraged the development of stable market economies in those areas. They also sought to further the ideal of national self-determination. But under the growing East-West tensions of the Cold War, both the Truman and the Eisenhower administrations often failed to recognize that indigenous national-ist or socialist movements in emerging nations had their own goals and were not necessarily under the control of either local Communists or the Soviet Union.

The Middle East, an oil-rich area that was playing an increasingly central role in the strategic planning of the United States and the Soviet Union, presented one of the most complicated challenges. Zionism, the Jewish nationalist movement, had long encouraged Jews to return to their ancient homeland of Israel (Palestine). After World War II, many Jewish survivors of the Nazi extermination camps had resettled in Palestine, which was still controlled by Britain under a World War I mandate (see Chapter 22). On November 29, 1947, the U.N. General Assembly voted to partition Palestine into two states, Jewish and Arab—a decision that Egypt, Jordan, and other Arab League states resisted. On May 14, 1948, the British mandate ended, and Zionist leaders proclaimed the state of Israel. President Truman quickly recognized the new state, alienating the Arabs but winning crucial support from Jewish voters in the 1948 election.

Egypt was another site of conflict with the Arab nations, one that reflected the way in which Third World countries became embroiled in the Cold War. When Gamal Abdel Nasser came to power in Egypt in 1954, two years after independence from Britain, he pledged to lead not just his country but the entire Middle East out of its dependent, colonial relationship through a form of pan-Arab socialism. Nasser obtained arms and promises of economic assistance from the Soviet Union, including help in building the Aswan Dam on the Nile, a major water and energy development project. Secretary of State Dulles countered with an offer of American assistance, but Nasser refused to distance himself from the Soviets, declaring Egypt's neutrality in the Cold War. Unwilling to accept this stance of nonalignment, Dulles abruptly withdrew his offer in July 1956.

A week later Nasser retaliated against the withdrawal of Western financial aid by seizing and nationalizing the Suez Canal, over which Britain had retained ad-ministrative authority and through which three-quarters of Western Europe's oil was transported. After several months of fruitless negotiation, Britain and France, in alliance with Israel, attacked Egypt and retook the canal. Their attack occurred at the same time as the Soviet repression of the Hungarian revolt, placing the United States in the potentially awkward position of denouncing Soviet aggression while tolerating a similar action by its own allies. Eisenhower and the United Nations forced France and Britain to pull back. Egypt retook the Suez Canal and built the Aswan Dam with Soviet support. In the end the Suez crisis increased Soviet influ-ence in the Third World, intensified anti-Western sentiment in Arab countries, and produced dissension among leading members of the NATO alliance.

In early 1957, in the aftermath of the Suez crisis, the president persuaded Congress to approve the Eisenhower Doctrine. Addressing concerns over declining

British influence in the Middle East, the policy stated that American forces would assist any nation in the region "requiring such aid, against overt armed aggression from any nation controlled by International Communism." Later that year Eisenhower invoked the doctrine when he sent the U.S. Sixth Fleet to the Mediterranean Sea to aid King Hussein of Jordan against a Nasser-backed revolt. A year later he landed 14,000 troops to back up a pro-U.S. government in Lebanon.

The attention that the Eisenhower administration paid to developments in the Middle East in the 1950s demonstrated how the desire for access to steady supplies of oil increasingly affected foreign policy. More broadly, attention to the Middle East confirmed the global scope of American interests. Just as the Korean War had stretched the application of containment from Europe to Asia, the Eisenhower Doctrine revealed U.S. intentions to influence events in the Middle East as well.

The Cold War at Home

As the Cold War took shape, Americans had to grapple with a new and often alarming world order. Fears about the menace of Soviet communism pervaded the culture, as did anxieties about the destructive capabilities of nuclear weaponry. These factors would have a powerful impact on domestic politics, especially in the hunt for internal Communist subversives, but other issues, including the conversion to a peacetime economy, the call for black civil rights, and the legacy of the New Deal, also influenced politics on the "home front" of the Cold War.

Postwar Domestic Challenges

The public's main fear in 1945—that the depression would return once war production had ended—proved unfounded. Despite a drop in government spending after the war, consumer spending increased; workers had amassed substantial wartime savings and were eager to spend them. The Servicemen's Readjustment Act of 1944, popularly known as the GI Bill, also put money into the economy by providing educational and economic assistance to returning veterans. Despite some temporary dislocations as war production shifted back to civilian production and veterans entered the workforce, unemployment did not soar.

But the transition was hardly trouble free. The main domestic problem was inflation. Consumers wanted to end wartime restrictions and price rationing, but Truman feared economic chaos if he lifted all controls immediately. In the summer of 1945, he eased industrial controls but retained the wartime Office of Price Administration (OPA). When he disbanded the OPA and lifted almost all the remaining controls in the following year, prices soared, producing an annual inflation rate of 18.2 percent. Rising prices and persistent shortages of food and household goods irritated consumers.

The rapidly rising cost of living prompted workers' demands for higher wages. Under government-sanctioned agreements the labor movement held the line on salary increases during the war. But after the war ended, union leaders expressed frustration. Corporate profits had doubled while real wages had declined as a result of inflation and the loss of overtime pay. Determined to make up for their war-induced sacrifices, workers mounted crippling strikes in the automobile, steel, and coal industries. General strikes effectively closed down business in more than half a dozen cities in 1946. By the end of that year, 5 million workers had idled factories and mines for a total of 107,476,000 workdays.

Truman responded dramatically. In the face of a devastating railway strike, he used his executive authority to place the nation's railroad system under federal control and asked Congress for the power to draft striking workers into the army—a move that infuriated labor leaders but pressured strikers to go back to work. Three days later he seized control of the nation's coal mines to end a strike by the United Mine Workers. Such actions won Truman support from many Americans but outraged organized labor, an important partner in the Democratic coalition.

These domestic upheavals did not bode well for the Democrats at the polls. In 1946 the Republicans gained control of both houses of Congress and set about undoing New Deal social welfare measures, especially targeting labor legislation. In 1947 Congress passed the Taft-Hartley Act, a rollback of several provisions of the 1935 National Labor Relations Act. Unions especially disliked Section 14b of Taft-Hartley, which outlawed the closed shop and allowed states to pass "right-to-work" laws that further limited unions' operations. The act also restricted unions' political power by prohibiting use of their dues for political activity and allowed the president to declare an eighty-day cooling-off period in strikes that had a national impact. Truman issued a ringing veto of the Taft-Hartley bill in June 1947, calling it "bad for labor, bad for management, and bad for the country." Congress easily overrode the veto, but Truman's actions countered some of workers' hostility to his earlier antistrike activity and kept labor in the Democratic fold.

Most observers believed that Truman faced an impossible task in the presidential campaign of 1948. The Republicans were united, and with Thomas E. Dewey, the politically moderate governor of New York, as their candidate once again, they had a good chance of attracting traditional Democratic voters. To increase their appeal in the West, the Republicans nominated Earl Warren, governor of California, for vice president. In their platform they promised to continue most New Deal reforms and to support a bipartisan foreign policy.

Truman, in contrast, led a party in disarray. Both the left and the right wings of the Democratic Party split off and nominated their own candidates. Henry A. Wallace, a former New Deal liberal whom Truman had fired as secretary of commerce in 1946 because he was perceived as too "soft" on communism, ran as the candidate of the new Progressive Party. Wallace advocated increased government intervention in the economy, more power for labor unions, and cooperation with the Soviet Union. The right-wing challenge came from the South. At the

Truman Triumphant

In one of the most famous photographs in American political history, Harry S Truman gloats over an inaccurate headline in the *Chicago Daily Tribune.* Pollsters had predicted an overwhelming victory for Thomas E. Dewey. Their primitive techniques, however, did not reflect the dramatic surge in support for Truman during the last days of the campaign.

© Bettmann / Corbis.

Democratic national convention, northern liberals such as Mayor Hubert H. Humphrey of Minneapolis had pushed through a platform calling for the repeal of the Taft-Hartley Act and increased federal commitment to civil rights. Southern Democrats, unwilling to tolerate federal interference in race relations, bolted the convention and created the States' Rights Party, popularly known as the "Dixiecrats." They nominated Governor J. Strom Thurmond of South Carolina for president.

Truman responded to these challenges with one of the most effective presidential campaigns ever waged. He launched a strenuous cross-country speaking tour in which he hammered away at the Republicans' support for the antilabor Taft-Hartley Act. He also criticized Republicans for opposing legislation for housing, medical insurance, and civil rights. By combining these issues with attacks on the Soviet menace abroad, Truman began to salvage his troubled campaign. At his rallies enthusiastic listeners shouted, "Give 'em hell, Harry!"

Truman won a remarkable victory, receiving 49.6 percent of the vote to Dewey's 45.1 percent. The Democrats also regained control of both houses of Congress. Strom Thurmond carried only four southern states, and Henry Wallace failed to win any electoral votes. Truman retained the support of organized labor. Jewish and Catholic voters in the big cities and black voters in the North offset his losses to the Dixiecrats. Most important, Truman appealed effectively to people like himself from the farms, towns, and small cities in the nation's heartland.

Fair Deal Liberalism

Shortly after becoming president Truman proposed to Congress a twenty-one-point plan for expanded federal programs based on individual "rights," including the right to a "useful and remunerative" job, controls over monopolies, good housing, "adequate medical care," "protection from the economic fears of old age," and a "good education." Later Truman added support for civil rights and in his 1949 State of the Union address christened his program the Fair Deal. Although to some extent the Fair Deal represented an extension of the New Deal's liberalism—with faith in the positive influence of government and the use of federal power to ensure public welfare—it also took some new directions. Its attention to civil rights reflected the growing importance of African Americans to the Democratic Party's coalition of urban voters. And the desire to extend a high standard of living and other benefits of capitalism to an ever-greater number of citizens reflected a new liberal vision of the role of the state. Economically, the liberals of Truman's era were more moderate than the Progressive Era and New Deal reformers who had proposed extensive federal regulation of corporations and intrusive planning of the economy. They believed that the essential role of the federal government was to manage the economy indirectly through fiscal policy. Drawing on the Keynesian notion of using government spending to spur economic growth, they expected that welfare programs not only would provide a safety net for disadvantaged citizens but also would maintain consumer purchasing power, keeping the economy healthy.

Truman's agenda met with a generally hostile Congress, despite the Democratic majority. The same conservative coalition that had blocked Roosevelt's initiatives in his second term and dismantled or cut popular New Deal programs during wartime continued to fight against Truman's proposals. Only parts of the Fair Deal won adoption: the minimum wage was raised; the Social Security program was extended to cover 10 million new workers; and Social Security benefits were increased by 75 percent. The National Housing Act of 1949 called for the construction of 810,000 units of low-income housing, but only half that number were actually built.

Interest groups successfully opposed other key items in the Fair Deal. The American Medical Association (AMA) quashed a labor-backed movement for national health insurance by denouncing it as the first step toward "socialized medicine." Catholics successfully opposed aid to education because it did not include subsidies for parochial schools. Trade associations, the National Association of Manufacturers, and other business groups also actively opposed what they called "creeping socialism." Though most corporate leaders recognized that some state involvement in the economy was necessary and even beneficial to business interests, they felt the Fair Deal went too far. As a lobbyist for the National Association of Real Estate Boards explained, "In our country we prefer that government activity shall take the form of assisting and aiding private business rather than undertake great public projects of a governmental character." Through extensive lobbying and public relations campaigns, business groups agitated not only to defeat specific pieces of Fair Deal legislation but also to forestall increased taxes, antitrust activity, and other unwanted federal interference in corporate affairs. Their activities helped to block support for enlarged federal responsibilities for economic and social welfare. The outbreak of the Korean War in 1950 also limited the chances of the Fair Deal's being passed by diverting national attention and federal funds from domestic affairs. The nation's growing paranoia concerning internal subversion, the most dramatic manifestation of the Cold War's effect on American life, also undermined the Fair Deal.

The Great Fear

As American relations with the Soviet Union deteriorated, fear of communism at home fueled a widespread campaign of domestic repression. Americans often call this phenomenon "McCarthyism," after Senator Joseph R. McCarthy of Wisconsin, the decade's most vocal anti-Communist, but more was involved than the work of just one man. The "Great Fear" built on the long-standing distrust of radicals and foreigners that had exploded in the Red Scare after World War I. Worsening Cold War tensions intersected with both those deep-seated anxieties and partisan politics to spawn an obsessive concern with internal subversion. Ultimately, few Communists were found in positions of power; far more Americans became innocent victims of false accusations and innuendos.

The roots of postwar anticommunism dated back to 1938, when Congressman Martin Dies of Texas and other conservatives launched the House Committee on Un-American Activities (HUAC) to investigate alleged Fascist and Communist influence in labor unions and New Deal agencies. HUAC gained heightened visibility after the war, especially after revelations in 1946 of a Soviet spy ring operating in Canada accentuated U.S. fears of Soviet subversion.

In 1947 HUAC helped spark the Great Fear by holding widely publicized hearings on alleged Communist infiltration in the film industry. A group of writers and directors, soon dubbed the Hollywood Ten, went to jail for contempt of Congress when they cited the First Amendment while refusing to testify about their past associations. Hundreds of other actors, directors, and writers whose names had been mentioned in the HUAC investigation or whose associates and friends the committee had labeled as "reds" were unable to get work, victims of an unacknowledged but very real **blacklist** honored by industry executives. HUAC also investigated playwrights, authors, university professors, labor activists, organizations, and government officials thought to be "left wing."

Although HUAC bore much of the responsibility for spawning the witch hunt, its effects spread far beyond the congressional committee. In March 1947 President Truman issued an executive order initiating a comprehensive investigation into the loyalty of federal employees. Following Washington's lead many state and local governments, universities, political organizations, churches, and businesses undertook their own antisubversion campaigns, including the requirement that employees take loyalty oaths. In the labor movement, which Communists had been active in organizing in the 1930s, charges that Soviet-led Communists were taking over American unions led to a purge of Communist members. Civil rights organizations such as the NAACP and the National Urban League also expelled Communists or "fellow travelers"—words used to describe people viewed as left-wing or as Communist sympathizers who were not members of the Communist Party. Thus the Great Fear was particularly devastating to the political left; accusations of guilt by association affected progressives of all stripes.

The anti-Communist crusade intensified in 1948 when HUAC began an investigation of Alger Hiss, a former New Dealer and a State Department official who had accompanied Franklin Roosevelt to Yalta. A former Communist, Whittaker Chambers, claimed that Hiss was a member of a secret Communist cell operating within the government and had passed him classified documents in the 1930s. Hiss categorically denied the allegations and denied even knowing Chambers. HUAC's investigation was orchestrated by freshman Republican congressman Richard M. Nixon of California. Because the statute of limitations on the crime of which Hiss was accused had expired, he was charged instead with perjury for lying about his Communist affiliations and acquaintance with Chambers. In early 1950 Hiss was found guilty and sentenced to five years in federal prison. The decision was contested at the time and debated for years afterwards. Although recently released evidence from the former Soviet archives has helped to harden the case against Hiss, the question of his guilt continues to be a contentious one among historians and journalists.

Hiss's conviction fueled the paranoia about a Communist conspiracy in the federal government, contributing to the meteoric rise of Senator Joseph McCarthy of Wisconsin. In February 1950 McCarthy delivered a bombshell during a speech in Wheeling, West Virginia: "I have here in my hand a list of the names of 205 men that were known to the Secretary of State as being members of the Communist Party and who nevertheless are still working and shaping the policy of the State Department." McCarthy later reduced his numbers, first to fifty-seven, then to one "policy risk," and he never released any names or proof, but he had gained the attention he sought. For the next four years, he was the central figure in a virulent campaign of anticommunism. Like other Republicans in the late 1940s, McCarthy leveled accusations of Communist subversion in the government to embarrass President Truman and the Democratic Party. Critics who disagreed with him exposed themselves to charges of being "soft" on communism. Because McCarthy charged that his critics were themselves part of "this conspiracy so immense," few political leaders challenged him. Truman called McCarthy's charges "slander, lies, character assassination" but could do nothing to curb them. When Republican Dwight D. Eisenhower was elected president in 1952, he refrained from publicly challenging his party's most outspoken senator.

McCarthy failed to identify a single Communist in government, but a series of national and international events allowed him to retain credibility. Besides the Hiss case, the sensational 1951 espionage trial of Julius and Ethel Rosenberg fueled McCarthy's allegations. Convicted of passing atomic secrets to the Soviet Union in a highly controversial trial, the Rosenbergs were executed in 1953. The Korean War, which embroiled the United States in a frustrating fight against communism in a faraway land, also made Americans susceptible to McCarthy's claims. Blaming disloyal individuals rather than complex international factors for the problems of the Cold War undoubtedly helped many Americans make sense of a disordered world of nuclear bombs, "police actions," and other world crises that seemed to come with alarming regularity.

In early 1954 McCarthy overreached himself by launching an investigation into possible subversion in the U.S. Army. When lengthy hearings—the first of its kind broadcast on the new medium of television—brought McCarthy's smear tactics and leering innuendos into the nation's living rooms, support for him declined. The end of the Korean War and the death of Stalin in 1953 also undercut public interest in McCarthy's red-baiting campaign. In December 1954 the Senate voted 67 to 22 to censure McCarthy for unbecoming conduct. He died from an alcohol-related illness three years later at the age of forty-eight, his name forever attached to a period of political repression of which he was only the most flagrant manifestation.

"Modern Republicanism"

At the height of the Great Fear, Dwight D. Eisenhower became president. Having secured the 1952 Republican nomination, he asked Senator Richard M. Nixon of California to be his running mate. Nixon, young, tirelessly partisan, and with a strong anti-Communist record from his crusade against Alger Hiss, brought an aggressive campaign style as well as regional balance to the Republican ticket. The new administration set the tone for what historians have called "modern

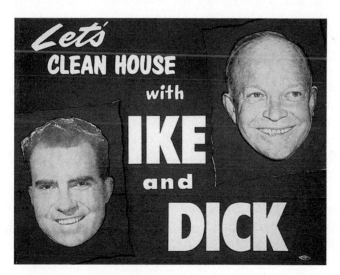

The 1952 Presidential Campaign

The 1952 Republican ticket of Dwight D. Eisenhower and Richard M. Nixon launched an effective attack on the Democratic leadership by stressing the Truman administration's involvement in bribery and influence-peddling scandals and by capitalizing on Truman's failure to end the war in Korea. Collection of Janice L. and David J. Frent.

Republicanism," an updated party philosophy that emphasized a slowdown, rather than a dismantling, of federal responsibilities. Compared with their predecessors in the 1920s and their successors in the 1980s and 1990s, modern Republicans were more tolerant of government intervention in social and economic affairs, though they did seek to limit the scope of federal action.

The Democrats never seriously considered renominating Harry Truman, who by 1952 was a thoroughly discredited leader. Lack of popular enthusiasm for the Korean War had dealt the most severe blow to Truman's support, but a series of scandals, including federal officials accused of bribery and influence-peddling schemes, also had caused a public outcry. With a certain relief the Democrats turned to Governor Adlai E. Stevenson of Illinois, who enjoyed the support of respected liberals, such as Eleanor Roosevelt, and of organized labor. To appease southern voters who feared Stevenson's liberal agenda, the Democrats nominated Senator John A. Sparkman of Alabama for vice president.

Throughout the 1952 campaign Stevenson advocated New Deal and Fair Deal policies with an almost literary eloquence. But Eisenhower's artfully unpretentious speeches and "I Like Ike" slogan were more effective with voters. Eager to win the support of the broadest electorate possible, Eisenhower played down specific questions of policy. Instead, he attacked the Democrats with the "K_1C_2" formula— "Korea, Communism, and Corruption."

That November Eisenhower won 55 percent of the popular vote, carrying all the northern and western states and four southern states. Republican candidates for Congress did not fare quite as well. They regained the Senate from the Democrats but took the House of Representatives by a slender margin of only four seats. In 1954 they would lose control of both houses to the Democrats. (The Democrats would hold a majority in the House until 1995.) Even though the enormously popular Eisenhower would easily win reelection over Adlai Stevenson in 1956, the Republicans would remain in the minority in Congress.

Seeking a middle ground between liberalism and conservatism, Eisenhower did his best as president to set a quieter national mood, hoping to decrease the need for federal intervention in social and economic issues, while avoiding conservative demands for a complete rollback of the New Deal.

He nonetheless presided over new increases in federal activity. When the Soviet Union launched the first satellite, *Sputnik*, in 1957, Eisenhower, who initially had opposed the space program, supported a U.S. effort to catch up in this new Cold War competition. The National Aeronautics and Space Administration (NASA) was founded the following year. Alarmed that the United States was falling behind the Soviets in technological expertise, the president also persuaded Congress to appropriate additional money for college scholarships and for research and development at universities and in industry. After 1954, when the Democrats took control over Congress, the Eisenhower administration also acceded to legislation promoting social welfare. Federal outlays for veterans' benefits, unemployment compensation, housing, and Social Security were increased, and the minimum wage was raised from 75 cents an hour to $1. The creation of the new Department of Health, Education, and Welfare (HEW) in 1953 consolidated government control of social welfare programs, confirming federal commitments in that area. Congress also passed the Interstate Highway Act of 1956, which authorized $26 billion over a ten-year period for the construction of a nationally integrated highway system (see Map 28.1, p. 853). This enormous public works program surpassed anything undertaken during the New Deal.

Thus Republicans, though they resisted the unchecked expansion of the state, had become part of a broad **liberal consensus** in American politics and did not generally cut back federal power. In social welfare programs and defense expenditures, modern Republicanism signaled a moderation of the traditional Republican commitment to limited government. When Eisenhower retired from public life in 1961, the federal government had become an even greater presence in everyday life than it had been when he took office. Some of the most controversial federal initiatives occurred in the area of civil rights.

The Emergence of Civil Rights as a National and International Issue

The civil rights movement was arguably the most important force for change in postwar America, and its accelerating momentum had profound implications for the federal government. The movement built upon a long tradition of African American protest but was also shaped by the climate of the Cold War that so pervaded American politics and society.

Civil Rights under Truman

Beginning with World War II, the National Association for the Advancement of Colored People (NAACP) had redoubled its efforts to combat segregation in housing, transportation, and other areas. Black demands for justice continued into the postwar years, spurred by symbolic victories such as Jackie Robinson's breaking through the color line in major league baseball by joining the Brooklyn Dodgers in 1947. African American leaders were cautiously optimistic about extracting support from President Truman. Although capable of using racist language in private, Truman was moderately sympathetic to civil rights on moral grounds, a sympathy that was reinforced by the realization that black voters were playing an increasingly large role in the Democratic Party as they migrated from the South, where they were effectively disenfranchised, to northern and western cities. Truman was also concerned about America's image abroad, especially since the Soviet Union often compared the segregation of southern blacks with the Nazis' treatment of the Jews. The desire to gain the allegiance of emerging African nations and of India provided further incentive for the United States to address the problem of racial discrimination.

Lacking a popular mandate on civil rights, Truman turned to executive action. In 1946 he appointed a National Civil Rights Commission. Basing its arguments on moral, economic, and international grounds, its 1947 report called for an expanded federal role in civil rights that foreshadowed much of the civil rights legislation of the 1960s. Truman also ordered the Justice Department to prepare an amicus curiae (friend of the court) brief in the Supreme Court case of *Shelley v. Kraemer* (1948), which ruled that states that enforced restrictive covenants maintaining residential segregation by barring home buyers of a certain race or religion violated the Fourteenth Amendment. In this and other briefs, the Justice Department explicitly referred to the way in which "the United States has been embarrassed in the conduct of foreign relations by acts of discrimination taking place in this country." Also in 1948, under pressure from the Committee Against Jim Crow in Military Service organized by World War II's March on Washington's founder, A. Philip Randolph, Truman signed an executive order desegregating the armed forces. His administration also proposed a federal antilynching law, federal protection of voting rights (such as an end to poll taxes), and a permanent federal agency to guarantee equal employment opportunity, but a filibuster by southern conservatives blocked the legislation.

Challenging Segregation

In addition to exerting pressure on white politicians like Truman, civil rights leaders in the early 1950s continued their long-standing battle to challenge segregation in the courts and adopted a new strategy of nonviolent protest. They were determined to overturn the legal segregation of the races that still governed southern society in the early 1950s. In most southern states whites and blacks could not eat in the same rooms at restaurants and luncheonettes or use the same waiting rooms and toilets at bus and train stations. All forms of public transportation were rigidly segregated by custom or by law. Even drinking fountains were labeled "White" and "Colored."

The first significant victory came in 1954, when the Supreme Court handed down its most far-reaching decision in *Brown v. Board of Education of Topeka*. The NAACP's chief legal counsel, Thurgood Marshall, had argued that the segregated schools mandated by the Board of Education in Topeka, Kansas, were inherently unconstitutional because they stigmatized an entire race, denying black children the "equal protection of the laws" guaranteed by the Fourteenth Amendment. In a unanimous decision announced on May 17, 1954, the Supreme Court, following the lead of Chief Justice Earl Warren (see Chapter 30), agreed with Marshall and overturned the long-standing "separate but equal" doctrine of *Plessy v. Ferguson* (see Chapter 19).

Over the next several years, in response to NAACP suits, the Supreme Court used the *Brown* precedent to overturn segregation at city parks, public beaches, and golf courses; in interstate and intrastate transportation; and in public housing. In the face of these Court decisions, white resistance to integration solidified. In 1956,

Integration at Little Rock, Arkansas

With chants such as "Two-four-six-eight, we ain't gonna integrate," angry crowds taunted Elizabeth Eckford (shown here walking past white students and National Guardsmen) and eight other black students who tried to register at the previously all-white Central High School in Little Rock, Arkansas, on September 4, 1957. The court-ordered integration proceeded only after President Eisenhower reluctantly mobilized the Arkansas National Guard to protect the students.
Francis Miller/Timepix/Getty Images.

101 members of Congress signed the Southern Manifesto, denouncing the *Brown* decision as "a clear abuse of judicial power" and encouraging their constituents to defy it. That same year, 500,000 southerners joined White Citizens' Councils dedicated to blocking school integration and other civil rights measures. Some whites revived old tactics of violence and intimidation, swelling the ranks of the Ku Klux Klan to levels not seen since the 1920s.

Unlike Harry Truman, Eisenhower showed little interest in civil rights. Though he proved extremely reluctant to intervene in what was widely seen as a state issue, entrenched southern resistance to federal authority eventually forced his hand. In 1957 in response to the *Brown* decision, racial moderates on the Little Rock, Arkansas, school board had designed a desegregation plan. But pressure from White Citizens' Councils and other groups led the governor of Arkansas, Orval Faubus, to defy a federal court order to desegregate Little Rock's Central High School. Faubus called out the National Guard to bar nine black students who were attempting to enroll in the all-white school. When scenes of vicious mobs harassing the determined students aired on television, the crisis rocked the nation and provoked a storm of criticism abroad. President Eisenhower—concerned about the nation's international image and Faubus's defiance of federal authority—reluctantly intervened, sending 1,000 federal troops and 10,000 nationalized members of the Arkansas National Guard to protect the students. Eisenhower thus became the first president since Reconstruction to use federal troops to enforce the rights of blacks.

White resistance to the *Brown* decision, as well as Eisenhower's hesitancy to act in Little Rock, showed that court victories were not enough to overturn segregation. In 1955 a single act of defiance gave black leaders an opportunity to implement a new strategy—nonviolent protest. On December 1 Rosa Parks, a seamstress and a member of the NAACP in Montgomery, Alabama, refused to give up her seat on a city bus to a white man. "I felt it was just something I had to do," Parks stated. She was promptly arrested and charged with violating a local segregation ordinance. When the black community in Montgomery met to discuss the proper response, they turned to the Reverend Martin Luther King Jr., who had become the pastor at a local church the year before. King endorsed a plan by a Montgomery black women's organization to boycott the city's bus system until it was integrated. For the next 381 days, members of a united black community formed carpools or walked to work. The bus company neared bankruptcy, and downtown stores saw their business decline. But not until the Supreme Court ruled in November 1956 that bus segregation was unconstitutional did the city of Montgomery finally relent, prompting one woman boycotter to proclaim, "My feets is tired, but my soul is rested."

The Montgomery bus boycott catapulted King to national prominence. In 1957, with the Reverend Ralph Abernathy and other southern black clergy, King founded the Southern Christian Leadership Conference (SCLC), based in Atlanta. The black church had long been the center of African American social and cultural life. Through the SCLC the church lent its moral and organizational strength, as well as the voices of its most inspirational preachers, to the civil rights movement. Black churchwomen flocked to the movement, transferring the skills they had honed through years of church work to the fight for racial change. Soon the SCLC joined the NAACP as one of the major advocates for racial justice. While the two groups achieved only limited victories in the 1950s, they laid the organizational groundwork for the dynamic civil rights movement that would become one of the defining issues of the 1960s and would open the door to wide-ranging dissent from America's Cold War culture of consensus and conformity.

The Impact of the Cold War

The Cold War extended to the most distant areas of the globe, but it also had powerful effects on the national economy, politics, and cultural values of the United States. It permeated domestic politics, helped to shape the response to the civil rights movement, and created an atmosphere that stifled dissent. Moreover, the implications of the nation's extensive military mobilization, even in times of peace, were far ranging. For the first time in the nation's history, there was a peacetime draft. In the past the armed forces had shrunk to a skeleton volunteer force at the end of each war or foreign engagement. But when World War II ended, the draft was kept in place to meet the military commitments associated with the Cold War: occupation forces in defeated Axis countries, missile deployment operations in Europe, and counterinsurgency forces in the Third World.

The postwar expansion of the military produced a dramatic shift in the country's economic priorities, as military spending took up a greater percentage of national income. Between 1900 and 1930, except for the two years that the United States fought in World War I, the country spent less than 1 percent of its gross domestic product (GDP) for military purposes. When Eisenhower left office in January 1961, the figure was closer to 10 percent, fully half of the federal budget. Even though the country was at peace during most of his administration, the economy and the government operated practically on a war footing.

Nuclear Proliferation

One of the most alarming aspects of the nation's militarization was the dangerous cycle of nuclear proliferation that would outlive the Soviet-American conflict that spawned it. The nuclear arms race affected all Americans by fostering a climate of fear and uncertainty. Bomb shelters and civil defense drills provided a daily reminder of the threat of nuclear war, and atomic research and testing had a devastating impact on human health. In the late 1950s a small but growing number of citizens became concerned about the effects of radioactive fallout from aboveground bomb tests. In later years federal investigators documented a host of illnesses, deaths, and birth defects among families of veterans who had worked on weapons tests and among "downwinders"—people who lived near nuclear test sites and weapons. The most shocking revelations, however, came to light in 1993, when the Department of Energy released millions of previously classified documents on human radiation experiments conducted in the late 1940s and 1950s under the auspices of the Atomic Energy Commission (AEC) and other federal agencies. Many of the subjects were irradiated without their consent or understanding.

By the late 1950s, public concern over nuclear testing and fallout had become a high-profile issue, and new antinuclear groups such as SANE (the National Committee for a Sane Nuclear Policy) and Physicians for Social Responsibility called for an international test ban. Eisenhower himself had second thoughts about a nuclear policy based on the premise of annihilating the enemy even if one's own country was destroyed—the aptly named MAD (Mutually Assured Destruction) policy. He also found spiraling arms expenditures a serious hindrance to balancing the federal budget, one of his chief fiscal goals. Consequently, Eisenhower tried to negotiate an arms-limitation agreement with the Soviet Union. Progress along those lines was cut short, however, when on May 5, 1960, the Soviets shot down an American U-2 spy plane over their territory and captured and imprisoned its pilot, Francis Gary Powers. Eisenhower at first denied that the plane was engaged in espionage but later

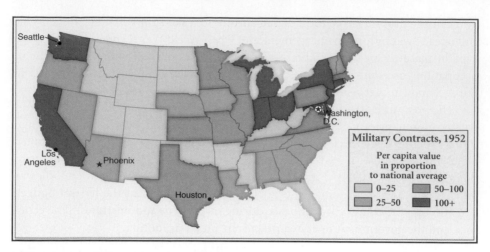

MAP 27.4 The Military-Industrial Complex

The development and expansion of military facilities and defense contracting during the Cold War helped boost the populations and economies of Los Angeles and other Sun Belt cities. Large defense contracts made the economies of California and other states highly dependent on defense expenditures.

admitted that he had authorized the mission and other secret flights over the Soviet Union. In the midst of the dispute, a proposed summit meeting with Khrushchev was canceled, and Eisenhower's last chance to negotiate an arms agreement evaporated.

The Military-Industrial Complex

The nuclear arms buildup had domestic implications as well. With its headquarters at the sprawling Pentagon in Arlington, Virginia, the Department of Defense evolved into a massive bureaucracy that profoundly influenced the postwar economy. Federal money underwrote 90 percent of the cost of research on aviation and space and also subsidized the scientific instruments, automobile, and electronics industries. Pentagon spending created a powerful defense industry. Aircraft companies such as Boeing and Lockheed did so much of their business with the government that they became dependent on Defense Department orders. In the South and West, where much of the new military activity was concentrated, dependence on federal defense contracts was even greater. That increased spending put money in the pockets of the millions of people working in defense-related industries, but it also limited the resources available for domestic needs.

In his final address to the nation, Eisenhower warned against the power of what he called the "military-industrial complex," which by then was employing 3.5 million Americans (Map 27.4). Its pervasive influence, he said, "is felt in every city,

AMERICAN VOICES

Memories of a Cold War Childhood

RON KOVIC

T he menacing threat of the atom bomb, the looming presence of the Soviet Union, and the fear of internal subversion were part of everyday life in the 1950s. In his autobiography, Born on the Fourth of July, *Ron Kovic conveys the anxiety Americans felt when the Soviets launched the satellite* Sputnik, *revealing that Americans were behind in the race to conquer outer space.*

We joined the cub scouts and marched in parades on Memorial Day. We made contingency plans for the Cold War and built fallout shelters out of milk cartons. We wore spacesuits and space helmets. We made rocket ships out of cardboard boxes. And one Saturday afternoon in the basement Castiglia [a friend] and I went to Mars on the couch we had turned into a rocket ship. . . . And the whole block watched a thing called the space race begin. On a cold October night Dad and I watched the first satellite, called *Sputnik*, moving across the sky above our house like a tiny bright star. I still remember standing out there with Dad looking up in amazement at that thing moving in the sky above Massapequa. It was hard to believe that this thing, this *Sputnik*, was so high up and moving so fast around the world, again and again. Dad put his hand on my shoulder that night and without saying anything I quietly walked back inside and went to my room thinking that the Russians had beaten America into space and wondering why we couldn't even get a rocket off the pad. . . .

The Communists were all over the place back then. And if they weren't trying to beat us into outer space, Castiglia and I were certain they were infiltrating our schools, trying to take over our classes and control our minds. We were both certain that one of our teachers was a secret Communist agent and in our next secret club meeting we promised to report anything new he said during our next history class. We watched him very carefully that year.

SOURCE: Ron Kovic, *Born on the Fourth of July* (New York: Pocket Books, 1976), 56–57.

every statehouse, every office of the federal government." Even though his administration had fostered this growth in the defense establishment to contain the Soviet threat, Eisenhower was gravely concerned about its implications for a democratic people: "We must guard against the acquisition of unwarranted influence, whether sought or unsought, by the military-industrial complex," he warned. "We must never let the weight of this combination endanger our liberties or democratic processes." With those words Dwight Eisenhower showed how well he understood the major transformations that the Cold War had brought to American life (see American Voices, "Memories of a Cold War Childhood," above).

TIMELINE

1945	Yalta and Potsdam Conferences	**1950–**	Korean War
	Harry S Truman succeeds Roosevelt as president	**1953**	
	End of World War II	**1950**	Joseph McCarthy's "list" of Communists in government
	Senate approves U.S. participation in United Nations		NSC-68 calls for permanent mobilization
1946	George Kennan sends "Long Telegram" outlining containment policy	**1952**	Dwight D. Eisenhower elected president
	Baruch Plan for international control of atomic weapons fails	**1954**	Army-McCarthy hearings on army subversion
			Brown v. Board of Education of Topeka
1947	Taft-Hartley Act limits union power	**1955**	Montgomery bus boycott begins
	Jackie Robinson becomes first black player in major league baseball	**1956**	Crises in Hungary and at Suez Canal
	House Un-American Activities Committee (HUAC) investigates film industry		Southern Manifesto defies *Brown* decision
			Interstate Highway Act
	Truman Doctrine promises aid to governments resisting communism	**1957**	Eisenhower Doctrine commits aid to Middle East
	Marshall Plan aids economic recovery in Europe		Eisenhower sends U.S. troops to enforce integration of Little Rock Central High School
1948	Communist coup in Czechoslovakia		
	Truman signs executive order desegregating armed forces		Southern Christian Leadership Conference founded
	State of Israel created		Soviet Union launches *Sputnik*
	Stalin blockades West Berlin; Berlin airlift begins	**1958**	National Aeronautics and Space Administration (NASA) established
1949	North Atlantic Treaty Organization (NATO) founded		
	Soviet Union detonates atomic bomb		
	Mao Zedong establishes People's Republic of China		

For Further Exploration

An excellent overview of the diplomatic history of the Cold War is Stephen Ambrose and Douglas Brinkley, *Rise to Globalism* (8th ed., 1997). A good introduction to the Great Fear is the collection of documents in Ellen Schrecker, ed., *The Age of McCarthyism* (1994), which offers primary sources covering court cases, Hollywood, spy scandals, the Rosenbergs, and other topics. Another valuable set of sources that helps to explain the early stages of the Cold War is Ernest R. May, ed., *American Cold War Strategy: Interpreting NSC-68* (1993), which includes essays by both American and foreign scholars. David Halberstam's *The Fifties* (1993) offers a brief but searing account of CIA covert activities in Iran and Guatemala. For a powerful fictional account of growing up with the bomb, see Tim O'Brien, *The Nuclear Age* (1996). Taylor Branch's biography of Martin Luther King Jr., *Parting the Waters: America in the King Years, 1954–1963* (1988), while focusing on King's leadership, provides an engaging account of the early civil rights movement.

The Woodrow Wilson International Center for Scholars has established the Cold War International History Project at <http://wwics.si.edu/index.cfm?topic_id=1409&fuseaction=topics.home>, an exceptionally rich Web site offering documents on the Cold War, including materials from former communist-bloc countries. The Center for the Study of the Pacific Northwest's site, The Cold War and Red Scare in Washington State, at <http://www.washington.edu/uwired/outreach/cspn/curcan/main.html>, provides detailed information on how the Great Fear operated in one state. Its bibliography includes books, documents, and videos. Project Whistlestop: Harry Truman at <http://www.trumanlibrary.org/whistlestop/student_guide.htm>, a program sponsored by the U.S. Department of Education, is a searchable collection of images and documents from the Harry S Truman Presidential Library. The site is organized into categories such as the origins of the Truman Doctrine, the Berlin airlift, the desegregation of the armed forces, and the 1948 presidential campaign. Users can also browse through the president's correspondence.

Korea + 50: No Longer Forgotten is cosponsored by the Harry S Truman and Dwight D. Eisenhower Presidential Libraries: <http://www.trumanlibrary.org/korea/>. It offers official documents, oral histories, and photographs connected to the Korean War. It also features an audio recording of President Truman's recollections of his firing of General MacArthur in 1951.

The Arkansas *Democrat Gazette* has compiled materials from two Arkansas newspapers covering the Central High School Crisis at <http://www.ardemgaz.com/prev/central/>. Editorials and daily news coverage, including photographs, are featured, as well as later commentary by such diverse political figures as former president Bill Clinton and Governor Orval Faubus.

For definitions of key terms boldfaced in this chapter, see the glossary at the end of the book.

To assess your mastery of the material covered in this chapter, see the Online Study Guide at **bedfordstmartins.com/henrettaconcise**.

For map resources and primary documents, see **bedfordstmartins.com/henrettaconcise**.

Chapter 28

THE AFFLUENT SOCIETY AND THE LIBERAL CONSENSUS 1945–1965

> The nation of the well-off must be able to see through the wall of affluence and recognize the alien citizens on the other side. And there must be vision in the sense of purpose, of aspiration. . . . [T]here must be a passion to end poverty, for nothing less than that will do.
>
> MICHAEL HARRINGTON, *THE OTHER AMERICA* (1962)

In 1959 Vice President Richard Nixon traveled to Moscow to open the American National Exhibit, one of several efforts to reduce Cold War tensions in the period. While touring the kitchen of a model American home, Nixon and Soviet Premier Nikita Khrushchev got into a heated debate about the relative merits of Soviet and American societies. Instead of discussing rockets, submarines, and missiles, however, they talked dishwashers, toasters, and televisions. In what was quickly dubbed the "kitchen debate," Nixon used the exhibit and its representation of American affluence and mass consumption to assert the superiority of capitalism over communism and inevitable American victory in the Cold War.

During the postwar era millions of Americans, enjoying the highest standard of living in the nation's history, pursued the promise of consumer society in the burgeoning suburbs. But affluence was never as widespread as the Moscow exhibit implied. The middle-class suburban lifestyle was beyond the reach of many poor and nonwhite Americans, particularly those in the decaying inner cities. Hoping to spread the abundance of a flourishing economy to greater numbers of Americans, the Democratic administrations of John F. Kennedy and—to a much greater extent—Lyndon B. Johnson in the early 1960s pressed for the expansion of New Deal social welfare programs. Promoting a liberal agenda, they tried to use federal power to ensure the public welfare in areas such as health care, education, and civil rights.

Kennedy and Johnson also pursued an activist stance abroad. Continuing and in some cases expanding the Cold War policies of Truman and Eisenhower, their administrations took aggressive action against Communist influence in Europe, the Caribbean, Vietnam (see Chapter 29), and other areas. The growing financial and political costs of that ambitious agenda, however, hampered further progress on the domestic front and revealed ominous cracks in the postwar liberal consensus.

The Affluent Society

By the end of 1945, war-induced prosperity had made the United States the richest country in the world, a preeminence that would continue unchallenged for twenty years. U.S. military policy and foreign aid, as well as the absence of major economic competitors, were vital factors in extending the global reach of American corporate capitalism, which enjoyed remarkable growth in productivity and profits. American economic leadership abroad translated into affluence at home. As many Americans, especially whites, moved to home ownership in new suburban communities, it was clear that domestic prosperity was benefiting a wider segment of society than anyone would have dreamed possible in the dark days of the Great Depression.

Economic Expansion and the Affluent Society

The predominant thrust of modern corporate life in this period was the consolidation of economic and financial resources by oligopolies—a few large producers that controlled the national and, increasingly, the world market. In 1970, for example, the top four American automobile manufacturers produced 91 percent of the motor vehicles sold in the domestic market. Large firms maintained their dominance by diversifying. Combining companies in unrelated industries, these conglomerates ensured for themselves protection from instability in any single market, making them more effective international competitors. International Telephone and Telegraph became a diversified conglomerate by acquiring companies in unrelated industries, including Sheraton Hotels, Avis Rent-a-Car, Levitt and Sons home builders, and Hartford Fire Insurance. This pattern of corporate acquisition developed into a great wave of mergers that peaked in the 1960s.

The development of giant corporations also depended on the penetration of foreign markets. Unlike the Soviet Union, Western Europe, and Japan, America emerged physically unscathed from the war, with its defense industries eager to convert to consumer production. The weakness of the competition enabled American business to enter foreign regions when domestic markets became saturated or when American recessions cut into sales. Soon American companies provided products and services for war-torn European and Asian markets, giving the nation a trade surplus close to $5 billion in 1960.

The Growing Middle Class

Postwar affluence resulted in an unprecedented standard of living for the rapidly expanding middle class of the 1950s and 1960s. This 1951 photograph shows DuPont worker Steve Czekalinski and his family amid a year's supply of food. Prior to the 1950s, most families relied on a diet of starches and smoked meats. The newfound prosperity of the growing middle class enabled families like the Czekalinskis to enrich their diets with fresh meats and vegetables and frozen food. The cost to the Czekalinskis in 1951 for a year's supply of food: $1,300.
Alexander Henderson / Hagley Museum and Library.

FOR MORE HELP ANALYZING THIS IMAGE, see the Online Study Guide at **bedfordstmartins.com/henrettaconcise**.

American global supremacy rested in part on decisions made at a U.N. economic conference held in Bretton Woods, New Hampshire, in July 1944, which established the U.S. dollar as the capitalist world's principal reserve currency. The International Bank for Reconstruction and Development (commonly known as the World Bank) provided private loans for the reconstruction of war-torn Europe as well as for the development of Third World countries. The International Monetary Fund (IMF), designed to stabilize the value of currencies, helped to guide the world economy after the war. Backed by U.S. money and influence, these organizations tended to favor

American-style internationalism over the economic nationalism traditional in most countries.

U.S. economic supremacy abroad helped boost the domestic economy, creating millions of new jobs. One of the fastest-growing groups was salaried office workers, whose numbers increased by 61 percent between 1947 and 1957. Growing corporate bureaucracies and increased access to a college education through the GI Bill helped expand the male white-collar ranks. These "organization men," as sociologist William Whyte called them, were joined by millions of women who moved into clerical work and other lower-paying service-sector occupations. Although the percentage of blue-collar manufacturing jobs declined slightly during this period, the power of organized labor reached an all-time high. In 1955 the Congress of Industrial Organizations made a formal alliance with its old adversary, the American Federation of Labor. That merger created a single organization—the AFL-CIO—which represented more than 90 percent of the nation's 17.5 million union members. In exchange for labor peace and stability—that is, fewer strikes—corporate managers often cooperated with unions, agreeing to contracts that gave many workers secure and steadily rising incomes, guaranteeing them a share in the new prosperity. In 1950 General Motors and the United Automobile Workers signed a contract containing two novel provisions: an escalator clause, providing that wages would be adjusted to reflect changes in the cost of living, and a productivity clause, guaranteeing that wages would rise as productivity in the industry increased.

As the income of many American workers grew, consumer spending soared. That spending, combined with federal outlays for defense and domestic programs, seemed to promise a continuously rising standard of living. The gross domestic product (GDP) grew from $213 billion in 1945 to more than $500 billion in 1960. With a 25 percent rise in real income between 1946 and 1959, American home ownership rates soared: in 1940, 43 percent of American families owned their homes; by 1960, 62 percent owned them. The postwar boom was marred, however, by periodic bouts of recession and unemployment that particularly hurt low-income and nonwhite workers. Moreover, the rising standard of living was not accompanied by a noticeable redistribution of income: the top 10 percent of Americans still earned more than the bottom 50 percent. Nevertheless, most Americans had more money to spend than ever before.

The Suburban Explosion

Although Americans had been gravitating toward urban areas throughout the twentieth century, the postwar period was characterized by two new patterns: one was a shift away from older cities in the Northeast and Midwest and toward newer urban centers in the South and West; the other, a mass defection from the cities to the suburbs. Both processes were stimulated by the dramatic growth of a car culture and the federal government's support of housing and highway initiatives.

At the end of World War II, many cities were surrounded by pastures and working farms, but just five to ten years later those cities were encircled by tract housing, factories, and shopping centers. By 1960 more Americans lived in suburbs than in cities. Few new dwellings had been built during the depression or war years, and the returning veterans and their families faced a critical housing shortage. The difficulty was partly resolved by an innovative Long Island building contractor, Arthur Levitt, who revolutionized the suburban housing market by applying mass-production techniques to home construction. Levitt's company could build 150 homes per week. In Levittown a basic four-room house, complete with kitchen appliances and an attic that a handy home owner could convert into two additional bedrooms, was priced at less than $10,000 in 1947. Other developers soon followed suit in subdivisions all over the country, hastening the exodus from the farm and the city center.

Many families financed their homes with mortgages from the Federal Housing Administration (FHA) and the Veterans Administration at rates dramatically lower than those offered by private lenders. In 1955 those two agencies wrote 41 percent of all nonfarm mortgages. Such lending demonstrated the quiet yet revolutionary way in which the federal government was entering and influencing daily life.

The new suburban homes—and much of the FHA and Veterans Administration loan funds—were reserved almost exclusively for whites. Levittown home owners had to sign a **restrictive covenant** prohibiting occupation "by members of other than the Caucasian Race"; Levitt did not sell houses directly to blacks until 1960. Other communities adopted similar covenants to exclude Jews or Asians. Although the Supreme Court had ruled in *Shelley v. Kraemer* (1948) that restrictive covenants were illegal, the custom continued informally until the civil rights laws of the 1960s banned private discrimination.

The new patterns of growth and development were most striking in the South and the West, where open space allowed for sprawling suburban-style expansion. Fueled by World War II defense spending, the postwar development of the southern and western cities accelerated as industry took advantage of inexpensive land, unorganized labor, low taxes, and warm climates (now made more livable through the new technology of air conditioning). Some of the most explosive growth occurred in Florida, Texas, and California—states that would become the industrial leaders of the emerging Sun Belt economy. Between 1940 and 1970 Miami's metropolitan population increased by 79 percent with the addition of more than a million new residents, many of them older or retired. Texas cities, especially Houston and Dallas, grew as the petrochemical industry expanded rapidly after 1945. Spurred by massive defense spending, California grew the most rapidly, adding 2.6 million people in the 1940s and 3.1 million more in the 1950s.

Automobiles were essential both to suburban growth and to the development of the Sun Belt. The layout of suburban communities required cars to get to work and to take children to school, piano lessons, and sporting events. In 1945 Americans owned 25 million cars; by 1965 the number had tripled to 75 million. As the car culture that first emerged in the 1920s expanded dramatically in the 1950s, cars—extravagant gas guzzlers with elaborate tail fins and ostentatious chrome detail—became symbols of status and success. More cars required more highways, which were funded largely by the federal government. In 1947 Congress

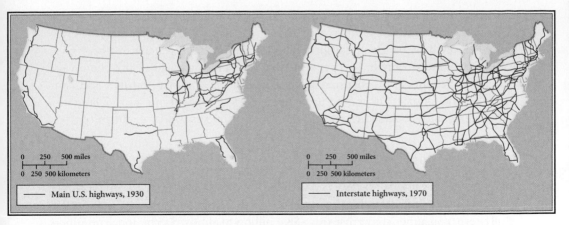

MAP 28.1 Connecting the Nation: The Interstate Highway System, 1930 and 1970

The 1956 Interstate Highway Act paved the way for an extensive network of federal highways throughout the nation. The act pleased American drivers and enhanced their love affair with the automobile, and also benefited the petroleum, construction, trucking, real estate, and tourist industries. The new highway system promoted the nation's economic integration and contributed to the erosion of distinct regional identities within the United States.

authorized the construction of 37,000 miles of highways; the National Interstate and Defense Highway Act of 1956 increased this commitment by another 42,500 miles (Map 28.1). One of the largest civil-engineering projects in world history, the new interstate system would link the entire country with roads at least four lanes wide. The interstate system changed both the cities and the countryside. It rerouted traffic away from small towns and through rural areas, creating isolated pockets of gas stations, fast-food outlets, and motels along highway exits. In urban areas new highways cut wide swaths through old neighborhoods and caused air pollution and traffic jams.

Highway construction had far-reaching effects on patterns of consumption and shopping. Instead of taking a train into the city or walking to a corner grocery store, people drove to the new suburban shopping malls and supermarkets. The first mall appeared in Kansas City in the 1920s, and there were still only eight in 1945; by 1960 the number mushroomed to almost 4,000. When a 110-store complex at Roosevelt Field on suburban Long Island opened in 1956, it was conveniently situated at an expressway exit and had parking for 11,000 cars. Downtown department stores and other retail outlets soon declined, helping to precipitate the decay of American inner cities.

American Life during the Baby Boom

Hula hoops and poodle skirts, sock hops and rock 'n' roll, and shiny cars and gleaming appliances—all signify the "fifties," a period that really stretched from 1945 through the early 1960s. The postwar years are remembered as a time of affluence and stability, a time when Americans enjoyed an optimistic faith in progress and technology and a serene family-centered culture, reflected in a booming birthrate known as the baby boom and enshrined in television sitcoms such as *Father Knows Best*. This powerful myth, like many myths, has some truth to it, but there were other sides to the story. Focusing solely on affluence, popular culture, and consumption does not do justice to this complex period of economic and social transformation, which included challenges to the status quo as well as conformity.

Consumer Culture

The new prosperity of the 1950s was aided by a dramatic increase in consumer credit, which enabled families to stretch their incomes. Between 1946 and 1958 short-term consumer credit rose from $8.4 billion to almost $45 billion. The Diners Club introduced the first credit card in 1950, followed by the American Express card and Bank Americard in 1959. By the 1970s the omnipresent plastic credit card had revolutionized personal and family finances.

Aggressive advertising contributed to the massive increase in consumer spending. In 1951 businesses spent more on advertising ($6.5 billion) than taxpayers did on primary and secondary education ($5 billion). The 1950s gave Americans the Marlboro man; M&Ms that "melt in your mouth, not in your hand"; and Wonder Bread "to build strong bodies in twelve ways."

Consumers also had more free time than ever before in which to spend their money. In 1960 the average worker put in a five-day week, with eight paid holidays a year (double the 1946 standard) plus a two-week paid vacation. Americans took to the interstate highway system by the millions, encouraging dramatic growth in motel chains, roadside restaurants, and fast-food eateries. (The first McDonald's restaurant opened in 1954 in San Bernardino, California; the Holiday Inn motel chain started in Memphis in 1952.) Among the most popular destinations were state and national parks and Disneyland, which opened in Anaheim, California, in 1955.

Perhaps the most significant hallmark of postwar consumer culture was television. Television's leap to cultural prominence was swift and overpowering. In 1947 there were only ten broadcasting stations in the country and 7,000 sets in American homes. By 1960, 87 percent of American families had at least one television set. Television quickly supplanted radio as the chief diffuser of popular culture, its national programming promoting shared interests and tastes and reducing regional and ethnic differences.

What Americans saw on television, besides the omnipresent commercials, was an overwhelmingly white, middle-class world of nuclear families living in suburban homes. *Leave It to Beaver, Ozzie and Harriet,* and similar situation comedies (sitcoms) featured characters who adhered to clear-cut gender roles and plots based on minor family crises that were always happily resolved by the end of the show. Programs such as *The Honeymooners*, starring Jackie Gleason as a Brooklyn bus driver, and *Life of Reilly*, a sitcom featuring a California aircraft worker, were rare in their treatment of working-class lives. Nonwhite characters appeared mainly as servants, such as comedian Jack Benny's black "houseboy" Rochester or the Latino gardener with the anglicized name "Frank Smith" on *Father Knows Best*. Although the new medium did offer some serious programming, notably live theater and documentaries, Federal Communications Commissioner Newton Minow concluded in 1963 that television was "a vast wasteland." Its reassuring images of family life and postwar society, however, dovetailed with the social expectations of many Americans.

The Search for Security: Religion and the Family

The dislocations of the depression and war years made many Americans yearn for security and a reaffirmation of traditional values. Some of this sentiment was expressed in a renewed emphasis on religion. Church membership rose from 49 percent of the population in 1940 to 69 percent in 1960. All the major denominations shared in the growth, which was accompanied by an ecumenical movement to bring Catholics, Protestants, and Jews together. The stress on religion meshed with Cold War Americans' view of themselves as a righteous people opposed to "godless communism." In 1954 the phrase "under God" was inserted into the Pledge of Allegiance, and in 1956 Congress added "In God We Trust" to all U.S. coins.

Beyond patriotism, religion also served more deeply felt needs. In his popular television program, Catholic bishop Fulton Sheen asked, "Is life worth living?" He and countless others optimistically answered in the affirmative. None was more positive than Norman Vincent Peale, whose best-selling book *The Power of Positive Thinking* (1952) embodied the trend toward the therapeutic use of religion to assist men and women in coping with the stresses of modern life. Evangelical religion also experienced a resurgence, most evident in the dramatic rise to popularity of the Reverend Billy Graham, who used television, radio, advertising, and print media to spread the gospel. Although critics suggested that middle-class interest in religion stemmed not so much from a renewed spirituality as from a surging impulse toward conformity, the revival nonetheless spoke to Americans' search for spiritual meaning in uncertain times.

Another indication of the desire for stability in the postwar era was the emphasis Americans placed on the family and children. As one popular advice book put it, "The family is the center of your living. If it isn't, you've gone far astray." Family demographics between 1940 and 1960 reversed depression- and war-era trends. Marriages were remarkably stable; not until the mid-1960s did the divorce rate begin to rise sharply. The average age at marriage fell during the period, to twenty-two for men and twenty for women. In 1951 a third of all women were married by age nineteen. The drop in the average age at marriage resulted in a surge of young married couples who produced a bumper crop of children. After a century and a half of declining family size, the birthrate shot up and peaked in 1957: more babies were born between 1948 and 1953 than had been born in the previous thirty years. As a result of this trend and a lengthened life expectancy because of improvements in diet, public health, and medicine, the American population rose dramatically from 140 million in 1945 to 179 million in 1960 and to 203 million in 1970.

A Woman's Dilemma in Postwar America

This 1959 cover of the *Saturday Evening Post* depicts some of the difficult choices facing women in the postwar era. Women's consignment to low-paid, dead-end jobs in the service sector encouraged many to become full-time homemakers. Once back in their suburban homes, however, many middle-class women felt isolated and trapped amid endless rounds of cooking, cleaning, and diaper changing.

Daydreaming by Constantin Alajalov © 1959 SEPS: Licensed by Curtis Publishing Company, Indianapolis, IN. All rights reserved. www.curtispublishing.com

The baby boom had a broad and immediate impact on American society. It prompted a major expansion of the nation's educational system: by 1970 school expenditures were double those of the 1950 level. In addition, babies' consumer needs fueled the economy as families bought food, diapers, toys, and clothing for their expanding broods. Together with federal expenditures on national security, family spending on consumer goods fueled the unparalleled prosperity and economic growth of the 1950s and 1960s.

Contradictions in Women's Lives

In addition to providing for their children materially and emotionally, the parents of baby boomers were expected to adhere to rigid gender roles as a way of maintaining the family and undergirding the social order. The mass media, educators, and experts urged men to conform to a masculine ideal that emphasized their traditional role as responsible breadwinners. Women's proper place, they advised, was in the home. Endorsing what Betty Friedan has called the "feminine mystique" of the 1950s—the ideal that "the highest value and the only commitment for women is the fulfillment of their own femininity "—many psychologists pronounced motherhood the only "normal" female gender role and berated mothers who worked outside the home, charging that they damaged their children's development.

Though the power of these ideas stunted the lives of many women, not all housewives were unhappy or neurotic, as Friedan would later charge in her 1963 best-seller, *The Feminine Mystique*. Many working-class women embraced their new roles as housewives; unlike their mothers and unmarried sisters, they were not compelled to take low-paid employment outside the home. But not all Americans could, or did, live by the norms of suburban domesticity, ideals that were out of reach of or irrelevant to many racial minorities, inner-city residents, recent immigrants, rural Americans, and homosexuals. At the height of the postwar period, more than one-third of American women held jobs outside the home (see American Voices, "A Woman Encounters the Feminine Mystique," p. 858). The increase in the number of working women coincided with another significant change—a dramatic rise in the number of older, married, middle-class women who took jobs.

How could the society of the 1950s cling so steadfastly to the domestic ideal while an increasing number of wives and mothers worked? Often women justified their jobs as an extension of their family responsibilities, enabling their families to enjoy more of the fruits of the consumer culture. Working women also still bore full responsibility for child care and household management, allowing families and society to avoid facing the social implications of their new roles. Thus the reality of women's lives departed significantly from the cultural stereotypes glorified in advertising, sitcoms, and women's magazines.

Youth Culture and Challenges to Conformity

Beneath the surface of family togetherness lay other tensions—those between parents and children. Dating back to the 1920s, the emergence of a mass youth culture had its roots in the democratization of education and the increasing purchasing power of teenagers in an age of affluence. Eager to escape the climate of suburban conformity of their parents, youth became a distinct new market that advertisers eagerly exploited. In 1956 advertisers projected an adolescent market of $9 billion for items such as transistor radios (introduced in 1952), clothing, and fads such as hula hoops (1958).

What really defined this generation's youth culture, however, was its music. Rejecting the rigid boundaries of traditional popular music, teenagers in the 1950s discovered rock 'n' roll, an amalgam of white country and western music and the black urban music known as rhythm and blues. The Cleveland disc jockey Alan Freed played a major role in introducing white America to the new African American sound by playing rhythm and blues records on white radio stations

AMERICAN VOICES

~

A Woman Encounters the Feminine Mystique

*T*he power of the feminine mystique in the 1950s made it difficult for middle-class women who challenged the view that women's proper place was in the home. In this oral history, "Sylvia" describes her struggle to pursue a career as an ophthalmologist. She began her medical training in nursing, even though she knew when she entered college at Adelphi University that she wanted to become a doctor.

We sat on a bench in the middle of the lobby there—I remember it looked like a train station—and he [her professor] said, "Do you plan to get pregnant or married?" I promised him I wouldn't do either. I felt like I was about ten years old. They gave me a year's trial in the research department and after that I could get a residency. Most people there, the men, had a three-year residency. I was only the second woman they'd ever accepted, and I was the only woman out of twenty men.

I had a fellowship, so when I finished with my work I'd have to go over to see how my research projects were coming along. I never, never, goofed off. These guys were watching me all the time and complaining that I wasn't doing my work. It was hard enough to be a first-year resident, where you're the bottom person who gets kicked by everybody. I had no friends. My fellow physicians were constantly telling me I should switch to obstetrics or pediatrics, I should be home having babies, that a man could earn a wonderful living for his family in my place. Finally I was at my wits' end and I called my old ophthalmology professor and told him I didn't know if I could psychologically take this for another two and a half years. He said, "You know, if you give up now I'll never be able to get another woman in there." So I went on.

SOURCE: *The Fifties: A Women's Oral History.* Copyright © 1993 by Brett Harvey. Reprinted by permission of the author.

---

beginning in 1954. Young white performers such as Bill Haley, Buddy Holly, and especially Elvis Presley incorporated the new mixture into their own music and capitalized on the new youth market. Between 1953 and 1959 record sales increased from $213 million to $603 million, with 45-rpm rock 'n' roll records as the driving force. The new teen music shocked many white adults, who saw rock 'n' roll as an invitation to race-mixing, sexual promiscuity, and juvenile delinquency.

The youth rebellion was only one aspect of a broader undercurrent of discontent with the conformist culture of the 1950s. In major cities across the nation, gay men and women, many of whom had served in the military during World War II, fought back against homophobic laws and personal attacks. In Los Angeles homosexual men founded the Mattachine Society, a gay rights organization, in 1951, and in 1954 lesbians established the Daughters of Bilitis. While for the most part the gay subculture remained closeted, this did not stop gay baiting or local police raids on

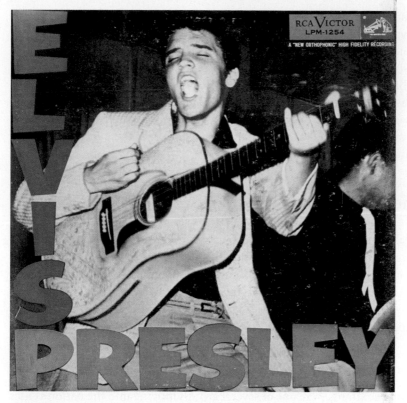

Elvis Presley

The young Elvis Presley, shown here on the cover of his first album in 1956, embodied cultural rebellion against the conservatism and conformity of adult life in the 1950s. ©1956 BMG Music.

gay bars. And because homosexuals were viewed as emotionally unstable or vulnerable to blackmail, they were assumed to be security risks. As a result of publicity attached to raids, as well as government investigations, many gays lost their jobs, a testament to the perceived threat they represented to mainstream sexual and cultural norms.

Postwar artists, musicians, and writers expressed their alienation from mainstream society through intensely personal, introspective art forms. In New York Jackson Pollock and other painters rejected the social realism of the 1930s for an unconventional style that became known as abstract expressionism. Swirling and splattering paint onto giant canvases, Pollock emphasized self-expression in the act of painting, capturing the chaotic atmosphere of the nuclear age.

A similar trend developed in jazz, as black musicians originated a hard-driving improvisational style known as "bebop." Black jazz musicians found eager fans not only in the African American community but among young white Beats in New York and San Francisco. Disdaining middle-class conformity, corporate capitalism, and suburban materialism, the Beats were a group of writers and poets who were both literary innovators and outspoken social critics. In his poem *Howl* (1956), which became a manifesto of the Beat generation, Allen Ginsberg lamented: "I saw the best minds of my generation destroyed by madness, starving hysterical naked, dragging themselves through the angry negro streets at dawn looking for an angry fix." In works such as Jack Kerouac's novel *On the Road* (1957), the Beats glorified spontaneity, sexual adventurism, drug use, and spirituality. Although they were most often apolitical, they inspired a new generation of rebels in the 1960s who would champion both cultural and political change.

The Other America

As middle-class whites flocked to the suburbs, a diverse group of poor and working-class migrants, many of them nonwhite, moved into the inner cities. With jobs and financial resources flowing to the suburbs, urban newcomers inherited a declining economy and a decaying environment. To those enjoying new prosperity, "the Other America "—as the social critic Michael Harrington called it in 1962—remained largely invisible.

International and Domestic Migration to Cities

Newly arrived immigrants were one of several groups moving into the nation's cities in the postwar era. Although until 1965 U.S. immigration policy followed the restrictive national origins quota system set up in 1924 (see Chapter 23), Congress modified the law during and after World War II. The War Brides Act of 1945, permitting the entry and naturalization of the wives and children of Americans living abroad (mainly servicemen), brought thousands of new immigrants between 1950 and 1965, including some 17,000 Koreans. Three years later the Displaced Persons Act admitted approximately 415,000 European refugees. The repeal of the Chinese Exclusion Act in 1943, in deference to America's wartime alliance with China, and the passage of the McCarran-Walter Act in 1952 ended the exclusion of Chinese, Japanese, Korean, and Southeast Asian immigrants. Finally, in recognition of the freeing of the Philippines from American control in 1946, Filipinos received their own quota.

One of the largest groups of postwar migrants came from Mexico. Nearly 275,000 Mexicans came in the 1950s and almost 444,000 in the 1960s. They moved primarily to western and southwestern cities such as Los Angeles, El Paso, and Phoenix. Before World War II most Mexican Americans had lived in rural areas and engaged in agricultural work; by 1960 a majority were living in urban areas where they joined more settled communities of service and manufacturing workers.

Part of the stimulus for Mexican immigration was the reinstitution of the Bracero Program from 1951 to 1964. Originally devised as a means of importing temporary labor during World War II, the program brought 450,000 Mexican workers to the United States at its peak in 1959. But even as the federal government welcomed braceros, it deported those who stayed on illegally. In response to the recession of 1953–1954 and the resulting high rate of unemployment throughout the nation, federal authorities deported nearly 4 million Mexicans in a program called "Operation Wetback." The deportations discouraged illegal immigration for a few years, but the level increased again after the Bracero Program ended.

Another group of Spanish-speaking migrants came from the American-controlled territory of Puerto Rico. Residents of that island had been American citizens since 1917, so their migration was not subject to immigration laws. The inflow from the territory increased dramatically after World War II, when mechanization of the island's sugarcane industry pushed many rural Puerto Ricans off the land. When airlines began to offer cheap direct flights between San Juan and New York City (in the 1940s the fare was about $50, or two weeks' wages), Puerto Ricans—most of whom settled in New York—became this country's first group to immigrate by air.

Cuban refugees constituted the third large group of Spanish-speaking immigrants. In the six years after Communist Fidel Castro's overthrow of the Batista dictatorship in 1959 (see p. 865), an estimated 180,000 people fled Cuba for the United States. The Cuban refugee community grew so quickly that it turned Miami into a cosmopolitan, bilingual city almost overnight. Unlike most new immigrants, Miami's Cubans prospered, in large part because they had arrived with more resources.

Internal migration from rural areas also brought large numbers of people to the cities, especially African Americans, continuing a trend that had begun during World War I (see Chapter 22). Although both whites and blacks left the land in large numbers, the starkest decline was among black farmers. Their migration was hastened by the transformation of southern agriculture, especially by the introduction of innovations like the mechanical cotton picker, which significantly reduced the demand for farm labor. Some of the migrants settled in southern cities, where they found industrial jobs. White southerners from Appalachia moved north to "hillbilly" ghettos such as Cincinnati's Over the Rhine neighborhood and Chicago's Uptown. As many as 3 million blacks headed to Chicago, New York, Washington, Detroit, Los Angeles, and other cities between 1940 and 1960. So pervasive were the migrants that certain sections of Chicago seemed like the Mississippi Delta transplanted. By 1960 about half of the nation's black population was living outside the South, compared with only 23 percent before World War II.

In western cities Native Americans also contributed to the rise in the nonwhite urban population. Seeking to end federal responsibility for Indian affairs, Congress in 1953 authorized a "termination" program aimed at liquidating the reservation system and integrating Native Americans into mainstream society. Reflecting the Cold War preoccupation with conformity and assimilation, the program enjoyed strong support from mining, timber, and agricultural interests that wanted to open reservation lands for private development. The Bureau of Indian Affairs encouraged voluntary relocation to urban areas with a program subsidizing moving costs and establishing relocation centers in San Francisco, Denver, Chicago, and other cities. The relocation program proved problematic, however, as many Native Americans found it difficult to adjust to an urban environment and culture. Although forced termination was halted in 1958, by 1960 some 60,000 Native Americans had moved to the cities, mostly living in poor urban neighborhoods alongside other nonwhite groups.

The Urban Crisis

American cities thus saw their nonwhite populations swell at the same time that many whites were flocking to the suburbs. From 1950 to 1960 the nation's twelve largest cities lost 3.6 million whites and gained 4.5 million nonwhites. As affluent whites left the cities, urban tax revenues shrank, leading to the decay of services and infrastructure, which, coupled with growing racial fears, accelerated "white flight" to the suburbs in the 1960s.

By the time that blacks, Latinos, and Native Americans moved to the inner cities, urban America was in poor shape. Housing continued to be a crucial problem. City planners, politicians, and real estate developers responded with **urban renewal** programs, razing blighted city neighborhoods to make way for modern construction projects. Redevelopment programs often produced grim high-rise housing projects that destroyed community bonds and created anonymous open areas that were vulnerable to crime. Between 1949 and 1967 urban renewal demolished almost 400,000 buildings and displaced 1.4 million people.

Postwar urban areas were increasingly becoming places of last resort for the nation's poor. Lured to the cities by the promise of plentiful jobs, migrants found that many of those opportunities had relocated to the suburban fringe, putting steady employment out of reach for those who needed it most. Migrants to the city, especially blacks, also faced racial hostility and institutional barriers to mobility—biased school funding, hiring and promotion decisions, and credit practices. Two separate Americas were emerging: a largely white society in suburbs and peripheral areas and an inner city populated by blacks, Latinos, and other disadvantaged groups.

The stereotypes of boundless affluence and contentment in the 1950s—of "Happy Days"—are thus misleading, for they hide those persons who did not share equally in the American dream—displaced factory workers, destitute old people, female heads of households, blacks, and other racial minority groups. In the turbulent decade to come, the contrast between suburban affluence and the "other America"; between the lure of the city for the poor and minorities and its grim, segregated reality; and between a heightened emphasis on domesticity and the widening opportunities for women would spawn growing demands for social change that the nation's leaders in the 1960s could not ignore.

John F. Kennedy and the Politics of Expectation

In his 1961 inaugural address President John Fitzgerald Kennedy challenged a "new generation of Americans" to take responsibility for the future: "Ask not what your country can do for you, ask what you can do for your country." With his New Frontier program, Kennedy promised to "get America moving again" through vigorous governmental activism at home and abroad.

The New Politics

The Republicans would have been happy to renominate Dwight D. Eisenhower for president, but the Twenty-second Amendment prevented them from doing so. Passed in 1951 by a Republican-controlled Congress to prevent a repetition of Franklin Roosevelt's four-term presidency, the amendment limited future presidents to two full terms. So in 1960 the Republicans turned to Vice President Richard M. Nixon, who campaigned for an updated version of Eisenhower's policies but was hampered by lukewarm support from the popular president.

The Democrats chose Senator John F. Kennedy of Massachusetts, with the Senate majority leader, Lyndon B. Johnson of Texas, as the vice presidential nominee. First elected to Congress in 1946, John Kennedy moved to the Senate in 1952. Ambitious and hard driven, Kennedy launched his campaign in 1960 with a platform calling for civil rights legislation, health care for the elderly, aid to education, urban renewal, expanded military and space programs, and containment of communism abroad.

At forty-three Kennedy was poised to become the youngest man ever elected to the presidency and the nation's first Catholic chief executive. Turning his age into a powerful campaign asset, Kennedy practiced what came to be called the "new politics," an approach that emphasized youthful charisma, style, and personality more than issues and platforms. Using the power of the media—particularly television—to reach voters directly, practitioners of the new politics relied on professional media consultants, political pollsters, and mass fund-raising.

A series of four televised debates between the two principal candidates, a major innovation of the 1960 campaign, showed how important television was becoming to political life. Nixon, far less photogenic than Kennedy, looked sallow and unshaven under the intense studio lights. Kennedy, in contrast, looked vigorous, cool, and self-confident on screen. Polls showed that television did sway political perceptions: voters who listened to the first debate on the radio concluded that Nixon had won, but those who viewed it on television judged in Kennedy's favor.

Despite the edge Kennedy enjoyed in the debates, he won only the narrowest of electoral victories, receiving 49.7 percent of the popular vote to Nixon's 49.5 percent. Kennedy attracted large numbers of Catholic and black voters and a significant sector of the middle class; the vice presidential nominee, Lyndon Johnson, brought

The Kennedy Magnetism

John Kennedy, the Democratic candidate for president in 1960, used his youth and personality to attract voters. Here, the Massachusetts senator draws an enthusiastic crowd on a campaign stop in Elgin, Illinois. Wide World Photos, Inc.

in southern white Democrats. Yet only 120,000 votes separated the two candidates, and the shift of a few thousand votes in key states such as Illinois (where there were confirmed cases of voting fraud) would have reversed the outcome.

Activism Abroad

Kennedy's greatest priority as president was foreign affairs. A resolute cold warrior, Kennedy took a hard line against Communist expansionism. In contrast to Eisenhower, whose cost-saving New Look program had built up the American nuclear arsenal at the expense of conventional weapons, Kennedy proposed a new policy of "**flexible response**," stating that the nation must be prepared "to deter all wars, general or limited, nuclear or conventional, large or small." Congress quickly granted Kennedy's military requests, and by 1963 the defense budget reached its highest level as a percentage of total federal expenditures in the Cold War era, greatly expanding the military-industrial complex.

Flexible response measures were designed to deter direct attacks by the Soviet Union. To prepare for a new kind of warfare, evident in the wars of national liberation that had broken out in many developing countries, Kennedy adopted a new military doctrine of **counterinsurgency**. Soon U.S. Army Special Forces, called "Green Berets" for their distinctive headgear, were receiving intensive training in repelling the random, small-scale attacks typical of guerrilla warfare. The growing war in Vietnam would soon provide a testing ground for counterinsurgency techniques (see Chapter 29).

Another of Kennedy's projects, the Peace Corps, established in 1961, embodied the commitment to public service that the president had called for in his inaugural address. Thousands of men and women agreed to devote two or more years to programs that had them teaching English to Filipino schoolchildren or helping African villagers obtain adequate supplies of water. Exhibiting the idealism of the early 1960s, the Peace Corps was also a Cold War weapon intended to bring developing countries into the American orbit and away from Communist influence.

Another way of pursuing this aim was through programs of economic assistance to developing countries (Map 28.2). The State Department's Agency for International Development coordinated foreign aid for the Third World, and its Food for Peace program distributed surplus agricultural products. In 1961 the president proposed a "ten-year plan for the Americas" called the Alliance for Progress, a $20 billion partnership between the United States and the republics of Latin America. Designed to reduce the appeal of communism, the alliance provided funds for food, education, medicine, and other services but did little to enhance economic growth or improve social conditions in Latin America during the 1960s.

Latin America was the site of Kennedy's first major foreign-policy initiative and one of his biggest failures—an effort to overthrow the new Soviet-supported regime in Cuba. The United States had long exercised nearly total economic and political dominance of the island. But in 1959, the revolutionary Fidel Castro overthrew the corrupt and unpopular dictator Fulgencio Batista. When Castro began agrarian reforms and nationalized American-owned banks and industries, relations with Washington deteriorated. By early 1961 the United States had declared an embargo on all exports to Cuba, cut back on imports of Cuban sugar, and broken off diplomatic relations with Castro's regime.

Isolated by the United States, Cuba turned increasingly toward the Soviet Union for economic and military support. Concerned about Castro's growing friendliness with the Soviets, in early 1961 Kennedy used plans originally drawn up by the Eisenhower administration to dispatch Cuban exiles living in Nicaragua to foment an anti-Castro uprising. Although the invaders had been trained by the Central Intelligence Agency (CIA), they were ill prepared for their task and had little popular support. After landing at Cuba's Bay of Pigs on April 17, the tiny force of 1,400 men was crushed by Castro's troops.

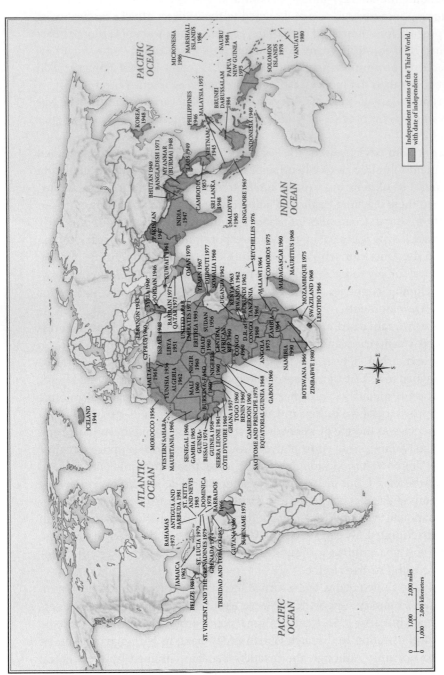

MAP 28.2 Decolonization and the Third World, 1943–1990

Instigated by the upheaval of World War II and continuing for several decades, peoples throughout the globe challenged the long-standing colonial order and demanded independence. After 1945, movements for national self-determination swept across Africa, India, Southeast Asia, and other parts of the "third world," a Cold War term designating countries not formally aligned with the United States ("first world") or the Soviet Union ("second world"). Courted with weapons and promises of aid by both the United States and the Soviet Union, many Third World nations like Vietnam and Angola became key battlegrounds of the Cold War, often with disastrous results for the local populations.

Already weakened by the Bay of Pigs invasion, U.S.-Soviet relations deteriorated further in June 1961 when Soviet premier Khrushchev deployed soldiers to isolate Communist-controlled East Berlin from the western sector of the city controlled by West Germany. With congressional approval Kennedy responded by adding 300,000 troops to the armed forces and promptly dispatching 40,000 of them to Europe. In mid-August, to stop the exodus of East Germans to the West, the Soviets ordered construction of the Berlin Wall and East German guards began policing the border. Until it was dismantled in 1989, the Berlin Wall remained the supreme symbol of the Cold War.

The climactic confrontation of the Cold War came in October 1962. After the failed Bay of Pigs invasion, the Kennedy administration increased economic pressure against Cuba and resumed covert efforts to overthrow the Castro regime. In response the Soviets stepped up military aid to Cuba, including the installation of nuclear missiles. In early October American reconnaissance planes photographed Soviet-built bases for intermediate-range ballistic missiles (IRBMs), which could reach U.S. targets as far as 2,200 miles away. Some of those weapons had already been installed, and more were on the way.

In a somber televised address on Monday, October 22, Kennedy confronted the Soviet Union and announced that the United States would impose a "quarantine on all offensive military equipment" intended for Cuba. As the two superpowers went on full military alert, people around the world feared that the confrontation would end in nuclear war. Americans living within range of the missiles restocked their bomb shelters or calculated the fastest route out of town. When Khrushchev denounced the quarantine, tension mounted. But as the world held its breath, ships carrying the Soviet-made missiles turned back. After a week of tense negotiations, both Kennedy and Khrushchev made concessions: Kennedy pledged not to invade Cuba, and Khrushchev promised to dismantle the missile bases.

Although the risk of nuclear war was greater during the Cuban missile crisis than it was at any other time in the postwar period, it led to a slight thaw in U.S.-Soviet relations. In the words of national security advisor McGeorge Bundy, "Having come so close to the edge, the leaders of the two governments have since taken care to keep away from the cliff." Kennedy softened his Cold War rhetoric and began to strive for peaceful coexistence. Soviet leaders, similarly chastened, were willing to talk. In August 1963 the three nuclear powers—the United States, the Soviet Union, and Great Britain—agreed to ban the testing of nuclear weapons in the atmosphere, in space, and under water. Underground testing, however, was allowed to continue. The new emphasis on peaceful coexistence also led to the establishment of a Washington-Moscow telecommunications "hotline" in 1963 so that leaders could contact each other quickly in the event a new crisis emerged.

But no matter how often American leaders talked about opening channels of communication with the Soviets, the preoccupation with the Soviet military threat to American security remained a cornerstone of U.S. policy. And Soviet leaders did not moderate their concern over the threat that they believed the United States posed to the survival of the Soviet Union. The Cold War, and the escalating arms race that accompanied it, would continue for another twenty-five years.

The New Frontier at Home

The expansive vision of presidential leadership that Kennedy and his advisors brought to the White House worked less well at home than it did abroad. Hampered by the lack of a popular mandate in the 1960 election, Kennedy could not mobilize public support for the domestic agenda of the New Frontier. He managed to push through legislation raising the minimum wage and expanding Social Security benefits, but a conservative coalition of southern Democrats and western and midwestern Republicans effectively stalled most liberal initiatives. On such issues as federal aid to education, wilderness preservation, federal investment in mass transportation, and medical insurance for the elderly, he ran into determined congressional opposition from both Republicans and dissenters in his own party.

One program that did win both popular and congressional support was increased funding for the National Aeronautics and Space Administration (NASA), whose Mercury space program had begun in 1958. On May 5, 1961, just three months after Kennedy took office, Alan Shepard became the first American in space. (The Soviet cosmonaut Yuri Gagarin became the first person in space when he made a 108-hour flight in April 1961.) The following year, American astronaut John Glenn manned the first space mission to orbit the earth. At the height of American fascination with space flight, Kennedy proposed that the nation commit itself to landing a man on the moon within the decade. To support this mission (accomplished in 1969), Kennedy persuaded Congress to greatly increase NASA's budget.

Kennedy's most striking domestic achievement was his use of modern economic theory to shape government **fiscal policy**. New Dealers had gradually moved away from the ideal of a balanced budget, turning instead to deliberate deficit spending to stimulate economic growth. In addition to relying on federal spending to create the desired deficit, Kennedy and his advisors proposed a reduction in income taxes. A tax cut, they argued, would put more money in the hands of taxpayers, who would spend it, thereby creating more jobs, raising incomes, and generating higher tax revenues.

Congress balked at this unorthodox proposal, and the measure failed to pass. But Lyndon Johnson pressed for it after Kennedy's assassination, signing it into law in February 1964. The Kennedy-Johnson tax cut—the Tax Reduction Act (1964)—marked a milestone in the use of fiscal policy to encourage economic growth, an approach that Republicans and other fiscal conservatives would later embrace.

New Tactics for the Civil Rights Movement

Perhaps the most notable failure of the Kennedy administration was its reluctance to act on civil rights—the most important domestic issue of the 1960s. Building on the strategy of nonviolent direct action pioneered by Martin Luther King Jr. and the Montgomery bus boycotters in the 1950s, a younger generation of activists in the 1960s initiated new, more assertive tactics such as sit-ins, freedom rides, and voter registration campaigns.

This new phase of the civil rights movement began in Greensboro, North Carolina, on February 1, 1960, when four black college students took seats at the "whites-only" lunch counter of a local Woolworth's, determined to "sit in" until they were served. Although the protesters were arrested, the sit-in tactic worked—the Woolworth lunch counter was desegregated—and sit-ins quickly spread to other southern cities. A few months later Ella Baker, an administrator with the Southern Christian Leadership Conference (SCLC), helped to organize the Student Non-Violent Coordinating Committee (SNCC, known as "Snick") to facilitate student sit-ins. By the end of the year, about 50,000 people had participated in sit-ins or other demonstrations, and 3,600 of them had been jailed. But lunch counters had been desegregated in 126 cities throughout the South (see American Voices, "We Would Like to Be Served," p. 870).

The success of SNCC's unorthodox tactics encouraged the Congress of Racial Equality (CORE), an interracial group founded in 1942, to organize a series of freedom rides in 1961 on interstate bus lines throughout the South, riding in integrated groups to call attention to the continuing segregation of public transportation. The activists who rode the buses, mostly young and both black and white, were brutally attacked by white mobs in Anniston, Montgomery, and Birmingham, Alabama. Governor John Patterson refused to intervene, claiming, "I cannot guarantee protection for this bunch of rabble rousers."

Although the Kennedy administration generally opposed the freedom riders' activities, films of their beatings and the bus burning shown on the nightly news prompted Attorney General Robert Kennedy to send federal marshals to Alabama to restore order. Faced with Department of Justice intervention against those who defied the Interstate Commerce Commission's prohibition of segregation in interstate vehicles and facilities, most southern communities quietly acceded to the changes. And civil rights activists learned that nonviolent protest could succeed if it provoked vicious white resistance and generated publicity. Only when forced to, it appeared, would the federal authorities act.

This lesson was confirmed in Birmingham, Alabama, when Martin Luther King Jr. and the Reverend Fred Shuttlesworth called for a protest against conditions in what King called "the most segregated city in the United States." In April 1963 thousands of black demonstrators marched downtown to picket Birmingham's department stores. They were met by Eugene ("Bull") Connor, the city's commissioner of public safety, who used snarling dogs, electric cattle prods, and high-pressure fire hoses to break up the crowd. Television cameras captured the scene for the evening news.

President Kennedy, realizing that he could no longer postpone decisive action, decided to step up the federal government's role in civil rights. On June 11, 1963, Kennedy went on television to promise major legislation banning discrimination in public accommodations and empowering the Justice Department to enforce

AMERICAN VOICES

We Would Like to Be Served

ANNE MCODY

*B*orn in rural Mississippi in 1940, Anne Moody was one of thousands of black college students, many of them women, who joined the Student Non-Violent Coordinating Committee in the early 1960s. In her senior year she participated in a sit-in at a Woolworth's lunch counter in Jackson, Mississippi, which she describes in her autobiography.

Our waitress walked past us a couple of times before she noticed we had started to write our own orders down and realized we wanted service. She asked us what we wanted. We began to read to her from our order slips. She told us that we would be served at the back counter, which was for Negroes.

"We would like to be served here," I said. . . .

At noon, students from a nearby white high school started pouring in to Woolworth's. When they first saw us they were sort of surprised. They didn't know how to react. A few started to heckle and the newsmen [who had arrived earlier] became interested again. Then the white students started chanting all kinds of anti-Negro slogans. We were called a little bit of everything. The rest of the seats except the three we were occupying had been roped off to prevent others from sitting down. A couple of the boys took one end of the rope and made it into a hangman's noose. Several attempts were made to put it around our necks. . . .

Memphis suggested that we pray. We bowed our heads, and all hell broke loose. A man rushed forward, threw Memphis from his seat, and slapped my face. Then another man who worked in the store threw me against an adjoining counter.

Down on my knees on the floor, I saw Memphis lying near the lunch counter with blood running out of the corners of his mouth. As he tried to protect his face, the man who'd thrown him down kept kicking him against the head. . . .

. . . The mob started smearing us with ketchup, mustard, sugar, pies, and everything on the counter. Soon Joan [Trumpauer, a white college student and NAACP member] and I were joined by John Salter, but the moment he sat down he was hit on the jaw with what appeared to be brass knuckles. Blood gushed from his face and someone threw salt into the open wound. . . .

. . . The mob took spray paint from the counter and sprayed it on the new demonstrators. The high school student had on a white shirt; the word "nigger" was written on his back with red spray paint.

We sat there for three hours taking a beating when the manager decided to close the store because the mob had begun to go wild with stuff from other counters. . . .

After the sit-in, all I could think of was how sick Mississippi whites were. They believed so much in the segregated Southern way of life, they would kill to preserve it. I sat there in the NAACP office and thought of how many times they had killed when this way of life was threatened. I knew that the killing had just begun. . . .

SOURCE: *Coming of Age in Mississippi* by Anne Moody. Copyright © 1968 by Anne Moody. Used by permission of Doubleday, a division of Random House, Inc.

The March on Washington

The Reverend Martin Luther King Jr. (1929–1968) was one of the most eloquent advocates of the civil rights movement. For many, his "I have a dream" speech of the 1963 March on Washington was the high point of the event, but the focus on the charismatic King has meant that the importance of other civil rights leaders is frequently overlooked. Bob Adelman / Magnum Photos, Inc.

desegregation. Black leaders hailed the speech as the "Second Emancipation Proclamation," but for one person Kennedy's speech came too late. That night, Medgar Evers, president of the Mississippi chapter of the NAACP, was shot in the back and killed in his driveway in Jackson. The martyrdom of Evers became a spur to further action.

To rouse the conscience of the nation and to marshal support for Kennedy's bill, civil rights leaders adopted a tactic that A. Philip Randolph had first suggested in 1941 (see Chapter 26): a massive march on Washington. Martin Luther King Jr. of the SCLC, Roy Wilkins of the NAACP, Whitney Young of the National Urban League, and the black Socialist Bayard Rustin were the principal organizers. On August 28, 1963, about 250,000 black and white demonstrators gathered at the Lincoln Memorial. The march culminated in the memorable "I have a dream" speech delivered by King, in the evangelical style of the black church. He ended with an exclamation from an old Negro spiritual: "Free at last! Free at last! Thank God almighty, we are free at last!"

King's eloquence and the sight of blacks and whites marching solemnly to-gether did more than any other event to make the civil rights movement acceptable to white Americans. The March on Washington marked the high point of the civil rights movement and confirmed King's position, especially among white liberals, as the leading speaker for the black cause. In 1964 King won the Nobel Peace Prize for his leadership.

The attention focused on King, however, has often obscured the dynamics of the civil rights movement, especially the importance of thousands of activists work-ing within their communities, particularly women in church groups and organiza-tions like SNCC. It also has minimized the role of other leaders, including Bayard Rustin, Roy Wilkins, and Ella Baker, as well as the young activists in SNCC like Bob Moses, and those such as John Lewis, who were more radical than King and be-coming impatient with the federal government's failure to act decisively to protect black lives and rights. At the march Lewis was pressured to modify the militant tone of the speech he was to give, and the episode foreshadowed the conflicts among black activists over tactics and goals that were to transform the civil rights move-ment in the next few years (see Chapter 29).

Although the March on Washington had a positive impact on public opinion about King and the civil rights movement, it changed few congressional votes. Southern senators continued to block Kennedy's legislation by threatening a fili-buster. Even more troubling was a new outbreak of violence by white extremists who were determined to oppose equality for blacks at all costs. In September a Baptist church in Birmingham was bombed and four black Sunday-school students were killed. The violence shocked the nation and stiffened the resolve of civil rights activists to escalate their demands for change. Two months later President Kennedy was assassinated.

The Kennedy Assassination

Although the first two years of Kennedy's presidency had been plagued by foreign-policy crises and domestic inaction, many political observers believed that by 1963 Kennedy was maturing as a national leader. On November 22, 1963, Kennedy went to Texas on a political trip. As he and his wife, Jacqueline, rode in an open car past the Texas School Book Depository in Dallas, he was shot through the head and neck by a sniper. Kennedy died a half hour later. (Whether accused killer Lee Harvey Oswald, a twenty-four-year-old loner who had spent three years in the Soviet Union, was the sole gunman is still a matter of controversy.) Before Air Force One left Dallas to take the president's body back to Washington, a grim-faced Lyndon Johnson was sworn in as president. Kennedy's stunned widow, still wearing her bloodstained pink suit, looked on.

Kennedy's youthful image, the trauma of his assassination, and the collective sense that Americans had been robbed of a promising leader contributed to a powerful mystique. This romantic aura has overshadowed a mixed record of accomplishments. Kennedy exercised bold presidential leadership in foreign affairs, and some historians, using newly available sources such as Oval Office tapes and Soviet archives, have praised his skill in handling the Cuban missile crisis. Others remain critical of his belligerent stance toward the Soviet Union and lack of attention to domestic issues. Kennedy's proposals for educational aid, medical insurance, and other liberal reforms stalled, and his tax-cut bill languished in Congress until after his death.

Lyndon B. Johnson and the Great Society

Lyndon Baines Johnson, a seasoned politician who was best at negotiating in the back rooms of power, was no match for the Kennedy style, but less than a year after assuming office, Johnson won the 1964 presidential election in a landslide that far surpassed Kennedy's meager mandate in 1960. Johnson then used his astonishing energy and genius for compromise to bring to fruition many of Kennedy's stalled programs and more than a few of his own. Those legislative accomplishments— Johnson's "Great Society"—fulfilled and in many cases surpassed the New Deal liberal agenda of the 1930s.

The Momentum for Civil Rights

On assuming the presidency, Lyndon Johnson promptly pushed the passage of civil rights legislation as a memorial to his slain predecessor—an ironic twist in light of Kennedy's lukewarm support for the cause. Johnson's motives were a combination of the political and the personal. As a politician he hoped to maintain the loyalty of African Americans and northern white liberals to the Democratic Party. As an unelected president from the South, he sought to appeal to a broad national audience, especially on the issue of race. Achieving historic civil rights legislation would not only be an impressive legislative accomplishment, but also would, he hoped, place his mark on the presidency.

The Civil Rights Act, narrowly passed in June 1964, was a landmark in the history of American race relations. Its keystone, Title VII, outlawed discrimination in employment on the basis of race, religion, national origin, or sex. Another section barred discrimination in public accommodations. But while the act forced the desegregation of public facilities throughout the South, including many public schools, obstacles to black voting rights remained.

To meet this challenge, in 1964 black organizations and churches mounted a major civil rights campaign in Mississippi. Known as "Freedom Summer," the effort drew several thousand volunteers from across the country, including many idealistic white college students. Freedom Summer workers established freedom schools, which taught black children traditional subjects as well as their own history; conducted a major voter registration drive; and organized the Mississippi Freedom Democratic Party, a political alternative to the all-white Democratic organization in Mississippi. Some white south-erners reacted swiftly and violently to those efforts. Fifteen civil rights workers were murdered; only about 1,200 black voters were registered that summer.

The need for federal action to support voting rights became even clearer in March 1965, when Martin Luther King Jr. and other black leaders called for a mas-sive march from Selma, Alabama, to the state capital in Montgomery to protest the murder of a voting-rights activist. As soon as the marchers left Selma, mounted state troopers attacked them with tear gas and clubs. The scene was shown on national television that night. Calling the episode "an American tragedy," President Johnson redoubled his efforts to persuade Congress to pass the pending voting-rights legis-lation. In a televised speech to a joint session of Congress on March 15, quoting the best-known slogan of the civil rights movement, "We shall overcome," he pro-claimed voting rights a moral imperative.

On August 6 Congress passed the Voting Rights Act of 1965, which suspended the literacy tests and other measures most southern states used to prevent blacks from registering to vote. The act authorized the attorney general to send federal ex-aminers to register voters in any county where less than 50 percent of the voting-age population was registered. Together with the adoption in 1964 of the Twenty-fourth Amendment to the Constitution, which outlawed the poll tax in federal elections, and successful legal challenges to state and local poll taxes, the Voting Rights Act al-lowed millions of blacks to register and vote for the first time. Congress reautho-rized the Voting Rights Act in 1970, 1975, and 1982.

In the South the results were stunning. In 1960 only 20 percent of blacks of voting age had been registered to vote; by 1964 the figure had risen to 39 percent, and by 1971 it was 62 percent (Map 28.3). As Hartman Turnbow, a Mississippi farmer who risked his life to register in 1964, later declared, "It won't never go back where it was."

Enacting the Liberal Agenda

Johnson's success in pushing through the 1965 Voting Rights Act stemmed in part from the 1964 election, in which he won the presidency in his own right by defeating the conservative Republican senator Barry Goldwater of Arizona. With his running mate, Senator Hubert H. Humphrey of Minnesota, Johnson achieved one of the largest mar-gins in history, 61.1 percent of the popular vote. And Johnson's coattails were long—his sweeping victory brought Democratic gains in both Congress and the state legislatures. Thus strengthened politically, he used this mandate not only to promote a civil rights agenda but also to bring to fruition what he called the "Great Society."

Like most New Deal liberals, Johnson took an expansive view of presidential leadership and the role of the federal government. During his presidency, those who lived below the poverty line—three-fourths of whom were white—made up about a quarter of the American population. They included isolated farmers and miners in Appalachia, blacks and Puerto Ricans in urban ghettos, Mexican Americans in migrant labor camps and urban barrios, and Native Americans on reservations.

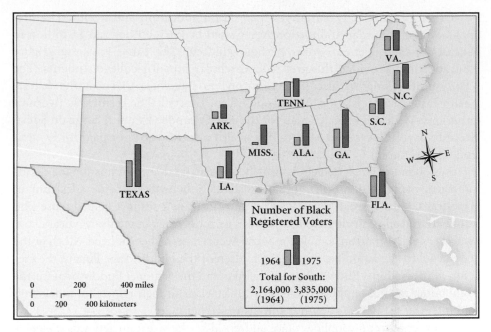

MAP 28.3 Black Voter Registration in the South, 1964 and 1975

After passage of the Voting Rights Act of 1965, black registration in the South increased dramati
cally. The bars on the map show the number of blacks registered in 1964, before the act was passed,
and in 1975, after it had been in effect for ten years. States in the Deep South, such as Mississippi,
Alabama, and Georgia, had the biggest rises.

Wherever he acted, Johnson pursued an ambitious goal of putting "an end to
poverty in our time."

To reduce poverty, the Johnson administration expanded social insurance, welfare, and public works programs established by earlier administrations, especially
Franklin Roosevelt's New Deal. It broadened Social Security to include waiters and
waitresses, domestic servants, farmworkers, and hospital employees. Social welfare expenditures increased rapidly, especially for Aid to Families with Dependent Children
(AFDC), as did public housing and rent subsidy programs and food stamps. As during the New Deal, these social welfare programs developed in piecemeal fashion, without overall coordination.

The Office of Economic Opportunity (OEO), established by the Economic
Opportunity Act of 1964, was the Great Society's showcase in the War on Poverty.
OEO programs produced some of the most innovative measures of the Johnson administration. Head Start provided free nursery schools to prepare disadvantaged
preschoolers for kindergarten. The Job Corps, Upward Bound, and Volunteers in
Service to America (VISTA), modeled on the Peace Corps, provided poor youths
with training and jobs. The Community Action Program encouraged the poor to
demand "maximum feasible participation" in decisions that affected them.

Other Great Society initiatives focused on education and health. The Elementary and Secondary Education Act, passed in 1965, authorized $1 billion in federal funds to benefit impoverished children. The same year the Higher Education Act provided the first federal scholarships for college students. The Eighty-ninth Congress also gave Johnson enough votes to enact the federal health insurance legislation first proposed by Truman. The result was two new programs: Medicare, a health plan for the elderly funded by a surcharge on Social Security payroll taxes, and Medicaid, a health plan for the poor paid for by general tax revenues.

Although the Great Society is usually associated with programs for the disadvantaged, many of Johnson's initiatives actually benefited a wide spectrum of Americans. Federal urban renewal and home mortgage assistance helped those who could afford to live in single-family homes or modern apartments. Medicare covered every elderly person eligible for Social Security, regardless of need. Much of the federal aid to education benefited the children of the middle class. Finally, the creation of the National Endowment for the Arts and the National Endowment for the Humanities in 1965 supported artists and historians in their efforts to understand and interpret the nation's cultural and historical heritage.

Another aspect of public welfare addressed by the Great Society was the environment. President Johnson pressed for expansion of the national park system, improvement of the nation's air and water, and increased land-use planning. At the insistence of his wife, Lady Bird Johnson, he promoted the Highway Beautification Act of 1965. His approach marked a significant break with past conservation efforts, which had tended to concentrate on maintaining natural resources and national wealth. Under Secretary of the Interior Stewart Udall, Great Society programs emphasized quality of life, battling the problem "of vanishing beauty, of increasing ugliness, of shrinking open space, and of an overall environment that is diminished daily by pollution and noise and blight."

Taking advantage of the Great Society's reform climate, liberal Democrats also brought about significant changes in immigration policy. The Immigration Act of 1965 abandoned the quota system of the 1920s that had discriminated against Asians and southern and Eastern Europeans, replacing it with more equitable numerical limits on immigration from Europe, Africa, Asia, and countries in the Western Hemisphere. Since close relatives of individuals who were already legal residents of the United States could be admitted over and above the numerical limits, the legislation led to an immigrant influx far greater than anticipated, with the heaviest volume coming from Asia and Latin America.

By the end of 1965, the Johnson administration had compiled the most impressive legislative record of liberal reforms since the New Deal. It had put issues of poverty, justice, and access at the center of national political life, and it had expanded the federal government's role in protecting citizens' welfare. Yet the Great Society never quite measured up to the extravagant promises made for it, and by the end of the decade, many of its programs were under attack.

In part the political necessity of bowing to pressure from various interest groups hampered Great Society programs. For example, the American Medical Association (AMA) used its influence to shape the Medicare and Medicaid programs to ensure that Congress did not impose a cap on medical expenses. Its intervention produced escalating federal expenditures and contributed to skyrocketing medical costs. And Democratic-controlled urban political machines criticized VISTA and Community Action Program agents who encouraged poor people to demand the public services long withheld by unresponsive local governments. In response to such political pressure, the Johnson administration gradually phased out the Community Action Program and instead channeled spending for housing, social services, and other urban poverty programs through local municipal governments.

Another inherent problem was the limited funding of Great Society programs. The annual budget for the War on Poverty was less than $2 billion. Despite the limited nature of the program, the statistical decline in poverty during the 1960s suggests that the Great Society was successful on some levels. From 1963 to 1968 the proportion of Americans living below the poverty line dropped from 20 percent to 13 percent. Among African Americans economic advancement was even more marked. In the 1960s the black poverty rate was cut in half and millions of blacks moved into the middle class. But critics charged that the reduction in the poverty rate was due to the decade's booming economy and not to the War on Poverty. Another criticism was that while the nation's overall standard of living increased during this period, distribution of wealth remained uneven. The poor were better off in an absolute sense, but they remained far behind the middle class in a relative sense.

Other factors also hampered the success of the Great Society. Following in the steps of Roosevelt's New Deal coalition, Kennedy and Johnson had gathered an extraordinarily diverse set of groups—middle-class and poor; white and nonwhite; Protestant, Jewish, and Catholic; urban and rural—in support of an unprecedented level of federal activism. For a brief period between 1964 and 1966, the coalition held together. But inevitably the demands of certain groups—such as blacks' demands for civil rights and the urban poor's demands for increased political power—conflicted with the interests of other Democrats, such as white southerners and northern political bosses. In the end the Democratic coalition could not sustain a consensus on the purposes of governmental activism powerful enough to resist a growing challenge of conservatives, who increasingly resisted expanded civil rights and social welfare legislation.

At the same time, Democrats were plagued by disillusionment over the shortcomings of their reforms. In the early 1960s the lofty rhetoric of the New Frontier and the Great Society had raised unprecedented expectations for social change. But competition for federal largesse was keen, and the shortage of funds for the War on Poverty left many promises unfulfilled, especially after 1965 when the escalation of the Vietnam War siphoned funding away from domestic programs. In 1966 the government spent $22 billion on the Vietnam War and only $1.2 billion on the War on Poverty. Ultimately, as Martin Luther King Jr. put it, the Great Society was "shot down on the battlefields of Vietnam."

TIMELINE

1944	Bretton Woods economic conference	**1962**	Michael Harrington's *The Other America*
	World Bank and International Monetary Fund (IMF) founded		Cuban missile crisis
		1963	Betty Friedan's *The Feminine Mystique*
1947	Levittown, New York, built		Civil rights protest in Birmingham, Alabama
1953– 1958	Operation Wetback and Indian reservation termination programs		March on Washington
			Nuclear test-ban treaty
1954	*Brown v. Board of Education of Topeka*		John F. Kennedy assassinated; Lyndon B. Johnson assumes presidency
1955	AFL and CIO merge		
	Montgomery bus boycott	**1964**	Freedom Summer
			Civil Rights Act
1956	National Interstate and Defense Highway Act		Economic Opportunity Act inaugurates War on Poverty
1957	Peak of postwar baby boom		Johnson elected president
	School desegregation battle in Little Rock, Arkansas	**1965**	Immigration Act abolishes national quota system
	Southern Christian Leadership Conference (SCLC) founded		Civil rights march from Selma to Montgomery
1960	Sit-ins in Greensboro, North Carolina		Voting Rights Act
	John F. Kennedy elected president		Medicare and Medicaid programs established
1961	Peace Corps established		Elementary and Secondary Education Act
	Freedom rides		
	Bay of Pigs invasion		
	Berlin Wall erected		

For Further Exploration

Two engaging introductions to postwar society are Paul Boyer, *Promises to Keep* (1995), and James T. Patterson, *Grand Expectations* (1996). Elaine Tyler May, *Homeward Bound* (1988), is the classic introduction to postwar family life. For youth culture, see William Graebner, *Coming of Age in Buffalo* (1990). For insightful essays on the impact of television see Karal Ann Marling, *As Seen on TV* (1996). Powerful literary works of the period include Jack Kerouac, *On the Road* (1957); Allen Ginsberg, *Howl and Other Poems* (1996); and Arthur Miller, *Death of a Salesman* (1949). An excellent award-winning memoir of the Beat generation is Joyce Johnson, *Minor Characters* (1983). Good starting points for understanding Kennedy's presidency are W. J. Rorabaugh, *Kennedy and the Promise of the Sixties* (2002), and David Halberstam, *The Best and the Brightest* (1972). For Lyndon Johnson see Robert Dallek, *Flawed Giant* (1998), and Doris Kearns, *Lyndon Johnson and the American Dream* (1976). There are many engaging accounts of the civil rights movement, including Henry Hampton and Steve Fayer's oral history, *Voices of Freedom* (1991), and Harvard Sitkoff, *The Struggle for Black Equality* (2nd ed., 1993).

The John F. Kennedy Library and Museum's site at <http://www.jfklibrary.org/> provides a large collection of records from Kennedy's presidency. The Reference Desk area contains frequently requested information, including transcripts and recordings of JFK's speeches, a database of his executive orders, and a number of other resources. The Avalon Project at the Yale Law School's site, Foreign Relations of the United States: 1961–1963 Cuban Missile Crisis and Aftermath, at <http://www.yale.edu/lawweb/avalon/diplomacy/forrel/cuba/cubamenu.htm> contains almost three hundred official documents related to the crisis, including State Department memoranda, records of telephone conversations, transcripts of conversations in the White House, and CIA reports.

Civil Rights in Mississippi Digital Archive, at <http://www.lib.usm.edu/~spcol/crda/oh/index.html>, is maintained by the University of Southern Mississippi Center for Oral History. It offers 150 oral histories relating to the civil rights movement in Mississippi. Audio clips are also included, as are short biographies, photographs, newsletters, FBI documents, and arrest records.

Literary Kicks: The Beat Generation, at <http://www.charm.net/~brooklyn/LitKicks.html>, is an independent site created by New York writer Levi Asher devoted to the literature of the Beat generation. The site includes writings by Jack Kerouac, Allen Ginsberg, Neal Cassady, and others; material on Beats, music, religion, and film; an extensive bibliography; biographical information; and photographs.

For definitions of key terms boldfaced in this chapter, see the glossary at the end of the book.

To assess your mastery of the material covered in this chapter, see the Online Study Guide at **bedfordstmartins.com/henrettaconcise**.

For map resources and primary documents, see **bedfordstmartins.com/henrettaconcise**.

Chapter 29

WAR ABROAD AND AT HOME: THE VIETNAM ERA
1961–1975

In our excessive involvement in the affairs of other countries, we are not only living off our assets and denying our own people the proper enjoyment of their resources; we are also denying the world the example of a free society enjoying its freedom to the fullest. This is regrettable indeed for a nation that aspires to teach democracy to other nations.

SENATOR J. WILLIAM FULBRIGHT, 1966

On June 16, 1972, mourners assembled at Arlington National Cemetery for the funeral of John Paul Vann, a well-known army lieutenant colonel who had died in a helicopter crash in Vietnam. Though he supported the U.S. commitment to the war, Vann had publicly criticized the way it was being fought. Politicians and military leaders closely associated with the war effort—General William Westmoreland, Secretary of State William Rogers—were very much in evidence but so were Daniel Ellsberg, a former Pentagon official who had turned against the war, and Senator Edward Kennedy, another war opponent. Vann's family also showed the rifts over Vietnam. His wife, Mary Jane, requested her husband's favorite piece of music: the upbeat "Colonel Bogie March" from the film *The Bridge on the River Kwai* but added the haunting antiwar ballad "Where Have All the Flowers Gone?" to voice her own antiwar stance. One of his sons expressed his sentiments by tearing his draft card in two at the funeral, placing half of it on his father's casket. Although unusually public, the Vann funeral provides a dramatic example of the ruptures the Vietnam War brought to families, institutions, and the American social fabric.

Vietnam spawned a vibrant antiwar protest movement, which intersected with a broader youth movement that questioned traditional American political and cultural values. The challenges posed by youth, together with the revival of feminism, the rise of the black- and Chicano-power movements, the Kennedy and King assassinations, and explosive riots in the cities, produced a profound sense of social disorder at home. Vietnam split the Democratic Party and shattered the liberal consensus. The high monetary cost of the war diverted resources from domestic uses, spelling an end to the Great Society. Beyond its domestic impact the war wreaked extraordinary damage on Vietnam and undermined U.S. credibility abroad. For the first time average Americans began to question their assumptions about the nation's Cold War objectives and the beneficence of American foreign policy.

Into the Quagmire, 1945–1968

Like many new nations that emerged from the dissolution of European empires after World War II, Vietnam encompassed a volatile mix of nationalist sentiment, religious and cultural conflict, economic need, and political turmoil. The rise of communism there was just one phase of the nation's larger struggle, which would eventually climax in a bloody civil war. But American policymakers viewed these events through the lens of the Cold War, interpreting them as part of an international Communist movement toward global domination. Their failure to understand the complexity of Vietnam's internal conflicts led to a long and ultimately disastrous attempt to influence the course of the war.

America in Vietnam: From Truman to Kennedy

Vietnam had been part of the French colony of Indochina since the late nineteenth century but had been occupied by Japan during World War II. When the Japanese surrendered in August 1945, Ho Chi Minh and the Vietminh, the Communist nationalist group that had led Vietnamese resistance to the Japanese, with the encouragement of U.S. officials, took advantage of the resulting power vacuum. With words drawn from the American Declaration of Independence, Ho proclaimed an independent republic of Vietnam that September. The next year, when France rejected his claim and reasserted control over the country, an eight-year struggle ensued that the Vietminh called the Anti-French War of Resistance. Appealing to American anticolonial sentiment, Ho called on President Truman to support the struggle for Vietnamese independence. Truman ignored his pleas and instead offered covert financial support to the French, in hopes of stabilizing the politically chaotic region and rebuilding the French economy.

By the end of the decade Cold War developments had prompted the United States to step up its assistance to the French. After the Chinese revolution of 1949, the United States became concerned that China—along with the Soviet Union—might actively support anticolonial struggles in Asia and that newly independent countries might align themselves with the Communists. At the same time Republican charges that the Democrats had "lost" China influenced Truman to take a firmer stand against perceived Communist aggression in Korea and Vietnam. Truman also wanted to maintain good relations with France, whose support was crucial to the success of the new NATO alliance. Finally, Indochina played a strategic role in Secretary of State Dean Acheson's plans for an integrated Pacific Rim economy centered on a reindustrialized Japan.

For all these reasons, when the Soviet Union and the new Chinese leaders recognized Ho's republic early in 1950, the United States recognized the French-installed puppet government of Bao Dai. Subsequently, both the Truman and the Eisenhower administrations provided substantial military support to the French in Vietnam. President Eisenhower argued that such aid was essential to prevent the collapse of all non-Communist governments in the area, in a chain reaction he called the domino effect: "You have a row of dominoes set up, you knock over the first one, and what will happen to the last one is the certainty that it will go over very quickly."

Despite joint French-American efforts, the Vietminh forces gained strength in northern Vietnam. In the spring of 1954, they seized the isolated administrative fortress of Dienbienphu after a fifty-six-day siege. The spectacular victory gave the Vietminh negotiating leverage in the 1954 Geneva Accords, which partitioned Vietnam temporarily at the seventeenth parallel (Map 29.1) and committed France to withdraw its forces from the area north of that line. The accords also provided that within two years, in free elections, the voters in the two sectors would choose a unified government. The United States considered the agreements a "disaster," especially provisions for elections that it feared would be won by the Communists, and refused to sign the accords.

Eisenhower had no intention of allowing a Communist victory in Vietnam's upcoming election. With the help of the Central Intelligence Agency (CIA), he made sure that a pro-American government took power in South Vietnam in June 1954, just before the accords were signed. Ngo Dinh Diem, an anti-Communist Catholic who had spent eight years in the United States, returned to Vietnam as the premier of the French-backed South Vietnamese government. The next year, in a rigged election, Diem became president of an independent South Vietnam. Realizing that the popular Ho Chi Minh would easily win in both the North and the South, Diem called off the reunification elections that were scheduled for 1956—a move the United States supported.

In March 1956 the last French soldiers left Saigon, the capital of South Vietnam, and the United States replaced France as the dominant foreign power in the region. American policymakers quickly asserted that a non-Communist South Vietnam was vital to U.S. security interests. In reality, Vietnam was too small a country to upset the international balance of power, and its Communist movement was regional and nationalistic rather than directed by Moscow. Nevertheless, the Cold War consensus shared by Eisenhower and subsequent U.S. presidents saw Vietnam as part of the larger struggle to contain the Soviet Union and the Communist threat to the free world. Between 1955 and 1961 the Eisenhower administration sent Diem an average of $200 million a year in aid and stationed approximately 675 American military advisors in

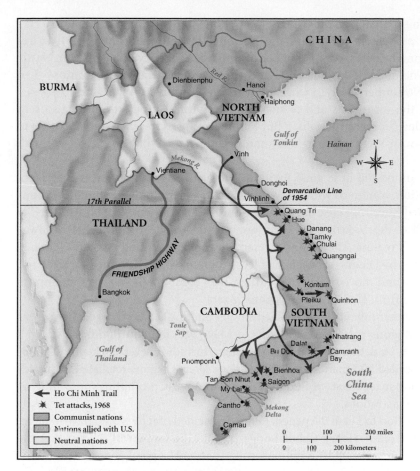

MAP 29.1 The Vietnam War, 1954–1975

The Vietnam War was a guerrilla war, fought in skirmishes and inconclusive encounters rather than decisive battles. Supporters of the National Liberation Front filtered into South Vietnam along the Ho Chi Minh Trail, which wound through Laos and Cambodia. In January 1968 Vietcong forces launched the Tet offensive, a surprise attack on several South Vietnamese cities and provincial centers. American vulnerability to these attacks served to undermine U.S. credibility and fueled opposition to the war. After a 1973 cease-fire was signed, the United States withdrew its troops, and in 1975 South Vietnam fell to the northern forces. The country was reunited under Communist rule in April of that year.

Saigon. Having stepped up U.S. involvement there considerably, Eisenhower left office, passing the Vietnam situation to his successor, John F. Kennedy.

President Kennedy saw Vietnam as an ideal testing ground for the counterinsurgency techniques that formed the centerpiece of his military policy (see Chapter 28). But he first had to prop up Diem's unpopular and repressive regime, which faced a growing military threat. In December 1960 the Communist Party in

North Vietnam organized most of Diem's opponents in South Vietnam into a revolutionary movement known as the National Liberation Front (NLF). In response, Kennedy increased the number of American military "advisors" (an elastic term that included helicopter units and special forces), raising it to more than 16,000 by November 1963. To win the "hearts and minds" of Vietnamese peasants away from the insurgents and to increase agricultural production, he also sent economic development specialists. But Kennedy refused to send combat troops to assist the South Vietnamese in what had become a guerrilla-style civil war with the North.

American aid did little good in South Vietnam. Diem's political inexperience and corruption, combined with his Catholicism in a predominantly Buddhist country, prevented him from creating a stable popular government. The NLF's guerrilla forces—called the Vietcong by their opponents—made considerable headway against Diem's regime. They found a receptive audience among peasants who had been alienated by Diem's "strategic hamlet" program, which uprooted families and whole villages and moved them into barbed-wire compounds in a vain attempt to separate them from Ho Chi Minh's sympathizers.

Anti-Diem sentiment also flourished among Buddhists, who charged the government with religious persecution. Starting in May 1963, militant Buddhists staged a dramatic series of demonstrations against Diem, including several self-immolations that were recorded by American television crews. Diem's regime retaliated with raids on temples and mass arrests of Buddhist priests in August, prompting more antigovernment demonstrations.

As opposition to Diem deepened, Kennedy decided that he would have to be removed. Ambassador Henry Cabot Lodge Jr. let it be known in Saigon that the United States would support a military coup that had "a good chance of succeeding." On November 1, 1963, Diem was driven from office and assassinated by officers in the South Vietnamese army. America's role in the coup reinforced the links between the United States and the new regime in South Vietnam, making the prospect of withdrawal from the region less acceptable to U.S. policymakers.

Less than a month later, Kennedy was assassinated. When Lyndon Johnson became president, he retained many of Kennedy's foreign-policy advisors and continued Kennedy's acceleration of U.S. involvement in the conflict. Afraid of sparking another round of McCarthy-style charges of being soft on communism, Johnson asserted that he was "not going to be the President who saw Southeast Asia go the way China went," and quickly declared he would maintain U.S. support for South Vietnam.

Escalation: The Johnson Years

The removal of Diem did not improve the viability of the Saigon government. Secretary of Defense Robert McNamara and other top advisors argued that only a rapid, full-scale deployment of U.S. forces could prevent the imminent defeat of the South Vietnamese. But Johnson would need at least tacit congressional support, perhaps even a declaration of war, to commit U.S. forces to an offensive strategy. During the summer of 1964, the president saw his opportunity to get congressional support to commit U.S. forces to an offensive strategy. American naval forces were conducting surveillance missions off the North Vietnamese coast to aid amphibious attacks by the South Vietnamese. When the North Vietnamese resisted the attacks, President Johnson told the nation that North Vietnamese torpedo boats had fired on American destroyers in international waters. At Johnson's request, Congress authorized him to "take all necessary measures to repel any armed attack against the forces of the United States and to prevent further aggression." On August 7 the Gulf of Tonkin resolution passed both houses of Congress overwhelmingly. Johnson's deceptive characterization of the unverified attack gave him a sweeping mandate to conduct operations in Vietnam as he saw fit. The only formal approval of American intervention in Vietnam that Congress ever granted, the Tonkin resolution represented a significant expansion of presidential power.

Once congressional support was assured and the 1964 elections had passed (see Chapter 28), the Johnson administration moved toward the total Americanization of the war with Operation Rolling Thunder, a protracted bombing campaign. Begun in March 1965, by 1968 it had dropped a million tons of bombs on North Vietnam. The several hundred captured American pilots downed in the raids then became pawns in negotiations with the North Vietnamese over the fate of prisoners of war.

To the amazement of American advisors, the bombing had little effect on the ability of the Vietnamese to wage war. The flow of troops and supplies to the South continued unabated as the North Vietnamese quickly rebuilt roads and bridges, moved munitions plants underground, and constructed a network of tunnels and shelters. Instead of destroying enemy morale and bringing the North Vietnamese to the bargaining table, Operation Rolling Thunder intensified their will to fight. The bombing continued nevertheless.

A week after the launch of Operation Rolling Thunder, the United States sent its first official ground troops into combat duty. Soon U.S. Marines were skirmishing with the enemy. Over the next three years, the number of American troops in Vietnam grew dramatically. Although U.S. troops were accompanied by military forces from Australia, New Zealand, and South Korea, the war increasingly became an American war, fought for American aims. By 1966 more than 380,000 American soldiers were stationed in Vietnam; by 1967, 485,000; and by 1968, 536,000.

The massive commitment of troops and air power threatened to destroy Vietnam's countryside. Besides the bombardment, a defoliation campaign had seriously damaged agricultural production, undercutting the economic and cultural base of Vietnamese society. After one devastating but not unusual engagement, a commanding officer reported, using the logic of the time, "It became necessary to destroy the town in order to save it." Graffiti on a plane that dropped defoliants read "Only you can prevent forests." (In later years defoliants such as Agent Orange were found to have highly toxic effects on both humans and the environment.) The destruction was not limited to North Vietnam; South Vietnam, America's ally,

The Longest War

American combat troops fought in Vietnam from 1965 to 1973, making it the longest war in the nation's history. Ambushed during a search-and-destroy mission, these soldiers await the arrival of a medical evacuation helicopter. The red smoke, produced by a grenade, designated the clearing in the jungle where the helicopter could land. More than 58,000 Americans lost their lives in the conflict, while another 300,000 were injured. © Tim Page / Corbis.

FOR MORE HELP ANALYZING THIS IMAGE, see the Online Study Guide at **bedfordstmartins.com/henrettaconcise**.

absorbed more than twice the bomb tonnage dropped on the North, as U.S. forces tried to flush out Vietcong sympathizers. In Saigon and other South Vietnamese cities, the influx of American soldiers and dollars distorted local economies, spread corruption and prostitution, and triggered uncontrollable inflation and black-market activity.

But the dramatically increased American presence in Vietnam failed to turn the tide of the war. Some advisors argued that military intervention could accomplish little without simultaneous reform in Saigon and increased popular support in the countryside. Other critics claimed that the United States never fully committed it-self to a "total victory"—although what that term meant was never settled. Military strategy was inextricably tied to political considerations. For domestic reasons policy-makers often searched for an elusive "middle ground" between all-out invasion of North Vietnam (and the possibility of sparking a nuclear exchange with China) and the politically unacceptable alternative of disengagement. Hoping to win a **war of attrition**, the Johnson administration assumed that American superiority in per-sonnel and weaponry would ultimately triumph. But that limited commitment was never enough to ensure victory—however it was defined.

American Soldiers' Perspectives on the War

Approximately 2.8 million Americans served in Vietnam. At an average age of only nineteen, most of those servicemen and -women were too young to vote or drink (the voting age was twenty-one until passage of the Twenty-sixth Amendment in 1971), but they were old enough to fight and die. Some were volunteers, including 7,000 women enlistees. Many others served because they were drafted. Until the nation shifted to an all-volunteer force in 1973, the draft stood as a concrete re-minder of the government's impact on the lives of ordinary Americans. Blacks were drafted and died roughly in the same proportion as their share of the draft-age population (about 12 to 13 percent), although early in the war black casualty rates were significantly higher than average. Even more than in other recent wars, sons of the poor and the working class shouldered a disproportionate amount of the fighting, forming an estimated 80 percent of the enlisted ranks. Young men from more affluent backgrounds were more likely to avoid combat through stu-dent deferments, medical exemptions, and appointments to National Guard and reserve units—alternatives that made Johnson's Vietnam policy more acceptable to the middle class.

At first many draftees and enlistees, children of the Cold War, shared common assumptions about the need to fight communism and the superiority of the American military. However, their experience in Vietnam quickly challenged simple notions of patriotism and the inevitability of victory (see American Voices, "A Vietnam Vet Remembers," p. 888). In "Nam" long days of boring menial work were punctuated by brief flashes of intense fighting. "Most of the time, nothing happened," a soldier recalled, "but when something did, it happened instantaneously and without warning." Rarely were there large-scale battles as in World War II, only skirmishes; rather than front lines and conquered territory, there were only daytime operations in areas the Vietcong controlled at night.

Racism was a fact of everyday life. Because differentiating between friendly South Vietnamese and Vietcong sympathizers was difficult, many soldiers lumped them together as "gooks." As a draftee noted of his indoctrination, "The only thing they told us about the Vietcong was they were gooks. They were to be killed. Nobody

AMERICAN VOICES

A Vietnam Vet Remembers

DAVE CLINE

B orn in 1947, Dave Cline grew up in a working-class family outside Buffalo, New York. *Drafted by the army in 1967, Cline was eager to help fight Communist aggression in Vietnam. But after his arrival in Da Nang seven months later, his attitude toward the war quickly changed. Cline described this transformation in an interview conducted in 1992.*

I went to basic training at Fort Dix. . . . Down there, they used to give you basically two raps on why you were going to Vietnam. One was that rap about we're going to help the heroic South Vietnamese people. We're going to go fight for freedom [and repel] communist aggression. They'd show you the maps and stuff, the domino theory, the Red Chinese are trying to engulf all of southeast Asia. The other rap was: killing communists was your duty. . . .

First thing you do when you get in-country is, they give you these indoctrination classes and they say, "Forget all that shit they told; you can't trust any of these people. They're not really people anyway; they're gooks." . . . In other words: You see anyone with slant eyes, that's your potential enemy—don't trust them. That sort of blows away any "help the people" thing. . . .

I got wounded the last time out near the Cambodian border. This happened on December 20, 1967. . . . The north Vietnamese launched a massive human wave attack. . . .

A guy came running up to my foxhole. We saw him coming from the next hole over and we didn't know if it was an American retreating over to us or a Vietnamese, because it was two in the morning. . . . I was sitting there with my rifle waiting to see, and all of a sudden he stuck his rifle in. I saw the front side of an AK-47 and a muzzle flash, and then I pulled my trigger. I shot him through the chest. I blacked out initially, but then I came to and found a round went right through my knee. . . .

They carried me over to this guy I had shot. . . . He was dead. The sergeant started giving me this pep talk, "Here's the gook you killed!" . . .

The kid looked about the same age as me. The first thing I started thinking was, Why is he dead and I'm alive? . . .

Then after going into the hospital, I started thinking about that guy. I wonder if his mother knows he's dead? I wonder if he had a girlfriend? Looking back, I think I was retaining the sense that he was a human being.

SOURCE: *Winter Soldiers: An Oral History of the Vietnam Veterans Against the War* by Richard Stacewicz. Copyright 1997, Twayne Publishers. Reprinted by permission of the Gale Group.

sits around and gives you their historical and cultural background. They're the enemy. Kill, kill, kill."

Fighting and surviving under such conditions took its toll. One veteran explained that "the hardest thing to come to grips with was the fact that making it through Vietnam—surviving—is probably the only worthwhile part of the experience. It wasn't going over there and saving the world from communism or defending the country." Cynicism and bitterness were common. The pressure of waging war under such conditions drove many soldiers to seek escape in alcohol or drugs, which were cheap and readily available.

The women who served in Vietnam shared many of these experiences. As WACs, nurses, and civilians serving with organizations such as the USO, women volunteers witnessed death and mutilation on a massive scale. Though they tried to maintain a professional distance, as a navy nurse recalled, "It's pretty damn hard not getting involved when you see a nineteen- or twenty-year-old blond kid from the Midwest or California or the East Coast screaming and dying. A piece of my heart would go with each."

The Cold War Consensus Unravels

In the twenty years following World War II, despite widespread affluence and confidence in the nation's Cold War leadership, there had emerged a variety of challenges to the status quo. From the nonconforming Beats came a critical assault on corporate capitalism. Teenagers' embrace of rock 'n' roll defied the cultural norms of their elders. African Americans' boycotts, sit-ins, and freedom rides signaled a rising wind of protest against racial injustice (see Chapter 28). By 1965 such angry expressions of disaffection from mainstream America had multiplied dramatically. Criticism of the war in Vietnam mounted, as youthful protesters rebelled against traditional respect for the "system." The civil rights movement took on a more militant thrust and expanded beyond African Americans to other minority groups, while the feminist movement revived to challenge social values and the family structure itself. Together the various movements forced Americans to reassess basic assumptions about the nature of their society.

Public Opinion on Vietnam

President Kennedy and at first President Johnson enjoyed broad support for their conduct of foreign affairs. Both Democrats and Republicans approved Johnson's escalation of the war, and public opinion polls in 1965 and 1966 showed strong popular support for his policies. But in the late 1960s, public opinion began to turn against the war. In July 1967 a Gallup poll revealed that for the first time a majority of Americans disapproved of Johnson's Vietnam policy and believed the war had reached a stalemate. Television had much to do with these attitudes. Vietnam was

A Televised War

This harrowing scene from Saigon during the Tet offensive in 1968 was broadcast on U.S. network news. The NBC bureau chief described the film in a terse telex message: "A VC officer was captured. The troops beat him. They bring him to [Brigadier General Nguyen Ngoc] Loan who is head of South Vietnamese national police. Loan pulls out his pistol, fires at the head of the VC, the VC falls, zoom on his head, blood spraying out. If he has it all it's startling stuff." Wide World Photos, Inc.

the first war in which television brought film of the fighting directly into the nation's living rooms.

Despite the glowing reports filed by the media and the administration on the progress of the war, by 1967 many administration officials had privately reached a more pessimistic conclusion. In November Secretary of Defense Robert McNamara sent a memo to the president arguing that continued escalation "would be dangerous, costly in lives, and unsatisfactory to the American people," but President Johnson refused to break with the Cold War consensus and insisted that victory in Vietnam was vital to U.S. national security and prestige. Journalists, especially those who had spent time in Vietnam, soon began to warn that the Johnson administration suffered from a "credibility gap." The administration, they charged, was concealing important and discouraging information about the war's progress. In February 1966 television coverage of hearings by the Senate Foreign Relations Committee (chaired by J. William Fulbright, an outspoken critic of the war) raised further questions about the administration's policy.

Economic developments put Johnson and his advisors even more on the defensive. In 1966 the federal deficit was $9.8 billion; in 1967 the Vietnam War cost the taxpayers $27 billion, and the deficit jumped to $23 billion. Although the war consumed just 3 percent of the gross national product (GNP), its costs became more evident as the growing federal deficit nudged the inflation rate upward. Only in the summer of 1967 did Johnson ask for a 10 percent surcharge on individual and corporate income taxes, an increase that Congress did not approve until 1968. By then the inflationary spiral that would plague the U.S. economy throughout the 1970s was well under way.

As a result of these troubling political and economic developments, more Americans began to question the war effort in Vietnam. After the escalation in the spring of 1965, various antiwar coalitions, swelled by growing numbers of students, clergy, housewives, politicians, artists, and others opposed to the war, organized several mass demonstrations in Washington, bringing out 20,000 to 30,000 people at a time. Participants in these rallies shared a common skepticism about the means and aims of U.S. policy. The war was morally wrong, they argued, and antithetical to American ideals; the goal of an independent, anti-Communist South Vietnam was unattainable; and American military involvement would not help the Vietnamese people.

Student Activism

Youth were among the key protesters of the era. Not all youth challenged authority in the 1960s, but those who did had a powerful impact. It was black college students in Greensboro, North Carolina, who sparked the wave of sit-ins that did so much to challenge segregation in the South (see Chapter 28). Inspired by their model and galvanized by the struggle for racial justice, white students—many of whom had been raised in a privileged environment, showered with consumer goods, and inculcated with faith in American institutions and leaders—began to question U.S. foreign and domestic policy and middle-class morals and conformity.

In June 1962 forty students from Big Ten and Ivy League universities, disturbed by the gap they perceived between the ideals they had been taught to revere and the realities in American life, met in Port Huron, Michigan, to found Students for a Democratic Society (SDS). Tom Hayden wrote their manifesto, the Port Huron Statement, which expressed their disillusionment with the consumer culture and the gulf between the prosperous and the poor. These students rejected Cold War ideology and foreign policy, including but not limited to the Vietnam conflict. The founders of SDS referred to their movement as the "New Left" to distinguish themselves from the "Old Left"—Communists and Socialists of the 1930s and 1940s. Consciously adopting the activist tactics pioneered by members of the civil rights movement, they turned to grassroots organizing in cities and on college campuses.

The first major student demonstrations erupted in the fall of 1964 at the University of California at Berkeley, after administrators banned political activity in Sproul Plaza, where student groups had traditionally distributed leaflets and recruited volunteers. In protest the major student organizations formed a coalition called the Free Speech Movement (FSM) and organized a sit-in at the administration building. The FSM owed a strong debt to the civil rights movement. Some students had just returned from Freedom Summer in Mississippi, radicalized by their experience. Mario Savio spoke for many of them when he compared the conflict in Berkeley to what was happening in the South: "The same rights are at stake in both places—the right to participate as citizens in a democratic society and to struggle against the same enemy." Emboldened by the Berkeley movement, students across the nation were soon protesting their universities' academic policies and then, more passionately, the Vietnam War.

Many protests centered on the draft, especially after the Selective Service system abolished automatic student deferments in January 1966. To avoid the draft some young men enlisted in the National Guard or the reserves; others declared themselves conscientious objectors. Several thousand young men ignored their induction notices, risking prosecution for draft evasion. Others left the country, most often for Canada or Sweden. In public demonstrations of civil disobedience, opponents of the war burned their draft cards, closed down induction centers, and on a few occasions broke into Selective Service offices and destroyed records.

As antiwar and draft protests multiplied, students realized that their universities were deeply implicated in the war effort. In some cases as much as 60 percent of a university's research budget came from government contracts, especially those of the Defense Department. Protesters blocked recruiters from the Dow Chemical Company, the producer of napalm and Agent Orange. Arguing that universities should not train students for war, they demanded that the Reserve Officer Training Corps (ROTC) be removed from college campuses.

After 1967, nationwide student strikes, mass demonstrations, and other organized protests became commonplace. In October 1967 more than 100,000 antiwar demonstrators marched on Washington, D.C., as part of "Stop the Draft Week." The event culminated in a "siege of the Pentagon," in which protesters clashed with police and federal marshals. Hundreds of people were arrested and several demonstrators beaten. Lyndon Johnson, who had once dismissed antiwar protesters as "nervous Nellies," rebellious children, or Communist dupes, now had to face the reality of large-scale public opposition to his policies.

The Counterculture

While the New Left took to the streets in protest, a growing number of young Americans embarked on a general revolution against authority and middle-class respectability. The "hippie"—attired in ragged blue jeans, tie-dyed T-shirt, beads, and army fatigues, with long, unkempt hair—symbolized the new counterculture, a youthful movement that glorified liberation from traditional social strictures.

Not surprisingly, given the importance of rock 'n' roll to 1950s youth culture, popular music helped define the counterculture. Folksinger Pete Seeger set the tone for the era's political idealism with songs such as the antiwar ballad "Where Have All the Flowers Gone?" Another folksinger, Joan Baez, gained national prominence for her rendition of the African American protest song "We Shall Overcome" and other folk and political anthems she performed at protest rallies in the mid-1960s. In 1963, the year of the Birmingham demonstrations and President Kennedy's assassination, Bob Dylan's "Blowin' in the Wind" reflected the impatience of people whose faith in "the system" was wearing thin.

Other winds of change in popular music came from the Beatles, four English working-class youths who burst onto the American scene early in 1964. The Beatles' music, by turns lyrical and driving, was remarkably successful, spawning a commercial and cultural phenomenon called "Beatlemania." American youths' eager embrace of the Beatles deepened the generational divide between teenagers and their elders already set in motion by the popularity of rock 'n' roll in the 1950s. The Beatles also helped to pave the way for the more rebellious, angrier music of other British groups, notably the Rolling Stones.

Drugs intertwined with music as a crucial element of the youth culture. Their recreational use of drugs—especially marijuana and lysergic acid diethylamide, the hallucinogen popularly known as LSD or "acid"—was celebrated in popular music. San Francisco bands such as the Grateful Dead and Jefferson Airplane and musicians like the Seattle-born guitarist Jimi Hendrix developed a musical style known as "acid rock," which was characterized by long, heavily amplified guitar solos accompanied by psychedelic lighting effects. In August 1969, 400,000 young people journeyed to Bethel, New York, to "get high" on music, drugs, and sex at the three-day Woodstock Music and Art Fair. Despite torrential rain and numerous drug overdoses, most enjoyed the festival, the biggest of its kind to date.

For a brief time adherents of the counterculture believed a new age was dawning. They experimented in communal living and glorified uninhibited sexuality. In 1967 the "world's first Human Be-In" drew 20,000 people to Golden Gate Park in San Francisco. The Beat poet Allen Ginsberg "purified" the site with a Buddhist ritual, and the LSD advocate Timothy Leary, a former Harvard psychology instructor, urged the gathering to "turn on to the scene, tune in to what is happening, and drop out." That summer—dubbed the "Summer of Love"—San Francisco's Haight-Ashbury, New York's East Village, and Chicago's Uptown neighborhoods swelled with young dropouts, drifters, and teenage runaways dubbed "flower children" by observers. Their faith in instant love and peace quickly turned sour, however, as they suffered bad drug trips, sexually transmitted diseases, loneliness, and violence. Although many young people kept their distance from both the counterculture and the antiwar movement, extensive media coverage made it seem to many adult observers that all of American youth were rejecting political, social, and cultural norms.

The Widening Struggle for Civil Rights

The counterculture and the antiwar movement were not the only social movements to challenge the status quo in the 1960s. The frustration and anger of blacks boiled over in a new racial militance as the civil rights struggle moved outside the South

Jimi Hendrix at Woodstock

The three-day outdoor "Woodstock" concert in August 1969 was a defining moment in the counterculture as 400,000 young people journeyed to Bethel, New York, for music, drugs, and sex. Jimi Hendrix closed the show with an electrifying version of "The Star-Spangled Banner." More overtly political than most counterculture music, Hendrix's rendition featured sound effects that seemed to evoke the violence of the Vietnam War. Michael Wadleigh, who directed the documentary *Woodstock*, called Hendrix's performance "his challenge to American foreign policy."

Allan Koss / Image Bank.

and took on the more stubborn problems of entrenched poverty and racism. The rhetoric and tactics of the emerging black-power movement shattered the existing civil rights coalition and galvanized white opposition.

Once the system of legal, or *de jure*, segregation had fallen (see Chapter 28), the civil rights movement turned to the more difficult task of eliminating the *de facto* segregation, enforced by custom, that made blacks second-class citizens throughout the nation. Outside the South racial discrimination was less flagrant, but it was pervasive, especially in education, housing, and employment. Although the *Brown* decision outlawed separate schools, it did nothing to change the educational system in areas where schools were all black or all white because of residential segregation. Not until 1973 did federal judges begin to extend the desegregation of schools, which had begun in the South two decades earlier, to the rest of the country.

As civil rights leaders confronted northern racism, the movement fractured along generational lines. Some younger activists, eager for confrontation and rapid change, questioned the very goal of integration into white society. Black separatism, espoused by earlier black leaders such as Marcus Garvey in the 1920s (see Chapter 23), was revived in the 1960s by the Nation of Islam, a religious group with more than 10,000 members and many more sympathizers. Popularly known as the Black Muslims, the organization was hostile to whites and stressed black pride, unity, and self-help.

The Black Muslims' most charismatic figure was Malcolm X. A brilliant debater and spellbinding speaker, Malcolm X preached a philosophy quite different from Martin Luther King's. He advocated militant protest and separatism, though he condoned the use of violence only for self-defense. Hostile to the traditional civil rights organizations, he caustically referred to the 1963 March on Washington as the "Farce on Washington." In 1964, after a power struggle with the founder of the Black Muslims, Elijah Muhammad, Malcolm X broke with the Nation of Islam. Following a pilgrimage to Mecca and a tour of Africa, he embraced the liberation struggles of all colonized peoples. But before he could fully pursue his new agenda, he was assassinated while delivering a speech at the Audubon Ballroom in Harlem on February 21, 1965. Three Black Muslims were later convicted of his murder.

A more secular black nationalist movement emerged in 1966 when young black SNCC and CORE activists, following the lead of Stokely Carmichael, began to call for black self-reliance and racial pride under the banner of "Black Power." Amid growing distrust of white domination, SNCC ejected its white members. In the same year Huey Newton and Bobby Seale, two college students in Oakland, California, founded the Black Panthers, a militant self-defense organization dedicated to protecting local blacks from police violence. The Panthers' organization quickly spread to other cities, where members undertook a wide range of community organizing projects, including interracial efforts, but their affinity for Third World revolutionary movements and armed struggle became their most publicized attribute.

Among the most significant legacies of black power was the assertion of racial pride. Many young blacks insisted on using the term *Afro-American* rather than *Negro,* a term they found demeaning because of its historical association with slavery and racism. Rejecting white tastes and standards, blacks wore African clothing and hairstyles and helped to awaken interest in black history, art, and literature. By the 1970s many colleges and universities were offering programs in black studies.

The new black assertiveness alarmed many white Americans. They had been willing to go along with the moderate reforms of the 1950s and early 1960s but became wary when blacks began demanding immediate access to higher-paying jobs, housing in white neighborhoods, proactive integration of public schools, and increased political power. Another major reason for the erosion of white support was a wave of riots that struck the nation's cities. Lacking education and skills, successive generations of blacks had moved out of the rural South in search of work that

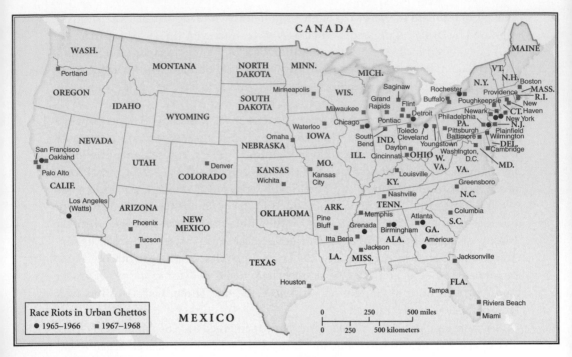

MAP 29.2 Racial Unrest in America's Cities, 1965–1968

American cities suffered through four "long hot summers" of rioting in the mid-1960s. In 1967, the worst year, riots broke out across the United States, including numerous locations in the South and the West. The riots' major impact on white America was to create a climate of fear that helped drain support from the larger civil rights movement.

FOR MORE HELP ANALYZING THIS MAP, see the Online Study Guide at **bedfordstmartins.com/henrettaconcise**.

paid an adequate wage. In the North many remained unemployed. Resentful of white landlords, who owned the substandard housing they were forced to live in, and white shopkeepers, who denied them jobs in their neighborhoods, many blacks also hated police, whose violent presence in black neighborhoods seemed that of "an occupying army."

The first "long hot summer" began in July 1964 in New York City, when police shot a young black criminal suspect in Harlem. Angry youths looted and rioted there for a week. Over the next four years, the volatile issue of police brutality set off riots in dozens of cities. In August 1965 the arrest of a young black motorist in the Watts section of Los Angeles sparked six days of rioting that left thirty-four blacks dead. The riots of 1967 were the most serious, engulfing twenty-two cities in July and August (Map 29.2). The most devastating outbreaks occurred in Newark and Detroit. Forty-three people were killed in Detroit alone, nearly all of them black, and $50 million worth of property was destroyed.

On July 29, 1967, President Johnson appointed a special commission to investigate the riots. The final report of the National Advisory Commission on Civil Disorders (also known as the Kerner Commission), released in March 1968, detailed the continuing inequality and racism of urban life. It also issued a warning: "Our nation is moving toward two societies, one black, one white—separate and unequal. . . . What white Americans have never fully understood—but what the Negro can never forget—is that white society is deeply implicated in the ghetto. White institutions created it, white institutions maintain it, and white society condones it."

On April 4, 1968, barely a month after the Kerner Commission released its report, Martin Luther King Jr. was assassinated in Memphis, Tennessee, where he had gone to support a strike by predominantly black sanitation workers. King's death set off an explosion of urban rioting, with major violence breaking out in more than a hundred cities. At the time of his death, King was only thirty-nine years old. During the last years of his life, he had moved toward a broader view of the structural problems of poverty and racism faced by blacks in contemporary America. He spoke out eloquently against the Vietnam War, and in 1968 he was planning a poor people's campaign to raise issues of economic injustice and inequality. With King's assassination, the civil rights movement lost the black leader best able to stir the conscience of white America.

King had lived to see permanent, indeed revolutionary, changes in American race relations. Jim Crow segregation was overturned and federal legislation passed to ensure protection of black Americans' most basic civil rights. The enfranchisement of blacks in the southern states ended political control by all-white state Democratic Parties and allowed black candidates to enter the political arena. White candidates who had once been ardent segregationists began to court the black vote. In time Martin Luther King Jr.'s greatness was recognized even among whites in the South; in 1986 his birthday became a national holiday. Yet much remained undone. The more entrenched forms of segregation and discrimination persisted. African Americans, particularly those in the central cities, continued to make up a disproportionate number of the poor, the unemployed, and the undereducated. As the civil rights movement gradually splintered, its agenda remained unfinished.

The Rights Revolution

Despite its limitations, the black civil rights movement provided an innovative model for social change. Although Mexican Americans had been working actively for civil rights since the 1930s (see Chapter 24), poverty, an uncertain legal status, and language barriers made their political mobilization difficult. That situation began to change when the Mexican American Political Association (MAPA) mobilized support for John F. Kennedy. Over the next four years, MAPA and other organizations worked successfully to elect Mexican American candidates such as Edward Roybal of California and Henry González of Texas to Congress.

Younger Mexican Americans quickly grew impatient with MAPA, however. The barrios of Los Angeles and other western cities produced the militant Brown Berets, modeled on the Black Panthers (who wore black berets). Rejecting the assimilationist approach of their elders, 1,500 Mexican American students met in Denver in 1969 to hammer out a new nationalist political and cultural agenda. They proclaimed a new term, *Chicano*, to replace *Mexican American*, and later organized a new political party, La Raza Unida (The United Race), to promote Chicano interests and candidates. In California and other southwestern states, students staged demonstrations and boycotts to press for bilingual education, the hiring of more Chicano teachers, and the creation of Chicano studies programs. By the 1970s dozens of such programs were offered at universities throughout the region.

Chicano strategists also pursued economic objectives. Working in the fields around Delano, California, labor leader César Chávez organized the United Farm Workers (UFW), the first union to represent migrant workers successfully. A 1965 grape pickers' strike and a nationwide boycott of table grapes brought Chávez and his union national publicity and won support from the AFL-CIO and from Senator Robert F. Kennedy of New York. Victory came in 1970 when California grape growers signed contracts recognizing the UFW.

North American Indians also found a model in the civil rights movement. Numbering nearly 800,000 in the 1960s, Native Americans were an exceedingly diverse group, divided by language, tribal history, region, and degree of integration into the mainstream of American life. The termination policy that had begun in the 1950s had accelerated the breakdown of tribal life and the dispersal of Native American populations. As a group, they shared an unemployment rate ten times the national average as well as the worst poverty, the most inadequate housing, the highest disease rates, and the least access to education of any group in the United States.

As early as World War II, the National Congress of American Indians had lobbied for reform. In the 1960s some Indian groups became more assertive. Like the young militants in the black civil rights movement, they challenged the accommodationist approach of their elders. Proposing a new name for themselves— Native Americans— and embracing the concept of "Red Power," they organized protests and demonstrations to build support for their cause. In 1968 several Chippewas from Minnesota organized the militant American Indian Movement (AIM).

In November 1969 a group calling themselves "Indians of All Tribes" seized the deserted federal penitentiary on Alcatraz Island in San Francisco Bay, offering the government $24 worth of trinkets to pay for it, supposedly the sum the Dutch had paid the native inhabitants for Manhattan Island in 1626. The occupation of Alcatraz lasted until the summer of 1971. A year later a thousand protesters occupied the headquarters of the Federal Bureau of Indian Affairs in Washington, D.C., which was to many Native Americans a hated symbol of the inconsistent federal policy on tribal welfare (see American Voices, "The Trail of Broken Treaties," p. 899).

AMERICAN VOICES

The Trail of Broken Treaties

MARY CROW DOG

*I*n November 1972, nineteen-year-old Mary Crow Dog traveled to Washington, D.C., with several hundred other Sioux from the Rosebud and Pine Ridge reservations in South Dakota. As she explains in her autobiography, their group was one of several caravans participating in a protest known as the Trail of Broken Treaties, which ended in a six-day occupation of the Bureau of Indian Affairs (BIA) headquarters. Their demands included restoration of native lands and resources, reinstitution of the treaty-making rights of the Indian Nations, and replacement of the BIA with an agency more attuned to their rights and cultures.

We had been promised food and accommodation, but due to government pressure many church groups which had offered to put us up and feed us got scared and backed off. . . .

Somebody suggested, "Let's all go to the BIA." It seemed the natural thing to do, to go to the Bureau of Indian Affairs building on Constitution Avenue. . . . It was "our" building after all. Besides, that was what we had come for, to complain about the treatment the bureau was dishing out to us. . . . Next thing I knew we were in it. We spilled into the building like a great avalanche. Some people put up a tipi on the front lawn. . . . The building finally belonged to us and we lost no time turning it into a tribal village. . . .

We pushed the police and guards out of the building. . . . We had formulated twenty Indian demands. These were all rejected by the few bureaucrats sent to negotiate with us. . . . Soon we listened to other voices as the Occupation turned into a siege. I heard somebody yelling, "The pigs are here." . . . A fight broke out between the police and our security. Some of our young men got hit over the head with police clubs and we saw the blood streaming down their faces. . . .

From then on, every morning we were given a court order to get out by six P.M. Come six o'clock and we would be standing there ready to join battle. I think many brothers and sisters were prepared to die right on the steps of the BIA building. . . .

In the end a compromise was reached. The government said . . . they would appoint two high administration officials to seriously consider our twenty demands. . . . Of course, our twenty points were never gone into afterward. . . . But morally it had been a great victory. We had faced White America collectively, not as individual tribes. We had stood up to the government and gone through our baptism of fire.

SOURCE: Mary Crow Dog, *Lakota Woman* (New York: Grove Weidenfeld, 1990), 84–85, 88–91.

In February 1973, 200 Sioux organized by AIM leaders began an occupation of the tiny village of Wounded Knee, South Dakota, the site of an army massacre of the Sioux in 1890 (see Chapter 16). They were protesting the light sentences given white men convicted of killing a Sioux in 1972. The protesters took eleven hostages and occupied several buildings. But when a gun battle with the FBI left one protester

Wounded Knee Revisited

In 1973 members of the American Indian Movement staged a seventy-one-day protest at Wounded Knee, South Dakota, the site of the 1890 massacre of 200 Sioux by U.S. soldiers. (See Map 16.2, The Sioux Reservations in South Dakota, 1868–1889, p. 488.) The takeover was sparked by the murder of a local Sioux by a group of whites but quickly expanded to include demands for basic reforms in federal Indian policy and tribal governance. © Bettmann / Corbis.

dead and another wounded, the seventy-one-day siege collapsed. Although the new Native American activism helped to alienate many white onlookers, it did spur government action on tribal issues (see Chapter 30).

Civil rights activism also sparked a new awareness among some predominantly white groups. Americans of Polish, Italian, Greek, and Slavic descent, most of them working class and Catholic, proudly embraced their ethnic identities. Through groups like the Grey Panthers, elderly Americans organized to demand better health, Social Security, and other benefits. Homosexual men and women also banded together to protest legal and social oppression based on their sexual orientation. In 1969 the gay liberation movement gained momentum in the "Stonewall riot" in New York City, when patrons of a gay bar fought back against police harassment. The assertion of gay pride that followed the incident drew heavily on the language and tactics of the civil rights movement. Activists took the new name of *gay* rather than *homosexual*; founded advocacy groups, newspapers, and political organizations to challenge discrimination and prejudice; and offered emotional support to those who "came out" and publicly affirmed their homosexuality. For gays as well as members of various ethnic and cultural groups, political activism based on heightened group identity represented one of the most significant legacies of the African American struggle.

The Revival of Feminism

The black civil rights movement also helped to reactivate feminism, a movement that had been languishing since the 1920s. Just as the abolition movement had been the training ground for women's rights advocates in the nineteenth century, the black struggle became an inspiration for young feminists in the 1960s. But the revival of feminism also sprang from social and demographic changes that affected women young and old. By 1970, 42.6 percent of women were working, and four out of ten working women were married. Especially significant was the growth in the number of working women with preschool children—up from 12 percent in 1950 to 30 percent in 1970.

Another significant change was increased access to education for women. Immediately after World War II, the percentage of college students who were women declined, as the GI Bill gave men a temporary advantage in access to higher education. At the height of the baby boom, many college women dropped out of school to marry and raise families. By 1960, however, the percentage of college students who were women had risen to 35 percent; in 1970 it reached 41 percent (by 2004 women had become a majority).

The meaning of marriage was changing, too. The baby boom was only a temporary interruption of a century-long decline in the birthrate. The introduction of the birth control pill, first marketed in 1960, and the intrauterine device (IUD) helped women control their fertility. Women had fewer children, and because of an increased life expectancy (seventy-five years in 1970, up from fifty-four years in 1920), they devoted proportionally fewer years to raising children. At the same time the divorce rate, which had risen slowly throughout the twentieth century, rose markedly as the states liberalized divorce laws. These changes undermined traditional gender expectations. American women's lives now usually included work and marriage, often childrearing and a career, and possibly bringing up children alone after a divorce. Those changing social realities created a major constituency for the emerging women's movement of the 1960s.

Older, politically active professional women sought change by working through the political system. This group was galvanized in part by a report by the Presidential Commission on the Status of Women (1963), which documented the employment and educational discrimination women faced. More important than the report's rather conservative recommendations was the rudimentary nationwide network of women in public life that formed in the course of the commission's work.

Another spark that ignited the revival of feminism was Betty Friedan's pointed indictment of suburban domesticity, *The Feminine Mystique*, published in 1963 (see Chapter 28). White, college-educated, middle-class women particularly responded enthusiastically to Friedan's book. The book sold 3 million copies and was excerpted in many women's magazines. *The Feminine Mystique* gave women a vocabulary with which to express their dissatisfaction and promoted women's self-realization through employment, continuing education, and other activities outside the home.

Like so many other constituencies in postwar America, women's rights activists looked to the federal government for help. The Civil Rights Act of 1964 had as great an impact on women as it did on blacks and other minorities. Title VII, which barred discrimination in employment on the basis of race, religion, national origin, or sex, eventually became a powerful tool in the fight against sex discrimination. At first, however, the Equal Employment Opportunity Commission (EEOC) avoided implementing it. Dissatisfied with the commission's reluctance to defend women's rights, Friedan and others founded the National Organization for Women (NOW) in 1966. Modeled on the NAACP, NOW aimed to be a civil rights organization for women. Under Friedan, who served as NOW's first president, membership grew from 1,000 in 1967 to 15,000 in 1971. Men made up a fourth of NOW's early membership. The group is still the largest feminist organization in the United States.

Another group of new feminists, the women's liberationists, came to the women's movement through their civil rights work. White college women had made up about half the students who went south with SNCC in the Freedom Summer project of 1964. These women developed self-confidence and organizational skills working in the South, and they found role models in older southern women like Ella Baker and Virginia Foster Durr, who were prominent in the civil rights movement. Yet women volunteers also began to question what would later be called the sexism of the male-dominated leadership.

After 1965 black militants made whites unwelcome in the civil rights movement. But when white women transferred their energies to the antiwar groups that were emerging in that period, they found the New Left even more male dominated. When the antiwar movement adopted draft resistance as a central strategy, women found themselves marginalized. Those women who tried to raise feminist issues at conventions were shouted off the platform with jeers such as "Move on, little girl, we have more important issues to talk about here than women's liberation."

Around 1967 the contradiction between the New Left's lip service to egalitarianism and women's treatment by male leaders caused women radicals to realize that they needed their own movement. In contrast to groups such as NOW, which had traditional organizational structures and dues-paying members, these women formed loose collectives whose shifting membership often lacked any formal structure. They organized independently in five or six different cities, including Chicago, San Francisco, and New York.

Members of the women's liberation movement (or "women's lib," as it was dubbed by the somewhat hostile media) went public in 1968 in a protest at the Miss America pageant. Their demonstration featured a "freedom trash can" into which they encouraged women to throw false eyelashes, hair curlers, brassieres, and girdles—all of which they branded as symbols of female oppression. An activity with a more lasting impact was "consciousness raising"—group sessions in which women shared their experiences of being female. Swapping stories about being passed over for a promotion, needing a husband's signature on a credit card application, or enduring the whistles and leers of men while walking down the street helped participants to realize that their individual problems were part of a wider pattern of oppression.

Women's Liberation

Arguing that beauty contests were degrading to women, members of the National Women's Liberation Party staged a protest against the Miss America pageant held in Atlantic City, New Jersey, in September 1968. Wide World Photos, Inc.

By 1970 a growing convergence of interests began to blur the distinction between women's rights and women's liberation. Radical women realized that key feminist goals—child care, equal pay, and abortion rights—could best be achieved in the political arena. At the same time more traditional activists developed a broader view of the women's movement, tentatively including divisive issues such as abortion and lesbian rights. Although the movement remained largely white and middle class, feminists were beginning to think of themselves as part of a broad, growing, and increasingly influential social crusade that would continue to grow.

The Long Road Home, 1968–1975

The United States in 1968 was deeply polarized. Riots in the cities, black and Chicano power, campus unrest, and a host of protests and challenges were, in the eyes of many citizens, tearing the country in two. But Vietnam remained the central domestic and foreign-policy issue, and the war became the prism through which many of the nation's ills came to be seen. Although the Johnson administration insisted that there was "light at the end of the tunnel," the reality was otherwise. The war would continue, at home and in Vietnam, for another five years.

1968: A Year of Shocks

In 1968, as Lyndon Johnson planned his reelection campaign, antiwar protests and rising battlefield casualties had begun to erode public support for a war that seemed to have no end. Since Diem's assassination in 1963, South Vietnam had undergone a confusing series of military coups and countercoups. In the spring of 1966, the Johnson administration pressured the unpopular South Vietnamese government to adopt democratic reforms, including a new constitution and popular elections. In September 1967 U.S. officials helped to elect General Nguyen Van Thieu president of South Vietnam. Thieu's regime, the administration hoped, would stabilize politics in South Vietnam, advance the military struggle against the Communists, and legitimize the South Vietnamese government in the eyes of the American public.

The administration's hopes evaporated on January 30, 1968, when the Vietcong unleashed a massive, well-coordinated assault on major urban areas in South Vietnam. Known as the "Tet" offensive, the assault was timed to coincide with the lunar new year, a Vietnamese holiday. Vietcong forces struck thirty-six of the forty-four provincial capitals and five of the six major cities, including Saigon, where they raided the supposedly impregnable U.S. embassy (see Map 29.1). In strict military terms the Tet offensive was a failure for the Vietcong since it did not provoke the intended collapse of the South Vietnamese government. But in the long term the daring attack made a mockery of official pronouncements that the United States was winning the war and swung American public opinion more strongly against the conflict. Just before the offensive a Gallup poll found that 56 percent of Americans considered themselves "hawks" (supporters of the war), while only 28 percent identified with the "doves" (war opponents). Three months after Tet the doves outnumbered the hawks 42 to 41 percent. This turnaround in public opinion did not mean that a majority of Americans supported the peace movement, however. Many who called themselves doves had simply concluded that the war was unwinnable and were therefore opposed to it on pragmatic rather than moral grounds. As a housewife told a pollster, "I want to get out, but I don't want to give up."

The growing opposition to the war spilled over into the 1968 presidential campaign. Even before Tet, Senator Eugene J. McCarthy of Minnesota had entered the Democratic primaries as an antiwar candidate. President Johnson won the early New Hampshire primary, but McCarthy received a stunning 42.2 percent of the vote. His strong showing against the president reflected profound public dissatisfaction with the course of the war, even among those who were hawks. To make matters worse for the president, McCarthy's showing propelled Senator Robert Kennedy (a younger brother of John F. Kennedy and former U.S. attorney general) into the race on an antiwar platform.

Johnson realized that his political support was evaporating. At the end of an otherwise mundane televised address on March 31, he stunned the nation by announcing that he would not seek reelection. Johnson had already reversed his policy of incremental escalation of the war. Now he called a partial halt to the bombing and vowed to devote his remaining months in office to the search for peace. On May 10, 1968, preliminary peace talks between the United States and North Vietnam opened in Paris.

Just four days after Johnson's withdrawal from the presidential race, Martin Luther King Jr. was assassinated in Memphis. The ensuing riots in cities across the country left forty-three people dead. Soon afterward, students protesting Columbia University's plans for expanding into a neighboring ghetto, thus displacing its residents, occupied several campus buildings. The brutal response of the New York City police helped to radicalize even more students. The next month a massive strike by students and labor unions toppled the French government. Student unrest seemed likely to become a worldwide phenomenon.

Then came the final tragedy of the year. On June 5, 1968, Robert Kennedy was shot dead as he celebrated his victory in the California primary. The assailant was a young Palestinian who was thought to oppose Kennedy's pro-Israeli stance. Robert Kennedy's assassination shattered the dreams of many who had hoped that social change could be achieved by working through the political system. His death also weakened the Democratic Party. In his brief but dramatic campaign, Kennedy had excited and energized the traditional members of the New Deal coalition, including blue-collar workers and black voters.

The Democratic Party never fully recovered from Johnson's withdrawal and Kennedy's assassination. McCarthy's campaign limped along, while Senator George S. McGovern of South Dakota entered the Democratic race in an effort to keep the Kennedy forces together. Meanwhile, Vice President Hubert H. Humphrey lined up pledges from traditional Democratic constituencies—unions, urban machines, and state political organizations. Democrats found themselves on the verge of nominating not an antiwar candidate but a public figure closely associated with Johnson's war policies.

At the August Democratic nominating convention, the political divisions generated by the war consumed the party. Most of the drama occurred not in the convention hall but outside on the streets of Chicago. Led by activists Jerry Rubin and Abbie Hoffman, around 10,000 protesters descended on the city, calling for an end to the war, the legalization of marijuana, and the abolition of money. To mock those inside the convention hall, these "Yippies," as the group called themselves, nominated a pig for president. Their stunts, geared toward maximizing their media exposure, diverted attention from the more serious and far more numerous antiwar activists who had come to Chicago as convention delegates or volunteers.

Richard J. Daley, the Democratic mayor of Chicago who had grown increasingly angry as protesters disrupted his convention, called out the police to break up the demonstrations. Several nights of skirmishes between protesters and police culminated on the evening of the nominations. In what an official report later described as a "police riot," patrolmen attacked protesters with Mace, tear gas, and clubs as demonstrators chanted, "The whole world is watching!" Television networks broadcast a film of the riot as the nominating speeches were being made, cementing a popular impression of the Democrats as the party of disorder. Inside the hall the Democrats dispiritedly nominated Hubert H. Humphrey, who chose Senator Edmund S. Muskie of Maine as his running mate. The delegates approved a middle-of-the-road platform that endorsed continued fighting in Vietnam while the administration explored diplomatic means of ending the conflict.

The disruptions at the Democratic convention unleashed a backlash against antiwar protesters. The general public did not differentiate between the disruptive antics of the Yippies and the more responsible behavior of those activists who were trying to work within the system. Polls showed overwhelming support for Mayor Daley and the police.

The turmoil surrounding the civil rights and the antiwar movements strengthened support for proponents of "law and order," which became a conservative catch phrase for the next several years. Indeed, many Americans, though opposed to the war, were fed up with protest and dissent. Governor George C. Wallace of Alabama, a third-party candidate, skillfully exploited their growing disapproval of the antiwar movement by making student protests and urban riots his chief campaign issues. But Wallace, who in 1963 had promised to enforce "segregation now . . . segregation tomorrow . . . and segregation forever," also exploited the mounting backlash against the civil rights movement. Articulating the resentments of many working-class whites, he combined attacks on liberal intellectuals and government elites with strident denunciations of school desegregation and forced busing.

Even more than George Wallace, Richard Nixon tapped the increasingly conservative mood of the electorate. After his unsuccessful presidential campaign in 1960 and his loss in the California gubernatorial race in 1962, Nixon engineered an amazing political comeback and in 1968 won the Republican presidential nomination. As part of what his advisors called the "southern strategy," he chose Spiro Agnew, the conservative governor of Maryland, as his running mate to help him make inroads into the once solidly Democratic South. Nixon hoped to attract southern voters, especially Wallace supporters, who opposed Democratic civil rights legislation. He also used traditional populist appeals, pledging to represent the "quiet voice" of the "great majority of Americans, the forgotten Americans, the nonshouters, the nondemonstrators."

Despite the Democratic debacle in Chicago, the election was a close one. In the last weeks of the campaign, Humphrey rallied by gingerly disassociating himself from Johnson's war policies. Then in a televised address on October 31, President Johnson announced a complete halt to the bombing of North Vietnam. Nixon countered by intimating that he had his own plan to end the war—although in reality no such plan

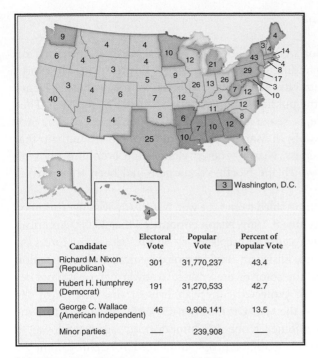

Candidate	Electoral Vote	Popular Vote	Percent of Popular Vote
Richard M. Nixon (Republican)	301	31,770,237	43.4
Hubert H. Humphrey (Democrat)	191	31,270,533	42.7
George C. Wallace (American Independent)	46	9,906,141	13.5
Minor parties	—	239,908	—

MAP 29.3 Presidential Election of 1968

With Lyndon B. Johnson's surprise decision not to run for another term and, less than three months later, the assassination of the party's most charismatic contender for the presidential nomination, Robert Kennedy, the Democrats faced the election of 1968 in disarray. Controversy over the Vietnam War fractured the party, as did the appeal of Governor George Wallace of Alabama, who left the Democrats to run as a third-party candidate and campaigned on the backlash against the civil rights movement. As late as mid-September Wallace held the support of 21 percent of the voters. But in November he received only 13.5 percent of the vote, winning five states and showing that the South was no longer solidly Democratic. Republican Richard M. Nixon, who like Wallace emphasized "law and order" in his campaign, defeated Hubert H. Humphrey with only 43.4 percent of the popular vote.

existed. On election day Nixon received 43.4 percent of the vote to Humphrey's 42.7 percent, defeating him by a scant 510,000 votes out of the 73 million that were cast (Map 29.3). Wallace finished with 13.5 percent of the popular vote. Though Nixon owed his election largely to the split in the Democratic coalition, the success of his southern strategy presaged the emergence of a new Republican majority. In the meantime, however, the Democrats retained a majority in both houses of Congress.

The closeness of the 1968 election suggested how polarized American society had become. Nixon appealed to a segment of society that came to be known as the silent majority—hardworking, nonprotesting, generally white Americans. Although his victory suggested a growing consensus among voters who were "unblack, unpoor, and unyoung," heated protest and controversy would persist until the war ended.

Nixon's War

Vietnam, long Lyndon Johnson's war, now became Richard Nixon's. At first Nixon sought to end the war by expanding its scope, as a means of pressuring the North Vietnamese to negotiate. But Nixon and his national security advisor, Henry Kissinger, soon realized that the public would not support such an approach. Thus shortly after Nixon took office, he sent a letter to the North Vietnamese leaders proposing mutual troop withdrawals. In March 1969, to convince North Vietnam that the United States meant business, Nixon ordered clandestine bombing raids on neutral Cambodia, through which the North Vietnamese had been transporting supplies and reinforcements.

When the intensified bombing failed to end the war, Nixon and Kissinger adopted a policy of Vietnamization. On June 8, 1969, Nixon announced that 25,000 American troops would be withdrawn by August and replaced by South Vietnamese forces. As the U.S. ambassador to Vietnam, Ellsworth Bunker, noted cynically, Vietnamization was just a matter of changing "the color of the bodies." Antiwar demonstrators denounced the new policy, which protected American lives at the expense of the Vietnamese but would not end the war. On October 15, 1969, in cities across the country, millions of Americans joined a one-day "moratorium" against the war. A month later more than a quarter of a million people mobilized in Washington in the largest antiwar demonstration to date.

To discredit his critics Nixon denounced student demonstrators as "bums" and stated that "North Vietnam cannot defeat or humiliate the United States. Only Americans can do that." On April 30, 1970, the bombing of Cambodia, which Nixon had kept secret from both the public and from Congress, culminated in an "incursion" into Cambodia by American ground forces to destroy enemy havens there. The invasion proved only a short-term setback for the North Vietnamese. More critically, the American action in Cambodia—along with the ongoing North Vietnamese intervention there—destabilized the country, exposing it to a takeover by the ruthless Pol Pot and his Communist regime, the Khmer Rouge, later in the 1970s.

When the *New York Times* uncovered the secret invasion of Cambodia, outraged antiwar leaders organized a national student strike. On May 4 at Kent State University outside Cleveland, panicky National Guardsmen fired into a crowd of students at an antiwar rally. Four people were killed and eleven more wounded. Only two of those who were killed had been attending the demonstration; the other two were just passing by on their way to class. Soon afterward, National Guardsmen stormed a dormitory at Jackson State College in Mississippi, killing two black students. More than 450 colleges closed in protest, and 80 percent of all campuses experienced some kind of disturbance. In June 1970, immediately after the Kent State slayings, a Gallup poll identified campus unrest, not the war, as the issue that most troubled Americans.

At the same time, however, dissatisfaction with the war continued to spread. Congressional opposition to the war, which had been growing since the Fulbright hearings in 1966, intensified with the invasion of Cambodia. In June 1970 the

Senate expressed its disapproval by voting to repeal the Gulf of Tonkin resolution and by cutting off funding for operations in Cambodia. Even the soldiers in Vietnam were showing mounting opposition to their mission. The number of troops who refused to follow combat orders increased steadily, and thousands of U.S. soldiers deserted. Among the majority who fought on, many sewed peace symbols on their uniforms. In the heat of battle, a number of overbearing junior officers were sometimes "fragged"—killed or wounded in grenade attacks by their own soldiers. At home, members of a group called Vietnam Veterans Against the War turned in their combat medals at demonstrations outside the U.S. Capitol.

In 1971 Americans were appalled by revelations of the sheer brutality of the war when Lieutenant William L. Calley was court-martialed for atrocities committed in the village of My Lai. In March 1968, acting under orders from his superiors, Calley and the platoon under his command had apparently murdered 350 Vietnamese villagers in retaliation for casualties sustained in an earlier engagement. The incident came to light because one member of the platoon refused to go along with a military cover-up; investigative reporter Seymour Hersh of the *New York Times* broke the story in November 1969. The military court sentenced Calley to life in prison for his part in the massacre. Yet George Wallace and some congressional conservatives called him a hero. President Nixon had Calley's sentence reduced; he was paroled in 1974.

After a final outbreak of protest and violence following the incident at Kent State, antiwar activism began to ebb. The antiwar movement was weakened in part by internal divisions within the New Left. In the late 1960s SDS and other antiwar groups fell victim to police harassment, and Federal Bureau of Investigation (FBI) and CIA agents infiltrated and disrupted radical organizations. After 1968 the New Left splintered into factions, its energy spent. Nixon's Vietnamization policy also played a role in the decline of antiwar protest by dramatically reducing the number of soldiers in combat. Nixon's promise to continue troop withdrawals, end the draft, and institute an all-volunteer army by 1973 further deprived the antiwar movement of important organizing issues, particularly on college campuses.

Withdrawal from Vietnam and Détente

At the same time Nixon had been prosecuting the war in Vietnam, ostensibly to halt the spread of communism, he had been formulating a new policy toward the Soviet Union and China. Known as **détente** (the French word for a relaxation of tensions), Nixon's policy was to seek peaceful coexistence with the two Communist powers and to link his overtures of friendship with a plan to end the Vietnam War. In his talks with Chinese and Soviet leaders, Nixon urged them to reduce their military aid as a means of pressuring the North Vietnamese to the negotiating table.

A lifelong anti-Communist crusader, Nixon was better able to reach out to the two Communist superpowers without arousing American mistrust than a Democratic president would have been. Since the Chinese revolution of 1949, the

United States had refused to recognize the government of the People's Republic of China. Instead, the State Department had recognized the Nationalist Chinese government in Taiwan. Nixon moved away from that policy, reasoning that the United States could exploit the growing rift between the People's Republic of China and the Soviet Union. In February 1972 Nixon journeyed to China in a symbolic visit that set the stage for the establishment of formal diplomatic relations in 1979.

In a similar spirit Nixon journeyed to Moscow in May 1972 to sign the first Strategic Arms Limitations Treaty (SALT I) between the United States and the Soviet Union. Although SALT I fell far short of ending the arms race, it did limit the production and deployment of intercontinental ballistic missiles (ICBMs) and antiballistic missile systems (ABMs). The treaty also signified that the United States could no longer afford the massive military spending that would have been necessary to attain the nuclear and military superiority it had enjoyed immediately following World War II. By the early 1970s inflation, domestic dissent, and the decline in American hegemony had limited and reshaped U.S. aims and options in international relations. Most of all Nixon hoped that a rapprochement with the Soviets would help to resolve the prolonged crisis in Vietnam.

The Paris peace talks had been in stalemate since 1968. Though the war had been "Vietnamized," and American casualties had decreased, the South Vietnamese military proved unable to hold its own. In late 1971, as American troops withdrew from the region, Communist forces stepped up their attacks on Laos, Cambodia, and South Vietnam. The next spring North Vietnamese forces launched a major new offensive against South Vietnam. In April, as the fighting intensified, Nixon ordered B-52 bombing raids against North Vietnam, and a month later he approved the mining of North Vietnamese ports.

That spring the increased combat activity and growing political pressure at home helped revive the Paris peace negotiations. Nixon hoped to undercut antiwar critics by making concessions to the North Vietnamese in the peace talks. In October Henry Kissinger and the North Vietnamese negotiator Le Duc Tho reached a cease-fire agreement calling for the withdrawal of the remaining U.S. troops, the return of all American prisoners of war, and the continued presence of North Vietnamese troops in South Vietnam. Nixon and Kissinger also promised the North Vietnamese substantial aid for postwar reconstruction. On the eve of the 1972 presidential election, Kissinger announced "peace is at hand," and Nixon returned to the White House with a resounding electoral victory (see Chapter 30).

The peace initiative, however, soon stalled, and with negotiations deadlocked, Nixon stepped up military action once more. In late December 1972, American planes subjected North Vietnamese civilian and military targets to the most devastating bombing of the war. Finally, on January 27, 1973, representatives of the United States, North and South Vietnam, and the Vietcong signed a cease-fire in Paris. But the Paris Peace Accords did not fulfill Nixon's promise of "peace with honor." Basically, they mandated the unilateral withdrawal of American troops in exchange for the return of American prisoners of war from North Vietnam. For most Americans that was enough.

Without massive U.S. military and economic aid and with North Vietnamese guerrillas operating freely throughout the countryside, the South Vietnamese government of General Nguyen Van Thieu soon fell to the more disciplined and popular Communist forces. In March 1975 North Vietnamese forces launched a final offensive. Horrified American television viewers watched as South Vietnamese officials and soldiers struggled with American embassy personnel to board the last helicopters that would fly out of Saigon before North Vietnamese troops entered the city. On April 29, 1975, Vietnam was reunited, and Saigon was renamed Ho Chi Minh City in honor of the Communist leader who had died in 1969.

The Legacy of Vietnam

Spanning nearly thirty years, the American involvement in Vietnam occupied administrations from Truman to Nixon's successor, Gerald Ford. U.S. troops fought in Vietnam for more than eleven years, from 1961 to 1973. In human terms the nation's longest war exacted an enormous cost. Some 58,000 U.S. troops died, and another 300,000 were wounded. Even those who returned unharmed encountered a sometimes hostile or indifferent reception. Arriving home alone without the fanfare that had greeted soldiers of America's victorious wars, most Vietnam veterans found the transition to civilian life abrupt and disorienting. The psychological tensions of serving in Vietnam and the difficulty of reentry sowed the seeds of what is now recognized as post-traumatic stress disorder—recurring physical and psychological problems that often lead to divorce, unemployment, and suicide. Only in the 1980s did America begin to make its peace with those who had served in the nation's most unpopular war.

In Southeast Asia the damage was far greater. The war claimed an estimated 1.5 million Vietnamese lives and devastated the country's physical and economic infrastructure. Neighboring Laos and Cambodia also suffered, particularly Cambodia, where between 1975 and 1979 the Khmer Rouge killed an estimated 2 million Cambodians—a quarter of the population—in a brutal relocation campaign. All told, the war produced nearly 10 million refugees, many of whom immigrated to the United States. Among them were thousands of Amerasians, the offspring of American soldiers and Vietnamese women. Spurned by their fathers and by most Vietnamese, more than 30,000 Amerasians arrived in the 1990s.

The defeat in Vietnam prompted Americans to think differently about foreign affairs and to acknowledge the limits of U.S. power abroad. The United States became less willing to plunge into overseas military commitments, a controversial change that conservatives dubbed the "Vietnam syndrome." In 1973 Congress declared its hostility to undeclared wars like those in Vietnam and Korea by passing the War Powers Act, which required the president to report any use of military force within forty-eight hours and directed that without a declaration of war by Congress hostilities must cease within sixty days. On those occasions when Congress did agree to foreign intervention, as in the Persian Gulf War of 1990 to 1991, American

The Vietnam Veterans' Memorial

Conceived and funded by a small group of veterans, the Vietnam Veterans' Memorial was dedicated in Washington, D.C., in November 1982. The memorial, designed by Maya Ling Lin, a Yale architecture student, consists of two walls of black granite inscribed with the names of 58,183 men and women who died in the war. The wall of names has tremendous emotional impact on viewers and has become one of the most popular tourist destinations in the nation's capital. Peter Marlow / Magnum Photos, Inc.

leaders would insist on obtainable military objectives and carefully channeled information to the news media. In the future any foreign entanglement would be evaluated in terms of its potential to become "another Vietnam."

The Vietnam War also distorted American economic and social affairs. At a total price of over $150 billion, the war siphoned resources from domestic needs, added to the deficit, and fueled inflation. Lyndon Johnson's Great Society programs had been pared down, and domestic reform efforts slowed thereafter. Moreover, the war shattered the liberal consensus that had supported the Democratic coalition. Even more seriously, the conduct of the war—the questionable representation of events in the Gulf of Tonkin, the lies about American successes on the battlefield, the secret war in Cambodia—spawned a deep distrust of government among American citizens. The discrediting of liberalism, the increased cynicism toward government, and the growing social turmoil that accompanied the war would continue into the next decade, paving the way for a resurgence of the Republican Party and a new mood of conservatism.

TIMELINE

1946	War begins between French and Vietminh over control of Vietnam	**1967**	Hippie counterculture's Summer of Love
			Race riots in Detroit and Newark
1950	United States recognizes French-backed government of Bao Dai and sends military aid		100,000 march in antiwar protest in Washington, D.C.
		1968	Tet offensive dashes American hopes of victory
1954	French defeat at Dienbienphu		Martin Luther King Jr. and Robert F. Kennedy assassinated
	Geneva Accords partition Vietnam at seventeenth parallel		Riot at Democratic National Convention in Chicago
1962	Students for a Democratic Society (SDS) founded		Women's liberation movement emerges
1963	Coup ousts Ngo Dinh Diem in South Vietnam		American Indian Movement (AIM) organized
	Presidential Commission on the Status of Women	**1969**	Stonewall riot leads to gay liberation movement
			Woodstock Music and Art Fair
1964	Free Speech Movement at Berkeley		Vietnam moratorium called in protest of war
	Gulf of Tonkin resolution authorizes military action in Vietnam	**1970**	Nixon orders invasion of Cambodia; renewed antiwar protests
1965	Malcolm X assassinated		Killings at Kent State and Jackson State
	Operation Rolling Thunder escalates war through mass bombing campaigns		
	First U.S. combat troops arrive in Vietnam	**1972**	Nixon visits People's Republic of China
	Race riot in Watts district of Los Angeles		SALT I Treaty with Soviet Union
1966	National Organization for Women (NOW) founded	**1973**	Paris Peace Accords
	Stokely Carmichael proclaims black power		War Powers Act
		1975	Fall of Saigon

For Further Exploration

Two insightful overviews of the 1960s are David Farber, *The Age of Great Dreams* (1994), and Maurice Isserman and Michael Kazin, *America Divided: The Civil War of the 1960s* (1999). The period is unusually rich in compelling primary accounts. *Takin' It to the Streets* (1995), edited by Alexander Bloom and Wini Breines, offers an impressive array of documents that encompass the war, counterculture, civil rights, feminism, gay liberation, and other issues. Henry Hampton and Steve Fayer's oral history, *Voices of Freedom* (1991), and *The Autobiography of Malcolm X* (1995), cowritten with Alex Haley, provide insight into black-power movements. Mary Crow Dog recounts her experiences as a Native American activist in *Lakota Woman* (1990). Memoirs of Vietnam are numerous. Secretary of Defense Robert McNamara offers an insider's view and belated apologia in his *In Retrospect* (1995); in *An*

American Requiem: God, My Father, and the War That Came Between Us (1996), the antiwar former priest James Carroll writes eloquently of the fissures Vietnam created in his family and the culture more generally; and Ron Kovic's *Born on the Fourth of July* (1976) is one soldier's powerful account of the war experience and its aftermath. Documents concerning the My Lai massacre may be found in James S. Olson and Randy Roberts, eds., *My Lai* (1999).

The Sixties Project, which is hosted by the University of Virginia at Charlottesville, offers personal narratives, special exhibits, and a bibliography of articles published in Vietnam Generation, at <http://lists.village.virginia.edu/sixties/>. A useful Vietnam site is edited by Professor Vincent Ferraro of Mount Holyoke College and includes state papers and official correspondence from 1941 to the fall of Saigon in 1975: <http://www.mtholyoke.edu/acad/intrel/vietnam.htm>. The University of California Library's site, Free Speech Movement: Student Protest–U.C. Berkeley, 1964–65" at <http://www.lib.berkeley.edu/ BANC/FSM/>, offers newsletters, oral histories, student newspaper accounts, legal defense material, and audio recordings, as well as good links to related sites. Historians at the University of Michigan maintain A Study and Timeline of the Lakota Nation, at <http://www-personal.umich.edu/~jamarcus/>, which includes material on the American Indian Movement, the occupation of Wounded Knee in 1973, and the confrontation at the Bureau of Indian Affairs Office in 1972.

Trial of the Chicago Seven, created by Douglas Linder of the University of Missouri, Kansas City, School of Law, explores this 1969–1970 trial of a group of radicals accused of conspiring to incite a riot at the 1968 Democratic National Convention in Chicago. The site provides a text of the trial as well as other legal documents. In addition, it offers biographies and audio clips of a wide range of people involved in the case. Access it at <http://www.law.umkc.edu/faculty/projects/ftrials/Chicago7/chicago7.html>.

For definitions of key terms boldfaced in this chapter, see the glossary at the end of the book.

To assess your mastery of the material covered in this chapter, see the Online Study Guide at **bedfordstmartins.com/henrettaconcise**.

For map resources and primary documents, see **bedfordstmartins.com/henrettaconcise**.

Chapter 30

THE LEAN YEARS
1969–1980

We've always believed in something called progress. We've always
had a faith that the days of our children would be better than our
own. Our people are losing that faith, not only in government itself
but in their ability as citizens to serve as the ultimate rulers and
shapers of our democracy.

JIMMY CARTER, 1979

"The United States Steel Corporation announced yesterday that it was
closing 14 plants and mills in 8 states. About 13,000 production and white-collar
workers will lose their jobs." "Weyerhaeuser Co. may trim about 1,000 salaried employees from its 11,000 member workforce over the next year." "Philadelphia: Food
Fair Inc. plans to close 89 supermarkets in New York and Connecticut." Newspaper
articles in the 1970s told the story of the widespread downsizing that cost millions
of workers their jobs when rising oil prices, runaway inflation, declining productivity, and stagnating incomes caused the biggest economic downturn in three
decades, which in turn created a widespread sense of disillusionment about the nation's future. Already reeling from the nation's withdrawal from Vietnam and its implications for the United States as an international power, many people also grew
disenchanted with their political leadership in the 1970s, as one public official after
another, including President Richard Nixon, resigned for misconduct. In the wake
of Nixon's resignation, the lackluster administrations of Presidents Gerald Ford and
Jimmy Carter failed to provide the leadership necessary to cope with the nation's
economic and international insecurities—failure that fed Americans' growing skepticism about government and its capacity to improve people's lives.

Paradoxically, in the midst of this growing disaffection and skepticism, a commitment to social change persisted. Some of the social movements born in the
1960s, such as feminism and environmentalism, had their greatest impact in the
1970s. As former student radicals moved into the political mainstream, they took
their struggles with them, from streets and campuses into courts, schools, workplaces,
and community organizations. But like the civil rights and antiwar movements of the

1960s, the social activism of the 1970s stirred fears and uncertainties among many Americans. Furthermore, the darkening economic climate of the new decade undercut the sense of social generosity that had characterized the 1960s, fueling a new conservatism that would become a potent political force by the decade's end.

The Nixon Years

Richard Nixon set the stage for the conservative political resurgence. His election gave impetus to the Republicans' desire to trim back the expansion of the federal government brought about by the New Deal and the Great Society and shift some federal responsibilities back to the states. At the same time facing a Democratic Congress, Nixon, like "modern Republican" Dwight D. Eisenhower (see Chapter 27), embraced the use of federal power—within limits—to uphold governmental responsibility for social welfare, environmental protection, and economic stability. The president's domestic accomplishments, however, as well as his international initiatives with the USSR and China, were ultimately overshadowed by the Watergate

Nixon Triumphant

One of the most resilient political figures in American history, Richard Nixon won the presidential elections of 1968 and 1972 after losing campaigns for president in 1960 and for governor of California in 1962. Even after his resignation in 1974, Nixon reemerged as an elder statesman and was frequently consulted for his views on foreign affairs. Here, he exults in an enthusiastic welcome from supporters in Savannah, Georgia, in 1970.

© Bettmann / Corbis.

scandal, which swept him from office in disgrace and undermined Americans' confidence in their political leaders.

The Republican Domestic Agenda

In a 1968 campaign pledge to "the average American," Nixon vowed to "reverse the flow of power and resources from the states and communities to Washington and start power and resources flowing back . . . to the people." One example of Nixon's approach was the 1972 revenue-sharing program, which distributed a portion of federal tax revenues to the states as block grants to be spent as state officials saw fit. In later years revenue sharing would become a key Republican strategy for reducing federal social programs and federal bureaucracy.

Nixon also worked to scale down certain government programs that had grown dramatically during the Johnson administration. Viewing many Great Society programs as bloated and inefficient, he reduced funding for most of the War on Poverty and dismantled the Office of Economic Opportunity altogether in 1971. Nixon also impounded (refused to spend) billions of dollars appropriated by Congress for urban renewal, pollution control, and other environmental initiatives. Although his administration claimed to support civil rights, Nixon adopted a cautious approach toward racial issues so as not to alienate southern white voters. Nixon also vetoed a 1971 bill to establish a comprehensive national child-care system, fearing that such "communal approaches to child rearing" would "Sovietize" American children.

As an alternative to Democratic social legislation, the administration put forward its own antipoverty program in an ambitious attempt to overhaul the jerry-built welfare system. In 1969 Nixon proposed a Family Assistance Plan that would provide a family of four a small but guaranteed annual income. The appeal of this proposal lay in its simplicity: it would eliminate the multiple layers of bureaucrats (caseworkers, local and state officials, and federal employees) who administered Aid to Families with Dependent Children (AFDC), the nation's largest welfare program. But the bill floundered in the Senate: conservatives attacked it for putting the federal government too deeply into the welfare business, and liberals and social welfare activists opposed it for not going far enough. Welfare reform would remain a contentious political issue for the next thirty years.

Although Nixon sought to streamline or scale back certain antipoverty programs, he presided over the expansion of the federal government in other ways. He agreed to the growth of major **entitlement programs** such as Medicare, Medicaid, and Social Security. In 1970 he signed a bill establishing the Environmental Protection Agency (EPA) and in 1972 approved legislation creating the Occupational Safety and Health Administration (OSHA) and the Consumer Products Safety Commission. The inconsistency apparent in Nixon's enhancing the federal government in some arenas, while vehemently insisting upon its curtailment in others, can be explained in part by political realities: he faced Democratic majorities in both houses of Congress who pushed for much of the social legislation passed during his administration. Personality comes into play as well: despite his opposition to federal bureaucracy, Nixon wanted to be an "activist" president, but one who was fiscally moderate and practical.

Nixon demonstrated his conservative social values most clearly in his appointments to the Supreme Court. The liberal thrust of the Court under the direction of Chief Justice Earl Warren (1953–1969) had disturbed many conservatives. Its *Brown v. Board of Education* decision in 1954 requiring the desegregation of public schools (see Chapter 27) was followed by other landmark decisions in the 1960s. The *Miranda v. Arizona* (1966) decision reinforced defendants' rights by requiring arresting officers to notify suspects of their legal rights. In *Baker v. Carr* (1962) and *Reynolds v. Sims* (1964), the Court put forth the doctrine of "one person, one vote," meaning that all citizens' votes should have equal weight, no matter where they lived, a challenge to disproportionately weighted rural voting districts. The ruling substantially increased the representation in state legislatures and Congress of both suburban and urban areas (with their concentrations of African American and Spanish-speaking residents) at the expense of rural regions. One of the most controversial decisions was *Engel v. Vitale* (1962), which banned organized prayer in public schools as a violation of the First Amendment. When Justice Warren retired in 1969, President Nixon took the opportunity to begin reshaping the Court and nominated conservative Warren Burger to become chief justice. After some difficulties in getting nominees confirmed by the Senate, Nixon eventually named three other justices: Harry Blackmun (who proved more liberal than expected), Lewis F. Powell Jr., and William Rehnquist.

Nixon's appointees did not always hand down decisions the president approved, however. Despite attempts by the Justice Department to halt further desegregation in the face of determined white opposition, the Court ordered busing of public school students to nonneighborhood schools in order to achieve racial balance. In 1972 it issued restrictions on the implementation of capital punishment, though it did not rule the death penalty unconstitutional. And in the controversial 1973 case *Roe v. Wade*, Justice Blackmun wrote the decision that struck down laws prohibiting abortion in Texas and Georgia.

The 1972 Election

Nixon's reelection in 1972 was never much in doubt. In May the threat of a conservative third-party challenge from Alabama governor George Wallace ended abruptly when an assailant shot Wallace, paralyzing him from the waist down. With Wallace out of the picture, Nixon's strategy of wooing southern white voters away from the Democrats got a boost. Nixon also benefited from the disarray of the Democratic Party. Divided over Vietnam and civil rights, the Democrats were plagued by tensions between their newer, more liberal constituencies—women, minorities, and young adults—and the old-line officeholders and labor-union leaders who had always dominated the party. Recent changes in the party's system of selecting delegates and candidates benefited the newer groups, and they helped to nominate Senator George McGovern of South Dakota, a noted liberal and an outspoken opponent of the Vietnam War.

Nixon's campaign took full advantage of the Democrats' weaknesses. Although the president had yet to end the war, his Vietnamization policy had virtually eliminated American combat deaths by 1972. Henry Kissinger's premature declaration that "peace is at hand" raised voters' hopes for a negotiated settlement (see Chapter 29). Not only did those initiatives rob the Democrats of their greatest appeal—their antiwar stance—but a short-term upturn in the economy further favored the Republicans. Nixon won handily, receiving nearly 61 percent of the popular vote and carrying every state except Massachusetts and the District of Columbia. Yet the president failed to kindle strong loyalty in the electorate. Only 55.7 percent of eligible voters bothered to go to the polls, and the Democrats maintained control of both houses of Congress.

Watergate

Watergate, one of the great constitutional crises of the twentieth century, was a scandal that began with a break-in at the Democratic National Committee's headquarters at the Watergate apartment complex in Washington, D.C. Its origins were rooted in Nixon's ruthless political tactics, his secretive style of governing, and his obsession with the antiwar movement. Many Americans saw Watergate as consisting of only the evil deeds of one person (Richard Nixon) and one unlawful act (obstruction of justice), but Watergate was not an isolated incident. It was part of a broad pattern of illegality and misuse of power that flourished in the crisis atmosphere of the Vietnam War.

During Nixon's first administration, the White House, obsessed with the antiwar movement, repeatedly authorized illegal surveillance—opening mail, tapping phones, arranging break-ins—of citizens such as Daniel Ellsberg, a former Defense Department analyst who in 1971 had leaked the so-called Pentagon Papers to the *New York Times*. This secret study, commissioned by Secretary of Defense McNamara in 1967, detailed so many American blunders in Vietnam that, after reading it, McNamara had commented, "You know, they could hang people for what is in there." To discredit Ellsberg, White House underlings broke into his psychiatrist's office in an unsuccessful search for damaging personal information. When their break-in was revealed, the court dismissed the government's case against Ellsberg.

In another abuse of presidential power, the White House had established a clandestine intelligence group known as the "plumbers" that was supposed to plug leaks of government information. The plumbers relied on tactics such as using the Internal Revenue Service to harass the administration's opponents. These secret and highly questionable activities were financed by massive illegal fund-raising efforts by Nixon's Committee to Re-Elect the President (known as CREEP). CREEP raised over $20 million, a portion of which was used to finance the plumbers' "dirty tricks," including the Watergate break-in.

Early in the morning of June 17, 1972, police arrested five men carrying cameras, wiretapping equipment, and a large amount of cash and charged them with breaking into the Democratic National Committee's headquarters at the Watergate apartment complex in Washington, D.C. Two accomplices were apprehended soon afterward. Three of the men had worked in the White House or for CREEP, and four had CIA connections. Although Nixon later claimed that "no one on the White House staff, no one in this administration, presently employed, was involved in this very bizarre incident," subsequent investigations revealed that shortly after the break-in the president had ordered his chief of staff, H. R. Haldeman, to instruct the CIA to tell the FBI not to probe too deeply into connections between the White House and the burglars.

The cover-up of the White House's involvement began to unravel when one of the convicted burglars began to talk. Two tenacious investigative reporters at the *Washington Post* traced the cover-up back to the White House. Reports of CREEP's dirty tricks and illegal fund-raising soon compounded the public's suspicions about the president. In February 1973 the Senate established an investigative committee which began holding nationally televised hearings in May. In June Assistant Secretary of Commerce Jeb Magruder testified before the committee, confessing his guilt and implicating former Attorney General John Mitchell, White House counsel John Dean, and others. Dean, in turn, implicated Nixon in the plot. Even more startling testimony from a Nixon aide revealed that Nixon had installed a secret taping system in the Oval Office.

The president steadfastly "stonewalled" the committee's demand that he surrender the tapes, citing executive privilege and national security. Archibald Cox, a **special prosecutor** whom Nixon had appointed to investigate the case, successfully petitioned a federal court to order the president to hand the tapes over, but Nixon refused to comply. After receiving additional federal subpoenas in April 1974, Nixon finally released a heavily edited transcript of the tapes, peppered with the words "expletive deleted." Senate Republican leader Hugh Scott called the transcripts "deplorable, disgusting, shabby, immoral." Most suspicious was an eighteen-minute gap in the tape covering a crucial meeting between Nixon and his staff on June 20, 1972—three days after the break-in.

The Watergate affair moved into its final phase when on June 30 the House of Representatives's Judiciary Committee voted three articles of impeachment against Richard Nixon: obstruction of justice, abuse of power, and acting to subvert the Constitution. Under duress, on August 5 Nixon released the unexpurgated tapes, which contained evidence that he had ordered the cover-up as early as six days after the break-in. Facing certain conviction if impeached, on August 9, 1974, Nixon became the first U.S. president to resign.

The next day Vice President Gerald Ford was sworn in as president. Ford, a former Michigan congressman and House minority leader, had replaced Vice President Spiro Agnew in 1973 after Agnew himself had resigned under indictment for accepting kickbacks on construction contracts while governor of Maryland. The transfer of power proceeded smoothly. A month later, however, Ford stunned the nation by granting Nixon a "full, free, and absolute" pardon "for all offenses he had committed or might have committed during his presidency." Ford took that action, he said, to spare the country the agony of rehashing Watergate in a criminal prosecution. Twenty-five members of Nixon's administration went to prison, but up to his death in 1995 Nixon refused to admit guilt for what had happened, conceding only that he had made an error in judgment.

In response to the abuses of the Nixon administration and to contain the power of what became known as "the imperial presidency," Congress adopted several reforms. In 1974 a strengthened Freedom of Information Act gave citizens greater access to files federal agencies had amassed on them. The Fair Campaign Practices Act of 1974 limited campaign contributions and provided for stricter accountability and public financing of presidential campaigns. Ironically, because the act allowed an unlimited number of political action committees (PACs) to donate up to $5,000 per candidate, corporations and lobbying groups found they could actually increase their influence by making multiple donations. By the end of the 1970s, close to 3,000 PACs were playing an increasingly pivotal—and some would argue unethical—role in national elections, and campaign finance reform would become a major political issue in the decades ahead.

Perhaps the most significant legacy of Watergate was the wave of cynicism that swept the country in its wake. Beginning with Lyndon Johnson's "credibility gap" during the Vietnam War, public distrust of government had risen steadily with the disclosure of the secret bombing of Cambodia and the illegal surveillance and harassment of antiwar protesters and other political opponents. The saga of Watergate confirmed what many Americans had long suspected: that politicians were hopelessly corrupt and that the federal government was out of control (see American Voices, "Watergate Diary," p. 922).

Lean Economic Times

Economic difficulties compounded Americans' political disillusionment. Growing international demand for natural resources, coupled with unstable access to foreign oil supplies wreaked havoc with the American economy. At the same time, foreign competitors in varied industries recovered from the devastation of World War II and successfully expanded their share of the world market, edging out American-made products. The resulting sharp downturn in the domestic economy marked the end of America's twenty-five-year dominance of the world economy.

Energy Crisis

During World War II the nation had produced two-thirds of the world's oil, but by 1972 its share had fallen to only 22 percent, even though domestic production had

AMERICAN VOICES

Watergate Diary

ELIZABETH DREW

J ournalist Elizabeth Drew kept a diary during the Watergate crisis. This passage, written on August 5, 1974, shortly after President Nixon was forced to release some exceptionally damaging tape transcripts, explores the implications of the revelations for Americans' faith in the presidency.

For those who believed that the President was aware of, and even directed, the cover-up, it must still be a shock to read his conversation about it. . . .

There is an inexplicable difference between the experiences of suspecting a lie and being whacked in the face with the evidence of one. Many Americans had become accustomed to thinking of the President as a liar, and had alternately suspended belief in, scoffed at, or become enraged at his statements. But I wonder whether the enormity of his lying has sunk in yet—whether we have, or can, come to terms with the thought that so much of what he said to us was just noise, words, and that we can no longer begin by accepting any of it as the truth. This is a total reversal of the way we were brought up to think about Presidents, a departure from deeply ingrained habits. One's mind resists the thought of our President as a faithless man, capable of looking at us in utter sincerity from the other side of the television camera and telling us multiple, explicit, barefaced lies. One is torn between the idea that people must be able to have some confidence in their leaders and the idea that in this day of image manipulation a certain skepticism may serve them well. I do not think there is much comfort to be taken from the fact that eventually Nixon's lies—like Johnson's— caught up with him. It took a long time, and a great deal of damage was done meanwhile.

SOURCE: *Washington Journal: The Events of 1973–1974* by Elizabeth Drew. Copyright © 1974, 1975 by Elizabeth Drew. Used by permission of Random House, Inc.

---

continued to rise. By the late 1960s the United States was buying more and more of its oil on the world market to keep up with shrinking domestic reserves and growing demand. The imported oil came primarily from the Middle East, where production had increased a stupendous 1,500 percent in the twenty-five years following 1945. The rise of nationalism and the corresponding decline of colonialism in the postwar era had encouraged the Persian Gulf nations to wrest control from the European and American oil companies. In 1960, joining with other oil-producing developing countries, they had formed the Organization of Petroleum Exporting Countries (OPEC). Just five of the founding countries—the Middle Eastern states of Saudi Arabia, Kuwait, Iran, and Iraq, plus Venezuela—were the source of more than 80 percent of the world's crude oil exports. During the early 1970s, when world demand climbed and oil reserves fell, they took advantage of market forces to maximize their profits. Between 1973 and 1975 OPEC raised the price of a barrel of oil from $3 to $12. By the end of the decade, the price had peaked at $34 a barrel, compounding the economic problems caused by the Vietnam War and setting off a round of furious inflation in the oil-dependent United States.

OPEC members also found that oil could be used as a weapon in global politics. Tensions had escalated in the Middle East in 1967 when Israel attacked Egypt and Jordan, seizing the Gaza Strip, the West Bank of the Jordan River, and the Sinai Peninsula. In 1973, in the Yom Kippur War, Egypt and Syria invaded Israel, regaining some of the land lost in 1967. In both instances, the Soviets had assisted the Arab nations, while the United States had aided Israel with arms and funds. In retaliation for their aid to Israel during the Yom Kippur War, OPEC instituted an oil embargo against the United States, Western Europe, and Japan. The embargo lasted six months and forced Americans to curtail their driving or spend long hours in line at the pumps; in a matter of months, gas prices climbed 40 percent. Since the U.S.

No Gas

During the energy crisis of 1973 to 1974, American motorists faced widespread gasoline shortages for the first time since World War II. Although gas was not rationed, gas stations were closed on Sundays, and some communities instituted further restrictions such as creating systems by which motorists with license plates ending in even numbers could purchase gas on certain days, with alternate days being reserved for odd numbers.

Tony Korody/Sygma/Corbis.

automobile industry had little to offer except "gas-guzzlers" built to run on cheap fuel, Americans turned to cheaper, more fuel-efficient foreign cars manufactured in Japan and West Germany. Soon the auto industry was in a slump, further weakening the American economy.

The energy crisis was an enormous shock to the American psyche. Americans felt like hostages to economic forces that were beyond their control. Yet despite an extensive public conservation campaign and a second gas shortage in 1979 caused by the Iranian revolution, Americans would not wean themselves from foreign oil. In fact, they used even more foreign oil after the energy crisis than they had before— a testimony to the enormous thirst of modern industrial and consumer societies for petroleum (Figure 30.1).

Economic Woes

Other developments also undercut the U.S. economy. The high cost of the Vietnam War and the Great Society had contributed to a steadily growing federal deficit and

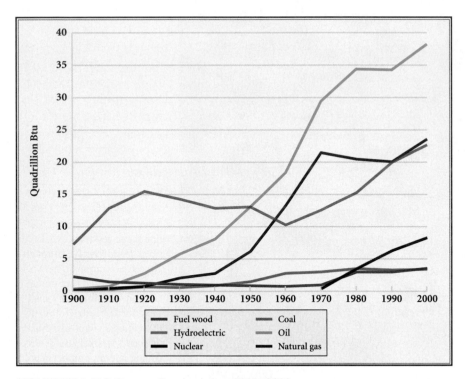

FIGURE 30.1 U.S. Energy Consumption, 1900–2000

Coal was the nation's primary source of energy until the 1950s, when oil and natural gas became the dominant fuels. The use of nuclear and hydroelectric power also rose substantially in the postwar era. During the 1980s fuel-efficient automobiles and conservation measures reduced total energy use, but in the 1990s energy consumption rose significantly. *Source: World Almanac 2002.*

spiraling inflation. A business downturn in 1970 had led to rising unemployment and declining productivity. In the industrial sector the reviving economies of West Germany and Japan over time had reduced demand for American goods worldwide. As a result, in 1971 the dollar fell to its lowest level on the world market since 1949, and the United States posted its first trade deficit, importing more than it exported, in almost a century.

Overall economic growth, as measured by the gross domestic product (GDP), had averaged 4.1 percent per year in the 1960s; in the 1970s it dropped to only 2.9 percent, contributing to a noticeable decline in most Americans' standard of living. At the same time galloping inflation forced consumer prices upward. Housing prices, in particular, rose rapidly: the average cost of a single-family home more than doubled in the 1970s, making home ownership inaccessible to a growing segment of the working and middle classes.

The inflationary crisis helped to forge new attitudes about saving and spending. With bank savings accounts' interest rates unable to keep up with inflation, many Americans turned to the stock market, taking advantage of the appearance of new discount brokerage firms like Charles Schwab. The money-market mutual fund also emerged in this decade, offering investors uninsured but relatively safe investment opportunities. By 1982 more than $200 billion dollars were invested in mutual funds. While investors sought new ways to fight inflation and increase their savings, millions of Americans dispensed with savings altogether. Putting aside the fear of indebtedness so evident in people who had lived through the Great Depression, now Americans coped with inflation and their declining purchasing power by going into debt. By mid-1975 consumer borrowing totaled $167 billion, but by 1979 it had skyrocketed to $315 billion, helped by a dramatic increase in the use of credit cards.

In addition to inflation, young adults in particular faced a constricted job market in the late 1970s as a record number of baby boomers competed for a limited number of jobs. Unemployment peaked at around 9 percent in 1975 and hovered at 6 to 7 percent in the late 1970s. A devastating combination of inflation and unemployment termed **stagflation** bedeviled presidential administrations from Nixon to Reagan, whose remedies, such as deficit spending and tax reduction, failed to eradicate the double scourge.

American economic woes were most acute in the industrial sector, which entered a prolonged period of decline, or deindustrialization. Investors who had formerly bought stock in basic U.S. industries like automobiles and steel began to speculate on the stock market or put their money into mergers or foreign companies. Many U.S. firms relocated overseas, partly to take advantage of cheaper labor and production costs. By the end of the 1970s, the hundred largest multinational corporations and banks were earning more than a third of their overall profits abroad.

The most dramatic consequences of deindustrialization occurred in the older manufacturing regions of the Northeast and Midwest, which came to be known as

Symbol of the Rust Belt

A padlock on the gate of Youngstown, Ohio's United States Steel mill symbolizes the creation of the Rust Belt when economic hard times in the 1970s led to widespread plant closures in the industrial areas of the Midwest and Northeast. Bettmann/Corbis.

FOR MORE HELP ANALYZING THIS IMAGE, see the Online Study Guide at **bedfordstmartins.com/henrettaconcise**.

the "Rust Belt" (Map 30.1). There the dominant images of American industry in the mid-twentieth century—huge factories such as Ford's River Rouge plant outside Detroit and the United States Steel Corporation compound in Gary, Indiana—were fast becoming relics.

When a community's major employer closed up shop and left town, the effect was devastating and led to widespread unemployment. Many of the displaced workers relocated to the Sun Belt, which continued its postwar expansion with the spectacular growth of cities like Houston, Los Angeles, San Diego, and Atlanta (see Chapter 28). The growth of the Sun Belt owed much to federal spending for defense contracts, military bases, and the space program in the region. The oil industry and agribusiness also benefited from federal subsidies and tax breaks. Equally important, however, in the creation of new jobs were low labor costs. "Right-to-work" laws that made it difficult to build strong labor unions made these states, unlike those of the Rust Belt, inhospitable to organized labor.

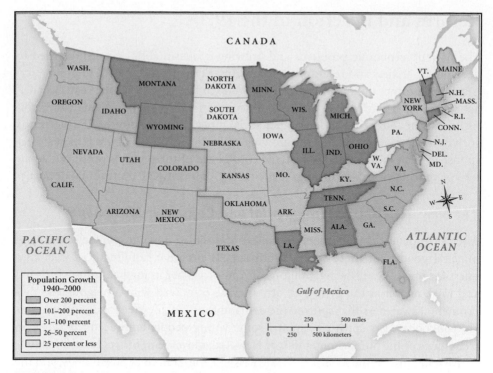

MAP 30.1 From Rust Belt to Sun Belt, 1940–2000

One of the most significant developments of the post–World War II era was the growth of the Sun Belt. Sparked by federal spending for military bases, the defense industry, and the space program, states of the South and Southwest experienced an economic boom in the 1950s. This growth was further enhanced in the 1970s, as the heavily industrialized regions of the Northeast and Midwest declined, and migrants from what was quickly dubbed the "Rust Belt" headed to the South and West in search of jobs. Rising political influence accompanied the economic and demographic growth of the Sun Belt: since Lyndon B. Johnson, all presidents but Gerald Ford have hailed from a Sun Belt state, and the region has provided an important base for the conservative wing of the Republican Party.

Deindustrialization, the population shift to the Sun Belt, and the changing economic conditions of the 1970s posed a critical problem for the labor movement. In the heyday of labor during the 1940s and 1950s, American managers had often cooperated with unions; with profits high there was room for accommodation. But as foreign competition cut into corporate profits in the 1970s, industry became less willing to bargain, and the labor movement's power declined. In the 1970s union membership dropped from 28 to 23 percent of the American workforce. In the South membership was 14 percent. By the end of the 1980s, only 16 percent of American workers were organized. Operations moving abroad also hurt labor, as the new overseas workforce was beyond American labor's power to influence. In a competitive global environment, labor's prospects seemed dim.

Reform and Reaction in the 1970s

The nation's economic problems and growing cynicism about government led to deep public anxiety and resentment. Many Americans turned inward to private satisfactions, prompting the journalist Tom Wolfe to label the 1970s the "Me Decade." Yet such a label hardly does justice to a decade in which environmentalism, feminism, lesbian and gay rights, and other social movements blossomed. Furthermore, such characterizations neglect the growing social conservatism that was in part a response to such movements. In fact, the confluence of these trends produced a pattern of shifting crosscurrents that made the 1970s a complex transitional decade.

The New Activism: Environmental and Consumer Movements

After 1970 many baby boomers left college and settled down to pursue careers and material goods, but these young adults sought personal fulfillment as well. In a quest for physical well-being, millions of Americans began jogging, riding bicycles, and working out at the gym. The fitness craze coincided with a heightened environmental awareness that spurred the demand for pesticide-free foods and vegetarian cookbooks. For spiritual support some young people embraced the self-help techniques of the human-potential, or New Age, movement; others turned to alternative religious groups such as the Hare Krishna, the Church of Scientology, and the Unification Church of Reverend Sun Myung Moon.

A few baby boomers continued to pursue the unfinished social and political agendas of the 1960s. Moving into law, education, social work, medicine, and other fields, these former radicals continued their activism on a grassroots level. Some joined the left wing of the Democratic Party; others helped to establish community-based organizations, including health clinics, food co-ops, and day-care centers. On the local level, at least, the progressive spirit of the 1960s lived on.

Many of these activists helped to invigorate the emerging environmental movement that had been energized by the publication in 1962 of Rachel Carson's *Silent Spring*, a powerful analysis of the impact of pesticides on the food chain. Activists brought their radical political sensibilities to the movement, using sit-ins and other protest tactics developed in the sixties to mobilize mass support and infuse environmentalism with new life.

Other issues that galvanized public opinion included the environmental impact of industrial projects such as an Alaskan oil pipeline and the harmful effects of chlorofluorocarbons and increased carbon dioxide levels on the earth's atmosphere. In January 1969 a huge oil spill off the coast of Santa Barbara, California, provoked an outcry, as did the discovery in 1978 that a housing development outside Niagara Falls, New York, had been built on a toxic waste site, with a spike in instances of cancer in the people who lived there.

Nuclear energy became the subject of citizen action in the 1970s, when rising prices and oil shortages led to the expansion of nuclear power, pitting environmental concerns against the need for alternative energy sources. By January 1974 forty-two nuclear power plants were in operation, and over a hundred more were planned. The proliferation of nuclear power plants and reactors, which had gone largely unchallenged in the 1950s and 1960s, raised public concerns about safety. Activists protested plans for new reactors, citing inadequate evacuation plans and the unresolved problem of the disposal of radioactive waste.

Their fears seemed to be confirmed in March 1979 when a nuclear plant at Three Mile Island near Harrisburg, Pennsylvania, came critically close to a meltdown of its central core reactor. A prompt shutdown of the plant brought the problem under control before significant radioactive material seeped into the environment, but as a member of the panel who investigated the accident admitted, "We were damn lucky." The accident at Three Mile Island alarmed the American people and caused them to rethink whether nuclear power could be a viable solution to the nation's energy needs. Grassroots activism, combined with public fear of the potential dangers of nuclear energy, convinced many utility companies to abandon nuclear power, despite its short-term economic advantages.

Americans' concerns about nuclear power, chemical contamination, and other environmental issues helped to turn environmentalism into a mass movement. The first Earth Day was held on April 22, 1970, and 20 million citizens gathered in communities across the country to express their concern for the endangered planet. Their efforts helped to create bipartisan support for a spate of new federal legislation. In 1969 Congress had passed the National Environmental Policy Act, which required the developers of public projects to file an environmental impact statement. The next year Nixon established the Environmental Protection Agency (EPA) and signed the Clean Air Act, which toughened standards for auto emissions in order to reduce smog and air pollution. And in 1973 the Endangered Species Act expanded the protection provided by the Endangered Animals Act of 1964, granting species such as snail darters and spotted owls protected status. Thus environmental protection joined social welfare, defense, and national security as areas of federal intervention.

The environmental movement did not go uncontested. The EPA-mandated fuel-economy standards for cars provoked criticism for threatening the health of the auto industry as it struggled to keep up with foreign competitors. Corporations resented environmental regulations, but so did many of their workers, who believed that tightened standards threatened their jobs and privileged nature over human beings. "IF YOU'RE HUNGRY AND OUT OF WORK, EAT AN ENVIRONMENTALIST" read one labor union's bumper sticker. In a time of rising unemployment and deindustrialization, activists clashed head-on with proponents of economic development, full employment, and global competitiveness.

Paralleling the rise of environmentalism was a growing consumer-protection movement to eliminate harmful products and curb dangerous practices by American corporations. The consumer movement had originated in the Progressive Era with the founding of government agencies such as the Food and Drug Administration (see Chapter 20). After decades of inertia, the consumer movement reemerged in the

1960s under the leadership of Ralph Nader, a young Harvard-educated lawyer whose book *Unsafe at Any Speed* (1965) attacked General Motors for putting flashy style ahead of safe handling and fuel economy in its engineering of the Chevrolet Corvair.

In 1969 Nader launched a Washington-based consumer-protection organization that gave rise to the Public Interest Research Group, a national network of consumer groups that focused on issues ranging from product safety to consumer fraud and environmental pollution. Staffed by a handful of lawyers and hundreds of student volunteers known as "Nader's Raiders," the organization pioneered legal tactics such as the class-action suit, which allowed people with common grievances to sue as a group. Nader's organization became a model for dozens of other groups that emerged in the 1970s and afterward to combat the health hazards of smoking, unethical insurance and credit practices, and other consumer problems. The establishment of the federal Consumer Products Safety Commission in 1972 reflected the growing importance of consumer protection in American life.

Challenges to Tradition: The Women's Movement and Gay Rights

Feminism proved the most enduring movement to emerge from the 1960s. In the next decade the women's movement grew more sophisticated, generating an array of services and organizations, from rape crisis centers and battered women's shelters to feminist health collectives and women's bookstores. In 1972 Gloria Steinem and other journalists founded *Ms.* magazine, the first consumer magazine aimed at a feminist audience. Formerly all-male bastions, such as Yale, Princeton, and the U.S. Military Academy, admitted women undergraduates for the first time, and the proportion of women attending graduate and professional schools rose markedly. Several new national women's organizations emerged, and established groups such as the National Organization for Women (NOW) continued to grow. In 1977, 20,000 women went to Houston for the first National Women's Conference. Their "National Plan of Action" represented a hard-won consensus on topics ranging from violence against women to homemakers' rights, the needs of older women, and most controversially, abortion and other reproductive issues.

Women were also increasingly visible in politics and public life. The National Women's Political Caucus, founded in 1971, actively promoted the election of women to public office. Their success stories included Shirley Chisholm, Patricia Schroeder, and Geraldine Ferraro, all of whom served in Congress, and Ella T. Grasso, who won election as Connecticut's governor in 1974.

Women's political mobilization produced significant legislative and administrative gains. With the passage of Title IX of the Educational Amendments Act of 1972, which broadened the 1964 Civil Rights Act to include educational institutions, Congress prohibited colleges and universities that received federal funds from discriminating on the basis of sex, a change that particularly benefited women athletes. Another federal initiative was **affirmative action**. Originally instituted in 1966 under

Lyndon Johnson's administration to redress a history of discrimination against nonwhites in employment and education, affirmative action procedures—hiring and enrollment goals and recruitment training programs—were extended to women the following year and gave many women, especially those who were educated and white, more opportunities for educational and career advancement. In 1972 Congress authorized child-care deductions for working parents; in 1974 it passed the Equal Credit Opportunity Act, which significantly improved women's access to credit.

The Supreme Court also significantly advanced women's rights. In several rulings the Court gave women more control over their reproductive lives by reading a right of privacy into the Ninth and Fourteenth Amendments' concept of personal liberty. In 1965 *Griswold v. Connecticut* had overturned state laws against the sale of contraceptive devices to married adults, an option that was later extended to single persons. In 1973, in *Roe v. Wade*, the Court struck down Texas and Georgia statutes that allowed an abortion only if the mother's life was in danger. According to this seven-to-two decision, states could no longer outlaw abortions performed during the first trimester of pregnancy.

Roe v. Wade nationalized the liberalization of state abortion laws, which had begun in New York in 1970, but also fueled the development of a powerful antiabortion movement. Charging that the rights of a fetus took precedence over a woman's right to decide whether or not to terminate a pregnancy, abortion opponents worked to circumvent or overturn *Roe v. Wade*. In 1976 they convinced Congress to deny Medicaid funds for abortions for poor women, one of the opening rounds in a protracted legislative and judicial campaign to overturn the *Roe* decision.

Another battlefront for the women's movement was the proposed Equal Rights Amendment (ERA) to the Constitution. The ERA, first introduced in Congress in 1923 by the National Woman's Party, stated in its entirety, "Equality of rights under the law shall not be denied or abridged by the United States or any State on the basis of sex." In 1971 feminists pressured Congress to revive the amendment and it was submitted to the states for ratification. Thirty-four states quickly passed the ERA between 1972 and the end of 1974, but then the momentum stopped (Map 30.2). Congress extended the deadline for ratification until June 30, 1982, but the Equal Rights Amendment still fell short of the required three-fourths majority for ratification.

The fate of the ERA and the battle over abortion rights showed that by the mid-1970s the women's movement was beginning to weaken. Increasingly its members were divided by issues of race, class, age, and sexual orientation. For many nonwhite and working-class women, the feminist movement seemed to stand for the interests of self-seeking, white career women. At the same time, the women's movement faced growing social conservatism among Americans in general. Although 63 percent of women polled in 1975 said they favored "efforts to strengthen and change women's status in society," a growing minority of both sexes expressed concern over what seemed to be revolutionary changes in women's traditional roles.

Lawyer Phyllis Schlafly, long active in conservative causes, led the antifeminist backlash. Despite the active career she had pursued while raising five children,

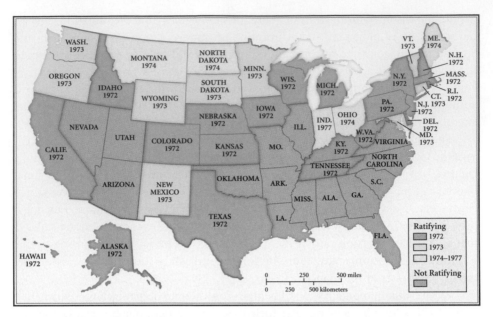

MAP 30.2 States Ratifying the Equal Rights Amendment, 1972–1977

The Equal Rights Amendment (ERA) quickly won support in 1972 and 1973 but then stalled. ERAmerica, a coalition of women's groups formed in 1976, lobbied extensively, particularly in Florida, North Carolina, and Illinois, but failed to sway the conservative legislatures in those states. After Indiana ratified in 1977, the amendment still lacked three votes toward the three-fourths majority needed to pass. Efforts to revive the ERA in the 1980s were unsuccessful, and it remains a dead issue.

Schlafly advocated traditional roles for women. Schlafly's STOP ERA organization claimed that the amendment would create a "unisex society" in which women could be drafted, homosexuals could be married, and separate toilets for men and women would be prohibited. Alarmed, conservative women in grassroots networks mobilized, showing up at statehouses with home-baked bread and apple pies, symbols of their traditional domestic role. As labels on baked goods at one anti-ERA rally expressed it, "My heart and hand went into this dough / For the sake of the family please vote no." Their message, that women would lose more than they would gain if the ERA passed, resonated with many men and women, especially those who were troubled by the rapid pace of social change.

Despite challenges to feminism, women's lives did not return to the patterns of the 1950s. Because of increasing economic pressures, the proportion of women in the paid workforce continued to rise, from 44 percent in 1970 to 51 percent in 1980. In their private lives easier access to birth control permitted married and unmarried women to enjoy greater sexual freedom (although they also became more vulnerable to male pressure and sexually transmitted diseases). With a growing number of career options available to them, many women, particularly educated white women, stayed single or delayed marriage and childrearing. With the baby boom over, the birthrate continued its twentieth-century decline, reaching an all-time low in the mid-1970s. At the same time the divorce rate rose 82 percent in the 1970s, as more men and women elected to leave unhappy marriages.

Although such changes brought increased autonomy for many women, they also caused new hardships, particularly in poor and working-class families. Divorce left many women with low-paying jobs and inadequate child care. Meanwhile, more tolerant attitudes toward premarital sex, along with other social and economic factors, had contributed to rising teenage pregnancy rates. The rise in divorce and adolescent pregnancy produced a sharp increase in the number of female-headed families, contributing to the "feminization" of poverty. By 1980 women accounted for 66 percent of adults who lived below the poverty line, a development that fueled a growing wave of social reaction.

Another major focus of social activism, the gay liberation movement, achieved heightened visibility in the 1970s. Thousands of gay men and lesbians "came out," publicly proclaiming their sexual orientation (see American Voices, "The Real Score: A Gay Athlete Comes Out," p. 934). In New York's Greenwich Village, San Francisco's Castro neighborhood, and other urban enclaves, growing gay communities gave rise to hundreds of new gay and lesbian clubs, churches, businesses, and political organizations. In 1973 the National Gay Task Force launched a campaign to include gay men and lesbians as a protected group under laws covering employment and housing rights. Such efforts were most successful on the local level; during the 1970s Detroit, Boston, Los Angeles, Miami, San Francisco, and other cities passed laws barring discrimination on the basis of sexual preference. By 2004 the legality of gay marriage would become a major national issue.

Like abortion and the ERA, gay rights came under attack from conservatives, who believed that granting gay lifestyles legal protection would encourage immoral behavior. When the Miami city council passed a measure banning discrimination against gay men and lesbians in 1977, the singer Anita Bryant led a campaign to repeal the law by popular referendum. Later that year voters overturned the measure by a two-to-one majority, prompting similar antigay campaigns around the country.

Racial Minorities

Although the civil rights movement was in disarray by the late 1960s, continued minority-group protests brought social and economic gains in the next decade. Native Americans realized some of the most significant changes. In 1971 the Alaska Native Land Claims Act restored 40 million acres to Eskimos, Aleuts, and other native peoples, along with $960 million in compensation. Most important, the federal government abandoned the tribal termination program of the 1950s (see Chapter 28). Under the Indian Self-Determination Act of 1974, Congress restored the tribes' right to govern themselves and gave them authority over federal programs on their reservations (Map 30.3).

The Real Score: A Gay Athlete Comes Out

DAVID KOPAY

F or ten years David Kopay played professional football for the San Francisco Forty-Niners, the Detroit Lions, the Washington Redskins, the New Orleans Saints, and the Green Bay Packers. In 1975, at the end of his playing career, Kopay publicly acknowledged his homosexuality, creating a national furor in the sports world.

I always knew I was a bit different, but I kept it kind of quiet. I didn't think of myself as queer. In fact I couldn't even say that word for years and years. . . .

When I thought about the future, I assumed I'd be able to get a job in coaching because I was a player-coach my last few years playing. I was always working behind the scenes with the young ballplayers, coaching them. But I wasn't getting any interviews. There were all kinds of rumors about me being gay. . . .

By the time I spoke out, I really had nothing left to lose. It felt like I didn't have a choice—I just had to do it. Then one morning in 1975 I saw an article in the *Washington Star* about homosexual athletes and why they had everything to lose. There was an interview in the article with Jerry Smith [Washington Redskins tight end who died of AIDS in 1986]. . . .

So I called Lynn Rosellini, who was the reporter for the article that quoted Jerry Smith. Lynn was doing an entire series on gay athletes. . . .

Everybody said there was going to be a terrible backlash against me when Lynn's article was published. But there wasn't a backlash against me personally: There was a backlash against all the television shows and radio stations that I went on. And the newspapers. The *Washington Star* said they had never received more negative mail for anything they'd ever done—hundreds of horrible hate letters. . . . The letters said things like, "It doesn't belong on the sports page as a model for our young boys and girls." "How could the *Washington Star* run an article like this?" I got letters that said, "I hope you never get a coaching job. Yours in Christ. Love. . . ." Just horrible things.

I never did get a coaching job. . . . No one would hire me to be a coach, I think, because of the image problem. They didn't think I could fill the role of the coach as guardian of the morals of the young students—the father figure. I also knew that I probably wouldn't get that really good sales-rep job that a lot of the other guys got. I had to make a spot for myself somehow, so I wound up working with Perry Young for a year on my book, *The Dave Kopay Story.* . . .

A lot of kids still write. They say that the book meant so much to them. They remember that it changed them a lot or made a difference.

SOURCE: Eric Marcus, *Making History* (New York: Harper Collins, 1992), 275–77.

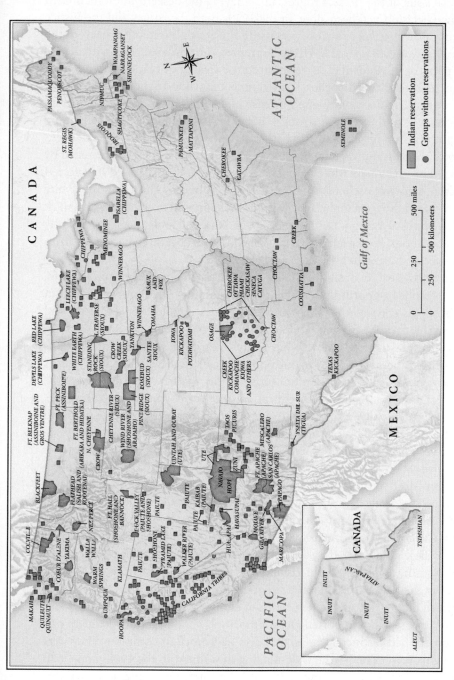

MAP 30.3 American Indian Reservations

Although Native Americans have been able to preserve small enclaves in the northeastern states, most Indian reservations are in the West. Beginning in the 1970s various nations filed land claims against federal and state governments.

FOR MORE HELP ANALYZING THIS MAP, see the Online Study Guide at **bedfordstmartins.com/henrettaconcise.**

The busing of children to achieve school desegregation proved the most disruptive social issue of the 1970s. Progress in achieving the desegregation mandated by the *Brown* decision had been slow. In the 1970s both the courts and the Justice Department pushed for more action, not just in the South but in other parts of the country. In *Milliken v. Bradley* (1974), the Supreme Court ordered cities with deeply ingrained patterns of residential segregation to use busing of black and white students from segregated neighborhoods to nonneighborhood schools to integrate their classrooms. The decision sparked intense and sometimes violent opposition. In Boston in 1974 and 1975, the strongly Irish-Catholic working-class neighborhood of South Boston responded to the arrival of African American students from Roxbury with mob action reminiscent of that in Little Rock in 1957. Threatened by court-ordered busing, many white parents rejected "forced busing" and transferred their children to private schools or moved to the suburbs. The resulting "white flight" exacerbated the racial imbalance busing was supposed to redress. Some black parents also opposed busing, calling instead for better schools in predominantly black neighborhoods. By the late 1970s federal courts had begun to back away from their insistence on busing to achieve racial balance.

Almost as divisive as busing was the issue of affirmative action procedures, which had expanded opportunities for blacks and Latinos. The number of African American students enrolled in colleges and universities doubled between 1970 and 1977 to 1.1 million, or 9.3 percent of total student enrollment. A small but growing number of African Americans moved into white-collar professions in corporations and universities. Others found new opportunities in civil service occupations such as law enforcement or entered apprenticeships in the skilled construction trades. Latinos experienced similar gains in education and employment. On the whole, however, both groups enjoyed only marginal economic improvement, since poor and working-class nonwhites bore the brunt of job loss and unemployment in the 1970s.

Nevertheless, many whites, who were also feeling the economic pinch, came to resent affirmative action programs as an infringement of their rights. White men especially complained of "reverse discrimination" against them. In 1978 Allan Bakke, a white man, sued the University of California Medical School at Davis for rejecting him in favor of less qualified minority candidates. The Supreme Court ruling in *Bakke v. University of California* was inconclusive. Though it branded the medical school's strict quota system illegal and ordered Bakke admitted, it stated that racial factors could be considered in hiring and admission decisions, thus upholding the principle of affirmative action. But the *Bakke* decision was a setback for proponents of affirmative action, and it prepared the way for subsequent efforts to eliminate those programs.

Though activists who supported racial minorities, women, gays, consumers, and the environment had distinct agendas, they also had much in common. They were part of "a rights revolution"—the wide-ranging movement in the 1960s and 1970s to bring issues of social justice and welfare to the forefront of public policy (see Chapter 29). Influenced by the Great Society's liberalism, they invariably turned to the federal government for protection of individual rights and—in the case of environmentalists—the world's natural resources. The activists of this period made substantial progress in widening the notion of the federal government's responsibilities, but by the end of the 1970s their movements faced growing opposition.

The Growth of Conservatism

Together with the rapidly growing antiabortion movement, the often violent public opposition to busing, affirmative action, gay rights ordinances, and the Equal Rights Amendment constituted a broad challenge to the social changes of the previous decade. This resurgent climate of conservatism was also fueled by a major revival in evangelical Christianity that would soon become a potent force in American culture and politics.

In the 1970s, many Americans came to believe that their interests had been slighted by the rights revolution and resented a federal government that supported legal rights for criminals, protected women who sought abortions, or minorities who benefited from affirmative action. The economic changes of the 1970s, which left many working- and middle-class Americans with lower disposable incomes, rising prices, and higher taxes, further fueled resentment against "special-interest groups" (women, minorities, gays, and so on) and growing expenditures on social welfare. Special groups and programs, conservatives believed, robbed other Americans of educational and employment opportunities and saddled the working and middle classes with an extra financial burden.

One manifestation of this resentment was a wave of local taxpayers' revolts. In 1978 California voters passed Proposition 13, a measure that reduced property taxes and eventually undercut local governments' ability to maintain schools and other essential services. Promising tax relief to middle-class home owners and reduced funding for busing and other programs to benefit the poor—who were invariably assumed to be nonwhite—Proposition 13 became the model for similar tax measures around the country in the late 1970s and the 1980s.

A different source for conservatism was religion. Fundamentalist groups that fostered a "born-again" experience had been growing steadily since World War II, under the leadership of charismatic preachers such as Billy Graham. According to a Gallup poll conducted in 1976, some 50 million Americans—about a quarter of the population—were affiliated with evangelical movements. The most prominent born-again Christian of the decade was Jimmy Carter, who publicly discussed his spirituality in the 1976 presidential campaign. Evangelical groups set up their own school systems and newspapers. Through innovative media outlets like the Christian Broadcasting Network, founded by the Virginia preacher Pat Robertson, a new breed of televangelists such as Jerry Falwell built vast and influential electronic ministries.

Many of these evangelicals spoke out on a broad range of issues, denouncing abortion, busing, sex education, pornography, feminism, and gay rights and bringing their religious values to a wider public. In 1979 Falwell founded the Moral

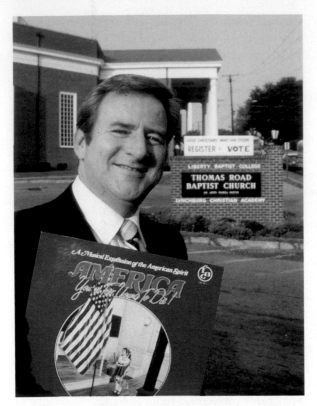

Jerry Falwell

The resurgence of evangelical religion in the 1970s was accompanied by a conservative movement
in politics known as the "New
Right." Founded in 1979 by tele-
vangelist Jerry Falwell, the Moral
Majority was one of the earliest
New Right groups, committed to
promoting "family values" in
American society and politics.
Wally McNamee / Corbis.

Majority, a political pressure group that promoted Christian "family values"—
traditional gender roles, heterosexuality, family cohesion—and staunch anticommunism. The extensive media and fund-raising networks of the Christian right
contributed to the organizational base for a larger conservative movement known
as the "**New Right**."

The New Right's constituency was complex. Conservatives of the early Cold
War era had focused on resisting creeping socialism at home and abroad and were
often identified with corporate business interests. In the 1970s they were joined not
only by evangelical Christian groups but by "neoconservatives," intellectuals who
criticized affirmative action, the welfare state, and changing gender and sexual values; they helped to give conservative values a heightened respectability. The New
Right's diverse constituents shared hostility toward a powerful federal government
and a fear of declining social morality. Backed by wealthy corporate interests and
using sophisticated computerized mass-mailing campaigns, a variety of New Right
political groups mobilized thousands of followers and millions of dollars to support
conservative candidates and causes. They laid a foundation for a movement that not
only helped to elect Ronald Reagan as president in 1980, but also powerfully affected national politics for decades to come.

Politics in the Wake of Watergate

The New Right had no monopoly on its criticism of big government. In the wake of Watergate many citizens from a wide range of the political spectrum had become cynical about the federal government and about politicians in general. "Don't vote. It only encourages them" read one bumper sticker during the 1976 campaign. Nixon's successors, Gerald Ford and Jimmy Carter, plagued by foreign-policy crises and continued economic woes, did little to restore public confidence. In the 1980 elections voter apathy persisted, but Ronald Reagan's lopsided presidential victory signified a hope that the charismatic former actor could restore America's traditional values and its economic and international power.

Ford's Caretaker Presidency

During the two years Gerald Ford held the nation's highest office, he failed to establish his legitimacy as president. Ford's pardon of Nixon hurt his credibility as a political leader, but an even bigger problem was his handling of the economy, which was reeling from inflation. In 1974 the inflation rate soared to almost 12 percent, and in the following year the economy entered its deepest downturn since the Great Depression. Though many of the nation's economic problems were beyond the president's control, Ford's failure to take more vigorous action made him appear timid and powerless.

In foreign policy Ford was equally lacking in leadership. He maintained Nixon's détente initiatives by asking Henry Kissinger to stay on as secretary of state. Though Ford met with Soviet leaders hoping to hammer out the details of a SALT II (Strategic Arms Limitation Treaty) agreement, he made little progress. Ford and Kissinger also continued Nixon's policy of increasing assistance to the shah of Iran, ignoring the bitter opposition and anti-Western sentiment that the shah's policy of rapid modernization was provoking among the growing Muslim fundamentalist population.

Jimmy Carter: The Outsider as President

The 1976 presidential campaign was one of the blandest in years. President Ford chose as his running mate the conservative senator Robert J. Dole of Kansas. The Democratic choice, James E. (Jimmy) Carter, governor of Georgia, shared the ticket with Senator Walter F. Mondale of Minnesota. Avoiding issues and controversy, Carter played up his role as a Washington outsider, pledging to restore morality to government. Carter won the election with 50 percent of the popular vote to Ford's 48 percent.

Despite his efforts to overcome the post-Watergate climate of skepticism and apathy, Carter never became an effective leader. His outsider strategy distanced him from traditional sources of power, and he did little to close the breach. Moreover, he proved ineffective in combating inflation, the nation's major domestic challenge. When he took office, the country was still recovering from the severe recession of

1975 and 1976, but Carter's fiscal policy eroded both business and consumer confidence. To counter inflation the Federal Reserve Board raised interest rates repeatedly; in 1980 the prime interest rate that banks charged their best customers topped 20 percent, a historic high.

The Carter administration expanded the federal bureaucracy in some cases and limited its reach in others. Carter enlarged the cabinet by creating the Departments of Energy and Education and approved new environmental protection measures, such as the $1.6 billion "Superfund" to clean up chemical pollution sites as well as new park and forest lands in Alaska. But he continued President Nixon's efforts to reduce the scope of federal activities by reforming the civil service and deregulating the airline, trucking, and railroad industries. With **deregulation**, prices often dropped, but the resulting cutthroat competition drove many firms out of business and encouraged corporate consolidation.

Carter's attempt to resolve the energy crisis also faltered. He failed in his effort to decontrol oil and natural gas prices as a spur to domestic production and conservation. In a famous 1979 address popularly known as the "the malaise" speech because he focused on the deep-seated problems besetting the country, Carter called energy conservation efforts "the moral equivalent of war"—a phrase the media reduced to "MEOW," suggesting the weakness of the president's leadership. In early 1979 a revolution in Iran curtailed oil supplies, leading to raised oil prices. In the first six months of 1979, the pump price increased by 55 percent and gas lines again reminded Americans of their dependence on foreign oil. That summer, Carter's approval rating dropped to 26 percent—lower than Richard Nixon's during the worst part of the Watergate scandal.

Carter and the World

In foreign affairs President Carter made human rights the centerpiece of his policy. He criticized the suppression of dissent in the Soviet Union and withdrew economic and military aid from Argentina, Uruguay, Ethiopia, and other countries that violated human rights. Carter also established the Office of Human Rights in the State Department. Unable to change the internal policies of longtime U.S. allies who were serious violators such as the Philippines, South Korea, and South Africa, he did manage to raise public awareness of the human rights issue, making it one future administrations would have to address.

In Latin America Carter's most important contribution was the resolution of the lingering dispute over control of the Panama Canal. In a treaty signed on September 7, 1977, the United States agreed to turn over control of the canal to Panama on December 31, 1999. In return the United States retained the right to send its ships through the canal in case of war, even though the canal itself would be declared neutral territory. Despite a conservative outcry that the United States was giving away more than it got, the Senate narrowly approved the treaty.

Though Carter had campaigned to free the United States from its "inordinate fear of Communism," relations with the Soviet Union soon became tense, largely because of problems surrounding arms-limitation talks. Eventually the Soviet leader Leonid Brezhnev signed SALT II (1979), but hopes for Senate ratification of the treaty collapsed when the Soviet Union invaded Afghanistan that December. In response, Carter canceled American participation in the 1980 summer Olympics in Moscow and, like his successor Ronald Reagan, provided covert assistance to an Afghan group who called themselves *mujahideen* (holy warriors). With funding provided by Saudia Arabia and Pakistan, the CIA supported these radical Islamic fundamentalists (whose numbers would eventually include Osama bin Laden) in their efforts to drive the Russians from Afghanistan in the 1980s, thereby helping to establish the now infamous Taliban.

It was in the Middle East that President Carter achieved both his most stunning success and his greatest failure. Relations between Egypt and Israel had remained tense since the 1973 Yom Kippur War. In 1978 Carter helped to break the diplomatic stalemate by inviting Israel's prime minister, Menachem Begin, and Egyptian president Anwar el-Sadat to Camp David, the presidential retreat in Maryland. Two weeks of discussions and Carter's promise of additional foreign aid to Egypt persuaded Sadat and Begin to adopt a "framework for peace." The agreement included Egypt's recognition of Israel's right to exist and Israel's return of the Sinai Peninsula, which it had occupied since 1967. Transfer of the territory to Egypt took place from 1979 to 1982.

Dramatically less successful was U.S. foreign policy toward Iran. Ever since the CIA had helped to install Muhammad Reza Pahlavi on the throne in 1953 (see Chapter 27), the United States had counted Iran as a faithful ally in the troubled Middle East. Overlooking the repressive tactics of Iran's CIA-trained secret police, SAVAK, Carter followed in the footsteps of previous Cold War policymakers for whom access to Iranian oil reserves and the shah's consistently anti-Communist stance outweighed all other considerations.

Early in 1979, however, the shah's government was overthrown and driven into exile by a revolution led by fundamentalist Muslim leader Ayatollah Ruhollah Khomeini. In late October 1979 the Carter administration admitted the deposed shah, who was suffering from incurable cancer, to the United States for medical treatment. In response, on November 4, 1979, militants under Khomeini's direction seized the U.S. embassy in Tehran, taking Americans hostage in a flagrant violation of the principle of diplomatic immunity. The hostage takers demanded that the shah be returned to Iran for trial and punishment, but the United States refused. Instead, President Carter suspended arms sales to Iran, froze Iranian assets in American banks, and threatened to deport Iranian students in the United States.

For the next fourteen months, the Iranian hostage crisis paralyzed Jimmy Carter's presidency. Night after night, humiliating pictures of blindfolded hostages appeared on television newscasts. The extensive media coverage and Carter's insistence that the safe return of the fifty-two hostages was his top priority enhanced the

A Framework for Peace

President Jimmy Carter's greatest foreign-policy achievement was the personal diplomacy he exerted to persuade President Anwar el-Sadat of Egypt (left) and Prime Minister Menachem Begin of Israel (right) to sign a peace treaty in 1978. The signing of the Camp David Accords marked an important first step in constructing a framework for peace in the Middle East. In 2002 Carter received the Nobel Peace Prize in recognition of his "untiring effort to find peaceful solutions to international conflicts, to advance democracy and human rights, and to promote economic and social development." David Rubinger / TimeLife Pictures / Getty Images.

value of the hostages to their captors. An attempt to mount a military rescue of the hostages failed miserably in April 1980, six months into the crisis, because of helicopter equipment failures in the desert. The abortive rescue mission reinforced the public's view of Carter as a bumbling and ineffective executive.

The Reagan Revolution

With Carter embroiled in the hostage crisis, the Republicans gained momentum by nominating former California governor Ronald Reagan. A movie actor from the late 1930s to the early 1950s, Reagan had been active in the postwar anti-Communist crusade in Hollywood. He began his political career as governor of California from 1967 to 1975. After losing a bid for the Republican nomination in 1976, Reagan secured it easily in 1980 and chose former CIA director George Bush as his running mate.

In the final months of the campaign, Carter took on a defensive tone, while Reagan remained upbeat and decisive. The Republicans benefited from superior financial resources, but Reagan also had a powerful issue to exploit: the hostage stalemate. He hinted that he would take strong action to win the hostages' return. More important, Reagan effectively appealed to the American insecurities that flourished in the 1970s. In a televised debate between the candidates, Reagan emphasized the economic plight of working- and middle-class Americans when he posed the rhetorical question, "Are you better off today than you were four years ago?"

In November Reagan won easily, with 51 percent of the popular vote to Carter's 41 percent. The landslide also gave the Republicans control of the Senate for the first time since 1954, though the Democrats maintained their hold on the House. Voter turnout, however, was at its lowest since the 1920s: only 53 percent of those eligible to vote went to the polls. Many poor and working-class voters stayed home. Nevertheless, the election confirmed the growth in the power of the Republican Party since Richard Nixon's victory in 1968.

Superior campaign funds and a realignment of the electorate contributed to the Republican resurgence of the 1970s. While the Democratic Party saw its key constituency--organized labor—dwindle, the GOP's financial superiority enabled it to make sophisticated and effective use of television and direct mail to reach voters. This aggressive outreach helped bring about a realignment of the electorate. The core of the Republican Party that elected Ronald Reagan remained the upper-middle-class, white, Protestant voters who supported balanced budgets, disliked government activism, feared crime and communism, and believed in a strong national defense. But new groups had gravitated toward the Republican vision: southern whites disaffected by big government and black civil rights gains; blue-collar workers, especially culturally conservative Catholics; young voters who identified themselves as conservatives; and residents in the West, especially those in the rapidly growing suburbs. By wooing these "Reagan Democrats," the Republican Party made deep inroads into Democratic territory, eroding that party's New Deal coalition of southerners, blacks, laborers, and urban ethnics.

The New Right was another significant contributor to the Republican victory, especially the religious right, associated with groups like the Moral Majority, whose emphasis on traditional values and Christian morality dovetailed well with conservative Republican ideology. In 1980 these concerns formed the basis for the party's platform, which called for a constitutional ban on abortion, voluntary prayer in public schools, and a mandatory death penalty for certain crimes. The Republicans also demanded an end to court-mandated busing and for the first time in forty years opposed the Equal Rights Amendment. A key factor in the 1980 election, the New Right contributed to the rebirth of the Republican Party under Ronald Reagan.

On January 20, 1981, at the moment Carter turned over the presidency to Ronald Reagan, the Iranian government released the American hostages. After 444 days of captivity, the hostages returned home to an ecstatic welcome, a reflection of the public's frustration over their long ordeal. The hostage crisis in Iran came to symbolize the loss of America's power to control world affairs. Its psychological impact was enhanced by its occurrence at the end of a decade that had witnessed Watergate, the American defeat in Vietnam, and the OPEC embargo.

To a great extent, the decline in American influence had been magnified by the unusual predominance the United States had enjoyed after World War II—an advantage that could not have lasted forever. The return of Japan and Western Europe to economic and political power, the control of vital oil resources by Middle Eastern countries, and the industrialization of some developing nations had widened the cast of characters on the international stage. Still, many Americans retained a core belief in the economic and political supremacy of the United States born in the postwar years. Ronald Reagan rode their frustrations to victory in 1980.

T I M E L I N E

1968	Richard Nixon elected president	**1974– 1975**	Busing controversy in Boston
1970	Earth Day first observed		
	Environmental Protection Agency established	**1975– 1976**	Recession
1971	Pentagon Papers published		Jimmy Carter elected president
	Nixon suspends Bretton Woods system		First National Women's Conference in Houston
	Swann v. Charlotte-Mecklenburg institutes busing		Voters overturn a Miami city council's gay rights measure
1972– 1974	Watergate investigation		Carter brokers Camp David Accords between Egypt and Israel
			Proposition 13 reduces California taxes
1972	Revenue sharing begins		*Bakke v. University of California* limits affirmative action
	Watergate break-in; Nixon reelected		
	Congress passes Equal Rights Amendment		Love Canal crisis begins
	Ms. magazine founded	**1979**	Three Mile Island nuclear accident
			Moral Majority founded
1973	Spiro Agnew resigns; Gerald Ford appointed vice president		Second oil crisis triggered by revolution in Iran
	Roe v. Wade legalizes abortion		Hostages seized at American embassy in Tehran, Iran
	Endangered Species Act		Soviet Union invades Afghanistan
1973– 1974	Arab oil embargo; gas shortages	**1980**	"Superfund" created to clean up chemical pollution
1974	Nixon resigns; Ford becomes president and pardons Nixon		Ronald Reagan elected president
	Freedom of Information Act strengthened		
	Fair Campaign Practices Act passed		

For Further Exploration

Peter N. Carroll, *It Seemed Like Nothing Happened* (1982), provides a general overview of the period. Gary Wills, *Nixon Agonistes* (rev. ed. 1990), judges Nixon to be a product of his times. For Watergate, a starting point is the books by the *Washington Post* journalists who broke the scandal, Carl Bernstein and Bob Woodward: *All the President's Men* (1974) and *The Final Days* (1976). Stanley Kutler, *Abuse of Power: The Nixon Tapes* (1997), is a collection of transcripts from the White House tapes relating to Watergate and other Nixon-era scandals. Gary Sick, a Jimmy Carter White House advisor on Iran, offers an insider's account of the hostage crisis in *All Fall Down: America's Tragic Encounter with Iran* (1986). For documents on the Carter presidency and his "malaise" speech, see Daniel Horowitz, *Jimmy Carter and the Energy Crisis of the 1970s* (2005). Thomas Byrne Edsall with Mary D. Edsall, *Chain Reaction: The Impact of Race, Rights, and Taxes on American Politics* (1991), examines some of the divisive social issues of the 1970s. J. Anthony Lukas, *Common Ground* (1985), tells the story of the Boston busing crisis through the biographies of three families. Barbara Ehrenreich examines the backlash against feminism in *Hearts of Men* (1984).

For the Watergate scandal see the National Archives and Record Administration's Watergate Trial Tapes and Transcripts, at <http://www.nara.gov/nixon/tapes/trial&transcripts.html>, which provides transcripts of the infamous tapes as well as other useful links to archival holdings concerning Richard Nixon's presidency. Watergate, at <http://vcepolitics.com/watergate/>, is a textual, visual, and auditory survey of the scandal. Created by Australian political science professor Malcolm Farnsworth, the site's materials include a Nixon biography with speech excerpts, a Watergate chronology, an analysis of the significance of the "Deep Throat" informant, and an assessment of the Watergate legacy. Relevant links provide access to primary documents. The Oyez Project at Northwestern University, at <http://oyez.nwu.edu/>, is an invaluable resource for over one thousand Supreme Court cases, with audio transcripts, voting records, and summaries. For this period, see, for example, its materials on *Roe v. Wade*, *Bakke v. University of California*, and *Griswold v. Connecticut*. Documents from the Women's Liberation Movement, culled from the Duke University Special Collections Library, emphasize the women's movement of the late 1960s and early 1970s. This searchable site, at <http://scriptorium.lib.duke.edu/wlm/>, includes books, pamphlets, and other written materials on categories that include theoretical writings, reproductive health, women of color, and women's work and roles.

For definitions of key terms boldfaced in this chapter, see the glossary at the end of the book.

To assess your mastery of the material covered in this chapter, see the Online Study Guide at **bedfordstmartins.com/henrettaconcise**.

For map resources and primary documents, see **bedfordstmartins.com/henrettaconcise**.

Chapter 31

A NEW DOMESTIC AND WORLD ORDER
1981–2004

> September 11 will be commemorated this year as a day of national and private grief, but it is also a political anniversary. One year ago, the post–Cold War era came to an end and a new phase in our country's history began. What this new phase will be—whether the September 11 attacks will stand as an isolated episode or initiate a longer and perhaps more dreadful chain of events—we cannot possibly know.
>
> PAUL STARR, *THE AMERICAN PROSPECT*, SEPTEMBER 2002

On November 9, 1989, millions of television viewers worldwide watched jubilant Germans swarm through the Berlin Wall after the East German government lifted all restrictions on passage between the eastern and western sectors of the city. The wall, which had divided the city since 1961, was the foremost symbol of Communist repression and the Cold War division of Europe. Twelve years later, in September 2001, a stunned world television audience would watch as New York's World Trade Center's two towers collapsed after being rammed by airplanes hijacked and piloted by terrorists associated with Al Qaeda, a militant Islamic organization based in Afghanistan.

These two dramatic events frame the shifting patterns of international politics at the close of the twentieth century and dawn of the twenty-first. When the Berlin Wall came down, it brought communism's grip over Eastern Europe down with it. The Soviet Union would dissolve in 1991, ending the Cold War. But new sources of conflict soon erupted—including instability in developing nations, ethnic conflict, and above all, international terrorism—that would pose continued threats to world peace and security. As U.S. leaders forged policies to address the changing international scene, Americans also came to recognize that in the new world order their nation was increasingly linked to a global economy. At the same time, they grappled with serious domestic issues of racial, ethnic, and cultural conflict; crime; and economic inequities. Heated debates about the role of the federal government and a disenchantment with political leaders' failure to solve many of the nation's pressing

946

social and economic problems would continue into the twenty-first century, and will no doubt shape America's history for decades to come.

Reagan-Bush Domestic Policy, 1981–1993

First elected at age sixty-nine, Ronald Reagan was the oldest man ever to serve as president, yet he conveyed a sense of physical vigor. By capitalizing on his skills as an actor and a public speaker and by winning the support of the emerging New Right within the Republican Party, Reagan became one of the most popular presidents of the twentieth century. George H. W. Bush, Reagan's vice president for two terms before he became president in his own right in 1989, paled in comparison. Bush's one term as president often seems indistinguishable from the two terms of his predecessor, in part because he was overshadowed by Reagan's extraordinary charisma but also because he followed the basic policies of the previous administration. Distrustful of the federal government, both Bush and Reagan turned away from the state as a source of solutions to America's social problems, calling into question almost half a century of governmental activism. "Government is not the solution to our problem," Reagan declared. "Government is the problem."

Festive Times at the Reagan White House

Since Ronald and Nancy Reagan were both former actors, perhaps they thought of 1930s dancing stars Fred Astaire and Ginger Rogers when they struck this pose at a White House state dinner in May 1985. Some former White House staffers now suspect that Reagan was showing signs of early Alzheimer's disease by that point.

Photo by Harry Benson. Cover courtesy VANITY FAIR. © 1985 by Condé-Nast Publications, Inc.

Reaganomics

The economic and tax policies that emerged under Reagan, quickly dubbed Reaganomics, were based on supply-side economics theory. According to the theory, high taxes siphoned off capital that would otherwise be invested, stimulating growth. Tax cuts would therefore promote private investment launching an economic expansion that would increase tax revenues. Together with reductions in government spending, tax cuts would also shrink the federal budget deficit. The Economic Recovery Tax Act passed in 1981 reduced income tax rates by 25 percent over three years. The reductions were supposed to be linked to drastic cutbacks in federal expenditures. But while cuts were made in food stamps, unemployment compensation, and welfare programs such as Aid to Families with Dependent Children (AFDC), congressional resistance kept the Social Security and Medicare programs intact. The net impact of Reaganomics was to further the redistribution of income from the poor to the wealthy. During the 1980s, the average income of the nation's wealthiest 1 percent grew by 75 percent while for families in the bottom 90 percent, income increased by only 7 percent.

Another tenet of Reaganomics was the assertion that many federal regulations impeded economic growth and productivity. The administration moved to abolish or reduce federal regulation of the workplace, health care, consumer protection, and the environment, thus eroding many of the legislative victories of the New Deal and Great Society programs of the 1930s and 1960s (see Chapters 25 and 28). The responsibility for and cost of such regulations were transferred to the states, making regulatory oversight impossible because of local budget constraints. One of the results of this policy was the deinstitutionalization of many of the mentally ill, forcing them onto the streets and increasing the homeless population to levels not seen since the Great Depression.

The money saved by these means—and more—was redirected into a five-year, $1.2 trillion defense buildup. This huge increase fulfilled Reagan's campaign pledge to "make America number one again," a slogan that tapped anxieties about the nation's foreign-policy failures, most recently symbolized by the Iranian hostage crisis (see Chapter 30). The B-1 bomber, which President Carter had canceled, was resurrected, and development of a new missile system, the MX, was begun. Reagan's most ambitious and controversial weapons plan, proposed in 1983, was the Strategic Defense Initiative (SDI), popularly known as "Star Wars." A computerized satellite and laser shield for detecting and intercepting incoming missiles, SDI would, if it worked, render nuclear war obsolete. (Because of serious questions about the technology and resistance by many nations, SDI would never be deployed.)

Reagan's programs benefited from the Federal Reserve Board's tight money policies as well as a drop in world oil prices, which reduced the disastrous inflation rates that had bedeviled the nation in the 1970s. Between 1980 and 1982 the inflation rate dropped from 12.4 percent to just 4 percent. Unfortunately, the Fed's tightening of the money supply also brought on the "Reagan recession" of 1981 to 1982, which put some 10 million Americans out of work. But as the recession bottomed out in early 1983, the economy began to grow, and for the rest of the decade, inflation remained low. Despite rather unexceptional growth in the Gross Domestic Product (GDP), the Reagan administration presided over what was then the longest peacetime economic expansion in American history.

Reagan's Second Term

Economic growth played a critical role in the 1984 elections, and Reagan campaigned on the theme "It's Morning in America," suggesting that a new day of prosperity and pride was dawning. The Democrats nominated former vice president Walter Mondale of Minnesota. With strong ties to labor unions, minority groups, and party leaders, Mondale epitomized the New Deal coalition that had dominated the Democratic Party since Franklin Roosevelt. To appeal to women voters, Mondale selected Representative Geraldine Ferraro of New York as his running mate—the first woman to run on a major party ticket. Nevertheless, Reagan won a landslide victory, carrying the entire nation except for Minnesota and the District of Columbia. Democrats, however, held onto the House and in 1986 would regain control of the Senate.

A major scandal marred Reagan's second term when in 1986 news leaked out that the administration had negotiated an "arms-for-hostages" deal with the revolutionary government of Iran—the same government Reagan had denounced during the 1980 hostage crisis. In an attempt to gain Iran's help in freeing some American hostages held by pro-Iranian forces in Lebanon, the United States had covertly sold arms to Iran. Some of the profits generated by the arms sales were diverted to the Contras, counterrevolutionaries in Nicaragua, whom the administration supported in their attempt to overthrow the leftist regime of the Sandinistas. The covert diversion of funds, which was both illegal and unconstitutional, seemed to have been the idea of marine lieutenant colonel Oliver North, a National Security Council aide at the time. One key memo linked the White House to his plan. But when Congress investigated the mounting scandal in 1986 and 1987, White House officials testified that the president knew nothing about the diversion. Reagan's defense remained simple and consistent: "I don't remember."

The scandal bore many similarities to Watergate, including the possibility that the president had acted illegally. In 1993, Lawrence Walsh, special prosecutor for the investigation, concluded: "President Reagan, the secretary of state, the secretary of defense, and the director of central intelligence and their necessary assistants committed themselves, however reluctantly, to two programs contrary to congressional policy and contrary to national policy. They skirted the law, some of them broke the law, and almost all of them tried to cover up the President's willful activities." Yet early in Reagan's administration, one of his critics had coined the phrase "Teflon presidency" to describe Reagan's resiliency: bad news did not stick; it just rolled off. The public seemed untroubled that the president was often confused or ill informed. Reagan weathered "Iran-Contragate," but the scandal weakened his presidency.

As a result, Reagan proposed no bold domestic policy initiatives in his last two years in office. He had promised to place drastic limits on the federal government and to give free-market forces freer rein, but despite reordering the federal government's priorities, he failed to reduce its size or scope. Social Security and other entitlement programs remained untouched, and the dramatic military buildup counteracted cuts in other programs. Nevertheless, those spending cuts and Reagan's antigovernment rhetoric shaped the terms of political debate for the rest of the century.

One of Reagan's most significant legacies was his conservative judicial appointments. In 1981 he appointed Sandra Day O'Connor, the first woman ever to serve on the Supreme Court. In his second term he appointed two more justices, Antonin Scalia (1986) and Anthony Kennedy (1988), both far more conservative than the moderate O'Connor. Justice William Rehnquist, a noted conservative, was elevated to chief justice of the United States in 1986. Under his leadership the Court, often by a bare majority, chipped away at the Warren Court's legacy in decisions on individual liberties, affirmative action, and the rights of criminal defendants (see Chapter 30).

Ironically, though Reagan had promised to balance the budget by 1984, his most enduring legacy was the national debt, which tripled during his two terms. The huge deficit reflected the combined effects of increased military spending, tax reductions for high-income taxpayers, and the Democratic-controlled Congress's refusal to approve deep cuts in domestic programs. By 1989 the national debt had climbed to $2.8 trillion—more than $11,000 for every American citizen.

The annual deficit in America's trade with other nations skyrocketed as well. Exports had been falling since the 1970s, when American products began to encounter increasing competition in world markets. In the early 1980s a high exchange rate for dollars made U.S. goods more expensive for foreign buyers and imports more affordable for Americans. The budget and trade deficits contributed to a major shift in 1985: for the first time since 1915, the United States became a debtor rather than a creditor nation.

The First Bush Presidency

George Bush won the Republican nomination in 1988 and chose for his vice president a young conservative Indiana senator, Dan Quayle. In the Democratic primaries the most important contest was between Governor Michael Dukakis of Massachusetts and the charismatic civil rights leader Jesse Jackson, whose populist Rainbow Coalition had embraced the diversity of Democratic constituencies. Dukakis received the party's nomination and chose Senator Lloyd Bentsen of Texas as his running mate.

Bush beat Dukakis in an exceptionally negative campaign, but it was the judiciary rather than the executive branch that determined some of the more significant domestic trends of the Bush era. Under Reagan's appointees the Supreme Court continued to move away from the liberal activism of the Warren Court and toward a more conservative stance, especially on the issue of abortion. The 1989 *Webster v. Reproductive Health Services* decision upheld the right of states to limit the use of public funds and institutions for abortions, and the next year the Court upheld a federal regulation barring personnel at federally funded health clinics from discussing abortion with their clients. In 1992 the Court upheld a Pennsylvania law mandating informed consent and a twenty-four-hour waiting period before an abortion could be performed. Nevertheless, the justices also reaffirmed the "essential holding" in *Roe v. Wade*: women had a constitutional right to abortion.

Like Reagan, Bush also had an opportunity to shape the Supreme Court. In 1990 David Souter, a little-known federal judge from New Hampshire, easily won confirmation to the Court. But the next year a major controversy erupted over President Bush's nomination of Clarence Thomas, an African American conservative with little judicial experience. Just as Thomas's confirmation hearings were drawing to a close, a former colleague, Anita Hill, testified publicly that Thomas had sexually harassed her in the early 1980s. After widely watched and highly debated televised testimony by both Thomas and Hill before the all-male Senate Judiciary Committee, the Senate confirmed Thomas by a narrow margin. In the wake of the hearings, national polls confirmed the pervasiveness of sexual harassment on the job: four out of ten women said that they had been the object of unwanted sexual advances from men at work.

Bush's efforts to promote economic growth were crippled by his predecessor's policies, especially the budget deficit. The Gramm-Rudman Act, passed in 1985, had mandated automatic cuts if budget targets were not met in 1991. Facing the prospect of a halt in nonessential government services and the layoff of thousands of government employees, Congress resorted to new spending cuts and one of the largest tax increases in American history. Bush signed the tax increase, and his failure to keep his "No New Taxes" promise, a cornerstone of his 1992 campaign strategy, earned him the enmity of Republican conservatives and dramatically hurt his chances for reelection in 1992.

Reagan's decision to shift the cost of many federal programs—including housing, education, public works, and social services—to state and local governments also caused problems for Bush. In 1990 a recession began to erode state and local tax revenues. As incomes declined and industrial and white-collar layoffs increased, poverty and homelessness rose sharply. In 1991 unemployment approached 7 percent nationwide. To save money, state and local governments laid off workers even as demand for social services climbed. In 1992 these persistent economic problems would prove a crucial factor in denying George Bush a second term as president.

Foreign Relations under Reagan and Bush

The collapse of détente during the Carter administration, after the Soviet invasion of Afghanistan, prompted Reagan's confrontational approach to what he called the "evil empire." Backed by Republican hard-liners and determined to reduce Communist influence in developing nations, Reagan articulated some of the harshest anti-Soviet rhetoric since the 1950s. The collapse of the Soviet Union in 1991 removed that nation as a credible threat, but new post–Cold War challenges quickly appeared.

Interventions in Developing Countries and the End of the Cold War

As the Cold War ran its course, not all the significant international events during the Reagan presidency involved U.S.-Soviet confrontations. International terrorism emerged as an alarming trend to be reckoned with. In 1983, after Israel invaded Lebanon, the U.S. embassy in Beirut was bombed by Islamic fundamentalists, killing 241 marine peacekeepers barracked in the city. Around the world, terrorist assassins struck down Indira Gandhi in India and Anwar el-Sadat in Egypt. But it was the airplane hijackings and numerous terrorist incidents in the Middle East that led Reagan in 1986 to order air strikes against one highly visible source of state-sponsored terrorism, Muammar al-Qaddafi of Libya.

The administration applied its most concerted attention to Central America. Halting what was seen as the spread of communism in that region became an obsession. In 1983 Reagan ordered the marines to invade the tiny Caribbean island of Grenada, claiming that its Cuban-supported Communist regime posed a threat to other states in the region. Reagan's top priority, however, was to topple the leftist Sandinista government in Nicaragua (Map 31.1). In 1981 the United States suspended aid to Nicaragua, charging that the Sandinistas were supplying arms to rebels against a repressive but non-Communist right-wing regime in El Salvador. At the same time the CIA began to provide extensive covert support to the Nicaraguan opposition, the Contras, whom Reagan called "freedom fighters." Congress, wary of the assumption of unconstitutional powers by the executive branch, responded in 1984 by passing the Boland Amendment, which banned the CIA and other intelligence agencies from providing military support to the Contras—a provision violated in the Iran-Contra affair.

Despite Reagan's heated rhetoric, his second term brought a reduction in tensions with the Soviet Union. In 1985 Reagan met with the new Soviet premier, Mikhail Gorbachev, at the first superpower summit meeting since 1979. Two years later the two leaders agreed to eliminate all intermediate-range nuclear missiles based in Europe. During the Bush administration even more dramatic changes abroad brought an end to the Cold War. In 1989 the grip of communism on Eastern Europe eroded in a series of mostly nonviolent revolutions that climaxed in the destruction of the Berlin Wall in November. Soon the Soviet Union itself began to

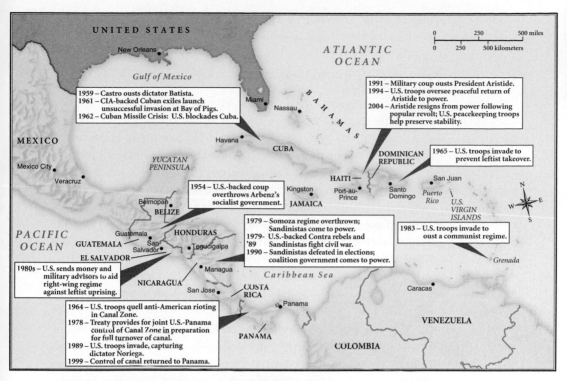

MAP 31.1 U.S. Involvement in Latin America and the Caribbean, 1954–2004

Ever since the Monroe Doctrine (1823), the United States has claimed a special interest in Latin America. During the Cold War, U.S. foreign policy throughout Latin America focused on containing instability and the appeal of communism in a region plagued by poverty and military dictatorships. Providing foreign aid was one approach to addressing social and economic needs, but more typically, U.S. policy concentrated on supporting American business interests. The desire for stability and governments friendly to the United States also led to repeated military interventions, both overt and covert, throughout the Cold War decades.

succumb to the forces of change. The background for these dramatic upheavals was established by Gorbachev. His policies of glasnost (openness) and perestroika (economic restructuring) after 1985 signaled a willingness to tolerate significant changes in Soviet society.

Alarmed by Gorbachev's shift, on August 19, 1991, Soviet military leaders seized Gorbachev and attempted unsuccessfully to oust him. The failure of the coup broke the Communist Party's dominance over the Soviet Union. In December the Union of Soviet Socialist Republics formally dissolved to make way for an eleven-member Commonwealth of Independent States (CIS). Gorbachev resigned, and Boris Yeltsin, president of the new state of Russia, the largest and most populous republic, became the preeminent leader in the region.

The unexpected collapse of the Soviet Union and the end of the Cold War stunned America and the world. In the absence of bipolar superpower confrontations, future international conflicts would arise from varied regional, religious, and ethnic differences. Suddenly, the United States faced unfamiliar military and diplomatic challenges.

War in the Persian Gulf, 1990–1991

The greatest challenge had already surfaced in the Middle East. On August 2, 1990, Iraq, led by Saddam Hussein, invaded Kuwait, its small but oil-rich neighbor, and threatened Saudi Arabia, the site of one-fifth of the world's known oil reserves (see Voices from Abroad, "Calling for a Holy War against the United States," p. 955). Concerned about this threat to Middle East stability as well as U.S. access to oil, President Bush sponsored a series of resolutions in the UN Security Council condemning Iraq, calling for its withdrawal, and imposing an embargo and trade sanctions. When Hussein showed no signs of yielding, Bush prodded the United Nations to create a legal framework for a military offensive against the man he called "the butcher of Baghdad." In November the Security Council voted to use force if Iraq did not withdraw by January 15. In a close vote of 52 to 48 on January 12, the U.S. Senate authorized military action. Four days later President Bush announced to the nation that "the liberation of Kuwait has begun."

The forty-two-day war was a resounding success for the UN coalition forces, which were predominantly American. Under the leadership of General Colin Powell, chairman of the Joint Chiefs of Staff, and the commanding general, H. Norman Schwarzkopf, Operation Desert Storm opened with a month of air strikes to crush communications, destroy armaments, and pummel Iraqi ground troops. A land offensive followed. Within days, thousands of Iraqi troops had fled or surrendered, and the fighting quickly ended, although Hussein was allowed to remain in power (Map 31.2). As the war ended, the United Nations passed Resolution 687, which imposed economic santions against Iraq until it had submitted to unfettered weapons inspections, had destroyed all biological and chemical weapons, and had unconditionally agreed not to develop nuclear capability.

Operation Desert Storm's success and low U.S. casualties (145 Americans were killed in action) produced a euphoric reaction at home. For many Americans, victory over a vastly inferior fighting force seemed to banish the ghost of Vietnam. "By God, we've kicked the Vietnam syndrome once and for all," Bush gloated. The president's approval rating shot up precipitously but declined almost as quickly when a new recession showed that the easy victory in war could not hide the country's serious economic problems.

Uncertain Times: Economic and Social Trends at the Turn of the Millennium

Opinion polls taken in the early 1990s showed that Americans were deeply concerned about the future. They worried about crime in the streets, increases in

VOICES FROM ABROAD

Calling for a Holy War against the United States

SADDAM HUSSEIN

A fter Iraq invaded Kuwait in August 1990, President Saddam Hussein of Iraq justified the action in the language of jihad, or Muslim holy war. Coming from a secular ruler committed to the suppression of religion in public life, Hussein's call for a holy war against the United States suggested the ways in which Islamic fundamentalism had become part of the larger political discourse of the Arab world, particularly in political relations with Western nations.

This great crisis started on the 2nd of August, between the faithful rulers and presidents of these nations—the unjust rulers who have abused everything that is noble and holy until they are now standing in a position which enables the devil to manipulate them. This is the great crisis of this age in this great part of the world where the material side of life has surpassed the spiritual one and the moral one. . . . This is the war of right against wrong and is a crisis between Allah's teachings and the devil.

Allah the Almighty has made his choice—the choice for the fighters and the strugglers who are in favor of principles, God has chosen the arena for this crisis to be the Arab World, and has put the Arabs in a progressive position in which the Iraqis are among the foremost. And to confirm once more the meaning that God taught us ever since the first light of faith and belief, which is that the arena of the Arab World is the arena of the first belief and Arabs have always been an example and a model for belief and faith in God Almighty and are the ones who are worthy of true happiness.

It is now your turn, Arabs, to save all humanity and not just save yourselves, and to show the principles and meanings of the message of Islam, of which you are all believers and of which you are all leaders.

It is now your turn to save humanity from the unjust powers who are corrupt and exploit us and are so proud of their positions, and these are led by the United States of America. . . .

For, as we know out of a story from the Holy Koran, the rulers, the corrupt rulers, have always been ousted by their people for it is a right on all of us to carry out the holy jihad, the holy war of Islam, to liberate the holy shrines of Islam. . . .

We call upon all Arabs, each according to his potentials and capabilities within the teachings of Allah and according to the Muslim holy war of jihad, to fight this U.S. presence of nonbelievers. . . . And we hail the people of Saudi Arabia who are being fooled by their rulers, as well as the people of dear Egypt, as well as all the people of the Arab nations who are not of the same position as their leaders, and they believe in their pride and their sovereignty over their land. We call on them to revolt against their traitors, their rulers, and to fight foreign presence in the holy lands. And we support them, and more important, that God is with them.

SOURCE: *The New York Times*, September 6, 1990, p. A19. Copyright © 1990 The New York Times, Reprinted by permission.

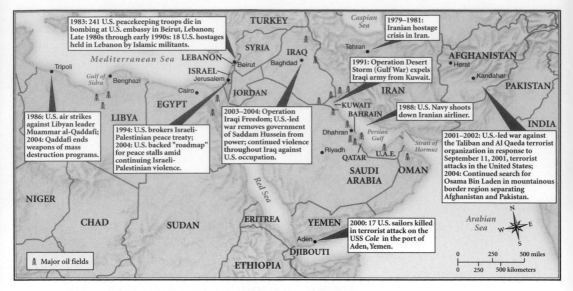

MAP 31.2 U.S. Involvement in the Middle East, 1979–2004

The United States has long played an active role in the Middle East, pursuing the twin goals of protecting Israel's security and ensuring a reliable supply of low-cost oil from the Persian Gulf states. In 1991, with the blessing of the United Nations, President George Bush sent 540,000 American troops to liberate Kuwait from Iraq. In 2003 the United States again fought Iraq, this time driving Saddam Hussein from power and occupying the country. The Middle East has also been the site of terrorist activities targeting U.S. interests, most notably the suicide attack, presumably by Al Qaeda operatives, on the USS *Cole* while it was refueling in Yemen. Al Qaeda terrorism against sites in the United States on September 11, 2001, provoked a U.S.-led United Nations attack on Afghanistan that overthrew the Islamic fundamentalist Taliban government.

For more help analyzing this map, see the Online Study Guide at **bedfordstmartins.com/henrettaconcise**.

poverty and homelessness, the decline of the inner cities, illegal immigration, the environment, the failure of public schools, the unresolved abortion issue, and AIDS. But above all they worried about their own economic security—whether they would be able to keep their jobs in an era of increasing global competition.

The Economic Roller Coaster

Between 1980 and 2000, the nation's economic mood swung from despairing to optimistic and back again. At the beginning of this period, Americans struggled with a growing trade deficit, declining productivity, increased international competition, and a widening gap between rich and poor. By 2000 productivity had improved, the federal deficit had disappeared, and the stock market boomed. Despite Americans' optimism, however, many observers warned of danger signs that threatened to reverse the country's future economic outlook.

Women at War

Women played key and visible roles in the Persian Gulf War, comprising approximately 10 percent of the American troops. Increasing numbers of women are choosing military careers, despite widespread reports of sexual harassment and other forms of discrimination. Luc Delahaye / SIPA Press.

FOR MORE HELP ANALYZING THIS IMAGE, see the Online Study Guide at **bedfordstmartins.com/ henrettaconcise**.

In the 1980s and early 1990s, Americans viewed with alarm the economic success of Germany and Japan, the growing U.S. trade deficit, and the infusion of foreign workers and investment money into the United States. While other nations improved their competitive edge, Americans grappled with a worrisome decline in productivity. In contrast to the period of 1945 to 1973, when productivity had grown 2.8 percent annually, in the next quarter century that figure had dropped to less than 1 percent.

As productivity declined, economic inequality increased: the rich got richer, the poor got poorer, and the middle class shrank. By 1996 the United States was the most economically stratified industrial nation in the world. Statistics from the Congressional Budget Office showed that the richest 1 percent of American families reaped most of the gains of Reaganomics. Even relatively well-advantaged Americans felt a sense of diminished expectations, in part from changes in the job market. Following an established pattern, the number of minimum-wage service jobs continued to grow, while the number of union-protected manufacturing jobs shrank. One-fifth of the labor force in 1994 held only part-time or temporary work. Moreover, in the 1980s and 1990s the downsizing trend, in which companies deliberately shed permanent workers to cut wage costs, spread to middle management. Although most laid-off middle managers eventually found new jobs, many took a large pay cut.

These economic trends put even more pressure on women to seek paid employment. In 1994, 58.8 percent of women were in the labor force, up from 38 percent in 1962, compared with 75.1 percent of men. The stereotypical nuclear family of employed father, homemaker wife, and children characterized less than 15 percent of U.S. households. Although women continued to make inroads in traditionally male-dominated fields—medicine, law, law enforcement, the military, and skilled trades—one out of five held a clerical or secretarial job, the same proportion as in 1950. Women's pay lagged behind men's; for black women and Latinas, the gender gap in pay was especially wide.

At the same time, the labor movement—hurt by downsizing, foreign competition, fear of layoffs, government hostility during the Reagan-Bush years, and its own failure to organize unskilled workers—continued to decline. In 1981, in response to a strike by the Professional Air Traffic Controllers Organization (PATCO), Reagan used his authority to fire all who refused to return to work, and the failure of the strike became symbolic of labor's weakened position. The number of union members dropped from 20 million in 1978 to 16.2 million in 1998, representing only 13.9 percent of the labor force. Although union membership was more than one-third female and one-fifth black, union leadership remained overwhelmingly white and male.

The discouraging economic picture began to improve by the mid-1980s. To compete with the economic success of Germany and Japan, American corporations had adopted new technologies, including microelectronics, biotechnology, computers, and robots and in the late 1990s saw their competitiveness return. By 1997 U.S. economic growth measured 4 percent and was among the healthiest in the world. In contrast, the Japanese economy, one of America's most serious competitors in the 1980s, limped along with only a 1.1 percent growth rate. Working Americans benefited from these developments: unemployment dropped from 7.5 percent in 1992 to barely over 4 percent in the first half of 2000. A booming stock market, energized by a flow of funds into the high-tech sector and the highly touted emergence of e-commerce (firms doing business over the Internet), seemed to reach new highs daily and fueled the wealth and retirement savings of middle- and upper-income Americans. By 2000, as a result of the economy's strong performance and the spending cuts in the federal budget, the nagging deficit was wiped out: the Congressional Budget Office projected an astonishing surplus of $4.6 trillion in the next ten years.

But there were downsides to the picture as well. Many economic analysts worried that a steep drop in the stock market might create a recession, although the country weathered a stunning market plunge of 554 points in 1997. Moreover, prosperity was not equally distributed. A federal survey released in January 2000 reported that the earnings of the top one-fifth of Americans grew 15 percent in the preceding decade, while the bottom one-fifth grew less than 1 percent. By the end of 2000, the collapse of many e-commerce enterprises and the declining value of many technology stocks signaled that the boom was over. In the final quarter of that year, economic growth slowed to 2.2 percent, a pattern that would intensify in 2001, especially after the devastating terrorist attacks against the World Trade Center and the Pentagon on September 11.

Globalization

As Americans grappled with these economic swings, many recognized that their financial well-being was linked to a significant development in the world economy that is generally termed **globalization**. A process begun in the 1970s, it heated up in the 1990s, in part as a result of the end of the Cold War and the shattering of political barriers that had restrained international trade. As the flow of capital and trade expanded, regional economies became more integrated. The nations that joined the European Union in 1991 created a strong free-trade zone and by 2002 had converted to a single currency, the euro. In East Asia an informal bloc also emerged that included Japan, South Korea, Taiwan, Singapore, and China. In the Americas, meanwhile, the United States, Canada, and Mexico signed the North American Free Trade Agreement (NAFTA), in which they agreed to make all of North America a free-trade zone, an agreement Congress ratified in 1993.

Multinational corporations drive globalization. During the last decades of the twentieth century, these businesses increased dramatically, to an estimated 37,000 by 2000. Multinationals tend to be dominated by American-based firms, but they draw upon a complex mixture of regions for their raw materials, labor force, and markets, and increasingly view political boundaries of nation-states as irrelevant to their pursuit of profits and productivity.

"McWorld" and Globalization in Saudi Arabia

Many of the leading multinational corporations transforming the world's economy are purveyors of American-style consumer goods like Nike and Disney products. So successful was McDonald's in extending its international markets—with 25,000 outlets worldwide—that many critics refer to the results of globalization in general as "McWorld." AP/Wide World Photos.

While many observers trumpet globalization for spurring productivity that will in turn raise living standards and promote democracy, others emphasize the costs. Growth has been uneven, and poorer nations—such as those in sub-Saharan Africa and much of Latin America and Asia—have not enjoyed the benefits of the global economy. The spread of consumer culture and its acquisitive values also have tended to sharpen the dividing lines between the haves and the have-nots. Because multinationals are able to take advantage of cheap labor in nations such as India and Vietnam, some categories of skilled and semiskilled jobs are increasingly "outsourced" from more prosperous countries, such as the United States, a process that is restructuring the job market and further eroding the strength of organized labor. The increased integration of world economies also means that political crises or economic instability in one region can have devastating effects elsewhere in the world.

Another serious issue is the environment. Underdeveloped nations eager to modernize their economies have rapidly despoiled their natural resources. In the countries of the former Soviet Union economic modernization has been pursued with little concern for environmental repercussions. In Latin America, in a thirty-year period, roughly a third of the rain forests were cleared to make way for agricultural production. At the same time, economically advanced nations like the United States use far more of the world's resources and contribute the vast majority of carbon emissions that scientists believe are creating global warming, or the greenhouse effect. Ozone depletion produced by chlorofluorocarbons (CFCs)—compounds used in industrial cleaning agents, refrigerators, and aerosol cans—is another serious environmental hazard linked to industrial nations' pursuit of economic growth. Despite some progress in controlling pollution and promoting conservation, many Americans have paid little attention to the limited nature of the world's resources. Even though energy experts warned that a tightening of oil supplies and higher prices were inevitable—a prediction that came true in 2000—few consumers changed their lifestyles by reducing energy consumption, and indeed, the popularity of gas-guzzling SUVs (sport-utility vehicles) suggests a widespread American indifference to the problem of declining fuel resources.

That the environment is a truly global issue was symbolized by the 1987 Montreal Protocol, in which thirty-four nations, including the United States, agreed to phase out ozone-damaging CFCs by 1999. In June 1992 delegates from 170 countries at the UN Earth Summit in Rio de Janeiro adopted a treaty on global warming, and in 1994 the United States joined sixty-three other countries in signing the Basel Convention, which banned the export of hazardous wastes from industrialized to developing countries. In 1997, reflecting continuing concern about global warming, the international community drafted the Kyoto accord, which would require industrialized countries to reduce greenhouse-gas emissions over the next fifteen years, while leaving the problem of developing nations' emissions unresolved. In 1998 President Bill Clinton signed the Kyoto Treaty, but it was never ratified by the U.S. Senate and was rejected by President George W. Bush's administration in

2001, primarily out of fear that the United States, which was responsible for 36.1 percent of the industrialized nations' emissions, would be hurt economically.

Popular Technology

As globalization created a sense of an interconnected economic world, technological developments also enhanced Americans' communications with each other and the world. Beginning in the 1980s, the television industry was transformed by cable and satellite dishes, and by the mid-1990s, viewers could choose from well over a hundred channels, including upstarts such as Ted Turner's Cable News Network (CNN). That station's live coverage of the Gulf War marked a turning point in the world's access to dramatic events as they happened.

Technology also reshaped the home in the late twentieth century. The 1980s saw the introduction of videocassette recorders (VCRs), compact disc (CD) players, cellular telephones, and inexpensive fax machines. Video was everywhere—stores, airplanes, tennis courts, operating rooms. With the introduction of camcorders, the family photo album could be supplemented by inexpensive video of a high school graduation, a marriage, or a birth immediately available on the home television screen. After 2000, digital video discs (DVDs) became the newest technology for viewing movies, but an even hotter item was the cell phone. By 2002, 62 percent of American adults carried these portable devices.

But it was the personal computer that revolutionized the home and office. The big breakthrough came in 1977 when the Apple Computer Company offered the Apple II personal computer for $1,195—a price middle-class Americans could afford. When the Apple II became a runaway success, other companies scrambled to get into the market. IBM offered its first personal computer in the summer of 1981. Software companies such as Microsoft, whose founder Bill Gates is now the richest and most powerful single player in the global economy, grew rapidly by providing operating systems and other software for the expanding personal-computer market. By 2000, 77 percent of American households had at least one personal computer.

More than any other technological advance, the computer created the modern electronic office. Even the smallest business could afford to keep its records and do all its correspondence, billing, and other business on a single desktop machine. The very concept of the office changed as a new class of telecommuters worked at home via computer, fax machine, and electronic mail (e-mail). Today, new technologies utilizing fiber optics, microwave relays, and satellites can transmit massive quantities of information to and from almost any place on earth and even outer space.

The importance of the personal computer would grow even more significant with the popularization of the Internet, which almost 600 million people worldwide were using by 2003. At first scientists and other professionals, who communicated with their peers through a UNIX or text-based e-mail system, were the primary users of the Internet. But the debut of the graphics-based World Wide Web in 1991 enhanced the Internet's commercial possibilities. The Web allowed companies, organizations, and even the White House to create their own "home pages," incorporating visual, audio, and textual information. Businesses and entrepreneurs began to use the Internet to sell their products and services. Political campaigns like that of Democrat Howard Dean during the 2004 presidential primaries illustrated the power of the Internet as a grassroots organizational and fund-raising tool.

The glories of cyberspace are still limited mostly to those who can afford them: in 2003, estimates were that 62 percent of adult Americans used the Internet, but for people with incomes less than $30,000 only 38 percent had access. Internet use is also linked to age. In 2002, one survey found that 14 percent of people over 65 used the Internet, while for children between twelve and seventeen years of age the figure was 78 percent. Many of these were students who benefited from programs to wire public schools and libraries. In 2000, 63 percent of public classrooms were connected to the Internet. Although most observers are sure that the Internet has profoundly transformed the way Americans obtain news and political information, shop, do business, and communicate with each other, the long-term implications of this new technology remain to be seen. Will it have a democratizing effect on politics in the United States and the rest of the world, or will its major impact be to speed along the process of globalization?

An Increasingly Pluralistic Society

As technological change reshaped the nation, significant demographic developments emerged as well. Ethnic and racial diversity, always a source of conflict in American culture, became a defining theme of the 1990s. Between 1981 and 1996 almost 13.5 million immigrants entered the country. The greatest number of newcomers were Latinos. Although Mexico continued to provide the largest group of Spanish-speaking immigrants, many also arrived from El Salvador, Guatemala, and the Dominican Republic. The Latino population grew at a rate of 18 percent in the 1990s to reach 35.3 million in the 2000 census, surpassing African Americans (34 million) as the largest minority group. Once concentrated in California, Texas, and New Mexico, Latinos now lived in urban areas throughout the country and made up about 16 percent of the population of Florida and New York (Map 31.3). Their growing numbers have increased their significance as consumers and voters and have led advertisers and politicians alike to vie for their loyalty.

Asia was the other major source of new immigrants. Asian migration, which increased almost 108 percent from 1980 to 1990, consisted mainly of people from China, the Philippines, Vietnam, Laos, Cambodia, Korea, India, and Pakistan. More than 700,000 Indochinese refugees came to escape upheavals in Southeast Asia in the decade following the Vietnam War. The first arrivals, many of them well educated, adapted successfully to their new homeland. Later refugees lacked professional or vocational skills and took low-paying jobs where they could find them.

The new immigrants' impact on the country's social, economic, and cultural landscape has been tremendous. In many places they have created thriving ethnic

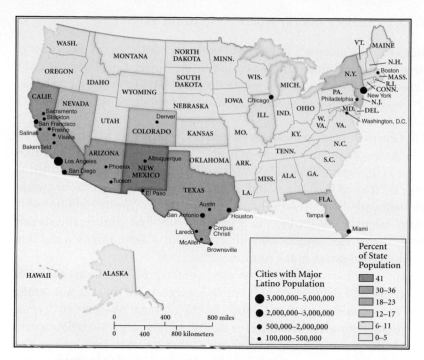

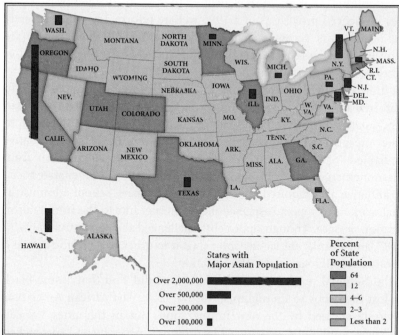

MAP 31.3 Latino Population and Asian Population, 2000

In 2000 Latinos made up over 11 percent of the U.S. population and Asian Americans 4 percent. Demographers predict that Latinos will overtake African Americans as the largest minority group early in the twenty-first century and that by the year 2050 only about half of the U.S. population will be composed of non-Latino whites.

communities, such as Koreatown in Los Angeles. In the 1980s tens of thousands of Jews fleeing religious and political persecution in the Soviet Union created Little Odessa in Brooklyn, New York. Ethnic restaurants and shops have sprung up across the country, while some three hundred specialized periodicals serve immigrant readers.

The U.S. Census Bureau predicts that in the year 2050, whites will make up 52.7 percent of the American population (down from 75.7 percent in 1990), with Latinos accounting for 21.1 percent, blacks 15 percent, and Asians 10.1 percent. If projected intermarriage is factored in (Latinos and Asians marry outside their racial groups much more frequently than blacks), the estimated white "majority" will probably slip to a white "minority." At the beginning of the twenty-first century, already one out of twenty-five married couples were interracial and at least 3 million children were of mixed-race parentage in the country.

While many Americans celebrated the nation's ethnic pluralism as a source of strength, others viewed the new immigrants as scapegoats for all that was wrong with the United States. Though a 1997 study by the National Academy of Science reported that immigration has benefited the nation, adding some $10 billion a year to the economy, many American-born workers felt threatened by immigrants. The unfounded assumption that immigrants were lured to the United States by generous public services influenced provisions of a 1996 welfare reform act, which severely curtailed legal immigrants' access to welfare benefits, especially food stamps (see p. 970). Also in 1996, Congress enacted legislation that increased the financial requirements for sponsors of new immigrants.

The most dramatic challenges to immigrants have emerged at the state level. In the 1980s California absorbed far more immigrants than any other state: more than a third of its population growth in that decade came from foreign immigration. In 1994 California voters overwhelmingly approved Proposition 187, a ballot initiative provocatively named "Save Our State," which barred undocumented aliens from public schools, nonemergency care at public health clinics, and all other state social services. The initiative also required law enforcement officers, school administrators, and social workers to report suspected illegal immigrants to the Immigration and Naturalization Service. Though opponents challenged the constitutionality of Proposition 187, anti-immigrant feeling soon spread to other parts of the country, becoming a hotly debated issue in the 1996 election.

Though the National Academy of Sciences report did find that "some black workers have lost their jobs to immigrants," for the most part African Americans were not adversely affected by the new immigration. But in the cities, African Americans and new immigrants were forced by economic necessity and entrenched segregation patterns to fight for space in decaying, crime-ridden ghettos, where unemployment rates sometimes hit 60 percent. Overcrowded and underfunded, inner-city schools had fallen into disrepair and were unable to provide a proper education.

In April 1992 the frustration and anger of impoverished urban Americans erupted in five days of race riots in Los Angeles. The worst civil disorder since the

1960s, the violence took sixty lives and caused $850 million in damage. The riot was set off by the acquittal (on all but one charge) of four white Los Angeles police officers accused of using excessive force in arresting a black motorist, Rodney King. A graphic amateur video showing the policemen kicking, clubbing, and beating King had not swayed the predominantly white jury. Three of the officers were later convicted on federal civil rights charges.

The Los Angeles riot exposed the rifts in urban neighborhoods. Trapped in the nation's inner cities, many blacks resented recent immigrants who were struggling to get ahead and often succeeding. As a result some blacks had targeted Korean-owned stores during the arson and looting. Latinos were also frustrated by high unemployment and crowded housing conditions. According to the Los Angeles Police Department, Latinos accounted for more than half of those arrested and a third of those killed during the rioting. Thus the riots were not simply a case of black rage at white injustice; they contained a strong element of class-based protest against the failure of the American system to address the needs of all poor people.

One of the ways federal and state governments tried to help poor blacks and Latinos was through the establishment of affirmative action programs in government hiring, contracts, and university admissions. In 1995, however, under pressure from the Republican governor, Pete Wilson, the regents of the University of California voted to scrap the university's twenty-year-old policy of affirmative action, despite protests from the faculty and from university presidents. In 2003 the U.S. Supreme Court continued to uphold the principle of affirmative action when it considered two cases involving the University of Michigan. By a narrow margin the Court confirmed the value of a diverse student body, but insisted that admissions' affirmative action policies be "narrowly tailored" to achieve racial diversity.

One reason affirmative action became a political issue in the 1990s was that many people, including prominent conservatives like George F. Will, William Bennett, and Patrick Buchanan, saw it as a threat to core American values. Lumping affirmative action together with multiculturalism—the attempt to represent the diversity of American society and its peoples—critics feared that all this counting by race, gender, sexual preference, and age would lead to a "balkanization," or fragmentation, of American society. Attempts to revise American history textbooks along multicultural lines aroused much anger, as did efforts by universities such as Stanford to revise college curricula to include the study of non-European cultures. Conservatives also took aim at the antiracist and antisexist regulations and speech codes that had been adopted by many colleges. Arguing for the need to protect First Amendment rights, conservatives derided the attempt to regulate hate speech as "politically correct" (PC).

Backlash against Women's and Gay Rights

Conservative critics also targeted the women's movement. In the widely read *Backlash: The Undeclared War on American Women* (1991), the journalist Susan Faludi described a powerful reaction against the gains American women had won in the 1960s and 1970s. Spearheaded by New Right leaders and aided by the media, conservatives held the women's movement responsible for every ill afflicting modern women, from infertility to rising divorce rates. Yet polls showed strong support for many feminist demands, including equal pay, reproductive rights, and a more equitable distribution of household and child-care responsibilities.

Feminism was also weakened by racial and generational fault lines. Despite the attempts of prominent feminist organizations such as the National Organization for Women (NOW) to focus on racial and ethnic differences among women, African Americans and other women of color continued to feel themselves to be tokens in a predominantly white movement. Many young women felt that the movement had become too obsessed with identifying females as passive victims (of date rape, discrimination, sexual harassment, the media's beauty myth, and so forth) rather than offering women models of empowerment. Others, influenced by women's studies programs and the explosion of feminist scholarship, forged a third wave of feminism in the 1990s.

The deep national divide over abortion, one of the main issues associated with feminism, continued to polarize the country. In the 1980s and 1990s, harassment and violence toward those who sought or provided abortions became common. In 1994 two workers were fatally gunned down at Massachusetts abortion clinics and five people were wounded in the attacks. Although only a fraction of antiabortion activists supported such extreme acts, disruptive confrontational tactics made receiving what was still a woman's legal right more dangerous.

Gay rights was another field of battle. As gays and lesbians gained legal protection against housing and job discrimination across the country, Pat Robertson, North Carolina senator Jesse Helms, and others denounced these civil rights gains as undeserved "special rights." To conservatives, gay rights threatened America's traditional family values. In 1992 Coloradans passed a referendum (overturned by the Supreme Court in 1996) that barred local jurisdictions from passing ordinances protecting gays and lesbians. Across the nation, "gay bashing" and other forms of violence against homosexuals continued. The debate over legal rights for gays and lesbians was reignited in 2003 when the Massachusetts Supreme Court held that same-sex couples were entitled to the "protections, benefits and obligations of civil marriage," a decision that provoked outrage among conservatives. Tensions further escalated when officials in a number of states, including New York, California, and Oregon, began performing highly publicized gay marriages in early 2004 as a prelude to court challenges over the issue. The controversies over gay rights, the women's movement, and affirmative action were revealing signs of the cultural divide that characterized the American people at the turn of the twenty-first century.

A grim backdrop to gay men's struggle against discrimination was the AIDS epidemic. Acquired immune deficiency syndrome (AIDS) was first recognized by physicians in 1981 in the gay male population and its cause identified as the human immunodeficiency virus (HIV). At first, little government funding was directed toward AIDS research or treatment; critics charged that the lack of attention to the syndrome reflected society's antipathy toward gay men. Only when heterosexuals, such as hemophiliacs who had received the virus through blood transfusions, began to be affected did AIDS gain significant public attention. The death of the film star Rock Hudson from AIDS in 1985 finally broke the barrier of public apathy. Another galvanizing moment came in 1991, when the basketball great Earvin "Magic" Johnson announced that he was HIV positive.

To date more Americans have died of AIDS than were killed in the Korean and Vietnam Wars combined. Between 1995 and 1999, however, deaths from AIDS in the United States dropped 30 percent. This decline—in part the result of new treatment strategies using a combination of drugs, or a "cocktail"—has led to cautious optimism about controlling the disease. Yet the drugs' high costs limit their availability and make distribution particularly limited in poor nations. As AIDS deaths decline in developed countries like the United States, the epidemic has reached crisis proportions in sub-Saharan Africa, which accounts for 28 million of the 40 million infections worldwide. Approximately 95 percent of people infected with HIV live in the developing world.

Restructuring the Domestic and International Order: Public Life, 1992–2004

In the 1990s American politics continued to focus on the economy, the environment, and the deep social cleavages surrounding race, gender, and sexual orientation, but after September 11, 2001, foreign affairs would dominate all else. Low voter turnout in the 1992 presidential elections and the strong showing of independent candidates signaled a deep dissatisfaction with the American political system that would continue throughout the decade. One thing was certain: on the domestic front, Americans continued to support the rollback of federal power begun by Reagan, although what programs and responsibilities would be trimmed remained hotly debated.

Clinton's First Term

As the 1992 election campaign got under way, the economy was the overriding issue, for the recession that had begun in 1990 showed no sign of abating. George Bush easily won renomination as the Republican candidate. To solidify the support of the New Right, his running mate, J. Danforth (Dan) Quayle, spoke out strongly for "family values" and other conservative social agendas. William Jefferson (Bill) Clinton, the longtime governor of Arkansas, won the Democratic nomination, and as his running mate he chose Albert (Al) Gore Jr., a senator from Tennessee. At age forty-four Gore was a year and a half younger than Clinton, making the two men the first of the baby-boom generation to occupy the national ticket. Texas billionaire H. Ross Perot, hoping to capitalize on voters' desire for a change from politics as usual, ran as an independent candidate. On election day Clinton received

43 percent of the popular vote to Bush's 38 percent and Perot's 19 percent. The Democrats retained control of both houses of Congress, ending twelve years of divided government.

The liberals who supported Clinton hoped that a Democratic presidency could erase the Reagan-Bush legacy and oversee the creation of a new Democratic social agenda. Initially, Clinton seemed to fulfill that promise. He nominated the liberal Ruth Bader Ginsburg for a seat on the Supreme Court; she was confirmed. The president also appointed Janet Reno as attorney general—the first woman to head the Department of Justice. Other trailblazing cabinet appointments included Secretary of Health and Human Services Donna E. Shalala and, in Clinton's second term, Secretary of State Madeleine Albright. Clinton chose an African American, Ron Brown, as secretary of commerce, and two Latinos, Henry Cisneros and Frederico Peña, to head the Department of Housing and Urban Development (HUD) and the Department of Transportation, respectively.

Clinton's early legislative and administrative record was mixed. In early 1993 he signed into law the Family and Medical Leave Act, twice vetoed by Bush, which provided workers with up to twelve weeks of unpaid leave to tend to a newborn or an adopted child or to respond to a family medical emergency. But when Clinton tried to implement a campaign promise to lift the ban on gays serving in the armed forces, he ran into such ferocious opposition that he backed off, offering instead a weak compromise policy—"Don't ask, don't tell, don't pursue." The solution was an ineffective palliative at best, one that called into question Clinton's willingness to stand firm on issues of principle.

Clinton staked his political fortunes on his campaign promise of universal health care. Though the United States spent more on medical care than any other country in the world, it remained the only major industrialized country not to provide national health insurance to all. Spiraling medical costs and rising insurance premiums had brought the health-care system to a crisis. The president chose his wife, attorney Hillary Rodham Clinton, to head the task force that would draft the legislation—a controversial move since no First Lady had ever played a formal role in policymaking. The resulting proposal was based on the idea of managed competition: market forces, not the government, would control health-care costs and expand citizen's access to medical care. But even this mild form of social engineering ran into intense opposition from the well-financed pharmaceutical and insurance industries. By September 1994 congressional leaders admitted that health reform was dead. In 1995 an estimated 40.3 million Americans had no health insurance; by 2002, 43.6 million, or 15.2 percent of the population, lacked coverage.

Limiting the Federal Government

In the 1994 midterm elections, Republicans gained control of both houses of Congress, winning the House of Representatives for the first time since 1954. In the House the centerpiece of the new Republican majority was the "Contract with

A Bipartisan Balanced Budget

On August 5, 1997, a smiling President Clinton signed the balanced budget bill, surrounded by congressional leaders including House Speaker Newt Gingrich of Georgia (second from right) and House Budget Committee Chairman John Kasich of Ohio (far right). Also looking on with satisfaction was Vice President Al Gore, who already had hopes for the presidency in 2000.

Ron Edmonds / Wide World Photos, Inc.

America," a list of proposals that Newt Gingrich of Georgia, the new Speaker of the House, vowed would be voted on in the first one hundred days of the new session. The contract included constitutional amendments to balance the budget and set term limits for congressional office, significant tax cuts, reductions in welfare and other entitlement programs, anticrime initiatives, and cutbacks in federal regulations. President Clinton, bowing to political reality, acknowledged in his State of the Union message in January 1996 that "the era of big government is over." For the rest of his presidency, he attempted to co-opt Republican issues by moving his own administration to a centrist position and representing himself as a "New Democrat."

Despite Clinton's concessions, Republicans were frustrated in their commitment to cut taxes and balance the budget because both practical and political considerations made many items in the budget immune to serious reductions. Interest on the national debt had to be paid. Defense spending had declined only slightly in the post–Cold War world, and Social Security was politically untouchable. After protracted conflict with Clinton and the Democrats in Congress, the Republicans extracted a pledge from the president that he was committed to ending the budget deficit in 2002 and compromised on a budget that cut $23 billion from discretionary spending.

As part of the Contract with America, House Republicans were especially determined to cut welfare, a joint federal-state program that represented a fairly small part of the budget. The benefits of the main welfare program, Aid to Families with Dependent Children (AFDC), were small: the average annual payment to families (including food stamps) was $7,740, well below the established poverty line. Still, in the 1990s both Democratic and Republican statehouses sought ways to change the behavior of welfare recipients by imposing work requirements or denying benefits for additional children born to women on AFDC. In August 1996, after vetoing two Republican-authored bills, President Clinton signed into law the Personal Responsibility and Work Opportunity Act, a historic overhaul of federal entitlements. The 1996 law ended the federal guarantee of cash assistance to poor children by abolishing AFDC, required most adult recipients to find work within two years, set a five-year limit on payments to any one family, and gave states wide discretion in running their welfare programs.

The Republican takeover of Congress had one unintended consequence: it united the usually fractious Democrats behind the president. Unopposed in the 1996 primaries, Clinton was able to burnish his image as a moderate. He also benefited from the continuing strength of the economy. Economic indicators released shortly before election day showed that the "misery index"—a combination of the unemployment rate and inflation—was the lowest it had been in twenty-seven years. The Republicans settled on Senate Majority Leader Bob Dole of Kansas as their presidential candidate. Dole made a 15 percent across-the-board tax cut the centerpiece of his campaign, while Clinton emphasized the improved economy. With only 49 percent of the eligible voters casting ballots, the lowest voter turnout since Calvin Coolidge won the presidency in 1924, Clinton became the first Democrat since Franklin Roosevelt to win reelection. Republicans retained a majority of the nation's statehouses and strengthened their control of Congress. In his second term, Clinton's key to success would be his ability, as a Democratic president, to work with a Republican-dominated Congress.

Clinton's Impeachment

Clinton's attempt to shape a bipartisan political agenda would unravel halfway through his second term when a sex scandal led to his impeachment. In January 1998 attorneys representing Paula Jones, who claimed that the then-governor

Clinton had propositioned her when she was an Arkansas state employee, revealed that they planned to depose a former White House intern, Monica Lewinsky, about an alleged affair with President Clinton. Kenneth Starr, the independent counsel initially charged with investigating the Whitewater scandal—a dubious Arkansas real estate deal involving both President and Mrs. Clinton—widened his investigation to explore whether Clinton or his aides had encouraged Lewinsky to lie in her statement. Clinton consistently denied having a sexual relationship with Lewinsky—both on national television and in deposition before a federal grand jury.

In September 1998, after Starr issued a report that concluded that the president had committed impeachable offenses, the House of Representatives began its inquiry. On December 19 the House narrowly approved two articles of impeachment against Clinton: one for perjury before a grand jury concerning his liaison with Lewinsky and a second for obstruction of justice, in which he was accused of encouraging others to lie on his behalf. Yet on the evening of the House vote, a CBS news poll reported that 58 percent of its respondents opposed impeachment, while only 38 percent supported it.

Throughout the ensuing trial conducted by the Senate, Clinton's approval rating remained exceptionally high, perhaps because most Americans questioned the political motives of his attackers and almost certainly because a strong economy kept most citizens content with the president's performance, even if they disapproved of his personal morality. Finally, after a five-week trial and hours of televised debate, with Democrats voting solidly against conviction and enough Republicans breaking with their party, the Senate acquitted Clinton on both charges. Like Andrew Johnson, the only other president to be impeached (see Chapter 15), Bill Clinton survived the process, but the scandal, the trial, and the profoundly partisan sentiments that surrounded it limited his effectiveness as president and deepened public cynicism about politics and its practitioners.

For if Clinton had been hampered by the controversy, so too had Republicans. Despite polls that indicated that Americans did not place much emphasis on the Lewinsky scandal, during the 1998 elections many Republicans made Clinton's moral character the focus of their campaigns. The Democrats, in contrast, focused on issues like Social Security and education. They also employed vigorous get-out-the-vote drives, particularly among traditional Democratic constituencies—labor unions and African Americans. When the ballots were counted, for the first time since 1934 the party of the incumbent president gained seats—five—in a midterm election, shrinking the Republican majority in Congress to twelve. Although a variety of factors influenced voting patterns, including the improving economy, many observers pointed to a backlash against the drive for impeachment.

Clinton's Foreign Policy

A major dilemma facing the Clinton administration was how to conceptualize and implement the U.S. role in the post–Cold War world. The end of the superpower rivalry presented unexpected opportunities to resolve some long-standing conflicts and created some new ones. In Haiti the threat of a U.S. invasion in October 1993 led to the restoration of the exiled president, Jean-Bertrand Aristide, who had been ousted by a military coup in 1991. In South Africa the end of a fifty-year policy of racial separation was capped in May 1994 by the election of the rebel leader Nelson Mandela, who had spent twenty-seven years in prison for challenging apartheid, as the country's first black president. And in a move that was seen as the symbolic end to the American experience in Vietnam, the United States established diplomatic relations with Hanoi in July 1995, two decades after the fall of Saigon (see Chapter 29).

Clinton scored some modest successes in his efforts to mediate long-standing conflicts. In 1998 he facilitated an agreement in Northern Ireland between Protestants and Catholics. In 1994 he brought Israeli prime minister Yitzhak Rabin and Yasir Arafat, chairman of the Palestine Liberation Organization, together in Washington to sign an agreement allowing limited Palestinian self-rule in the Gaza Strip and Jericho. The optimism about this breakthrough was short-lived, however. In 1995 Rabin was assassinated, and in 1996 Benjamin Netanyahu was elected prime minister of Israel. His hard-line policy against the Palestinians contributed to escalating tensions. Clinton would make several more efforts to move the peace process along, including an unsuccessful last-ditch effort in the remaining weeks of his presidency.

Nothing seemed more intractable than the problems that engulfed the former state of Yugoslavia, which had split into five independent states in 1991. The province of Bosnia and Herzegovina, made up largely of Muslims and committed to a multiethnic state—Serb, Croat, and Muslim—had declared its independence in 1992. But Bosnian Serbs, supported financially and militarily by what remained of Yugoslavia, formed their own breakaway state and began a siege of the Bosnian capital, Sarajevo. In the countryside the Serbs launched a ruthless campaign of "ethnic cleansing," driving Bosnian Muslims and Croats from their homes and into concentration camps or shooting them in mass executions. Clinton was unwilling initially to involve the United States, but in November 1995 America facilitated a peace accord. A NATO-led peacekeeping force, backed by 20,000 American troops, would end the fighting, at least temporarily.

A new crisis emerged in the region in March 1999 in Kosovo, a province of the Serbian-dominated Federal Republic of Yugoslavia. NATO, strongly influenced by the United States, intervened to protect ethnic Albanians from the Serbians who were determined to drive them out of the region. This was NATO's first offensive war since its establishment in 1947 and it succeeded in restoring order to the region, but no long-term solutions were found to the problems generated by ethnic conflict.

In the post–Cold War era, terrorism constituted yet another challenge to world peace. In 1993 foreign terrorists bombed the World Trade Center in New York City. Five men, associated with Islamic extremists, were later sentenced to life in prison. In October 2000 a suicide attack on the USS *Cole*, a navy guided-missile destroyer that was refueling in the Yemeni port of Aden, blew a huge hole in the ship's hull, killing seventeen sailors. The United States immediately blamed Saudi exile and

Islamic extremist Osama bin Laden, who was also suspected in the 1993 World Trade Center attack. The Balkan crises, as well as terrorist activity, served as potent reminders that despite the end of the Cold War and regardless of the U.S. position as the most powerful nation in the world, America was limited in its ability to achieve its foreign-policy aims.

An Unprecedented Election

In 2001 foreign affairs and particularly the issue of international terrorism would come to dominate American politics, but in the 2000 campaign domestic issues predominated. The Democrats nominated Vice President Al Gore, who chose Connecticut senator Joseph I. Lieberman as his running mate. The Republicans selected Governor George W. Bush of Texas, son of the former president, to head their ticket and Richard Cheney for their vice presidential nominee. Although both Bush and Gore were considered moderate centrists, they had ideological differences over the role of the federal government and how best to use the large projected budget surpluses. Bush proposed a major tax cut, a partial privatization of Social Security, and the use of government-issued vouchers to pay for private education. Gore argued for using the surplus to shore up the Social Security funds, for a tax-break incentive for college tuition, and for expansion of Medicare. The two candidates disagreed on the abortion issue, with Bush opposing abortion and Gore in support of a woman's right to choose. While conservative Pat Buchanan of the Reform Party fared poorly, Ralph Nader, the Green Party candidate, did appeal to many in the left wing of the Democratic Party who were disenchanted with Gore's centrist position. Nader received over two and a half million votes and detracted enough ballots from Gore in New Hampshire, New Mexico, and Florida to give those states to Bush. Nader's 97,419 votes in Florida (2 percent) contributed to making that state's presidential election a virtual tie between Bush and Gore.

As Florida hung in the balance, returns from the rest of the country showed that Gore had a lead of 337,000 in the popular vote and had won the District of Columbia and twenty states, with 267 electoral votes, while Bush had triumphed in twenty-nine states, with 246 electoral votes. In four states, however, fewer than 7,500 votes separated the two major candidates. In such a tight election, the results in Florida became crucial because the electoral college victory would come down to which candidate could claim that state's twenty-five electoral votes.

Almost immediately, a controversy erupted over "butterfly ballots" that had apparently misled some Gore voters into voting for Buchanan and "under votes" (ballots not clearly marked), which resulted from antiquated voting machines and inattentive voters (see American Voices, "We Marched to Be Counted," p. 974). To make certain all votes were tabulated, Gore forces demanded hand recounts in several counties. When Florida secretary of state Katherine Harris halted the recount process and declared Governor Bush the winner by a mere 537 votes, Gore turned

AMERICAN VOICES

We Marched to Be Counted

JOHN LEWIS

*E merging from the furor over apparent voting irregularities in Florida in the 2000 presi-
dential election was a concern that uncounted and disqualified voters were more likely to
be poor people, especially African Americans. John Lewis, a civil rights activist who had
marched from Selma to Montgomery in 1965 to demonstrate for African American voting
rights in Alabama, reflects on the relationship between the 1960s civil rights movement and the
Florida voting controversy. Lewis is now a congressman from Atlanta.*

What's happening in Florida and in Washington is more than a game for pundits. The
whole mess reminds African Americans of an era when we had to pass literacy tests, pay
poll taxes, and cross every *t* and dot every *i* to get to be able to vote. . . . For all the political
maneuvering and legal wrangling, many people have missed an important point: the story
of the 2000 election is about more than George W. Bush and Al Gore. It's about the right
to vote. And you cannot understand the true implications of this campaign and the subsequent litigation without grasping how deeply many minorities feel about the seemingly
simple matter of the sanctity of the ballot box.

   There is a lot of troubling new talk of "political profiling"—allegations that officials
tried to suppress the black vote on Election Day and may be maneuvering now to make
sure it isn't counted. There are reports that officials put new voting machines in white areas
but not black ones and that African Americans were asked to present two, not just one,
forms of identification to be allowed to vote. These charges should be looked into. But I like
to believe that no one met in some smoke-filled room and said, "We're going to keep black
voters out, we're going to keep Jewish voters out." . . .

   My greatest fear today is that the perception our votes were not counted may usher in a
period of great cynicism. On the other hand—and I bet this is more likely—it may give
people a greater sense of the importance of voting and of vigilance. The vote, after all, is the
real heart of the movement. Younger people shouldn't think civil rights was just about water
fountains or stirring speeches on TV. Late in the summer of 1961, after the Freedom Rides,
we realized it was not enough to integrate lunch counters and buses. We had to get the vote.

SOURCE: *Newsweek*, December 11, 2000. Reprinted by permission of Congressman John Lewis.

to the Florida Supreme Court in an attempt to get a hand recount. When that court
ordered the hand count to continue, Bush went to the U.S. Supreme Court.

   Finally, on December 12, a deeply divided Supreme Court, in a 5-to-4 decision
marked by acrimonious dissenting opinions, declared that the equal protection clause
of the Fourteenth Amendment required that all ballots had to be counted in the same
way and that time did not permit a statewide hand count. Justice Stephen G. Breyer,
in dissent, angrily pointed out that the majority's opinion was clearly a political one
that ran "the risk of undermining the public's confidence in the Court itself." On the

following day Vice President Gore gave his concession speech, and George W. Bush announced his victory to become the forty-third president. It took thirty-seven dramatic days and the intervention of the Supreme Court to resolve the controversies surrounding the Florida vote and determine the new president, making the election one of the most remarkable in American history.

George W. Bush's Early Presidency and September 11

In his first seven months in office, Bush compiled a mixed record of success. He pleased the right wing of his party on his first day when he banned the use of foreign-aid funds for family-planning programs abroad that included abortion counseling among their services. Then, despite vigorous opposition, he secured Senate approval for his appointment of John Ashcroft—noted for his conservative social values concerning homosexuality, abortion, and religion—as attorney general. Other major Bush appointees were Donald Rumsfeld as secretary of defense, a position he had also filled under President Gerald Ford, and two highly regarded African Americans, Gulf War hero and former chairman of the Joint Chiefs of Staff Colin Powell as secretary of state, and Stanford University professor Condoleezza Rice as national security advisor.

Bush also made good on his campaign pledge to cut taxes, which he claimed would stimulate the slowing economy. The Economic Growth and Tax Relief Reconciliation Act of 2001 refunded money retroactively to taxpayers ($300–$600 per person); however, it failed to immediately stimulate the economy and contributed to the rapid decline of the federal budget surplus. His economic headaches intensified when the stock market took two steep dives and economic indicators revealed a jump in unemployment figures and slowing economic growth. Other financial woes emerged in the summer, when sharply escalating gasoline prices alarmed consumers and severe power shortages on the West Coast led to rolling blackouts and increased energy costs there. President Bush resisted calls for federal price controls and emphasized instead the need for the creation of more power plants and for oil drilling in Alaska and the Arctic, a move that infuriated environmentalists. The political fallout was compounded by complaints that President Bush's and Vice President Cheney's close personal ties to the energy industry were guiding administration policies.

Abroad, Bush took steps to heighten his credibility as a world leader, a task made difficult both by the controversial nature of his election and his inexperience in foreign affairs. Indeed, before he took office, he had barely been outside the United States. His major initiatives called for maintaining UN sanctions against Iraq, which had been put in place at the end of the Gulf War, and for increased efforts to destabilize Saddam Hussein's regime. In contrast to his predecessor, Bush decided that the United States would withdraw from active participation in negotiations in the Palestinian-Israeli conflict.

The domestic and foreign issues that shaped the Bush administration in its first months would soon take a backseat to a sobering challenge when terrorists hijacked four commercial airliners on September 11, 2001. Two plowed into New York's World

September 11, 2001

This image of the New York World Trade Center's twin towers being engulfed in flames after Al Qaeda terrorists rammed hijacked commercial jets into them on September 11, 2001, shocked the world as it demonstrated the horrific destruction terrorism could wreak in the world's most powerful nation. Of the estimated 2,900 people who died in the attacks, 2,605 were at the World Trade Center. Robert Clarke / AURORA.

Trade Center, destroying its twin towers and killing over 2,600 persons. A third plane seriously damaged the Pentagon and killed almost 200 people; the fourth, presumably headed for the White House, crashed in Pennsylvania when passengers fought back and thwarted the hijackers' efforts. Within hours, the United States had traced the origins of the attack to a militant Muslim sect, Al Qaeda, led by Osama bin Laden and supported by Taliban leaders in Afghanistan. The Taliban was itself a fundamentalist Muslim organization that had seized control of Afghanistan in 1996, following the overthrow of a Soviet-backed regime by forces supplied and assisted by the United States in the heat of the Cold War.

In response to the attacks, President George W. Bush and his advisors proclaimed a "war on terrorism" and successfully called upon a multinational force to support military strikes against Osama bin Laden and the Taliban in Afghanistan. Within weeks, the United States and its allies, relying on massive air power and deployment of special forces, routed the Taliban and rolled up the Al Qaeda network's center of operations. Despite these successes in the war on terrorism, however, as of this writing U.S. officials believe Osama bin Laden to be alive and the Al Qaeda network to be active in a "holy war" against the United States and its allies.

In his State of the Union address on January 29, 2002, President Bush signaled his intention to carry the war against terrorism to nations that harbor terrorists or develop weapons of mass destruction—hence his characterization of Iran, Iraq, and North Korea as "an axis of evil." By the first anniversary of September 11, the president was threatening to attack Iraq, a controversial plan that divided his advisors and provoked heated public debate. Bush presented his case to the United Nations, and on November 8, the Security Council approved Resolution 1441, which included the return of UN weapons inspectors to Iraq (Hussein had expelled the inspectors in 1998) and a requirement that Saddam Hussein's government submit to the Security Council a full account of its weapons, stockpiles, facilities, and de-livery capabilities. As weapons inspections proceeded in December 2002, the Bush administration continued its war preparations, and when it failed to obtain UN-sanctioned support for an immediate preemptive strike, the United States and Britain launched an armed attack against Iraq without it.

President Bush declared victory in May 2003, but even with the dramatic capture of Hussein in December 2003, the prolonged resistance to U.S. occupation by Iraqis that continued even after the formal turnover of power to an interim government in June 2004 leaves the long-term result of the war an open question. In April 2004 graphic evidence of widespread prisoner abuse at Baghdad's Abu Ghraib prison by the U.S. military in violation of the Geneva Conventions surfaced and damaged America's moral position abroad. Moreover, the bombing of Afghanistan and the invasion of Iraq did not halt terrorism, which experts note is not limited to Al Qaeda but encompasses many groups organized throughout the world. In November 2003 more than twenty people died from bombs targeting the British

Continuing Violence in Iraq

In spring 2004, U.S. troops faced mounting opposition from Iraqi rebels, especially those associated with the charismatic Shiite cleric Moqtada al-Sadr. A battle in the city of Al Ramadi, near Fallujah, left more than a dozen Americans dead. Here a marine from the Second Battalion sits at the wheel of his Humvee. In the wake of high casualties in April (with 120 U.S. dead), the Pentagon was under criticism for not having provided American soldiers with heavier vehicles—such as the Stryker or Bradley tanks—that could offer more protection from explosions from grenades, land mines, and other devices than the "thin-skinned" Humvees could. AP.

consulate in Istanbul, and in March 2004, a well-coordinated series of explosions on trains in Madrid left over two hundred dead. In August 2004 a bipartisan congressional committee issued a report on its 9/11 investigations that severely criticized the intelligence community's failures to prepare the nation for terrorist attacks. Its recommendations for enhancing counterterrorist measures became one of many hotly contested issues in the presidential campaign, with Democratic nominee John Kerry claiming that President Bush was not doing enough to protect the nation.

Related to the spread of terrorism is the deep-seated resentment by militant Islamic fundamentalists of long-standing U.S. support of the state of Israel. The crisis in the Middle East over Israeli resistance to demands for a Palestinian homeland deepened after the 9/11 attacks on the United States, with both sides adopting a harder position, particularly regarding Israeli settlements in the West Bank and the Palestinian use of terrorism, including suicide bombings against Israeli citizens. The Bush administration reversed its earlier decision to disengage from the Middle East peace process, and worked with Russia, the European Union, and the United Nations to create a Middle East "Roadmap" in June 2003, which set out a step-by-step plan to bring a halt to the violence and create an independent Palestinian state. Although the suicide bombings in Israel have abated somewhat, the attacks continue and the Israelis have been slow to close their controversial settlements in the West Bank. In the spring of 2004, Israeli prime minister Ariel Sharon stepped up an effort to eliminate the leadership of Hamas, a militant Islamic terrorist organization responsible for many of the suicide bombings, and the Israeli military successfully assassinated Sheikh Ahmad Yassin and Abdel Aziz al-Rantissi. In the Middle East, the "Roadmap" has stalled and peace remains elusive.

Politics and the Economy after 9/11

From a political standpoint, the crisis caused by the September 11 attacks gave George W. Bush's administration an immense boost. Prior to the attacks, Bush was lampooned in the media for the "dyselection of 2000." Jokes that Vice President Dick Cheney, a far more experienced and sophisticated policymaker, was the real president abounded. Opinion polls in Europe indicated that Bush was not taken seriously as a world leader, while the president's approval rating at home sagged steadily during the summer of 2001, registering only 52 percent in early July. By January 2002, however, Bush's approval rating had soared to an exceptional 83 percent. Some critics flinched at Bush's promotion of strident nationalism, but the majority of the public approved of the president's handling of the crisis.

As during any war, the power and influence of the executive clearly increased, and many observers agreed that Bush's demeanor became more "presidential." Beyond the direction of foreign policy, however, Bush's new political strength affected domestic policy as well. In the November 2002 elections, the Republicans gained two seats in the Senate and reestablished a majority that they had lost briefly when Republican Jim Jeffords announced that he was leaving the Republicans to become an independent. Republicans also picked up five seats in the House, increasing their majority to 228 out of the total of 435 representatives. The election results were striking, as this was the first time since 1934 that the party of the president scored gains in both houses of Congress in his administration's first midterm election.

Trust in the president's leadership, coupled with fears about future terrorism, permitted the Bush administration significant leeway in implementing new domestic security measures. The USA PATRIOT (Uniting and Strengthening America by Providing Appropriate Tools Required to Intercept and Obstruct Terrorism) Act of 2002, which passed with only one dissenting vote, gave unparalleled powers to the federal government to investigate and detain immigrants suspected of terrorist activity, all surrounded by a high degree of secrecy in the name of national security. Another important domestic initiative created the Office of Homeland Security, which Congress approved in November 2002. Combining approximately twenty-two different government departments into a single cabinet-level agency operating with a budget of $40 billion, this centralized agency became responsible for the protection of American life and property from terrorist activities and for controlling the nation's borders. Although supporters hope that this monumental reorganization will bring efficiency to the myriad government agencies engaged in national security, critics worry that it will create an unwieldy bureaucracy. They also warn that it will lead to vastly enhanced governmental authority and the reduction of Americans' civil liberties and privacy rights.

President Bush's popularity and Republican political success also allowed him to continue domestic policies that emphasized tax cuts, increased military spending, rollbacks of government regulations (especially those concerning the environment), and reductions in expenditures for social welfare. An exception to the latter was to back Medicare reform legislation that provided prescription drug benefits to America's elderly. Taking the issue from the Democrats, whose version of reform included efforts to put a cap on drug costs, the Republicans passed legislation in December 2003 that would provide over $400 billion dollars in benefits. The expenditures add to what will become an important legacy of Bush's economic policies: the return to enormous budget deficits that the White House has projected to be $450 billion for the year 2004.

Despite Republican political successes since 9/11, the state of the economy has been a persistent trouble spot. Economic indicators show that the economy was in recession months before the terrorist attacks, which contributed significantly to the financial woes, most noticeably in damage to the airline industry. But the fragility of the airlines paled in comparison to broader problems that were unconnected to the terrorist attacks. Just weeks after the destruction of the Twin Towers, the energy giant Enron, a Houston-based company that brokered electricity and natural gas, collapsed on Wall Street after its announcement of a $618 million third-quarter loss. The Securities and Exchange Commission discovered that the auditing firm Arthur Andersen, which handled Enron's accounts, had been shredding and destroying documents that revealed immense irregularities. During the summer of 2002, other corporate giants fell—including WorldCom and Adelphia Communications—costing thousands of jobs and threatening the nation's economy. By midsummer the unemployment rate stood at 5.9 percent as compared to 4.6 percent the previous year. The accompanying decline in the stock market wiped out $7.7 trillion of paper wealth—an outcome devastating for many Americans, roughly half of whom owned stock. As falling stock prices depleted 401(k) accounts and retirement funds, the elderly found their real incomes reduced and for many their hopes of retirement put on hold.

By the end of 2003, despite concerns about the growing deficit and its impact on the strength of the dollar in international markets, economic signs, including modest growth in GDP and a slight drop in unemployment, looked more promising. Experts were divided over whether this was a long-term trend or an anomaly tied to tax rebates and a boon in mortgage refinancing spurred by record-low interest rates. They particularly debated whether lower-income Americans had benefited from the growth and whether they would be able to participate in the consumer spending necessary to sustain a solid economic recovery, a recovery that still seemed elusive by the end of 2004.

Entering the presidential election that year, the nation was profoundly divided. The war in Iraq bogged down as Iraqi resistance intensified. Over one thousand GIs had died, and no clear plans for ending the conflict had emerged. But President Bush ran for reelection with a confidence that proclaimed his war leadership, his record in defending the country against terrorist attacks, and improvements in the economy that he claimed benefited from his tax cuts, which he vowed to make permanent in his second term. The Democratic candidate John Kerry and his running mate Senator John Edwards of North Carolina argued that the tax cuts had overwhelmingly benefited the wealthy. They proposed a program to stop jobs from drifting overseas, provide health-care insurance for everyone, increase funding for public education, and safeguard Social Security benefits for the elderly. But the underlying issues were the Vietnam-era military records of the two leaders, the debate over legalizing gay marriages, and most significantly the public's perception of the candidates' religious and moral values. These issues revealed a deep cultural divide in the nation that helped spur a turnout of 59 percent of eligible voters—the highest percentage since 1968. The close election ended with President Bush the clear victor in both the popular vote and the Electoral College, while the Republican Party gained a greater majority in both houses of Congress. The impact of this victory on policy remained to be seen, but most analysts agreed that healing the nation's divisions would be one of the country's most formidable tasks.

George W. Bush Wins a Second Term

George W. Bush and his wife, Laura, greet supporters on November 3, 2004, at the Ronald Reagan Center in Washington, D.C., following his reelection victory in the 2004 presidential contest.

© Gary Hershorn/Reuters/Corbis.

TIMELINE

1981	Sandra Day O'Connor nominated to Supreme Court MTV premieres Beginning of AIDS epidemic IBM markets its first personal computer	1992	Los Angeles riots Earth Summit in Rio de Janeiro Bill Clinton elected president
1981–1983	Recession	1993	Family and Medical Leave Act North American Free Trade Agreement (NAFTA)
1981–1989	National debt triples	1994	Health-care reform fails Republicans gain control of Congress
1983	Star Wars proposed	1995	U.S. troops enforce peace in Bosnia
1985	Gramm-Rudman Balanced Budget Act United States becomes a debtor nation Mikhail Gorbachev takes power in Soviet Union	1996	Personal Responsibility and Work Opportunity Act Clinton reelected
1986	Iran-Contra affair	1998–1999	Bill Clinton impeached and acquitted
1987	Montreal environmental protocol Stock market collapse	2000	Terrorists attack USS Cole in Yemen George W. Bush elected president in contested election
1988	George H. W. Bush elected president	2001	Worst stock market loss in eleven years Terrorists destroy New York's World Trade Center and attack Pentagon USA Patriot Act gives federal government sweeping new powers
1989	Savings and loan crisis Webster v. Reproductive Health Services		
1990–1991	Persian Gulf War	2002	Department of Homeland Security created
1990–1992	Recession	2003–2004	U.S.-led war against Iraq overthrows government of Saddam Hussein
1991	Dissolution of Soviet Union ends Cold War		

For Further Exploration

Two valuable overviews of the period are by Haynes Johnson: *Sleepwalking through History: America in the Reagan Years* (1992) and *Divided We Fall: Gambling with History in the Nineties* (1995). Richard A. Posner, *An Affair of State: The Investigation, Impeachment, and Trial of President Clinton* (1999), stresses the legal issues involved in Bill Clinton's impeachment and acquittal. An engaging book that uses census data to counter the emphasis on American decline in the 1980s and 1990s is Reynolds Farley, *The New American Reality: Who We Are, How We Got There, Where We Are Going* (1996). On foreign policy Stephen Ambrose and Douglas Brinkley, *Rise of Globalism* (8th ed., 1997), offers a solid assessment and Richard A. Melanson, *American Foreign Policy since the Vietnam War* (1991) deals specifically with the era of Nixon through Clinton. A lively collection of essays debating the new immigration is Nicolaus Mills, ed., *Arguing Immigration: The Debate over the Changing Face of America* (1994). On work, women, and families, see Arlie Hochschild, *The Second Shift: Working Parents and the Revolution at Home* (1989).

Jurist, the Law Professors' Network, provides Guide to Impeachment and Censure Materials Online at <http://jurist.law.pitt.edu/impeach.htm#Public>, which offers extensive links to materials on the constitutional issues raised by impeachment and on public-opinion polls, documents, and analysis specific to the Clinton impeachment.

The Gallup Organization has been conducting public-opinion surveys since 1935. Its site, at <http://www.gallup.com>, provides access to recent polls on politics, the family, religion, crime, and lifestyles. This searchable site is an invaluable guide to contemporary American opinion. The U.S. Census Bureau's Web page, at <http://www.census.gov/population/www/>, offers a rich variety of data—on health insurance, racial and ethnic composition, poverty, work environment, and marriage and family—that provides insight into the major demographic changes transforming American society.

The *New York Times*'s AIDS at 20, at <http://www.nytimes.com/library/national/science/aids/aids-index.html>, provides more than 350 selected *New York Times* articles from 1981 to 2001 on the epidemic, including material on its course of devastation in Africa.

The Gulf War, at <http://www.pbs.org/wgbh/pages/frontline/gulf/>, is an online documentary treatment of the conflict. A companion to the Gulf War documentary produced by the PBS series *Frontline*, the site includes maps, a chronology, interviews with decision makers and soldiers from the various sides of the conflict, audio clips, and a section on weapons and technology.

The September 11 Digital Archive, at <http://911digitalarchive.org/>, is cosponsored by the American Social History Project at the City University of New York Graduate Center and the Center for History and New Media at George Mason University. The site is part of an ongoing project to collect and preserve firsthand accounts of Americans' responses to the terrorist attack of September 11, 2001. The site includes oral histories, video and still images, and a valuable guide to Web sites on the topic.

For definitions of key terms boldfaced in this chapter, see the glossary at the end of the book.

To assess your mastery of the material covered in this chapter, see the Online Study Guide at **bedfordstmartins.com/henrettaconcise**.

For map resources and primary documents, see **bedfordstmartins.com/henrettaconcise**.

DOCUMENTS

The Declaration of Independence

The Unanimous Declaration of the Thirteen United States of America

When in the Course of human events, it becomes necessary for one people to dissolve the political bands which have connected them with another, and to assume among the Powers of the earth, the separate and equal station to which the Laws of Nature and of Nature's God entitle them, a decent respect to the opinions of mankind requires that they should declare the causes which impel them to the separation.

We hold these truths to be self-evident, that all men are created equal, that they are endowed by their Creator with certain unalienable rights, that among these are Life, Liberty, and the pursuit of Happiness. That to secure these rights, Governments are instituted among Men, deriving their just powers from the consent of the governed. That whenever any Form of Government becomes destructive of these ends, it is the Right of the People to alter or to abolish it, and to institute new Government, laying its foundation on such principles and organizing its powers in such form, as to them shall seem most likely to effect their Safety and Happiness. Prudence, indeed, will dictate that Governments long established should not be changed for light and transient causes; and accordingly all experience hath shown, that mankind are more disposed to suffer, while evils are sufferable, than to right themselves by abolishing the forms to which they are accustomed. But when a long train of abuses and usurpations, pursuing invariably the same Object evinces a design to reduce them under absolute Despotism, it is their right, it is their duty, to throw off such Government, and to provide new Guards for their future security. —Such has been the patient sufferance of these Colonies; and such is now the necessity which constrains them to alter their former Systems of Government. The history of the present King of Great Britain is a history of repeated injuries and usurpations, all having in direct object the establishment of an absolute Tyranny over these States. To prove this, let Facts be submitted to a candid world.

He has refused his Assent to Laws, the most wholesome and necessary for the public good.

He has forbidden his Governors to pass Laws of immediate and pressing importance, unless suspended in their operation till his Assent should be obtained; and, when so suspended, he has utterly neglected to attend to them.

He has refused to pass other Laws for the accommodation of large districts of people, unless those people would relinquish the right of Representation in the Legislature, a right inestimable to them and formidable to tyrants only.

He has called together legislative bodies at places unusual, uncomfortable, and distant from the depository of their public Records, for the sole purpose of fatiguing them into compliance with his measures.

He has dissolved Representative Houses repeatedly, for opposing with manly firmness his invasions on the rights of the people.

He has refused for a long time, after such dissolutions, to cause others to be elected; whereby the Legislative powers, incapable of Annihilation, have returned to the People at large for their exercise; the State remaining in the mean time exposed to all the dangers of invasion from without and convulsions within.

He has endeavoured to prevent the population of these States; for that purpose obstructing the Laws of Naturalization of Foreigners; refusing to pass others to encourage their migrations hither, and raising the conditions of new Appropriations of Lands.

He has obstructed the Administration of Justice, by refusing his Assent to Laws for establishing Judiciary powers.

He has made Judges dependent on his Will alone, for the tenure of their offices, and the amount and payment of their salaries.

He has erected a multitude of New Offices, and sent hither swarms of Officers to harass our People, and eat out their substance.

He has kept among us, in times of peace, Standing Armies without the Consent of our legislature.

He has combined with others to subject us to a jurisdiction foreign to our constitution, and unacknowledged by our laws; giving his Assent to their Acts of pretended Legislation:

For quartering large bodies of armed troops among us:

For protecting them, by a mock Trial, from Punishment for any Murders which they should commit on the Inhabitants of these States:

For cutting off our Trade with all parts of the world:

For imposing taxes on us without our Consent:

For depriving us in many cases, of the benefits of Trial by jury:

For transporting us beyond Seas to be tried for pretended offences:

For abolishing the free System of English Laws in a neighbouring Province, establishing therein an Arbitrary government, and enlarging its Boundaries so as to render it at once an example and fit instrument for introducing the same absolute rule into these Colonies:

For taking away our Charters, abolishing our most valuable Laws, and altering fundamentally the Forms of our Governments:

For suspending our own Legislatures, and declaring themselves invested with Power to legislate for us in all cases whatsoever.

He has abdicated Government here, by declaring us out of his Protection and waging War against us.

He has plundered our seas, ravaged our Coasts, burnt our towns, and destroyed the lives of our people.

He is at this time transporting large armies of foreign mercenaries to compleat the works of death, desolation, and tyranny, already begun with circumstances of Cruelty & perfidy scarcely paralleled in the most barbarous ages, and totally unworthy the Head of a civilized nation.

He has constrained our fellow Citizens taken Captive on the high Seas to bear Arms against their Country, to become the executioners of their friends and Brethren, or to fall themselves by their Hands.

He has excited domestic insurrections amongst us, and has endeavoured to bring on the inhabitants of our frontiers, the merciless Indian Savages, whose known rule of warfare, is an undistinguished destruction of all ages, sexes, and conditions.

In every stage of these Oppressions We have Petitioned for Redress in the most humble terms: Our repeated petitions have been answered only by repeated injury. A Prince, whose character is thus marked by every act which may define a Tyrant, is unfit to be the ruler of a free people.

Nor have We been wanting in attention to our British brethren. We have warned them from time to time of attempts by their legislature to extend an unwarrantable jurisdiction over us. We have reminded them of the circumstances of our emigration and settlement here. We have appealed to their native justice and magnanimity, and we have conjured them by the ties of our common kindred to disavow these usurpations, which, would inevitably interrupt our connections and correspondence. They too have been deaf to the voice of justice and of consanguinity. We must, therefore, acquiesce in the necessity, which denounces our Separation, and hold them, as we hold the rest of mankind, Enemies in War, in Peace Friends.

We, therefore, the Representatives of the United States of America, in General Congress, Assembled, appealing to the Supreme Judge of the world for the rectitude of our intentions, do, in the Name, and by Authority of the good People of these Colonies, solemnly publish and declare, That these United Colonies are, and of Right ought to be FREE AND INDE-PENDENT STATES; that they are Absolved from all Allegiance to the British Crown, and that all political connection between them and the State of Great Britain, is and ought to be totally dissolved; and that as Free and Independent States, they have full Power to levy War, conclude Peace, contract Alliances, establish Commerce, and to do all other Acts and Things which Independent States may of right do. And for the support of this Declaration, with a firm reliance on the Protection of Divine Providence, we mutually pledge to each other our Lives, our Fortunes, and our sacred Honor.

John Hancock

Button Gwinnett	George Wythe	James Wilson	Josiah Bartlett
Lyman Hall	Richard Henry Lee	Geo. Ross	Wm. Whipple
Geo. Walton	Th. Jefferson	Caesar Rodney	Saml. Adams
Wm. Hooper	Benja. Harrison	Geo. Read	John Adams
Joseph Hewes	Thos. Nelson, Jr.	Thos. M'Kean	Robt. Treat Paine
John Penn	Francis Lightfoot Lee	Wm. Floyd	Elbridge Gerry
Edward Rutledge	Carter Braxton	Phil. Livingston	Step. Hopkins
Thos. Heyward, Junr.	Robt. Morris	Frans. Lewis	William Ellery
Thomas Lynch, Junr.	Benjamin Rush	Lewis Morris	Roger Sherman
Arthur Middleton	Benja. Franklin	Richd. Stockton	Sam'el Huntington
Samuel Chase	John Morton	Jno. Witherspoon	Wm. Williams
Wm. Paca	Geo. Clymer	Fras. Hopkinson	Oliver Wolcott
Thos. Stone	Jas. Smith	John Hart	Matthew Thornton
Charles Carroll of Carrollton	Geo. Taylor	Abra. Clark	

The Articles of Confederation and Perpetual Union

Between the states of New Hampshire, Massachusetts Bay, Rhode Island and Providence Plantations, Connecticut, New York, New Jersey, Pennsylvania, Delaware, Maryland, Virginia, North Carolina, South Carolina, Georgia.*

ARTICLE 1
The stile of this confederacy shall be "The United States of America."

ARTICLE 2
Each State retains its sovereignty, freedom and independence, and every power, jurisdiction, and right, which is not by this confederation expressly delegated to the United States, in Congress assembled.

ARTICLE 3
The said states hereby severally enter into a firm league of friendship with each other for their common defence, the security of their liberties and their mutual and general welfare; binding themselves to assist each other against all force offered to, or attacks made upon them, or any of them, on account of religion, sovereignty, trade, or any other pretence whatever.

ARTICLE 4
The better to secure and perpetuate mutual friendship and intercourse among the people of the different states in this union, the free inhabitants of each of these states, paupers, vagabonds, and fugitives from justice excepted, shall be entitled to all privileges and immunities of free citizens in the several states; and the people of each State shall have free ingress and regress to and from any other State, and shall enjoy therein all the privileges of trade and commerce, subject to the same duties, impositions, and restrictions, as the inhabitants thereof respectively; provided, that such restrictions shall not extend so far as to prevent the removal of property, imported into any State, to any other State of which the owner is an inhabitant; provided also, that no imposition, duties, or restriction, shall be laid by any State on the property of the United States, or either of them.

If any person guilty of, or charged with treason, felony, or other high misdemeanor in any State, shall flee from justice and be found in any of the United States, he shall, upon demand of the governor or executive power of the State from which he fled, be delivered up and removed to the State having jurisdiction of his offence.

Full faith and credit shall be given in each of these states to the records, acts, and judicial proceedings of the courts and magistrates of every other State.

ARTICLE 5
For the more convenient management of the general interests of the United States, delegates shall be annually appointed, in such manner as the legislature of each State shall direct, to

---

*This copy of the final draft of the Articles of Confederation is taken from the *Journals*, 9:907–25, November 15, 1777.

meet in Congress, on the 1st Monday in November in every year, with a power reserved to each State to recall its delegates, or any of them, at any time within the year, and to send others in their stead for the remainder of the year.

No State shall be represented in Congress by less than two, nor by more than seven members; and no person shall be capable of being a delegate for more than three years in any term of six years; nor shall any person, being a delegate, be capable of holding any office under the United States, for which he, or any other for his benefit, receives any salary, fees, or emolument of any kind.

Each State shall maintain its own delegates in a meeting of the states, and while they act as members of the committee of the states.

In determining questions in the United States, in Congress assembled, each State shall have one vote.

Freedom of speech and debate in Congress shall not be impeached or questioned in any court or place out of Congress: and the members of Congress shall be protected in their persons from arrests and imprisonments, during the time of their going to and from, and attendance on Congress, except for treason, felony, or breach of the peace.

ARTICLE 6

No State, without the consent of the United States, in Congress assembled, shall send any embassy to, or receive any embassy from, or enter into any conference, agreement, alliance, or treaty with any king, prince, or state; nor shall any person, holding any office of profit or trust under the United States, or any of them, accept of any present, emolument, office or title, of any kind whatever, from any king, prince, or foreign state; nor shall the United States, in Congress assembled, or any of them, grant any title of nobility.

No two or more states shall enter into any treaty, confederation, or alliance, whatever, between them, without the consent of the United States, in Congress assembled, specifying accurately the purposes for which the same is to be entered into, and how long it shall continue.

No state shall lay any imposts or duties which may interfere with any stipulations in treaties entered into by the United States, in Congress assembled, with any king, prince, or state, in pursuance of any treaties already proposed by Congress to the courts of France and Spain.

No vessels of war shall be kept up in time of peace by any State, except such number only as shall be deemed necessary by the United States, in Congress assembled, for the defence of such State or its trade; nor shall any body of forces be kept up by any State, in time of peace, except such number only as, in the judgment of the United States, in Congress assembled, shall be deemed requisite to garrison the forts necessary for the defence of such State; but every State shall always keep up a well regulated and disciplined militia, sufficiently armed and accoutred, and shall provide, and constantly have ready for use, in public stores, a due number of field pieces and tents, and a proper quantity of arms, ammunition and camp equipage.

No State shall engage in any war without the consent of the United States, in Congress assembled, unless such State be actually invaded by enemies, or shall have received certain advice of a resolution being formed by some nation of Indians to invade such State, and the danger is so imminent as not to admit of a delay till the United States, in Congress assembled, can be consulted; nor shall any State grant commissions to any ships or vessels of war, nor letters of marque or reprisal, except it be after a declaration of war by the United States, in Congress assembled, and then only against the kingdom or state, and the subjects thereof, against which war has been so declared, and under such regulations as shall be established by the United States, in Congress assembled, unless such State be infested by pirates, in which case vessels of war may be fitted out for that occasion, and kept so long as the danger shall continue, or until the United States, in Congress assembled, shall determine otherwise.

ARTICLE 7

When land forces are raised by any State for the common defence, all officers of or under the rank of colonel, shall be appointed by the legislature of each State respectively, by whom such forces shall be raised, or in such manner as such State shall direct; and all vacancies shall be filled up by the State which first made the appointment.

ARTICLE 8

All charges of war and all other expences, that shall be incurred for the common defence or general welfare, and allowed by the United States, in Congress assembled, shall be defrayed out of a common treasury, which shall be supplied by the several states, in proportion to the value of all land within each State, granted to or surveyed for any person, as such land and the buildings and improvements thereon shall be estimated according to such mode as the United States, in Congress assembled, shall, from time to time, direct and appoint.

The taxes for paying that proportion shall be laid and levied by the authority and direction of the legislatures of the several states, within the time agreed upon by the United States, in Congress assembled.

ARTICLE 9

The United States, in Congress assembled, shall have the sole and exclusive right and power of determining on peace and war, except in the cases mentioned in the 6th article; of sending and receiving ambassadors; entering into treaties and alliances, provided that no treaty of commerce shall be made, whereby the legislative power of the respective states shall be restrained from imposing such imposts and duties on foreigners as their own people are subjected to, or from prohibiting the exportation or importation of any species of goods or commodities whatsoever; of establishing rules for deciding, in all cases, what captures on land or water shall be legal, and in what manner prizes, taken by land or naval forces in the service of the United States, shall be divided or appropriated; or granting letters of marque and reprisal in times of peace; appointing courts for the trial of piracies and felonies committed on the high seas, and establishing courts for receiving and determining, finally, appeals in all cases of captures; provided, that no member of Congress shall be appointed a judge of any of the said courts.

The United States, in Congress assembled, shall also be the last resort on appeal in all disputes and differences now subsisting, or that hereafter may arise between two or more states concerning boundary, jurisdiction or any other cause whatever; which authority shall always be exercised in the manner following: whenever the legislative or executive authority, or lawful agent of any State, in controversy with another, shall present a petition to Congress, stating the matter in question, and praying for a hearing, notice thereof shall be given, by order of Congress, to the legislative of executive authority of the other State in controversy, and a day assigned for the appearance of the parties by their lawful agents, who shall then be directed to appoint, by joint consent, commissioners or judges to constitute a court for hearing and determining the matter in question; but, if they cannot agree, Congress shall name three persons out of each of the United States, and from the list of such persons each party shall alternately strike out one, the petitioners beginning, until the number shall be reduced to thirteen; and from that number not less than seven, nor more than nine names, as Congress shall direct, shall, in the presence of Congress, be drawn out by lot; and the persons whose names shall be so drawn, or any five of them, shall be commissioners or judges to hear and finally determine the controversy, so always as a major part of the judges who shall hear the cause shall agree in the determination; and if either party shall neglect to attend at the day appointed, without shewing reasons which Congress shall judge sufficient, or, being present, shall refuse to strike, the Congress shall proceed to nominate three persons out of each State, and the secretary of Congress shall strike in behalf of such party absent or refusing; and the judgment and sentence of the court to be appointed, in the manner before prescribed, shall be final and conclusive; and if any of the parties shall refuse to submit to the authority of such court, or to appear or defend their claim or cause, the court shall nevertheless proceed to pronounce sentence or judgment, which shall, in like manner, be final and decisive, the judgment or sentence and other proceedings begin, in either case, transmitted to Congress, and lodged among the acts of Congress for the security of the parties concerned: provided, that every commissioner, before he sits in judgment, shall take an oath, to be administered by one of the judges of the supreme or superior court of the State where the cause shall be tried, "well and truly to hear and determine the matter in question, according to the best of his judgment, without favour, affection, or hope of reward:" provided, also, that no State shall be deprived of territory for the benefit of the United States.

All controversies concerning the private right of soil, claimed under different grants of two or more states, whose jurisdictions, as they may respect such lands and the states which passed such grants, are adjusted, the said grants, or either of them, being at the same time claimed to have originated antecedent to such settlement of jurisdiction, shall, on the petition of either party to the Congress of the United States, be finally determined, as near as may be, in the same manner as is before prescribed for deciding disputes respecting territorial jurisdiction between different states.

The United States, in Congress assembled, shall also have the sole and exclusive right and power of regulating the alloy and value of coin struck by their own authority, or by that of the respective states; fixing the standard of weights and measures throughout the United States; regulating the trade and managing all affairs with the Indians not members of any of the states; provided that the legislative right of any State within its own limits be not infringed or violated; establishing and regulating post offices from one State to another throughout all the United States, and exacting such postage on the papers passing through the same as may be requisite to defray the expences of the said office; appointing all officers of the land forces in the service of the United States, excepting regimental officers; appointing all the officers of the naval forces, and commissioning all officers whatever in the service of the United States; making rules for the government and regulation of the said land and naval forces, and directing their operations.

The United States, in Congress assembled, shall have authority to appoint a committee to sit in the recess of Congress, to be denominated "a Committee of the States," and to consist of one delegate from each State, and to appoint such other committees and civil officers as may be necessary for managing the general affairs of the United States, under their direction; to appoint one of their number to preside; provided that no person be allowed to serve in the office of president more than one year in any term of three years; to ascertain the necessary sums of money to be raised for the service of the United States, and to appropriate and apply the same for defraying the public expences; to borrow money or emit bills on the credit of the United States, transmitting, every half year, to the respective states, an account of the sums of money so borrowed or emitted; to build and equip a navy; to agree upon the number of land forces, and to make requisitions from each State for in quota, in proportion to the number of white inhabitants in such State; which requisitions shall be binding; and thereupon, the legislature of each State shall appoint the regimental officers, raise the men, and cloathe, arm, and equip them in a soldier-like manner, at the expence of the United States; and the officers and men so cloathed, armed, and equipped, shall march to the place appointed and within the time agreed on by the United States, in Congress assembled; but if the United States, in Congress assembled, shall, on consideration of circumstances, judge proper that any State should not raise men, or should raise a smaller number than its quota, and that any other State should raise a greater number of men than the quota thereof, such extra number shall be raised, officered, cloathed, armed, and equipped in the same manner as the quota of such State, unless the legislature of such State shall judge that such extra number cannot be safely spared out of the same, in which case they shall raise, officer, cloathe, arm, and equip as many of such extra number as they judge can be safely spared. And the officers and men so cloathed, armed, and equipped, shall march to the place appointed and within the time agreed on by the United States, in Congress assembled.

The United States, in Congress assembled, shall never engage in a war, nor grant letters of marque and reprisal in time of peace, nor enter into any treaties or alliances, nor coin money, nor regulate the value thereof, nor ascertain the sums and expences necessary for the defence and welfare of the United States, or any of them: nor emit bills, nor borrow money on the credit of the United States, nor appropriate money, nor agree upon the number of vessels of war to be built or purchased, or the number of land or sea forces to be raised, nor appoint a commander in chief of the army or navy, unless nine states assent to the same; nor shall a question on any other point, except for adjourning from day to day, be determined, unless by the votes of a majority of the United States, in Congress assembled.

The Congress of the United States shall have power to adjourn to any time within the year, and to any place within the United States, so that no period of adjournment be for a longer duration than the space of six months, and shall publish the journal of their proceedings monthly, except such parts thereof, relating to treaties, alliances or military operations, as, in their judgment, require secrecy; and the yeas and nays of the delegates of each State on any question shall be entered on the journal, when it is desired by any delegate; and the delegates of a State, or any of them, at his, or their request, shall be furnished with a transcript of the said journal, except such parts as are above excepted, to lay before the legislatures of the several states.

ARTICLE 10
The committee of the states, or any nine of them, shall be authorized to execute, in the recess of Congress, such of the powers of Congress as the United States, in Congress assembled, by the consent of nine states, shall, from time to time, think expedient to vest them with; provided, that no power be delegated to the said committee, for the exercise of which, by the articles of confederation, the voice of nine states, in the Congress of the United States assembled, is requisite.

ARTICLE 11
Canada acceding to this confederation, and joining in the measures of the United States, shall be admitted into and entitled to all the advantages of this union; but no other colony shall be admitted into the same, unless such admission be agreed to by nine states.

ARTICLE 12

All bills of credit emitted, monies borrowed and debts contracted by, or under the authority of Congress before the assembling of the United States, in pursuance of the present confederation, shall be deemed and considered as a charge against the United States, for payment and satisfaction whereof the said United States and the public faith are hereby solemnly pledged.

ARTICLE 13

Every State shall abide by the determinations of the United States, in Congress assembled, on all questions which, by this confederation, are submitted to them. And the articles of this confederation shall be inviolably observed by every State, and the union shall be perpetual; nor shall any alteration at any time hereafter be made in any of them, unless such alteration be agreed to in a Congress of the United States, and be afterwards confirmed by the legislatures of every State.

These articles shall be proposed to the legislatures of all the United States, to be considered, and if approved of by them, they are advised to authorize their delegates to ratify the same in the Congress of the United States; which being done, the same shall become conclusive.

The Constitution of the United States

We the People of the United States, in Order to form a more perfect Union, establish Justice, insure domestic Tranquility, provide for the common defence, promote the general Welfare, and secure the Blessings of Liberty to ourselves and our Posterity, do ordain and establish this Constitution for the United States of America.

ARTICLE I

Section 1
All legislative Powers herein granted shall be vested in a Congress of the United States, which shall consist of a Senate and a House of Representatives.

Section 2
The House of Representatives shall be composed of Members chosen every second Year by the People of the several States, and the Electors in each State shall have the Qualifications requisite for Electors of the most numerous Branch of the State Legislature.

No Person shall be a Representative who shall not have attained to the Age of twenty-five Years, and been seven Years a Citizen of the United States, and who shall not, when elected, be an Inhabitant of that State in which he shall be chosen.

Representatives and direct Taxes shall be apportioned among the several States which may be included within this Union, according to their respective Numbers, *which shall be determined by adding to the whole Number of free Persons, including those bound to Service for a Term of Years, and excluding Indians not taxed, three fifths of all other Persons.* The

---

Note: The Constitution became effective March 4, 1789. Provisions in italics have been changed by constitutional amendment.

*Changed by Section 2 of the Fourteenth Amendment.

actual Enumeration shall be made within three Years after the first Meeting of the Congress of the United States, and within every subsequent Term of ten Years, in such Manner as they shall by Law direct. The Number of Representatives shall not exceed one for every thirty Thousand, but each State shall have at Least one Representative; and *until such enumeration shall be made, the State of New Hampshire shall be entitled to chuse three, Massachusetts eight, Rhode Island and Providence Plantations one, Connecticut five, New-York six, New Jersey four, Pennsylvania eight, Delaware one, Maryland six, Virginia ten, North Carolina five, South Carolina five, and Georgia three.*

When vacancies happen in the Representation from any State, the Executive Authority thereof shall issue Writs of Election to fill such Vacancies.

The House of Representatives shall chuse their Speaker and other Officers; and shall have the sole Power of Impeachment.

Section 3

The Senate of the United States shall be composed of two Senators from each State, *chosen by the Legislature thereof,** for six Years; and each Senator shall have one Vote.

Immediately after they shall be assembled in Consequence of the first Election, they shall be divided as equally as may be into three Classes. The Seats of the Senators of the first Class shall be vacated at the Expiration of the second Year, of the second Class at the Expiration of the fourth Year, and of the third Class at the Expiration of the sixth Year, so that one-third may be chosen every second Year; *and if Vacancies happen by Resignation, or otherwise, during the Recess of the Legislature of any State, the Executive thereof may make temporary Appointments until the next Meeting of the Legislature, which shall then fill such Vacancies.*†

No person shall be a Senator who shall not have attained to the Age of thirty Years, and been nine Years a Citizen of the United States, and who shall not, when elected, be an Inhabitant of that State for which he shall be chosen.

The Vice President of the United States shall be President of the Senate, but shall have no Vote, unless they be equally divided.

The Senate shall chuse their other Officers, and also a President pro tempore, in the absence of the Vice President, or when he shall exercise the Office of President of the United States.

The Senate shall have the sole Power to try all Impeachments. When sitting for that Purpose, they shall be on Oath or Affirmation. When the President of the United States is tried, the Chief Justice shall preside: And no Person shall be convicted without the Concurrence of two thirds of the Members present.

Judgment in Cases of Impeachment shall not extend further than to removal from Office, and disqualification to hold and enjoy any Office of honor, Trust or Profit under the United States: but the Party convicted shall nevertheless be liable and subject to Indictment, Trial, Judgment and Punishment, according to Law.

Section 4

The Times, Places and Manner of holding Elections for Senators and Representatives, shall be prescribed in each State by the Legislature thereof, but the Congress may at any time by Law make or alter such Regulations, except as to the Places of Chusing Senators.

---

*Changed by Section 1 of the Seventeenth Amendment.

†Changed by Clause 2 of the Seventeenth Amendment.

The Congress shall assemble at least once in every Year, and such Meeting *shall be on the first Monday in December, unless they shall by Law appoint a different Day.**

Section 5

Each House shall be the Judge of the Elections, Returns and Qualifications of its own Members, and a Majority of each shall constitute a Quorum to do Business; but a smaller number may adjourn from day to day, and may be authorized to compel the Attendance of absent Members, in such Manner, and under such Penalties, as each House may provide.

Each House may determine the Rules of its Proceedings, punish its Members for disorderly Behavior, and, with the Concurrence of two thirds, expel a Member.

Each House shall keep a Journal of its Proceedings, and from time to time publish the same, excepting such Parts as may in their Judgment require Secrecy; and the Yeas and Nays of the Members of either House on any question shall, at the Desire of one-fifth of those Present, be entered on the Journal.

Neither House, during the Session of Congress, shall, without the Consent of the other, adjourn for more than three days, nor to any other Place than that in which the two Houses shall be sitting.

Section 6

The Senators and Representatives shall receive a Compensation for their Services, to be ascertained by Law, and paid out of the Treasury of the United States. They shall in all Cases, except Treason, Felony and Breach of the Peace, be privileged from Arrest during their Attendance at the Session of their respective Houses, and in going to and returning from the same; and for any Speech or Debate in either House, they shall not be questioned in any other Place.

No Senator or Representative shall, during the Time for which he was elected, be appointed to any civil Office under the Authority of the United States, which shall have been created, or the Emoluments whereof shall have been increased, during such time; and no Person holding any Office under the United States, shall be a Member of either House during his Continuance in Office.

Section 7

All Bills for raising Revenue shall originate in the House of Representatives; but the Senate may propose or concur with Amendments as on other Bills.

Every Bill which shall have passed the House of Representatives and the Senate, shall, before it becomes a Law, be presented to the President of the United States; If he approve he shall sign it, but if not he shall return it, with his Objections to that House in which it shall have originated, who shall enter the Objections at large on their Journal, and proceed to reconsider it. If after such Reconsideration two thirds of that House shall agree to pass the Bill, it shall be sent, together with the Objections, to the other House, by which it shall likewise be reconsidered, and if approved by two thirds of that House, it shall become a Law. But in all such Cases the Votes of both Houses shall be determined by Yeas and Nays, and the Names of the Persons voting for and against the Bill shall be entered on the Journal of each House respectively. If any Bill shall not be returned by the President within ten Days (Sundays excepted) after it shall have

---

*Changed by Section 2 of the Twentieth Amendment.

been presented to him, the Same shall be a Law, in like Manner as if he had signed it, unless the Congress by their Adjournment prevent its Return, in which Case it shall not be a Law.

Every Order, Resolution, or Vote to which the Concurrence of the Senate and the House of Representatives may be necessary (except on a question of Adjournment) shall be presented to the President of the United States; and before the Same shall take Effect, shall be approved by him, or being disapproved by him, shall be repassed by two thirds of the Senate and House of Representatives, according to the Rules and Limitations prescribed in the Case of a Bill.

Section 8

The Congress shall have Power To lay and collect Taxes, Duties, Imposts and Excises, to pay the Debts and provide for the common Defence and general Welfare of the United States; but all Duties, Imposts and Excises shall be uniform throughout the United States;

To borrow money on the credit of the United States;

To regulate Commerce with foreign Nations, and among the several States, and with the Indian Tribes;

To establish an uniform Rule of Naturalization, and uniform Laws on the subject of Bankruptcies throughout the United States;

To coin Money, regulate the Value thereof, and of foreign Coin, and fix the Standard of Weights and Measures;

To provide for the Punishment of counterfeiting the Securities and current Coin of the United States;

To establish Post Offices and post Roads;

To promote the Progress of Science and useful Arts, by securing for limited Times to Authors and Inventors the exclusive Right to their respective Writings and Discoveries;

To constitute Tribunals inferior to the supreme Court;

To define and punish Piracies and Felonies committed on the high Seas, and Offenses against the Law of Nations;

To declare War, grant Letters of Marque and Reprisal, and make Rules concerning Captures on Land and Water;

To raise and support Armies, but no Appropriation of Money to that Use shall be for a longer Term than two Years;

To provide and maintain a Navy;

To make Rules for the Government and Regulation of the land and naval Forces;

To provide for calling forth the Militia to execute the Laws of the Union, suppress Insurrections and repel Invasions;

To provide for organizing, arming, and disciplining the Militia, and for governing such Part of them as may be employed in the Service of the United States, reserving to the States respectively, the Appointment of the Officers, and the Authority of training the Militia according to the discipline prescribed by Congress;

To exercise exclusive Legislation in all Cases whatsoever, over such District (not exceeding ten Miles square) as may, by Cession of particular States, and the acceptance of Congress, become the Seat of Government of the United States, and to exercise like Authority over all Places purchased by the Consent of the Legislature of the State in which the Same shall be, for the Erection of Forts, Magazines, Arsenals, dock-Yards, and other needful Buildings;—And

To make all Laws which shall be necessary and proper for carrying into Execution the foregoing Powers, and all other Powers vested by this Constitution in the Government of the United States, or in any Department or Officer thereof.

Section 9

The Migration or Importation of such Persons as any of the States now existing shall think proper to admit, shall not be prohibited by the Congress prior to the Year one thousand eight hundred and eight but a tax or duty may be imposed on such Importation, not exceeding ten dollars for each Person.

The privilege of the Writ of Habeas Corpus shall not be suspended, unless when in Cases of Rebellion or Invasion the public Safety may require it.

No Bill of Attainder or ex post facto Law shall be passed.

No capitation, or other direct, Tax shall be laid, unless in Proportion to the Census or Enumeration herein before directed to be taken.*

No Tax or Duty shall be laid on Articles exported from any State.

No Preference shall be given by any Regulation of Commerce or Revenue to the Ports of one State over those of another: nor shall Vessels bound to, or from, one State, be obliged to enter, clear, or pay Duties in another.

No Money shall be drawn from the Treasury, but in Consequence of Appropriations made by law; and a regular Statement and Account of the Receipts and Expenditures of all public Money shall be published from time to time.

No Title of Nobility shall be granted by the United States: And no Person holding any Office of Profit or Trust under them, shall, without the Consent of the Congress, accept of any present, Emolument, Office, or Title, of any kind whatever, from any King, Prince, or foreign State.

Section 10

No State shall enter into any Treaty, Alliance, or Confederation; grant Letters of Marque and Reprisal; coin Money; emit Bills of Credit; make any Thing but gold and silver Coin a Tender in Payment of Debts; pass any Bill of Attainder, ex post facto Law, or Law impairing the Obligation of Contracts, or grant any Title of Nobility.

No State shall, without the Consent of the Congress, lay any Imposts or Duties on Imports or Exports, except what may be absolutely necessary for executing its inspection Laws: and the net Produce of all Duties and Imposts, laid by any State on Imports or Exports, shall be for the Use of the Treasury of the United States; and all such Laws shall be subject to the Revision and Control of the Congress.

No State shall, without the Consent of the Congress, lay any duty of Tonnage, keep Troops, or Ships of War in time of Peace, enter into any Agreement or Compact with another State, or with a foreign Power, or engage in War, unless actually invaded, or in such imminent Danger as will not admit of delay.

ARTICLE II

Section 1

The executive Power shall be vested in a President of the United States of America. He shall hold his Office during the Term of four Years, and, together with the Vice President, chosen for the same Term, be elected, as follows:

Each State shall appoint, in such Manner as the Legislature thereof may direct, a Number of Electors, equal to the whole Number of Senators and Representatives to which the

---

*Changed by the Sixteenth Amendment.

State may be entitled in the Congress; but no Senator or Representative, or Person holding an Office of Trust or Profit under the United States, shall be appointed an Elector.

The Electors shall meet in their respective States, and vote by Ballot for two Persons, of whom one at least shall not be an Inhabitant of the same State with themselves. And they shall make a List of all the Persons voted for, and of the Number of Votes for each; which List they shall sign and certify, and transmit sealed to the Seat of the Government of the United States, directed to the President of the Senate. The President of the Senate shall, in the Presence of the Senate and House of Representatives, open all the Certificates, and the Votes shall then be counted. The Person having the greatest Number of Votes shall be the President, if such Number be a Majority of the whole Number of Electors appointed; and if there be more than one who have such Majority, and have an equal Number of Votes, then the House of Representatives shall immediately chuse by Ballot one of them for President; and if no Person have a Majority, then from the five highest on the List the said House shall in like Manner chuse the President. But in chusing the President, the Votes shall be taken by States, the Representation from each State having one Vote; a quorum for this Purpose shall consist of a Member or Members from two thirds of the States, and a Majority of all the States shall be necessary to a Choice. In every Case, after the Choice of the President, the Person having the greatest Number of Votes of the Electors shall be the Vice President. But if there should remain two or more who have equal Votes, the Senate shall chuse from them by Ballot the Vice President.*

The Congress may determine the Time of chusing the Electors, and the Day on which they shall give their Votes; which Day shall be the same throughout the United States.

No Person except a natural born Citizen, or a Citizen of the United States, at the time of the Adoption of this Constitution, shall be eligible to the Office of President; neither shall any Person be eligible to that Office who shall not have attained to the Age of thirty five Years, and been fourteen years a Resident within the United States.

In Case of the Removal of the President from Office, or of his Death, Resignation, or Inability to discharge the Powers and Duties of the said Office, the same shall devolve on the Vice President, *and the Congress may by Law provide for the Case of Removal, Death, Resignation, or Inability, both of the President and Vice President, declaring what Officer shall then act as President, and such Officer shall act accordingly, until the Disability be removed, or a President shall be elected.*†

The President shall, at stated Times, receive for his Services a Compensation, which shall neither be increased nor diminished during the Period for which he shall have been elected, and he shall not receive within that Period any other Emolument from the United States, or any of them.

Before he enter on the Execution of his Office, he shall take the following Oath or Affirmation:—"I do solemnly swear (or affirm) that I will faithfully execute the Office of President of the United States, and will to the best of my Ability, preserve, protect and defend the Constitution of the United States."

Section 2

The President shall be Commander in Chief of the Army and Navy of the United States, and of the Militia of the several States, when called into the actual Service of the United States; he may require the Opinion, in writing, of the principal Officer in each of the executive

---

*Superseded by the Twelfth Amendment.

†Modified by the Twenty-fifth Amendment.

Departments, upon any Subject relating to the Duties of their respective Offices, and he shall have Power to Grant Reprieves and pardons for Offences against the United States, except in Cases of Impeachment.

He shall have Power, by and with the Advice and Consent of the Senate, to make Treaties, provided two thirds of the Senators present concur; and he shall nominate, and by and with the Advice and Consent of the Senate, shall appoint Ambassadors, other public Ministers and Consuls, Judges of the supreme Court, and all other Officers of the United States, whose Appointments are not herein otherwise provided for, and which shall be established by Law: but the Congress may by Law vest the Appointment of such inferior Officers, as they think proper, in the President alone, in the Courts of Law, or in the Heads of Departments.

The President shall have Power to fill up all Vacancies that may happen during the Recess of the Senate, by granting Commissions which shall expire at the End of their next Session.

Section 3
He shall from time to time give to the Congress Information of the State of the Union, and recommend to their Consideration such Measures as he shall judge necessary and expedient; he may, on extraordinary Occasions, convene both Houses, or either of them, and in Case of Disagreement between them, with Respect to the Time of Adjournment, he may adjourn them to such Time as he shall think proper; he shall receive Ambassadors and other public Ministers; he shall take Care that the Laws be faithfully executed, and shall Commission all the Officers of the United States.

Section 4
The President, Vice President and all civil Officers of the United States, shall be removed from Office on Impeachment for, and Conviction of, Treason, Bribery, or other high Crimes and Misdemeanors.

ARTICLE III

Section 1
The judicial Power of the United States, shall be vested in one supreme Court, and in such inferior Courts as the Congress may from time to time ordain and establish. The Judges, both of the supreme and inferior courts, shall hold their Offices during good Behaviour, and shall, at stated Times, receive for their Services a Compensation, which shall not be diminished during their Continuance in Office.

Section 2
The judicial Power shall extend to all Cases, in Law and Equity, arising under this Constitution, the Laws of the United States, and Treaties made, or which shall be made, under their Authority;—to all Cases affecting Ambassadors, other public Ministers and Consuls;—to all Cases of admiralty and maritime Jurisdiction;—to Controversies to which the United States shall be a Party;—to Controversies between two or more States;—*between a State and Citizens of another State,**—between Citizens of different States;—between Citizens of the

---

*Restricted by the Eleventh Amendment.

same State claiming Lands under Grants of different States, and between a State, or the Citizens thereof, and foreign States, Citizens or Subjects.

In all Cases affecting Ambassadors, other public Ministers and Consuls, and those in which a State shall be Party, the supreme Court shall have original Jurisdiction. In all the other Cases before mentioned, the supreme Court shall have appellate Jurisdiction, both as to Law and Fact, with such Exceptions, and under such Regulations as the Congress shall make.

The trial of all Crimes, except in Cases of Impeachment, shall be by Jury; and such Trial shall be held in the State where said Crimes shall have been committed; but when not committed within any State, the Trial shall be at such Place or Places as the Congress may by Law have directed.

Section 3

Treason against the United States, shall consist only in levying War against them, or in adhering to their Enemies, giving them Aid and Comfort. No Person shall be convicted of Treason unless on the Testimony of two Witnesses to the same overt Act, or on Confession in open Court.

The Congress shall have Power to declare the Punishment of Treason, but no Attainder of Treason shall work Corruption of Blood, or Forefeiture except during the Life of the Person attainted.

ARTICLE IV

Section 1

Full Faith and Credit shall be given in each State to the public Acts, Records, and judicial Proceedings of every other State. And the Congress may by general Laws prescribe the Manner in which such Acts, Records, and Proceedings shall be proved, and the Effect thereof.

Section 2

The Citizens of each State shall be entitled to all Privileges and Immunities of Citizens in the several States.

A Person charged in any State with Treason, Felony, or other Crime, who shall flee from Justice, and be found in another State, shall on demand of the executive Authority of the State from which he fled, be delivered up, to be removed to the State having Jurisdiction of the Crime.

*No Person held to Service or Labour in one State, under the Laws thereof, escaping into another, shall, in Consequence of any Law or Regulation therein, be discharged from such Service or Labour, but shall be delivered up on Claim of the Party to whom such Service or Labour may be due.**

Section 3

New States may be admitted by the Congress into this Union; but no new State shall be formed or erected within the Jurisdiction of any other State; nor any State be formed by the

---

*Superseded by the Thirteenth Amendment.

Junction of two or more States, or parts of States, without the Consent of the Legislatures of the States concerned as well as of the Congress.

The Congress shall have Power to dispose of and make all needful Rules and Regulations respecting the Territory or other Property belonging to the United States; and nothing in this Constitution shall be so construed as to Prejudice any Claims of the United States, or of any particular State.

Section 4

The United States shall guarantee to every State in this Union a Republican Form of Government, and shall protect each of them against Invasion; and on Application of the Legislature, or of the Executive (when the Legislature cannot be convened) against domestic Violence.

ARTICLE V

The Congress, whenever two thirds of both Houses shall deem it necessary, shall propose Amendments to this Constitution, or, on the Application of the Legislatures of two thirds of the several States, shall call a Convention for proposing Amendments, which, in either Case, shall be valid to all Intents and Purposes, as Part of this Constitution, when ratified by the Legislatures of three fourths of the several States, or by Conventions in three fourths thereof, as the one or the other Mode of Ratification may be proposed by the Congress; Provided that no Amendment which may be made prior to the Year One thousand eight hundred and eight shall in any Manner affect the first and fourth Clauses in the Ninth Section of the first Article; and that no State, without its Consent, shall be deprived of its equal Suffrage in the Senate.

ARTICLE VI

All Debts contracted and Engagements entered into, before the Adoption of this Constitution, shall be as valid against the United States under this Constitution, as under the Confederation.

This Constitution, and the Laws of the United States which shall be made in Pursuance thereof; and all Treaties made, or which shall be made, under the Authority of the United States, shall be the supreme Law of the Land; and the Judges in every State shall be bound thereby, any Thing in the Constitution or Laws of any State to the Contrary notwithstanding.

The Senators and Representatives before mentioned, and the Members of the several State Legislatures, and all executive and judicial Officers, both of the United States and of the several States, shall be bound by Oath or Affirmation, to support this Constitution; but no religious Test shall ever be required as a Qualification to any Office or public Trust under the United States.

ARTICLE VII

The Ratification of the Conventions of nine States shall be sufficient for the Establishment of this Constitution between the States so ratifying the Same.

Done in Convention by the Unanimous Consent of the States present the Seventeenth Day of September in the Year of our Lord one thousand seven hundred and Eighty seven and of the Independence of the United States of America the Twelfth. In Witness whereof We have hereunto subscribed our Names.

Go. Washington

President and deputy from Virginia

New Hampshire	New Jersey	Delaware	North Carolina
John Langdon	Wil. Livingston	Geo. Read	Wm. Blount
Nicholas Gilman	David Brearley	Gunning Bedford jun	Richd. Dobbs Spaight
	Wm. Paterson	John Dickenson	Hu Williamson
Massachusetts	Jona. Dayton	Richard Bassett	
Nathaniel Gorham		Jaco. Broom	South Carolina
Rufus King	Pennsylvania		J. Rutledge
	B. Franklin	Maryland	Charles Cotesworth
Connecticut	Thomas Mifflin	James McHenry	Pickney
Wm. Saml. Johnson	Robt. Morris	Dan. of St. Thos. Jenifer	Pierce Butler
Roger Sherman	Geo. Clymer	Danl. Carroll	
	Thos. FitzSimons		Georgia
New York	Jared Ingersoll	Virginia	William Few
Alexander Hamilton	James Wilson	John Blair	Abr. Baldwin
	Gouv. Morris	James Madison, Jr.	

Amendments to the Constitution

AMENDMENT I [1791]*

Congress shall make no law respecting an establishment of religion, or prohibiting the free exercise thereof; or abridging the freedom of speech, or of the press; or the right of the people peaceably to assemble, and to petition the Government for a redress of grievances.

AMENDMENT II [1791]

A well regulated Militia, being necessary to the security of a free State, the right of the people to keep and bear Arms shall not be infringed.

AMENDMENT III [1791]

No Soldier shall, in time of peace, be quartered in any house, without the consent of the Owner, nor in time of war, but in a manner to be prescribed by law.

AMENDMENT IV [1791]

The right of the people to be secure in their persons, houses, papers, and effects, against unreasonable searches and seizures, shall not be violated, and no Warrants shall issue, but upon probable cause, supported by Oath or affirmation, and particularly describing the place to be searched, and the persons or things to be seized.

AMENDMENT V [1791]

No person shall be held to answer for a capital or otherwise infamous crime, unless on a presentment or indictment of a Grand Jury, except in cases arising in the land or naval forces,

---

*The dates in brackets indicate when the amendments were ratified.

or in the Militia, when in actual service in time of War or public danger; nor shall any person be subject for the same offence to be twice put in jeopardy of life or limb; nor shall be compelled in any criminal case to be a witness against himself, nor be deprived of life, liberty, or property, without due process of law; nor shall private property be taken for public use, without just compensation.

AMENDMENT VI [1791]

In all criminal prosecutions, the accused shall enjoy the right to a speedy and public trial, by an impartial jury of the State and district wherein the crime shall have been committed, which district shall have been previously ascertained by law, and to be informed of the nature and cause of the accusation; to be confronted with the witnesses against him; to have compulsory process for obtaining witnesses in his favor, and to have the Assistance of Counsel for his defence.

AMENDMENT VII [1791]

In suits at common law, where the value in controversy shall exceed twenty dollars, the right of trial by jury shall be preserved, and no fact tried by a jury, shall be otherwise reexamined in any Court of the United States, than according to the Rules of the common law.

AMENDMENT VIII [1791]

Excessive bail shall not be required, nor excessive fines imposed, nor cruel and unusual punishments inflicted.

AMENDMENT IX [1791]

The enumeration in the Constitution, of certain rights, shall not be construed to deny or disparage others retained by the people.

AMENDMENT X [1791]

The powers not delegated to the United States by the Constitution, nor prohibited by it to the States, are reserved to the States respectively, or to the people.

AMENDMENT XI [1798]

The Judicial power of the United States shall not be construed to extend to any suit in law or equity, commenced or prosecuted against one of the United States by Citizens of another State, or by Citizens or subjects of any foreign state.

AMENDMENT XII [1804]

The Electors shall meet in their respective States and vote by ballot for President and Vice-President, one of whom, at least, shall not be an inhabitant of the same State with themselves; they shall name in their ballots the person voted for as President, and in distinct ballots the person voted for as Vice-President, and they shall make distinct lists of all persons voted for as President, and of all persons voted for as Vice-President, and of the number of votes for each, which lists they shall sign and certify, and transmit sealed to the seat of the government of the United States, directed to the President of the Senate;—the President of the Senate shall, in the presence of the Senate and House of Representatives, open all the certificates and the votes shall then be counted;—The person having the greatest number of votes for President, shall be the President, if such number be a majority of the whole number of Electors appointed; and if no person have such majority, then from the persons having the highest numbers not exceeding three on the list of those voted for as President, the House of Representatives shall choose immediately, by ballot, the President. But in choosing the President, the votes shall be taken by States, the representation from each State having one vote; a quorum for this purpose shall consist of a member or members from two-thirds of the States, and a majority of all the States shall be necessary to a choice. And if the House of Representatives shall not choose a President whenever the right of choice shall devolve upon them, before *the fourth day of March* next following, then the Vice-President shall act as President, as in the case of the death or other constitutional disability of the President.*—The person having the greatest number of votes as Vice-President, shall be the Vice-President, if such number be a majority of the whole number of Electors appointed, and if no person have a majority, then from the two highest numbers on the list, the Senate shall choose the Vice-President; a quorum for the purpose shall consist of two-thirds of the whole number of Senators, and a majority of the whole number shall be necessary to a choice. But no person constitutionally ineligible to the office of President shall be eligible to that of Vice-President of the United States.

AMENDMENT XIII [1865]

Section 1
Neither slavery nor involuntary servitude, except as a punishment for crime whereof the party shall have been duly convicted, shall exist within the United States, or any place subject to their jurisdiction.

Section 2
Congress shall have power to enforce this article by appropriate legislation.

AMENDMENT XIV [1868]

Section 1
All persons born or naturalized in the United States, and subject to the jurisdiction thereof, are citizens of the United States and of the State wherein they reside. No State shall make or enforce any law which shall abridge the privileges or immunities of citizens of the United States; nor shall any State deprive any person of life, liberty, or property, without due process of law; nor deny to any person within its jurisdiction the equal protection of the laws.

Section 2
Representatives shall be apportioned among the several States according to their respective numbers, counting the whole number of persons in each State, excluding Indians not taxed. But when the right to vote at any election for the choice of electors for President and Vice-President of the United States, Representatives in Congress, the Executive and Judicial officers of a State, or the members of the Legislature thereof, is denied to any of the male inhabitants of such State, being twenty-one years of age, and citizens of the United States, or

---

*Superseded by Section 3 of the Twentieth Amendment.

in any way abridged, except for participation in rebellion, or other crime, the basis of representation therein shall be reduced in the proportion which the number of such male citizens shall bear to the whole number of male citizens twenty-one years of age in such State.

Section 3

No person shall be a Senator or Representative in Congress, or elector of President and Vice-President, or hold any office, civil or military, under the United States, or under any State, who, having previously taken an oath, as a member of Congress, or as an officer of the United States, or as a member of any State legislature, or as an executive or judicial officer of any State, to support the Constitution of the United States, shall have engaged in insurrection or rebellion against the same, or given aid or comfort to the enemies thereof. Congress may by a vote of two-thirds of each house, remove such disability.

Section 4

The validity of the public debt of the United States, authorized by law, including debts incurred for payment of pensions and bounties for services in suppressing insurrection or rebellion, shall not be questioned. But neither the United States nor any State shall assume or pay any debt or obligation incurred in aid of insurrection or rebellion against the United States, or any claim for the loss or emancipation of any slave; but all such debts, obligations and claims shall be held illegal and void.

Section 5

The Congress shall have power to enforce, by appropriate legislation, the provisions of this article.

Amendment XV [1870]

Section 1

The right of citizens of the United States to vote shall not be denied or abridged by the United States or by any State on account of race, color, or previous condition of servitude—

Section 2

The Congress shall have power to enforce this article by appropriate legislation.

Amendment XVI [1913]

The Congress shall have power to lay and collect taxes on incomes, from whatever source derived, without apportionment among the several States, and without regard to any census or enumeration.

Amendment XVII [1913]

The Senate of the United States shall be composed of two Senators from each State, elected by the people thereof, for six years; and each Senator shall have one vote. The electors in each State shall have the qualifications requisite for electors of the most numerous branch of the State legislatures.

When vacancies happen in the representation of any State in the Senate, the executive authority of such State shall issue writs of election to fill such vacancies: *Provided*, That the legislature of any State may empower the executive thereof to make temporary appointments until the people fill the vacancies by election as the legislature may direct.

This amendment shall not be so construed as to affect the election or term of any Senator chosen before it becomes valid as part of the Constitution.

Amendment XVIII [1919]

Section 1
After one year from the ratification of this article the manufacture, sale, or transportation of intoxicating liquors within, the importation thereof into, or the exportation thereof from the United States and all territory subject to the jurisdiction hereof for beverage purposes is hereby prohibited.

Section 2
The Congress and the several States shall have concurrent power to enforce this article by appropriate legislation.

Section 3
This article shall be inoperative unless it shall have been ratified as an amendment to the Constitution by the legislatures of the several States, as provided by the Constitution, within seven years from the date of submission hereof to the States by the Congress.*

Amendment XIX [1920]
The right of citizens of the United States to vote shall not be denied or abridged by the United States or by any State on account of sex.

Congress shall have power to enforce this article by appropriate legislation.

Amendment XX [1933]

Section 1
The terms of the President and Vice-President shall end at noon on the 20th day of January, and the terms of Senators and Representatives at noon on the 3d day of January, of the years in which such terms would have ended if this article had not been ratified; and the terms of their successors shall then begin.

Section 2
The Congress shall assemble at least once in every year, and such meeting shall begin at noon on the 3d day of January, unless they shall by law appoint a different day.

Section 3
If, at the time fixed for the beginning of the term of the President, the President elect shall have died, the Vice-President elect shall become President. If a President shall not have been chosen before the time fixed for the beginning of his term, or if the President elect shall have failed to qualify, then the Vice-President elect shall act as President until a President

---

*Repealed by Section 1 of the Twenty-first Amendment.

shall have qualified; and the Congress may by law provide for the case wherein neither a President elect nor a Vice-President elect shall have qualified, declaring who shall then act as President, or the manner in which one who is to act shall be selected, and such person shall act accordingly until a President or Vice-President shall have qualified.

Section 4
The Congress may by law provide for the case of the death of any of the persons from whom the House of Representatives may choose a President whenever the right of choice shall have devolved upon them, and for the case of the death of any of the persons from whom the Senate may choose a Vice-President whenever the right of choice shall have devolved upon them.

Section 5
Sections 1 and 2 shall take effect on the 15th day of October following the ratification of this article.

Section 6
This article shall be inoperative unless it shall have been ratified as an amendment to the Constitution by the legislatures of three-fourths of the several States within seven years from the date of its submission.

Amendment XXI [1933]

Section 1
The eighteenth article of amendment to the Constitution of the United States is hereby repealed.

Section 2
The transportation or importation into any State, Territory, or possession of the United States for delivery or use therein of intoxicating liquors, in violation of the laws thereof, is hereby prohibited.

Section 3
This article shall be inoperative unless it shall have been ratified as an amendment to the Constitution by conventions in the several States, as provided in the Constitution, within seven years from the date of submission hereof to the States by the Congress.

Amendment XXII [1951]

Section 1
No person shall be elected to the office of President more than twice, and no person who has held the office of President, or acted as President, for more than two years of a term to which some other person was elected President shall be elected to the office of the President more than once. But this Article shall not apply to any person holding the office of President when this Article was proposed by the Congress, and shall not prevent any person who may be holding the office of President, or acting as President, during the term within which this Article becomes operative from holding the office of the President or acting as President during the remainder of such term.

Section 2

This article shall be inoperative unless it shall have been ratified as an amendment to the Constitution by the legislatures of three-fourths of the several States within seven years from the date of its submission to the States by the Congress.

Amendment XXIII [1961]

Section 1

The District constituting the seat of Government of the United States shall appoint in such manner as the Congress may direct:

A number of electors of President and Vice-President equal to the whole number of Senators and Representatives in Congress to which the District would be entitled if it were a State, but in no event more than the least populous State; they shall be in addition to those appointed by the States, but they shall be considered, for the purposes of the election of President and Vice-President, to be electors appointed by a State; and they shall meet in the District and perform such duties as provided by the twelfth article of amendment.

Section 2

The Congress shall have power to enforce this article by appropriate legislation.

Amendment XXIV [1964]

Section 1

The right of citizens of the United States to vote in any primary or other election for President or Vice-President, for electors for President or Vice-President, or for Senator or Representative in Congress, shall not be denied or abridged by the United States or any State by reason of failure to pay any poll tax or other tax.

Section 2

The Congress shall have power to enforce this article by appropriate legislation.

Amendment XXV [1967]

Section 1

In case of the removal of the President from office or of his death or resignation, the Vice-President shall become President.

Section 2

Whenever there is a vacancy in the office of the Vice-President, the President shall nominate a Vice-President who shall take office upon confirmation by a majority vote of both houses of Congress.

Section 3

Whenever the President transmits to the President pro tempore of the Senate and the Speaker of the House of Representatives his written declaration that he is unable to discharge the powers and duties of his office, and until he transmits to them a written declaration to the contrary, such powers and duties shall be discharged by the Vice-President as Acting President.

Section 4

Whenever the Vice-President and a majority of either the principal officers of the executive departments or of such other body as Congress may by law provide, transmit to the President pro tempore of the Senate and the Speaker of the House of Representatives their written declaration that the President is unable to discharge the powers and duties of his office, the Vice-President shall immediately assume the powers and duties of the office as Acting President.

Thereafter, when the President transmits to the President pro tempore of the Senate and the Speaker of the House of Representatives his written declaration that no inability exists, he shall resume the powers and duties of his office unless the Vice-President and a majority of either the principal officers of the executive department or of such other body as Congress may by law provide, transmit within four days to the President pro tempore of the Senate and the Speaker of the House of Representatives their written declaration that the President is unable to discharge the powers and duties of his office. Thereupon Congress shall decide the issue, assembling within forty-eight hours for that purpose if not in session. If the Congress, within twenty-one days after receipt of the latter written declaration, or, if Congress is not in session, within twenty-one days after Congress is required to assemble, determines by two-thirds vote of both Houses that the President is unable to discharge the powers and duties of his office, the Vice-President shall continue to discharge the same as Acting President; otherwise, the President shall resume the powers and duties of his office.

Amendment XXVI [1971]

Section 1

The right of citizens of the United States, who are eighteen years of age or older, to vote shall not be denied or abridged by the United States or by any state on account of age.

Section 2

The Congress shall have power to enforce this article by appropriate legislation.

Amendment XXVII [1992]

No law varying the compensation for services of the Senators and Representatives, shall take effect, until an election of Representatives shall have intervened.

APPENDIX

Territorial Expansion

Territory	Date Acquired	Square Miles	How Acquired
Original states and territories	1783	888,685	Treaty of Paris
Louisiana Purchase	1803	827,192	Purchased from France
Florida	1819	72,003	Adams-Onís Treaty
Texas	1845	390,143	Annexation of independent country
Oregon	1846	285,580	Oregon Boundary Treaty
Mexican cession	1848	529,017	Treaty of Guadalupe Hidalgo
Gadsden Purchase	1853	29,640	Purchased from Mexico
Midway Islands	1867	2	Annexation of uninhabited islands
Alaska	1867	589,757	Purchased from Russia
Hawaii	1898	6,450	Annexation of independent country
Wake Island	1898	3	Annexation of uninhabited island
Puerto Rico	1899	3,435	Treaty of Paris
Guam	1899	212	Treaty of Paris
The Philippines	1899–1946	115,600	Treaty of Paris; granted independence
American Samoa	1900	76	Treaty with Germany and Great Britain
Panama Canal Zone	1904–1978	553	Hay–Bunau-Varilla Treaty
U.S. Virgin Islands	1917	133	Purchased from Denmark
Trust Territory of the Pacific Islands*	1947	717	United Nations Trusteeship

*A number of these islands have recently been granted independence: Federated States of Micronesia, 1990; Marshall Islands, 1991; Palau, 1994.

The Labor Force (thousands of workers)

Year	Agriculture	Mining	Manufacturing	Construction	Trade	Other	Total
1810	1,950	11	75	—	—	294	2,330
1840	3,570	32	500	290	350	918	5,660
1850	4,520	102	1,200	410	530	1,488	8,250
1860	5,880	176	1,530	520	890	2,114	11,110
1870	6,790	180	2,470	780	1,310	1,400	12,930
1880	8,920	280	3,290	900	1,930	2,070	17,390
1890	9,960	440	4,390	1,510	2,960	4,060	23,320
1900	11,680	637	5,895	1,665	3,970	5,223	29,070
1910	11,770	1,068	8,332	1,949	5,320	9,041	37,480
1920	10,790	1,180	11,190	1,233	5,845	11,372	41,610
1930	10,560	1,009	9,884	1,988	8,122	17,267	48,830
1940	9,575	925	11,309	1,876	9,328	23,277	56,290
1950	7,870	901	15,648	3,029	12,152	25,870	65,470
1960	5,970	709	17,145	3,640	14,051	32,545	74,060
1970	3,463	516	20,746	4,818	15,008	34,127	78,678
1980	3,364	979	21,942	6,215	20,191	46,612	99,303
1990	3,186	730	21,184	7,696	24,269	60,849	118,793
2000	3,382	524	20,256	9,591	28,140	74,998	136,891

Source: Historical Statistics of the United States, Colonial Times to 1970 (1975), 139; Statistical Abstract of the United States, 2003, Table 619.

Changing Labor Patterns

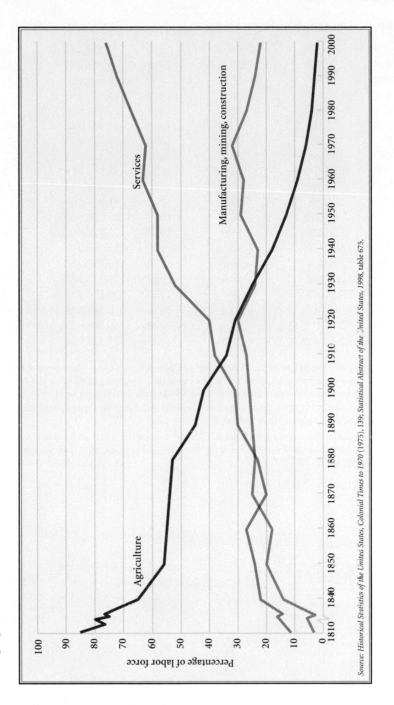

Source: Historical Statistics of the United States, Colonial Times to 1970 (1975), 139; Statistical Abstract of the United States, 1998, table 675.

American Population

Year	Population	Percent Increase	Year	Population	Percent Increase
1610	350	—	1810	7,239,881	36.4
1620	2,300	557.1	1820	9,638,453	33.1
1630	4,600	100.0	1830	12,866,020	33.5
1640	26,600	478.3	1840	17,069,453	32.7
1650	50,400	90.8	1850	23,191,876	35.9
1660	75,100	49.0	1860	31,443,321	35.6
1670	111,900	49.0	1870	39,818,449	26.6
1680	151,500	35.4	1880	50,155,783	26.0
1690	210,400	38.9	1890	62,947,714	25.5
1700	250,900	19.2	1900	75,994,575	20.7
1710	331,700	32.2	1910	91,972,266	21.0
1720	466,200	40.5	1920	105,710,620	14.9
1730	629,400	35.0	1930	122,775,046	16.1
1740	905,600	43.9	1940	131,669,275	7.2
1750	1,170,800	29.3	1950	150,697,361	14.5
1760	1,593,600	36.1	1960	179,323,175	19.0
1770	2,148,100	34.8	1970	203,235,298	13.3
1780	2,780,400	29.4	1980	226,545,805	11.5
1790	3,929,214	41.3	1990	248,709,873	9.8
1800	5,308,483	35.1	2000	281,421,906	13.2

Note: These figures largely ignore the Native American population. Census takers never made any effort to count the Native American population that lived outside their political jurisdictions and compiled only casual and incomplete enumerations of those living within their jurisdictions until 1890. In that year the federal government attempted a full count of the Indian population: the Census found 125,719 Indians in 1890, compared with only 12,543 in 1870 and 33,985 in 1880.

Source: Historical Statistics of the United States, Colonial Times to 1970 (1975); *Statistical Abstract of the United States,* 1999; Bureau of the Census, 2001 <http://blue.census.gov/dmd/www/resapport/states/unitedstates.pdf>.

Presidential Elections

Year	Candidates	Parties	Percentage of Popular Vote	Electoral Vote	Percentage of Voter Participation
1789	**George Washington**	No party designations	*	69	
	John Adams[†]			34	
	Other candidates			35	
1792	**George Washington**	No party designations		132	
	John Adams			77	
	George Clinton			50	
	Other candidates			5	
1796	**John Adams**	Federalist		71	
	Thomas Jefferson	Democratic-Republican		68	
	Thomas Pinckney	Federalist		59	
	Aaron Burr	Democratic-Republican		30	
	Other candidates			48	
1800	**Thomas Jefferson**	Democratic-Republican		73	
	Aaron Burr	Democratic-Republican		73	
	John Adams	Federalist		65	
	Charles C. Pinckney	Federalist		64	
	John Jay	Federalist		1	
1804	**Thomas Jefferson**	Democratic-Republican		162	
	Charles C. Pinckney	Federalist		14	
1808	**James Madison**	Democratic-Republican		122	
	Charles C. Pinckney	Federalist		47	
	George Clinton	Democratic-Republican		6	
1812	**James Madison**	Democratic-Republican		128	
	De Witt Clinton	Federalist		89	
1816	**James Monroe**	Democratic-Republican		183	
	Rufus King	Federalist		34	
1820	**James Monroe**	Democratic-Republican		231	
	John Quincy Adams	Independent Republican		1	
1824	**John Quincy Adams**	Democratic-Republican	30.5	84	26.9
	Andrew Jackson	Democratic-Republican	43.1	99	
	Henry Clay	Democratic-Republican	13.2	37	
	William H. Crawford	Democratic-Republican	13.1	41	
1828	**Andrew Jackson**	Democratic	56.0	178	57.6
	John Quincy Adams	National Republican	44.0	83	
1832	**Andrew Jackson**	Democratic	54.5	219	55.4
	Henry Clay	National Republican	37.5	49	
	William Wirt	Anti-Masonic	8.0	7	
	John Floyd	Democratic	‡	11	
1836	**Martin Van Buren**	Democratic	50.9	170	57.8
	William H. Harrison	Whig		73	
	Hugh L. White	Whig		26	
	Daniel Webster	Whig	49.1	14	
	W. P. Mangum	Whig		11	
1840	**William H. Harrison**	Whig	53.1	234	80.2
	Martin Van Buren	Democratic	46.9	60	

*Prior to 1824, most presidential electors were chosen by state legislators rather than by popular vote.

†Before the Twelfth Amendment was passed in 1804, the electoral college voted for two presidential candidates; the runner-up became vice president.

‡Percentages below 2.0 have been omitted. Hence the percentage of popular vote might not total 100 percent.

Year	Candidates	Parties	Percentage of Popular Vote	Electoral Vote	Percentage of Voter Participation
1844	**James K. Polk**	Democratic	49.6	170	78.9
	Henry Clay	Whig	48.1	105	
	James G. Birney	Liberty	2.3	0	
1848	**Zachary Taylor**	Whig	47.4	163	72.7
	Lewis Cass	Democratic	42.5	127	
	Martin Van Buren	Free Soil	10.1	0	
1852	**Franklin Pierce**	Democratic	50.9	254	69.6
	Winfield Scott	Whig	44.1	42	
	John P. Hale	Free Soil	5.0	0	
1856	**James Buchanan**	Democratic	45.3	174	78.9
	John C. Frémont	Republican	33.1	114	
	Millard Fillmore	American	21.6	8	
1860	**Abraham Lincoln**	Republican	39.8	180	81.2
	Stephen A. Douglas	Democratic	29.5	12	
	John C. Breckinridge	Democratic	18.1	72	
	John Bell	Constitutional Union	12.6	39	
1864	**Abraham Lincoln**	Republican	55.0	212	73.8
	George B. McClellan	Democratic	45.0	21	
1868	**Ulysses S. Grant**	Republican	52.7	214	78.1
	Horatio Seymour	Democratic	47.3	80	
1872	**Ulysses S. Grant**	Republican	55.6	286	71.3
	Horace Greeley	Democratic	43.9	0	
1876	**Rutherford B. Hayes**	Republican	48.0	185	81.8
	Samuel J. Tilden	Democratic	51.0	184	
1880	**James A. Garfield**	Republican	48.5	214	79.4
	Winfield S. Hancock	Democratic	48.1	155	
	James B. Weaver	Greenback-Labor	3.4	0	
1884	**Grover Cleveland**	Democratic	48.5	219	77.5
	James G. Blaine	Republican	48.2	182	
1888	**Benjamin Harrison**	Republican	47.9	233	79.3
	Grover Cleveland	Democratic	48.6	168	
1892	**Grover Cleveland**	Democratic	46.1	277	74.7
	Benjamin Harrison	Republican	43.0	145	
	James B. Weaver	People's	8.5	22	
1896	**William McKinley**	Republican	51.1	271	79.3
	William J. Bryan	Democratic	47.7	176	
1900	**William McKinley**	Republican	51.7	292	73.2
	William J. Bryan	Democratic; Populist	45.5	155	
1904	**Theodore Roosevelt**	Republican	57.4	336	65.2
	Alton B. Parker	Democratic	37.6	140	
	Eugene V. Debs	Socialist	3.0	0	
1908	**William H. Taft**	Republican	51.6	321	65.4
	William J. Bryan	Democratic	43.1	162	
	Eugene V. Debs	Socialist	2.8	0	
1912	**Woodrow Wilson**	Democratic	41.9	435	58.8
	Theodore Roosevelt	Progressive	27.4	88	
	William H. Taft	Republican	23.2	8	
1916	**Woodrow Wilson**	Democratic	49.4	277	61.6
	Charles E. Hughes	Republican	46.2	254	
	A. L. Benson	Socialist	3.2	0	

Year	Candidates	Parties	Percentage of Popular Vote	Electoral Vote	Percentage of Voter Participation
1920	**Warren G. Harding**	Republican	60.4	404	49.2
	James M. Cox	Democratic	34.2	127	
	Eugene V. Debs	Socialist	3.4	0	
1924	**Calvin Coolidge**	Republican	54.0	382	48.9
	John W. Davis	Democratic	28.8	136	
	Robert M. La Follette	Progressive	16.6	13	
1928	**Herbert C. Hoover**	Republican	58.2	444	56.9
	Alfred E. Smith	Democratic	40.9	87	
1932	**Franklin D. Roosevelt**	Democratic	57.4	472	56.9
	Herbert C. Hoover	Republican	39.7	59	
1936	**Franklin D. Roosevelt**	Democratic	60.8	523	61.0
	Alfred M. Landon	Republican	36.5	8	
1940	**Franklin D. Roosevelt**	Democratic	54.8	449	62.5
	Wendell L. Willkie	Republican	44.8	82	
1944	**Franklin D. Roosevelt**	Democratic	53.5	432	55.9
	Thomas E. Dewey	Republican	46.0	99	
1948	**Harry S Truman**	Democratic	49.6	303	53.0
	Thomas E. Dewey	Republican	45.1	189	
1952	**Dwight D. Eisenhower**	Republican	55.1	442	63.3
	Adlai E. Stevenson	Democratic	44.4	89	
1956	**Dwight D. Eisenhower**	Republican	57.6	457	60.6
	Adlai E. Stevenson	Democratic	42.1	73	
1960	**John F. Kennedy**	Democratic	49.7	303	64.0
	Richard M. Nixon	Republican	49.5	219	
1964	**Lyndon B. Johnson**	Democratic	61.1	486	61.7
	Barry M. Goldwater	Republican	38.5	52	
1968	**Richard M. Nixon**	Republican	43.4	301	60.6
	Hubert H. Humphrey	Democratic	42.7	191	
	George C. Wallace	American Independent	13.5	46	
1972	**Richard M. Nixon**	Republican	60.7	520	55.5
	George S. McGovern	Democratic	37.5	17	
1976	**Jimmy Carter**	Democratic	50.1	297	54.3
	Gerald R. Ford	Republican	48.0	240	
1980	**Ronald W. Reagan**	Republican	50.7	489	53.0
	Jimmy Carter	Democratic	41.0	49	
	John B. Anderson	Independent	6.6	0	
1984	**Ronald W. Reagan**	Republican	58.4	525	52.9
	Walter F. Mondale	Democratic	41.6	13	
1988	**George H. W. Bush**	Republican	53.4	426	50.3
	Michael Dukakis	Democratic	45.6	111*	
1992	**William J. Clinton**	Democratic	43.7	370	55.1
	George H. W. Bush	Republican	38.0	168	
	H. Ross Perot	Independent	19.0	0	
1996	**William J. Clinton**	Democratic	49	379	49.0
	Robert J. Dole	Republican	41	159	
	H. Ross Perot	Reform	8	0	
2000	**George W. Bush**	Republican	47.9	271	51.3
	Albert A. Gore	Democratic	48.4	266†	
	Ralph Nader	Green Party	2.7	0	
2004	**George W. Bush**	Republican	51.0	286	59.0
	John F. Kerry	Democratic	48.0	252	

*One Dukakis elector cast a vote for Lloyd Bentsen.
†One Gore elector abstained.

GLOSSARY

This list of terms will help you with the vocabulary of history. Many of these terms refer to broad, enduring concepts that appear not only in your textbook but also in further studies of history and in discussions of current events. The terms appear in bold print at their first use in each volume. The glossary notes the pages on which the terms first appear in bold print. Check the index to look up the terms' uses in other historical eras and different contexts. For definitions and discussions of other unfamiliar words and concepts, consult the book's index or a dictionary.

affirmative action Government mandates beginning in the 1970s that required unions, businesses, and educational institutions to make a deliberate effort to achieve a better measure of racial and gender equality in their recruitment and hiring. While the civil rights movement had achieved significant legal and political victories, historic patterns of racial and gender discrimination proved difficult to overcome without the assistance of the government. (p. 930)

American System A mercantilist system of national economic development advocated by Henry Clay and supported by John Quincy Adams. It had three interrelated parts: a national bank to manage the financial system; protective tariffs to encourage American industry and provide revenue; and a nationally funded system of internal improvements, such as roads, canals, and railroads. (p. 325)

anarchism The advocacy of a stateless society achieved by revolutionary means. Feared for their views, anarchists became the scapegoats for the 1886 Haymarket Square bombing. (p. 527)

Anglo-Saxonism A theory widely held in the late nineteenth century that the English-speaking peoples were racially superior and for that reason justified in colonizing and dominating the peoples of less-developed areas of the world. Combined with Social Darwinism, Anglo-Saxonism fueled American expansionism in the late nineteenth century. (p. 636)

appeasement Pacifying an enemy by making concessions. In the context of the coming of World War II, it refers specifically to the agreement reached at Munich in 1938 in which England and France agreed to allow Hitler to annex the Sudetenland in exchange for his promise not to take more territory. (p. 782)

Benevolent Empire A broad-ranging campaign of moral and institutional reform inspired by evangelical Christian ideals and created by middle-class men and women in the 1820s. "Benevolence" became a seminal concept in American spiritual and social thought during the Second Great Awakening. Promoters of benevolent reform suggested that people who had experienced saving grace should provide charity to the less fortunate. (p. 314)

bills of exchange Credit slips that British manufacturers, West Indian planters, and American merchants used to trade among themselves in the eighteenth century. (p. 96)

Black Codes Laws passed by southern states after the Civil War denying ex-slaves the civil rights enjoyed by whites and intended to force blacks back to the plantations. (p. 445)

blacklist Procedure used by employers throughout the nineteenth century to label and identify workers affiliated with unions. In the 1950s, blacklists were utilized to exclude alleged Communists from jobs in government service, the motion picture business, and many industries and unions. (pp. 345, 835)

Bolsheviks Members of Russia's Communist revolutionary party in the early twentieth century. Led by Vladimir Lenin, they took Russia out of the war in early 1917, giving up huge territories to the Germans in the Treaty of Brest-Litovsk. After World War I, Americans often used this term to describe anyone they viewed as radical. (p. 670)

broker state An activist government that mediates between contending pressure groups seeking power and benefits. In the United States, Franklin D. Roosevelt's New Deal in the 1930s marked the clear emergence of the broker state. (p. 765)

business cycle The periodic rise and decline of business activity characteristic of capitalist-run, market economies. A quest for profit stimulates a level of production that exceeds demand and prompts a decline in output. In the United States, major periods of expansion during 1802–1818, 1824–1836, 1846–1856, 1865–1873, 1896–1914, and 1922–1928 were followed by either relatively short financial panics (1819–1822 and 1857–1860) or extended depressions (1837–1843, 1873–1896, and 1929–1939). (pp. 247, 723)

capitalism, capitalist The system of economic production based on the private ownership of property and the contractual exchange for profit of goods, labor, and money (capital). Although some elements of capitalism existed in the United States before 1820, a full-blown capitalist economy and society emerged only with the market revolution of the mid-nineteenth century and reached its pinnacle during the final decades of the century. (p. 228)

carpetbaggers A derisive name given by Southerners to Northerners who moved to the South during Reconstruction. Former Confederates despised these Northerners as transient exploiters. Carpetbaggers actually were a varied group, including Union veterans who had served in the South, reformers eager to help the ex-slaves, and others looking for business opportunities. (p. 457)

caste system A relatively rigid system of social status based primarily on birth. (p. 29)

chattel slavery A system of bondage in which enslaved people have the legal status of property and, hence, may be bought and sold in a manner similar to other forms of property. (p. 50)

civic humanism A political and civil outlook that stressed virtuous service to the community and its government. During the Renaissance, this idea of selfless service was thought to be critical in a republic where authority lay in the hands of the citizenry. (p. 19)

civil religion A term used to describe the sacred, religious-like allegiance that many Americans gave to their republican political institutions. (p. 214)

clan A group of related families who share a common ancestor. In the sixteenth century many native peoples north of the Rio Grande organized their societies around these groups, which often combined to form tribes. (p. 10)

closed shop Workplace in which a job seeker had to be a union member to gain employment. In the nineteenth century, the closed shop was favored by craft unions as a method of keeping out incompetent and lower-wage workers and of strengthening their bargaining position with employers. (p. 526)

closed-shop agreement A labor contract in which an employer agrees to hire only union members. Many employers strongly opposed such agreements and instituted court cases to have them declared illegal by the judiciary. (p. 345)

collective bargaining A process of negotiation between labor unions and employers, particularly favored by the American Federation of Labor (AFL). Led by Samuel Gompers, the AFL accepted the new industrial order, but fought for a bigger share of the profits for the workers. (p. 530)

collective security A peacekeeping concept whereby nations ally to protect one another from aggression. The post–World War I League of Nations, in Article X, was the first international body to mandate collective security. Unwillingness to accept Article X contributed to U.S. failure to join the League. In 1945, after World War II, the United States joined the United Nations, thereby agreeing to the principle of collective security. (p. 687)

Columbian Exchange The sixteenth-century transfer of agricultural products and diseases among the continents. The foodstuffs of the Western Hemisphere—maize, tomatoes, potatoes, manioc—moved eastward, as did a new variety of syphilis; and African and Eurasian crops, animals, and diseases, particularly smallpox and measles, moved to the Americas. (p. 28)

common law Centuries-old body of English law based on custom and judicial interpretation, not legislation, and evolving case by case on the basis of precedent. The common law was transmitted to America along with English settlement and became the foundation of American law at the state and local levels. In the United States, even more than in Britain, the common law gave the courts supremacy over the legislatures in many areas of law. (pp. 142, 611)

companionate marriage Reflecting republican ideas, some men and women in the early nineteenth century tried to create marriages based on mutual equality and respect. Although husbands retained significant legal powers, they increasingly viewed their wives as loving partners rather than as inferiors or dependents. (p. 201)

conservation, conservationist Advocacy for protection of the natural environment for sustained use. As applied by Theodore Roosevelt at the start of the twentieth century, conservation accepted development of public lands, provided this was in the public interest and not wastefully destructive. In contrast, preservationists valued wilderness in its natural state and were more broadly opposed to development. (p. 613)

containment American Cold War policy designed to prevent Soviet expansionism, articulated most forcefully in 1946 by American diplomatic advisor George Kennan. For over forty years, American defense policy was guided by Kennan's argument that the Soviets would stop only when met with "unanswerable force." (p. 820)

counterinsurgency A military operation using specially trained forces to defend against guerrilla warfare. The U.S. military created the Green Berets in the early 1960s to fight this type of nontraditional warfare, characteristic of the conflict in Vietnam. (p. 865)

court injunction A directive issued by a judge that prohibits certain conduct until a dispute is legally adjudicated. During labor disputes, probusiness judges routinely issued injunctions that prevented labor unions from striking or picketing and imposed stringent penalties against individuals and unions who defied the injunction. (p. 347)

covert interventions Secret undertakings by a country in pursuit of foreign-policy goals, as evidenced by the Central Intelligence Agency, started in the 1950s, when operating in the interests of the United States. Knowledge of these acts, like U.S. participation in the overthrow of the government of Guatemala in 1954 and support for the Contras in Nicaragua in the 1980s, was kept from the American people and most members of Congress. (p. 828)

cultural pluralism A term coined in 1924 that posits that diversity, especially religious and ethnic diversity, can be a source of strength in a democratic nation and thus cultural differences should be respected and valued. (p. 771)

deficit spending High government spending in excess of tax revenues based on the ideas of economist John Maynard Keynes, who proposed in the 1930s that governments should be prepared to go into debt to stimulate a stagnant economy. (p. 764)

deflation The sustained decline of prices, generally accompanying an economic depression, but in the United States after the Civil War, the result of rapidly rising productivity, market competition, and a tight money supply. (p. 591)

Deism, Deist The belief, popular in the eighteenth century among educated Americans urban artisans, that God made the world but subsequently exerted no influence on it or its people. This doctrine was radical because it repudiated the belief of many Christians that God intervened directly in human affairs. (p. 113)

deregulation Process of removing or limiting federal regulatory mechanisms, justified on the basis of promoting competition and streamlining government bureaucracy. President Carter began deregulation in the 1970s, starting with the airline, banking, and communications industries. The process continued under subsequent administrations. (p. 940)

détente From the French word for a relaxation of tension, this term was used to signify the new foreign policy of President Nixon, which sought a reduction of tension and hostility between the United States and the Soviet Union and China in the early 1970s. (p. 909)

direct primary The selection of party candidates by a popular vote rather than by the party convention, this progressive reform was especially pressed by Robert La Follette, who viewed it as an instrument for breaking the grip of machines on the political parties. In the South, where it was limited to whites, the primary was a means of disfranchising blacks. (p. 604)

division of labor A system of manufacture that assigned specific tasks to different workers. It improved efficiency and productivity but also eroded the workers' control over the conditions of labor. This system began around 1800 in the shoe industry and soon became the general practice throughout the manufacturing sector of the economy. (p. 293)

dollar diplomacy Policy adopted by President Taft emphasizing the connection between America's economic and political interests overseas. The benefits would flow in both directions. Business would gain from diplomatic efforts in its behalf, while the strengthened American economic presence overseas would give added leverage to American diplomacy. (p. 652)

domino theory An American Cold War concept associated with the containment policy that posited that Communist incursions into nations must be stopped before communism spread to neighboring countries and enveloped entire regions. The term was first used by President Eisenhower, who warned of the "falling domino" principle. (p. 820)

dower, dower right A legal right originating in medieval Europe and carried to the American colonies that extended to a widow the use of one-third of the family's land and goods during her lifetime. (p. 17)

enclosure acts The laws passed in England in the sixteenth century that allowed landowners to fence in the open fields surrounding many peasant villages and set sheep to graze on them. The acts left many peasants without land to cultivate and forced them to work as wage laborers or as wool spinners and weavers. (p. 34)

encomenderos Privileged Spanish landholders in America who held land grants from the Spanish crown and the right to collect tribute from the resident Native American population, both in goods and through forced labor. (p. 39)

encomiendas Land grants in America given by the Spanish kings to reward conquistadors and others in the sixteenth century. The *encomiendas* also gave the landholders legal control over the native population who lived on or near their estates. (p. 27)

entitlement programs Government programs that provide financial benefits to which recipients are entitled by law. Examples include Social Security, Medicare, unemployment compensation, and agricultural price supports. (p. 917)

established church, establishment A church that enjoys a government-bestowed preferred legal status. Historically, established churches in Europe and America were supported by public taxes and sometimes were the only legally permitted religious institutions in a nation or colony. (p. 193)

ethnocultural Refers to the distinctive social characteristics of immigrants and religious groups, especially in determining their party loyalties and stance on political issues touching personal behavior and public morality. (p. 575)

fascism Right-wing antidemocratic totalitarian movements that began in Europe after World War I and which were characterized by strong dictators backed by the military. The dictatorships of Benito Mussolini in Italy, Adolf Hitler in Germany, and Francisco Franco in Spain represent three Fascist states. (p. 766)

feminism, feminist Doctrine advanced in the early twentieth century by women activists that women should be equal to men in all areas of life. Earlier women activists and suffragists had accepted the notion of separate spheres for men and women, but feminists sought to overcome all barriers to equality and full personal development. (p. 602)

fiscal policy The manipulation of government expenditure and taxation aimed at affecting a nation's allocation of economic resources, the distribution of income, and the level and general growth of economic activity. (p. 868)

flexible response A strategy adopted by the Kennedy administration in the early 1960s that called for a military establishment that was prepared to fight any foe—large or small, with conventional or nuclear arms—that was seen as a threat to American interests. (p. 864)

Fourteen Points President Wilson proposed these as a basis for peace negotiations at Versailles in 1919. Included in the points were open diplomacy, freedom of the seas, free trade, territorial integrity, arms reduction, national self-determination, and establishment of the League of Nations. (p. 683)

franchise The right to vote. It was extended to all adult white males in the 1820s and 1830s by most states, to black men in 1870 by the Fifteenth Amendment to the U.S. Constitution, and to women in 1920 by the Nineteenth Amendment. (p. 323)

free soil A political movement of the 1840s that opposed the expansion of slavery in order to allow white farm families to settle the western territories and install democratic republican values and institutions there. The short-lived Free-Soil Party stood for "free soil, free labor, free men," which subsequently became the program of the Republican Party. (p. 395)

freehold Property owned in its entirety, without feudal dues or landlord obligations. Freeholders have the legal right to improve, transfer, or sell their property. The first settlers of New England instituted this landholding system in an effort to escape exploitative leaseholds and feudal obligations. (p. 52)

fundamentalists, fundamentalism Conservative Protestants who believe in a literal interpretation of the Bible. In the 1920s, fundamentalists opposed modernist Protestants, who tried to reconcile Christianity with Darwin's theory of evolution and recent technological and scientific discoveries. Fundamentalists' promotion of antievolution laws for public schools led to the famous *Scopes* trial of 1925. (p. 713)

gang-labor system A system of work discipline used on Southern cotton plantations in the mid-nineteenth century. White overseers or black drivers constantly supervised gangs of enslaved laborers in order to enforce work norms and secure greater productivity. (p. 383)

general strike A strike that draws in all the workers in a society, with the intention of shutting the entire system down. Radical groups like the International Workers of the World (IWW), in the early twentieth century, saw the general strike as the means for initiating a social revolution. (p. 533)

gentry A class of English men and women who were substantial landholders but lacked the social privileges and titles of nobility that marked the aristocracy. During the Price Revolution of the sixteenth century, the relative wealth and status of the gentry rose while that of the aristocracy declined. (p. 34)

globalization As the flow of capital and trade expands, regional economies become more integrated; national political and economic borders become less significant; and multinational corporations dominate world trade. This process began in the 1970s and heated up in the 1990s, in part as a result of the end of the Cold War and the shattering of political barriers that had restrained international trade. (p. 959)

gold standard An international monetary standard in which the values of national currencies of participating countries are fixed in terms of gold and, therefore, in terms of each other. (p. 726)

habeas corpus A legal writ (Latin for "bring forth the body") used in English common-law courts to force government authorities to justify their arrest and detention of an individual. It was given the status of a formal privilege in the U.S. Constitution

(Art. I, Sec. 9), which also allows its suspension in cases of invasion or insurrection. During the Civil War, Lincoln suspended habeas corpus to stop protests against the draft and disloyal activities. The USA PATRIOT Act (2001) likewise suspends this privilege in cases of suspected terrorism, but the act's constitutional legitimacy has not yet been decided by the courts. (p. 424)

hegemony Dominance in global affairs by a nation. The United States and the Soviet Union emerged from World War II as the world's leading powers, each exercising a tremendous influence, or hegemony, within their respective spheres of influence. (p. 718)

heresy, heresies Religious doctrines inconsistent with the teaching of an established, official Christian Church. Some of the Crusades between 1096 and 1291 stand as examples of Christians attempting to crush groups spreading these "unauthorized" doctrines. (p. 18)

home rule A rallying cry used by southern Democrats painting Reconstruction governments as illegitimate—imposed on the South—and themselves as the only party capable of restoring the South to "home rule." By 1876, northern Republicans were inclined to accept this claim. (p. 469)

homespun Yarn and cloth spun and woven by American women and long worn by poor colonists. During political boycotts in the 1760s, the wearing of homespun clothes by higher social classes took on a political meaning. It also substituted for the textiles previously imported from Britain and provided women with the opportunity to contribute directly to the Patriot movement. (p. 148)

ideology A systematic philosophy or political theory that purports to explain the character of the social world or to prescribe a set of values or beliefs. (p. 19)

impeachment First step in the constitutional process for removing the president from office, in which charges of wrongdoing (articles of impeachment) are passed by the House of Representatives. A trial is then conducted by the Senate to determine whether the impeached president is guilty of the charges. (p. 453)

indenture, indentured servants A seventeenth-century labor contract that required service for a period of time in return for passage to North America. Indentures were typically for a term of four or five years, provided room and board in exchange for labor, and granted free status at the end of the contract period. (p. 50)

indulgences Certificates granted by the Catholic Church that allegedly pardoned sinners from punishments in the afterlife. In his *Ninety-five Theses*, written in 1517, Martin Luther condemned the sale of indulgences, a common practice among Catholic clergy. (p. 30)

injunction, court injunction An order by a judge halting a specified activity by a party to a legal dispute on the grounds that potential injury to the other party would be irreparable. Injunctions are not subject to normal due-process proceedings but are emergency measures instituted prior to the resolution of the dispute. Injunctions were widely used in early-twentieth-century labor disputes. (p. 610)

isolationism, isolationist A foreign-policy stance supporting the withdrawal of the United States from involvement with other nations, especially an avoidance of entangling diplomatic relations. The common view of post–World War I U.S. foreign policy is that it was isolationist, but in fact the United States played an active role in world affairs, particularly in trade and finance. (p. 701)

Jim Crow A term first heard in antebellum minstrel shows to designate black behavior and used in the age of segregation to designate facilities restricted to blacks, such as Jim Crow railway cars. (p. 585)

jingoism This term came to refer to the super-patriotism that took hold during the mid-1890s during the American dispute with Spain over Cuba. Jingoes were enthusiastic about a military solution as a way of showing the nation's mettle and, when diplomacy failed, they got their wish with the Spanish-American War of 1898. (p. 637)

joint-stock company A financial arrangement established by the British around 1550 that subsequently facilitated the colonization of North America. These agreements allowed merchants to band together as stockholders, raising large amounts of money while sharing the risks and profits in proportion to their part of the total investment. (p. 44)

judicial review The claim by the judiciary that it has the legitimate authority to judge the constitutionality of laws passed by Congress and the state legislatures. This power is implicit in the federal Constitution and was first practiced by the Supreme Court with respect to congressional legislation in *Marbury v. Madison* in 1803. The Court's review of legislation became particularly significant between 1874 and 1937. (p. 238)

Keynesian economics Originally developed by John Maynard Keynes in the 1930s, this theory stresses that aggregate (or total) demand for goods and services is the primary determinant of the level of overall economic activity. (p. 764)

labor theory of value The belief that the price of a product should reflect the work that went into making it and should be paid mostly to the person who produced it. This idea was popularized by the National Trades' Union and other labor organizations in the mid-nineteenth century. (p. 300)

laissez-faire In French, literally "let do" or "leave alone," the term refers to the principle that the less government does, the better, in particular as related to interference with the economy. This was the dominant philosophy of American government in the late nineteenth century and the guiding light of conservative politics in the twentieth. (p. 571)

liberal consensus Refers to widespread agreement in the decades of the 1950s and 1960s that government power could be used to stimulate the economy to bring about extensive affluence; protect the rights of disadvantaged minorities; and promote social welfare in general. The liberal consensus supported an optimistic belief in a prosperous, harmonious future that also assumed U.S. world activism to contain communism. (p. 839)

lien (crop lien) A legal device enabling a creditor to take possession of the property of a borrower, including the right to have it sold in payment of the debt. Furnishing merchants took such liens on cotton crops as collateral for supplies advanced to sharecroppers during the growing season. This system trapped farmers in a cycle of debt and made them vulnerable to exploitation by the furnishing merchant. (p. 462)

literacy test The requirement that an ability to read be demonstrated as a qualification for the right to vote. It was a device easily used by registrars to prevent blacks from voting, whether they could read or not, and was widely adopted across the South beginning with Mississippi in 1890. (p. 577)

machine tools Cutting, boring, and drilling machines used to produce standardized metal parts that will then be assembled into products like sewing machines. The development of machine tools by American inventors in the early nineteenth century facilitated the rapid spread of the Industrial Revolution. (p. 523)

Manifest Destiny Term coined by John L. O'Sullivan in 1845 describing the idea that Euro-Americans were fated by God to settle the North American continent from the Atlantic to the Pacific and supplant the Native Americans. Adding geographic and secular dimensions to the Second Great Awakening, Manifest Destiny implied that the spread of American republican institutions and Protestant churches across the continent was part of God's plan for the world. With the completion of the westward movement in the late nineteenth century, the focus of "manifest destiny" expanded and began to encompass American overseas expansion. (pp. 387, 636)

manorial, manorial system The quasi-feudal system of landholding in the Hudson River Valley in which wealthy landlords leased out thousands of acres to tenant farmers. In return, the tenants owed their landlords rent, a quarter of the value of all improvements, and a number of days of personal service. (p. 69)

manumission A word from Latin meaning literally "to release from the hand." The legal act whereby owners relinquished their property rights in slaves. In 1782 the Virginia assembly passed an act allowing manumission and within a decade planters had freed 10,000 slaves. Worried that a large free black population would threaten the institution of slavery, the assembly repealed the law in 1792. (p. 189)

margin buying The purchase of stocks or securities with a small down payment while financing the rest with a broker loan. When stock prices started to fall in 1929, brokers requested repayment of such loans; the funds were often not forthcoming, contributing to the crash of the stock market in October of that year. (p. 724)

Market Revolution The dramatic increase between 1820 and 1850 in the exchange of goods and services in market transactions. The Market Revolution resulted from the combined impact of the increased output of farms and factories, the entrepreneurial activities of traders and merchants, and the development of a transportation network of roads, canals, and railroads. (p. 301)

mass production A system of factory production that, through the use of sophisticated machinery, turns out vast quantities of identical goods at a low cost. In the nineteenth century the textile industry was a pioneer of mass production, which eventually became the standard mode for making consumer goods such as cigarettes, cars, and many electronic items—such as telephones, radios, televisions, and computers. (p. 307)

matrilineal A system of family organization in which social identity and property descend through the female line. Children are usually raised by their mother's brother (their uncle), not their biological father. (p. 14)

mechanics A term used in the nineteenth century to refer to skilled craftsmen and inventors who built and improved machinery and developed machine tools for industry. They developed a professional identity and established institutes to spread their skills and knowledge. (p. 295)

mercantilism A set of policies that regulated colonial commerce and manufacturing for the enrichment of the mother country. These policies insured that the American colonies produced agricultural goods and raw materials, which would then be carried to Britain, where they would be re-exported or made into finished goods. (pp. 20, 70)

mestizo A person of mixed blood, the offspring of intermarriage or sexual liaison between white Europeans and native people, usually a white man and an Indian woman. In sixteenth-century Mesoamerica, nearly 90 percent of the Spanish settlers were men who took Indian women as wives or mistresses; the result was a substantial mixed-race population. (p. 29)

Middle Passage The brutal sea voyage from Africa to the Americas in the eighteenth and nineteenth centuries during which nearly a million enslaved Africans lost their lives. (p. 80)

military-industrial complex A term first used by President Eisenhower in his farewell address in 1961, it refers to the interlinkage of the military and the defense industry that emerged with the arms buildup of World War II and the Cold War and continues to this day. Eisenhower particularly warned against the "unwarranted influence" that the military-industrial complex might exert on public policy. (p. 780)

Minutemen In the imperial crisis of the 1770s, colonists reorganized their voluntary militia units so that they were ready to mobilize on short notice. Militiamen formed the core of the armed citizenry army that met the British at Lexington and Concord in 1775. (p. 158)

modernist movement A literary and artistic style and movement in the early twentieth century that broke sharply with past traditions and was marked by skepticism and stylistic experimentation. Modernist writers include Gertrude Stein, T. S. Eliot, and John Dos Passos. (p. 716)

muckrakers Journalists in the early twentieth century whose stock-in-trade was exposure of the corruption of big business and government. Theodore Roosevelt gave them the name as a term of reproach. The term comes from a character in *Pilgrim's Progress*, a religious allegory by John Bunyan. (p. 599)

national debt The financial obligations of the U.S. government for money borrowed from its citizens and foreign investors. Alexander Hamilton thought that the national debt, owed to wealthy Americans, would insure their support for the new national government. For similar reasons, in recent decades the U.S. government encouraged individuals and institutions in crucial foreign nations, such as Saudi Arabia and Japan, to invest billions of dollars in the American national debt. (p. 211)

national self-determination This concept holds that nations have the right to be sovereign states with political and economic autonomy. A central component of Woodrow Wilson's World War I Fourteen Points, it challenged the existing colonial empires. The right of national self-determination continues to be invoked by nationalist, usually ethnic, groups, such as the Basques in Spain, the Kurds in Turkey and Iraq, and the Palestinians in Israel. (p. 684)

nativism Antiforeign sentiment in the United States that fueled a drive against immigration. Nativism directed at the Chinese led to the 1882 Chinese Exclusion Act. Nativist anxiety about "hyphenated Americans" became particularly strong in the World War I era and led to legislation in 1924 that restricted immigration from Europe by use of a quota system and prohibited all Asian immigrants. (p. 709)

New Right Conservative political movement that achieved considerable success beginning in the 1970s, helping to elect Ronald Reagan president in 1980 and enabling the Republican Party to retake both houses of Congress in the 1994 elections.

The New Right has a diverse constituency, including evangelical Christians, concerned primarily about moral issues, and conservatives hostile to federal activism. (p. 938)

nullification The constitutional argument that a state could void (nullify) a law enacted by Congress. This idea had its origin in the Kentucky and Virginia Resolutions of 1798, which were drafted by Thomas Jefferson and James Madison, and received its fullest exposition in John C. Calhoun's *Exposition and Protest* in 1828 and South Carolina's attempt at nullifying the tariff in 1832. (p. 333)

open-door policy U.S. foreign policy articulated in the Open Door notes sent by the secretary of state in 1899 to Japan, Russia, Germany, and France—all of whom were establishing spheres of influence in China—asking that China remain open to trade on equal terms by all nations. Because it was not participating in the assault on China's territorial integrity, an open door was crucial if the United States was to be assured access to China's large markets. (p. 651)

outwork A system of manufacturing, also known as "putting out," used in the English woolen industry. Merchants in the sixteenth and seventeenth centuries bought wool and provided it to landless peasants, who spun and wove it into cloth, which the merchants in turn sold in English and foreign markets. (p. 33)

patriarchy A family system in which the father is the dominant authority, usually both by legal right and customary practice. (p. 87)

patronage The power of elected officials to grant government jobs. Beginning in the early nineteenth century, politicians systematically used—and abused—patronage to create and maintain strong party loyalties. After 1870, political reformers gradually introduced merit-based civil service systems in the federal and state governments. (pp. 324, 567)

peasant A farm laborer who often worked land owned by a landlord. In 1450 Europe, these laborers sometimes owned or leased a small plot in the town and worked collectively with other village laborers on the common lands of the community. (p. 14)

peonage (debt peonage) As cotton prices declined during the 1870s, many sharecroppers fell into permanent debt. Merchants often conspired with landowners to make the debt a pretext for forced labor, or peonage. (p. 462)

pocket veto Presidential way to kill a piece of legislation without issuing a formal veto. When congressional Republicans passed the Wade-Davis Bill in 1864, a harsher alternative to President Lincoln's restoration plan, Lincoln used this method to kill it by simply not signing the bill and letting it expire after Congress adjourned. (p. 443)

political machine Nineteenth-century term for highly organized groups operating within and intending to control political parties. Machines were regarded as antidemocratic by political reformers and were the target especially of Progressive era leaders such as Robert La Follette. The direct primary was the favored antimachine instrument because it made the selection of party candidates the product of a popular ballot rather than conventions that were susceptible to machine control. (pp. 324, 556, 576)

poll tax A tax paid for the privilege of voting, used in the South beginning during Reconstruction to disfranchise freedmen. Nationally, the northern states used poll taxes to keep immigrants and others deemed unworthy from the polls. (pp. 455, 584)

popular sovereignty The republican principle that ultimate power resides in the hands of the electorate. Following the principle of popular sovereignty, voters directly or indirectly ratify the constitutions of the state and national governments and amendments to those fundamental laws. During the 1850s Congress applied the principle of popular sovereignty to the western lands by enacting legislation giving residents the authority to determine the status of slavery in their territory. (p. 397)

pragmatism Philosophical doctrine developed primarily by William James that denied the existence of absolute truths and argued that ideas should be judged by their practical consequences. Problem solving, not ultimate ends, was the proper concern of philosophy, in James's view. Pragmatism provided a key intellectual foundation for progressivism. (p. 599)

praying towns Native American settlements in New England that were supervised by Puritan ministers. These seventeenth-century settlements were intended to introduce Indians to Christianity, in part through an Algonquian-language Bible. (p. 61)

predestination The idea that God had chosen certain people for salvation even before they were born. This strict belief was preached by John Calvin in the sixteenth century and became a fundamental tenet of Puritan theology. (pp. 30, 55)

preservationists, preservation Early-twentieth-century activists, like John Muir, who fought to protect the natural environment from commercial exploitation, particularly in the American West. They should be distinguished from conservationists, who accepted development but on a regulated basis, so as not to be wastefully destructive of the nation's resources. Preservationists were the first to advocate the establishment of national parks like Yellowstone and Yosemite. (p. 613)

Price Revolution A term that describes the significance of the high rate of inflation in Europe in the mid-1500s. The inflation resulted from Spain's importation of American gold and silver, which doubled the money supply in Europe, at a time when the population was also increasing. It brought about profound social changes by reducing the political power of the aristocracy and leaving many peasant families on the brink of poverty, setting the stage for a substantial migration to America. (p. 34)

primogeniture An inheritance practice by which a family's land was passed on to the eldest son. Although republican-minded Americans of the Revolutionary era felt this practice was unfair, they did not prohibit it. However, most state legislatures passed laws providing that, if the father died without a will, the estate would be distributed equally among his children. (p. 17)

probate inventory The inventory of a person's property taken by legal officials at death. These inventories are of great value to historians because they provide detailed lists of personal property, household items, and financial debts and credits. (p. 90)

Prohibition, prohibitionists Forbids sale of alcohol by law, thus using legal means to enforce temperance. The Anti-Saloon League, founded in 1893, embarked on a national campaign for Prohibition, which eventually led to the passage of the Eighteenth Amendment, ratified in 1919, which prohibited the "manufacture, sale, or transportation of intoxicating liquors." The Prohibition amendment was repealed in 1933, although some states continued to have Prohibition laws. (p. 680)

propaganda The spreading of ideas that support a particular cause. Although this process does not require a distortion of the facts, it usually involves a misrepresentation of the views or policies of one's opponents. During World War I, the U.S. Committee on Public Information, led by George Creel, published literature and sponsored speeches to increase public hostility toward Germany. (p. 662)

proprietors Groups of settlers who received land grants from the General Courts of Massachusetts Bay and Connecticut, mostly between 1630 and 1720. The proprietors distributed the land among themselves, usually on the basis of social status and family need. This system encouraged widespread ownership of land. (p. 58)

pump priming Term first used during the Great Depression of the 1930s to describe the practice of increased government spending in the hope that it would generate additional economic activity throughout the system. It is the beginning of a process that is supposed to lead to significant economic recovery. (p. 745)

Radical Whigs Eighteenth-century faction in the British Parliament that protested against corruption in government, the growing cost of the British empire, and the rise of a wealthy class of government-related financiers. (p. 93)

reconquista The centuries-long campaign by Spanish Catholics to drive North African Moors (Muslim Arabs) from the European mainland. After a long effort to recover their lands, the Spanish defeated the Moors at Granada in 1492 and secured control of all of Spain. (p. 24)

red-baiting Tactics used to identify, accuse, or raise suspicion of Communist sympathies. In the 1930s critics of the New Deal charged the Federal Theatre Project with being under the influence of Communists, leading to its termination in 1939. These tactics were also widely evident in the "Red Scares" following World Wars I and II. (p. 775)

Renaissance A great revival of classical learning that began in Italy around 1400 and spread after 1500 to northern Europe. Drawing inspiration from ancient Greek and Rome and patronized by wealthy merchants and churchmen, European artists and writers created brilliant works of painting, architecture, and literature. Their work shaped European culture well into the nineteenth century. (p. 18)

republican motherhood The idea that the main political role of American women would be to instill the values of patriotic duty and republican virtue in their children and mold them into exemplary citizens. (p. 262)

republicanism A political ideology that repudiates rule by kings and princes and celebrates a representative system of government and a virtuous, public-spirited citizenry. Historically, most republics have limited active political participation to those with a significant amount of property. After 1800, the United States became a democratic republic, with widespread participation by white adult men of all social classes. (p. 171)

restrictive covenant Limiting clauses in real estate transactions intended to prevent the sale or rental of properties to classes of the population considered "undesirable," such as African Americans, Jews, or Asians. Such clauses were declared unenforceable by the Supreme Court decision in *Shelley v. Kraemer* (1948), but continued to be instituted informally in spite of the ruling. (p. 852)

revivals, revivalism An intense outburst of religious enthusiasm, often prompted by the preaching of a charismatic Baptist or Methodist minister. Revivalism swept across the United States in waves between the 1790s and 1850s and imparted a deep religiosity to American culture. Subsequent revivals in the 1880s and 1890 and in the late twentieth century helped to maintain a strong Protestant evangelical culture. (p. 277)

rotten boroughs Tiny electoral districts for Parliament whose voters were controlled by wealthy aristocrats or merchants. In the 1760s Radical Whig John Wilkes called for their elimination to make Parliament more representative of the property-owning classes. (p. 134)

rural ideal Concept advanced by the landscape architect Andrew Jackson Downing urging the benefits of rural life, it was especially influential among middle-class Americans making their livings in cities but attracted to the suburbs. (p. 540)

salutary neglect British colonial policy during the reigns of George I (r. 1714–1727) and George II (r. 1727–1760). Relaxed supervision of internal colonial affairs by royal bureaucrats contributed significantly to the rise of American self-government. (p. 92)

scalawags Southern whites who joined the Republicans during Reconstruction and were ridiculed by ex-Confederates as worthless traitors. They included ex-Whigs and yeomen farmers who had not supported the Confederacy and who believed that an alliance with the Republicans was the best way to attract northern capital and rebuild the South. (p. 457)

scientific management A system of organizing work, developed by Frederick W. Taylor in the late nineteenth century, designed to get the maximum output from the individual worker and reduce the cost of production, using methods such as the time-and-motion study to determine how factory work should be organized. The system was never applied in its totality in any industry, but it contributed to the rise of the "efficiency expert" and the field of industrial psychology. (p. 524)

segregation The policy of racial separation primarily associated with the southern states, which first began passing segregation laws aimed at African Americans in the 1880s. Also known as Jim Crow laws, these statutes required segregation in every type of public facility. These laws were not overturned until after the civil rights movement of the 1950s and 1960s. (p. 791)

self-made man The nineteenth-century ideal that celebrated men who rose to wealth or social prominence from humble origins through self-discipline, hard work, and temperate habits. (pp. 312, 748)

sentimentalism European cultural movement that emphasized feelings, emotions, and a physical appreciation of God, nature, and other people. Sentimentalism came to the United States in the early nineteenth century and accounted, in part, for marriages being based on love rather than on financial considerations. (p. 260)

separate spheres Term used by historians to describe the nineteenth-century view that men and women had different gender-defined characteristics and that, consequently, the sexes inhabited—and should inhabit—different social worlds, with men in the public sphere of politics and economics and women in the private sphere of home and family. In mid-nineteenth-century America this cultural understanding was sharply defined and hotly contested. (pp. 374, 578)

sharecropping The labor system by which freedmen agreed to exchange a portion of their harvested crops with the landowner for use of the land, a house, and tools. A compromise between freedmen and white landowners, this system developed in the cash-strapped South because the freedmen wanted to work their own land but lacked the money to buy it, while the white landowners needed agricultural laborers but did not have money to pay wages. (p. 462)

Social Darwinism The application of Charles Darwin's biological theory of evolution by natural selection to the development of society, this late-nineteenth-century principle encouraged the notion that societies progress as a result of competition and the "survival of the fittest." Intervention by the state in this process was counterproductive because it impeded healthy progress. Social Darwinists justified the increasing inequality of late-nineteenth-century, industrial American society as natural. (p. 571)

Sons of Liberty The members of the (usually) well-disciplined mobs that, after 1763, protested against the new British measures of taxation and control. Most Sons of Liberty were minor merchants and middling artisans. (p. 139)

special prosecutor An attorney, not employed by the government, who is appointed by Congress or the Justice Department to investigate a federal official suspected of misconduct. Archibald Cox was the special prosecutor in the Watergate scandal. The appointment is similar to that of independent counsel, the position held by Kenneth Starr, who investigated the scandals connected to President Clinton's impeachment. (p. 920)

spoils system The widespread award of public jobs to political supporters following an electoral victory. Underlying this practice was the view that in a democracy rotation in office was preferable to a permanent class of officeholders. In 1829 Andrew Jackson began this practice on the national level and it became a central, and corrupting, feature of American political life. (pp. 332, 567)

stagflation An economic condition that results when inflation and unemployment rise at the same time. This condition does not respond to traditional governmental remedies, such as deficit spending and tax reduction. (p. 925)

states' rights An interpretation of the Constitution that exalts the sovereignty of the states and circumscribes the authority of the national government. Expressed first by the Antifederalists and then in the Virginia and Kentucky Resolutions of 1798, the philosophy of states' rights became the basis for Southern resistance to the high tariffs of the 1820s and 1830s, legislation to limit the spread of slavery, and attempts by the national government in the mid-twentieth century to end "Jim Crow" practices. (p. 224)

subtreasury system A scheme deriving from the Texas Exchange, a cooperative in the 1880s, through which cotton farmers received cheap loans and marketed their crops. When the Texas Exchange failed in 1891, Populists proposed that the federal government take over these functions on a national basis through a "subtreasury," which would have the added benefit of increasing the stock of money in the country and thus push up prices. (p. 588)

suffrage The right to vote. In the early national period suffrage was limited by property restrictions. Gradually state constitutions gave the vote to all white men over the age of twenty-one. Over the course of American history, suffrage has expanded as barriers of race, gender, and age have fallen. In the late nineteenth and early twentieth centuries, women activists on behalf of the vote were known as "suffragists." (pp. 210, 451)

tariff A tax on imports, which has two purposes: raising revenue for the government and protecting domestic products from foreign competition. A hot political issue throughout much of American history, in the late nineteenth century the tariff became particularly controversial as protection-minded Republicans and pro-free-trade Democrats made the tariff the centerpiece of their political campaigns. (pp. 207, 569)

task system A system of slave labor used primarily in the rice fields of South Carolina. Unlike the gang-labor system in which an overseer supervised workers, the task system allowed slaves to work at their own pace but required them to complete an assigned daily task. Once the task was finished, slaves could cultivate their own small plots. (p. 271)

temperance movement A long-running series of reform organizations that have encouraged individuals and governments to limit the consumption of alcoholic beverages. Leading temperance groups include the American Temperance Society of the 1830s, the Washingtonian Association of the 1840s, the Women's Christian Temperance Union of the late nineteenth century, and Alcoholics Anonymous in the mid-twentieth century. (pp. 317, 681)

Third World This term came into usage in the post–World War II era to describe developing or ex-colonial nations that were not aligned with either the First World, meaning the Western capitalist countries, or the Second World, referring to the socialist states of Eastern Europe. It is currently used in reference to developing countries in Asia, Africa, Latin America, and the Middle East. (p. 829)

total war A form of warfare, characteristic of nineteenth and twentieth century conflicts, that mobilized all of a society's resources—economic, political, cultural—in support of the military effort. Armies grew dramatically in size and now were composed of civilian conscripts rather than professional soldiers. Moreover, the civilians and industries that supported the war effort increasingly became the object of enemy attack; examples include Sherman's march through Georgia in the Civil War and the massive American firebombing of Dresden, Hamburg, and Tokyo during World War II. (p. 423)

totalitarianism, totalitarian Centralized regimes that systematically repress dissent and exercise dictatorial control over public and private life, usually through the use of force and propaganda. A twentieth-century phenomenon, it is represented by both the Fascist regime of Germany's Adolph Hitler and the Communist rule of the USSR's Joseph Stalin. (p. 781)

town meeting The system of local government in New England. The meeting included all male heads of households and was the main governing body. It elected the selectmen, levied local taxes, and regulated markets, roads, and schools. (p. 59)

trade slaves Those unfree West Africans who were sold from one African kingdom to another and not considered members of the society that had enslaved them. For centuries Arab merchants had carried trade slaves to the Mediterranean region; around 1440, Portuguese ship captains joined in this trade by buying slaves from African princes and warlords. (p. 23)

transcendentalism A nineteenth-century intellectual movement that postulated the importance of an ideal world of mystical knowledge and harmony beyond the world of the senses. As articulated by Ralph Waldo Emerson and Henry David Thoreau, transcendentalism called for a critical examination of society and emphasized individuality, self-reliance, and nonconformity. (p. 353)

trusts A term originally applied to a specific form of business organization enabling participating firms to assign the operation of their properties to a board of trustees, but by the early twentieth century, the term applied more generally to corporate mergers and business combinations that exerted monopoly power over an industry. It was in this latter sense that progressives referred to firms like United States Steel and Standard Oil as trusts. (p. 615)

urban renewal Process by which city planners, politicians, and real estate developers leveled urban tenements and replaced them with modern construction projects in the 1950s and 1960s. High-rise housing projects, however, destroyed community bonds and led to an increase in crime. (p. 862)

vice-admiralty courts Legal tribunals presided over by a judge and without a jury (as in common law courts). The Sugar Act of 1764 required that offenders be tried in vice-admiralty courts rather than in common law tribunals, thereby provoking protests from merchant-smugglers accustomed to acquittal by sympathetic local juries. (p. 136)

virtual representation Claim made by British politicians that the interests of the American colonists were "represented" in Parliament by merchants who traded with the colonies and by absentee landlords (mostly West Indian sugar planters) who held property there. (p. 137)

voluntarism The view that citizens should act among themselves to improve their lives, rather than rely on the efforts of the state. Especially favored by Samuel Gompers, voluntarism was a key idea within the labor movement, but one it gradually abandoned in the course of the twentieth century. (p. 610)

war of attrition A military strategy of small-scale attacks used, usually by the weaker side, to sap the resources and the morale of the adversary. Examples include the southern resistance of the Patriot forces commanded by General N. Greene during the American War of Independence and the tactics of the Vietcong and North Vietnamese during the Vietnam War. (pp. 182, 887)

welfare capitalism A system of labor relations that stresses management's responsibility for employees' well-being. Originating in the 1920s, welfare capitalism offered such benefits as stock plans, health care, and old-age pensions and was designed to maintain a stable workforce and undercut the growth of trade unions. (p. 698)

welfare state A nation that provides for the basic needs of its citizens, including such provisions as old-age pensions, unemployment compensation, child-care facilities, education, and other social programs. Unlike the major European countries, such provisions appeared in the United States only with the coming of the New Deal in the 1930s. (pp. 601, 761)

yellow journalism Term that refers to newspapers that specialize in sensationalistic reporting. The name came from the ink used in Hearst's *New York Journal* to print the first comic strip to appear in color in 1895 and is generally associated with the inflammatory reporting leading up to the Spanish-American War of 1898. (p. 561)

yellow-dog contract An agreement by a worker, as a condition of employment, not to join a union. Employers in the late nineteenth century used this along with the blacklist and violent strikebreaking to fight unionization of their workforce. (p. 528)

yeoman In medieval England, a farmer below the level of gentry but above the peasantry. A freeholder, he owned his own land, which released him from economic obligations to a landlord. In America, Thomas Jefferson envisioned a nation based on democracy and a thriving agrarian society, built on the labor and prosperity of the yeomen. (p. 15)

CREDITS

CHAPTER 13

"Mary Boykin Chesnut: A Slaveholding Woman's Diary." From *Mary Chesnut's Civil War* by C. Vann Woodward. Copyright © 1981 by C. Vann Woodward. Reprinted by permission of Yale University Press.

"Axalla John Hoole: 'Bleeding Kansas': A Southern View." From "A Southerner's Viewpoint of the Kansas Situation, 1856–1857" from *Kansas Historical Quarterly* 3 (1934), edited by William Stanley Hoole. Reprinted by permission of the publisher.

CHAPTER 15

"Jourdon Anderson: Relishing Freedom." From *Looking for America*, 2nd edition, Volume 1, by Stanley I. Kutler. Copyright © 1979, 1976 by Stanley I. Kutler. Used by permission of W. W. Norton & Company, Inc.

CHAPTER 16

"Ida Lindgren: Swedish Emigrant in Frontier Kansas." From *Letters from the Promised Land: Swedes in America, 1840–1914*, edited by H. Arnold Barton. Copyright © 1975 by H. Arnold Barton. Reprinted by permission of the University of Minnesota Press.

"Baron Joseph Alexander von Hübner: A Western Boom Town." From *This Was America*, edited by Oscar Handlin. Reprinted by permission.

CHAPTER 17

"Count Vay de Vaya und Luskod: Pittsburgh Inferno." From *This Was America*, edited by Oscar Handlin. Reprinted by permission.

CHAPTER 20

"James Bryce: America in 1905: 'Business Is King.'" From *America through British Eyes*, edited by Allan Nevins. Copyright © 1968 by Allan Nevins. Reprinted by permission of Peter Smith Publisher, Gloucester, MA.

CHAPTER 21

"George W. Prioleau: Black Soldiers in a White Man's War." From *Smoked Yankees and the Struggle for Empire, 1898–1902* by Willard Gatewood. Copyright © 1987 by the Board of Trustees of the University of Arkansas. Reprinted by permission of the University of Arkansas Press.

"Jean Hess, Émile Zola, and Ruben Dario: American Goliath." Hess excerpt from "On American Expansion" in *The Anti-Imperialist Reader: A Documentary History of Anti-Imperialism in the United States*, volume 1, edited by Philip S. Foner and Robert C. Winchester. Published by Holmes & Meier Publishers, 1984. Copyright © 1984 by Philip S. Foner and Robert C. Winchester. Reprinted by permission. Ten lines from *Selected Poems of Ruben Dario* by Ruben Dario, translated by Lysander Kemp. Copyright © 1965, renewed 1993. Reprinted by permission of the University of Texas Press.

CHAPTER 24

"Larry Van Dusen: A Working Class Family Encounters the Great Depression." From *Hard Times* by Studs Terkel. Copyright © 1986 by Studs Terkel. Reprinted by permission of Donadio & Olson, Inc.

CHAPTER 25

"Americans Respond to the Fireside Chats." From *The People and the President* by Lawrence W. Levine. Copyright © 2002 by Lawrence W. Levine and Cornelia Roettcher Levine. Reprinted by permission of Beacon Press, Boston.

"Susana Archuleta: A Chicana Youth Gets New Deal Work." From *Las Mujeres: Conversations from a Hispanic Community* by Nan Elsasser. Copyright © 1980 by Susana Archuleta. Reprinted by permission of the Feminist Press at the City University of New York. www.feministpress.org.

INDEX

A note about the index: Names of individuals appear in boldface; biographical dates are included for major historical figures. Letters in parentheses following pages refer to: *(f)* figures, including charts and graphs; *(i)* illustrations, including photographs and artifacts; *(m)* maps; and *(t)* tables.

Abbott, Grace, 761
Abbott, Jacob, 549
Abbott, John, 264
Abenaki (or Abnaki) Indians, 75
Abernathy, Ralph, 842
Ableman v. Booth (1857), 400
abolition, 189–190, 192*(m)*. *See also* emancipation; Emancipation Proclamation
   as central war aim, 428–429
   economic consequences of, 460–464
   government power and, 442
   opposition to, 412, 429
   Radical Republicans and, 428–429, 451
   of slave trade, 210, 267–268, 271, 275, 371, 398
   support for, 417, 432
abolitionism, 367–374
   African resettlement and, 268
   attacks on, 371–372
   evangelical, 368–371, 374
   free blacks and, 272, 274–275, 367
   Fugitive Slave Acts and, 398, 399–400
   and Garrison, 352
   in Kansas, 382, 402–403
   Lincoln and, 407, 412, 428–429
   politics and, 372, 382–383, 390–391, 394–396, 402
   Radical Republicans and, 451
   religion and, 268, 284, 368–371
   slavery and, 327*(i)*, 344
   in the South, 382–383
   transcendentalism and, 358, 371, 374
   Uncle Tom's Cabin and, 400
   women and, 370, 372, 373*(m)*, 376–378, 456, 457, 901

abortion, 933, 973, 975
   feminism and, 966
   Great Depression and, 730
   1980 elections and, 943
   in 1990s, 956
   opposition to, 937
   right to, 903
   Roe v. Wade and, 918, 931, 951
   Supreme Court on, 951
   violence and, 966
abstract expressionism, 859
Abu Ghraib prison, abuses at, 977
Abyssinian Baptist Church, 717
Acadia, 75, 76*(m)*, 179. *See also* Nova Scotia
Acadians, 121
accommodationism, 605, 783
Acoma pueblo, destruction of, 40
Acts of Trade and Navigation. *See* Navigation Acts
Adams, Abigail, 188
   on equality of women, 199, 200, 201
Adams, Brooks, 635
Adams, Charles Francis, 393, 396, 432, 645
Adams, Charles Francis, Jr., 577
Adams, Henry, 428
Adams, Hugh Grant, 698
Adams, John (1735–1826), 325
   Abigail Adams and, 188, 200
   appointment of Marshall to Supreme Court (1801), 251
   as Boston lawyer, 136, 142
   on Boston Tea Party, 152
   death of, 257
   as diplomat, 183–184, 207
   on elite politics, 92
   foreign policy of, 222
   "midnight appointments" of, 237–238
   peace negotiations and, 183
   political theory of, 114
   as president (1797–1801), 222, 237–238
   republicanism and, 282, 284
   Second Continental Congress and, 167
   on Sons of Liberty, 139, 142

Adams, John (*cont.*)
  as vice president, 215
  view of legislature, 197–198
  women's rights and, 200, 260
Adams, John Quincy (1767–1848), 393
  American System and, 327–328, 336, 342
  ceding of Florida and, 244–245
  1824 elections and, 318(*m*), 325, 326
  1828 elections and, 328–330
  Indian policy of, 328–329
  as president (1825–1829), 326–330
  slavery and, 327(*i*)
  Treaty of Ghent and, 244
Adams, Samuel (1722–1803), 207
  Committees of Correspondence and,
    151–152
  Constitution and, 213
  pre-Revolutionary views of, 143–144,
    150, 167
Adams, Samuel Hopkins, 618
Adamson eight-hour law for railroad
    workers, 625
Adams-Onís Treaty (1819), 245, 386
Addams, Jane, 599, 601–602, 606, 645
Adelphia Communications, 979
adolescence, 549. *See also* juvenile delinquency;
    youth
  pregnancy in, 933
advertising
  brand names and, 513, 513(*i*)
  consumer culture and, 703
  gender stereotypes in, 857
  Great Depression and, 731(*i*)
  mass marketing and, 513, 513(*i*)
  in 1950s, 854
  radio and, 706
  by railroads, 482, 501
  religion and, 855
  WWII and, 794
  youth culture and, 857–858
AFDC. *See* Aid to Families with Dependent
    Children
affirmative action, 930–931, 936, 966
  opposition to, 937, 965
  Supreme Court on, 950
affluent society (1950s), 849–853
Afghanistan, 946, 977
  Soviet invasion of, 941, 952, 976
  U.S. aid to, 941
  U.S. attack on, 956(*m*)

AFL-CIO, 851, 898. *See also* American
    Federation of Labor; Congress of
    Industrial Organizations
Africa. *See also* West Africa
  African American migration to, 718
  AIDS in, 967
  anticolonialism in, 829
  Arab civilization in, 18
  Atlantic slave trade with, 6, 7, 21(*m*), 23,
    78(*m*), 271
  colonization by freed slaves in, 268, 407
  decolonization in, 866(*m*)
  gender relations in, 80
  globalization and, 960
  Guinea company in, 33
  jazz and, 705
  migration from. *See* Middle Passage
  North, 799, 800(*m*)
  post-WWI colonialism in, 684
  Protestant missions in, 283(*m*)
  slave trade in, 20, 21(*m*), 23
  society of, 20–21, 80
  trade with, 14, 20
  U.S. civil rights and, 839
African Americans. *See also* abolition;
    abolitionism; civil rights movement;
    desegregation; free blacks; racism;
    segregation; slavery; slaves
  activists among, 606, 607
  affirmative action and, 936, 965
  alleged inferiority of, 384, 385
  Atlanta boycott by, 586–587, 610
  Baptists and, 118, 277–278, 280–281
  in baseball, 707
  Black Power and, 880, 894
  as buffalo soldiers, 487
  in cattle industry, 481, 481(*i*)
  changing demographics and, 962–965,
    963(*m*), 964
  citizenship for, 432, 446, 450
  civil rights movement and, 839, 842, 889,
    893, 896(*m*), 915
  Civil War and, 412, 432–433
  in Cleveland, Ohio, 552
  in colonial America, 99, 104, 106, 107,
    109, 117
  community of, 84–86
  Congressional Delegation (1872) of, 459(*i*)
  culture of slavery and, 84–86, 271–273
  decay of inner cities and, 862

Democratic Party and, 457–458, 777, 833, 971

discrimination against, 494, 499, 515–517, 521, 581–584, 788, 789, 791, 852, 897

disfranchisement of, 584

Dred Scott and, 405–406

economic expansion and (1920s), 697

education of, 265, 284, 461(*i*)

emancipation and, 446–450

employment and, 552

equality of, 272–275, 277–278, 280–281, 581–587

Ethiopian Regiment, 167

as Exodusters, 485

and Fair Deal, 834

feminism and, 966

Fourteenth Amendment and, 573, 581, 586

Fifteenth Amendment and, 455(*t*), 456, 581, 584, 586, 605–606

in France, 716

Fugitive Slave Acts and, 399–400

Great Depression and, 728, 735–737

Great Migration of, 676–678, 677(*m*)

Great Society and, 877

Harlem Renaissance and, 717–718

hostility to, 424, 465–467

in industrial jobs, 676–678

jazz and, 705, 706(*i*)

JFK and, 863

John Brown and, 409

labor unions and, 526, 766

LBJ and, 873

leadership of, 458, 460

lynchings of, 587, 587(*i*), 688

Methodism and, 268, 274, 277–281

middle class and, 552, 555(*i*)

militancy of, 688, 718, 894–896, 902

in military, 641–643, 642(*i*), 671–672, 788, 789

music of, 857–858, 859

Muslim, 895

New Deal and, 756, 768–769, 777–778

in New South, 515–516, 581–584

1936 elections and, 763

nominating process and, 605

northern, 694

northward migration of, 552, 676–678, 677(*m*), 708(*m*)

origins of, 271–272

as percent of population, 172, 552

political activism and, 900

post-WWI, 688

in public life, 349

Reconstruction and, 444, 470

Republican Party and, 457–460, 569, 694

resettlement in Africa of, 268, 407

revivalism and, 277–281

Revolutionary War and, 157–158, 167–168, 172, 180–182, 188–191, 192(*m*)

rights of, 395. *See also* civil rights

rock 'n' roll and, 857–858

sex ratio of, 85

Shakers and, 360

sharecropping and, 463(*m*)

social class and, 50–51

Social Security Act and, 761

in South Carolina, 333

and Southern primaries, 605

in Spanish-American War, 641–643, 642(*i*)

stereotypes of, 458

on Supreme Court, 951

on television, 855

terms for, 895

in Union Army, 433(*i*)

urban, 552, 554, 554(*i*)

urban migration of, 707–708, 708(*m*), 717, 736, 777, 861

urban rioting of, 880, 895–896, 896(*m*), 905

Vietnam War and, 887

violence against, 445, 450, 451, 452(*i*), 465–467, 587, 587(*i*), 688, 869

voting districts and, 918

voting rights and, 371, 569, 584–585, 585(*m*), 695, 974

War on Poverty and, 877

white supremacy movement and, 584–588

white women as caretakers of, 384, 385

women, 695, 730, 735, 767, 958

WWII and, 780, 795–796

youth of, 796

African Methodist Episcopal Church (AME), 268, 274, 460

African School, 274(*i*)

Afrika Korps, 800

Agency for International Development, 865

Agent Orange, 885, 892

The Age of Innocence (Wharton), 716

Agnew, Spiro, 906, 920

Agreda, Maria de Jesus de, 40(*i*)

Agricultural Adjustment Act (AAA), 756, 763

Agricultural Marketing Act (1929), 744
agricultural societies, 7–9, 14–16, 20–21
agriculture. *See also* corn; cotton; farmers;
    freehold society; grain; sugar; tobacco;
    wheat
    African, 20–21, 83–84, 85
    in California, 497, 499–500, 501
    capital for, 486
    capitalists in, 106
    Columbian Exchange and, 28
    commercialized, 740
    cotton, 462
    crop-lien system in, 462, 464
    crop rotation in, 235
    dry-farming, 485
    in Dust Bowl, 740
    in the East, 235
    in England, 33
    in English colonies, 37, 46–50, 48(*i*), 51
    in Europe, 14–16
    evangelicalism and, 114, 116, 283(*m*)
    expansion of, 232–237
    exports of, 104, 110, 123, 124, 135, 150, 292,
        308–309
    farm life and, 101–106, 116
    Granger movement and, 588
    Great Depression and, 724, 744
    on Great Plains, 477(*m*), 477–478, 482–486
    household mode of production and,
        100–101, 104
    irrigation for, 9, 11, 485, 501
    laborers in, 102, 297. *See also* farmers
    land as commodity and, 482
    mechanization of, 861
    medieval methods of, 14–16
    in Middle Atlantic colonies, 104–106
    migrant labor and, 497, 499–500
    of Mormons, 364
    Native Americans and, 9–14, 230, 478, 490
    Native American women and, 12, 14, 231
    natural disasters and, 483(*i*), 485, 490. *See
        also* drought
    nesters and, 482
    New Deal and, 777–778
    in New England, 100–104
    in 1920s, 697
    orchards and, 497, 499, 501
    outwork and, 106
    in Pacific Northwest, 491
    post-WWII, 816

prices for, 588
rain forests and, 960
of Shakers, 360
in the South, 308, 515, 516(*m*), 735–736, 861
in Southwest, 496–497
subsidies to, 926
subtreasury system and, 588
tariffs and, 295
technology for, 105–106, 233, 235, 294,
    307–308, 485
in Texas, 496, 497
transportation and, 302–305
TVA and, 772
in Vietnam, 885
in the West, 270
westward migration for, 484
Aguinaldo, Emilio, 644, 644(*i*)
AIDS (acquired immune deficiency
    syndrome)/HIV (human
    immunodeficiency virus), 956, 966–967
Aid to Dependent Children (ADC), 875
Aid to Families with Dependent Children
    (AFDC), 875, 917, 948, 970
airline industry, 861, 979
air traffic controllers' strike, 958
Aix-la-Chapelle, Treaty of (1748), 95
Alabama
    admission to Union of (1818), 268
    coal mining in, 507
    migration to, 233, 269(*m*), 270, 303(*m*)
    Reconstruction and, 452, 457, 465
    secession and, 398, 413, 414(*m*)
    slavery in, 268–270, 276(*m*), 383
    voter registration in, 875(*m*)
    voting rights in, 259, 259(*m*)
Alabama (Confederate warship), 432, 629
the Alamo, 387, 388(*i*)
Alaska, 388, 391, 631–632
    oil drilling in, 928, 975
    parks in, 940
    purchase of, 631
    radar in, 828
Alaska Native Land Claims Act (1971), 933
Albanians, 972
Albany, New York, 175, 234
    Dutch in, 43
    Erie Canal and, 303–304, 306(*m*)
Albany Argus (newspaper), 324
Albany Congress (1754), 119, 137
Albany Plan (Plan of Union; 1754), 119, 154

Albany Regency (Albany, New York), 324
Albemarle, duke of, 68
Albemarle County, Virginia, rebellion in, 69
Albemarle Sound, 45(i)
Albright, Madeline, 968
Alcatraz Island, 898
alcohol. *See also* Prohibition
    blue laws and, 575–576
    taxes on, 568
    temperance and, 314, 316–319, 575–576,
      578–579
Aldrich, Nelson W., 620
Aleut peoples, 7
Alexandria, Egypt, 19
Algeciras Conference, 655
Alger, Horatio, 571, 572(i)
Algonquian Indians, 42–44
    "praying towns" of, 61
Alien and Sedition Acts (1798), 224, 237
Alien Land Law (1913; California), 710
Aliquippa, Pennsylvania, 536
Allegheny River, 63
Allen, Gracie, 735
Allen, James, 367
Allen, Richard, 268, 274
Allen, Thomas, 458
Alliance for Progress, 865
Allies (World War II), 784, 799, 806
alphabet-soup agencies (New Deal), 757
Al Qaeda, 916, 956(m), 976
Al Ramadi, Iraq, 977(i)
Alsberg, Henry, 775
Alton, Illinois, 372
Alzheimer's disease, 947(i)
America First Committee, 784
American and Foreign Anti-Slavery Society,
    372, 395
American Anti-Slavery Society, 370
American Automobile Association (AAA), 704
American Bible Society (1816), 282
American Civil Liberties Union (ACLU),
    Scopes trial and, 714
American colonies. *See also* colonization;
    individual colonies by name
    agriculture in, 37–39, 46–50, 48(i), 51,
      103–106, 247–249
    Anglicanism in, 108, 108(m), 112, 117–118,
      158
    British reform measures in (1763–1765),
      131–138

    British Restoration and, 69–72
    British troops in, 132, 133, 137–138
    colonial assemblies in, 91–92
    constitutional rights of, 136–138, 145–146
    control of trade by, 89(m)
    economic growth in, 123–124
    elite in, 91–92
    Enlightenment in (1740–1765), 112–118,
      143
    European spheres of influence in, 120(m)
    evangelicalism in, 117–118
    freehold society in, 103–104, 105(m),
      117, 125
    French and Indian War and, 119–122, 155
    governments of, 44, 46–48, 53–56, 58–59
    independence of. *See* Revolutionary War
    land conflicts in, 124–125
    mercantilism and, 33, 70–72, 89(m), 94–96
    Navigation Acts and, 95
    patronage in, 87, 94
    proprietary, 69, 73
    royal, 69
    salutary neglect and, 92–94, 94(i), 96
    seaport society in, 90–91
    self-government in, 91–96, 131
    slave labor in, 76–91
    tenant farmers in, 104–106, 125
    tobacco in, 47–52
    urban growth in, 88–90
    women in, 57–58, 89–90
American Colonization Society, 268, 369
The American Commonwealth (Bryce), 566,
    616–617
American Education Society (1815), 282
American Expeditionary Force (AEF), 669
American Federation of Labor (AFL),
    528–529, 743, 766, 851
    Bill of Grievances (1906) of, 610
American Home Missionary Society (1826),
    282, 283(m)
American Indian Movement (AIM), 898–900
American Indians, National Council of, 898
American Legion, 673
American Lyceum, 355
American Medical Association (AMA)
    birth control and, 730
    Medicare and Medicaid and, 877
American Party. *See* Know-Nothing Party
American Philosophical Society, 113
American Plan, 699

American Protective League, 682
American Railway Union (ARU), 531
American Red Cross, 425
"The American Scholar" (Emerson), 355
American Slavery as It Is: Testimony of a Thousand Witnesses, 370
American Sunday School Union (1824), 282
American System (Clay), 325, 349, 391, 426
    Jackson and, 329–330, 332–334, 336, 340–342
    John Q. Adams and, 327–328, 336, 342
American Tobacco Company, 616
American Union against Militarism, 667
The American Woman's Home (C. Beecher), 546
American Woman Suffrage Association, 457
Ames, Adelbert, 467
Ames, Fisher, 206
amusement parks, 560
    Disneyland, 854
Anabaptists, 30
anarchism, 527
Anasazi Indians, 11
Anderson, Jourdon, 447
Anderson, Robert, 415
Andover, Massachusetts, 58, 60(*m*)
Andros, Edmund, 72, 73
Angelou, Maya, 735
Anglicanism (Church of England), 31, 47, 53–54, 56, 127
    in American colonies, 69–70, 72, 108, 108(*m*), 117–118, 158, 193
    Columbia University and, 116
    as established church, 73, 117
Anglo-Saxonism, 636
Angola, West Africa, 20, 866(*m*)
Anthony, Susan B. (1820–1906), 379–380, 456, 457
anti-Americanism, 978
Antiballistic Missile Treaty (1972), 910
Anti-Comintern Pact, 782
anticommunism, 820, 830–832, 835–837. *See also* **McCarthy, Joseph R.**
    in Hollywood, 942
Antietam, battle of, 419(*m*), 420, 421(*i*), 423, 429
Antifederalists, 212–215
Anti-French War of Resistance, 881. *See also* Vietnam War
Antigua, 464
anti-imperialism, 644–645, 648–649
Anti-Imperialist Leagues, 645

anti-Masonry, 344
Anti-Saloon League, 681
anti-Semitism. *See also* Jews: discrimination against
    Holocaust and, 802
    racism and, 790
Anti-Slavery Conventions of American Women, 370
Anti-Slavery Society, 372
antitrust laws, 693
    Fair Deal and, 834
    New Deal and, 756
    Sherman Antitrust Act (1890), 610, 615–617, 620, 624
    wartime suspension of, 674
antiwar movement (Vietnam War), 880, 889, 918–919, 921
    in 1970s, 915
    backlash against, 906
    Chicago Democratic convention (1968) and, 905–906
    decline of, 909
    draft and, 892, 902
    Kent State and, 908
    student protests and, 891–892
    women in, 902
ANZUS (Australia, New Zealand, United States; 1951), 829(*m*)
A & P (Great Atlantic and Pacific Tea Company), 513
Apache Indians, 7, 486, 487
Apalachee Indians, 12, 38
apartheid, 972
Appalachia
    migration from, 861
    War on Poverty and, 874
Appalachian Mountains, 59, 204, 228, 232, 235
    western expansion and, 125, 126(*m*), 133(*m*), 270, 301
    as western frontier, 119, 122, 133(*m*), 154(*m*)
An Appeal . . . to the Colored Citizens of the World (Walker), 367, 368
appeasement (World War II), 782
Apple Computer Company, 961
Appleton, Nathan, 295
Appomattox Court House, Virginia, 440, 442
Arab League, 830
Arabs, 18–20. *See also* Middle East; Muslims
    effect on Europe of, 18–19
    Islamic fundamentalism and, 955

Mediterranean commerce and, 18
  scholarship of, 18, 19, 19(*i*)
Arapaho Indians, 478, 486
Arawak Indians, 24–25
architecture
  Aztec, 9, 10
  building codes, 540
  Chicago school of, 539
  downtown, 540, 542
  Federal style, 220
  mission style, 501
  skyscraper, 539
  suburban, 545
  tenements, 540
  urban, 544
Archuleta, Susana, 770
Arctic, oil drilling in, 975
Argentina, 940
Arikara Indians, 478
Aristide, Jean-Bertrand, 972
Aristocratic-Republicanism, 257, 266–277, 281
Aristotle, 355
Arizona, 11, 38
  copper mining in, 497
  Hispanic settlement in, 497
  Japanese internment in, 797
  Latino immigrants in, 860
Arkansas
  in Civil War, 430
  drought in, 737
  Japanese internment in, 797
  migration to, 302, 303(*m*)
  Reconstruction and, 465
  secession and, 414
  slavery in, 386
Arkansas National Guard, 841(*i*), 842
Arkwright, Richard, 295
arms control, 952. *See also* weapons of mass
    destruction
  Carter and, 941
  nuclear test ban treaty (1963), 867
  SALT I, 910
  SALT II, 939, 941
  Washington Naval Arms Conference (1921),
    701
arms race, 816. *See also* atomic bomb; nuclear
    weapons
  nuclear, 817(*i*), 819, 843–844
  nuclear proliferation and, 843–844
Armstrong, Louis, 705

Army, U.S., 628
  anticommunism and, 837
  frontier posts of, 479
  Indian wars and, 479, 487, 490
  in Philippines, 645
  in Pullman strike, 531
  racial segregation in, 671–672
  racial violence in, 672
  Special Forces of, 865
Army Corps of Engineers, U.S., 648
Army of Northern Virginia, 431
Army of the Potomac, 419, 420, 430, 434
Arnold, Benedict, 182
art. *See also* Mayas
  in cities, 562–563
  cultural dissent and, 859
  modernist, 716
  museums and, 562
  Native American, 9, 11
  New Deal and, 773–776
  in 1920s, 716–717
  Renaissance, 20
Arthur, Chester A. (1829–1886), as president
    (1881–1885), 567, 630
Arthur Anderson Company, 979
Articles of Confederation (1777)
  provisions of, 202–205
  revision of, 208–211
artisan republicanism, 345
artisans, 247–249, 345. *See also* mechanics
  among free blacks, 274
  in colonial America, 104, 106, 109, 113, 116
  education for, 264
  European, 20
  in industrial age, 297, 299–301, 319, 506,
    517, 521–522
  Native American, 9, 11, 12, 65
  as new Democrats, 329, 336
  on plantations, 266
  Shaker, 360
  as Sons of Liberty, 139–140, 152
  South Atlantic system and, 90
  taxation on, 258
  trade unionism and, 526
Asante people, 80
Ashby, Robert, 118
Ashcroft, John D., 975
Asia, 6, 20, 23, 401. *See also individual countries*
  anticolonialism in, 829
  European empires in, 633, 650, 651(*m*)

Asia (cont.)
    free trade in, 959
    globalization and, 960
    immigrants from, 962–965
    post-WWI colonialism in, 684
    U.S. foreign investment in, 701
Asian Americans, 631(i)
    discrimination against, 852
    in Great Depression, 742–743
    increase of, 962–965, 963(m)
    intermarriage of, 964
assemblies, colonial, 91–92
    restrictions on, 146, 153
    self-government and, 132, 137–138, 146
    struggle with royal government and, 119,
        132–133, 137–138, 146
assembly line, 293, 294, 294(i)
assimilation, cultural, 489, 771–772, 861–862
    Franciscans and, 38–40
    Native Americans and, 29, 37–41, 228
Astaire, Fred, 733, 947(i)
Astor, John Jacob, 246
Astor, Mrs. William, 543
astronomy
    Arabic, 19(i)
    Mayan, 9
Aswan Dam, 830
asylum reform, 459
    Dix and, 375
    Reconstruction and, 459
    women's rights and, 375
Atchison, David R., 402
Atherton, Joshua, 213
Atlanta, Georgia, 434
    fall of (1864), 438(m)
    as railroad hub, 307(m)
Atlanta Compromise (1895; Booker T.
        Washington), 605
Atlantic Charter (1941), 785, 786(m), 799, 806
Atlantic Monthly, 563
atomic bomb, 780, 816, 818, 823, 826
    fears of, 845
    Soviet Union and, 821
    U.S., 808–810
    use of, 805(m)
Atomic Energy Commission (AEC), 843
Attucks, Crispus, 150
Augsberg, Peace of (1555), 30
Auschwitz concentration camp, 802
Austin, Moses, 386

Austin, Stephen F., 386
Australia, 632
    Chinese immigration to, 497
    gold rush in, 492
    in SEATO, 828
    secret ballot from, 577
    Vietnam War and, 885
    WWII and, 803
An Australian Looks at America (Adams), 698
Austria, 684, 783
Austria-Hungary, 663–664
Autobiography (Franklin), 113, 312
automobile
    culture of, 703–704, 851, 852–853
    foreign, 924
    fuel-efficient, 924(f)
    interstate highways and, 853(m)
    1950s culture and, 854
    rural life and, 703, 709
    suburbs and, 851, 852–853
automobile industry
    consumer culture and, 702, 703
    energy crisis and, 924
    environmentalism and, 929
    labor unions and, 766
    mass production in, 698, 703
    in 1920s, 697–698
Axis, Rome-Berlin (WWII), 782
Azores, 20
Aztecs
    culture of, 9–10, 12
    European diseases and, 26–27
    human sacrifice among, 10, 12
    social structure of, 9–10, 25
    Spanish conquest of, 25–28, 28(i)

Babcock, Orville, 468
baby-boom generation, 853–860, 925, 933, 967
Backlash: The Undeclared War on American
        Women (Faludi), 965
Backus, Isaac, 116, 194
Bacon, Nathaniel, 52–53, 61
Bacon's Rebellion (1676), 52–53, 69, 87
Bad Axe Massacre, 337
Baez, Joan, 892
Bahamas, 24
Baker, Ella, 869, 872, 902
Baker, Josephine, 716
Baker v. Carr (1962), 918
Bakke, Allan, 936

Bakke v. University of California (1978), 936
balance of power, 647, 652
balance of trade. *See under* trade, foreign
Balboa, Vasco Núñez de, 25
Balfour Declaration, 684
Balkans, 663
   conflicts in, 654
   ethnic nationalism in, 687
Ball, Charles, 281
Ballinger, Richard A., 620
Baltimore, Lord. *See* **Calvert, Cecilius;**
   Calvert, George
Baltimore, Maryland
   British attack on (1812), 242, 243*(m)*
   business elite of, 310
   free blacks in, 274
   population of, 536*(t)*
   secessionists in, 416
   transportation and, 305, 309
   West Indian trade and, 88–89
bank holiday, 754
Banking Acts
   of 1863, 591
   of 1935, 758
Bank of England, 346
Bank of North America, 246
Bank of the United States, 238
   First, 246, 426
   Jackson's attack on Second, 334–336
   Second, 251, 252, 325, 328, 334–335, 335*(i)*,
      347, 349, 426
   Washington and, 217
banks
   American System and, 327–328, 336, 341
   bankers and, 308–310
   central, 623
   charters for, 324, 335
   in Civil War, 426
   economic expansion and (1920s), 697
   failures of, 724–725
   gold standard and, 592
   Great Depression and, 724–725,
      744–745, 749
   Hamilton on, 216–217
   investment, 343, 510
   national, 347, 349, 391
   National Banking Acts and, 427, 591
   New Deal and, 754, 758
   private, 345
   reform of, 623–624

   regulation of, 325, 334–336
   savings, 316
Bank War, 325, 328, 334–336, 335*(i)*, 347, 349
Banneker, Benjamin, 274
Bao Dai, Emperor of Vietnam, 882
Baptists, 127, 189, 190
   abolitionism and, 368, 376
   African Americans and, 118, 277–278, 280–281
   Brown University and, 116
   child rearing and, 264
   in colonial America, 102, 108, 108*(m)*, 111, 116
   egalitarianism of, 117–118, 277–278, 280*(i)*,
      284
   evangelicalism of, 277–278, 279–281, 280*(i)*,
      283*(m)*, 285
   National Convention of, 460
   separation of church and state and, 116
Barbados, 69, 77, 80, 81, 82, 464
Barbary States, 238
Barnum, P. T., 561
Barrow Plantation, 463*(m)*
Barry, Leonora M., 526
Barton, Clara, 425
Baruch, Bernard, 674–675, 756
Baruch Plan, 818–819
baseball, 560–561, 707
   segregation in, 839
   stadiums, 561
Basel Convention (1994), 960
Bataan death march, 803
Batista, Fulgencio, 861, 865
Bayard, James, 225
Bayard, Thomas F., 629
Bay of Pigs invasion (1961), 865, 867
Beard, Ithamar A., 313
the Beatles, 893
Beats, 859, 889
Beauregard, P.G.T., 393, 418, 421
bebop, 859
Beckley, John, 241
Beckwith, Abijah, 395
Beecher, Catharine, 375, 546
Beecher, Henry Ward, 346, 558, 563
Beecher, Lyman, 282, 314, 315
Begin, Menachem, 941, 942*(i)*
Beirut, Lebanon, 952
Belgium, 663–664, 784
   decolonization and, 829
   in NATO, 821
Bell, Alexander Graham, 539

Bell, John, 405(*m*), 410
Belle, Anne, 425(*i*)
Belleau Wood, Battle of, 670
Bellini, Jacopo, 20
Bellow, Saul, 775
Bellows, Henry W., 352
Benevolent Empire activities, 314–317
Benezet, Anthony, 190
Benin, Africa, 80, 81, 82
Bennett, James Gordon, 561
Bennett, William, 965
Bennington, Vermont, 174(*m*), 176
Benny, Jack, 735, 855
Benton, Thomas Hart, 336
Bentsen, Lloyd, 950
Bergen, Edgar, 735
Berger, Victor, 610, 683
Bering Strait, 7
Berkeley, William, 52–53
Berlin, Germany, 801(*m*), 802, 821
    Chicago, Illinois and, 541
    division of, 806, 819(*m*)
    JFK and, 867
Berlin Airlift, 821
Berlin Conference (1884), 634
Berlin Wall, 867
    fall of, 946, 952
Bernard, Francis, 137
Bernard, Thomas, 262
Bessemer, Henry, 507
Bethel African Methodist Episcopal Church,
    268
Bethune, Joanna, 315
Bethune, Mary McLeod, 768
Beveridge, Alfred J., 637
Bevin, Ernest, 822
The Bible against Slavery (Weld), 370
Bidault, Georges, 822
Biddle, Nicholas, 334–335, 335(*i*)
Big Foot, Chief of Minneconjous, 490
Bill for Establishing Religious Freedom (1786),
    193
Bill of Rights, 406. *See also* First Amendment
    Madison and, 215, 241
    ratification of Constitution and, 213, 215
    of William and Mary, 73
Bingham, Caleb, 264
Bingham, William, 246
bin Laden, Osama, 973, 976
    aid to Afghanistan and, 941

Birmingham, Alabama
    church bombing in, 872
    racial violence in, 869
    steel production in, 508(*m*)
Birney, James G., 372, 391
birth control, 932
    declining birth rate and, 261–262, 285, 901
    Great Depression and, 730
    women's rights and, 933
Birth of a Nation (film), 711
birth rate. *See also* population
    Colonial era and, 101(*i*)
    declining, 261–262, 285, 901
    of European peasants, 16
    Great Depression and, 730
    increasing, 511
    in 1950s, 855–856
    women and, 100–101, 261–262
    women's rights and, 933
Black, Hugo, 764
Black Ball Line, 309
black churches, 268, 274, 277, 281, 460, 552,
    717, 872. *See also individual*
    denominations under African Americans
Black Codes, 445, 459
Black Death, 14
Blackfoot Indians, 478
Black Hawk (1767–1838), 337–338, 339(*i*)
Black Hills, South Dakota, gold in, 488, 492
blacklist
    meaning of, 835
    workers' rights and, 345
Blackmun, Harry, 918
Black Muslims, 895
black nationalism, 718
Black Panthers, 895, 898
Black Robes. *See* Jesuits
Black Star Line steamship company, 718
black studies, black power movement and, 895
"Black Thursday" (Oct. 24, 1929), 724
"Black Tuesday" (Oct. 29, 1929), 724
Blaine, James G., 569, 571, 576, 630
Blair, Francis Preston, 332
Bland, Richard, 136
Bland-Allison Act (1878), 591
"Bleeding Kansas," 403, 404
The Blithedale Romance (Hawthorne), 358
blitzkrieg, 784
Board of Trade, British, 119, 121, 132, 146
Boland Amendment, 952

Bolivia, 630
Bolshevism, 670, 684, 689, 696. *See also*
   communism
Bonaparte, Charles J., 604
Bonus Army (1932), 747–748
Bonus Bill (1817), 251, 328
The Book of Mormon (Smith), 363
Book-of-the-Month Club, 705
Booth, John Wilkes, 442
Booth, Nathaniel, 258
Borah, William E., 687
Born on the Fourth of July (Kovic), 845
Bosnia, 663, 972
Boston, Absalom, 274(i)
Boston, Massachusetts
   British troops in, 149, 149(m), 153, 155, 158
   elite in, 542–543
   news of Glorious Revolution in, 73
   popular power in, 92
   population of, 536(t)
   school busing in, 936
   South Atlantic system and, 89(m)
   transportation and, 306, 306(m), 307(m),
      309
   West Indian trade and, 88, 89(m)
Boston Guardian, 606
Boston Manufacturing Company, 295–296,
   297, 308
Boston Massacre, 150
Boston Tea Party, 140(i), 152
Bourke-White, Margaret, 776
Bow, Clara, 704
Bowdoin, James, 207
the Bowery, New York City, 560
Bowie, Jim, 387
Boxer rebellion (China; 1900), 650–651,
   651(m)
Boyce, Ed, 533
boycotts. *See also* nonimportation
   of 1765, 139, 145, 147(i), 148, 156
   of 1768, 145, 148
   by Atlanta African Americans, 586–587
   of California grapes, 898
   civil rights movement and, 889
   effects of, 145, 148
   pre-Revolutionary War, 145, 146, 147(i), 148,
      150, 156
   Pullman, 531
   railroad strike of 1894 and, 531
Boyleston, Nicholas, 113

Boyleston, Thomas, 187
Bracero Program, 860–861
Braddock, Edward, 121
Bradford, Perry, 706(i)
Bradford, William, 54
Bradley, Joseph P., 470
Brady, Matthew, 408(i)
Brandeis, Louis D., 601, 603, 624
Brant, Joseph (Thayendanegea; Chief Joseph;
      Mohawk chief), 172, 173(i)
Braxton, Carter, 202
Brazil, 77, 80, 82
   African slaves in, 44
   economy of, 464
   trade with, 309
breadlines, women in, 727, 727(i)
Breckinridge, John C., 405(m), 409, 410
Brest-Litovsk, Treaty of, 670
Bretton Woods system, 850
Breyer, Stephen G., 974
Brezhnev, Leonid, 941
Brisbane, Arthur, 361
Briscoe v. Bank of Kentucky (1837), 341
British Columbia, gold in, 492
British East India Company, 33, 122, 151–153
British Empire. *See also* England; Great Britain
   in America (1660–1750), 68–98, 132–138
   in Boston, 150, 155, 158
   colonial land grants and, 103
   debts of, 124, 132, 134, 144, 155
   expansion of, 99, 119–122, 133(m)
   impressment and, 141
   in India, 121, 122, 152
   Industrial Revolution in, 123
   mercantilism and, 94–96
   Navigation Acts and, 135–137
   navy and, 121–122, 132, 141, 155
   politics of, 91–96
   profits of, 121
   reforms in, 131–138, 143, 145
   taxation and, 134–153
   trade in, 135. *See also* trade, Anglo-American
   in West Africa, 121–122
   WWII and, 806
British Guiana, 464
Brook Farm, 357–358, 359(m)
Brooklyn, New York, 964
   population of, 536(t)
Brooks, Phillips, 558
Brooks, Preston, 382

Brown, John, 403
  raid of (1859), 409
Brown, Joseph, 424
Brown, Moses, 295
Brown, Ron, 968
Brown, Susan, 296–297
Brown Berets, 898
Brownson, Orestes, 345
Brown University, founding of, 116
Brown v. Board of Education (1954), 840–842,
  894, 918, 936
Bruce, Blanche K., 458
Bruce, William, 709
Brunelleschi, Filippo, 20
Brush, Charles F., 539
Bryan, Charles W., 694
Bryan, William Jennings, 592–593, 594(*m*),
  620, 645, 655–656, 714
Bryant, Anita, 933
Bryce, James, 566, 569, 632
  on America, 616–617
Buchanan, James (1791–1868), 400
  Mormons and, 366
  as president (1857–1861), 403, 405, 406,
    414–415
  as Secretary of State, 392, 395
  on slave vs. free state conflict, 397, 405, 406
Buchanan, Patrick, 965, 973
Buchenwald concentration camp, 802
Buck, Pearl, 735
buffalo
  hunting of, 478–479, 480
  Native Americans and, 478
  slaughter of, 480
Buffalo, New York, 234
  population of, 536(*t*)
  transportation and, 304–305, 306(*m*), 307(*m*)
Buffalo Bill. *See* Cody, William F.
buffalo soldiers, 487
building codes, 540
Bulge, Battle of, 802
Bulkley, William Lewis, 607
Bull Moose Party, 621
Bull Run (Manassas Creek), battle of, 418, 420
Bundy, McGeorge, 867
Bunker, Ellsworth, 908
Bunyan, John, 599
Burger, Warren, 918
Burgess, John W., 605
Burgoyne, John, 174(*m*), 175–176, 183

burial mounds, Native American, 11, 12
Burke, Edmund, 92
Burkitt, Frank, 584
Burma, 803
Burns, George, 735
Burnside, Ambrose E., 420
Burr, Aaron, 218(*i*), 224
  duel with Hamilton, 240
Burroughs, Edgar Rice, 548
Bush, George H. W. (1924–), 942, 956(*m*)
  labor unions and, 958
  Persian Gulf War and, 954
  as president (1989–1993), 950–951
  vs. Reagan, 947
  renomination of, 967
  vetoes of, 968
Bush, George W. (1946–)
  9/11 and, 976, 978
  approval ratings of, 978
  energy industry and, 975
  Kyoto Treaty and, 960
  as president (2001–), 975, 976–980
  State of the Union address of 2002, 976
  2000 elections and, 973–975
  2004 elections and, 980
Bushnell, Horace, 563
business. *See also* corporations
  big, 511–514
  credit for, 745
  failures in, 726
  government cooperation with, 693–701,
    720, 765
  Great Depression and, 745
  mobilization for war and, 787–788
  modern management and, 514, 523–524,
    696, 697
  New Deal and, 756, 761, 763
  in 1920s, 696–699
  U.S. interventions and, 953(*m*)
busing, school, 918, 936
  1980 elections and, 943
  opposition to, 937
Bussell, Joshua H., 360(*i*)
Bute, Lord, 134
Butler, Andrew P., 382
Butler, Benjamin, 428
Butler, Pierce, 209
Butterfield Overland Mail, 389(*m*)
butterfly ballots, 973
Byzantine civilization, 19

Cagney, James, 734
Cahan, Abraham, 557
Cahill, Holger, 774
Cahokia (Mississippian civilization), 11–12
calendar
   Catholic, 17
   Mayan, 9
Calhoun, John C. (1782–1850), 241, 382, 406, 413
   Bonus Bill and, 251
   expansionism and, 395
   on majority rule, 333
   as presidential candidate, 325
   as secretary of state, 391
   on slave vs. free state conflict, 397
   as vice president, 333, 336
   as vice presidential candidate, 329
   Whig Party and, 342
California, 41
   affirmative action in, 936, 965
   agricultural strikes in, 741, 741(i)
   agriculture in, 497, 499–500, 501, 740
   annexation of, 390, 395, 403
   Asian Americans in, 742–743
   attempt to buy, 392
   British and, 391
   Catholic missions in, 400–501
   Chicano movement in, 898
   China trade and, 389
   climate of, 501
   Compromise of 1850 and, 398, 399(m)
   culture of, 500–501
   gay marriage in, 966
   gold rush in (1849–1857), 396, 397(i), 491–495, 492(m), 497–498
   immigration to, 710, 962, 964
   internal migration to, 390, 479, 491–495, 739(m), 739–740, 756, 795, 852
   Japanese internment in, 797
   labor movement in, 499
   Mexican culture in, 390
   Mexican War and, 392, 393
   migrant workers in, 739–740
   military-industrial complex in, 844(m)
   mining frontier and, 491–492, 492(m)
   movie industry in, 704
   national parks in, 501
   Proposition 13 in, 937
   statehood for, 396, 398, 401
   voting rights in, 456

California Trail, 389(m)
Californios, 390, 496
Calley, William, 909
Calvert, Benedict, 73
Calvert, Cecilius (Cecil; 2nd Baron Baltimore), 47, 71(i)
Calvert, George (1st Baron Baltimore), 69, 71(i)
Calvert, Leonard, 48
Calvin, John, 30–31
Calvinism, 32, 55, 315
   in Europe, 30–31
   Jonathan Edwards and, 114
   predestination and, 278, 281, 284
   Quakers and, 70
   transcendentalism and, 354
Cambodia
   immigrants from, 962
   Khmer Rouge in, 908, 911
   secret bombing of, 921
   Vietnam War and, 883(m), 908, 910, 911, 912
Cambridge, Massachusetts, 158
Camden, South Carolina, 180–182, 185
Camino Real, 389(m)
campaign finance reform, 921
Camp David accords (1978), 941, 942(i)
camp followers, 175
Canada, 13, 41, 629. *See also* Montreal; Quebec
   African Americans in, 367
   American invasion of, 167
   British conquest of (1754–1760), 121–122, 132–133
   Burgoyne's army and, 176
   Civil War and, 432
   draft evaders and, 892
   French loss of, 179
   immigrants from, 301
   Loyalist emigration to, 187
   NAFTA and, 959
   in NATO, 819(m), 821
   radar in, 828
   settlement of boundaries with, 243(m), 244, 647
   Soviet spies in, 835
   War of 1812 and, 241, 242, 243(m), 244, 245(m)
   WWII and, 802
canals, 293, 308, 324, 325, 327–328, 508
   Erie, 235, 283(m), 302–305, 304(i), 306(m), 309, 315–316, 316(i), 363

canals (*cont.*)
   foreign investment in, 303, 305, 346
   labor for, 303, 304(*i*), 316
Canary Islands, 20, 23
Canby, Henry Seidel, 546
Cane (Toomer), 717
Cane Ridge revival, 278, 283(*m*)
Cannon, "Uncle Joe", 620
Cape of Good Hope, 23
capital goods, 507
capitalism
   in agriculture, 106
   business cycles in, 723
   communalism and, 358, 361
   communism and, 817, 848
   corporate, 849, 859, 889
   and Fair Deal, 834
   Fourierism and, 361
   free-market, 246–249, 342, 344
   industrialization and, 505–514
   Mormons and, 363, 366
   New Deal and, 754, 758–759, 765
   1932 elections and, 749(*m*)
   in 1950s, 848
   Oneida Community and, 362
   Social Darwinism and, 571–572
   welfare, 698
   WWII and, 788
capital punishment, 918, 943
Capra, Frank, 734
captives, Indian, 63–65
carbon emissions, 960–961
Caribbean Islands (West Indies)
   American dominance in, 647
   Columbus in, 24
   communism in, 849
   economy of, 464
   expansionist foreign policy and, 401
   French, 95–96, 179, 180, 182, 219, 220, 240
   governance of, 25
   Molasses Act and, 96
   Navigation Acts and, 95
   Revolutionary War and, 167, 179, 180, 182, 183, 184, 187
   slavery in, 68, 76–77, 78, 80, 83, 86, 333, 398, 401, 415
   South Atlantic system in, 77–80
   sugar and, 106, 122, 133(*m*), 135, 156
   trade with, 69, 88, 89(*m*), 206, 246
   U.S. as power in, 637

   U.S. intervention in, 953(*m*)
   War of Austrian Succession and, 95
Caribbean Sea
   "policing" of, 649, 650(*m*)
   strategic importance of, 634, 635
Carib Indians, 24
Carmichael, Stokely, 895
Carnegie, Andrew, 507, 530, 562, 571, 645
Carolinas, 69, 74, 77. *See also* North Carolina; South Carolina
carpetbaggers, 457, 458
Carranza, Venustiano, 653–654
Carroll, Charles, 52, 85
Carson, Rachel, 928
Cartagena, Colombia, 95
Carter, Jimmy (James E.; 1924–), 915
   Camp David accords and, 941, 942(*i*)
   defeat of, 943
   defense spending of, 948
   evangelical Christianity and, 937
   as president (1977–1981), 939–942
Carter, Robert, III, 88
Cartier, Jacques, 41
cartoons, political, 156(*i*), 221(*i*), 335(*i*), 343(*i*), 568(*i*), 609(*i*), 618(*i*), 758(*i*)
Cartwright, Peter, 302
Casablanca (film), 794
Cass, Lewis, 395, 396, 397, 400, 405(*m*)
Castro, Fidel, 861, 865
Catharine of Aragon, 31
Catholicism
   in America, 38–39, 41, 43, 47–48, 65, 73
   Americanism and, 557–558, 558(*i*)
   birth control and, 730
   in California, 390
   in colonial America, 108(*m*)
   conversions to, 40, 40(*i*), 41
   Democratic party and, 342
   ethnic identity and, 557–558, 558(*i*), 900
   in Europe, 17–18
   and Fair Deal, 834
   immigration and, 557–558, 558(*i*)
   in Ireland, 972
   Irish, 557
   in Maryland, 73
   missions of, 37–40, 65
   mob revolt against, 320
   1928 elections and, 719–720
   parochial schools and, 557
   presidential elections and, 86, 749

vs. Protestantism, 29–33, 47–48
  rhetoric against, 387, 570
  of slaves, 86
  Spanish conquest and, 29
  and Vietnam War, 882, 884
Catholics, 108, 110, 277
  Acadians and, 121
  anti-Catholicism and, 153, 154, 319–320
  California missions and, 500–501
  Democratic Party and, 574–576, 575(f),
    833, 943
  discrimination against, 719–720
  immigration restriction and, 709
  JFK and, 863
  Know-Nothing Party and, 402, 403
  Ku Klux Klan and, 712
  1936 elections and, 763
  in 1950s, 855
  prejudice against, 141, 153, 154, 154(m),
    319–320
  in Southwest, 496
Catt, Carrie Chapman, 602, 680
cattle industry. *See also* meatpacking industry;
    ranching
  African Americans in, 481, 481(i)
  on Great Plains, 480–482, 481(i), 486
  Hispanics in, 481, 481(i)
  Long Drive and, 480–481
Caucasus, 799
Caverly, Azariah, 312(i)
Cayuga Indians, 63
"The Celebrated Jumping Frog of Calaveras
    County" (Twain), 500
cell phones, 961
Cemetery Ridge, 431, 431(m)
CENTO. *See* Central Treaty Organization
Central America. *See also* Mesoamerica
  U.S. intervention in, 952
Central Intelligence Agency (CIA)
  Afghanistan and, 941
  antiwar movement and, 909
  covert operations of, 828, 952
  creation of, 823
  Cuba and, 865
  Iran and, 941
  Nixon's dirty tricks and, 920
  Vietnam and, 882
Central Pacific Railroad, 493(i)
  building of, 480
  Chinese labor for, 498, 498(i), 499

Central Treaty Organization (CENTO), 829(m)
A Century of Dishonor (Jackson), 489
Cervera, Pascual, 639
Chaco Canyon, 11, 12
Chambers, Whittaker, 836
Champlain, Samuel de, 41
Chancellorsville, Virginia, 430, 431(m)
Chandler, Samuel, 103
Channing, William Ellery, 281
Chaplin, Charlie, 702, 704
charitable activities
  of Benevolent Empire, 314–317, 349
  Great Depression and, 728, 745, 749
  New Deal and, 757
  Progressivism and, 600
  of women, 262, 315, 349
Charles I, king of England (r. 1625–1649), 54,
    56, 138
Charles II, king of England (r. 1660–1685), 56,
    68–70, 124
Charles River Bridge Co. v. Warren Bridge Co.
    (1837), 341
Charles Schwab (company), 925
Charleston, South Carolina, 180, 181(m), 188,
    234(i)
  free blacks in, 274–275
  South Atlantic system and, 89(m)
  transportation and, 306(m), 307(m), 309
  West Indian trade and, 89
Charlestown, Massachusetts, 158, 320
charters, 249, 253
Chase, Salmon P., 398, 409, 426, 428, 454
Chastellux, marquis de, 266
Chateau-Thierry, Battle of, 670
Chatham, earl of. *See* **Pitt, William**
Chattanooga, Tennessee, 434, 438(m)
chattel slavery, meaning of, 50
Chauncy, Charles, 116
Chautauqua, New York, 561
Chávez, César, 741, 898
checks and balances, 212, 454
Cheever, John, 775
Cheney, Richard, 973, 975, 978
Cheney Family, 101(i)
Cherokee Indians, 12, 125, 172, 487
  removal of, 337, 339, 340(m)
Cherokee Nation v. Georgia (1831), 337
Chesapeake (ship), 240
Chesapeake Bay
  class in, 87–88

Chesapeake Bay (*cont.*)
  colonies of, 38, 47–51
  economy of, 219, 233
  governance of, 69
  peoples of, 46–47, 52
  plantations in, 49(*i*)
  planters of, 104, 118, 157, 267(*i*), 269(*m*),
    269–270
  Revolutionary War and, 176, 181(*m*), 182,
    185
  slavery in, 80, 83, 85, 104, 190, 192(*m*),
    267(*i*), 269(*m*), 269–271
  tobacco in, 47–52
  in War of 1812, 242, 243(*m*)
Chesnut, James, 385
Chesnut, Mary Boykin, 385
Cheyenne, Wyoming, 480
Cheyenne Indians, 478, 486, 487
Chiang Kai-shek (Jiang Jieshi), 823
Chicago, Illinois, 230, 310, 535, 536(*t*)
  African Americans in, 552, 708(*m*)
  Berlin and, 541
  as center of meat industry, 486, 512, 536
  expansion in, 538(*i*)
  fire of 1871, 539
  jazz and, 705
  mass transit in, 538(*i*)
  migration to, 708(*m*), 861
  race riots in, 688
  skyline of, 539
  skyscrapers in, 539
  transportation and, 306, 306(*m*), 307(*m*),
    309, 481, 486
Chicago Columbian Exposition (1893), 509,
  541
Chicago Democratic Convention (1968),
  905–906
Chicano movement, 880, 898. *See also* Mexican
  Americans
Chickasaw Indians, 12, 337, 487
Chigabe (Chippewa chief), 14
Child, Lydia Maria, 282, 457
child care programs
  in 1970s, 931
  Nixon and, 917
child labor, 296(*i*), 296–297, 515, 521, 522(*i*)
  New Deal and, 756, 764
children
  attitudes toward, 549
  as indentured servants, 102

  interracial, 964
  in medieval Europe, 16–17
  in 1950s culture, 855–856
  rearing of, 260–265, 263(*i*), 285
  republicanism and, 263(*i*), 263–265
  republican motherhood and, 261–265,
    263(*i*), 374
  Sheppard-Towner Act and, 695–696
  social reform and, 375
Children's Bureau (Labor Department), 601,
  761
Chile, 630
China, 14, 23, 464. *See also* People's Republic of
    China; Taiwan
  Boxer rebellion in, 650–651, 651(*m*)
  civil war in, 823
  European spheres of influence in, 633, 634,
    650–651, 651(*m*)
  Japanese invasion of, 781, 785
  lobby for, 824
  Nationalist, 650, 652, 823, 826, 910
  trade with, 389, 633, 650–651
  United Nations and, 806
  WWI and, 664
  in WWII, 799, 804(*m*), 805(*m*)
Chinatown, San Francisco, 498
Chinese Exclusion Act (1882), 499, 743
  repeal of, 860
Chinese immigrants, 397(*i*), 456, 962
  discrimination against, 494, 499, 796
  Great Depression and, 743
  immigration restriction and, 499, 710, 743,
    860
  as migrant workers, 740
  in the West, 493(*i*), 494, 497–500, 498(*i*)
Chipewyan Indians, 229, 229(*i*)
Chippewa Indians, 14
Chisholm, Shirley, 930
Chittendon, Ebenezer, 100
Choctaw Indians, 337, 487
Chou En-lai (Zhou Enlai), 823
Christiana, Pennsylvania, 400
Christian Broadcasting Network, 937
The Christian Evangelist (periodical), 317
Christianity. *See also* evangelicalism; Protestant
    Reformation; revivalism; *individual
    denominations*
  African American, 118, 268, 274, 277–281,
    460, 552, 555, 557
  in Europe, 16–18

French Revolution and, 220
fundamentalist, 713, 718, 937–938
Inquisition and, 24
vs. Islam, 18, 20, 29
vs. Judaism, 29
muscular, 559
Native Americans and, 230–231, 232(i)
in New World, 24, 37–41
vs. paganism, 17–18
slave imports and, 83
Christian missionaries, 630
church and state, separation of, 190, 193–194,
   257, 557
Churchill, Winston
Atlantic Charter and, 785, 786(m)
at Potsdam Conference, 818
wartime planning and, 799, 800
at Yalta, 806, 807(i)
Church of England. See Anglicanism
Church of Jesus Christ of Latter-day Saints. See
   Mormons
Church of Scotland, 31
Churubusco, battle of (1847), 393
Cíbola (mythical seven golden cities), 38
Cincinnati, Ohio, 236, 367
migration to, 861
population of, 536(t)
slaughterhouses of, 293, 294(i)
transportation and, 306(m), 307(m), 308
CIO. See Congress of Industrial Organizations
Cisneros, Henry, 968
cities. See also urbanization
African American migration to, 707–708,
   708(m), 717, 718, 735–736, 777, 861
American vs. European, 541
amusements in, 560–561
in art and literature, 563
building codes, 540
churches in, 552, 555
as commercial hubs, 308–309
congestion in, 538, 542
decaying inner, 853, 860, 862, 956, 964
Democratic Party and, 694, 749, 765,
   793–794
downtowns of, 537
entertainment in, 560–563
gay communities in, 933
Great Depression protests in, 747
growth of, 89–90, 535–537, 536(t), 538(i),
   551–555

high culture in, 561–563
immigrants in, 535, 537, 551(i), 551–555,
   553(i), 554(i), 556, 962
industrialization and, 476, 536–542
jazz and, 705
Ku Klux Klan in, 711
lighting in, 539
Mexican Americans in, 741–742
move to suburbs from, 851
1928 elections and, 719
1932 elections and, 749
park planning and, 541
political machines in, 694
population growth and, 308–309, 535
population shift to, 707–708, 708(m), 756,
   860–862
poverty in, 310, 313–314, 319–320, 964
private/public, 539–541
Prohibition in, 714
revivalism in, 559, 714
riots in, 688, 796, 880, 895–896, 896(m),
   905, 906, 964–965
skyscrapers in, 539
social divisions within, 310–314
Summer of Love (1967) in, 893
in Sun Belt, 852
ten largest U.S., 536(t)
transportation in, 537–539, 538(i), 544
urban development and, 876
urban renewal and, 862, 917
voting districts and, 918
West Indian trade and, 88
women's movement in, 902
city-states, 14, 19
civic humanism, 19
civil defense, 843
Civil Defense Agency, 817(i)
civil disobedience, 356
draft and, 892
Civilian Conservation Corps (CCC), 756,
   762(m)
environment and, 773
Mexican Americans and, 770
Native Americans and, 771
WWII and, 793
civil rights, 839–842, 979. See also natural
   rights
conservative opposition to, 877, 965
disfranchisement and, 584
Eisenhower and, 841–842

civil rights (*cont.*)
  Fourteenth Amendment and, 450–451, 453, 455(*t*), 573, 581, 586
  Fifteenth Amendment and, 455(*t*), 456, 581, 584, 586, 605, 606
  of freed slaves, 449–450
  for homosexuals, 900, 903
  individual, 73
  JFK and, 863, 873
  land and, 464
  LBJ and, 873–874
  for Mexican Americans, 897–898
  for Native Americans, 898–900
  New Deal and, 768, 777–778
  Niagara Movement and, 606
  in 1970s, 943
  1972 elections and, 918
  1980 elections and, 943
  Nixon and, 917
  nonviolent protest and, 840, 842, 869
  Reconstruction and, 446
  Truman and, 839–840
  white primaries and, 605
  for women, 901–903, 915
  WWII and, 780, 790–792, 791(*i*), 796–798, 810
Civil Rights Act (1866), 446, 450, 455(*t*)
Civil Rights Act (1964), 873
  Title IX and, 930
  women and, 901–902
Civil Rights Bill (1870), 468
Civil Rights Commission, National, 840
civil rights movement, 868–872, 893–897
  African Americans and, 839, 842, 889, 893, 896(*m*), 915
  anticommunism and, 835
  Cold War and, 816, 833, 839, 842
  conflicts within, 872
  federal government and, 869
  Freedom Summer and, 892, 902
  Harlem Renaissance and, 718
  and housing discrimination, 852
  in 1970s, 933
  school busing and, 906
  sit-ins and, 869
  television and, 869, 874
  2000 elections and, 974
  violence against, 869, 870
  WWII and, 792
Civil Service Commission, 567

civil service reform, 567, 612
Civil War (1861–1865), 412–441
  African Americans and, 412, 432–433
  Antietam, 419(*m*), 420, 421(*i*), 429
  black soldiers in, 432–433, 433(*i*)
  Bull Run, 418, 420
  casualties of, 420, 440
  civilians in, 423–425, 435
  Constitution and, 207
  cost of, 427, 440
  crisis of Union and, 382–411
  disease in, 423, 424–425
  Eastern campaigns of, 419(*m*)
  financing of, 591
  Gettysburg, 412, 424, 430–431, 431(*m*)
  martial law in, 424
  military draft in, 423–424
  mobilizing resources in, 426–428
  nurses in, 424–425
  Reconstruction and, 442, 470
  roles of France and Britain in, 629
  Shiloh, 421
  slavery and, 412, 417, 428–430, 432–433
  taxation in, 427
  as total war, 423–428
  trench warfare in, 434
  turning point of (1863), 428–432
  Union victory in (1864–1865), 432–440
  Virginia campaign (1864–1865), 435(*m*)
  war bonds in, 427
  in the West, 420–423, 422(*m*), 430
  women in, 424–425
Civil Works Administration (CWA), 757
  Native Americans and, 771
  women and, 768
Clark, William, 240
Clarke, Edward H., 547
Clarke family, 104
class. *See* social structure
class-action suits, 930
Clay, Henry, 268, 400, 413, 415
  American System of, 325–330, 332–334, 336, 340–342, 391, 426
  Compromise of 1850 and, 398
  1824 elections and, 318(*m*), 325–326
  1832 elections and, 336
  1840 elections and, 347
  1844 elections and, 391
  freemasonry and, 344
  Missouri Compromise and, 276

national mercantilism and, 426
  Second Bank and, 250–251, 335–336
  War of 1812 and, 244
Clayton Antitrust Act (1914), 624
Clean Air Act (1970), 929
Clemenceau, Georges, 684
Clemens, Samuel. *See* **Twain, Mark**
Clermont (ship), 305
Cleveland, Grover (1837–1908), 615
  1884 elections and, 569, 577
  as passive president (1885–1889), 568(*i*)
  as president (1885–1889; 1893–1897),
    567–569, 568(*i*), 577, 588, 592,
    630–631, 637
  Pullman strike and, 531, 592
  as reformer, 569
Cleveland, Ohio
  population of, 536(*t*)
  transportation and, 306(*m*), 307(*m*), 309
Cline, Dave, 888
Clinton, Bill (William Jefferson; 1946–)
  approval rating of, 971
  balanced budget and, 969(*i*)
  big government and, 969–970
  first term of, 967–968
  gays in the military and, 968
  impeachment of, 970–971
  Kyoto Treaty and, 960
  as president (1992–1999), 967–973
  scandals in administration of, 970–971
Clinton, De Witt, 242, 303
Clinton, George, 212
Clinton, Henry, 180
Clinton, Hillary Rodham, 968, 971
closed-shop agreements, 345, 347
CNN (Cable News Network), 961
coal mining, 507, 508(*m*), 611
  breaker boys and, 522(*i*)
  decline of (1920s), 697
  in New South, 516(*m*)
  strikes and, 625
Cobbett, William (Peter Porcupine), 223(*i*)
Cody, William F. (Buffalo Bill), 480
Coercive Acts (1774), 153, 155, 157, 171, 174
Coeur d'Alene, Idaho, 492, 532–533
Cohan, George M., 669
Cohen, Lizabeth, 702
Colbert, Claudette, 794
Colden, Cadwallader, 141
Cold Harbor, battle of, 434, 435(*m*)

Cold War, 816–847
  9/11 and, 946
  affluent society and, 848
  in Afghanistan, 976
  anticommunism in, 835–837
  arms race in, 867–868
  beginning of, 817–819
  Berlin Wall and, 867
  civil rights movement and, 816, 831, 833,
    839, 842
  consensus of, 889–903
  Cuba in, 865
  culture of, 842
  domestic front of, 831–839
  domino effect and, 882, 888
  economy and, 877
  end of, 946, 952, 971–972, 973
  in Europe, 819(*m*)
  foreign relations and, 817–831
  globalization and, 959
  impact of, 842–845
  Iran and, 941
  in Middle East, 820
  mutual defense treaties in, 829(*m*)
  nuclear test ban treaties and, 867
  Peace Corps and, 865
  tactics of, 976
  Third World and, 866(*m*)
  Vietnam War and, 880–914
  WWII and, 781, 799, 810
  Yalta and, 807(*i*)
Cole, USS, attack on, 956(*m*), 972
Coleridge, Samuel Taylor, 353
collective security, 785, 829(*m*)
College of New Jersey. *See* Princeton College
College of Rhode Island. *See* Brown University
Collier, John, 771, 771(*i*)
Collier's magazine, 599, 618
Collins, R. M., 412
Collins, Samuel W., 299
Colombia, 647
colonialism, 817
  opposition to, 829, 881
  WWII and, 806
colonization. *See also* British Empire; Dutch
  colonization; English colonization; French
  colonization; Spanish colonization
  of African Americans in Africa, 718
  end of, 866(*m*)
  of Florida, 122, 132, 133(*m*)

colonization (*cont.*)
  by freed slaves in Africa, 268, 407
  Portuguese, 18–22, 21(*m*)
  of Quebec, 122, 132, 133(*m*)
  slavery and, 268, 407
  by Spain, 495–497
Colorado
  drought in, 737
  gay rights in, 966
  Japanese internment in, 797
  mining in, 499
  nuclear testing in, 828
Colored Farmers' Alliance, 582
Colored Women's Clubs, National Association
  of, 607–608
Colt, Samuel, 294
Columbia, South Carolina, 437
Columbia Broadcasting Service (CBS), 706
Columbian Exchange, 28
Columbia River, 240
Columbia University, 131
  founding of, 116
  student demonstrations at, 905
Columbus, Christopher, 6
  slave trade and, 24
Columbus, Ohio, 520(*i*)
Comanche Indians, 478
Committee Against Jim Crow in Military
  Service, 840
Committee on Public Information, 682
Committees of Correspondence, 151–152, 153
Committees of Safety and Inspection, 156
Committee to Defend America by Aiding the
  Allies, 784
Committee to Re-Elect the President (CREEP),
  919, 920
common law, 136, 142, 253
  inheritance and, 263
  women and, 102
  worker's rights and, 300, 345, 347
Common Sense (Paine), 170–171
Commonwealth of Independent States (CIS),
  953. *See also* Russia
commonwealth system, 249–250
Commonwealth v. Hunt (1842), 347
communalism. *See* utopian communities
communal living, 893
communism. *See also* anticommunism
  vs. capitalism, 817, 848
  Carter and, 941

Chinese, 823, 881
Cold War and, 881–884, 887–889, 909–910
conservative opposition to, 938
containment of, 819–823
in developing countries, 849, 952
European economy and, 820
fear of, 816, 835–837, 845
in Germany, 781
godless, 855
Great Fear of, 835–837
Greece and, 820
international, 824, 827, 831
Iran and, 941
JFK and, 863, 864, 873
Peace Corps and, 865
Soviet, 831, 835–837, 952–953
U.S. interventions and, 953(*m*)
Vietnam War and, 880–914
in WWII, 796
Communist Labor Party, 689
Communist Party
  in Great Depression, 747
  influence of, 775
  labor unions and, 766
  1932 elections and, 748–749, 749(*m*)
  in Soviet Union, 953
  in U.S., 689
  in Vietnam, 883–884
Community Action Program, 875, 877
Comprehensive Orders for New Discoveries
  (1573), 38
Compromise of 1850, 398, 399(*m*)
  political realignment and, 405(*m*)
computer technology, 961–962
Comstock Lode (1859), 494
concentration camps, 782, 802
Concord, Massachusetts, 249, 354, 355
  British troops in, 158
  Patriot movement in, 156, 158
  Revolutionary War battle (1775), 167, 185
Conestoga Indians, 125
Confederate States of America, 416, 424, 425,
  432, 453(*m*). *See also* Civil War;
  secession
  collapse of, 440
  inflation in, 427–428
  proclamation of, 413
Confiscation Acts (1861 and 1862), 428, 429
conglomerates, rise of, 849
Congo, Africa, 20

Congregationalism, 55, 193–194, 575(f)
  abolitionism and, 369
  in British colonies, 72
  in colonial America, 101, 108(m), 114
  "separatists" and, 116
  social reform and, 314
  women in, 284
  women's rights and, 376
Congreso Nacional del Pueblo de Habla
    Español (National Congress of Spanish-
    Speaking Peoples), 769
Congress, U.S. See also House of
    Representatives, U.S.; Senate, U.S.
  abolitionism and, 371, 372, 373(m)
  civil rights movement and, 872
  Crisis of 1877 and, 469–470
  Democratic control of, 833, 917, 919, 968, 978
  1848 elections and, 393
  1864 elections and, 437
  FDR and, 763–764
  Gulf of Tonkin Resolution (1964), 909, 912
  isolationism in, 782–783
  JFK and, 864
  Ku Klux Klan and, 465, 466
  labor unions and, 790
  Mormons and, 363, 366
  New Deal and, 756, 758
  9/11 report of, 978
  1946 elections and, 832
  vs. President, 450–452
  Reconstruction and, 443–452
  Republicans in, 978–979
  secession and, 415
  slavery and, 428
  slave vs. free states and, 397–398, 405–406, 408
  Supreme Court and, 694
  term limits in, 969
  Vietnam War and, 884–885, 908–909
  War Powers Act (1973), 911
  Wilmot Proviso and, 395
  women in, 669
  in WWII, 793
Congress of Industrial Organizations (CIO),
    766–767, 851, 898
  Democratic Party and, 794
  Mexican Americans and, 769
Congress of Racial Equality (CORE), 792, 869, 895
Conkling, Roscoe, 468, 571
Connecticut, 730
  claims to Western lands, 202

  as corporate colony, 72
  land grants in, 103
  Litchfield Law School in, 261
  migration from, 124
  voting rights in, 324
Connecticut River Valley, 56
  religious revival in, 114–116
Connor, Eugene ("Bull"), 869
conquistadors, 25, 27
conscience Whigs, 393, 402
conscription, 669. See also draft, military
conservation. See also environment
  JFK and, 868
  LBJ and, 876
  New Deal and, 772–773
  T. Roosevelt and, 613–614
conservatism, 967, 973, 975
  affirmative action and, 965
  vs. feminism, 931–932, 933
  gay rights and, 933
  Great Society and, 877
  in 1970s, 916, 928, 937–938, 943
  1980 elections and, 943
  resurgence of, 906, 912, 916
  Sun Belt and, 927(m)
  on Supreme Court, 951
Constitution, 207–215, 237
  abolitionism and, 373
  acquired territories and, 646
  Bill of Rights and, 213, 215
  Civil War and, 207
  contract clause of, 253
  evolution of, 251
  Federalism and, 212–215, 224
  Garrison and, 369
  impeachment and, 454
  implementation of, 214–215
  on interstate commerce, 252
  New Deal and, 759
  ratification of, 211, 214(m), 215
  Reconstruction and, 445
  revision of, 244
  secession and, 443
  slave vs. free states and, 397, 398, 407
Constitutional amendments, 397, 415, 457,
    470, 680–681. See also First Amendment;
    Fourteenth Amendment; Fifteenth
    Amendment
  Fifth, 406
  Thirteenth, 437, 445, 455(t)

Constitutional amendments (*cont.*)
  Eighteenth (Prohibition), 681, 714
  Nineteenth, 680
  Twentieth (1933), 749
  Twenty-second (1951), 863
  Twenty-fourth (1964), 874
  Twenty-sixth (1971), 887
Constitutional Convention (1787), 207–211,
    253, 277
  Great Compromise in, 210
  New Jersey Plan of, 209
  protest against, 211–214
  Virginia Plan of, 208–209
Constitutional Crisis (1798–1800),
    222–225
constitutional monarchy, 91
constitutional rights, 150, 155
  of colonies, 136–138, 145–146
  and republicanism, 257
  of Southern states, 275–277
Constitutional Union Party, 405(*m*), 410
constitutions, state, 197–199, 224,
    341, 454
construction industry, 507, 509, 726
consumerism, 124, 702–704
  foreign investment and, 699
  globalization and, 960
  Great Depression and, 731(*i*)
  industrial expansion and, 696–697
  interstate highways and, 853
  leisure and, 702, 707
  in literature, 716
  mail order, 512
  in 1920s, 692
  in 1950s, 848, 854–855, 877
  railroads and, 511
  student activism and, 891
  women and, 549, 857
consumer price index (CPI), 726
Consumer Products Safety Commission,
    917, 930
consumers
  goods for, 506
  protection of, 618, 948
  rights of, 929–930
Consumers' League, National, 601
consumer spending
  advertising and, 854
  economic development and, 856
  postwar, 851

consumption, rates of
  Great Depression and, 726
  WWII and, 795
containment, policy of
  in Asia, 823–827, 831
  meaning of, 819–820
  militarization of (NSC-68), 823
  Third World and, 829
Continental army, 172–183, 185, 202
Continental Congress, First (1774), 153,
    155–156, 158
Continental Congress, Second (1775), 185
  affairs of colonies and, 202, 207
  alliance with France, 179–180
  Articles of Confederation and, 202–205
  Britain and, 167–168, 171, 172, 175, 176,
    178, 180
  delegates to, 208
  finances of, 178
  independence and, 171–172
  new governing institutions and, 197
contrabands, 428, 432
Contras, 949, 952
Conwell, Russell H., 571
Cooke, Jay, 427, 468, 480
Coolidge, Calvin, 688
  Boston police strike (1919) and, 688
  on factories, 697
  Garvey and, 718
  as president (1923–1929), 694
  as vice-presidential candidate, 693
  on wartime debts, 699
Cooper, Thomas, 328
Cooperstown, New York, 560
Coosas Indians, 38
Copernicus, 112
Copland, Aaron, 775
Copley, John Singleton, 201(*i*)
Coral Sea, Battle of, 804, 804(*m*)
CORE. *See* Congress of Racial Equality
Corinne, Utah, 493(*i*)
Corliss engine, 509(*i*)
corn, 8, 9, 14. *See also* grain
  on Great Plains, 478
  production of, 103–104, 270, 302–303,
    303(*m*)
Cornish, Samuel D., 367
Cornwallis, Charles, Lord, 180, 181(*m*),
    182, 183
Corona, Bert, 742

Coronado, Francisco Vásquez de, 38, 39(m)
corporations. See also business
    campaign contributions of, 921
    consolidation of, 697, 940
    consumer rights movement and, 929–930
    corruption in, 979
    downsizing of, 915, 957, 958
    foreign competition and, 849, 927
    foreign investment and, 699
    mergers of, 615, 849
    multinational, 925, 959
    new technology and, 958
    power of, 597, 622–624
    rise of, 509
    taxation of, 612, 674
Corporations, Bureau of, 615, 616, 617
Corrigan, Michael A., 557
corruption
    corporate, 979
    in Harding administration, 693–694
    Ku Klux Klan and, 712
    in Nixon administration, 919–920
    political, 324, 460, 468, 469, 597
    in Truman administration, 837(i), 838
    and Vietnam War, 886
Cortés, Hernán, 25
Costa Rica, 701
cost-plus provisions, 788
cotton, 516(m)
    Civil War and, 426
    as diplomatic weapon, 426
    exports of, 219, 292, 308, 426
    Panic of 1837 and, 346
    prices for, 588
    production of, 383–386, 462, 497, 588
    Reconstruction and, 458
    sharecropping and, 462, 464
    slavery and, 233, 267(i), 268–270, 269(m),
        383–386
    the South and, 268–270, 269(m), 295, 301,
        303(m), 308, 343, 383–386
    tariff battle and, 328
    technology for, 233, 295–299
    in Texas, 485, 497, 586, 588
    textile industry and, 294–298
cotton gin, 219
Coughlin, Father Charles, 759–760
Council for Mutual Economic Assistance
    (COMECON), 821
Council of National Defense, 784

counterculture
    drugs and, 893
    of 1950s, 857–860
    of 1960s, 889, 892–893
    1970s activism and, 928
    vs. social conformity, 880
counterinsurgency, 865, 883
counterterrorism, 978
Country Party (England), 134
Court of International Justice (World Court),
    701
court system, 215, 237–238. See also judiciary;
    Supreme Court
    trial by jury and, 136, 138–139, 142, 274
    vice-admiralty, 136, 142, 146
covenant, meaning of, 55
Coventry, Alexander, 191(i)
covert interventions, 828
cowboys, 480–482, 481(i), 496
Cox, Archibald, 920
Cox, Ida, 705
Cox, James M., 693
Coxey, Jacob S., 592
craftsmen. See artisans
Crane, Stephen, 485, 563
Crawford, William H., 318(m), 325, 326
Crazy Horse, 487
credit. See also debt
    consumer, 854, 925
    Great Depression and, 745
    vertical integration and, 512
Creek Indians, 12, 74, 75, 242, 243(m),
    328–329, 337, 339, 340(m), 487
Creel, George, 682
Crèvecoeur, St. Jean de, 258
The Crisis (magazine), 606, 607(i), 717–718
Crittenden Plan, 415
Croats, 972
Crocker, Charles, 499
Crockett, Davy, 387
Cromwell, Oliver, 56, 72
crop-lien system, 462, 464
crops. See agriculture
Crow Dog, Mary, 899
Crow Indians, 478
Crusades, 18
Crystal Palace Exhibition, London, 299
Cuba, 74, 122, 391
    Bay of Pigs in, 865, 867
    economy of, 464

Cuba (*cont.*)
  expansionism and, 395, 401, 630
  Grenada and, 952
  independence of, 638
  JFK and, 865, 867, 873
  refugees from, 861
  right-wing regime in, 828
  sensationalist journalism and, 637
  vs. Spain, 636, 637–642
  Spanish "reconcentration" camps in, 636,
    638
  U.S. relations with, 648–649, 650(*m*), 782
Cuban missile crisis (1962), 867, 873
Cullen, Countee, 717
cultural values
  automobile and, 703–704
  conflict and, 707–716
  conservative (1920s), 693
  industrialization and, 707–708
culture. *See also* multiculturalism; popular
    culture
  automobile, 703, 851, 852–853
  of California, 500–501
  conformist, 842, 861
  dissent and, 857–860
  elitism and, 563
  feminization of, 563
  modern American (1920s), 702–708
  national, 702–708
  of 1950s, 853–860
  urban, 535, 549–563
  and Vietnam War, 881
  of work, 521, 522
Cumberland River, 421
Cummins, Albert B., 604
currency
  free silver and, 590–591
  globalization and, 959
  land banks and, 96
  paper, 177(*i*), 177–178, 187, 206, 427, 428
  postwar value of, 850
  state, 341
  U.S., 850, 925, 980
Currency Acts
  of 1751, 96
  of 1764, 134
Currier and Ives, 459(*i*)
Curtin, Harry, 666
Custer, George Armstrong, Battle of Little Big
    Horn and, 487

cyberspace, 962
Czechoslovakia, 684, 820, 821, 828
  German invasion of, 783
Czekalinski, Steve, 850(*i*)
Czolgosz, Leon F., 612

D. E. Loewe & Company, 610
Dachau concentration camp, 782, 802
Dahomey, Africa, 78(*m*), 79
Dakota territory, Indian reservations in, 486,
    488(*m*), 899–900
Dale, Thomas, 46
Daley, Richard J., 906
Damrosch, Leopold, 562
Danbury, Connecticut, 522
Danbury Hatters case (1908), 610
The Dangers of an Unconverted Ministry
    (Tennent), 116
Daniel, Jackson, 429
Dario, Ruben, 648–649
Darrow, Clarence, 713
Dartmouth (ship), 152
Dartmouth, Lord, 155
Dartmouth College v. Woodward (1819), 253, 341
Darwin, Charles, 571, 635, 713–714
Daughters of Bilitis, 858
Daughters of Liberty, 147(*i*), 148. *See also* Sons
    of Liberty
The Dave Kopay Story (Kopay and Young), 934
Davis, David, 469
Davis, Jefferson (1808–1889), 409
  black soldiers and, 438
  as Confederate president, 413
  1863 elections and, 431
  on Emancipation Proclamation, 429
  expansionism and, 395
  Fort Sumter and, 415
  General Sherman and, 438
  inauguration of (1861), 418
  resources of the South and, 423, 427
  strategy of, 430
Davis, John W., 694
Davis, Robert, 177
Dawes, Charles G., 699–700
Dawes Plan (1924), 699–700
Dawes Severalty Act (1887), 490, 771
Day, William R., 642
D-Day (June 6, 1944), 801, 801(*m*)
Dean, Howard, 962
Dean, John, 920

death. *See also* disease
    AIDS and, 967
    Civil War, 420, 440
    seasonal patterns of, 16
    slavery and, 78(*m*), 80, 81, 83
Debs, Eugene V., 531–532, 575, 622, 667, 683
debt
    British Empire and, 124, 132, 134, 144, 155
    of colonists, 119, 124, 206
    consumer, 702, 854, 925
    of farmers, 207
    foreign, 207–208, 211, 699–700
    imprisonment for, 197, 206–207, 323, 345
    of Mexico, 391
    national, 211, 216, 238, 250. *See also* deficit
        spending
    public, 206–211
    of southern states, 460
    war, 216–217
Declaration of Independence, 171, 184, 197, 222
    and Vietnam War, 881
    women's rights and, 378, 457
Declaration of Rights (1689), 91
Declaration of Rights and Grievances (1774),
    155
Declaration of Sentiments (1848; Seneca Falls),
    378
Declaration of the Causes and Necessities of
    Taking Up Arms, 167
Declaratory Act (1766), 145, 155
decolonization, 866(*m*), 922
Deere, John, 307
Defense Department, creation of, 823
defense spending, 827, 970
    Bush (George W.) and, 979
    Cold War, 843
    economy and, 789, 795, 877, 881, 926,
        927(*m*)
    Eisenhower and, 843, 845, 864
    JFK and, 864–865
    postwar development and, 852
    Reagan and, 948, 950
    Republicans and, 839
    Vietnam War and, 912
    WWII, 784, 788
deficit spending. *See also* debt
    Bush (George W.) and, 979
    economy and, 924–925, 951, 958
    meaning of, 764
    in New Deal, 868

by Nixon, 925
    Reaganomics and, 948, 950
    Vietnam War and, 890–891, 912
    WWII and, 787
deflation, 506, 506(*f*)
deindustrialization, 925–926, 926(*i*), 927
    environmentalism and, 929
deinstitutionalization of mentally ill, 948
deism, 113
de Kooning, Willem, 774
Delaware, 70, 416
    free blacks in, 274
    secession and, 414, 418
Delaware Indians, 119, 121, 122, 125, 229
Delaware Iron Works, 307
Delaware River, 63
De Leon, Daniel, 532
De Lesseps, Ferdinand, 630
de Lôme, Dupuy, 638
democracy
    Civil War and, 413
    demagogues and, 760
    direct, 604
    in education, 857
    in England, 91
    globalization and, 960
    immigrants and, 417
    Internet and, 962
    meaning of, 322
    and military-industrial complex, 845
    movies and, 704, 733–734
    Native Americans and, 771–772
    political evolution of, 323–330
    transcendentalism and, 355
    views of, 196, 322, 357
    WWII as defense of, 785
Democracy in America (Tocqueville), 254(*i*),
    322, 566
Democratic Party. *See also* elections; Peace
    Democrats
    African Americans and, 736–737, 839
    anticommunism and, 836
    black political leaders and, 458
    Catholics and, 574–576, 575(*f*)
    Chicago convention of (1968), 905–906
    China policy and, 909
    coalition of, 765–766, 777, 793–794, 864,
        877, 943
    Compromise of 1850 and, 398
    in Congress, 919

Democratic Party (*cont.*)
  control of Congress by, 833, 917, 919, 968, 978
  Crisis of 1877 and, 469–470
  divisions in, 400, 402
  1848 elections and, 396
  1852 elections and, 401
  1858 elections and, 408, 409
  1862 elections and, 430
  1868 elections and, 456
  in 1870s, 467, 469–470
  FDR and, 765
  free trade and, 569
  impeachment and, 454
  Ku Klux Klan and, 465
  labor and, 347, 625, 767–768, 833
  LBJ and, 873
  leadership of, 978–979
  left wing of, 928
  liberalism and, 881, 912
  and loss of China, 881
  "Lost Cause" and, 569, 581
  Mexican Americans and, 769–771
  Mexican War and, 393, 394
  National Committee of, 919, 920
  New Deal and, 776–778, 905
  in New South, 584–587
  1910 elections and, 622
  1928 elections and, 719–720
  1932 elections and, 748–749
  1936 elections and, 763
  1952 elections and, 837–838
  1972 elections and, 918–919
  1980 elections and, 943
  1984 elections and, 949
  1998 elections and, 971
  Nixon's dirty tricks and, 919, 920
  Northern, 416, 424
  Oregon and, 391
  origins of, 324, 329
  presidency and, 693
  progressive politics and, 620
  Reagan and, 943
  realignment of, 405(*m*)
  Reconstruction and, 444, 464–465, 467
  slave vs. free states and, 396, 397, 398, 409
  social welfare and, 848
  in the South, 409, 764, 777–778, 833, 864, 868
  split in (1948), 832–833

  states' rights and, 568
  Texas and, 387
  Vietnam War and, 889
  vs. Whigs, 255, 322, 330 (*f*), 342–345, 347–349
  Whitman and, 356
  working class and, 905, 943
  in WWII, 793–794
Democratic-Republicans, 219, 258–265. *See also* Republican Party
  political equality and, 258–259, 286
Democratic Review (periodical), 387
Dempsey, Jack, 707
Denmark, 784
  in NATO, 821
Dennison, William, 415
deportation, 861
  Mexican American activism and, 740–741
  of radicals during 1919 Red Scare, 689
depressions, 358, 361. *See also* Great Depression; panics; recessions
  of 1837–1843, 346
  of 1839, 347
  of 1857, 301
  of 1873, 468–469
  of 1890s, 615
deregulation, 940
  under Reagan, 948
desegregation, 873, 894, 895
  of armed forces, 826(*i*), 840
  resistance to, 840–842
  school busing and, 918, 936, 937, 943
  Supreme Court on, 918
Deseret, Mormon state of, 364(*m*), 366
détente, 909
Detroit, Michigan, 122, 230, 242
  riots in, 796, 896
  tranportation and, 307(*m*), 308
Dewey, George, 639, 640, 641(*m*), 646
Dewey, Thomas E., 793, 832–833
DeWitt, John, 796
Dewson, Molly, 767
The Dial (journal), 356
Dias, Bartholomeu, 23
Díaz, Bernal, 29
Dickinson, G. Lowes, 562
Dickinson, John, 147, 167
Diedrich Knickerbocker's History of New York (Irving), 265
Diem, Ngo Dinh, 882–884, 904

Dienbienphu (Vietnam), 882
Dies, Martin, 835
dime novels, 481(*i*)
Dinwiddie, Robert, 119, 121
diplomacy. *See also* international relations
    Carter and, 940–942
    cotton and, 426
    dollar, 652
    economic, 633, 782
    in Latin America, 630
    in Revolutionary War, 183–184
    U.S. expansion and, 629–632
    wartime, 806
discount rate, 725
discrimination, 966. *See also* racism
    affirmative action and, 930–931
    against African Americans, 494, 499,
        515–517, 521, 581–584, 788, 789, 791,
        852, 897
    against Asian Americans, 852
    against Catholics, 719–720
    against Chinese, 494, 499, 796
    in cities, 552
    against Hispanics, 494, 497
    against homosexuals, 858–859
    against Japanese, 499–500
    Mexican American activism and, 740–742
    against Mexican Americans, 769–770
    in military, 788, 789
    reverse, 936
    U.S. civil rights and, 839
    against women, 901–903
    against women in military, 957(*i*)
    against women in workforce, 789
disease. *See also* smallpox
    AIDS, 966–967
    cholera, 319
    in Civil War, 423, 424–425
    dysentery, 16, 23
    effect on Native Americans, 26–27, 37–41,
        43, 54, 61, 63, 65
    environment and, 45–46, 49
    epidemic, 80, 83, 112, 113, 319, 478
    of Europeans in Africa, 23
    influenza, 27
    influenza epidemic (1918–1919), 670, 673(*i*)
    malaria, 23
    measles, 27, 112, 478
    Native Americans and, 478
    seasonal cycle and, 16

sexually transmitted, 680
    smallpox, 478
    tuberculosis, 11–12
    yellow fever, 23
disfranchisement, 584
    laws of, 599, 605
    in the New South, 585(*m*)
Disney (company), globalization and, 959(*i*)
Displaced Persons Act, 860
Dissertation on the English Language (Webster),
    265
Distant Early Warning system, 828
District of Columbia (Washington, D.C.),
    419(*m*)
    abolitionism and, 371, 373
    as capital, 272
    in Civil War, 430
    Compromise of 1850 and, 398
    slavery in, 268, 407, 429
    War of 1812 and, 242, 243(*m*)
Divine, Father, 736
Divine Peace Mission, 736
divine right, 73
divorce, 730, 855, 933
Dix, Dorothea (1802–1887), 375, 425
Dixiecrats. *See* States' Rights Party
documentary impulse during the Great
    Depression, 775–776
Doeg Indians, 52
the dole, 757. *See also* welfare
Dole, Robert J. (Bob), 939, 970
dollar-a-year men, 787
Domestic Manners of the Americans (Trollope),
    279, 322
domestic manufacture, 106, 148. *See also*
    household production
Dominican Republic, 24
    immigrants from, 962
    U.S. military intervention in, 701
Dominion of New England, 72–74, 92, 138
domino theory, 820
Doniphan, Alfred A., 394(*m*)
Dorr, Retha Childe, 578
Dorsey, Tommy, 735
Dos Passos, John, 716, 775
Doubleday, Abner, 560
Douglas, Stephen A. (1813–1861), 408(*i*), 416
    Compromise of 1850 and, 398
    debates with Lincoln, 408
    1852 elections and, 400

Douglas, Stephen A. (*cont.*)
  1860 elections and, 405(*m*), 409–410
  expansionism and, 395
  on Kansas, 406
  Kansas-Nebraska Act and, 401–402
  popular sovereignty and, 397–398, 402
  on slave vs. free state conflict, 397, 398
Douglas, William O., 764
Douglass, Frederick (1818–1895), 370, 428,
    432, 605
  Free-Soil Party and, 395
  Fugitive Slave Acts and, 400
  women's rights and, 456, 457
Dow Chemical Company, 892
dower right, 102
Downing, Andrew Jackson, 544
draft, military
  avoidance of, 887, 892
  Civil War, 423–424, 433, 438
  peacetime, 842–843
  Selective Service Act (1917), 669
  Vietnam War and, 887, 892, 902, 909
  women in, 932
  WWII and, 784, 788
draft riots (Civil War), 424
Dred Scott decision (*Dred Scott v. Sandford*;
    1857), 252, 405–406, 408
Dreiser, Theodore, 535, 543
Drew, Elizabeth, 922
drought
  conservation and, 772–773
  in Dust Bowl, 737–740
  on Great Plains, 485, 490, 737–738
  in Texas, 571
Dry Dock Bank, 346
Du Bois, W. E. B., 606–607, 607(*i*), 717
Duck Soup (film), 733
Duer, William, 217
Dukakis, Michael, 950, 951
Duke, James B., 515
Dulles, John Foster, 828, 830
Dunmore, Lord, 180
DuPont Corporation, 616
Durr, Virginia Foster, 902
Dust Bowl (Oklahoma, Texas, New Mexico,
    Colorado, Arkansas, Kansas), 737–740,
    738(*m*)
  conservation and, 772
Dutch colonization, 116, 117
  vs. British, 44, 51, 68, 182
  commercial activities and, 33, 122, 152
  fur trade and, 43–44, 63, 65
  in Hudson River Valley, 104, 124–125
  Navigation Acts and, 69
  New Amsterdam, 43–44
  New Netherlands, 33, 43–44, 68, 69, 71, 104,
    105(*m*)
  in New World, 6, 33
  slavery and, 191(*i*)
  sugar plantations and, 77
Dutch East India Company, 43
Dutch Reformed Protestants
  in colonial America, 104, 116, 117
  Rutgers University and, 117
Dutch West India Company, 104
Duveyier de Hauranne, Ernest, 417
Dwight, Timothy, 102
Dylan, Bob, 893

Early, Jubal, 435
Earth Day, 929
Earth Summit, UN (1992), 960
Eastern Europe, 818, 821, 827
  containment in, 829
  end of Cold War and, 946, 952
  Germany and, 782
  Soviet Union and, 806
eastern woodland Indians. *See under* Native
    Americans
East Germany. *See* German Democratic
    Republic
East India Company. *See* British East India
    Company
East Indians
  as migrant workers, 740
  as strikebreakers, 743
East Indies, 18, 121–122
  Japanese invasion of, 795
East St. Louis, Illinois, 688
Eaton, Peggy, 336
Eckford, Elizabeth, 841(*i*)
e-commerce, 958
economic development, 249, 250. *See also*
    agriculture; industrialization;
    manufacturing; mining; ranching
  capital goods and, 507
  in Civil War, 426
  colonial, 100, 104–106, 123–124
  consumerism and, 854
  consumer spending and, 856

eastern, 227–228
government spending and, 831
industrial capitalism and, 505–533
Jackson and, 341–342
John Q. Adams and, 327–328, 329
and Marshall Plan, 821
nonimportation and, 147(i), 148, 150, 155, 156
in South America, 865
in Sun Belt, 851, 852
tax cuts and, 868
of Third World countries, 830, 850
Whig program for, 426, 568
Economic Growth and Tax Relief
    Reconciliation Act (2001), 975
Economic Opportunity, Office of (OEO), 875,
    917
economic policy, 186–187, 329, 403
Economic Recovery Tax Act (1981), 948
economic sanctions, 418
    against Japan, 785, 786
    Persian Gulf War and, 954
    in South America, 782
economic theory
    Keynesian, 764
    supply-side, 948
    tax cuts and, 868
economy. See also business; capitalism;
        depressions; inflation; market economy;
        mercantilism; panics; recessions; trade;
        trade, foreign
    agricultural, 77, 219, 232–237, 308, 464, 506
    balanced budget and, 753, 868, 943, 969,
        969(i), 970
    British imperial, 76–94, 249
    budget deficits and, 948, 950, 958
    under (George H. W.) Bush, 951
    business cycles in, 723
    business-government partnership and, 692–
        693, 696
    as campaign issue, 967, 969, 970, 971, 980
    change in U.S., 674
    changing (1790–1820), 232–237
    Civil War destruction of, 437, 440
    commonwealth system, 249–250
    of communal utopias, 358, 360, 362
    concentration of, 615–617
    cotton, 383–387
    and defense spending, 843
    of diminished expectations, 957
    downsizing and, 915, 957, 958

Embargo Act of 1807 and, 241
entrepreneurial enterprise and, 247, 342
environment and, 960–961
expansionism and, 632–634
federal role in, 776, 787–791
Ford and, 939
free-market capitalist, 246–249, 342, 344
of Germany, 781
globalization and, 958–961
Great Deflation and, 506, 506(f)
growth of, 949, 956–957, 958
industrial, 597
inequality and, 105–106
international, 699–700, 701, 725–726, 921,
    922, 927, 946
Japanese, 805
laissez-faire, 342, 347, 571, 590
living standards and, 237, 352
mergers and, 615
mass-consumption, 723
merchant-based, 246–249
of Mexico, 392
Middle Atlantic (1720–1765), 104–106
military power and, 71
of Mormons, 366
in 1920s, 692, 696–699
1928 elections and, 720
in 1950s, 857
in 1970s, 915–945, 943
1972 elections and, 919
In 1990s, 956–958
Nixon and, 917
Northern maritime, 88–91
Pacific Rim, 882
plantation, 383–387, 402
politics and, 91, 391
postwar, 849–851
productivity in, 956, 957, 960
Reagan and, 948–949
Reconstruction and, 458–459
reform and, 352
regulation of, 693, 776
Republicans and, 979–980
slave, 76–91, 266–277, 267(i), 269(m),
    280–281
slowing, 975
social structure and, 90–91
South Atlantic system, 76–80
Southern, 219, 308, 458–459, 464
structural weaknesses of, 724

economy *(cont.)*
  tobacco, 48–52
  "trickle down," 745
  U.S. dominance of international, 921, 925,
    944
  of Vietnam, 881, 884, 885
  Vietnam War and, 890–891, 912
  War on Poverty and, 877
  West German, 821
  westward migration and, 235–237
  women in, 425
  women's rights and, 932–933
  WWII and, 787–791, 810
Ederle, Gertrude, 707
Edgar Thompson Works, 507
Edison, Thomas A., 537, 539
education
  affirmative action in, 936, 965
  of African Americans, 265, 284, 368, 461*(i)*
  bilingual, 898
  in cities, 964
  computer technology and, 962
  democratization of, 857
  elementary, 197, 201–202
  federal aid to, 831
  free blacks and, 367
  GI Bill and, 793, 851, 901
  Great Depression and, 732–733
  Japanese internment and, 798
  JFK and, 863, 868, 873
  LBJ and, 876
  middle class culture and, 311
  in New England, 264, 266
  in 1950s, 856
  in 1990s, 956
  in 1998 elections, 971
  popular, 355
  prayer in public schools and, 918
  public, 264–265, 375, 460
  reforms in, 265, 369, 375
  republicanism and, 258, 263–265
  school segregation and, 581, 894, 895
  states and, 951
  teachers and, 265, 286
  vouchers and, 973
  of women, 199–202, 262, 284–286, 375,
    547*(i)*, 549, 930
Education, Department of, 940
Educational Amendments Act (1972), Title IX,
    930

Edwards, Jonathan, 101, 114, 116
Egypt, 426, 830
  Camp David accords and, 941, 942*(i)*
  invasion of Israel by, 923
  Iraq and, 955
Eisenhower, Dwight D. (1890–1969), 863
  Bonus Army and, 747–748
  civil rights and, 841*(i)*, 841–842
  Cold War policies of, 864
  communism and, 827, 828
  covert intervention and, 828
  Cuba and, 865
  defense spending and, 843, 845, 864
  domino theory and, 820
  foreign policies of, 848
  Korea and, 827
  McCarthy and, 836
  on military-industrial complex, 844–845
  New Look in foreign policy of, 827–829,
    864
  1952 elections and, 837–838
  as president (1953–1961), 827–829, 836,
    838–839
  Suez crisis and, 830
  U-2 spy plane and, 843–844
  Vietnam and, 882
  in WWII, 800, 801
Eisenhower Doctrine, 830
elderly
  poverty and, 862
  in stock market, 980
elections. *See also* presidential elections
  Crisis of 1877 and, 469–470
  in Eastern Europe, 806, 818
  local, 322–323
  in Vietnam, 882
  voter turnout for, 576, 694–695
  Mormons and, 363, 365
  1800, 224
  1818, 253
  1824, 318*(m)*, 325–326
  1828, 328–330, 330*(f)*
  1832, 335–336
  1836, 344
  1840, 347–349, 348*(i)*
  1844, 390–391
  1846, 393
  1848, 394, 395–396, 405*(m)*
  1852, 400–401, 405*(m)*
  1856, 403–406, 405*(m)*

1858, 407–408
1860, 405(m), 408(i), 409–410, 412, 413
1862, 429, 430
1863, 431
1864, 434, 436–437
1866, 450–451, 452
1868, 455–456
1872, 468
1875, 467
1876, 469–470
1896, 597
1916, 668
1938, 765
1942, 793
1968, 904–907
1994, 968
1998, 971
2002, 978–979
electoral college, 210, 215, 224, 456, 469, 784
    abolition of, 694
    1824 elections and, 318(m), 325, 326
    1828 elections and, 326, 330
    1836 elections and, 344
    1860 elections and, 409–410
    2000 elections and, 973
electricity, 507, 509(i)
    downtowns and, 539, 541
electrification
    consumer culture and, 703
    TVA and, 772, 773(m)
Elementary and Secondary Education Act
        (1965), 876
Elgin, Lord, 307(m)
Eliot, John, 61
Eliot, T. S., 716
elite, 91–92. See also middle class; nobility;
        social structure
    African American intellectual, 717–718
    business, 301, 309–310, 342
    national, 543
    1928 elections and, 719
    planter-merchant, 77
    Reconstruction and, 444, 458
    Southern, 87–88, 384
    taxation of, 459–460
    urban, 542–543, 562
Elizabeth I, queen of England (r. 1558–1603),
        31, 32(i), 44, 70
Elkins Act (1903), 617
Ellington, Edward "Duke," 705, 735

Ellison, Ralph, 775
Ellsberg, Daniel, 816, 880, 919
El Paso, Texas, 495, 860
El Salvador, 952, 962
Ely, Ezra Stiles, 282, 284
e-mail, 961
emancipation, 267–268, 281, 333. See also
        abolition; abolitionism
    African Americans and, 446–450
    antiabolitionism and, 372
    in Caribbean, 267, 464
    Civil War and, 428–430, 437
    Democratic Party and, 436
    gradual, 192(m), 368, 418, 464
    Lincoln and, 407
    Missouri crisis and, 275–276
    Reconstruction and, 442, 458
    Revolutionary War and, 188–190, 192(m)
    state legislation for, 368
Emancipation Proclamation (1862), 429–430,
        437
    outcome of, 432, 464
Embargo Act (1807), 241
Emergency Banking Act (1933), 754
Emerson, Ralph Waldo (1803–1882), 265, 322,
        354(i), 362, 549
    at Brook Farm, 358
    on industrial revolution, 293
    literary influence of, 355–357
    on slavery, 371
    transcendentalism and, 353–355
emigration. See also immigrants; immigration;
        migration
    of Loyalists, 187–188
eminent domain, 250
empiricism, 112
employment. See also unemployment
    changing patterns of, 957–958
    discrimination in, 873
    equal opportunity in, 840
    and Fair Deal, 834
    gay rights and, 933
    homosexuals and, 859
    of women, 789, 851, 856(i), 857, 858, 901,
        932–933, 957–958
    in WWII, 780
enclosure acts, 34
encomenderos (land owners), 39
encomiendas (grants), 27
Endangered Species Act (1973), 929

energy, 975. *See also* oil industry
　alternative sources of, 929
　consumption of, 924(*f*)
　electrical, 507, 509(*i*)
　for manufacturing, 507
　nuclear, 924(*f*), 928–929
Energy, Department of, 843, 940
energy crisis (1973–1974), 921–924, 923(*i*),
　　928, 940
energy prices, shortages (2000), 975
Engel v. Vitale (1962), 918
England. *See also* British empire; Great Britain
　agriculture in, 33
　democracy in, 91, 323
　vs. Dutch, 44, 51, 68, 182
　duties on goods and, 135–136
　enclosure acts of, 34
　France and, 74
　Industrial Revolution and, 123, 292
　industry in, 34
　mercantilism in, 33
　merchants in, 150
　migration to America from, 33, 34, 37,
　　44–47
　new world trade monopolies of, 51
　Price Revolution in, 33–34
　Protestant Reformation and, 29–31
　Puritan exodus from, 53–56
　religious civil war in, 56, 69, 72–73
　vs. Spain, 32–33, 38
　Whig Party in, 91–93, 134, 143
English colonization, 120(*m*)
　colonial self-government and, 131, 132
　early attempts, 44–59
　fur trade and, 63, 65
　migration of ideas and traditions and, 33,
　　34, 37, 54–56
　Native Americans and, 6, 59–63
　in New England, 53–61, 60(*m*), 100–104
　population growth and, 99
　social causes of, 33–34
English language, 85
Enlightenment, 170, 171, 193, 204, 219
　in American colonies (1740–1765),
　　112–118, 141
　American revolutionary thought and, 141
　child rearing and, 264
　religious thought and, 281
　slavery and, 189–190
　transcendentalism and, 353

witchcraft accusations and, 58
　women's rights and, 376
Enrollment Act (1863), 424
Enron Corporation, 979
entitlement programs, 917
entrepreneurial enterprise, 247, 342
environment, 9, 27, 249, 967. *See also* national
　　park system
　Bush (George W.) and, 979
　Dust Bowl and, 738
　effects of fur trade on, 65
　effects of mining on, 501
　federal government and, 916
　globalization and, 960–961
　of Great Plains, 477(*m*), 477–478
　health and, 45–46, 49
　LBJ and, 876
　legislation on, 876, 929
　modernization and, 960
　New Deal and, 772–773
　in 1990s, 956
　Nixon and, 917
　preservation of, 501–502, 502(*i*), 612
　Reagan and, 948
　urban, 540–542
environmentalism, 501–502, 967
　Bush (George W.) and, 975
　in 1970s, 915, 928–929, 936–937, 940
　Sierra Club and, 501
Environmental Policy Act, National (1969), 929
Environmental Protection Agency (EPA), 917,
　　929
Episcopal Church, 127, 264, 277, 278. *See also*
　　Anglicanism
Equal Credit Opportunity Act (1974), 931
Equal Employment Opportunity Commission
　　(EEOC), 902
equality
　of African Americans, 272, 274–275,
　　277–278, 280–281, 446, 581–587
　antiabolitionism and, 372
　before the law, 446, 450, 465
　within marriage, 258, 260–261
　of opportunity, 840
　Quakers and, 109, 310
　republicanism and, 257–260, 281, 286
equal opportunity
　Jackson and, 336
　Whig ideal of, 343, 344
equal rights, 345, 349

Equal Rights Amendment (ERA), 931–932, 932(*m*)
  1980 elections and, 943
  opposition to, 937
Equal Rights Association, 457
Equiano, Olaudah (Gustavus Vassa), 81
Era of Good Feeling, 255
Erdman Mediation Act (1898), 597
Erie Canal, 235, 283(*m*), 302–305, 304(*i*), 306(*m*), 309
  Mormons and, 363
  revivalism on, 315–316, 316(*i*)
Erie Indians, 63
Erie Railroad, 306, 510
Espionage Act (1917), 682
Essay Concerning Human Understanding (Locke), 112–113
Estonia, 684
Ethiopia, 781, 940
Ethiopian Regiment, 167
ethnic cleansing, 972
ethnic conflict, 946
  in the Balkans, 972, 973
ethnic diversity, 70, 99, 104, 106, 108–111
  in mythic West, 481(*i*), 481–482
  in 19th century America, 517, 517(*f*), 519, 575(*f*)
  politics and, 574–576, 575(*f*), 593, 594
ethnicity, 551, 555, 900. *See also* race
  consumer culture and, 702
  Democratic Party and, 749, 765, 777, 793
  Great Depression and, 728
  immigration restriction and, 709, 711
  politics and, 718, 719
  television and, 854–855
  urbanization and, 719
Europe, 14–20. *See also* immigrants; migration; Protestant Reformation; *individual countries*
  agriculture in, 697
  American colonies and, 37–66
  American politics and, 322–323
  American writers in, 716
  artisans in, 20
  Chinese spheres of influence and, 633, 634, 640, 650–651, 651(*m*)
  communism in, 849
  economic recovery of, 944
  Great Depression and, 725–726
  immigration from, 99–103, 106, 108
  immigration restriction and, 709
  impact on new world of, 37–40
  jazz and, 705
  maritime expansion and, 18–20
  medieval era in, 14–18
  movies in, 704
  nineteenth-century alliances in, 654
  oil embargo vs., 923
  opinion polls in, 978
  political innovation and, 20
  vs. postwar U.S., 849
  Price Revolution in, 33–34
  reconstruction of, 850
  refugees from, 860
  religion in, 16–18, 29–31
  Renaissance in, 18–20
  rural life in, 14–16
  social values of, 17–18
  transcendentalism and, 353
  U.S. foreign investment in, 701
  war reparations of, 744
  welfare system in, 776
  WWII in, 778, 799–802, 800(*m*), 801(*m*), 806
European Union (EU), 959, 978
evangelicalism, 559. *See also* Protestantism; revivalism
  abolitionism and, 368–371, 374
  camp meetings and, 278–279, 280(*i*), 283(*m*)
  child rearing and, 264, 285
  Great Awakening and, 112–118, 141, 281, 282
  in Middle Atlantic colonies, 117–118
  in New England, 114–116, 278, 283(*m*)
  in 1950s, 855
  in 1970s, 937–938, 943
  Oneida Community and, 361–362
  political freedom and, 116–117, 141
  Presbyterian, 324
  republicanism and, 281–282, 284
  Second Great Awakening and, 257, 277–284, 283(*m*), 315, 319
  slavery and, 315
  social reform and, 315–318, 353
  Whigs and, 342, 344
  women's rights and, 278, 280–281, 284–286, 457
  women's role and, 100–102, 116, 278, 280–281, 284–286, 317
Evans, Oliver, 294
Evans, Walker, 776

Everett, Edward, 342
Evers, Medgar, 871
"evil empire," 952
evolution, 714
Ewell, Richard B., 430
exceptionalism, of U.S., 663
Executive Order 8802 (FEPC), 790
Executive Order 9066 (Japanese internment),
    796
executive privilege, 920
expansionism. *See also* westward expansion
    economy of, 632–634
    as foreign policy, 394, 401, 629–632
    ideology of, 636
    Manifest Destiny and, 383–391, 636
    opposition to, 644–645
    Ostend Manifesto and, 401
    roots of, 629–632
    slavery and, 392–398
exports, 632–633. *See also* trade
    colonial, 104, 110, 123–124, 135, 155, 292
    cotton, 219, 292, 308, 426
    grain, 103–104, 110, 308
    manufactured goods, 294
    rice, 123–124
    sugar, 135–136
    tobacco, 123–124

factory system. *See also* industrialization;
    manufacturing; mills
    assembly line and, 293, 294(*i*)
    division of labor and, 293–294, 294(*i*)
    industrialization and, 476, 536–537
    mass-production techniques in, 307–308
    technology and, 293–299, 294(*i*)
    women in, 425
Fairbanks, Douglas, 704
Fair Campaign Practices Act (1974), 921
Fair Deal, 833–835, 838
Fair Employment Practices Commission
    (FEPC), 790–791
Fairfax, Lord, 125
Fair Labor Standards Act (FLSA; 1938), 764, 768
Fall, Albert, 694
Fallen Timbers, battle of, 229(*i*), 230
Faludi, Susan, 965
Falwell, Jerry, 938, 938(*i*)
family, 84–85, 101(*i*). *See also* birth control;
    children; patriarchy; women
    changing patterns in, 957

child rearing and, 260–265, 263(*i*), 285
farm life and, 100–103
feminism and, 889, 932–933
Great Depression and, 728–733
inheritance and, 100, 102–103, 260–262, 310
labor system and, 515
marriage and, 102, 108–109, 111, 260–263,
    263(*i*)
middle class, 311, 312(*i*), 545–546
in 1950s, 854, 855–856
nuclear, 546
pre-industrial, 545
republican motherhood and, 261–265,
    263(*i*), 285
slavery and, 270–273
working-class, 519–521
WWI insurance for, 680
Family and Medical Leave Act (1993), 968
Family Assistance Plan (Nixon), 917
family values, 938, 938(*i*), 967
    gay rights and, 966
family wage, 519, 521
A Farewell to Arms (Hemingway), 716
Farmer, James, 792
farmers. *See also* agriculture; tenant farmers;
        yeomen farmers
    African American, 768
    bankruptcy of, 126, 128
    debt of, 207, 235
    economic problems of, 708
    education for, 264
    evangelicalism and, 112, 116
    Great Depression and, 724, 745–746
    Jackson and, 329, 335, 336
    land sales for, 302, 303(*m*)
    as loyalists, 157
    New Deal and, 756
    1936 elections and, 763
    politics and, 199, 212, 588, 590, 593
    Populism and, 532, 588–589
    protests by, 745–746
    Republican Party and, 694
    Revolutionary War and, 175, 177, 178, 182, 188
    Social Security and, 776
    tariffs and, 327, 328, 329
    taxation and, 140, 155
    War on Poverty and, 877
    Western migration of, 233
Farmers' Alliance of the Northwest, 588
Farm Holiday Association, 746

farming. *See* agriculture
Farm Security Administration (FSA), 723, 776
Farragut, David G., 423
fascism, 766, 781–782. *See also* Nazi (National
    Socialist) Party
    in movies, 794
Fast Horse, Fred, 672(*i*)
Father Knows Best (TV program), 854, 855
Faubus, Orval, 841–842
Faucit, Walter, 111
Faulkner, William, 716–717
Fauset, Jessie, 717
FBI. *See* Federal Bureau of Investigation
FDR. *See* Roosevelt, Franklin Delano
Federal Art Project (WPA), 773–774
Federal Bureau of Investigation (FBI), 899, 909
    Nixon's dirty tricks and, 920
Federal Deposit Insurance Corporation,
    (FDIC), 756
Federal Emergency Relief Administration
    (FERA), 757, 762, 771
Federal Farm Loan Act (1916), 625
federal government, 19
    abolition and, 442
    activism of, 619, 863, 877, 943
    AIDS and, 966
    automobile and, 703
    big, 968–970
    as broker state, 765
    bureaucracy of, 625, 765, 776, 787, 810, 917,
        940, 979
    business and, 693–702, 720, 765
    Carter and, 940
    centralized system of, 210–211
    civil rights and, 468
    civil rights movement and, 869, 874
    discrimination against women by, 731
    economy and, 674–675, 696, 787–791, 831,
        834
    environmental legislation and, 929, 940
    expansion of, 674–675, 745, 752, 761, 765,
        776, 787, 794, 810, 876
    Fuel Administration of, 675
    Great Depression and, 744–745
    highways and, 852–853
    homosexuals and, 859
    housing and, 851, 852
    Indian removal and, 336–339, 340(*m*)
    Ku Klux Klan and, 465
    LBJ and, 874, 876, 877

mining interests and, 532–533
New Deal and, 752, 761, 765
New Right and, 938
in 1970s, 936–937, 943
Nixon and, 916, 917
photography and, 776
postwar reforms and, 679
powers of, 329–330, 400, 415, 442, 451, 675,
    967, 979
public cynicism and, 915, 921, 928, 939
radio and, 706
railroads and, 508, 531, 573
Reagan and, 947, 948
regulatory powers of, 617–618
Republican Party and, 916, 917
resentment of, 937, 938
role of, 838–839, 943, 973
Second Bank and, 334–336
shrinking of, 946, 950, 967, 973
slavery and, 407
small, 341–342
states and, 252, 916, 917
Supreme Court and, 573
voting rights and, 456
wartime propaganda of, 681–683
welfare capitalism and, 699
WWII and, 787, 793, 794
Federal Housing Administration (FHA), 852
The Federalist, 212
Federalists, 259–260, 265, 325
    commonwealth idea and, 250–251
    Constitution and, 212–215, 224
    declaration of War of 1812 and, 241–242
    decline of, 253, 255
    financial policy and, 216–219
    the judiciary and, 237–238
    New England, 240, 242, 244
    opening of West and, 227
    pro-British foreign policy of, 241
    vs. Republicans, 218–219, 221–222, 224
Federal Music Project, 774–775
Federal Reserve Act (1913), 624
Federal Reserve system, 674, 776
    Great Depression and, 725
    inflation and, 940, 948
    New Deal and, 758
    1970s recessions and, 940
    1980s recessions and, 948
    Roosevelt recession and, 764
    tariff reform and, 624

Federal Theatre Project (FTP), 775
Federal Trade Commission (FTC), 624, 693
Federal Writers' Project (FWP), 775
Fell, Margaret, 70
fellow travelers, 836
Female Charitable Society, 262, 316
Female Guardian Society, 375
Female Moral Reform Society, 375
feminine mystique, 856, 857, 858
The Feminine Mystique (Friedan), 857,
    901–902
feminism, 457, 915. *See also* women's rights
    backlash against, 965–966
    consciousness raising and, 902
    in 1970s, 928, 930–933
    opposition to, 931–932, 937
    revival of, 880, 889, 901–903
    rise of, 602–604
    third-wave, 966
FEPC. *See* Fair Employment Practices
    Commission
Ferdinand, king of Spain (r. 1474–1516), 24
Ferraro, Geraldine, 930, 949
Field, David Dudley, 352
Field, Stephen J., 573
Field Workers Union, 743
Fifteenth Amendment, 455(*t*), 456, 581, 584,
    586, 605–606
fifties. *See* affluent society (1950s)
"Fifty-four forty or fight!", 391, 393
Filipinos. *See also* Philippines
    Great Depression and, 743
    as migrant workers, 740
    wartime treatment of, 645–646
Fillmore, Millard (1800–1874), 398, 403, 405
    as president (1850–1853), 307(*m*)
Finland, 684
Finley, James, 278
Finney, Charles Grandison, 315–317, 316(*i*),
    355, 361, 369, 375
Finney, Lydia, 316, 375
firearms industry, 294, 299. *See also* guns
fireside chats, 753–754, 755
First Amendment, 224, 835
    political correctness and, 965
    prayer in public schools and, 918
Fish, Nathaniel, 59
fishing industry, 88, 135, 495
Fiske, John, 636
Fithian, Philip, 103

Fitzgerald, F. Scott, 716, 723
Fitzhugh, George, 385
Five Nations, Iroquois, 14, 41, 63. *See also*
    Iroquois Indians
Flanagan, Hallie, 775
flappers, 704, 707
Fletcher v. Peck (1810), 253
flexible response policy, 864–865
Florentine Codex: General History of New Spain
    (Sahagún), 26
Florida
    British colonization of, 122, 132, 133(*m*)
    ERA and, 932(*m*)
    Latino immigration to, 962
    migration to, 852
    Reconstruction and, 453(*m*), 457
    Republican government in, 467, 469
    as sanctuary for escaped slaves, 272
    secession of, 413
    Seminole Indians in, 337, 339, 340(*m*)
    slavery and, 69, 182
    Spain and, 25, 38, 39(*m*), 41, 69, 74, 86, 184,
        245
    2000 elections in, 973–975
Foch, Ferdinand, 670
Food Administration (World War I), 675
Food and Drug Administration (FDA), 619,
    929
Food for Peace program, 865
Food Stamps, 875, 948, 964, 970
Foote, Edward Bliss, 548
Forbes, John Murray, 509
Force Bill (1833), 334
Ford, Gerald R. (1913–), 911, 915, 920–921,
    975
    as president (1974–1977), 939
    Sun Belt and, 927(*m*)
Ford, Henry, 667, 697
Ford Model T
    consumer culture and, 702, 703
    sexuality and, 704
Ford Motor Company, 926
    foreign investment and, 701
    mass production and, 698, 703
    strikes at, 747
Fordney-McCumber Tariff (1922), 699
foreign aid, 820, 823, 849, 865, 953(*m*). *See also*
    foreign investment; Marshall Plan
*Foreign Conspiracy against the Liberties of the
    United States* (Morse), 319

foreign investment, 699
in Asia, 701
in Europe, 701
Great Depression and, 726
in South America, 700–701
foreign policy, 222, 224. *See also* international
relations
acquisition of territories and, 646
anti-imperialism in, 644–645
in Asia, 650–652
bipartisan, 832, 889
Bush (George H. W.), 954
Bush (George W.), 975–978
Carter, 940–942
Cold War and, 881
crises in, 972
1852 elections and, 401
Eisenhower, 827–829
expansionist, 394, 401, 630–632
Ford, 939
globalization and, 634, 646
imperial experiment in, 642–643
JFK, 864–868, 873
"large," 634–635
New Deal and, 778
in 1920s, 699–702
1928 elections and, 720
of nonalignment, 629
oil and, 830, 831
post-Cold War, 971–973
pro-British, 221, 241
Reagan, 948, 952
trade and, 634, 650
Venezuela and, 635
Wilson's philosophy of reform and, 652
Forrest, Nathan Bedford, 465
Fort Beauséjour, Nova Scotia, 120(*m*), 121
Fort Bridger, 364(*m*)
Fort Donelson, 421
Fort Duquesne, 120(*m*), 121–122. *See also*
Pittsburgh, Pennsylvania
Fort Fisher, 433(*i*)
Fort George, 141
Fort Hall, 479
Fort Henry, 421
Fort McHenry, 242
Fort Orange, 43
Fortounescere, Vito, 555
Fort Pitt. *See* Pittsburgh, Pennsylvania
Fort Stanwix, Treaty of (1784), 229

Fort Sumter, 440
secession and, 414(*m*)
seizure of, 415, 416
Fort Ticonderoga, 176
Fort Wagner, 433
Forten, James, 367
"forty-niners," 396, 397(*i*), 500. *See also* gold
rush
Forty-ninth parallel, 244, 245
Foster, William Z., 748
The Four Hundred, 543
Fourier, Charles (1777–1837), 361
Fourierism, 361, 366(*i*)
Four-Power Conference (1947), 822
Fourteenth Amendment (1868), 454, 840, 974
abortion rights and, 931
civil rights and, 450–451, 453, 455(*t*), 573,
581, 586
Fowler, Philemon, 374
Fox, George, 70
Fox, Henry, 346
Fox Indians, 65, 337, 338, 339(*i*)
Frame of Government (1681; Pennsylvania), 70
France, 685. *See also* French colonization; New
France; Paris, France; Paris, Treaty of;
Versailles, Treaty of
American alliance with, 178–184, 181(*m*)
American writers in, 716
decolonization and, 829
England and, 68, 74, 94–95
Germany and, 782, 783, 784, 806
in Indochina, 881–882
jazz and, 705
liberation of, 801–802
loan from, 178
Marshall Plan and, 822
migration to New World from, 41–43
in NATO, 821
occupation of Germany by, 818
peace talks with, 183–184
slave trade and, 77, 78
vs. Spain, 38
Spanish civil war and, 783
student protests in, 905
Suez Canal and, 830
sugar islands and, 122, 135
Texas and, 386
U.S. isolationism and, 784
War of Austrian Succession and, 95
Washington Naval Arms Conference and, 701

France (*cont.*)
  WWI and, 663–664, 699
  WWII role of, 799
  XYZ Affair in, 221(*i*), 222
Franciscan friars
  cultural assimilation and, 38–41
  exploitation of Native Americans by, 38–40
Franco, Francisco, 781, 783
Franco-Prussian War (1870), 654
Frankfurter, Felix, 690, 764
Franklin, Benjamin (1706–1790), 111, 125,
    171, 186
  Albany Plan (Plan of Union) and, 119
  Constitution and, 207, 211
  as diplomat, 179, 183, 207
  in England, 137, 143, 147
  Enlightenment and, 113–114, 193
  George III and, 170
  pre-Revolutionary views of, 147–148,
    150–151
  as scientist, 297
  on slavery, 113
  on work ethic, 312, 317
Franklin Institute, 297
Franz Ferdinand, Archduke of Austria,
    assassination of (1914), 663
fraternalism, 525
Fredericksburg, Virginia, 420, 430
Free African Society, 274
free blacks, 86, 272–275
  abolitionism and, 272, 274–275, 367
  accomplishments of, 272, 274–275
  black churches and, 268, 274, 460
  in Charleston, 274–275
  Dred Scott and, 406
  education of, 461(*i*)
  Fugitive Slave Acts and, 399, 400
  labor of, 304(*i*), 445, 448(*i*)
  Patriot cause and, 189
  prejudice against, 268
  Reconstruction and, 443, 445–446, 458
  sharecropping and, 462–464
  as tenant farmers, 272
  terrorism against, 465–467
  voting rights for, 259–260, 272, 371, 456
  women, 462
Freed, Alan, 857
Freedman's Savings and Trust Company, 469
Freedmen's Bureau, 445–446, 448, 449, 450,
    458, 461

Freedom of Information Act, 921
freedom of speech, 224, 891–892. *See also* First
    Amendment
  limits on, 682–683
Freedom Rides, 869, 974
Freedom's Journal, 367
Freedom Summer (1964), 873–874, 892, 902
freehold society
  in Middle Atlantic colonies, 105, 105(*m*),
    117, 125
  in New England, 100–104
  property rights and, 100–104, 105(*m*),
    124–125
  republicanism and, 156
Freeman, Elizabeth, 189(*i*)
Freemasonry, Order of, 344
Freeport Doctrine (Douglas), 408
Free Presbyterian Church, 316
free silver, 590–593, 622
Free-Soil Party, 395–396, 398
  "Bleeding Kansas" and, 403
  elections and, 401
  political realignment and, 405(*m*)
  Republican Party and, 402
Free Speech Movement (FSM), 891–892
Frelinghuysen, Theodore Jacob, 114
Frémont, John C., 392, 393, 394(*m*), 405, 417
French and Indian War, 119–122, 172. *See also*
    Seven Years' War
French colonization, 6, 12, 14, 99, 119–122,
    120(*m*), 132–133, 135, 136
  British Empire and, 96
  Christianization and, 41, 43, 63, 65
  fur trade and, 41–44
  Iroquois and, 63, 65
  in Louisiana, 13, 41
  in West Indies, 71, 96, 179, 180, 182,
    219, 220
French Revolution
  division of Americans and, 219–221
  ideological impact of, 220, 223(*i*)
Freudian psychology, 716
Frick, Henry Clay, 530, 563
Friedan, Betty, 856, 857, 901–902
frontier
  concept of, 636
  end of, 476, 502
  mythic, 480, 481, 502(*i*)
Frost, Robert, 716
Fuel Administration, 675

Fugitive Slave Acts
  of 1793, 371
  of 1850, 398
  resistance to, 399–400
Fulani Indians, 22(i)
Fulbright, J. William, 880, 890, 908
Fuller, Margaret (1810–1850), 356, 357
Fulton, Robert, 305
Fundamental Constitutions (Carolina; 1669), 69
fur trade, 37, 38, 119
  British, 388
  Dutch, 43–44, 63, 65
  environmental effects of, 65
  French, 41–43
  Indian wars and, 41–43, 63–65
  inland peoples and, 63–65
F.W. Woolworth Company, 513

Gadsden, James, 401
Gagarin, Yuri, 868
Gage, Thomas, 125, 138, 141, 149, 155, 158
gag rule, 372
Gallatin, Albert, 238, 244, 248
Galloway, Joseph, 154
Gallup polls. See opinion polls
Gama, Vasco da, 23
Gandhi, Indira, assassination of, 952
Gandhi, Mahatma, 806
gang-labor system, 352, 383, 448, 449, 461, 464
Garfield, James A. (1831–1881), 567
  assassination of (1881), 567
Garland, Hamlin, 484, 549
Garrison, William Lloyd (1805–1879), 352,
     368–370, 369(i)
  Free-Soil Party and, 395
Garsed, Richard, 297
Garvey, Amy Jacques, 718
Garvey, Marcus, 718, 895
Gary, Elbert H., 617
Gaspée (ship), 151
Gassaway, Robert, 166
Gates, Bill, 961
Gates, Horatio, 174(m), 176, 180
gay marriage, 930, 933, 966
gay rights, 900, 903, 928, 930, 931, 933. See also
     homosexuals
  in military, 968
  opposition to, 937, 965
  in sports, 934
Gay Task Force, National, 933

Gaza Strip, 923, 972
Gazette of the United States, 224
Gellhorn, Martha, 775
gender
  Great Depression and, 727
  stereotypes and, 857
  wages and, 519–521, 520(i), 521, 580,
     933, 958
gender roles, 548, 901. See also women
  in Africa, 80
  conservative view of, 938
  employment and, 728–732
  feminism and, 931–932
  of free blacks, 449
  Great Depression and, 728–732
  Hispanic, 496–497
  in military, 788–789
  Mormons and, 366(i)
  Native American, 12–14, 231–232, 478
  New Deal and, 768, 776–777
  in 1950s, 856–857
  reform and, 352, 353
  separate spheres of, 374
  sex-typing and, 519–521, 520(i)
  on television, 854
  traditional, 817(i)
  transcendentalism and, 356
  utopian communalism and, 358, 360,
     361, 362
  in the West, 496–497
  wives and, 546–547
  women's rights and, 374, 376
General Union for Promoting the Observance
     of the Christian Sabbath, 315
Geneva, Switzerland, 30, 31
Geneva Accords (1954), 882
Geneva Conventions, Abu Ghraib and, 977
Genius of Universal Emancipation (newspaper),
     369
Gentle Measures in the Management and
     Training of the Young (Abbott), 549
gentlemen's agreements, 617
gentry class, 69, 87–88. See also elite
  defined, 34
George, David Lloyd, 684, 687
George, Henry, 499
George I, king of England (r. 1714–1727),
     92, 94(i)
George II, king of England (r. 1727–1760),
     92, 94(i)

George III, king of England (r. 1760–1820), 167, 168(i), 170, 179, 188, 253
  Declaration of Independence and, 171
  policies of, 132, 138, 143–145, 151–152
  rebellion against, 138
  repeal of Stamp Act and, 168
Georgia
  antiabolitionism in, 372
  as colony, 94–95, 153
  economy of, 219
  evangelicals in, 118
  freed slaves in, 446
  Ku Klux Klan in, 465
  migrants from, 386
  Native Americans and, 337, 339
  plantations in, 233
  Reconstruction and, 456, 458
  secession and, 398, 413, 414(m)
  sharecropping in, 463(m)
  Sherman's march through, 437
  slavery in, 94, 118, 268, 269(m), 276(m), 383
  voter registration in, 875(m)
  war with Spain and, 94–95
Germain, George, 175
German Americans, in WWII, 796
German Democratic Republic (East Germany), 818, 821
  Berlin Wall and, 867
German immigrants, 126, 309, 314, 349, 402, 497, 517, 517(f), 551
  in Civil War, 416, 417
  in colonial America, 104–106
  cultural conflict and, 317, 319
  draft and, 424
  as Loyalists, 157
  in Maryland, 110(i)
  in Pennsylvania, 70, 106–109, 157
  Pietism and, 114
  political activism of, 527, 532, 575, 575(f)
  unionism of, 526
Germantown, Pennsylvania, 70
Germany, 30, 95. See also Berlin; German Democratic Republic
  after WWI, 684
  anti-Semitism in, 790
  automobile industry in, 924
  cartels in, 625
  colonies of, 781
  declaration of war on U.S. by, 787
  defeat of, 817

  division of, 806
  economic growth of, 957, 958
  Japan and, 782
  Mexico and, 668
  Nazis in, 781–782
  Soviet Union and, 783, 785
  Spanish civil war and, 782
  war reparations of, 685, 699, 781, 806
  welfare system in, 761
  in WWI, 663–664
  in WWII, 780, 806
  zones of occupation in, 818, 821
Germany, Federal Republic of (West Germany), 818, 821
  Berlin Wall and, 867
  economy of, 924, 925
  in NATO, 819(m)
Geronimo, Chief, 487
Gettysburg, battle of (1863), 412, 424, 430–431, 431(m), 434
Ghent, Treaty of (1814), 244
ghettoes, 551(i), 552, 556, 557. See also cities
ghost dance, 490
Gibbons, Thomas, 252
Gibbons v. Ogden (1824), 252, 305
GI Bill of Rights (Servicemen's Readjustment Act; 1944), 793, 831, 851, 901
Gibraltar, 75, 180, 184
Gibson, Charles Dana, 549
Gibson girl, 549
Giddings, Joshua, 393
Gilbert, Humphrey, 44
Gilbert Islands, 804(m)
Gilded Age (late 19th century), 562–563, 598, 604, 629–632
The Gilded Age (Twain and Warner), 562
Giles, John, 118
Gilman, Charlotte Perkins, 602
Gingrich, Newt, 969, 969(i)
Ginsberg, Allen, 860, 893
Ginsburg, Ruth Bader, 968
glasnost, 953
Glass, Carter, 623
Glass-Steagall Banking Act (1932), 744–745, 756
Gleason, Jackie, 854
Glenn, John, 868
globalization, 927, 946, 958–961. See also economy: international
  foreign policy and, 634, 646
  Internet and, 962

global warming, 960
Glorious Revolution (1688), 72–74, 91, 93,
    96, 143
Godey's Lady's Book, 375
Godkin, Edwin L., 542, 543, 577
Godwyn, Morgan, 68
gold
    Spanish conquests and, 24, 28, 33, 38, 39*(m)*
    trade in, 20, 21*(m)*
    Virginia company and, 45
gold mining, 488, 491–495, 492*(m),* 497–498
gold rush (California; 1849–1857), 396, 397*(i),*
    491–495, 492*(m),* 497–498
gold standard, 592–593, 726, 757
Goldwater, Barry, 874
Goliad, Texas, 386, 387*(m)*
Gompers, Samuel, 527–528, 528*(i),* 610, 645
Gone with the Wind (Mitchell), 735
González, Henry, 897
The Good Earth (Buck), 735
Good Housekeeping (magazine), 546
Goodman, Benny, 735
Good Neighbor Policy, 782
Gorbachev, Mikhail, 952–953
Gore, Albert (Al), Jr., 967, 969*(i),* 973–975
Gorges, Ferdinando, 44
Gough, John (1817–1886), 318
Gould, Jay, 510, 527
Graham, Billy, 855, 937
Graham, Isabella, 315
grain. *See also* corn; Price Revolution; rice;
    wheat
    exports of, 103–104, 110, 308
    production of, 105–106, 485–486
    transportation for, 304–309
Gramm-Rudman Act (1985), 951
Grand Alliance, 818
Grand Canyon, 38
Grange, Red, 707
Granger movement, 588
Grant, Ulysses S. (1822–1885), 418
    1868 elections and, 455–456
    Ku Klux Klan Act (1871) and, 465
    Lee's surrender and, 440
    at Petersburg, 436
    as president (1869–1877), 467, 468,
        575–576, 630
    Reconstruction and, 454, 460, 469
    Richmond campaign (1864) and, 435*(m)*
    scorched earth campaign of, 435

Sherman and, 439
Shiloh and, 421, 423
as Union Army commander, 433–435
Vicksburg campaign of, 430
in the West, 421, 430, 434
The Grapes of Wrath (Steinbeck), 739*(i),* 740
Grasso, Ella T., 930
Grateful Dead, 893
Great American Desert, 479, 482. *See also* Great
    Plains
Great Atlantic and Pacific Tea Company
    (A & P), 513
Great Awakening, 112–118, 141, 277, 281, 282.
    See also evangelicalism; revivalism; Second
    Great Awakening
    Edwards and, 114
    George Whitefield and, 114–116
    political aspects of, 116–117
    religious fervor of, 114–117
Great Britain, 635. *See also* British Empire;
    England; English colonization
    American Civil War and, 432
    American empire of (1713), 76*(m)*
    appeasement of Hitler (1938) by, 782, 783,
        818
    boundaries of western lands and, 243*(m),*
        244, 245*(m)*
    civil war in, 56, 69, 72–73
    colonial trade of, 68
    Confederacy and, 426, 432
    control of trade by, 89*(m)*
    decolonization and, 829
    division of Germany and, 806
    France and, 74
    Greece and, 820
    Iraq war and, 977
    Marshall Plan and, 822
    Mexico and, 391
    Middle East oil and, 828
    in NATO, 821
    19th century immigration from, 318–319, 497
    nuclear test ban treaties and, 867
    Oregon and, 388, 393
    Palestine and, 830
    slave trade and, 77
    Spain and, 74, 86
    Spanish civil war and, 783
    Suez Canal and, 830
    territorial disputes with, 237
    U.S. aid to, 784–785

Great Britain (*cont.*)
  U.S. relations with, 647, 784
  War of Austrian Succession and, 95
  war on terrorism and, 977
  Washington Naval Arms Conference and, 701
  welfare system in, 761
  West Indian trade and, 88
  WWI and, 663, 699
  WWII role of, 799, 806
Great Deflation (late nineteenth century), 506
Great Depression, 611, 723–751
  African Americans in, 735–737
  beginning of, 724–725
  causes of, 724–725
  debt and, 925
  discontent and, 745–746
  fiscal policy and, 745
  Harlem Renaissance and, 718
  Hoover and, 744–745
  immigration and, 711
  intellectual life and, 717
  1920s economy and, 697
  Prohibition and, 716
  Republican Party and, 720
  WWII and, 780, 781, 795
Greater East Asia Co-Prosperity Sphere, 785
The Great Gatsby (Fitzgerald), 716
Great Lakes, 11, 63, 184, 230, 244, 344, 507
  migration to, 302, 303(*m*)
  transportation to, 304–305, 306(*m*)
Great Migration, 676–678, 677(*m*)
Great Plains, 28, 386, 389
  aridity of, 477(*m*), 485
  buffalo extermination on, 480
  climate of, 477(*m*), 477–478, 482, 485
  drought on, 485, 490, 737–738
  ecosystem of, 477(*m*), 477–478, 485–486
  European emigration to, 484
  as Great American Desert, 479, 482
  homesteaders on, 482–486, 488
  as Indian country, 479, 486–490
  marketing of, 481, 482
  railroads and, 479–481, 486, 488, 511(*m*)
  ranching on, 480–482, 481(*i*), 486
  settlement of, 476–490
  sheep raising on, 482
  shelter on, 478, 485
  sod houses on, 485
  wildlife on, 477–478

Great Salt Lake, 485
Great Society, 873–877, 881, 912
  declining economy and, 917
  funding for, 877
  in 1970s, 936
  Nixon and, 916, 917
  Reagan and, 948
Great Strike of 1877, 505–506
Great War for Empire. *See* Seven Years' War
Greece, 19, 820, 822
Greeley, Horace, 361, 428, 468, 477, 479
greenbacks, 427, 591. *See also* currency
Greene, Nathanael, 182
greenhouse effect, 960
Greenleaf, Simon, 377
Green Party, 973
Greensboro, North Carolina, 869, 891
Greenville, Treaty of (1795), 229(*i*), 230, 231(*i*)
Grenada, 952
Grenville, George, 134–138, 135(*i*)
Gresham, Walter Q., 634
Grey Panthers, 900
Griffin, James B., 423
Griffith, Beatrice, 769
Grimes County, Texas, 586–587
Grimké, Angelina, 370, 372, 376, 377
Grimké, Sarah, 370, 372, 376, 377
Grimké, Thomas, 262
Griswold v. Connecticut (1965), 931
Gropper, William, 758(*i*)
gross domestic product (GDP), 632
  decline of, 925
  postwar, 851
  under Reagan, 949
  Roosevelt recession and, 764
  WWII and, 788
Grund, Francis, 292
Guadalupe Hidalgo, Treaty of (1848), 395
Guam, 640–642, 646, 803
Guantanamo Bay, Cuba, 644, 649, 650(*m*), 782
Guatemala, 7, 9, 630, 701, 828, 962
guerrilla warfare, 865
guilds, 20
Guinea Company, 33
Guiteau, Charles, 567
Gulf of Mexico, 11, 41
Gulf of Tonkin Resolution (1964), 909, 912
Gullah dialect, 84–85, 271

guns, 294
   Gatling machine, 487
   Remington rifles, 299
   repeating rifle, 487
   Rifle Clubs and, 467
   rifle-muskets, 426, 431
Guttridge, Molly, 185*(i)*
Guy Fawkes Day, 141
Guzman, Jacobo Arbenz, 828
Gypsies, Holocaust and, 782, 802

Haas, Philip, 327*(i)*
habeas corpus, meaning of, 424
Hague Peace Conference (1899), 655
Haiti, 24, 238, 630, 972
   economy of, 464
   slave revolt in, 267, 464
   U.S. military intervention in, 701
Haldeman, H. R., 920
Haldimand, General, 152
Haley, Bill, 858
Halifax, Lord, 121
Hall, Basil, 322
Hall, G. Stanley, 548
Hall, John H., 299
Hall, Prince, 367
Haller, Albrecht von, 37
Hamilton, Alexander (1755–1804)
   assumption plan of, 217
   banking system and, 336
   Constitution and, 252
   duel with Aaron Burr, 240
   The Federalist and, 212
   fiscal program of, 216–219
   Jefferson and, 217–219, 218*(i)*
   on national bank, 216–217
   at Philadelphia Convention, 208
   plan for Northern Confederacy and, 240
   pro-British foreign policy of, 221
   program of national mercantilism, 250
   on public credit, 216
   as secretary of the treasury, 216–218
Hamilton, Alice, 612–613
Hamilton Manufacturing Company, 313
Hammond, James, 266
Hammond, John Henry, 384
Hancock, John, 136, 142
Handsome Lake (Seneca chief), 230
Hanna, Mark, 593, 597
Hard, William, 599

Harding, Chester, 251*(i)*
Harding, Warren G. (1865–1923)
   corruption and, 693–694
   as president (1921–1923), 693
Hare Krishnas, 928
Harlan County, Kentucky, 746–747
Harlem, New York City, 552
   depression in, 736
   race riot in, 736
Harlem Renaissance, 717–718
Harper, Frances, 457
Harpers Ferry, Virginia, 299, 420, 426
   Brown's raid on (1859), 409
Harriman, Averell, 822
Harrington, Michael, 848, 860
Harris, Anna, 270
Harris, David, 438
Harris, Jim, 428
Harris, Katherine, 973
Harris, William, 62–63
Harrison, Benjamin (1833–1901)
   1892 elections and, 567–568, 568*(i)*, 594*(m)*
   as president (1889–1893), 574, 579*(i)*,
      588, 635
   on protective tariffs, 569
Harrison, William Henry (1773–1841), 241,
      242, 568*(i)*
   death of, 349
   1836 elections and, 344
   1840 elections and, 347–349, 348*(i)*
   as president (1841), 349
Harte, Bret, 500
Hartford, Connecticut, 56, 185, 244
   manufacturing in, 294
   transportation and, 308
Harvard College, 144
hat making, 249
Hatters' Union, 610
Hawaii, 283*(m)*
   annexation of, 640, 646
   Chinese immigration to, 497
   Japanese internment and, 797
   strategic importance of, 635
   sugarcane in, 630–631, 631*(i)*
   treaties with, 630–631
Hawikuh Indians, 39
Hawley-Smoot Tariff (1930), 699, 726
Hawthorne, Nathaniel, 304, 357, 358
Hay, John, 650
Hayden, Tom, 891

Hayes, Rutherford B. (1822–1893)
    1876 elections and, 567
    as president (1877–1881), 469, 470
    Strike of 1877 and, 505
Haymarket affair, 527–528
Hay-Pauncefote Agreement (1901), 647
A Hazard of New Fortunes (Howells), 563
Head Start, 875
Health, Education, and Welfare, Department of
        (HEW), 839
health care
    in 1950s, 855
    attempts to reform, 968
    for elderly, 863
    JFK and, 863
    1970s fitness craze and, 928
    socialized, 834
health insurance, 611
    and Fair Deal, 834
    Great Society and, 876
    JFK and, 868, 873
    national, 761, 834, 968
    Social Security and, 776
    welfare capitalism and, 699
Hearst, William Randolph, 561, 637
Heaton, Hannah, 101–102, 115
hegemony, 816
Helms, Jesse, 966
Helper, Hinton, 414
Hemingway, Ernest, 716
Henderson, Charles, 612
Hendrix, Jimi, 893, 894(*i*)
Henrietta Maria, queen of England
        (r. 1625–1649), 47
Henry, Patrick (1736–1799), 138–139, 139(*i*),
        150, 157, 167, 208
    church taxes and, 193
    on Hamilton's financial program, 216
    on ratification of Constitution, 213, 221
Henry, prince of Portugal (r. 1394–1460), 20
Henry VIII, king of England
        (r. 1509–1547), 31
Hepburn Railway Act (1906), 618
heresy, 18, 30, 58
Hernandes, Harriet, 466
Hersh, Seymour, 909
Herzegovina, 663, 972
Hess, Jean, 648
HEW. *See* Health, Education, and Welfare,
        Department of

Hickok, Lorena, 775
Hicks, Clarence J., 611
Higginson, Francis, 37
Higginson, Thomas Wentworth, 432–433
Higher Education Act (1965), 876
Highway Act, National Interstate and Defense
        (1956), 853, 853(*m*)
Highway Beautification Act (1965), 876
highways
    automobile and, 703
    interstate, 852–853, 853(*m*)
    move to suburbs and, 851
    1950s culture and, 854
    postwar growth of, 852–853, 853(*m*)
    Route 66, 738(*m*)
Hill, Anita, 951
Hill, James J., 510
Hillsborough, Lord, 148–150
Hilton, James, 735
hippies, 892–893. *See also* counterculture
Hirabayashi v. United States (1943), 798
Hiroshima, 805(*m*), 808, 808(*i*), 823
Hispanics. *See* Latinos
Hispaniola, 24, 25, 27
Hiss, Alger, 836, 837
"The History of the Standard Oil Company"
        (Tarbell), 600(*i*)
Hitler, Adolph, 781–782, 802, 818
HIV. *See* AIDS
Hoar, George F., 645
Ho Chi Minh, 685, 881, 882, 911
Hoff, John, 247
Hoffman, Abbie, 905
hog production, 270, 293–294, 294(*i*), 302, 305
Hohokam culture, 11
Holiday Inn, 854
Holland. *See* Dutch colonization
Holland Land Company, 235
Holloway, Houston H., 442
Holly, Buddy, 858
Hollywood, 942. *See also* Los Angeles,
        California; movies
Hollywood Ten, 835
Holmes, Isaac, 271
Holmes, Oliver Wendell, Jr., 683
Holocaust, 780, 782, 802
Holy Roman Empire, 30
Home Insurance Building, 539
Homeland Security, Office of, 979
homelessness (1990s), 951, 956

Home Owners Loan Corporation, 756
Homestead Act (1862), 426–427,
    482–484, 488
homesteaders, 482–486
Homestead steel strike (1892), 476, 530
homosexuals, 975. *See also* gay rights; lesbians
    cultural dissent and, 858–859
    gay liberation movement and, 933
    Holocaust and, 782, 802
    marriages of, 930, 933, 966
    in military, 788
    1950s culture and, 857
    terms for, 900
    urban culture and, 560
    violence against, 966
Honduras, 701
The Honeymooners (TV program), 854
Hong Kong, 803, 804(*m*), 805(*m*)
Hood, John B., 436, 438(*m*)
Hooker, Joseph ("Fighting Joe"), 420, 430
Hooker, Thomas, 56
Hoole, Axalla John, 382, 404
Hoover, Herbert (1874–1964), 675
    at Department of Commerce, 693
    Great Depression and, 725, 744–745, 752
    New Deal and, 752–753
    as president (1929–1933), 720, 744–745
    Roosevelt recession and, 764
Hoovervilles, 747(*i*)
Hopewell Indians, 10–11
Hopi Indians, 11
Hopkins, Harry, 757, 762
Hopkins, Samuel, 282
horsecar, 537, 538(*i*)
horses, 27–28, 478
Horseshoe Bend, battle of (1814), 242,
    243(*m*)
House, Edward, 667
House Committee on Un-American Activities
    (HUAC), 835–836
household production
    in colonial America, 100, 104, 148
    outwork and, 106, 148, 293, 300
Houseman, John, 775
House of Burgesses, Virginia, 46–47, 51–53
House of Commons, England, 34, 137–138, 144
House of Lords, England, 34
House of Representatives, U.S.
    abolitionism and, 372
    Democratic control of, 949

impeachment and, 454
    Know-Nothing Party in, 402
    Republican Party and, 409, 968, 970, 979
    Wilmot Proviso and, 395
housing
    in cities, 862
    discrimination in, 852
    gay rights and, 933
    inflation and, 925
    lack of, 951, 956
    LBJ and, 877
    legislation on, 764, 834
    postwar boom in, 849, 851
    public, 875
    states and, 951
    wartime migration and, 795–796
Housing and Urban Development, Department
    of (HUD), 968
housing codes, 540
Houston, Sam, 387
Howard, Oliver O., 446
Howe, Frederic, 592
Howe, Julia Ward, 457
Howe, Marie Jenny, 602
Howe, William, 172–175
Howells, William Dean, 563
"Howl" (Ginsberg), 860
HUAC. *See* House Committee on Un-
    American Activities
Hübner, Joseph Alexander von, 493(*i*)
HUD. *See* Housing and Urban Development,
    Department of
Hudson, Henry, 43
Hudson, Rock, 967
Hudson Bay, 75
Hudson River, 41, 63, 172–173, 176, 252
    Erie Canal and, 235
    manors on, 105, 105(*i*), 234
Hudson River Valley
    Dutch in, 104–105, 124–125
    land conflicts in, 124–125, 126(*m*)
    loyalists in, 157
    settlement of, 105(*m*)
Hudson's Bay Company, 388
Huerta, Victoriano, 653
Hughes, Charles Evans, 668
Hughes, Langston, 716, 717, 718, 735
Huguenots, 31, 41, 108–109
Hull, Cordell, 782
Hull House, 601, 612

human rights
    Carter and, 940
    Fair Deal and, 833–834
Human Rights, Office of, 940
human sacrifice, 10, 12
Hume, David, 143
Humphrey, Hubert H., 833, 874
    1968 elections and, 906–907, 907(m)
Hundred Days (New Deal), 754–757
Hungarian immigrants, 516, 517, 517(f), 518(i)
Hungary, 684, 821, 827, 830
hunter-gatherers, 7
Huntington, Susan, 101
Huron Indians, 41–43, 63, 65
Hurston, Zora Neale, 717, 775
Hus, Jan, 30
Hussein, King of Jordan, 831
Hussein, Saddam, 954, 955, 975, 977
Hutcheson, Francis, 143
Hutchinson, Anne, 55–56
Hutchinson, Thomas, 139, 151–152, 155
hydrogen bomb, 823, 828. *See also* nuclear
    weapons

IBM Corporation, 961
Icaria, Texas, 359(m)
Ice Age, 7, 8(m)
Iceland, in NATO, 821
Ickes, Harold, 754, 757, 762(m), 771
Idaho
    gold in, 493(i)
    Japanese internment in, 797
    mining in, 493(i), 499, 532–533
idealism, 865
    progressive, 599
Illinois, 230. *See also* Chicago
    1960 elections and, 864
    Civil War and, 418
    ERA and, 932(m)
    internal migration to, 795
    Lincoln and, 407–408
    migration to, 301, 303(m)
    Mormons and, 363, 364(m), 365
    slaves in, 405
    voting rights in, 258, 259(m), 322
Illinois Indians, 65
immigrants, 222. *See also* Chinese immigrants;
    German immigrants; Irish immigrants;
    migration
    Asian, 742–743, 876, 962

    in British America, 102, 104–105
    Canadian, 301
    as cheap labor, 519
    in cities, 535, 537, 551(i), 551–552, 553(i),
        554(i), 556, 962
    class distinctions and, 309–310, 319–320
    cultural conflict and, 707
    democracy and, 417
    Democratic Party and, 574–576, 575(f),
        749, 777
    deportation of, 740–741, 861
    discrimination against, 719, 876
    draft and, 424
    earliest, 7, 8(m)
    Eastern European, 876
    English, 31, 33, 34, 37–38, 44–59,
        318–319, 497
    European, 99–103, 106, 108, 516–517,
        517(f), 519, 551(i), 551–552, 553(i),
        554(i), 556
    experience of, 710
    Filipino, 740, 860
    French Canadian, 301
    hostility to, 964
    Hungarian, 516, 517, 517(f), 518(i)
    illegal, 712(i)
    Italian, 517, 517(f), 519, 551(i), 552, 556
    Japanese, 499–500, 709–710, 860
    Jewish, 709, 964
    Know-Nothing Party and, 402
    Korean, 860, 962, 964
    Latino, 860–861, 962–965
    Mexican, 495–497, 500, 709–711, 712(i),
        740–742, 962
    movies and, 704
    New Deal and, 769
    newspapers and, 552
    from New York City, 774(i)
    in New York City, 537
    19th century, 318–319, 495–500
    Norwegian, 484
    Patriot Act and, 979
    politics and, 719
    poverty of, 310, 313–314, 319–320
    Puerto Rican, 861
    Puritan, 53–61
    Red Scare and, 709
    Scandinavian, 517, 517(f)
    South American, 709–711, 876
    Southeast Asian, 860, 962

U.S. fear of anarchy and, 688–690
voting rights and, 456
from Western Hemisphere, 709
immigration
    to California, 710, 962, 964
    changing demographics and, 962–965
    Democratic Party and, 694
    to Florida, 962
    Great Depression and, 711
    to Hawaii, 497
    legislation on, 876
    in 1920s, 697
    in 1950s, 857, 860–861
    in 1990s, 956, 979
    opposition to, 964
    rates of, 711(f)
    restrictions on, 694, 709, 711, 860, 876
Immigration Act (1965), 876
Immigration and Naturalization Service (INS),
    964
immigration laws, 222, 224, 237, 238
    LBJ and, 876
    in 1950s, 860
    quota system in, 860, 876
impeachment, 454
    Clinton, 970–971
    Johnson, 971
    Nixon, 920
imperialism, U.S., 628, 642–644
    opposition to, 644–645, 648–649
imports, 110, 123, 295. See also boycotts;
    exports; nonimportation; trade
impoundment, 917
impressment, 267. See also draft, military
Inca civilization, 27
incorporation, 509
indentured servants, 34, 109, 134, 168, 175,
    210, 292
    in Chesapeake, 50–53
    children sold as, 102
    laws against, 497
    vs. slavery, 464
Independence, Missouri, 390
Independent Order of Good Templars, 375
Independent Treasury Act (1840), 347
India, 18, 23, 426
    as British colony, 121, 152
    decolonization in, 866(m)
    globalization and, 960
    immigrants from, 962

indentured servants from, 464
Protestant mission in, 283(m)
U.S. civil rights and, 839
WWII and, 803, 806
Indiana, 230
    Ku Klux Klan in, 712
    migration to, 234, 301, 303(m)
    revivals in, 317
    Shakers in, 284
    voting rights in, 258, 259(m), 322
Indian Affairs, Federal Bureau of, 862, 898, 899
Indian Affairs, Office of, 486, 487, 489
Indian Ocean, 23
Indian Removal Act (1830), 337, 339(i)
Indian Reorganization Act (1934), 771
Indian reservations. See Native Americans:
    reservation system and
Indian Rights Association, 489
Indian Self-Determination Act (1974), 933
indigo, 124, 269(m)
individualism, 353–358, 616–617
    big business and, 697–698
    Great Depression and, 728, 745
    ideology of, 571–572
    mass production and, 698
    meaning of, 353
    Mormons and, 363, 366
    in movies, 733
    1928 elections and, 719
    Prohibition and, 715
    technology and, 707
    transcendentalism and, 353–355
    utopian communalism and, 357–358, 361
Indochina, 827. See also Cambodia; Vietnam
    France in, 881–882
    Japanese invasion of, 785
Indonesia, 18, 23
industrialization, 426. See also factory system;
    manufacturing; mills
    accumulation of wealth and, 573
    artisans and, 297, 299–301, 319
    Civil War and, 434
    environmental pollution and, 540
    immigrant labor and, 516–517, 517(f),
        518(i), 519
    integrated systems within, 512, 513, 514
    intellectual life and, 716
    in late 19th century, 476, 485(i), 505–514,
        509(i), 536–542
    market economy and, 317

industrialization (*cont.*)
  middle class and, 544, 546
  mining and, 494–495
  in New South, 515, 516(*m*)
  1928 elections and, 719
  in the North, 536–542
  post-WWII, 816
  Republican Party and, 402
  reversal of, 925–926, 927
  skills for, 515, 517
  traditional values and, 707
  transcendentalism and, 355, 358
  unemployment and, 301, 309, 319
  urbanization and, 308–309, 536–542
  U.S. dominance and, 944
  voting patterns and, 719
  working conditions and, 353
Industrial Revolution, 172, 349
  in America, 292–301
  in England, 123, 247, 292
  labor for, 293, 295–298, 296(*i*)
  political parties and, 324
  social structure and, 292–293, 309–314, 312(*i*)
  U.S. Patent Office and, 297
  Whig policy and, 342
industrial unionism, 766. *See also* labor unions
Industrial Workers of the World (IWW;
      Wobblies), 533, 683, 689
industry. *See also* industrialization
  decline of, 925–926, 927
  development of, 616–617, 852
  employment in, 851
  gender roles in, 731–732
  Great Depression and, 724–725, 749
  growth of, 629
  interstate highways and, 853(*m*)
  labor unions and, 766–767
  Mexican Americans in, 741–742
  New Deal and, 756
  new techniques in, 696
  postwar, 821, 851, 852
  product standardization in, 693
  wage and price controls in, 693
inflation, 34, 831, 832
  during American Revolution, 186–187
  in Confederacy, 427–428
  elections and, 970
  energy crisis and, 923
  excess of currency and, 177–178, 187
  federal goverment and, 915

  housing and, 925
  in 1920s, 696
  in 1970s, 939, 940
  oil crisis and, 923
  postwar, 851
  Reagan and, 948–949
  Roosevelt recession and, 764
  Vietnam War and, 886, 891, 910, 912
  in wartime, 676
  WWII and, 790
The Influence of Seapower upon History
      (Mahan), 634
influenza, 27
  epidemic (1918–1919), 670, 673(*i*)
Ingersoll, Jared, 140
inheritance, 102–103, 310
  marriage and, 102, 260–262
  primogeniture and, 263
  women's rights to, 260–261
In His Steps (Sheldon), 559
inland Indians. *See* Native Americans: inland
Inquisition, 24
In Re Jacobs (1885), 573
installment plans, 702. *See also* credit
Institutes of the Christian Religion (Calvin), 30
Inter-American Treaty of Reciprocal Assistance
      (Rio Treaty; 1947), 829(*m*)
interest rates, 980
Internal Revenue Service (IRS), 919. *See also*
      taxation
International Bank for Reconstruction and
      Development (World Bank), 850
internationalism, 781, 793. *See also*
      globalization; isolationism
  economic, 816, 851
International Labor Defense (ILD), 737(*i*)
International Monetary Fund (IMF), 850
international relations. *See also under*
      individual countries
  Cold War, 817–831, 829(*m*)
  desegregation and, 841–842
  economic, 699, 701
  JFK, 873
  overseas bases and, 643
  Truman and, 818
  U.S. civil rights and, 839–840
  U.S. dominance in, 646–649, 670, 690
  Vietnam War and, 910, 911
International Telephone and Telegraph
      Corporation, 849

Internet, 961–962
  economy and, 958
Interstate Commerce Commission (ICC), 617–618
  segregation and, 869
Interstate Highway Act (1956), 839
Intolerable Acts (1774), 153
Inuit Indians, 7
investment banks, 510
Iowa, 302, 303(m)
Iran, 19, 820, 976
  British oil in, 828
  modernization in, 939
  oil production in, 922, 941
  revolution in, 924, 940
  right-wing regime in, 828
  shah of, 939, 941
Iran-Contra affair, 949, 952
Iranian hostage crisis, 941–944
  1980 elections and, 942, 943–944
  Reagan and, 948
Iraq
  interim government in, 977
  invasion of Kuwait by, 954, 955
  oil production in, 922
  Persian Gulf War and (1990–1991), 911,
    954, 956(m)
  preemptive strike against, 977
  UN sanctions against, 975, 976–977
  U.S. occupation of, 977(i), 980
  violence in, 977(i)
Iraq War (2003–), 977–978
  casualties in, 977(i)
Ireland, 155, 972
  famine in, 319, 516
Ireland, John, 557
Irish immigrants, 110, 222, 349. See also
    Scots-Irish
  cultural conflict and, 319–320
  Democratic Party and, 575–576, 575(f)
  draft and, 424
  1852 elections and, 402
  19th century, 301, 303, 304, 304(i), 309, 314,
    317, 319–320, 497, 516–517, 517(f), 551,
    556, 557
Irish Test Act (1704), 110
iron industry, 299, 307, 342
  coal in, 508(m)
  in New South, 516(m)
  steel and, 507, 508(m)
  tariffs on, 295, 328

Iroquois Indians, 7, 19, 119, 121, 229
  adopted captives of, 63, 65
  "covenant chain" of military alliances, 75
  Five Nations of, 14, 41, 63
  French and, 63, 65, 75
  fur trade wars of, 41–44, 63, 65
  Six Nations of, 75, 172, 173(i), 176
irrigation, 9, 11, 83, 485, 497, 501–502
Irving, Washington, 265
Isabel, queen of Spain (r. 1474–1516), 24
Islam, 24, 85
  African American, 895
  vs. Christianity, 18, 20
  fundamentalist, 939, 941, 943–944, 946, 952,
    955, 956(m), 972, 978
  militant, 946
isolationism, 629, 632, 655
  opposition to, 784–785
  post-WWI, 701–702
  Republican Party and, 793
  retreat from, 783–785
  WWII and, 781, 782–785
Israel
  Camp David accords and, 941, 942(i)
  in international politics, 923
  in Lebanon, 952
  oil embargo and, 923
  Palestinians and, 830, 956(m), 972, 975, 978
  RFK and, 905
  Suez crisis and, 830
  West Bank and, 978
Issei (first-generation Japanese Americans),
    797
Istanbul, Turkey, attacks on British embassy in,
    977–978
Isthmus of Darien (Panama), 25
Italian Americans, in WWII, 796
Italian Revolution (1848), 356
Italy, 19, 356, 663
  fall of, 800–801
  immigration from, 517, 517(f), 519, 551(i),
    552, 556
  invasion of Ethiopia by, 781
  in NATO, 821
  Spanish civil war and, 782, 783
  Washington Naval Arms Conference
    and, 701
  WWII and, 781, 782, 787, 800(m)
Iwo Jima, 805, 805(m), 806
IWW. See Industrial Workers of the World

Jackson, Andrew (1829–1836)
  abolitionism and, 372
  American System and, 329–330, 332–334,
    336, 340–342
  antimonopoly policies of, 329, 341
  Democratic Party and, 324, 347
  1824 elections and, 318(m), 325–326
  1828 elections and, 328–330
  freemasonry and, 344
  inauguration of, 331
  Indian Removal Act of, 337, 340(m)
  as military commander, 242, 243(m), 244
  Native Americans and, 329, 336–340
  nullification and, 333–334, 343, 415
  as president (1829–1837), 331–342, 332 (i),
    335(i), 343(i), 387
  Second Bank and, 334–336
  on states' rights, 329, 333–334, 341
  Supreme Court and, 341
Jackson, Helen Hunt, 489, 500
Jackson, Jesse, 950
Jackson, Patrick Tracy, 295
Jackson, Rebecca Cox, 360
Jackson, Thomas J. ("Stonewall"), 419(m), 420
Jacksonian Democrats, 324
Jackson State College, killing at, 908
Jacobins, 220
Jamaica, 77
James, duke of York, 69
James, Henry, 563
James, William, 598–599, 645–646
James I, king of England (r. 1603–1625), 44, 54
James II, king of England (r. 1685–1688), 72,
    73, 138
James River, 46, 49(i), 182
Jamestown, 46, 53
Japan, 24, 401, 633–634
  automobile industry in, 924
  containment of, 701
  defeat of, 817
  economy of, 924, 925, 944, 957, 958
  Germany and, 782
  globalization and, 959
  invasion of China by, 781, 785
  invasion of Manchuria by, 781
  oil embargo vs., 923
  Pearl Harbor and, 785–787
  postwar constitution of, 823
  vs. postwar U.S., 849
  and racial equality, 684
  and Russia, 651–652
  Soviet Union and, 799
  surrender of, 810
  U.S. occupation of, 823
  U.S. relations with, 650–652, 742
  Washington Naval Arms Conference and, 701
  WWII and, 778, 780, 781, 802–806, 808–810
Japanese Americans
  Great Depression and, 742
  internment of, 780, 796–798, 798(m)
  Issei (first-generation), 797
  Nisei (second-generation), 797
Jay, John (1745–1829), 323
  The Federalist and, 212
Jay's Treaty (1795), 230
jazz, 705, 706(i), 717, 859
Jazz Age (1920s), 705, 723
The Jazz Singer (film), 704
Jefferson, Thomas (1743–1826), 86, 157
  agrarian vision of, 218–219
  Bill for Establishing Religious Freedom
    (1786), 193
  Constitution and, 239
  death of, 257
  Declaration of Independence and, 171–172,
    184
  as diplomat, 208
  on education, 264–265
  Embargo act and, 241
  Enlightenment and, 143
  Hamilton and, 217–219, 218(i), 224
  on John Q. Adams, 328
  on manufacturing, 219, 297
  on Missouri crisis, 277
  Mormons and, 365
  Northwest Ordinance and, 204
  as president (1801–1809), 237–240
  primacy of statute law and, 252
  republicanism and, 218–219, 282, 284
  Revolution of 1800 and, 237
  slavery and, 190, 219, 367
  states' rights and, 224, 333, 335
  the West and, 239–240
Jefferson Airplane, 893
Jeffords, Jim, 978
Jenkins' Ear, War of (1740), 95
Jenney, William, 539
Jericho, Israel, 972
Jerome, Chauncey, 292
Jesuits, 43, 65

Jewish Daily Forward, 552
　bintel brief (bundle of letters) of, 554(*i*)
Jews, 24, 108(*m*)
　culture of, 557
　Democratic Party and, 833
　discrimination against, 719, 760, 782, 792, 852
　Holocaust and, 802
　immigration of, 552, 553(*i*), 554(*i*), 556,
　　557, 964
　immigration restrictions and, 709
　Ku Klux Klan and, 712
　on Lower East Side, New York City, 553(*i*)
　national home for, 684
　Nazi view of, 782
　1936 elections and, 763
　in 1950s, 855
　religious practices of, 557
　U.S. civil rights and, 839
　voting rights and, 974
　Yiddish theater and, 552
Jiang Jieshi (Chiang Kai-shek), 823
jihad, 955
Jim Crow laws, 585–587, 605, 695, 897
jingoism, 637
Job Corps, 875
Joffre, Joseph, 669
Johnson, Andrew (1808–1875), 442
　campaigning by, 451
　vs. Congress, 450–452
　Fourteenth Amendment and, 450–451
　impeachment of, 454, 971
　as Lincoln's running mate, 436
　as president (1865–1869), 444–446
　Reconstruction plan of, 444(*i*), 444–446,
　　450–451, 461
　veto of civil rights bill by, 450
　veto of Reconstruction Act by, 454
Johnson, Earvin "Magic", 967
Johnson, Gabriel, 92–93
Johnson, Hiram W., 604, 687
Johnson, Lady Bird, 876
Johnson, Lyndon B. (1908–1973), 863, 872
　affirmative action and, 931
　civil rights movement and, 874
　credibility gap of, 921, 922
　Democratic coalition of, 877
　foreign policies of, 848–849
　Great Society of, 873–877, 912
　as president (1963–1969), 873–877, 884–887
　social welfare programs and, 848

Sun Belt and, 927(*m*)
　tax cuts and, 868
　Vietnam policy of, 884–887, 892, 904–906, 908
Johnson, Samuel, 188
Johnson, Sir William, 99, 119
Johnston, Albert Sidney, 421
Johnston, Joseph E., 436
Johnston, Joshua, 272
Jolson, Al, 704
Jones, Bobby, 707
Jones, Nathaniel, 166
Jones, Paula, 970
Jones Act (1916; 1917), 646
Jones and Laughlin Steel Company, 536
Jordan, 831, 923
Joseph, Chief (Mohawk chief). *See* **Brant, Joseph**
Joseph, chief of Nez Percé, 487
journalism. *See also* mass media
　national culture and, 705
　photo, 775
　reform and, 599–600, 618
　sensationalist, 637
　yellow, 561
J.P. Morgan & Co., 510
Judaism. *See* Jews
judicial review, 252, 253
　meaning of, 238
judicial supremacy, 572–574
judiciary, 198. *See also* common law; court
　　system; laws; Supreme Court
　on rights of private property, 572–573
　trial by jury and, 136, 138–139, 142, 274
Judiciary Acts (1789, 1801), 215, 237, 238
Julian, George W., 451
July Fourth, 257
　Lincoln's speech on, 418
The Jungle (Sinclair), 618
the Junta (Cuban exiles), 637
Justice Department, U.S., 968
　civil rights and, 869
juvenile delinquency, 780
　music and, 858
　WWII and, 796

Kaiser Corporation, 795
kamikaze missions, 806
Kansas, 38
　abolitionism in, 382
　admission of, 406
　African American exodus to, 485

Kansas (*cont.*)
  African American regiments in, 432
  "Bleeding Kansas," 403, 404
  drought in, 737
  popular sovereignty in, 399(*m*)
Kansas City, 480, 541
  first mall in, 853
Kansas-Nebraska Act (1854), 399(*m*),
    401–403, 407
Kant, Immanuel, 353
Kasich, John, 969(*i*)
Kawai, Kazuo, 710
Kearney, Denis, 499
Kearney, Stephen, 394(*m*)
Keaton, Buster, 704
Keegan, John, 799
Kelley, Abby, 372
Kelley, Florence, 601
Kellogg-Briand Peace Pact (1928), 701
Kempe, John Tabor, 187
Kendall, Amos, 332
Kendall, Keziah, 377
Kennan, George F., 822
  containment theory of, 820
Kennedy, Anthony, 950
Kennedy, Jacqueline, 872
Kennedy, John Fitzgerald (1917–1963),
    864(*i*), 905
  assassination of, 872–873, 880, 884, 893
  civil rights and, 868–872
  Democratic coalition of, 877
  domestic policies of, 868
  foreign policy of, 848–849, 864–868
  Mexican Americans and, 897
  as president (1961–1963), 863–873
  social welfare programs and, 848
  Vietnam policy and, 883–884, 889
Kennedy, Robert F., 869, 898
  assassination of, 905, 907(*m*)
Kennesaw Mountain, battle of, 436
Kent State University, killings at, 909
Kentucky, 233, 234
  migration from, 302, 303(*m*)
  revivals in, 278, 283(*m*)
  secession and, 414, 416, 418, 421
  Shakers in, 284
  slavery in, 268, 276(*m*)
  westward migration from, 390
Kerner Commission (1968; National Advisory
    Commission), 897

Kerouac, Jack, 860
Kerry, John, 978, 980
Keynes, John Maynard, 764, 834
Khmer Rouge, 908, 911
Khomeini, Ayatollah Ruhollah, 941
Khrushchev, Nikita, 827, 844, 848, 867
Kickapoo Indians, 65
Kim Il Sung, 824
King, Charles Bird, 339(*i*)
King, Martin Luther, Jr. (1929–1968), 842,
    869, 871, 871(*i*), 874, 877
  assassination of, 880, 897, 905
  philosophy of, 895, 897
King, Rodney, 965
King George's War (War of the Austrian
    Succession; 1740–1748), 95
King Philip's War (Metacom's Rebellion),
    61–63, 62(*i*)
King's Canyon National Park, 501
King's College. *See* Columbia University
King's Mountain, South Carolina, 182
Kiowa Indians, 478
Kissinger, Henry, 919, 939
  Vietnam cease fire agreement and, 908, 910
"kitchen debate" (Nixon-Khrushchev), 848
Knickerbocker Trust Company, 623
Knights of Labor, 525–529
Knowland, William S., 824
Know-Nothing (American) Party, 402, 403,
    405, 405(*m*)
Knox, Henry, 207, 215, 228
Knox, John, 31
Knox, William, 133
Kongo, Africa, 86
Kopay, David, 934
Korea. *See also* North Korea; South Korea
  communism in, 881
  demilitarized zone in, 825(*m*), 827
  immigrants from, 860, 962, 965
  Japanese and Chinese claims to, 633
  thirty-eighth parallel in, 824–825, 825(*m*)
Korean War (1950–1953), 824–827, 825(*m*),
    826(*i*), 831, 911
  beginning of, 824, 834–835
  end of, 827, 837
  impact of, 827, 836
  public support in U.S. for, 825, 838
  veterans of, 793
Korematsu v. United States (1944), 798
Kosovo, 972

Kovic, Ron, 845
Kuhn Loeb & Co., 510
Ku Klux Klan, 455(*t*), 465–467, 467(*i*), 841
   Democratic Party and, 694–695
   revival of, 711–713
   women in, 466, 712–713, 713(*i*)
Ku Klux Klan Act (1871), 455(*t*)
   failure to enforce, 465, 467
Kuwait
   Iraq's invasion of, 954, 955
   oil production in, 922
   Persian Gulf War and, 954, 956(*m*)
Kyoto accord (1997), 960

labor. *See also* indentured servants; labor
    unions; slavery
   Adamson eight-hour law for, 625
   of African Americans, 445
   antiunion movement and, 676
   capital and, 343–344, 505–533
   division of, 293–294, 294(*i*)
   eight-hour day and, 527, 625
   family system of, 515
   forced, 40, 462
   free black, 304(*i*), 445, 448(*i*)
   gang, 352, 383, 448, 461, 464
   globalization and, 960
   Industrial Revolution and, 293, 295–298,
    296(*i*)
   manufacturing and, 295, 309
   overseas, 925, 927
   Reconstruction and, 442
   restricted output, 521
   sex-typing and, 519–521, 520(*i*)
   shortage of, 789, 797
   slavery and, 402, 417
   systematic control of, 523–524
   wage, 343, 361, 448(*i*), 449, 461–462, 464
   of women, 449
   working conditions and, 608, 611, 612–613
   work week and, 697, 707, 854
   in WWII, 789–792
   yellow-dog contracts and, 528
laborers
   Chinese, 740
   education for, 264–265
   farm, 102, 297
   Jewish garment, 523, 529(*i*)
   as journeymen, 299–300
   Mexican, 497, 500, 740–742

   migrant, 497, 499–500, 740–742, 860–861, 898
   Pietism and, 112
   and politics, 588, 590, 593
   railroad, 625
   rights of, 300, 345–347
   as Sons of Liberty, 141, 152
   urbanization and, 310, 313–314, 319, 336
   women, 301
Labor's Nonpartisan League, 767
labor theory of value, 300–301
labor unions, 525–533, 838. *See also* American
    Federation of Labor (AFL); Congress of
    Industrial Organizations (CIO)
   AFL-CIO, 851, 898
   African Americans in, 526
   Amalgamated Association of Iron and Steel
    Workers, 530
   Asian Americans in, 743
   Brotherhood of Locomotive Firemen, 532
   Brotherhood of Sleeping Car Porters, 790
   in California, 499
   closed-shop agreements and, 345, 347, 526
   Cold War and, 832
   collective bargaining and, 530
   communism and, 835
   decline of, 958
   Democratic Party and, 777, 794, 833, 918, 971
   emergence of, 299–301, 345–347, 525–529
   employer attacks on, 688
   environmentalism and, 929
   and Fair Deal, 834
   French, 905
   in Germany, 781
   globalization and, 960
   identification with radicals of, 688–689
   immigration and, 711
   industrial unions and, 532
   Mexican Americans and, 741–742, 898
   in mining industry, 494
   movie industry and, 704
   need for, 525
   New Deal and, 756–757, 761, 766 767
   1936 elections and, 763
   1980 elections and, 943
   1984 elections and, 949
   in 1990s, 958
   Panic of 1837 and, 346
   political activism of, 610
   Populist Party and, 590
   post-WWI antiunion movement and, 676, 688

labor unions (*cont.*)
  Progressive Party and, 694
  public image of, 688–689
  reform and, 525–529
  seniority systems in, 766
  social legislation and, 610
  strength of, 676, 851
  strikes and, 300, 301
  in Sun Belt, 926–927
  trade unionism and, 525–529
  wages and, 789–790
  welfare capitalism and, 698–699
  Western Federation of Miners (WFM), 532–533
  women in, 526, 529(*i*), 742
  working hours and, 300, 347, 527, 625
  WWII and, 789–790
Ladies' Home Journal, 546, 705, 731(*i*)
Lafayette, marquis de, 181(*m*), 182
La Follette, Robert M., 598, 605, 611, 620,
      687, 694
Lake Champlain, 63
  battle of, 243(*m*), 244
Lake Erie, 242
Lake Texcoco, 9
Lakota. *See* Sioux
Lancaster, Pennsylvania, 90, 250
Lancaster Turnpike Company, 250
land
  for freed slaves, 451
  grants of, 103, 119, 124
  ownership of, 446, 449, 461, 464. *See also*
      freehold society; property rights
  policies on, 46, 51–52, 58–59
  public, 461
  taxation of, 384
Land Act (1820), 239
land banks, 96
land grants
  for railroads, 479–480, 508
  from Spain, 496
Landon, Alfred M., 763
Land Ordinance (1785), 463(*m*)
Lane, Dutton, 118
Lane Theological Seminary (Cincinnati, Ohio),
      369
Lange, Dorothea, 739(*i*), 775
Lansing, John, 209
Laos
  immigrants from, 962
  Vietnam War and, 883(*m*), 910, 911

Larcom, Lucy, 296, 298
Larkin, Thomas Oliver, 390, 392
La Salle, Robert de, 41
Latin America. *See* South America
Latinos
  affirmative action and, 936, 965
  in cattle industry, 481, 481(*i*)
  culture of, 501
  decay of inner cities and, 862
  increase of, 963(*m*), 964
  intermarriage of, 964
  migration to cities of, 860–861
  migratory work and, 497
  as percentage of population, 491
  race riots and, 965
  in Southwest, 481(*i*), 481–482, 495–497
  on television, 855
  in Texas, 495–497
  voting districts and, 918
  women, 958
  youth gangs of, 796
Latter-day Saints, Church of Jesus Christ of.
      See Mormons
Latvia, 684
Laud, William, 54, 56
Laurens, Henry, 185
The Law of Civilization and Decay (B. Adams),
      635
Lawrence, Kansas, 403
Lawrence, William, 571
laws. *See also* common law; court system;
      immigration laws; judiciary; Supreme
      Court
  anti-immigrant, 710
  antilynching, 695
  antitrust, 610, 615, 624, 674, 693, 756
  blue, 575–576
  child labor, 601, 621
  eight-hour, 625
  equality before, 446, 450, 465
  homestead, 482–484, 488
  Jim Crow, 585–587, 695, 897
  minimum wage, 601, 604, 621, 834,
      838–839
  Nuremberg, 802
  right-to-work, 832
  statute, 252
lawyers, 142
lead mining, 494
lead poisoning, 612–613

League of Nations, 684–687, 818, 829(m)
    Democratic Party and, 693
    U.S. and, 686–687, 701
    WWII and, 781
League of United Latin American Citizens
        (LULAC), 791
League of Women Voters, 695
Leahy, William D., 806
Leary, Timothy, 893
Lease, Mary Elizabeth, 589–590
Leave It to Beaver (TV program), 854
Leaves of Grass (Whitman), 356
Lebanon, 831, 949
    Israeli invasion of, 952
Lecompton constitution (Kansas), 402–403, 406
Lee, Mother Ann, 284
Lee, Richard Henry, 171, 188
Lee, Robert E., 419(m)
    black soldiers and, 438
    Gettysburg and, 430–431
    Grant and, 434, 435(m)
    invasion of North by, 420, 431(m)
    Lincoln and, 416
    in Mexican War, 393
    surrender of, 435(m), 440
Leeward Islands, 77
Legal Tender Act (1862), 427
Leggett, William, 345
Leibowitz, Samuel, Scottsboro case and,
        737(i)
Leisler, Jacob, 73–74
Leisler's revolt (1689), 73–74, 129
leisure
    automobile and, 704
    consumerism and, 702
    in Great Depression, 735
    mass media and, 704–707
    national culture and, 707
    in 1920s, 692, 697
    urban, 560–561
Lemke, William, 763
Lend-Lease Act (1941), 785, 786(m)
Lenglen, Suzanne, 707
Lenin, Vladimir Ilych, 670
Leningrad, Soviet Union, 800(m)
Leo X, Pope (1513–1521), 29
lesbians, 928, 933
Le Temps (newspaper), 646
Letters from a Farmer in Pennsylvania
        (Dickenson), 147

Letters from an American Farmer
        (Crèvecoeur), 258
Levant Company (Turkey), 33
Levitt, Arthur, 852
Levittown, Long Island, 852
Lewinsky, Monica, 971
Lewis, John (civil-rights movement), 872, 974
Lewis, John L. (labor movement), 766, 790
Lewis, Meriwether, 240
Lexington, battle of (1775), 158, 185
Leyte Gulf, Battle of, 804
Libby, Owen, 214(m)
liberalism, 881
    Democratic Party and, 918, 968
    Fair Deal, 833–835
    1970s activism and, 936
    role of the state and, 834, 838, 839
    urban, 608–610, 696
    Vietnam War and, 912
The Liberator (newspaper), 370, 374
Liberia, Africa, 268
Liberty League, 759
Liberty Party, 372–373, 391, 395
libraries, public, 562, 735
Libya, 952
Lieberman, Joseph, 973
Life magazine, 775
The Life of George Washington (Weems), 265
Life of Reilly (TV program), 854
Liliuokalani, Queen of Hawaii (r. 1891–1893),
        631
Lin, Maya Ling, 912(i)
Lincoln, Abraham (1809–1865), 408(i). See
        also Civil War; Emancipation
        Proclamation
    assassination of, 442
    debates with Douglas of, 408
    early life of, 407
    1860 elections and, 405(m), 409–410, 412
    1864 presidential campaign of, 436–437, 456
    Grant and, 421, 434
    McClellan and, 419, 420
    national mercantilism under, 426
    as president (1860–1865), 442, 443–444
    Reconstruction and, 442, 470
    Republican Party and, 402, 406–410
    slavery and, 409, 410, 412
    the South and, 412
    speeches of, 408, 413, 418, 442
    states' rights and, 334

Lincoln, Abraham (*cont.*)
  suspension of habeas corpus by, 424
  Union victory and, 432–440
Lincoln, Benjamin, 180
Lincoln, Mary Todd, 407
Lincoln Brigade, American, 783
Lindbergh, Charles, 707, 784
Lindgren, Ida, 482, 483(*i*)
Lisbon, Portugal, 23
Litchfield Law School, 261
literacy, 368, 402, 456, 458
  voting rights and, 874
literature
  antislavery, 385, 400
  cultural dissent and, 859–860
  documentary, 775
  genteel tradition in, 563
  modernist, 716
  in 1920s, 716–717
  republican, 265
  transcendental, 355–357
Lithuania, 684
Little Big Horn, Battle of (1876), 487
Little Rock, Arkansas, 841(*i*), 841–842
Little Round Top, 430
Little Turtle (Miami chief), 230
living standards
  decline of, 925
  and Fair Deal, 834
  globalization and, 960
  Great Society and, 877
  improved nutrition and, 850(*i*)
  postwar, 816, 848, 851
Livingston, Robert, 239
Livingston family, 104–105, 124
Loan, Nguyen Ngoc, 890(*i*)
Locke, Alain, 717
Locke, John, 73, 112–113, 189, 264
  on natural rights, 113, 143, 184
Loco-Foco (Equal Rights) Party, 345
Lodge, Henry Cabot, 634, 640, 643,
  686, 687
Lodge, Henry Cabot, Jr., 884
log cabin campaign (1840), 348(*i*)
London, England, 14
London Times (newspaper), 646
Long, Huey, 759–760
  assassination of, 760(*i*)
  New Deal and, 761
Long, Stephen H., 386, 479

Long Island, New York, 44, 73, 853
  battle of, 173, 185
  Levittown in, 852
Longstreet, James, 430
Look magazine, 775
Lorentz, Pare, 775
Los Alamos, New Mexico, 808
Los Angeles, California
  Latino immigrants in, 860, 861
  movie industry in, 704
  population in, 495(*m*)
  real estate boom in, 501
  riots in, 896, 964–965
  youth gangs in, 796, 797(*i*)
lost colony. *See* Roanoke
Lost Horizon (Hilton), 735
Louisbourg, siege of (1745), 95, 122
Louisiana, 11
  Acadians in, 121
  admission to Union, 245, 268
  African American regiments in, 432
  in Civil War, 430
  Emancipation Proclamation and, 429
  as French colony, 13, 41
  migration to, 233, 302, 303(*m*)
  Napoleon and, 239
  Reconstruction and, 443, 453(*m*), 457, 461
  Republican government in, 467, 470
  secession of, 413
  slavery in, 268–271, 269(*m*), 276(*m*), 437
  voting rights in, 323
Louisiana Purchase (1803), 227, 239–240, 245(*m*)
  slavery and, 276(*m*), 397, 401
  Texas and, 245, 386
Louisville, Kentucky, 306(*m*), 307(*m*), 308
Louis XIV, king of France (r. 1643–1715), 41,
  72, 94
Louis XVI, king of France (r. 1774–1792), 179,
  182, 221(*i*), 223(*i*)
  execution of, 220
L'Ouverture, Toussaint, 239
Love Canal, Niagara Falls, New York, 928
Lovejoy, Elijah P., 372
Low, Thomas, 265
Lowell, Francis Cabot, 295
Lowell, Josephine Shaw, 600–601
Lowell, Massachusetts, 296–298, 301, 308, 342,
  521
Loyalists, 157
  British strategies and, 172–176, 180–182

emigration of, 187–188
  vs. Patriots, 166, 167, 172, 176
Loyalists, Spanish, 783
loyalty oaths, 835
Luce, Henry R., 824
"The Luck of Roaring Camp" (Harte), 500
lumber industry, 135
  in New South, 516(m)
  in Pacific Northwest, 494–495
Lundy, Benjamin, 369
Lunt, Dolly Summer, 439
Luther, Martin, 30, 116
Lutheranism, 277
  in colonial America, 104, 108, 108(m)
Luxembourg, 784, 821
Luzon (Philippines), 643
lynching, 736
  laws against, 695, 840
  New Deal and, 768
  in New South, 587, 587(i)
Lynd, Helen Merrell, 692, 728
Lynd, Robert, 692, 728
Lynn, Massachusetts, 247, 300

McAdoo, William, 674
MacAllister, Alexander, 99
McAllister, Ward, 543
MacArthur, Douglas (1897–1978), 823, 824
  Bonus Army and, 747–748
  Truman and, 826
  in WWII, 804
McCallum, Daniel C., 514
McCarran-Walter Act (1952), 860
McCarthy, Eugene, 904–905
McCarthy, Joseph R., 835, 836–837
  censure of, 837
McCarthyism, 835, 836, 884
McClellan, George B., 416, 418–420, 436, 437
McClure's magazine, 599
McColl, Ada, 484(i)
McCormick, Cyrus, 294, 309
McCormick and Hussey, 308
McCormick industries, strike at, 527
McCulloch v. Maryland (1819), 252
McDonald's, 854, 959(i)
McDougall, Alexander, 141
McDowell, Irwin, 418
McDuffie, George, 476
McGovern, George, 919
  1968 election and, 905, 907(m)

McGready, James, 278
McGuire, Thomas B., 525
Machiavelli, Niccolò, 20
machinery, 507. See also technology
  industrialization and, 294(i), 294–296, 296(i)
  interchangeable parts and, 292
  tool making and, 299
machinists, 517, 521, 523
McKay, Claude, 717
McKinley, William (1843–1901), 597, 612,
    615, 619(i)
  1896 elections and, 593–594, 594(m)
  as president (1897–1901), 637–639,
    645–646
  war aims of, 639–640
McKinley Tariff (1890), 588, 592, 631
MacLeish, Archibald, 780
McNamara, Robert, 884, 890, 919
Macon, Nathaniel, 275
McPherson, Aimee Semple, 714
McWorld, 959(i)
MAD (Mutually Assured Destruction policy),
    843
Madeira Islands, 20, 23
Madero, Francisco, 653
Madison, James (1751–1836), 157–158, 168,
    208–209. See also Virginia Plan
  Bill of Rights and, 215, 241
  Bonus Bill and, 251, 328
  Embargo Act and, 241
  First Bank and, 247
  on Hamilton's financial plan, 216, 217
  Marbury case and, 238
  political theory of, 114
  as president (1809–1817), 237, 238,
    241–242
  religion and, 193
  as secretary of state, 238, 241
  on slavery, 267
  states' rights and, 333
Madrid, Spain, terrorist attacks in, 978
magazines, 707, 775, 930
  gender stereotypes in, 857
  reform journalism in, 599, 606–607, 607(i),
    618
Maggie: Girl of the Streets (Crane), 563
Magna Charta, 142
Magnum, W. P., 344
Magruder, Jeb Stuart, 920
Mahan, Alfred T., 634, 643

Maine, 44, 360(i)
  admission as free state, 275–276,
    276(m)
  Massachusetts and, 73
  settlement of, 233
  temperance movement and, 382
  voting rights in, 272
  women's rights in, 378
Maine (battleship), 638
"Maine Law," 382
maize, 8, 9. See also corn
Malaya, 701, 803
Malaysia, 795
Malcolm, John, 140(i)
Malcolm X, 895
management techniques, 524, 696
Manassas Creek (Bull Run), 418, 420
Manchuria, 781
Mandan Indians, 478, 479
Mandela, Nelson, 972
Manhattan Island, 43. See also New York City
Manhattan Project, 808
Manifest Destiny, 383–391, 636
  origin of term, 387–388
Manifesto and Declaration of the Indians
    (Bacon), 53
Mann, Horace, 375
Mansfield, Sir James, 143
manufacturing. See also factory system;
    industrialization; mills
  American System and, 327–328
  business elite and, 301, 310
  distribution for, 512–513
  education and, 265
  energy for, 507
  labor force for, 515–519, 517(f)
  mass production and, 523–524
  in Midwest, 307–308, 309
  mining and, 494–495
  in Northeast, 292–301
  rural, 247–249
  time-and-motion studies in, 524
  water power and, 294, 295, 308
Mao Zedong (Mao Tse-tung), 823
Marbury, William, 238
Marbury v. Madison (1803), 238, 252
March on Washington (1963), 871–872
March on Washington (WWII), 840
Marcy, William L., 332, 401
margin buying, 724, 758

Marianas Islands, 640
Marion, Francis (Swamp Fox), 182
market economy, 349, 830
  big business and, 615
  class divisions and, 292–293, 309–314,
    312(i), 317
  cycles of, 358
  expansion of, 301–309
  industrialization and, 319
  mass marketing and, 513, 513(i)
  trade with Native Americans and, 479
Marquette, Jacques, 41
marriage. See also women
  arranged, 102, 260–261
  vs. bachelorhood, 548
  companionate, 260–261
  complex, 362
  divorce and, 261, 901
  domestic abuse and, 261
  dower right and, 102
  equality within, 258, 260–261
  within ethnic group, 109, 111
  farming's dual economy and, 484
  gay, 930, 933, 966
  Great Depression and, 728
  inheritance and, 102, 260–262
  interracial, 371, 412–413, 964
  in late 20th century, 901
  medieval, 16–17
  Mormons and, 366(i)
  in 1950s, 855
  polygamous, 363, 366, 366(i)
  republican, 260–261, 263(i)
  slaves and, 271, 449
  utopian communalism and, 358, 359, 362
  women's rights and, 374, 378, 546–548,
    732, 933
marriage portion, 102
Married Women's Property Acts (1839–1845),
    378
Marshall, George C., 820, 822
Marshall, John (1755–1835), 240, 250–253,
    251(i), 305. See also Supreme Court
  on commerce clause, 341
  death of, 341
  Fletcher v. Peck (1810), 253
  McCulloch v. Maryland (1819), 252, 253
  Marbury v. Madison (1803), 238, 252
  Native American cases and, 339
  three principles of, 251

Marshall Islands, 804(m)
Marshall Plan, 820–822
Martin, Henry Byam, 234(i)
Martin, Joseph J., 826
Martin, Josiah, 168
Martineau, Harriet, 322
Martinique, 122
Marx, Groucho, 733
Marx, Karl, 532
Marx Brothers, 733
Marxism, 532. *See also* communism
Mary II, queen of England (r. 1688–1694),
    72–74, 91
Maryland, 448. *See also* Baltimore, Maryland
    Catholicism in, 47–48, 73
    Civil War and, 416, 420
    claims to western lands and, 202
    as colony, 47–48, 52, 69, 73, 85
    emancipation in, 429, 437
    freed slaves in, 448
    ratification of Constitution and, 213
    revolts in, 73
    Scots-Irish in, 110
    secession and, 414, 418
    Second Bank and, 252
    slavery in, 80, 83, 85, 270
    South Atlantic system and, 89–90
    voting rights in, 258, 259(m), 323
    wheat production in, 124
Maryland Gazette, 233, 265
masculinity, cult of, 548
Mason, George, 193, 210
Masons. *See* Freemasonry, Order of
Massachusetts
    birth control in, 730
    claims to Western lands, 202
    free blacks in, 272
    Fugitive Slave Acts and, 400
    gay rights in, 966
    Know-Nothing Party in, 402
    1928 elections and, 719
    ratification convention in, 213
    revivals in, 278
    separation of Maine from, 275
    transportation in, 235
    voting rights in, 324
    women in, 199–201, 375, 378
Massachusetts Bay Colony. *See also* Boston,
    Massachusetts
    assembly of, 91

    Dominion of New England and, 72–74
    General Court of, 54, 132
    government of, 54–55
    House of Representatives in, 136–138,
        158
    land grants in, 103
    Native American attacks on, 75
    Navigation Acts and, 71–72
    religious intolerance in, 55–56
    revolts in, 73–74
    "taxation without representation" and,
        136–137, 149, 150
Massachusetts Gazette, 148
Massachusetts Spy, 152
Massacre of Saint George Fields, 150
Massatamohtnock. *See* **Opechancanough**
mass media. *See also* magazines; movies;
        newspapers; radio; television
    Chicago convention and, 905–906
    cities and, 707–708
    counterculture and, 893
    vs. feminism, 856, 857, 902, 966
    gender stereotypes in, 857
    Great Depression and, 731
    Holocaust and, 802
    Iranian hostage crisis and, 941
    JFK's elections and, 863
    leisure and, 704–707
    1980 elections and, 943
    WWII and, 784
mass production
    of automobiles, 523, 698, 703
    big business and, 696
    critique of, 698
    in housing, 852
    industrial expansion and, 696
    in manufacturing, 523–524
    WWII and, 788
Mather, Cotton, 58, 112, 113
matrilineal societies, 14
Mattachine Society, 858
Maxim, Hiram, 664
Maximilian, Ferdinand, Archduke of Mexico
        (r. 1864–1867), 629
Mayas, 9, 12
Mayflower Compact, 54
Mayor of New York v. Miln (1837), 341
Meade, George G., 393, 430, 431, 431(m)
Meat Inspection Act, 619
meatpacking industry, refrigeration and, 512

mechanics, 295, 297, 313. *See also* artisans
    trade union for, 523
    unemployment and, 319
Mechanics' Union of Trade Association, 300
mechanization, 523–524
Medicaid, 876, 877
    abortion rights and, 931
    Nixon and, 917
Medicare, 876, 877, 973
    Nixon and, 917
    Reagan and, 948
    reform of, 979
medieval period, 14–18
    agriculture in, 14–16
    marriage in, 16–17
    religion in, 17–18
    seasonal cycle in, 15–16
    social order in, 16–17
Mediterranean Sea, 18–21, 21(m)
Mein Kampf (Hitler), 782
Melbourne, Australia, gold rush in, 492
Mellon, Andrew W., 693, 725
Melville, Herman, 357
Memphis, Tennessee, 450
Mennonites, 109
mercantilism, 89(m), 94–96. *See also* South
    Atlantic system
    American, 249–250, 426
    British, 33, 94–95
    in British colonies, 70–72
    commonwealth system and, 249–250
    meaning of, 20, 33
    politics of, 94–95, 97–98
merchant marine, 634
merchants, 89(m), 106. *See also*
    shopkeepers
    as business elite, 301, 308–310
    Dutch, 70, 122
    education and, 265
    in England, 150
    Enlightenment and, 112, 113
    as loyalists, 147(i), 148, 150, 158
    Navigation Acts and, 95
    of New England, 135–136
    revolution and, 139, 141, 142, 152, 157
    sharecropping and, 462, 464
    Six Companies and, 498
    South Atlantic system and, 88–91
    textile industry and, 293
    trade with Britain and, 123–124

Mesabi Range, 507
Mesoamerica, 7, 8(m), 9–12, 27. *See also* Aztecs
    trade with, 95
mestizos, 29, 390, 496
Metacom's Rebellion (King Philip's War),
    61–63, 62(i)
Metcalf, Seth, 131
Methodism, 114, 575(f), 576
    abolitionism and, 368, 376
    African Americans and, 268, 274, 277–281
    child rearing and, 264
    evangelical, 277–281, 283(m)
Meuse-Argonne campaign, 670–671
Mexican American Political Association
    (MAPA), 897
Mexican Americans. *See also* Latinos
    in cities, 861
    civil rights for, 897–898
    discrimination against, 494, 677
    Great Depression and, 728, 735
    labor activism of, 741–742, 766
    as migrant workers, 497, 500, 740–742
    in military, 788
    movement into industrial jobs, 676–677
    New Deal and, 769–771
    race riots and, 796
    strikes by, 741(i)
    terms for, 898
    War on Poverty and, 874
    women, 768
    WWII and, 780
Mexican Revolution (1911–1917), 668, 711
    U.S. intervention in, 653–654, 701
Mexican War (1846–1848), 382, 392–394,
    394(m)
    Democratic Party and, 393, 396
    presidential candidates and, 400
    slavery and, 371
    victory in, 393–396
Mexico, 7, 9, 245(m), 630
    California and, 390
    cession of land from, 398
    economy of, 392
    foreign debts of, 391
    independence of, 386
    Mexican Americans and, 769
    Mormons in, 363, 364, 364(m)
    NAFTA and, 959
    purchase of land from, 401
    Spanish civil war and, 783

Spanish conquests in, 25, 27
Texas and, 386–387
U.S. involvement in, 653–654, 701
Mexico City, 9, 393
Miami, Florida, Cuban refugees in, 861
Miami Indians, 65
Miantonomi (Narragansett chief), 37
Michelangelo, 20
Michigan, 302, 303(m), 361, 795
Micmac Indians, 10
Microsoft Corporation, 961
Middle Atlantic colonies (1720–1765)
    economic inequality in, 104–106
    religious diversity in, 99, 104–111, 108(m)
Middlebury Female Seminary, 285
middle class
    African American, 717–718, 877
    birth control and, 730
    Civil War and, 424, 427
    conformity of, 859
    conservatism of, 937
    consumerism of, 702, 703
    culture of, 311, 312(i), 317
    Democratic Party and, 777
    education legislation and, 876
    family life of, 545(i), 545–546
    in government, 342, 344
    Great Depression and, 724, 728, 754
    Great Society and, 877
    housing and, 925
    industrial expansion and, 697
    JFK and, 863
    Lincoln and, 402, 407
    movie industry and, 704
    1936 elections and, 763
    in 1970s, 943
    1980 elections and, 943
    in 1990s, 957
    politics and, 323–324, 336
    postwar, 848, 850(i)
    Protestant, 694
    racism and, 372
    reform and, 353
    Republican Party and, 402, 694
    salaried, 544
    South Atlantic system and, 90
    strikes and, 767
    student activism and, 891
    suburban, 544–545, 860
    taxes and, 427

    on television, 854
    transcendentalism and, 354(i), 355
    women of, 311, 312(i), 375, 857, 858
    women's rights and, 903
Middle East. *See also individual countries*
    Carter and, 941
    Cold War in, 820, 826, 829–831
    crisis in, 978
    declining British influence in, 830–831
    oil production in, 922, 941, 944
    post-WWI colonialism in, 684
    "Roadmap" for, 978
    U.S. involvement in, 956(m)
    in WWI, 664
    WWII in, 784
Middle Passage, 78(m), 81, 82(i), 267(i)
Middlesex County Congress (1774), 158
Middletown (Lynd and Lynd), 692, 728
Midway, Battle of, 804, 804(m)
the Midwest
    democracy in, 323
    Jackson and, 329
    John Q. Adams and, 327
    manufacturing in, 307–308, 309
    migration from, 756
    migration to, 234, 298, 301–302, 303(m)
    wheat production in, 302–305, 303(m)
migrant labor, 497, 499–500
migration. *See also* emigration; immigrants
    to Africa, 718
    African American, 552, 676–678, 677(m),
      708(m), 717, 718, 735–736, 777–778,
      861
    Asian, 497
    to California, 390, 479, 491–492, 495(m),
      496, 497–500, 501, 738(m), 739–741, 756,
      795, 852
    difficulties of, 482–485, 483(i)
    from dust bowl, 737
    of farmers, 756
    to Florida, 852
    internal, 8(m), 232–235, 861–862
    to and from Midwest, 234, 298, 301–302,
      303(m), 756
    Native American, 7
    from New England, 124–125, 233–234, 298,
      301–302, 303(m), 307
    to old Southwest, 267(i), 268, 269(m),
      301–302, 303(m)
    postwar, 852

migration (*cont.*)
  religious conflict and, 31
  social causes of, 16, 33–34
  to and from the South, 232–233, 302,
    303(*m*), 515–517
  to Sun Belt, 851, 852
  trans-Appalachian, 122, 126(*m*), 133(*m*),
    262, 283(*m*), 301–302, 303(*m*)
  urban, 735–736, 777–778, 860–862. *See also*
    urbanization
  to the West, 323, 383, 386, 387–390, 389(*m*),
    491–502, 495(*m*), 851, 852, 860–861,
    926–927, 927(*m*)
  west to east, 492
  WWII and, 795–796
military. *See also* Army, U.S.; Army of Northern
    Virginia; Army of the Potomac; defense
    spending; draft, military; missiles; Navy,
    U.S.; weapons of mass destruction
  African Americans in, 432–433, 433(*i*), 438,
    440, 641–643, 642(*i*), 671–672, 788, 789,
    791
  Americanization in, 671
  Cold War and, 842–843
  Defense Department and, 823
  economic growth and, 926, 927(*m*)
  gays in, 968
  growth of, 628
  Japanese internment and, 798
  JFK and, 863, 864–865
  politics and, 887
  racism in, 641–643, 671–672, 788
  segregation in, 671–672, 780, 788, 789,
    791, 798
  U.S. interventions and, 953(*m*)
  women in, 957(*i*)
  WWII mobilization of, 788–789
military-industrial complex, 780,
    828, 844(*m*), 844–845, 865
  WWII and, 788, 810
militia, 185. *See also* Minutemen
  colonial, 121, 128–129, 132, 158
  mob control and, 320
  service in, 259(*m*), 324
Militia Act (1862), 424
Mill Dam Act (1795), 250
Miller, Arthur, 775
Miller, Lewis, 267(*i*)
Millerites, 379(*i*)
Milliken v. Bradley (1974), 936

mills, 520. *See also* factory system
  colonial, 106
  steel, 507, 517, 518(*i*), 519
  textile, 294–298, 301, 308, 515, 516(*m*)
  on waterways, 247
Mimbres Valley, 11
minimum wage
  JFK and, 868
  laws on, 601, 604, 621, 834, 838–839
  New Deal and, 756, 764
  Supreme Court on, 763
  for women, 621, 768
mining
  in Arizona, 497
  boom towns and, 491–495
  capital for, 494
  Chinese labor for, 497–499
  coal, 507, 508(*m*), 516(*m*)
  copper, 494
  environmental pollution of, 501
  gold, 488, 491–495, 492(*m*), 497–498
  immigrant labor and, 517, 517(*f*)
  industrialization of, 494–495
  labor force for, 517(*f*)
  migrant labor and, 497
  1902 strike and, 602, 615
  silver, 492(*m*), 494, 591
  strikes and, 528(*i*), 532–533, 590, 602, 615
  technology for, 494
  zinc, 494
Minneconjou Indians, 490
minorities. *See also individual groups*
  consumer culture and, 702
  Great Depression and, 728, 732
  1950s culture and, 857
  rights of, 933–937
  women, 768
Minow, Newton, 855
Minutemen, 158
Miranda v. Arizona (1966), 918
Miss America pageant, 902, 903(*i*)
missiles
  in Cold War, 843
  intercontinental ballistic (ICBMs), 828, 910
  intermediate-range ballistic (IRBMs), 867
  Polaris, 828
  "Star Wars" and, 948
missionaries. *See also* Jesuits
  Catholic, 37–40, 65
  missions of, 38–40

to Native Americans, 37–41, 43, 65
Protestant, 282, 283(m)
Mississippi, 233, 467
admission to Union, 268
Freedom Summer in, 873–874
migration to, 302, 303(m)
Reconstruction and, 456, 457, 458, 465
secession and, 398, 413
slavery in, 268, 269(m), 270–271, 276(m), 383
voter registration in, 875(m)
women's rights in, 378
Mississippian civilization, 13, 27
Mississippi Freedom Democratic Party, 873
Mississippi River, 244
Civil War and, 416, 420–421, 422(m), 423, 430
early explorers and, 41, 63
navigation of, 184, 236
resettlement of Indians and, 337–340, 340(m)
Treaty of Paris and, 184
Mississippi River Valley
cotton production in, 268–270, 269(m)
land sales in, 303(m)
Native Americans in, 6, 9, 11, 13, 119, 120(m)
Missouri
Civil War and, 416, 417
emancipation in, 429, 437
migration to, 301–302, 303(m)
Mormons in, 364(m), 365
racism in, 409
secession and, 414, 418
slavery in, 383, 386
statehood for, 275–277, 276(m)
westward migration from, 390
Missouri Compromise (1821), 275–277, 276(m), 397, 415
Dred Scott and, 406
Kansas-Nebraska Act and, 401
Missouri River, 240, 420
Mitchell, John, 615, 920
Mitchell, Margaret, 735
Mittelberger, Gottlieb, 111
mobs. See also draft riots; race riots; riots; Sons of Liberty
antiabolitionist, 371–372
antiblack, 367
anti-Catholic, 320
anti-Chinese, 499

anti-Mormon, 363
in Britain, 150
British troops and, 128–129, 141, 150
colonial land rights and, 125, 128
colonial taxation and, 131, 134, 139, 140(i), 141–142
Moby-Dick (Melville), 357
Moctezuma, 25, 26
A Modern Instance (Howells), 563
modernism, 716
Protestant, 713
Mogollon culture, 11
Mohawk Indians, 44, 62–63, 75
Mohawk River, 63
Mohegan Indians, 62
Molasses Act (1733), 96, 132, 135–136
Moley, Raymond, 754
Molotov, Vyacheslav, 818, 822
Mondale, Walter F., 939, 949
Mongolia, 18
Monnet, Jean, 822
monopolies, chartered, 341, 345
Monroe, James (1758–1831), 268
Era of Good Feeling and, 255
Louisiana Purchase and, 239
as president (1817–1825), 237, 245
Monroe Doctrine (1823), 635, 953(m)
Roosevelt Corollary to, 649
Montana, 492, 493(i), 499
Montauk Indians, 37
Monterrey, Mexico, 393
Montesquieu, Charles-Louis de, 143, 212
Montgomery, Alabama, 874
Bus Boycott in, 842
Montgomery Ward, 512
Montreal, capture of (1760), 122
Montreal protocol (1987), 960
Moody, Anne, 870
Moody, Dwight L., 559
Moody, Paul, 295
Moon, Reverend Sun Myung, 928
Moore, John Bassett, 646
Moore, Marianne, 716
Moore's Creek Bridge, battle of, 168, 169
Moral Majority, 937–938, 938(i)
1980 elections and, 943
Morgan, Daniel, 182
Morgan, J. P., 592, 615, 619(i)
Morgan, William, 344
Morgenthau, Henry, Jr., 754

Mormons, 359(m), 362–366, 364(m), 485, 491,
    493(i)
  polygamy of, 363, 364, 366
  in Utah, 364, 366
  violence against, 363
Mormon Trail, 389(m)
Moroccan crisis, 655
Morris, Gouverneur (1752–1814), 105(m),
    210, 211(i), 253
Morris, Robert, 178, 186, 202–204, 207, 208, 234
Morris, Samuel, 117
Morris, Thomas, 329, 394
Morristown, New Jersey, 185
Morse, Samuel F. B., 319
Morton, Ferdinand "Jelly Roll", 705
Morton, Oliver, 451
Moscow, Soviet Union, in WWII, 799
Moses, Robert, 872
Mossadegh, Muhammad, 828
Mother's Magazine, 285
Mott, Lucretia, 370, 372, 378
mound building, 11, 12
movies
  blacklist in, 835
  documentary, 775
  in Great Depression, 733–734
  lobbyists portrayed in, 733
  mass culture and, 704–707
  politicians in, 733
  self-censorship of, 733
  women and, 704
  WWII and, 794–795
Mr. and Mrs. Isaac Newton Phelps Stokes
    (painting; Sargent), 550(i)
Mr. Smith Goes to Washington (film), 734
Ms. magazine, 930
muckrakers, 599–600, 610
Mugwumps, 577–578, 604, 612, 645
Muhammad, Elijah, 895
Muir, John, 501–502, 613
mujahideen (holy warriors), 941
Mulberry Street, New York City, 551(i)
Muller v. Oregon (1908), 601, 603, 624
multiculturalism, 965. See also ethnic diversity
Muncie, Indiana, 692
Mundt, Karl, 824
Munich Conference (1938), 783
Murray, Judith Sargent, 201, 201(i)
Murrow, Edward R., 795
museums, 562

music
  African American, 857–858, 859
  the Beatles, 893
  bebop, 859
  of counterculture, 889, 892–893
  country, 740, 857
  cultural dissent and, 857–858, 859
  documentaries and, 775
  folk, 892–893
  institutions for, 562
  jazz, 705
  modernist, 716
  New Deal and, 774–775
  Okie, 740
  rhythm and blues, 857
  rock 'n' roll, 889, 892–893
  of youth culture, 857–858, 859
Muskie, Edmund S., 906
Muslims, 18, 20, 21, 29, 972. See also Arabs;
    Islam
  African American, 895
  fundamentalist, 939, 941, 943–944, 952, 955,
    956(m), 978
  militant, 946
Mussolini, Benito, 781, 801
mutual aid societies, 552
Mutual Benefit Society, 300
mutual funds, 925
My Lai massacre, 909
My Life in the South (Stroyer), 273
mysticism, 354

NAACP. See National Association for the
    Advancement of Colored People
Nader, Ralph, 930, 973
NAFTA. See North American Free Trade
    Agreement
Nagasaki, 805(m), 808, 823
Nanking, sack of (1937), 785
Nantucket, Massachusetts, 274(i)
Napoleon Bonaparte, 239
Napoleonic Wars (1802–1815), 240
Narragansett Indians, 37, 55, 61–62
NASA. See National Aeronautics and Space
    Administration
Nashoba, Mississippi, 359(m)
Nashville, Tennessee, 444
Nasser, Gamal Abdel, 830, 831
Nast, Thomas, 452(i)
Natchez Indians, 6, 12, 13

National Advisory Commission (Kerner Commission; 1968), 897
National Aeronautics and Space Administration (NASA), 838, 868
National Association for the Advancement of Colored People (NAACP), 601, 607, 607(i), 717, 737, 870, 871, 902
  Communists and, 835
  formation of (1909), 606
  segregation and, 839, 840, 842
  on segregation in military, 788
  in WWII, 792
National Banking Acts (1863, 1864), 427
National Broadcasting Company (NBC), 706
National Defense Advisory Commission, 784
National Endowment for the Arts (NEA), 876
National Endowment for the Humanities (NEH), 876
national forests, 613, 614(m). See also national park system
National Guard
  at Kent State, 908
  Vietnam War and, 887, 892
National Housing Acts
  of 1937, 764
  of 1949, 834
National Industrial Recovery Act (NIRA; 1933), 756
  Supreme Court on, 759
nationalism, 207, 922, 978
  black, 718
  Cold War and, 829, 830
  economic, 851
  jingoistic, 637
  New, 621–622
  and Vietnam War, 881
National Labor Relations Act, 832
National Labor Relations Board (NLRB), 761
national liberation, wars of, 865
National Liberation Front (NLF), 883(m), 884
National Organization for Women (NOW), 902, 930, 966
National Origins Act (1924), 709, 712
national park system, 501, 502, 502(i), 614(m), 854, 876, 940
National Progressive Republican League, 621
National Recovery Administration (NRA), 756
  Supreme Court on, 761, 763
  women and, 768
National Road, 302, 328, 333

National Security Council (NSC), 823
National Trades' Union, 300
National Union for Social Justice, 759
National Union Party, 436, 451
National Urban League, 607, 871
  Communists and, 835
National War Labor Board (NWLB), 789–790
National Woman Suffrage Association, 457
National Youth Administration (NYA), 732
  Mexican Americans and, 770
  WWII and, 793
Nation of Islam, 895
Native American Clubs, 319–320
Native Americans, 6–14, 636. See also individual peoples/tribes
  adopted prisoners of, 63, 65
  agriculture of, 9–14, 230–232, 479, 490
  alleged inferiority of, 388
  art of, 9, 11
  assimilation of, 38–41, 489, 771–772, 861–862
  buffalo and, 478–479
  in California, 390
  in Carolina, 45(i)
  changed world of, 59–65
  citizenship for, 489
  civil rights of, 898–900, 933, 935
  and conformist culture, 861
  cultural destruction of, 27–28, 37–43, 65
  cultural diversity of, 63–65
  decay of inner cities and, 862
  defense against, 132, 149(m)
  of eastern woodlands, 12–14, 65
  education of, 489, 489(i), 898
  encounters with immigrants and, 99, 109, 111
  English settlers and, 46–47, 59, 61
  European diseases and, 26–27, 37, 39, 40, 41, 43, 54, 61, 63, 65
  vs. European military technology, 25
  European wars and, 74–75
  as farmers, 27
  French and Indian War and, 122
  fur trade and, 41–44, 63, 65
  on Great Plains, 476, 477(m), 478–479, 486–490
  horses and, 478
  inland, 63–65
  Kansas-Nebraska Act and, 401
  land of, 11, 52, 227–230, 231(m)

Native Americans (*cont.*)
  languages of, 44
  Marshall Court and, 337, 339
  matrilineal societies of, 14
  medicine men of, 478
  in Mesoamerica, 7, 8(*m*), 9, 10, 12, 27
  migrations of, 7
  migration to cities of, 861–862
  in military, 670, 788
  as minority populations, 490
  missionaries to, 37–40, 65
  mission life and, 501
  in Mississippi valley, 6, 9, 11, 13
  mixed-blood, 337
  Mormons and, 364(*m*)
  mythic West and, 490
  New Deal and, 771, 771(*i*)
  policies towards, 328–329
  political status of, 349
  Pontiac's uprising and, 122, 123(*i*), 132
  population changes of, 52, 63, 65
  Puritan treatment of, 61
  religions of, 9, 10, 13, 478
  removal of (1820–1843), 336–339, 340(*m*)
  reservation system and, 486–490, 488(*m*),
    861–862, 898, 899, 935(*m*)
  resistance of, 46–47, 52, 61, 228–232
  Revolutionary War and, 172, 173(*i*), 176, 184
  self-government and, 771–772
  in southwest U.S., 11–12
  Spanish conquest of, 25–29, 38–40
  termination policy and, 898
  trade with, 69, 75, 479
  treaty violations and, 486, 488
  tribal land holdings, 478
  tribal politics of, 65
  unemployment among, 898
  War on Poverty and, 874
  as warriors, 478, 486–487, 490
  wars with, 52, 61, 476, 487, 490
  women's role among, 12–14, 65, 478
Native Son (Wright), 775
nativism, 319–320, 708–711. *See also* Know-
  Nothing Party
  anti-Catholic, 402
  politics and, 718
NATO. *See* North Atlantic Treaty Organization
Naturalization Act (1798), 222, 238
natural resources. *See* environment
natural rights, 113, 143, 184, 189–190

Nauvoo, Illinois, 363, 365
Navajo Code Talkers, 788
Navajo Indians, 7, 487, 496
naval power, 639–641. *See also* Navy, U.S.
Naval War College, 630
Navigation Acts (Acts of Trade and Navigation;
  1651–1751), 51, 147, 249
  British Empire and, 135–137
  British mercantilism and, 68, 70–72, 95
  resistance to, 95, 97–98
  South Atlantic system and, 77, 89–90
  vice-admiralty courts and, 136–137
  West Indian trade and, 95, 206
Navy, U.S., 628, 629–630
  battleships and, 640, 640(*i*)
  building of, 634–635, 647
  power of, 634–635, 647, 653
  strategy of, 639–640
Nazi (National Socialist) Party, 781
Nebraska, 399(*m*)
Neel, Alice, 774
Negro Labor Relations League, 791(*i*)
Negro leagues, 707
Negro World, 718
neoconservatives, 938
Neolin, 122
Nestor, Agnes, 602
Netanyahu, Benjamin, 972
Netherlands. *See also* Dutch colonization
  decolonization and, 829
  German invasion of, 784
  in NATO, 821
neutrality, 665, 667
Neutrality Acts
  of 1935, 783
  of 1937, 784
Nevada, nuclear testing in, 828
Nevelson, Louise, 774
New Amsterdam, 43, 44. *See also*
  New York City
Newark, New Jersey, rioting in, 896
New Deal (1933–1939), 680, 752–778, 816, 905
  and 1940 elections, 784
  African Americans and, 756, 768–769
  anticommunism and, 835
  art and, 773–774, 775
  Asian Americans and, 743
  attacks on, 758–760
  banks and, 754, 758
  business and, 756, 761, 763

capitalism and, 754, 758–759, 765
cartoons of, 758(i)
coalition of, 877, 949
conservation and, 772–773
deficit spending and, 868
Democratic Party and, 719
first (1933–1935), 752–760
gender roles and, 768, 776–777
Great Society and, 873, 875
labor unions and, 756–757, 761, 766–767
legacies of, 776–778, 831, 832
Mexican Americans and, 769–771
Native Americans and, 771(i), 771–772
Nixon and, 916
postwar programs and, 848
Reagan and, 948
Republican Party and, 760, 778, 832
rollback of, 838
second (1935–1938), 761–778
society and, 765–778
stalemate in, 763–765
Supreme Court on, 759, 761, 778
vs. Truman's Fair Deal, 834
women and, 767–768, 776–777
WWII and, 793
New England
    agriculture in, 100–104
    black tenant farmers in, 272
    California and, 390
    China trade and, 389
    Currency Act and, 96
    Dominion of, 72–74, 92, 138
    economy of, 88–91
    education in, 264, 266
    elite politics in, 92
    English colonization in, 53–61,
        60(m), 100–104
    evangelicalism in, 114–116, 278,
        281–282, 283(m)
    farm life in, 100–104
    fishing industry in, 185
    freehold society in, 100–104
    governance of, 69, 72
    manufacturing in, 292–301
    merchants of, 135–136
    migration from, 124–125, 233–234, 298,
        301–302, 303(m), 307
    population of, 99, 103
    Puritans in, 100, 103–104, 114, 121, 131,
        141, 143, 148, 153. See also Pietism

republicanism and, 141, 148
    Shakers in, 360
    tenant farmers in, 102
    textile industry in, 247–249, 293–298, 301,
        308, 342
    transcendentalism in, 353–358
    utopian communities in, 362
    War of 1812 and, 242, 243(m), 244
    women's rights in, 377
New England Anti-Slavery Society, 369
New England Emigrant Aid Society, 402
Newfoundland, 44, 75, 76(m), 184
    as British colony, 122, 149(m),
        153, 154(m)
New France, 41. See also Canada
New Freedom, 622, 625
New Frontier, 863, 868, 877
New Guinea, 804, 804(m)
New Hampshire, 103, 233, 253, 973
    constitution of, 184
    migration from, 301, 303(m)
    ratification of Constitution by, 213
    as royal colony, 72
    Shakers in, 284
    South Atlantic system and, 89–90
New Harmony, Indiana, 359(m)
New Jersey, 185, 252, 896
    as colony, 69, 72, 91
    land disputes in, 125
    popular power in, 91, 92
    Quaker settlements in, 106, 109
    revivalism in, 114
    in Revolutionary War, 174(m), 177
    settlement of, 104, 106
    voting rights in, 201, 259(m), 260
Newlands Reclamation Act, 613
New Left, 891, 902, 909. See also Students for a
    Democratic Society
New Lights, 115–116, 117, 118, 127, 170
New Mexico, 11, 38–41
    annexation of, 395
    attempt to buy, 392
    Compromise of 1850 and, 398, 399(m)
    drought in, 737
    grazing rights in, 496–497
    Hispanic culture in, 495–497
    immigration to, 962
    Mexican War and, 393
    2000 elections and, 973
New Nationalism, 621–622

New Negro, 717

The New Negro, 717

New Netherlands, 33, 43–44, 68. *See also*
    New York

    British occupation of, 69, 71

New Orleans, battle of, 243(*m*), 244

New Orleans, Louisiana, 41, 239, 243(*m*),
    244, 423

    business elite of, 274–275

    Emancipation Proclamation and, 429

    free blacks in, 274–275

    jazz in, 705

    population of, 536(*t*)

    railroad connections to, 480

    Reconstruction and, 443

    transportation and, 305, 306(*m*),
        307(*m*), 308

Newport, Rhode Island, 55, 88, 89(*m*), 182

New Right, 938, 938(*i*), 967

    vs. feminism, 966

    1980 elections and, 943

    Reagan and, 947

New Spain, 495

newspapers, 143, 646. *See also* journalism; *New
    York Times*; *New York Tribune*

    abolitionist, 369, 370, 374

    baseball and, 561

    circulation of, 562(*t*)

    immigrants and, 552

    New York, 561, 637

    political cartoons in, 156(*i*), 221(*i*), 335(*i*),
        343(*i*), 568(*i*), 609(*i*), 618(*i*), 758(*i*)

    politics and, 324, 329, 335(*i*)

Newton, Huey, 895

Newton, Isaac, 112

New York

    British occupation of, 69, 71, 185

    colonial, 14, 43–44, 69, 71, 72, 73–74

    Dutch in, 43–44, 104, 105(*m*)

    Erie Canal, 302–305, 304(*i*), 306(*m*)

    gay marriage in, 966

    Hudson River manors, 104, 105(*m*)

    immigration to, 962

    land disputes in, 124–125

    land in, 104

    machine politics in, 569

    Mormons in, 364(*m*)

    New England immigrants, 302

    politics in, 324

    popular power in, 92

    ratification of Constitution by, 213

    representative assembly in, 74

    revivals in, 283(*m*)

    revolts in, 73–74

    in Revolutionary War, 172–176, 174(*m*), 185

    utopian communities in, 360, 361, 362

    voting rights in, 259(*m*), 260, 324

    West Indian trade and, 88, 89

    wheat production in, 124

    women's rights in, 375, 378, 380

New York Central Railroad, 509

New York City

    African American migration to, 708(*m*)

    business elite of, 310

    colonial, 43, 44, 73

    corruption in, 469

    draft riots in (1863), 424

    foreign trade and, 309

    Great Depression in, 747(*i*)

    immigrants from, 774(*i*)

    immigrants in, 537, 551(*i*), 551–552, 553(*i*),
        554(*i*), 556

    jazz and, 705

    liberalism in, 696

    Lower East Side in, 553(*m*)

    national elite and, 543

    Panic of 1837 and, 346

    population of, 536(*t*)

    Prohibition in, 714–715

    reform movement in, 317

    during Revolutionary era, 149(*m*), 182, 185

    riots in, 896

    slavery in, 90

    slums of, 313

    Stonewall riot in, 900

    subway in, 539

    as transportation hub, 303–306, 306(*m*),
        307(*m*)

    on V-J Day, 780

    West Indian trade and, 88, 89, 89(*m*)

New York Herald, 561

New York Humane Society, 282

New York Journal, 637

New York Sun, 561

New York Times

    Pentagon Papers and, 919

    Vietnam War and, 908, 909

New York Tribune, 309, 458, 468

    Fourierism and, 361

    Fuller and, 356

New York World, 561, 637
New Zealand, 828, 885
Nez Percé Indians, 487
Niagara Falls, New York, Love Canal, 928
Niagara Movement, 606
Nicaragua
    Contras in, 949
    right-wing regime in, 828
    U.S. intervention in, 701, 952
Nicholson, Lieutenant Governor, 73
nickelodeons, 560
Nike (company), 959(*i*)
Niles' Weekly Register (periodical), 292
Nimitz, Chester W., 804
9/11. *See* September 11, 2001, terrorist attacks
Ninety-eighth meridian, 476, 485
Ninety-five Theses (Luther), 30
Nipmuck Indians, 61
NIRA. *See* National Industrial Recovery Act
Nisei (second-generation Japanese
    Americans), 798
Nixon, Richard M. (1913–1994), 915, 943
    Alger Hiss and, 836
    antiwar movement and, 919, 921
    approval ratings of, 940
    as Eisenhower's running mate, 837
    environment and, 916, 929
    "kitchen debate" and, 848
    1968 elections and, 906–907, 907(*m*), 916(*i*)
    pardon of, 921, 939
    as president (1969–1974), 916(*i*), 916–921
    recognition of China, 910
    resignation of, 920
    on television, 863
    Vietnamization and, 908, 909, 910
    Watergate and, 916, 919–921, 922
nobility
    in medieval Europe, 16
    Price Revolution and, 34
Nonaggression Pact, Nazi-Soviet (1939),
    783, 785
nonimportation, 147(*i*), 148, 155. *See also*
    boycotts
Normandy, France, D-Day (June 6, 1944) in,
    801(*m*), 801–802
the North
    African American migration to, 552,
        676–678, 677(*m*), 708(*m*), 735–736
    civil rights movement and, 894, 896
    communal experiments in, 359(*m*)
    Compromise of 1850 and, 398
    economy of, 88–91, 459
    education in, 375
    Fugitive Slave Acts and, 399–400
    population of, 426
    racism in, 367
    Republican Party and, 402, 410
    slave vs. free states and, 396–398,
        401–403, 404
    vs. the South, 383, 413, 449
    Uncle Tom's Cabin and, 400
North, Lord, 172, 174, 182
    compromises of, 149–150
    naval blockade and, 155
North, Oliver, 949
North Africa, WWII in, 800, 800(*m*)
North American Free Trade Agreement
    (NAFTA), 959
North Anna, battle of, 435(*i*)
North Atlantic Treaty Organization (NATO),
    819(*m*), 828, 829(*m*), 830, 882
    creation of (1949), 821
    division of Europe under, 821
    Kosovo and, 972
    peacekeeping forces of, 972
North Carolina
    as colony, 44, 69, 75, 91
    ERA and, 932(*m*)
    freed slaves in, 449
    industrial capacity in, 426
    Ku Klux Klan in, 465
    land disputes in, 126, 128–129
    migration from, 301–302, 303(*m*)
    ratification of Constitution by, 213
    Regulators in, 125–126, 126(*m*), 128(*i*),
        128–129, 180, 233
    revivalism in, 317
    salutary neglect and, 92–93
    secession and, 414, 416
    slave labor in, 270, 276(*m*), 384
    voting rights in, 324
the Northeast. *See also* New England; New York
    Jackson and, 329
    John Q. Adams and, 327–328
    manufacturing in, 292–301
Northern Pacific Railroad, 468
Northern Securities Company, 615
North Korea, 824, 827, 976
Northwest Ordinance, 203(*m*), 204, 405, 406
Northwest Territory, 221

Norton, Charles Eliot, 645
Norway, 784, 821
Norwood (H. W. Beecher), 563
notables, 323–324
Notes on the State of Virginia (Jefferson),
    219, 239
Nova Scotia (Acadia), 10, 75, 76(*m*), 179, 184
    as British colony, 121, 149(*m*), 153, 154(*m*)
    control of fisheries off, 184
Noyes, John Humphrey (1811–1886), 361–362
NRA. *See* National Recovery Administration
NSC-68 (report of National Security
    Council), 823
nuclear power, 924(*f*)
    environmentalism and, 928–929
nuclear weapons, 823, 828, 831, 837, 864, 910.
    See also atomic bomb
    radioactive fallout from, 843
    U.S. monopoly of, 819
Nueces River, 392
nuevo mundo (new world), 24–25
nullification of tariffs, 333–334, 336, 343, 415
Nuremberg Laws, 802
nurses
    Civil War, 424–425, 425(*i*)
    in military, 789
Nye, Gerald P., 782–783

Oberlin College, 316(*i*)
Occupational Disease Commission, 612
occupational hazards, 612–613
Occupational Safety and Health
    Administration (OSHA), 917
Ochasteguins. *See* Huron Indians
O'Connor, Sandra Day, 950
Ogden, Aaron, 252
Oglethorpe, Georgia, 311
Ohio, 10, 230, 234, 795, 980
    migration to, 234, 301–302, 303(*m*)
    Shakers in, 360
    slavery in, 386
    utopian communities in, 361, 362
    voting rights in, 259(*m*), 260, 323–324
    westward migration from, 388
Ohio Company, 119–121, 126(*m*)
Ohio River, 63, 65, 236, 241, 416, 420,
    421, 422(*m*)
Ohio River Valley
    expansion of Quebec and, 153–154
    French and Indian War and, 119–121, 120(*m*)

oil
    embargo on (1970s), 944
    energy use and, 960
    foreign policy and, 828, 830, 831
    in Mexico, 701
    in Middle East, 944, 956(*m*)
    in Persian Gulf, 922
    prices of, 940, 948
oil industry
    energy consumption and, 924(*f*)
    energy crisis and, 915, 921–922
    environmentalism and, 928
    foreign investment and, 701
    markets for, 512
    subsidies to, 926
    in Sun Belt, 926
oil spills, 928
Okies, 739–740. *See also* Dust Bowl
Okinawa, 805, 805(*m*), 806
Oklahoma
    drought in, 737
    Indian reservations in, 486–487, 488
    Ku Klux Klan in, 712
Old Age Revolving Pension Plan, 759
Old Lights, 116
Old Republicans, 328
Old Southwest (Alabama, Mississippi,
    Louisiana), 233
    migration to, 267(*i*), 268, 269(*m*),
    301–302, 303(*m*)
Old Whigs, 145. *See also* Whig
    Party (England)
oligopolies, 697, 849
Oliver, Andrew, 139
Oliver, Robert, 246
Olmec Indians, 9
Olmsted, Frederick Law, 540–541
Olney, Richard, 531, 597, 635
Olsen, Tillie, 775
Olympics, boycotts of, 941
Omaha, Nebraska, 480
    Mormons in, 364(*m*)
Oñate, Juan de, 40
Oneida Community, 359(*m*), 361–362
Oneida Indians, 63
O'Neill, Eugene, 717
Onondaga Indians, 63
"On The Equality of the Sexes"
    (Murray), 201
On the Origin of Species (Darwin), 571

On the Road (Kerouac), 860
OPA. *See* Price Administration, Office of
OPEC. *See* Organization of Petroleum
   Exporting Countries
Opechancanough, 46–47, 61
open-door policy, 650–651, 785
Operation Desert Storm, 954
Operation Rolling Thunder, 885
Operation Wetback, 861
opinion polls, 777, 781, 978. *See also* public
   opinion
   on evangelical Christianity, 937
   Vietnam War and, 889, 904, 908
Orange, New Jersey, 522
Order of the Star-Spangled Banner, 402
Ordinance of Nullification, 333–334
Oregon, 389*(m)*, 393, 395
   annexation of, 391
   economy of, 494–495
   1844 elections and, 391
   gay marriage in, 966
   Japanese internment in, 797
   Ku Klux Klan in, 712
   migration to, 388, 389–390
Oregon territory
   British ceding of, 479
   settlement of, 479, 494, 495*(m)*
Oregon Trail, 364*(m)*, 389*(m)*, 390, 479
Organization of Petroleum Exporting
   Countries (OPEC), 922–923
Orlando, Vittorio, 684
Orpen, William, 686
Orphan Asylum Society, 315
Ostend Manifesto (1854), 401
Ostram, Mary Walker, 374
O'Sullivan, John L., 387–388
Oswald, Lee Harvey, 872
The Other America (Harrington), 848
Otis, James, 138, 142
Ottawa Indians, 65, 122, 123*(i)*, 229, 229*(i)*
"The Outcasts of Poker Flat" (Harte), 500
outsourcing, 960
outwork system, 247–248
   in agriculture, 106
   household production and, 106, 148, 293
Ovington, Mary White, 606, 607
Owens Valley, California, 502
"Oxford Pledge," 732
ozone depletion, 960. *See also* environment
Ozzie and Harriet (TV program), 854

pachuco (youth) gangs, 796
Pacific Mail Steamship Company, 499
Pacific region
   U.S. in, 631, 646, 650–652, 651*(m)*
   WWII in, 802–806
Pacific slope, 495*(m)*
   ranches in, 495, 496–497
pacifism
   abolitionism and, 372
   Garrison and, 352
   in Pennsylvania, 70
   Quakers and, 109, 111, 125, 157
Pago Pago (Samoa), 632
Pahlavi, Muhammad Reza, shah of Iran, 828, 941
Paige, Satchel, 707
Paine, Sarah Cobb, 185
Paine, Thomas (1737–1809), 166, 170–171,
   173. *See also Common Sense*
   attack on George III, 170
   on word "republic," 184
Paiute Indians, 490
Pakistan
   Afghanistan and, 941
   immigrants from, 962
   in SEATO, 828
Palestine, 830, 978
Palestine Liberation Organization (PLO), 972
Palestine Mandate, 684
Palestinian-Israeli conflict, 956*(m)*, 975, 978
Palladio, Andrea, 20
Palmer, A. Mitchell, 689
Palmer raids (1919–1920), 689
Panama (Isthmus of Darien), 25, 630
Panama Canal, 647–648
   Colombia and, 647
   U.S. return of, 940
Pan American conference, 630
Pan-Americanism, 630
Pan-American Union, 630
panics. *See also* depressions; Great Depression
   of 1819, 247
   of 1837, 346, 358, 361
   of 1857, 301, 311
   of 1873, 468, 480, 505
   of 1893, 588, 592, 634
pantheism, 355
Paris, France, 14
   liberation of, 802
Paris, Treaty of (1763), 133*(m)*, 154*(m)*, 184,
   228, 230

Paris, Treaty of (1783), 231(*m*)
    western lands and, 227, 228, 229, 230,
        231(*m*)
Paris, Treaty of (1899), 644
Parker, Alton B., 616
parks
    Central Park, New York City, 541
    national, 501, 502, 502(*i*), 614(*m*),
        854, 876, 940
    urban planning and, 541
Parks, Rosa, 842
Parliament, English, 34
    taxation and, 132–138
patent medicine, 618
Paterson, William, 209
patriarchy, 16–17, 87, 100–103
    vs. republicanism, 260–261
Patriots, 131, 138–140. *See also* Sons of Liberty
    alliance with France and, 179–180
    ideological roots of, 142–143, 151
    vs. Loyalists, 166, 167, 172, 176
    Radical Whig, 175, 216
patronage, 567, 576
    in colonies, 87, 94, 132
    John Q. Adams and, 329
    Van Buren and, 324
Patterson, John, 869
Patton, George S., 747–748, 800
Paul, Alice, 602, 680
Pawnee Indians, 478, 479
Paxton Boys, 125, 126(*m*)
Payne-Aldrich Tariff Act (1909), 620
Peace Corps, 865, 875
Peace Democrats, 436
peaceful coexistence, 827, 867, 909
peace movement, 655. *See also* antiwar
    movement
Peale, Charles Willson, 173(*i*), 263(*i*)
Peale, James, 263(*i*)
Peale, Norman Vincent, 855
Pearce, Charles H., 460
Pearl Harbor, attack on (December 7, 1941),
        631, 780, 785–787, 803, 804(*m*)
peasants, 9, 14–17, 272
peddlers, 247, 248(*i*), 551(*i*)
Pelham, Henry, 121
Peña, Frederico, 968
Pendleton, Edmund, 168
Pendleton Act (1883), 567
Penn, John, 125

Penn, William, 70, 91, 124
Pennsylvania, 127
    assembly of, 91
    coal mining in, 507, 522(*i*)
    as colony, 70
    German immigrants in, 70, 106–111, 157
    internal migration to, 795
    Know-Nothing Party in, 402
    Quakers in, 70, 106–109
    revivalism in, 114, 317
    transportation in, 235
    voting rights in, 258, 259(*m*)
    West Indian trade and, 90
    wheat production in, 124
Pennsylvania Gazette, 114
Pennsylvania Railroad, 505, 507
Pentagon, September 11, 2001 attack on, 976
Pentagon Papers, 919
peonage (forced labor), 462
People's Party. *See* Populist Party
People's Republic of China
    establishment of (1949), 823, 881
    globalization and, 959
    Korean War and, 824–825
    Nixon and, 916
    support for Vietnam by, 881, 882, 887
    United Nations and, 824
    U.S. recognition of, 909–910
    Vietnam War and, 888
Peoria Indians, 43
Pequot Indians, 59, 61
perestroika, 953
perfectionism, 361–362
Perkins, Frances, 608, 754, 761, 767
Perot, H. Ross, 967
Perry, Oliver Hazard, 242
Pershing, John J., 654, 654(*i*), 669–670
Persia. *See* Iran
Persian Gulf, 922
Persian Gulf War (1990–1991), 911, 954,
        956(*m*)
    sanctions and, 975
    television and, 961
    women in, 957(*i*)
Personal Responsibility and Work Opportunity
        Act (1996), 970
Peru, 7, 9, 27, 28(*m*), 630
Petersburg, Virginia, 434, 435, 436
petrochemical industry, 852
petroleum industry. *See* oil industry

phalanxes (Fourierist communities), 361
Philadelphia, Pennsylvania, 72
    abolitionist convention in (1830), 367–368
    agitation against George III in, 170
    antiabolitionism in, 372
    Committee of Resistance in, 170
    Committee on Prices in, 186
    Continental Army in, 176
    free blacks in, 268
    Howe's attack on, 174(m), 176
    industrial development in, 535, 537
    Patriot traders in, 188
    population of, 536(t)
    during Revolutionary era, 149(m)
    slavery in, 90
    South Atlantic system and, 89–90
    Tom Paine in, 170
    transportation and, 250, 305–306,
        306(m), 307(m)
    unions in, 300
    West Indian trade and, 88–90, 89(m)
    women of, 376
Philadelphia Centennial (1876), 509(i)
Philadelphia Convention (1787), 266
Philadelphia Female Anti-Slavery Society, 370
philanthropy, 562–563. See also charitable
    activities
Philip, King (Metacom; Wamponoag chief),
    61–62, 62(i)
Philippines, 122. See also Filipinos
    acquisition from Spain of, 642–644
    human rights in, 940
    immigrants from, 743, 860, 962
    independence of, 646, 860
    right-wing regime in, 828
    in SEATO, 828
    Spanish-American war in, 639, 641(m),
        642–646
    vs. United States, 645–646
    U.S. foreign investment in, 701
    in WWII, 803, 804(m), 805(m)
Phillip II, king of Spain (r. 1556–1598),
    31–33, 33, 38
Phillips, David Graham, 599
Phillips, Wendell, 368, 429
phonograph, 705
photography, 723, 735, 775
photojournalism, 775
Physicians for Social Responsibility, 843
Pickett, George E., 431

Pickford, Mary, 704
Piedmont region, 123
Pierce, Franklin (1804–1869), 400–401
    as president (1853–1857), 402
Pietism, 99, 112, 114–115, 574
Pike, James M., 468
Pike's Peak, 494
Pilgrims, 53–56. See also Puritans
Pilgrim's Progress (Bunyan), 599
Pinchot, Gifford, 620
Pinckney, Thomas, 446
Pinckney's Treaty (1795), 239
Pine Bluff, Arkansas, 449–450
Pine Ridge reservation, South Dakota, 899
Pinkerton Detective Agency, 530
Pitt, William, 121–122, 137, 145–146, 155
Pittsburgh, Pennsylvania, 536, 540. See also
        Fort Duquesne
    coal mining in, 508(m)
    railroad strike and, 505
    steel production and, 507
    transportation and, 305, 306(m),
        307(m), 308
Pius IX, Pope, 319
Pizarro, Francisco, 27
Plain Home Talk on Love, Marriage, and
        Parentage (Foote), 548
Plains Indians. See Native Americans: on Great
        Plains
planning
    suburban, 541
    urban, 540–541
plantations, 123–124. See also the South
    cotton and, 302, 308, 383–384
    culture of, 124
    impact of sharecropping on, 464(m)
    Kansas-Nebraska Act and, 402
    religion of, 112, 117, 118
    river, 49(i)
    sharecropping on, 463(m)
    slavery and, 80–83, 266–273, 267(i), 269(m),
        280–281
    Southern gentry and, 87
    sugar and, 630–631, 631(i)
    sugar production and, 77
Platt, Orville, 632
Platt Amendment, 648
    repeal of, 782
Pledge of Allegiance, 855
Plessy v. Ferguson (1896), 586, 840

PLO. *See* Palestine Liberation Organization
plumbers, Watergate, 919
Plunkitt, George Washington, 556
pluralism. *See also* ethnic diversity
    cultural, 962–965
    ethnic, 709, 962–965
    religious, 99, 104, 108*(m)*, 108–111
Plymouth colony, 72, 73
    legal code in, 54
Poague, William, 416
los pobros (the poor ones), 497
Pocahontas, 46
Poland, 684, 818, 821
    German invasion of, 783, 784
    Holocaust in, 802
    Yalta and, 806
Poland Hill, Maine, 360*(i)*
police action. *See* Korean War
police brutality
    American Indian movement and, 899
    civil rights movement and, 896
    at Democratic convention, 906
    gay rights movement and, 900
Polish immigrants, 552
political action committees (PACs), 921
political campaigns. *See also* elections;
    presidential elections
    economy as issue in, 967, 970, 971, 980
    finance reform and, 921
    fundraising for, 921
    Internet and, 962
    presidential, 837*(i)*, 837–838, 967
    television and, 863, 943
political crisis of 1790s, 215–225
political parties. *See also* elections; *individual*
    parties
    nineteenth-century changes in, 398–406
    boss system and, 556
    fragmentation of, 409–410
    loyalty to, 574
    male-dominated, 579*(i)*
    new, 401–402
    and political machine, 324
    political machines and, 556, 569, 576–577
    priorities of, 568–569
    realignment of (1848–1860), 405*(m)*
    regional vs. national, 405*(m)*
    rise of, 221–222, 323–325
    workingmen's, 345
political theory, 113

politics
    abolitionism and, 372, 382–383
    African Americans and, 446, 556
    American, 322–323
    biracial, 581–584
    British, 91–96
    class, 577
    corruption in, 324, 460, 468, 469, 597. *See*
      also patronage
    Depression-era movies on, 733–734
    direct primary in, 604, 605
    elite, 91, 92
    energy crisis and, 923–924
    of expectation, 863–873
    farmer-labor, 588, 590, 593
    government-business cooperation in,
      692–693
    imperial, 68–76
    initiative and recall in, 605
    international, 923–924
    Ku Klux Klan and, 712
    labeling in, 619
    labor unions in, 767
    of late nineteenth century, 566–596
    machine, 569, 576–577, 597, 604
    middle class and, 323–324, 336
    new, 863–864
    in "New Era" (1920s), 693–697
    newspapers and, 329
    post-Watergate, 939–944
    power, 604–605
    race and, 581–584
    reform in, 577
    religion and, 324
    of resentment, 937–938, 943
    rise of popular, 323–330
    sharecropping and, 464
    slavery and, 383, 396–398
    students in, 732
    ward, 555–556
    women in, 348–349, 695–696, 930
    in WWII, 793–794
Polk, James K. (1795–1849), 396
    expansionism of, 391, 392, 394, 395, 401
    as president (1845–1849), 392–395
Pollock, Jackson, 774, 859
poll taxes, 258
    voting rights and, 456, 584, 840, 874
pollution. *See also* environmentalism
    highways and, 853

at Love Canal, 928
from mining, 501
Pol Pot, 908
Ponce de León, Juan, 25
Pontiac (Ottawa chief), 123(*i*)
    rebellion of, 122, 132
Pony Express, 389(*m*), 479
Poor Richard's Almanack (Franklin), 113
Popé (shaman), 40
popular culture. *See also* advertising; mass
    media; movies; television
    of 1950s, 854
    Great Depression and, 733–735
    intellectual life and, 717
    leisure and, 707
    WWII and, 794–795
popular front, Communist, 766
popular sovereignty, 252, 339
    original meaning of, 197
    slavery decisions and, 397–398, 399(*m*), 400,
        401–402, 403, 407, 408
population
    changes in, 962–965, 963(*m*)
    in colonial America, 99, 103, 124, 126(*m*)
    disease and, 26–27
    in England, 33
    environment and, 9
    first census (1790) and, 228
    Great Depression and, 730
    immigration and, 511, 551
    life expectancy and, 855
    in Middle Atlantic colonies, 104
    Native American, 9, 26–27, 63, 65
    of North vs. South, 426
    patterns of, 708
    seasonal patterns and, 15–16
    Spanish conquests and, 27, 28
    in Sun Belt, 852
    urbanization and, 308–309
    in the West, 491–495, 495(*m*)
    WWII and, 810
Populism
    of American West, 532–533
    among farmers, 532, 588–589, 589(*i*)
    Father Coughlin and, 759
    one party rule and, 584–591
    women's rights and, 589–590
Populist Party, 589
    free silver and, 590–591
    platform of (1892), 590

Port Bill (1774), 153
Port Hudson, Louisiana, 430
Port Huron Statement (1962), 891
Portland, Oregon, 494, 495(*m*)
Portugal, 6, 23, 32, 77, 821
    maritime expansion and, 18–22, 21(*m*)
Postlethwayt, Malachy, 68
Post Office Act (1792), 305
Potomac River, 419
Potsdam Conference, 818
Pottawatomie massacre (1856), 403
Potter, Helen, 580
poverty
    Bush (George H. W.) and, 951
    in cities, 964, 965
    civil rights movement and, 894, 897
    of elderly, 862
    feminization of, 933
    Hoover on, 745
    of immigrants, 310, 313–314, 319–320
    LBJ's war on, 874–877
    New Deal and, 777
    1928 elections and, 719
    in 1950s, 860–862
    in 1990s, 951, 956
    of women, 313, 315
Powderly, Terence V., 525–526, 529
Powell, Adam Clayton, Sr., 717
Powell, Colin, 954, 975
Powell, Lewis F., Jr., 918
The Power of Positive Thinking (Peale), 855
Powers, Francis Gary, 843
Powhatan, 46
POWs. *See* prisoners of war
pragmatism, 599
prairies, 476–478, 477(*m*)
    destruction by cattle, 481, 482
    short grama grass, 477(*m*), 477–478
praying towns, 61. *See also* Algonquian Indians
predestination, 55
Preemption Act (1841), 349
Presbyterians, 31, 193
    abolitionism and, 369
    in colonial America, 104, 108, 108(*m*),
        110–111, 114
    egalitarianism of, 117, 310
    Enlightenment and, 264
    evangelical, 324
    New Lights, 115–118, 127, 170
    Old Lights, 116

Presbyterians (*cont.*)
  Princeton and, 116
  social reform and, 314–317, 374
  synods of, 277
prescription drug benefits, 979
presidency
  control of, 693
  expanded powers of, 754
  FDR and, 763
  imperial, 921
  LBJ and, 874, 885
  New Deal and, 752
  Watergate and, 921
Presidential Commission on the Status of
    Women (1963), 901
presidential elections
  of 2004, 980
  radio and, 705–706
  Adams, John (1796), 222
  Adams, John Quincy (1824), 318(*m*),
    325–326
  Arthur, Chester A. (1880), 567
  Buchanan, James (1856), 403–405
  Bush, George H. W. (1988), 950–951
  Bush, George W. (2000), 973–975
  Bush, George W. (2004), 980
  Carter, James E. (1976), 937
  Cleveland, Grover (1884), 567–569,
    570(*m*), 577
  Cleveland, Grover (1888), 570(*m*)
  Cleveland, Grover (1892), 567, 568(*i*),
    594(*m*)
  Clinton, William Jefferson (1992), 967–968
  Clinton, William Jefferson (1996), 964, 970
  Coolidge, Calvin (1924), 694
  Eisenhower, Dwight D. (1952), 827, 837(*i*),
    837–838
  Garfield, James A. (1880), 567
  Grant, Ulysses S. (1868), 455–456
  Grant, Ulysses S. (1872), 468, 576–577
  Harding, Warren G. (1920), 693
  Harrison, Benjamin (1888), 567, 568(*i*),
    570(*m*), 588
  Harrison, William Henry (1840), 347–349,
    348(*i*)
  Hayes, Rutherford B. (1876), 469, 567
  Hoover, Herbert (1928), 719–720,
    720(*m*), 744
  Jackson, Andrew (1832), 335–336
  Jefferson, Thomas (1800), 224, 237

  Johnson, Lyndon B. (1964), 873, 874, 885
  Johnson, Lyndon B. (1968), 904, 905
  Kennedy, John F. (1960), 863–864
  Lincoln, Abraham (1860), 405(*m*),
    408(*i*), 409–410
  Lincoln, Abraham (1864), 434, 436–437
  McKinley, William (1896), 593–594, 594(*m*),
    619(*i*), 645
  Madison, James (1808), 237
  Madison, James (1812), 237, 242
  Nixon, Richard M. (1968), 906–907, 907(*m*),
    916(*i*), 917
  Nixon, Richard M. (1972), 910, 916(*i*),
    918–919
  Pierce, Franklin (1852), 400–401
  Polk, James K. (1844), 391
  Reagan, Ronald (1980), 938, 942–943
  Reagan, Ronald (1984), 949
  Roosevelt, Franklin D. (1932), 748–749,
    749(*m*)
  Roosevelt, Franklin D. (1936), 760, 763
  Roosevelt, Franklin D. (1940), 784
  Roosevelt, Franklin D. (1944), 793
  Roosevelt, Theodore (1904), 616,
    617–618, 619(*i*)
  Taft, William Howard (1908), 652
  Taylor, Zachary (1848), 396, 405(*m*)
  Truman, Harry S. (1948), 832–833
  Van Buren, Martin (1836), 344
  Washington, George (1788), 215
  Wilson, Woodrow (1912), 623(*m*), 652
  Wilson, Woodrow (1916), 668
presidios (forts), 390, 496
Presley, Elvis, 858, 859(*i*)
Price Administration, Office of (OPA),
    795, 831
Price Revolution, 33–34
prices. *See also* consumer price index
  agricultural, 588
  controls on, 693, 831, 975
  inflation and, 925
  New Deal and, 757
  of oil, 940, 948
  WWII and, 831
primogeniture, 17, 263
The Prince (Machiavelli), 20
Princeton, New Jersey, battle of, 173, 174(*m*)
Princeton College, founding of, 116
Princip, Gavrilo, 663
Principia Mathematica (Newton), 112

printing industry, 113, 142, 143, 148
Prioleau, George W., 643
Prison Discipline Society, 314
prisoners of war (POWs)
    Bataan death march and, 803
    German, 792
    in Vietnam War, 885, 910
prisons
    abolition of, 352, 372
    debtors', 197, 206–207, 323, 345
    as reforming institutions, 314–315
    reform of, 372, 375, 459
Privy Council (British), 146, 152
Proclamation for Suppressing Rebellion and
    Sedition, 167
Proclamation Line (1763), 122, 132–133,
    133(m), 154(m), 157
Production Code Administration, 733
Professional Air Traffic Controllers
    Organization (PATCO), 958
Progressive Era (1890–1914), 563,
    597–627, 834
    academic expertise in, 598
    consumer rights and, 929
    end of, 693
    New Deal and, 776
Progressive Party, 694
    new, 621, 832, 833
progressivism
    and environment, 614(m)
    fracturing of Republican, 620–621
    national politics and, 611–621
    of 1970s, 928–930
    Prohibition and, 680–681
    reform and, 679–681
    science and, 598
    white supremacy and, 605, 607
    women and, 600–601, 679–680
    in WWI, 679–681
Prohibition, 578–579, 715(i)
    Al Smith on, 749
    Democratic Party and, 694
    Eighteenth Amendment on, 681, 714
    politics and, 718
    progressive reform and, 680–681
    repeal of (1933), 756
    rural areas vs. cities in, 681
    WWI impetus for, 681
Prohibitory Act (1775), 180
Promontory Point, Utah, 480

propaganda
    vigilante groups and, 682
    wartime, 681–683
property
    common ownership of, 353, 358, 359, 361
    ownership of, 233, 446, 448
    political rights and, 91
    private, 246, 251, 252–253
    protection of, 210, 448, 461
    slaves as, 449
    taxation of, 459
    voting rights and, 92, 322–324, 456, 464
property rights, 197, 199, 251, 252–253
    abolitionism and, 371
    in Confederacy, 428
    conflicts over, 125–129
    corporate, 253
    Dred Scott and and, 406
    freeholders and, 100–104, 105(m)
    inheritance and, 102, 260
    Mormons and, 366
    Reconstruction and, 461
    slavery and, 383, 418, 429
    of women, 87, 100, 102, 109, 378,
        379, 380
Prophetstown, Indiana, 241
Proposition 13 (California), 937
Proposition 187 (California), 964
proprietorships, 69–70, 73, 74
prospectors, 492(m), 492–494, 498
Prosser, Gabriel, 190, 272
Prosser, Martin, 272, 281
prostitution, 375, 559, 560, 680
The Prostrate State (Pike), 468
protectionism, 569, 592, 620, 699. *See also*
    tariffs: protective
Protestantism, 73, 85. *See also* evangelicalism;
    individual denominations
    accumulation of wealth and, 571
    anti-Catholicism of, 141, 153, 154(m),
        319–320
    evangelical, 559
    French (Huguenots), 31, 41, 108–109
    immigration and, 558–559
    in Ireland, 972
    Know-Nothing Party and, 402
    Manifest Destiny and, 388
    missionary action and, 282, 283(m)
    modernist vs. fundamentalist, 713–714
    muscular Christianity and, 559

Protestantism (*cont.*)
  in New World, 37, 38, 41, 47–48
  in 1950s, 855
  in North, 558–559
  Republican Party, 574–576, 575(*f*)
  social reform and, 277, 282, 314, 599
  Whigs and, 342
  women and, 262, 284–286
  work ethic and, 311, 692
Protestant Reformation, 29–31. *See also*
    Calvinism; Luther, Martin
  in England, 31
  in Holland, 31, 32
  Roman Catholic Church and, 29–33
Providence, Rhode Island, 55, 88, 295
public assistance. *See* welfare
Public Interest Research Group, 930
public opinion
  on civil rights, 872
  in 1990s, 955–956
  presidential use of, 619(*i*)
  WWII and, 781
public works, 540, 541
  Great Depression and, 744–745
  Long and, 759
  in New Deal, 757, 762(*m*), 768
  Roosevelt recession and, 764
  states and, 951
  War on Poverty and, 875
Public Works Administration (PWA), 757,
    762(*m*), 768
publishing industry, 718, 735
Pueblo Indians, 11–12, 27, 38–40, 496
  revolt of, 40
Puerto Ricans, 874
Puerto Rico
  annexation of, 642, 646
  immigrants from, 861
Puget Sound, 389
Pulitzer, Joseph, 561, 637
Pullman, George M., 531
Pullman strike (1894), 531, 592, 597
pump priming, 745
Pure Food and Drug Act, 619
Puritans, 31, 53–61, 103–104, 131
  coercive policies of, 54–56
  vs. English government, 56
  as freeholders, 100
  during French and Indian War, 121
  Great Awakening and, 113, 114–115

  vs. hierarchichal institutions, 56
  Mormons and, 363
  Plymouth colony and, 53–54, 72, 73
  republicanism and, 143, 148, 282
  Revolution of, 56, 138, 141
  seizure of Indian lands by, 55, 59
  transcendentalism and, 353
  witchcraft fears of, 57–58
  women and, 55–56, 100–102
putting-out system, 247

al-Qaddafi, Muammar, 952
Quaker Oats Company, 513(*i*)
Quakers, 102, 104, 106–109, 278
  abolitionism and, 189–190, 368,
    370, 376
  Calvinism and, 70
  as merchants, 309
  in Nantucket, 274(*i*)
  in New Jersey, 106, 109
  pacifism of, 109, 111, 125, 157, 284
  in Pennsylvania, 70, 106–109
  social equality and, 106, 109, 310
  women of, 70
Quartering Acts
  of 1765, 138, 146
  of 1774, 153
Quayle, Dan, 950, 967
Quebec, 6, 41, 42, 63, 75
  battle for (1758), 122
  capture of (1759), 122
  colonization of, 122, 132, 133(*m*)
Quebec Act (1774), 153, 154(*m*), 157
Queen Anne's War (War of the Spanish
    Succession; 1702–1713), 74, 76(*m*)
Queen's College. *See* Rutgers University
Queen's Own Loyal Virginians, 167
Quetzalcoatl, 25
Quinn, Anthony, 794

Rabin, Yitzhak, 972
race. *See also* ethnicity; *individual groups*
  Democratic coalition and, 777
  feminism and, 931, 966
  Great Depression and, 728
  in Japan, 684
  lynchings and, 688
  in military, 671–672
  reform and, 352
  status and, 29, 51

race riots
    African Americans and, 880, 895–896,
        896(m), 903, 906
    in Chicago, 688
    in Harlem (1935), 736
    Latinos and, 965
    in Los Angeles, 964–965
    Mexican Americans and, 796
    post-WWI, 688
    social structure and, 965
    Springfield (1908), 606
    WWII and, 795–796
racism, 80, 268, 272–275, 408. See also
        lynching; segregation
    abolitionism and, 371–372
    anti-Asian, 652, 742
    anti-Semitic, 790
    anti-Vietnamese, 887–889
    atomic bomb and, 809
    in California, 499–500
    in cities, 552, 862
    civil rights movement and, 897
    cultural conflict and, 707–708
    France and, 716
    Free-Soil Party and, 395
    immigration restriction and, 652, 709, 711
    interracial marriage and, 371, 412–413
    Jim Crow laws and, 585–587, 897
    Ku Klux Klan and, 712
    Manifest Destiny and, 388
    Mexican Americans and, 740, 741–742
    middle-class, 371–372
    in military, 433, 641–643, 671–672, 788
    National Advisory Commission (1968)
        and, 897
    in New South, 581–584, 587(i)
    Ninth Cavalry experience of, 643
    opposition to, 889, 891, 893–897
    Philippine annexation and, 645
    post-WWI, 688
    Reconstruction and, 450
    reform and, 605, 606, 607
    Scottsboro case and, 736
    in the South, 485, 581–584, 897
    in Spanish-American War, 641–643,
        642(i)
    in suburbs, 852
    voting rights and, 257, 259–260
    in WWI, 671–672
    in WWII, 780, 792

radar, 828
radicalism, 531–533
    fear of, 688–689
    in the West, 532–533
Radical movement, southern, 409–410, 413
Radical Republicans, 443, 445, 451–452,
        461, 468–470
radio
    Father Coughlin on, 759
    FDR and, 753–754
    in Great Depression, 734(m), 734–735
    JFK-Nixon debates on, 863
    music and, 857
    national culture and, 705–706
    religion and, 855
    television and, 854
    WWII and, 795
radioactive fallout, 843
railroads, 293, 307(m), 426, 434. See also Central
        Pacific Railroad; Union Pacific Railroad
    Adamson eight-hour law and, 625
    advertising by, 482, 488
    Baltimore and Ohio, 505
    bankruptcy of, 588
    Brotherhood of Locomotive Firemen, 532
    cattle industry and, 480–481, 486
    Chicago, Burlington, and Quincy, 509
    completion of transcontinental (1869), 480
    construction of, 479–480
    destruction of, 436
    development of California and, 494–495,
        497, 498, 501
    elevated, 538, 538(i)
    entepreneurship and, 536
    Erie, 306, 510
    expansion of, 305–307, 306(m), 307(m)
    federal government and, 531, 573
    freight rates for, 510
    government support for, 508, 531, 567, 573
    Great Depression and, 725
    Great Northern, 510
    in Great Plains, 479–481, 486, 488, 511(m)
    hub for, 307(m)
    immigrant labor and, 498(i), 498–499
    industrialization and, 505–511, 508(m)
    investment in, 301, 341, 343, 508–510
    labor unions and, 531, 597
    land grants for, 479–480, 508
    Missouri Pacific, 480, 510
    nationalization of, 694

railroads (*cont.*)
New York Central, 509
Northern Pacific, 468, 480
Pennsylvania, 505, 507
Pullman strike (1894) of, 531, 592, 597
Reconstruction and, 458, 459
regulation of, 567, 618
Rock Island, 482
Santa Fe, 480, 501
segregation laws and, 581, 585
in the South, 516(*m*)
Southern Pacific, 480, 501
in Southwest, 496, 497
strikes against, 505, 531, 590, 832
track gauge, 510
transcontinental, 401, 403, 479–480, 493(*i*), 498, 498(*i*)
Wabash, 510
Wall Street and, 510
western expansion and, 479–482, 488, 501, 511(*m*)
Railroad War Board, 675
Rainbow Coalition, 950
Rainey, Ma, 705
rain forests, 960
Raleigh, Walter, 44, 45(*i*)
Ramona (Jackson), 500
Ramsay, David, 166, 227
ranching. *See also* cattle industry
barbed wire and, 485
cattle, 305, 390
on Great Plains, 480–482, 485–486
range right and, 481
sheep, 482, 486, 496
in Texas, 480–481, 496, 497
in the West, 495, 496–497
Randolph, A. Philip, 667, 790, 840, 871
Randolph, Edward, 71
Ranke, Leopold von, 196
Rankin, Christopher, 275
Rankin, Jeannette, 669, 787
al-Rantissi, Abdel Aziz, 978
Raphael, 20
rapid transit. *See* transportation system
Raskob, John J., 724
ratification conventions, 208–211
rationing, World War II, 794, 795
Rauschenbush, Walter, 599
La Raza Unida (The United Race), 898
Readjusters, 582

Reagan, Nancy, 947(*i*)
Reagan, Ronald (1911–2004), 925, 938, 939, 942–944
air traffic controllers and, 958
Alzheimer's of, 947(*i*)
domestic policies of, 947–951
Iran-Contra Affair and, 949
labor unions and, 958
as president (1981–1989), 947–950
rollback of federal power and, 967
Teflon presidency of, 949
Reagan Democrats, 943
Reaganomics, 948–949, 957
budget deficits and, 948, 950
recessions, 979. *See also* depressions; panics
of FDR, 764
foreign trade and, 851
vs. Great Depression, 724–725
migrant workers and, 861
of 1920–1921, 696–697, 724
of 1975–1976, 939
of 1990s, 951, 954, 967
postwar, 851
of Reagan (1981–1982), 948
reconquista, 24
Reconstruction (1865–1877), 442–471, 605
end of (1877), 581
Fourteenth Amendment and, 573
Presidential, 443–452
quest for land in, 460–464
Radical, 452–464, 453(*m*), 468–470
Republicans and, 442, 568–569
role of black churches in, 460
southern resistance to, 485
undoing of, 464–470
violence and, 451
Reconstruction Act (1867), 453, 455(*t*)
Reconstruction Finance Corporation (RFC), 745
red-baiting, 775. *See also* anticommunism
Red Cloud, Chief of the Sioux, 486
Red Cross, 680
Redeemers, 465, 467
home rule and, 581–582
one party system and, 581
redemptioners, 109
Red Jacket (Sagoyewatha; c.1758–1830), 230, 232(*i*)
Redmond, Juanita, 803
Red River Valley, North Dakota, 485, 487

Red Scare, 689. *See also* anticommunism
  nativism and, 709
  power of federal government and, 696
Red Shirts, 467
reform, 597–599. *See also* social reform
  British (1763–1765), 131–137, 143, 146
  economic, 353
  educational, 265, 375
  government, 341–342
  labor, 608–610
  moral, 375, 575–576, 680–681
  progressive, 719
  racism and, 605, 606
  Republican Party and, 403, 620–621
  tariff, 623
Reform Bill of 1832 (England), 323
Reform Party, 973
refugees
  Cuban, 861
  European, 860
  Holocaust and, 802
  in 1950s, 861
regionalism, 318(*m*), 405(*m*)
  interstate highways and, 853(*m*)
  television and, 854
regulation. *See also* deregulation
  of economy, 693, 776
  of railroads, 567, 618
Regulators, 157
  in North Carolina, 125–126, 126(*m*), 128(*i*),
    128–129, 180, 233
Rehnquist, William, 918, 950
relief. *See* welfare
religion, 37–41, 53–56. *See also* evangelicalism;
    Great Awakening; Protestant Reformation;
    revivalism; Second Great Awakening;
    individual denominations
  abolitionism and, 268, 284, 368–371, 374
  African, 85
  African American, 117–118, 268, 274,
    277–281, 460, 552, 555, 717, 872
  anti-Masonry and, 344
  Cold War and, 829
  conservative social values and, 975
  Crusades and, 18
  cultural conflict and, 707–708, 713–714
  diversity of, 99, 104, 108(*m*), 108–111
  English civil war and, 56, 69, 72–73
  Enlightenment and, 281
  established church and, 257

  in Europe, 17–18, 29–33
  freedom of, 55, 70, 190, 193–194
  intolerance and, 55–56
  justification of slavery and, 384
  vs. laws of nature, 58
  leisure and, 735
  medieval, 17–18
  in Middle Atlantic colonies (1720–1765), 99,
    104, 108(*m*), 108–111
  Native American, 9, 10, 12, 13, 40, 42, 43
  New Age, 928
  in 1950s, 855
  Okie, 740
  parochial schools and, 575–576
  on plantations, 112, 117–118
  politics and, 324
  prayer in public schools and, 918, 943
  progressive idealism and, 599
  reform and, 352–381
  separation of church and state, 190,
    193–194, 257
  social meaning and, 557, 559
  society and, 54–56
  taxation and, 193–194
  and Vietnam War, 881
  wars of, 18, 56
  women's rights and, 374
Religious Right, 1980 elections and, 943
Renaissance
  American, 265
  impact of, 18–20
  Muslim influences on, 18–19
Reno, Janet, 968
Reorganized Church of Jesus Christ of
    Latter-day Saints, 364
representative government, 136–141
republic, meaning of, 171, 184–185
republicanism, 171, 184–194. *See also*
    constitutional rights
  artisan, 345
  charters and, 250
  Civil War and, 413
  condemnation of, 319
  definition of, 322
  education of children and, 263–265
  evangelical Christianity and, 281–282, 284
  ideals of, under wartime pressure, 184–187
  institutions of, 196–215
  literary culture of, 265
  modern, 837–839

republicanism (*cont.*)
  of Puritans, 143, 148, 282
  religion and, 190, 193–194
  as representative government, 257
  rights of women and, 260–263, 263(*i*), 281
  social classes and, 258, 310, 342
  the South and, 458
  testing of, 184–187
  Virginia Plan and, 208–209
republican motherhood, 261–262, 263(*i*),
      285, 374
Republican Party (Jeffersonian), 251
  agricultural expansion and, 237, 239
  commonwealth idea and, 250
  factions of, 255, 325
  vs. Federalists, 219, 221–222, 253, 255
  War of 1812 and, 241
Republican Party (1850s-on), 668
  anticommunism and, 836
  on big government, 839
  candidates of, 967
  Clinton and, 971
  in Congress, 978–979
  conservative, 906, 907(*m*), 912, 927(*m*)
  constituents of, 694
  "Contract with America" and, 968–969, 970
  Crisis of 1877 and, 469–470
  Crittenden Plan and, 415
  defense expenditures and, 839
  Democrats and, 329, 436–437
  domestic policies of, 917–918, 947–951
  draft riots and, 424
  1858 elections and, 408, 409
  1860 elections and, 409–410
  1862 elections and, 430
  1863 elections and, 431
  free silver and, 597
  free-soil policy of, 426
  Halfbreeds in, 576
  isolationism in, 820
  JFK and, 868
  Ku Klux Klan and, 465, 467
  law and order campaign of, 906, 907(*m*)
  Lincoln and, 406–410, 423
  and loss of China, 881
  as majority party, 694, 943
  modern, 837–839
  Mugwumps and, 576
  national mercantilism and, 426
  New Deal and, 760, 778, 832
  1928 elections and, 719–720
  1932 elections and, 748–749
  1936 elections and, 763
  1938 elections and, 765
  1946 elections and, 832
  1952 elections and, 837–838
  1968 elections and, 906–907
  1980 elections and, 943
  origins of, 402
  Peace Democrats and, 436, 437
  pietism and, 574
  presidency and, 693
  protectionism and, 569, 699
  Protestants and, 574–576, 575(*f*)
  Reagan and, 947
  realignment of, 405(*m*)
  Reconstruction and, 442, 443–446, 450–452,
      460, 461, 468–470
  reform and, 620–621
  in Senate, 978
  silent majority and, 906, 907
  slavery and, 409, 412, 415
  social welfare and, 839
  in the South, 457–460, 469, 907, 917, 918
  Stalwarts in, 576
  Sun Belt and, 927(*m*)
  Theodore Roosevelt and, 611–613, 621–622
  veterans' benefits and, 569
  Vietnam War and, 889
  white supremacy and, 605
  women's rights groups and, 457, 459
  in WWII, 793
Reserve Officer Training Corps (ROTC), 892
Resettlement Administration, 776
  African Americans and, 768
"Resistance to Civil Government"
      (Thoreau), 371
Restoration (Great Britain), 69–72
Restraining Act (1767), 146
restrictive covenants, 852
retailing, 512–513
  women in, 522
Revels, Hiram, 459(*i*)
Revenue Acts
  of 1673, 71
  of 1762, 132
  of 1767, 146
  of 1935, 763
  of 1942, 787
  tax cuts and, 693

revenue-sharing program, 917
Revere, Paul, 158
revivalism, 316(i), 349. *See also* evangelicalism;
    Great Awakening; Second Great
    Awakening
    abolitionism and, 370
    in colonial America, 114–118
    in post-colonial America, 257, 260
    Second Great Awakening and, 257, 277–284,
        283(m), 315, 319
    social reform and, 315–318, 316(i)
    urban, 559, 714
    women's rights and, 374
Revolutionary War
    armies and strategies in, 174–175
    battles in, 158, 167, 172–182, 174(m),
        181(m), 185
    British strategies in, 172–176, 180–182
    causes of. *See* Revolutionary War (prewar
        events)
    diplomatic triumph in, 183–184
    financial crisis in, 177–178
    in the North, 172–176, 174(m)
    paper money in, 427
    partisan warfare in Carolinas, 180–182
    political legacy of, 199
    publishing and, 143
    response in Britain to, 183
    rights of man and, 112–113, 142–143
    social and financial perils in, 176–178
    in the South, 180–182, 181(m)
    Treaty of Alliance with France (1778), 179
    women in, 185(i)
Revolutionary War (prewar events)
    Boston Massacre, 150
    Boston Tea Party, 140(i), 152
    boycotts, 139, 145, 147(i), 148, 150, 153
    Committees of Correspondence, 151–153
    Daughters of Liberty, 147(i), 148
    Intolerable Acts (1774), 153
    Loyalists, 157
    militia, 121–122, 128–129, 158
    Quartering Acts, 138, 146, 153
    Sons of Liberty, 139–142, 140(i), 147(i), 152
    Stamp Act (1765), 131, 137–147, 150
    taxation, 131–138, 155–157
    Tea Act (1773), 151–152
Reynolds v. Sims (1964), 918
Rhee, Syngman, 824
Rhett, Robert Barnwell, 409, 413

Rhode Island, 55, 203, 208, 211, 213, 719
    currency in, 96
    revocation of corporate charters, 72
    voting rights in, 324
Rhodes, Elisha Hunt, 412, 423
rice
    African knowledge of, 83
    exports of, 123–124
    production, 269(m), 270–272
    slavery and, 83
    in South Carolina, 83, 94, 126
    Southern production of, 269(m), 270–272
Rice, Condoleezza, 975
Richelieu River (River of the Iroquois), 63
Richmond, Virginia, 419(m), 537
    in Civil War, 418, 426, 428, 434, 436, 440
    food riots in, 428
    free blacks in, 274
    manufacturing in, 299, 306(m), 307(m), 308
Rio Grande River, 11, 392, 495, 496
Rio Grande Valley, Hispanic settlement in,
    495, 496
Rio Treaty (Inter-American Treaty of
    Reciprocal Assistance; 1947), 829(m)
riots. *See also* mobs; race riots
    anti-U.S., 630
    armory construction and, 505–506
    in Detroit, 796, 896
    in Los Angeles, 896, 964–965
    in Newark, 896
    rent, 747
    in San Francisco, 499
    school busing and, 936
    Stonewall, 900
    urban, 880, 895–896, 903, 906, 964–965
The Rise of David Levinsky (Cahan), 557
The Rise of Silas Lapham (Howells), 563
Riverside Indian School, Oklahoma, 489(i)
Roanoke (lost colony), 44
Roanoke Island, 45(i)
Roaring Twenties, 714
Robertson, Pat, 937, 966
Robespierre, Maximilien, 220
Robinson, Edward G., 734
Robinson, Jackie, 839
Robinson, John, 56
Rochambeau, Comte de, 182
Rochester, New York
    revivalism in, 316–317
    transportation and, 305, 307(m)

Rockefeller, John D., 512, 600(*i*)
Rockingham, Lord, 145
rock 'n' roll, 857–858, 889, 892–893
Rockwell, Norman, 789
Rocky Mountains, 11, 240, 245, 477
Rodgers, John, 282
Roe v. Wade (1973), 918, 931, 951
Rogers, Ginger, 733, 947(*i*)
Rogers, Robert, 123(*i*)
Rogers, William, 880
Rolfe, John, 46
Rolling Stones, 893
Roman Catholic Church. *See* Catholicism;
    Catholics
Romanticism, 260, 353
Rome, ancient, 18–19
Rommel, Erwin, 800
Roosevelt, Eleanor, 748, 768
    civil rights and, 790
    Great Depression and, 728, 730
    Stevenson and, 838
    Truman and, 816
Roosevelt, Franklin Delano (1882–1945),
    774(*i*), 816. *See also* New Deal
    aid to Britain and, 784–785
    Alger Hiss and, 836
    Atlantic Charter and, 785, 786(*m*)
    death of, 807, 818
    four terms of, 863
    Great Depression and, 728
    Holocaust and, 802
    isolationism and, 782, 783
    Japanese internment and, 796
    labor unions and, 767, 790
    leadership of, 753–754
    New Deal of, 875, 877, 949
    1932 elections and, 748–749
    on Pearl Harbor, 787
    popularity of, 753(*i*), 753–754
    presidency and, 763
    as president (1933–1945), 748–749, 749(*m*),
        752–778, 780–810
    reforms of, 793
    second term of, 834
    Stalin and, 817
    third term of, 784–785
    as vice-presidential candidate, 693
    wartime planning and, 799
    WWII and, 781, 793
    at Yalta, 806, 807, 807(*i*)

Roosevelt, New Jersey, 774(*i*)
Roosevelt, Theodore (1858–1919), 548, 578,
    599, 611–623, 634, 636, 668
    attack on legal system, 621
    balance of power philosophy of, 647, 652
    "bully pulpit" of, 619(*i*)
    conservation and, 613–614
    national parks system and, 614(*m*)
    presidency and, 754
    as president (1901–1909), 646–649, 652
    public opinion use by, 619(*i*)
    as rancher, 481
    Republican Party and, 611–613
    as "Rough Rider," 639, 641
    social justice and, 621, 622
    Spanish-American War and, 639, 641
    Square Deal of, 619, 619(*i*)
    Taft and, 620–621
    trust-busting and, 616–617, 621
    Wall Street Giants and, 618(*i*)
Roosevelt Corollary (to Monroe Doctrine),
    649
Roosevelt family, 105(*m*)
Roosevelt Field (Long Island, New York), 853
Root, Elihu, 648, 655
Root-Talahira Agreement, 652
Rosebud reservation, South Dakota, 899
Rosellini, Lynn, 934
Rosenberg, Ethel, 836
Rosenberg, Julius, 836
Rosie the Riveter, 789
Rough Riders, 639, 641
Route 66, 738(*m*). *See also* highways
Rowlandson, Mary, 64
Royal African Company, 78
Roybal, Edward, 897
Rubin, Jerry, 905
Ruffin, Thomas, 384
rule of reason, judicial, 616, 621
rum, 88, 96
Rumsfeld, Donald, 975
Rural Electrification Administration, 772
rural life
    of African Americans, 86
    automobile and, 703
    in Europe, 14–16
    as ideal, 535, 540, 544
    Ku Klux Klan in, 711
    manufacturing and, 247–249
    mass media and, 709

Prohibition and, 681
urbanization and, 708–709
Rush, Benjamin, 163, 170, 185, 262, 264
Rush-Bagot Treaty, 244
Russia. *See also* Soviet Union
    Alaska and, 391
    claims on China of, 634
    Germany and, 670
    immigration restriction and, 709
    1917 revolution in, 670, 689
    post-Soviet Union, 952–953, 978
    war on terrorism and, 978
    in WWI, 663–664, 670
Russian immigrants, 516, 517(*f*)
Russo-Japanese War (1904–1905), 651(*m*),
    651–652
Russwurm, John, 367
Rust Belt, 926, 927(*m*)
Rustin, Bayard, 871, 872
Rutgers University, founding of, 116
Ruth, Babe, 707

Sacco, Nicola, 689–690
Sacco-Vanzetti case, 689–690
Sackville-West, Lionel, 628
Sacramento, California, 480, 495(*m*)
Sacramento Valley, California, 392
el-Sadat, Anwar
    assassination of, 952
    Camp David accords and, 941, 942(*i*)
al-Sadr, Moqtada, 977(*i*)
Sahagún, Friar Bernardino de, 26
Saigon, Vietnam, 882, 884, 886,
    890(*i*), 904
    fall of, 911
St. Augustine, 38, 39, 39(*m*)
St. Lawrence River, 41, 122
St. Leger, Colonel Barry, 171(*m*), 176
St. Louis, Missouri, 11
    population of, 536(*t*)
    transportation and, 306(*m*), 307(*m*),
        308–309
St. Louis Post-Dispatch, 561
St. Mary's City (first settlement), 47
St. Paul, Minnesota, 480
Salem, Massachusetts, 55
    popular power in, 92
    witchcraft trials in, 58
Salisbury, Stephan, 206
Salmagundi (Irving), 265

saloons, 314. *See also* taverns
    temperance movement and, 578–579
    in Wild West, 492, 494
SALT. *See* Strategic Arms Limitation Treaties
Salter, John, 870
Salt Lake City, Utah, 493(*i*)
salutary neglect, 92, 94(*i*), 96, 132, 136
Salvation Army, 559
Samoa, 632
    U.S. acquisition of (1900), 646
San Diego, California
    population in, 495(*m*)
    tourism in, 501
Sandinistas, 949, 952
SANE (National Committee for a Sane Nuclear
    Policy), 843
San Francisco, California
    Alcatraz Island in, 898
    Anglo migration to, 496
    anti-Chinese mobs in, 499
    Asian Americans in, 498, 499, 743
    earthquake (1906) in, 539
    Eastern connections of, 480
    as economic hub of the West, 495
    elite in, 542
    gold rush in (1849–1857), 396, 491–492,
        495, 496, 498
    growth of, 491–492, 495
    Mexican War and, 382
    population of, 536(*t*)
    water needs of, 502
Sanger, Margaret, 730
Sanitary Commission, U.S., 424, 425
San Jacinto, battle of (1836), 387
San Juan Hill, Battle of (1898), 612, 641,
    641(*m*), 642(*i*)
Santa Anna, Antonio López de, 386–387, 393,
    394(*m*)
Santa Fe, New Mexico, 39(*m*), 40, 393
    Hispanic culture of, 495, 496, 501
Santa Fe Railroad, 480, 501
Santa Fe Trail, 389(*m*)
Santiago, Cuba, 641–642
Santiago de Cuba, Battle of (1898), 640(*i*)
Santo Domingo, 630
Sarajevo, Serbia, 663, 972
Saratoga, battle of (1777), 174(*m*), 175–176,
    179, 183, 185
Sargent, John Singer, 550(*i*)
Saturday Evening Post, 856(*i*)

Saudi Arabia
  Afghanistan and, 941
  globalization and, 959(*i*)
  Iraq and, 955
  oil production in, 922
  Persian Gulf War and, 954
Sauk Indians, 65, 337, 338, 339(*i*)
Savage, Augusta, 717
Savannah, Georgia, 180, 181(*m*), 188, 437
Savio, Mario, 892
scalawags, 457, 458
Scalia, Antonin, 950
The Scarlet Letter (Hawthorne), 357
Schechter v. United States, 759, 763
Schenck, Charles T., 683
Schenck v. United States (1919), 683
Schlafly, Phyllis, 931–932
Schneebeli, Heinrich, 109
Schneiderman, Rose, 529(*i*), 602
Schroeder, Patricia, 930
Schurz, Carl, 577, 645
Schuyler, Philip, 175
Schwarzkopf, H. Norman, 954
science
  of management, 524
  progressivism and, 598
Scientology, Church of, 928
SCLC. *See* Southern Christian Leadership
  Conference
Scopes, John T., 714
Scopes ("monkey") trial (1925), 714
Scots-Irish, 104
  in colonial America, 99, 110, 117, 119
  merchant credit of, 123–124
  in Middle Atlantic colonies, 110–111, 114,
    123–124
  in Pennsylvania colony, 106
Scott, Hugh, 920
Scott, Winfield, 339, 393, 394(*m*), 416, 418
  as presidential nominee, 400
Scottsboro case, 736, 737(*i*)
Scudder, Vida, 546, 548
Sea Islands, 446, 448
Seale, Bobby, 895
Seamen's Act (1916), 625
Sears, Isaac, 141
Sears, Roebuck, 486, 512
SEATO. *See* Southeast Asia Treaty
  Organization
Seattle, Washington, 495, 495(*m*)

secession, 412–441
  Compromise of 1850 and, 398
  Constitution and, 443
  Democratic Party and, 409
  elite southerners and, 444
  insurrection and, 415
  Lincoln and, 410
  process of, 414(*m*)
  Reconstruction and, 445
  Republican Party and, 405
  slave vs. free state conflict and, 397, 398
  southern leaders and, 410
  Upper South states and, 414, 414(*m*),
    416, 418
Second Bank of the United States, 251, 252
  war against, 334–336, 335(*i*)
Second Great Awakening (1820–1860), 257,
    277–284, 283(*m*), 315, 319, 352. *See also*
    evangelicalism; Great Awakening;
    revivalism
  abolitionism and, 367
  child rearing and, 264
  women's rights and, 374
Second Party System, 342–344, 348(*i*)
  end of, 398–406
secret ballot, 577
secularism, evolution and, 713
Securities and Exchange Commission (SEC),
    757, 979
Sedalia, Missouri, 480
Sedition Act (1918), 682
Seeger, Charles, 775
Seeger, Pete, 892
Seeger, Ruth Crawford, 775
segregation, 891, 906. *See also* busing, school;
    desegregation
  in cities, 964
  disfranchisement and, 584
  Jim Crow and, 585–587, 897
  laws supporting, 581
  in military, 780, 788, 791, 798
  opposition to, 839, 840
  residential, 736
  school, 792
  of transportation, 869
  Woodrow Wilson, 605
Selassie, Haile, 781
Selective Service Act (1917), 669
self-determination, national, 684, 806, 830
  Atlantic Charter and, 785

movements for, 866(m)
Yalta and, 806
self-government. See also democracy;
    representative government; republicanism
    colonial assemblies and, 137–138, 146, 150,
        154, 158
Sellars, John, 297
Sellars, Samuel, 297
Selma, Alabama, civil rights protests in, 874
Seminole Indians, 12, 272, 337, 339, 340(m), 487
Senate, U.S.
    Clinton's impeachment trial and, 971
    conduct of diplomacy and, 630
    Democratic Party control of, 949
    impeachment and, 454, 971
    Kyoto Treaty and, 960
    Lincoln and, 407
    Republican control of, 943
    Republican gains in, 968–969, 970, 978
    Watergate Committee of, 920
    Wilmot Proviso and, 395
Seneca Falls convention (1848), 680
Seneca Falls Declaration (1848), 378
Seneca Indians, 14, 63, 229, 230, 232(i), 772
Senegal, Africa, 20
Scnegambia, Africa, 23
sentimentalism, 260
Seoul, South Korea, 824, 825
separation of powers, 212, 764. See also checks
    and balances
September 11, 2001, terrorist attacks (9/11),
    946, 956(m), 967, 975–976, 976(i)
    economy and, 958, 979
Sequoia National Park, 501
Sequoyah, 337
Serbia, 663, 972
Servicemen's Readjustment Act (GI Bill; 1944),
    793, 831
settlement houses, 599, 601
Seven Years' War, 121–122. See also French and
    Indian War
Sewall, Samuel, 57
Seward, William H., 398, 406, 409, 630
Sex in Education (Clarke), 547(i)
sexual harassment, 951
    feminism and, 966
    against women in military, 957(i)
    in WWII, 789
sexuality
    automobile and, 704

changing views of, 546–549
counterculture and, 893
disease and, 680
flapper and, 704
jazz and, 705
music and, 858
Oneida Community and, 361–362
rock 'n' roll and, 858
Shakers and, 359, 360
utopian communities and, 362
women's rights and, 374–375, 932–933
Seymour, Horatio, 429, 456
Shahn, Ben, 774, 774(i), 776
Shakers, 284, 358–360, 359(m), 366(i)
Shakespeare, William, 563
Shalala, Donna E., 968
shaman, 40
sharecropping, 462–464
    African Americans and, 735, 768
    New Deal and, 756, 777
Share Our Wealth Society, 760, 760(i), 763
Sharon, Ariel, 978
Sharpsburg, Maryland, 420
Shaw, Lemuel, 347
Shawnee Indians, 119, 125, 229(i), 230, 232, 241
Shays, Daniel, 206–207, 213
Shaysites, 220
Shays's Rebellion, 206–207, 208, 220
Sheen, Bishop Fulton, 855
Shelburne, earl of, 99, 146
Sheldon, Charles M., 539
Sheldon, Lucy, 236(i)
Shelley v. Kraemer (1948), 840, 852
shell shock, 665(i)
Shepard, Alan, 868
Sheppard-Towner Act (1921), 695–696
Sheridan, Philip H., 435, 480, 629
Sheridan, Robert, 272
Sherman, William Tecumseh (1820–1891),
    434, 446, 469
    capture of Atlanta, 436, 437
    land for liberated slaves and, 446
    march to the sea, 437–438, 438(m)
    total war and, 437–438
Sherman Antitrust Act (1890), 610, 615, 620,
    621, 624
Sherman Silver Purchase Act (1890), 592
Shiloh, battle of, 421, 423
shipbuilding industry, 88–90
    arms control and, 701

shoemaking, 293

shopkeepers, 104, 106, 141

shopping malls, 853

Shuttlesworth, Fred, 869

Siberia, 7

Sicily, WWII in, 800, 800(*m*)

Sierra Club, 501

Sierra Leone, Africa, 188

Sierra Nevada mountains, 480, 491–492,
    498(*i*), 501

*The Significance of the Frontier in American
    History* (Turner), 636

Silent Spring (Carson), 928

silver mining, 532–533

Sinai Peninsula, 923, 941

Singapore, globalization and, 959

Singer Sewing Machine Company, 299,
    512, 632

Sino-Japanese War (1894–1895), 633–634, 651

Sioux Indians, 478–479

    AIM and, 899, 900(*i*)

    Battle of Little Big Horn and, 487

    expropriation of territories, 488(*m*)

    religion of, 478

    wars with, 486–487

    Wounded Knee massacre and, 490

Sister Carrie (Dreiser), 535

sitcoms, 857

sit-ins, 891

    civil rights movement and, 869

    1970s activism and, 928

Sitting Bull, Chief of Sioux, 487

Six Companies, 498

Six Nations, Iroquois, 75, 172, 173(*i*), 176.
    See also Iroquois Indians

skyscrapers, 539

Slater, Samuel, 295

"Slave-Power" conspiracy, 395, 401, 402, 403,
    407

slave rebellion, 85–86, 267, 272, 281, 409

    abolitionism and, 367–368

    Emancipation Proclamation and, 429

    fear of, 333, 384, 412

    in Haiti, 239

slavery, 76–91, 189(*i*). *See also* abolition;
        cotton; emancipation; Middle Passage;
        plantations; the South

    abolition of, 188–192, 327(*i*), 344, 437, 442,
        443, 464

    among Native Americans, 86, 337

antislavery movement and. *See* abolitionism

British Empire and, 68, 96

in Chesapeake colony, 80, 83, 104, 267(*i*),
    269(*m*), 269–271

Civil War and, 412, 417, 428–430, 432–433

in colonial America, 50–51, 53, 99, 117–118,
    126, 157–158

colonization and, 268, 407

communal experiments and, 359(*m*)

Constitutional Convention and, 210

cotton and, 233, 267(*i*), 268–270, 269(*m*),
    383–384

culture of, 329

economics of, 313

in 1800, 192(*m*)

evangelicism and, 315

expansion of, 204, 267(*i*), 268–270, 269(*m*),
    302, 303(*m*), 392–398, 399(*m*), 402

family life and, 270–273

fugitive slave laws and, 267

justifications for, 384

legalization of, 53

Lincoln and, 407–408, 409

Mexican War and, 395

in Mexico, 386

in Middle Atlantic colonies, 104, 106

military service and, 433

Mormons and, 366

Northwest Ordinance and, 204

politics and, 391, 396–398, 405(*m*), 409, 410

popular education and, 355

positions on, 113, 329

in post-colonial America, 266–277, 267(*i*),
    269(*m*), 276(*m*)

property rights and, 275–276

protection of, 409, 415

Quakers and, 109

reform movement and, 352, 353

republicanism and, 188–190, 192(*m*)

Republican Party and, 402

resettlement to old Southwest and, 267(*i*),
    268, 269(*m*), 302, 303(*m*)

Revolutionary War and, 167–168, 172, 180,
    182, 188–191, 192(*m*)

secession and, 414(*m*), 429

slave vs. free states and, 396–398, 405–406

in the South, 317, 343

Union threat to, 427

in West Indies, 68, 77, 80, 83, 86, 333

westward expansion and, 390–391, 401–402

white south and, 582
women and, 83, 385
slaves
  African, 24, 50–51, 53
  arming, 438, 440
  auctions of, 234(i)
  British and, 188
  in Civil War, 426, 427
  denial of education to, 85, 368
  draft and, 423
  Dutch and, 77
  emancipation of, 188–190, 192(m),
    267–268, 275–276, 281, 333, 437, 442,
    446–450, 458, 464
  freed, 376
  fugitive, 210, 398, 428, 430, 432
  Indian peoples and, 86
  labor gang system and, 352, 383, 448,
    461, 464
  manumission of, 189, 190
  in Middle Atlantic colonies, 104, 106
  Muslim beliefs and, 85
  Native American, 47
  as percentage of population, 172, 228
  as property, 210, 428, 429
  relocation of, 267(i), 268, 269(m), 302
  resettlement of freed, 268, 407
  resistance by, 85–86, 384–385
  three-fifths rule for, 210
  westward migration and, 233
slave trade
  abolition of, 210, 267–268, 271, 275,
    371, 398
  in Africa, 20, 21(m), 23
  with Africa, 6, 20–23, 21(m), 78(m),
    89(m), 271
  South Atlantic system and, 76(m), 76–80, 90
Slave Trader, Sold to Tennessee, 267(i)
Slavs
  discrimination against, 517
  Holocaust and, 782, 802
Slidell, John, 392
Sloan, John, 715(i)
Sloat, John, 393, 394(m)
Slocumb, Mary Hooks, 169
smallpox, 26, 27, 54, 59, 63, 113, 478
Smallwood, William, 175
Smith, Adam, 77, 219
Smith, Alfred E. (Al), 608, 696, 719–720, 749
Smith, Bessie, 705

Smith, Jerry, 934
Smith, Joseph (1805–1844), 363, 364(m), 365
Smith, Joseph, III, 364
Smith, Mamie, 705, 706(i)
Smith, Margaret Bayard, 331
Smith, Melancton, 212
Smith, Seba (Major Jack Downing), 335(i)
Smith, William, 276
Smith-Connally Labor Act (1943), 790
smuggling, 96, 134, 136
SNCC. See Student Non-Violent Coordinating
    Committee
Social Chaos on the Carolina Frontier
    (Woodmason), 126, 127
Social Darwinism, 598, 635
The Social Destiny of Man (Brisbane), 361
social insurance, 610–611. See also health
    insurance; welfare
socialism, 361, 531–533
  Cold War and, 829, 830
  conservative opposition to, 938
  "creeping," 834
  New Deal and, 759
  pan-Arab, 830
  women activists and, 532
Socialist Labor Party (1877), 532
Socialist Party, 610, 623(m), 667, 689
  1932 elections and, 748–749, 749(m)
Socialist Party of America (1901), 532
social mobility
  African, 51
  downward, 728
  Great Depression and, 733
  as republican ideal, 258
  Republican Party and, 402
  work ethic and, 311–312, 317
social realism, 859
social reform
  asylums and, 375
  blue laws and, 575–576
  children and, 375
  evangelicalism and, 315–318, 353
  of nineteenth century, 314–319
  in 1920s, 693, 695–696
  in 1970s, 915–916, 928–938, 943
  opposition to, 696, 937–938
  prisons and, 314–315, 372, 375
  Protestantism and, 277, 282, 314
  religion and, 352–381
  revivalism and, 315–318, 316(i)

social reform (*cont.*)
  sexually transmitted diseases and, 680
  urban liberalism and, 696
  women and, 375
  women's rights and, 375, 380, 679–680
  WWII and, 793
Social Register, 543
Social Security Act (1935), 759, 761
  limitations of, 776
  Supreme Court on, 763
  women and, 768
Social Security system
  in Clinton administration, 970, 971
  expansion of, 875
  increase in, 838
  JFK and, 868
  Nixon and, 917
  Reagan and, 948, 950
  in Truman administration, 834
social structure, 544. *See also* elite; gentry class;
    middle class; working class
  in Africa, 21
  African Americans and, 50–51
  anarchy and, 597
  Aztec, 9–10, 25
  of British colonies, 69
  in Chesapeake colonies, 87–88
  Confederacy and, 438
  English, 34
  European medieval, 14–18, 19, 20
  Great Depression and, 728–730
  hierarchy in, 16–17
  immigrants and, 309–310, 319–320
  Inca, 27
  Industrial Revolution and, 292–293,
    309–314, 312(*i*)
  market economy and, 292–293, 309–314,
    312(*i*), 317
  matrilineal societies and, 12–14
  Native American, 9, 12
  Oneida Community and, 362
  peasants in, 34
  politics and, 322–324, 577
  race and, 29, 51, 372
  race riots and, 965
  Republican Party and, 402
  revolt and, 51–53
  slavery and, 402
  social order and, 542
  in the South, 257, 266, 320, 384, 582, 584–585

South Atlantic system and, 88–91
  in Spanish America, 27, 29
  yeomen in, 34, 51–52, 58–59
social values, in new world, 53–56
Society for Promoting Christian Knowledge, 284
Society for the Free Instruction of African
    Females, 284
Society for the Promotion of Industry, 315
Society for the Relief of Poor Widows, 284, 315
Society of Friends. *See* Quakers
Society of Journeymen Tailors, 345
socioeconomic status. *See* social structure
*Sociology for the South; or, the Failure of Free
    Society* (Fitzhugh), 385
sod houses, 485
Sokoloff, Nicholas, 743
Solemn League and Covenant, 156
Solomon Islands, 803, 804(*m*)
Sons of Liberty, 139–142, 140(*i*), 147(*i*), 152,
    157, 220. *See also* mobs
Soto, Hernán de, 12, 38, 39(*m*)
The Souls of Black Folk (Du Bois), 606
The Sound and the Fury (Faulkner), 716–717
sound money, 590–593
Souter, David, 951
the South. *See also* Civil War; cotton;
    plantations; slavery
  abolitionism and, 372, 376, 382–383
  African American migration from, 676–678,
    677(*m*), 717
  African Americans in, 735–736
  agricultural economy of, 308
  American System and, 325
  civil rights movement and, 869, 870, 874,
    891, 892, 894
  Civil War destruction of, 437, 440
  class distinctions in, 257, 266, 320, 343–344,
    582, 584–585
  communal experiments in, 359(*m*)
  Compromise of 1850 and, 398
  debt of, 460
  Democratic Party in, 409, 694, 749, 763, 777,
    833, 864
  disfranchisement in, 584
  economic growth of, 926, 927, 927(*m*)
  economy of, 458–459, 464
  1860 elections and, 409–410
  elite life in, 384
  Fugitive Slave Acts and, 399–400
  gentry class in, 87–88

home rule for, 469
Jim Crow laws in, 585–587, 897
labor unions in, 926–927
Lower vs. Upper, 414(m), 416, 418
low wages in, 515, 582
migration to and from, 232–233, 301–302,
    303(m), 515–517, 756, 851, 852, 861,
    926–927, 927(m)
New Deal and, 768
New South (1900) and, 515, 516(m), 585(m)
1928 elections and, 718
1936 elections and, 763
1968 elections and, 906–907
1980 elections and, 943
Nixon and, 917, 918
vs. the North, 383, 413, 449
policies of John Q. Adams and, 328
popular education in, 355
population of, 426
Populism in, 584–591, 587
race in, 257
racism in, 581–584, 897
Reconstruction and, 442
Republican Party and, 405
segregation in, 581, 906
sharecropping and, 464
slavery in, 266–277, 267(i), 317, 329,
    343, 417
slave vs. free states and, 396–398,
    401–403, 404
tariffs and, 328–329, 333–334
tenant farmers of, 266, 582
urbanization of, 708(m)
voter registration in, 875(m)
westward expansion and, 390–391
South Africa
    apartheid in, 972
    human rights in, 940
South America, 29. See also Mesoamerica
    Chinese immigration to, 497
    economic development in, 865
    environmental pollution in, 960
    foreign aid in, 865
    foreign investment in, 700–701
    globalization and, 960
    immigrants from, 709, 711, 876
    slavery in, 415
    trade with, 309
    U.S. intervention in, 630, 633, 701, 953(m)
    U.S. relations with, 782, 940

South Atlantic system, 76–80
    Navigation Acts and, 95
    social structure and, 88–91
    urbanization and, 88, 90–91
South Carolina
    abolitionism and, 382
    African American regiments in, 432
    Civil War and, 437
    class in, 87, 88
    as colony, 69–70, 75, 83–85
    economy of, 219
    evangelicals in, 118
    freed slaves in, 446, 448(i)
    indigo production in, 124
    kinship in, 85
    Ku Klux Klan in, 465, 466
    migration to and from, 233, 301–302,
        303(m)
    nullification and, 333–334, 336, 343
    ratification of Constitution and, 213
    Reconstruction and, 453(m), 457, 458, 460
    Regulators and, 125–126, 126(m), 128–129
    Republican government in, 467, 469, 470
    revivals in, 278
    rice in, 83, 94
    secession and, 398, 413, 415
    slavery in, 83, 85, 86, 118, 266, 269(m),
        269–273, 276, 276(m), 333, 383, 384
    tariffs and, 333–334
    voting rights in, 258, 259(m)
    war with Spain and, 95
The South Carolina Exposition and Protest
    (Calhoun), 333
Southeast Asia
    communism in, 884
    decolonization in, 866(m)
    in WWII, 804(m)
Southeast Asia Treaty Organization (SEATO),
    828, 829(m)
Southern Christian Leadership Conference
    (SCLC), 842, 869
Southern Homestead Act (1866), 461
Southern Manifesto, 841
Southern Rights Democrats, 398, 409
Southern Tenant Farmers Union (STFU), 736
Southgate, Eliza, 261
South Korea, 824–825, 827
    globalization and, 959
    human rights in, 940
    Vietnam War and, 885

South Vietnam, 828. *See also* Vietnam War
Southwest
    Anglo-Hispanic conflict in, 496–497
    economic growth of, 926–927, 927(*m*)
    Hispanic settlement in, 482, 495–497, 500, 501
Southwest, Old (Alabama, Mississippi,
        Louisiana), migration to, 267(*i*), 268,
        269(*m*), 296, 301–302, 303(*m*)
Soviet Union, 684. *See also* Russia
    in Afghanistan, 941, 952, 976
    arms-limitation agreements with, 843–844
    arms race with, 909–910
    atomic bomb and, 809, 821
    Carter and, 939, 941
    collapse of (1991), 817, 946, 952–953
    communism in, 796, 831, 835–837, 952–953
    Cuba and, 865
    Eastern Europe and, 806
    environmental pollution in, 960
    fears of, 845
    Germany and, 782, 783, 785, 806
    Greece and, 820
    immigrants from, 964
    intraparty struggle in, 827
    Israel and, 923
    Japan and, 799
    JFK and, 865–868, 873
    Marshall Plan and, 821
    military-industrial complex and, 845
    mutual defense treaties and, 829(*m*)
    Nasser and, 830
    Nixon and, 916
    nuclear test ban treaties and, 865
    Oswald and, 872
    vs. postwar U.S., 849
    satellite states of, 806
    space program of, 838
    Spanish civil war and, 783
    Third World and, 830
    U.S. recognition of, 782
    U.S. relations with, 816, 817–819, 823, 824,
        843–844
    on U.S. civil rights, 839
    Vietnam and, 881, 882
    war in Pacific and, 799, 805(*m*), 806
    in WWII, 799, 800(*m*)
space program, 868
    economic growth and, 926, 927(*m*)
    JFK and, 863
    Soviet, 838

Spain
    acquisition of territories from, 642–644
    Cuba and, 391, 401, 636, 637–642
    vs. England, 32–33, 38, 94–95
    vs. France, 38
    Islam in, 18
    maritime expansion of, 18, 24
    Mexican independence from, 386
    missions of, 38–40
    Napoleon and, 239
    in North America, 495
    peace talks with, 183–184
    Portugal and, 32
    vs. Protestantism, 31–33
    in Revolutionary War, 180, 183–184
    South American empire of, 636
    territorial disputes with, 237
    Texas and, 386
    wars with, 86, 94–95
    the West and, 245(*m*), 390
    WWII and, 781, 782
Spanish-American War (1898), 612, 628,
        636–642, 647, 690, 782
Spanish Armada, 33
Spanish civil war (1936–1939), 782, 783
Spanish colonization, 24, 39(*m*), 75, 272
    Catholicism and, 29, 38–41
    conquest of Aztecs and Incas, 9, 25–29,
        28(*i*), 28(*m*)
    Florida and, 69
    gold and, 24, 28, 33, 38
    in Mexico, 25–28
    in North America, 99, 120(*m*), 121, 132,
        154(*m*), 245(*m*)
    in Texas, 245
Spanish Netherlands, 32. *See also* Dutch
    colonization
Sparkman, John A., 838
speakeasies, 714–715, 715(*i*)
Special Forces, Army, 865
special interest groups, 937
specie, 334, 346, 591. *See also* currency
Specie Circular (1836), 347
Spencer, Herbert, 571–572
spheres of influence
    in American colonies, 120(*m*)
    in China, 634, 640, 650–651, 651(*m*)
    in Korea, 824
    meaning of, 818
spinning, 248

Spirit of St. Louis (airplane), 707
spoils system, 332, 342, 349, 567
Spokane Indians, 6
sports
    baseball, 560–561, 707
    gay rights and, 934
    national culture and, 707
    radio and, 707
    rise of, 548
    Title IX and, 930
Spotsylvania Court House, battle of, 434,
    435(*i*)
Sprague, Frank J., 537, 538
Springfield race riot (1908), 606
Sputnik (Soviet satellite), 838, 845
Square Deal, 619, 619(*i*)
squatter sovereignty, 395, 397
stagflation, 925
Stalin, Joseph
    Berlin blockade and, 821
    death of, 827, 837
    FDR and, 817, 818
    Kim Il Sung and, 824
    wartime planning and, 799
    at Yalta, 805(*m*), 806, 807(*i*)
Stalingrad, Battle of, 800, 800(*m*)
Stamp Act (1765), 131, 137–147, 180, 206
    repeal of, 145, 168
    resistance to, 137–142
Stamp Act Congress (1765), 138, 142
Standard Oil case (1911), 621
Standard Oil Company, 512, 616, 632
    monopoly of, 599
    of New Jersey, 701
Stanford University, 965
Stanley, Ann Lee (Mother Ann), 358–360
Stanton, Edward M., 454
Stanton, Elizabeth Cady, 372, 380,
    456, 457
    Seneca Falls and, 378
Starr, Ellen Gates, 601
Starr, Kenneth, 971
Starr, Paul, 946
"Star Wars" (Strategic Defense Initiative;
    SDI), 948
State Department, U.S., 630, 836
state governments
    business and, 693
    vs. federal, 765
    Great Depression and, 728

shift of costs to, 948, 951
shift of powers to, 917
Social Security and, 776
states
    block grants to, 917
    constitutions of, 197–199, 224, 341, 454
    formation and Indian cessions, 231(*m*)
    governments of, 249–250, 341–342
    secession of, 405
    slave vs. free, 382–383, 393–394, 396–398,
        401–403, 404, 405–406
    voting rights and, 456
    welfare and, 970
    women's rights and, 378
states' rights, 275–277, 341, 343, 349
    Calhoun on, 333
    Confederacy and, 427
    draft and, 424
    Fourteenth Amendment and, 573
    Fugitive Slave Acts and, 400
    Indian removal and, 337, 339
    interstate commerce and, 305
    Reconstruction and, 445, 450
    Second Bank and, 334–335, 335(*i*)
    slavery and, 382
States' Rights Party (Dixiecrats), 833
steam power, 507, 536, 538
    manufacturing and, 294
    steamboats and, 305, 308–309, 519
steel industry
    Bessemer furnace and, 507
    Homestead strike and, 530
    labor unions and, 766–767
    in late nineteenth century, 506–507,
        508(*m*), 530
    mills for, 506–507, 508(*m*)
Steel Workers Organizing Committee
    (SWOC), 767
Steffens, Lincoln, 599
Stein, Gertrude, 716
Steinbeck, John, 739(*i*), 740, 775
Steinem, Gloria, 930
Stephens, Alexander, 418, 436, 445
Stephenson, David, 712
Steuben, Baron von, 178
Stevens, Thaddeus, 428–429, 451
Stevens, Wallace, 716, 719
Stevenson, Adlai E., 838
Stewart, Maria W., 376
Stiles, Ezra, 129, 196

Stimson, Henry, 788
stock market, 975
    crash of (1929), 724, 744, 754
    elderly and, 980
    government regulation of, 776
    Great Depression and, 724
    growth in, 958
    increased investment in, 925
    margin buying in, 724, 758
Stone, Lucy, 457
Stone, Samuel, 259
Stonewall riot (1969), 900
Stono Rebellion (1739), 86, 95
Story, Joseph, 251, 330
Stowe, Harriet Beecher, 376, 385, 400
Strategic Air Command, 828
Strategic Arms Limitation Treaties
    SALT I, 910
    SALT II, 939, 941
Strategic Defense Initiative (SDI; "Star
    Wars"), 948
strikes, 300, 301
    agricultural, 741, 741(*i*), 743
    arbitration in, 615
    by Asian Americans, 743
    in automobile industry, 747
    Boston police (1919), 688
    craft worker, 523
    of 1877, 505–506
    general, 533
    in Great Depression, 746–747
    Haymarket affair, 527–528
    Homestead (1892), 476, 530
    injunctions against, 610
    by Mexican Americans, 741(*i*)
    middle class and, 767
    in mining industry, 528(*i*),
        532–533, 590, 615, 620, 625
    New Deal and, 761
    in 1902, 615, 620
    in 1919, 688, 766–767
    post-WWII, 851
    Pullman, 531, 592, 597
    railroad, 505, 531, 590, 832
    sit-down, 766
    in steel industry, 766–767
    strikebreakers in, 743
    by suffrage movement, 680
    in textile industry, 625
    welfare capitalism and, 698

women and, 523, 741(*i*)
    in WWII, 790
Strong, Josiah, 536
Stroyer, Jacob, 272
Student Non-Violent Coordinating Committee
    (SNCC), 869, 870, 895, 902
Students for a Democratic Society (SDS), 891,
    909. *See also* New Left
Student Strike against War (1936), 732
Stuyvesant, Peter, 44
submarines, 667–668
    nuclear, 828
    in WWII, 786(*m*), 799
suburbs, 544–545, 848, 849, 851–853
    automobile and, 704, 852–853
    decay of inner cities and, 860, 862
    mass transit and, 538(*i*), 542
    in 1950s, 860
    planning of, 541
    racism in, 852
    voting districts and, 918
    white flight to, 936
Sudetenland, German invasion of, 783
Suez Canal, 630, 799, 830
suffrage. *See* voting rights
suffrage movement, 589–590, 603(*m*), 695. *See
    also* voting rights
    activists in, 578–580, 579(*i*), 602
    American politics and, 602
    hunger strikes and, 680
    organizations in, 578–579, 602, 680
    revival of, 602–603
sugar, 461
    Asian laborers and, 631(*i*)
    duties on, 135–137
    migrant labor and, 497
    Molasses Act and, 96
    plantations and, 77, 80, 630–631,
        631(*i*)
    planter-merchant elite and, 77
    Puerto Rican immigrants and, 861
    related industries and, 78–79
    slavery and, 68, 76(*m*), 76–80, 83, 86
    in the South, 268, 269(*m*)
    U.S. foreign investment in, 701
    West Indies trade and, 88, 89(*m*), 106,
        135–136
    WWI rationing of, 795
Sugar Act (1764), 135–138, 145, 180
Sumatra, 701

A Summary View of the Rights of British America (Jefferson), 171
Sumner, Charles, 382, 385, 428, 451, 457, 468
Sumner, Willliam Graham, 572–573
Sun Belt, 851, 852
  migration to, 926–927, 927*(m)*
  military-industrial complex in, 844*(m)*
Sun Dance, 478
Sunday, Billy, 559, 713–714
Superfunds, 940
supply and demand, 506, 506*(f)*
supply-side economics, 948
Supreme Court, 210, 215, 224, 237–238, 250–253, 454, 968
  abortion rights and, 918, 931. *See also Roe v. Wade*
  on affirmative action, 936
  Civil Rights Bill (1870) and, 468
  Congress and, 694
  conservatism of, 951
  Dred Scott and, 405–406, 407–408
  FDR and, 763–764
  Fugitive Slave Acts and, 400
  gay rights and, 966
  Gibbons v. Ogden, 252, 305
  on housing discrimination, 852
  interstate trade and, 305
  on Japanese internment, 798
  labor unions and, 767
  Marshall and, 250–253
  Native American cases and, 337, 339
  New Deal and, 759, 761, 778
  on New York subway, 540
  Nixon appointments to, 918
  on prayer in public schools, 918
  Reagan and, 950
  Roger Taney and, 341
  rule of reason and, 616, 621
  school busing and, 936
  Scottsboro case and, 736
  segregation and, 840, 842
  slavery and, 407–408
  strikes and, 767
  2000 elections and, 974–975
  welfare capitalism and, 698–699
Susquehanna Company, 124
Susquehannock Indians, 52, 63
Sutter, John A., 396
Sutter's Mill, discovery of gold (1848) at, 494
Swamp Fox. *See* Marion, Francis

Sweden, 44
  draft evaders and, 892
  homesteaders from, 482, 483*(i)*, 484
Swedish immigrants, 551
Swift, Gustavus F., 512
syndicalism, 533
Syria, invasion of Israel by, 923

Taft, William Howard (1857–1930), 605, 619–622
  as Philippine governor general, 645
  as president (1909–1913), 652
  Roosevelt and, 620–621
Taft-Hartley Act, 832, 833
Taino Indians, 24
Taiwan, 823, 826, 910. *See also* China: Nationalist
  globalization and, 959
Taliban, 941, 956*(m)*, 976
Talleyrand, Charles, 222
Tallmadge, James, 275
Tammany Hall, 556, 608, 694
  1928 elections and, 719
Taney, Roger B., 332, 341
  Dred Scott and, 406
  Fugitive Slave Acts and, 400
  Second Bank and, 336
Taos, New Mexico, 501
Tappan, Arthur, 317, 370, 371
Tappan, Lewis, 317, 370, 372
Tarbell, Ida, 599, 600*(i)*
Tardieu, Andre, 656
Tariff of Abominations, 328, 329, 333
tariffs, 207, 213, 217
  of 1816, 328, 334
  of 1828, 328, 333
  in Civil War, 426, 427
  Jackson and, 329, 333–334, 336
  during John Q. Adams' administration, 327–328
  Know-Nothing Party and, 403
  for manufacturing, 295, 297
  and Marshall Plan, 821
  nullification of, 333–334, 336
  post-WWI, 699
  protective, 336, 342, 347, 349, 569, 592, 620
  for road and canal building, 325, 327
  textile industry and, 310
Tarzan of the Apes (Burroughs), 548
Tatch, Kitty, 502*(i)*

taverns, 140
taxation. *See also* Shays's Rebellion
   Articles of Confederation and, 202
   under Bush (George H. W.), 951
   of business, 693
   in Civil War, 427
   in Cold War, 823
   in colonial America, 131–138,
      155–157
   colonial assemblies and, 91
   Confederacy and, 202, 206, 427
   Constitution and, 206
   of corporations, 674
   decay of inner cities and, 862
   excess-profits, 674
   excise levies and, 134, 217, 238, 310, 568
   exemption for churches, 193
   federal surplus and, 568
   Great Depression and, 725, 744
   hidden currency, 187
   of income, 573, 674, 675–676
   increases in, 73, 674, 696, 951
   Jefferson and, 238
   land, 384
   Long on, 759–760
   mass, 787
   in New England colonies, 71, 73
   1988 campaign and, 951
   occupation tax, 258
   political rights and, 91
   poll tax, 258, 584, 874
   power of, 252
   of property, 459–460
   Reaganomics and, 948, 950
   rebellion and, 69
   Reconstruction and, 459–460
   reductions in, 693, 868, 873, 925, 948, 950,
      969, 970, 973, 975, 980
   religion and, 193–194
   Revolutionary War and, 175, 178, 183
   self-government and, 257
   smuggling and, 134, 136, 152
   Southern gentry and, 87
   of stocks and bonds, 345
   taxpayers' revolts against, 937
   Vietnam War and, 891
   of wealthy, 345
   without representation, 136–139, 377
   women's rights and, 377
   WWII and, 787

Tax Reduction Act (1964), 868
Taylor, Frederick W., 598
   scientific management and, 524
Taylor, Zachary (1784–1850), 392
   1848 elections and, 396, 405(*m*)
   Mexican War and, 393, 394(*m*)
   as president (1849–1850), 396
   slave vs. free states and, 396
Tea Act (1773), 151–152, 180
Teapot Dome scandal (1924), 693–694
technology. *See also* machinery
   abolitionism and, 370
   advances in, 523–524
   in agriculture, 105–106, 294, 307–308, 485
   alternative, 929
   computer, 961–962
   consumer culture and, 703
   cotton production and, 233, 295–299
   economic growth and, 958
   in factories, 293–299, 294(*i*)
   fundamentalists and, 713
   individualism and, 707
   in mining, 494
   1950s culture and, 854
   in 1990s, 961–962
   postwar development and, 852
   in railroad system, 510
   Republican values and, 219
   in steel production, 507
   textile industry and, 219
   tidal, 83
Tecumseh (Shawnee chief), 241, 242
Teedyuscung, 75
teenagers. *See* adolescence; youth
Tehran conference (1943), 799
Tejanos, 497
telecommuters, 961
telegraph, 487
   transcontinental (1861), 479, 629
telephone company, 520(*i*)
television
   civil rights movement and, 869, 874
   Clinton and, 971
   desegregation and, 841
   JFK-Nixon debates on, 863
   JFK's elections and, 863
   McCarthy and, 837
   1950s culture and, 854–855
   1980 elections and, 943
   religion and, 855

sitcoms on, 854
as "vast wasteland," 855
in Vietnam, 884
Watergate and, 920, 922
Teller, Henry M., 639
temperance movement, 316–319, 344, 349,
    578–579, 681
    abolitionism and, 369
    free blacks and, 367
    in Maine, 382
    reform and, 353
    societies of, 314, 317
    women's rights and, 375, 379
tenant farmers, 232–235. *See also* sharecropping
    African American, 735, 768
    in England, 149–150
    in Hudson River Valley, 105(*m*), 124–125, 157
    in Middle Atlantic colonies, 104–105
    New Deal and, 756
    in New England, 102, 272
    in Pennsylvania, 106
    Populist party and, 582
    in Virginia, 117–118, 266
Tenderloin District, New York City, 560
Tenement House Law (1901; New York), 540
Tennent, Gilbert, 114, 116, 170
Tennent, William, 114
Tennessee, 233, 242, 414, 416, 430
    emancipation in, 429, 437
    industrial capacity in, 426
    Ku Klux Klan in, 465
    public education in, 460
    Reconstruction and, 445, 453
    revivals in, 278, 317
    Scopes trial in, 714
    secession and, 414, 414(*m*)
    westward migration from, 390
Tennessee Coal and Iron Company, 621
Tennessee River, 236, 421, 422(*m*)
Tennessee Valley Authority (TVA), 756,
    772–773, 773(*m*)
    Supreme Court on, 763
Tenochtitlán, 9, 10, 25, 27, 28
Ten Percent Plan, 443
Tenskwatawa (Lalawethika), 241
Tenure of Office Act (1867), 454, 455(*t*)
Teotihuacán culture, 9, 14
tepees, 478
Terkel, Studs, 729, 780
term limits, 969

terrorism, 946
    against blacks, 465–467
    in Civil War, 435
    fears about, 979
    in Middle East, 956(*m*)
    of 9/11, 956(*m*), 967, 975–976, 976(*i*), 979
    in 1980s, 952
    1993 World Trade Center bombing, 972, 973
    Palestinian use of, 978
    spread of, 978
    USS *Cole* attack, 956(*m*), 972
    war on, 976
Terry, Eli, 292
Texas
    admission to Union of, 382
    American settlement in, 386–387, 387(*m*),
        389(*m*)
    annexation of, 391, 392
    cattle ranching in, 480–481, 496, 497
    in Civil War, 430
    Compromise of 1850 and, 398
    cotton production in, 485, 497
    drought in, 737
    farming in, 485, 496–497
    Hispanics in, 496–497
    immigration and, 712(*i*), 962
    independence of, 386–387
    migration to, 852
    rebellion in, 386–387
    Reconstruction and, 456, 465
    secession of, 413
    segregation in, 791
    slavery in, 386, 387, 398
    Spanish, 245
textile industry
    British competition and, 294–297
    decline of (1920s), 697
    Great Depression and, 724–725
    growth of, 308
    innovations in, 294–299
    Jewish garment workers and, 523, 529(*i*)
    Navigation Acts and, 95
    in New England, 342
    in the South, 515, 516(*m*)
    strikes in, 625
    tariffs and, 310, 328
    technological innovation and, 219
    trade in, 78, 247–248
    women in, 293, 296(*i*), 296–298, 301, 309,
        315, 515, 519–520

Thailand, 828
Thames, battle of the, 242
Thayendanegea (Mohawk chief). *See* **Brant, Joseph**
Thayer, Webster, 690
theater
    in New Deal, 775
    vaudeville, 560
    Yiddish, 552
Their Eyes Were Watching God (Hurston), 775
Thieu, Nguyen Van, 904, 911
Third World
    AIDS in, 967
    black power movement and, 895
    Cold War and, 830, 843
    decolonization in, 866*(m)*
    development of, 850
    meaning of, 866*(m)*
    Soviet influence in, 830
    U.S. intervention in, 952
Tho, Le Duc, 910
Thomas, Clarence, 951
Thomas, M. Carey, 547*(i)*
Thomas, Norman, 748
Thomas, Theodore, 562
Thompson, Virgil, 775
Thoreau, Henry David (1817–1862), 355–356, 357, 371, 409
Thoughts on Female Education (Rush), 262
Thoughts on Government (John Adams), 198, 212
Three Mile Island, Pennsylvania, 929
Thurmond, J. Strom, 833
Tidewater region, 117, 123
Tikal, 9
Tilden, Bill, 707
Tilden, Samuel J., 469
Tillman, Ben, 585
timber industry. *See* lumber industry
Time (magazine), 707
time zones, establishment of, 510, 511*(m)*
Timucua Indians, 12
Tippecanoe, battle of, 241, 347
The Titan (Dreiser), 543
Title IX, Educational Amendments Act (1972), 930
tobacco, 73, 77–79, 80, 83
    colonial production of, 157
    decline of, 268
    duties on, 134, 568
    economy based on, 48–52

exports of, 124
    Southern gentry and, 87
    Southern production of, 268, 269*(m)*, 270, 516*(m)*
    trade in, 89*(m)*
    transportation for, 306*(m)*
Tobago, 184
Tocqueville, Alexis de, 254*(i)*, 322, 353
    on American democracy, 566
Tojo, Hideki, 786
Toleration Act (1649), 48
Toomer, Jean, 717
Tory Association, 158
totalitarianism, 780, 781
town meetings, 58–59
Townsend, Francis, 759, 761, 763
Townshend, Charles, 96, 145–146
Townshend Act (1767), 145–148, 147*(i)*, 151–152
Tracy, Benjamin F., 634
Tracy, Spencer, 794
trade, 19. *See also* exports; imports; South Atlantic system; *individual commodities*
    Anglo-American, 119, 123–124, 135–136, 145, 148, 150, 155
    British empire and, 121
    with California, 390
    of Confederacy, 426, 427
    with Confederacy, 415
    control of, 89*(m)*
    duties on, 110, 135–137
    free, 322, 785, 851, 959
    of manufactured goods, 309–310
    New York City and, 309
    restraint of, 625
    slave, 71, 76–83, 82*(i)*, 233, 234*(i)*
    West Indian, 88, 106, 135–137, 155
trade, foreign, 652
    automobile and, 924
    balance of, 632–633, 633*(f)*, 726, 849, 925. *See also* trade deficits
    corporations and, 927
    globalization and, 959
    Great Depression and, 726
    with Japan, 785
    and Marshall Plan, 821
    in 1970s, 944
    postwar, 821, 849, 851
    recessions and, 851
    restrictions on, 726
    surpluses in, 849

trade deficits, 925
  in 1990s, 957
  Reaganomics and, 950
trade routes, 20, 21(m), 24
trade unionism. See labor unions
Trail of Tears, 339
transcendentalism, 353–355, 362
  abolitionism and, 371, 374
  industrialization and, 358
Trans-Missouri case (1897), 616
Transportation, Department of, 968
transportation system. See also airline industry;
    canals; highways; railroads
  automobile and, 703
  bottleneck in, 235–237
  emergence of mass, 537–539, 538(i)
  employment and, 542, 544–545
  financing of roads and canals, 293, 302, 324,
    325, 327–328, 333, 341, 344
  freight lines and, 479
  JFK and, 868
  rapid transit, 539
  revolution in, 293, 302–308, 304(i), 306(m)
  segregation in, 840, 869
  subways, 539
  trolley and, 507
  water, 235–236, 507–508
Treasury Department, U.S., 754
treaties. See also arms control; individual
    treaties by name
  mutual defense, 829(m)
  nuclear test ban, 865
  Strategic Arms Limitation, 910, 939, 941
Treatise on Domestic Economy (Beecher), 375
Tredegar Iron Works, 299, 426
Treitschke, Heinrich von, 541
trench warfare, 664–666, 665(i)
Trenton, battle of, 173, 174(m), 184(m)
trial by jury, 136, 138–139, 142, 274
Triangle Shirtwaist factory fire, 606, 607,
    608, 609(i)
tribal termination program, 933
Tri-Partite Pact (Germany, Japan, Italy; 1940),
    785
Triple Alliance, 654, 663
Triple Entente, 655, 663
Triumphant Democracy (Carnegie), 571
Trollope, Frances, 279, 322
Trotter, William Monroe, 606
Troup, George M., 329

Truman, Harry S (1884–1972), 793
  atomic bomb and, 808, 809
  civil rights and, 834, 839–840
  communism and, 824, 830
  death of Roosevelt and, 816
  desegregation of armed forces and,
    826(i), 840
  Fair Deal of, 833–835, 838, 848
  foreign policies of, 848
  health insurance and, 876
  Korean War and, 824–826
  loyalty program of, 835
  Marshall Plan and, 820
  McCarthy and, 836
  NATO and, 821
  1948 election of, 832–833, 833(i)
  1949 State of the Union address, 834
  postwar price controls and, 831
  at Potsdam, 818
  as president (1945–1953), 816–823,
    835–836
  railroad strike and, 832
  recognition of Israel, 830
  Soviet Union and, 818
  veto of Taft-Hartley bill, 832
  Vietnam policy of, 881, 882, 911
Truman Doctrine (1947)
  containment and, 819–823
  National Security Act and, 823
Trumbull, Lyman, 445, 446, 450
Trumpauer, Joan, 870
trust-busting, 615–617. See also antitrust laws
Truth, Sojourner, 379(i), 457
Tryon, William, 128–129
Tubman, Harriet, 370–371
Tucson, Arizona, 495
Tunney, Gene, 707
Turkey, 19(i), 33, 820, 822
  colonies of, 781
Turnbow, Hartman, 874
Turner, Frederick Jackson, 636
Turner, Henry M., 449
Turner, Nat, 368
Turner, Randolph, 382
Turner, Ted, 961
turnpikes, 293, 302
Tuscarora Indians, 7, 75
Tuskegee Institute, 606
Twain, Mark (Samuel Clemens), 500, 562, 577
  on New York, 537, 539, 550

Tweed, William Marcy, 556
"Tweed Days in St. Louis" (Steffens), 599
Two Treatises on Government (Locke), 73, 113
Tydings-McDuffie Act (1934), 743
Tyler, James G., 640*(i)*
Tyler, John (1790–1862), 347
    1844 elections and, 391
    as president (1841–1845), 349
Typographical Union (1852), 526

U-2 spy plane incident (1960), 843–844
Udall, Stewart, 876
Ukraine, 799
Uncle Sam, 758*(i)*
Uncle Tom's Cabin (Stowe), 376, 385, 400
underground railroad, 370–371
Underwood Company, 311
Underwood Tariff Act (1913), 623
unemployment, 301, 309, 313, 316, 319, 346
    African American, 736
    Asian American, 742–743
    baby boom and, 925
    Bush (George H. W.) and, 951
    in cities, 965
    compensation for, 611, 761, 838
    decay of inner cities and, 862
    decline of, 958
    declining economy and, 925
    Democratic Party and, 777
    environmentalism and, 929
    in Germany, 781
    Great Depression and, 728, 745, 748
    in late 19th century, 588
    migrant workers and, 861
    Native American, 771, 898
    New Deal and, 757
    in 1920s, 696
    postwar, 851
    Reagan and, 948
    rise in, 949, 975, 980
    Roosevelt recession and, 764
    in Rust Belt, 926
    of women, 732, 743
    workers' compensation and, 610–611
    WWII and, 789, 793
Unification Church, 928
Union. *See* Civil War
Union Army, 433–435
    African Americans in, 433*(i)*
    black veterans of, 448, 458

Unionists, 416
Union Pacific Railroad, 493*(i)*, 509, 510
    building of, 480
Union Party, 1936 elections and, 763
unions. *See* labor unions
Union Stock Yards, Chicago, 512
Unitarianism, 353, 354
United Automobile Workers (UAW), 766
United Cloth Hat and Cap Makers Union,
    529*(i)*
United Farm Workers (UFW), 898
United Fruit Company, 700–701, 828
United Mine Workers (UMW), 615, 766,
    790, 832
United Nations, 818
    China and, 824
    founding of, 806–807
    General Assembly of, 830
    Iraq and economic sanctions, 975
    Iraq and Resolution 1441, 976
    Korean War and, 824, 825*(m)*
    partitioning of Palestine, 830
    peacekeeping forces of, 824, 825*(m)*, 972
    Persian Gulf War and, 954, 956*(m)*
    Security Council of, 806–807, 824
    Suez Canal and, 830
United Nations Earth Summit (1992), 960
United States Steel Corporation, 617, 621, 926
    strikes against, 766–767
United States v. Minoru Yasui (1943), 798
*United States v. One Package of Japanese
    Pessaries* (1936), 730
Universalists, 278, 283*(m)*, 324
Universal Negro Improvement Association
    (UNIA), 718
University of California
    affirmative action and, 965
    Free Speech Movement and, 891–892
University of Michigan
    affirmative action and, 965
    antiwar movement at, 891
Unsafe at Any Speed (Nader), 930
Upward Bound, 875
urbanization, 536–563, 708*(m)*. *See also* cities
    in American colonies, 88–90
    ethnicity and, 719
    individualism and, 355
    industrialization and, 308–309, 536–542
    intellectual life and, 716
    labor and, 310, 313–314, 319, 336

postwar, 851
  South Atlantic system and, 88, 90–91
  in the West, 491–495
U'Ren, Harold, 604
Uruguay, 940
USA PATRIOT (Uniting and Strengthening
    America by Providing Appropriate Tools
    Required to Intercept and Obstruct
    Terrorism) Act (2002), 979
USA trilogy (Dos Passos), 716, 775
Utah
  Compromise of 1850 and, 398, 399(m)
  Japanese internment in, 797
  Mormons in, 364, 364(m), 366, 366(i)
  nuclear testing in, 828
Ute Indians, 487
Utica, New York, 372, 374
utopian communities, 357–366
  Brook Farm, 357–358, 359(m)
  Fourierist, 361
  Mormon, 359(m), 362–366, 364(m)
  Oneida, 359(m), 361–362
  Shaker, 284, 358–360, 359(m), 361
Utrecht, Treaty of (1713), 75, 76(m)

Valley Forge, Pennsylvania, 178
Valparaiso (Chile), anti-U.S. riot in, 630
Van Buren, Martin (1782–1862), 387
  1836 elections and, 344
  1840 elections and, 347–348
  1844 elections and, 391
  1848 elections and, 396, 405(m)
  1852 elections and, 401
  Independent Treasury Act of 1840 and, 347
  Jackson and, 328, 329
  party government and, 323–325
  party politics and, 322–325
  patronage and, 324
  as president (1837–1841), 339, 347
  as vice presidential candidate, 336
  Wilmot Proviso and, 395
Vance, Zebulon, 424
Vanderbilt, Cornelius, 509, 563
Vanderbilt, George W., 563
Van Dusen, Larry, 729
Vann, James, 337
Vann, John Paul, 880
Vann, Mary Jane, 880
Van Rensselaer, Kiliaen, 43
Van Rensselaer family, 124

Vanzetti, Bartolomeo, 689–690
Vassa, Gustavus (Olaudah Equiano), 81
vaudeville, 560
Vaya, Count Vay de, 517(f), 518(i)
V-E (Victory in Europe) Day, 802
Venezuela, 309, 630, 635
  oil production in, 922
  U.S. foreign investment in, 701
Venice, Italy, 19
Vergennes, Comte de, 179
Vermont
  land grants in, 103
  migration from, 301, 303(m)
  settlement of, 233
  voting rights in, 258, 259(m), 272
Versailles, Treaty of (1783), 184
Versailles, Treaty of (1919), 686(i), 829(m)
  racial equality and, 684
  Senate refusal to ratify, 686–687
  WWII and, 781, 782
vertical integration, 512, 513, 514, 615
Vesey, Denmark, 272
Vespucci, Amerigo, 24–25
veterans
  benefits for, 611, 793, 838
  GI Bill and, 793
  protests by, 747–748
Veterans Administration, 852
Vicksburg, Mississippi, 430, 431, 432, 434
Victory gardens, 794
Vietcong, 884, 886, 887, 904, 910
Vietminh, 881, 882
Vietnam
  Cold War and, 866(m)
  communism in, 849
  diplomatic relations with, 972
  globalization and, 960
  immigrants from, 962
  strategic hamlet program in, 884
Vietnam syndrome, 911
Vietnam Veterans Against the War, 909
Vietnam Veterans Memorial, 912(i)
Vietnam War (1961–1975), 880–914, 944. See
    also antiwar movement
  African Americans in, 887
  aftermath of, 911–912
  Agent Orange and, 885, 892
  bombing campaigns in, 885, 906, 910, 911
  Buddhist opposition to, 884
  Cambodian attacks and, 908, 909, 910

Vietnam War (*cont.*)
  casualties in, 886(*i*), 911
  civil rights movement and, 897
  credibility gap in, 890
  desertions during, 909
  détente and, 909–911
  economy and, 923, 924
  Eisenhower administration and, 882–883
  fall of Saigon and, 911
  Ford administration and, 911
  Great Society and, 881
  guerrilla tactics in, 883(*m*), 884
  Gulf of Tonkin resolution and, 884–885,
    909, 912
  immigration and, 962
  Johnson administration and, 884–887, 892
  Kennedy administration and, 883–884, 889
  legacy of, 911–912
  mass media and, 889–890, 890(*i*), 908, 909,
    911, 912
  music and, 894(*i*)
  My Lai massacre and, 909
  1968 elections and, 904–907, 907(*m*)
  1972 elections and, 918–919
  Nixon administration and, 908–909, 911
  Operation Rolling Thunder and, 885
  opposition to. *See* antiwar movement
  Paris peace talks and, 910
  peace talks in, 905
  Persian Gulf War and, 954
  poverty and, 877
  prisoners of war in, 885, 910
  public cynicism and, 889–891, 921
  Tet offensive and, 890(*i*), 904
  troops in, 887–889, 909
  veterans and, 888, 889, 909, 911, 912(*i*)
  Vietnamization policy in, 908, 909, 910, 919
  as war of attrition, 887
  War on Poverty and, 877
  women in, 887, 889
vigilantism, WWI, 682
Villa, Pancho, 653–654, 654(*i*)
Vinci, Leonardo da, 20
violence
  abortion rights and, 966
  against civil rights movement, 872
  desegregation and, 841
Virginia
  vs. Chesapeake peoples, 46–47, 52
  claims to Western lands, 202, 233
  as colony, 44–52
  elite politics in, 92
  Emancipation Proclamation and, 429
  end of Civil War and, 440
  evangelicals in, 117–118
  House of Burgesses of, 51–53, 87, 138, 148,
    151, 157
  industrial capacity in, 426
  land disputes in, 125
  migration from, 302, 303(*m*)
  presidency and, 237
  ratification of Constitution and, 213
  Reconstruction and, 453(*m*), 456
  river plantations in, 49(*i*)
  Scots-Irish in, 110
  secession and, 414, 414(*m*), 416
  slavery in, 50–51, 80, 81, 83, 86, 157–158,
    281, 368
  tenant farmers of, 117–118, 266
  voting rights in, 324
  wheat production in, 124
Virginia City, Nevada, 493(*i*), 494
Virginia Company, 44–46
The Virginian (Wister), 548
Virginia Plan, 208–209
Virginia planters. *See also* plantations
  culture of, 113, 117–118
  revolution and, 157
Virgin of Guadalupe, 29
V-J (Victory over Japan) Day (August 15,
    1945), 780
voluntarism
  trade unions and, 610
  in WWI, 674–675
Volunteers in Service to America (VISTA), 875
voter registration
  civil rights movement and, 840, 869,
    873–874
  labor unions and, 794
  in the South, 875(*m*)
voting patterns
  changes in, 330(*f*)
  ethnicity and, 719
  in 1998 election, 971
  in 2000 election, 973
  urbanization and, 719
voting rights. *See also* Fifteenth Amendment
  African American, 446, 451, 453, 454, 457,
    464, 467, 581–584, 585(*m*), 873–874, 897
  federal protection of, 840

for free blacks, 272, 371
intimidation and, 466, 467
Know-Nothing Party and, 402
literacy tests and, 584
movement for, 379, 457
poll tax and, 584
property qualifications for, 92, 197, 199
republicanism and, 258–260, 259(m), 285–286
Southern gentry and, 87
Supreme Court on, 918
2000 elections and, 974
universal, 322, 349
white male, 258–259, 259(m), 322–324, 341
for women, 379, 456–457. See also suffrage
    movement
Voting Rights Act (1965), 874, 875(m)

WAACs (Women's Auxiliary Army Corps), 789
Wade-Davis Bill (1864), 443
Wadleigh, Michael, 894(i)
Wadsworth, Benjamin, 100
wages. See also minimum wage
    abolitionism and, 371
    controls on, 693
    family, 519, 521
    gender gap in, 519–521, 520(i), 580, 933, 958
    inflation and, 832
    labor for, 361, 448(i), 449, 461–462, 464
    labor unions and, 790
    in postwar economy, 851
    slavery and, 402
    in the South, 515, 582
    of women, 375, 380
Wagner, Robert F., 608, 609, 761
Wagner Act (1935), 761
    labor unions and, 767
    Supreme Court on, 763
wagon trains, 479, 491, 493(i)
Wake Island, 803
Walden, or Life in the Woods (Thoreau), 355–356
Walden Pond, 355
Walker, David (1785–1830), 367–368
Walker, John, 275
Wallace, George C., 906, 907(m), 909, 918
Wallace, Henry A., 754, 784, 793, 832
Waller, John, 118
Wall Street, New York City. See also stock
    market
    gold purchases on, 592
    railroad building and, 510

Walpole, Sir Robert, 92–95, 94(i)
Walsh, Lawrence, 949
Waltham plan, 296
Wampanoag Indians, 54, 61. See also
    Metacom's Rebellion
Wanamaker, John, 513
Wappinger Indians, 124–125
War Brides Act (1945), 860
War Industries Board, 674–675, 756
War Information, Office of (OWI), 794
War Manpower Commission, 789
Warner, Charles Dudley, 562
War of 1812, 237, 347
    causes of, 242
    Congressional vote on declaration of, 242
    emancipation and, 268
    Indian peoples and, 337
    Jackson and, 325
    terms of, 268
    Washington, D.C. and, 242, 243(m)
War of the Austrian Succession (King George's
    War; 1740–1748), 95
War of the Spanish Succession (Queen Anne's
    War; 1702–1713), 74
War on Poverty, 874–877, 917
War Powers Acts
    of 1941, 787
    of 1973, 911
War Production Board (WPB), 787–788
War Refugee Board, 802
War Relocation Authority, 797
Warren, Earl, 832, 840, 918, 950, 951
Warren, Joseph, 143
Warren, Mercy Otis, 260
War Revenue Bills (1917, 1918), 674
War Risk Insurance Act (1917), 680
Warsaw Pact, 819(m), 827
Washington, Booker T., 605–606
Washington, George (1732–1799), 157
    in battle of Long Island, 173
    cabinet of, 215
    church taxes and, 193
    on closing of Boston Harbor, 153
    as commander of Continental army, 167,
        175–176, 183
    creation of national bank and, 217
    as delegate to Constitutional Convention,
        208
    on expansion of West, 227
    Federalists and, 222

Washington, George (*cont.*)
on foreign alliances, 829(*m*)
freemasonry and, 344
in French and Indian War, 121
John Jay and, 220
nationalist faction and, 207
on national system of taxation, 202
Native American resistance and, 230
as president (1789–1797), 215
Proclamation of Neutrality, 219
return to plantation, 196
soldiers' pensions and, 179
southern strategy of, 182
at Valley Forge, 178
Whiskey Rebellion and, 220
Zachary Taylor and, 396
Washington Globe, 332
Washington Naval Arms Conference (1921),
701
Washington Post, Watergate and, 920
Washington Star, gay rights and, 934
Washington state, Japanese internment
in, 797
WASPs (Women Airforce Service Pilots), 789
Washington, D.C. *See* District of Columbia
The Waste Land (Eliot), 716
Watergate scandal, 919–921, 944
Iran-Contra and, 949
water power, 507
manufacturing and, 294, 295, 297,
298, 308
mills and, 247
water resources
agriculture and, 485, 497, 501
dams and, 502
transportation and, 507–508
Waters, Ethel, 705
Watson, Tom, 582–583, 585
WAVES (Women Accepted for Volunteer
Emergency Service), 789
Wayne, John, 794
Wayne, "Mad Anthony", 230
wealth. *See also* economy
of business elite, 301, 309–310
creed of individualism and, 571
distribution of, 877, 948, 957, 958, 960
increase of, 616–617
inheritance and, 310
per capita income and, 293, 308, 506, 795
unequal distribution of, 725, 760

The Wealth of Nations (Smith), 77, 219
weapons of mass destruction (WMD), 976. *See
also* atomic bomb; nuclear weapons
Weaver, James B., 589, 594(*m*)
Webster, Daniel, 242, 253, 342, 413
Compromise of 1850 and, 398
1836 elections and, 344
1840 elections and, 347, 349
on Jackson, 330
Second Bank and, 335
Whig Party and, 347, 349
Webster, Noah, 265
Webster v. Reproductive Health Service (1989),
951
Weed, Thurlow, 344
Weems, Parson Mason, 265
Weld, Theodore, 369, 372
welfare
and arms race, 828
Asian Americans and, 743
categorical, 761
conservative opposition to, 877
cuts in, 948, 969, 970
Democratic Party and, 848
in Europe, 776
and Fair Deal, 834
federal involvement with, 838–839, 917
Great Depression and, 745, 748
immigrants and, 964
labor unions and, 767
legislation on, 969, 970
maternalist, 601
Nixon and, 917
reform of, 917, 964, 969, 970, 979
Republican Party and, 839
resentment of, 937
states and, 970
of Truman, 834
War on Poverty and, 875
welfare capitalism, 698, 766
welfare state, 601, 776–777
conservative opposition to, 937
New Deal and, 761
in 1970s, 943
WWII and, 793
Welles, Orson, 775
The Well-Ordered Family (Wadsworth), 100
Wells, David A., 511
Wells, Ida B., 587, 587(*i*)
Wentworth, Governor, 158

Wesley, John, 114
the West, 184, 202–205. *See also* westward
    expansion
    American sovereignty and, 241
    American System and, 325
    Asian Americans in, 742
    cession to U.S. of, 244–245
    Civil War in, 420–423, 430
    claims to, 202–204, 203(*m*)
    closing of frontier in, 636
    communal experiments in, 359(*m*)
    economic growth of, 926–927, 927(*m*)
    ethnic diversity in, 481(*i*), 481–482, 485
    Free-Soil Party and, 395
    geology of, 477, 491, 492, 492(*m*)
    Jackson as first president from, 330
    migration to, 323, 383, 387–390, 389(*m*),
        851, 852, 861, 926–927, 927(*m*)
    myth vs. reality of, 480, 481(*i*)
    1928 elections and, 718
    1932 elections and, 749
    1980 elections and, 943
    opening up of, 202–204, 227–237
    removal of Indians to, 337–340, 340(*m*)
    Second Bank and, 336
    settlement of, 227, 232–237, 476–502
    slavery in, 398
    transmountain, 492(*m*), 502(*i*). *See also*
        California; Pacific slope
    urbanization of, 708(*m*)
West, Mae, 733
West Africa, 84. *See also* Africa
    as British colony, 121
    culture of, 20–22
    Dutch trade in, 43
    Mediterranean trade and, 21, 21(*m*)
    slave trade in, 21(*m*), 23
West Bank, 923
Western Confederacy (Shawnees, Miamis, and
    Potawatomis), 229(*i*), 230, 241
Western Federation of Miners (WFM),
    532–533
Western Front (World War I), 663–664,
    670, 671(*m*)
Western Hemisphere, immigration from, 709
Western Trail (periodical), 482
West Germany. *See* Germany, Federal
    Republic of
West India Company, 33, 43
West Indies. *See* Caribbean Islands

Westinghouse, George, 510
Westinghouse turbine, 509(*i*)
Westmoreland, William, 880
West Virginia
    creation of, 416
    secession and, 414(*m*), 418
westward expansion, 126(*m*), 132, 153–154,
        157, 227–237, 240, 253. *See also*
        migration
    Louisiana Purchase and, 276(*m*)
    Manifest Destiny and, 383–391
    migration and, 119, 122, 232–237, 301–302,
        303(*m*), 323, 383, 387–390, 389(*m*)
    Missouri Compromise and, 275–277,
        276(*m*)
    Native Americans and, 99, 119–121, 125
    postcolonial, 262
    of slavery to old Southwest, 233, 267(*i*), 268,
        269(*m*), 302, 303(*m*)
    slave vs. free states and, 396–398, 401–402,
        406
    Treaty of Paris and, 133(*m*), 154(*m*)
Wethersfield, Connecticut, 56, 60(*m*)
Wetmore, Ephraim, 206
Weyler, Valeriano, 636, 638
whaling industry, 274(*i*)
Wharton, Edith, 542, 716
wheat
    in California, 499
    colonial production of, 103, 110(*i*), 124
    exports of, 124, 135, 292
    on Great Plains, 485–486
    Midwest production of, 302–305, 303(*m*)
    from North in Civil War, 432
    prices of, 219, 588
    western, 235
Wheeler, Adam, 206
Whig Party, 426
    Compromise of 1850 and, 398
    creation of, 342
    decline of, 400–401
    vs. Democratic Party, 255, 322, 330 (*f*), 344,
        345, 349
    economic program of, 403
    1844 elections and, 391
    evangelical moralism and, 342, 344
    first national convention of, 347
    ideology of, 342–344
    Lincoln in, 407
    Mexican War and, 393, 395

Whig Party (*cont.*)
    Radical, 134, 141, 143, 150, 175, 216
    realignment of, 405(*m*)
    salutary neglect and, 92
    slave vs. free states and, 396, 398, 402
    support in the South, 343–344
Whig Party (England), 91–93, 134, 143,
        145, 198
Whiskey Rebellion (1794), 220, 238
Whiskey Ring, 468
White, Hugh L., 344
White, John, 45(*i*)
White, William Allen, 574, 784
White Citizens' Councils, 841
white collar jobs. *See* middle class
Whitefield, George, 114–116, 115(*i*), 117,
        278, 284
White Man's Union, 586
white supremacy, 408, 413, 445, 450, 465–467,
        584–588. *See also* Ku Klux Klan; racism
    in Progressive vein, 605, 607
Whitewater investigation, 971
Whitlock, Brand, 574
Whitman, Walt (1819–1892), 356–357, 396
Whitney, Eli, 233, 299
Whyte, William, 851
Wickersham, George, 621
Wilderness, battle of the, 434, 435(*i*)
Wilhelm II, Emperor of Germany
        (r. 1888–1918), 655
Wilkes, John, 134, 150
Wilkins, Roy, 871, 872
Wilkinson, Eliza, 199
Wilkinson, James, 240
Wilkinson, Jemima, 284
Will, George F., 965
Willamette Valley, Oregon, 388, 479, 494
Willard, Emma, 285
Willard, Frances, 578–579
William III, king of England, 91
Williams, Roger, 55, 56
Williams, William Carlos, 716
Williams v. Mississippi (1898), 586
Willkie, Wendell, 784
Wills, Helen, 707
Wilmot, David, 394
Wilmot Proviso, 394–395, 396, 407, 429
Wilson, Charles E., 828
Wilson, Edith Bolling Galt, 687
Wilson, Pete, 965

Wilson, Woodrow (1856–1924), 693
    African Americans and, 605
    banks and, 624
    as Democratic Party nominee, 622
    "Fourteen Points" of, 683–684, 785
    isolationism and, 783–784
    League of Nations and, 683–687
    neutrality in WWI and, 665, 667
    the New Freedom and, 622–623
    presidency and, 754
    as president (1913–1921), 652–656,
        667–669, 674, 675, 680–687
    social program of, 625
    trusts and, 624
Wilson-Gorman Tariff (1894), 592
Windsor, Connecticut, 56
The Winning of the West (T. Roosevelt), 636
Winthrop, James, 212
Winthrop, John, 54, 59
Wisconsin, 11, 41
    Fugitive Slave Acts and, 400
    slaves in, 405
    utopian communities in, 361
Wise, John, 113
Wissler, Clark, 478
Wister, Owen, 548
witchcraft executions, 58
WMD. *See* weapons of mass destruction
Wobblies. *See* Industrial Workers of the World
Wolfe, James, 122, 132
Wolfe, Tom, 928
Wollstonecraft, Mary, 262
Wolof Indians, 23
Woman in the Nineteenth Century (Fuller), 356
Woman's Party, National, 602, 680, 931
Woman Suffrage Association, National, 457
Woman Suffrage Association, National
        American (NAWSA), 578, 602, 679–680
women. *See also* children; gender roles;
        marriage
    abolitionism and, 370, 371, 372, 373(*m*),
        376–378, 379(*i*), 457, 901
    African American, 462, 695, 705, 731, 735
    in antiwar movement, 902
    Baptists and, 118, 280–281
    birth rates and, 100–101, 261–262, 901
    in breadlines, 727(*i*)
    changing roles of, 932–933
    charitable institutions and, 315, 349
    in civil rights movement, 842, 872

in Civil War, 424–425, 425(i)
in colonies, 58
in Congress, 669
consumer culture and, 703
Democratic Party and, 918
discrimination against, 731
divorce and, 261, 901
as domestic servants, 319, 519
dower right and, 102
education of, 199–202, 262, 284–286, 547(i),
    549, 732
emancipation and, 449
employment of, 730–732
equality of, 199–202, 372, 669, 679–680
evangelicalism and, 101–102
on farms, 100–101, 109, 110(i), 148
feminism and, 457
feminist movement and, 457, 880, 889,
    901–903, 915
Fourierism and, 361
free black, 462
Free-Soil Party and, 395
Garrison and, 369(i)
gentry, 87–88
in government, 669
Great Depression and, 728–732, 731(i)
in Hispanic culture, 496–497
as homemakers, 546
household production and, 185–186
intellect of, 546, 547(i)
jazz and, 705
Ku Klux Klan and, 466, 712–713
labor of, 449
labor unions and, 526, 529(i), 742
legal status of married, 546
in medieval Europe, 16–17
Mexican American, 742, 796
middle class, 311, 312(i), 703, 858
in military, 789, 957(i)
minimum wage for, 621, 768
minority, 768
moral reform and, 375
Native American, 12–14, 64, 65, 231–232
New Deal and, 767–768, 776–777
in 1920s, 695–696
in 1950s, 856(i), 856–857
1984 elections and, 949
in the North, 375
Oneida Community and, 361, 362
opportunities for, 862

opposition to marriage and, 546
political status of, 199–202, 348–349,
    695–696
poverty and, 313, 315
as Progressives, 600–601
prostitution and, 492, 494, 498
Puritan, 55–56, 100–101
Quaker, 70
Radical Reconstruction program and,
    456–457, 459
republican motherhood and, 261–262,
    263(i), 285
in Revolutionary War, 185, 185(i)
role of, 101(i), 273–274, 278, 280–281,
    284–286, 317
slavery and, 83, 173, 385
social reform and, 375, 532
Social Security Act and, 761
in South Atlantic system, 90
strikes and, 741(i)
as teachers, 286
in textile industry, 293, 296(i), 296–298, 301,
    309, 315, 515, 519–520
transcendentalism and, 356
unemployment of, 742–743
utopian communalism and, 361, 362
Vietnam War and, 887, 889
wage gap and, 519–521, 520(i), 580, 958
in wartime jobs, 677, 679, 679(i)
westward migration and, 390, 483(i), 484
in workforce, 789, 851, 856(i), 857, 858, 901,
    932–933, 957–958
WWII and, 780, 789
women activists
    Dorr, Retha Childe, 578
    Friedan, Betty, 901–902
    Lease, Mary Elizabeth, 589–590
    Potter, Helen, 580
    Schneiderman, Rose, 529, 529(i)
    Steinem, Gloria, 930
    Wells, Ida B., 587, 587(i)
    Willard, Frances, 578–579
Women's Bureau (Labor Department), 601
Women's Christian Temperance Union
    (WCTU), 578–579, 681
Women's Conference, National (1977), 930
Women's Division of Democratic National
    Committee, 767, 777
Women's International League for Peace and
    Freedom, 701

Women's Joint Congressional Committee, 695
Women's Liberation Party, National, 903(i)
Women's Peace Party, 667
Women's Political Caucus, National, 930
women's rights, 366(i). See also feminism;
    suffrage movement
  Abigail Adams on, 199, 200, 201
  activists in movement for, 526, 578–580, 590
  child care and, 903
  Douglass on, 456, 457
  economic, 519–521, 520(i), 579–580, 957–958
  equal, 732
  evangelicalism and, 116, 278, 280–281,
    284–286
  feminist movement and, 901–903
  Garrison and, 352
  German settlers and, 109
  in Great Depression, 732
  inheritances and, 260–261
  John Adams on, 260
  in labor force, 301, 526, 529(i)
  media and, 902, 966
  movement for, 374–380
  to property, 100, 102, 109
  sex-typing and, 519–521, 520(i)
  social reform and, 375
  Title IX and, 930
  Title VII and, 902
  voting, 260, 262, 456–457, 578–580, 579(i),
    679–680
  women's liberation and, 902–903, 903(i)
women's studies, 966
Women's Trade Union League, National, 602
Wood, Jethro, 308
Woodstock, rock concert at, 893, 894(i)
Woolman, John, 189
Woolworth Building, 539
Worcester, Massachusetts, 379
Worcester v. Georgia (1832), 339
work, culture of, 521, 522
work ethic, 311–312, 317
  Protestant, 692
working class, 612, 613. See also laborers
  African American, 718
  birth control and, 730
  conservatism of, 937
  Democratic Party and, 905, 943
  ethnic identities and, 900
  feminism and, 931, 933
  Great Depression and, 729
    housing and, 925
    movie industry and, 704
    in 1950s, 860
    in 1970s, 915
    1980 elections and, 943
    and politics, 588, 590, 593
    school busing and, 936
    on television, 854
    Vietnam War and, 887, 888
    Wallace and, 906
    women, 857
Working Men's Party, 300, 499
Works Progress Administration (WPA),
    762, 762(m)
  African Americans and, 768
  environment and, 773
  Federal One of, 773–774
  Roosevelt recession and, 764
World Anti-Slavery Convention (London;
    1840), 378
World Bank (International Bank for
    Reconstruction and Development), 850
WorldCom, 979
World Court (Court of International
    Justice), 701
World's Fairs. See Chicago Columbian
    Exposition (1893)
World's Work (periodical), 687
World Trade Center, 975–976. See also
    September 11, 2001, terrorist attacks
  1993 bombing of, 972, 973
World War I (1914–1918), 434, 663–683, 818
  Allied Powers in, 663
  business-government partnership and,
    692–693
  Central Powers in, 663
  civilians in, 664
  civil rights in, 682–683
  and defense spending, 843
  domestic efforts during, 675
  Dust Bowl and, 738
  ethnic loyalties during, 667
  European alliances in, 664(m)
  federal government and, 662, 696
  growth of trade during, 667
  immigration and, 709
  intellectual life and, 716
  international balance of power and,
    663–664, 670
  isolationism and, 782–783

liberty bonds of, 674
Lusitania and, 667–668
modern bureaucratic state and, 675
mutual defense treaties and, 829(*m*)
neutrality on the seas in, 667
new military technology in, 664–665
1920s and, 692
progressive reforms and, 681
Prohibition and, 681
propaganda in, 681–683
quasi-vigilantism in, 682
racism in, 671–672
Red Scare after, 835
reparations for, 699
scope of, 663–664
ship convoys in, 669
social divisions and, 662
student activism and, 732
trench warfare in, 664–666, 665(*i*), 670
U-boats in, 667
Uncle Sam and, 731(*i*)
unresolved issues of, 687
U.S. involvement in, 669–670, 782
Verdun, battles of, 665, 670
veterans of, 747
voluntarism in, 674, 675
war profiteers in, 783
Western Front in, 663–664, 670, 671(*m*)
WWII and, 687, 781, 787, 799
World War II (1939–1945), 420,
  780–810
  African American rights and, 737
  black market in, 795
  casualties in, 799, 808(*i*)
  decolonization and, 866(*m*)
  defense spending and, 784, 788
  in Europe (1941–1943), 800(*m*)
  in Europe (1944–1945), 801(*m*)
  federal budget and, 787, 810
  as "good war," 780
  Great Depression and, 723, 764
  on home front, 794–798
  homosexuals in, 858
  mobilization for, 787–794
  mutual defense treaties after, 829(*m*)
  in North Atlantic, 786(*m*)
  in Pacific, 804(*m*), 805(*m*)
  postwar world and, 780–781
  prelude to, 781–787
  rationing in, 794, 795

reparations and, 818
second front in, 799
strategies of, 799
U.S. power and, 781
U.S. role in, 799, 816, 843
WWI and, 687, 781, 787, 799
World Wide Web, 961. *See also* Internet
Wounded Knee, South Dakota
  massacre at, 476, 490
  occupation of (1973), 899–900, 900(*i*)
Wovoka, Indian holy man, 490
Wright, Richard, 775
Wyandot Indians, 229
Wyoming
  gold in, 492
  Japanese internment in, 797
Wyoming Valley, Pennsylvania, 124, 126(*m*)

Yale College, 283(*m*)
Yalta meeting (1945), 805(*m*), 806, 807, 807(*i*),
  818, 836
Yalu River, 824
Yamasee people, 69
Yancey, William Lowndes, 409
Yassin, Sheikh Ahmad, 978
Yates, Robert, 209
Yellow Bird, Sioux medicine man, 490
The Yellow Kid (comic strip), 561
Yellowstone National Park, 614(*m*)
Yellowstone region, 11
Yeltsin, Boris, 953
Yemen, 956(*m*), 972
yeomen farmers, 34, 52, 53, 235, 384, 414,
  444, 458
  draft and, 423
  Free-Soil Party and, 395
  Lincoln and, 407, 409
  migration to America, 34
  Reconstruction and, 444
  secession and, 414(*m*), 416
  slavery and, 393, 395
  social structure of, 58–59, 260
  Southern, 87, 343, 458
  taxes and, 427
  westward expansion and, 386
Yiddish language, 552
yippies, 905, 906
YMCA. *See* Young Men's Christian
  Association
Yom Kippur War (1973), 923, 941

Yorktown, battle of (1781), 181(m), 182
Yosemite National Park, 501, 502, 502(i)
Yosemite Valley, 501, 502(i)
Young, Brigham, 364, 364(m), 366
Young, Perry, 934
Young, Whitney, 871
Young Men's Christian Association (YMCA), 559, 680
Young Women's Christian Association (YWCA), 559, 680
youth, 549, 875, 933. *See also* National Youth Administration
  counterculture movement and, 880
  Great Depression and, 732–733
  WWII and, 780, 796

youth culture, 549. *See also* counterculture
  music of, 857–858, 859
  in 1950s, 857–859
Yucatán peninsula, 9, 11
Yugoslavia, 684, 685
  Federal Republic of (FRY), 972
YWCA. *See* Young Women's Christian Association

Zhou Enlai (Chou En-lai), 823
Zimmerman, Arthur, 668
Zionism, 830
Zoffany, Johann, 168
Zola, Émile, 648
zoot suits, 796, 797(i)
Zuni Indians, 11

Understanding History through Maps

Working with maps deepens your understanding of the basic issues of geography and how they relate to historical studies. Understanding these five themes — location, place, region, movement, and interaction — will enrich your readings of maps and the historical situation they depict.

Location

"When?" and "where?" are the first questions asked by historians and cartographers. Every event happens somewhere and at some point in time, and maps are the best devices to show a particular location at a particular time.

Place

Human activity creates places. Locations exist on their own without the presence of people, but they become places when people use the spots in some way. As human enterprise thickens and generation after generation use a place, it accumulates artifacts, develops layers of remains, and generates a variety of associations held in a society's history and memory.

Region

A region highlights common elements, tying certain places together as a group distinguishable from other places. Perceiving regional ties helps the reader of historical maps because they suggest the forces binding individual interests together and encouraging people to act in common.

Movement

All historical change involves movement. People move in their daily activities, in seasonal patterns, and in migration to new places of residence. To understand a map fully, the reader must always envision it as one part of a sequence, not unlike a "still" excerpted from a motion picture.

Interaction

The interaction between people and the environment goes both ways. On the one hand, people change their environment to suit their needs. Human ingenuity has found ways to put almost all places to some use. On the other hand, climate and topography present constraints on how people use the land and force people to change their behavior and culture as they adapt to their natural surroundings.